REFERENCE

DOES NOT CIRCULATE

2000

# HISTORIC
# DOCUMENTS
OF
# 2000

# HISTORIC DOCUMENTS

## OF

# 2000

Cumulative Index, 1996–2000

CQ PRESS

A Division of Congressional Quarterly Inc.

# Historic Documents of 2000

*Editors:* Martha Gottron, John Felton, Bruce Maxwell
*Production and Associate Editor:* Kerry V. Kern
*Indexer:* Victoria Agee


CQ Press
A Division of Congressional Quarterly Inc.
1414 22nd Street, N.W.
Washington, D.C. 20037
(202) 822-1475; (800) 638-1710
www.cqpress.com

Printed and bound in the United States of America
05 04 03 02 01   5 4 3 2 1

⊗ The paper used in this publication meets the minimum requirements of the
American National Standard for Information Sciences—Permanence of Paper
for Printed Library Materials, ANSI Z39.48-1992.


**The Library of Congress cataloged the first issue of this
title as follows:**

Historic documents. 1972—
    Washington. Congressional Quarterly Inc.

    1. United States—Politics and government—1945– —Yearbooks.
2. World politics—1945– —Yearbooks. I. Congressional Quarterly Inc.

E839.5H57                          917.3'03'9205                          72-97888

ISBN 1-56802-491-6
ISSN 0892-080X

# PREFACE

The United States, which likes to preach the virtues of democracy to authoritarian regimes around the world, in 2000 found itself in the uncomfortable position of having its democratic system become the object of derision abroad and dissension at home. For thirty-six days after the November 7 elections, the world watched as the United States engaged in its messiest and most contentious fight over the presidency since 1876. Suddenly, the magisterial process by which the world's oldest democracy routinely transferred power through the ballot box became enmeshed in bitter disputes over the failures of the electoral process in Florida. At issue were "hanging chads," dysfunctional voting machines, confusing ballots, and allegations that some black voters had been intimidated at the polls.

Many foreign observers were inclined at first to mock the spectacle, but as it dragged on, the giggles were replaced by fears that maybe cracks were appearing in the vaunted political stability of the United States. Most Americans also were fascinated and mystified by the process—except for the partisans who were convinced that the other side was plotting to steal the election. Democrats were convinced that the Republican political establishment in Florida, led by Governor Jeb Bush, was distorting legal procedures in an effort to protect a razor-thin lead of a few hundred votes held by Republican presidential candidate George W. Bush, the governor's brother. By winning Florida and its twenty-five electoral votes, Bush would capture the presidency, even though he had lost the popular vote to Democrat Al Gore. For their part, Republicans believed that Democrats were determined to manufacture just enough votes for Vice President Gore to overcome Bush's slim lead in Florida.

In the end, the vote that mattered most was that of the U.S. Supreme Court, which on December 12 halted the counting of disputed ballots—the ballots that Gore was convinced would give him the election and that Bush insisted were invalid. The Court itself was divided in its decision, one of the most controversial it had ever rendered. On the central question before the Court, five justices sided with Bush and four with Gore. The decision meant that Bush would carry Florida by 537 votes, out of 6 million cast in the state, and win the presidency. A clearly frustrated Gore conceded the following day. The outcome kept the nation's political system intact, but it did not totally calm the

---

## How to Use This Book

The documents are arranged in chronological order. If you know the approximate date of the report, speech, statement, court decision, or other document you are looking for, glance through the titles for that month in the table of contents.

If the table of contents does not lead you directly to the document you want, turn to the index at the end of the book. There you may find references not only to the particular document you seek but also to other entries on the same or a related subject. The index in this volume is a five-year cumulative index of *Historic Documents* covering the years 1996–2000. There is a separate volume, *Historic Documents Index, 1972–1995*, which may also be useful.

The introduction to each document is printed in italic type. The document itself, printed in roman type, follows the spelling, capitalization, and punctuation of the original or official copy. Where the full text is not given, omissions of material are indicated by the customary ellipsis points.

New to this volume, Internet URL addresses noting where the documents have been obtained appear at the end of each introduction. If documents were not available on the Internet, this also has been noted.

---

partisan anger that had arisen during the five-week dispute. While Democrats fumed, Bush prepared to take office in January 2001 as the first president since Rutherford B. Hayes to have come in second in the popular vote.

Bush, who had claimed during his campaign to be a "uniter, not a divider," promised conciliation and a bipartisan approach to governing. It was clear that many of the issues on the national agenda would be resolved only through a spirit of cooperation that had been lacking in Washington during much of the eight years of Democrat Bill Clinton's presidency. The central questions facing Bush would be the health of the economy and the role of the federal government in national affairs. Within days of the Supreme Court decision awarding him the election, Bush and his vice president-elect, Richard B. Cheney, began warning of softness in the economy. The nation was in its ninth year of economic expansion, the longest in history, but Bush said he saw signs of a possible slowdown. Bush said he had a cure for that possible economic illness: the $1.6 trillion, across-the-board tax cut that had been the centerpiece of his campaign. Democrats thought they smelled a rat. Bush, they said, was "talking down" the economy in hopes of pressuring Congress to enact a tax cut that had generated little excitement among voters during the campaign.

One campaign issue that had excited voters, at least older voters, was a call by both Bush and Gore for insurance covering prescription drugs for senior citizens. Numerous studies and anecdotal evidence showed that millions of seniors were unable to pay for the prescription drugs that had become necessary facts of life for the nation's aging population. Drug prices were rising well above the rate of overall inflation, spurring a dramatic increase in the cost of health insurance as well. Medicare, the successful but financially troubled system of health insurance for seniors, did not cover prescription drugs. Responding to the public's demands on the issue, Bush suggested providing prescription drug coverage for seniors through private insurance plans. Gore, by contrast, proposed expanding the existing Medicare program to accommodate prescription drugs.

Hope that scientists would someday be able to cure many of the illnesses and ailments that affected people of every age took a step forward in June with the announcement that two competing teams had nearly completed sequencing the human genome—determining the order and arrangement of the roughly 3 billion bits of DNA contained in every ordinary human cell. Among the "bits" were thousands of genes—no one yet knew exactly how many—that made each individual human being unique. Scientists had long predicted that once they understood how the human genome functioned, they would be able to use that knowledge to revolutionize the diagnosis, prevention, and treatment of disease.

The presidential election contest was the second media circus in Florida in 2000. The first involved a highly unusual custody battle that turned into an international incident. The story began in November 1999, when a five-year-old Cuban boy, Elian Gonzalez, was rescued off the coast of Florida. The boat in which he had fled from Cuba capsized, drowning his mother and several others. The boy quickly became the pawn in a battle between the federal government and Elian's Cuban American relatives in Miami, who had temporary custody of him. The government said Elian should be returned to the custody of his father; the relatives, some of whom had themselves fled communist Cuba, refused to turn him over if it meant his return to Cuba. The government eventually won the battle but only after staging a commando raid to snatch Elian away from his Miami relatives.

On the international front, the year 2000 was remarkable for the unusual number of dramatic political transitions, even in countries with long histories of one-party rule. In fact, both of the world's longest-ruling political parties lost power during the year. Number one in that category was the Institutional Revolutionary Party (known as the PRI) in Mexico, which had controlled the presidency since 1929 and had run the country pretty much as a one-party state until the late 1980s. Vicente Fox, a businessman turned politician representing the center-right National Action Party, won the presidency in the July 2 election and took office December 1. Fox owed his election in large part to electoral reforms pushed through in 1996 by his PRI predecessor, Ernesto Zedillo, who managed to portray the defeat of his own party as a victory for democracy in Mexico.

Fox's victory followed the surprising defeat of the world's second-longest ruling party, the Nationalist Party in Taiwan. Chen Shui-bian, leader of the

Democratic Progressive Party, narrowly won the presidency on March 18 in a three-man race. Chen's victory was all the more remarkable in that he became the first opposition figure elected to the top national office in the 5,000 years of Chinese history. Mainland China had never held truly free elections, and Taiwan was just a few years into its experiment with real democracy after a half century of Nationalist Party domination. Chen's rise to power upset the communist rulers in Beijing for a different reason: he had long advocated independence for Taiwan, which the mainland rulers claimed was part of China. Chen struck a conciliatory posture after he took office on May 20, but there was no reciprocal response from Beijing.

Two other countries underwent dramatic political transformations during the year, both the result of elections that had been rigged by presidents who feared entrusting their futures to unalloyed democracy. Peruvian president Alberto Fujimori nearly got away with his heavy-handed attempt to win a third term in office despite a strong challenge by opposition leader Alejandro Toledo. Fujimori at first tried to maneuver a first-round electoral victory in April. When that attempt failed because of international pressure, Fujimori made it clear that he was determined to win the second round in May at any cost, prompting Toledo to withdraw. But Fujimori had no time to savor his victory. His intelligence chief, Vladimiro Montesinos, was shown on television bribing an opposition legislator, setting off a political furor that ultimately drove Fujimori into exile in Japan, from where he faxed his resignation. An interim president took office in November and pledged honest elections in 2001.

In international terms, an even more important turnover occurred in Yugoslavia, where President Slobodan Milosevic tried just a little too hard to hold onto power. Apparently believing that he was invulnerable politically, Milosevic called presidential elections for September 2000, even though he had a year left in office. The unofficial results showed that he lost to Voislav Kostunica, a lawyer who represented a coalition of opposition parties. But Milosevic refused to concede the election and insisted that a second round was necessary. Demonstrating an unprecedented degree of unity and power, opposition forces mounted nationwide protests, culminating in a massive demonstration in Belgrade on October 5. Discovering that he could no longer rely on the army, which had fought losing wars on his behalf in Bosnia and Kosovo, Milosevic reluctantly stepped aside, and Kostunica took office on October 7 as Yugoslavia's first freely elected president. In December his coalition swept Milosevic's allies from power in the republic of Serbia, the dominant partner in the Yugoslav federation.

The United States and its western European allies immediately offered economic aid to Yugoslavia, hoping that the departure of Milosevic finally would bring peace to the Balkans. Even so, serious challenges remained in the two provinces that Milosevic had set ablaze during the 1990s. In Bosnia, United Nations administrators and NATO peacekeepers were still struggling to keep intact a fragile balance of Croatians, Muslims, and Serbs. The task of peacekeeping was equally difficult in Kosovo, where the Muslim majority was agitating for independence from Serbia. Albanian moderates won provincial elections in Kosovo in October, but at year's end NATO peacekeepers were concerned about attacks by Albanian guerrillas along the southern boundary between Kosovo and Serbia proper. The fear was that the fighting could spread into neighboring Macedonia, another ethnic tinderbox.

Yugoslavia's former close ally, Russia, was still struggling with its own transition from communism to democracy and capitalism. Vladimir Putin, who in mid-1999 had been plucked from obscurity by President Boris Yeltsin to become Russia's prime minister, took over as acting president after Yeltsin's surprise resignation on the last day of 1999. Putin then easily won election in his own right in March, becoming the first person to be elected to succeed an elected president of Russia. Despite his electoral success and his promises to respect the country's fragile democratic process, many of Putin's actions during the year led critics to suggest that he was returning to the authoritarian ways of Russia's past czars and commissars. The Russian economy continued on its downward slide, as did the military, which suffered an excruciatingly painful embarrassment in August when a nuclear submarine, the *Kursk*, sank in the Barents Sea, killing all 118 aboard. As much as any other event in recent years, the loss of the *Kursk* seemed to symbolize Russia's loss of power and prestige since the collapse of the Soviet Union.

A transition of a different sort was under way on the Korean peninsula, where North Korean leader Kim Jong Il appeared to be starting the process of dragging his country out of its shell. Kim held an emotional summit meeting in June with South Korean president Kim Dae-jung, and the two signed a document vaguely pledging Korean unification in the future. In October the North Korean Kim also hosted U.S. secretary of state Madeleine K. Albright for meetings in Pyongyang, but plans for a landmark visit by President Clinton fell through in December.

The one continent where little progress was visible during the year was Africa. The AIDS pandemic continued its deadly march across sub-Saharan Africa, killing tens of thousands of people each year and slicing decades off the expected average life spans in several countries. Thousands more died in the region's bloody wars, most notably the massive conflict in the Democratic Republic of the Congo. Six nations and a host of guerrilla groups and militias were battling for control of Africa's third biggest country, frustrating the diligent peacekeeping efforts by the United Nations.

With the lessons of such wars in mind, more than 150 world leaders gathered at UN headquarters in New York early in September for a "millennium summit." It was the biggest gathering ever of presidents, kings, prime ministers, and other leaders. They held elegant dinner parties and made many pledges, including a series of promises to try to reduce global poverty by 2015.

These are only some of the topics of national and international interest chosen by the editors for *Historic Documents of 2000*. This edition marks the twenty-ninth volume of a Congressional Quarterly project that began with *Historic Documents of 1972*. The purpose of the series is to give students, librarians, journalists, scholars, and others convenient access to documents on a wide range of topics that set forth some of the most important issues of the year. In our judgment, the official statements, news conferences, speeches, special studies, and court decisions presented here will be of lasting interest.

Each document is preceded by an introduction that provides context and background material and, when relevant, an account of continuing developments during the year. We believe these introductions will become increasingly useful as memories of current events fade.

John Felton and Martha Gottron

# CONTENTS

## January

## February

## March

Thomas Young, a former executive at NASA and the Lockheed Martin Corporation, and released March 28, 2000, by NASA.

# April

# May

# June

fessions could not be admitted into evidence against criminal defendants who had not been warned of their rights to remain silent and to have an attorney present during questioning.

# July

# August

# September

# October

# November

# December

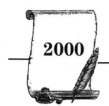

# January

# PRESIDENT'S Y2K COUNCIL ON SUCCESS OF YEAR 2000 CONVERSION
## January 2 and March 29, 2000

*One of the biggest disasters in modern history did not happen at midnight on January 1, 2000. For several years in the late 1990s there had been widespread predictions that millions of computers would crash at the start of the year 2000, popularly known as Y2K, because they could not recognize the rollover from 1999 to 2000. But a concerted worldwide effort by governments, businesses, and millions of private citizens corrected most potential problems before they occurred. Around the world, thousands of minor computer problems were reported early in the year, but there was not a single major failure of any duration.*

*The Y2K problem surfaced because, until the late 1980s, most computers and software programs used only two digits for the year: 1999 was shown as 99. During the early decades of the computer era, annual dates were put in two digits to save computer memory. It was widely assumed that the computers and software programs would be replaced well before the new century. But millions of these computer systems proved more durable than anyone had anticipated, and by the mid-1990s it was widely recognized that when 2000 came around, those systems would recognize the date as 1900 unless they were corrected. As a result, computers would spit out inaccurate data or simply shut down.*

*The federal government and major industries launched massive efforts to update their computer systems, either by rewriting old software programs to recognize dates starting with 2000 or by buying new computers and programs. The Clinton administration in 1998 began a public awareness campaign to encourage state and local governments, small businesses, and individuals to locate and fix problems with their computers. Some computer experts warned that all those efforts to avoid the so-called Y2K bug would not work, and so the world would be faced with weeks or even months of industrial shutdowns. A few economists had even warned that a collapse of computer systems might cause a worldwide recession.*

*John A. Koskinen, the chairman of President Bill Clinton's Council on Year 2000 Conversion, said on January 2 that dealing with the Y2K prob-*

3

*lem had been the "most significant management challenge the world has faced in fifty years," since the end of World War II. Koskinen said the federal government spent $8.5 billion to upgrade its computers so they would keep working in 2000. Estimates for the overall cost of Y2K computer fixes for governments, businesses, and individuals in the United States ranged from $100 billion to more than $300 billion. The estimates varied so widely, in part, because of differences in what were included. Some estimates of Y2K spending included all computer upgrades that were directly or indirectly linked to the year 2000 rollover; other, more conservative, estimates counted only those costs that were directly related to correcting Y2K problems.*

*In addition, there appeared to be no reliable estimates of the total costs incurred by governments and businesses in the rest of the world. Estimates of how much Russia spent on Y2K conversions, for example, varied from a low of $200 million to a high of more than $1 billion.* (Y2K preparations, Historic Documents of 1997, p. 534; Historic Documents of 1998, p. 543; Historic Documents of 1999, p. 760)

## *Problems Were Minor*

*The work to fix computers before January 1, 2000, paid off. As midnight came and went around the world, governments and businesses reported no major problems and a surprisingly limited number of minor computer problems. Among the most significant problems reported in the United States were:*

- *A Defense Department spy satellite system went on the blink after the January 1 rollover because of a failure in the ground-based system that received and processed information from the satellite. Pentagon officials said the problem was fixed within a few hours.*
- *An estimated 4,000 small businesses that had failed to update their credit card processing systems were unable to transact business in the first days of the new year. Koskinen estimated that sales to some 40,000 customers were affected.*
- *A Y2K failure at a Chicago area bank temporarily interrupted electronic Medicare payments to some hospitals and health care providers.*
- *Systems that alerted airports to potential wind-shear problems failed in New York, Chicago, Atlanta, and several other cities but were quickly corrected.*

*Similar problems surfaced on February 29, a date that had to be programmed into many computers because of the convergence of a leap year with the switch from 1999 to 2000. Koskinen's council reported, for example, that several hotel chains were unable to issue electronic room keys because their computers would not recognize the February 29 date. Even Koskinen himself was not exempt from minor Y2K-related problems. He said he received a rental car contract in March that would have charged him an extra $10 a day as an underage driver because the company's computer software showed his birth date as 2039, rather than 1939.*

## *How Big a Problem Was It?*

*In the first days and weeks of the new year, many observers asked two questions about the Y2K problem: Were the warnings about widespread computer failures overblown, and why weren't there more failures in countries, especially developing countries, that had done little to prepare for the year 2000 rollover? Koskinen's answer to the first question was that predictions of widespread calamity were exaggerated. Numerous experts had been warning people to stock up on flashlights and canned goods—and even to buy portable electrical generators—because of expected widespread failures of computer systems that ran electrical power plants and other public utilities. Throughout 1999 Koskinen had discounted such predictions but had urged computer users, both big and small, to make sure their systems would work in 2000.*

*Koskinen and other officials rejected a contention, made by some critics, that much of the money spent on Y2K corrections had been wasted. He told reporters on March 1 that "it was important to do the work, because that's why there were minor glitches. I think it is fairly clear that if more significant work had not been done there would have been more glitches, which would have made them more difficult and more significant ones." In its March 29 report, Koskinen's council said that criticism in hindsight of the spending on Y2K was "a little like saying you could have saved money spent on building safer roads when fewer accidents occur."*

*In its March 29 report, the president's council sought to correct what it said was a misperception that many countries had failed to take the Y2K problem seriously. By mid-1999, the council said, "virtually every country had a Y2K program in place and was devoting a high level of attention to the problem. In many cases, the fact that some countries may have spent the bulk of their funds in a concentrated effort the last six to nine months of 1999 was largely ignored."*

*The council also noted that most of the world's countries were much less dependent on computer technology than were the United States, Canada, Japan, and major European nations. As a result, fixing Y2K problems in many countries was relatively easier than in the United States because their computer systems were less complex and had been installed more recently, after hardware and software manufacturers began taking account of the year 2000 problem. The Gartner Group, an international consulting group that in 1999 had predicted "significant disruptions" around the world, acknowledged in 2000 that it probably had "overstated" the reliance on computer technology in many countries.*

*Following are excerpts from a news conference held January 2, 2000, by John A. Koskinen, chairman of the President's Council on Year 2000 Conversions, and the "Results" and "Conclusions" sections of* The Journey to Y2K: Final Report of the President's Council on Year 2000 Conversion, *issued March 29, 2000, which described various efforts by governments, private businesses,*

5

*and individuals to prevent computer failures resulting from the*
*rollover to the year 2000. These documents were not available on*
*the Internet at the time of publication.*

# Y2K NEWS CONFERENCE

**John A. Koskinen:** Good morning. All right, anybody who has had more than five hours sleep since the last briefing has to leave the room.

We are here to give you the latest update on the world's transition into the year 2000. Since we briefed earlier this morning at 2:00, obviously all the time zones have been covered in the United States. So at this juncture, the entire world has not only gone to the year 2000, but parts of the world are now into January 2.

Since we last briefed, major infrastructure systems in the rest of the United States have made an apparent successful transition to the year 2000. Critical systems in areas such as electric power, telecommunications, transportation and finance continue to function normally at this time with very few reports of difficulties related to the date change.

Around the world, industry information centers and government agencies worldwide. . . .

**John Leonard** (U.S. Postal Service): Excuse me, Mr. Koskinen.

**Koskinen:** This is actually—it looks staged, but this is an actual Fed Ex package mailed to me last night by the Postal Service from Los Angeles. And the question was, would it work and would it process through the systems.

This is John Leonard of the Postal Service. Postal carriers are better dressed these days than they used to be. And so it says for noon delivery, and if you open it—we did pre-stage in fact that we would ask them to mail it to see if it worked. You get stamps—Celebrate the Century in a very—do I get to keep these stamps?

**Leonard:** You sure do.

**Koskinen:** Wow! With a whole range of 1900s, '10s, '20s, '30s, '40s, '50s, '60s and '70s. If you pay more, you get the '80s, '90s and the year 2000.

John, thank you.

**Leonard:** You're welcome. Happy New Year.

**Koskinen:** Thank you.

So, in all seriousness, a package did come, and was mailed to us last night from Los Angeles, again, to test the system. Now the question is, would we have told you if it didn't arrive?

And we'll leave that to others to determine. But it is a good sign, because it does demonstrate that the basic systems in the United States continue to operate.

And as noted earlier, and we'll test again on Monday more of them, systems depend upon each other. Obviously this is a system that depended upon the

Postal Service, depended upon the air traffic system, depended on local transportation systems to operate effectively.

In any event, as noted the information centers and government agencies worldwide are reporting normal operations for critical systems in areas such as power, telecommunications, finance and transportation. . . .

We are now as I say continuing to receive reports from all 50 states, six territories, the 10 FEMA [Federal Emergency Management Agency] regions, and the 11 industrial national information centers who are operating. We are beginning to talk with the states today about the ongoing operation of their emergency centers and their reporting process because again, they are finding no significant problems. Most states are reporting to us through their emergency centers and so we will discussing with them today the level of their ongoing reporting as we move through the next several days.

Looking at a few specific areas, the Internet as you know has been an issue that everyone has focused on. Operations there continue to be normal. There are issues that may arise because a number of organizations, as we discussed, turned off their systems to avoid security or potential Y2K problems.

And some of those systems may experience delays as they are restarted, so it won't be a Y2K issue or a virus issue, it's just that mail systems cue up messages that have been destined for systems taken off line, so when you bring the system back on line, not only do you have mail, you may have a lot of mail and it may actually slow down the processing as you go.

And, in fact, in some cases, as the Internet society and others warned, if you haven't taken a major system down for some time and you shut it down, you may have the usual glitch problems of starting it up. Although as we have gotten reports thus far from federal operations, OPM [Office of Personnel Management], as you know, took its Internet-based system off line for a matter of hours over the rollover period and as of 7:00 o'clock this morning, they report that the web site is fully operational and ready for use by the public. So they were able to take it down and bring it back up without difficulty.

But I would note the difference between the web site and an Internet operation is that the web site will not necessarily cue the mail. If it's down, you don't get access to it. Whereas, if you are an Internet address and somebody sends you mail and you're not there, it just cues up and goes forward. But in any event, that process has worked for OPM without difficulty.

In the energy sector, electricity, oil and gas industries all report continued, successful transitions through the Y2K rollover. While we have focused our conversations with you about developing countries and monitoring those services in the critical infrastructure for gradual degradation over time, we also are monitoring for the same situation here, although we have no concerns of any significance about that because of the quality and the depth of the work that's been done. But it's not a division that it's only somebody else's systems that could have that problem.

So we are continually monitoring that but, again, the way degradation of service will occur in some developing countries if it does is because they will lose control of their ability to monitor and manage those systems.

Our national industry centers here are monitoring exactly that set of potential glitches and are finding none thus far. So we think that it is extremely unlikely that we will experience any of those difficulties over the next few days, but we will continue to monitor that.

The Nuclear Regulatory Commission has reported that five licensees reported very minor Y2K-related problems with computer systems used for support functions, not operations of any plants, including things like physical plant, access control, the monitoring of operating data and calculating meteorological data, none of those glitches affected anything to do with operations of the—or safe operations.

And most were corrected almost immediately after discovery. But again, they're the kind of monitoring or processing glitches that may occur across systems generally. And as we talked in earlier briefings, in a lot of companies you may never know about that. Again, with the Nuclear Regulatory Commission, no matter how small the glitch, there's an obligation on the part of the operators to report those. So we'll have more minor reporting issues probably coming along than most companies would report.

In the transportation section, the system is functioning normally. The U.S. and European air traffic control systems rolled over successfully. There are no reports of difficulties there.

The FAA [Federal Aviation Administration]—in the last 24 hours or so has had about a dozen equipment problems reported. But as they note, that's about half the daily average. In other words, they have—the system is operating more robustly during this rollover period than on a normal day. In all but one instance, the problems were corrected very quickly, ranging from a matter of minutes to one or two hours. They—FAA is investigating each of these to determine whether any of them are Y2K related. Again, because of the low number of them and the fact that they're fewer than they normally have. They suspect most of them are not, but they are pursuing that in any event.

In one situation that they are pursuing, it may be a Y2K-related one, again, not affecting air traffic safety. The system that distributes certain notices to airmen has experienced electronic problems. It's the one system that didn't immediately get restored. They expect to have a patch for that system corrected today. In the meantime, the information is readily available through other computer paths for pilots. It's a way of providing standard notifications to pilots. So, the one system is being corrected, but the information continues to flow to the pilots.

So again, because of the sensitive nature of the FAA and its operations, we will have more information about very minor and modest glitches there than we might have in an industrial or commercial operation that doesn't have the same reporting requirements.

There was a minor Y2K problem discovered at Amtrak's control center. The system would not retain train symbols—which are basically the train numbers—as the train progressed through the system. But those symbols were inserted manually and the date was reset and the system is now functioning as expected.

And the San Francisco regional office reported that the Bay Area Rapid Transit system, the BART system, experienced a failure of two maintenance-related computers used for time clocks at their facility, nothing to do with the operation of the trains.

There was no impact on the operations and it was not a Y2K failure, and it has been fixed. As you can tell, we are trying to tell you everything we know about glitches. And in fact, what we think we will do for the 3:00 briefing to sort of keep your interest is collect for you all of the incidents that we have been tracking—Y2K related or not, unfounded rumor or not, if they've been reported—and give you in effect a status report of all of those incidences.

And obviously, as federal agencies are testing systems today and others are, we may have other reported minor issues. If there is any significant one, we obviously will report that. But it occurred to us as we are tracking down all of these things that it would probably be helpful to put them all together in one place for you. And you can take a look at what will be, not a very large list, but it will be everything that we have been able to confirm has been a glitch in operations. And we'll identify those that we know were definitely not Y2K, those that were Y2K and those that are still under investigation. . . .

But as you can tell by this report, the problems as we warned—or predicted in advance are out there on a daily basis glitches. We are talking about a very now small handful in ongoing operations of the basic infrastructure of the United States.

So we continue to be very pleased with the success we're having in making this transition. But we also continue to note that we're going to continue to monitor this for the next two or three days. And we would encourage everyone else to do that before we sign off on this problem. . . .

On the international level, with the rollover now of all of Latin America and Canada, as I noted, not only is the entire world in the year 2000, but that means that 100 percent of the world's oil and natural gas production has successfully reached the year 2000, and we have had no reports of any difficulty in any of those operations.

At 8:00 this morning, we received reports from a total of 164 of our overseas posts. The weather-vane reports an hour after rollover. Now many of them are now reporting on the 12 hours after rollover, and they have found no reports of any significant Y2K operations in any of those 164 reports. . . .

# COUNCIL'S FINAL REPORT

## IV. Results

The United States and the rest of the world made a successful transition into the Year 2000. This did not happen by accident. The positive outcome was the result of a tremendous, world-wide mobilization of people and resources to meet the common challenge presented by the date change.

Domestically, key infrastructure sectors such as electric power, telecommunications, finance, and transportation put forth an extraordinary effort to prepare systems for the Year 2000. Toward the end of 1999, system operators in these areas stated they were basically done with their Y2K work. The Council reported this information in its final quarterly assessment and, as expected, there were no major infrastructure failures—nationally or regionally—in the United States. For the most part, the lights stayed on, the phones and ATMs worked, and rail, transit and air transport systems functioned normally. Scattered Y2K glitches that did arise were relatively isolated and did not have a cumulating or cascading effect on other systems.

Government was ready for the Year 2000 as well. Thanks to the hard work of thousands of dedicated public servants, the Federal Government made dramatic strides toward Y2K readiness in the two years leading up to the transition. As noted, the consensus when the Council began its work in early 1998 was that it would be impossible for the Federal Government to be ready for the date change. But two weeks before the New Year, to the surprise, or consternation, of some, 99.9 percent of the Government's more than 6,000 mission-critical systems were Y2K ready. Agencies also had been conducting thorough end-to-end tests with States and other partners for key programs that have a significant impact on the public, including unemployment insurance, Medicaid, and Food Stamps. While there were a few Y2K-related problems in government systems, they did not have an impact on the major services and benefits provided to the American people.

It is worth noting that, in both government and the private sector, organizations understood the value of contingency plans to make sure that Y2K-related failures, if they did occur, would not force work to grind to a halt. Businesses and governments formulated or updated contingency plans and strategies to allow for the continuation of important functions in the event of Y2K problems. Equally important, most organizations spent the last weeks of 1999 training employees in the implementation of their contingency plans. Thus, when glitches did surface, most organizations were able to rely upon back-up processes as they worked to restore normal operations. Since most problems were fixed very quickly, customers and constituents were not seriously inconvenienced and, in most cases, were unaware of the difficulties.

Internationally, after a slow start by many countries, most made a concerted effort to ensure that critical systems would be ready for the date change. Many of the 120 countries attending the first UN meeting on Y2K in December 1998 weren't exactly sure why they were there. At the second meeting, in June 1999, none of the more than 170 countries in attendance believed Y2K was not a critical problem. By that time, most countries had participated in at least two meetings within their respective regions to share Y2K information in critical areas such as power, telecommunications and transportation. As a general matter, major infrastructure systems abroad, including those in less-developed countries, did not experience Y2K-related disruptions during the rollover. Financial markets around the world, which were closely monitored, conducted normal operations in business days after January 1. There were also no reports of Y2K-related problems that affected trade between the United States and its major economic partners.

## Retrospective on the Magnitude of the Problem

There is general agreement that the Year 2000 rollover went more smoothly than expected. The incredible success of the transition has prompted a number of questions about the effort and the results it produced.

### Was Y2K an insignificant, over-hyped problem?

In the weeks since the rollover, some have expressed doubt about the magnitude of the Y2K problem and whether or not the significant investment of time and money to avoid disruptions was necessary. However, it has been difficult to find executives who worked on Y2K in a major bank, financial institution, telephone company, electric power company or airline who believe that they did not confront—and avoid—a major risk of systemic failure.

One indication of the difficulty of the Y2K problem is the fact that many large, sophisticated users of information technology revealed in regular filings with the Securities and Exchange Commission that they had been required to increase the funds allocated to their Y2K programs. These increases, which in some cases were in the hundreds of millions of dollars, were not for public relations purposes. Rather, they reflected the difficult effort of remediating large, complicated and often antiquated IT [information technology] systems.

The Federal Government experienced a similar phenomenon. Cumulative agency estimates for the costs to solve the Y2K problem increased over four years from under $3 billion to the $8.5 billion that was actually spent. This was still significantly less than the $20 to $30 billion estimated by outsiders. But here too, the job of ensuring Y2K compliance proved to be more challenging than initially expected.

The range of actual failures during the January 1 and February 29 (Leap Day) rollovers served as a reminder of the major economic and operating disruptions that had been avoided by the development of Y2K compliant IT systems:

- A classified Defense Department intelligence satellite system was totally inoperable for several hours during the rollover period. The problem originated not in the satellite itself but in the ground-based switching and software equipment used to download and process information from the satellite.
- Bank credit card companies identified a Y2K-glitch involving some credit card transactions. Merchants that did not make use of free upgrades provided during 1999 for a particular software package charged customers for orders every day after a single purchase was made. The problem affected primarily smaller retailers since most major retailers use their own customized software.
- A Y2K computer glitch at a Chicago-area bank temporarily interrupted electronic Medicare payments to some hospitals and other health care providers. As a work- around, Medicare contractors—private insurance companies that process and pay Medicare claims—were forced to send diskettes containing processed claims to the bank by courier or Federal Express so that the payments could be made in a timely manner.

- Florida and Kentucky unemployment insurance benefit systems encountered a Y2K glitch in an automated telephone call processing system. The Y2K glitch in customized code prevented some claimants from claiming earned income for the week ending 01/01/2000. Claimants reporting the problem had to be given an alternative means for filing their claims pursuant to State contingency plans.
- Low-level Windshear Alert Systems (LLWAS) failed at New York, Tampa, Denver, Atlanta, Orlando, Chicago O'Hare and St. Louis airports during the date rollover. The systems displayed an error message. Air transportation system specialists at each site were forced to reboot LLWAS computers to clear the error. Fortunately, the weather was mild across the United States.
- Seven nuclear power plant licensees reported problems with plant computer systems used for supporting physical plant access control, monitoring operating data, and calculating meteorological data. The affected systems did not have an impact on the safety of operations at the plants.
- During the Leap Day rollover, several hotels reportedly were unable to issue room keys to guests because of a failure in hotel key-producing software.
- The Council Chair [John A. Koskinen], traveling in March, received a car rental contract that included a $10 daily charge as an underage driver since the software indicated he was born in 2039.

These and other glitches would have been more serious had they occurred in an environment in which a wide range of other Y2K problems had also surfaced. If there had been a flurry of other difficulties, some glitches would have gone undetected for a longer period of time. Glitches also could have had a multiplier effect by creating problems through interfaces to other systems or could have resulted in a gradual degradation of service. As it happened, organizations were able to focus all of their attention on the relatively few problems that did occur, which resulted in much faster restoration of normal operations.

Some of the failed expectations about more serious Y2K problems can be traced to the skepticism and disbelief with which some people greeted company and government progress reports on Y2K, believing that these institutions were inevitably covering up the possibilities of major Y2K failures. However, as the Council noted on numerous occasions, individuals in positions of responsibility who were claiming success in their Y2K efforts would be easily found after January 1, and held accountable, if subsequent system failures proved that they had misrepresented the facts. But many people continued to assume the worst would materialize even as much of the self-reporting pointed to a fairly orderly transition into the new millennium.

### Why weren't there more Y2K-related problems abroad, especially in less-developed nations?

Some of those who have discounted, after the fact, the significance of the Y2K threat point to the relative lack of major disruptions abroad as evidence of how exaggerated the problem was. How did countries that appeared to have spent so little, and were thought to be relatively unprepared, emerge unscathed?

A number of factors created the mismatch between perception about the Y2K readiness of foreign countries and the actual outcome. Chief among them was the difficulty in obtaining accurate status reports internationally on a fast moving issue such as Y2K. Information three months old was out of date, and much of the international information reported was second hand and anecdotal. But, in many cases, this was the best information available until countries began to report more publicly on their Y2K work. Without more current, detailed reports, people often relied on such older information and were then surprised when it was overtaken by subsequent progress. A report about risks from April or June 1999 was assumed to still be operative in December.

A related problem was the stereotype of countries doing nothing to prepare for Y2K. While this was probably true for three-quarters of the countries in the world in early 1998, by mid-1999 virtually every country had a Y2K program in place and was devoting a high level of attention to the problem. In many cases, the fact that some countries may have spent the bulk of their funds in a concentrated effort the last six to nine months of 1999 was largely ignored. For some commentators, therefore, it has been easier to suggest that the problem was overstated rather than to consider the possibility that perceptions before the rollover were inaccurate.

Additionally, outside of the world's largest users of information technology B countries like the United States, Canada, Japan, and the United Kingdom— the reliance upon IT drops off quickly. In many of these less IT-dependent countries, other factors also made for an easier transition into the Year 2000. Fixes in these countries were frequently more straightforward than in the United States since the technology being used was more likely to be "off the shelf," and not customized. Also, unlike the United States, countries such as Spain and Italy that had moved into IT more recently were not saddled with old legacy systems that were built with antiquated, customized code by people who had long since retired. Countries starting later also had the benefit of lessons learned by those who had been working on Y2K for several years. The sharing of technical information about problems, products, fixes and testing techniques that was encouraged by international organizations and the Council paid enormous dividends. Elevators provide a good example. In 1998, everyone was testing to see if elevator-specific systems had a Y2K problem. Once it became clear that they did not, no one else had to spend time and money pursuing the issue. Similar experiences took place in industries such as banking, finance, telecommunications, air traffic and electric power where information was being exchanged and shared globally in a way never seen before. And in many industries, large multi-national companies actually worked directly with their local counterparts and host countries to fix basic systems.

Finally, technology itself helped countries that had gotten a late start on Y2K. One the reasons those that started late spent less on their Year 2000 efforts was that the technology to fix the problem improved dramatically. By 1999, automated tools could fix millions of lines of code quickly and at a dramatically lower cost than was possible just two years earlier. This technology helped late-starting countries to fix the problem quickly—and more cheaply.

## Why weren't there more problems among small businesses?

Small business was another area about which many, including the Council, had expressed concerns. While there were relatively few reports of Y2K-related failures among small businesses, for firms large and small, there is a natural inclination not to report problems that are fixed in very short time frames. This phenomenon was revealed before the rollover when surveys showed that over 70 percent of companies reported they had experienced Y2K glitches, even though the public was unaware of virtually all of them. Some said the number of failures indicated the pervasive nature of the Y2K problem. The Council believed that the experience of companies with Y2K failures before January 1, 2000 also demonstrated that most Y2K problems could be fixed without people being inconvenienced or even knowing that anything had happened.

The lack of information about how small businesses were doing was an ongoing challenge for the Council and others following Y2K. The sheer number of these companies—over 23 million—and the absence of regular reporting relationships that made it difficult to gather information on the progress of small businesses prior to January 1, also made it difficult to determine how many actually experienced Y2K difficulties after the date change.

## What happened to fears of overreaction by the public?

While a very small, but visible, minority engaged in excessive stockpiling of goods in advance of the New Year, most Americans took Y2K in stride. Anxiety about the date change, which seemed to peak in 1998, declined throughout 1999 as more and more information became available about organizations that were completing their Y2K work. By the end of the year, there was very little evidence of overreaction among the general public to the potential consequences of Y2K. The availability of information—both positive and negative—about Y2K efforts played a major role in reversing the trend toward overreaction. The Council's position was that people are more inclined to panic when they lack information, which can lead to a general feeling that the system is out of control. But, given the facts, whatever they are, people have great common sense and will respond appropriately. Even when the information about industry and government Y2K efforts revealed that there was still substantial work left to do, people were not alarmed. Instead, they seemed reassured in the knowledge that organizations were treating the problem seriously, were working together to solve it, and would keep the public informed about their progress. Americans knew Y2K was an important problem, but they also knew that organizations were spending large amounts of time and money to minimize any difficulties that could have been created by the date change.

## Was the money well spent?

In hindsight, it is always easy to see what was not a problem and say that less money could have been spent. It's a little like saying you could have saved money spent on building safer roads when fewer accidents occur. But part of the reason for the smooth transition, in the face of thoughtful analyses noting that IT projects generally finish late and over budget with remediation work creating errors as well as removing them, was that people did test, retest, and then test their systems once again. Never before had so much independent verification and validation been done for IT work—and it showed in the positive results and the on-time performance.

Ultimately each organization had to make its own judgement about the potential implications of failures and the appropriate cost necessary to minimize such problems. Any organization that cut back on its work to save money and subsequently experienced serious system failures would have been pilloried as badly managed and foolish. . . .

# V. Conclusion

The Year 2000 problem was an extraordinary challenge for businesses and governments around the world that is not likely to be duplicated. The success that resulted from efforts to prepare systems for the date change is a tribute to the skill, dedication, and hard work of the countless professionals who made Y2K their cause. The story of Y2K is one of diverse organizations—industry associations, companies, and government agencies that often had opposing agendas and interests—coming together to recognize the power of information sharing and collaboration to achieve a commonly held goal. In its two years of operation, the President's Council on Year 2000 Conversion worked to serve as a catalyst and facilitator for this activity, which helped the United States make a smooth transition to the new millennium.

# STATE OF THE UNION ADDRESS AND REPUBLICAN RESPONSE

## January 27, 2000

*A year after he escaped forced removal from office, and just one year be-
fore he was to leave office at the end of eight years, President Bill Clinton delivered his last State of the Union address to Congress on January 27, 2000.
Clinton said the state of the union had never been better, and he recited a
long list of statistics on the economy, health, and welfare to prove his point.*

*Clinton's address to a generally enthusiastic Congress lacked the drama
of his appearance in 1999, when the Senate was preparing to hear impeachment charges that had been lodged against him by the House of Representatives. The Senate acquitted Clinton of all the charges of perjury and
obstruction of justice that arose from his illicit affair with White House
intern Monica Lewinsky.* (Grand jury testimony, Historic Documents of 1998,
p. 564; 1999 State of the Union speech, Historic Documents of 1999, p. 41; Clinton acquittal, Historic Documents of 1999, p. 15)

*With impeachment behind him, Clinton's priorities in 2000 clearly were
to burnish his legacy and to improve the electoral chances for his chosen
successor, Vice President Al Gore, and for Democrats seeking to grasp control of Congress from the Republicans. Clinton offered dozens of legislative
proposals for tax cuts and new government programs—all targeted to specific sectors of the public that were important to the Democrat's hopes in November.* (Elections, pp. 895, 1025)

*Clinton had told reporters two days earlier that he believed some of his
high-priority proposals had a "better than 50-50 chance" of approval by
Congress. As it turned out, the president's legendary political skills did not
win him anywhere near that level of legislative success. The Republican
leaders in Congress—especially in the Senate—were in no mood, during an
election year, to hand Clinton victories that would make him look better in
the history books. Nor were they interested in promoting the fortunes of
Gore or of Democratic congressional candidates. Congressional Democrats,
for their part, refused to cooperate with Republican efforts on many of the
issues Clinton had raised. Ultimately, Congress became so bogged down in
political posturing before the election that it was unable to finish even its*

*necessary business and was forced to return for two lame-duck sessions: a brief meeting right after the election and a final one in December.*

## *Clinton's Major Proposals*

*At ninety minutes, it was Clinton's longest State of the Union speech. In fact, it was the longest one ever, breaking Clinton's own record of eighty-one minutes, set in 1995, when he was at the low point of his presidency following the Republican takeover of Congress. Democrats, at least, liked what they heard; they broke into Clinton's speech with applause about one hundred times—better than once a minute. Naturally, Republicans were much less enthusiastic, except when the president touched on one of their favorite themes, such as reducing the "marriage penalty" in the income tax code.*

*Clinton wasted no time in getting to the supposed purpose of the annual presidential speech to Congress: outlining how the republic was faring at home and abroad. "We are fortunate to be alive at this moment in history," he said to applause. "Never before has our nation enjoyed, at once, so much prosperity and social progress with so little internal crisis and so few external threats."*

*From that lofty point, the president went on to detail the specifics of low unemployment, low inflation, government surpluses, and the longest sustained period of economic growth in the nation's history. "My fellow Americans," he said, "the state of our union is the strongest it has ever been."*

*A State of the Union address is by its nature a political speech, and Clinton used his last one to make a political point by drawing a sharp contrast between the nation's posture in 2000 and that of eight years earlier. In 1992, Clinton recalled, "our nation was gripped by economic distress, social decline, political gridlock." Clinton mentioned no names, but he did not need to remind his audience that the president in 1992 was a Republican named George Bush whose son, George W. Bush, was the leading candidate for the Republican presidential nomination in 2000.*

*In the details of his speech, Clinton offered several dozen specific proposals, nearly all of them for incremental changes. There were no sweeping calls for grand ideas, such as ending poverty or bringing peace to the world. Instead, Clinton acknowledged that "great goals are reached step by step, building on our progress, always gaining ground."*

*Perhaps as significant as anything Clinton said was what he did not say. He dropped what had been the political centerpiece of his previous two State of the Union addresses—a demand that Congress "save Social Security first" when it considered what to do with budget surpluses. In part, this was because Clinton was himself proposing to dip into the expected surpluses to finance his proposals. The president's shift of rhetorical emphasis also reflected the fact that projections of the budget surpluses were increasingly upbeat, giving him more elbow room for spending proposals. As of January, the administration was projecting cumulative surpluses by 2010 of $4.2 trillion.*

*Most of the single-step gains that Clinton proposed involved politically popular ideas that Democrats saw as working to their advantage in the elec-*

*tion year, in part because the proposals had been resisted by many Republicans. Among the most important proposals were: allowing patients to sue their health insurance companies when they were unfairly denied coverage; creating a new prescription drug benefit under Medicare for senior citizens; increasing the minimum hourly wage, currently $5.25, by $1; and boosting federal spending on education. Clinton also endorsed several proposals that Gore had advanced in his campaign, including federal funding for pay raises for public school teachers, and requiring prospective buyers of hand guns to have licenses issued by the states.*

*In addition to spending proposals, Clinton suggested tax breaks—although few were of the variety most favored by Republican leaders. He suggested expanding the earned income tax credit for low-wage earners by $21 billion over ten years and new spending and tax incentives for health programs costing an estimated $110 billion over ten years, including one to encourage health insurance for children. Clinton also proposed an estimated $30 billion in subsidies and tax breaks for college tuition.*

*Clinton embraced one of the Republicans' favorite themes: the unfairness of the so-called marriage penalty, the additional income tax that most couples paid once they were married. Republicans had long demanded eliminating the penalty. Clinton suggested a more limited step of increasing the standard deduction for those who did not itemize their returns, a proposal that would benefit primarily low-income couples. In another bow to Republicans, Clinton endorsed what was called a "new markets initiative," which involved tax credits and other incentives for business investment in low-income rural and urban communities. That plan had been a leading priority for House Speaker Dennis Hastert, an Illinois Republican.*

*Of those proposals, only the new markets initiative made it through Congress intact during 2000. Some items were approved by one of the chambers, or even by both—but in most cases the results were unsatisfactory to one or more parties and never became law. Republican leaders refused to negotiate with their Democratic counterparts or the White House on tax issues, and so Clinton vetoed Republican-sponsored bills to eliminate the marriage penalty and the estate tax. The House also passed a bill (HR 2614) raising the minimum wage by $1 over two years, but refused to negotiate with the White House on a variety of tax cuts also in the bill—and so neither item was enacted. Both houses passed legislation offering patients additional rights to health insurance coverage, but a conference committee failed to resolve differences on the matter.*

*If any single event signified the level of partisan rancor in Washington just prior to the election it was the failure of a bipartisan agreement reached in the early morning hours of October 30 on an appropriations bill covering the departments of labor, education, and health and human services. Leaders of the House and Senate Appropriations committees negotiated a compromise on a Republican demand to delay federal regulations that were intended to reduce repetitive-motion injuries in the workplace. Top Republican leaders later disowned the compromise, and Clinton, in anger, vetoed an unrelated bill containing appropriations for the legislative branch. With the election just days away, Republicans and Democrats accused each other of negotiating in bad faith.*

*Congress finally finished its business in a lame duck session during the first two weeks of December. An omnibus spending bill, cleared on December 15 (PL 106–554) covered the last three appropriations bills that had not been enacted, including those for the legislative branch and for the labor, education, and health and human services departments.*

*Except in times of international crisis, State of the Union addresses rarely focused on foreign policy, and so Clinton spent little time on overseas affairs. He did emphasize one issue that involved domestic politics as much as foreign affairs: a trade agreement between the United States and China then pending in Congress. Signed in 1999, the agreement established normal trade relations between the two countries for the first time and was necessary for China's admission into the World Trade Organization. Major business interests supported the agreement, but labor unions, many human rights advocates, and leading congressional conservatives staunchly opposed it. Clinton ultimately prevailed on the issue, with the House approving the agreement in May and the Senate following suit in September.* (China trade, p. 213)

*Normally one of the most self-assured speakers on the American political scene, Clinton blew one line in his address, not once but twice. In one of several laudatory references to Gore, Clinton said the vice president had "launched a new effort to make communities more liberal"—then he immediately corrected himself to say "livable." With members of Congress laughing and applauding, Clinton came back to say, "That's this year's agenda; last year was livable, right?" Moments later, he repeated his mistake, saying he was asking Congress "to make American communities more liberal—livable." To more laughter and applause, he said: "I've done pretty well with this speech, but I can't say that."*

## Republican Responses

*Republicans—who for years had been united on little other than their intense dislike of Clinton—managed to offer a unified response to the president's last State of the Union address. Without exception, Republican leaders denounced Clinton's spending programs as excessive and his proposed tax cuts as inadequate. Texas governor Bush lead that charge in a statement: "The litany of spending programs the president announced tonight proves my point that if you leave a large surplus in Washington, the money will be spent on bigger government." Furthermore, Bush said, "the president's tax cut is too small, and it will not help the economy grow or make the tax code more fair."*

*The Republican Party's official, nationally televised responses to Clinton on January 27 came from Senators Susan Collins of Maine and Bill Frist of Tennessee. Both in their forties, Collins and Frist represented a new generation of moderate Republican leaders who chose to focus on issues that had long been dominated by Democrats. Collins specialized in education and Frist, a medical doctor, in health care.*

*In her address, Collins generally ignored Clinton's State of the Union speech and instead focused on a Republican "four-point plan for educational excellence." The points centered on boosting federal funding for education but allowing state and local authorities to decide how the money should be spent. "Republicans want what all parents want for their children's schools: more federal help but less federal interference," she said.*

*Frist took a more aggressively partisan approach, denouncing the president's health care plan as "just as bad" as his ill-fated 1993 proposal for universal health care insurance—a plan Frist likened to "socialized medicine" in Great Britain and Canada. Clinton's latest plan "makes government even bigger and more bloated because each new program we heard about—and there were about eleven of them in health care alone—comes with its own massive bureaucracy," he said. Even so, Frist said Republicans would offer legislation on two issues Clinton had championed: giving patients a "bill of rights" enabling them, under certain circumstances, to sue their health insurance companies if denied coverage, and improving insurance coverage to senior citizens for prescription drugs.*

*Following are texts of President Bill Clinton's State of the Union address, delivered to a joint session of Congress on January 27, 2000, and the Republican response by Senators Susan Collins of Maine and Bill Frist of Tennessee. The documents were obtained from the Internet at http://www.pub.whitehouse.gov/uri-res/ I2R?pdi://oma.eop.gov.us/2000/01/27/15.text.1.*

# STATE OF THE UNION ADDRESS

Mr. Speaker [Dennis Hastert], Mr. Vice President [Al Gore], members of Congress, honored guests, my fellow Americans:

We are fortunate to be alive at this moment in history. Never before has our nation enjoyed, at once, so much prosperity and social progress with so little internal crisis and so few external threats. Never before have we had such a blessed opportunity—and, therefore, such a profound obligation—to build the more perfect union of our founders' dreams

We begin the new century with over 20 million new jobs; the fastest economic growth in more than 30 years; the lowest unemployment rates in 30 years; the lowest poverty rates in 20 years; the lowest African American and Hispanic unemployment rates on record; the first back-to-back budget surpluses in 42 years. And next month, America will achieve the longest period of economic growth in our entire history.

We have built a new economy.

And our economic revolution has been matched by a revival of the American spirit: crime down by 20 percent, to its lowest level in 25 years; teen births down seven years in a row; adoptions up by 30 percent; welfare rolls cut in half to their lowest levels in 30 years.

My fellow Americans, the state of our union is the strongest it has ever been. As always, the real credit belongs to the American people. My gratitude also goes to those of you in this chamber who have worked with us to put progress over partisanship.

Eight years ago, it was not so clear to most Americans there would be much to celebrate in the year 2000. Then our nation was gripped by economic distress, social decline, political gridlock. The title of a best-selling book asked: "America: What Went Wrong?"

In the best traditions of our nation, Americans determined to set things right. We restored the vital center, replacing outmoded ideologies with a new vision anchored in basic, enduring values: opportunity for all, responsibility from all, a community of all Americans. We reinvented government, transforming it into a catalyst for new ideas that stress both opportunity and responsibility, and give our people the tools they need to solve their own problems. With the smallest federal work force in 40 years, we turned record deficits into record surpluses, and doubled our investment in education. We cut crime, with 100,000 community police and the Brady law, which has kept guns out of the hands of half a million criminals.

We ended welfare as we knew it—requiring work while protecting health care and nutrition for children, and investing more in child care, transportation, and housing to help their parents go to work. We've helped parents to succeed at home and at work, with family leave, which 20 millions Americans have now used to care for a newborn child or a sick loved one. We've engaged 150,000 young Americans in citizen service through AmeriCorps, while helping them earn money for college.

In 1992, we just had a road map; today, we have results.

But even more important, America again has the confidence to dream big dreams. But we must not let this confidence drift into complacency. For we, all of us, will be judged by the dreams and deeds we pass on to our children. And on that score, we will be held to a high standard, indeed, because our chance to do good is so great.

My fellow Americans, we have crossed the bridge we built to the 21st century. Now, we must shape a 21st century American revolution—of opportunity, responsibility and community. We must be now, as we were in the beginning, a new nation.

At the dawn of the last century, Theodore Roosevelt said, "the one characteristic more essential than any other is foresight . . . it should be the growing nation with a future that takes the long look ahead." So, tonight, let us take our long look ahead—and set great goals for our nation.

To 21st century America, let us pledge these things: Every child will begin school ready to learn and graduate ready to succeed. Every family will be able to succeed at home and at work, and no child will be raised in poverty. We will meet the challenge of the aging of America. We will assure quality, affordable health care, at last, for all Americans.

We will make America the safest big country on Earth. We will pay off our national debt for the first time since 1835. We will bring prosperity to every American community. We will reverse the course of climate change and leave a safer, cleaner planet. America will lead the world toward shared peace and prosperity, and the far frontiers of science and technology. And we will become at last what our founders pledged us to be so long ago—one nation, under God, indivisible, with liberty and justice for all.

These are great goals, worthy of a great nation. We will not reach them all this year. Not even in this decade. But we will reach them. Let us remember that the first American Revolution was not won with a single shot; the continent was not settled in a single year. The lesson of our history—and the lesson of the last seven years—is that great goals are reached step by step, always building on our progress, always gaining ground.

Of course, you can't gain ground if you're standing still. And for too long this Congress has been standing still on some of our most pressing national priorities. So let's begin tonight with them.

Again, I ask you to pass a real patients' bill of rights. I ask you to pass common-sense gun safety legislation. I ask you to pass campaign finance reform. I ask you to vote up or down on judicial nominations and other important appointees. And, again I ask you—I implore you—to raise the minimum wage.

Now, two years ago—let me try to balance the seesaw here two years ago, as we reached across party lines to reach our first balanced budget, I asked that we meet our responsibility to the next generation by maintaining our fiscal discipline. Because we refused to stray from that path, we are doing something that would have seemed unimaginable seven years ago. We are actually paying down the national debt.

Now, if we stay on this path, we can pay down the debt entirely in 13 just years now and make America debt-free for the first time since Andrew Jackson was President in 1835.

In 1993, we began to put our fiscal house in order with the Deficit Reduction Act, which you'll all remember won passages in both Houses by just a single vote. Your former colleague, my first Secretary of the Treasury, led that effort and sparked our long boom. He's here with us tonight. Lloyd Bentsen, you have served America well, and we thank you.

Beyond paying off the debt, we must ensure that the benefits of debt reduction go to preserving two of the most important guarantees we make to every American—Social Security and Medicare. Tonight, I ask you to work with me to make a bipartisan down payment on Social Security reform by crediting the interest savings from debt reduction to the Social Security Trust Fund so that it will be strong and sound for the next 50 years. But this is just the start of our journey. We must also take the right steps toward reaching our great goals. First and foremost, we need a 21st century revolution in education, guided by our faith that every single child can learn. Because education is more important than ever, more than ever the key to our children's future, we must make sure all our children have that key. That means quality preschool and after-school, the best trained teachers in the classroom, and college opportunities for all our children.

For seven years now, we've worked hard to improve our schools, with opportunity and responsibility—investing more, but demanding more in turn. Reading, math, college entrance scores are up. Some of the most impressive gains are in schools in very poor neighborhoods.

But all successful schools have followed the same proven formula: higher standards, more accountability, and extra help so children who need it can get it to reach those standards. I have sent Congress a reform plan based on that formula. It holds states and school districts accountable for progress, and rewards them for results. Each year, our national government invests more than $15 billion in our schools. It is time to support what works and stop supporting what doesn't.

Now, as we demand more from our schools, we should also invest more in our schools. Let's double our investment to help states and districts turn around their worst-performing schools, or shut them down. Let's double our investments in after-school and summer school programs, which boost achievement and keep people off the streets and out of trouble. If we do this, we can give every single child in every failing school in America—everyone— the chance to meet high standards.

Since 1993, we've nearly doubled our investment in Head Start and improved its quality. Tonight, I ask you for another $1 billion for Head Start, the largest increase in the history of the program.

We know that children learn best in smaller classes with good teachers. For two years in a row, Congress has supported my plan to hire 100,000 new qualified teachers to lower class size in the early grades. I thank you for that, and I ask you to make it three in a row.

And to make sure all teachers know the subjects they teach, tonight I propose a new teacher quality initiative—to recruit more talented people into the classroom, reward good teachers for staying there, and give all teachers the training they need.

We know charter schools provide real public school choice. When I became President, there was just one independent public charter school in all America. Today, thanks to you, there are 1,700. I ask you now to help us meet our goal of 3,000 charter schools by next year.

We know we must connect all our classrooms to the Internet, and we're getting there. In 1994, only 3 percent of our classrooms were connected. Today, with the help of the Vice President's E-rate program, more than half of them are. And 90 percent of our schools have at least one Internet connection.

But we cannot finish the job when a third of all our schools are in serious disrepair. Many of them have walls and wires so old, they're too old for the Internet. So tonight, I propose to help 5,000 schools a year make immediate and urgent repairs; and again, to help build or modernize 6,000 more, to get students out of trailers and into high-tech classrooms. I ask all of you to help me double our bipartisan Gear-Up program, which provides mentors for disadvantaged young people. If we double it, we can provide mentors for 1.4 million of them. Let's also offer these kids from disadvantaged backgrounds the same chance to take the same college test-prep courses wealthier students use to boost their test scores.

To make the American Dream achievable for all, we must make college affordable for all. For seven years, on a bipartisan basis, we have taken action toward that goal: larger Pell grants, more affordable student loans, education IRAs, and our HOPE scholarships, which have already benefited 5 million young people.

Now, 67 percent of high school graduates are going on to college. That's up 10 percent since 1993. Yet millions of families still strain to pay college tuition. They need help.

So I propose a landmark $30-billion college opportunity tax cut—a middle class tax deduction for up to $10,000 in college tuition costs. The previous actions of this Congress have already made two years of college affordable for all. It's time to make four years of college affordable for all. If we take all these steps, we'll move a long way toward making sure every child starts school ready to learn and graduates ready to succeed. We need a 21st century revolution to reward work and strengthen families, by giving every parent the tools to succeed at work and at the most important work of all—raising children. That means making sure every family has health care and the support to care for aging parents, the tools to bring their children up right, and that no child grows up in poverty.

From my first days as President, we've worked to give families better access to better health care. In 1997, we passed the Children's Health Insurance Program—CHIP—so that workers who don't have coverage through their employers at least can get it for their children. So far, we've enrolled 2 million children; we're well on our way to our goal of 5 million.

But there are still more than 40 million of our fellow Americans without health insurance—more than there were in 1993. Tonight I propose that we follow Vice President Gore's suggestion to make low income parents eligible for the insurance that covers their children. Together with our children's initiative—think of this—together with our children's initiative, this action would enable us to cover nearly a quarter of all the uninsured people in America.

Again, I want to ask you to let people between the ages of 55 and 65—the fastest growing group of uninsured—buy into Medicare. And this year I propose to give them a tax credit to make that choice an affordable one. I hope you will support that, as well.

When the baby boomers retire, Medicare will be faced with caring for twice as many of our citizens; yet, it is far from ready to do so. My generation must not ask our children's generation to shoulder our burden. We simply must act now to strengthen and modernize Medicare.

My budget includes a comprehensive plan to reform Medicare, to make it more efficient and competitive. And it dedicates nearly $400 billion of our budget surplus to keep Medicare solvent past 2025. And, at long last, it also provides funds to give every senior a voluntary choice of affordable coverage for prescription drugs.

Lifesaving drugs are an indispensable part of modern medicine. No one creating a Medicare program today would even think of excluding coverage for prescription drugs. Yet more than three in five of our seniors now lack dependable drug coverage which can lengthen and enrich their lives. Millions of older Americans who need prescription drugs the most pay the highest prices for them. In good conscience, we cannot let another year pass without extending to all our seniors this lifeline of affordable prescription drugs.

Record numbers of Americans are providing for aging or ailing loved ones at home. It's a loving, but a difficult and often very expensive choice. Last year, I proposed a $1,000 tax credit for long-term care. Frankly, it wasn't enough. This year, let's triple it, to $3,000. But this year, let's pass it.

We also have to make needed investments to expand access to mental health care. I want to take a moment to thank the person who led our first White House Conference on Mental Health last year, and who for seven years has led all our efforts to break down the barriers to decent treatment of people with mental illness. Thank you, Tipper Gore. Taken together, these proposals would mark the largest investment in health care in the 35 years since Medicare was created—the largest investment in 35 years. That would be a big step toward assuring quality health care for all Americans, young and old. And I ask you to embrace them and pass them.

We must also make investments that reward work and support families. Nothing does that better than the Earned Income Tax Credit—the EITC. The "E" in the EITC is about earning, working, taking responsibility and being rewarded for it. In my very first address to you, I asked Congress to greatly expand this credit; and you did. As a result, in 1998 alone, the EITC helped more than 4.3 million Americans work their way out of poverty toward the middle class. That's double the number in 1993.

Tonight, I propose another major expansion of the EITC: to reduce the marriage penalty, to make sure it rewards marriage as it rewards work, and also, to expand the tax credit for families that have more than two children. It punishes people with more than two children today. Our proposal would allow families with three or more children to get up to $1,100 more in tax relief. These are working families; their children should not be in poverty.

We also can't reward work and family unless men and women get equal pay for equal work. Today, the female unemployment rate is the lowest it has been in 46 years. Yet, women still only earn about 75 cents for every dollar men earn. We must do better, by providing the resources to enforce present equal pay laws; training more women for high-paying, high-tech jobs; and passing the Paycheck Fairness Act.

Many working parents spend up to a quarter—a quarter—of their income on child care. Last year, we helped parents provide child care for about 2 million children. My child care initiative, before you now, along with funds already secured in welfare reform, would make child care better, safer and more affordable for another 400,000 children. I ask you to pass that. They need it out there—

For hard-pressed middle-income families, we should also expand the child care tax credit. And I believe strongly we should take the next big step and make that tax credit refundable for low-income families. For people making under $30,000 a year, that could mean up to $2,400 for child care costs. You know, we all say we're pro-work and pro-family. Passing this proposal would prove it.

Tens of millions of Americans live from paycheck to paycheck. As hard as they work, they still don't have the opportunity to save. Too few can make use of IRAs and 401-K plans. We should do more to help all working families save and accumulate wealth. That's the idea behind the Individual Development Accounts, the IDAs. I ask you to take that idea to a new level, with new Retirement Savings Accounts that enable every low- and moderate-income family in America to save for retirement, a first home, a medical emergency, or a college education. I propose to match their contributions, however small, dollar for dollar, every year they save. And I propose to give a major new tax credit to any small business that will provide a meaningful pension to its workers. Those people ought to have retirement as well as the rest of us.

Nearly one in three American children grows up without a father. These children are five times more likely to live in poverty than children with both parents at home. Clearly, demanding and supporting responsible fatherhood is critical to lifting all children out of poverty. We've doubled child support collections since 1992. And I'm proposing to you tough new measures to hold still more fathers responsible. But we should recognize that a lot of fathers want to do right by their children, but need help to do it. Carlos Rosas of St. Paul, Minnesota, wanted to do right by his son, and he got the help to do it. Now he's got a good job and he supports his little boy. My budget will help 40,000 more fathers make the same choices Carlos Rosas did. I thank him for being here tonight. Stand up, Carlos. Thank you.

If there is any single issue on which we should be able to reach across party lines, it is in our common commitment to reward work and strengthen families, similar to what we did last year. We came together to help people with disabilities keep their health insurance when they go to work. And I thank you for that. Thanks to overwhelming bipartisan support from this Congress, we have improved foster care. We've helped those young people who leave it when they turn 18, and we have dramatically increased the number of foster care children going into adoptive homes. I thank all of you for all of that.

Of course, I am forever grateful to the person who has led our efforts from the beginning, and who's worked so tirelessly for children and families for 30 years now: my wife, Hillary. And I thank her.

If we take the steps I've just discussed, we can go a long, long way toward empowering parents to succeed at home and at work, and ensuring that no child is raised in poverty. We can make these vital investments in health care, education, support for working families, and still offer tax cuts to help pay for college, for retirement, to care for aging parents, to reduce the marriage penalty. We can do these things without forsaking the path of fiscal discipline that got us to this point here tonight.

Indeed, we must make these investments and these tax cuts in the context of a balanced budget that strengthens and extends the life of Social Security and Medicare and pays down the national debt.

Crime in America has dropped for the past seven years—that's the longest decline on record—thanks to a national consensus we helped to forge on community police, sensible gun safety laws, and effective prevention. But nobody—nobody here, nobody in America—believes we're safe enough. So again, I ask you to set a higher goal. Let's make this country the safest big country in the world.

Last fall, Congress supported my plan to hire, in addition to the 100,000 community police we've already funded, 50,000 more, concentrated in high-crime neighborhoods. I ask your continued support for that.

Soon after the Columbine tragedy, Congress considered common-sense gun legislation, to require Brady background checks at the gun shows, child safety locks for new handguns, and a ban on the importation of large-capacity ammunition clips. With courage—and a tie-breaking vote by the Vice President—the Senate faced down the gun lobby, stood up for the American people, and passed this legislation. But the House failed to follow suit.

Now, we have all seen what happens when guns fall into the wrong hands. Daniel Mauser was only 15 years old when he was gunned down at Columbine. He was an amazing kid—a straight-A student, a good skier. Like all parents who lose their children, his father Tom has borne unimaginable grief. Somehow he has found the strength to honor his son by transforming his grief into action. Earlier this month, he took a leave of absence from his job to fight for tougher gun safety laws. I pray that his courage and wisdom will at long last move this Congress to make common-sense gun legislation the very next order of business.

Tom Mauser, stand up. We thank you for being here tonight. Tom. Thank you, Tom.

We must strengthen our gun laws and enforce those already on the books better. Federal gun crime prosecutions are up 16 percent since I took office. But we must do more. I propose to hire more federal and local gun prosecutors and more ATF agents to crack down on illegal gun traffickers and bad-apple dealers. And we must give them the enforcement tools that they need, tools to trace every gun and every bullet used in every gun crime in the United States. I ask you to help us do that.

Every state in this country already requires hunters and automobile drivers to have a license. I think they ought to do the same thing for handgun purchases. Now, specifically, I propose a plan to ensure that all new handgun buyers must first have a photo license from their state showing they passed the Brady background check and a gun safety course, before they get the gun. I hope you'll help me pass that in this Congress.

Listen to this—listen to this. The accidental gun rate—the accidental gun death rate of children under 15 in the United States is nine times higher than in the other 25 industrialized countries combined. Now, technologies now exist that could lead to guns that can only be fired by the adults who own them. I ask Congress to fund research into smart gun technology, to save these children's lives. I ask responsible leaders in the gun industry to work with us on smart guns, and other steps to keep guns out of the wrong hands, to keep our children safe.

You know, every parent I know worries about the impact of violence in the media on their children. I want to begin by thanking the entertainment industry for accepting my challenge to put voluntary ratings on TV programs and video and Internet games. But, frankly, the ratings are too numerous, diverse and confusing to be really useful to parents. So tonight, I ask the industry to accept the First Lady's challenge to develop a single voluntary rating system for all children's entertainment that is easier for parents to understand and enforce. The steps I outline will take us well on our way to making America the safest big country in the world.

Now, to keep our historic economic expansion going—the subject of a lot of discussion in this community and others—I believe we need a 21st century revolution to open new markets, start new businesses, hire new workers right here in America—in our inner cities, poor rural areas, and Native American reservations. Our nation's prosperity hasn't yet reached these places. Over the last six months, I've traveled to a lot of them, joined by many of you, and many far-sighted business people, to shine a spotlight on the enormous potential in communities from Appalachia to the Mississippi Delta, from Watts to the Pine Ridge Reservation. Everywhere I go, I meet talented people eager for opportunity, and able to work. Tonight I ask you, let's put them to work. For business, it's the smart thing to do. For America, it's the right thing to do. And let me ask you something—if we don't do this now, when in the wide world will we ever get around to it?

So I ask Congress to give businesses the same incentives to invest in America's new markets they now have to invest in markets overseas. Tonight, I propose a large New Markets tax credit and other incentives to spur $22 billion in private-sector capital to create new businesses and new investments in our inner cities and rural areas. Because empowerment zones have been creating these opportunities for five years now, I also ask you to increase incentives to invest in them and to create more of them. And let me say to all of you again what I have tried to say at every turn—this is not a Democratic or a Republican issue. Giving people a chance to live their dreams is an American issue.

Mr. Speaker, it was a powerful moment last November when you joined Reverend Jesse Jackson and me in your home state of Illinois, and committed to working toward our common goal, by combining the best ideas from both sides of the aisle. I want to thank you again, and to tell you, Mr. Speaker, I look forward to working with you. This is a worthy, joint endeavor. Thank you.

I also ask you to make special efforts to address the areas of our nation with the highest rates of poverty—our Native American reservations and the Mississippi Delta. My budget includes $110-million initiative to promote economic development in the Delta, and a billion dollars to increase economic opportunity, health care, education and law enforcement for our Native American communities. In this new century—we should begin this new century by honoring our historic responsibility to empower the first Americans. And I want to thank tonight the leaders and the members from both parties who've expressed to me an interest in working with us on these efforts. They are profoundly important. There's another part of our American community in trouble tonight—our family farmers. When I signed the Farm Bill in 1996, I said there was great danger it would work well in good times, but not in bad. Well, droughts, floods, and historically low prices have made these times very bad for the farmers. We must work together to strengthen the farm safety net, invest in land conservation, and create some new markets for them by expanding our programs for bio-based fuels and products. Please, they need help—let's do it together.

Opportunity for all requires something else today—having access to a computer and knowing how to use it. That means we must close the digital divide between those who've got the tools and those who don't. Connecting classrooms and libraries to the Internet is crucial, but it's just a start. My budget ensures that all new teachers are trained to teach 21st century skills, and it creates technology centers in 1,000 communities to serve adults. This spring, I'll invite high-tech leaders to join me on another New Markets tour, to close the digital divide and open opportunity for our people.

I want to thank the high-tech companies that already are doing so much in this area. I hope the new tax incentives I have proposed will get all the rest of them to join us. This is a national crusade. We have got to do this, and do it quickly.

Now, again I say to you, these are steps, but step by step, we can go a long way toward our goal of bringing opportunity to every community.

To realize the full possibilities of this economy, we must reach beyond our own borders, to shape the revolution that is tearing down barriers and building new networks among nations and individuals, and economies and cultures: globalization. It's the central reality of our time. Of course, change this profound is both liberating and threatening to people. But there's no turning back. And our open, creative society stands to benefit more than any other—if we understand, and act on, the realities of interdependence. We have to be at the center of every vital global network, as a good neighbor and a good partner. We have to recognize that we cannot build our future without helping others to build theirs.

The first thing we have got to do is to forge a new consensus on trade. Now, those of us who believe passionately in the power of open trade, we have to ensure that it lifts both our living standards and our values, never tolerating abusive child labor or a race to the bottom in the environment and worker protection. But others must recognize that open markets and rule-based trade are the best engines we know of for raising living standards, reducing global poverty and environmental destruction, and assuring the free flow of ideas.

I believe as strongly tonight as I did the first day I got here, the only direction forward for America on trade—the only direction for America on trade is to keep going forward. I ask you to help me forge that consensus.

We have to make developing economies our partners in prosperity. That's why I would like to ask you again to finalize our groundbreaking African and Caribbean Basin trade initiatives.

But globalization is about more than economics. Our purpose must be to bring together the world around freedom and democracy and peace, and to oppose those who would tear it apart. Here are the fundamental challenges I believe America must meet to shape the 21st century world.

First, we must continue to encourage our former adversaries, Russia and China, to emerge as stable, prosperous, democratic nations. Both are being held back today from reaching their full potential: Russia by the legacy of communism, an economy in turmoil, a cruel and self-defeating war in Chechnya; China by the illusion that it can buy stability at the expense of freedom. But think how much has changed in the past decade: 5,000 former Soviet nuclear weapons taken out of commission; Russian soldiers actually serving with ours in the Balkans; Russian people electing their leaders for the first time in a thousand years; and in China, an economy more open to the world than ever before.

Of course, no one, not a single person in this chamber tonight, can know for sure what direction these great nations will take. But we do know for sure that we can choose what we do. And we should do everything in our power to increase the chance that they will choose wisely, to be constructive members of our global community.

That's why we should support those Russians who are struggling for a democratic, prosperous future; continue to reduce both our nuclear arsenals; and help Russia to safeguard weapons and materials that remain.

And that's why I believe Congress should support the agreement we negotiated to bring China into the WTO, by passing Permanent Normal Trade Relations with China as soon as possible this year.

I think you ought to do it for two reasons. First of all, our markets are already open to China; this agreement will open China's markets to us. And, second, it will plainly advance the cause of peace in Asia and promote the cause of change in China. No, we don't know where it's going. All we can do is decide what we're going to do. But when all is said and done, we need to know we did everything we possibly could to maximize the chance that China will choose the right future.

A second challenge we've got is to protect our own security from conflicts that pose the risk of wider war and threaten our common humanity. We can't prevent every conflict or stop every outrage. But where our interests are at stake and we can make a difference, we should be, and we must be, peacemakers.

We should be proud of our role in bringing the Middle East closer to a lasting peace; building peace in Northern Ireland; working for peace in East Timor and Africa; promoting reconciliation between Greece and Turkey and in Cyprus; working to defuse these crises between India and Pakistan; in defending human rights and religious freedom. And we should be proud of the men and women of our Armed Forces and those of our allies who stopped the ethnic cleansing in Kosovo, enabling a million people to return to their homes.

When Slobodan Milosevic unleashed his terror on Kosovo, Captain John Cherrey was one of the brave airmen who turned the tide. And when another American plane was shot down over Serbia, he flew into the teeth of enemy air defenses to bring his fellow pilot home. Thanks to our Armed Forces' skill and bravery, we prevailed in Kosovo without losing a single American in combat. I want to introduce Captain Cherrey to you. We honor Captain Cherrey, and we promise you, Captain, we'll finish the job you began. Stand up so we can see you.

A third challenge we have is to keep this inexorable march of technology from giving terrorists and potentially hostile nations the means to undermine our defenses. Keep in mind, the same technological advances that have shrunk cell phones to fit in the palms of our hands can also make weapons of terror easier to conceal and easier to use. We must meet this threat by making effective agreements to restrain nuclear and missile programs in North Korea; curbing the flow of lethal technology to Iran; preventing Iraq from threatening its neighbors; increasing our preparedness against chemical and biological attack; protecting our vital computer systems from hackers and criminals; and developing a system to defend against new missile threats—while working to preserve our ABM missile treaty with Russia. We must do all these things.

I predict to you, when most of us are long gone, but some time in the next 10 to 20 years, the major security threat this country will face will come from the enemies of the nation state: the narco-traffickers and the terrorists and the organized criminals, who will be organized together, working together, with increasing access to ever-more sophisticated chemical and biological weapons.

And I want to thank the Pentagon and others for doing what they're doing right now to try to help protect us and plan for that, so that our defenses will be strong. I ask for your support to ensure they can succeed.

I also want to ask you for a constructive bipartisan dialogue this year to work to build a consensus which I hope will eventually lead to the ratification of the Comprehensive Nuclear Test Ban Treaty.

I hope we can also have a constructive effort to meet the challenge that is presented to our planet by the huge gulf between rich and poor. We cannot accept a world in which part of humanity lives on the cutting edge of a new economy, and the rest live on the bare edge of survival. I think we have to do our part to change that—with expanded trade, expanded aid, and the expansion of freedom. This is interesting—from Nigeria to Indonesia, more people got the right to choose their leaders in 1999 than in 1989, when the Berlin Wall fell. We've got to stand by these democracies—including, and especially tonight, Colombia, which is fighting narco-traffickers, for its own people's lives and our children's lives. I have proposed a strong two-year package to help Colombia win this fight. I want to thank the leaders in both parties in both Houses for listening to me and the President of Colombia about it. We have got to pass this. I want to ask your help. A lot is riding on it. And it's so important for the long-term stability of our country, and for what happens in Latin America.

I also want you to know I'm going to send you new legislation to go after what these drug barons value the most—their money. And I hope you'll pass that as well.

In a world where over a billion people live on less than a dollar a day, we also have got to do our part in the global endeavor to reduce the debts of the poorest countries, so they can invest in education, health care and economic growth. That's what the Pope and other religious leaders have urged us to do. And last year, Congress made a down payment on America's share. I ask you to continue that. I thank you for what you did, and ask you to stay the course.

I also want to say that America must help more nations to break the bonds of disease. Last year in Africa, 10 times as many people died from AIDS as were killed in wars—10 times. The budget I give you invests $150 million more in the fight against this and other infectious killers. And today, I propose a tax credit to speed the development of vaccines for diseases like malaria, TB and AIDS. I ask the private sector and our partners around the world to join us in embracing this cause. We can save millions of lives together, and we ought to do it.

I also want to mention our final challenge, which, as always, is the most important. I ask you to pass a national security budget that keeps our military the best-trained and best-equipped in the world, with heightened readiness and 21st century weapons; which raises salaries for our servicemen and women; which protects our veterans; which fully funds the diplomacy that keeps our soldiers out of war; which makes good on our commitment to pay our U.N. dues and arrears. I ask you to pass this budget.

I also want to say something, if I might, very personal tonight. The American people watching us at home, with the help of all the commentators, can tell from who stands and who sits, and who claps and who doesn't, that there's still modest differences of opinion in this room. But I want to thank you for something, every one of you. I want to thank you for the extraordinary support you have given—Republicans and Democrats alike—to our men and women in uniform. I thank you for that.

I also want to thank, especially, two people. First, I want to thank our Secretary of Defense, Bill Cohen, for symbolizing our bipartisan commitment to national security. Thank you, sir. Even more, I want to thank his wife, Janet, who, more than any other American citizen, has tirelessly traveled this world to show the support we all feel for our troops. Thank you, Janet Cohen. I appreciate that. Thank you.

These are the challenges we have to meet so that we can lead the world toward peace and freedom in an era of globalization.

I want to tell you that I am very grateful for many things as President. But one of the things I'm grateful for is the opportunity that the Vice President and I have had to finally put to rest the bogus idea that you cannot grow the economy and protect the environment at the same time.

As our economy has grown, we've rid more than 500 neighborhoods of toxic waste, ensured cleaner air and water for millions of people. In the past three months alone, we've helped preserve 40 million acres of roadless lands in the national forests, created three new national monuments.

But as our communities grow, our commitment to conservation must continue to grow. Tonight, I propose creating a permanent conservation fund, to restore wildlife, protect coastlines, save natural treasures, from the California redwoods to the Florida Everglades.

This Lands Legacy endowment would represent by far the most enduring investment in land preservation ever proposed in this House. I hope we can get together with all the people with different ideas and do this. This is a gift we should give to our children and our grandchildren for all time, across party lines. We can make an agreement to do this. Last year, the Vice President launched a new effort to make communities more liberal—livable—liberal, I know. Wait a minute, I've got a punchline now.

That's this year's agenda; last year was livable, right? That's what Senator Lott is going to say in the commentary afterwards. To make our communities more livable. This is big business. This is a big issue. What does that mean? You ask anybody that lives in an unlivable community, and they'll tell you. They want their kids to grow up next to parks, not parking lots; the parents don't have to spend all their time stalled in traffic when they could be home with their children.

Tonight, I ask you to support new funding for the following things, to make American communities for liberal—livable. I've done pretty well with this speech, but I can't say that.

One, I want you to help us to do three things. We need more funding for advanced transit systems. We need more funding for saving open spaces in places of heavy development. And we need more funding—this ought to have bipartisan appeal—we need more funding for helping major cities around the Great Lakes protect their waterways and enhance their quality of life. We need these things and I want you to help us.

The greatest environmental challenge of the new century is global warming. The scientists tell us the 1990s were the hottest decade of the entire millennium. If we fail to reduce the emission of greenhouse gases, deadly heat waves and droughts will become more frequent, coastal areas will flood, and economies will be disrupted. That is going to happen, unless we act. Many people in the United States—some people in this chamber—and lots of folks around the world still believe you cannot cut greenhouse gas emissions without slowing economic growth. In the Industrial Age that may well have been true. But in this digital economy, it is not true anymore. New technologies make it possible to cut harmful emissions and provide even more growth.

For example, just last week, automakers unveiled cars that get 70 to 80 miles a gallon—the fruits of a unique research partnership between government and industry. And before you know it, efficient production of bio-fuels will give us the equivalent of hundreds of miles from a gallon of gasoline.

To speed innovation in these kind of technologies, I think we should give a major tax incentive to business for the production of clean energy, and to families for buying energy-saving homes and appliances and the next generation of super-efficient cars when they hit the showroom floor. I also ask the auto industry to use the available technologies to make all new cars more fuel-efficient right away.

And I ask this Congress to do something else. Please help us make more of our clean energy technology available to the developing world. That will create cleaner growth abroad and a lot more new jobs here in the United States of America.

In the new century, innovations in science and technology will be the key not only to the health of the environment, but to miraculous improvements in the quality of our lives and advances in the economy. Later this year, researchers will complete the first draft of the entire human genome, the very blueprint of life. It is important for all our fellow Americans to recognize that federal tax dollars have funded much of this research, and that this and other wise investments in science are leading to a revolution in our ability to detect, treat, and prevent disease.

For example, researchers have identified genes that cause Parkinson's, diabetes, and certain kinds of cancer—they are designed precision therapies that will block the harmful effect of these genes for good. Researchers already are using this new technique to target and destroy cells that cause breast cancer. Soon, we may be able to use it to prevent the onset of Alzheimer's. Scientists are also working on an artificial retina to help many blind people to see—and listen to this—microchips that would actually directly stimulate damaged spinal cords in a way that could allow people now paralyzed to stand up and walk.

These kinds of innovations are also propelling our remarkable prosperity. Information technology only includes 8 percent of our employment, but now it counts for a third of our economic growth—along with jobs that pay, by the way, about 80 percent above the private sector average. Again, we ought to keep in mind, government-funded research brought supercomputers, the Internet, and communications satellites into being. Soon researchers will bring us devices that can translate foreign languages as fast as you can talk; materials 10 times stronger than steel at a fraction of the weight; and—this is unbelievable to me—molecular computers the size of a tear drop with the power of today's fastest supercomputers.

To accelerate the march of discovery across all these disciplines in science and technology, I ask you to support my recommendation of an unprecedented $3 billion in the 21st Century Research Fund, the largest increase in civilian research in a generation. We owe it to our future. Now, these new breakthroughs have to be used in ways that reflect our values. First and foremost, we have to safeguard our citizens' privacy. Last year, we proposed to protect every citizen's medical record. This year, we will finalize those rules. We've also taken the first steps to protect the privacy of bank and credit card records and other financial statements. Soon I will send legislation to you to finish that job. We must also act to prevent any genetic discrimination whatever by employers or insurers. I hope you will support that.

These steps will allow us to lead toward the far frontiers of science and technology. They will enhance our health, the environment, the economy in ways we can't even imagine today. But we all know that at a time when science, technology and the forces of globalization are bringing so many changes into all our lives, it's more important than ever that we strengthen the bonds that root us in our local communities and in our national community.

No tie binds different people together like citizen service. There's a new spirit of service in America—a movement we've tried to support with Ameri-Corps, expanded Peace Corps, unprecedented new partnerships with businesses, foundations, community groups. Partnerships, for example, like the one that enlisted 12,000 companies which have now moved 650,000 of our fellow citizens from welfare to work. Partnerships to battle drug abuse, AIDS, teach young people to read, save America's treasures, strengthen the arts, fight teen pregnancy, prevent violence among young people, promote racial healing. The American people are working together.

But we should do more to help Americans help each other. First, we should help faith-based organizations to do more to fight poverty and drug abuse, and help people get back on the right track, with initiatives like Second Chance Homes that do so much to help unwed teen mothers. Second, we should support Americans who tithe and contribute to charities, but don't earn enough to claim a tax deduction for it. Tonight, I propose new tax incentives that would allow low- and middle-income citizens who don't itemize to get that deduction. It's nothing but fair, and it will get more people to give.

We should do more to help new immigrants to fully participate in our community. That's why I recommend spending more to teach them civics and English. And since everybody in our community counts, we've got to make sure everyone is counted in this year's census. Within 10 years—just 10 years—there will be no majority race in our largest state of California. In a little more than 50 years, there will be no majority race in America. In a more interconnected world, this diversity can be our greatest strength. Just look around this chamber. Look around. We have members in this Congress from virtually every racial, ethnic, and religious background. And I think you would agree that America is stronger because of it.

You also have to agree that all those differences you just clapped for all too often spark hatred and division even here at home. Just in the last couple of years, we've seen a man dragged to death in Texas just because he was black. We saw a young man murdered in Wyoming just because he was gay. Last year, we saw the shootings of African Americans, Asian Americans, and Jewish children just because of who they were. This is not the American way, and we must draw the line.

I ask you to draw that line by passing without delay the Hate Crimes Prevention Act and the Employment Non-Discrimination Act. And I ask you to reauthorize the Violence Against Women Act.

Finally tonight, I propose the largest-ever investment in our civil rights laws for enforcement, because no American should be subjected to discrimination in finding a home, getting a job, going to school, or securing a loan. Protections in law should be protections in fact.

Last February, because I thought this was so important, I created the White House Office of One America to promote racial reconciliation. That's what one of my personal heroes, Hank Aaron, has done all his life. From his days as our all-time home run king to his recent acts of healing, he has always brought people together. We should follow his example, and we're honored to have him with us tonight. Stand up, Hank Aaron.

I just want to say one more thing about this, and I want every one of you to think about this the next time you get mad at one of your colleagues on the other side of the aisle. This fall, at the White House, Hillary had one of her millennium dinners, and we had this very distinguished scientist there, who is an expert in this whole work in the human genome. And he said that we are all, regardless of race, genetically 99.9 percent the same.

Now, you may find that uncomfortable when you look around here. But it is worth remembering. We can laugh about this, but you think about it. Modern science has confirmed what ancient faiths have always taught: the most important fact of life is our common humanity. Therefore, we should do more than just tolerate our diversity—we should honor it and celebrate it.

My fellow Americans, every time I prepare for the State of the Union, I approach it with hope and expectation and excitement for our nation. But tonight is very special, because we stand on the mountain top of a new millennium. Behind us we can look back and see the great expanse of American achievement; and before us we can see even greater, grander frontiers of possibility. We should, all of us, be filled with gratitude and humility for our present progress and prosperity. We should be filled with awe and joy at what lies over the horizon. And we should be filled with absolute determination to make the most of it.

You know, when the framers finished crafting our Constitution in Philadelphia, Benjamin Franklin stood in Independence Hall and he reflected on the carving of the sun that was on the back of a chair he saw. The sun was low on the horizon. So he said this—he said, "I've often wondered whether that sun was rising or setting. Today," Franklin said, "I have the happiness to know it's a rising sun." Today, because each succeeding generation of Americans has kept the fire of freedom burning brightly, lighting those frontiers of possibility, we all still bask in the glow and the warmth of Mr. Franklin's rising sun.

After 224 years, the American revolution continues. We remain a new nation. And as long as our dreams outweigh our memories, America will be forever young. That is our destiny. And this is our moment.

Thank you, God bless you, and God bless America.

# REPUBLICAN RESPONSE

**Senator Collins:** Good evening. I'm Susan Collins of Maine. Tonight, Senator Bill Frist of Tennessee and I would like to talk with you about issues that are vital to all of us.

Our Republican agenda is driven by the simple but powerful truth that America will continue to lead the world as long as our government allows opportunity, initiative, and freedom to flourish. Letting people create what they can dream has transformed our economy.

As we reflect on our economic health, we should never forget that America's recent success is, above all, a triumph of values. Americans will never let our country become rich in things and poor in spirit.

The achievements of the "dotcom" generation rest on the foundation built by our parents and grandparents. They prevailed through the Depression, defeated the forces of fascism, and made personal freedom the hallmark of countries around the globe.

To pay tribute to those great Americans on whose shoulders we stand, we are honor-bound to keep our promise to protect Social Security. Last year, for the first time in thirty-nine years, the federal budget was balanced without dipping into the Social Security trust fund.

We'll do it again this year, and we'll pay down even more of the national debt. We've already paid off 150 billion dollars in the last two years. Now, our goal is to eliminate the 3.6 trillion-dollar debt entirely in the next 15 years.

To promote job growth, we'll continue to help our small businesses. That means reducing burdens like the federal "death tax"—so that when parents work their whole lives to leave their children a family business, it won't have to be sold just to pay the IRS.

Taxes, in general, are simply too high. We will continue to fight for tax relief for American families so that they can keep more of what they earn.

We'll honor our commitment to our brave men and women in uniform. Last year, the Republican Congress approved the largest increase in military pay in more than a decade. And to protect our country from terrorist nations, we will build a shield against missile attack.

As important as all these issues are, there's something else that is vital to securing our future, and that is education. Prior to coming to the Senate, I worked at Husson College in Bangor, Maine. I know first-hand the difference that education can make.

We live in a time of unparalleled prosperity. But between Silicon Valley and Wall Street, many Americans still live in the shadows of the new prosperity. New technologies, unimagined a decade ago, provide exciting opportunities for some but pose unsettling challenges to others.

As we enter the 21st Century, every young American must be educated to adapt to a changing workplace, and many in our current workforce must be provided with new skills to succeed in the new economy.

A good education is the ladder of opportunity. It turns dreams into reality. That's why education is at the top of the Republican agenda.

Tonight, I ask the President to join with Republicans in our commitment to bring a good education to all our children. Our "Four-Point Plan for Educational Excellence" will ensure that all children have an equal opportunity to reach their full potential.

First, we will continue to increase federal funds for elementary and secondary education. Last year, the Republicans boosted education spending by 500 million dollars more than the President's budget, and we added funds for children with special needs.

Second, rather than Washington dictating to communities how they should run their schools, we should listen to those who know best: our parents, teachers, and local school boards.

The debate in Washington is not about money. It is about who makes the decisions. We need a change of approach—one that recognizes that local schools, not Washington offices, are the heart and home of education. We will empower states and communities to use federal education dollars in the ways children need most.

I've watched my younger brother Sam serve on the school board in our hometown of Caribou, Maine. He is motivated by the same goal as parents everywhere: to get the world's best education for their children. Doesn't it make sense to have the people who know your children's names decide how best to educate them?

Republicans want what all parents want for their children's schools: more federal help but less federal interference. Instead of imposing a "one-size fits all" straitjacket, our plan recognizes that one community may need more math teachers, while another may need better reading programs—and still others, new computers. It should be your community's decision, not Washington's.

In return for that flexibility, the Republican plan requires real accountability—not more paperwork, but better results. Schools will be held responsible for what is truly important—improving student achievement.

Third, our plan will strengthen teaching excellence.

America's teachers need our help. About one-third of our new teachers get so discouraged that they leave the profession. Many are prevented from doing their very best because they don't have a chance to get enough training in the subject they teach.

We will increase federal grants to states and communities and give them the freedom to use that money to better prepare, recruit, and retain good teachers. The lessons are clear—we must encourage talented people to choose teaching as a career and keep them in the classroom.

Fourth, our plan will continue the long-time Republican support for higher education. Last year, we increased Pell grants and student loans to open the doors to college for more low- and middle-income families. This year, we will increase the amount that families can contribute to education savings accounts to make higher education more affordable.

Education today is America's broadband to the future—a powerful conduit for achievement and success. Let us work together to ensure that all Americans have the educational opportunity for a bright future.

Now I'd like to call upon my friend and colleague, Dr. Bill Frist, the Senate's only physician.

**Senator Frist:** I'm Bill Frist. I'm a senator from the state of Tennessee, but I've spent the better part of my life working in hospitals, caring for people with heart disease.

I've learned a lot by listening to my patients and to the people who work in hospitals.

Earlier tonight we heard the President talk about his latest health care proposals. The last time he proposed a health plan was seven years ago. And then it amounted to a federal government takeover of our entire health system. It would have forced every American into a Washington-run HMO and denied them the right to choose their own doctor.

In the end, thank goodness, it was soundly defeated by Democrats and Republicans alike. Now tonight, 84 months later, the President has unveiled a similar plan just as bad as the first. It makes government even bigger and more bloated because each new program we heard about tonight—and there were about 11 of them in health care alone—comes with its own massive bureaucracy. And each will cost you, the taxpayer, billions more of your tax dollars—more than $1,000 for every man, woman, and child.

During my surgical fellowship, I worked in England for the British "National Health Service," and I saw firsthand the rationing, the lack of choice, the long waits, and the denial of care for seniors.

I learned that socialized medicine—whether in England or in Canada, where patients are fleeing to the US for treatment—just does not work.

In fact, if David Letterman had lived in Canada, he'd still be waiting for his heart surgery!

But I think we all know that America's health care system can be better. Costs are climbing. Too many people can't get insurance or breakthrough drugs. Too many heavy handed HMOs tell doctors how to do their jobs.

And yet we should remember that Americans still enjoy the best and most advanced health care in the world. That's why people from all over the globe come here for the latest treatments. If you have diabetes, or arthritis, or high blood pressure, chances are your medicines weren't even around 10 years ago. Today, we live longer, and stay healthier, than ever before.

So a lot is good. A lot is working. But we still have to make it even better.

As Republicans in Congress we're determined not to be guided by bigger government, but by your freedom to choose your kind of health care and to select the doctor of your choice. Already because of Republican efforts, five million more children now have access to health care; if you change jobs, you can now take your health insurance with you; new mothers can leave the hospital when their doctor, not some bureaucrat, says they're ready. And we're doubling medical research for more and better cures.

A great start, but not enough.

As a doctor, I've cared for thousands of seniors. I know Medicare is their lifeline, their security.

But this 35-year-old program, with 130,000 pages of regulations creates waste and abuse, and leaves our seniors with confusing red tape and heartache. Worst of all, Medicare doesn't even include the mainstay of modern medicine—outpatient prescription drugs.

The answer is NOT government-dictated price controls that stop life-saving research, or forcing the 65 percent of seniors who now have drug coverage to pay more or give up what they have.

Instead, both Republicans and Democrats in Congress have come together with a plan to build on two simple principles: choice and security. It lets people choose the type of medical plan that is best for them, including prescription drugs. No senior citizen, no mother, no person with a disability will ever be told by a bureaucrat what plan to pick, what doctor to see, or what service they can receive.

But just last year the President said "No" to this plan put forth by the National Bipartisan Medicare Commission—the very commission the President and Congress appointed to save Medicare.

However, I'm proud to say that I've asked for and received full assurances today from our Majority Leader Trent Lott, that he is prepared to bring this needed bipartisan legislation to the Senate floor within two weeks. For this to happen, Mr. President, all we need is for you to tell the American people "Yes" to this Democrat and Republican plan to fix Medicare.

And tonight, to show you that we are sincere and that we mean business, Republicans take a first step toward making Medicare stronger. To guarantee that seniors can rely on Medicare forever, we will add it to the Social Security lockbox, which will lock away the surplus for both Social Security and Medicare. We will not let anyone spend your Medicare money.

We believe that neither HMO's nor the government should be practicing medicine. That's why Congress will, for the first time, send the President a real "Patients' Bill of Rights," with strong patient protections. In our plan, if you're denied the treatment that you and your doctor decide is right, you'll get a quick appeal to an independent doctor.

Unlike the President, we see lawsuits as a last resort, not the first. Because as every American knows, your sick child needs to see a doctor, not a lawyer.

During the Clinton years, the number of individuals without health insurance has increased by six million people. But with the plan we announced yesterday, we will finally make it easier for low- and middle-income families to buy the coverage of their choice.

I believe we will dramatically improve medical care in America. How could anyone not be hopeful, with what we've seen? Just look at our ability to correct heart defects in children, halt the progression of osteoporosis, and treat breast and prostate cancer. Soon we'll see revolutionary new treatments for conditions like Alzheimer's, sickle cell anemia, and schizophrenia.

But all of these innovations require freedom, because progress and freedom go hand in hand.

You know, my father was a family doctor for 55 years. As a young boy making housecalls with him, I remember his stethoscope, his doctor's bag, and best of all his wonderful and compassionate heart. But these were his only tools. Just one generation later, he would join me on my rounds and he'd witness the miraculous new technologies and medicines that allowed us to transplant hearts and to give new life.

It's all possible because Americans are blessed with the spirit to dream, the freedom to explore, and the work ethic to produce.

And so tonight, Mr. President, I ask you to put your trust in the American people—in their creativity, in their resourcefulness, in their ability to achieve—free of government interference.

Mr. President, please, no more red tape.

Instead, give us a health care plan that includes choice and security.

The American people deserve no less.

On behalf of Senator Collins and myself, thank you for being with us. Good night, and may God bless all of you and our great nation.

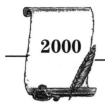

# February

# PRESIDENT'S ECONOMIC REPORT, ECONOMIC ADVISERS' REPORT
## February 10, 2000

*President Bill Clinton took office in January 1993 just as the economy was beginning to recover from recession. Eight years later, as he entered the last year of his second term, Clinton could boast that his administration had presided over the longest economic expansion in the nation's history— one that appeared to be reaching people of all races and at every income level. Inflation and unemployment were both low, family income was rising overall, and poverty rates were declining. The federal government was running a huge surplus and beginning to pay down the national debt.*

*The expansion of the 1990s entered its 107th month in February 2000, surpassing the 106-month record of a recession-free economy set in the 1960s. The latest expansion was remarkable not only for its length, but also for its refusal to follow typical patterns. In the past, for example, low unemployment had led to wage inflation, which in turn contributed to price inflation, higher interest rates, lower investment, and eventually a slackening of productivity. In the current expansion, productivity had grown fast enough to accommodate low jobless rates and low inflation simultaneously. The booming economy was also unusual in that it appeared to do little to help Clinton's vice president, Al Gore, in his bid for the presidency. In the past voters were quick to change parties when the economy was in trouble, but they usually stayed with the party in power during boom times.*

*Perhaps voters were concerned by signs that the expansion might be slowing—or even coming to an end. Although inflation and the jobless rate were holding steady, growth slowed in the third quarter and was expected to slow even further in the fourth. Corporate earnings, particularly in high-technology companies, failed to meet expectations, sending both the stock market and consumer confidence downward. As the year ended, some economists and business analysts were predicting a possible recession in 2001. President-elect George W. Bush suggested that quick approval of his proposed tax-cut package, the centerpiece of his presidential campaign, might jump-start the economy. But he and others could hardly fail to note the irony: the defeat of the president-elect's father, George Bush, for reelection in 1992 was generally attributed to economic problems that turned into a recession, which was followed by eight years of robust economic growth under the Democratic successor, which in turn appears to be followed by renewed economic troubles as the younger Bush entered the White House.*

## Clinton's Proud Record

*In his annual formal economic message to Congress, released February 10, 2000, President Clinton proudly listed the achievements of the economy during his administration—the creation of more than 20 million new jobs, the lowest unemployment rate in thirty years, the lowest core inflation rate (excluding food and energy) since 1965, and the largest dollar surplus in the federal budget in the nation's history. Clinton said the government had paid off $140 billion in national debt in the last two years and was on track to eliminate the $3.4 trillion debt by 2013.*

*Clinton said those achievements were not the result of accident but of his administration's unwavering commitment to a three-prong economic strategy: federal fiscal discipline to help lower interest rates and stimulate business investment; continuous investment in education, health care, science, and technology to ensure that Americans were prepared for the challenges of the twenty-first century; and opening foreign markets to American goods and services. "As a result," Clinton reported, "the American economy is not only strong today; it is well positioned to continue to expand and to widen the circle of opportunity for more Americans."*

## The Economic Year in Review

*In its annual report accompanying the president's message, the Council of Economic Advisers affirmed the good performance of the economy in 1999. Real (inflation-adjusted) gross domestic product (GDP), a measure of overall productivity, grew at a rate of 4.2 percent in 1999, only slightly slower than the 4.6 percent rate recorded in 1998. Inflation increased 2.7 percent in 1999, largely because of increases in energy prices. But core inflation, which did not take food and energy prices into account, increased 1.9 percent in 1999, slightly below the 2.2 percent increase in 1998. Unemployment averaged 4.2 percent in 1999, compared with 4.5 percent in 1998.*

*A key component of the economy's growth was household spending, which grew at an annual rate of 5.4 percent in 1999. The strong stock market and the overall rise in value of housing contributed to a "wealth effect" that made households willing to spend a greater share of their income. Sales of houses, new cars, and trucks all reached record levels in 1999. Real business investment, particularly in computers, telecommunications, and other information technology, continued to boom. Brisk sales kept inventories at "lean levels," the report said, adding that this was probably related to the adoption of "just-in-time" inventory management and other information technology techniques that allowed companies to operate without having to stockpile large quantities of inventory over relatively long periods of time.*

*Although real federal spending and investment were up in 1999 com-*

*pared with 1998, the surplus continued to grow, reaching $124 billion (on a unified budget basis) in fiscal 1999, compared with a deficit of $290 billion in fiscal 1992. The last time the federal government ran back-to-back surpluses was in fiscal years 1956 and 1957. Like the president, the economic advisers stressed the importance of paying down the national debt to help ensure continued low interest rates and more capital for investment.*

*One dark note was the relatively low demand for U.S. exports. Although foreign growth was clearly on the rebound after the financial crisis that began in East Asia in 1997, U.S. export growth rose only 4 percent in 1999, while real spending on imported goods and services rose 13 percent. As a result, the U.S. trade deficit widened to about $90 billion, or about 2.8 percent of GDP.* (Asian crisis, Historic Documents of 1997, p. 832)

*For 2000 the economic advisers predicted that real GDP growth would slow to 2.9 percent, a decline from its annual average rate of 4.3 percent in 1996–1999, but nonetheless a respectable rate of growth. Inflation was expected to remain flat, while unemployment was expected to edge up to 5.2 percent by 2003. The economic advisers expected export growth to pick up but cautioned that the trade deficit was likely to worsen in the near term as demand for imports continued at its high rates. Seeing "no obvious signs of an imminent slowdown," the economic advisers said that "the most likely prognosis is therefore the same as last year's: sustained job creation and continued noninflationary growth."*

## Signs of a Slowdown

*For the first two quarters of 2000, the economic advisers' growth forecast looked too conservative. Gross domestic product grew at a rate of 4.8 percent in the first quarter and 5.6 percent in the second. Concerned for some time that the fast growth would touch off inflation, the board of governors of the Federal Reserve had raised interest rates six times between June 1999 and May 2000, pushing real interest rates to their highest levels in fifteen years.*

*At the same time, the air began to go out of the stock market. High-tech stocks were the first to fall, plummeting in April following the announcement that Microsoft had failed to settle the government's antitrust suit against it and a report by a respected analyst that high-tech stocks were overvalued. That analysis was validated throughout the year as one high-tech company after another reported lower-than-expected earnings. Many, such as Amazon.com, an Internet retailer of books and other items, showed no profit, and still others went out of business altogether. By the end of the year, the NASDAQ composite, heavily influenced by high-technology stocks, had lost 39 percent of its value compared with 1999, when it gained nearly 86 percent. Microsoft lost 63 percent of its value.* (Digital economy, p. 299)

*The old economy did much better overall, as utilities, energy, health care, tobacco, and banking stocks all did well. But the old economy also suffered losses. The Dow Jones industrial average was off 6.2 percent, and the Standard and Poor's index declined 10.1 percent. Big losers were Xerox, which lost 80 percent of its value, and AT&T, which registered a 66 percent loss.*

*By the end of the year the faltering stock market, as well as soaring prices for gasoline and home heating fuel, especially natural gas, appeared to be undermining consumer confidence and business investment. The business community repeatedly called on the Federal Reserve to lower interest rates, charging that the earlier rate hikes had slowed the economy too much and might tip it into recession. Many economists cautioned, however, that the fundamental health of the economy was still sound and that talk of recession was unwarranted.*

*Whatever the health of the economy, political skirmishing was already under way. Both President-elect Bush and Vice President-elect Dick Cheney repeatedly raised the specter of a recession. Democrats complained that the incoming Republican administration was "talking down the economy" so that the Clinton administration would be blamed if in fact a recession did develop and to pump up support for Bush's massive tax cut proposal. Speaking on* Fox News Sunday *on December 24, Gene Sperling, Clinton's White House economic adviser, warned the incoming administration that it "shouldn't, just to support a political agenda, risk hurting confidence in [the] economy by talking about a worst-case scenario. One of the things that you do when you go to make a transition from a campaign to governing is realize that when you are president-elect or vice president-elect, your words actually have an impact on the economy itself."*

*Following are excerpts from the Economic Report of the President and excerpts from Chapter 1 of the Annual Report of the Council of Economic Advisers, both released February 10, 2000. The documents were obtained from the Internet at http://w3 .access.gpo.gov/eop.*

# ECONOMIC REPORT OF THE PRESIDENT

*To the Congress of the United States:*

Today, the American economy is stronger than ever. We are on the brink of marking the longest economic expansion in our Nation's history. More than 20 million new jobs have been created since Vice President Gore and I took office in January 1993. We now have the lowest unemployment rate in 30 years—even as core inflation has reached its lowest level since 1965.

This expansion has been both deep and broad, reaching Americans of all races, ethnicities, and income levels. African American unemployment and poverty are at their lowest levels on record. Hispanic unemployment is likewise the lowest on record, and poverty among Hispanics is at its lowest level since 1979. A long-running trend of rising income inequality has been halted in the last 7 years. From 1993 to 1998, families at the bottom of the income distribution have enjoyed the same strong income growth as workers at the top.

In 1999 we had the largest dollar surplus in the Federal budget on record and the largest in proportion to our economy since 1951. We are on course to achieve more budget surpluses for many years to come. We have used this unique opportunity to make the right choices for the future: over the past 2 years, America has paid down $140 billion in debt held by the public. With my plan to continue to pay down the debt, we are now on track to eliminate the Nation's publicly held debt by 2013. Our fiscal discipline has paid off in lower interest rates, higher private investment, and stronger productivity growth.

These economic successes have not been achieved by accident. They rest on the three pillars of the economic strategy that the Vice President [Al Gore] and I laid out when we took office: fiscal discipline to help reduce interest rates and spur business investment; investing in education, health care, and science and technology to meet the challenges of the 21st century; and opening foreign markets so that American workers have a fair chance to compete abroad. As a result, the American economy is not only strong today; it is well positioned to continue to expand and to widen the circle of opportunity for more Americans.

## The Administration's Economic Strategy

Our economic strategy was based on a commitment, first, to fiscal discipline. When the Vice President and I took office, the U.S. Government had a budget deficit of $290 billion. Today we have a surplus of $124 billion. This fiscal discipline has helped us launch a virtuous circle of strong investment, increasing productivity, low inflation, and low unemployment.

Second, we have remained true to our commitment to invest in our people. Because success in the global economy depends more than ever on highly skilled workers, we have taken concerted steps to make sure all Americans have the education, skills, and opportunities they need to succeed. That is why, even as we maintained fiscal responsibility, we expanded our investments in education, technology, and training. We have opened the doors of college to all Americans, with tax credits, more affordable student loans, education IRAs, and the HOPE Scholarship tax credits. So that working families will have the means to support themselves, we have increased the minimum wage, expanded the Earned Income Tax Credit (EITC), provided access to health insurance for people with disabilities, and invested in making health insurance coverage available to millions of children.

Third, we have continued to pursue a policy of opening markets. We have achieved historic trade pacts such as the North American Free Trade Agreement and the Uruguay Round agreements, which led to the creation of the World Trade Organization. Negotiations in the wake of the Uruguay Round have yielded market access commitments covering information technology, basic telecommunications, and financial services. We have engaged in bilateral initiatives with Japan and in regional initiatives in Europe, Africa, Asia, the Western Hemisphere, and the Middle East. We have also actively protected our rights under existing trade agreements through the World Trade Organization and helped maintain the Internet as a tax-free zone.

## Meeting the Challenges of the Future

Despite the economy's extraordinary performance, we must continue working to meet the challenges of the future. Those challenges include educating our children, improving the health and well-being of all our citizens, providing for our senior citizens, and extending the benefits of the economic expansion to all communities and all parts of this Nation.

We must help our children prepare for life in a global, information-driven economy. Success in this new environment requires that children have a high-quality education. That means safe, modern schools. It means making sure our children have well-trained teachers who demand high standards. It means making sure all schools are equipped with the best new technologies, so that children can harness the tools of the 21st century.

First and foremost, our children cannot continue trying to learn in schools that are so old they are falling apart. One-third of all public schools need extensive repair or replacement. By 2003 we will need an additional 2,400 schools nationwide to accommodate these rising enrollments. That is why, in my State of the Union address, I proposed $24.8 billion in tax credit bonds over 2 years to modernize up to 6,000 schools, and a $1.3 billion school emergency loan and grant proposal to help renovate schools in high-poverty, high-need school districts.

Second, if our children are to succeed in the new digital economy, they must know how to use the tools of the 21st century. That is why the Vice President and I have fought for initiatives like the E-rate, which is providing $2 billion a year to help schools afford to network their classrooms and connect to the Internet. The E-rate and our other initiatives in education technology have gone a long way toward giving all children access to technology in their schools. But there is still a great "digital divide" when children go home. Children from wealthy families are far more likely to have access to a computer at home than children from poor or minority families. That is why, in my budget, I propose a new Digital Divide initiative that will expand support for community technology centers in low-income communities; a pilot project to expand home access to computers and the Internet for low-income families; and grants and loan guarantees to accelerate the deployment of high-speed networks in underserved rural and urban communities.

Third, we must continue to make college affordable and accessible for all Americans. I have proposed a college opportunity tax cut, which would invest $30 billion over 10 years in helping millions of families who now struggle to afford college for their children. When fully phased in, this initiative would give families the option to claim a tax deduction or a tax credit on up to $10,000 of tuition and fees for any postsecondary education in which their members enroll, whether college, graduate study, or training courses. I have proposed increases in Pell grants, Supplemental Educational Opportunity Grants, and Work Study. I have also proposed creating new College Completion Challenge Grants to encourage students to stay in college.

We have seen dramatic advances in health care over the course of the 20th century, which have led to an increase in life expectancy of almost 30 years.

But much remains to be done to ensure that all have and maintain access to quality medical care. That is why my budget expands health care coverage, calls for passing a strong and enforceable Patients' Bill of Rights, strengthens and modernizes Medicare, addresses long-term care, and continues to promote life-saving research.

My budget invests over $110 billion over 10 years to improve the affordability, accessibility, and quality of health insurance. It will provide a new, affordable health insurance option for uninsured parents as well as accelerate enrollment of uninsured children who are eligible for Medicaid and the State Children's Health Insurance Program. The initiative will expand health insurance options for Americans facing unique barriers to coverage. For example, it will allow certain people aged 55–65 to buy into Medicare, and it will give tax credits to workers who cannot afford the full costs of COBRA [Consolidated Omnibus Budget Reconstruction Act] coverage after leaving a job. Finally, my initiative will provide funds to strengthen the public hospitals and clinics that provide health care directly to the uninsured. If enacted, this would be the largest investment in health coverage since Medicare was created in 1965, and one of the most significant steps we can take to help working families.

As our Nation ages and we live longer, we face new challenges in Medicare and long-term care. Despite improvements in Medicare in the past 7 years, the program begins this century with the disadvantages of insufficient funding, inadequate benefits, and outdated payment systems. To strengthen and modernize the program, I have proposed a comprehensive reform plan that would make Medicare more competitive and efficient and invest $400 billion over the next 10 years in extending solvency through 2025 and adding a long-overdue, voluntary prescription drug benefit.

The aging of America also underscores the need to build systems to provide long-term care. More than 5 million Americans require long-term care because of significant limitations due to illness or disability. About two-thirds of them are older Americans. That is why I have proposed a $27 billion investment over 10 years in long-term care. Its centerpiece is a $3,000 tax credit to defray the cost of long-term care. In addition, I propose to expand access to home-based care, to establish new support networks for caregivers, and to promote quality private long-term care insurance by offering it to Federal employees at group rates.

We must continue to make this economic expansion reach out to every corner of our country, leaving no town, city, or Native American reservation behind. That is why I am asking the Congress to authorize two additional components of our New Markets agenda. The first is the New Markets Venture Capital Firms program, geared toward helping small and first-time businesses. The second is America's Private Investment Companies, modeled on the Overseas Private Investment Corporation, to help larger businesses expand or relocate to distressed inner-city and rural areas. Overall the New Markets initiative could spur $22 billion of new equity investment in our underserved communities.

I am also proposing a new initiative called First Accounts, to expand access to financial services for low- and moderate-income Americans. We will work with private financial institutions to encourage the creation of low-cost bank accounts for low-income families. We will help bring more automated teller machines to safe places in low-income communities, such as the post office. And we will educate Americans about managing household finances and building assets over time.

To further increase opportunities for working families, I am proposing another expansion of the EITC to provide tax relief for 6.4 million hard-pressed families—with additional benefits for families with three or more children. We have seen the dramatic effects that our 1993 expansion of the EITC had in reducing poverty and encouraging work: 4.3 million people were directly lifted out of poverty by the EITC in 1998 alone. More single mothers are working than ever before, and the child poverty rate is at its lowest since 1980.

Our initiatives to open overseas markets will continue. We have successfully concluded bilateral negotiations on China's accession to the World Trade Organization and now seek congressional action to provide China with permanent normal trade relations. The United States will also work to give the least developed countries greater access to global markets. We will participate in the scheduled multilateral talks to liberalize trade in services and agriculture and will continue to press our trading partners to launch a new round of negotiations within the World Trade Organization.

We have a historic opportunity to answer the challenges ahead: to increase economic opportunity for all American families; to provide quality, affordable child care, health care, and long-term care; and to give our children the best education in the world. Working together, we can meet these great challenges and make this new millennium one of ever-increasing promise, hope, and opportunity for all Americans.

William J. Clinton
The White House
February 10, 2000

# THE ANNUAL REPORT OF THE
# COUNCIL OF ECONOMIC ADVISERS

## Growth and Inequality: A Century-Long Perspective

Over the past century the U.S. economy has recorded spectacular performance. It has found the 2 percent answer to the American dream: if living standards rise at 2 percent annually, they double every 35 years. This means that by the time they reach their mid-30s, parents can provide their children with a standard of living that is twice the level that they themselves enjoyed as children. By maintaining an annual average increase in gross national product (GNP) per capita of about 2.1 percent over the whole century, the U.S. economy exceeded this target. . . . When incomes grow at this pace, each generation experiences a far more affluent lifestyle than the previous one, and over the course of a lifetime, Americans can expect, on average, a fourfold increase in living standards.

How much richer are Americans today than at the turn of the century? Despite the uncertainties in the data, it is clear that total growth of the economy has been remarkable. In 1999 the economy produced almost 30 times the volume of goods and services that it did in 1899, and it employed about 5 times as many workers in doing so. (That it took 5 rather than 30 times as many workers is tribute to another great accomplishment, namely, enormous increases in productivity.) Measured in 1999 dollars, average income per capita in 1899 was a little less than $4,200. With an average 1999 income of $33,740, Americans today can acquire (and businesses can produce) more than eight times as many goods and services as could Americans living in 1899. But this simple comparison grossly understates the true improvement in living standards for three important reasons. First, it fails to fully account for the vast array of goods and services that were simply unavailable in the past: aircraft, antibiotics, air conditioners, radio and television, and computers, to name only a few. Second, it fails to account for a substantial increase in leisure, as the typical workweek has fallen to 35 hours. Third, it fails to account for the impact of the improved health of the population in raising life expectancy from 47.3 years in 1900 to about 77 years today, while also improving the quality of those added years. (However, the improvement in living standards may be overstated to the extent that workers, particularly women, have shifted from nonmarket work at home, which is not captured in the GNP measure, to market activity, which is.)

Through sustained economic growth, the United States has been able to accomplish much both at home and abroad. Although poverty rates still remain too high, growth has been the driving force lifting many of the poorest members of society out of poverty. Growth has created more opportunities and made it much easier to tackle the challenges of supporting a growing number of retirees. By maintaining solid growth, the United States moved to a position of global economic leadership sometime near the start of the century and remains in that position today. Recent World Bank data show that U.S. income per capita is 27 percent greater than income per capita in Japan, and 47 percent greater than that in Germany (based on purchasing power parities).

. . . [P]rogress over the century has not always been smooth. In the century's first half, growth was punctuated by several deep recessions and by the disaster of the Great Depression. Fewer workers were employed in 1939 than in 1929. Nonetheless, despite economic instability and two world wars, in the first 50 years of the century income per capita more than doubled, and income inequality declined.

## The Golden Years of Equitable Growth

The quarter century after World War II was a period of rapid increase in productivity growth, and the resulting rise in living standards was remarkable. From the cyclical peak of 1948 to that of 1973, business sector output per hour rose by more than 3 percent per year, as innovative technologies, strong capital investment, and a more skilled and educated work force proved mutually reinforcing. . . . Recessions interrupted this growth, but median family income rose by 3.0 percent per year on average, and the gains were widely shared. The average income of the poorest fifth of families rose 3.4 percent annually, whereas that of the top quintile grew at a 2.8 percent annual rate. On average, living standards in 1973 were 82 percent higher than in 1948. These were years when the American dream seemed achievable for all.

## Growth Undermined: Stagflation, Rising Inequality, and Deficits

The two decades after 1973 were a rude awakening. It appeared as if the early postwar vision of continuously rising incomes for all had indeed been just a dream. The economy's performance deteriorated noticeably in several dimensions. First, there was much greater economic instability than in the early postwar period. Spurred by rising oil prices, inflation jumped to 11 percent in 1974, and a deep recession followed. After a few years of recovery, inflation then soared to new heights, hitting 13.5 percent in 1980. When, in response, monetary policy made a dedicated effort to bring inflation under control, the economy entered the deepest recession of the postwar period: unemployment rose to 10.8 percent in November 1982. Between 1973 and 1983 the U.S. economy recorded average yearly inflation and unemployment rates of 8.4 and 7.2 percent, respectively—this was the period of the infamous stagflation. The economy did grow strongly in the mid-1980s, but exploding Federal deficits, caused by a lack of fiscal discipline, together with the crisis in the savings and loan industry, undermined that success. Inflation again started to rise, and the economy was already teetering on the edge of recession in 1990 when declining consumer confidence following the Iraqi invasion of Kuwait pushed it over the edge.

Second, growth in productivity lost its momentum. Between 1973 and 1990, growth in business sector output per hour rose at 1½ percent per year—about half its rate from 1948 to 1973. Slower productivity growth in turn affected wages. Between 1973 and 1993, annual growth in real compensation per hour averaged 0.8 percent. Real earnings declined at the end of the 1980s expansion and continued to decline in the 1990-91 recession. The economy did sustain a 1.9 percent annual increase in income per capita over the 1973–90 period, but this was due primarily to rapid labor force growth as more women and baby-boomers went to work.

Third, the years between 1973 and 1993 also saw a marked increase in inequality: not only were real income gains meager, but they were also unevenly shared. Those at the top did far better than those at the bottom. After adjusting for consumer price inflation, income for the top quintile of families increased at a 1.3 percent annual pace, but growth was minimal for the middle class and markedly negative for the less well off. These income data were partly driven by developments in earnings: between 1979 and 1993, real earnings in the lowest decile declined by 0.6 percent, whereas those in the highest decile rose 0.3 percent. The premium earned by college graduates over high school graduates increased from about 40 percent to 70 percent. Moreover, the dispersion of earnings increased even for workers with similar education and demographic characteristics. Finally, the poverty rate of 13.5 percent at the cyclical peak in 1990 was considerably higher than at the peak in 1973.

## The Return to Broad-Based Growth in a Record-Breaking Expansion

The expansion that began hesitantly in 1991 found its stride and has been sustained. It will in all likelihood have become the longest expansion in U.S. history—107 months free of recession—in February 2000. Since the beginning of 1993, payroll employment has increased by more than 20 million jobs. Boosted by higher employment and faster productivity growth, output growth has been strong, with GNP per capita rising at an average rate of 2.7 percent per year between the first quarter of 1993 and the third quarter of 1999. Participation in the labor force has increased to a record 67 percent of the working-age population, yet the annual unemployment rate has declined to 4.2 percent—a level not seen in 30 years. After remaining sluggish in the early years of the expansion, output per hour has accelerated, to an average annual growth rate of 2.8 percent between the fourth quarter of 1995 and the third quarter of 1999. In response, solid real compensation gains have been recorded. . . .

The benefits of this growth have been widely shared as well. Some observers focus on changes over a decade or two and conclude that inequality is still rising, but they ignore the recent trends. Between 1993 and 1998, real average household incomes have grown by between 9.9 and 11.7 percent for every quintile of the income distribution, and the median African American household has seen a 15 percent increase in real income. Between 1993 and 1998, family incomes in the lowest quintile rose at a 2.7 percent annual rate, slightly faster than the 2.4 percent rate recorded by the top quintile. . . . This recent experience contrasts sharply with the performance from 1973 to 1993. Similar breadth is evident in the growth of earnings. Although wage inequality continued to widen through 1994, for the past 5 years weekly earnings growth has been broad-based.

The economy is increasingly providing workers with good employment opportunities. A recent analysis by the Council of Economic Advisers and the Department of Labor found that 81 percent of new jobs created from 1993 to 1999 are located in industry and occupation categories that pay wages above the median. These good jobs have not gone only to the professional elite: even when professional occupations were excluded from the sample, the study found that 71 percent of new jobs were in categories paying above the median wage. Nor are workers with college degrees the only ones gaining ground. Among workers with only a high school education, an overwhelming proportion of job growth was found to occur in those industry and occupation categories in which these workers earn the highest wages.

Data on poverty also show progress. The proportion of Americans living in poverty fell from 15.1 percent in 1993 to 12.7 percent in 1998. The poverty rate for African Americans in 1998, although still high at 26.1 percent, was the lowest ever recorded, and that for Hispanics is the lowest it has been since 1979.

Since 1993, African American unemployment has declined from 13.0 percent to 8.0 percent, and Hispanic unemployment has fallen from 10.7 percent to 6.4 percent. For both groups these represent the lowest rates on record. Meanwhile the unemployment rate for females aged 16 and over has dropped to 4.3 percent, the lowest in 46 years.

Data on the probability of job displacement, which showed a rise in the late 1980s and early 1990s, show a drop since then. The share of all workers with 3 or more years of job tenure who became displaced from their jobs was 3.9 percent in the 1991–92 period but declined to 2.9 percent in the 1995–96 period. And because the labor market has been so robust in the 1990s, the rate of reemployment following displacement has been higher in this decade, as have earnings after displacement, than at comparable levels of unemployment during the 1980s. Workers' fears of job loss have also eased in recent years: the share of workers who believe they are likely to lose their jobs declined from 12 percent in 1993 to 8 percent in 1998.

## The Engines of the 1990s Expansion

The performance of the economy over this expansion has surprised most observers. Two decades of slow growth and rising inequality have ended. In their place is a record-breaking expansion that has brought strong and equitable growth. The gloomy view of long-term U.S. prospects so popular in the 1970s and 1980s has proved decidedly misguided. The record of the past 7 years suggests that it may be time to reappraise what one popular book at the turn of the last decade called the Nation's "diminished expectations." Before undertaking such a reappraisal, however, it is useful to identify the principal engines of this expansion, and to see how these have resulted in an expansion that is unusual in important respects from previous long expansions. In this section we look at the policy and private sector drivers of growth under four headings: technology; trade and competition; education and skills; and pro-investment policies.

### Information and Other Technology

The economy is clearly in the ferment of rapid technological change. . . . One powerful contributor to the strength of this expansion has been investment in plant and equipment, particularly computers and information technology. Prices of computers and semiconductors, adjusted for quality improvements, have been falling particularly rapidly. Investment in information processing equipment and software took off in the 1990s, growing at a rate of 19 percent per year from 1993 to 1999. . . . More broadly, the share of real investment in GDP has risen dramatically, as has the share of high-technology investment in total investment. Real spending on research and development (R&D) increased at an estimated annual rate of 5 percent between 1993 and 1999.

For many years it seemed that the information technology revolution was not paying off in higher productivity, but that now seems to be changing. Companies have learned to use the new technology to operate more efficiently. New ways of producing and delivering goods and services have been developed. Venture capitalists provide both funds and expertise to new companies with bold ideas. And of course, the improvements in communications technologies have been as dramatic as those in computers. The diffusion and development of the Internet promise continued productivity payoffs still to come.

The revolution in information technology is the most visible and probably the most important technological trend, but it is far from the only one. Materials science, biotechnology, and medical technology have all advanced rapidly and are generating their own economic benefits. America hosts many of the preeminent scientific research institutions in the world, which have pioneered numerous advances and trained the people who are now leading these technological revolutions.

Over the years, government support of scientific research and education has been a vital element in the success of U.S. technology. Going forward, the increased funding proposed in the President's science and technology initiative is important to sustaining growth in the years to come.

## Competition and Trade

Industries in which companies compete vigorously tend to be more productive. Conventional economic logic argues that companies operate efficiently and innovate whenever there is the chance of a profit payoff. In practice, however, companies can become complacent and keep doing things the old way even when new, more profitable methods are available. The pressures of competition encourage change and force companies to adopt the more productive methods. And even as it keeps the pressure on businesses to improve and innovate, competition exposes them to best-practice technologies that will help them to do so.

Competition in the global economy adds benefits beyond those from domestic competition. The economy benefits from trade as firms face new incentives, and resources shift to the most productive industries. In addition, companies that face global competition are exposed to best practices worldwide, challenging them to reach for the highest possible performance themselves. The U.S. economy has become increasingly open to overseas trade in the course of this expansion. Indeed, its importance in GDP has grown even more than in previous long expansions. Between 1991 and 1999, trade (measured as the sum of exports and imports) in goods and services as a share of GDP rose by 4.8 percentage points, compared with increases of 1.5 and 3.5 percentage points during the expansions of the 1960s and the 1980s, respectively.

The Administration's antitrust and regulatory policies have fostered competition at home. At the same time, its trade policies have worked to expand trade and open markets through major regional and multilateral agreements.

## Education, Skills, and Work Incentives

Dazzling new technologies, redesigned business systems, new services—the promise of these sources of economic growth can be realized only if people have the skills and the knowledge to use them. To take advantage of the benefits of trade in expanding those industries where the United States has comparative advantage, workers must acquire the necessary skills. Workers who lose their jobs when industries contract, whether because of foreign competition or because of technological advance, must often be retrained in order to reenter the productive economy at a comparable living standard.

Strong job growth and low unemployment have been possible in this expansion only because people have found that work has paid off. Providing work incentives is an essential element in strong economic growth. With one of the most highly educated, skilled, and motivated work forces in the world, the United States has also been able to take advantage of growth opportunities worldwide.

Policies to increase access to education and training and make work pay have been a central theme of economic policy in this expansion.

## Pro-Investment Policies

Output growth in this expansion has gone predominantly to households and businesses rather than for government purchases. One can measure how the growth of GDP over time has been allocated among the components of GDP: consumption, investment, government purchases (Federal, State, and local), and net exports. . . . When this is done, the current expansion stands out for the strong contribution of private investment spending. The contribution of government purchases of goods and services to growth has been only 7 percent, about a third of what it was in the two previous long expansions.

Government purchases of goods and services reflect the direct use of economic resources. But Federal spending also includes Social Security payments and other transfers to households and businesses. On this broader basis, the current expansion also shows evidence of fiscal restraint. Federal outlays in 1991 were 22.3 percent of GDP. By fiscal 1999 this ratio had fallen to 18.7 percent, as efforts to restrain spending combined with strong economic growth. This decline in spending of 3.6 percentage points of GDP is much greater than the 1.3-percentage-point decline during the 1982–90 expansion. Since this measure typically declines as the economy moves out of recession—and the deeper the recession, the greater the decline—the comparison between the two expansions is striking given that the current expansion was launched from a much shallower recession. Moreover, this decline in spending occurred even as revenues were rising. . . .

According to the Administration forecast, assuming implementation of policy as proposed by the President, Federal outlays are forecast to fall to 16.7 percent of GDP by 2010. This reduction results in part from a decline in interest costs as debt is paid off.

But perhaps the most dramatic illustration of how unusual budget policy has been in this expansion comes from estimates of the structural budget deficit by the Congressional Budget Office (CBO). The structural budget deficit adjusts the actual deficit to take out the effect of fluctuations in the business cycle. It estimates what the budget deficit would have been if GDP had been at its potential. According to the CBO's estimates, structural deficits were pervasive during the long expansion of the 1960s, except at the very beginning. . . . And those deficits increased sharply until the tax increase of 1968.

Throughout its duration, the expansion of the 1980s was also associated with large structural deficits—and large actual deficits as well. This expansionary fiscal policy was accompanied by a tight monetary policy, and this combination of policies contributed to relatively high real interest rates and declining net national saving and domestic investment.

The current expansion, by contrast, started with a large structural deficit and turned it around, to the point that there is now a structural surplus, as Federal spending has been kept in check while revenues have risen. Monetary policy, meanwhile, has been given the freedom to encourage real growth while keeping inflation low. Interest rates, as a result, have been lower than they would have been. Indeed, real interest rates in this expansion have been considerably lower than in the 1980s expansion. Using survey data to measure inflation expectations suggests that real short-term interest rates have been about half what they were in the 1980s expansion, and real long-term rates are about a third lower. Lower interest rates have stimulated investment spending, and this investment has, in turn, boosted capacity growth and raised productivity—two key factors that have helped keep inflation in check.

Although the current account (the balance of trade in goods and services plus net factor income and net transfers) moved into deficit in both the 1980s and the 1990s, the forces behind these shifts were different. In the 1980s both net national saving and net domestic investment declined as a percentage of GDP, so that foreign borrowing was used, directly or indirectly, to finance consumption and Federal budget deficits rather than investment. In the 1990s, by contrast, net national saving increased, and the capital inflow has helped finance an investment boom.

## Key Features of the Expansion

Driven by technological advance, more open markets, and investment in physical capital and human skills—all with the ongoing support of Federal policy—this expansion is on track to become the longest ever. In 1999, the ninth year of the expansion, GDP grew by 4.0 percent, and 2.7 million payroll jobs were created. The expansion remained youthful-looking and vigorous despite its chronological age. How did the engines of this expansion, just described, translate their energy into such a sustained performance?

## Productivity Growth

The start of an expansion is usually a period of rapid productivity growth. Companies set up factories and offices that are designed to produce a certain target level of output. In a recession, output falls below this target, plants operate less efficiently, and productivity falls. Companies may also retain valued workers that are not needed today but will be needed when the upturn comes, and this, too, lowers average productivity. The surge of productivity growth at the start of an expansion occurs as businesses are again able to make better use of their workers and their physical capital.

The magnitude of this surge varies from expansion to expansion and tends to be greater, the deeper the recession that preceded it. After a deep recession, there is more ground that can be made up before the economy returns to its long-term potential. After a while, however, this productivity surge ends, and the economy moves closer to its normal or trend rate of productivity growth, which is determined by the rates of capital accumulation, technological change, and enhancement of skills. Finally, in the last year or so of an expansion, productivity growth often slows again in what has been called an end-of-expansion effect. This likely results from diminishing returns, as capacity becomes strained and a shortage of experienced and skilled workers develops.

. . . [T]he expansions of the 1960s and the 1980s very much followed this pattern. Productivity growth was rapid in the first 2-year period of the expansion but then started to fall off. It had dropped off sharply by the seventh year of expansion in both cases. But the pattern for the current expansion looks very different. After the initial productivity surge, growth fell for a couple of years, but since then it has actually been accelerating. Instead of looking like an old expansion suffering from diminishing returns, this one has been getting stronger. This pattern of strong productivity growth at a mature stage of the cycle is a key reason why this expansion is set to become the longest on record. And that is exactly the result one would expect from policies that have stimulated investment, technology development, and skill enhancement.

## Inflation

Accelerating inflation poses a threat to expansions and, unless kept under control, eventually brings them to a halt. . . . The 1960s expansion was marked by 5 years of strong economic growth with low inflation. Administration policies in those years restored prosperity and full employment after bouts with recession between 1957 and 1961. But during the mid-1960s, the pressures of expenditure at the time of the Vietnam War stretched industrial capacity too much, causing inflation to accelerate rapidly, until rising interest rates and monetary restraint brought the expansion to an end.

The 1980s expansion started with very high unemployment and slack resources, which helped restrain inflation in the early years of the expansion, as did the collapse of oil prices and a strong dollar. But eventually the inflation path flattened out and started to turn up as the economy reached lower levels of unemployment.

The pattern of inflation over the current expansion is surprising: core inflation has been low and stable, when not actually declining, even as unemployment has approached 4 percent. . . . [S]everal factors . . . have contributed to this combination of low inflation and low unemployment. Certainly the pattern of productivity described earlier and the rapid expansion of capacity have been important. The importance of investment for productivity growth was noted above, but rapid investment growth has also been the driver of capacity expansion. . . .

## Questioning the Causes of Inequality

Three of the major driving forces behind the economy's recent success—rapid technological change, increased trade, and tight fiscal policy—have all in the past been viewed by some as sources of greater inequality of income. It is remarkable, therefore, that even though these forces have been particularly powerful in the current expansion, the trend toward greater inequality that began in the 1970s has been arrested, and income gains are now being shared equally across income groups.

Economists are sometimes said to agree on very little, but there is a broad consensus among them that the most important cause of rising earnings inequality in the 1970s and 1980s was technological change. It was simply a matter of supply and demand. The supply of highly skilled and well-educated workers was growing relatively rapidly during these years. Between 1973 and 1992, for example, the share of the civilian labor force with some college education increased from 29.4 percent to 51.6 percent—or 3 percent a year on average. But the relative earnings of these workers were rising even as their supply was expanding, because demand was growing even faster. Something, it was argued, must be shifting the relative demand for skilled and unskilled workers, raising demand for the former and lowering it for the latter. Some attributed this skill bias to the impact of new capital investment in general and computers in particular; others saw changes in management approaches and the adoption of new, more flexible production methods as the cause. In either case, technological change was seen as at the root of the wage disparity.

A second cause of inequality has been said to be international trade, although most economists believed its contribution was far smaller than that of technological change. Expanded trade benefits all countries that take part, but within each country some people and industries may be hurt. Those who maintain that trade had increased inequality made the following argument. As developing countries with many low-skilled workers increasingly participate in trade, they put downward pressure on world prices of products intensive in low-skilled labor. If the United States then opens up to trade with these countries, low-skilled workers here become less scarce in the world market, and their relative wages fall. Some claimed that globalization imposes painful consequences on relatively underskilled workers: accept lower wages, as in the United States, or suffer higher unemployment, as in many European countries. In addition, the threat of foreign outsourcing by firms and of increased international competition was said to have reduced labor's bargaining power—a factor also sometimes held responsible for the slow rise in real wages.

Still other institutional and structural changes in the economy have been implicated in increasing inequality. The decline in union membership, for example, is seen as a factor reducing the bargaining power of U.S. workers. A second source has been changes in the mix of industries, in particular the relative decline in manufacturing employment for reasons other than international trade. A third element was the decline in the real minimum wage.

To be sure, some of these proposed explanations are not mutually exclusive. Indeed, they may be interrelated. International competition may have stimulated technological change. It has also been invoked to help explain the declining share of manufacturing employment. Some also blame technology and trade for higher structural unemployment: both may bring about structural change in the economy, as employment rises in some industries but falls in others. Workers who have developed skills in one field are forced to make a difficult transition into another.

Finally, there is a view that the rise in inequality could be attributed to cuts in government social expenditure. The reductions in poverty in the 1960s, in this view, were not simply the result of faster economic growth. The expansion of social programs, particularly Social Security for the elderly, played an important role. By contrast, cutbacks in social spending were seen as hurting the poor in the 1980s.

In light of these explanations, the recent direction of trends in inequality is surprising. As reflected in the data on investment and productivity growth, technological change appears to have accelerated over the past 5 years. Trade and international investment have expanded at rapid rates, the price pressures from this increased trade have been considerable, and the trade deficit has grown. Yet over this same period, real average hourly earnings have increased, and income gains have been widely shared, in contrast to the 1980s. Moreover, research shows that the hourly wages of lower wage groups have increased about as much as or more than the wages of upper wage groups.

This remarkable turnaround shows that rapid growth in an open economy can occur without worsening inequality. There always was a nagging doubt associated with blaming technological change for rising inequality. Why, during the 1980s, was technological change apparently contributing little or nothing to productivity growth, yet at the same time causing major shifts in relative wages? Likewise, the explanation that ascribes a role to trade was always controversial, because the evidence in support of these claims either was weak or suggested that any impacts were small. This is not surprising, because most U.S. workers are in domestic industries where there is little or no international trade. Moreover, a large proportion of U.S. trade is with countries such as Canada, Germany, and Japan, where wages are not very different from those in the United States. Only a small fraction of U.S. workers compete directly against very low wage workers overseas. To be sure, in some economic models, international competition in even a few industries is the sole determinant of relative wages across the economy, but the evidence is that many domestic factors have an important influence on relative wages.

Whatever the explanation for the growth in inequality during the 1980s, the recent experience suggests that it is time to reappraise the inevitability of the allegedly adverse impacts of technology and trade. It is time to look at the ways in which they may actually help foster growth with equity, and to recognize that a flexible economy can adjust to these changes.

Rapid productivity growth and openness to trade—and the policies that have supported them—have allowed the U.S. economy to operate and sustain a high-employment economy. And in this high-employment economy, employers have been recruiting workers at all skill levels and training many who lack the necessary skills. Moreover, faster productivity growth may allow firms to pay higher wages without raising prices, thus dampening the inflationary impact of higher levels of employment. Similarly, falling import prices will increase purchasing power, enabling real wages to rise without accelerating inflation; surplus global capacity can also help reduce inflationary pressures.

It is also quite possible that the shocks due to technology and trade have been dissipated over time by responses in the economy itself. One possibility is that the direction of technological change responds to economic incentives. As the relative cost of workers who are less well educated falls, firms have an increased incentive to employ them. Similarly, as international competitive pressures increase, firms either figure out new strategies (improved technology, new products, or higher quality of existing products) that allow them to compete, or they exit. Those firms that survive can compete successfully with low-wage countries and thus are less affected by pressures to reduce wages. The result is a far more resilient economy.

Finally, the connection between aggregate government spending and poverty reduction is too simplistic. Determined deficit reduction in the 1990s has not hurt efforts to reduce poverty, because spending has been more carefully targeted. Increased funding for the Earned Income Tax Credit and for education and training programs has played an important role. Also important have been increases in the minimum wage. Certainly a higher minimum wage has raised wages at the bottom of the income distribution, and it has not had a noticeably negative impact on employment of the lowest paid workers.

Taken as a whole, the evidence on inequality suggests that policy has been doing the right things. In addition, it provides an optimistic message. We remain masters of our fate. We are not, as some suggest, condemned to be buffeted by hostile global or technological forces, in the face of which we are helpless. To be sure, two qualifications to this proposition are in order. First, the final verdict on the impact of these forces is not yet in. The strongest test will be whether these more recent trends are sustained if there is slower growth at home and a global economic environment with less excess capacity. And second, we must not become complacent. Although the trend of rising inequality has been stopped, it has not been reversed. Similarly, although progress has been made in reducing poverty, poverty rates remain far too high. There remains much for policy to do, but the turnaround so far is heartening.

## Is the Dream Restored?

[There are] reasons to believe that the level of unemployment at which the economy will experience strong inflationary pressures has declined. But far more important over the long run is the question of whether productivity growth has increased. Certainly a great deal of anecdotal evidence suggests that technological change has been particularly rapid and widespread, but until recently the official data offered scant proof that these changes had boosted productivity. Over the past few years, as this chapter has noted, productivity growth has clearly increased, but the full implications of the economy's recent performance remain difficult to interpret because we have not seen the end of the current expansion.

One favorable interpretation of the unusual behavior of productivity growth in this cycle is that is not part of a typical cycle at all, but rather reflects a shift to a new wave of innovation. Typically, when a technology is first introduced, inexperience prevents users from extracting its full potential. Over time, however, users learn by doing and productivity accelerates. Similarly, it is possible that the innovations in the current technological wave are interrelated, so that breakthroughs in some areas yield benefits in many others. But we cannot be certain how long the current growth spurt can be sustained.

A conservative approach is to measure the change in productivity not from 1995 but from the previous cyclical peak in 1990, so that the last recession, the initial sluggish recovery, and the subsequent acceleration are all included. On that basis, it is striking that growth in GNP per capita at 2.1 percent per year, and that of GNP per worker at 1.8 percent per year, have matched the pace recorded for the century as a whole. . . . One cannot say for certain, therefore, that the past decade has witnessed the emergence of a new economy that will generate historically unprecedented growth. But we can be more confident that we have at least returned to the pace of growth sustained over most of the 20th century, which gave us the 2 percent answer to the American dream and the more than eightfold increase in output per worker over the 20th century. This, moreover, is a conservative view. There is certainly support, if not yet overwhelming evidence, for the view that the future could be even more prosperous. . . .

As we enter the 21st century, the principal challenges we face are to sustain the extraordinary progress that America has made in this record-breaking expansion, and to make sure that all Americans share in the strong economy. The goal should be to make the accomplishments of this new century even better than those of the last. New policy issues will surely emerge, but the policy framework that has worked so well—maintaining fiscal discipline, investing in people, and opening international markets—is the right one to take us forward.

# CLINTON ON U.S. SUPPORT FOR AFRICA
## February 17, 2000

*In a landmark speech on Africa policy, delivered February 17, 2000, to a National Summit on Africa, held in Washington, D.C., President Bill Clinton made a forceful case for the United States to play a larger role in the African affairs. "Because we want to live in a world which is not dominated by a division of people who live on the cutting edge of a new economy and others who live on the bare edge of survival, we must be involved in Africa," he said. "Because we want to broaden global growth and expand markets for our own people, we must be involved in Africa. Because we want to build a world in which our security is not threatened by the spread of armed conflict in which bitter ethnic and religious differences are resolved by the force of argument, not the force of arms, we must be involved in Africa."*

*Clinton in August paid his second visit to sub-Saharan Africa in as many years, attempting to promote a positive role for the United States in the troubled region. The Clinton administration, especially in its later years, devoted substantially more time, attention, and energy to Africa than had most previous U.S. administrations. But by the end of 2000 it was unclear how much impact the United States was having on events in the region. Only one of Africa's numerous wars appeared to be nearing an end, moves in some countries toward democracy and political stability appeared to be matched by backward steps in other countries, and the region lagged far behind the rest of the world in economic development. Moreover, there was little good news about the AIDS pandemic that was sweeping through much of Africa, infecting and killing millions of people. By 2000 experts were predicting that AIDS would reduce the average life expectancy in sub-Saharan Africa by twenty years. (African wars, pp. 449, 978, 1072; AIDS in Africa, p. 410)*

*Clinton won congressional approval during the year for two significant pieces of legislation intended to provide broad economic benefits to low-income nations in Africa and other regions. One bill was intended to stimulate development of textile industries in African and Caribbean nations by allowing duty-free imports into the United States of clothing made in those nations. The other expanded U.S. participation in an international program to forgive the massive debts accumulated during previous decades by developing countries in Africa, Asia, and Latin America. As of December 22, 2000, eighteen African countries had become eligible for debt relief, according to the World Bank and International Monetary Fund.* (Debt relief, p. 475)

## Clinton Trip to Nigeria, Tanzania

*In some respects, Clinton's three-day visit to two African nations at the end of August was symbolic of the problems faced both by Africa and by the United States when it tried to influence events there. Clinton visited Nigeria on August 26–27, signaling U.S. support for Olusegun Obasanjo, whose election as president in 1999 ended two decades of military dictatorship. On August 28 Clinton traveled to Tanzania, where he had hoped to witness the signing of a political agreement settling conflict between the Tutsi and Hutu ethnic groups in neighboring Burundi. But despite the determined mediating efforts of former South African president Nelson Mandela, Clinton witnessed continued discord, not a peace agreement.*

*Clinton had bypassed Nigeria—Africa's most populous nation, with nearly 120 million people—during his historic two-week visit to Africa in 1998, which was the most extensive trip taken to the region by a sitting U.S. president. At the time, Nigeria was ruled by the dictatorial regime of General Sani Abacha. Obasanjo, elected president in 1999 about nine months after Abacha's sudden death, had himself been a former military leader of Nigeria in the 1970s. But he had won widespread plaudits by handing power over to an elected civilian regime in 1979; he was later imprisoned by Abacha.* (Obasanjo election, Historic Documents of 1999, p. 272)

*During his visit to Nigeria, Clinton lavished praise both on Obasanjo and on the Nigerian people for what he called "the most important democratic transition in Africa since the fall of apartheid" in South Africa in the early 1990s. Clinton did not dwell on Nigeria's domestic political difficulties, which had potential to threaten the new democracy. Obasanjo for months had been battling the National Assembly, which he called corrupt and incompetent. When Clinton addressed the assembly, Obasanjo refused to attend. Obasanjo also had faced disputes between his central government, which controlled revenues from the country's oil industry, and the state governments, especially those in the oil-producing Niger Delta region, which demanded a greater share of oil money. Moreover, Nigerians were divided by the efforts of several states to impose strict Islamic law. Several local politicians said they were disturbed that Clinton was showering so much attention on Obasanjo, an action they said could ultimately undermine democracy by placing too much emphasis on the role of one leader, the so-called big man in many African societies.*

*On August 28 Clinton traveled to the resort city of Arusha, Tanzania, for what was supposed to have been a historic ceremony symbolizing the end to bloody civil war in Burundi. Like its neighbor Rwanda, Burundi for nearly four decades had been torn by conflict between the majority Hutu and the minority Tutsi; since the most recent outbreak of fighting in 1993, an estimated 200,000 people had been killed in Burundi.*

*Mandela, universally considered Africa's most distinguished citizen, had been mediating the conflict for more than a year and had succeeded in winning a general agreement among most of the nearly twenty parties involved. But shortly before the signing ceremony—scheduled so Clinton could be on hand—several of the Tutsi parties backed out. Mandela harshly denounced all sides to the Burundi conflict, saying they were responsible for continuing a "slaughter of innocent people." Clinton used his visit to Arusha as an opportunity to step up the international pressure for peace. "If you don't do it, what is the price?" Clinton said. "If you don't do it, what is the chance that the progress you have made will unravel? If you come back in five or ten years, will the issues change? The gulf between you will not narrow, but the gulf between Burundi and the rest of the world will grow greater if you let this moment slip away."*

*The eloquence of Mandela and Clinton appeared to have little impact, however. By year's end, there still seemed little chance that the Hutu and Tutsi parties in Burundi would end their conflict.*

## *Africa, Caribbean Trade Bill*

*Clinton had some success during the year in convincing Congress that aiding the economies of Africa was a good economic and political investment. Two years after Clinton first asked for it, Congress in May approved a trade measure offering concessions for low-income countries in sub-Saharan Africa and the Caribbean. The trade bill (PL 106–200) fell far short of the sweeping "free trade" measures that some African leaders had hoped for, but it did offer a promise that some countries in the region could substantially boost their exports to the United States. For African countries the most important provision of the bill eliminated, for eight years, quotas and tariffs on U.S. imports of clothing made from African-made fabrics and yarns. This provision would remain in effect so long as the imports from Africa did not initially exceed 1.5 percent of all U.S.-imported apparel and 3.5 percent of the national total during the eight-year period of the bill. The Clinton administration estimated that this provision, if fully used, could boost African clothing exports to the United States from about $250 million a year to as much as $4.2 billion annually.*

*The bill also eliminated, for a four-year period, quotas and tariffs on African clothing made from fabrics produced outside Africa or the United States so long as the annual per capita income of the African country where the clothing was made did not exceed $1,500. That provision would enable African manufacturers to import low-cost fabric from Asian countries, convert it into finished clothing, and export the product to the United States duty-free. The provision was intended to encourage investments in clothing manufacturing facilities in Africa's poorest countries.*

*U.S. government officials and representatives of importing firms said they expected the primary beneficiaries of the bill, at least initially, would be South Africa and the island nation of Mauritius, both of which had well-*

*established clothing manufacturers. The bill established eligibility criteria that effectively ruled out countries that were dictatorships and were not moving toward market economies. Clinton on October 2 signed a procla-mation designating thirty-four sub-Saharan countries as being eligible for the bill's provisions; among the major countries excluded from that list were the Democratic Republic of Congo (formerly Zaire), the Ivory Coast, and Zimbabwe. Clinton included Sierra Leone on the list of eligible countries but delayed the effective date until the U.S. special trade representative de-termined that the country fully met the bill's provisions.*

> *Following are excerpts from the text of a speech delivered Febru-ary 17, 2000, by President Bill Clinton to the National Summit on Africa, in Washington, D.C., in which he called for closer co-operation between the United States and the countries of Africa. The document was obtained from the Internet at http://www.pub .whitehouse.gov/uri-res/I2R?urn:pdi://oma.eop.gov.us/2000/ 2/17/9.text.1*

Secretary Salim [Salim Salim, secretary-general of the Organization of Afri-can Unity] said Africa lacks a strong constituency in the United States. Well, I open this National Summit on Africa with a simple message: Africa does mat-ter to the United States.

Of whatever background Americans claim—Leonard Robinson told me when I came here, we even have 17 delegates from Utah here. There they are, you see? Africa matters not simply because 30 million Americans trace their heritage to Africa, though that is profoundly important. Not simply because we have a strong interest in a stable and prosperous Africa—though 13 per-cent of our oil comes from Africa, and there are 700 million producers and consumers in sub-Saharan Africa, though that is important. Africa's future matters because the 21st century world has been transformed, and our views and actions must be transformed accordingly.

For most of history, the central reality in international relations was that size and location matter most. If you were a big country or on a trade or inva-sion route, you mattered. If not, you are marginalized. The average American child growing up in the past saw African nations as colorful flags and exotic names on a map, perhaps read books about the wonderful animals and great adventures. When colonialism ended, the colors on the flags were changed and there were more names on the map. But the countries did not seem nearer to most Americans.

That has all changed now. For the central reality of our time is global-ization. It is tearing down barriers between nations and people; knowledge, contact and trade across borders within and between every continent are ex-ploding. And all this globalization is also, as the barriers come down, making us more vulnerable to one another's problems: to the shock of economic tur-moil, to the spread of conflict, to pollution and, as we have painfully seen, to disease; the terrorists, the drug traffickers, the criminals who can also take advantage of new technologies and globalization, the openness of societies and borders.

Globalization means we know more about one another than ever before. You may see the Discovery Channel in Africa. I was thinking of that when that little film was on. The Discovery Channel followed me to Africa and talked about how they were building communications networks in African schools to share knowledge and information. We can find out within seconds now what the weather is in Nairobi, how a referendum turned out in Zimbabwe, how Cameroon's indomitable Lions performed in the latest soccer match. We can go online and read the Addis Tribune, the Mirror of Ghana, the East African, or dozens of other African newspapers. We sit in front of a television and watch people in a South African township line up to vote.

We also, now, bear witness to the slaughter of innocents in Rwanda, or the ravages of AIDS in scores of lands, or the painful coincidence of remarkable growth and abject poverty in nation after nation. In other words, it is no longer an option for us to choose not to know about the triumphs and the trials of the people with whom we share this small planet. Not just America and Africa; I would imagine millions of Africans identified with the Muslims of Kosovo when they were run out of their country, all of them at one time. We know about each other; we can no longer choose not to know. We can only choose not to act, or to act.

In this world, we can be indifferent or we can make a difference. America must choose, when it comes to Africa, to make a difference. Because we want to live in a world which is not dominated by a division of people who live on the cutting edge of a new economy and others who live on the bare edge of survival, we must be involved in Africa. Because we want to broaden global growth and expand markets for our own people, we must be involved in Africa. Because we want to build a world in which our security is not threatened by the spread of armed conflict, in which bitter ethnic and religious differences are resolved by the force of argument, not the force of arms, we must be involved in Africa.

Because we want to build a world where terrorists and criminals have no place to hide, and where those who wish harm to ordinary people cannot acquire the means to do them harm, we must be involved in Africa. Because we want to build a world in which we can harness our natural resources for economic growth without destroying the environment, so that future generations will also have the chance to do the same, we must be involved in Africa.

That is why I set out in 1993, at the beginning of my presidency, to build new ties between the United States and Africa; why we had the first White House conference, the ministerial and that wonderful trip in the spring of 1998, that I will remember for the rest of my life.

I went to Africa as a friend, to create a partnership. And we have made significant progress. There are challenges that are profound, but in the last two years we have seen thousands of triumphs large and small. Often, they don't make the headlines because the slow, steady progress of democracy and prosperity is not the stuff of headlines.

But, for example, I wish every American knew that last year the world's fastest-growing economy was Mozambique. Botswana was second, Angola fourth. I wish every American knew that and understood that that potential is in every African nation. It would make a difference. We must know these things about one another.

People know all about Africa's conflicts, but how many know that thousands of African soldiers are trying to end those conflicts as peacekeepers—and that Nigeria alone, amidst all its difficulties, has spent $10 billion in these peacekeeping efforts?

For years, Africa's wealthiest country, South Africa, and its most populous, Nigeria, cast long, forbidding shadows across the continent. Last year, South Africa's remarkable turnaround continued as its people transferred power from one elected president to another. Nigeria inaugurated a democratically elected president for the first time in decades. It is working to ensure that its wealth strengthens its people, not their oppressors. These are good news stories. They may not be in the headlines, but they should be in our hearts and our minds as we think of the future.

No one here, no one in our government, is under any illusions. There is still a lot of work to be done. Hardly anyone disagrees about what is needed: genuine democracy, good government, open markets, sustained investment in education and health and the environment—and more than anything, widespread peace. All depend, fundamentally and first, on African leadership. These things cannot be imported, and they certainly cannot be imposed from outside.

But we must also face a clear reality: even countries making the right policy choices still have to struggle to deliver for their people. Each African government has to walk down its own road to reform and renewal. But it is a hard road. And those of us who are in a position to do so must do our part to smooth that road, to remove some of the larger barriers, so that Africa can fully share in the benefits and the responsibilities of globalization.

I tell the American people all the time, and they're probably tired of hearing it now, that I have a very simple political philosophy: everybody counts, everybody has a role to play, everybody deserves a chance. And we all do better when we help each other. That is a rule we ought to follow with Africa.

There are five steps in particular I believe we must take. First, we must build an open world trading system which will benefit Africa alongside every other region in the world. Open markets are indispensable to raising living standards. From the 1970s to the 1990s, developing countries that chose trade grew at least twice as fast as those that chose not to open to the world.

Now, there are some who doubt that the poorest countries will benefit if we continue to open markets, but they should ask themselves: what will happen to workers in South Africa and Kenya without the jobs that come from selling the fruit of their labors abroad? What will happen to farmers in Zimbabwe and Ghana if protectionist farm subsidies make it impossible for them to sell beyond their borders?

Trade must not be a race to the bottom, whether we're talking about child labor, harsh working conditions or environmental degradation. But neither can we use fear to keep the poorest part of the global community stuck at the bottom forever. Africa has already taken important steps, forming regional trade blocks like ECOWAS, the East Africa Community, and SADC. But we can do more. That is why our Overseas Private Investment Corporation in Africa is working to support three times as many business projects in 1999 than it did in 1998, to create jobs for Africans and, yes, for Americans as well. That is why we are working with African nations to develop the institutions to sustain future growth—from efficient telecommunications to the financial sector.

And that is why, as soon as possible, we must enact in our Congress the bipartisan Africa Growth and Opportunity Act. This bill has passed in one version in our House and another version in our Senate. I urge the Congress to resolve the differences and send me a bill for signature by next month. And I ask every one of you here who just clapped—and those who didn't, but sympathize with the clapped—to contact anyone you know in the United States Congress and ask them to do this. This is a job that needs to be done.

We must also realize that trade alone cannot conquer poverty or build a partnership we need. For that reason, a second step we must take is to continue the work now underway to provide debt relief to African nations committed to sound policies. Struggling democratic governments should not have to choose between feeding and educating their children and paying interest on a debt. Last March, I suggested a way we could expand debt relief for the world's poorest and most indebted countries, most of which are African, and ensure the resources would be used to improve economic opportunity for ordinary African citizens. Our G-7 partners embraced that plan.

Still, I felt we should do more. So in September, I announced that we would completely write off all the debts owed to us by the countries that qualified for the G-7 program—as many as 27 African nations in all. The first countries, including Uganda and Mauritania, have begun to receive the benefits. Mozambique, Benin, Senegal and Tanzania are expected to receive benefits soon. Mozambique's debt is expected to go down by more than $3 billion. The money saved will be twice the health budget—twice the health budget—in a country where children are more likely to die before the age of five than they are to go on to secondary school.

Last year, I asked Congress for $970 million for debt relief. Many of you helped to persuade our Congress to appropriate a big share of that. Keep in mind, this is a program religious leaders say is a moral imperative, and leading economists say is a practical imperative. It's not so often that you get the religious leaders and the economists telling us that good business is good morals. It's probably always true, but they don't say it all that often.

We must finish the job this year; we must continue this work to provide aggressive debt relief to the countries that are doing the right thing, that will take the money and reinvest it in their people and their future. I ask you, especially the Americans in this audience, if you believe in what brought you here, help us to continue this important effort.

A third step we must take is to give better and deeper support to African education. Literacy is crucial—to economic growth, to health, to democracy, to securing the benefits of globalization. Sub-Saharan Africa has the developing world's lowest school enrollment rate. In Zambia, over half the schoolchildren lack a simple notebook. In rural parts of Tanzania, there is one textbook for every 20 children. That's why I proposed in our budget to increase by more than 50 percent the assistance we provide to developing countries to improve basic education, targeting areas where child labor is prevalent. I ask other nations to join us in this.

I'll never forget the schools I visited on my trip to Africa—the bright lights in the eyes of the children, how intelligent they were, how eager they were. It is wrong for them to have to look at maps of nations that no longer exist, without maps of nations in their own continent that do exist. It is wrong for them to be deprived the same opportunities to learn that our young people have here. If intelligence is equally distributed throughout the human race—and I believe it is—then every child in the human race ought to have a chance to develop his or her intelligence in every country in the world.

A fourth step we must take is to fight the terrible diseases that have afflicted so many millions of Africans, especially AIDS and also TB and malaria. Last year, ten times as many people died of AIDS in Africa as were killed in all the continent's wars combined. It will soon double child mortality and reduce life expectancy by 20 years.

You all laughed when Andy Young said that I was going to get out of the presidency as a young man. Depending on the day, I sometimes feel young or I feel that I'm the oldest man my age in America. The life expectancy in this country has gone from 47 to 77 in the 20th century. An American who lives to be 65 has a life expectancy in excess of 82 years. AIDS is going to reduce the life expectancy in Africa by 20 years. And even that understates the problem, because the people that escape it will live longer lives as African economies grow and strengthen.

The worst burden in life any adult can bear is to see a child die before you. The worst problem in Africa now is that so many of these children with AIDS have also already lost their parents. We must do something about this. In Africa there are companies that are hiring two employees for every job on the assumption that one of them will die. This is a humanitarian issue, a political issue and an economic issue.

Last month, Vice President [Al] Gore opened the first-ever United Nations Security Council session on health issues, on a health issue, by addressing the AIDS crisis in Africa. I've asked Congress for another $100 million to fight the epidemic, bringing our total to $325 million. I've asked my administration to develop a plan for new initiatives to address prevention, the financial dimensions of fighting AIDS, the needs of those affected, so that we can make it clear to our African partners that we consider AIDS not just their burden but ours, as well.

But even that will not be enough. Recently, Uganda's Health Minister pointed out that to provide access to currently available treatments to every Ugandan afflicted with AIDS would cost $24 billion. The annual budget of Uganda is $2 billion.

The solution to this crisis, and to other killer diseases like malaria and TB, has to include effective and expensive vaccines. Now, there are four major companies in the world that develop vaccines, two in the United States and two in Europe. They have little incentive to make costly investments in developing vaccines for people who cannot afford to pay for them. So in my State of the Union address, I proposed a generous tax credit that would enable us to say to private industry, if you develop vaccines for AIDS, malaria and TB, we will help to pay for them. So go on and develop them, and we'll save millions of lives.

But I have to tell you, my speech—and I don't want anybody else but me to be responsible; my speechwriters were so sensitive, they didn't put this in the speech. But I want to say this: AIDS was a bigger problem in the United States a few years ago than it is today. AIDS rates are not going up in African countries, all African countries. They're actually going down in a couple of African countries.

Now, I know that this is a difficult and sensitive issue. I know there are cultural and religious factors that make it very difficult to tackle this issue from a preventive point of view. We don't have an AIDS vaccine yet. We have drugs that will help to prevent the transmission from pregnant mothers to their children, which I want to be able to give out. We have other drugs that have given people with AIDS in our country normal lives, in terms of their health and the length of their lives. I want those to be available.

But the real answer is to stop people from getting the HIV virus in the first place.

I got to see firsthand some of the things that were being done in Uganda that were instrumental in driving down the AIDS rate. Now, I don't care how hard or delicate or difficult this is; this is your children's lives we're talking about. You know, we who are adults, when our children's lives are at stake, have to get over whatever our hang-ups or problems are and go out there and do what is necessary to save the lives of our children.

And I'll help you do that, too. That's not free; that costs money. Systems have to be set up. But we shouldn't pretend that we can give injections and work our way out of this. We have to change behavior, attitudes. And it has to be done in an organized, disciplined, systematic way. And you can do more in less time for less money in a preventive way, to give the children of Africa their lives back, and the nations of Africa their futures back, with an aggressive prevention campaign than anything else. And there is no excuse for not doing it; it has to be done.

Finally, let me say there is one more huge obstacle to progress in Africa, that we are committed to doing our part to overcome. We must build on the leadership of Africans to end the bloody conflicts killing people and killing progress.

You know the toll: tens of thousands of young lives lost in the war between Ethiopia and Eritrea; thousands killed and disfigured at unbelievably young ages in the civil war that nearly destroyed Sierra Leone; 2 million killed by famine and war in Sudan, where government sees diversity as a threat rather than a strength, and denies basic relief to citizens it claims to represent.

Most of the world's conflicts pale in complexity before the situation in the Congo. At least seven nations and countless armed groups are pitted there against each other in a desperate struggle that seems to bring no one victory, and everyone misery—especially the innocent people of the Congo. They deserve a better chance. Secretary [Madeleine] Albright has called the Congo struggle Africa's first world war. As we search for an end to the conflict, let us remember the central lesson of the First World War: the need for a good peace. If you mess up the peace, you get another world war.

A year ago, I said if the nations of the region reached an agreement that the international community could support, I would support a peacekeeping operation in the Congo. The region has now done so. The Lusaka cease-fire agreement takes into account the sovereignty and territorial integrity of Congo; the withdrawal of foreign forces; the security of Congo's neighbors; the need for dialogue within the nation; and most important, the need for the countries within Central Africa to cooperate in managing the region's security. It is more than a cease-fire; it is a blueprint for building peace. Best of all, it is a genuinely African solution to an African problem.

There is still fighting in Congo. Peace will not happen overnight. It will require steady commitment from the parties and the unwavering support of the international community. I have told our Congress that America intends to do its part by supporting the next phase of the U.N.'s peacekeeping operation in the Congo, which will send observers to oversee the implementation of the agreement.

We need to think hard about what is at stake here. African countries have taken the lead—not just the countries directly affected, either. They are not asking us to solve their problems or to deploy our military. All they have asked is that we support their own efforts to build peace, and to make it last. We in the United States should be willing to do this. It is principled and practical.

I know—I see the members of Congress here. I say again—I see Congressman [Donald] Payne [D-N.J.], Congresswoman Sheila Jackson-Lee [D-Texas], Congresswoman Barbara Lee [D-Calif.], Congressman [Ed] Royce [R-Calif.]—we need to stand by the people of Africa who have decided how to solve this most complex and troubling problem. We have learned the hard way in the United States, over decades and decades, that the costliest peace is far cheaper than the cheapest war. And we need to remember that as we approach our common responsibilities in central Africa.

Finally, let me say that I intend to continue to work hard on these things for every day that I am President. For me, the remarkable decade of the 1990s began with the liberation symbolized by Nelson Mandela's first steps from Robben Island. In a few days, I will have the opportunity to join by satellite the conference in Tanzania that President Mandela is organizing to build peace in Burundi.

A lot of people look at Africa and think, oh, these problems are just too complicated. I look at Africa and I see the promise of Africa, and think, if the problems are complicated now, think how much worse they'll be if we continue to ignore them.

Other people grow frustrated by bad news, and wish only to hear good news. But empty optimism does Africa no more service than groundless cynicism. What we need is not empty optimism or groundless cynicism, but realistic hope. We need to see the promise, the beauty, the dreams of Africa. We need to see the problems clear and plain, and stop ignoring the evident responses. We in the United States need to understand that our obligations to be good partners with Africa are not because we are certain that everything will turn out all right, but because it is important. Because we're human beings, we can never expect everything to turn out all right.

Africa is so incredibly diverse. Its people speak nearly 3,000 languages. It is not a single, monolithic place with single, monolithic truths. A place of many places, each defined by its own history and aspirations, its own successes and failures. I was struck on my trip to Africa by the differences between Ghana and Uganda, Botswana and Senegal—between Capetown and Soweto. I was also struck by what bound people together in these places.

In George Washington's first draft of his Farewell Address, he wrote, "We may all be considered as the children of one common country." The more I think about globalization and the interdependence it promises and demands, the more I share that sentiment. Now, we must think of ourselves as children of one common world. If we wish to deepen peace and prosperity and democracy for ourselves, we must wish it also for the people of Africa. Africa is the cradle of humanity, but also a big part of humanity's future.

I leave you with this thought: when I think of the troubles of Africa, rooted in tribal differences; when I think of the continuing troubles in America, across racial lines, rooted in the shameful way we brought slaves here from West Africa so long ago, and our continuing challenges as we integrate wave after wave after wave of new immigrants from new places around the world; I am struck by the fact that life's greatest joy is our common humanity, and life's greatest curse is our inability to see our common humanity.

In Africa, life is full of joy and difficulty. But for too long, the African people have lacked for friends and allies to help the joys overcome the difficulties. The United States will be a friend for life.

Thank you.

73

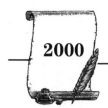

# March

# THE POPE ON THE ERRORS OF THE ROMAN CATHOLIC CHURCH
## March 12, 2000

*In an unprecedented moment in the history of the Roman Catholic Church, Pope John Paul II asked God's forgiveness for the errors committed by Roman Catholics throughout its two thousand-year history. This extraordinary public act of repentance for religious intolerance and mistreatment of Jews, women, and ethnic and racial groups came during a "Day of Pardon" mass in St. Peter's Basilica on March 12, 2000, the first Sunday of Lent, the season of penitence leading up to the celebration of the crucifixion and resurrection of Jesus Christ. The pontiff had described the sweeping apology as a key element of a churchwide "purification of memory" as the church prepared to enter its third millennium.*

*Little more than a week later, John Paul made his first visit as pope to the Holy Land. The Vatican billed the pope's visit to sites in Israel, Jordan, and Palestine that figured prominently in the life of Jesus as a personal pilgrimage. But the pope also met with political as well as religious leaders in all three jurisdictions in an effort to promote political and religious reconciliation in the region. He visited sites of immense importance to Arabs and Jews, including a Palestinian refugee camp on the West Bank and the Yad Vashem Holocaust memorial in Jerusalem. Although the pope neither apologized for the church's silence during the Holocaust, as many Jews hoped he would, nor endorsed Palestinian refugee claims that they be returned to their historic homelands, the presence of the aging and ailing pontiff lent new symbolic weight to his calls for reconciliation.*

*The "Day of Pardon" and the trip to the Holy Land were highlights of the Roman Catholic Holy Year in which the pope sought to kindle a "new evangelism" among Catholics and to give new vigor to the concept of clemency. Bowing to the pope's wishes, the Italian government in June pardoned Mehmet Ali Agca, the man who tried to assassinate the pope in 1981. John Paul had also hoped to effect a reconciliation between the Roman Catholic Church and the Orthodox Christian churches, which had split apart nearly a thousand years earlier, in 1054. His failure to do so was thought to be a*

*major disappointment for the pope. At the same time, a Vatican edict, is-
sued in September, declared that individuals could attain full salvation only
through the Catholic Church, a statement at sharp odds with the pope's calls
for reconciliation.*

## The "Day of Pardon"

*"Let us ask pardon for the divisions which have occurred among Chris-
tians, for the violence some have used in the service of truth and for the distrustful and hostile attitudes sometimes taken toward followers of other
religions," the pope said in his homily seeking divine forgiveness for the
sins of the Catholic Church. Although the pope's homily did not name
specific groups that the church had sinned against, special prayers said
during the mass alluded to the church's intolerance or mistreatment of Jews,
ethnic and racial groups, and women, among others.*

*Dressed in the purple robes symbolic of the Lenten season, the pope was
assisted in the mass by five cardinals and two bishops, each of whom confessed to a specific category of sin, for which the pope then asked for forgiveness. In addition to a general confession, the prelates confessed to sins
"committed in the service of truth," referring to the brutal treatment of Jews,
Muslims, and others during the Inquisition and the Crusades; sins that
"have harmed the unity of the body of Christ," a reference to the schisms between the Catholic Church and Protestants and Orthodox Christians; sins
against "the people of Israel"; sins "committed in actions against love,
peace, the rights of peoples, and respect for cultures and religions," in references to forced conversions; sins "against the dignity of women and the
unity of the human race"; and sins "in relation to the fundamental rights of
the person," referring to the church's failure to feed the poor and prevent
abortions, among other lapses.*

*Many observers hailed the mass as one of John Paul's most important
acts. "In the future," one Vatican official said, "when everyone has forgotten
communism, he will be remembered as the pope who asked for forgiveness."
John Paul had been thinking about making such a blanket apology for several years and had laid out the groundwork for it in a 1994 apostolic letter
called "The Coming of the Third Millennium." The mass was also preceded
by a document prepared by the International Theological Commission,
which sought to place the apology on firm theological footing.*

*This was not the first apology the pope had issued. Perhaps the most no-
table was the 1998 report repenting for the failure of many Catholics to help
Jews during the Holocaust, or Shoah. Although Jewish leaders generally welcomed the church's acknowledgement of complicity in the Holocaust, many
also said the report, entitled "We Remember: A Reflection on the Shoah," did
not go far enough in admitting either the historical anti-Semitic teachings
of the church, which many Jews said set the stage for the Holocaust, or the
failure during World War II of church leaders, including Pope Pius XII, to
take aggressive steps against the Nazi tyranny.* (Catholic Church on the
Holocaust, Historic Documents of 1998, p. 121)

*Jewish leaders had a similar reaction to the pope's "day of pardon" mes-*

*sage. "It's a positive and courageous act, we hope it enters into the mentality of other Christians," said the head of the Union of Jewish Communities in Italy. "But it remains primarily theological, when the problems between Jews and Christians are historic, social, and political." Rabbi Marvin Hier, dean of the Simon Wiesenthal Center, said the apology was a "bold and important step forward," but regretted that the pope had not referred explicitly to the Holocaust. "The church still wants to steer clear of dealing with the role of the Vatican during World War II," he said.*

*Controversy over the role of Pope Pius XII during World War II continued throughout the year. In October a panel created by the Vatican and several Jewish organizations to respond to allegations that the pope had not spoken out strongly enough against the Holocaust issued an interim report stating that the eleven volumes of materials published by the Vatican did not "put to rest significant questions about the role" the church played during the Holocaust. The International Catholic-Jewish Commission listed forty-seven questions that it said were still unanswered and asked the Vatican to give it access to closed archives pertaining to the war. The six scholars, three Catholic and three Jewish, added that "no serious historian could accept that the published, edited volumes could put us at the end of the story." The Vatican's only immediate response was to acknowledge the commission's request. At year's end the panel was still waiting for an answer, and many observers predicted they would have a long wait.*

## The Pope's Visit to the Holy Land

*John Paul's visit to the Holy Land, which began in Amman, Jordan, on March 20 and ended in Tel Aviv on March 26, was the first he had made as pontiff. As bishop of Cracow, Poland, the pope had made a pilgrimage to the area in 1963. The pope's visit to the Holy Land was billed as a personal religious pilgrimage to sites that had figured prominently in the life of Jesus. In Jordan he visited Mt. Nebo, where Moses saw the "promised land" before his death, and a site in the Jordan Valley that may have been the place where Jesus was baptized. In Bethlehem on March 22 the pope said mass in Manger Square outside the Basilica of the Nativity; on March 23 he visited the site in Jerusalem where Jesus is said to have eaten the Last Supper. During the next three days he said a mass for youth near the site of the Sermon on the Mount; visited the Grotto of the Annunciation in Nazareth, where Jesus's parents lived, and the Basilica of the Garden of Gesthemane, where Jesus is said to have prayed on the eve of his arrest; and said mass in Jerusalem's Church of the Holy Sepulcher, commemorating Jesus's crucifixion, death, burial, and resurrection.*

*The pope's trip to a land torn by religious and political hostilities was also filled with immense symbolic significance, as John Paul sought to use his moral stature as head of the church to press for reconciliation and peace among Christians, Jews, and Muslims. In separate meetings with King Abdullah II of Jordan, Palestinian leader Yasir Arafat, and Israeli prime minister Ehud Barak and other Israeli politicians, the pope did not go beyond already stated Vatican policy toward the region: support for a Palestinian*

homeland on the one hand, and recognition of the state of Israel and acknowledgement of the Holocaust on the other.

The pope's clear empathy with the plight of the Palestinians as well as for
the sorrows experienced by the Jews during the Holocaust underscored his
message of reconciliation and brotherhood. "By saying right here on Palestinian soil that he was praying for the Palestinians who are homeless, the
pope abridged the whole Palestinian story," said an editorial in a Palestinian daily after the pope appeared with Yasir Arafat at the Palestinian
refugee camp, Deheisheh, on the West Bank. At the Yad Vashem Holocaust
memorial, John Paul spoke with such eloquence that many Israelis put
aside their disappointment that he had not offered an official apology from
the church. "I thought he sounded almost Jewish," the chairman of the Yad
Vashem Council told the New York Times.

In a meeting with Israel president Ezer Weizman on March 23, the pope
blessed Israel, an act widely seen as the Vatican's full acknowledgement of
the Israeli state. Although the Vatican did not oppose the creation of Israel
in 1948, it did not establish diplomatic relations with the government until 1994. When Pope Paul VI visited Israel briefly in 1964, he did not use the
word Israel, nor did he address the Israeli president by his title—slights
that many Israelis had not forgotten. In perhaps the most symbolic gesture
of his visit, the pope on March 26, the final day of his visit, tucked a note to
God into a crevice of the Western Wall of the Old City in Jerusalem, the remains of the Second Temple, destroyed in 70 A.D., and perhaps the holiest
site in Judaism. Based on his prayers during the "Day of Pardon" mass, the
note read: "God of our fathers, you chose Abraham and his descendants to
bring your name to the nations. We are deeply saddened by the behavior of
those who in the course of history have caused these children of yours to suffer. And asking your forgiveness, we wish to commit ourselves to genuine
brotherhood with the people of the covenant."

The tensions could not be totally submerged, however. At the Deheisheh
refugee camp on the West Bank, John Paul expressed support for an estimated 3 million Palestinian refugees uprooted from their homes and separated from their families. Immediately after he left the area, however, violent
clashes broke out between the police and some of the refugees, who had long
been concerned that Palestinian leaders would agree to a peace plan that
would not allow them to return to their traditional homelands. An interfaith
meeting with Christian, Jewish, and Muslim religious leaders was side-
tracked when participants wrangled over the status of Jerusalem, the city
holy to all three religions and claimed by Palestinians and Israelis as the
capital of each. The Vatican sought international recognition of Jerusalem
as a holy city—what the pope at one stop referred to as "a part of the common patrimony" of Christianity, Island, and Judaism. On his last day John
Paul met with Jerusalem's chief Islamic cleric at Al Aksa Mosque. But instead of engaging in a conversation, the cleric, Sheik Ikrima Sabri, lectured
the pope, demanding an end to the Israeli occupation of Jerusalem.

Any relaxation of tensions that John Paul may have achieved during his
visit to the Middle East may have been undercut by a Vatican dictum, issued

*September 5, stating that individuals could attain full salvation for their sins only through the Roman Catholic Church. Although the statement was a reaffirmation of the church's centuries-old claim to primacy, it drew responses of dismay from leaders of other faiths. The statement was "a jump backwards in terms of ecumenism and with dialogues with other religions," said the Reverend Valdo Benecchi, president of the Methodist Evangelical Churches of Italy. Others said the statements would be seen as a rejection of the dialogue on a variety of religious issues that had been taking place between Catholics and other religions.*

*Following are excerpts from the "Day of Pardon" homily delivered by Pope John Paul II on March 12, 2000, followed by the "Universal Prayer" in which the pope, assisted by seven prelates, asked forgiveness for the historical sins committed by Roman Catholics. The documents were obtained from the Internet at http://www .vatican.va/holy_father/john_paul_ii/homilies/documents/ hf_jp-ii_hom_20000312_pardon_en.html.*

# HOMILY OF THE HOLY FATHER

## "Day of Pardon"

1. *"We implore you, in Christ's name: be reconciled to God! For our sake God made him who did not know sin to be sin, so that in him we might become the righteousness of God"* (2 *Cor* 5: 20–21).

These are words of St Paul which the Church rereads every year on Ash Wednesday, at the beginning of Lent. In the Lenten season, the Church desires to be particularly united to Christ, who, moved inwardly by the Holy Spirit, began his messianic mission by going into the wilderness and fasting there for 40 days and 40 nights (cf. *Mk* 1: 12–13). . . .

2. *"He made him who did not know sin to be sin"* (2 *Cor* 5: 21). A few moments ago, in the second reading, we heard this surprising assertion made by the Apostle. What do these words mean? They seem, and in effect are, a paradox. How could God, who is holiness itself, "make" his Only-begotten Son, sent into the world, "to be sin"? Yet this is exactly what we read in the passage from St Paul's Second Letter to the Corinthians. We are in the presence of a mystery: a mystery which at first sight is baffling, but is clearly written in divine Revelation.

Already in the Old Testament, the Book of Isaiah speaks of it with inspired foresight in the fourth song of the Servant of Yahweh: "We had all gone astray like sheep, each following his own way; but the Lord laid upon him the guilt of us all" (*Is* 53: 6).

Although Christ, the Holy One, was absolutely sinless, he agreed to take our sins upon himself. He agreed in order to redeem us; he agreed to bear our sins

81

to fufil the mission he had received from the Father, who—as the Evangelist John writes—"so loved the world that he gave his only Son, that whoever believes in him . . . may have eternal life" (*Jn* 3: 16).

3. Before Christ who, out of love, took our guilt upon himself, we are all invited to make a profound examination of conscience. One of the characteristic elements of the Great Jubilee is what I described as the "purification of memory". . . . As the Successor of Peter, I asked that "in this year of mercy the Church, strong in the holiness which she receives from her Lord, should kneel before God and implore forgiveness for the past and present sins of her sons and daughters". . . . Today, the First Sunday of Lent, seemed to me the right occasion for the Church, gathered spiritually round the Successor of Peter, to implore divine forgiveness for the sins of all believers. *Let us forgive and ask forgiveness!*

This appeal has prompted a thorough and fruitful reflection, which led to the publication several days ago of a document of the International Theological Commission, entitled: *"Memory and Reconciliation: The Church and the Faults of the Past."* I thank everyone who helped to prepare this text. It is very useful for correctly understanding and carrying out the authentic request for pardon, based on the *objective responsibility* which Christians share as members of the Mystical Body, and which spurs today's faithful to recognize, along with their own sins, the sins of yesterday's Christians, in the light of careful historical and theological discernment.

Indeed, "because of the bond which unites us to one another in the Mystical Body, all of us, though not personally responsible and without encroaching on the judgement of God who alone knows every heart, bear the burden of the errors and faults of those who have gone before us". . . . The recognition of past wrongs serves to *reawaken our consciences to the compromises of the present,* opening the way to conversion for everyone.

4. *Let us forgive and ask forgiveness!* While we praise God who, in his merciful love, has produced in the Church a wonderful harvest of holiness, missionary zeal, total dedication to Christ and neighbour, we cannot fail to recognize *the infidelities to the Gospel committed by some of our brethren,* especially during the second millennium. Let us ask pardon for the divisions which have occurred among Christians, for the violence some have used in the service of the truth and for the distrustful and hostile attitudes sometimes taken towards the followers of other religions.

Let us confess, even more, *our responsibilities as Christians for the evils of today.* We must ask ourselves what our responsibilities are regarding atheism, religious indifference, secularism, ethical relativism, the violations of the right to life, disregard for the poor in many countries.

We humbly ask forgiveness for the part which each of us has had in these evils by our own actions, thus helping to disfigure the face of the Church.

At the same time, as we confess our sins, *let us forgive the sins committed by others against us.* Countless times in the course of history Christians have suffered hardship, oppression and persecution because of their faith. Just as the victims of such abuses forgave them, so let us forgive as well. The Church today feels and has always felt obliged to *purify her memory* of those sad events from every feeling of rancour or revenge. In this way the Jubilee becomes for everyone a favourable opportunity for a profound conversion to the Gospel. The acceptance of God's forgiveness leads to the commitment to forgive our brothers and sisters and to be reconciled with them.

5. But what does the word "reconciliation" mean to us? To grasp its precise sense and value, we must first recognize the possibility of division, of separation. Yes, man is the only creature on earth who can have a relationship of communion with his Creator, but he is also *the only one who can separate himself from him.* Unfortunately, he has frequently turned away from God.

Fortunately many people, like the prodigal son spoken of in the Gospel of Luke (cf. *Lk* 15: 13), after leaving their father's house and squandering their inheritance, reach the very bottom and realize how much they have lost (cf. *Lk* 15: 13–17). Then they set out to return home: "I will arise and go to my father, and I will say to him, 'Father, I have sinned.' . . ." (*Lk* 15: 18).

God, clearly represented by the father in the parable, welcomes every prodigal child who returns to him. He welcomes him through Christ, in whom the sinner can once again become "righteous" with the righteousness of God. He welcomes him, because for our sake he made his eternal Son to be sin. Yes, only through Christ can we become the righteousness of God (cf. *2 Cor* 5: 21). . . .

Mary, Mother of forgiveness, help us to accept the grace of forgiveness which the Jubilee generously offers us. Make the Lent of this extraordinary Holy Year an acceptable time, a time of reconciliation, a time of salvation for all believers and for everyone who is searching for God!

# THE UNIVERSAL PRAYER

## Confession of Sins and Asking for Forgiveness

*The Holy Father:*
Brothers and Sisters,
let us turn with trust to God our Father,
who is merciful and compassionate,
slow to anger, great in love and fidelity,
and ask him to accept the repentance of his people
who humbly confess their sins,
and to grant them mercy. . . .

## I. Confession of Sins in General

*A representative of the Roman Curia*
Let us pray that our confession and repentance
will be inspired by the Holy Spirit,
that our sorrow will be conscious and deep,
and that, humbly viewing the sins of the past
in an authentic "purification of memory,"
we will be committed to the path of true conversion. . . .

*The Holy Father:*
Lord God,
your pilgrim Church,
which you ever sanctify in the blood of your Son,
counts among her children in every age
members whose holiness shines brightly forth
and members whose disobedience to you
contradicts the faith we profess and the Holy Gospel.
You, who remain ever faithful,
even when we are unfaithful,
forgive our sins
and grant that we may bear true witness to you
before all men and women.
We ask this through Christ our Lord. . . .

## II. Confession of Sins Committed in the Service of Truth

*A representative of the Roman Curia:*
Let us pray that each one of us,
looking to the Lord Jesus, meek and humble of heart,
will recognize that even men of the Church,
in the name of faith and morals,
have sometimes used methods not in keeping with the Gospel
in the solemn duty of defending the truth. . . .

*The Holy Father:*
Lord, God of all men and women,
in certain periods of history
Christians have at times given in to intolerance
and have not been faithful to the great commandment of love,
sullying in this way the face of the Church, your Spouse.
Have mercy on your sinful children
and accept our resolve
to seek and promote truth in the gentleness of charity,
in the firm knowledge that truth
can prevail only in virtue of truth itself.
We ask this through Christ our Lord. . . .

## III. Confession of Sins Which Have Harmed the Unity of the Body of Christ

*A representative of the Roman Curia:*
Let us pray that our recognition of the sins
which have rent the unity of the Body of Christ
and wounded fraternal charity
will facilitate the way to reconciliation
and communion among all Christians. . . .

*The Holy Father:*
Merciful Father,
on the night before his Passion
your Son prayed for the unity of those who believe in him:
in disobedience to his will, however,
believers have opposed one another, becoming divided,
and have mutually condemned one another and fought against one another.
We urgently implore your forgiveness
and we beseech the gift of a repentant heart,
so that all Christians, reconciled with you and with one another
will be able, in one body and in one spirit,
to experience anew the joy of full communion.
We ask this through Christ our Lord. . . .

## IV. Confession of Sins Against the People of Israel

*A representative of the Roman Curia:*
Let us pray that, in recalling the sufferings
endured by the people of Israel throughout history,
Christians will acknowledge the sins
committed by not a few of their number
against the people of the Covenant and the blessings,
and in this way will purify their hearts. . . .

*The Holy Father:*
God of our fathers,
you chose Abraham and his descendants
to bring your Name to the Nations:
we are deeply saddened by the behaviour of those
who in the course of history
have caused these children of yours to suffer,
and asking your forgiveness we wish to commit ourselves
to genuine brotherhood
with the people of the Covenant.
We ask this through Christ our Lord. . . .

## V. Confession of Sins Committed in Actions Against Love, Peace, The Rights of Peoples, and Respect for Cultures and Religions

*A representative of the Roman Curia:*
Let us pray that contemplating Jesus,
our Lord and our Peace,
Christians will be able to repent of the words and attitudes
caused by pride, by hatred,
by the desire to dominate others,
by enmity towards members of other religions
and towards the weakest groups in society,
such as immigrants and itinerants. . . .

*The Holy Father:*
Lord of the world, Father of all,
through your Son
you asked us to love our enemies,
to do good to those who hate us
and to pray for those who persecute us.
Yet Christians have often denied the Gospel;
yielding to a mentality of power,
they have violated the rights of ethnic groups and peoples,
and shown contempt for their cultures and religious traditions:
be patient and merciful towards us, and grant us your forgiveness!
We ask this through Christ our Lord. . . .

## VI. Confession of Sins Against the Dignity of Women and the Unity of the Human Race

*A Representative of the Roman Curia:*
Let us pray for all those who have suffered offences
against their human dignity and whose rights have been trampled;
let us pray for women, who are all too often humiliated and emarginated,
and let us acknowledge the forms of acquiescence in these sins
of which Christians too have been guilty. . . .

*The Holy Father:*
Lord God, our Father,
you created the human being, man and woman,
in your image and likeness
and you willed the diversity of peoples
within the unity of the human family.
At times, however, the equality of your sons
and daughters has not been acknowledged,
and Christians have been guilty of attitudes
of rejection and exclusion,
consenting to acts of discrimination
on the basis of racial and ethnic differences.
Forgive us and grant us the grace to heal the wounds
still present in your community on account of sin,
so that we will all feel ourselves to be your sons and daughters.
We ask this through Christ our Lord. . . .

## VII. Confession of Sins in Relation to the Fundamental Rights of the Person

*A Representative of the Roman Curia:*
Let us pray for all the men and women of the world,
especially for minors who are victims of abuse,
for the poor, the alienated, the disadvantaged;
let us pray for those who are most defenceless,

the unborn killed in their mother's womb
or even exploited for experimental purposes
by those who abuse
the promise of biotechnology
and distort the aims of science. . . .

*The Holy Father:*
God, our Father,
you always bear the cry of the poor.
How many times have Christians themselves not recognized you
in the hungry, the thirsty and the naked,
in the persecuted, the imprisoned,
and in those incapable of defending themselves,
especially in the first stages of life.
For all those who have committed acts of injustice
by trusting in wealth and power
and showing contempt for the "little ones"
who are so dear to you, we ask your forgiveness:
have mercy on us and accept our repentance.
We ask this through Christ our Lord. . . .

## Concluding Prayer

*The Holy Father:*
Most merciful Father,
your Son, Jesus Christ, the judge of the living and the dead,
in the humility of his first coming
redeemed humanity from sin
and in his glorious return he will demand an account of every sin.
Grant that our forebears, our brothers and sisters,
and we, your servants, who by the grace of the Holy Spirit
turn back to you in whole-hearted repentance,
may experience your mercy and receive
the forgiveness of our sins.
We ask this through Christ our Lord.

*R[esponse].* Amen.

# INDEPENDENT NASA REPORT ON MARS MISSION FAILURES
## March 28, 2000

*The National Aeronautics and Space Administration (NASA) cut corners and took unacceptable risks with missions to Mars, resulting in the high-profile failures of three missions late in 1999. These were the basic conclusions of a series of reports issued during the first half of 2000 by panels commissioned by NASA to probe the Mars failures, which had threatened to undermine public support for the nation's entire space program.*

*Each of the investigations concluded that there was nothing fundamentally wrong with NASA's overall approach toward its space mission. Known as "faster, better, cheaper," that approach, adopted by NASA administrator Daniel S. Goldin in 1992, was intended to mount space missions more quickly, each with a more specific focus and slimmer budget than in the past, when missions cost billions of dollars each and took decades to complete.*

*The problem, according to the reports, was that NASA and its various components in too many instances emphasized speed and cost cutting at the expense of quality. The results were inadequate management of space programs and lapses in the design and testing of mission hardware and software, leading in turn to the failure of some missions.*

*NASA officials took a number of steps during the year in response to the reports. Most important, the agency appointed new management for its Mars programs and revised its schedule for key Mars missions in the first decade of the twenty-first century. Goldin acknowledged to a House panel on June 20 that the Mars programs were not adequately funded, but he insisted that NASA itself had an adequate budget. The mistakes that led to the Mars program failures could be corrected with improved training and internal procedures requiring only "negligible or modest costs," he said.*

*Congressional leaders said in 2000 that they were monitoring NASA to make sure the agency made the changes called for in the various reports. Congress placed no serious restrictions on NASA's Mars programs, however, and it provided full funding for the space agency. In October Congress sent President Bill Clinton authorizing legislation for NASA (PL 106–391), marking the first time since 1992 that either chamber had passed a regular*

*authorization bill for the agency (as opposed to annual appropriations).
The bill allowed $42.4 billion for the agency in fiscal years 2001–2003, an
increase over the Clinton administration's request. Congress appropriated
$14.3 billion for NASA in fiscal 2001, an increase of $684 million over the
previous year (PL 106–377).*

## Mission Successes and Failures

*NASA had two sensational successes with Mars missions in the mid-
1990s, both of which incorporated elements of the "faster, better, cheaper"
philosophy. The* Mars Global Surveyor, *launched in 1996, reached orbit
around Mars in 1997 and in 1998 began sending back to Earth detailed
photographs and measurements of the planet's surface and atmosphere. The*
Global Surveyor's *main mission was to look for evidence of water on Mars;
its reports suggested that large reservoirs of liquid water might be hidden
under the planet's dry surface. (Global Surveyor reports, p. 379)*

*The Mars* Pathfinder, *also launched in 1996, landed on Mars in 1997 and
deposited a remote-controlled unit called* Sojourner. *For several weeks Sojourner roamed the Martian surface, collecting and examining geological
samples and sending detailed reports back to Earth. (Pathfinder mission,*
Historic Documents of 1997, p. 509)

*Then, on September 23, 1999, a follow-up mission, the* Mars Climate Orbiter, *failed to achieve a proper orbit of Mars and apparently was destroyed.
A subsequent investigation by an independent panel found that a misunderstanding between Lockheed Martin Astronautics, the Denver-based
contractor that built the* Orbiter, *and the Jet Propulsion Laboratory in
Pasadena, California, which managed the $125 million mission, concern-
ing one measurement on the craft had led it to go dangerously off course.*

*Just ten weeks later, on December 3, another mission—the* Mars Polar-
Lander—*disappeared during its planned descent to the Martian surface.
That craft was carrying two miniature robot probes, known as* Deep Space
2, *that were supposed to dig into the Martian soil and send reports back to
Earth. After the descent, NASA never received any signals from either the*
Mars Polar Lander *or the probes, leading the agency eventually to conclude
that the craft had crashed into the surface and been destroyed. (Climate Or-
biter and Polar Lander failures,* Historic Documents of 1999, p. 711)

*A special review board, appointed by the Jet Propulsion Laboratory to
examine the failure of the* Polar Lander-Deep Space 2 *missions, issued a report on March 22 concluding that it was probable that the* Polar Lander's *engines shut down prematurely during the descent because switches on the
landing legs sent false signals that the craft had landed. As a result, the craft
almost certainly crashed onto the Martian surface. A "design error" that
caused this malfunction might have been caught if NASA had done adequate
testing before the mission was launched, the panel reported. The panel said
it could not make a definitive finding on why the* Deep Space 2 *probes had
failed, but it noted that NASA, for schedule and budget reasons, had not conducted some of the standard tests on the probes before they were loaded onto
the* Polar Lander.

## *Assessment Reports*

*In addition to the March 22 report on the* Polar Lander-Deep Space 2 *failure, NASA in March released three reports containing broad criticisms of the space agency's implementation of its "faster, better, cheaper" philosophy, particularly as it was applied to the Mars missions.*

*Two of the reports were released on March 13. The first, by the Mars Climate Orbiter Mishap Investigation Board, was a general follow-up to an earlier report, issued in November 1999, on the failure of that mission. The board, chaired by Arthur G. Stephenson, director of the Marshall Space Flight Center in Alabama, addressed a wide range of issues dealing with NASA's management of space projects. A second report released on March 13 was written by Tony Spear, a former Jet Propulsion Laboratory official best known as the project manager of the successful Mars* Pathfinder *mission. NASA administrator Goldin had asked Spear to examine the overall "faster, better, cheaper" concept.*

*NASA on March 28 released a third report reviewing the agency's entire Mars program. That review was conducted by an independent assessment team chaired by Thomas Young, a former NASA executive who had also been executive vice president of the Lockheed Martin Corporation, one of the agency's chief private contractors.*

*In general, all three reports said NASA should not abandon the "faster, better, cheaper" philosophy but should put the "better" component on an equal footing with the other two. In too many cases, the reports said, NASA and its contractors had rushed programs, imposed unrealistic budget limits, failed to carry out adequate tests, and relied on inexperienced managers. Each of these factors had, in varying degrees, created excessive risks leading to the specific problems that caused the failures of the Mars missions in late 1999, the reports said.*

*The Stephenson committee, composed of senior representatives from NASA and agencies that carried out NASA missions, used the failure of the* Mars Climate Orbiter *as a case study of NASA management. NASA did many things right with the program, the panel said, but excessive cost cutting, inadequate communication among offices responsible for various components of the program, and inexperienced management combined to create a climate in which the "root cause" of the* Orbiter's *failure developed. The root cause, the panel said, was that Lookheed Martin improperly used Anglo-American measurements (such as pounds and inches) for a key system, while the Jet Propulsion Laboratory assumed the measurements were in metric units (such as grams and centimeters). This misunderstanding might have been caught by a more experienced management team, the panel said.*

*Stephenson's panel suggested a new vision for NASA, "Mission Success First," in which all other considerations, including cost and schedule, would be secondary to the ability of each mission to carry out it stated goals. A central element for every program, the panel said, should be "testing, testing, and more testing, conducted as early as possible in the work plans."*

*An eighteen-page report by Spears, the former Mars* Pathfinder *executive, assessed NASA's fundamental concept of developing missions "faster, better, cheaper." After meeting with several hundred officials and employees of NASA and its affiliates, Spears said he found conflicting definitions of the concept. Within NASA, he said there was no agreement on whether the three elements were equally important. And some in the NASA community argued that it was possible to have two of the three elements (most notably, faster and cheaper), but not all three. Spears said he also found widespread misunderstanding of another of Goldin's precepts: "It's OK to fail."*

*Several NASA missions undertaken in the early years of the "faster, better, cheaper" concept were successful, Spears said, in part because employees and contractors rose to the challenge that Goldin had posed. But in later years—especially during the preparation of the* Climate Orbiter *and the* Polar Lander *projects—the drive to cut costs intensified even as more tasks were added to the missions. "The cost cap challenges were made too great, along with a mix of unstable funding and escalating requirements," he said.*

*While endorsing the overall "faster, better, cheaper" philosophy, Spears offered this modification as a solution to NASA's problems: "We need to slow down some, not rush too quickly into important programs and projects, plan and implement them more carefully, and move away from fixations on cost and near term gain." As a former manager of a major NASA project, Spears said it was up to each project manager to take full responsibility for the work of his or her team, even if that meant declaring "that the project is not doable for the available resources."*

*The Stephenson and Spears reports were followed two weeks later by release of the Young committee's detailed analysis of NASA's Mars program during the last half of the 1990s. In addition to Young, the panel included administrators and scientists from within NASA and its affiliated agencies, academic experts, industry executives, and two retired air force generals.*

*Like its counterparts, the Young committee endorsed Goldin's overall "faster, better, cheaper" approach as the best way for NASA to develop and manage space exploration programs within a limited budget. But the committee said it found "significant flaws" in the execution of Mars programs, especially the failed* Climate Orbiter, Polar Lander, *and* Deep Space 2 *missions. However, the flaws could be corrected—in a timely manner—so Mars exploration could continue, the committee said.*

*All three missions, the committee said, were led by "competent but inexperienced managers." The panel noted that the Jet Propulsion Laboratory—which ran all of the missions—did not have enough experienced managers for the number of projects assigned to it. Earlier in the 1990s the laboratory typically managed one to four projects in any given year; under the "faster, better, cheaper" concept the number of projects rose to between ten and fifteen annually. NASA could have compensated for this lack of experience by providing oversight by senior management, but failed to do so. NASA compounded its management problem, the panel said, by dividing respon-*

*sibility for the* Climate Orbiter *and* Polar Lander *projects into two phases: development and postlaunch operations. The result was a lack of "continuity" in decision making.*

*The Young committee endorsed the finding of Stephenson's panel that the* Climate Orbiter *failed because of the misunderstanding over how one piece of equipment was to be measured. This mistake could have been prevented by better project management, testing, and independent analysis, the committee said. Young's panel placed some of its harshest criticism on the* Deep Space 2 *mission. Components of that mission "were not adequately tested and were not ready for launch," the committee said. The committee suggested adding an element to NASA's basic credos: "If not ready, do not launch."*

*The committee said the* Climate Orbiter, Polar Lander, *and* Deep Space 2 *programs (costing a total of about $190 million) were "underfunded by at least 30 percent." All space programs run risks, some of which involve unknown factors, such as the exact terrain of the place on Mars where a spacecraft is supposed to land. But NASA, with its cost-cutting and inadequate management, had allowed the Mars missions to proceed despite an "unacceptable level of risk," the committee said.*

### Mars Mission Changes

*Goldin and his key aides accepted and endorsed the findings of the various committees and pledged to make changes in response to the reports. In a March 29 speech to employees of the Jet Propulsion Laboratory, Goldin said that "in my effort to empower people, I pushed too hard and, in so dong, stretched the system too thin."*

*The NASA official directly in charge of the space programs—Edward Weiler, the associate administrator for space science—announced two major changes on March 28, the day the Young report was released. First, Weiler appointed Scott Hubbard to a new position as director of all Mars programs at NASA headquarters. Hubbard had been director of astrobiology and space programs at NASA's Ames Research Center in Mountain View, California. Weiler said the appointment, coupled with changes planned in NASA's relationship with the Jet Propulsion Laboratory, would improve communication and clarify lines of authority in the Mars programs.*

*Weiler also announced an overall reassessment of future Mars missions, starting with the postponement of a mission that had been scheduled for launch in 2001, to land another spacecraft on Mars. The change was certain to delay what had been planned as the centerpiece mission: the landing in 2006 of a robot craft that would collect samples of the Martian soil and bring them back to Earth. "That's not going to be a five- or six-year program," Weiler said. "That's going to be a decade-long program." NASA later disbanded the team that had been working on that project. Weiler said plans would proceed for the launch in April 2001 of an orbiting craft. NASA announced on September 28 that the orbiter would be called the* 2001 Mars Odyssey, *in honor of the book by Arthur C. Clarke and movie by Stanley Kubrick,* 2001: A Space Odyssey.

*On August 10 Hubbard announced that NASA had decided to launch missions in the spring of 2003 that would place two robots, called "rovers," on the Martian surface in January 2004. The robots would send radio reports back to Earth but would not bring back samples of what they found. NASA officials acknowledged that the plan for twin Martian rovers posed substantial management, budgetary, technological, and scientific hurdles. But Hubbard and others said NASA was determined to learn from the mistakes that had caused the mission failures in 1999. For example, they said the rover programs would be subjected to more frequent and rigorous testing than any previous Mars missions.*

*Finally, on October 26 top NASA officials announced a long-term plan for six Mars missions during the first decade of the twenty-first century, starting with the launch of the twin rovers in 2003. In 2005 NASA planned to launch the Mars Reconnaissance Orbiter, which would take close-up photographs of the planet. Officials said high-resolution cameras would be able to photograph rocks the size of beach balls. As early as 2007 NASA would launch a long-range, long-duration mobile science laboratory, which would land on Mars. NASA also planned to develop a new series of smaller missions, called the "Scout" program, that would be selected from proposals submitted by the scientific community. The first mission was to be ready for launch in 2007. These missions were expected to cost $400 million to $450 million annually during the first five years of the decade—about what NASA had previously projected for its Mars program.*

*The Planetary Society, a private organization that advocated exploration of Mars, praised the space agency's new schedule of missions. But, in an October 26 statement, Louis Friedman, the society's executive director, expressed disappointment that NASA appeared to have abandoned a previous policy calling for a "permanent robotic presence on Mars." Friedman also said that public interest in Mars exploration—and therefore extensive funding—would be lacking until NASA made a commitment for manned missions to the planet.*

## *Space Shuttle Report*

*In a related development, an internal NASA study warned that budget cuts were threatening the safety of the agency's space shuttle program. A thirteen-member committee of experts, headed by Henry McDonald, director of the Ames Research Center in California, critiqued the work of the United Space Alliance, a Houston-based joint project of the Boeing Corporation and Lockheed Martin. NASA in 1996 contracted with United Space Alliance to manage the maintenance of the four space shuttles and the preparation for shuttle launches. NASA commissioned McDonald and his colleagues to study the shuttle program after a series of maintenance problems caused trouble with the July 1999 flight of the* Columbia. *All four shuttles were grounded for several months for repairs.*

*McDonald's panel said turning shuttle operations over to the United Space Alliance had resulted in lower costs and more efficient operations—but at the expense of safety. Most important, the panel said the contractors had reduced the number of safety checks to save money. The panel said NASA needed to be more directly involved in monitoring the work of the alliance.*

*Joseph H. Rothenberg, NASA associate administrator for space flight, said the agency had made some of the changes recommended by the McDonald committee and was studying others. But he said some of the panel's suggested changes appeared to be more appropriate to the aviation industry generally than to the space shuttle program. A spokesman for the United Space Alliance told the* Washington Post *that many of the McDonald committee recommendations had "already been addressed."*

> *Following are excerpts from the "Mars Program Independent Assessment Team Summary Report," compiled by an eighteen-member committee chaired by Thomas Young, a former executive at NASA and the Lockheed Martin Corporation, and released March 28, 2000, by NASA. The document was obtained from the Internet at http://www.nasa.gov/newsinfo/mpiat_summary.pdf.*

Mars Climate Orbiter failed to achieve Mars orbit on September 23, 1999. On December 3, 1999, Mars Polar Lander and two Deep Space 2 microprobes failed. As a result, the NASA Administrator established the Mars Program Independent Assessment Team (MPIAT) with the following charter:

Review and Analyze Successes and Failures of Recent Mars and Deep Space Missions
  - Mars Global Surveyor
  - Mars Climate Orbiter Pathfinder
  - Mars Polar Lander
  - Deep Space 1
  - Deep Space 2
Examine the Relationship Between and Among
  - NASA Jet Propulsion Laboratory (JPL)
  - California Institute of Technology (Caltech)
  - NASA Headquarters
  - Industry Partners.
Assess Effectiveness of Involvement of Scientists.
Identify Lessons Learned From Successes and Failures.
Review Revised Mars Surveyor Program to Assure Lessons Learned Are Utilized.
Oversee Mars Polar Lander and Deep Space 2 Failure Reviews.
Complete by March 15, 2000.

In-depth reviews were conducted at NASA Headquarters, JPL, and Lockheed Martin Astronautics (LMA). Structured reviews, informal sessions with numerous Mars Program participants, and extensive debate and discussion within the MPIAT establish the basis for this report. The review process began on January 7, 2000, and concluded with a briefing to the NASA Administrator on March 14, 2000.

This report represents the integrated views of the members of the MPIAT who are identified in the appendix. In total, three related reports have been produced: this report, a more detailed report titled "Mars Program Independent Assessment Team Report" (dated March 14, 2000), and the "Report on the Loss of the Mars Polar Lander and Deep Space 2 Missions" (dated March 22, 2000).

## Review and Analyze Successes and Failures of Recent Mars and Deep Space Missions

The Mars and deep space missions, reviewed and analyzed by this team, were implemented over a period of about 6 years (1994–present). Mars Global Surveyor (MGS) was launched in 1996 and was the first Mars mission to employ some tenets of Faster, Better, Cheaper (FBC). MGS is an extraordinary success and continues to be a highly productive science mission.

Mars Pathfinder was launched in 1996, landed on Mars on July 4, 1997, and captured the excitement of the public with lander and rover operations on the Mars surface. It was the first complete Mars FBC mission and was an engineering, science, and public success.

Deep Space 1 (DS-1) was a successful technology mission launched in 1998. It provided a space demonstration of numerous new technologies, including ion propulsion and onboard autonomous operations. These technologies are now space proven and available for future deep space missions.

Mars Climate Orbiter (MCO) was launched in late 1998, followed by Mars Polar Lander (MPL) and Deep Space 2 launched in early 1999. MCO failed to achieve Mars orbit because of a navigation error, resulting in the spacecraft entering the Mars atmosphere instead of going into the planned orbit. The "Report on the Loss of the Mars Climate Orbiter Mission," dated November 11, 1999, and the "MCO Mishap Investigation Board Phase I Report," dated November 10, 1999, provide details on the failure cause and corrective action.

The following is a summary of the MCO findings. Spacecraft operating data needed for navigation were provided to the JPL navigation team by prime contractor Lockheed Martin in English units rather than the specified metric units. This was the direct cause of the failure. However, it is important to recognize that space missions are a "one strike and you are out" activity. Thousands of functions can be correctly performed and one mistake can be mission catastrophic. Mistakes are prevented by oversight, test, and independent analysis, which were deficient for MCO.

Specifically, software testing was inadequate. Equally important, the navigation team was understaffed, did not understand the spacecraft, and was inadequately trained. Navigation anomalies (caused by the same units error) observed during cruise from Earth to Mars were not adequately pursued to determine the cause, and the opportunity to do a final trajectory correction maneuver was not utilized because of inadequate preparation.

MPL and the two Deep Space 2 microprobes were integrated on a common cruise stage for the trip from Earth to Mars. Separation of the microprobes and the lander was planned to occur about 10 minutes prior to the planned Mars landings. The design of the lander precluded any communications from the period shortly before separation from the cruise stage until after Mars landing. The planned communications after landing did not occur, resulting in the determination that the MPL mission had failed. Extensive reviews, analyses, and tests have been conducted to determine the most probable cause of the MPL failure. This is documented in the "Report on the Loss of the Mars Polar Lander and Deep Space 2 Missions." Several possible failure causes are presented, which include loss of control due to spacecraft dynamic effects or fuel migration, local characteristics of the landing site beyond the capabilities of the lander, and the parachute covering the lander after touchdown. Extensive tests have demonstrated that the most probable cause of the failure is that spurious signals were generated when the lander legs were deployed during descent. The spurious signals gave a false indication that the lander had landed, resulting in a premature shutdown of the lander engines and the destruction of the lander when it crashed into the Mars surface.

Without any entry, descent, and landing telemetry data, there is no way to know whether the lander reached the terminal descent propulsion phase. If it did successfully reach this phase, it is almost certain that premature engine shutdown occurred.

It is not uncommon for sensors involved with mechanical operations, such as the lander leg deployment, to produce spurious signals. For MPL, there was no software requirement to clear spurious signals prior to using the sensor information to determine that landing had occurred. During the test of the lander system, the sensors were incorrectly wired due to a design error. As a result, the spurious signals were not identified by the systems test, and the systems test was not repeated with properly wired touchdown sensors. While the most probable direct cause of the failure is premature engine shutdown, it is important to note that the underlying cause is inadequate software design and systems test.

Deep Space 2 (DS-2) was a technology mission to demonstrate microprobe technology for future applications in exploring various solid bodies in our solar system. The DS-2 design provided no data from the time it was integrated on the cruise stage at the launch site until after the Mars landing; therefore, there is no knowledge of probe health following cruise stage integration. No communications were received after the expected landings, resulting in the determination that the two DS-2 microprobes failed. Reviews and analyses of the DS-2 development process have been performed and are documented in the earlier referenced "Report on the Loss of the Mars Polar Lander and Deep Space 2 Missions."

DS-2 had an inadequate test program that deviated significantly from the proven practice of "test-as-you-fly, fly-as-you-test." No "most probable cause" has been identified for the DS-2 microprobes; however, it is clear that the microprobes were not adequately tested and were not ready for launch.

The discussion on the previous pages summarizes the three successful and three unsuccessful Mars and deep space missions reviewed and analyzed by the MPIAT. The important question is: "What are the lessons learned from these successes and failures?"

There are common characteristics of the successful missions and of the unsuccessful missions. The following summarizes the lessons learned from the MPIAT review of these missions.

**Experienced project management or mentoring is essential.**

Deep space missions are inherently difficult. These difficulties include long-duration operations, precision navigation, hazardous environments, landing sites with unknown hazards at the scale of the lander, and, in many situations, the first use of sophisticated hardware and software. Launch schedules typically have little flexibility. As an example, Mars launch opportunities are approximately 1 month long and are separated by about 26 months.

The management challenges are enormous. MGS and Pathfinder had experienced project managers who contributed significantly to their successes. DS-1 had a competent, but inexperienced, project manager who was augmented by senior JPL management. MCO, MPL, and DS-2 had competent, but inexperienced, project managers. The lack of senior management involvement to compensate for the lack of experience contributed to the MCO, MPL, and DS-2 failures.

The number of JPL projects has increased significantly. There are not enough experienced managers for the large number of projects for which JPL is currently responsible. This situation requires significant involvement by senior management to compensate for the lack of experience.

**Project manager must be responsible and accountable for all aspects of mission success.**

For MGS, Pathfinder, DS-1, and DS-2, the project managers were responsible for all aspects of their projects, from project formulation through completion of mission operations. The MCO and MPL project manager was responsible for development only, with a separate organization and project manager responsible for operations after launch. This arrangement contributed to the MCO failure.

**Unique constraints of deep space missions demand adequate margins.**

Deep space missions are characterized by a fixed launch date (which fixes the schedule), a given launch vehicle (which fixes the available weight), competitively selected science payloads (which establish the performance requirements), and for the missions that were analyzed, fixed cost. When these four constraining parameters are fixed, there are only two remaining variables: margins and risk. If adequate margins are available, risk can be effectively managed; if not, risk will grow to an unacceptable level.

MGS and Pathfinder had adequate margins, and the risks were effectively managed, contributing to successful missions. The technology mission, DS-1, did not have adequate margins; however, relief was provided because this was not a science-driven planetary mission with a fixed launch opportunity. DS-1 performance requirements were effectively descoped, and the launch schedule was delayed several months. Without this performance and schedule flexibility, DS-1 would have had excessive risk.

MCO, MPL, and DS-2 did not have adequate margins. MCO and MPL were managed as a single Mars '98 project. The project was significantly underfunded from the start for the established performance requirements. By comparison, MGS was a single orbiter with science instruments and several subsystems developed for an earlier mission (Mars Observer). The development cost plus the estimated value of the inheritance was approximately $250 million. Pathfinder is the standard for a Mars FBC mission. Development cost for Pathfinder was about $200 million, including $25 million for the rover. Mars '98, which included an orbiter, a lander, and about three times as much science as Pathfinder, cost about $190 million. All costs are constant-year 1999 dollars to allow for a direct comparison.

Mars '98 (which included both MCO and MPL) cost approximately the same as Pathfinder. This clearly indicates the significant lack of sufficient budget for Mars '98. It was underfunded by at least 30 percent. There were many reasons for the underfunding, including an aggressive proposal from LMA.

The selection of a launch vehicle with little margin, some growth in the science payload, and the fixed planetary launch window also contributed to inadequate margins. The result was analysis and testing deficiencies as well as inadequate preparations for mission operations. These resulted in excessive risk and contributed to the failures. . . .

**Appropriate application of institutional expertise is critical for mission success.**

For more than four decades, significant investments have been made in developing the deep space capabilities at JPL. As a result, JPL is a center of excellence for deep space exploration. A primary reason for doing deep space missions at JPL is to take advantage of this unique capability. This expertise was effectively used for MGS, Pathfinder, and (to some degree) DS-1, resulting in a significant contribution to the success of these missions. Use of the JPL capabilities was significantly curtailed on Mars '98 largely because of funding limitations. Consequently, a significant opportunity was missed that may have resulted in recognition of inadequate margins and excessive risk in the Mars '98 project. JPL institutional support for DS-2 varied considerably, but was inadequate for the technical complexity of the microprobes.

National capabilities can also contribute to the success of deep space missions. As an example, the atmospheric entry expertise at NASA's Langley Research Center, Ames Research Center, and LMA was the primary source of this capability for Pathfinder. The air bag technology for Pathfinder came from Sandia National Laboratory. Industry, academia, NASA Centers, and other Government organizations were also important participants in DS-1.

**A thorough test and verification program is essential for mission success.**

FBC encourages taking prudent risk in utilizing new technology and pursuing important science objectives and innovation. However, risk associated with deviating from sound principles should not be allowed. Sound principles include:

Efficient, competent, independent reviews;
Oversight, analysis, and test to "eliminate" a single human mistake from
    causing mission failure;
Clear definition of responsibilities and authority;
Prudent use of redundancy;
Test-as-you-fly, fly-as-you-test;
Risk assessment and management.

This is not an exhaustive list, but rather important examples.

MGS and Pathfinder rigorously followed sound principles. DS-1 execution was mixed. DS-2 deviated to such a degree that it leads to the conclusion that the microprobes were not ready to launch. Mars '98 did the best that could be done with the limited resources, but deviated significantly in analysis, testing, and the conduct of reviews.

**Effective risk identification and management are critical to assure successful deep space missions.**

Risk is inherent in deep space missions. Effective identification and management of risk are critical responsibilities of project management and often determine whether a mission will be successful. This was clearly a problem in the implementation of MCO, MPL, and DS-2.

Faster, Better, Cheaper encourages taking prudent risk where justified by the return. The MPIAT found that the lack of an established definition of FBC and policies/procedures to guide implementation resulted in project managers having different interpretations of what is prudent risk. Senior management needs to establish that risk associated with new high-return technology and innovation is acceptable as is risk associated with pursuing high-value science. Risk associated with deviating from sound principles is unacceptable. Risk must be assessed and accepted by all accountable parties, including senior management, program management, and project management. All projects should utilize established risk management tools such as fault tree analysis and failure effects and criticality analysis.

**Institutional management must be accountable for policies and procedures that assure a high level of mission success.**

**Institutional management must assure project implementation consistent with required policies and procedures.**

Senior management is responsible and accountable to establish standards for the conduct of deep space missions; to assure that these standards are being followed; to assure that adequate resources, including institutional expertise, are available and used; and to assure that projects are being implemented with prudent risk. In the case of Mars '98, this did not happen at NASA Headquarters, JPL, or LMA. A clear example is the absence of critical entry, descent, and landing telemetry on MPL.

MGS and Pathfinder success can be directly attributed to the experienced project managers and their effective use of expertise from numerous sources. JPL senior management contributed significantly to the success of DS-1.

**Telemetry coverage of critical events is necessary for analysis and ability to incorporate information in follow-on projects.**

The lack of communications (telemetry) to provide entry, descent, and landing data for MPL was a major mistake. Absence of this information prevented an analysis of the performance of MPL and eliminated any ability to reflect knowledge gained from MPL in future missions. It is a prime example of the Mars Program being treated as a collection of individual projects as opposed to an integrated program.

The final observation that needs to be made is:

**If not ready—do not launch.**

Planetary launch opportunities are typically separated by periods of many months or years; Mars launch opportunities are approximately every 26 months. Not being ready for a scheduled launch opportunity is serious, but not as serious as proceeding without being ready. Senior management needs to make it unambiguously clear that "if not ready, do not launch."

## Interfaces and Relationships

The MPIAT charter includes an examination of relationships among JPL, Caltech, NASA Headquarters, and Lockheed Martin. An assessment of the effectiveness of the involvement of scientists was also required. Among the interfaces and relationships reviewed, two significant areas of concern were identified: "The interface between NASA Headquarters and JPL" and "The interface between JPL and Lockheed Martin."

The interface between NASA Headquarters and JPL was found to be highly ineffective. . . .

NASA Headquarters provided objectives, requirements, and constraints for the Mars Program and projects to JPL. They appropriately considered this a Headquarters responsibility. JPL interpreted these objectives, requirements, and constraints as launch vehicle, cost, schedule, and performance mandates. As an example, for Mars '98, the JPL management perception was that no cost increase was possible. The response from JPL was more one of advocacy for the program and presenting a positive image to the customer (NASA Headquarters) than a rigorous risk assessment with appropriate concerns expressed. What NASA Headquarters understood was JPL agreement with the objectives, requirements, and constraints. The result was an ineffective interface that did not resolve issues or manage risk. This directly contributed to inadequate margins for Mars '98, which in turn contributed to the MCO and MPL failures. The lessons learned from an analysis of this relationship are:

**Frank communication of objectives, requirements, constraints, and risk assessment throughout all phases of the program is critical to successful program/project implementation.**

**Senior management must be receptive to communications of problems and risks.**

Another aspect of the interface was the absence of a single Mars Program interface at NASA Headquarters responsible for all requirements, including those from other NASA organizations. Absence of a single interface resulted in multiple inputs to the JPL Mars Program that were in some instances conflicting and in general added to the confusion and poor communications. The lesson learned is:

**A dedicated single interface at NASA Headquarters for the Mars Program is essential. This individual should have responsibility for all requirements (including human exploration) and funds. The position should report to the Associate Administrator for Space Science.**

The day-to-day relationship between JPL and LMA was positive during the conduct of the Mars '98 project. However, the relationship was ineffective when it came to informing senior management about risk. Lockheed Martin senior management did not formally identify risk or deviations from acceptable practice. The lesson learned is:

**Contractor (Lockheed Martin) responsibilities must include formal notification to the customer (NASA/JPL) of project risk and deviations from acceptable practice.**

## Mars Program Implementation

The final responsibility identified by the charter is a review of the Mars Program to assure that the identified lessons learned are utilized.

JPL has historically been responsible for individual projects. With NASA delegating program management responsibilities from NASA Headquarters to the NASA Centers in 1996, JPL was assigned this responsibility for the Mars Surveyor Program.

The MPIAT does not believe that the Mars Program has been effectively managed. It has been managed as a collection of individual projects rather than as an integrated framework in which projects fit to accomplish more than the sum of individual projects. Not including entry, descent, and landing telemetry is a prime example of this deficiency.

As a result of moving to the FBC concept, the number of flight projects at JPL has increased over a 3-year period from a historical average of 1 to 4 in a given year to a current level of 10 to 15 at the same time. This increase is a result of the FBC approach, which has as its objective smaller spacecraft with more frequent missions. This increase in the number of projects requires additional capable project managers. There has been a loss of experienced, successful project managers through retirement. The net effect is to use competent, but inexperienced, managers for the increased number of projects. An earlier lesson learned is the need for senior management involvement and mentoring to compensate for the lack of experience.

Currently, all flight projects, the Mars Program, and numerous other instrument and program responsibilities are in one organization at JPL. This results in an extraordinary workload and span of control for this organization.

The conclusion of the MPIAT is that the current organization at JPL is not appropriate to successfully manage the Mars Program in combination with other commitments for the reasons discussed above.

The following organizational changes would be responsive to this concern:

**Establish an integrated Mars Program Office at JPL reporting to the Laboratory Director.**

**Establish a new, independent organization at the Directorate level dedicated to implementing major flight projects.**

## Summary

Based upon intensive review by the MPIAT, there are several general observations important to the future Mars Program:

**Mars Exploration Is an Important National Goal That Should Continue.**

**Deep Space Exploration Is Inherently Challenging. The Risks Are Manageable and Acceptable.**

**NASA, JPL, and Industry Have the Required Capabilities to Implement a Successful Mars Exploration Program.**

**JPL Is a Center of Excellence for Deep Space Exploration with Unique Capabilities.**

**Faster, Better, Cheaper, Properly Applied, Is an Effective Concept for Guiding Program Implementation that Should Continue.**

**Significant Flaws Were Identified in the Formulation and Execution of the Mars Program.**

**All Identified Flaws Are Correctable in a Timely Manner to Allow a Comprehensive Mars Exploration Program to Successfully Continue.**

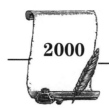
# April

# DISTRICT COURT ON MICROSOFT'S ILLEGAL MONOPOLY ACTIONS
## April 3, 2000

*A federal judge ruled on April 3, 2000, that the Microsoft Corporation engaged in illegal "predatory" behavior during the 1990s that was intended to bolster the company's monopoly in operating systems for personal computers. The finding by Judge Thomas Penfield Jackson set the stage for his ruling two months later, on June 7, that Microsoft be broken into two separate companies.* (Remedy ruling, p. 308)

*Jackson had already ruled, in November 1999, that Microsoft was a monopoly company that had gone to extraordinary steps to protect its overwhelming position in the market for key elements of personal computer software. The judge's rulings during 2000 came after the Seattle-based company and the plaintiffs in the case—the federal government and attorneys general representing nineteen states and the District of Columbia—failed to agree on a compromise settlement.* (Monopoly ruling, Historic Documents of 1999, p. 654)

*Jackson's three rulings, taken as a whole, represented one of the most significant uses ever of the Sherman Antitrust Act, enacted by Congress in 1890 to curtail the power of giant industrial monopolies that then controlled much of the U.S. economy. Just as important, in a contemporary setting, the Microsoft case had the potential to alter the future of the computer technology industry worldwide, if only because of the company's dominance in its market. Even so, developments in technology and the marketplace were moving so quickly that some of the issues raised by the case were likely to be considered moot by the time it was finally settled.*

*In addition to any legal or technological implications, the Microsoft case had an immediate impact on the financial markets. Microsoft shares tumbled on the stock markets even before Jackson released his April 3 ruling, and shares of most other computer-related businesses followed suit. Within a few days, Microsoft founder and chairman William H. Gates and many of his colleagues had lost billions of dollars in wealth. Microsoft stock gradually inched back up later in the year.*

## *Failure of Settlement Effort*

*Immediately after issuing his initial ruling in November 1999, Jackson pushed the parties to reach a settlement before the case moved to the next phase of determining whether Microsoft had violated the antitrust law. He took the extraordinary step of recruiting an influential appellate court judge—Richard Posner, chief judge of the U.S. Court of Appeals for the Seventh Circuit in Chicago—to mediate negotiations among Microsoft, the U.S. Justice Department, and the states.*

*According to news reports, Microsoft and the plaintiffs traded nineteen proposals and counterproposals during four months of on-and-off negotiations. While the last proposal put on the table by the Justice Department reportedly would have placed restrictions on Microsoft's business activities, it would have left the company intact. Microsoft rejected that proposal as extreme, arguing that it imposed too many restraints on the company's ability to continue improving its computer operating system, known as "Windows." Likewise, several of the state attorneys general involved in the case said the proposal was too weak because it allowed Microsoft to continue as a single company with a monopoly in its market.*

*With no apparent prospect for a resolution of the case, Posner notified the parties on Saturday, April 1, that he was ending his mediation efforts. The following Monday Jackson issued his ruling.*

## *Judge Jackson's Main Findings*

*The heart of the case involved claims by the government that Microsoft went to illegal lengths to protect its monopoly over operating systems for personal computers—especially computers known as "Intel-compatible" because they used semiconductors made by the Intel Corporation and its competitors. As of 2000, according to Jackson's ruling, more than 90 percent of all personal computers (not counting the relatively small number of Macintosh computers produced by the Apple Corporation) relied on Microsoft's Windows programs for their basic operating system.*

*The government argued, and Jackson concurred, that Microsoft had taken several actions, beginning in 1995, that illegally pressured Microsoft competitors, most notably the Netscape Communications Corporation and Sun Microsystems. In essence, Jackson ruled that Microsoft was determined to preserve what he called the "applications barrier to entry": the nearly insurmountable hurdle that any company faced in gaining market acceptance of an operating system to compete with Windows. The hurdle, or applications barrier, arose from Microsoft's insistence on exclusive contracts and other deals with computer makers to ensure that Windows was the dominant operating system. Because of that dominance, thousands of computer applications (such as word processing and accounting programs) had been written to work only with Windows. Consumers would not switch to a competing system unless they had a choice of applications to work with it, but software developers would not write such applications until they could be sure that a consumer market existed for a competitor to Windows.*

*When it developed its "Navigator" program to "browse" the Internet's World Wide Web in late 1994, Netscape became a potential competitor to Microsoft. That was because Navigator, as originally envisioned, could have served as what was called a* platform *for software applications, conceivably eliminating the need for Windows. Sun Microsystems in 1995 developed its "Java" computer language that posed a similar challenge to Windows.*

*In his November 1999 "findings of fact," and again in his April 3 ruling, Jackson detailed numerous steps Microsoft took during the 1990s to block Netscape and Sun Microsystems from competing with Windows. Perhaps the key action took place in mid-1995, when Microsoft attempted to pressure Netscape into making its Navigator browser incompatible with Windows. When Netscape resisted that pressure, Microsoft undermined Netscape's marketing efforts by offering consumers its own Internet Explorer browser for free. Microsoft also incorporated, or "bundled," Internet Explorer into its Windows 95 and Windows 98 operating systems, thus making it much easier for consumers to use Internet Explorer than Netscape's Navigator.*

*Jackson's April 3 ruling found that Microsoft acted illegally in three central ways. First, the company successfully and illegally used "anticompetitive means" to protect its monopoly in personal computer operating systems. Using legal language drawn from Section Two of the Sherman Antitrust Act and subsequent court decisions, Jackson said Microsoft maintained its monopoly "through exclusionary acts that lacked procompetitive justification"; in other words, the company had no basis for arguing that its actions promoted, rather than discouraged, true competition in the marketplace.*

*Second, Jackson ruled that Microsoft illegally used its Windows monopoly to attempt to establish a monopoly in a second market, that for Internet browser software. This also violated Section Two of the Sherman Antitrust Act, he ruled. Through its various schemes to undermine market acceptance of Netscape's Navigator, Jackson said, Microsoft intended to create a monopoly for its own Internet Explorer. In 1995, when Microsoft first moved against Netscape, Navigator was the dominant Internet browser, with about a 70 percent market share, Jackson said. By 2000 Internet Explorer was the dominant browser with more than 50 percent of the market, and it was expected to exceed 60 percent by January 2001, he said. "The predatory course of conduct Microsoft has pursued since June of 1995 has revived the dangerous probability that Microsoft will attain monopoly power in a second market," Jackson wrote.*

*Third, Jackson ruled that Microsoft illegally "tied" or "bundled" Internet Explorer with its Windows operating systems as a means of blunting competition. After its initial effort to pressure Netscape failed in 1995, Microsoft began incorporating Internet Explorer into its Windows 95 and Windows 98 systems. The company insisted that Internet Explorer had become an integral part of Windows, a claim that was repeatedly undermined during courtroom testimony in 1998 and 1999. Jackson wrote: "This court concludes that Microsoft's decision to offer only the bundled 'integrated' ver-*

*sion of Windows and Internet Explorer derived not from technical necessity or business efficiencies; rather, it was the result of a deliberate and purposeful choice to quell incipient competition before it reached truly minatory [threatening] proportions." Jackson said Microsoft's action had violated Section One of the Sherman Antitrust Act, the so-called restraint of trade clause.*

*In a sweeping summation of the case, Jackson argued that Microsoft had done "violence" to business competition. "In essence, Microsoft mounted a deliberate assault upon entrepreneurial efforts that, left to rise or fall on their own merits, could well have enabled the introduction of competition into the market for Intel-compatible PC operating systems," he wrote. "While the evidence does not prove that they would have succeeded absent Microsoft's actions, it does reveal that Microsoft placed an oppressive thumb on the scale of competitive fortune, thereby effectively guaranteeing its continuing dominance in the relevant market. More broadly, Microsoft's anti-competitive actions trammeled the competitive process through which the computer software industry generally stimulates innovation and conduces to the optimum benefit of consumers."*

*The fact that Microsoft in some cases gave up the opportunity to make money—for example, when it offered consumers Internet Explorer at no charge—merely underscored the company's absolute determination to maintain its monopoly, Jackson ruled. He cited Supreme Court rulings to bolster his contention that underpricing a competitor to drive him out of business constitutes a predatory action by a monopoly.*

### One Win for Microsoft

*Surprising many observers, Jackson sided with Microsoft on one key issue: whether the company violated Section One of the Sherman Antitrust Act when it pressured computer manufacturers and other elements of the computer industry not to put Netscape Navigator on their products. Section One of the law prohibited "every contract, combination . . , or conspiracy, in restraint of trade or commerce."*

*In his November 1999 findings of fact, Jackson had cited numerous contracts that Microsoft had negotiated with Compaq, America Online, and other firms making Internet Explorer the exclusive Web browser. These contracts had the effect, Jackson said, of blocking Netscape from "the most efficient channel" for getting its Navigator browser into the hands of consumers.*

*But Microsoft's deals did not constitute a "restraint of trade," Jackson ruled, because they did not totally prevent consumers from having access to Netscape Navigator. He noted that consumers could download Navigator from the Internet, could purchase it in retail stores, or could request a copy through the mail. In 1998 alone, he noted, Netscape distributed 160 million copies of Navigator.*

*Despite this portion of the ruling, Jackson noted that Microsoft's actions in thwarting Netscape did contribute to the company's illegal maintenance of its monopoly, as prohibited by Section Two of the Sherman Antitrust act.*

## *Jackson vs. the Appeals Court*

*Jackson noted that one important element of his ruling conflicted with a related finding by his immediate superiors, the U.S. Court of Appeals for the District of Columbia. In 1998, acting in a previous version of the Microsoft case, a three-judge panel of the appellate court had overturned an order by Jackson requiring Microsoft to "unbundle" or separate Internet Explorer from the Windows operating system. The appellate panel ruled that Microsoft had not violated Section one of the Sherman Antitrust Act by incorporating its Web browser into Windows. The Appeals Court said Microsoft could claim compliance with the law if it could make a "plausible claim" that its action was based on "valid business reasons" or "some advantage" to consumers.*

*In his April 3 ruling, Jackson took the unusual step—for a lower court judge—of directly criticizing and rejecting the finding by the Appeals panel. But he did so by linking his position with that of an even higher authority, the U.S. Supreme Court.*

*The 1998 Appeals Court ruling, Jackson wrote, was "inconsistent" with the Supreme Court's own approach in two similar cases,* Jefferson Parish Hospital District No. 2 v. Hyde *(1984) and* Eastman Kodak v. Image Technical Services Inc. *(1992). Citing those cases, Jackson offered several objections to the Appeals Court ruling, most notably that it "views the market from the defendant's [Microsoft's] perspective, or more precisely, as the defendant would like to have the market viewed."*

*Most analysts said Jackson was employing a risky strategy in attacking the Appeals Court, if only because that panel might cooperate with Microsoft's obvious game plan of delaying a final decision in the case. But these analysts noted that Jackson's argument might find a more receptive audience at the Supreme Court.*

## *Reaction to the Ruling*

*Reaction to Judge Jackson's ruling fell along virtually the same lines as that to his prior "findings of fact" in November 1999. Attorney General Janet Reno praised the ruling in lavish terms: "Microsoft has been held accountable for its illegal conduct by a court of law," she said. "We are pleased that the court agreed with the [Justice] department that Microsoft abused its monopoly power that it violated antitrust laws and that it harmed consumers." Similar views were expressed by the state attorneys general involved in the case, most notably the lead state official, Tom Miller of Iowa. He called the ruling a "broad-based and compelling finding of liability, of law-breaking" by Microsoft.*

*Microsoft executives heatedly denounced the ruling and promised to fight the government's case to the end. "This ruling turns on its head the reality that consumers know, that our software has helped make PC's more accessible and more affordable to millions," Gates said. Steve Ballmer, the Microsoft president, said: "Until the appeal's over, nothing's settled. We've learned that through experience."*

*As in the past, other software industry executives offered split opinions, depending in part on whether they were close business partners with Microsoft or competitors. Alan Cooper, president of Cooper Interaction Design in Palo Alto, California, said the case against Microsoft was a mistake. "Our federal government and our Justice Department don't have an understanding of the digital universe and are miscomprehending it," he told the* New York Times. *"Their actions will backfire." But Scott McNealy, chairman of Sun Microsystems, said Jackson's ruling demonstrated why his firm was unhappy with Microsoft. "Every time we sign a deal, they [Microsoft] go in behind us and make an investment," he said. "It's beyond blatant."*

> *Following are excerpts from the ruling issued April 4, 2000, by U.S. District Court Judge Thomas Penfield Jackson in the case,* United States of America v. Microsoft Corporation, *in which Microsoft was found to have committed three violations of the Sherman Antitrust Act. The document was obtained from the Internet at http://usvms.gpo.gov/conclusions_index.html.*

The United States, nineteen individual states, and the District of Columbia ("the plaintiffs") bring these consolidated civil enforcement actions against defendant Microsoft Corporation ("Microsoft") under the Sherman Antitrust Act, [Sections 1 and 2]. The plaintiffs charge, in essence, that Microsoft has waged an unlawful campaign in defense of its monopoly position in the market for operating systems designed to run on Intel-compatible personal computers ("PCs"). Specifically, the plaintiffs contend that Microsoft violated Section 2 of the Sherman Act by engaging in a series of exclusionary, anticompetitive, and predatory acts to maintain its monopoly power. They also assert that Microsoft attempted, albeit unsuccessfully to date, to monopolize the [World Wide] Web browser market, likewise in violation of Section 2. Finally, they contend that certain steps taken by Microsoft as part of its campaign to protect its monopoly power, namely tying its browser to its operating system and entering into exclusive dealing arrangements, violated Section 1 of the Act.

Upon consideration of the Court's Findings of Fact ("Findings"), filed herein on November 5, 1999, as amended on December 21, 1999, the proposed conclusions of law submitted by the parties, the briefs of amici curiae, and the argument of counsel thereon, the Court concludes that Microsoft maintained its monopoly power by anticompetitive means and attempted to monopolize the Web browser market, both in violation of Section 2. Microsoft also violated Section 1 of the Sherman Act by unlawfully tying its Web browser to its operating system. The facts found do not support the conclusion, however, that the effect of Microsoft's marketing arrangements with other companies constituted unlawful exclusive dealing under criteria established by leading decisions under Section 1.

The nineteen states and the District of Columbia ("the plaintiff states") seek to ground liability additionally under their respective antitrust laws. The Court is persuaded that the evidence in the record proving violations of the Sherman Act also satisfies the elements of analogous causes of action arising under the laws of each plaintiff state. For this reason, and for others stated below, the Court holds Microsoft liable under those particular state laws as well.

# I. Section Two of the Sherman Act

## A. Maintenance of Monopoly Power by Anticompetitive Means

Section 2 of the Sherman Act declares that it is unlawful for a person or firm to "monopolize . . . any part of the trade or commerce among the several States, or with foreign nations. . . ." This language operates to limit the means by which a firm may lawfully either acquire or perpetuate monopoly power. Specifically, a firm violates Section 2 if it attains or preserves monopoly power through anticompetitive acts. . . .

### 1. Monopoly Power

The threshold element of a Section 2 monopolization offense being "the possession of monopoly power in the relevant market,". . . the Court must first ascertain the boundaries of the commercial activity that can be termed the "relevant market.". . . Next, the Court must assess the defendant's actual power to control prices in—or to exclude competition from—that market. . . .

In this case, the plaintiffs postulated the relevant market as being the worldwide licensing of Intel-compatible PC operating systems. Whether this zone of commercial activity actually qualifies as a market, "monopolization of which may be illegal," depends on whether it includes all products "reasonably interchangeable by consumers for the same purposes." . . .

The Court has already found, based on the evidence in this record, that there are currently no products—and that there are not likely to be any in the near future—that a significant percentage of computer users worldwide could substitute for Intel-compatible PC operating systems without incurring substantial costs. The Court has further found that no firm not currently marketing Intel-compatible PC operating systems could start doing so in a way that would, within a reasonably short period of time, present a significant percentage of such consumers with a viable alternative to existing Intel-compatible PC operating systems. From these facts, the Court has inferred that if a single firm or cartel controlled the licensing of all Intel-compatible PC operating systems worldwide, it could set the price of a license substantially above that which would be charged in a competitive market—and leave the price there for a significant period of time—without losing so many customers as to make the action unprofitable. This inference, in turn, has led the Court to find that the licensing of all Intel-compatible PC operating systems worldwide does in fact constitute the relevant market in the context of the plaintiffs' monopoly maintenance claim.

The plaintiffs proved at trial that Microsoft possesses a dominant, persistent, and increasing share of the relevant market. Microsoft's share of the worldwide market for Intel-compatible PC operating systems currently exceeds ninety-five percent, and the firm's share would stand well above eighty percent even if the Mac OS [operating system] were included in the market. The plaintiffs also proved that the applications barrier to entry protects Microsoft's dominant market share. This barrier ensures that no Intel-compatible PC operating system other than Windows can attract significant consumer demand, and the barrier would operate to the same effect even if Microsoft held its prices substantially above the competitive level for a protracted period of time. Together, the proof of dominant market share and the existence of a substantial barrier to effective entry create the presumption that Microsoft enjoys monopoly power. . . .

At trial, Microsoft attempted to rebut the presumption of monopoly power with evidence of both putative constraints on its ability to exercise such power and behavior of its own that is supposedly inconsistent with the possession of monopoly power. None of the purported constraints, however, actually deprive Microsoft of "the ability (1) to price substantially above the competitive level and (2) to persist in doing so for a significant period without erosion by new entry or expansion.". . . Furthermore, neither Microsoft's efforts at technical innovation nor its pricing behavior is inconsistent with the possession of monopoly power.

Even if Microsoft's rebuttal had attenuated the presumption created by the prima facie showing of monopoly power, corroborative evidence of monopoly power abounds in this record: Neither Microsoft nor its OEM customers [original equipment manufacturers, such as computer makers] believe that the latter have—or will have anytime soon—even a single, commercially viable alternative to licensing Windows for pre-installation on their PCs. . . . Moreover, over the past several years, Microsoft has comported itself in a way that could only be consistent with rational behavior for a profit-maximizing firm if the firm knew that it possessed monopoly power, and if it was motivated by a desire to preserve the barrier to entry protecting that power.

In short, the proof of Microsoft's dominant, persistent market share protected by a substantial barrier to entry, together with Microsoft's failure to rebut that prima facie showing effectively and the additional indicia of monopoly power, have compelled the Court to find as fact that Microsoft enjoys monopoly power in the relevant market.

## 2. Maintenance of Monopoly Power by Anticompetitive Means

In a Section 2 case, once it is proved that the defendant possesses monopoly power in a relevant market, liability for monopolization depends on a showing that the defendant used anticompetitive methods to achieve or maintain its position. . . . Prior cases have established an analytical approach to determining whether challenged conduct should be deemed anticompetitive in the context of a monopoly maintenance claim. The threshold question in this analysis is whether the defendant's conduct is "exclusionary"—that is, whether it has restricted significantly, or threatens to restrict significantly, the ability of other firms to compete in the relevant market on the merits of what they offer customers. . . .

If the evidence reveals a significant exclusionary impact in the relevant market, the defendant's conduct will be labeled "anticompetitive"—and liability will attach—unless the defendant comes forward with specific, pro-competitive business motivations that explain the full extent of its exclusionary conduct. . . .

If the defendant with monopoly power consciously antagonized its customers by making its products less attractive to them—or if it incurred other costs, such as large outlays of development capital and forfeited opportunities to derive revenue from it—with no prospect of compensation other than the erection or preservation of barriers against competition by equally efficient firms, the Court may deem the defendant's conduct "predatory." As the D.C. Circuit stated in *Neumann v. Reinforced Earth Co.*,

> [P]redation involves aggression against business rivals through the use of business practices that would not be considered profit maximizing except for the expectation that (1) actual rivals will be driven from the market, or the entry of potential rivals blocked or delayed, so that the predator will gain or retain a market share sufficient to command monopoly profits, or (2) rivals will be chastened sufficiently to abandon competitive behavior the predator finds threatening to its realization of monopoly profits.

Proof that a profit-maximizing firm took predatory action should suffice to demonstrate the threat of substantial exclusionary effect; to hold otherwise would be to ascribe irrational behavior to the defendant. Moreover, predatory conduct, by definition as well as by nature, lacks procompetitive business motivation. . . . In other words, predatory behavior is patently anticompetitive. Proof that a firm with monopoly power engaged in such behavior thus necessitates a finding of liability under Section 2.

In this case, Microsoft early on recognized middleware as the Trojan horse that, once having, in effect, infiltrated the applications barrier, could enable rival operating systems to enter the market for Intel-compatible PC operating systems unimpeded. Simply put, middleware threatened to demolish Microsoft's coveted monopoly power. Alerted to the threat, Microsoft strove over a period of approximately four years to prevent middleware technologies from fostering the development of enough full-featured, cross-platform applications to erode the applications barrier. In pursuit of this goal, Microsoft sought to convince developers to concentrate on Windows-specific APIs [application programming interfaces, which link application programs, such as word processing, with the operating system] and ignore interfaces exposed by the two incarnations of middleware that posed the greatest threat, namely, Netscape's Navigator Web browser and Sun's [Microsystems] implementation of the Java technology. Microsoft's campaign succeeded in preventing—for several years, and perhaps permanently—Navigator and Java from fulfilling their potential to open the market for Intel-compatible PC operating systems to competition on the merits. Because Microsoft achieved this result through exclusionary acts that lacked procompetitive justification, the Court deems

Microsoft's conduct the maintenance of monopoly power by anticompetitive means.

*a. Combating the Browser Threat.*   The same ambition that inspired Microsoft's efforts to induce Intel, Apple, RealNetworks and IBM to desist from certain technological innovations and business initiatives—namely, the desire to preserve the applications barrier—motivated the firm's June 1995 proposal that Netscape abstain from releasing platform-level browsing software for 32-bit versions of Windows. This proposal, together with the punitive measures that Microsoft inflicted on Netscape when it rebuffed the overture, illuminates the context in which Microsoft's subsequent behavior toward PC manufacturers ("OEMs"), Internet access providers ("IAPs"), and other firms must be viewed.

When Netscape refused to abandon its efforts to develop Navigator into a substantial platform for applications development, Microsoft focused its efforts on minimizing the extent to which developers would avail themselves of interfaces exposed by that nascent platform. Microsoft realized that the extent of developers' reliance on Netscape's browser platform would depend largely on the size and trajectory of Navigator's share of browser usage. Microsoft thus set out to maximize Internet Explorer's share of browser usage at Navigator's expense. The core of this strategy was ensuring that the firms comprising the most effective channels for the generation of browser usage would devote their distributional and promotional efforts to Internet Explorer rather than Navigator. Recognizing that pre-installation by OEMs and bundling with the proprietary software of IAPs led more directly and efficiently to browser usage than any other practices in the industry, Microsoft devoted major efforts to usurping those two channels.

**i. The OEM Channel.** With respect to OEMs, Microsoft's campaign proceeded on three fronts. First, Microsoft bound Internet Explorer to Windows with contractual and, later, technological shackles in order to ensure the prominent (and ultimately permanent) presence of Internet Explorer on every Windows user's PC system, and to increase the costs attendant to installing and using Navigator on any PCs running Windows. Second, Microsoft imposed stringent limits on the freedom of OEMs to reconfigure or modify Windows 95 and Windows 98 in ways that might enable OEMs to generate usage for Navigator in spite of the contractual and technological devices that Microsoft had employed to bind Internet Explorer to Windows. Finally, Microsoft used incentives and threats to incentives and threats induce especially important OEMs to design their distributional, promotional and technical efforts to favor Internet Explorer to the exclusion of Navigator.

Microsoft's actions increased the likelihood that pre-installation of Navigator onto Windows would cause user confusion and system degradation, and therefore lead to higher support costs and reduced sales for the OEMs. Not willing to take actions that would jeopardize their already slender profit margins, OEMs felt compelled by Microsoft's actions to reduce drastically their distribution and promotion of Navigator. The substantial inducements that Microsoft held out to the largest OEMs only further reduced the distribution and promotion of Navigator in the OEM channel. The response of OEMs to Microsoft's efforts had a dramatic, negative impact on Navigator's usage share. The drop in usage share, in turn, has prevented Navigator from being the vehicle to open the relevant market to competition on the merits.

Microsoft fails to advance any legitimate business objectives that actually explain the full extent of this significant exclusionary impact. The Court has already found that no quality-related or technical justifications fully explain Microsoft's refusal to license Windows 95 to OEMs without version 1.0 through 4.0 of Internet Explorer, or its refusal to permit them to uninstall versions 3.0 and 4.0. The same lack of justification applies to Microsoft's decision not to offer a browserless version of Windows 98 to consumers and OEMs, as well as to its claim that it could offer "best of breed" implementations of functionalities in Web browsers. With respect to the latter assertion, Internet Explorer is not demonstrably the current "best of breed" Web browser, nor is it likely to be so at any time in the immediate future. The fact that Microsoft itself was aware of this reality only further strengthens the conclusion that Microsoft's decision to tie Internet Explorer to Windows cannot truly be explained as an attempt to benefit consumers and improve the efficiency of the software market generally, but rather as part of a larger campaign to quash innovation that threatened its monopoly position.

To the extent that Microsoft still asserts a copyright defense, relying upon federal copyright law as a justification for its various restrictions on OEMs, that defense neither explains nor operates to immunize Microsoft's conduct under the Sherman Act. As a general proposition, Microsoft argues that the federal Copyright Act endows the holder of a valid copyright in software with an absolute right to prevent licensees, in this case the OEMs, from shipping modified versions of its product without its express permission. In truth, Windows 95 and Windows 98 are covered by copyright registrations. But the validity of Microsoft's copyrights has never been in doubt; the issue is what, precisely, they protect. Microsoft has presented no evidence that the contractual (or the technological) restrictions it placed on OEMs' ability to alter Windows derive from any of the enumerated rights explicitly granted to a copyright holder under the Copyright Act. Instead, Microsoft argues that the restrictions "simply restate" an expansive right to preserve the "integrity" of its copyrighted software against any "distortion," "truncation," or "alteration," a right nowhere mentioned among the Copyright Act's list of exclusive rights, thus raising some doubt as to its existence. . . .

It is also well settled that a copyright holder is not by reason thereof entitled to employ the perquisites in ways that directly threaten competition. . . . Even constitutional privileges confer no immunity when they are abused for anticompetitive purposes. . . . The Court has already found that the true impetus behind Microsoft's restrictions on OEMs was not its desire to maintain a somewhat amorphous quality it refers to as the "integrity" of the Windows platform, nor even to ensure that Windows afforded a uniform and stable platform for applications development. Microsoft itself engendered, or at least countenanced, instability and inconsistency by permitting Microsoft-friendly modifications to the desktop and boot sequence, and by releasing updates to

Internet Explorer more frequently than it released new versions of Windows. Add to this the fact that the modifications OEMs desired to make would not have removed or altered any Windows APIs, and thus would not have disrupted any of Windows' functionalities, and it is apparent that Microsoft's conduct is effectively explained by its foreboding that OEMs would pre-install and give prominent placement to middleware like Navigator that could attract enough developer attention to weaken the applications barrier to entry. In short, if Microsoft was truly inspired by a genuine concern for maximizing consumer satisfaction, as well as preserving its substantial investment in a worthy product, then it would have relied more on the power of the very competitive PC market, and less on its own market power, to prevent OEMs from making modifications that consumers did not want.

**ii. The IAP Channel.** Microsoft adopted similarly aggressive measures to ensure that the IAP channel would generate browser usage share for Internet Explorer rather than Navigator. To begin with, Microsoft licensed Internet Explorer and the Internet Explorer Access Kit to hundreds of IAPs for no charge. Then, Microsoft extended valuable promotional treatment to the ten most important IAPs in exchange for their commitment to promote and distribute Internet Explorer and to exile Navigator from the desktop. Finally, in exchange for efforts to upgrade existing subscribers to client software that came bundled with Internet Explorer instead of Navigator, Microsoft granted rebates—and in some cases made outright payments—to those same IAPs. Given the importance of the IAP channel to browser usage share, it is fair to conclude that these inducements and restrictions contributed significantly to the drastic changes that have in fact occurred in Internet Explorer's and Navigator's respective usage shares. Microsoft's actions in the IAP channel thereby contributed significantly to preserving the applications barrier to entry.

There are no valid reasons to justify the full extent of Microsoft's exclusionary behavior in the IAP channel. A desire to limit free riding on the firm's investment in consumer-oriented features, such as the Referral Server and the Online Services Folder, can, in some circumstances, qualify as a procompetitive business motivation; but that motivation does not explain the full extent of the restrictions that Microsoft actually imposed upon IAPs. Under the terms of the agreements, an IAP's failure to keep Navigator shipments below the specified percentage primed Microsoft's contractual right to dismiss the IAP from its own favored position in the Referral Server or the Online Services Folder. This was true even if the IAP had refrained from promoting Navigator in its client software included with Windows, had purged all mention of Navigator from any Web site directly connected to the Referral Server, and had distributed no browser other than Internet Explorer to the new subscribers it gleaned from the Windows desktop. Thus, Microsoft's restrictions closed off a substantial amount of distribution that would not have constituted a free ride to Navigator.

Nor can an ostensibly procompetitive desire to "foster brand association" explain the full extent of Microsoft's restrictions. If Microsoft's only concern had been brand association, restrictions on the ability of IAPs to promote Navigator likely would have sufficed. It is doubtful that Microsoft would have paid

IAPs to induce their existing subscribers to drop Navigator in favor of Internet Explorer unless it was motivated by a desire to extinguish Navigator as a threat. More generally, it is crucial to an understanding of Microsoft's intentions to recognize that Microsoft paid for the fealty of IAPs with large investments in software development for their benefit, conceded opportunities to take a profit, suffered competitive disadvantage to Microsoft's own OLS [online service] and gave outright bounties. Considering that Microsoft never intended to derive appreciable revenue from Internet Explorer directly, these sacrifices could only have represented rational business judgments to the extent that they promised to diminish Navigator's share of browser usage and thereby contribute significantly to eliminating a threat to the applications barrier to entry. Because the full extent of Microsoft's exclusionary initiatives in the IAP channel can only be explained by the desire to hinder competition on the merits in the relevant market, those initiatives must be labeled anticompetitive.

In sum, the efforts Microsoft directed at OEMs and IAPs successfully ostracized Navigator as a practical matter from the two channels that lead most efficiently to browser usage. Even when viewed independently, these two prongs of Microsoft's campaign threatened to "forestall the corrective forces of competition" and thereby perpetuate Microsoft's monopoly power in the relevant market. . . . Therefore, whether they are viewed separately or together, the OEM and IAP components of Microsoft's anticompetitive campaign merit a finding of liability under Section 2.

**iii. ICPs, ISVs and Apple.** No other distribution channels for browsing software approach the efficiency of OEM pre-installation and IAP bundling. Nevertheless, protecting the applications barrier to entry was so critical to Microsoft that the firm was willing to invest substantial resources to enlist ICPs [Internet content providers], ISVs [Internet service providers], and Apple in its campaign against the browser threat. By extracting from Apple terms that significantly diminished the usage of Navigator on the Mac OS, Microsoft helped to ensure that developers would not view Navigator as truly cross-platform middleware. By granting ICPs and ISVs free licenses to bundle Internet Explorer with their offerings, and by exchanging other valuable inducements for their agreement to distribute, promote and rely on Internet Explorer rather than Navigator, Microsoft directly induced developers to focus on its own APIs rather than ones exposed by Navigator. These measures supplemented Microsoft's efforts in the OEM and IAP channels.

Just as they fail to account for the measures that Microsoft took in the IAP channel, the goals of preventing free riding and preserving brand association fail to explain the full extent of Microsoft's actions in the ICP channel. With respect to the ISV agreements, Microsoft has put forward no procompetitive business ends whatsoever justify their exclusionary terms. Finally, Microsoft's willingness to make the sacrifices involved in canceling Mac Office [a suite of business applications for the Mackintosh computer] , and the concessions relating to browsing software that it demanded from Apple, can only be explained by Microsoft's desire to protect the applications barrier to entry from the threat posed by Navigator. Thus, once again, Microsoft is unable to justify the full extent of its restrictive behavior.

*b. Combating the Java Threat.*     As part of its grand strategy to protect the applications barrier, Microsoft employed an array of tactics designed to maximize the difficulty with which applications written in Java [a computer language developed by Sun Microsystems] could be ported from Windows to other platforms, and vice versa. The first of these measures was the creation of a Java implementation for Windows that undermined portability and was incompatible with other implementations. Microsoft then induced developers to use its implementation of Java rather than Sun-compliant ones. It pursued this tactic directly, by means of subterfuge and barter, and indirectly, through its campaign to minimize Navigator's usage share. In a separate effort to prevent the development of easily portable Java applications, Microsoft used its monopoly power to prevent firms such as Intel from aiding in the creation of cross-platform interfaces.

Microsoft's tactics induced many Java developers to write their applications write their applications using Microsoft's developer tools and to refrain from distributing Sun-compliant JVMs [Java Virtual Machine] to Windows users. This stratagem has effectively resulted in fewer applications that are easily portable. What is more, Microsoft's actions interfered with the development of new cross-platform Java interfaces. It is not clear whether, absent Microsoft's machinations, Sun's Java efforts would by now have facilitated porting between Windows and other platforms to a degree sufficient to render the applications barrier to entry vulnerable. It is clear, however, that Microsoft's actions markedly impeded Java's progress to that end. The evidence thus compels the conclusions that Microsoft's actions with respect to Java have restricted significantly the ability of other firms to compete on the merits in the market for Intel-compatible PC operating systems.

Microsoft's actions to counter the Java threat went far beyond the development of an attractive alternative to Sun's implementation of the technology. Specifically, Microsoft successfully pressured Intel, which was dependent in many ways on Microsoft's good graces, to abstain from aiding in Sun's and Netscape's Java development work. Microsoft also deliberately designed its Java development tools so that developers who were opting for portability over performance would nevertheless unwittingly write Java applications that would run only on Windows. Moreover, Microsoft's means of luring developers to its Java implementation included maximizing Internet Explorer's share of browser usage at Navigator's expense in ways the Court has already held to be anticompetitive. Finally, Microsoft impelled ISVs, which are dependent upon Microsoft for technical information and certifications elating to Windows, to use and distribute Microsoft's version of the Windows JVM rather than any Sun-compliant version.

These actions cannot be described as competition on the merits, and they did not benefit consumers. In fact, Microsoft's actions did not even benefit Microsoft in the short run, for the firm's efforts to create incompatibility between its JVM for Windows and others' JVMs for Windows resulted in fewer total applications being able to run on Windows than otherwise would have been written. Microsoft was willing nevertheless to obstruct the development of Windows-compatible applications if they would be easy to port to other platforms and would thus diminish the applications barrier to entry.

*c. Microsoft's Conduct Taken As a Whole.*    As the foregoing discussion illustrates, Microsoft's campaign to protect the applications barrier from erosion by network-centric middleware can be broken down into discrete categories of activity, several of which on their own independently satisfy the second element of a Section 2 monopoly maintenance claim. But only when the separate categories of conduct are viewed, as they should be, as a single, well-coordinated course of action does the full extent of the violence that Microsoft has done to the competitive process reveal itself. . . . In essence, Microsoft mounted a deliberate assault upon entrepreneurial efforts that, left to rise or fall on their own merits, could well have enabled the introduction of competition into the market for Intel-compatible PC operating systems. While the evidence does not prove that they would have succeeded absent Microsoft's actions, it does reveal that Microsoft placed an oppressive thumb on the scale of competitive fortune, thereby effectively guaranteeing its continued dominance in the relevant market. More broadly, Microsoft's anticompetitive actions trammeled the competitive process through which the computer software industry generally stimulates innovation and conduces to the optimum benefit of consumers.

Viewing Microsoft's conduct as a whole also reinforces the conviction that it was predacious. Microsoft paid vast sums of money, and renounced many millions more in lost revenue every year, in order to induce firms to take actions that would help enhance Internet Explorer's share of browser usage at Navigator's expense. These outlays cannot be explained as subventions to maximize return from Internet Explorer. Microsoft has no intention of ever charging for licenses to use or distribute its browser. Moreover, neither the desire to bolster demand for Windows nor the prospect of ancillary revenues from Internet Explorer can explain the lengths to which Microsoft has gone. In fact, Microsoft has expended wealth and foresworn opportunities to realize more in a manner and to an extent that can only represent a rational investment if its purpose was to perpetuate the applications barrier to entry. Because Microsoft's business practices "would not be considered profit maximizing except for the expectation that . . . the entry of potential rivals" into the market for Intel-compatible PC operating systems will be "blocked or delayed" [citation from *Neumann v. Reinforced Earth Co.*, 1986], Microsoft's campaign must be termed predatory. Since the Court has already found that Microsoft possesses monopoly power, the predatory nature of the firm's conduct compels the Court to hold Microsoft liable under Section 2 of the Sherman Act.

## B. Attempting to Obtain Monopoly Power in a Second Market by Anticompetitive Means

In addition to condemning actual monopolization, Section 2 of the Sherman Act declares that it is unlawful for a person or firm to "attempt to monopolize . . . any part of the trade or commerce among the several States, or with foreign nations. . . ." Relying on this language, the plaintiffs assert that Microsoft's anticompetitive efforts to maintain its monopoly power in the market for Intel-compatible PC operating systems warrant additional liability as an illegal attempt to amass monopoly power in "the browser market." The Court agrees.

In order for liability to attach for attempted monopolization, a plaintiff generally must prove "(1) that the defendant has engaged in predatory or anticompetitive conduct with (2) a specific intent to monopolize," and (3) that there is a "dangerous probability" that the defendant will succeed in achieving monopoly power. . . . Microsoft's June 1995 proposal that Netscape abandon the field to Microsoft in the market for browsing technology for Windows, and its subsequent, well-documented efforts to overwhelm Navigator's browser usage share with a proliferation of Internet Explorer browsers inextricably attached to Windows, clearly meet the first element of the offense.

The evidence in this record also satisfies the requirement of specific intent. Microsoft's effort to convince Netscape to stop developing platform-level browsing software for the 32-bit versions of Windows was made with full knowledge that Netscape's acquiescence in this market allocation scheme would, without more, have left Internet Explorer with such a large share of browser usage as to endow Microsoft with de facto monopoly power in the browser market.

When Netscape refused to abandon the development of browsing software for 32-bit versions of Windows, Microsoft's strategy for protecting the applications barrier became one of expanding Internet Explorer's share of browser usage—and simultaneously depressing Navigator's share—to an extent sufficient to demonstrate to developers that Navigator would never emerge as the standard software employed to browse the Web. While Microsoft's top executives never expressly declared acquisition of monopoly power in the browser market to be the objective, they knew or should have known, that the tactics they actually employed were likely to push Internet Explorer's share to those extreme heights. Navigator's slow demise would leave a competitive vacuum for only Internet Explorer to fill. Yet, there is no evidence that Microsoft tried—or even considered trying—to prevent its anticompetitive campaign from achieving overkill. Under these circumstances, it is fair to presume that the wrongdoer intended "the probable consequences of its acts.". . . Therefore, the facts of this case suffice to prove the element of specific intent.

Even if the first two elements of the offense are met, however, a defendant may not be held liable for attempted monopolization absent proof that its anticompetitive conduct created a dangerous probability of achieving the objective of monopoly power in a relevant market. The evidence supports the conclusion that Microsoft's actions did pose such a danger.

At the time Microsoft presented its market allocation proposal to Netscape, Navigator's share of browser usage stood well above seventy percent, and no other browser enjoyed more than a fraction of the remainder. Had Netscape accepted Microsoft's offer, nearly all of its share would have devolved upon Microsoft, because at that point, no potential third-party competitor could either claim to rival Netscape's stature as a browser company or match Microsoft's ability to leverage monopoly power in the market for Intel-compatible PC operating systems. In the time it would have taken an aspiring entrant to launch a serious effort to compete against Internet Explorer, Microsoft could have erected the same type of barrier that protects its existing monopoly power by adding proprietary extensions to the browsing software under its control and by extracting commitments from OEMs, IAPs and others similar to the ones discussed in Section I.A.2. In short, Netscape's assent to Microsoft's market division proposal would have, *instanter*, resulted in Microsoft's attainment of monopoly power in a second market. It follows that the proposal itself created a dangerous probability of that result. . . . Although the dangerous probability was no longer imminent with Netscape's rejection of Microsoft's proposal, "the probability of success at the time the acts occur" is the measure by which liability is determined.

This conclusion alone is sufficient to support a finding of liability for attempted monopolization. The Court is nonetheless compelled to express its further conclusion that the predatory course of conduct Microsoft has pursued since June of 1995 has revived the dangerous probability that Microsoft will attain monopoly power in a second market. Internet Explorer's share of browser usage has already risen above fifty percent, will exceed sixty percent by January 2001, and the trend continues unabated. . . .

## II. Section One of the Sherman Act

Section 1 of the Sherman Act prohibits "every contract, combination . . . or conspiracy, in restraint of trade or commerce. . . ." Pursuant to this statute, courts have condemned commercial stratagems that constitute unreasonable restraints on competition. . . . Tying arrangements have been found unlawful where sellers exploit their market power over one product to force unwilling buyers into acquiring another. . . . Where agreements have been challenged as unlawful exclusive dealing, the courts have condemned only those contractual arrangements that substantially foreclose competition in a relevant market by significantly reducing the number of outlets available to a competitor to reach prospective consumers of the competitor's product. . . .

### A. Tying

Liability for tying under Section 1 exists where (1) two separate "products" are involved; (2) the defendant affords its customers no choice but to take the tied product in order to obtain the tying product; (3) the arrangement affects a substantial volume of interstate commerce; and (4) the defendant has "market power" in the tying product market. The Supreme Court has since reaffirmed this test in *Eastman Kodak Co. v. Image Technical Services, Inc.* [1992]. All four elements are required, whether the arrangement is subjected to a per se or Rule of Reason analysis.

The plaintiffs allege that Microsoft's combination of Windows and Internet Explorer by contractual and technological artifices constitute unlawful tying to the extent that those actions forced Microsoft's customers and consumers to take Internet Explorer as a condition of obtaining Windows. While the Court agrees with plaintiffs, and thus holds that Microsoft is liable for illegal tying under Section 1, this conclusion is arguably at variance with a decision of the U.S. Court of Appeals for the D.C. Circuit in a closely related case, and must therefore be explained in some detail. Whether the decisions are indeed inconsistent is not for this Court to say.

The decision of the D.C. Circuit in question is *United States v. Microsoft Corp.* [1998 —"*Microsoft II*"], which is itself related to an earlier decision of the same Circuit, *United States v. Microsoft Corp.*, [1995 —"*Microsoft I*"]. The history of the controversy is sufficiently set forth in the appellate opinions and need not be recapitulated here, except to state that those decisions anticipated the instant case, and that *Microsoft II* sought to guide this Court, insofar as practicable, in the further proceedings it fully expected to ensue on the tying issue. Nevertheless, upon reflection this Court does not believe the D.C. Circuit intended *Microsoft II* to state a controlling rule of law for purposes of this case. As the *Microsoft II* court itself acknowledged, the issue before it was the construction to be placed upon a single provision of a consent decree that, although animated by antitrust considerations, was nevertheless still primarily a matter of determining contractual intent. The court of appeals' observations on the extent to which software product design decisions may be subject to judicial scrutiny in the course of Section 1 tying cases are in the strictest sense obiter dicta, and are thus not formally binding. Nevertheless, both prudence and the deference this Court owes to pronouncements of its own Circuit oblige that it follow in the direction it is pointed until the trail falters.

The majority opinion in *Microsoft II* evinces both an extraordinary degree of respect for changes (including "integration") instigated by designers of technological products, such as software, in the name of product "improvement," and a corresponding lack of confidence in the ability of the courts to distinguish between improvements in fact and improvements in name only, made for anticompetitive purposes. Read literally, the D.C. Circuit's opinion appears to immunize any product design (or, at least, software product design) from antitrust scrutiny, irrespective of its effect upon competition, if the software developer can postulate any "plausible claim" of advantage to its arrangement of code.

This undemanding test appears to this Court to be inconsistent with the pertinent Supreme Court precedents in at least three respects. First, it views the market from the defendant's perspective, or, more precisely, as the defendant would like to have the market viewed. Second, it ignores reality: The claim of advantage need only be plausible; it need not be proved. Third, it dispenses with any balancing of the hypothetical advantages against any anticompetitive effects.

The two most recent Supreme Court cases to have addressed the issue of product and market definition in the context of Sherman Act tying claims are *Jefferson Parish* [*Jefferson Parish Hospital District No. 2 v. Hyde*, decided in 1984] and *Eastman Kodak* [*Eastman Kodak Co. v. Image Technical Services Inc.*, decided in 1992]. In *Jefferson Parish*, the Supreme Court held that a hospital offering hospital services and anesthesiology services as a package could not be found to have violated the anti-tying rules unless the evidence established that patients, i.e. consumers, perceived the services as separate products for which they desired a choice, and that the package had the effect of forcing the patients to purchase an unwanted product. In *Eastman Kodak* the Supreme Court held that a manufacturer of photocopying and micrographic equipment, in agreeing to sell replacement parts for its machines only to those customers who also agreed to purchase repair services from it as well, would be guilty of tying if the evidence at trial established the existence of consumer demand for parts and services separately.

Both defendants asserted, as Microsoft does here, that the tied and tying products were in reality only a single product, or that every item was traded in a single market. In *Jefferson Parish*, the defendant contended that it offered a "functionally integrated package of services"—a single product—but the Supreme Court concluded that the "character of the demand" for the constituent components, not their functional relationship, determined whether separate "products" were actually involved. In *Eastman Kodak*, the defendant postulated that effective competition in the equipment market precluded the possibility of the use of market power anticompetitively in any after-markets for parts or services: Sales of machines, parts, and services were all responsive to the discipline of the larger equipment market. The Supreme Court declined to accept this premise in the absence of evidence of "actual market realities," ultimately holding that "the proper market definition in this case can be determined only after a factual inquiry into the 'commercial realities' faced by consumers."

In both *Jefferson Parish* and *Eastman Kodak*, the Supreme Court also gave consideration to certain theoretical "valid business reasons" proffered by the defendants as to why the arrangements should be deemed benign. In *Jefferson Parish*, the hospital asserted that the combination of hospital and anesthesia services eliminated multiple problems of scheduling, supply, performance standards, and equipment maintenance. The manufacturer in *Eastman Kodak* contended that quality control, inventory management, and the prevention of free riding justified its decision to sell parts only in conjunction with service. In neither case did the Supreme Court find those justifications sufficient if anticompetitive effects were proved. Thus, at a minimum, the admonition of the D.C. Circuit in *Microsoft II* to refrain from any product design assessment as to whether the "integration" of Windows and Internet Explorer is a "net plus," deferring to Microsoft's "plausible claim" that it is of "some advantage" to consumers, is at odds with the Supreme Court's own approach.

The significance of those cases, for this Court's purposes, is to teach that resolution of product and market definitional problems must depend upon proof of commercial reality, as opposed to what might appear to be reasonable. In both cases the Supreme Court instructed that product and market definitions were to be ascertained by reference to evidence of consumers' perception of the nature of the products and the markets for them, rather than to abstract or metaphysical assumptions as to the configuration of the "product" and the "market." In the instant case, the commercial reality is that consumers today perceive operating systems and browsers as separate "products," for which there is separate demand. This is true notwithstanding the fact that the software code supplying their discrete functionalities can be commingled in virtually infinite combinations, rendering each indistinguishable from the whole in terms of files of code or any other taxonomy.

Proceeding in line with the Supreme Court cases, which are indisputably controlling, this Court first concludes that Microsoft possessed "appreciable economic power in the tying market,". . . which in this case is the market for Intel-compatible PC operating systems. . . . While courts typically have not specified a percentage of the market that creates the presumption of "market power," no court has ever found that the requisite degree of power exceeds the amount necessary for a finding of monopoly power. . . Because this Court has already found already found that Microsoft possesses monopoly power in the worldwide market for Intel-compatible PC operating systems (i.e., the tying product market), the threshold element of "appreciable economic power" is a fortiori met.

Similarly, the Court's Findings strongly support a conclusion that a "not insubstantial" amount of commerce was foreclosed to competitors as a result of Microsoft's decision to bundle Internet Explorer with Windows. The controlling consideration under this element is "simply whether a total amount of business" that is "substantial enough in terms of dollar-volume so as not to be merely de minimis" is foreclosed. . . .

Although the Court's Findings do not specify a dollar amount of business that has been foreclosed to any particular present or potential competitor of Microsoft in the relevant market, including Netscape, the Court did find that Microsoft's bundling practices caused Navigator's usage share to drop substantially from 1995 to 1998, and that as a direct result Netscape suffered a severe drop in revenues from lost advertisers, Web traffic and purchases of server products. It is thus obvious that the foreclosure achieved by Microsoft's refusal to offer Internet Explorer separately from Windows exceeds the Supreme Court's de minimis threshold. . . .

The facts of this case also prove the elements of the forced bundling requirement. Indeed, the Supreme Court has stated that the "essential characteristic" of an illegal tying arrangement is a seller's decision to exploit its market power over the tying product "to force the buyer into the purchase of a tied product that the buyer either did not want at all, or might have preferred to purchase elsewhere on different terms.". . . In that regard, the Court has found that, beginning with the early agreements for Windows 95, Microsoft has conditioned the provision of a license to distribute Windows on the OEMs' purchase of Internet Explorer. The agreements prohibited the licensees from ever modifying or deleting any part of Windows, despite the OEMs' expressed desire to be allowed to do so. As a result, OEMs were generally not permitted, with only one brief exception, to satisfy consumer demand for a browserless version of Windows 95 without Internet Explorer. Similarly, Microsoft refused to license Windows 98 to OEMs unless they also agreed to abstain from removing the icons for Internet Explorer from the desktop. Consumers were also effectively compelled to purchase Internet Explorer along with Windows 98 by Microsoft's decision to stop including Internet Explorer on the list of programs subject to the Add/Remove function and by its decision not to respect their selection of another browser as their default.

The fact that Microsoft ostensibly priced Internet Explorer at zero does not detract from the conclusion that consumers were forced to pay, one way or another, for the browser along with Windows. Despite Microsoft's assertion that the Internet Explorer technologies are not "purchased" since they are included in a single royalty price paid by OEMs for Windows 98, . . . it is nevertheless clear that licensees, including consumers, are forced to take, and pay for, the entire package of software and that any value to be ascribed to Internet Explorer is built into this single price. . . . Moreover, the purpose of the Supreme Court's "forcing" inquiry is to expose those product bundles that raise the cost or difficulty of doing business for would-be competitors to prohibitively high levels, thereby depriving consumers of the opportunity to evaluate a competing product on its relative merits. It is not, as Microsoft suggests, simply to punish firms on the basis of an increment in price attributable to the tied product. . . .

As for the crucial requirement that Windows and Internet Explorer be deemed "separate products" for a finding of technological tying liability, this Court's Findings mandate such a conclusion. Considering the "character of demand" for the two products, as opposed to their "functional relation," Web browsers and operating systems are "distinguishable in the eyes of buyers." Consumers often base their choice of which browser should reside on their operating system on their individual demand for the specific functionalities or characteristics of a particular browser, separate and apart from the functionalities afforded by the operating system itself. Moreover, the behavior of other, lesser software vendors confirms that it is certainly efficient to provide an operating system and a browser separately, or at least in separable form. Microsoft is the only firm to refuse to license its operating system without a browser. . . . This Court concludes that Microsoft's decision to offer only the bundled—"integrated"—version of Windows and Internet Explorer derived not from technical necessity or business efficiencies; rather, it was the result of a deliberate and purposeful choice to quell incipient competition before it reached truly minatory proportions.

The Court is fully mindful of the reasons for the admonition of the D.C. Circuit in *Microsoft II* of the perils associated with a rigid application of the traditional "separate products" test to computer software design. Given the virtually infinite malleability of software code, software upgrades and new application features, such as Web browsers, could virtually always be configured so as to be capable of separate and subsequent installation by an immediate licensee or end user. A court mechanically applying a strict "separate demand" test could improvidently wind up condemning "integrations" that represent genuine improvements to software that are benign from the standpoint of consumer welfare and a competitive market. Clearly, this is not a desirable outcome. Similar concerns have motivated other courts, as well as the D.C. Circuit, to resist a strict application of the "separate products" tests to similar questions of "technological tying.". . .

To the extent that the Supreme Court has spoken authoritatively on these issues, however, this Court is bound to follow its guidance and is not at liberty to extrapolate a new rule governing the tying of software products. Nevertheless, the Court is confident that its conclusion, limited by the unique circumstances of this case, is consistent with the Supreme Court's teaching to date.

## B. Exclusive Dealing Arrangements

Microsoft's various contractual agreements with some OLSs, ICPs, ISVs, Compaq and Apple are also called into question by plaintiffs as exclusive dealing arrangements under the language in Section 1 prohibiting "contract[s] . . . in restraint of trade or commerce. . . ." As detailed in Section I.A.2, each of these agreements with Microsoft required the other party to promote and distribute Internet Explorer to the partial or complete exclusion of Navigator. In exchange, Microsoft offered, to some or all of these parties, promotional patronage, substantial financial subsidies, technical support, and other valuable consideration. Under the clear standards established by the Supreme Court, these types of "vertical restrictions" are subject to a Rule of Reason analysis. . . .

Acknowledging that some exclusive dealing arrangements may have benign objectives and may create significant economic benefits, . . . courts have tended to condemn under the Section 1 Rule of Reason test only those agreements that have the effect of foreclosing a competing manufacturer's brands from the relevant market. More specifically, courts are concerned with those exclusive dealing arrangements that work to place so much of a market's available distribution outlets in the hands of a single firm as to make it difficult for other firms to continue to compete effectively, or even to exist, in the relevant market. . . .

To evaluate an agreement's likely anticompetitive effects, courts have consistently looked at a variety of factors, including: (1) the degree of exclusivity and the relevant line of commerce implicated by the agreements' terms; (2) whether the percentage of the market foreclosed by the contracts is substantial enough to import that rivals will be largely excluded from competition; (3) the agreements' actual anticompetitive effect in the relevant line of commerce; (4) the existence of any legitimate, procompetitive business justifications offered by the defendant; (5) the length and irrevocability of the agreements; and (6) the availability of any less restrictive means for achieving the same benefits. . . .

Where courts have found that the agreements in question failed to foreclose absolutely outlets that together accounted for a substantial percentage of the total distribution of the relevant products, they have consistently declined to assign liability. . . . This Court has previously observed that the case law suggests that, unless the evidence demonstrates that Microsoft's agreements excluded Netscape altogether from access to roughly forty percent of the browser market, the Court should decline to find such agreements in violation of Section 1. . . .

The only agreements revealed by the evidence which could be termed so "exclusive" as to merit scrutiny under the Section 1 Rule of Reason test are the agreements Microsoft signed with Compaq, AOL [America Online] and several other OLSs, the top ICPs, the leading ISVs, and Apple. The Findings of Fact also establish that, among the OEMs discussed supra, Compaq was the only one to fully commit itself to Microsoft's terms for distributing and promoting Internet Explorer to the exclusion of Navigator. Beginning with its decisions in 1996 and 1997 to promote Internet Explorer exclusively for its PC products, Compaq essentially ceased to distribute or pre-install Navigator at all in exchange for significant financial remuneration from Microsoft. AOL's March 12 and October 28, 1996 agreements with Microsoft also guaranteed that, for all practical purposes, Internet Explorer would be AOL's browser of choice, to be distributed and promoted through AOL's dominant, flagship online service, thus leaving Navigator to fend for itself. In light of the severe shipment quotas and promotional restrictions for third-party browsers imposed by the agreements, the fact that Microsoft still permitted AOL to offer Navigator through a few subsidiary channels does not negate this conclusion. The same conclusion as to exclusionary effect can be drawn with respect to Microsoft's agreements with AT&T WorldNet, Prodigy and CompuServe, since those contract terms were almost identical to the ones contained in AOL's March 1996 agreement.

Microsoft also successfully induced some of the most popular ICPs and ISVs to commit to promote, distribute and utilize Internet Explorer technologies exclusively in their Web content in exchange for valuable placement on the Windows desktop and technical support. Specifically, the "Top Tier" and "Platinum" agreements that Microsoft formed with thirty-four of the most popular ICPs on the Web ensured that Navigator was effectively shut out of these distribution outlets for a significant period of time. In the same way, Microsoft's "First Wave" contracts provided crucial technical information to dozens of leading ISVs that agreed to make their Web-centric applications completely reliant on technology specific to Internet Explorer. Finally, Apple's 1997 Technology Agreement with Microsoft prohibited Apple from actively promoting any non-Microsoft browsing software in any way or from pre-installing a browser other than Internet Explorer. This arrangement eliminated all meaningful avenues of distribution of Navigator through Apple.

Notwithstanding the extent to which these "exclusive" distribution agreements preempted the most efficient channels for Navigator to achieve browser usage share, however, the Court concludes that Microsoft's multiple agreements with distributors did not ultimately deprive Netscape of the ability to have access to every PC user worldwide to offer an opportunity to install Navigator. Navigator can be downloaded from the Internet. It is available through myriad retail channels. It can (and has been) mailed directly to an unlimited number of households. How precisely it managed to do so is not shown by the evidence, but in 1998 alone, for example, Netscape was able to distribute 160 million copies of Navigator, contributing to an increase in its installed base from 15 million in 1996 to 33 million in December 1998. As such, the evidence does not support a finding that these agreements completely excluded Netscape from any constituent portion of the worldwide browser market, the relevant line of commerce.

The fact that Microsoft's arrangements with various firms did not foreclose enough of the relevant market to constitute a Section 1 violation in no way detracts from the Court's assignment of liability for the same arrangements under Section 2. As noted above, all of Microsoft's agreements, including the non-exclusive ones, severely restricted Netscape's access to those distribution channels leading most efficiently to the acquisition of browser usage share. They thus rendered Netscape harmless as a platform threat and preserved Microsoft's operating system monopoly, in violation of Section 2. But virtually all the leading case authority dictates that liability under Section 1 must hinge upon whether Netscape was actually shut out of the Web browser market, or at least whether it was forced to reduce output below a subsistence level. The fact that Netscape was not allowed access to the most direct, efficient ways to cause the greatest number of consumers to use Navigator is legally irrelevant to a final determination of plaintiffs' Section 1 claims.

Other courts in similar contexts have declined to find liability where alternative channels of distribution are available to the competitor, even if those channels are not as efficient or reliable as the channels foreclosed by the defendant. In *Omega Environmental, Inc. v. Gilbarco, Inc.* (1997), for example, the Ninth Circuit found that a manufacturer of petroleum dispensing equipment "foreclosed roughly 38% of the relevant market for sales." Nonetheless, the Court refused to find the defendant liable for exclusive dealing because "potential alternative sources of distribution" existed for its competitors. Rejecting plaintiff's argument (similar to the one made in this case) that these alternatives were "inadequate substitutes for the existing distributors," the Court stated that "[c]ompetitors are free to sell directly, to develop alternative distributors, or to compete for the services of existing distributors. Antitrust laws require no more."

## III. The State Law Claims

In their amended complaint, the plaintiff states assert that the same facts establishing liability under Sections 1 and 2 of the Sherman Act mandate a finding of liability under analogous provisions in their own laws. The Court agrees. The facts proving that Microsoft unlawfully maintained its monopoly power in violation of Section 2 of the Sherman Act are sufficient to meet analogous elements of causes of action arising under the laws of each plaintiff state. The Court reaches the same conclusion with respect to the facts establishing that Microsoft attempted to monopolize the browser market in violation of Section 2, and with respect to those facts establishing that Microsoft instituted an improper tying arrangement in violation of Section 1.

The plaintiff states concede that their laws do not condemn any act proved in this case that fails to warrant liability under the Sherman Act. . . . Accordingly, the Court concludes that, for reasons identical to those stated in Section II.B, the evidence in this record does not warrant finding Microsoft liable for exclusive dealing under the laws of any of the plaintiff states.

Microsoft contends that a plaintiff cannot succeed in an antitrust claim under the laws of California, Louisiana, Maryland, New York, Ohio, or Wisconsin without proving an element that is not required under the Sherman Act, namely, intrastate impact. Assuming that each of those states has, indeed, expressly limited the application of its antitrust laws to activity that has a significant, adverse effect on competition within the state or is otherwise contrary to state interests, that element is manifestly proven by the facts presented here. The Court has found that Microsoft is the leading supplier of operating systems for PCs and that it transacts business in all fifty of the United States. It is common and universal knowledge that millions of citizens of, and hundreds, if not thousands, of enterprises in each of the United States and the District of Columbia utilize PCs running on Microsoft software. It is equally clear that certain companies that have been adversely affected by Microsoft's anticompetitive campaign—a list that includes IBM, Hewlett-Packard, Intel, Netscape, Sun, and many others—transact business in, and employ citizens of, each of the plaintiff states. These facts compel the conclusion that, in each of the plaintiff states, Microsoft's anticompetitive conduct has significantly hampered competition.

Microsoft once again invokes the federal Copyright Act in defending against state claims seeking to vindicate the rights of OEMs and others to make certain modifications to Windows 95 and Windows 98. The Court concludes that these claims do not encroach on Microsoft's federally protected copyrights and, thus, that they are not pre-empted under the Supremacy Clause. The Court already concluded in Section I.A.2. that Microsoft's decision to bundle its browser and impose first-boot and start-up screen restrictions constitute independent violations of Section 2 of the Sherman Act. It follows as a matter of course that the same actions merit liability under the plaintiff states' antitrust and unfair competition laws. Indeed, the parties agree that the standards for liability under the several plaintiff states' antitrust and unfair competition laws are, for the purposes of this case, identical to those expressed in the federal statute. . . . Thus, these state laws cannot "stand[] as an obstacle to" the goals of the federal copyright law to any greater extent than do the federal antitrust laws, for they target exactly the same type of anticompetitive behavior. . . . The Copyright Act's preemption clause provides that "[n]othing in this title annuls or limits any rights or remedies under the common law or statutes of any State with respect to . . . activities violating legal or equitable rights that are not equivalent to any of the exclusive rights within the general scope of copyright as specified by section 106. . . . ." Moreover, the Supreme Court has recognized that there is "nothing either in the language of the copyright laws or in the history of their enactment to indicate any congressional purpose to deprive the states, either in whole or in part, of their long-recognized power to regulate combinations in restraint of trade.". . .

The Court turns finally to the counterclaim that Microsoft brings against the attorneys general of the plaintiff states under 42 U.S.C. [1983]. In support of its claim, Microsoft argues that the attorneys general are seeking relief on the basis of state laws, repeats its assertion that the imposition of this relief would deprive it of rights granted to it by the Copyright Act, and concludes with the contention that the attorneys general are, "under color of" state law, seeking to deprive Microsoft of rights secured by federal law—a classic violation of 42 U.S.C. [1983]. Having already addressed the issue of whether granting the relief sought by the attorneys general would entail conflict with the Copyright Act, the Court rejects Microsoft's counterclaim on yet more fundamental grounds as well: It is inconceivable that their resort to this Court could represent an effort on the part of the attorneys general to deprive Microsoft of rights guaranteed it under federal law, because this Court does not possess the power to act in contravention of federal law. Therefore, since the conduct it complains of is the pursuit of relief in federal court, Microsoft fails to state a claim under 42 U.S.C. [1983]. Consequently, Microsoft's request for a declaratory judgment against the states under 28 U.S.C. [2201 and 2202] is denied, and the counterclaim is dismissed.

Thomas Penfeld Jackson
U.S. District Judge

# FEDERAL REPORT ON
# PRESCRIPTION DRUG PRICES
## April 10, 2000

*The rising price of prescription drugs, especially for seniors, supplanted a patients' bill of rights as the most closely watched health issue of the year—and one of the most hotly contested on the campaign trail. The issue, which had been festering for some time, came to a head early in the year with the release of two reports showing not only that prices were rising, but also that people without drug insurance coverage, primarily the elderly and the poor, typically paid a higher price than others for prescription drugs*

*Seeing the election year as an opportunity, senior citizen and consumer advocacy groups as well as an unusual coalition of big business and big labor mounted campaigns seeking price relief and better insurance coverage. Democrats led by President Bill Clinton were quick to jump on the bandwagon, forcing Republican leaders, who had hoped to put off the issue until the next session of Congress, to act or be accused of being insensitive to the needs of an important voting block. The two parties disagreed on how best to offer relief, and the issue quickly became one of the pivotal factors differentiating presidential contenders George W. Bush and Al Gore.*

*At year's end Congress had adopted a stop-gap measure designed to lower prices paid by seniors for some drugs, but the issue of broadening insurance coverage was left to another day. In the absence of comprehensive federal legislation, several state legislatures adopted their own relief measures. By the end of the year about half of the states had approved legislation offering some subsidy or discount, or both, on prescription drugs for eligible seniors and low-income residents. Several of those states used money from their tobacco settlement fund to help finance the drug subsidy.* (Tobacco settlement fund, Historic Documents of 1998, p. 842)

### *Genesis of the Problem*

*At the root of the problem was the changing role of drugs in medical care in the last three decades of the twentieth century. When Medicare was enacted in 1965 as one of President Lyndon Johnson's Great Society programs, prescription drugs were used mainly in medical crises to treat pain and in-*

131

*fection. By 2000 the pharmaceutical industry had developed a wide array of drugs to treat a variety of chronic conditions. Without these drugs, millions of people, particularly the elderly, would have shortened life expectancy and a poorer quality of life. According to one widely quoted calculation, the elderly made up 13 percent of the population but accounted for more than one-third of the nation's annual drug expenditures, estimated to reach $112 billion in 2000.*

*The millions of working-age Americans and their families covered by private health insurance were largely insulated from rising drug prices. Typically these Americans paid about $15 in copayments per prescription. Poor families on Medicaid also received drug benefits. But millions of other Americans did not have drug coverage. These included low-income workers who did not receive coverage through their employers and earned too much to qualify for Medicaid. By far the largest group without drug benefits was the elderly. While most Americans age sixty-five and older received health coverage under Medicare, the health program did not offer drug benefits, and efforts to provide such coverage had never passed Congress. Some Medicare recipients bought supplemental coverage to fill the gap, while others were covered under employer-sponsored plans for retirees.*

*According to a report prepared by the Department of Health and Human Services (HHS) and released April 10 by President Clinton, in 1996, the last year for which statistics were available, 28 percent of all Medicare recipients—11 million people—had no drug coverage for the entire year, while another 19 percent were covered for only part of the year. For those Medicare recipients with coverage, the benefits were shrinking as insurers raised the copayment amount the insured had to pay and imposed annual limits on the total amounts they would pay for any one person. The HHS report said that, in 1999, 70 percent of the plans—double the number in 1998—had caps of $1,000 or less. According to the Kaiser Family Foundation, about half of the elderly spent less than $500 a year on prescription drugs, 45 percent spent between $500 and $3,000, and 6 percent spent $3,000 or more.*

*A second report prepared for a consumer advocacy group found that prices for the fifty prescription drugs most frequently used by the elderly rose at nearly twice the rate of inflation in 1999. Moreover, the report said, thirty-nine of these drugs had been on the market for at least six years, and the prices of all but two of the thirty-nine had increased faster than the rate of inflation over the period. Prices for six of the thirty-nine increased at least five times faster than the rate of inflation. Although it was not a government report, the Families USA study was released by President Clinton at the White House on April 25 because its conclusion supported those in the HHS report.*

*Not only were the elderly facing rising prices, but those who paid for their prescription drugs totally out of pocket did not receive the discounts and rebates that bulk buyers such as HMOs, major insurers, and governments negotiated with the pharmaceutical manufacturers. According to the HHS report, the gap between drug prices for people with and without insurance discounts was 15 percent in 1999, up from 8 percent in 1996. (Because of data limitations the HHS study did not include information on rebates but estimated that they widened the price gap by an additional 2–35 percent.) As a result, the study said, the percentage of Medicare recipients without drug coverage who reported that they could not afford to buy prescribed drugs was about five times higher than those with drug coverage. Overall Medicare recipients without drug coverage bought about one-third fewer drugs than those with coverage, but they spent nearly twice as much out of pocket.*

*Moreover, American drugs were often sold in foreign countries, including Canada and Mexico, that imposed price controls and took other measures to make the drugs more affordable. According to one set of calculations, for example, the price of the same prescription of Prilosec, a popular ulcer medication, was $37.50 in Mexico, $49.80 in Canada, $58.73 for insured American consumers, and $117.56 for uninsured American consumers. "The most profitable industry in the country is charging the highest prices in the world to the Americans who can least afford it," said Rep. Tom Allen (D-Maine), who sponsored legislation to give all 39 million people on Medicare the same discounts the federal government negotiated for its employees.*

### *Comprehensive Legislation Delayed*

*Clinton used both the HHS study, which he had requested, and the independent Families USA Study, which was released at the White House on April 26, to urge the Republican-led Congress to pass legislation adding prescription drug coverage to Medicare. The House had not planned to act on the issue, but Republican leaders changed their minds after an assessment by a GOP pollster advised Republican lawmakers that passing some plan— any plan—was a "political imperative" for the party if it wished to keep control of the House after the November elections. Republicans had a thirteen-seat majority in the House going into the elections.*

*In June House Republicans unveiled a prescription drug proposal that relied on the private insurance market to develop coverage that seniors and others could purchase. Although the proposal included subsidies to help insurers cover their costs, the insurance industry surprised their longtime GOP allies by opposing the plan as unworkable. Industry officials said they could not develop or keep such policies at affordable rates, knowing that many of the prospective buyers of the insurance would be seniors who had the highest drug bills. The industry's opposition was a powerful blow, as was the lukewarm reception from the American Association of Retired Persons (AARP), the lobbying group representing millions of senior citizens. AARP said many elderly patients would not be able to afford either the premiums or the prescription copayments. The measure passed the House on June 28 by a three-vote margin, 217–214, nowhere near enough to override Clinton's promised veto.*

*The Senate took no action on that proposal; Senate Republican leaders said they preferred to add a prescription drug benefit in the context of a broad Medicare overhaul, which they said could not be accomplished in the final months of the 106th Congress. Legislators did approve language at-*

*tached to the agriculture appropriations bill for fiscal 2001 that would allow drug wholesalers and pharmacies to reimport American-manufactured prescription drugs that were sold abroad for less than the retail cost in the United States. Previously only pharmaceutical companies could reimport the drugs. Democrats generally opposed the reimportation amendment, charging that the language pushed through by House Republican leaders could be exploited by pharmaceutical companies to keep prices high. Clinton signed the appropriations bill (PL 106-387) despite misgivings over the reimportation provisions.*

## Massive Lobbying, Political Campaigns on Drug Prices

*Pressure in Congress and on the campaign trail to lower drug prices was remarkable. In an unusual alliance, Kaiser Permanente, General Motors, and the AFL-CIO joined with some sixty other groups to fight rising drug prices, which were pushing up health care costs for their employees and members. Presidential contenders Bush and Gore both had elaborate plans for helping seniors cope with prices. The Bush plan would give short-term help to states to help low-income elderly meet their prescription drug needs. In the long run, Bush wanted to fold drug reform into broader Medicare reform, which would rely on competition in the marketplace to control health care costs, including drug prices. Gore in contrast advocated the Democrat position of including a prescription drug benefit in Medicare. Saying repeatedly that he was not afraid to take on the drug industry, Gore also promised to make the industry more competitive by changing the patent laws and allowing less expensive generic drugs to come to market more quickly than they did under existing law.*

*For its part the pharmaceutical industry spent millions to ensure that if any legislation were passed it would provide drug coverage through private insurance rather than through Medicare. By one estimate the industry spent nearly $84 million on lobbying in 1999, and that amount was expected to be even higher in 2000. Underlying that position was the industry's desire to block any legislation that might regulate drug pricing. The major drug manufacturers, represented by the Pharmaceutical Research and Manufacturers Association, acknowledged that some drugs were expensive but argued that the value given by those drugs was worth it and that the prices were necessary to fund the development of better and more effective medicines. Manufacturers said that only one of every ten drugs developed reached the market and that a new drug cost an average of $500 million to develop and took twelve to fourteen years to reach the market.*

*Opponents dismissed those arguments as scare tactics. The industry had an 18.6 percent return on revenues in 1999, the highest of any industry in the United States. While it spent an estimated $22.5 billion on research and development in 2000, the industry spent nearly $14 billion on promotions in 1999, including $2 billion on direct consumer marketing. Furthermore, they said, the industry's research and development arguments did not explain the rising costs of existing drugs, many of which were protected by* *patents and did not have direct competition in the marketplace. "There is no sign of a living, breathing free market here," Alan Sager, professor of health services at Boston University, told the* Seattle Times.

> *Following is the executive summary from the "Report to the President: Prescription Drug Coverage, Spending, Utilization, and Prices," prepared by the Department of Health and Human Services and released April 10, 2000, by President Bill Clinton at a White House ceremony. The document was obtained from the Internet at http://aspe.hhs.gov/health/reports/drugstudy/index .htm.*

## Executive Summary

Prescription drugs play an ever-increasing role in modern medicine. New medications are improving health outcomes and quality of life, replacing surgery and other invasive treatments, and quickening recovery for patients who receive these treatments. As important as prescription drugs are, not everyone has access to them. The newest drugs are often the most expensive, and millions of Americans—especially elderly and disabled Medicare beneficiaries—have inadequate or no insurance coverage for drugs. Nearly a third of all Medicare beneficiaries have no financial protection for the costs of drugs, if they can obtain them at all. Many additional beneficiaries find themselves moving in and out of the protection provided by insurance over the course of a year.

Medicare has generally excluded coverage of outpatient prescription drugs, as was common in private health plans when the program was enacted in 1965. Since then drug coverage has become a standard feature of private insurance, and it has become clear that the omission of outpatient drug coverage represents a crucial gap in protection for the most vulnerable Medicare beneficiaries. As part of a broader plan to modernize Medicare, President Clinton has proposed a new, voluntary Medicare drug benefit that would offer all beneficiaries access to affordable, high-quality prescription drug coverage while maintaining the fiscal integrity of the program. In Congress, there has also been growing bipartisan interest in finding ways of extending drug coverage.

As policymakers consider options to ensure that every American can have access to innovative drug treatments, there is an urgent need for comprehensive and reliable information on drug coverage, drug spending, and drug prices. On October 25, 1999, the President directed the Secretary of Health and Human Services to study prescription drug costs and trends for Medicare beneficiaries. He asked that the study investigate:

- price differences for the most commonly used drugs for people with and without coverage;

- drug spending by people of various ages, as a percentage of income and of total health spending; and
- trends in drug expenditures by people of different ages, as a percentage of income and of total health spending.

This report is the Department's response to that request. It represents the work of individuals and agencies throughout the Department, including the Agency for Healthcare Research and Quality (AHRQ), the Food and Drug Administration (FDA), the Health Care Financing Administration (HCFA), and the Office of the Assistant Secretary for Planning and Evaluation (ASPE).

## Chapter 1: Prescription Drug Coverage

While today, over 85 percent of Medicare beneficiaries use at least one prescription drug annually, beneficiaries must obtain drug coverage through a supplemental policy, by enrollment in a Medicare + Choice plan which includes coverage for prescription drugs, or through Medicaid. The result has been a patchwork of coverage that is not dependable, affordable, or accessible to all beneficiaries. Chapter 1 uses survey data to examine the sources of drug coverage for both the Medicare and non-Medicare population, describes the economic and demographic characteristics of those who have drug coverage and those who do not, and analyzes current trends in drug coverage. Analysis of data on the duration of coverage for the Medicare population is also presented. Differences in coverage rates by alternative measures of health status are explored. Lastly, trends in drug coverage for the Medicare and non-Medicare population are analyzed.

Key findings include:

- Only 53 percent of Medicare beneficiaries had drug coverage for the entire year of 1996, although 69 percent had coverage for at least one month during the year.
- Most sources of drug coverage are potentially unstable. Almost 48 percent of beneficiaries with drug coverage through Medigap and 29 percent who were covered through Medicare HMOs had drug coverage for only part of the year. Additionally, while employer-sponsored retiree coverage, the most prevalent single source of drug benefits, covered 32 percent of Medicare beneficiaries in 1996, 14 percent of those beneficiaries had only part year coverage from their former employers.
- Drug benefits are becoming less generous. There is considerable evidence that cost sharing for prescription drugs is increasing and that overall caps on coverage are both becoming more common and are being set at lower levels. For example, Medicare + Choice plans generally have reduced drug benefits and increased enrollee out-of-pocket costs in 2000. Eighty-six percent of plans have annual dollar limits on drugs, including 70 percent of plans with annual caps of $1000 or less, and 32 percent with caps of $500 or less per enrollee—levels that are up from 35 percent and 19 percent in 1998.
- Drug coverage is likely to decline as fewer employers offer health benefits to future retirees. For example, one employer survey recorded a drop

from 40 percent in 1993 to 28 percent in 1999 in the number of large firms offering health benefits to Medicare eligible retirees. Additionally, employers have tightened eligibility rules and increased cost-shifting to retirees. Of those employers that still offer medical coverage, the survey found that 40 percent are requiring Medicare-eligible retirees to pay the full cost of their benefits, compared to 28 percent in 1995.

- Beneficiaries with incomes between 100 percent and 150 percent of poverty (that is, individuals age 65 or older with incomes between $7,527 and $11,287 in 1996) have the lowest rate of coverage. Although coverage varies by income, nearly one-fourth of beneficiaries with incomes over 400 percent of poverty lack coverage.

- Beneficiaries are less likely to have coverage if they are very old or live outside of a metropolitan area. About 37 percent of beneficiaries age 85 and above lacked coverage at any time during 1996 compared to 28 percent of beneficiaries age 65 through 69. About 43 percent of beneficiaries living in rural areas lacked drug coverage, compared to 27 percent of beneficiaries living in urban areas.

- Coverage rates vary little by self-reported health status, but are considerably higher for those with five or more chronic conditions. But by all measures, at least one-fourth of those in any category of health status lack coverage.

- Nearly one in four in the non-Medicare population never had any coverage for drugs in 1996. About 80 percent of those with full-year coverage got that coverage through employers.

## Chapter 2: Effects of Prescription Drug Coverage on Spending and Utilization

Insurance coverage for prescription drugs makes a major difference in the amount of drugs people obtain, in how much they spend on drugs out of pocket, and in how much is spent in total on their behalf. People with coverage not only fill more prescriptions than those without coverage; they are likely to have access to a broader array of therapies, including more costly therapies. People without drug coverage face greater financial burdens and may sometimes be unable to follow the courses of treatment ordered by their physicians. There are even some indications that physicians themselves may recommend different therapies to people with and without coverage. Coverage increases prescription drug utilization, and reduces financial burdens for all population groups. However, access to drug coverage is most important for the elderly, simply because they require more medications, including a higher prevalence of long-term maintenance drugs for chronic conditions.

Chapter 2 presents detailed comparisons of utilization and spending (including out-of-pocket spending) for Medicare beneficiaries and the total population with and without drug coverage. It also examines some of the possible reasons for those differences and considers the consequences of being without coverage. Finally, it summarizes trends in utilization and spending and some of the factors that influence these changes.

Key findings include:

- Medicare beneficiaries with coverage fill nearly one-third more prescriptions than those without coverage.
- Although total drug spending for beneficiaries with coverage is nearly two-thirds higher, those without coverage pay nearly twice as much out of pocket ($463 versus $253).
- On average, beneficiaries with coverage pay out of pocket for about one-third of their total spending on drugs. However, the share of spending paid out of pocket varies by source of coverage, from 58 percent for those with Medigap coverage to 20 percent for those with Medicaid.
- Differences in utilization and spending between Medicare beneficiaries with and without drug coverage generally hold up across different income levels, ages, health status, and other categories.
- Drug insurance makes an especially large difference in dollar terms for those in the poorest health. Among beneficiaries with five or more chronic conditions, those with coverage had much higher total spending ($1,402 versus $944) and much lower out-of-pocket spending ($412 versus $944) than beneficiaries without coverage.
- Self-selection does not explain the difference in spending between Medicare beneficiaries with and without drug coverage. Even among beneficiaries with the same poor health status, more prescriptions are filled by people with coverage.
- Among people who are not Medicare beneficiaries, similar differences in utilization and spending exist between prescription drug users with and without coverage. Those with coverage for drugs fill two-thirds more prescriptions but spend a third less out of pocket than those without coverage.
- About a third of Medicare beneficiaries accounted for three-fourths of beneficiaries' total drug spending in 1996. Only 13 percent had no spending at all. Spending on prescription drugs in the non-Medicare population is even less evenly distributed.
- Prescription drugs take up about one-sixth of all health spending by the elderly. Out-of-pocket spending for prescription drugs is a larger proportion of health spending for the elderly than for younger people. Prescription drug spending also accounts for a larger share of spending by people with low incomes than it does for people with higher incomes.
- The burden of prescription drug costs creates access problems for some beneficiaries. Among Medicare beneficiaries, 10 percent of those with only Medicare coverage report not being able to afford a needed drug, compared to 2 percent of those with a non-Medicaid supplement.
- Drug spending has grown more quickly than other health spending throughout the 1990's. Price increases, higher utilization, and the use of newer, more expensive drugs all play a part in increasing drug spending.

## Chapter 3: Prescription Drug Prices

In today's market for prescription drugs, most insurers obtain significant discounts on behalf of their insured beneficiaries. Individuals without coverage thus face not only the burden of paying for the entire cost of the drugs they need out of pocket, but they may also face higher prices for a given drug than do insurers and other large purchasers. Sorting out the differences in prices paid by those with and without coverage is not simple. The process by which prescription drug prices are determined is highly complex, involving numerous interactions and arrangements among manufacturers, wholesalers, retailers, insurers, pharmacy benefit managers (PBMs), and consumers.

In order to explain the complexity of this market, Chapter 3 begins with a description of the distribution channels for prescription drugs and how prices are established for different purchasers. It then offers an empirical analysis of whether prices paid for drugs at the retail level differ between cash customers and those with insurance coverage, using data from two sources: the Medical Expenditure Panel Survey (MEPS) and a widely used private sector data source on drug prices, IMS Health. A key limitation on the analysis of drug prices in this study, however, is our inability to incorporate the effect of rebates provided by manufacturers to insurers and PBMs. Given the greater market leverage of third party payers relative to individual consumers, it might be expected that cash customers will pay more than insurers for the same drugs at the retail pharmacy. Results from both sources, despite the absence of rebate data, support this hypothesis.

Key findings include:

- At the retail pharmacy level:

   Individuals without drug coverage pay a higher price at the retail pharmacy than the total price paid on behalf of those with drug coverage (based on analysis of MEPS data that do not include rebates but look across all drug purchases holding drug type, form, strength, and quantity constant). The differences generally held up when examining the Medicare and non-Medicare populations.

   Cash customers (including those without coverage and those with indemnity coverage) pay more for a given drug than those with third party payments at the point of sale (based on IMS Health data for over 90 percent of the most commonly prescribed drugs). In 1999, excluding the effect of rebates, the typical cash customer paid nearly 15 percent more than the customer with third party coverage. For a quarter of the most common drugs, the price difference between cash and third parties was even higher— over 20 percent. For the most commonly prescribed drugs, the price difference between cash customers and those with third party coverage grew substantially larger between 1996 and 1999.

The pattern of differences in the price paid by cash customers and those with third party payments is different for generic and brand name drugs (based on both MEPS and IMS Health data). Percentage differences in the price paid are often smaller for brand name drugs, but absolute differences may be larger because average prices for brand name drugs are considerably higher.

- Data on manufacturer rebates, if available, would reduce the total amount paid by the insurer or PBM on behalf of insured customers, increasing the difference in the total net price. Data on rebate arrangements, however, are confidential and unavailable to this study. In some instances, the amount of the rebate may be significantly more than the price differences observed at the retail pharmacy level. In other cases, the rebates may add only modestly to the observed differences.

- Various sources produce estimates of rebates ranging from 2 percent to 35 percent of drug sales prices. These rebates are not reflected in retail prices, but are instead paid directly to insurers and other organizations that manage drug benefits after they have already reimbursed the pharmacy.

This study presents a detailed examination of multiple factors relating to coverage, utilization, and spending for prescription drugs, particularly by the Medicare population. It also raises a variety of issues that are ripe for further investigation. Suggestive relationships between demographic factors, insurance status, and prescription drug use were revealed. However, we were unable to examine the more complex interrelationships among these factors. Future multivariate analyses will allow us to come to a more nuanced understanding of these relationships. Future research should explore what can be learned from using more sophisticated definitions of drug coverage status and severity of illness than were available for this study. In addition, if more data were available on elements of manufacturer pricing, such as rebates, further research could probe more fully the differences in prices paid by different customers. Finally, ongoing analyses will allow us to continue to use the most recent data—rapid change in the pharmaceutical market requires that analyses be refreshed and updated on a continuing basis. . . .

# GENERAL ACCOUNTING OFFICE ON SITUATION IN THE BALKANS
## April 24, 2000

*Bosnia and Kosovo, the two most ethnically divided remnants of the former Yugoslavia, remained wards of the international community through 2000. They were prevented from again erupting into violence only by the presence of thousands of peacekeeping troops. Bosnia held its fourth round of elections since a U.S.-brokered peace agreement in 1995 ended Europe's bloodiest war since World War II. But the election results appeared to offer little hope for improved relations among the republic's Croat, Muslim, and Serbian factions. One year after NATO warplanes forced the Yugoslav army out of the Serbian province of Kosovo, the ethnic Albanian majority and Serbian minority there remained locked in bitter hatred, and most Albanian Kosovars were still hoping to achieve independence from Serbia.*

*Despite the seemingly endless litany of bad news, the results of two elections appeared to offer some hope for long-term peace in the Balkans. First, in February, voters in Croatia ousted the hard-line nationalist party that had helped fuel the war in neighboring Bosnia. In that election, moderate Stjepan Mesic was elected as president to replace war leader Franjo Tudjman, who had died in December 1999. Then, in the fall, voters in Yugoslavia ousted President Slobodan Milosevic, who for years had fomented the ethnic wars in the Balkans as a way of maintaining his own political power. His successor, Voislav Kostunica, visited Sarajevo in December and gave official diplomatic recognition to Bosnia, an act of great symbolic importance that held some promise for improved relations in the region. (Yugoslav election, p. 833)*

*The departure of Milosevic came not a moment too soon for Western leaders, many of whom seemed to be growing weary of their peacekeeping chores in Bosnia and Kosovo. One important element of uncertainty was the attitude of the U.S. president-elect George W. Bush, who had called during his 2000 election campaign for a gradual withdrawal of American forces from the peacekeeping missions in Bosnia and Kosovo.*

*Congress in April received a report from its investigative arm, the General Accounting Office (GAO), warning that hard-line ethnic nationalists in*

*Kosovo and Bosnia had not given up the sectarian aims for which they fought during the region's wars. The GAO also cautioned that both territories probably would again become engulfed in war if the NATO-led peacekeepers were to withdraw.*

## Bosnia

*The 1992–1995 war in Bosnia was a savage conflict among three ethnic groups—Croats, Muslims, and Serbs—who in previous decades had managed an uneasy but peaceful coexistence. The war was the result of the dissolution of the former Yugoslav federation, starting in 1991, when communism was collapsing in eastern Europe. Tens of thousands of people were killed in the war; some estimates put the total at 200,000 or more. That war, along with a companion war between Croats and Serbs in the neighboring republic of Croatia, gave birth to the modern concept of "ethnic cleansing": the use of terror tactics, including murder, against civilians to capture territory occupied by members of an opposing ethnic group. The culminating act of the war was the slaughter, in July 1995, of an estimated 8,000 Bosnian Muslims in and around the town of Srebrenica by Serbian military and paramilitary forces. Four months later, the United States arranged a peace agreement that ended the war and divided Bosnia into two ethnic zones (one controlled by Serbs, the other by Croats and Muslims). Bosnia's peace was enforced by peacekeepers from the NATO allies and other countries; as of late 2000 some 22,000 peacekeepers were assigned to Bosnia, less than one-fourth of whom were American.* (Bosnia war, Historic Documents of 1995, p. 717; Srebrenica massacre, Historic Documents of 1999, p. 735)

*The end of the fighting in November 1995 did not restore ethnic harmony to Bosnia. Instead, according to most diplomats and observers, Bosnia during five years of peace saw ethnic nationalist leaders continuing to achieve their aims through other means. Croat, Muslim, and Serb leaders were manipulating for their own ends the government agencies put in place by the Western powers. Corruption was rampant, the economy was largely dependent on foreign aid, and nearly 2 million war refugees (most of them Muslims) were still unable or afraid to return to their homes.*

*The United States and other aid donors had poured more than $4 billion into reconstructing public services, roads, buildings, and other physical structures damaged during the war. But the massive reconstruction effort, coordinated by the United Nations, had been unable to get Bosnians to work together, much less live together in harmony. Moreover, dozens of war leaders responsible for ethnic murders during the war remained at large in Bosnia, some of whom continued to exercise considerable influence.*

*By 2000 Western leaders were concluding that they had failed to take the necessary steps to ensure long-term peace in Bosnia. There appeared to be an emerging consensus that the 1995 Bosnia peace agreement—brokered by U.S. diplomat Richard Holbrooke during negotiations in Dayton, Ohio—needed to be strengthened. Holbrooke was among those acknowledging the accord's flaws. Speaking at a November 17 ceremony in Dayton commemorating the fifth anniversary of the agreement, Holbrooke said the agreement had wrongly allowed each ethnic group to retain its own army. "A single country cannot have more than one army," he said. Unless the Bosnian military was united, he said, "NATO will be there indefinitely. With three armies, there is always a potential for conflict, and therefore, a need for outside forces."*

*Holbrooke and other observers noted that the political system created for Bosnia by the Dayton agreement was weak because the central government in Sarajevo (the capital) had no real power, and hard-line ethnic leaders controlled the two regional federations where most day-to-day decisions were made. In a report to the Security Council on November 30, UN Secretary-General Kofi Annan said progress "has been frustratingly slow and difficult, owing mainly to political obstruction by extremist nationalists who refuse to accept the reality of a sovereign and multi-ethnic state where the rights of all citizens are guaranteed not by ethnicity but by rule of law."*

*The Western powers with international responsibility for Bosnia—most importantly the United States, Great Britain, France, and Russia—had hoped that elections would help soothe some of the wounds from the war. The idea was that Bosnians were so tired of conflict that they would vote for moderates committed to coexistence and would deny power to the extremists who fomented hatred. Three rounds of elections prior to 2000 had produced ambiguous results, but a fourth round held on November 11 was little different. Moderates made slight gains in both of the two Bosnian regional entities: the Serb republic and the Muslim-Croat federation. But at year's end it appeared that the ethnic nationalist parties that had been responsible for the war would be able to exercise enough power to block major changes. A pessimistic assessment of the election, issued December 18 by the International Crisis Group, a private international research agency, said ethnic extremists had been "energized" by the voting—directly opposite of what the Western powers had intended.*

## *Kosovo*

*The southernmost province of Serbia (which in turn was the dominant republic in the Yugoslav federation), Kosovo long had been considered the tinderbox of the Balkans. Ethnic Albanian Muslims made up nearly 90 percent of the 2 million residents in Kosovo, and the rest were Serbs. But Serbs considered Kosovo an important part of their national heritage, largely because it was the site of Serbia's defeat in 1389 at the hands of the Turkish Ottoman Empire. The most recent round of conflict between Serbs and ethnic Albanians, who wanted independence for Kosovo, broke out in 1998. During the winter of 1998–1999 Serbian authorities launched a massive terror campaign that drove an estimated 700,000 Albanians from their homes. In late March 1999, after the United States and its European allies failed to arrange a diplomatic settlement, NATO began air strikes against Yugoslavia. The eleven-week air campaign ultimately forced Milosevic to give up his grip on Kosovo and to withdraw all Serbian and Yugoslav security forces from the province. By the end of the war an estimated 1.5 million*

143

*Kosovars—the vast majority of them Albanians—had been forced from their homes; about half fled to neighboring countries or to western Europe. Most of the refugees had returned by late 1999, many of them to homes and villages that had been destroyed.* (War in Kosovo, Historic Documents of 1999, pp. 134, 285, 802)

*Under a United Nations Security Council resolution ending the war, NATO established a peacekeeping force (with 50,000 troops in 1999, down to 35,000 by late 2000) to enforce security in Kosovo, and the United Nations took over responsibility for nearly all civil functions.*

*The peacekeepers, along with more than 4,000 police under UN command, confronted daily examples of violence between Kosovo's Albanian and Serbian communities. Although the Albanian guerrilla force that had fought for independence—the Kosovo Liberation Army—had officially disbanded in 1999 and transformed itself into a UN-sponsored police force, hundreds of former guerrillas kept their weapons and conducted periodic raids against Serb targets.*

*The peacekeepers in some regions often found themselves protecting the Serb minority from the Albanian majority. By late 2000 an estimated 100,000 Serbs—about half the prewar population—remained in or had returned to Kosovo. Nearly all the Serbs lived in small enclaves or in a section of northern Kosovo, including the ethnically divided city of Mitrovica. In the American-controlled sector in southeast Kosovo, soldiers spent many of their days escorting Serb civilians to and from workplaces and shops. The work was frustrating, and many soldiers said they could not be sure they were really accomplishing anything. But some peacekeepers must have found the experience rewarding because the units assigned to Kosovo and Bosnia had among the highest reenlistment rates in the U.S. military.*

*One worrisome development for international authorities was an upsurge of violence in the southern Presevo valley, a Serbian territory just outside Kosovo but with an ethnic Albanian majority. Albanian independence fighters based in Kosovo launched numerous attacks on Serbian targets in an apparent attempt to provoke an incident that would force a Serbian withdrawal from the region. U.S. peacekeepers, who were responsible for security in the adjoining region of Kosovo, tried with varying degrees of success to contain the violence.*

*While the peacekeepers tried to keep Kosovars from killing each other, the UN agency responsible for Kosovo (called the United Nations Mission in Kosovo, or UNMIK) grappled with a host of economic and social problems in a province that was poor before the war and absolutely impoverished afterward. The United States, western European nations, and international financial institutions had pledged more than $3 billion in aid for Kosovo, but money and supplies were much slower in arriving than were problems.*

*The chief crisis faced by the UN agency was a shortage of housing for the nearly 1.5 million Kosovars who had fled their homes before and during the war. UN administrators estimated that more than 120,000 housing units had been damaged during the war; approximately 80,000 homes had been destroyed and needed to be totally rebuilt. Officials said fewer than one-*

*fourth of the damaged houses could be repaired or replaced by the end of 2000, meaning that tens of thousands of refugees would be forced to continue living with relatives or friends, in "temporary" group shelters, or even in tents. UNMIK head Bernard Kouchner asked western European countries, which had taken in many Kosovar refugees, to slow the pace of refugees returning to Kosovo. But some of those countries, especially Germany, were anxious to be rid of the refugees.*

*Kosovo's agriculture-based economy was still in shambles in late 2000, but Kouchner was able to stimulate some entrepreneurial effort by making the German Deutschmark the official currency of the province. As much as any action taken since the end of the war, that step effectively delinked Kosovo from the floundering economy of Serbia proper and offered business people a reliable currency for making and receiving payments for goods and services. The UN mission was much slower to carry out a related pledge to privatize public utilities, factories, and other large businesses that had been owned by the Serbian government—a step that many observers said was needed to encourage foreign investment in Kosovo.*

*The central unresolved issue in Kosovo was its status relative to Serbia. UN Security Council Resolution 1244, which followed the 1999 air war, declared that Kosovo should have "substantial autonomy" from Serbia but did not offer independence as an option. Although it was clear that the vast majority of Kosovar Albanians wanted independence from Serbia, the United States and its western European allies were extremely reluctant to allow that step. The former Yugoslavia already had been partitioned into four separate countries (Bosnia, Croatia, the Yugoslav federation, and Slovenia), and the Western allies feared that additional partitioning could set off a cycle leading to a dozen or more ethnic ministates in the Balkan peninsula. Many western European countries also worried that allowing an independent Kosovo might encourage independence moves among their own ethnic or religious minorities, a prospect that raised fears of Europe being engulfed by the types of wars that had been distressingly common in previous centuries.*

*Ironically, many observers said the departure of Milosevic from power in Yugoslavia had the potential to inflame the aspirations for independence among Kosovar Albanians. When Milosevic was in power, the Kosovars were widely viewed as Belgrade's victims and received special attention from the Western powers. With Milosevic out of the picture, some Kosovar Albanians suggested that the West might forget them unless they pushed more aggressively for independence.*

*One significant ray of hope for Kosovo came with municipal elections held on October 28. The Democratic League of Kosovo, headed by a moderate nationalist, Ibrahim Rugova, claimed victory in the first free elections in the province's history. Representatives of Rugova's party won 58 percent of the vote and a majority of local council seats in twenty of the twenty-seven cities and towns where elections were held. They defeated representatives of the Democratic Party of Kosovo, which was aligned with the former guerrilla independence movement, the Kosovo Liberation Army. That party's leader, Hashim Thaqi, promised to accept the election results. Kouchner called the results a "victory for moderation and maturity." Kosovo's Serbs refused to participate in the elections, but UN officials planned to appoint Serb and other minority representatives to some town councils.*

*Less than a month after the election, however, Kosovo's latest political assassination raised new questions about prospects for democracy. One of Rugova's chief aides, Xhemail Mustafa, was gunned down as he entered his apartment building in Pristina, the capital, on November 23. Jock Covey, a U.S. diplomat assigned to the United Nations mission in Kosovo, told the* Washington Post: *"This is a contemptible and cowardly act by extremists who want to undermine Kosovo's move to democracy."*

> *Following are excerpts from "Balkans Security: Current and Projected Factors Affecting Regional Stability," a report prepared for the House Armed Services Committee by the General Accounting Office and dated April 24, 2000. The document was obtained from the Internet at http://frwebgate.access.gpo.gov/cgi-bin/useftp.cgi ?IPaddress=162.140.64.21&filename=ns00125b.txt&directory=/ diskb/wais/data/gao.*

## Current Situation in Kosovo and Bosnia

The large presence of NATO-led military personnel in the region—about 70,000 troops located in five countries—has greatly reduced the ability of the former warring parties in Kosovo and Bosnia to restart the conflicts in those locations. However, the former warring parties largely retain their wartime goals, and, according to western observers, would resume war if the NATO-led troops were withdrawn.

The NATO-led force in Kosovo continues to deter a resumption of hostilities there by (1) ensuring that uniformed Yugoslav security forces, who withdrew from Kosovo as scheduled, remain outside of the province; and (2) monitoring the demilitarization and transformation of the Kosovo Liberation Army into the civilian Kosovo Protection Corps. Although the NATO-led force considers the former Kosovo Liberation Army to be in compliance with its demilitarization agreement, KFOR [Kosovo Force, the NATO-led peace-keeping force] and U.N. international police said that they have detained members of the provisional protection corps for carrying unauthorized weapons and engaging in violence and intimidation against ethnic minorities. Moreover, a large number of undeclared weapons remain hidden. Further, according to western observers and their reports, the Kosovo Protection Corps—which is considered by its leadership to be the core of Kosovo's future army—has retained the army's overall structure and remained capable of resuming hostilities on short notice. In addition, armed Kosovar Albanian insurgent groups outside of the control of the former Kosovo Liberation Army continued to operate in the province, as did Serb paramilitaries, specifically, locally organized groups of armed Serbs.

The NATO-led force in Bosnia, SFOR [Special Force], has continued to enforce the cease-fire and ensure the separation and progressive reduction of the Bosniak [Bosnian Muslims], Bosnian Croat, and Bosnian Serb militaries, but paramilitaries—specifically, small groups of armed thugs organized and controlled by extremist political leaders—continued to operate in the country. SFOR also continued to provide a military presence in critical areas or "hot spots" where the international community expects violent resistance to Dayton implementation, for example, in locations where people are attempting to return to their prewar homes across ethnic lines.

Parties to the wars in Kosovo and Bosnia, largely supported by their respective ethnic groups, still retain their wartime goals. According to fall 1999 polls from the U.S. Information Agency, almost all Kosovar Albanians are willing to fight for the independence of Kosovo, while about half of Serbs in Serbia are willing to fight to retain Kosovo as part of Yugoslavia. Further, the vast majority of Bosnian Serbs and Bosnian Croats continued to want states separate from Bosnia, while almost all Bosniaks support a unified, multiethnic Bosnia, but, according to some observers, with Bosniaks in control.

Since the end of the NATO bombing campaign, according to reports of the Organization for Security and Cooperation in Europe and others, the overall level of violence in Kosovo has declined significantly, but retaliatory, ethnically related violent incidents still regularly occur and recently increased with the approach of spring. In many incidents, Kosovar Albanians harass or violently intimidate ethnic minority populations, such as Serbs and Roma (Gypsy), frequently forcing them to leave their homes for Serb-controlled areas of Kosovo or locations outside the province. In other cases, Serb paramilitaries or armed groups have harassed and intimidated Kosovar Albanians. In late February 2000, the U.N. international police reported increasing violence against Serbs in the province.

During early 2000, the city of Kosovska Mitrovica emerged as the most difficult "hot spot" in Kosovo after a series of escalating violent incidents among Kosovar Serbs and Albanians occurred there. According to U.N. and other reports, the incidents included (1) Albanians striking with an antitank rocket a U.N. bus transporting Kosovar Serbs, killing two elderly people on board; (2) a crowd of Serbs going on a retaliatory rampage in the predominately Serb northern side of Mitrovica, leading to the deaths of 8 ethnic Albanians and the exodus of another 1,650 from the northern part of the city; (3) both ethnic groups attacking KFOR personnel and U.N. property; and (4) violence associated with Kosovar Albanians returning home to northern Mitrovica. In public statements, U.S. and international officials blamed extremists from both ethnic groups for causing the incidents, while a U.S. government official also blamed Yugoslavia's leadership for using Yugoslav security forces to foment the security problems.

The continuing hostilities and lack of political and social reconciliation between Kosovar Albanians and non-Albanians have overshadowed positive developments that have occurred in Kosovo since the end of the NATO bombing campaign. For example, the U.N. mission has established a number of interim administrative structures for governing the province, including the provisional judicial panel and the provincewide Kosovo Transition Council formed by the U.N. mission in July 1999; however, Kosovar Serbs either have never joined or have withdrawn from them. Further, while at least 800,000 Kosovar Albanian refugees who had fled Kosovo during the conflict had returned there by December 1999, about 243,000 non-Albanians had left the province for other parts of Serbia and Montenegro by November 1999 and, as of February 2000, an estimated 10,000 to 15,000 Serbs were displaced from their homes within Kosovo as they had moved to Serb majority areas.

While SFOR has ensured an absence of war in Bosnia, political leaders of the country's three major ethnic groups continued to obstruct the implementation of the Dayton Agreement's [1995 peace agreement ending the wars in Bosnia and Croatia] political, humanitarian, and economic provisions. For example, institutions of the national government and the joint Bosniak-Croat Federation still largely do not function due to lack of cooperation among the parties. In addition, the Republika Srpska [Serb Republic in Bosni] government has been unstable since early March 1999, when the [United Nations] High Representative removed from office the entity's democratically elected President, a hard-line Serb nationalist, for his deliberate attempts to obstruct the implementation of the Dayton Agreement. Moreover, the economy remains stagnant, largely because Bosnia's political leaders continue to resist implementing meaningful economic reforms.

Further, people attempting to return home to areas controlled by another ethnic group continue to face sporadic attacks and violent intimidation in some locations, as well as political and legal obstruction. According to the SFOR Commander, in late 1999 and early 2000 the NATO-led force increased the number of "hot spots" its troops patrol, as well as the number of patrols in some areas, in response to violent incidents related to these returns. Recent polling data show that of those refugees and displaced persons who did not wish to return to their prewar homes, 58 percent said that the lack of security for themselves and their property is the primary reason they will not return. In contrast, many international officials in Bosnia, including the SFOR Commander, believe that the primary obstacle to minority returns is the poor economy, primarily unemployment and a lack of funding to repair homes, rather than a lack of personal security.

The number of "minority returns" in Bosnia—that is, people returning to their prewar homes across ethnic lines—continues to increase each year, though the number in 1999 was significantly lower than the 120,000 minority returns hoped for by the international community. About 9,500 minority returns occurred in 1996; 39,000 in 1997; 41,275 in 1998; and 42,500 in 1999 for a total of about 132,275 minority returns since the signing of the Dayton Agreement. According to the 1999 State Department Human Rights report and a senior SFOR officer, political leaders of all three ethnic groups have continued their attempts to take or maintain control of strategically important terrain through the return process. They may either organize or discourage the return of people from their own ethnic group to areas across ethnic lines or obstruct the return of people from other ethnic groups to their areas of control.

In an attempt to accelerate progress, the High Representative during 1999 and early 2000 continued to use his authority to revoke or amend existing laws, to impose new laws, and to remove government officials from office. For example, he imposed (1) a law that established a state border service after Bosnian Serb delegates to Bosnia's parliament refused to pass the law and (2) laws that instituted a judicial framework to combat crime and corruption in the Federation. Moreover, to help promote minority returns, in late November 1999 he removed 22 local officials from their positions for fostering "the poison of division" and obstructing Dayton implementation.

As originally envisioned by NATO planners, KFOR would conduct public security functions in Kosovo for a period of at least 3 months. After that, the U.N. international civilian police force would assume full responsibility for policing until the establishment of a local police service in Kosovo by the end of 2002. In November 1999, U.N. and KFOR officials were unable to specify a date by which the U.N. international police force would assume primary responsibility for public security in Kosovo. According to a senior KFOR officer, even after the public security function transitions to the United Nations, KFOR could reduce its presence by no more than one military police battalion of about 650 troops from each of the five military sectors, given the security situation and the force's other missions.

KFOR is still performing most of the tasks that were to have been transferred to the U.N. international police force by September 1999, largely because of delays in fully staffing the U.N. international police force, according to KFOR and U.N. officials. As of April 7, 2000, according to U.N. documents, the U.N. international police force was significantly understaffed at 2,886 personnel, about 1,830 fewer that the number authorized by the United Nations and almost 3,115 less than requested by the U.N. mission in Kosovo. Of these amounts, about 1,100 positions were for specialized police, that is, police trained in riot control duties. Because of these shortfalls, the U.N. police force had assumed primary responsibility for public security in only 4 of Kosovo's 29 municipalities as of January 2000.

The NATO-led forces in Kosovo and Bosnia both face a shortfall in their respective specialized police units, also known as "multinational specialized units." These units are intended to be specially trained and equipped military units that would assist regular soldiers in dealing with civil disturbances associated with events such as returns of refugees and displaced persons and installation of elected officials. SFOR's multinational specialized unit has been significantly understaffed since its establishment in late August 1998, operating with only 1 of 2 required battalions, or 450 of the required 750 personnel. Similarly, KFOR's multinational specialized unit is only partially staffed. According to a U.N. official, KFOR is in effect competing with the U.N. international police force for these specialized police assets, as the NATO-led force's multinational specialized unit consists of the same types of police personnel being sought by the United Nations.

In mid-July 1999, about the time most of KFOR was deploying into Kosovo, senior NATO officials told us that many allies were considering reducing their troop contributions to SFOR, largely because they could not provide resources for two concurrent military operations in the Balkans. Based on a study by NATO's military headquarters, the North Atlantic Council—NATO's political leadership—concluded in October 1999 that a significantly reduced SFOR could maintain a secure environment in Bosnia, assuming that the force would be restructured to allow a more flexible response to outbreaks of violence and would focus only on the force's key military tasks associated with controlling the Bosniak, Bosnian Croat, and Bosnian Serb militaries. About the same time, NATO revised KFOR's operations plan and force structure and authorized a reduction in its force levels, based on its assessment that improving security conditions in the province and the start-up of the U.N. mission in Kosovo allowed a modification to the force's mission and tasks.

The SFOR drawdown—from about 32,000 troops (as of September 1999) to about 20,000 troops (as of April 2000)—will substantially reduce the amount of assistance the force provides to civilian efforts, including general security for the operations of international organizations, area security for returns of people across ethnic lines, and support for the conduct of elections. After SFOR announced its drawdown and the U.N. mission in Bosnia decided on a more robust implementation strategy, the U.N. mission developed a request for U.N. authorization of an armed protection group; as of April 7, 2000, this request had not yet been approved by U.N. headquarters. The proposed group would consist of about 270 armed police and would provide protection for U.N. police monitors and other U.N. personnel. According to U.N. officials, with protection from the armed protection group, U.N. staff would be able to credibly and safely pursue more robust actions to remove political/criminal obstructionists and complete earlier its mission of local police reform and restructuring.

NATO is currently reviewing the KFOR statement of requirements, which could increase the force size or change the force composition, in response to changing conditions in and around Kosovo. After initially deploying a force of about 43,000 NATO nation troops to Kosovo, NATO nations contributing to KFOR reduced their troop strengths to 33,000 during the November 1999 troop rotation. However, after a rapid escalation of violent incidents occurred in Kosovska Mitrovica during February 2000, the Supreme Allied Commander, Europe, asked for two additional battalions for Kosovo. As of March 17, 2000, two NATO countries had agreed to provide the equivalent of one additional battalion for this purpose, and, according to DOD officials, the United States had agreed to deploy an additional 125 military personnel to the U.S. sector. According to executive branch officials, it may ultimately be necessary for NATO to consider reviewing the KFOR operations plan to (1) better meet the staffing demands of the force's existing public security mission and (2) control Kosovo's provincial boundary to prevent armed Albanian groups from operating in southern Serbia from bases in Kosovo.

The two NATO-led forces also operate within geographic and operational constraints placed on participating forces by their respective national command authorities. Participating countries allow their forces to participate in

SFOR and KFOR within specific areas and with specific rules of engagement. These restrictions at times could prevent the commanders of the NATO-led forces from deploying their troops outside of specific geographic areas or using them for certain tasks within assigned areas, thereby reducing the forces' ability to respond quickly and effectively.

U.N. efforts to establish a functioning civil administration and create a democratic, multiethnic society in Kosovo are hindered in part by a lack of civilian resources. For example, the U.N. mission [with more than 1,300 civilian personnel and about 2,390 civilian police] was tasked with creating municipal administrative structures based on democratic principles. However, according to U.N. officials in Kosovo, the U.N. mission was slower to deploy international administrators to the field than had been hoped, due largely to a lack of available personnel at the start of the endeavor. These officials told us that the slow deployment of U.N. staff allowed the Kosovo Liberation Army to gain control of municipal administrations in an undemocratic manner and made it difficult for U.N. administrators to effectively control them. Moreover, the United Nations was unable to do advance planning for the mission's operations, including staff deployment, because it was informed that it would be leading the mission only a short time before its start.

## Projected Security Situation in the Balkans

Throughout the Balkans, many of the region's major ethnic groups continue to dispute the definitions of what geographic territory and ethnic groups constitute their states. As discussed earlier, parties to the wars in Bosnia and Kosovo, largely supported by their respective ethnic groups, still retain their wartime goals. Croatia's former ruling nationalist party, which in early 2000 was defeated in parliamentary and presidential elections by democratic opposition groups, (1) politically, economically, and militarily supported Bosnian Croat aims to maintain a state separate from Bosnia; and (2) denied citizenship rights to and obstructed the return of Croatian Serb refugees. Over the past 2 years in Montenegro, as Slobodan Milosevic was consolidating Yugoslavia's federal power at the expense of the republic-level governments, segments of the population of Montenegro have begun calling for independence from Yugoslavia. In Albania, the U.S. Secretary of State told the Albanian parliament during mid-February 2000 that "the international community would no sooner accept a Greater Albania than it would a Greater Serbia or Croatia." According to some western observers, people in the region, especially in Macedonia, fear that Albanians in the region do support a "Greater Albania." In Macedonia, where political and social tensions have increased between the country's two largest ethnic groups, Macedonians and Albanians, neither group appears fully committed to developing a unified, multiethnic state.

Milosevic retains authoritarian power over both Yugoslav and republic of Serbia governmental structures—including their security forces—and uses their combined power to further his political goals in Kosovo, Montenegro, and other areas in the region, as described later in this section.

Economies in the region, many of which were poor before the wars, suffer from years of wars, sanctions against Yugoslavia, and limited progress on making market reforms. The destruction of infrastructure during the wars in Bosnia, Croatia, and Yugoslavia, as well as the months of civil unrest in Albania [in 1997], led to economic turmoil in each of these locations and put stress on neighboring economies that depended on these locations as trade routes and markets. U.S., European Union, and U.N. sanctions against Yugoslavia and Serbia's economic war against its neighbors have caused economic decline in Serbia and trade losses for the rest of the region, since Serbia represents a large market for many of the region's countries. Balkan countries generally have been unable to implement the free market reforms necessary to attract foreign investment, due to constant political instability or a lack of political will on the part of their leaders, according to international officials and observer reports.

. . . [A]pproximately 2.4 million refugees and displaced persons from the conflicts in Bosnia, Croatia, and Kosovo have not returned to their prewar homes or found durable solutions to their displacement. As of November 1999, about 97 percent of these people were residing within the Balkans region, either as refugees (624,630 people) or displaced persons within their own country (1.74 million people). The remaining 79,200 people were refugees located in countries outside of the Balkans region. According to observer reports and U.S. Information Agency polling data, the reasons for their continued displacement include the intransigence of political leaders, the lack of security for returnees, the unavailability of housing, and poor economic prospects. . . .

The international community has attempted to resolve political, social, and other problems throughout the region through a variety of programs intended to develop democratic institutions and practices; reform and regenerate economic systems; and provide humanitarian assistance for refugees, displaced persons, and others in need. In late July 1999, the international community formally established a regional assistance framework called the "Stability Pact for South Eastern Europe." The Stability Pact is intended to coordinate and prioritize economic and other assistance going to the region, including Romania and Bulgaria, and to accelerate and deepen the integration of a reformed region into the Euro-Atlantic community. . . .

## Prospects for Change in Croatia

Prior to its defeat in elections in early 2000, Croatia's nationalist ruling party destabilized the region by, among other things, providing economic, political, and military support to Bosnian Croat attempts to maintain a separate state and obstructing the return of Croatian Serb refugees. The leaders of Croatia's new government have publicly pledged to change many of the earlier policies. Specifically, the new President [Stipe Mesic] pledged that Croatia would allow the return of all Croatian citizens to the country, regardless of ethnicity; recognize that Croats form an element of Bosnia, make transparent its support for Bosnian Croats; and cut off funds for the military of their "quasi-state." In public statements, U.S. and international leaders welcomed the change in government as a positive step in establishing a democratic system and economic reforms in Croatia and in improving the country's relations with neighboring countries, as well as with the rest of Europe. Further, according to international officials in Bosnia, the elections signify to Bosnian Croats, whose political leaders belong to Croatia's former ruling nationalist party, that they must give up their hope of becoming part of Croatia.

In late February and early March 2000, Croatia's new government took steps toward changing government policies on Croatian Serb refugee returns and making transparent funding for Bosnian Croat institutions. For example, the new government announced a program for the return of 16,500 refugees to Croatia and reached an agreement with the Republika Srpska Prime Minister for the two-way return of Bosnian Croat and Croatian Serb refugees to their pre-war homes. Further, under U.S. auspices, Croatia's Defense Minister reached an agreement with the Federation Defense Minister (a Bosnian Croat) that provides for Croatia's continued financing of the Bosnian Croat army through the Standing Committee for Military Matters, an institution established by the Dayton Agreement to coordinate the activities of the three militaries in Bosnia.

Despite these moves, however, it is not clear (1) to what extent Croatia's new government will be able to implement these changes; (2) whether all of Croatia's political leaders have given up the dream of a "Greater Croatia"; or (3) how Bosnian Croats would react to significant changes, if any, in their relationship to Croatia. For example, Croatia's refugee return program and two-way return agreement with Republika Sprska may be obstructed by property laws that continue to favor Bosnian Croat refugees over Croatian Serbs and a lack of progress in returning Bosnian Croats to their homes in Bosnia. Further, if Croatia does threaten to cut all ties with Bosnian Croats, a significant number of them may react by choosing to revoke their Bosnian citizenship, retain their Croatian citizenship, and move to Croatia, instead of opting to effectively join Bosnia's institutions and become part of Bosnia. About 77 percent of Bosnian Croats want to join Croatia or become an independent state rather than remain part of Bosnia, according to late 1999 polling data from the U.S. Information Agency.

## Prospects for Change in Serbia

[This section reviewed the political situation in Serbia, focusing on speculation about the future of Yugoslav President Slobodan Milosevic, who was defeated for reelection in September, after this report was written.]

. . . [I]f the efforts to remove Milosevic from power and replace him with the Serbian opposition were to succeed, it is unclear to what extent the change would improve regional security. While a senior U.S. official stated that Milosevic's removal would result in Kosovar Albanians agreeing to remain in Yugoslavia, political leaders and people in the region told us that a change in Yugoslavia's leadership from Milosevic to the opposition would have no impact on the security or political situation in Kosovo. They and western observers in Kosovo explained that Serb opposition leaders strongly support continued Yugoslav sovereignty over Kosovo and would not agree to Kosovo's independence, the primary political demand of Kosovar Albanians during and after the war. Further, according to recent public statements, Serb opposition leaders have close links to Bosnian Serb political leaders who, while many of them are anti-Milosevic, are nationalists who retain the goal of maintaining "Serb unity" and a Serbian state separate from Bosnia.

Prospects for Violence Over the next 5 Years in Serbia, Kosovo, and Bosnia In Serbia, low-level violence has occurred regularly since late 1999 in the form of attacks against the republic's police in southern Serbia—a predominately ethnic Albanian area outside of Kosovo but near Kosovo's boundary—by ethnic Albanian insurgents who believe Kosovo's territory includes this area. In early March 2000, a U.N. official reported that 5,000–6,000 ethnic Albanians had fled southern Serbia since June 1999. Many of these people had reported an increase in Yugoslav forces in that area, stating that the security situation for ethnic Albanians there had deteriorated to such an extent that life had become intolerable. The U.N. official added that his agency is concerned that if the conflict between the ethnic Albanian extremist groups and Serbia's police is allowed to continue, there may be larger refugee flows from southern Serbia.

Current low-level violence in Kosovo and Bosnia is likely to continue and may escalate given the slow pace of political and social reconciliation in both locations. As long as KFOR maintains a credible deterrent presence, the likelihood of renewed armed conflict is low; however, low-level violence will likely continue and may escalate due to the unresolved political status of Kosovo, competition for power among ethnic Albanian political parties, and an absence of reconciliation among the province's ethnic groups. Further, the previously discussed violence in southern Serbia may also destabilize the security situation in Kosovo. The Commander of KFOR stated on March 10, 2000, that the situation in southeastern Serbia constitutes a threat to the peace and security of Kosovo and could develop into a regional security issue. He also stated that KFOR is prepared to take all action necessary to ensure Kosovo is not used as a staging base by either ethnic Albanians or Serbs wishing to "export violence" into southeastern Serbia.

According to U.S. and NATO officials, as long as SFOR remains, the force will continue to prevent an outbreak of war among the three militaries in Bosnia. However, as SFOR draws down, there will still be a requirement to maintain a presence significant enough to deter violence associated with people returning home across ethnic lines or against international civilian organizations operating in Bosnia. These types of violent incidents, according to a U.N. official, will likely increase as more people return to areas with few or no minority returns and as the international community attempts to implement other civil aspects of the Dayton Agreement. DOD [U.S. Department of Defense] officials told us that SFOR, as part of its transition strategy, will look more to the local police forces in Bosnia to provide security for these situations. According to the 1999 State Department Human Rights report, local police in Bosnia—which are still largely organized along ethnic lines—continue to use excessive force, or do not ensure security, to discourage minority resettlement in majority areas.

The security situation in Montenegro has become more volatile over the past year due to the controversy within the republic over its discreet moves toward greater autonomy or independence and the Yugoslav leadership's aggressive action against the republic. The ruling coalition government of Montenegro—which consists of people who support either greater autonomy or independence—controls the republic's 20,000-strong police force. The anti-independence movement is led by the former President of Montenegro (now the Prime Minister of Yugoslavia) and is supported by Milosevic, who controls the 14,000 Yugoslav army troops and 1,000 federal-level police in Montenegro and has used them and other federal institutions to intimidate the republic's coalition government. According to late 1999 polling data from the U.S. Information Agency, about 30 percent of Montenegro's population support independence, 36 percent greater autonomy for the republic within Yugoslavia, and 27 percent the status quo.

The likelihood and extent of armed conflict in Montenegro depend on a number of complex factors, such as how far the President of Montenegro is willing to push Milosevic to gain greater autonomy, whether Milosevic would intervene in Montenegro short of a referendum on independence, and whether the current governing coalition of Montenegro would stay together if a referendum on independence is not held this spring. Western observers in Montenegro hold differing views on whether developments in Montenegro would lead to armed conflict. Some believe that the past close relationship between the President of Montenegro and Milosevic would encourage them to reach an understanding before violence occurs, while others believe that the moves toward greater autonomy or independence will lead to possibly armed conflict.

While ethnic Macedonians and Albanians are currently working together in the ruling government coalition, several western observers told us that interethnic tensions between these two groups could ultimately result in armed conflict. Structures are in place on both sides that could serve as the basis for future ethnically based militaries. Specifically, Macedonia's military and internal security forces are predominantly ethnic Macedonian, and armed, radical Albanian groups are operating in Macedonia.

These observers offered a range of views about how soon and under what scenario armed conflict may occur in Macedonia. Armed conflict could develop (1) if ethnic Albanian parties pulled out of the coalition government due to a lack of progress in resolving political issues; according to a western observer, it would most likely occur sometime over the next year; or (2) if radical Albanian groups began to violently target Macedonian institutions, leading Macedonia's police to crack down on ethnic Albanians. A western observer in Macedonia is most concerned with this second threat in the near term, stating that these radical groups have been emboldened by what the Kosovo Liberation Army was able to accomplish. Either of these scenarios could lead to a spiral of violent incidents and ultimately armed conflict among the country's two major ethnic groups, similar to the violence that occurred in Kosovo. Other observers told us that ethnic tensions in Macedonia could result in violence between the two communities in 10 to 20 years. . . .

## Selected Issues Related to U.S. and International Operations in the Balkans

The executive branch has described U.S. interests in the Balkans in a number of ways. The National Security Strategy [issued by President Bill Clinton in December 1999]—the most authoritative statement on the President's definition of U.S. interests and military commitments worldwide—lays out three categories of national interests: vital, important, and humanitarian. The strategy directly links U.S. interests in the Balkans to two of these three types of interests, stating that the decision to use military force is dictated first and foremost by the definition of U.S. national interests.

- European stability is described in the strategy as a "vital" U.S. interest. Vital interests are of broad, overriding importance to the survival, safety, and vitality of the United States, for example, the physical security of territory belonging to the United States and U.S. allies. According to the strategy, the United States will do what it must to defend these interests, using military force decisively and, if necessary, unilaterally. The U.S. commitment to European security includes U.S. leadership in NATO and the forward presence of 100,000 military personnel in Europe.
- NATO operations to end the conflicts and restore peace in Bosnia and Kosovo are presented as "important" U.S. interests, rather than as vital interests. According to the strategy, important interests do not affect the survival of the United States but do affect national well-being and the character of the world in which Americans live. In cases where important U.S. interests are at stake, the strategy states that the use of military forces should be selective and limited.

The National Security Strategy indicates that United States has a continuing interest in "peace in the Balkans and Southeastern Europe" but does not directly link vital or important interests in the region to when, how, or for how long U.S. military forces would be employed there. The strategy states that continued instability in the region threatens European security, an area that it had previously defined as a vital U.S. interest. In commenting on our report, the Undersecretary of Defense for Policy reiterated that the National Security Strategy reads, "'The United States has an abiding interest in peace in this region because continued instability there threatens European security.' The identified interest here is clearly instability threatening European security—a vital interest in and of itself."

The National Security Strategy does not directly link humanitarian interests to the Balkans region, although executive branch officials on many occasions have cited humanitarian interests there. The report cites the following as examples of humanitarian and other interests that may require a U.S. military response: (1) natural and manmade disasters; (2) promoting human rights and seeking to halt gross violations of those rights; and (3) supporting democratization, adherence to the rule of law, and civilian control of the military. According to the strategy, the military is generally not the best tool for addressing humanitarian concerns, but under certain conditions it may be appropriate to use U.S. military forces for these purposes. The strategy states that such efforts by the United States will be limited in duration.

According to the National Security Strategy, U.S. military forces should be used when important interests are at stake only if, among other things, the costs and risks of their employment are commensurate with the importance of U.S. interests, and they are likely to accomplish their objectives. In making a determination on these matters, key issues to consider include (1) the appropriate level of the U.S. military contribution relative to that of other NATO countries, (2) whether strategic and operational objectives for operations in the region have been clearly defined, and (3) whether the international community is willing and able to provide the necessary military and civilian resources for the operations. . . .

# VERMONT LAW PERMITTING SAME-SEX CIVIL UNIONS
## April 26, 2000

*Vermont became the first state in the nation to grant all the rights and responsibilities of traditional marriage to same-sex couples who joined in civil union. The law, which went into effect July 1, 2000, was enacted in response to a state supreme court ruling in December 1999 holding that the Vermont constitution's equal protection guarantees required the state to extend the same rights and benefits to homosexual and lesbian couples as it did to heterosexual couples.*

*While gay rights advocates applauded the action in Vermont, they were dismayed by the results of a California referendum barring same-sex marriages in that state and by a U.S. Supreme Court ruling that the Boy Scouts of America could dismiss an adult leader because he was openly homosexual.*

*In addition, controversy continued to swirl around the U.S. military's "don't ask, don't tell" policy. Although the policy, in place since 1994, was intended to diminish prejudice against gays serving in the armed forces, a survey of more than 70,000 troops early in 2000 found that gay harassment was "commonplace" and "tolerated to some extent." Later in the year the Pentagon put into place a new "action plan" designed to curb such harassment.*

### Vermont Civil Unions

*In its ruling December 20, 1999, the Vermont Supreme Court left it to the state legislature to determine whether same-sex couples would be granted the rights and benefits of marriage through formal marriage or through a legal system of domestic partnerships. The state legislature took the latter option. As of July 1, gay and lesbian couples could obtain a license to enter a civil union from their town clerks, and their unions could be certified by a justice of the peace, a judge, or a clergy member. A dissolution of a civil union would be handled in family court, just as divorces. Partners in civil unions would be entitled to the same rights and benefits as married couples in the state, including the right to inherit from each other under the same state tax laws, the right to make medical decisions on the partner's behalf, and the right not to be compelled to testify against one's partner. Partners in civil unions would also bear the same responsibilities as married couples, including the assumption of each other's debts and the duty to pay child support.* (Vermont Supreme Court ruling, Historic Documents of 1999, p. 898)

*The more than three hundred rights and responsibilities granted under the civil union law were those conferred by the state of Vermont. Partners in civil unions were not entitled to federal benefits granted to married couples, such as spousal benefits under Social Security. It also seemed unlikely that other states would recognize the unions.*

*The civil union law won final approval from the Vermont house on April 25. The state senate had approved it a week earlier. "I think the powerful message is that in Vermont, we tend to value people for who they are, not what they are," Governor Howard Dean said after the House had acted. Dean signed the legislation into law on April 26 behind the closed doors of his office, with only a handful of aides present.*

*The three couples who had brought the successful suit in the Vermont Supreme Court were in the House when the final vote was taken. "This isn't marriage," said one, "but it's a huge and powerful bundle of rights that we've finally gotten." One of the couples was among the first to enter into a civil union on July 1. Yet in the first weeks that the law was in effect, more couples from out-of-state than from Vermont appeared to be joining in civil unions, even though they were unlikely to reap any of the benefits conferred by the law. Some of those couples were expected to use their civil union in Vermont law to seek similar laws in their own states or as proof of their relationship in situations such as medical emergencies.*

*Opposition to the civil union law was fierce both before and after passage of the law. The state population was almost evenly split on the issue, and public hearings and rallies occasionally turned ugly. After the law passed, its opponents mounted strong campaigns to oust Dean and other politicians who had supported it. Dean won election to a sixth term, but at least a dozen Democrats in the House lost their seats, turning control of the Vermont House over to Republicans. "The civil unions issue blew us out," one Democratic official said.*

## Supreme Court on Gays in the Boy Scouts

*In a 5–4 decision, the U.S. Supreme Court on July 28, 2000, ruled that the Boy Scouts of America was exercising its constitutionally protected right of "expressive association" when it ousted an adult leader because he was gay. The ruling overturned a decision by the New Jersey Supreme Court, which had ruled that the dismissal had violated the state's antidiscrimination laws. The Boy Scouts is a private organization that "believes that homosexual conduct is inconsistent with the values it seeks to instill in its youth members," Chief Justice William H. Rehnquist wrote for the majority. Requiring the Boy Scouts to accept an openly gay leader "would, at the very least, force the organization to send a message, both to the youth members and the world, that the Boy Scouts accepts homosexual conduct as a legitimate form of behavior."* (New Jersey ruling, Historic Documents of 1999, p. 901)

*The Boy Scouts and many churches and other groups that sponsored troops applauded the ruling. "It is important for the Boy Scouts of America and our church that private organizations retain the right to define their leadership criteria," the unit of the United Methodist Church that sponsored Boy Scout troops said in a written statement. James Dale, the leader who had been fired, said he was disappointed by the ruling but thought that the Boy Scouts and other groups that used the ruling to bar gays would be marginalized. "Dinosaurs became extinct because they didn't evolve," he said. "The Boy Scouts are making themselves extinct, and it's a very sad thing." Several school districts with rules barring discrimination on the basis of sexual orientation said they would have to reconsider their sponsorship of Boy Scout troops.*

## Gays in the Military

*A survey of attitudes toward gays in the U.S. military confirmed what many gay rights advocates and others had long claimed: the "don't ask, don't tell" policy instituted by the Clinton administration in 1994 apparently had done little to curb antigay sentiment. The survey, conducted by the Pentagon's inspector general, interviewed 71,570 service members on thirty-eight military bases and eleven naval vessels in late January and early February. The findings, released March 24, reported that 80 percent of those surveyed had heard offensive speech and derogatory remarks, names, or jokes about gays, and that 85 percent believed such comments "were tolerated to some extent." More than one-third—37 percent—said they had witnessed or experienced an incident of harassment based on perceived homosexuality. While 78 percent of all service members interviewed said they would feel free to report antigay harassment, only 16 percent of those who said they had witnessed or experienced such harassment actually reported it.*

*Under the "don't ask, don't tell" policy, homosexuals could still be discharged from the armed forces. But gay men and lesbians were allowed to serve if they did not openly acknowledge their homosexuality or engage in homosexual acts, and the armed forces were ordered to stop actively searching for gays. The policy also stipulated that harassment would not be tolerated. A chief complaint against the policy was that those who reported antigay harassment or threats often triggered an investigation of their conduct rather than of the alleged harassers.*

*The issue came to a head in December 1999 following the conviction of an army private for the July 5 beating death of Pfc. Barry Winchell in their barracks at Fort Campbell in Kentucky. At the trial it was revealed that Winchell, who was gay, had for months suffered taunts and threats that had gone unreprimanded by superiors and that one superior had participated in the taunting. Defense Secretary William S. Cohen immediately ordered spot checks of troops throughout the services to determine how to make the "don't ask, don't tell" policy more effective.*

On February 1, 2000, the Pentagon announced that it would require every member of the armed forces, from four-star generals to new recruits, to undergo training to broaden understanding of what the policy did and did not allow and to emphasize that harassment would not be tolerated.

In direct response to the findings of the survey, the Pentagon announced an "antiharassment action plan" on July 21 that would require military commanders to discipline service members who engaged in, condoned, or tolerated antigay harassment. The plan, which was drawn up by a panel of military and civilian leaders, emphasized that those complaining of harassment should not disclose their sexual orientation or be asked to do so. And it recommended that training on the policy be tailored to the rank of the troops receiving the training. Actual details for implementing the thirteen-point action plan had yet to be worked out.

On the same day, in back-to-back press conferences, the army announced that its internal investigation of Winchell's murder had found that the general climate of command at Fort Campbell, home of the 101st Airborne Division, was not homophobic, although Winchell's unit was an exception. Describing the sergeant who was Winchell's immediate superior as "abusive," the report said he had been relieved of his command and reassigned. All officers were exonerated of blame in the murder.

In a related event, the U.S. Senate on June 20 voted, 57–42, to make hate crimes against gays a federal crime. It was the first time that either chamber had taken a roll-call vote on the issue, thus forcing legislators to take a public stand on the issue. In 1999 the Senate passed a similar measure by unanimous consent, which did not require individual senators to record their vote. The House Republican leadership, which was adamantly opposed to the amendment, barred a House vote on the legislation in both years. But in 2000 the House voted, 232–190, to instruct House conferees to accept the Senate language, which was in the form of an amendment to the 2001 defense authorization bill. Despite the instruction, House conferees stood firmly against the language, and the provision was eventually dropped from the bill.

During the second presidential debate at Wake Forest University on October 11, the Democratic candidate, Vice President Al Gore, tried to draw out his Republican opponent, George W. Bush, on the issue, suggesting that Bush had blocked a hate crimes bill pending in the Texas legislature. Bush sidestepped that specific question but acknowledged that he did not support the language that the U.S. Senate had approved. (Presidential debates, p. 797)

## Other Events

Even as Vermont was considering legislation to permit civil unions, California voters resoundingly endorsed a referendum on March 8 to prohibit the state from recognizing the validity of same-sex marriages. The vote made California the thirty-first state to ban gay marriages. Republican state senator Pete Knight placed the proposition on the ballot, after the California legislature rejected it. The campaign was led and financed by religious conservatives. The text of the referendum was short and to the point: "Only marriage between a man and a woman is valid and recognized in California."

*The Central Conference of American Rabbis, an organization of Judaism's Reform movement, formally declared on March 29 that gay relationships were "worthy of affirmation" and that the rabbinical body would support Reform rabbis who officiated at same-sex ceremonies, just as it would support those rabbis who chose not to participate in such ceremonies. The announcement made the conference the largest group of clergy to support same-sex religious unions. The conference represented about 1,800 rabbis who led about 1.5 million Jews in the United States and Canada.*

*Three other, larger religious organizations all went on record as opposing church ceremonies blessing or affirming same-sex unions. In May the policymaking board of the United Methodist Church reaffirmed its church law prohibiting ministers from performing such unions. In June the Southern Baptist Convention called on all Christians to oppose homosexuality. In July the policymaking body of the Presbyterian Church adopted language prohibiting its ministers from conducting same-sex unions. That decision could not take effect, however, until it had been ratified by two-thirds of the church's regional jurisdiction. A similar prohibition failed to win ratification in 1994.*

*The "big three" domestic automakers—Ford, General Motors, and Daimler-Chrysler—announced on June 8 that starting August 1 they would offer full health benefits to the domestic partners of all employees who had shared "a committed relationship" for at least six months. The United Autoworkers had sought the new benefits in their contract talks. The automakers were not offering similar benefits to unmarried heterosexual couples.*

*According to the Human Rights Campaign, which tracked the companies offering domestic partner benefits, the joint announcement represented the first time that an entire sector had agreed to provide such benefits and would be an enormous boost to the group's efforts to solicit similar benefits from other employers. In September the group reported that some 3,500 companies, including more than 20 percent of Fortune 500 firms, offered domestic partner benefits. That number was up 25 percent from the number in 1999. "Employers have discovered that these benefits help attract and keep the best workers, a critical consideration in the current tight job market," said a spokesperson for the gay rights organization.*

*Elsewhere, the British government conceded to a ruling by the European Court of Human Rights and on January 12 announced that it would no longer bar openly gay men and women from serving in the military. In its place, the government set out a new code of conduct that applied to "unacceptable social conduct," whether engaged in by heterosexual or homosexual service members. Unacceptable conduct included sexual harassment, overt displays of affection, and taking sexual advantage of subordinates.*

*In response to another directive from the European Union (EU), the Dutch parliament's upper house on December 19 voted overwhelmingly to approve legislation allowing same-sex couples to marry and adopt children. The legislation was expected to take effect in April 2001. The Dutch action came after the EU's parliament adopted a nonbinding resolution in March urging member nations to grant same-sex couples equal rights to those of heterosexual couples.*

*Following is the text of "The Vermont Guide to Civil Unions," prepared by the office of the Vermont secretary of state upon the enactment on April 26, 2000, of a law permitting couples of the same sex to be joined in civil union that conferred upon them all of the rights and responsibilities given to married couples by Vermont law. The document was obtained from the Internet at http://www.sec.state.vt.us/pubs/civilunions.htm.*

Vermont's Civil Union law will go into effect July 1st, 2000. This law permits eligible couples of the same sex to be joined in civil union. The eligibility criteria are discussed in this pamphlet.

Parties to a civil union shall have all the same benefits, protections and responsibilities under Vermont law, whether they derive from statute, policy, administrative or court rule, common law or any other source of civil law, as are granted to spouses in a marriage.

In order to be joined in civil union the couple must complete the following steps:

1. Apply for a civil union license from the town clerk of the town where either party resides or, if neither is a resident of the state, from any Vermont town clerk. At least one of the parties must sign the license application and pay a $20.00 fee to the town clerk.
2. The couple must then deliver the license to an official authorized to certify a civil union: a judge, justice of the peace or member of the clergy. The civil union may be certified anywhere in the state.
3. The official must perform the certification within sixty days after the town clerk issues the license. The official must fill out and sign a portion of the civil union license. If the certification is delayed for more than sixty days a new license must be issued.
4. Within ten days of the certification, the official who certifies the union must return it to the town clerk who issued it. If the official delays returning the certification beyond the tenth day, the official may be penalized, but the civil union will still be valid. . . .

For civil unions, as for marriages, Vermont law requires no medical certificate, blood test or waiting period.

## Frequently Asked Questions

### Who may be joined in civil union?

To be joined in civil union a couple must satisfy all of the following criteria:

1. Not be a party to another civil union or a marriage or a party in a legal reciprocal beneficiary relationship.
2. Be of the same sex and therefore excluded from the marriage laws of this state.

3. Not be close family members: A woman may not enter into a civil union with her mother, grandmother, daughter, granddaughter, sister, brother's daughter, sister's daughter, father's sister or mother's sister. A man may not enter into a civil union with his father, grandfather, son, grandson, brother, brother's son, sister's son, father's brother or mother's brother.

4. Not be under 18 years of age;

5. Not be non compos mentis (of unsound mind);

6. Not be under guardianship, unless the guardian consents in writing. . . .

7. **PLEASE NOTE: The law permits non-residents to obtain a Vermont civil union.**

## What are the legal consequences of a civil union?

Parties to a civil union are given all the same benefits, protections and responsibilities under Vermont law, whether they derive from statute, administrative or court rule, policy, common law or any other source of civil law, as are granted to spouses in a marriage. These include:

1. Parties to a civil union shall be responsible for the support of one another to the same degree and in the same manner as prescribed under law for married persons.

2. The law of domestic relations, including annulment, separation and divorce, child custody and support, and property division and maintenance shall apply to parties to a civil union.

3. The rights of parties to a civil union, with respect to a child of whom either becomes the natural parent during the term of the civil union, shall be the same as those of a married couple, with respect to a child of whom either spouse becomes the natural parent during the marriage.

4. The following is a nonexclusive list of legal benefits, protections and responsibilities of spouses, which shall apply in like manner to parties to a civil union:

   a. laws relating to title, tenure, descent and distribution, intestate succession, waiver of will, survivorship, or other incidents of the acquisition, ownership, or transfer, inter vivos or at death, of real or personal property, including eligibility to hold real and personal property as tenants by the entirety (parties to a civil union meet the common law unity of person qualification for purposes of a tenancy by the entirety);

   b. causes of action related to or dependent upon spousal status, including an action for wrongful death, emotional distress, loss of consortium, dramshop, or other torts or actions under contracts reciting, related to, or dependent upon spousal status;

   c. probate law and procedure, including nonprobate transfer;

   d. adoption law and procedure;

   e. group insurance for state employees under 3 V.S.A. § 631, and continuing care contracts under 8 V.S.A. § 8005;

f.  spouse abuse programs under 3 V.S.A. § 18;

g.  prohibitions against discrimination based upon marital status;

h.  victim's compensation rights under 13 V.S.A. § 5351;

i.  workers' compensation benefits;

j.  laws relating to emergency and non-emergency medical care and treatment, hospital visitation and notification, including the Patient's Bill of Rights under 18 V.S.A. chapter 42 and the Nursing Home Residents' Bill of Rights under 33 V.S.A. chapter 73;

k.  terminal care documents under 18 V.S.A. chapter 111, and durable power of attorney for health care execution and revocation under 14 V.S.A. chapter 121;

l.  family leave benefits under 21 V.S.A. chapter 5, subchapter 4A;

m.  public assistance benefits under state law;

n.  laws relating to taxes imposed by the state or a municipality other than estate taxes;

o.  laws relating to immunity from compelled testimony and the marital communication privilege;

p.  the homestead rights of a surviving spouse under 27 V.S.A. § 105 and homestead property tax allowance under 32 V.S.A. § 6062;

q.  laws relating to loans to veterans under 8 V.S.A. § 1849;

r.  the definition of family farmer under 10 V.S.A. § 272;

s.  laws relating to the making, revoking and objecting to anatomical gifts by others under 18 V.S.A. § 5240;

t.  state pay for military service under 20 V.S.A. § 1544;

u.  application for absentee ballot under 17 V.S.A. § 2532;

v.  family landowner rights to fish and hunt under 10 V.S.A. § 4253;

w.  legal requirements for assignment of wages under 8 V.S.A. § 2235; and

x.  affirmance of relationship under 15 V.S.A. § 7.

Note that a party to a civil union is included, by law, in any definition or use of the terms "spouse," "family," "immediate family," "dependent," "next of kin," and other terms that denote the spousal relationship, as those terms are used throughout Vermont law.

## Can parties to a civil union modify the terms of the union?

Yes, parties to a civil union may modify the terms, conditions, or effects of their civil union in the same manner and to the same extent as married persons who execute an antenuptial agreement or other agreement recognized and enforceable under the law, setting forth particular understandings with respect to their union. . . . The family court determines the enforceability of such agreements.

## Who can certify a civil union in Vermont?

Civil unions may be certified by:

- **Judges:** A supreme court justices, a superior court judge, a district judge, a judge of probate, an assistant judge.

- **Justices of the Peace:** Performing ceremonies (marriage and civil union) are discretionary functions of this office. A justice may decide whether to perform a particular ceremony on a case by case basis, or may decline to perform all ceremonies or may decide only to perform ceremonies for family and friends. A justice may not discriminate on any basis prohibited by law (age, race, sex, national origin, religion, sexual orientation,) and must apply the same policy to both marriages and civil unions.
- **Clergy:** Clergy members residing in Vermont and ordained or licensed, or otherwise regularly authorized by the published laws or discipline of the general conference, convention or other authority of his or her faith or denomination, or by such a clergy person residing in an adjoining state or country, whose parish, church, temple, mosque or other religious organization lies wholly or in part in this state, or by a member of the clergy residing in some other state of the United States or in the District of Columbia, provided he or she has first secured from the probate court of the district within which the civil union is to be certified, a special authorization, authorizing him or her to certify the civil union if such probate judge determines that the circumstances make the special authorization desirable. Civil unions among the Friends or Quakers, the Christadelphian Ecclesia and the Baha'i Faith may be certified in the manner used in such societies. . . .

### What does a Vermont civil union ceremony have to include?

Vermont law is silent on the mechanics of both wedding and civil union ceremonies. Some authorities say that a minimum ceremony conducted by a judge or justice involves saying the words, "By the authority vested in me by the State of Vermont, I hereby join you in civil union." By signing the license the official is certifying that the parties entered into the civil union with mutual consent. Parties are free to discuss with the justice, judge or clergy member their own ideas of what they want in a ceremony.

**A possible ceremony for civil unions performed by a justice of the peace, judge or clergy includes the following:**

**JUSTICE OF THE PEACE:** We are here to join _____ and _____ in civil union. (Then to each in turn, giving names as appropriate) Will you ____ have ____ to be united as one in your civil union?

**RESPONSE:** I will.

**JUSTICE OF THE PEACE:** (Then to each in turn, giving names as appropriate): Then repeat after me: "I ____ take you ____ to be my spouse in our civil union, to have and to hold from this day on, for better, for worse, for richer, for poorer, to love and to cherish forever." (Then, if rings are used, each in turn says, as the ring is put on): "With this ring I join with you in this our civil union."

**JUSTICE OF THE PEACE:** By the power vested in me by the State of Vermont, I hereby join you in civil union.

### How can I prove that I am legally a party to a civil union?

A copy of the civil union certificate received from the town or county clerk, the commissioner of health or the director of public records shall be presumptive evidence of the civil union in all courts. . . .

### How are civil unions dissolved?

The Vermont family court has jurisdiction over all proceedings relating to the dissolution of civil unions. The dissolution of civil unions follows the same procedures and is subject to the same substantive rights and obligations that are involved in the dissolution of marriage, including any residency requirements. . . .

It is unclear how other states may handle a civil union dissolution; however, in Vermont, a residency requirement exists for dissolving either a marriage or a civil union. A complaint to dissolve a civil union in Vermont may be brought if either party to the civil union has resided within the state for a period of six months or more, but dissolution cannot be granted unless one of the parties has resided in the state at least one year preceding the date of the final hearing.

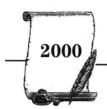

# May

# PUTIN ON HIS INAUGURATION
# AS PRESIDENT OF RUSSIA
## May 7, 2000

*Vladimir Putin, the hand-chosen successor of Boris Yeltsin, easily won election as president of Russia in the nation's third free election since the waning days of the Soviet Union. A former colonel in the Soviet secret police, Putin immediately began tightening Moscow's control over the eighty-nine regions that made up the Russian republic. Putin also sought to rein in the power of Russia's industrial and financial barons and to undermine the newfound independence of the news media. These actions raised a question at home and abroad about his motives: Was he using strong-arm tactics only as a temporary measure to save Russia's infant democracy, or was he assembling an updated, softer version of the authoritarianism Russians had experienced under both the czars and the commissars? The answer to that question was still not clear by the end of the year.*

*During Putin's first year in office the transformation of Russia into a civil society based on democracy and capitalism continued at about the same erratic pace it had in the preceding eight years, following the collapse of the Soviet Union at the end of 1991. The presidential election, despite its problems, bore at least some resemblance to the free exercise of citizen franchise that had become nearly a worldwide goal toward the end of the twentieth century. Aspects of a democratic government were functioning somewhat as intended, including the parliament, which managed to approve laws and budgets despite the frequent appearance of chaos. And the economy—buoyed by rising world oil and natural gas prices—showed limited signs of recovery from its low point in 1998, when the government was forced to renege on billions of dollars worth of internal debt and devalue the ruble.* (Russian economic troubles, Historic Documents of 1998, p. 601)

*Russia as a whole—and Putin in particular—received an embarrassing blow in August when a nuclear submarine, the* Kursk, *sank in the Barents Sea, killing all 118 sailors aboard. Russian officials offered confusing and contradictory explanations of the disaster. Putin refused to interrupt a vacation during the initial days of uncertainty about the fate of the sub-*

*marine's crew, fostering doubts about his sensitivity to the needs of public opinion and Russian national honor.* (*Kursk* disaster, p. 635)

## *Putin Elected*

*Putin's rapid rise to the center of power started in August 1999, when an ailing Yeltsin abruptly made the obscure Kremlin aide his prime minister and designated successor as president. Putin quickly rose to his first challenge: a series of bombings that killed dozens of people. Blaming the bombings on Muslim separatists in the republic of Chechnya, Putin launched a bloody military assault on Chechnya that proved to be enormously popular among Russians. Political parties aligned with Putin gained working control of parliament in elections in mid-December 1999. Less than two weeks later, on New Year's Eve, Yeltsin announced that he was resigning and turning the presidency—along with his legacy—over to Putin.* (Yeltsin resignation, Historic Documents of 1999, p. 917)

*Presidential elections had been scheduled for June 2000, but under Russian law, Yeltsin's resignation moved the voting to March. Putin was heavily favored to defeat his main challenger, Gennadi A. Zyuganov, leader of the Communist Party, who had lost the 1996 election to Yeltsin. But as the March 26 election date approached, many observers began to express doubts about the intensity of public support for Putin. Zyuganov appeared to be drawing unexpectedly strong backing, especially from the millions of Russians who had been impoverished by the country's headlong stumble from communism to capitalism starting in 1992. Putin also was challenged by a leading reformer, Grigory V. Yavlinsky, who threatened to draw off some of the noncommunist vote.*

*In the final weeks of the campaign, Putin acted partly like a Western politician—flying to distant parts of the republic for staged campaign appearances—and partly like a Kremlin boss during the Soviet era—making heavy-handed use of the media to attack his opponents and of government agencies to bolster his own support. Putin appeared intent on avoiding a runoff election, which would have been necessary if he had failed to capture less than a majority on March 26.*

*The final results showed that Putin narrowly succeeded in his goal of a first-round victory, with 52.6 percent of the vote. Zyuganov, the communist leader, came in second with 29.3 percent—above his standing in pre-election polls but a sharp drop-off from his showing against Yeltsin four years earlier. Yavlinsky drew slightly under 6 percent, with minor-party candidates accounting for the rest of the vote. Some analysts said the results might indicate that Russia was developing a two-party system, with the split representing the difference between those who approved of and benefited from the move away from communism and those who yearned for a return to the past.*

*Despite numerous reports of irregularities on election day, most outside observers declared the election to be free and fair. But the Communist Party alleged massive fraud, saying Putin's government had stolen at least 7 million votes. The* Moscow Times, *a newspaper often critical of the government, verified many of the opposition's claims in a detailed report on September 10. The newspaper said Putin got enough votes to avoid a run-off only through widespread vote buying, ballot stuffing, and tampering with returns. Even so, it seemed clear that Putin would have won election even in the second round.*

## *A Democrat or Dictator?*

*Putin was inaugurated as president on May 7, in a lavish Kremlin ceremony that sought to capture Russia's days of past glory. Yeltsin was there to emphasize the significance of the occasion: "For the first time in a hundred years, there is a lawful transition of power," he said in a brief speech. "We can be proud of that."*

*In his inaugural speech Putin laid out a vision of Russia as an economically successful democracy able to take its rightful place as a world power. "We want Russia to be free and flourishing, a rich, strong and civilized country of which its citizens are proud and which is respected in the world," he said. But he acknowledged that the working of building a democratic society "has not been completed. We have to preserve and develop democracy."*

*Putin named as his prime minister Mikhail Kasyanov, an economics specialist who supported free market reforms. Both men were in their forties—Putin was forty-seven, Kasyanov was forty-one—and they symbolized the transition of power to a younger generation. Except for the last Soviet leader, Mikhail Gorbachev, elderly or ailing rulers had controlled the Kremlin for decades. And except for Gorbachev and Yeltsin, none had been willing to challenge the communist system that had made the Soviet Union a military giant with a hollow economy.*

*Putin inherited a Russia still caught between the failures of the Soviet system and the lapses of the sudden transition to democracy and free markets. Yeltsin had moved swiftly in 1992 to turn the state-run economy over to private markets. The ensuing chaos enabled a small number of opportunistic Communist Party officials and entrepreneurs to gain control of giant state enterprises at a fraction of their value. Millions of people were thrown out of work, large sectors of the economy nearly stopped functioning, corruption was rampant at all levels of society, and the government was unable to collect enough tax revenue to pay its workers and soldiers. The collapse of the ruble in August 1998 focused world attention on Russia's woes and halted the massive infusion of Western aid and loans that had kept the economy afloat.*

*One of Putin's main challenges was to deal with the consequences of Yeltsin's rushed privatization, which had concentrated wealth in the hands of a few dozen industrial and financial barons known as the "oligarchs." The most flamboyant and controversial of them—Boris Berezovsky, who controlled numerous industrial enterprises—had aided Putin's rise to power. Many of the oligarchs were among the 1,000 or so invited guests at his inauguration, and they clearly were on the alert for any challenge to their newfound wealth and power.*

173

*Putin's government moved quickly to mount such a challenge, starting with Vladimir Gusinsky, one of the Kremlin's fiercest critics among the oligarchs. Gusinsky headed the Media-Most conglomerate, including the television channel NTV, which had been the sole Russian media outlet daring to provide critical coverage of the war in Chechnya.*

*In May, masked men—most likely representing the Russian secret service—raided Gusinsky's Moscow offices, leading to an international uproar over threats to press freedoms in Russia. On June 13 Gusinsky was arrested and imprisoned for three nights on multi-million-dollar fraud charges that were later dropped. Then in July Gusinsky came under intense pressure to sell his media holdings to his major creditor, Gazprom, the Russian natural gas monopoly that was effectively controlled by the Kremlin. Gusinsky fled the country, saying he feared for his life. But by late November he was forced to give Gazprom a major stake in Media-Most, raising fears that the Kremlin would be able to dictate editorial policy. At year's end Gusinsky was under house arrest in Spain, facing a second round of criminal charges brought by Russian prosecutors. Gusinsky also was trying to find a foreign buyer for his stake in Media-Most.*

*With Gusinsky on the run, the Kremlin mounted a broader challenge to the power of the oligarchs. Federal prosecutors launched investigations of several oligarchs and threatened to take actions that might undo some of the privatizations from the mid-1990s. On July 28 Putin summoned twenty-one of the oligarchs to a meeting at the Kremlin. Putin told them he was not seeking to reverse the privatizations or strip the oligarchs of their holdings, but he insisted that they begin paying taxes and made it clear that he—not they—would determine government policy. Most of the oligarchs appeared to accept Putin's demands. But Berezovsky, previously among Putin's staunchest supporters, angrily demurred, resigned his seat in parliament, and announced that he was forming an opposition movement. Federal prosecutors in November started an inquiry into Berezovsky's financial empire, and he went into exile in Europe.*

*Putin launched a parallel drive to gain control over the elected governors in the eighty-nine Russian republics, or regions. He appointed seven "presidential representatives" to monitor the regions; five of the seven were former generals or officials of the Federal Security Service (the domestic secret service). Putin also pushed legislation through parliament that gave him the right to fire the governors and stripped them of their automatic membership in the Federation Council—the appointed, upper chamber of parliament.*

*Critics in the news media, other than Gusinsky, also faced government intimidation, including a Moscow newspaper whose offices were raided after it published a satellite photograph of the Kursk. Moreover, journalists and government critics were alarmed in January when Putin signed a decree authorizing the Federal Security Service to monitor e-mails and Internet usage by private citizens.*

*If Putin's tactics unnerved domestic critics and caused deep concern in Western capitals, they proved to be popular with the Russian public. Opin-*

*ion polls consistently showed two-thirds or more of the public approving of how he was doing his job and endorsing his moves toward a strong central government.*

*Putin's economic policies during the year appeared aimed at maintaining the drive toward capitalism that Yeltsin had initiated in 1992. In his July 8 address to the nation Putin laid out six economic priorities: guaranteeing property rights, eliminating preferential treatment for state enterprises, ending unnecessary state intervention in the economy, lowering taxes, developing banks, and targeting welfare to those who needed it the most. Perhaps his most direct success during the year was in winning parliamentary passage of a flat 13 percent income tax—a measure he said was needed to encourage Russians to pay taxes, something most of them had not done for years.*

*As one of the world's largest producers of oil and natural gas, Russia benefited from surging world prices for both commodities. But inflation, which had been rampant before the 1998 ruble devaluation, began creeping up again during the last half of 2000. Putin acknowledged that many elements of the economy were barely functioning and would need to be reformed if Russia was to enjoy a sustained economic recovery.*

## *Chechen War*

*Still unresolved at the end of 2000 was the conflict in Chechnya, which Putin's government initiated in 1999 to wipe out Islamic "terrorists" said to be responsible for a series of bombings that killed more than three hundred people in Russia. The military's all-out assault on Chechnya caused massive damage and killed thousands of civilians—as well as fighters on both sides. Russian forces launched a full-scale assault on Grozny, the Chechen capital, in January and captured the bombed-out remains of the city on February 6. At the end of February Russian generals announced that large-scale resistance by Chechen independence forces had ended. Putin said in November that some 2,600 Russian soldiers had died in the conflict; most Western observers said the actual number of casualties was probably much higher.* (Chechnya war, Historic Documents of 1999, p. 909)

*Despite Russian claims of success, the war continued as a low-level conflict of attrition, with several thousand rebels launching periodic guerrilla raids from bases in remote mountain areas. An estimated 25,000 Russian soldiers remained on duty in the province throughout 2000, enough to keep the population under a limited degree of control but not enough to wipe out the rebels, who continued to harass the authorities with guerrilla attacks and bombings.*

*Human rights organizations accused the military of committing horrific atrocities against rebels and civilians alike. The United Nations Human Rights Commission in April criticized Russia's use of "disproportionate and indiscriminate" force in Chechnya, including attacks against civilians. It was the first time that a permanent member of the UN Security Council had been formally rebuked by the Human Rights Commission. In response, Kremlin officials said any abuses by Russians were simply in re-*

*taliation for those of the rebels. Moscow appointed administrators to run the province but provided little aid to help in the recovery effort. The United Nations pulled its aid workers from the province because of security concerns.*

*The clear losers in the war were the Chechen civilians, especially the 250,000 residents of Grozny, who had been forced into exile when most of the city was destroyed by Russian aerial bombing. By late 2000 more than 100,000 residents returned to Grozny, where they lived in the few remaining private homes or tents, makeshift shelters, and bombed-out apartment houses without electricity, heat, or running water. The city was an environmental disaster zone. According to an October 22 report by the* New York Times, *smoke spewed from dozens of oil wells that burned uncontrolled, and the groundwater under the city was seriously contaminated with byproducts from the petroleum industry that once had been the backbone of the local economy.*

*The Clinton administration made several efforts during the year to persuade Putin that the brutal war in Chechnya, while politically popular within Russia, was damaging the country's economy and its relations with the West. In a speech at Oxford University on January 22, Deputy Secretary of State Strobe Talbott called the war a "gruesome reminder of how hard it is for Russia to break free of its own past."*

*Following is the text of the speech delivered May 7, 2000, by Vladimir Putin upon his inauguration as president of the Russian Federation; translation was provided by the Russian presidential press service. The document was obtained from the Internet at http://www.russianembassy.org/RUSSIA/Speech-president.htm.*

Distinguished citizens of Russia, dear friends,

Today I am addressing you—no one but you—because it is you who have entrusted me with the highest government post in the country. I understand that I have taken on an enormous responsibility, and I know that in Russia the head of state has always been and will be the one responsible for everything that goes on in the land. Upon leaving the Kremlin, the first President of Russia, Boris Nikolayevich Yeltsin, said the words that got embedded in the memory of many people. He said—and today he repeated those words in this hall: "Take care of Russia." It is this job that I view as my paramount duty as president. It is the discharge of this duty that I will also demand from my co-workers, from people serving together with me. In this patriotic endeavor I also count on help from my countrymen, citizens of Russia, from all those who care for the fate of our Fatherland.

Today I would like to thank also my supporters, all those who cast their votes in the elections for me. You backed those first steps which had already been taken. You believed that together we would be able to change our life for the better. I am profoundly thankful to you for that.

I understand, however, that your support is only an advance payment to government as a whole and, of course, to me, who today is taking the oath as President of the country.

I am also addressing those who voted for other candidates. It is my conviction that you voted for our common future and for our common goals, for a better life and for a strong and prosperous Russia. Each of us has his or her own experience and views. But we must be together as we have a great deal to do by joint effort.

Today is a truly historic day. I would like to focus on this fact anew: indeed, for the first time in the history of our state, in the entire history of Russia supreme power in the country is passed on in the most democratic and most simple way—by the will of the people. It is passed on lawfully and peacefully. Any change of guard always is a test of the constitutional system, a test of its strength. Yes, in our country it is not the first test; clearly, perhaps, it is not the last one. But we have passed this test and this landmark in a dignified manner. We have proved that Russia is becoming a truly modern democracy. Peaceful succession of power is the most important element of political stability, stability which we all were dreaming about, seeking and working for.

The road to free society was not simple or easy. There were both dark and bright pages in our history. The building of a democratic state is far from complete. But a great deal has already been done. We must cherish what has been achieved and preserve and advance democracy. We must make sure that the government chosen by the people works in the interests of the people and protects the Russian citizen everywhere, both in our country and abroad, and serves the public. This is a position of principle, and a tough one. I have been standing up for it and shall do so in the future.

It is for today's solemn event that we have gathered here, in the Kremlin, this day. It is a sacred place for our people. Here, in the Kremlin, is the nexus of our national memory. Here, in the Kremlin, the history of our land has been decided over the centuries. And we have no right to be "Ivans denying our roots." We must remember everything. We must know our history, know it as it is. We must learn its lessons and always remember those who built the State of Russia, who upheld its dignity and who made it great, strong and powerful. We will carry on this memory, and we will preserve this continuity. And we will pass on to our successors everything the best of our history, everything the best.

Distinguished citizens of Russia! We believe in our strength. We believe that we can truly transform and change our country. We have common goals: we want our Russia to be a free, prosperous, wealthy, strong and civilized land, a land in which its citizens take pride and which commands respect in the world.

Over the past few months, here in Moscow and meeting people in Russia's regions, I have been sensing our understanding and your support. And it is fairly often that on the squares and streets of our cities I heard from people, from most ordinary people, very simple words—but words of great importance to me. They would say: "We trust you, we pin our hopes on you. Just don't fail us." I can assure you that in my actions I will guide myself exclusively by state interests. Perhaps, I will not avoid mistakes. But what I promise—what I can really promise and do promise—is that that I will work openly and honestly.

I believe it my sacred duty to cement the people of Russia together, to rally citizens around clear goals and tasks—and to remember every day and every minute of my service to the Fatherland that we have one homeland and one people, that all of us have one common future. Thank you.

# GENERAL ACCOUNTING OFFICE ON UNITED NATIONS REFORM
## MAY 10, 2000

*A broad program initiated in 1997 by Secretary General Kofi Annan to reform the United Nations had made some progress by 2000, the U.S. General Accounting Office (GAO) told Congress in May. But key elements of the reform plan had yet to be adopted, the GAO said, most notably a new budgeting system that was needed to ensure that UN spending produced concrete results in the field, not just meetings and diplomatic busywork.*

*The GAO's analysis came as the United Nations was undertaking its own assessment of its work, timed to coincide with a "Millennium Summit" of heads of state and government in September 2000. Annan on April 3 issued a report, "We the Peoples," offering his ideas for how the world body would confront what he called "the main challenges confronting humanity" in the twenty-first century. (Millennium summit, p. 700)*

*At year's end, UN diplomats negotiated an agreement revising the budget assessments paid to the world body by its 189 member nations. If fully supported in 2001 by Congress and the incoming administration of George W. Bush, the agreement would free up $582 million in back dues owed the UN by the United States.*

### Annan's Reforms

*Under pressure from member nations, most notably the United States, the United Nations in 1994 began a process of determining how to reform its operations to make them more efficient and cost-effective. Much of the pressure for reform was generated by Congress, which routinely refused to appropriate the full extent of U.S. assessments to the United Nations. Under a longstanding agreement, the United States was supposed to pay for 30 percent of the UN's basic budget and peacekeeping costs, but Congress voted in 1994 to limit the U.S. share to 25 percent and to demand sweeping management reforms at the United Nations.*

*Annan, who became secretary general at the beginning of 1997, initiated an internal study that produced sweeping recommendations for reforms at all levels of UN operations. Annan approved the reforms that were within*

179

*his power to initiate. The General Assembly approved many of the reforms in December 1997. As part of the reforms, the United Nations cut its basic operating budget in 1998 and 1999, for the first time ever, and eliminated about 1,000 staff positions, according to the U.S. Mission to the United Nations. The UN also beefed up the powers of its inspector general, the Office of Internal Oversight. In a report issued November 11, that office said it had identified $17 million in savings during 2000.*

*For many years, a frequent complaint about the United Nations was that its dozens of offices and agencies either refused or were unable to work together. The UN's lack of coordination started at the top—among senior officials who often seemed more interested in protecting their bureaucratic turf and battling for funding than in delivering services. This confusion and duplication of services extended all through the UN system, most observers agreed. At the field level, UN agencies often failed to cooperate with one another. The GAO cited, as an example, the situation in Mozambique, where two UN agencies—the World Health Organization (WHO) and the United Nations International Children's Emergency Fund (UNICEF)—both ran health programs but were unaware of each other's presence.*

*As part of his reforms, Annan mandated regular meetings among senior UN managers so they could coordinate activities of their agencies, discuss policy issues, and share information. Annan also grouped all UN operations into one of four "core" functions (peace and security, humanitarian affairs, economic and social affairs, and development operations), each coordinated by an executive committee. To emphasize the importance of human rights, Annan included the High Commission on Human Rights in all four executive committees—the only UN agency with such a broad mandate.*

*Annan's reforms also were supposed to extend to UN operations at the country level, the GAO said. UN agencies were expected to contribute to a "framework" for operations in each country and to coordinate their activities through a central office. After studying UN operations in Guatemala and Mozambique, the GAO said the effort to improve coordination appeared to have improved effectiveness in those countries. But the GAO said UN peacekeeping operations had not yet benefited from improved coordination. The agency quoted senior and mid-level UN officials in the Middle East and Guatemala as saying that coordination between the UN political affairs and peacekeeping departments remained at a "low level."*

*In his reforms, Annan also sought to streamline UN operations by consolidating duplicated or similar operations. The GAO cited two examples of successful streamlining. In one case, the Department of Humanitarian Affairs was abolished and replaced with a new Office for the Coordination of Humanitarian Affairs, which was given broad authority to coordinate the activities of various UN offices dealing with relief programs and humanitarian disasters. The UN also put several offices dealing with human rights issues under the jurisdiction of the High Commissioner for Human Rights, thus giving that agency more personnel and influence and reducing duplication in the UN system.*

*A substantial portion of the GAO report was devoted to Annan's various proposals to improve the UN's systems for hiring and managing personnel. The UN lacked basic information about its employees, their capabilities, and responsibilities, the GAO said. Because the UN required thirteen review and evaluation steps for hiring personnel, staff vacancies normally took many months to fill. The GAO said Annan's reforms had resulted in some improvements in the UN's personnel practices, but many more steps needed to be taken.*

*Perhaps the most important reform that had not been stalled was Annan's proposal for "performance-based" budgeting, the GAO said. Under that proposal, UN budgets would specify performance criteria—such as how many children had been immunized under a health program—and each office or agency would be measured by its effectiveness in meeting the criteria that applied to it. That proposal had run into stiff resistance in the General Assembly, where the representatives of many developing countries viewed it as a budget-cutting move engineered by the United States and other major donor nations. As part of an overall budget approved December 23, the General Assembly adopted a resolution allowing for the gradual introduction of Annan's performance-based budgeting proposal.*

*The GAO said Annan had been unable to convince the General Assembly to limit the number and scope of tasks it assigned to the UN Secretariat, the central bureaucracy that he headed. Each year the General Assembly passed dozens of resolutions calling on the secretary general and his staff to take certain actions. Some resolutions made specific demands, such as requiring the secretary general to submit reports poverty, refuges, and other broad issues. But many General Assembly resolutions contained vague or open-ended mandates, apparently because member states could not agree on specifics and settled on vaguely worded language as a compromise, the GAO said. Moreover, the General Assembly was making increasingly heavy demands on the secretariat, the GAO said, noting that the number of mandates more than doubled from 246 in 1997 to 587 in 1998.*

## Status of U.S. Dues

*Ever since the United Nations was founded in 1945, the United States had been its major financial contributor. For many years the United States subsidized half of the UN budget. In 1973 Washington's share of the regular UN budget was set at 25 percent. The United States also was expected to pay 30.4 percent of UN peacekeeping costs and was the largest single contributor to the budgets of major UN-related organizations, such as UNICEF, the UN Development Program, and the WHO. In 2000, according to U.S. figures, Washington was scheduled to pay UN agencies a total of nearly $3 billion, of which $830 million was for the regular UN budget and peacekeeping operations and the remainder was for voluntary contributions to UN agencies and programs.*

*In 1994 Congress demanded cutbacks in U.S. funding for the United Nations, insisting on a limit of 22 percent as the U.S. share of the UN's operating budget—down from the standard 25 percent. Congress also demanded* *a cut in the U.S. share of peacekeeping expenses from 30.4 percent to 25 percent. In subsequent years Congress reduced its annual appropriations for the UN to those limits, even though the UN had not agreed to them. As a consequence, by 1999 the UN estimated that the United States owed some $1.6 billion in unpaid contributions (the Clinton administration estimated the accumulated unpaid balance at less than $1 billion). Late in 1999 the Clinton administration and congressional leaders agreed on a compromise plan under which the United States would pay $926 million in overdue assessments to the UN. The payments were to be made in three segments, each conditioned on a presidential report to Congress on the status of various UN reforms. The Clinton administration made a first payment of $100 million in December 1999.*

*During 2000, a follow-up payment of $582 million (of which $107 represented forgiveness of debt that the United Nations owed the United States) was pending General Assembly approval of budget reforms demanded by Congress. The most controversial of those reforms were the congressional demands for lower U.S. shares of the budget. Intense negotiations at UN headquarters in New York resulted in an agreement, ratified by the General Assembly on December 23, lowering the U.S. share of the UN operating budget to 22 percent and the U.S. share of peacekeeping expenses to 28 percent in 2001 and 26 percent in 2002. Several nations—most notably South Korea, China, and Russia—were required to increase their contributions so the United States share could be reduced.*

*One novel aspect of the agreement was the involvement of Ted Turner, the founder of the Cable News Network and a major shareholder in the Time-Warner media conglomerate. Turner agreed to make a one-time-only payment of nearly $35 million to help subsidize the U.S. contribution in fiscal year 2001. Richard C. Holbrooke, the U.S. ambassador to the UN, praised Turner's action as "an extraordinary demonstration of how to use philanthropy money for leveraging effect."*

*Holbrooke expressed hope that Congress would endorse the UN budget agreement during 2001 even though Washington's share of UN peacekeeping expenses would be slightly higher than the 25 percent Congress had demanded. The prospects for congressional approval appeared to be heightened by the endorsement of the agreement by Senate Foreign Relations Committee Chairman Jesse Helms (R-N.C.), who for years had been one of the UN's most vociferous critics in Congress.*

> *Following are excerpts from the report, "United Nations Reforms Are Progressing but Overall Objectives Have Not Been Achieved," presented May 10, 2000, to the Senate Foreign Relations Subcommittee on International Operations by Harold J. Johnson, associate director for international relations and trade issues at the General Accounting Office. The document was obtained from the Internet at http://www.gao.gov/cgi-bin/getrpt?GAO/ T-NSIAD-00-169.*

# Background

The United Nations carries out a wide range of activities, including peace-keeping in locations such as Kosovo, East Timor, and the Congo; humanitarian and refugee operations in Sudan and Tajikistan; and thousands of development, economic, social, and human rights projects worldwide. Organizationally, the United Nations is comprised of three types of entities. First are the member states' governing or intergovernmental bodies, such as the Security Council and the General Assembly, which set U.N. objectives and mandate activities in accordance with the U.N. Charter. Second is the Secretariat, the central working unit of the United Nations, which carries out work mandated by the governing bodies. The Secretariat consists of the Secretary General, whom the U.N. Charter specifies as the chief administrative officer of the United Nations, and the staff necessary to carry out the mandated work. Third are the U.N. programs and funds, which the General Assembly authorized to address specific areas of work of continuing importance. Examples of the programs and funds are the U.N. Children's Fund and the U.N. Development Program. Many of the programs are authorized to have their own governing bodies and budgets (paid for by voluntary contributions from participating nations). Consequently, while the Secretary General is the U.N.'s highest-ranking official and his reform proposals influence these programs, he does not have authority to direct the programs to undertake reforms.

The expenses of the Secretariat are funded through regular budget assessments of the U.N. member states. The U.N. regular budget for the biennium 2000–2001 is $2.5 billion, of which the U.S. contribution is assessed at 25 percent. Member states are assessed separately for U.N. peacekeeping activities. For 2000–2001, the cost of U.N. peacekeeping operations is estimated to be $3.6 billion, of which the United States is to contribute 25 percent. Member states are also assessed for the costs of international tribunals on war crimes and genocide. Finally, the United Nations receives voluntary, or extrabudgetary, contributions for the funds and programs—estimated to be $3.7 billion for the 2000–20001 biennium. The United States has historically paid about 25 percent. . . .

## U.N. Leadership and Operations
## Substantially Restructured

The United Nations has substantially restructured its operations, and we found this has provided more cohesive and unified leadership for the organization. A major problem for the United Nations has been the fragmentation and lack of cooperation among the Secretariat departments and the programs. To begin addressing this problem, the Secretary General formed (1) the senior management group and (2) the executive committees. The Senior Management Group consists of the heads of all U.N. departments and programs and has been meeting weekly since September 1997 to collectively decide on unified U.N. policies. Previously, the heads of some of the programs met only once a year at the General Assembly. Now there is a regular mechanism for developing a single U.N. direction. The four executive committees are organized around the U.N.'s core missions—peace and security, development operations, humanitarian affairs, and economic and social issues. Human rights is a core issue that cuts across all U.N. missions. Consisting of the senior managers of the departments and programs in each area, the executive committees try to translate senior management group decisions into coordinated action by all U.N. entities. . . .

We found that these reform initiatives have resulted in a more coherent and unified leadership for the United Nations and have begun to reduce competition among the various U.N. agencies and to foster more coordinated actions in the field. The following examples help illustrate areas where the reforms have made a difference.

- During the Kosovo crisis, the Secretary General, the Deputy Secretary General, the Emergency Relief Coordinator, the High Commissioners for Refugees and Human Rights, and other senior managers used the senior management group to develop a single U.N. response. The High Commissioner for Refugees would regularly report to the group through video-conferencing and provide real-time information on the situation on the ground. Since the top-level managers were members of the group, the United Nations was able to develop a unified response and provide clear direction to the departments and programs. One initial direction was that the High Commissioner's office would lead the U.N.'s initial response to the crisis and other U.N. entities would support the Commissioner. As the U.N.'s role in Kosovo evolved, the Secretary General continued to work through the Senior Management Group to develop a unified concept for U.N. operations and to ensure that all departments and programs pooled their resources to support U.N. tasks in humanitarian affairs, civilian police, and civil administration. According to senior U.N. officials, the management group was also used to ensure that all heads of U.N. departments and programs had a consistent understanding of the U.N.'s mandate in Kosovo, particularly for their dealings with the Organization for Security and Cooperation in Europe and the World Bank, which were also responsible for tasks in Kosovo.

- Leadership by the executive committee on peace and security enabled various U.N. departments to integrate some peacekeeping efforts and has resulted in better planning for new missions. For example, in developing plans for the U.N. operation in East Timor in 1999, the Under Secretary General for Political Affairs provided the group a full and candid assessment of the political situation and strategies for conducting the referendum, according to members of the executive committee. According to a senior political officer in the Department of Political Affairs, his openness with his priorities paved the way for unified strategy and planning among his department, the Department of Peacekeeping Operations, the Human Rights Coordinator, and others on the committee. As a result, the plan for the East Timor operation was more comprehensive and better integrated than other U.N. peacekeeping plans we have examined in our past work, and resulted in deploying the mission more quickly and with fewer problems than past complex operations. I should add that these reforms do not address the capacity of the United Nations to undertake the scale of its current peacekeeping responsibilities or the organizational limits of the United Nations in leading operations calling for the use of force.

- In Guatemala, initiatives to integrate U.N. development activities under the development assistance framework have helped improve the effectiveness of U.N. support for the 1994 peace accords by coordinating the work of 17 separate U.N. agencies. The U.N.'s efforts to demobilize combatants, which officials of the U.S. Agency for International Development described as a model for international cooperation, resulted in U.N. agencies conducting joint planning and taking steps to avoid duplicative programming. For example, the U.N. Population Fund had incorporated reproductive health activities into the U.N. Children's Fund and the U.N. Development Program's development projects. In addition, all U.N. agencies fully coordinated their efforts in an effective response to Hurricane Mitch and in producing a country development report, which for the first time included a candid section on human rights. Although the government objected to this report, all U.N. agencies in country were united in defending the report.

Despite improvements in some of the areas, we also found that the reforms are still in process and that U.N. agencies do not fully coordinate their activities at the working levels and in the field. The following examples illustrate areas where we found some continuing weaknesses in U.N. cooperation.

- The improved policy coordination and information sharing apparent at the U.N.'s highest levels and on critical issues are less evident in day-to-day activities at working levels of the organization. Several U.N. officials who recently worked both in U.N. headquarters and in field peacekeeping operations confirmed the need for increased interdepartmental coordination and cooperation on day-to-day policy and operational matters. During our fieldwork in the Middle East and Guatemala, senior and mid-level peacekeeping and political officers told us that coordination between them remains at a low level and they are continuing their practice of following instructions respectively from both the Department of Peacekeeping Operations and the Department of Political Affairs. They do not see evidence from their instructions that these departments are coordinating their work on a day-to-day basis.
- We also found impediments to fully integrating country development activities. In Guatemala, the common country assessment was delayed because agencies sought to include development indicators in line with their own mandates and programming, rather than agreeing on overall indicators of U.N. success. In Mozambique, U.N. officials said that some of the country team's working groups were largely inactive—such as education and water and sanitation—because officials were reluctant to spend time working on issues not directly related to their agencies' pri-

orities. About one-third of the U.N. officials we interviewed had no requirement or job expectation to participate in the U.N. development assistance framework. According to these officials, their career, promotion, and reward paths are through their parent organizations, and their work on the framework is an adjunct to their agency duties.

## Reforms to Develop a Results-Oriented Human Capital System Partly in Place

The Secretariat has partly implemented initiatives to begin transforming its human resources culture into one that is results oriented, responsive, and accountable. Fundamental tasks remain to be completed, such as developing U.N. procedures that allow the organization to staff critical needs and fully automating its personnel database. Nonetheless, in comparison to the situation in 1994, when the human capital system was in crisis, positive steps have been taken, such as implementing a merit-based appraisal system and a U.N.-wide code of conduct. Also, the overall plan for reforming the human capital system shares the elements and values that are common to high-performing organizations. For example, a hallmark of high-performing organizations is that human capital procedures are directly linked to achieving organizational objectives. The Secretariat's new merit-based appraisal system requires that managers set performance expectations for all staff and that the expectations be linked to achieving U.N. objectives.

Implementation of the new appraisal system helps illustrate the progress the Secretariat has made in reforming its human capital system. The appraisal system is intended to help introduce a results-based culture to the Secretariat by providing honest feedback to staff about their performance. Ratings are based on a staff member's performance in meeting expectations, as measured by agreed-upon indicators. In comparison, the old appraisal did not set work expectations; ratings were uniformly high, with about 80 percent of staff receiving the highest rating; and the Secretariat did not routinely compile statistics on staff performance. . . .

The Secretary General has also followed up on the application of the appraisal system. For the 1998/99 appraisal cycle, the Deputy Secretary General sent letters to two departments that had ratings markedly higher than the other departments. The letters instructed the departmental chiefs to counsel supervisors on the requirements for fair and well-documented ratings. He also sent letters to the promotion board informing the board that the ratings in these departments might be inflated and to consider this in its promotion decisions. Finally, in November 1999, the Under Secretary General issued an administrative instruction that set out the consequences of receiving less than fully successful performance ratings, ranging from not receiving the annual salary pay increase to dismissal, depending on the length of time the staff member had not fully met expectations.

The United Nations plans to fully put into place its human capital reforms over the next 2–4 years. The following examples help illustrate some of the progress made and the tasks remaining.

- Beginning in 1999, the Department of Management extended the use of the Integrated Management Information System—the Secretariat's data system on budget, finances, management, and personnel—to the entire Secretariat. This provided the Office of Human Resources Management with basic data on all Secretariat staff with a contract of 1 year or longer, such as staff hiring date, current and past positions, work location and office, nationality, age, and gender. The office now generates regular reports of the Secretariat workforce, including projections of retirements by position, grade level, and type of employment for short-term planning. While this development provides the United Nations with a basic management tool, several steps need to be taken to make the personnel information system fully functional, including linking the databases electronically with all offices (currently the Secretariat has real-time access to personnel data for 48 percent of professional staff—those located at headquarters in New York and at the offices in Geneva and Vienna); completing an inventory of existing staff skills and knowledge; and automating a list of job qualifications for each Secretariat position.
- The Secretariat has begun identifying and filling critical needs projected for the next 2–4 years but has not begun developing a long-range workforce planning strategy. This will start once basic tools are in place and after the General Assembly debates the U.N.'s future role at the millennium assembly in the summer and fall of the year 2000.
- The Office of Human Resources Management has developed a comprehensive plan to improve recruitment and mobility, which includes lateral moves, job exchanges, temporary assignments, and job rotation systems within departments and field missions. The office discussed these proposals with staff committees during 1999 and plans to continue discussing the proposals through April 2000, as part of its policy to consider all staff views regarding human capital reforms. At the end of April 2000, the Office plans to complete a report on the proposal and submit it to the General Assembly, which must approve any changes to staff rules and regulations needed to implement the proposal.

## Reforms to Manage for Results Not Yet Adopted

A core element of the U.N. reform was to introduce processes to hold the U.N. Secretariat accountable for results by (1) focusing and clarifying the objectives member states expected the Secretariat to achieve; and (2) adopting performance-oriented programming and budgeting, that is, linking budgeted activities with performance expectations and measures. The United Nations is considering these initiatives, including the use of performance measures in its principal planning document—the medium-term plan. However, these proposals have not yet been adopted because some member states believe they are tactics to cut the budget. Another problem is that the Secretariat does not have an overall system to monitor and evaluate the results and impact of its programs. Such a system is necessary to implement performance management. . . .

The Secretary General proposed that the General Assembly focus the Secretariat's work by limiting the number of new work requirements or mandates for the Secretariat and clearly stating what it expected the Secretariat to do. These initiatives were not adopted. For 1997 and 1998, the most recent 2-year period for which information was available, we found that the number of new tasks mandated by the General Assembly increased from 246 to 587 and that 20 percent of these mandates had vague or open-ended expectations.

The Secretary General also proposed revising the budget process to focus on performance. He proposed that budgets would specify not only program costs but also expected program results and performance indicators. Member states could thus hold the Secretariat accountable for results. The Secretary General further proposed intermediate steps to prepare for and build confidence in this results-based approach, such as developing acceptable and reliable performance indicators; incorporating qualitative information in the performance measures; and pilot-testing proposed changes. The General Assembly is considering these proposals but has not yet approved them. Some member states are concerned that performance-oriented budgeting is a tactic to cut the U.N. budget. For example, in 1998, the Group of 77—a block of over 130 U.N. member states classified as developing countries took the position that results-based budgeting was a radical departure from accepted practices. They stated there should be no predetermined ceilings on budgets, that all mandates should be fully funded, and that any attempt to use results-based budgeting to cut the budget would be resisted. Although the General Assembly has not yet approved performance budgeting, it authorized the Secretariat to specify expected program accomplishments and performance indicators in its primary program planning document—the medium-term plan.

Member states were also concerned that the Secretariat lacked a system to monitor and evaluate program results and impact. Currently, numerous U.N. departments monitor their programs, and over 20 U.N. departments and offices have their own evaluation units. However, in the absence of results-oriented budgeting, monitoring largely involves counting outputs, such as the number of conferences held or staff years spent. Evaluations do not systematically provide information on program impact and whether objectives have been met. Furthermore, the United Nations has not developed a centralized strategy to improve monitoring and evaluation. Presently there is no centralized strategy that identifies limitations or gaps in existing efforts, employs guides to help provide some consistency and reliability in evaluation, or creates an approach to unify monitoring and evaluation functions to support performance-oriented budgeting.

## Conclusions and Recommendations

What distinguishes this U.N. reform from others tried in the past is the effort to transform the United Nations into a performance-based organization by implementing interrelated reform initiatives. The initiatives put into place thus far—substantially realigning the organization and introducing a merit-based appraisal system tied to U.N. objectives—are moving the United Nations in this direction. There is also evidence that these reforms are strengthening operations on the ground, where United Nations services and programs are actually delivered. However, without fully implementing programming, budgeting, and evaluation processes focused on performance, the U.N. will not have the management systems to sustain the gains made and transform the organization.

To help ensure that the United Nations maintains momentum in its overall reform efforts, our report recommends that the Secretary of State report annually to the Congress on the status of the Secretary General's reform plan, including an assessment of whether U.N. agencies and departments are effectively coordinating efforts at the country level, effectively implementing a results-oriented human capital system, and effectively implementing a performance-oriented management system.

Additionally, to support the United Nations in transforming the organization into one that is performance oriented and continuously improves, we recommend that the Secretary of State and the Permanent Representative of the United States to the United Nations work with other member states to

- take intermediate steps at the Secretariat to implement results-oriented budgeting, such as setting measurable goals and performance indicators for each section of the budget and
- require the Secretariat to develop an organizational strategy for monitoring and evaluating the results and impact of Secretariat activities.

The Department of State, the U.S. Mission to the United Nations, and the United Nations generally agreed with our findings on U.N. reform. State and the U.S. Mission also said they would report regularly to the Congress, in the context of the oversight process, on the status of the U.N. reform plan and would continue working on improving the U.N.'s planning, budgeting, and evaluation systems.

# CHEN ON HIS INAUGURATION
# AS PRESIDENT OF TAIWAN
## May 20, 2000

*Taiwan voters in March ended the half-century rule of the Nationalist Party, which had dominated the island since its leaders fled mainland China following the communist takeover there in 1949. Chen Shui-bian, an opposition leader who had espoused independence from China, was narrowly elected president on March 18, 2000. He became only the second man to win the Taiwanese presidency in direct popular elections—and the first opposition figure elected to office in the 5,000 years of Chinese history.*

*Chen's election alarmed China's leaders in Beijing, who considered Taiwan to be part of China and had threatened reprisals if the island moved toward any form of independence. Since 1949, there had been conflicting claims of who had sovereignty over Taiwan: the communist People's Republic of China, which controlled the mainland and had its capital in Beijing, or the Republic of China, which controlled only Taiwan and a handful of small islands and had its capital in Taipei.*

*Chen, leader of the Democratic Progressive Party, succeeded Lee Teng-hui, who during his dozen years as Nationalist Party chairman had moved both his party and Taiwan away from authoritarianism and toward democracy. Ironically, it was Lee—rather than his handpicked candidate defeated by Chen—who became the target of outraged Nationalist Party supporters after the election.*

## Chen's Rise to Power

*Chen was born in February 1951, two years after Nationalist government leader Chiang Kai-shek and his followers fled to Taiwan following the communist victory in a civil war on the mainland. After earning a law degree from Taiwan National University, Chen became active in opposition politics by defending pro-democracy figures who had been arrested by the repressive Nationalist Party regime. He was elected to the Taipei city council in 1981, and in 1986 he was imprisoned for eight months for his opposition activities.*

*Chen won a seat in the National Assembly in 1989, and four years later was elected mayor of Taipei, running as the candidate of the pro-independence Democratic Progressive Party. He aggressively tackled the corruption that had become entrenched in the island's politics during the half century of one-party control, but he also made many enemies with his authoritarian style of governing. Chen was defeated for reelection in 1998 by a popular Nationalist Party candidate, Ma Ying-jeou.*

*After that defeat, Chen adopted a more conciliatory style as he built a base of support for a run for the presidency. Chen's big break came when President Lee elbowed aside James Soong, a former close aide who was one of the Nationalist Party's most popular leaders, and chose Vice President Lien Chan as the party's presidential candidate. Soong ran as an independent, effectively splitting the Nationalist Party. That enabled Chen to emerge as a viable candidate for Taiwanese wanting new leadership and the elimination of political corruption.*

*Aside from his decidedly uncharismatic speaking style, Chen's biggest obstacle was the widespread perception that his party's pro-independent position might bring a violent reaction from Beijing. To soothe the nerves of voters, Chen promised that he would not provoke leaders on the mainland. Even so, Beijing allowed itself to be provoked. Chinese officials made several threats in the weeks before the election, apparently aimed at intimidating Taiwan voters into defeating Chen. China on February 21 issued a lengthy "white paper" explicitly threatening the use of military force against Taiwan if the island continued to delay reunification. Beijing's clumsy attempt to sway Taiwan's election against Chen failed. On election day, Chen won a plurality of the vote, 39 percent. Soong finished second with 36.5 percent, and Lien finished third in the five-candidate field with 23 percent.*

*Chen and his supporters were ecstatic, but the most dramatic reaction came from Nationalist Party faithful, several thousand of whom took to the streets the day after the election, surrounded the party headquarters building, and noisily denounced President Lee, who had been the island's most popular politician. Many of the demonstrators charged that Lee was responsible for splitting the party, and some even accused him of deliberately throwing the election to Chen. Lee was forced to barricade himself in the headquarters building for several hours until he could leave under a heavy police escort. One of his top lieutenants was pulled from a car and beaten by protesters.*

## The "One China" Issue

*Throughout the previous fifty years, the conflicting claims on Taiwan had poisoned relations between the island and the mainland. Until 1987 the Nationalist Party ruled Taiwan with an authoritarian hand, under the terms of martial law, but generally tried to avoid provoking China. In fact, by the 1980s the aging rulers of the Nationalist Party chose not to challenge Beijing's formulation that there was only "one China." For all practical purposes the Nationalist leaders had given up the pretense that their Republic of China still held sovereignty over the mainland as well as Taiwan. In-stead, many Nationalist Party leaders appeared to hope for a reconciliation between Taiwan and the mainland—but only after communism had died out in China, as they assumed was inevitable. In 1992 and 1993 representatives from the two sides held high-level, but unofficial, talks that raised expectations for an eventual settlement.*

*Lee, a native-born Taiwanese who became president in 1988, gradually moved away from established Nationalist Party doctrine and began seeking international recognition of Taiwan's government through a type of associate membership in the United Nations. When that approach failed, Lee sought, and eventually got, permission to visit the United States, on an unofficial basis. Beijing vigorously opposed his 1995 visit, claiming that the United States was retreating on its 1979 policy of not recognizing Taiwan's government. China in 1995 and 1996 also conducted war games and missile tests in the Taiwan Strait, apparently intended to influence Taiwan's legislative and presidential elections in those years. The Clinton administration sent two aircraft carrier battle groups into the strait as a show of force on Taiwan's behalf, and Lee handily won Taiwan's first-ever direct presidential election in 1996.*

*Lee again provoked a sharp reaction from Beijing in July 1999 when he called for "state to state" negotiations between Taiwan and the mainland. Chinese officials viewed that formulation as verging on a declaration of independence for Taiwan.*

*The days just before Taiwan's 2000 presidential election brought new warnings of potential trouble if Chen was elected. Chinese prime minister Zhu Rongji warned that "the people of China are ready to shed blood" if Taiwan declared independence. Chen's reaction was far from conciliatory: "Taiwan is an independent, sovereign country," he said. "It is not a part of the People's Republic of China." However, Chen said that as president he would not declare outright independence. But then on election night Chen declared that Taiwan "will never be a second Hong Kong or a second Macao"—the two city-states that had reverted to Chinese control in the late 1990s after the end of long-term leases held by Great Britain and Portugal, respectively.* (Hong Kong handover, Historic Documents of 1997, p. 501)

*In that tense atmosphere, Chen's election posed a problem for the United States, which had encouraged democracy in Taiwan but had wanted the island's leaders to avoid taking steps that would provoke Beijing. Four days after the election, Clinton sent former Rep. Lee H. Hamilton, a respected foreign affairs expert, to Taipei as an unofficial envoy. Hamilton carried a message urging restraint on Chen's part. Among other concerns, the Clinton administration worried that any precipitous action by Beijing would torpedo congressional support for pending legislation approving a U.S.-China trade agreement.* (China trade bill, p. 213)

*Chen's election came at a difficult time for the United States, as the Clinton administration was in the process of considering Taiwan's request to buy a weapons system that China considered to be provocative. The United States was Taiwan's major source of weapons, and China viewed Washing-*

ton's decisions on what to sell Taiwan as interfering with its internal affairs. Early in 2000 the issue was Taiwan's request for four advanced naval destroyers equipped with the sophisticated Aegis system of missiles and radar capable of tracking dozens of targets. Despite intense pressure from congressional Republican leaders to approve that sale, the Clinton administration on April 17 decided against it. Instead, the administration agreed to sell Taiwan several other defensive missile systems and a radar system intended to give Taiwan an early warning of an attack.

The actual impact of U.S. diplomacy at this stage was difficult to discern, but between the election and his May 20 inauguration Chen took a conciliatory stand toward China, offering to hold a peace summit and saying he was willing to consider some form of loose "confederation" between Taiwan and China. In his inaugural address, Chen repeated his preelection promise not to declare independence as long as China "has no intention to use military force against Taiwan."

Chen's approach did little to satisfy the leaders in Beijing, who complained that he was avoiding their "one China" formula. "Without accepting the one China principle, there is no foundation for talks and negotiations between the two sides," the official Chinese Xinhua News Agency said May 21. "Not only will a relaxation and improvement of relations be difficult, it could lead to conflict and provoke a crisis."

A month later, on June 20, Chen went somewhat beyond his previous stance, suggesting that he and Chinese president Jiang Zemin should emulate the dramatic peacemaking effort of North Korean leader Kim Jong-il and South Korean president Kim Dae-Jung, who had just held a historic summit meeting in Pyongyang. "If North and South Korea can, why can't the two sides of the [Taiwan] strait?" he said. (Korean talks, p. 359)

China rejected that overture, but a week later, on June 27, Chen took yet another conciliatory step. He told visiting American scholars that he recognized the "one China" principle, but in the context of a vague 1992 agreement between the two sides. Chen said he understood the 1992 accord as allowing China and Taiwan to interpret the "one China" principle as each saw fit. The Chinese government—in a June 29 statement rejecting Chen's latest move—said it viewed the 1992 agreement merely as leaving a precise definition of the "one China" principle unsettled for the time being. China repeated its position on November 29, accusing Chen of using "technicalities" to distort the 1992 agreement.

One small but potentially important step toward reconciliation came December 28, when Chinese officials accepted a Taiwanese plan for limited direct trade. In the past, Taiwan had required all exchanges with the mainland to go through Hong Kong (which was a British colony until 1997) or third countries. But a new plan accepted by China would allow some tourists, and limited quantities of trade goods, to travel between two of Taiwan's offshore islands (Quemoy and Matsu, both in the Taiwan Strait) and the mainland province of Fujian.

The year's diplomatic maneuvering made it clear that Taiwan and China were still far apart on the fundamental question of whether, or when, the is-

*land would again be united with China. Despite Beijing's occasional threats of military action to retake Taiwan, and despite the growing commercial ties between the island and the mainland, by the end of 2000 it seemed clear that few Taiwanese were ready to merge with the much less prosperous mainland, which was governed by one of the world's most authoritarian regimes.*

## *Chen's Difficult Months*

*Even setting aside the inevitable controversy over Taiwan-China relations, Chen's first months in office were not easy. The island's economy, which had generally survived the battering of the 1997 East Asian financial crisis, was facing a slump. The chief causes were a sharp drop in worldwide demand for computer chips and personal computers, which had been among the island's leading exports; the steady migration of Taiwanese business investments to the mainland, where operating costs were much lower; and a sharp decline in the real estate market, which coupled with the other factors led to a surge of bad loans held by Taiwanese banks. At year's end Taiwan was facing a banking crisis, potentially similar in magnitude to those that had undermined the economies of Thailand, Indonesia, Japan, and other Asian countries during the late 1990s.* (Asian financial crisis, Historic Documents of 1997, p. 832; Historic Documents of 1998, p. 722)

*Chen also created a huge storm of controversy when he followed through on his party's antinuclear power platform and announced plans to scrap a partially built $5.5 billion nuclear power plant that had been initiated by the previous Nationalist Party government. That action contributed to a run on the Taiwan stock market that trimmed nearly one-third of the value of its shares. A coalition of Nationalist Party members and other opposition parties, who controlled a majority of votes in the National Assembly, threatened in November to push through legislation forcing a national referendum on recalling Chen. But after Chen apologized for causing the crisis, polls showed strong majorities of the public opposing the recall move, and the drive to oust him from office fizzled—at least for the moment. Foiled on the recall front, Chen's opponents in December unleashed a blizzard of personal attacks on the president, accusing him of financial improprieties and conducting an affair with a female aide. By year's end those attacks apparently had succeeded in again damaging Chen's public support.*

*Following are excerpts from the text of the address delivered May 20, 2000, by Chen Shui-bian, upon his inauguration as president of the Republic of China (Taiwan). The document was obtained from the Internet at http://th.gio.gov.tw/pi2000/dow_1 .htm.*

Leaders of our friendly nations, distinguished guests and compatriots from Taiwan and abroad;

This is a glorious moment; this is also a solemn moment full of hope. I thank our distinguished guests, who have come here from afar, as well as those friends from around the world who love democracy and care about Taiwan, for sharing this glorious moment with us.

We are here today, not just to celebrate an inauguration, but to witness the flowering of hard-won democratic values and the dawn of a new era.

On the eve of the 21st century, the people of Taiwan have completed a historic alternation of political parties in power. This is not only the first of its kind in the history of the Republic of China, but also an epochal landmark for Chinese communities around the world. Taiwan has not only set a new model for the Asian experience of democracy, but has also added an inspiring example to the third wave of democracy the world over.

The election for the 10th-term president of the Republic of China has clearly shown the world that the fruits of freedom and democracy are not easy to come by. Twenty-three million people, through the power of determined will, have dispelled enmity with love, overcome intimidation with hope, and conquered fear with faith.

With our sacred votes we have proved to the world that freedom and democracy are indisputable universal values, and that peace is humanity's highest goal.

The outcome of Taiwan's year 2000 presidential election is not the victory of an individual or a political party. It is a victory of the people as well as a victory for democracy, because we have, while attracting global attention, transcended fear, threats and oppression and bravely risen to our feet together.

**Taiwan stands up, demonstrating a firm insistence on reason and a sturdy faith in democracy.**

**Taiwan stands up, representing the self-confidence of the people and the dignity of the country.**

**Taiwan stands up, symbolizing the quest for hope and the realization of dreams.**

Dear compatriots, let's always remember this moment; let's always remember to value and feel gratitude for it, because the fruits of democracy did not come out of the blue. We reaped the fruits only after we had been subjected to many perils and countless hardships. If not for the fearless sacrifice of our democratic forebears, if not for the unswerving faith of the tens of millions of Taiwanese people in freedom and democracy, we could not possibly be standing on our beloved land today and celebrating a glorious occasion that belongs to all the people.

Today, it is as if we are standing before a fresh new gate of history. In the process of democratization, the Taiwanese people have created a brand-new key to our shared destiny. The new century's gates of hope are soon to open. We are humble but not submissive. We are full of self-confidence but do not have the slightest bit of complacence.

Since that moment on March 18 when the election results came to light, I have accepted the mandate of all Taiwanese people in a most earnest and humble frame of mind, and have vowed to devote all my heart, knowledge and courage to assuming the heavy responsibility for our country's future.

I personally understand that the significance of the alternation of political parties and of the peaceful transition of power lies not in that it is a change of personnel or political parties. Nor in that it is a dynastic change. Rather, it is the return of state and government power to the people through a democratic procedure. The country belongs to the people, rather than to any individual or political party. The government and its officials, from the head of state down to the rank-and-file employees, exist for the service of the people.

The alternation of political parties does not mean an across-the-board negation of the past. We should be fair in evaluating the contributions made by those in power throughout the ages. Mr. Lee Teng-hui deserves our highest tribute and heartfelt gratitude for his promotion of democratic reforms and for his excellent performance during his twelve years of leadership.

Taiwan society has rallied and participated energetically in the election. Despite the diverse views and stances, all individuals share the same commitment—to come forward for the sake of their political ideas and the country's future. We believe that the end of an election is the beginning of reconciliation. After the curtain falls on emotional campaigns, rationality should prevail. Under the supreme principles of national interest and the welfare of the people, those in power and in opposition should both fulfill their mandates given by the people and realize the ideals of fair competition in multiparty politics, as well as the checks and balances of democratic politics.

A democratic society with fair competition, tolerance and trust is the strongest impetus for a nation's development. Placing national interests above those of political parties, we should solidify the will of the people and seek consensus among the ruling and opposition parties, to promote the country's progress and reforms.

"A government for all people" and "rule by the clean and upright" are promises I made to the people during the campaign period. They are also Taiwan's key to stepping over its fault lines and rising to a higher level in the future.

The spirit of "a government for all people" lies in the fact that "the government exists for the people." The people are the masters and shareholders of the state. The government should rule on the basis of majority public opinion. The interests of the people should reign supreme over those of any political party or individual.

I have always taken pride in being a member of the Democratic Progressive Party, but from the moment I take my oath and assume the presidency, I will put all my efforts into fulfilling my role as a "president for all people." As in the formation of the new government, we recruit people according to their talents and do not discriminate on the basis of ethnicity, gender or party affiliation. The welfare of the populace shall be our primary goal in the future.

"Rule by the clean and upright" has as its topmost priority the elimination of "black gold"—the involvement of organized crime and moneyed interests in politics—and the eradication of vote-buying. For a long time, the Taiwanese people have been deeply repelled by moneyed politics and the interference of organized crime. Vote-buying in grassroots elections has also robbed the people of their right to elect the wise and the able, and tainted the development of Taiwan's democracy.

Today, I am willing to promise hereby that the new government will eliminate vote-buying and crack down on "black gold" politics, so that Taiwan can rise above such sinking forces and ensure rule by the clean and upright. We must give the people a clean political environment.

In the area of government reforms, we need to establish a government that is clean, efficient, far-sighted, dynamic, highly flexible and responsive, in order to ensure Taiwan's competitiveness in the face of increasingly fierce global competition. The age of "large and capable" governments has now passed, replaced by one of "small and effective" governments, which have established partnership relations with the people. We should accelerate the streamlining of government functions and organization and actively expand the role of public participation.

This will not only allow the public to fully utilize its energy but also significantly reduce the government's burdens.

Similar partnership relations should also be set up between the central and local governments. We want to break the authoritarian and centralized control over both power and money. We want to realize the spirit of local autonomy, where the local and central governments share resources and responsibilities, where "the central government will not do what the local governments can." Whether in the east, west, north or south, or whether on Taiwan proper or on offshore islands, all will enjoy balanced, pluralistic development, and the gap between urban and rural areas will be reduced.

We should understand that the government is no panacea for all ills. The driving force for economic development and societal progress is the people. Over the past half-century, the Taiwanese people have toiled hard to create an economic miracle that has won global applause, and to lay the foundation for the survival and development of the Republic of China. Today, facing the impact of the fast-changing information technologies and trade liberalization, Taiwan must move toward a knowledge-based economy. High-tech industries need to be constantly innovative, while traditional ones have to undergo transformation and upgrading.

In the future, the government should not necessarily play the role of a "leader" or "manager." On the contrary, it should be the "supporter" and "service provider," as expected by private enterprises. The responsibility of a modern government is to raise administrative efficiency, improve the domestic investment environment, and maintain financial order and stock market stability, so as to allow the economy to move toward full liberalization and globalization through fair competition. Based on these principles, the vitality of the public will naturally bloom and create a new phase in Taiwan's economic miracle.

Apart from consolidating democratic achievements, promoting government reforms, and raising economic competitiveness, the new government should, as its foremost objective, closely watch the public opinion and implement reforms accordingly, so that the people on this land can live with more dignity, greater self-confidence and a better quality of life. . . .

We believe that the Republic of China, with its democratic achievements and technological and economic prowess, can certainly continue to play an indispensable role in the international community. In addition to strengthening the existing relations with friendly nations, we want to actively participate in all types of international nongovernmental organizations. Through humanitarian care, economic cooperation, cultural exchanges and various other ways, we will actively participate in international affairs, expand Taiwan's room for survival in the international arena, and contribute to the welfare of the international community.

Besides, we are also willing to commit a more active contribution in safeguarding international human rights. The Republic of China cannot and will not remain outside global human rights trends. We will abide by the Universal Declaration of Human Rights, the International Convention for Civil and Political Rights, and the Vienna Declaration and Program of Action. We will bring the Republic of China back into the international human rights system.

The new government will urge the Legislative Yuan to ratify the International Bill of Rights as a domestic law of Taiwan, so that it will formally become the "Taiwan Bill of Rights." We hope to set up an independent national human rights commission in Taiwan, thereby realizing an action long advocated by the United Nations. We will also invite two outstanding nongovernmental organizations, the International Commission of Jurists and Amnesty International, to assist us in our measures to protect human rights and make the Republic of China into a new indicator for human rights in the 21st century.

We firmly believe that at no time, nor in any corner of the world, can the meaning and values of freedom, democracy and human rights be ignored or changed.

The 20th century left us with a major lesson—that war is a failure of humanity. Waged for whatever lofty purposes or high-sounding reasons, war is the greatest harm to freedom, democracy and human rights.

Over the past one hundred plus years, China has suffered imperialist aggression, which left indelible wounds. Taiwan has had an even sadder fate, tormented by brute force and colonial rule. These similar historical experiences should bring mutual understanding between the people on the two sides of the Taiwan Strait, setting a solid foundation for pursuing freedom, democracy and human rights together. However, due to the long period of separation, the two sides have developed vastly different political systems and ways of life, obstructing empathy and friendship between the people on the two sides, and even creating a wall of divisiveness and confrontation.

Today, as the Cold War has ended, it is time for the two sides to cast aside the hostility left from the old era. We do not need to wait further because there is a new opportunity now for the two sides to create an era of reconciliation together.

The people on the two sides of the Taiwan Strait share the same ancestral, cultural, and historical background. While upholding the principles of democracy and parity, building upon the existing foundations, and constructing conditions for cooperation through good will, we believe that the leaders on both sides possess enough wisdom and creativity to jointly deal with the question of a future "one China."

I fully understand that, as the popularly elected 10th-term president of the Republic of China, I must abide by the Constitution, maintain the sovereignty, dignity and security of our country, and ensure the well-being of all citizens. Therefore, as long as the CCP regime has no intention to use military force against Taiwan, I pledge that during my term in office, I will not declare independence, I will not change the national title, I will not push forth the inclusion of the so-called "state-to-state" description in the Constitution, and I will not promote a referendum to change the status quo in regard to the question of independence or unification. Furthermore, there is no question of abolishing the Guidelines for National Unification and the National Unification Council.

History has proved that war will lead to more hatred and enmity, without the least help to the development of mutual relations. Chinese people emphasize the difference between statesmanship and hegemony, believing in the philosophy that a government which employs benevolence "will please those near and appeal to those from afar," and "when those from afar will not submit, then one must practice kindness and virtue to attract them." Such Chinese wisdom will remain a universal value.

Under the leadership of Mr. Deng Xiaoping and Mr. Jiang Zemin, the mainland has created a miracle of economic openness. In Taiwan, over a half century, not only have we created a miracle economy, we have also created the political marvel of democracy. On such a basis, as long as the governments and people on the two sides of the Taiwan Strait can interact more, following the principles of "goodwill reconciliation, active cooperation, and permanent peace," while at the same time respecting the free choice of the people and excluding unnecessary obstacles, both sides of the Strait can make great contributions to the prosperity and stability of the Asia-Pacific region. Both sides will also create a glorious civilization for humanity.

Dear compatriots, we hope so much to share the moving scene of this moment with all Chinese-speaking people around the world. The wide Ketagelan Boulevard before us was bristling with security guards only a few years ago. The building behind me used to be the Governor General's Mansion during the colonial era. Today, we gather here to extol the glory and joy of democracy with songs of the land and the voice of the people.

With a little reflection, our compatriots should be able to appreciate the deep and far-reaching meaning of this moment:

**Authoritarianism and force can only bring surrender for one time, while democracy and freedom are values that will endure forever.**

**Only by adhering to the will of the people can we pioneer the paths of history and build enduring architecture.**

Today, as the son of a tenant farmer with a poor family background, I have struggled and grown on this land and, after experiencing defeat and tribulation, I have finally won the trust of the people to take up the great responsibility of leading the country. My individual achievements are minor, but the message is valuable because each citizen of Formosa is a "child of Taiwan" just like me. In whatever difficult environment, Taiwan will be like a selfless, loving mother, who never stops giving her children opportunities and who helps them realize beautiful dreams.

The spirit of the "child of Taiwan" reveals to us that even though Taiwan, Penghu, Kinmen and Matsu are tiny islands on the rim of the Pacific, the map of our dreams knows no limits. The map extends all the way to the horizon as long as our 23 million compatriots fear no hardship and move forward hand in hand.

Dear compatriots, this magnificent moment belongs to all the people. All grace and glory belongs to Taiwan—our eternal Mother. Together, let's extend our gratitude to the earth and our respect to the people.

Long live freedom and democracy!

Long live the people of Taiwan!

We pray for the prosperity of the Republic of China, and for the health and happiness of all compatriots and all our distinguished guests!

# UNITED NATIONS CONFERENCE ON NUCLEAR NONPROLIFERATION
## May 20, 2000

*For the first time ever, the five original countries possessing nuclear weapons made an "unequivocal" pledge in 2000 to rid themselves of those weapons. The United States, Russia, Britain, China, and France did not set a specific time limit for nuclear disarmament, but their willingness to make the pledge was widely seen as a historic turning point in the fifty-five-year history of the nuclear era.*

*The disarmament pledge was one of the principal achievements of a month-long conference at United Nations headquarters in New York that reviewed the thirty-year-old nuclear nonproliferation treaty. The treaty was intended to halt the spread of nuclear weapons. Despite the end of the cold war a decade earlier, nuclear arms control efforts were making limited progress in 2000, and in some respects were sliding backwards. The United States and Russia, the two major nuclear powers, were no longer actively negotiating to reduce the size of their arsenals. A multilateral Conference on Disarmament, meeting in Geneva, Switzerland, was making no progress toward a treaty banning production of material necessary for nuclear weapons. India and Pakistan had conducted competing nuclear explosions in 1998, creating fears of a nuclear weapons race in South Asia. The United States and fifteen other nations were blocking implementation of a treaty banning all nuclear weapons tests. And the United States was testing elements of a system to defend itself against ballistic missile attacks, a move that was opposed even by close U.S. allies as endangering the nuclear balance of power that had prevented war among the major powers for a half century.*

### Treaty Background

*The nonproliferation treaty was negotiated during the height of the cold war in the 1960s and took effect in 1970. The central point of the treaty was a bargain between the five original nuclear powers (called the "nuclear weapons states") and the rest of the world (called the "nonnuclear weapons states"). The five nuclear powers promised in the treaty to give up their weapons eventually and to share technology for the peaceful uses of nuclear energy. The nonnuclear weapons states promised not to acquire such weapons nor to help any other state do so. The treaty established a complex series of procedures under which countries would allow their civil nuclear power facilities to be monitored by the International Atomic Energy Agency to ensure that nuclear technology and materials were not diverted to weapons.*

*To overcome the resistance of many countries—primarily those that did not possess nuclear weapons—negotiators originally put a twenty-five year limit on the treaty. A review conference in 1995 agreed to extend the treaty indefinitely, with follow-up reviews every five years afterward. A major element of the 1995 review was a promise by the nuclear powers to pursue "systematic and progressive efforts to reduce nuclear weapons globally, with the ultimate goal of eliminating those weapons." The key word in that phrase was "ultimate" because it allowed plenty of maneuvering room for any of the five powers that had no serious intention of eliminating its weapons.* (1995 Conference, Historic Documents of 1995, p. 233)

*By the time of the 2000 review conference, 187 countries had ratified the nonproliferation treaty and pledged to live by its terms. Cuba, India, Israel, and Pakistan were the only holdouts; of that group, only Cuba did not possess nuclear weapons. Under the treaty, India, Israel, and Pakistan were considered "unrecognized nuclear weapons states" because the rest of the world did not recognize the legality of their weapons.* (Indian and Pakistani weapons tests, Historic Documents of 1998, p. 326)

## Negotiations Toward an Agreement

*As they gathered in New York on April 24, conference delegates faced a host of difficult issues on the nuclear arms control agenda, most importantly the obvious lack of progress toward the disarmament that was supposed to be the ultimate goal of the nonproliferation treaty. Many of the countries that did not have nuclear weapons were becoming increasingly annoyed by that lack of progress, and they formed several groups to put pressure on the nuclear powers. Ultimately, the most successful of those groups was the New Agenda Coalition, which opened the conference with a strongly worded demand that the nuclear powers make "an unequivocal undertaking" to eliminate their nuclear weapons and engage in "an accelerated process of negotiations" toward that end during the next five years. Members of that coalition were Brazil, Egypt, Ireland, Mexico, New Zealand, South Africa, and Sweden.*

*To an outside observer, the coalition's demands might have seemed noncontroversial. But in the context of arms control negotiations, the five nuclear weapons states were willing to make unambiguous pledges—even pledges that they might not feel compelled to carry out—only if other countries were forced to make concessions as well.*

*Central to the conference negotiations were the difficult issues raised by the U.S. proposal to build a national defense that was intended to protect the country against ballistic missile attacks by "rogue" nations such as North Korea or Iraq. It was generally agreed, even by many supporters of such a defense system, that actual construction would violate the terms of the 1972 Anti-ballistic Missile (ABM) treaty between the United States and the then-Soviet Union. Every previous conference on the nonproliferation treaty had declared the ABM treaty to be an essential "cornerstone" of arms control. Russia, which inherited the Soviet Union's ABM treaty responsibilities, insisted on similar wording in 2000. Nearly all other countries rejected Washington's reasoning for its defense system and accepted the Russian position on the ABM treaty. China also opposed a U.S. defense system because its use of satellites would lead to the "weaponization" of space.* (Missile defense, p. 677)

*After three weeks of negotiations, delegates gradually worked out compromises on the issues that stood in the way of a disarmament pledge. They reaffirmed the importance of the ABM treaty as an arms control "cornerstone" and avoided any direct reference to the U.S. missile defense plan.*

*In the key disarmament language, the five nuclear weapons powers made "an unequivocal undertaking" to "accomplish the total elimination of their nuclear arsenals leading to nuclear disarmament." The diplomatic significance of that language was that it did not include such qualifiers as "ultimate" or "eventual" that had muddied all previous disarmament pledges. The nuclear powers also agreed to numerous "practical steps" toward that goal, including abiding by existing treaties, reducing their weapons stocks both through unilateral actions and through bilateral treaties (such as the U.S.-Russian strategic arms treaties), and negotiating new treaties such as a ban on producing nuclear weapons materials.*

## Regional Issues

*In addition to the overarching question of whether the original nuclear powers would agree unconditionally to disarmament, the conference faced several major disagreements on regional issues, any one of which could have prevented the conference from reaching an overall agreement. The most divisive of those issues involved three countries (India, Israel, and Pakistan) that had developed nuclear weapons but refused to join the nonproliferation treaty, and two countries (Iraq and North Korea) that had ratified the treaty but were widely suspected of trying to develop nuclear weapons anyway.*

*With their tests in 1998, India and Pakistan had jeopardized the entire rationale of the nonproliferation treaty, which was to halt the spread of nuclear weapons. Neither country had accepted the treaty, and both wanted to be recognized as nuclear powers, along with the five original nuclear states. The conference rejected that demand and instead voted to call on both India and Pakistan to accept the treaty and put their nuclear facilities under international supervision. In effect, the conference refused to accept the Indian and Pakistani weapons as legitimate under international law.*

*According to several observers, the single most troublesome issues con-*

*cerned Israel and Iraq. Several Arab states, led by Egypt, demanded that the conference denounce Israel's weapons as a threat to stability in the Middle East and call on Israel to accept the nonproliferation treaty—a step that would require its nuclear disarmament. The United States, Israel's most important ally, agreed to support the call on Israel to join the treaty. But the United States also wanted language noting that Iraq had failed to comply fully with United Nations Security Council resolutions requiring it to dismantle all its ballistic missiles and weapons of mass destruction, under UN supervision.*

*Because the United States and Iraq had suspended diplomatic relations at the outset of the 1991 Persian Gulf War, diplomats from the two nations could not negotiate with each other. Talks between the two nations were conducted through other diplomats, but there was little progress as the conference neared its scheduled end at midnight on May 19. At ten minutes to midnight, according to observers, the conference chairman, Abdallah Baali of Algeria, ordered the clock stopped. The indirect U.S.-Iraq negotiations continued until noon the next day, when the United States basically prevailed with its insistence on a call for Iraq to comply with the Security Council disarmament resolutions.*

*The United States and South Korea also insisted on including language demanding that North Korea live up to promises it had made in 1994 to turn over to international authorities all material it had developed for nuclear weapons. At U.S. insistence, North Korea had agreed to place all its nuclear programs under international observation, in return for a U.S.-led program to build two new nuclear power stations in the country. But as of 2000 U.S. officials were uncertain that North Korea actually had turned over all the weapons-grade nuclear material it had produced before 1994. (U.S.-North Korea talks, p. 866)*

## Assessments of the Conference

*UN Secretary General Kofi Annan hailed the conference agreement as "a significant step forward in humanity's pursuit of a more peaceful world—a world free of nuclear dangers, a world with strengthened global norms for nuclear nonproliferation and disarmament." And the chief U.S. representative, Robert Grey, said the conference affirmed that "strict observance of the [nonproliferation] treaty remains central to achieving its objectives."*

*Baali, the Algerian diplomat who chaired the conference, acknowledged that the outcome "may be seen as inadequate in view of the challenges before us." But using the standard language of diplomacy, he added: "It is in my view the best outcome we could have reached under the prevailing conditions."*

*Writing in the July-August edition of* Arms Control Today, *a publication of the U.S.-based Arms Control Association, Canadian nonproliferation expert Tariq Rauf noted that the conference reached an agreement only because nations "papered over deep differences" on such issues as national missile defense, the fate of the ABM treaty, and the need for disarmament.*

*Given the historic unwillingness of the nuclear powers to abandon their weapons, he said, "it is unlikely that the 'practical steps' agreed to" at the conference would be fulfilled by 2005, when the next conference was scheduled.*

## U.S.-Russian Arms Control

*Since the mid-1970s the most important element of nuclear arms control had been the relationship between the two nuclear superpowers: the United States and the Soviet Union. And the key to that relationship was a series of negotiations aimed at reducing the number of nuclear bombs and missiles in each country's arsenal. The Strategic Arms Limitation Treaty negotiated during the administration of Jimmy Carter and two Strategic Arms Reduction treaties (START) negotiated during the administrations of Ronald Reagan and George Bush stopped, and then reversed, the growth of the nuclear arsenals.*

*After the collapse of the Soviet Union at the end of 1991, arms control appeared to lose some of its urgency. President Bush and Russian president Boris Yeltsin signed the second START treaty (known as START II) in January 1993, but the U.S. Senate did not approve it until 1997. The Russian parliament withheld its approval until April 2000. That treaty called for each nation to reduce its arsenal of strategic missiles to between 3,000 and 3,500 warheads.*

*In 1997 President Bill Clinton and Yeltsin reached general agreement on terms for a START III treaty, which would reduce each country's arsenal to the range of 2,000–2,5000 warheads. But during the following three years there was little progress toward finishing the agreement. In 2000 the new Russian president, Vladimir Putin, began pushing for even deeper cuts in the two nuclear arsenals. He suggested that each side eliminate all but 1,500 warheads—about 10 percent of the total each country held before the first START treaty in the 1980s. Most analysts said Putin's proposal was driven by budgetary realities. Given its limited financial resources, Russia would be hard-pressed to maintain an up-to-date arsenal of more than about 1,500 warheads. Senior U.S. military officials reportedly opposed such a deep cut, and Clinton expressed hesitation on the matter during a June 4 summit meeting in Moscow. He said the step "would require us to change our strategic plan" and would need to be linked to development of a missile defense system.*

*Clinton's latter point, about the missile defense system, had become the major stumbling block in the U.S.-Russian strategic relationship. Moscow objected that the missile defense proposal would violate the ABM treaty and set off a new round of the nuclear arms race. Clinton administration officials said they believed the arms race issue could be addressed with diplomatic assurances and agreements. But they faced immediate diplomatic and legal hurdles under the ABM treaty, which allowed each superpower to build just one localized missile defense system—and banned a national system such as Clinton was considering.*

*The Clinton administration broached several ideas for modifying the ABM treaty to accommodate its proposed missile defense system but met with unrelenting opposition from Moscow. As an alternative, Putin proposed in May that the United States and Russia jointly develop an even more limited system to provide a defense against shorter-range ballistic missiles. At their June 4 summit meeting, Clinton and Putin failed to resolve the disagreement, and Putin held firm in opposing any change to the ABM treaty. "We are against having a cure that is worse than the disease," he said.*

*The issue became moot, at least for the moment, on September 1 when Clinton announced that he was deferring a decision on deploying the proposed missile defense system because of failures in Pentagon tests. Clinton's decision did not halt pressure for a missile defense from U.S. conservatives. His successor, George W. Bush, was committed to an even more ambitious system, regardless of what the Russians thought of the idea.*

*Following are excerpts from the "Final Document" approved May 20, 2000, by a consensus vote of the 2000 Review Conference of the Parties to the Treaty on the Nonproliferation of Nuclear Weapons, meeting at United Nations headquarters in New York, in which the 187 nations that had ratified the treaty reaffirmed its goals and issued an "unequivocal" call for the elimination of all nuclear weapons. The document was obtained from the Internet at http://www.un.org/Depts/dda/WMD/2000FD.pdf.*

## Articles I and II. . . .

1. The Conference reaffirms that the full and effective implementation of the Treaty and the regime of non-proliferation in all its aspects has a vital role in promoting international peace and security. The Conference reaffirms that every effort should be made to implement the Treaty in all its aspects and to prevent the proliferation of nuclear weapons and other nuclear explosive devices, without hampering the peaceful uses of nuclear energy by States Parties to the Treaty. The Conference remains convinced that universal adherence to the Treaty and full compliance of all Parties with its provisions are the best way to prevent the spread of nuclear weapons and other nuclear explosive devices.

2. The Conference recalls that the overwhelming majority of States entered into legally binding commitments not to receive, manufacture or otherwise acquire nuclear weapons or other nuclear explosive devices in the context, inter alia, of the corresponding legally binding commitments by the nuclear-weapon States to nuclear disarmament in accordance with the Treaty.

3. The Conference notes that the nuclear-weapon States reaffirmed their commitment not to transfer to any recipient whatsoever nuclear weapons or other nuclear explosive devices, or control over such weapons or explosive

devices directly, or indirectly, and not in any way to assist, encourage, or induce any non-nuclear-weapon State to manufacture or otherwise acquire nuclear weapons or other nuclear explosive devices, or control over such weapons or explosive devices.

4. The Conference notes that the non-nuclear-weapon States Parties to the Treaty reaffirmed their commitment not to receive the transfer from any transferor whatsoever of nuclear weapons or other nuclear explosive devices or of control over such weapons or explosive devices directly, or indirectly, not to manufacture or otherwise acquire nuclear weapons or other nuclear explosive devices, and not to seek or receive any assistance in the manufacture of nuclear weapons or other nuclear explosive devices. . . .

8. The Conference urges all States not yet party to the Treaty, namely Cuba, India, Israel and Pakistan, to accede to the Treaty as non-nuclear-weapon States, promptly and without condition, particularly those States that operate unsafeguarded nuclear facilities.

9. The Conference deplores the nuclear test explosions carried out by India and then by Pakistan in 1998. The Conference declares that such actions do not in any way confer a nuclear-weapon State status or any special status whatsoever. The Conference calls upon both States to undertake the measures set out in the United Nations Security Council resolution 1172 (1998).

10. The Conference also calls upon all State Parties to refrain from any action that may contravene or undermine the objectives of the Treaty as well as of the United Nations Security Council resolution 1172 (1998).

11. The Conference notes that the two States concerned have declared moratoriums on further testing and their willingness to enter into legal commitments not to conduct any further nuclear tests by signing and ratifying the Comprehensive Nuclear-Test-Ban Treaty. The Conference regrets that the signing and ratifying has not yet taken place despite their pledges to do so.

12. The Conference reiterates the call on those States that operate unsafeguarded nuclear facilities [those not monitored by the International Atomic Energy Agency, the IAEA] and that have not yet acceded to the Treaty on the Non-Proliferation of Nuclear Weapons to reverse clearly and urgently any policies to pursue any nuclear-weapon development or deployment and to refrain from any action which could undermine regional and international peace and security and the efforts of the international community towards nuclear disarmament and the prevention of nuclear weapons proliferation. . . .

## Article III. . . .

14. The Conference notes with concern that IAEA continues to be unable to verify the correctness and completeness of the initial declaration of nuclear material made by the Democratic People's Republic of Korea (DPRK) [North Korea], and is therefore unable to conclude that there has been no diversion of nuclear material in that country.

15. The Conference looks forward to the Democratic People's Republic of Korea (DPRK) fulfilling its stated intention to come into full compliance with its Treaty safeguards agreement with IAEA, which remains binding and in

force. The Conference emphasizes the importance of the Democratic People's Republic of Korea preserving and making available to IAEA all information needed to verify its initial declaration. . . .

34. The Conference, recalling the obligations of all States parties under articles I, II and III of the Treaty, calls upon all States parties not to cooperate or give assistance in the nuclear or nuclear-related field to States not party to the Treaty in a manner which assists them to manufacture nuclear weapons or other nuclear explosive devices. . . .

43. Expressing concern about the illicit trafficking of nuclear and other radioactive materials, the Conference urges all States to introduce and enforce appropriate measures and legislation to protect and ensure the security of such material. The Conference welcomes the activities in the fields of prevention, detection and response being undertaken by IAEA in support of efforts against illicit trafficking. The Conference acknowledges the Agency's efforts to assist member States in strengthening their regulatory control on the applications of radioactive materials, including its ongoing work on a registry of sealed sources. It also welcomes the Agency's activities undertaken to provide for the enhanced exchange of information among its Member States, including the continued maintenance of the illicit trafficking database. The Conference recognizes the importance of enhancing cooperation and coordination among States and among international organizations in preventing, detecting and responding to the illegal use of nuclear and other radioactive material. . . .

49. The Conference notes the agreement between the Russian Federation and the United States to convert in Russia 500 tonnes of high enriched uranium (HEU) from Russia's nuclear weapons to low enriched uranium for use in commercial reactors. It welcomes the conversion to date of over 80 tonnes of HEU in the framework of this agreement. The Conference also recognizes the affirmation by Presidents of the Russian Federation and the United States of the intention of each country to remove by stages approximately 50 tonnes of plutonium from their nuclear weapons programmes and convert it so that it can never be used in nuclear weapons. . . .

## Article VI. . . .

2. The Conference notes that, despite the achievements in bilateral and unilateral arms reduction, the total number of nuclear weapons deployed and in stockpile still amounts to many thousands. The Conference expresses its deep concern at the continued risk for humanity represented by the possibility that these nuclear weapons could be used.

3. The Conference takes note of the proposal made by the United Nations Secretary-General that the convening of a major international conference that would help to identify ways of eliminating nuclear dangers be considered at the Millennium Summit [held in September 2000].

4. The Conference reaffirms that the cessation of all nuclear weapon test explosions or any other nuclear explosions will contribute to the nonproliferation of nuclear weapons in all its aspects, to the process of nuclear disarmament leading to the complete elimination of nuclear weapons and, therefore, to the further enhancement of international peace and security.

5. The Conference welcomes the adoption by the General Assembly and subsequent opening for signature of the Comprehensive Nuclear-Test-Ban Treaty in New York on 24 September 1996, and notes that 155 States have signed it and that 56 of them, including 28 whose ratification is necessary for its entry into force, have deposited their instruments of ratification. The Conference welcomes the ratifications by France and the United Kingdom of Great Britain and Northern Ireland and the recent decision by the Duma of the Russian Federation to ratify the Treaty. The Conference calls upon all States, in particular on those 16 States [including the United States] whose ratification is a prerequisite for the entry into force of the Comprehensive Nuclear-Test-Ban Treaty, to continue their efforts to ensure the early entry into force of the Treaty. . . .

9. The Conference welcomes the significant progress achieved in nuclear weapons reductions made unilaterally or bilaterally under the Strategic Arms Reduction Treaty (START) process, as steps towards nuclear disarmament. Ratification of START II by the Russian Federation is an important step in the efforts to reduce strategic offensive weapons and is welcomed. Completion of ratification of START II by the United States remains a priority.

10. The Conference also welcomes the significant unilateral reduction measures taken by other nuclear-weapon States [a reference to France and the United Kingdom], including the close-down and dismantling of nuclear weapon related facilities. . . .

15. The Conference agrees on the following practical steps for the systematic and progressive efforts to implement Article VI of the Treaty on the Non-Proliferation of Nuclear Weapons and paragraphs 3 and 4(c) of the 1995 Decision on "Principles and Objectives for Nuclear Non-Proliferation and Disarmament":

1. The importance and urgency of signatures and ratifications, without delay and without conditions and in accordance with constitutional processes, to achieve the early entry into force of the Comprehensive Nuclear-Test-Ban Treaty.

2. A moratorium on nuclear-weapon-test explosions or any other nuclear explosions pending entry into force of that Treaty.

3. The necessity of negotiations in the Conference on Disarmament on a non-discriminatory, multilateral and internationally and effectively verifiable treaty banning the production of fissile material for nuclear weapons or other nuclear explosive devices in accordance with the statement of the Special Coordinator in 1995 and the mandate contained therein, taking into consideration both nuclear disarmament and nuclear non-proliferation objectives. The Conference on Disarmament is urged to agree on a programme of work which includes the immediate commencement of negotiations on such a treaty with a view to their conclusion within five years.

4. The necessity of establishing in the Conference on Disarmament an appropriate subsidiary body with a mandate to deal with nuclear disarmament. The Conference on Disarmament is urged to agree on a pro-

gramme of work which includes the immediate establishment of such a body.

5. The principle of irreversibility to apply to nuclear disarmament, nuclear and other related arms control and reduction measures.

6. An unequivocal undertaking by the nuclear-weapon States to accomplish the total elimination of their nuclear arsenals leading to nuclear disarmament to which all States parties are committed under Article VI.

7. The early entry into force and full implementation of START II and the conclusion of START III as soon as possible while preserving and strengthening the ABM Treaty as a cornerstone of strategic stability and as a basis for further reductions of strategic offensive weapons, in accordance with its provisions.

8. The completion and implementation of the Trilateral Initiative between the United States of America, the Russian Federation and the International Atomic Energy Agency.

9. Steps by all the nuclear-weapon States leading to nuclear disarmament in a way that promotes international stability, and based on the principle of undiminished security for all:
   • Further efforts by the nuclear-weapon States to reduce their nuclear arsenals unilaterally
   • Increased transparency [openness] by the nuclear-weapon States with regard to the nuclear weapons capabilities and the implementation of agreements pursuant to Article VI and as a voluntary confidence-building measure to support further progress on nuclear disarmament
   • The further reduction of non-strategic nuclear weapons, based on unilateral initiatives and as an integral part of the nuclear arms reduction and disarmament process
   • Concrete agreed measures to further reduce the operational status of nuclear weapons systems
   • A diminishing role for nuclear weapons in security policies to minimize the risk that these weapons ever be used and to facilitate the process of their total elimination
   • The engagement as soon as appropriate of all the nuclear-weapon States in the process leading to the total elimination of their nuclear weapons.

10. Arrangements by all nuclear-weapon States to place, as soon as practicable, fissile material designated by each of them as no longer required for military purposes under IAEA or other relevant international verification and arrangements for the disposition of such material for peaceful purposes, to ensure that such material remains permanently outside of military programmes.

11. Reaffirmation that the ultimate objective of the efforts of States in the disarmament process is general and complete disarmament under effective international control. . . .

13. The further development of the verification capabilities that will be required to provide assurance of compliance with nuclear disarmament agreements for the achievement and maintenance of a nuclear-weapon-free world. . . .

# Article VII

16. Regional issues
*The Middle East, particularly implementation of the 1995 Resolution on the Middle East. . . .*

6. The Conference invites all States, especially States of the Middle East, to reaffirm or declare their support for the objective of establishing an effectively verifiable Middle East zone free of nuclear weapons as well as other weapons of mass destruction, to transmit their declarations of support to the Secretary-General of the United Nations, and to take practical steps towards that objective. . . .

10. Bearing in mind the importance of full compliance with the Non-Proliferation Treaty, the Conference notes the statement of 24 April 2000 by the IAEA Director-General that, since the cessation of IAEA inspections in Iraq on 16 December 1998, the Agency has not been in a position to provide any assurance of Iraq's compliance with its obligations under UN Security Council Resolution 687. The Conference further notes that the IAEA carried out an inspection in January 2000 pursuant to Iraq's safeguards agreement with the IAEA during which the inspectors were able to verify the presence of the nuclear material subject to safeguards (low enriched, natural and depleted uranium). The Conference reaffirms the importance of Iraq's full continuous cooperation with the IAEA and compliance with its obligations.

*South Asia and other regional issues:*

11. The Conference emphasizes that nuclear disarmament and nuclear non-proliferation are mutually reinforcing.

12. With respect to the nuclear explosions carried out by India and then by Pakistan in May 1998, the Conference recalls Security Council Resolution 1172 (1998), adopted unanimously on 6 June 1998, and calls upon both States to take all of the measures set out therein. Notwithstanding their nuclear tests, India and Pakistan do not have the status of nuclear-weapon States.

13. The Conference urges India and Pakistan to accede to the Non-Proliferation Treaty as non-nuclear-weapon States and to place all their nuclear facilities under comprehensive Agency safeguards. The Conference further urges both States to strengthen their non-proliferation export control measures over technologies, material and equipment that can be used for the production of nuclear weapons and their delivery systems.

14. The Conference notes that India and Pakistan have declared moratoriums on further testing and their willingness to enter into legal commitments not to conduct any further nuclear testing by signing and

ratifying the Comprehensive Nuclear-Test-Ban Treaty. The Conference urges both States to sign the Treaty, in accordance with their pledges to do so.

15. The Conference notes the willingness expressed by India and Pakistan to participate in the negotiation in the Conference on Disarmament of a treaty banning the production of fissile material for nuclear weapons and other nuclear explosive devices. Pending the conclusion of a legal instrument, the Conference urges both countries to observe a moratorium on the production of such material. The Conference also urges both States to join other countries in actively seeking an early commencement of negotiations on this issue, in a positive spirit and on the basis of the agreed mandate, with a view to reaching early agreement.

16. The Conference notes with concern that, while the Democratic People's Republic of Korea remains a party to the Non-Proliferation Treaty, IAEA continues to be unable to verify the correctness and completeness of the initial declaration of nuclear material made by the Democratic People's Republic of Korea and is therefore unable to conclude that there has been no diversion of nuclear material in the Democratic People's Republic of Korea. The Conference looks forward to the fulfillment by the Democratic People's Republic of Korea of its stated intention to come into full compliance with its safeguards agreement with IAEA, which remains binding and in force. The Conference emphasizes the importance of action by the Democratic People's Republic of Korea to preserve and make available to IAEA all information needed to verify its initial inventory. . . .

# CLINTON ON HOUSE APPROVAL
# OF CHINA TRADE AGREEMENT
## May 24, 2000

*President Bill Clinton secured one of the most important achievements of his presidency in 2000 with congressional approval of legislation linked to a landmark U.S.-China trade agreement. The agreement was intended to open Chinese markets to U.S. goods and services and to pave the way for China's membership in the World Trade Organization (WTO), the Geneva-based organization that set the rules for world trade. Supported by business and farm groups but opposed by his own allies in labor, human rights, and environmental organizations, Clinton convinced both chambers of Congress that exposing China to the full force of world trade would be good for the U.S. economy and ultimately would force political reform in Beijing.*

*The key action came on May 24, 2000, when the House approved, by a 237–197 vote, legislation (PL 106–286) exempting China from a 1974 law giving Congress an annual opportunity to block normal trade relations with communist countries. The Senate adopted the legislation September 19 by a much broader 83–15 vote, and Clinton signed it into law on October 10.*

*Congressional approval of the legislation had the effect of endorsing a sweeping U.S.-China trade agreement reached in November 1999. That agreement—coupled with a comparable accord reached in June 2000 between China and the European Union—was a major step toward China's entry into the WTO.* (Trade agreement, Historic Documents of 1999, p. 724)

*Despite those developments, by late 2000 there was growing concern, both in Beijing and in Western capitals, that hard-line nationalist and communist factions within China might seek to block the country's entry into the WTO—or at least might stall Chinese compliance with key terms of WTO membership. Largely because of such concerns, Chinese entry into the WTO was postponed at least until early 2001.*

## *Lobbying the House*

*Ever since he convinced Congress in 1973 to support the North American Free Trade Agreement with Canada and Mexico, Clinton had argued that commerce would be the central component of U.S. involvement in the world in the post-cold war era. Free trade and open markets, Clinton said repeatedly in his travels both at home and abroad, would keep the U.S. economy strong, ensure good relations with friendly nations, and eventually lead to the triumph of democracy in nations with a history of dictatorship.* (North-American Free Trade Agreement, Historic Documents of 1993, p. 953)

*China was to be an important test of Clinton's argument. The adoption of economic reforms in the 1980s under the leadership of Deng Xiaoping had given China one of the fastest-growing economies in the world, but the country retained a rigid communist political system that stifled dissent and posed limits on the growth of free markets. The government's brutal suppression of student dissidents at Beijing's Tiananmen Square in 1989 led to international sanctions and a brief economic downturn, but by the early 1990s China's economy was again growing rapidly. After a 1994 international agreement created the WTO (as a successor to the post-World War II General Agreement on Tariffs and Trade), China's leaders decided to move to the next step of economic development by seeking membership in the new trade body.*

*Under WTO rules, China could join (or "accede to" in legal terminology) the WTO once it had negotiated bilateral trade agreements with a majority of the 130-some member nations and had agreed to accept WTO rules governing international trade; the most important of these rules required China to abandon state ownership of key industries and to allow free markets. A major step toward China's membership was the negotiation of a trade agreement with the United States, which had the world's biggest economy. The agreement signed on November 15, 1999, committed China to opening its markets to U.S. products and services, most importantly by reducing tariffs on imported goods from an average of 24.6 percent to an average of 9.4 percent. The agreement imposed no significant new requirements on the United States, which had opened its markets to Chinese trade two decades earlier.*

*Technically, Congress did not have to approve the trade agreement. But for the agreement to go into effect, and for the United States and China to have what was called "permanent normal trade relations," Congress needed to exempt China from the Jackson-Vanik amendment to the 1974 Trade Act (PL 93–618). That amendment, passed in reaction to the Soviet Union's refusal to allow emigration by its Jewish citizens, prohibited normal trade relations (at the time called "most favored nation" status) with any communist nation unless the president submitted an annual report to Congress stating that the country allowed free emigration. Congress could block the normal trade status by passing legislation overturning the president's report; in such a case, the United States would impose prohibitive tariffs on imports from that country. Congress had never rejected a presidential report, but the annual exercise was an embarrassment for China because it gave congressional critics regular opportunities to highlight that country's human rights abuses.*

*In that context, the 2000 debate on the China trade agreement had two components: a narrow issue of whether Congress would give up its leverage over China and a broader question of what the proper relationship should be between the United States and China. Much of the behind-the-scenes negotiating on Capitol Hill concerned the first issue, while most of the public debate concerned U.S.-Chinese economic and political relations. Clinton ultimately prevailed by making compromises on the narrow procedural issue while his administration—in collaboration with business groups—applied intense public pressure on Congress on the broader debate. Most attention focused on the House of Representatives, which was assumed to be narrowly divided on the matter. A strong majority of the Senate was on record as favoring the China trade bill.*

*The issue was one of the most heavily lobbied ones in recent years, with business and labor groups vying for the attention and support of a few dozen members who were undecided in the closing weeks before the vote. Business lobbies, led by the Chamber of Commerce of the United States and the Business Roundtable, spent nearly $10 million on television, magazine, and newspaper advertising favoring the bill. The campaign was reported to be the most expensive effort ever by American business to influence a single congressional vote. The AFL-CIO and its constituent labor unions also spent heavily on advertising and other lobbying tactics to oppose the bill. In the final week before the vote, the opposing sides flew business and labor leaders from members' congressional districts to Washington for one-on-one lobbying sessions. "We are sending so many people at these members that they can go home each night and tell their children they're famous," Chamber of Commerce President Thomas Donohue told the* New York Times.

*Both leading presidential candidates—Vice President Al Gore, the Democrat, and Texas governor George W. Bush, the Republican—supported the bill. Gore's position put him at odds with environmental groups with whom he had been allied for many years and with labor leaders whose support he desperately needed in his presidential race. As a consequence, the vice president played only a minor role in administration lobbying of Congress on the issue.*

*According to news reports, the Clinton administration made numerous promises to wavering members in the final days before the vote. In one of the most widely publicized episodes, the administration reportedly promised to continue sending business to a Northrop Grumman Corporation defense plant in Grand Prairie, Texas. The plant was the largest employer in the district of Rep. Martin Frost, a senior Democratic leader who had been wavering on the issue. Frost announced he would support the China trade bill on May 23, the day after the administration made the pledge to Northrop Grumman.*

*As with nearly all controversial issues on Capitol Hill, the China trade bill led to unusual alliances among politicians with little else in common. Perhaps the most startling was the Clinton administration's uncomfortable reliance on Rep. Tom DeLay, of Texas, the third-ranking House Republican, as its primary contact in rounding up Republican votes for the bill. Perhaps the most vociferous anti-Clinton Republican in Congress, DeLay generally was considered the driving force behind the House impeachment of the president in late 1998. Among the leaders of the opposition to the China bill were Barney Frank (D-Mass.), one of the most articulate and liberal members of the House, and Dana Rohrabacher (R-Calif.), one of the chamber's most conservative members.*

*Opponents offered a host of arguments reflecting the particular concerns of the group involved. Labor unions and their allies on Capitol Hill argued that many American manufacturers, attracted by the low wages and virtually nonexistent labor and environmental standards in China, would move their operations there, throwing hundreds of thousands of Americans out of work. Union officials also argued that China routinely used slave labor in its domestic industry, in violation of international treaties. Environmental groups said Chinese industrial concerns were among the world's worst polluters and that it was futile to hope that China would adopt Western-style environmental protections anytime soon. Human rights advocates and anticommunist conservatives pointed to China's refusal to permit dissent in any form as evidence that the Beijing government remained a dictatorship immune to Western influence.*

*One common argument among the opponents was that China had a long history of violating agreements on trade and other matters and could not be trusted to keep the promises it had made to gain entry into the WTO. As an example, opponents cited China's 1995 promise to crack down on the illegal duplication of U.S.-origin computer software programs, movies, music, and other items known as "intellectual property." Despite that pledge, the bootleg production of those items increased sharply in the latter part of the 1990s, and the government appeared unwilling or unable to stop the practice.*

*The Clinton administration and supporters of the trade bill argued that the 1999 U.S.-China agreement provided one of the best business opportunities of all time for American business. China, with its rapidly growing economy and 1.2 billion citizens, represented a vast untapped market for U.S. exporters of farm goods, consumer items, manufacturing equipment, and business services, supporters said. Because the trade agreement imposed dozens of conditions on Chinese behavior, and virtually no new conditions on the United States, supporters said it was a "no-lose" proposition.*

*Ultimately, the key to House passage of the bill was an amendment, drafted by Michigan Democrat Sander Levin and Nebraska Republican Doug Bereuter, that created a twenty-three-member commission, composed of representatives from Congress and the executive branch, that would monitor Chinese actions on human rights, labor standards, and religious freedoms. Any legislation recommended by the commission would be guaranteed expedited consideration in Congress. Another provision required the president to send Congress an annual report on China's compliance with its trade agreements. These provisions did not replace Congress's annual opportunity to block trade with China, but they did provide political cover for some two dozen House members who had wavered on the bill because of their concerns about human rights and other issues in China.*

*By the time the House began debate on the trade bill on May 23, supporters were confident of victory but predicted it would pass by a narrow margin. During the two days of debate the majority of members who had been wavering announced they would support the bill. As expected, Republicans provided the bulk of support for the bill: 164 of the 237 majority in favor, while Democrats provided 138 of the 197 votes in opposition.*

*President Clinton hailed the vote as "an important step for the kind of future I think we all want for our children; for an America that will be more prosperous and more secure; for a China that is more open to our products and more respectful of the rule of law at home and abroad."*

## Senate Action

*Supporters of the China trade bill urged the Senate to take up the measure shortly after the House vote. But the Senate's Republican leaders—most of whom supported the bill—appeared reluctant to give Clinton another easy victory, and they said the bill would have to fit in with other legislative priorities. The Senate's delay gave opponents yet another shot at derailing the bill. The opponents' only realistic option was to convince the Senate to adopt an amendment to the bill, thus sending it back to the House, where further delay might jeopardize chances for final passage.*

*The key vote in the Senate came September 13 on an amendment offered by Fred Thompson (R-Tenn.) and Robert G. Torricelli (D-N.J.) that would have imposed sanctions on Chinese companies that were caught exporting nuclear, chemical, or biological weapons in violation of international treaties. The two senators cited intelligence and news reports indicating that Chinese companies had exported materials for weapons of mass destruction to Pakistan and Iran. But their effort to amend the bill fell short, largely because the overwhelming majority of senators favored the underlying bill and feared delaying it. The Senate voted 65–32 to table, or kill, the amendment. Six days later, the Senate gave final approval to the bill, 83–15, with a majority of Democrats and Republicans supporting it.*

## China's WTO Entry Delayed

*As China came closer to WTO membership in late 2000, it became increasingly clear that the leaders in Beijing were coming under pressure from domestic factions worried about the consequences of opening the country's markets to the strong winds of international competition. Senior Chinese government officials repeatedly assured their Western counterparts that Beijing would honor its agreements and was still committed to joining the WTO. Toward the end of the year China was making little progress in negotiating final agreements needed for its WTO membership, including a bilateral trade agreement with Mexico and a broad WTO document called a "protocol" detailing all the commitments it had made in its trade agreements.*

*To a remarkable degree, worries in China about the ultimate impact of opening the country's markets to global trade mirrored concerns expressed in the United States and other industrialized countries about their trade with China. More than half of all Chinese workers—about 600 million— were farmers, and Chinese agriculture was very inefficient compared to mechanized farming in the United States. Similarly, many Chinese sectors of Chinese heavy industry, especially government-owned automobile, steel, and chemical factories, were notoriously inefficient. A growing number of Chinese economists and government officials reportedly worried that once China's economy was opened to full-scale international competition, these sectors almost certainly would falter, throwing millions of Chinese out of work and causing massive social dislocations.*

*These concerns prompted two reactions in China, according to numerous news reports. On the one hand, the government launched studies of ways to protect vulnerable Chinese industries from competition, either through legitimate means authorized by trade agreements (such as "antidumping" provisions to counter imports of items priced below world market levels) or through other protectionist measures that might violate the agreements but be difficult for outsiders to counteract. At the same time, hard-line communist and nationalist factions (sometimes calling themselves the "new left") began talking openly about the dangers facing China from unrestrained global capitalism.*

*As late as October senior Chinese and Western officials expressed hope that China might join the WTO by the end of the year. On October 26, for example, Chinese finance minister Xiang Huaiceng and U.S. Treasury secretary Lawrence H. Summers issued a statement, after a meeting in Beijing, saying China still planned on WTO membership during 2000. But within a month such hopes had faded, and at year's end China was still negotiating the necessary document for its entry into the WTO.*

## U.S.-China Talks on Missile Sales

*As the debate in Congress indicated, one pending issue between the United States and China in late 2000 was a dispute over Chinese sales of ballistic missile technology to Iran and Pakistan. Iran reportedly was attempting to develop a nuclear weapons capability, and Pakistan had exploded a nuclear device in 1998. U.S. officials said China had provided some items for ballistic missiles to both countries. If either nation was to develop a medium- or long-range ballistic missile capable of carrying nuclear weapons, the potential for instability in the Middle East or South Asia was significant. Under U.S. law, the Clinton administration was obliged to impose sanctions on any country that supplied missile technology to a country that was attempting to develop nuclear weapons.* (Pakistani nuclear bomb, Historic Documents of 1998, p. 326)

*During meetings in Beijing in mid-November, U.S. and Chinese officials negotiated an agreement under which China formally pledged not to supply parts of technology for missiles that could be used to deliver nuclear weapons. China made that pledge public on November 21. In return, the State De-*

*partment announced the same day that Clinton was waiving the required sanctions against China. State Department spokesman Richard Boucher said the United States would impose new sanctions, lasting for two years, against Iran and Pakistan for buying the Chinese missile components; in both cases, however, the sanctions generally duplicated existing trade restrictions.*

*Boucher said the agreement would help achieve "our common objective of preventing the spread of ballistic missiles that threaten regional and international security." But some congressional critics complained that the administration was accepting promises from a country that had violated previous commitments. "China has an abysmal track record at living up to nonproliferation agreements," Senator Thompson said.*

*Following is the text of a statement by President Bill Clinton on May 24, 2000, commending the House of Representatives for passing legislation granting permanent normal trading status to the People's Republic of China. The document was obtained from the Internet at http://www.pub.whitehouse.gov/uri-res/ I2R?urn:pdi://oma.eop.gov.us/2000/5/25/3.text.1.*

Good afternoon. Today, the House of Representatives has taken an historic step toward continued prosperity in America, reform in China, and peace in the world. If the Senate votes, as the House has just done, to extend permanent normal trade relations with China, it will open new doors of trade for America and new hope for change in China.

Seven years ago, when I became President, I charted a new course for a new economy—a course of fiscal discipline, investment in our people and open trade. I have always believed that by opening markets abroad, we open opportunities at home. We've worked hard to advance that goal of more open and more fair trade since 1993—all the way up to the landmark legislation I signed just a few days ago to expand trade with Africa and the Caribbean Basin.

Just this week, Speaker [Dennis] Hastert [R-Mich.] and I reached an agreement that many members of the House in both parties have already supported, to bring the same kinds of investment opportunity and jobs to America's new markets—to people and places here in this country who have not yet participated in our prosperity, in rural areas, inner cities, on our Native American reservations.

With more than a billion people, China is the largest new market in the world. Our administration has negotiated an agreement which will open China's markets to American products made on American soil—everything from corn to chemicals to computers. Today, the House has affirmed that agreement.

We will be exporting, however, more than our products. By this agreement, we will also export more of one of our most cherished values, economic freedom. Bringing China into the WTO and normalizing trade will strengthen those who fight for the environment, for labor standards, for human rights, for the rule of law. For China, this agreement will clearly increase the benefits of cooperation, and the costs of confrontation.

America, of course, will continue to defend our interests, but at this stage in China's development, we will have more positive influence with an out-stretched hand than with a clenched fist. The House today has affirmed that belief.

Now, I have spoken personally to many, many members of Congress. I have heard their concerns and those of their constituents. I know this, for many, was a difficult vote. Decisions like this one test our deepest beliefs. They challenge our hopes, and they call forth our fears. Though China may be changing, we all know it remains a one-party state, that it still denies people the rights of free speech and religious expression. We know that trade alone will not bring freedom to China or peace to the world. That's why permanent normal trade relations must also signal our commitment to permanent change.

America will keep pressing to protect our security and to advance our values. The vote today is a big boost to both efforts. For the more China liberalizes its economy, the more it will liberate the potential of its people—to work without restraint; to live without fear.

In January, I pledged an all-out effort to take this important step. I want to thank everyone who has joined in it. I want to express special gratitude to Speaker Hastert for his leadership, to Congressman [Bill] Archer [R-Texas] and Congressman [Charles] Rangel [D-N.Y.] of the Ways and Means Committee. I also want to acknowledge Congressman [Sander] Levin [D-Mich.] and Congressman [Doug] Bereuter [R-Neb.], who authored a provision on human rights that improves this bill and strengthens our ability to stand up for our values.

I thank all the others who spoke out for this action, including all our former Presidents, all the former Secretaries of State, Defense, trade ministers, other Cabinet members, all the military leaders. I thank those who worked for human rights and the rule of law who spoke out for this legislation.

And, of course, I want to thank all those who worked in this administration: Secretary [of Commerce William] Daley, for spearheading our campaign; [U.S. Trade Representative] Charlene Barshefsky and Gene Sperling [chairman of the National Economic Council], for their negotiation of the agreement; Steve Ricchetti, here in the White House, and Sandy Berger [of the National Security Council] and all the others who worked so hard for this agreement here. I appreciate what everyone has done.

Today, the House has taken an important step for the kind of future I think we all want for our children, for an America that will be more prosperous and more secure; for a China that is more open to our products and more respectful of the rule of law at home and abroad. The House has spoken, and now the eyes of the world turn toward the United States Senate. I am confident it, too, will act swiftly to advance these interests.

I will be speaking with many senators in the days ahead to ensure that we continue to move ahead to get this done as promptly as possible. This is one of the most important votes the Senate will face in this session. I hope we can build on our momentum on this issue and on other pressing priorities, as well. I still believe the Congress can act to add voluntary prescription drug coverage to Medicare; to invest more in our children's education; to pass the legislation to invest in these American markets here at home; to pass the common sense gun safety legislation; to raise the minimum wage.

Again, I thank the House and I look forward to working with the Congress in the days ahead.

This is a good day for America. And 10 years from now we will look back on this day and be glad we did this. We will see that we have given ourselves a chance to build the kind of future we want. This is a good economic agreement because we get all the economic benefits of lower tariffs and lowered access to the Chinese market. We get new protections against dumping of products in our own markets. What we have granted is full membership in the World Trade Organization, which brings China into a rule-based international system.

But I have said many times, and I'd just like to say once more, to me, the most important benefit of all is that we have given ourselves and the Chinese a chance—not a guarantee, but a chance—to build a future in the Asia Pacific region for the next 50 years very different from the last 50. We fought three wars in that part of the world. A lot of Americans died for freedom; a lot of sacrifice should not go unredeemed. We owe it to them, to their children, and to our children and grandchildren to give the world a chance to build a better and a different future. We have taken a big step toward giving them that chance today.

Thank you very much.

# SURGEON GENERAL ON
# ORAL HEALTH IN AMERICA
## May 25, 2000

*According to the first report on the nation's oral health ever issued by the office of the surgeon general, the United States made dramatic strides in curbing tooth decay and gum disease in the last half of the twentieth century. Nonetheless, Surgeon General David Satcher said, "profound disparities" in oral health still afflicted "those without the knowledge or resources to achieve good oral care"—the poor, especially poor children, the elderly, and minorities. As a result, Satcher said, a disproportionate number in these groups endured needless pain and other consequences of poor oral health, such as poor self-image and even chronic stress and depression. Moreover, advances in science were revealing a close relationship between oral health and general health that the general public, the health care profession, and policymakers were only beginning to recognize.*

*In 1900 most Americans could expect to lose their teeth by middle age. With the discovery that fluoride could prevent tooth decay, it became commonplace to add it to the public's drinking water. This, plus healthier diets, better personal hygiene, and advances in dentistry, helped to improve oral health markedly during the twentieth century. By 2000 most middle-aged and younger Americans expected to retain their teeth throughout their lives and not to have any serious oral health problems. Yet poor children, the elderly, and minorities were still experiencing "a silent epidemic" of oral diseases, the report said, an epidemic that caused "needless pain and suffering, complications that devastate overall health and well-being, and financial and social costs that diminish the quality of life and burden American society."*

*The report emphasized that good oral health was necessary for good general health. In addition to tooth decay (known as "dental caries") and gum disease, oral problems included oral infections (such as cold sores, which could occur at any age), birth defects (such as cleft palates and craniofacial injuries, which tended to affect the young), and chronic facial pain and oral cancers (which were seen primarily in older people). General health risks, such as smoking, excessive alcohol use, and poor dietary practices also af-*

*fected oral health, and some studies indicated that chronic oral infections might be linked to diabetes, heart and lung diseases, stroke, and premature, low birth-weight babies. Infections and other disorders in the mouth could also signal broader health problems, such as the presence of osteoporosis (loss of bone density) or HIV, the virus that caused AIDS (acquired immuno-deficiency syndrome). "Oral health means more than healthy teeth," Health and Human Services secretary Donna E. Shalala wrote in a preface to the report. "You cannot be healthy without oral health."*

*Shalala and Satcher released the findings of the report "Oral Health in America" before a group of first-graders at an elementary school in down-town Washington, D.C. The children were participants in a government-sponsored pilot program to teach youngsters about oral health. Using his own experience to underline the importance of his message, Satcher told the children that as the son of uneducated farmers in rural Alabama, his first visit to the dentist came as he was preparing to leave for college. "There are still too many families like that in this country," he said.*

*The 309-page report, which took three years to prepare, reached beyond simple dentistry to consider the entire craniofacial complex, which is made up not only of teeth and gums but also the hard and soft palate, the mucosal linings of the mouth and throat, the tongue, the lips, the salivary glands, the chewing muscles, the upper and lower jaws, as well as the nervous, im-mune, and vascular systems associated with the mouth. "These are the tis-sues whose functions we often take for granted," the report said, "yet they represent the very essence of our humanity. They allow us to speak and smile; sigh and kiss; smell, taste, touch, chew, and swallow; cry out in pain; and convey a world of feelings and emotions through facial expressions." Diet, nutrition, sleep, psychological well-being, social interaction, school and work could all be adversely affected by impaired oral and craniofacial health, the report said.*

## The "Silent Epidemic"

*Despite the remarkable strides made in preventing tooth decay, it was still the single most common chronic childhood disease—five times more common than asthma and seven times more common than hay fever. More than 50 percent of all children ages five to nine had at least one cavity or filling; this increased to 78 percent by age seventeen. Moreover, poor chil-dren had more cavities and more untreated cavities than did children from wealthier families. More than 30 percent of all poor children ages two through nine had untreated cavities, compared with 17 percent of children who were not poor. Approximately 25 percent of all poor children had not ever seen a dentist before entering kindergarten.*

*Among adults and older patients, oral health problems tended to shift away from tooth decay and toward gum disease, tooth loss, and other oral or craniofacial problems, including temporomandibular disorders affecting the lower jaw and osteoporosis. These disorders caused pain that could in-terfere with speaking, eating, and swallowing. While more than 60 percent of adults reported seeing a dentist within the previous year, those with in-*

*comes at or above the poverty level were twice as likely to have seen a dentist as those below the poverty level. About 5 percent of the elderly were living in nursing homes, where, according to the report, dental care was "problematic."*

*About 30,000 Americans, most of them elderly, were diagnosed with oral and pharyngeal (throat) cancers each year. The prognosis was poor for everyone, but worse for blacks than whites. The five-year survival rate was 56 percent for whites and 34 percent for blacks.*

*The reasons for these disparities were complex, Satcher said. The report cited a lack of education, poor overall health, and insufficient access to dental care as contributing factors. Lack of access was a broad category that ranged from lack of transportation to get to a clinic to lack of dental health care providers. While fluoridated drinking water benefited people of all ages and socioeconomic classes by helping to prevent cavities, only 62 percent of Americans hooked up to public water supplies received fluoridated water. Seven of the nation's fifty largest cities—including Portland, San Antonio, and San Diego—did not supply fluoridated water.*

*A major barrier to dental care was lack of dental insurance. While 44 million Americans did not have health insurance, more than twice that many—108 million—did not have dental health insurance, the report said. Many people lost their coverage upon retirement, and Medicare did not reimburse for routine dental care. Some states covered some dental care under Medicaid, but reimbursements tended to be low. For those with insurance, narrow definitions of "medically necessary dental care" limited the oral health services covered.*

*The costs of poor oral health were high. According to the report, Americans spent $53.8 billion in 1998 on dental services alone—4.7 percent of all health expenditures—and were expected to spend in excess of $60 billion in 2000. That figure did not include expenditures for oral and pharyngeal cancers, accidents to the head and face, and chronic disorders that affected the craniofacial region. Nor did it include the direct and indirect costs associated with absence from work or school because of acute dental conditions, losses from premature death caused by mouth and throat cancers, and the loss of self-image that could limit career and social opportunities.*

## Promoting Oral Health

*Many effective means of promoting oral health and preventing oral diseases were already known and widely available to people of all economic and social backgrounds, the report said. Most tooth decay could be avoided by the use of fluoride toothpaste daily, and gum diseases could be minimized by daily brushing and flossing. Fluoridation of community water supplies would help prevent tooth decay, and individuals could improve their overall oral health by not smoking and by reducing alcohol consumption. Many oral injuries could be avoided by the use of protective head and mouth gear during sports activities.*

*Increasing access to oral health care would require action on several fronts, the report said. Lack of dental insurance, public and private, was an obvious impediment that would require concerted effort to overcome, the report said. Another was the dwindling supply of dentists and oral health care providers. According to the report, the dentist-to-population ratio was declining, and 25 million Americans lived in areas without adequate dental care services.*

*The report called on the entire health care profession to be more aware of the role oral health played in overall general health. Achieving that goal would involve curriculum changes and multidisciplinary training for doctors and other health care providers. The report also called on legislators and public policymakers to include oral health services in health promotion and disease prevention programs, care delivery systems, and reimbursement schedules.*

*Although the report was short on specific suggestions for overcoming some of the seemingly more intractable obstacles to better oral care, such as the lack of health insurance, experts in the field said it would nonetheless serve a useful purpose. "We're the stepchild of health care in the United States," said the president of an organization of dentists' professional groups. "We think this report will help change that."*

*Following are excerpts from the executive summary of the report, "Oral Health in America: A Report of the Surgeon General," released May 25, 2000, by Surgeon General David Satcher. The document was obtained from the Internet at http://www.nidcr.nih .gov/sgr/oralhealth.htm.*

Publication of this first Surgeon General's Report on Oral Health marks a milestone in the history of oral health in America. The report elaborates on the meaning of oral health and explains why oral health is essential to general health and well-being. In the course of the past 50 years, great progress has been made in understanding the common oral diseases—dental caries (tooth decay) and periodontal (gum) diseases—resulting in marked improvements in the nation's oral health. Most middle-aged and younger Americans expect to retain their natural teeth over their lifetime and do not expect to have any serious oral health problems.

The major message of this Surgeon General's report is that oral health is essential to the general health and well-being of all Americans and can be achieved by all Americans. However, not all Americans are achieving the same degree of oral health. In spite of the safe and effective means of maintaining oral health that have benefited the majority of Americans over the past half century, many among us still experience needless pain and suffering, complications that devastate overall health and well-being, and financial and social costs that diminish the quality of life and burden American society. What amounts to "a silent epidemic" of oral diseases is affecting our most vulnerable citizens—poor children, the elderly, and many members of racial and ethnic minority groups. . . .

The word *oral* refers to the mouth. The mouth includes not only the teeth and the gums (gingiva) and their supporting tissues, but also the hard and soft palate, the mucosal lining of the mouth and throat, the tongue, the lips, the salivary glands, the chewing muscles, and the upper and lower jaws. Equally important are the branches of the nervous, immune, and vascular systems that animate, protect, and nourish the oral tissues, as well as provide connections to the brain and the rest of the body. The genetic patterning of development in utero further reveals the intimate relationship of the oral tissues to the developing brain and to the tissues of the face and head that surround the mouth, structures whose location is captured in the word craniofacial.

A major theme of this report is that *oral health means much more than healthy teeth*. It means being free of chronic oral-facial pain conditions, oral and pharyngeal (throat) cancers, oral soft tissue lesions, birth defects such as cleft lip and palate, and scores of other diseases and disorders that affect the oral, dental, and craniofacial tissues, collectively known as the craniofacial complex. These are tissues whose functions we often take for granted, yet they represent the very essence of our humanity. They allow us to speak and smile; sigh and kiss; smell, taste, touch, chew, and swallow; cry out in pain; and convey a world of feelings and emotions through facial expressions. They also provide protection against microbial infections and environmental insults.

The craniofacial tissues also provide a useful means to understanding organs and systems in less accessible parts of the body. The salivary glands are a model of other exocrine glands, and an analysis of saliva can provide telltale clues of overall health or disease. The jawbones and their joints function like other musculoskeletal parts. The nervous system apparatus underlying facial pain has its counterpart in nerves elsewhere in the body. A thorough oral examination can detect signs of nutritional deficiencies as well as a number of systemic diseases, including microbial infections, immune disorders, injuries, and some cancers. Indeed, the phrase the mouth is a mirror has been used to illustrate the wealth of information that can be derived from examining oral tissues.

New research is pointing to associations between chronic oral infections and heart and lung diseases, stroke, and low-birth-weight, premature births. Associations between periodontal disease and diabetes have long been noted. This report assesses these associations and explores mechanisms that might explain the oral-systemic disease connections.

The broadened meaning of oral health parallels the broadened meaning of health. In 1948 the World Health Organization expanded the definition of health to mean "a complete state of physical, mental, and social well-being, and not just the absence of infirmity." It follows that oral health must also include well-being. Just as we now understand that nature and nurture are inextricably linked, and mind and body are both expressions of our human biology, so, too, we must recognize that oral health and general health are inseparable. We ignore signs and symptoms of oral disease and dysfunction to our detriment. Consequently, a second theme of the report is that oral health is integral to general health. You cannot be healthy without oral health. Oral health and general health should not be interpreted as separate entities. Oral health is a critical component of health and must be included in the provision of health care and the design of community programs.

The wider meanings of oral and health in no way diminish the relevance and importance of the two leading dental diseases, caries and the periodontal diseases. They remain common and widespread, affecting nearly everyone at some point in the life span. What has changed is what we can do about them.

Researchers in the 1930s discovered that people living in communities with naturally fluoridated water supplies had less dental caries than people drinking unfluoridated water. But not until the end of World War II were the investigators able to design and implement the community clinical trials that confirmed their observations and launched a better approach to the problem of dental caries: prevention. Soon after, adjusting the fluoride content of community water supplies was pursued as an important public health measure to prevent dental caries.

Although this measure has not been fully implemented, the results have been dramatic. Dental caries began to decline in the 1950s among children who grew up in fluoridated cities, and by the late 1970s, decline in decay was evident for many Americans. The application of science to improve diagnostic, treatment, and prevention strategies has saved billions of dollars per year in the nation's annual health bill. Even more significant, the result is that far fewer people are edentulous (toothless) today than a generation ago.

The theme of prevention gained momentum as pioneering investigators and practitioners in the 1950s and 1960s showed that not only dental caries but also periodontal diseases are bacterial infections. The researchers demonstrated that the infections could be prevented by increasing host resistance to disease and reducing or eliminating the suspected microbial pathogens in the oral cavity. The applications of research discoveries have resulted in continuing improvements in the oral health of Americans, new approaches to the prevention and treatment of dental diseases, and the growth of the science.

The significant role that scientists, dentists, dental hygienists, and other health professionals have played in the prevention of oral disease and disability leads to a third theme of this report: safe and effective disease prevention measures exist that everyone can adopt to improve oral health and prevent disease. These measures include daily oral hygiene procedures and other lifestyle behaviors, community programs such as community water fluoridation and tobacco cessation programs, and provider-based interventions such as the placement of dental sealants and examinations for common oral and pharyngeal cancers. It is hoped that this Surgeon General's report will facilitate the maturing of the broad field of craniofacial research so that gains in the prevention of craniofacial diseases and disorders can be realized that are as impressive as those achieved for common dental diseases.

At the same time, more needs to be done to ensure that messages of health promotion and disease prevention are brought home to all Americans. In this regard, a fourth theme of the report is that general health risk factors, such as tobacco use and poor dietary practices, also affect oral and craniofacial health. The evidence for an association between tobacco use and oral diseases has been clearly delineated in almost every Surgeon General's report on tobacco since 1964, and the oral effects of nutrition and diet are presented in the Surgeon General's report on nutrition. . . . All the health professions can play a role in reducing the burden of disease in America by calling attention to these and other risk factors and suggesting appropriate actions. . . .

Scientists today [are] researching the intricacies of the craniofacial complex. They are using an ever-growing array of sophisticated analytic tools and imaging systems to study normal function and diagnose disease. They are completing the mapping and sequencing of human, animal, microbial, and plant genomes, the better to understand the complexities of human development, aging, and pathological processes. They are growing cell lines, synthesizing molecules, and using a new generation of biomaterials to revolutionize tissue repair and regeneration. More than ever before, they are working in multidisciplinary teams to bring new knowledge and expertise to the goal of understanding complex human diseases and disorders.

## The Challenge

This Surgeon General's report has much to say about the inequities and disparities that affect those least able to muster the resources to achieve optimal oral health. The barriers to oral health include lack of access to care, whether because of limited income or lack of insurance, transportation, or the flexibility to take time off from work to attend to personal or family needs for care. Individuals with disabilities and those with complex health problems may face additional barriers to care. Sometimes, too, the public, policymakers, and providers may consider oral health and the need for care to be less important than other health needs, pointing to the need to raise awareness and improve health literacy.

Even more costly to the individual and to society are the expenses associated with oral health problems that go beyond dental diseases. The nation's yearly dental bill is expected to exceed $60 billion in 2000. . . . However, add to that expense the tens of billions of dollars in direct medical care and indirect costs of chronic craniofacial pain conditions such as temporomandibular disorders, trigeminal neuralgia, shingles, or burning mouth syndrome; the $100,000 minimal individual lifetime costs of treating craniofacial birth defects such as cleft lip and palate; the costs of oral and pharyngeal cancers; the costs of autoimmune diseases; and the costs associated with the unintentional and intentional injuries that so often affect the head and face. Then add the social and psychological consequences and costs. Damage to the craniofacial complex, whether from disease, disorder, or injury, strikes at our very identity. We see ourselves, and others see us, in terms of the face we present to the world. Diminish that image in any way and we risk the loss of self-esteem and well-being.

Many unanswered questions remain for scientists, practitioners, educators, policymakers, and the public. This report highlights the research challenges as well as pointing to emerging technologies that may facilitate finding solutions. Along with the quest for answers comes the challenge of applying what is already known in a society where there are social, political, economic, behavioral, and environmental barriers to health and well-being. . . .

## Part One: What Is Oral Health?

The meaning of oral health is explored in Chapter 1, and the interdependence of oral health with general health and well-being is a recurrent theme throughout the volume.

Chapter 2 provides an overview of the craniofacial complex in development and aging, how the tissues and organs function in essential life processes, and their role in determining our uniquely human abilities. . . .

## Part Two: What Is the Status of Oral Health in America?

Chapter 3 is a primer describing the major diseases and disorders that affect the craniofacial complex. The findings include:

- Microbial infections, including those caused by bacteria, viruses, and fungi, are the primary cause of the most prevalent oral diseases. Examples include dental caries, periodontal diseases, herpes labialis, and candidiasis.
- The etiology and pathogenesis of diseases and disorders affecting the craniofacial structures are multifactorial and complex, involving an interplay among genetic, environmental, and behavioral factors.
- Many inherited and congenital conditions affect the craniofacial complex, often resulting in disfigurement and impairments that may involve many body organs and systems and affect millions of children worldwide.
- Tobacco use, excessive alcohol use, and inappropriate dietary practices contribute to many diseases and disorders. In particular, tobacco use is a risk factor for oral cavity and pharyngeal cancers, periodontal diseases, candidiasis, and dental caries, among other diseases.
- Some chronic diseases, such as Sjögren's syndrome, present with primary oral symptoms.
- Oral-facial pain conditions are common and often have complex etiologies.

Chapter 4 constitutes an oral health status report card for the United States, describing the magnitude of the problem. Where data permit, the chapter also describes the oral health of selected population groups, as well as their dental visit behavior. The findings include:

- Over the past five decades, major improvements in oral health have been seen nationally for most Americans.
- Despite improvements in oral health status, profound disparities remain in some population groups as classified by sex, income, age, and race/ethnicity. For some diseases and conditions, the magnitude of the differences in oral health status among population groups is striking.
- Oral diseases and conditions affect people throughout their life span. Nearly every American has experienced the most common oral disease, dental caries.

- Conditions that severely affect the face and facial expression, such as birth defects, craniofacial injuries, and neoplastic diseases, are more common in the very young and in the elderly.
- Oral-facial pain can greatly reduce quality of life and restrict major functions. Pain is a common symptom for many of the conditions affecting oral-facial structures.
- National and state data for many oral and craniofacial diseases and conditions and for population groups are limited or nonexistent. Available state data reveal variations within and among states in patterns of health and disease among population groups.
- Research is needed to develop better measures of disease and health, to explain the differences among population groups, and to develop interventions targeted at eliminating disparities.

### Part Three: What Is the Relationship Between Oral Health and General Health and Well-being?

Chapters 5 and 6 address key issues in the report's charge—the relationship of oral health to general health and well-being. Chapter 5 explores the theme of the mouth as reflecting general health or disease status. Examples are given of how oral tissues may signal the presence of disease, disease progression, or exposure to risk factors, and how oral cells and fluids are increasingly being used as diagnostic tools. This is followed by a discussion of the mouth as a portal of entry for infections that can affect local tissues and may spread to other parts of the body. The final sections review the literature regarding emerging associations between oral diseases and diabetes, heart disease and stroke, and adverse pregnancy outcomes. The findings include:

- Many systemic diseases and conditions have oral manifestations. These manifestations may be the initial sign of clinical disease and as such serve to inform clinicians and individuals of the need for further assessment.
- The oral cavity is a portal of entry as well as the site of disease for microbial infections that affect general health status.
- The oral cavity and its functions can be adversely affected by many pharmaceuticals and other therapies commonly used in treating systemic conditions. The oral complications of these therapies can compromise patient compliance with treatment.
- Individuals such as immunocompromised and hospitalized patients are at greater risk for general morbidity due to oral infections.
- Individuals with diabetes are at greater risk for periodontal diseases.
- Animal and population-based studies have demonstrated an association between periodontal diseases and diabetes, cardiovascular disease, stroke, and adverse pregnancy outcomes. Further research is needed to determine the extent to which these associations are causal or coincidental.

Chapter 6 demonstrates the relationship between oral health and quality of life, presenting data on the consequences of poor oral health and altered appearance on speech, eating, and other functions, as well as on self-esteem, social interaction, education, career achievement, and emotional state. The chapter introduces anthropological and ethnographic literature to underscore the cultural values and symbolism attached to facial appearance and teeth. An examination of efforts to characterize the functional and social implications of oral and craniofacial diseases reveals the following findings:

- Oral health is related to well-being and quality of life as measured along functional, psychosocial, and economic dimensions. Diet, nutrition, sleep, psychological status, social interaction, school, and work are affected by impaired oral and craniofacial health.
- Cultural values influence oral and craniofacial health and well-being and can play an important role in care utilization practices and in perpetuating acceptable oral health and facial norms.
- Oral and craniofacial diseases and their treatment place a burden on society in the form of lost days and years of productive work. Acute dental conditions contribute to a range of problems for employed adults, including restricted activity, bed days, and work loss, and school loss for children. In addition, conditions such as oral and pharyngeal cancers contribute to premature death and can be measured by years of life lost.
- Oral and craniofacial diseases and conditions contribute to compromised ability to bite, chew, and swallow foods; limitations in food selection; and poor nutrition. These conditions include tooth loss, diminished salivary functions, oral-facial pain conditions such as temporomandibular disorders, alterations in taste, and functional limitations of prosthetic replacements.
- Oral-facial pain, as a symptom of untreated dental and oral problems and as a condition in and of itself, is a major source of diminished quality of life. It is associated with sleep deprivation, depression, and multiple adverse psychosocial outcomes.
- Self-reported impacts of oral conditions on social function include limitations in verbal and nonverbal communication, social interaction, and intimacy. Individuals with facial disfigurements due to craniofacial diseases and conditions and their treatments can experience loss of self-image and self-esteem, anxiety, depression, and social stigma; these in turn may limit educational, career, and marital opportunities and affect other social relations.
- Reduced oral-health-related quality of life is associated with poor clinical status and reduced access to care.

## Part Four: How Is Oral Health Promoted and Maintained and How Are Oral Diseases Prevented?

The next three chapters review how individuals, health care practitioners, communities, and the nation as a whole contribute to oral health. Chapter 7 reviews the evidence for the efficacy and effectiveness of health promotion and disease prevention measures with a focus on community efforts in preventing oral disease. It continues with a discussion of the knowledge and practices of the public and health care providers and indicates opportunities for broad-based and targeted health promotion. The findings include:

- Community water fluoridation, an effective, safe, and ideal public health measure, benefits individuals of all ages and socioeconomic strata. Unfortunately, over one third of the US population (100 million people) are without this critical public health measure.
- Effective disease prevention measures exist for use by individuals, practitioners, and communities. Most of these focus on dental caries prevention, such as fluorides and dental sealants, where a combination of services is required to achieve optimal disease prevention. Daily oral hygiene practices such as brushing and flossing can prevent gingivitis.
- Community-based approaches for the prevention of other oral diseases and conditions, such as oral and pharyngeal cancers and oral-facial trauma, require intensified developmental efforts.
- Community-based preventive programs are unavailable to substantial portions of the under-served population.
- There is a gap between research findings and the oral disease prevention and health promotion practices and knowledge of the public and the health professions.
- Disease prevention and health promotion approaches, such as tobacco control, appropriate use of fluorides for caries prevention, and folate supplementation for neural tube defect prevention, highlight opportunities for partnerships between community-based programs and practitioners, as well as collaborations among health professionals.
- Many community-based programs require a combined effort among social service, health care, and education services at the local or state level.

Chapter 8 explores the role of the individual and the health care provider in promoting and maintaining oral health and well-being. For the individual, this means exercising appropriate self-care and adopting healthy behaviors. For the provider, it means incorporating the knowledge emerging from the science base in a timely manner for prevention and diagnosis, risk assessment and risk management, and treatment of oral diseases and disorders. The chapter focuses largely on the oral health care provider. The management of oral and craniofacial health and disease necessitates collaborations among a team of care providers to achieve optimal oral and general health. The findings include:

- Achieving and maintaining oral health require individual action, complemented by professional care as well as community-based activities.
- Individuals can take actions, for themselves and for persons under their care, to prevent disease and maintain health. Primary prevention of many oral, dental, and craniofacial diseases and conditions is possible with appropriate diet, nutrition, oral hygiene, and health-promoting behaviors, including the appropriate use of professional services. Individuals should use a fluoride dentifrice daily to help prevent dental caries and should brush and floss daily to prevent gingivitis.

- All primary care providers can contribute to improved oral and craniofacial health. Interdisciplinary care is needed to manage the oral health-
  general health interface. Dentists, as primary care providers, are uniquely
  positioned to play an expanded role in the detection, early recognition,
  and management of a wide range of complex oral and general diseases
  and conditions.
- Nonsurgical interventions are available to reverse disease progression
  and to manage oral diseases as infections.
- New knowledge and the development of molecular and genetically based
  tests will facilitate risk assessment and management, and improve the
  ability of health care providers to customize treatment.
- Health care providers can successfully deliver tobacco cessation and
  other health promotion programs in their offices, contributing to both
  overall health and oral health.
- Biocompatible rehabilitative materials and biologically engineered tissues are being developed and will greatly enhance the treatment options
  available to providers and their patients.

Chapter 9 describes the roles of dental practitioners and their teams, the
medical community, and public health agencies at local, state, and national
levels in administering care or reimbursing for the costs of care. These activities are viewed against the changing organization of US health care and trends
regarding the workforce in research, education, and practice.

- Dental, medical, and public health delivery systems each provide services that affect oral and craniofacial health in the US population. Clinical oral health care is predominantly provided by a private practice
  dental workforce.
- Expenditures for dental services alone made up 4.7 percent of the
  nation's health expenditures in 1998—$53.8 billion out of $1.1 trillion.
  These expenditures underestimate the true costs to the nation, however,
  because data are unavailable to determine the extent of expenditures and
  services provided for craniofacial health care by other health providers
  and institutions.
- The public health infrastructure for oral health is insufficient to address
  the needs of disadvantaged groups, and the integration of oral and general health programs is lacking.
- Expansion of community-based disease prevention and lowering of
  barriers to personal oral health care are needed to meet the needs of the
  population.
- Insurance coverage for dental care is increasing but still lags behind
  medical insurance. For every child under 18 years old without medical
  insurance, there are at least two children without dental insurance; for
  every adult 18 years or older without medical insurance, there are three
  without dental insurance.
- Eligibility for Medicaid does not ensure enrollment, and enrollment does
  not ensure that individuals obtain needed care. Barriers include patient
  and caregiver understanding of the value and importance of oral health

to general health, low reimbursement rates, and administrative burdens for both patient and provider.

- A narrow definition of "medically necessary dental care" currently limits oral health services for many insured persons, particularly the elderly.
- The dentist-to-population ratio is declining, creating concern as to the capability of the dental workforce to meet the emerging demands of society and provide required services efficiently.
- An estimated 25 million individuals reside in areas lacking adequate dental care services, as defined by Health Professional Shortage Area (HPSA) criteria.
- Educational debt has increased, affecting both career choices and practice location.
- Disparities exist in the oral health profession workforce and career paths. The number of under-represented minorities in the oral health professions is disproportionate to their distribution in the population at large.
- Current and projected demand for dental school faculty positions and research scientists is not being met. A crisis in the number of faculty and researchers threatens the quality of dental education; oral, dental, and craniofacial research; and, ultimately, the health of the public.
- Reliable and valid measures of oral health outcomes do not exist and need to be developed, validated, and incorporated into practice and programs.

## Part Five: What Are the Needs and Opportunities to Enhance Oral Health?

Chapter 10 looks at determinants of oral health in the context of society and across various life stages. Although theorists have proposed a variety of models of health determinants, there is general consensus that individual biology, the physical and socioeconomic environment, personal behaviors and lifestyle, and the organization of health care are key factors whose interplay determines the level of oral health achieved by an individual. The chapter provides examples of these factors with an emphasis on barriers and ways to raise the level of oral health for children and older Americans. The findings include:

- The major factors that determine oral and general health and well-being are individual biology and genetics; the environment, including its physical and socioeconomic aspects; personal behaviors and lifestyle; access to care; and the organization of health care. These factors interact over the life span and determine the health of individuals, population groups, and communities—from neighborhoods to nations.
- The burden of oral diseases and conditions is disproportionately borne by individuals with low socioeconomic status at each life stage and by those who are vulnerable because of poor general health.
- Access to care makes a difference. A complex set of factors underlies access to care and includes the need to have an informed public and poli-

cymakers, integrated and culturally competent programs, and resources
to pay and reimburse for the care. Among other factors, the availability
of insurance increases access to care.

- Preventive interventions, such as protective head and mouth gear and
  dental sealants, exist but are not uniformly used or reinforced.
- Nursing homes and other long-term care institutions have limited capacity to deliver needed oral health services to their residents, most of
  whom are at increased risk for oral diseases.
- Anticipatory guidance and risk assessment and management facilitate
  care for children and for the elderly.
- Federal and state assistance programs for selected oral health services
  exist; however, the scope of services is severely limited, and their reimbursement level for oral health services is low compared to the usual fee
  for care.

Chapter 11 spells out in greater detail the promise of the life sciences in improving oral health in the coming years in the context of changes in American—and global—society. The critical role of genetics and molecular biology
is emphasized.

Chapter 12, the final chapter, iterates the themes of the report and groups
the findings from the earlier chapters into eight major categories. . . .

# A Framework for Action

All Americans can benefit from the development of a National Oral Health
Plan to improve quality of life and eliminate health disparities by facilitating
collaborations among individuals, health care providers, communities, and
policymakers at all levels of society and by taking advantage of existing initiatives. Everyone has a role in improving and promoting oral health. Together
we can work to broaden public understanding of the importance of oral health
and its relevance to general health and well-being, and to ensure that existing and future preventive, diagnostic, and treatment measures for oral diseases and disorders are made available to all Americans. The following are the
principal components of the plan:

**Change perceptions regarding oral health and disease so that oral
health becomes an accepted component of general health.**

- *Change public perceptions.* Many people consider oral signs and symptoms to be less important than indications of general illness. As a result,
  they may avoid or postpone needed care, thus exacerbating the problem.
  If we are to increase the nation's capacity to improve oral health and reduce health disparities, we need to enhance the public's understanding of
  the meaning of oral health and the relationship of the mouth to the rest
  of the body. These messages should take into account the multiple languages and cultural traditions that characterize America's diversity.
- *Change policymakers' perceptions.* Informed policymakers at the local,
  state, and federal levels are critical in ensuring the inclusion of oral
  health services in health promotion and disease prevention programs,

care delivery systems, and reimbursement schedules. Raising awareness of oral health among legislators and public officials at all levels of government is essential to creating effective public policy to improve America's oral health. Every conceivable avenue should be used to inform policymakers—informally through their organizations and affiliations and formally through their governmental offices—if rational oral health policy is to be formulated and effective programs implemented.

• *Change health providers' perceptions.* Too little time is devoted to oral health and disease topics in the education of nondental health professionals. Yet all care providers can and should contribute to enhancing oral health. This can be accomplished in several ways, such as including an oral examination as part of a general medical examination, advising patients in matters of diet and tobacco cessation, and referring patients to oral health practitioners for care prior to medical or surgical treatments that can damage oral tissues, such as cancer chemotherapy or radiation to the head and neck. Health care providers should be ready, willing, and able to work in collaboration to provide optimal health care for their patients. Having informed health care professionals will ensure that the public using the health care system will benefit from interdisciplinary services and comprehensive care. To prepare providers for such a role will involve, among other factors, curriculum changes and multidisciplinary training.

**Accelerate the building of the science and evidence base and apply science effectively to improve oral health.** Basic behavioral and biomedical research, clinical trials, and population-based research have been at the heart of scientific advances over the past decades. The nation's continued investment in research is critical for the provision of new knowledge about oral and general health and disease for years to come and needs to be accelerated if further improvements are to be made. Equally important is the effective transfer of research findings to the public and health professions. However, the next steps are more complicated. The challenge is to understand complex diseases caused by the interaction of multiple genes with environmental and behavioral variables—a description that applies to most oral diseases and disorders—and translate research findings into health care practice and healthy lifestyles.

This report highlights many areas of research opportunities and needs in each chapter. At present, there is an overall need for behavioral and clinical research, clinical trials, health services research, and community-based demonstration research. Also, development of risk assessment procedures for individuals and communities and of diagnostic markers to indicate whether an individual is more or less susceptible to a given disease can provide the basis for formulating risk profiles and tailoring treatment and program options accordingly.

Vital to progress in this area is a better understanding of the etiology and distribution of disease. But as this report makes clear, epidemiologic and surveillance databases for oral health and disease, health services, utilization of care, and expenditures are limited or lacking at the national, state, and local levels. Such data are essential in conducting health services research, generating research hypotheses, planning and evaluating programs, and identifying emerging public health problems. Future data collection must address differences among the subpopulations making up racial and ethnic groups. More attention must also be paid to demographic variables such as age, sex, sexual orientation, and socioeconomic factors in determining health status. Clearly, the more detailed information that is available, the better can program planners establish priorities and targeted interventions.

Progress in elucidating the relationships between chronic oral inflammatory infections, such as periodontitis, and diabetes and glycemic control as well as other systemic conditions will require a similar intensified commitment to research. Rapid progress can also occur with efforts in the area of the natural repair and regeneration of oral tissues and organs. Improvements in oral health depend on multidisciplinary and interdisciplinary approaches to biomedical and behavioral research, including partnerships among researchers in the life and physical sciences, and on the ability of practitioners and the public to apply research findings effectively.

**Build an effective health infrastructure that meets the oral health needs of all Americans and integrates oral health effectively into overall health.** The public health capacity for addressing oral health is dilute and not integrated with other public health programs. Although the Healthy People 2010 objectives provide a blueprint for outcome measures, a national public health plan for oral health does not exist. Furthermore, local, state, and federal resources are limited in the personnel, equipment, and facilities available to support oral health programs. There is also a lack of available trained public health practitioners knowledgeable about oral health. As a result, existing disease prevention programs are not being implemented in many communities, creating gaps in prevention and care that affect the nation's neediest populations. Indeed, cutbacks in many state budgets have reduced staffing of state and territorial dental programs and curtailed oral health promotion and disease prevention efforts. An enhanced public health infrastructure would facilitate the development of strengthened partnerships with private practitioners, other public programs, and voluntary groups.

There is a lack of racial and ethnic diversity in the oral health workforce. Efforts to recruit members of minority groups to positions in health education, research, and practice in numbers that at least match their representation in the general population not only would enrich the talent pool, but also might result in a more equitable geographic distribution of care providers. The effect of that change could well enhance access and utilization of oral health care by racial and ethnic minorities.

A closer look at trends in the workforce discloses a worrisome shortfall in the numbers of men and women choosing careers in oral health education and research. Government and private sector leaders are aware of the problem and are discussing ways to increase and diversify the talent pool, including easing the financial burden of professional education, but additional incentives may be necessary.

**Remove known barriers between people and oral health services.** This report presents data on access, utilization, financing, and reimbursement of oral health care; provides additional data on the extent of the barriers; and points to the need for public-private partnerships in seeking solutions. The data indicate that lack of dental insurance, private or public, is one of several impediments to obtaining oral health care and accounts in part for the generally poorer oral health of those who live at or near the poverty line, lack health insurance, or lose their insurance upon retirement. The level of reimbursement for services also has been reported to be a problem and a disincentive to the participation of providers in certain public programs. Professional organizations and government agencies are cognizant of these problems and are exploring solutions that merit evaluation. Particular concern has been expressed about the nation's children, and initiatives such as the State Children's Health Insurance Program, while not mandating coverage for oral health services, are a positive step. In addition, individuals whose health is physically, mentally, and emotionally compromised need comprehensive integrated care.

**Use public-private partnerships to improve the oral health of those who still suffer disproportionately from oral diseases.** The collective and complementary talents of public health agencies, private industry, social services organizations, educators, health care providers, researchers, the media, community leaders, voluntary health organizations and consumer groups, and concerned citizens are vital if America is not just to reduce, but to eliminate, health disparities. This report highlights variations in oral and general health within and across all population groups. Increased public-private partnerships are needed to educate the public, to educate health professionals, to conduct research, and to provide health care services and programs. These partnerships can build and strengthen cross-disciplinary, culturally competent, community-based, and community-wide efforts and demonstration programs to expand initiatives for health promotion and disease prevention. Examples of such efforts include programs to prevent tobacco use, promote better dietary choices, and encourage the use of protective gear to prevent sports injuries. In this way, partnerships uniting sports organizations, schools, churches, and other community groups and leaders, working in concert with the health community, can contribute to improved oral and general health.

## Conclusion

The past half century has seen the meaning of oral health evolve from a narrow focus on teeth and gingiva to the recognition that the mouth is the center of vital tissues and functions that are critical to total health and well-being across the life span. The mouth as a mirror of health or disease, as a sentinel or early warning system, as an accessible model for the study of other tissues and organs, and as a potential source of pathology affecting other systems and organs has been described in earlier chapters and provides the impetus for extensive future research. Past discoveries have enabled Americans today to enjoy far better oral health than their forebears a century ago. But the evidence that not all Americans have achieved the same level of oral health and well-being stands as a major challenge, one that demands the best efforts of public and private agencies and individuals.

# REVISED FEDERAL
# NUTRITIONAL GUIDELINES
## May 27, 2000

*The federal government issued revised dietary guidelines on May 27, 2000, once again urging Americans to eat less and exercise more; to eat more whole grains, fruits, and vegetables; to moderate their consumption of sugar and alcohol; and to reduce their intake of salt and saturated fat. For the first time the guidelines distinguished among types of fat, recommending a diet moderate in total fat but low in saturated fat and trans fatty acids. A section on safe handling of food to prevent foodborne illness was also included for the first time. The guidelines emphasized the importance of physical activity in helping to reach and maintain a healthy weight and overall good health. "We want the public to know that you can't divorce physical activity from the diet. The two are intimately intertwined," said Cutberto Garza, releasing the proposed guidelines earlier in the year. Garza, a professor of nutrition at Cornell University, was the chairman of the panel that wrote the guidelines.*

*The panel took pains to make the guidelines more user-friendly than they had been in the past, offering more specific examples of recommended foods and ways to prepare them. The guidelines also implicitly acknowledged the ethnic diversity of the American people by highlighting how common Asian and Hispanic foods such as tofu and tortillas can fit into a healthy diet. "Eating is one of life's greatest pleasures," the guidelines declared. "Since there are many foods and many ways to build a healthy diet and lifestyle, there is lots of room for choice."*

*First issued in 1980, the guidelines were reviewed and revised every five years in light of new scientific findings on health and nutrition. The last revision was issued on January 2, 1996. Published jointly by the Agriculture Department and the Department of Health and Human Services, the guidelines formed the basis of federal nutrition policy, including the school lunch program. The food industry also used the guidelines in its consumer information labels on the nutritional content of various foods.* (Last guidelines revision, Historic Documents of 1996, p. 3)

*The eleven-member panel that drew up the revised guidelines worked for eighteen months reviewing scientific evidence and taking testimony both from experts in the field and the general public. Although the committee's recommendations were based largely on data widely accepted in the medical and nutrition communities, some issues—such as the appropriate levels of sugar, salt, and fat intake—were always controversial. Meat, sugar, beverage, and snack producers argued that the dangers of consuming sugar, salt, and animal fats were overblown and that the guidelines concerning those products were too strict. The committee was also criticized by some professional and consumer organizations for being culturally and racially biased. For example, the committee's recommendations on the consumption of milk and other dairy products were criticized because high proportions of African-Americans were lactose intolerant. One nonprofit group that promoted preventive medicine and a vegetarian lifestyle, the Physicians Committee for Responsible Medicine, charged that the some members of the committee had ties to industry that could have affected their judgments. It won a suit in federal district court in October to force the Agriculture Department to release the resumes of the 140 people who were nominated to serve on the guidelines panel; the physicians committee said it hoped to show that the most qualified people had not been selected to serve on the guidelines panel.*

## *Aiming for Fitness*

*In emphasizing the importance of a healthy weight and physical activity, the dietary guidelines were mirroring a growing concern in the health field with the problem of obesity, which had been implicated in numerous serious conditions, including high blood pressure, heart disease, stroke, and diabetes. By some measures, one in every three Americans was overweight, up from one in four at the beginning of the 1990s. The guidelines encouraged overweight Americans to lose weight but to do so gradually, at a rate of half a pound to two pounds a week. Repeatedly losing and regaining weight was less likely to improve health than reaching and maintaining a healthy weight.*

*To help maintain a healthy weight, the guidelines recommended that adults, including the elderly, try to get thirty minutes of physical activity every day. Moderate physical activity was defined as any activity that required the same amount of energy as walking two miles in thirty minutes. Whether a person preferred to participate in a formal exercise program or simply walk more and drive less was not as important as simply being active, the report said. People wishing to lose weight might have to exercise more vigorously to burn off unused calories. The report also encouraged children and teens to be physically active for at least an hour a day; it suggested that parents join their children in physical activities and limit inactive forms of play, such as television watching and computer games.*

*As it had in the past, the guidelines urged people to follow the Food Guide Pyramid to ensure that their diet contained the proper balance of nutrients required for good health. Americans should make a variety of grains, particularly whole grains, fruit, and vegetables, the foundation of their diets and "go easy on foods high in fat or sugars." In a departure from previous recommendations, which called on Americans to lower their intake of all fats, the 2000 guidelines distinguished between saturated fats and unsaturated fats. Saturated fats and dietary cholesterol, found in meat, high-fat dairy products, and some vegetable oils, increased blood cholesterol and were linked to an increased risk of coronary heart disease. In contrast, unsaturated fats, found in many vegetable oils, nuts, and fatty fish like salmon, helped to keep blood cholesterol low. The guidelines advised Americans to limit their intake of saturated fats and to keep total fat intake at no more than 30 percent of total calories.*

*The guidelines also advised people to "choose and prepare foods with less salt" and to "choose beverages and foods to moderate your intake of sugars." The expert panel that drafted the guidelines had recommended that Americans be advised to "limit" their intake of sugars, but when the sugar industry, backed by powerful members of Congress, objected to this language, the government overseers amended the wording to "moderate." The final guidelines also amended draft language that had linked the increased intake of calories in the United States to increased consumption of added sugars in nondiet soft drinks. The sugar industry claimed that these links had not been supported by a preponderance of the scientific evidence, the standard the drafters were required to use in developing the guidelines. The sugar growers, processors, and beverage manufacturers also argued that the tougher proposed standard could economically devastate the industry.*

*The recommendations on safe food handling were added in an effort to stem an increasing incidence of foodborne illnesses. Caused by harmful bacteria, viruses, parasites, and chemical contaminants, most such illnesses lasted only a few hours or days with no lasting side effects, but some foodborne illness could last for weeks or months and occasionally resulted in death. Although only about 15,000 cases of foodborne illness were diagnosed each year, estimates put the actual number at 6.5 million or more. The major steps in keeping food safe included washing hands and utensil and food preparation surfaces often and thoroughly; preventing cross-contamination from one food to another by keeping raw, cooked, and ready-to-eat foods separate from each other; cooking food to a safe temperature; refrigerating perishable foods promptly; and throwing out any food that might not have been prepared, served, or stored safely.* (Food safety, p. 880)

### *Rise in Diabetes Attributed to Increase in Obesity*

*In a related development, the Centers for Disease Control (CDC) reported on August 24 that the incidence of diabetes in the United States had increased significantly, rising from 4.9 percent of the population in 1990 to 6.5 percent in 1998. Researchers attributed much of the increase in diabetes to the rising incidence of obesity in the American population. The report showed that for every pound of excess weight, the risk of diabetes rose by 4 percent.*

*Between 90 and 95 percent of the cases were Type 2, or adult-onset diabetes, one cause of which was weight gain and inactivity. (Most of the remaining cases are Type 1 diabetes, which was caused by a malfunction in the immune system.) The CDC researchers said they were particularly troubled by a large increase in the incidence of diabetes among people in their thirties, from 2.1 percent in 1990 to 3.7 percent in 1998, and by the growing incidence of Type 2 diabetes among teenagers. In the past doctors saw adult-onset diabetes primarily in people age forty-five and older. In general, the longer a person had the disease, the more likely that person was to experience complications. Major complications from diabetes included blindness, kidney failure, and leg amputation; diabetes also substantially increased the risk of heart disease and stroke, the two leading causes of death in the United States.*

*The cost of diabetes, including treatment, was estimated at $98 billion a year. "Expensive as we think health care is today, with these chronic conditions coming on, it's going to be very threatening to quality of life as well as cost issues," said Frank Vinicor, director of the CDC's diabetes division and an author of the report, which appeared in the journal* Diabetes Care. *"We can't just view inactivity and overweight as purely a kind of cosmetic thing," he continued. "It's got to be viewed as a serious public health issue."*

*Following are excerpts from "Dietary Guidelines for Americans," the fourth revision of national nutritional guidelines, issued May 27, 2000, by the Departments of Agriculture and Health and Human Services. The document was obtained from the Internet at http://www.ars.usda.gov/dgac/dgac_ful.pdf.*

## Aim, Build, Choose—for Good Health

Eating is one of life's greatest pleasures. Since there are many foods and many ways to build a healthy diet and lifestyle, there is lots of room for choice. Use this [article] to help you and your family find ways to enjoy food while taking action for good health.

This [article] carries three basic messages—the ABC's for your health and that of your family:

- **A**im for fitness
- **B**uild a healthy base
- **C**hoose sensibly

Ten guidelines point the way to good health. These guidelines are intended for healthy children (ages 2 years and older) and adults of any age.

### Aim for fitness

- Aim for a healthy weight.
- Be physically active each day.

Following these two guidelines will help keep you and your family healthy and fit. Healthy eating and regular physical activity enable people of all ages to work productively, enjoy life, and feel their best. They also help children grow, develop, and do well in school.

### Build a healthy base

- Let the Pyramid guide your food choices.
- Choose a variety of grains daily, especially whole grains.
- Choose a variety of fruits and vegetables daily.
- Keep food safe to eat.

Following these four guidelines builds a base for healthy eating. Let the Food Guide Pyramid guide you so that you get the nutrients your body needs each day. Make grains, fruits, and vegetables the foundation of your meals. This forms a base for good nutrition and good health and may reduce your risk of certain chronic diseases. Be flexible and adventurous—try new choices from these three groups in place of some less nutritious or higher calorie foods you usually eat. Whatever you eat, always take steps to keep your food safe to eat.

### Choose sensibly

- Choose a diet that is low in saturated fat and cholesterol and moderate in total fat.
- Choose beverages and foods to moderate your intake of sugars.
- Choose and prepare foods with less salt.
- If you drink alcoholic beverages, do so in moderation.

These four guidelines help you make sensible choices that promote health and reduce the risk of certain chronic diseases. You can enjoy all foods as part of a healthy diet as long as you don't overdo it on fat (especially saturated fat), sugars, salt, and alcohol. Read labels to identify foods that are higher in saturated fats, sugars, and salt (sodium).

## Aim, Build, Choose—for Good Health

By following all of the guidelines in this [article], you can promote your health and reduce your risk for chronic diseases such as heart disease, certain types of cancer, diabetes, stroke, and osteoporosis. These diseases are leading causes of death and disability among Americans. Good diets can also reduce major risk factors for chronic disease—such as obesity, high blood pressure, and high blood cholesterol. Your food choices, your lifestyle, your environment, and your family history all affect your wellbeing. It is important for everyone to follow the 10 Dietary Guidelines in this [article]. If you are at higher risk for a chronic disease, it is especially important. So find out your family history of disease and your other risk factors for disease . . . to make more informed decisions about how to improve your health.

Together, the 10 guidelines in this [article] will help you build healthful eating patterns and take action for good health. This [article] tells you the reason each guideline is important and gives tips for following the guidelines. Use this [article] to find out some of the many ways to aim for fitness, to build a healthy base, and to choose sensibly.

## Aim for Fitness

### Aim for a Healthy Weight

Choose a lifestyle that combines sensible eating with regular physical activity. To be at their best, adults need to avoid gaining weight, and many need to lose weight. Being overweight or obese increases your risk for high blood pressure, high blood cholesterol, heart disease, stroke, diabetes, certain types of cancer, arthritis, and breathing problems. A healthy weight is key to a long, healthy life.

### Evaluate your body weight

For adults and children, different methods are used to find out if weight is about right for height. If you have concerns about your child's body size, talk with your health care provider. . . .

If you are an adult . . . evaluate your weight in relation to your height, or Body Mass Index (BMI). Not all adults who have a BMI in the range labeled "healthy" are at their most healthy weight. For example, some may have lots of fat and little muscle. A BMI above the healthy range is less healthy for most people; but it may be fine if you have lots of muscle and little fat. The further your BMI is above the healthy range, the higher your weight-related risk. . . . If your BMI is above the healthy range, you may benefit from weight loss, especially if you have other health risk factors. . . . BMI's slightly below the healthy range may still be healthy unless they result from illness.

If your BMI is below the healthy range, you may have increased risk of menstrual irregularity, infertility, and osteoporosis. If you lose weight suddenly or for unknown reasons, see a health care provider. Unexplained weight loss may be an early clue to a health problem.

Keep track of your weight and your waist measurement, and take action if either of them increases. If your BMI is greater than 25, or even if it is in the "healthy" range, at least try to avoid further weight gain. If your waist measurement increases, you are probably gaining fat. If so, take steps to eat fewer calories and become more active.

### Manage your weight

Our genes affect our tendency to gain weight. A tendency to gain weight is increased when food is plentiful and when we use equipment and vehicles to save time and energy. However, it is possible to manage your weight through balancing the calories you eat with your physical activity choices.

To make it easier to manage your weight, make long-term changes in your eating behavior and physical activity. To do this, build a healthy base and make sensible choices. Choose a healthful assortment of foods that includes vegetables, fruits, grains (especially whole grains), skim milk, and fish, lean meat, poultry, or beans. Choose foods that are low in fat and added sugars . . . most of the time. Whatever the food, eat a sensible portion size. . . .

Try to be more active throughout the day. The physical activity guideline . . . recommends that all adults get at least 30 minutes of moderate physical activity most or preferably all days of the week. To maintain a healthy weight after weight loss, adults will likely need to do more than 30 minutes of moderate physical activity daily. Over time, even a small decrease in calories eaten and a small increase in physical activity can keep you from gaining weight or help you lose weight.

High-fat foods contain more calories than the same amount of other foods, so they can make it difficult for you to avoid excess calories. However, *low fat* doesn't always mean low calorie. Sometimes extra sugars are added to low-fat muffins or desserts, for example, and they may be just as high in calories.

Your pattern of eating may be important. Snacks and meals eaten away from home provide a large part of daily calories for many people. Choose them wisely. Try fruits, vegetables, whole grain foods, or a cup of low-fat milk or yogurt for a snack. When eating out, choose small portions of foods. If you choose fish, poultry, or lean meat, ask that it be grilled rather than fried.

Like younger adults, overweight and obese older adults may improve their health by losing weight. The guidance of a health care provider is recommended, especially for obese children and older adults. Since older people tend to lose muscle mass, regular physical activity is a valuable part of a weight-loss plan. Building or maintaining muscle helps keep older adults active and reduces their risk of falls and fractures. Staying active throughout your adult years helps maintain muscle mass and bone strength for your later years.

## If you need to lose weight, do so gradually

If you are overweight, loss of 5 to 15 percent of your body weight may improve your health, ability to function, and quality of life. Aim to lose about 10 percent of your weight over about 6 months. This would be 20 pounds of weight loss for someone who weighs 200 pounds. Loss of ½ to 2 pounds per week is usually safe. Even if you have regained weight in the past, it's worthwhile to try again.

## Encourage healthy weight in children

Children need enough food for proper growth, but too many calories and too little physical activity lead to overweight. The number of overweight U.S. children has risen dramatically in recent years. Encourage healthy weight by offering children grain products; vegetables and fruits; low-fat dairy products; and beans, lean meat, poultry, fish, or nuts—and let them see you enjoy eating the same foods. Let the child decide how much of these foods to eat. Offer only small amounts of food high in fat or added sugars. Encourage children to take part in vigorous activities (and join them whenever possible). Limit the time they spend in sedentary activities like watching television or playing computer or video games.

Help children to develop healthy eating habits. Make small changes. For example, serve low-fat milk rather than whole milk and offer one cookie instead of two. Since children still need to grow, weight loss is not recommended unless guided by a health care provider.

### Serious eating disorders

Frequent binge eating, with or without periods of food restriction, may be a sign of a serious eating disorder. Other signs of eating disorders include preoccupation with body weight or food (or both—regardless of body weight), dramatic weight loss, excessive exercise, self-induced vomiting, and the abuse of laxatives. Seek help from a health care provider if any of these apply to you, a family member, or a friend.

## Advice for Today

- Aim for a healthy weight. If you are at a healthy weight, aim to avoid weight gain. If you are already overweight, first aim to prevent further weight gain, and then lose weight to improve your health.
- Build a healthy base by eating vegetables, fruits, and grains (especially whole grains) with little added fat or sugar. Select sensible portion sizes.
- Get moving. Get regular physical activity to balance calories from the foods you eat.
- Set a good example for children by practicing healthy eating habits and enjoying regular physical activities together.
- Keep in mind that even though heredity and the environment are important influences, your behaviors help determine your body weight.

## Aim for Fitness

### Be Physically Active Each Day

Being physically active and maintaining a healthy weight are both needed for good health, but they benefit health in different ways. Children, teens, adults, and the elderly—all can improve their health and wellbeing and have fun by including moderate amounts of physical activity in their daily lives. Physical activity involves moving the body. A moderate physical activity is any activity that requires about as much energy as walking 2 miles in 30 minutes.

Aim to accumulate at least 30 minutes (adults) or 60 minutes (children) of moderate physical activity most days of the week, preferably daily. If you already get 30 minutes of physical activity daily, you can gain even more health benefits by increasing the amount of time that you are physically active or by taking part in more vigorous activities. No matter what activity you choose, you can do it all at once, or spread it out over two or three times during the day.

### Make physical activity a regular part of your routine

Choose activities that you enjoy and that you can do regularly. . . . Some people prefer activities that fit into their daily routine, like gardening or taking extra trips up and down stairs. Others prefer a regular exercise program, such as a physical activity program at their worksite. Some do both. The important thing is to be physically active every day.

Most adults do not need to see their health care provider before starting to become more physically active. However, if you are planning to start a vigorous activity plan and have one or more of the conditions below, consult your health care provider:

- Chronic health problem such as heart disease, hypertension, diabetes, osteoporosis, or obesity.
- High risk for heart disease
- Over age 40 for men or 50 for women.

### Health benefits of physical activity

Compared with being very sedentary, being physically active for at least 30 minutes on most days of the week reduces the risk of developing or dying of heart disease. It has other health benefits as well. . . . No one is too young or too old to enjoy the benefits of regular physical activity.

Two types of physical activity are especially beneficial:

- *Aerobic activities.* These are activities that speed your heart rate and breathing. They help cardiovascular fitness.
- *Activities for strength and flexibility.* Developing strength may help build and maintain your bones. Carrying groceries and lifting weights are two strength-building activities. Gentle stretching, dancing, or yoga can increase flexibility.

### Physical activity and nutrition

Physical activity and nutrition work together for better health. For example, physical activity increases the amount of calories you use. For those who have intentionally lost weight, being active makes it easier to maintain the weight loss. However, 30 minutes of activity daily may not be enough to lose weight or maintain weight loss. . . .

Physical activity and nutrition work together in more ways than weight management. Increasing the calories you use allows you to eat more, which makes it easier to get the nutrients you need. Physical activity and nutrition work together for bone health, too. Calcium and other nutrients are needed to build and maintain strong bones, but physical activity is needed as well.

### Help children be physically active

Children and adolescents benefit from physical activity in many ways. They need at least 60 minutes of physical activity daily. . . . Parents can help:

- Set a good example. For example, arrange active family events in which everyone takes part. Join your children in physical activities.
- Encourage your children to be physically active at home, at school, and with friends by jumping rope, playing tag, riding a bike.
- Limit television watching, computer games, and other inactive forms of play by alternating with periods of physical activity.

## Older people need to be physically active too

Older persons also need to be physically active. Engage in moderate physical activity for at least 30 minutes most days of the week, preferably daily, and take part in activities to strengthen muscles and to improve flexibility. Staying strong and flexible can reduce your risk of falling and breaking bones, preserve muscle, and improve your ability to live independently. Lifting small weights and carrying groceries are two ways to include strength building into your routine.

### Advice for Today

- Engage in at least 30 minutes (adults) or 60 minutes (children) of moderate physical activity most, preferably all, days of the week.
- Become physically active if you are inactive. Maintain or increase physical activity if you are already active.
- Stay active throughout your life.
- Help children get at least 60 minutes of physical activity daily.
- Choose physical activities that fit in with your daily routine, or choose recreational or structured exercise programs, or both.
- Consult your health care provider before starting a new vigorous physical activity plan if you have a chronic health problem, or if you are over 40 (men) or 50 (women).

## Build a Healthy Base

### Let the Pyramid guide your food choices

Different foods contain different nutrients and other healthful substances. No single food can supply all the nutrients in the amounts you need. For example, oranges provide vitamin C and folate but no vitamin $B_{12}$; cheese provides calcium and vitamin $B_{12}$ but no vitamin C. To make sure you get all the nutrients and other substances you need for health, build a healthy base by using the Food Guide Pyramid . . . as a starting point. Choose the recommended number of daily servings from each of the five major food groups. . . . If you avoid all foods from any of the five food groups, seek guidance to help ensure that you get all the nutrients you need.

### Use plant foods as the foundation of your meals

There are many ways to create a healthy eating pattern, but they all start with the three food groups at the base of the Pyramid: grains, fruits, and vegetables. Eating a variety of grains (especially whole grain foods), fruits, and vegetables is the basis of healthy eating. Enjoy meals that have rice, pasta, tortillas, or whole grain bread at the center of the plate, accompanied by plenty of fruits and vegetables and a moderate amount of low-fat foods from the milk group and the meat and beans group. Go easy on foods high in fat or sugars.

### Keep an eye on servings

Compare the recommended number of servings . . . and the serving sizes . . . with what you usually eat. If you don't need many calories (because

249

you're inactive, for example), aim for the lower number of servings. Notice that some of the serving sizes . . . are smaller than what you might usually eat or see on food labels. For example, many people eat 2 slices of bread in a meal, which equal 2 servings. So it's easy to meet the recommended number of servings. Young children 2 to 3 years old need the same number of servings as others, but smaller serving sizes except for milk.

Also notice that many of the meals and snacks you eat contain items from several food groups. For example, a sandwich may provide bread from the grains group, turkey from the meat and beans group, and cheese from the milk group.

Choose a variety of foods for good nutrition. Since foods within most food groups differ in their content of nutrients and other beneficial substances, choosing a variety helps you get all the nutrients and fiber you need. It can also help keep your meals interesting from day to day.

### There are many healthful eating patterns

Different people like different foods and like to prepare the same foods in different ways. Culture, family background, religion, moral beliefs, the cost and availability of food, life experiences, food intolerances, and allergies affect people's food choices. Use the Food Guide Pyramid as a starting point to shape your eating pattern. It provides a good guide to make sure you get enough nutrients. Make choices from each major group in the Food Guide Pyramid, and combine them however you like. For example, those who like Mexican cuisine might choose tortillas from the grains group and beans from the meat and beans group, while those who eat Asian food might choose rice from the grains group and tofu from the meat and beans group.

If you usually avoid all foods from one or two of the food groups, be sure to get enough nutrients from other food groups. For example, if you choose not to eat milk products because of intolerance to lactose or for other reasons, choose other foods that are good sources of calcium, . . . and be sure to get enough vitamin D. Meat, fish, and poultry are major contributors of iron, zinc, and B vitamins in most American diets. If you choose to avoid all or most animal products, be sure to get enough iron, vitamin $B_{12}$, calcium, and zinc from other sources. Vegetarian diets can be consistent with the *Dietary Guidelines for Americans*, and meet Recommended Dietary Allowances for nutrients.

### Growing children, teenagers, women, and older adults have higher needs for some nutrients

Adolescents and adults over age 50 have an especially high need for calcium, but most people need to eat plenty of good sources of calcium for healthy bones throughout life. When selecting dairy products to get enough calcium, choose those that are low in fat or fat free to avoid getting too much saturated fat. Young children, teenage girls, and women of childbearing age need enough good sources of iron, such as lean meats and cereals with added nutrients, to keep up their iron stores. . . . Women who could become pregnant need extra folic acid, and older adults need extra vitamin D.

### Check the food label before you buy

Food labels have several parts, including the front panel, Nutrition Facts, and ingredient list. The front panel often tells you if nutrients have been added—for example, "iodized salt" lets you know that iodine has been added, and "enriched pasta" (or "enriched" grain of any type) means that thiamin, riboflavin, niacin, iron, and folic acid have been added.

The ingredient list tells you what's in the food, including any nutrients, fats, or sugars that have been added. The ingredients are listed in descending order by weight.

. . . Use the Nutrition Facts to see if a food is a good source of a nutrient or to compare similar foods—for example, to find which brand of frozen dinner is lower in saturated fat, or which kind of breakfast cereal contains more folic acid. Look at the % Daily Value (% DV) column to see whether a food is high or low in nutrients. If you want to limit a nutrient (such as fat, saturated fat, cholesterol, sodium), try to choose foods with a lower % DV. If you want to consume more of a nutrient (such as calcium, other vitamins and minerals, fiber), try to choose foods with a higher % DV.

As a guide, foods with 5% DV or less contribute a small amount of that nutrient to your eating pattern, while those with 20% or more contribute a large amount. Remember, Nutrition Facts serving sizes may differ from those used in the Food Guide Pyramid. . . . For example, 2 ounces of dry macaroni yields about 1 cup cooked, or two (½ cup) Pyramid servings.

### Use of dietary supplements

Some people need a vitamin/mineral supplement to meet specific nutrient needs. For example, women who could become pregnant are advised to eat foods fortified with folic acid or to take a folic acid supplement in addition to consuming folate-rich foods to reduce the risk of some serious birth defects. Older adults and people with little exposure to sunlight may need a vitamin D supplement. People who seldom eat dairy products or other rich sources of calcium need a calcium supplement, and people who eat no animal foods need to take a vitamin $B_{12}$ supplement. Sometimes vitamins or minerals are prescribed for meeting nutrient needs or for therapeutic purposes. For example, health care providers may advise pregnant women to take an iron supplement, and adults over age 50 to get their vitamin $B_{12}$ from a supplement or from fortified foods.

Supplements of some nutrients, such as vitamin A and selenium, can be harmful if taken in large amounts. Because foods contain many substances that promote health, use the Food Guide Pyramid when choosing foods. Don't depend on supplements to meet your usual nutrient needs.

Dietary supplements include not only vitamins and minerals, but also amino acids, fiber, herbal products, and many other substances that are widely available. Herbal products usually provide a very small amount of vitamins and minerals. The value of herbal products for health is currently being studied. Standards for their purity, potency, and composition are being developed.

## Advice for Today

- Build a healthy base: Use the Food Guide Pyramid to help make healthy food choices that you can enjoy.
- Build your eating pattern on a variety of plant foods, including whole grains, fruits, and vegetables.
- Also choose some low-fat dairy products and low-fat foods from the meat and beans group each day. It's fine to enjoy fats and sweets occasionally.

## Build a Healthy Base

### Choose a variety of grains daily, especially whole grains

Foods made from grains (like wheat, rice, and oats) help form the foundation of a nutritious diet. They provide vitamins, minerals, carbohydrates (starch and dietary fiber), and other substances that are important for good health. Grain products are low in fat, unless fat is added in processing, in preparation, or at the table. Whole grains differ from refined grains in the amount of fiber and nutrients they provide, and different whole grain foods differ in nutrient content, so choose a variety of whole and enriched grains. Eating plenty of whole grains, such as whole wheat bread or oatmeal, . . . as part of the healthful eating patterns described by these guidelines, may help protect you against many chronic diseases. Aim for at least 6 servings of grain products per day—more if you are an older child or teenager, an adult man, or an active woman . . . and include several servings of whole grain foods. . . .

### Why choose whole grain foods?

Vitamins, minerals, fiber, and other protective substances in whole grain foods contribute to the health benefits of whole grains. Refined grains are low in fiber and in the protective substances that accompany fiber. Eating plenty of fiber-containing foods, such as whole grains (and also many fruits and vegetables) promotes proper bowel function. The high fiber content of many whole grains may also help you to feel full with fewer calories. Fiber is best obtained from foods like whole grains, fruits, and vegetables rather than from fiber supplements for several reasons: there are many types of fiber, the composition of fiber is poorly understood, and other protective substances accompany fiber in foods. Use the Nutrition Facts Label to help choose grains that are rich in fiber and low in saturated fat and sodium.

### Enriched grains are a new source of folic acid

Folic acid, a form of folate, is now added to all enriched grain products (thiamin, riboflavin, niacin, and iron have been added to enriched grains for many years). Folate is a B vitamin that reduces the risk of some serious types of birth defects when consumed before and during early pregnancy. Studies are underway to clarify whether it decreases risk for coronary heart disease, stroke, and certain types of cancer. Whole grain foods naturally contain some folate, but only a few (mainly ready-to-eat breakfast cereals) contain added folic acid as well. Read the ingredient label to find out if folic acid and other nutrients have been added, and check the Nutrition Facts Label to compare the nutrient content of foods like breakfast cereals.

## Advice for Today

- Build a healthy base by making a variety of grain products a foundation of your diet.
- Eat 6 or more servings of grain products daily (whole grain and refined breads, cereals, pasta, and rice). Include several servings of whole grain foods daily for their good taste and their health benefits. If your calorie needs are low, have only 6 servings of a sensible size daily. . . .
- Eat foods made from a variety of whole grains—such as whole wheat, brown rice, oats, and whole grain corn—every day.
- Combine whole grains with other tasty, nutritious foods in mixed dishes.
- Prepare or choose grain products with little added saturated fat and a moderate or low amount of added sugars. Also, check the sodium content on the Nutrition Facts Label.

# Build a Healthy Base

## Choose a variety of fruits and vegetables daily

Fruits and vegetables are key parts of your daily diet. Eating plenty of fruits and vegetables of different kinds, as part of the healthful eating patterns described by these guidelines, may help protect you against many chronic diseases. It also promotes healthy bowel function. Fruits and vegetables provide essential vitamins and minerals, fiber, and other substances that are important for good health. Most people, including children, eat fewer servings of fruits and vegetables than are recommended. To promote your health, eat a variety of fruits and vegetables—at least 2 servings of fruits and 3 servings of vegetables—each day.

### Why eat plenty of different fruits and vegetables?

Different fruits and vegetables are rich in different nutrients. . . . Some fruits and vegetables are excellent sources of carotenoids, including those which form vitamin A, while others may be rich in vitamin C, folate, or potassium. Fruits and vegetables, especially dry beans and peas, also contain fiber and other substances that are associated with good health. Dark-green leafy vegetables, deeply colored fruits, and dry beans and peas are especially rich in many nutrients. Most fruits and vegetables are naturally low in fat and calories and are filling. Some are high in fiber, and many are quick to prepare and easy to eat. Choose whole or cutup fruits and vegetables rather than juices most often. Juices contain little or no fiber.

### Aim for Variety

Try many colors and kinds. Choose any form: fresh, frozen, canned, dried, juices. All forms provide vitamins and minerals, and all provide fiber except for most juices—so choose fruits and vegetables most often. Wash fresh fruits and vegetables thoroughly before using. If you buy prepared vegetables, check the Nutrition Facts Label to find choices that are low in saturated fat and sodium.

Try serving fruits and vegetables in new ways:

- raw vegetables with a low- or reduced-fat dip
- vegetables stir-fried in a small amount of vegetable oil
- fruits or vegetables mixed with other foods in salads, casseroles, soups, sauces (for example, add shredded vegetables when making meatloaf)

Find ways to include plenty of different fruits and vegetables in your meals and snacks.

- Buy wisely. Frozen or canned fruits and vegetables are sometimes best buys, and they are rich in nutrients. If fresh fruit is very ripe, buy only enough to use right away.
- Store properly to maintain quality. Refrigerate most fresh fruits (not bananas) and vegetables (not potatoes or tomatoes) for longer storage, and arrange them so you'll use up the ripest ones first. If you cut them up or open a can, cover and refrigerate afterward.
- Keep ready-to-eat raw vegetables handy in a clear container in the front of your refrigerator for snacks or meals-on-the-go.
- Keep a day's supply of fresh or dried fruit handy on the table or counter.
- Enjoy fruits as a naturally sweet end to a meal.
- When eating out, choose a variety of vegetables at a salad bar.

### Advice for Today

Enjoy five a day—eat at least 2 servings of fruit and at least 3 servings of vegetables each day. . . . Choose fresh, frozen, dried, or canned forms and a variety of colors and kinds. Choose dark-green leafy vegetables, orange fruits and vegetables, and cooked dry beans and peas often.

## Build a Healthy Base

### Keep food safe to eat

Foods that are safe from harmful bacteria, viruses, parasites, and chemical contaminants are vital for healthful eating. *Safe* means that the food poses little risk of foodborne illness. . . . Farmers, food producers, markets, food service establishments, and other food preparers have a role to keep food as safe as possible. However, we also need to keep and prepare foods safely in the home, and be alert when eating out.

Follow the steps below to keep your food safe. Be very careful with perishable foods such as eggs, meats, poultry, fish, shellfish, milk products, and fresh fruits and vegetables. If you are at high risk of foodborne illness, be extra careful. . . .

### Clean. Wash hands and surfaces often

Wash your hands with warm soapy water for 20 seconds (count to 30) before you handle food or food utensils. Wash your hands after handling or preparing food, especially after handling raw meat, poultry, fish, shellfish, or eggs. Right after you prepare these raw foods, clean the utensils and surfaces you used with hot soapy water. Replace cutting boards once they have become worn or develop hard-to-clean grooves. Wash raw fruit and vegetables under running water before eating. Use a vegetable brush to remove surface dirt if necessary. Always wash your hands after using the bathroom, changing diapers, or playing with pets. When eating out, if the tables, dinnerware, and restrooms look dirty, the kitchen may be, too—so you may want to eat somewhere else.

### Separate. Separate raw, cooked, and ready-to-eat foods while shopping, preparing, or storing

Keep raw meat, poultry, eggs, fish, and shellfish away from other foods, surfaces, utensils, or serving plates. This prevents cross-contamination from one food to another. Store raw meat, poultry, fish, and shellfish in containers in the refrigerator so that the juices don't drip onto other foods.

### Cook. Cook foods to a safe temperature

Uncooked and undercooked animal foods are potentially unsafe. Proper cooking makes most uncooked foods safe. The best way to tell if meat, poultry, or egg dishes are cooked to a safe temperature is to use a food thermometer. . . . Several kinds of inexpensive food thermometers are available in many stores.

Reheat sauces, soups, marinades, and gravies to a boil. Reheat leftovers thoroughly to at least 165° F. If using a microwave oven, cover the container and turn or stir the food to make sure it is heated evenly throughout. Cook eggs until whites and yolks are firm. Don't eat raw or partially cooked eggs, or foods containing raw eggs, raw (unpasteurized) milk, or cheeses made with raw milk. Choose pasteurized juices. The risk of contamination is high from undercooked hamburger, and from raw fish (including sushi), clams, and oysters. Cook fish and shellfish until it is opaque; fish should flake easily with a fork. When eating out, order foods thoroughly cooked and make sure they are served piping hot.

### Chill. Refrigerate perishable foods promptly

When shopping, buy perishable foods last, and take them straight home. At home, refrigerate or freeze meat, poultry, eggs, fish, shellfish, ready-to-eat foods, and leftovers promptly. Refrigerate within 2 hours of purchasing or preparation—and within 1 hour if the air temperature is above 90° F. Refrigerate at or below 40°, or freeze at or below 0° F. Use refrigerated leftovers within 3 to 4 days. Freeze fresh meat, poultry, fish, and shellfish that cannot be used in a few days. Thaw frozen meat, poultry, fish, and shellfish in the refrigerator, microwave, or cold water changed every 30 minutes. (This keeps the surface chilled.) Cook foods immediately after thawing. Never thaw meat, poultry, fish, or shellfish at room temperature. When eating out, make sure that any foods you order that should be refrigerated are served chilled.

## Follow the label

Read the label and follow safety instructions on the package such as **"keep refrigerated"** and the **"safe handling instructions."**

## Serve safely

Keep hot foods hot (140° F or above) and cold foods cold (40° F or below). Harmful bacteria can grow rapidly in the "danger zone" between these temperatures. Whether raw or cooked, never leave meat, poultry, eggs, fish, or shellfish out at room temperature for more than 2 hours (1 hour in hot weather 90° F or above). Be sure to chill leftovers as soon as your are finished eating. These guidelines also apply to carryout meals, restaurant leftovers, and home-packed meals-to-go.

## When in doubt, throw it out

If you aren't sure that food has been prepared, served, or stored safely, throw it out. You may not be able to make food safe if it has been handled in an unsafe manner. For example, a food that has been left at room temperature too long may contain a toxin produced by bacteria—one that can't be destroyed by cooking. So if meat, poultry, fish, shellfish, or eggs have been left out for more than 2 hours, or if the food has been kept in the refrigerator too long, don't taste it. Just throw it out. Even if it looks and smells fine, it may not be safe to eat. If you have doubt when you're shopping or eating out, choose something else. . . .

### Advice for Today

Build a healthy base by keeping food safe to eat.

- Clean. Wash hands and surfaces often.
- Separate. Separate raw, cooked, and ready-to-eat foods while shopping, preparing, or storing.
- Cook. Cook foods to a safe temperature.
- Chill. Refrigerate perishable foods promptly.
- Check and follow the label.
- Serve safely. Keep hot foods hot and cold foods cold.
- When in doubt, throw it out.

## Choose Sensibly

### Choose a diet that is low in saturated fat and cholesterol and moderate in total fat

Fats supply energy and essential fatty acids, and they help absorb the fat-soluble vitamins A, D, E, and K, and carotenoids. You need some fat in the food you eat, but choose sensibly. Some kinds of fat, especially saturated fats, increase the risk for coronary heart disease by raising the blood cholesterol. . . . In contrast, unsaturated fats (found mainly in vegetable oils) do not increase blood cholesterol. Fat intake in the United States as a proportion of total calories is lower than it was many years ago, but most people still eat too much saturated fat. Eating lots of fat of any type can provide excess calories.

### Choose foods low in saturated fat and cholesterol

. . . [Limit] the amount of saturated fat and cholesterol you get from your food. Taking these steps can go a long way in helping to keep your blood cholesterol level low.

. . . [K]eep your intake of saturated fat at less than 10 percent of calories. . . . [K]eep your cholesterol intake less than the Daily Value of 300 mg/day listed on the Nutrition Facts Label. . . . The maximum number of saturated fat grams depends on the amount of calories you get daily. Use Nutrition Facts Labels to find out how much saturated fat is in prepared foods. If you choose one food that is higher in saturated fat, make your other choices lower in saturated fat. This will help you stay under your saturated fat limit for the day.

### Keep total fat intake moderate

Aim for a total fat intake of no more than 30 percent of calories, as recommended in previous editions of the Guidelines. If you need to reduce your fat intake to achieve this level, do so primarily by cutting back on saturated and *trans* fats. . . . If you are at a healthy weight and you eat little saturated fat, you'll have leeway to eat some plant foods that are high in unsaturated fats. . . .

### Advice for children

Advice in the previous sections applies to children who are 2 years of age or older. It does not apply to infants and toddlers below the age of 2 years. Beginning at age 2, children should get most of their calories from grain products; fruits; vegetables; low-fat dairy products; and beans, lean meat and poultry, fish, or nuts. Be careful, nuts may cause choking in 2 to 3 year olds.

### Advice for Today

To reduce your intake of saturated fat and cholesterol:

- Limit use of solid fats, such as butter, hard margarines, lard, and partially hydrogenated shortenings. Use vegetable oils as a substitute.
- Choose fat-free or low-fat dairy products, cooked dry beans and peas, fish, and lean meats and poultry.
- Eat plenty of grain products, vegetables, and fruits daily.
- Use the Nutrition Facts Label to help choose foods lower in fat, saturated fat, and cholesterol.

## Choose Sensibly

### Choose beverages and foods to moderate your intake of sugars

Sugars are carbohydrates and a source of energy (calories). Dietary carbohydrates also include the complex carbohydrates starch and dietary fiber. During digestion all carbohydrates except fiber break down into sugars. Sugars and starches occur naturally in many foods that also supply other nutrients. Examples of these foods include milk, fruits, some vegetables, breads, cereals, and grains.

## Sugars and tooth decay

Foods containing sugars and starches can promote tooth decay. The amount of bacteria in your mouth and lack of exposure to fluorides also promote tooth decay. These bacteria use sugars and starches to produce the acid that causes tooth decay. The more often you eat foods that contain sugars and starches, and the longer these foods remain in your mouth before you brush your teeth, the greater your risk for tooth decay. Frequent eating or drinking sweet or starchy foods between meals is more likely to harm teeth than eating the same foods at meals and then brushing.

## Added sugars

Added sugars are sugars and syrups added to foods in processing or preparation, not the naturally occurring sugars in foods like fruit or milk. The body cannot tell the difference between naturally occurring and added sugars because they are identical chemically. Foods containing added sugars provide calories, but may have few vitamins and minerals. In the United States, the number one source of added sugars is nondiet soft drinks (soda or pop). Sweets and candies, cakes and cookies, and fruit drinks and fruit-ades are also major sources of added sugars.

Intake of a lot of foods high in added sugars, like soft drinks, is of concern. Consuming excess calories from these foods may contribute to weight gain or lower consumption of more nutritious foods. . . . Limit your use of these beverages and foods. Drink water to quench your thirst, and offer it to children.

Some foods with added sugars, like chocolate milk, presweetened cereals, and sweetened canned fruits, also are high in vitamins and minerals. These foods may provide extra calories along with the nutrients and are fine if you need the extra calories.

The Nutrition Facts Label gives the content of sugars from all sources (naturally occurring sugars plus added sugars, if any. . . ). You can use the Nutrition Facts Label to compare the amount of total sugars among similar products. To find out if sugars have been added, you also need to look at the food label ingredient list. . . .

## Sugar substitutes

Sugar substitutes such as saccharin, aspartame, acesulfame potassium, and sucralose are extremely low in calories. Some people find them useful if they want a sweet taste without the calories. Some foods that contain sugar substitutes, however, still have calories. Unless you reduce the total calories you eat or increase your physical activity, using sugar substitutes will not cause you to lose weight.

## Sugars and other health issues

*Behavior.* Intake of sugars does not appear to affect children's behavior patterns or their ability to learn. Many scientific studies conclude that sugars do not cause hyperactivity in children.

*Weight control.* Foods that are high in sugars but low in essential nutrients primarily contribute calories to the diet. When you take in extra calories and don't offset them by increasing your physical activity, you will gain weight. As you aim for a healthy weight and fitness, keep an eye on portion size for all foods and beverages, not only those high in sugars. . . .

## Advice for Today

- Choose sensibly to limit your intake of beverages and foods that are high in added sugars.
- Get most of your calories from grains (especially whole grains), fruits and vegetables, low-fat or nonfat dairy products, and lean meats or meat substitutes.
- Take care not to let soft drinks or other sweets crowd out other foods you need to maintain health, such as low-fat milk or other good sources of calcium.
- Drink water often.

## Choose and prepare foods with less salt

Many people can reduce their chances of developing high blood pressure by consuming less salt. Several other steps can also help keep your blood pressure in the healthy range. . . . In the body, sodium—which you get mainly from salt—plays an essential role in regulating fluids and blood pressure. Many studies in diverse populations have shown that a high sodium intake is associated with higher blood pressure.

There is no way to tell who might develop high blood pressure from eating too much salt. However, consuming less salt or sodium is not harmful and can be recommended for the healthy, normal person. . . .

At present, the firmest link between salt intake and health relates to blood pressure. High salt intake also increases the amount of calcium excreted in the urine. Eating less salt may decrease the loss of calcium from bone. Loss of too much calcium from bone increases the risk of osteoporosis and bone fractures.

## Salt is found mainly in processed and prepared foods

Salt (sodium chloride) is the main source of sodium in foods. . . . Only small amounts of salt occur naturally in foods. Most of the salt you eat comes from foods that have salt added during food processing or during preparation in a restaurant or at home. Some recipes include table salt or a salty broth or sauce, and some cooking styles call for adding a very salty seasoning such as soy sauce. Not all foods with added salt taste salty. Some people add salt or a salty seasoning to their food at the table. Your preference for salt may decrease if you gradually add smaller amounts of salt or salty seasonings to your food over a period of time.

## Aim for a moderate sodium intake

Most people consume too much salt, so moderate your salt intake. Healthy children and adults need to consume only small amounts of salt to meet their sodium needs—less than ¼ teaspoon of salt daily. The Nutrition Facts Label lists a Daily Value of 2,400 mg of sodium per day. . . . This is the amount of sodium in about 1 teaspoon of salt. . . .

## Advice for Today

Choose sensibly to moderate your salt intake. Choose fruits and vegetables often. They contain very little salt unless it is added in processing. Read the Nutrition Facts Label to compare and help identify foods lower in sodium— especially prepared foods. Use herbs, spices, and fruits to flavor food, and cut the amount of salty seasonings by half. If you eat restaurant foods or fast foods, choose those that are prepared with only moderate amounts of salt or salty flavorings.

# Choose Sensibly

### If you drink alcoholic beverages, do so in moderation

Alcoholic beverages supply calories but few nutrients. Alcoholic beverages are harmful when consumed in excess, and some people should not drink at all. Excess alcohol alters judgment and can lead to dependency and a great many other serious health problems. Taking more than one drink per day for women or two drinks per day for men . . . can raise the risk for motor vehicle crashes, other injuries, high blood pressure, stroke, violence, suicide, and certain types of cancer. Even one drink per day can slightly raise the risk of breast cancer. Alcohol consumption during pregnancy increases risk of birth defects. Too much alcohol may cause social and psychological problems, cirrhosis of the liver, inflammation of the pancreas, and damage to the brain and heart. Heavy drinkers also are at risk of malnutrition because alcohol contains calories that may substitute for those in nutritious foods. If adults choose to drink alcoholic beverages, they should consume them only in moderation . . . and with meals to slow alcohol absorption.

Drinking in moderation may lower risk for coronary heart disease, mainly among men over age 45 and women over age 55. However, there are other factors that reduce the risk of heart disease, including a healthy diet, physical activity, avoidance of smoking, and maintenance of a healthy weight.

Moderate consumption provides little, if any, health benefit for younger people. Risk of alcohol abuse increases when drinking starts at an early age. Some studies suggest that older people may become more sensitive to the effects of alcohol as they age.

### Who should not drink?

Some people should not drink alcoholic beverages at all. These include:

- *Children and adolescents.*
- *Individuals of any age who cannot restrict their drinking to moderate levels.* This is a special concern for recovering alcoholics, problem drinkers, and people whose family members have alcohol problems.
- *Women who may become pregnant or who are pregnant.* A safe level of alcohol intake has not been established for women at any time during

pregnancy, including the first few weeks. Major birth defects, including fetal alcohol syndrome, can be caused by heavy drinking by the pregnant mother. Other fetal alcohol effects may occur at lower levels.

- *Individuals who plan to drive, operate machinery, or take part in other activities that require attention, skill, or coordination.* Most people retain some alcohol in the blood up to 2 to 3 hours after a single drink.
- *Individuals taking prescription or over-the-counter medications that can interact with alcohol.* Alcohol alters the effectiveness or toxicity of many medications, and some medications may increase blood alcohol levels. If you take medications, ask your health care provider for advice about alcohol intake, especially if you are an older adult.

## Advice for Today

If you choose to drink alcoholic beverages, do so sensibly. Limit intake to one drink/day for women or two/day for men, and take with meals to slow alcohol absorption. Avoid drinking before or when driving, or whenever it puts you or others at risk.

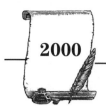

# June

# FEDERAL APPEALS COURT ON
# ASYLUM FOR ELIAN GONZALEZ
## June 1, 2000

*On November 25, 1999, a five-year old Cuban boy, Elian Gonzalez, was found clinging to an inner tube in the ocean waters near Fort Lauderdale, Florida. He was one of three survivors that had fled Cuba in a small boat; another ten, including his mother and stepfather, drowned when the boat capsized. Elian's great uncle, Lazaro Gonzalez, a Miami resident, was given temporary custody of the boy. On November 27, Elian's father, Juan Miguel Gonzalez, formally requested that his son be returned to him in Cuba. Lazaro, who in the early 1980s had fled the authoritarian regime in Cuba headed by President Fidel Castro, refused and instead filed an application for asylum on Elian's behalf.*

*Thus began a custody battle that during the next six months would embroil all three branches of government, American politics, and U.S. relations with Cuba. It also began a media frenzy surpassed in recent years only by President Bill Clinton's liaison with White House intern Monica Lewinsky and the deaths of Princess Diana and John F. Kennedy Jr. For more than six months television news crews chronicled every twist and turn of the unfolding story, and talk shows regularly discussed the case.*

*In the end Elian was reunited with his father and returned to Cuba—the outcome the Clinton administration had worked for from the beginning. But the Justice Department gained custody of Elian only by staging an armed raid on Lazaro's house, a move that touched off near-riots in Miami and appalled even those Americans who supported Elian's return to his father. For many Cuban Americans, Elian came to represent their quest to free their homeland from the authoritarian regime Castro had imposed on Cuba since taking power in 1959. They were not so opposed to reuniting Elian with his father as they were to returning him to a country where the government routinely suppressed human rights.*

*Ironically, the Cuban American community may have lost more than the custody battle. The incident may have revitalized, at least momentarily, Castro's political credibility among his people, who were suffering from a*

*weak economy and increasing isolation as the only communist regime re-
maining in the Western Hemisphere. At the same time, the strident and
unbending resistance that Elian's Miami relatives and their supporters
mounted against giving him to the authorities may have undermined the
political strength of the Cuban American lobby, which for years had successfully blocked lifting of American trade sanctions on Cuba. Whether the
incident had any lasting effect on the American political scene or on U.S. relations with Cuba remained to be seen. Although House Republican leaders
reluctantly acquiesced to legislation allowing direct food sales to Cuba, the
final version made it highly unlikely that much American food or medicine
would reach Cuba. President-elect George W. Bush indicated during his
campaign that he favored the continuation of trade sanctions against the
Castro government.*

## *The Custody Battle*

*The custody battle began in earnest on January 5, 2000, when the Immi-
gration and Naturalization Service (INS) rejected Lazaro's applications for
asylum on behalf of Elian and ruled that Elian should be returned to his
father. "Returning Elian to his father in Cuba was thus the right decision
legally; it's the right decision morally," said INS commissioner Doris M.
Meissner. "Both U.S. and international law recognize the unique relationship between parent and child and family reunification has long been a
cornerstone of both immigration and INS practice," she added.*

*In Miami, Elian's relatives said they would appeal the INS ruling to Attor-
ney General Janet Reno. At a demonstration outside INS offices in Miami,
Ileana Ros-Lehtinen, one of two Republican Cuban American representatives in the U.S. House, decried the INS ruling, charging that the Clinton
administration had decided to return the boy to his father to preserve its
policy of gradually improving relations with Cuba. Like many others in the
Cuban community, she also questioned whether the Castro regime allowed
Elian's father to speak his true feelings about what he thought would be best
for his son.*

*Reno upheld the INS decision on January 12, and on January 19 Elian's
great uncle Lazaro Gonzalez appealed the INS ruling in federal district
court. That suit was dismissed on March 21, and the Miami relatives immediately appealed the dismissal. Meanwhile Cuban Americans and Miami
officials threatened massive protests if the federal government intervened to
send Elian back to Cuba. Rumors were already circulating that the Justice
Department would seize Elian by force if his American relatives did not
give him up voluntarily. Demonstrators organized a round-the-clock watch
outside Lazaro's home and said they were ready to summon additional
demonstrators if the situation changed. The situation calmed for a few days
in late March when Castro announced that Juan Miguel would come to the
United States to take custody of his child, and the U.S. government agreed to
extend the relative's temporary custody for a few days.*

*By April the major sticking point in negotiations between the INS and the
Miami relatives was how the relatives would turn over Elian if they lost*

their appeal in federal circuit court. The uncle had said that once the INS revoked Elian's permission to stay in the country, he would not interfere with agents who came to pick up Elian. But Lazaro refused to agree to deliver Elian to federal authorities at some neutral location. Elian's relatives wanted assurances that they could retain custody of the boy if they decided to appeal to the Supreme Court, and they also sought psychological testing to determine if returning Elian to his father would cause him undue pain.

The stakes were raised on April 6, when Juan Miguel arrived in Washington, with his new wife and six-month old baby son. "This is Elian's true family, and we love him very much," Juan Miguel said at Dulles International Airport, while Cuban American demonstrators shouted "Welcome to freedom."

With Juan Miguel's arrival in the United States, talks between the Justice Department and the Miami relatives broke down. The relatives had said they would release Elian if they had a guarantee that the boy would remain in the United States until their legal appeal was decided. Once the father arrived, they said they would not turn over the boy because there was no guarantee that the Gonzalez family would remain in the country. On April 12 Attorney General Reno ordered the Florida relatives to turn Elian over to authorities.

The relatives continued to refuse. On April 22, after the family again refused to yield, armed federal agents seized a crying, frightened Elian from his relatives in a predawn commando-style raid that lasted only minutes. Elian was flown to Andrews Air Force Base outside Washington, where he was reunited with his father. Photographs taken shortly after the reunion showed a smiling, if tired-looking, Elian.

Only about fifty people were outside the Miami house when the raid occurred, but protest groups sprang up around the city throughout the day, backing up traffic throughout the city and blocking the roads to Miami International Airport. Police from both Dade County and Miami helped to restore peace. By late afternoon most of the crowds had broken up, but emotions continued to run high. On April 25 Cuban Americans staged a general strike in Miami.

President Clinton said he supported Reno's decision to mount the raid. "The law has been upheld and that was the right thing to do," he said. "She made the decision. She managed this. But I fully support what she did. . . . I think she did the right thing, and I'm very pleased with the way she handled it." Reno blamed the relatives for always changing the requirements. "Every time we thought we had achieved what was wanted, it wasn't enough," she said. Subsequent polls showed that a solid majority of the American people not only wanted to see Elian reunited with his father, but they also approved of the federal raid.

For the next few weeks Elian remained in seclusion with his family and several classmates who had been flown in from his school in Cuba, awaiting the decision of the federal Court of Appeals for the Eleventh Circuit on the validity of the original INS rejection of Lazaro's request for an asylum hearing for Elian. On June 1 the appeals court sustained the INS ruling that

*only Juan Miguel Gonzalez could speak for his son. The court also issued*
*an injunction keeping Elian in the United States pending an appeal to the*
*Supreme Court by the boy's Miami relatives. On June 28 the Supreme Court*
*announced that it had declined to hear arguments in the case, thus drawing*
*to a close the legal battle over Elian. Within hours Elian and his family had*
*returned to Cuba.*

### Complicated and Convoluted Politics

*Castro used the occasion of Elian's homecoming to stage a massive*
*demonstration on July 1 to protest the American trade embargo of Cuba,*
*which government officials said were costing the country billions of dollars*
*in economic damage. Castro may have been the one clear victor in the po-*
*litical fallout surrounding the Elian episode. "He got himself front and cen-*
*ter before the country on a daily basis," one foreign official in Cuba told the*
New York Times. *"He re-established himself . . . as the sole leader in Cuba*
*who still has the oomph and fire to carry on the revolution. He got an issue*
*he could [use to] mobilize the youth . . . a group that he had not had effec-*
*tive outreach to before."*

*Perhaps even more important, millions of Americans who had always*
*identified Cuba with its communist leader watched the unfolding events in*
*the Elian saga and began to notice, as one diplomat put it, that "there were*
*real people living in Cuba." At the same time, the unyielding stance and*
*stridency of the Cuban American community in Florida may have begun to*
*erode sympathy for the Cuban exile cause in the United States.*

*Some evidence of that became apparent on June 27, the day before Elian*
*returned to Cuba, when House Republican leaders grudgingly agreed to al-*
*low direct sales of food and medicine to Cuba and four other unfriendly*
*nations (Iran, Libya, North Korea, and Sudan). Farm-state legislators had*
*sought the amendment to the agricultural appropriations bill for fiscal*
*2001, arguing that it would open agricultural markets worth about $7 bil-*
*lion a year. American farmers and agricultural businesses had been barred*
*from selling their goods directly to Cuba since 1962. The agreement was a*
*major concession on the part of the GOP leadership, which had long sup-*
*ported the Cuban American lobby and backed the forty-year old sanctions on*
*food and medicine sales to Cuba. At the insistence of both the leaders and the*
*Cuban American lobby, the final version of the appropriations bill (PL 106–*
*387) barred public or private U.S. financing of Cuban agricultural pur-*
*chases, which made it unlikely that Cuba could afford much American food*
*or medicine. It also codified travel restrictions, previously implemented by*
*executive order, that prevented most Americans from traveling to Cuba.*

*Legislators from farm states and others saw the legislation as a break-*
*through and thought they might be able to win greater easing of sanctions*
*in a nonelection year. "You can no longer hold America's interest captive to*
*a small group of political interests, and that's essentially what the Cuban*
*American community has been doing," said Senator Chuck Hagel (R-Neb.),*
*who, together with Senator John Ashcroft (R-Mo.), sponsored the legislation*
*in the Senate. Republican presidential contender Bush opposed the initial*

*House action, arguing that sanctions should not be lifted until Castro stopped violating human rights. He also said he doubted that Castro would actually let food reach the people. "I like to remind people that this is a man who is tyrannical," Bush said June 27 during a campaign appearance.*

*Both Bush and his Democratic opponent, Vice President Al Gore, may have been mindful of the political clout of the Cuban American community in the key election state of Florida. Bush opposed the January INS ruling denying an asylum hearing to Elian. Elian's father should come to the United States and "get a taste of freedom . . . and then ought to make a decision about what's best for the boy," Bush said.*

*Gore kept his silence on the INS ruling, but on March 30 he took the Clinton administration—and many others—by surprise when he announced that he favored giving Elian and several family members permanent residency status so that the case could be transferred from INS jurisdiction into state family court, where it would be handled as a custody case rather than an immigration case. Many observers thought the Miami relatives were more likely to win a custody suit in the Florida state courts than an asylum case in federal court. Although Gore's decision might have been seen as a move to appeal to the large Cuban American population in the nation's fourth-largest state, several Democrats said they did not understand either Gore's timing or his reasoning. "If Gore did it because he's trying to get the anti-Castro Cubans . . . they're not going to vote for him anyway. They're Republicans," said Rep. Maxine Waters, a liberal California Democrat who said she was reconsidering her support for Gore. "And number two, the last polls I saw a month ago showed the American public is on the side of sending Elian back to his father." Whatever Gore's reasoning in March, his position on the Elian issue apparently was not a significant factor in the November election in Florida or in the vote-counting controversy that followed.* (Presidential election, p. 1025)

*Several legislators from Florida introduced legislation to give Elian permanent residency status or make him a naturalized citizen, but congressional leaders soon backed away, fearing that many conservatives who might normally have taken the opportunity to elicit an anti-Castro vote felt it was more important to keep a family intact and reunite Elian with his father. "I'm not sure this is something that Congress should step into," Senate majority leader Trent Lott said on April 3. Following the FBI raid on Lazaro Gonzalez's home, several Republican legislators referred to the agents as "jack-booted thugs" and "storm troopers" and called for congressional hearings into Reno's decision. That talk faded after the INS released information showing that as many as two dozen people, many with permits to carry concealed weapons, had organized into a security force to prevent the INS from taking Elian. After polls showed that more than 60 percent of the public was opposed to congressional hearings, the issue was quietly abandoned.*

*Following are excerpts from the opinion of the Eleventh U.S. Circuit Court of Appeals for the Eleventh District, handed down*

*June 1, 2000, holding that the father of Elian Gonzalez had sole
authority to speak for his son and thus the power to withdraw the
asylum application filed by Elian's great uncle Lazaro Gonzalez.
The document was obtained from the Internet at http://www.ins
.usdoj.gov/graphics/publicaffairs/Elianappeal.htm.*

## D.C. Docket No. 00-00206-CV-KMM

ELIAN GONZALEZ, a minor, by and through LAZARO GONZALEZ, as next
friend, or, alternatively, as temporary legal custodian, Plaintiffs-Appellants,

versus

JANET RENO, Attorney General of the United States; DORIS MEISSNER,
Commissioner, United States Immigration and Naturalization Service; ROB-
ERT WALLIS, District Director, United States Immigration and Naturalization
Service; UNITED STATES IMMIGRATION AND NATURALIZATION SER-
VICE; and UNITED STATES DEPARTMENT OF JUSTICE, Defendants-
Appellees, JUAN MIGUEL GONZALEZ, Intervenor.

Appeal from the United States District Court for the Southern District of
Florida

(June 1, 2000)
Before EDMONDSON, DUBINA and WILSON, Circuit Judges.

**EDMONDSON, Circuit Judge:** This case, at first sight, seems to be about
little more than a child and his father. But, for this Court, the case is mainly
about the separation of powers under our constitutional system of government: a statute enacted by Congress, the permissible scope of executive discretion under that statute, and the limits on judicial review of the exercise
of that executive discretion. Elian Gonzalez ("Plaintiff"), a six-year-old Cuban
child, arrived in the United States alone. His father in Cuba demanded that
Plaintiff be returned to Cuba. Plaintiff, however, asked to stay in the United
States; and asylum applications were submitted on his behalf. The Immigration and Naturalization Service ("INS")—after, among other things, consulting with Plaintiff's father and considering Plaintiff's age—decided that
Plaintiff's asylum applications were legally void and refused to consider their
merit.

Plaintiff then filed this suit in federal district court, seeking on several
grounds to compel the INS to consider and to determine the merit of his asylum applications. The district court dismissed Plaintiff's suit. . . . Plaintiff appeals, and we affirm.

## I.

[Several paragraphs setting out the facts in the case are omitted. The section detailed the arrival of Elian Gonzalez (the plaintiff) in the United States,

the INS decision to parole Elian into the case of his great uncle, Lazaro Gonzalez, and the decision to file three applications for asylum, one signed by Elian, and two signed by Lazaro acting on Elian's behalf both before and after a state court granted Lazaro temporary custody of Elian. The section further described Juan Miguel Gonzalez's request to have his son returned to him in Cuba, as well as two meetings Immigration and Naturalization Service (INS) agents had with the father in Cuba, in which he asserted that he wanted Elian returned, that he was not being coerced by the Cuban government, and that he had not authorized Lazaro to seek asylum in behalf of Elian.]

The INS Commissioner, on 5 January 2000, rejected Plaintiff's asylum applications as legally void. The Commissioner—concluding that six-year-old children lack the capacity to file personally for asylum against the wishes of their parents—determined that Plaintiff could not file his own asylum applications. Instead, according to the Commissioner, Plaintiff needed an adult representative to file for asylum on his behalf. The Commissioner—citing the custom that parents generally speak for their children and finding that no circumstance in this case warranted a departure from that custom—concluded that the asylum applications submitted by Plaintiff and Lazaro were legally void and required no further consideration. Plaintiff asked the Attorney General to overrule the Commissioner's decision; the Attorney General declined to do so. Plaintiff then, by and through Lazaro as his next friend, filed a complaint in federal district court seeking to compel the INS to consider the merits of his asylum applications. In his complaint, Plaintiff alleged, among other things, that the refusal to consider his applications violated 8 U.S.C.–1158 and the Fifth Amendment Due Process Clause. The district court rejected both claims and dismissed Plaintiff's complaint. Plaintiff appeals.

## II.

On appeal, Plaintiff argues that the district court erred (1) by dismissing Plaintiff's claim under 8 U.S.C.–1158, (2) by dismissing Plaintiff's due process claim, and (3) by failing to appoint a guardian ad litem to represent Plaintiff's interests. We have reviewed carefully the record and the briefs filed by all parties. We conclude that Plaintiff's due process claim lacks merit and does not warrant extended discussion. . . . Plaintiff's guardian ad litem claim, because Plaintiff was ably represented in district court by his next friend, also lacks merit and similarly does not warrant extended discussion. . . . We, accordingly, affirm the district court's dismissal of the constitutional claim and the district court's refusal to appoint a guardian ad litem. We now turn, however, to a more difficult question: the district court's dismissal of Plaintiff's statutory claim.

## III.

Plaintiff contends that the district court erred in rejecting his statutory Claim. . . . Section 1158 provides that "[a]ny alien . . . may apply for asylum.". . . Plaintiff says that, because he is "[a]ny alien," he may apply for asylum. Plaintiff insists that, by the applications signed and submitted by himself and Lazaro, he, in fact, did apply for asylum within the meaning of section 1158. In addition, Plaintiff argues that the summary rejection by the INS of his applications as invalid violated the intent of Congress as set out in the statute.

The INS responds that section 1158 is silent about the validity of asylum applications filed on behalf of a six-year-old child, by the child himself and a non-parental relative, against the wishes of the child's parent. The INS argues that, because the statute does not spell out how a young child files for asylum, the INS was free to adopt a policy requiring, in these circumstances, that any asylum claim on Plaintiff's behalf be filed by Plaintiff's father. As such, the INS urges that the rejection of Plaintiff's purported asylum applications as legally void was lawful. According to the INS, because the applications had no legal effect, Plaintiff never applied at all within the meaning of the statute. Guided by well-established principles of statutory construction, judicial restraint, and deference to executive agencies, we accept that the rejection by the INS of Plaintiff's applications as invalid did not violate section 1158.

## A.

Our consideration of Plaintiff's statutory claim must begin with an examination of the scope of the statute itself. . . . Section 1158 is neither vague nor ambiguous. The statute means exactly what it says: "[a]ny alien . . . may apply for asylum.". . . That "[a]ny alien" includes Plaintiff seems apparent. . . . Section 1158, therefore, plainly would permit Plaintiff to apply for asylum. When an alien does apply for asylum within the meaning of the statute, the INS—according to the statute itself and INS regulations—must consider the merits of the alien's asylum claim. . . . The important legal question in this case, therefore, is not whether Plaintiff may apply for asylum; that a six-year-old is eligible to apply for asylum is clear. The ultimate inquiry, instead, is whether a six-year-old child has applied for asylum within the meaning of the statute when he, or a non-parental relative on his behalf, signs and submits a purported application against the express wishes of the child's parent.

About this question, more important than what Congress said in section 1158 is what Congress left unsaid. In reading statutes, we consider not only the words Congress used, but the spaces between those words. Section 1158 is silent on the precise question at issue in this case. Although section 1158 gives "[a]ny alien" the right to "apply for asylum," the statute does not command how an alien applies for asylum. The statute includes no definition of the term "apply." The statute does not set out procedures for the proper filing of an asylum application. Furthermore, the statute does not identify the necessary contents of a valid asylum application. In short, although the statute requires the existence of some application procedure so that aliens may apply for asylum, section 1158 says nothing about the particulars of that procedure. . . .

## B.

Because the statute is silent on the issue, Congress has left a gap in the statutory scheme. From that gap springs executive discretion. As a matter of law, it is not for the courts, but for the executive agency charged with enforcing the statute (here, the INS), to choose how to fill such gaps. . . . Moreover, the authority of the executive branch to fill gaps is especially great in the context of immigration policy. . . . Our proper review of the exercise by the executive branch of its discretion to fill gaps, therefore, must be very limited. . . .

That the courts owe some deference to executive policy does not mean that the executive branch has unbridled discretion in creating and in implementing policy. Executive agencies must comply with the procedural requirements imposed by statute. . . . Agencies must respect their own procedural rules and regulations. . . . And the policy selected by the agency must be a reasonable one in the light of the statutory scheme. . . . To this end, the courts retain the authority to check agency policymaking for procedural compliance and for arbitrariness. But the courts cannot properly reexamine the wisdom of an agency-promulgated policy. . . . In this case, because the law—particularly section 1158—is silent about the validity of Plaintiff's purported asylum applications, it fell to the INS to make a discretionary policy choice. The INS, exercising its gap-filling discretion, determined these things: (1) six-year-old children lack the capacity to sign and to submit personally an application for asylum; (2) instead, six-year-old children must be represented by an adult in immigration matters; (3) absent special circumstances, the only proper adult to represent a six-year-old child is the child's parent, even when the parent is not in this country; and, (4) that the parent lives in a communist-totalitarian state (such as Cuba), in and of itself, does not constitute a special circumstance requiring the selection of a non-parental representative. Our duty is to decide whether this policy might be a reasonable one in the light of the statutory scheme. . . .

. . . We accept that the INS policy at issue here comes within the range of reasonable choices. First, we cannot say that the foundation of the policy—the INS determination that six-year-old children necessarily lack sufficient capacity to assert, on their own, an asylum claim—is unreasonable. . . . Because six-year-old children must have some means of applying for asylum, . . . and because the INS has decided that the children cannot apply personally, the next element of the INS policy—that a six-year-old child must be represented by some adult in applying for asylum—necessarily is reasonable.

The INS determination that ordinarily a parent (even one outside of this country)—and, more important, only a parent—can act for his six-year-old child (who is in this country) in immigration matters also comes within the range of reasonable choices. In making that determination, INS officials seem to have taken account of the relevant, competing policy interests: the interest of a child in asserting a non-frivolous asylum claim; the interest of a parent in raising his child as he sees fit; and the interest of the public in the prompt but fair disposition of asylum claims. The INS policy—by presuming that the parent is the sole, appropriate representative for a child—gives paramount consideration to the primary role of parents in the upbringing of their children. But we cannot conclude that the policy's stress on the parent-child relationship is unreasonable. . . .

We are not untroubled by the degree of obedience that the INS policy appears to give to the wishes of parents, especially parents who are outside this country's jurisdiction. . . . We recognize that, in some instances, the INS policy of deferring to parents—especially those residing outside of this country—

might hinder some six-year-olds with non-frivolous asylum claims and prevent them from invoking their statutory right to seek asylum. But, considering the well-established principles of judicial deference to executive agencies, we cannot disturb the INS policy in this case just because it might be imperfect. . . . And we cannot invalidate the policy—one with international-relations implications—selected by the INS merely because we personally might have chosen another. . . . Because we cannot say that this element of the INS policy—that, ordinarily, a parent, and only a parent, can act for a six-year-old child in immigration matters—is unreasonable, we defer to the INS policy.

The final aspect of the INS policy also worries us some. According to the INS policy, that a parent lives in a communist-totalitarian state is no special circumstance, sufficient in and of itself, to justify the consideration of a six-year-old child's asylum claim (presented by a relative in this country) against the wishes of the non-resident parent. We acknowledge, as a widely-accepted truth, that Cuba does violate human rights and fundamental freedoms and does not guarantee the rule of law to people living in Cuba. . . . Persons living in such a totalitarian state may be unable to assert freely their own legal rights, much less the legal rights of others. Moreover, some reasonable people might say that a child in the United States inherently has a substantial conflict of interest with a parent residing in a totalitarian state when that parent—even when he is not coerced—demands that the child leave this country to return to a country with little respect for human rights and basic freedoms.

Nonetheless, we cannot properly conclude that the INS policy is totally unreasonable in this respect. The INS policy does take some account of the possibility of government coercion: where special circumstances—such as definite coercion directed at an individual parent—exist, a non-parental representative may be necessary to speak for the child. In addition and more important, in no context is the executive branch entitled to more deference than in the context of foreign affairs. . . . This aspect of the INS policy seems to implicate the conduct of foreign affairs more than any other. Something even close to a per se rule—that, for immigration purposes, no parent living in a totalitarian state has sufficient liberty to represent and to serve the true, best interests of his own child in the United States—likely would have significant consequences for the President's conduct of our Nation's international affairs: such a rule would focus not on the qualities of the particular parent, but on the qualities of the government of the parent's country. As we understand the legal precedents, they, in effect, direct that a court of law defer especially to this international-relations aspect of the INS policy. We are obliged to accept that the INS policy, on its face, does not contradict and does not violate section 1158, although section 1158 does not require the approach that the INS has chosen to take.

## C.

. . . But whatever we personally might think about the decisions made by the Government, we cannot properly conclude that the INS acted arbitrarily or abused its discretion here. The application signed and submitted by Plaintiff himself, insofar as the INS has decided that six-year-old children cannot file for asylum themselves, necessarily was a nullity under the INS policy. As we have explained, the INS's per se rule—prohibiting six-year-old children from personally filing asylum applications against their parents1 wishes—is entitled to deference under the law. The INS, therefore, did not act arbitrarily or abuse its discretion in rejecting Plaintiff's own purported asylum application as void.

Plaintiff contends that, even if the INS policy is facially reasonable under Chevron, the INS decision to reject the applications submitted by Lazaro was arbitrary. Plaintiff asserts that two special circumstances—the alleged coercion of Juan Miguel by the Cuban government and the objective basis of Plaintiff's asylum claim—bear negatively upon Juan Miguel's fitness to represent Plaintiff in immigration matters. The INS, according to Plaintiff, was therefore required to recognize some other adult representative—namely, Lazaro—to act on Plaintiff's behalf. We, however, conclude that the INS adequately considered these circumstances in reaching its ultimate decision.

The INS first determined that Juan Miguel, in fact, was not operating under coercion from the Cuban government or that, even if he was, his honest and sincere desires were aligned with those of the Cuban government. That determination was not clearly wrong and was no abuse of discretion. An INS official, on two occasions, interviewed Juan Miguel in person in Cuba. Aware of the possibility that Juan Miguel might be under some kind of coercion, the INS official took steps to ensure that Juan Miguel could express freely his genuine wishes about Plaintiff's asylum claim. The INS official, after meeting with Juan Miguel face-to-face, concluded—based upon her observations of his demeanor—that Juan Miguel's statement was not the result of duress or coercion. We, therefore, cannot say that the INS's rejection of Plaintiff's contention about coercion was arbitrary. The INS also preliminarily assessed the objective basis of Plaintiff's asylum claim and concluded that his claim for asylum probably lacked merit. Again, we cannot conclude that the INS's determination was arbitrary or an abuse of discretion. In making this assessment, the INS considered the information contained in the asylum applications and information provided to the INS by Plaintiff's lawyers. In addition, the INS interviewed Lazaro and inquired about the basis for Plaintiff's asylum claim. The essence of Plaintiff's asylum claim was that, if he is returned to Cuba: (1) he will not enjoy the freedom that he has in the United States; (2) he might be forced to undergo "re-education" and indoctrination in communist theory; and (3) he might be used by the Cuban government for propaganda purposes. No one should doubt that, if Plaintiff returns to Cuba, he will be without the degree of liberty that people enjoy in the United States. Also, we admit that re-education, communist indoctrination, and political manipulation of Plaintiff for propaganda purposes, upon a return to Cuba, are not beyond the realm of possibility. Nonetheless, we cannot say that the INS's assessment of Plaintiff's asylum claim—that it probably lacked merit—was arbitrary. To make a meritorious asylum claim, an asylum applicant must show that he has a "well-founded fear of persecution" in his native land. . . . Congress largely has left the task of defining with precision the phrase "well-founded fear of persecution" to the INS. . . .

Plaintiff points to no earlier INS adjudications or judicial decisions where a person, in circumstances similar to Plaintiff1s, was found to have established a "well-founded fear of persecution." Political conditions "which affect the populace as a whole or in large part are generally insufficient to establish [persecution].". . . We cannot say that the INS had to treat education and indoctrination as synonymous with "persecution.". . . Not all exceptional treatment is persecution. The INS's estimate of the purported applications—as applications that were not strong on their merits—is not clearly inaccurate.

We have not the slightest illusion about the INS's choices: the choices— about policy and about application of the policy—that the INS made in this case are choices about which reasonable people can disagree. Still, the choices were not unreasonable, not capricious and not arbitrary, but were reasoned and reasonable. The INS's considerable discretion was not abused.

## Conclusion

As policymakers, it is the duty of the Congress and of the executive branch to exercise political will. Although courts should not be unquestioning, we should respect the other branches1 policymaking powers. The judicial power is a limited power. It is the duty of the judicial branch not to exercise political will, but only to render judicial judgment under the law.

When the INS was confronted with Plaintiff's purported asylum applications, the immigration law of the United States provided the INS with no clear answer. The INS accordingly developed a policy to deal with the extraordinary circumstances of asylum applications filed on behalf of a six-year-old child, by the child himself and a non-parental relative, against the express wishes of the child's parents (or sole parent). The INS then applied this new policy to Plaintiff's purported asylum applications and rejected them as nullities. Because the preexisting law compelled no particular policy, the INS was entitled to make a policy decision. The policy decision that the INS made was within the outside border of reasonable choices. And the INS did not abuse its discretion or act arbitrarily in applying the policy and rejecting Plaintiff's purported asylum applications. The Court neither approves nor disapproves the INS's decision to reject the asylum applications filed on Plaintiff's behalf, but the INS decision did not contradict 8 U.S.C.–1158. The judgment of the district court is

*AFFIRMED.*

# REPORT OF NATIONAL COMMISSION ON TERRORISM
## June 5, 2000

*A commission established by Congress argued in 2000 that the United States needed to take more aggressive action against international terrorist groups—especially those that might be taking aim at U.S. targets at home or abroad. The National Commission on Terrorism, in a report released June 5, 2000, called for increased U.S. government spending on antiterrorism programs and suggested the loosening of some restrictions on federal agencies that fought terrorists.*

*Congress mandated the commission in 1998 following the bombings of U.S. embassies in Nairobi, Kenya, and Dar es Salaam, Tanzania. The bombings, which the Clinton administration attributed to an anti-U.S. organization headed by wealthy Saudi exile Osama bin Laden, killed more than 250 people and injured more than 2,000, most of them African civilians.* (Embassy bombings, Historic Documents of 1998, p. 555)

*The commission did not call for sweeping changes in U.S. antiterrorism policy. Instead, the panel suggested a series of incremental changes in tactics and procedures, coupled with increased spending on antiterrorism programs. Commission chairman L. Paul Bremer III said the thrust of the proposals was to counter the growing threat of terrorism to the United States.*

*A reminder of the continuing threat of terrorism came October 12, 2000, when a bomb damaged the USS Cole, a Navy destroyer docked at the harbor in Aden, Yemen. The blast killed seventeen sailors and wounded thirty-five others. U.S. officials said they suspected the bombing was the work of bin Laden's organization.* (Cole bombing, p. 861)

### Changing Terrorism Threat

*The committee said the global threat of terrorism had changed somewhat in the decade since the collapse of the Soviet Union. Terrorist groups were no longer as dependent on state sponsorship and were motivated more by ideological or religious philosophies than by political goals. Moreover, the committee said, terrorists in the 1990s seemed more willing than in the past to launch strikes with no apparent purpose other than to kill large numbers of perceived enemies. As examples of current terrorist actions, the panel cited the 1993 bombing of the World Trade Center in New York City, which apparently was intended to kill tens of thousands of civilians, and the 1998 bombings of the two U.S. embassies in Africa, which killed many more African civilians than Americans.*

*The result of these trends, Bremer told reporters, was that "the threat of international terrorism is becoming more deadly, and terrorist organizations are becoming more diffuse, more difficult to detect, to penetrate, and to disrupt." Bremer was the State Department's ambassador-at-large for counterterrorism during the administration of President George Bush.*

*The committee said it was particularly worried about the prospect that one or more terrorist groups could attempt to use chemical or biological weapons against the United States. Those types of weapons were much easier to acquire and deploy than nuclear weapons and could cause widespread damage, the committee said. The panel acknowledged that the Aum Shinrikyo group in Japan had failed in its 1995 effort to release chemical agents in the Tokyo subway, despite having spent millions of dollars for help from skilled experts. But even a limited attack in the United States could "challenge significantly Americans' sense of safety and confidence," the committee said.*

## CIA Recruitment Rules

*To deal with the shifting environment of terrorism, the committee recommended several changes in U.S. government procedures and policies. Perhaps the commission's most controversial and highly publicized recommendation was that the Clinton administration drop restrictions on recruitment by the Central Intelligence Agency (CIA) of individuals who might have been involved in terrorist activities. In 1995 then CIA director John M. Deutch established a procedure requiring senior agency officials to approve the recruitment for counterterrorism efforts of any individuals suspected of having been involved in serious criminal activities, such as abusing human rights. Deutch imposed the rule following the CIA's admission that for many years it had working relationships in Guatemala with military officers who were responsible for serious human rights abuses.*

*The commission said the Deutch rule had discouraged the recruitment of "potentially useful informants," had forced the United States to rely too heavily on foreign intelligence services, and had undermined morale within the CIA, leading "a significant number" of agency case officers to retire early or resign. One commission member, James Woolsey—who preceded Deutch as CIA director—said the rule had gone too far. "One cannot prowl the back streets of states where terrorist incidents occur and recruit only nice people in order to inform on terrorist groups," he said.*

*CIA spokesman Bill Harlow said the agency stood by the Deutch rule and denied that it had hindered antiterrorism efforts or dampened morale within the agency. "The bottom line is, CIA headquarters has never turned down a request to use someone, even someone with a human rights record, if we thought that person could be valuable to our overall counterterrorism program," he told the* Washington Post. *Other CIA sources told news organizations that the guidelines helped protect agents in the field by putting the responsibility on high-ranking officials for establishing contacts with questionable individuals.*

*Representatives of several human rights organizations expressed concerns about the commission recommendation. Among them, Susan C. Peacock, senior associate for the Washington Office on Latin America, said the CIA should be even more cautious than it had been about using people who had committed human rights abuses.*

## Other Recommendations

*The committee also offered procedural recommendations concerning antiterrorism work by the Federal Bureau of Investigation (FBI). Existing guidelines were complex and confusing for FBI agents in the field and should be clarified, the panel said. In addition, the committee called for a "higher priority" for funding antiterrorism programs within the FBI, the CIA, and the National Security Agency (the secret agency responsible for monitoring radio and telephone transmissions overseas). The committee made no specific budget recommendations but said U.S. counterterrorism efforts lacked adequate funding to do their jobs in an age of rapidly changing information technology.*

*Treading into sensitive diplomatic territory, Bremer's committee suggested that the Clinton administration should cite Greece and Pakistan, two longtime allies, for "not cooperating fully" with U.S. antiterrorism efforts. The Greek government, the committee said, "has been disturbingly passive in response to terrorist activities." Since 1975, 146 terrorist attacks in Greece had targeted Americans or American interests. Of those, only one case had been solved and a succession of Greek governments had not undertaken a "meaningful investigation" into any of the other cases.*

*Pakistan had occasionally cooperated with U.S. antiterrorism efforts but provided "safe haven, transit, and moral, political and diplomatic support to several groups engaged in terrorism," the committee said. As an example, the panel cited Pakistan's backing for the Harakat-ul-Mujahidin group, widely believed to have kidnapped and murdered tourists in Kashmir as part of a campaign to gain independence for Muslims there. Kashmir was claimed by both Pakistan and India. In its annual report on international terrorism, the State Department in April said Pakistan had sent "mixed messages," especially with its support of the Kashmiri separatists. Michael Sheehan, the State Department coordinator for counterterrorism, said at a May 2 news conference that Pakistan was "a friendly country" that did "cooperate with us on numerous terrorist issues," even if the leaders there "need to improve their efforts."*

*The commission also said the Clinton administration had not put enough pressure on Iran to cooperate in an investigation into the 1996 bombing of a Saudi Arabian apartment complex that killed 19 U.S. servicemen and wounded 500 other people. Despite evidence that Iran played a role in the bombing, the United States had not worked diligently enough with its allies and international organizations to force Iranian cooperation with an investigation, the panel said. Furthermore, the committee said the Clinton administration's expression of support for political reform in Iran following the 1997 election of President Mohammed Khatami "could be misinterpreted in Iran or by U.S. allies as a signaling a weakening of resolve on counterterrorism." For that reason, the president "should not make further concessions to Iran" until it stopped supporting terrorism and cooperated fully in the Saudi bombing case, the committee said.*

*Citing Afghanistan's harboring of bin Laden, the committee said the United States should designate that country as a sponsor of terrorism and impose appropriate sanctions. The Clinton administration had listed Afghanistan as a country "not cooperating fully" with U.S. antiterrorism efforts—one step short of declaring that country to be a state sponsor of terrorism. The administration had done so for the diplomatic reason that the more serious designation might be interpreted as U.S. recognition of the Taliban regime as the government there, something the administration had refused to do. Clinton in July 1999 issued an executive order freezing any U.S.-based assets of the Taliban government and banning all trade, except for humanitarian goods, between the United States and Afghanistan. Those sanctions—coupled with worldwide economic sanctions imposed by the United Nations Security Council—were to remain in effect until the Afghan government turned over bin Laden to a jurisdiction where he could face U.S. charges arising out of the African embassy bombings.*

*The commission said the administration and Congress should give "higher priority" to funding counterterrorism programs within the CIA, FBI, and National Security Agency. In particular, the panel said, the agencies needed more money to upgrade their information technology systems so they could process and assign priorities to the enormous quantity of data they collected. The commission cited several programs within those agencies that it said needed more money, but it did not specify how much additional money needed to be spent. The White House said total U.S. spending on antiterrorism and related programs was about $10 billion in fiscal year 2000.*

*One commission recommendation that sparked some controversy and confusion concerned the monitoring of foreign students in the United States. The panel noted that several thousand people from countries designated as state sponsors of terrorism were studying at U.S. colleges and universities. While the vast majority of those people raised no security concerns, some of them might be related to terrorist organizations; as an example, the panel noted that one of the defendants in the World Trade Center bombing had entered the United States on a student visa and had remained in the country illegally after dropping out of school.*

*The commission said the administration should consider extending nationwide a pilot program that collected information about foreign students at twenty southern universities. Such a program could be used, for example, to monitor "useful and current information," such as when a student from a terrorism-supporting country changed his or her major from English literature to nuclear physics, the commission said. Representatives of civil liberties and some education groups objected to the student-monitoring proposal as an excessive intrusion on student privacy.*

## Second Gilmore Commission Report

*Another congressionally mandated commission—this one appointed in 1998 by Defense Secretary William S. Cohen—on December 11 called for the creation of a single high-level agency to coordinate the federal government's widespread antiterrorism efforts. The commission was called the Congressional Advisory Panel to Assess Domestic Response Capabilities for Terrorism Involving Weapons of Mass Destruction. Chaired by Virginia governor Jim Gilmore, a Republican, the committee issued a preliminary report in 1999, a follow-up report in December 2000, and was scheduled to make final recommendations in December 2001.* (Background, Historic Documents of 1999, p. 502)

*"The issue of who is in charge at the federal level is one of the key questions that must be addressed in order to develop a sensible, comprehensive national policy on how we can best respond to, and recover from, a terrorist attack inside our borders," Gilmore said in a September 29 statement after his panel took a consensus vote favoring a single agency. The panel suggested establishing the Office of Domestic Preparedness for Terrorism Management within the White House. "Some federal agencies have good places and operational strategies, but there is little or no strategic guidance because there is no one agency or entity in charge," Gilmore said.*

## Stimson Center Report

*An independent assessment of the domestic threat posed by terrorists using chemical or biological weapons was issued October 25 by the Henry L. Stimson Center, a Washington research group named after the World War II secretary of war. The center called its 319-page report "Ataxia: the Chemical and Biological Terrorism Threat and the U.S. Response." Its principal author was Amy E. Smithson, the center's expert on weapons of mass destruction.*

*Smithson argued that terrorists would face numerous hurdles in the development and deployment of chemical or biological weapons in the United States. Acquiring the necessary materials for those types of weapons was more expensive and time-consuming than was commonly assumed, she said. Any terrorist organization would need assistance from highly trained experts before it could assemble a large enough arsenal of chemical or biological weapons to inflict mass casualties.*

*Smithson argued that some observers had drawn the wrong conclusion from the March 1995 chemical weapons attack on the Tokyo subway by an apocalyptic sect, Aum Shinrikyo. While frightening in its implications, that attack nevertheless showed that even a well-financed, highly organized terrorist group could have trouble making effective use of chemical weapons. The failure of the Japanese group to achieve its apparent goal of killing thousands of people, Smithson said, tended to disprove "assertions that acquiring and spreading these [chemical and biological weapons] is shake-n-bake easy."*

*Smithson's report also harshly criticized the federal government's numerous programs intended to help state and local agencies prepare for chemical and biological hazards, whether posed by terrorism or industrial accidents. Between January 1999 and September 2000 Smithson interviewed health care personnel, emergency personnel, and other officials in thirty cities in twenty-five states. In general, she said these "front-line" personnel said hospitals and other local resources would not be able to handle the consequences of a major catastrophe caused by chemical or biological weapons or other hazardous materials. Federal programs to train local personnel had been ineffective and inordinately expensive, she said.*

### Vulnerability of National Monuments

*A study commissioned by the National Park Service said that nearly all the famous national monuments on the Mall in Washington, D.C., were vulnerable to terrorist attacks, according to a story in the July 2 edition of the* Washington Post. *Quoting from the study, which reportedly was labeled "sensitive" and not made public, the newspaper said the vulnerable monuments included some of the most heavily visited sites in Washington: the Washington Monument, the Lincoln Memorial, the Thomas Jefferson Memorial, and the Vietnam Veterans Memorial.*

*"The high potential for an unacceptable loss of life and property exists, along with the severe degradation of the public image and confidence in the ability of the United States to protect its people and its treasures," the* Post *quoted the study as saying. Of particular concern, the study said, was a shortage of manpower and resources for the U.S. Park Police, which was assigned to protect the monuments. The study was conducted by the Booz-Allen & Hamilton consulting firm, under contract to the National Park Service.*

*Several security experts quoted by the* Washington Post *said the threat of terrorism at the monuments was not as severe as the study claimed. Bruce Hoffman, a counterterrorism authority at the Rand Corp., said the monuments were vulnerable to attack because of their very nature of being open to the public. "It comes to a point where you have to accept that we can't have a risk-free society," he told the newspaper.*

*Following are the "foreword" and "executive summary" portions from the report, "Countering the Changing Threat of International Terrorism," issued June 5, 2000, by the National Com-*

*mission on Terrorism. The document was obtained from the Internet at http://www.fas.org/irp/threat/commission.html.*

# Foreword

Six months ago, the National Commission on Terrorism began its Congressionally mandated evaluation of America's laws, policies, and practices for preventing and punishing terrorism directed at American citizens. After a thorough review, the Commission concluded that, although American strategies and policies are basically on the right track, significant aspects of implementation are seriously deficient. Thus, this report does not attempt to describe all American counterterrorism activities, but instead concentrates on problem areas and recommended changes. We wish to note, however, that in the course of our assessment we gained renewed confidence in the abilities and dedication of the Americans who stand on the front lines in the fight against terrorism.

Each of the 10 commissioners approached these issues from a different perspective. If any one commissioner had written the report on his or her own, it might not be identical to that which we are presenting today. However, through a process of careful deliberation, we reached the consensus reflected in this report.

Throughout our deliberations, we were mindful of several important points:

- The imperative to find terrorists and prevent their attacks requires energetic use of all the legal authorities and instruments available.
- Terrorist attacks against America threaten more than the tragic loss of individual lives. Some terrorists hope to provoke a response that undermines our Constitutional system of government. So U.S. leaders must find the appropriate balance by adopting counterterrorism policies which are effective but also respect the democratic traditions which are the bedrock of America's strength.
- Combating terrorism should not be used as a pretext for discrimination against any segment of society. Terrorists often claim to act on behalf of ethnic groups, religions, or even entire nations. These claims are false. Terrorists represent only a minuscule faction of any such group.
- People turn to terrorism for various reasons. Many terrorists act from political, ideological, or religious convictions. Some are simply criminals for hire. Others become terrorists because of perceived oppression or economic deprivation. An astute American foreign policy must take into account the reasons people turn to terror and, where appropriate and feasible, address them. No cause, however, justifies terrorism.

Terrorists attack American targets more often than those of any other country. America's pre-eminent role in the world guarantees that this will continue to be the case, and the threat of attacks creating massive casualties is growing. If the United States is to protect itself, if it is to remain a world leader, this nation must develop and continuously refine sound counterterrorism policies appropriate to the rapidly changing world around us.

Ambassador L. Paul Bremer III
*Chairman*

Maurice Sonnenberg
*Vice Chairman*

## Executive Summary

**International terrorism poses an increasingly dangerous and difficult threat to America.** This was underscored by the December 1999 arrests in Jordan and at the U.S./Canadian border of foreign nationals who were allegedly planning to attack crowded millennium celebrations. Today's terrorists seek to inflict mass casualties, and they are attempting to do so both overseas and on American soil. They are less dependent on state sponsorship and are, instead, forming loose, transnational affiliations based on religious or ideological affinity and a common hatred of the United States. This makes terrorist attacks more difficult to detect and prevent.

**Countering the growing danger of the terrorist threat requires significantly stepping up U.S. efforts.** The government must immediately take steps to reinvigorate the collection of intelligence about terrorists' plans, use all available legal avenues to disrupt and prosecute terrorist activities and private sources of support, convince other nations to cease all support for terrorists, and ensure that federal, state, and local officials are prepared for attacks that may result in mass casualties. The Commission has made a number of recommendations to accomplish these objectives:

**Priority one is to prevent terrorist attacks. U.S. intelligence and law enforcement communities must use the full scope of their authority to collect intelligence regarding terrorist plans and methods.**

- CIA guidelines adopted in 1995 restricting recruitment of unsavory sources should not apply when recruiting counterterrorism sources.
- The Attorney General should ensure that FBI is exercising fully its authority for investigating suspected terrorist groups or individuals, including authority for electronic surveillance.
- Funding for counterterrorism efforts by CIA, NSA, and FBI must be given higher priority to ensure continuation of important operational activity and to close the technology gap that threatens their ability to collect and exploit terrorist communications.
- FBI should establish a cadre of reports officers to distill and disseminate terrorism-related information once it is collected.

**U.S. policies must firmly target all states that support terrorists.**

- Iran and Syria should be kept on the list of state sponsors until they stop supporting terrorists.

- Afghanistan should be designated a sponsor of terrorism and subjected to all the sanctions applicable to state sponsors.
- The President should impose sanctions on countries that, while not direct sponsors of terrorism, are nevertheless not cooperating fully on counter-terrorism. Candidates for consideration include Pakistan and Greece.

**Private sources of financial and logistical support for terrorists must be subjected to the full force and sweep of U.S. and international laws.**

- All relevant agencies should use every available means, including the full array of criminal, civil, and administrative sanctions to block or disrupt nongovernmental sources of support for international terrorism.
- Congress should promptly ratify and implement the International Convention for the Suppression of the Financing of Terrorism to enhance international cooperative efforts.
- Where criminal prosecution is not possible, the Attorney General should vigorously pursue the expulsion of terrorists from the United States through proceedings which protect both the national security interest in safeguarding classified evidence and the right of the accused to challenge that evidence.

**A terrorist attack involving a biological agent, deadly chemicals, or nuclear or radiological material, even if it succeeds only partially, could profoundly affect the entire nation. The government must do more to prepare for such an event.**

- The President should direct the preparation of a manual to guide the implementation of existing legal authority in the event of a catastrophic terrorist threat or attack. The President and Congress should determine whether additional legal authority is needed to deal with catastrophic terrorism.
- The Department of Defense [DoD] must have detailed plans for its role in the event of a catastrophic terrorist attack, including criteria for decisions on transfer of command authority to DoD in extraordinary circumstances.
- Senior officials of all government agencies involved in responding to a catastrophic terrorism threat or crisis should be required to participate in national exercises every year to test capabilities and coordination.
- Congress should make it illegal for anyone not properly certified to possess certain critical pathogens and should enact laws to control the transfer of equipment critical to the development or use of biological agents.
- The President should establish a comprehensive and coordinated long-term research and development program for catastrophic terrorism.
- The Secretary of State should press for an international convention to improve multilateral cooperation on preventing or responding to cyber attacks by terrorists.

**The President and Congress should reform the system for reviewing and funding departmental counterterrorism programs to ensure that the activities and programs of various agencies are part of a comprehensive plan.**

- The executive branch official responsible for coordinating counterterrorism efforts across the government should be given a stronger hand in the budget process.
- Congress should develop mechanisms for a comprehensive review of the President's counterterrorism policy and budget.

# SUPREME COURT ON THE RIGHTS OF GRANDPARENTS
## June 5, 2000

*The Supreme Court took a cautious step toward resolving a question more often dealt with in state family courts: how to balance the right of parents to make decisions about their children against the rights of grandparents and others to have access to those children. By a vote of 6–3, the Court on June 5, 2000, ruled that a Washington state law was so broad that it infringed on parents' "fundamental right" to rear their children. But the six justices did not agree on a single set of reasons supporting their decision, thus leaving lower courts considerable leeway for dealing with what Justice Sandra Day O'Connor called "the changing realities of the American family."*

*Over the four previous decades those realities had come to include a high incidence of divorce, remarriage, and single-parent families. As a result, millions of children were now reared or substantially cared for by family members other than their parents—grandparents, stepparents, and a gay parent's partner, for example—and disputes over visitation and custody had also risen. Since the mid-1960s all fifty states had adopted laws permitting third parties to sue for visitation rights under certain circumstances, typically the death of a parent or divorce. The Washington state law was especially broad, allowing "any person" to petition the courts "at any time" for visitation rights and permitting a court to order such visitations if they were determined to be in the "best interests" of the child.*

## A Sad Tug-of War

*The case,* Troxel v. Granville, *began in 1993 when Jennifer and Gary Troxel petitioned a Washington state court to grant them more visitation time with their two young granddaughters, who were the children of their son Brad Troxel and Tommie Granville. The couple had never married, and when they separated in 1991 Granville became the primary caregiver, but Brad kept the girls from time to time, sometimes at his parents' home. Brad committed suicide in 1993. After Brad's death Granville did not deny the*

*Troxels time with their granddaughters, but she was not willing to permit as many visits as the Troxels requested. The Troxels petitioned for more visits under the Washington statute. In 1995 the state court agreed to some visits but not as many as the Troxels had requested. In 1997 the Washington Court of Appeals reversed the trial court, ruling that grandparents had no standing to sue under the state law unless a custody proceeding was pending. (In the interim Granville had married and her husband had formally adopted the two girls.)*

*The Troxels then appealed to the Washington Supreme Court, which, on a 5–4 vote, ruled that the state law was unconstitutional because it interfered with parents' constitutionally protected "fundamental rights" to rear their children. Not only was the statute too broadly written, the court said, but it also failed to set a high enough standard for state intervention, namely, the presence of harm or potential harm to the children. The Troxels then appealed to the U.S. Supreme Court.*

*The case drew broad attention. The senior citizens advocacy group, the American Association of Retired Persons (AARP), sided with the grandparents. Based on a survey, AARP said that about 3 percent of the nation's 60 million grandparents reported that they were raising a grandchild, while another 8 percent said they provided day care on a regular basis. More than 80 percent of those questioned said they had seen their grandchildren within the previous month.*

*Siding with the mother was an unusual alliance of religious groups, which sought to preserve the traditional notions of family, and civil liberties groups, which argued that courts had no right to interfere with parental decisions about who their children could see. Seeking a middle course were gay and lesbian groups, who wanted to protect gay parents from challenges by third parties claiming to know what was best for a child while at the same time preserving visitation rights for gays who still had a significant relationship with their former partner's children. "The case is definitely a victory for parental rights, but it wasn't a broad-based attack on third-party visitation rights," David L. Hudson, of the First Amendment Center at Vanderbilt University, told the* Washington Post. *"It does not sound the death knell of grandparent visitation rights."*

## A Decision Resolving Little

*Justice O'Connor began her announcement of the decision on June 5 by acknowledging the justices' own divisions. "Unfortunately, the members of this court were no more able to reach a resolution than the parties to this case," she said. The decision stopped short of declaring the Washington law unconstitutional. Instead, O'Connor said in the main opinion only that the statute "as applied to Granville and her family in this case" unconstitutionally infringed on her "fundamental parental right" concerning the care, custody, and control of her children.*

*O'Connor stressed that the Troxels had not claimed that Granville was an unfit parent, that Granville had never refused the Troxels all visitation, and* that the Washington trial court had given no special weight to Granville's views. The judge's order, O'Connor said, "directly contravened the traditional presumption that a fit parent will act in the best interest of his or her child." Given the breadth of the statute, O'Connor said that the Court did not have to decide whether a nonparental visitation statute must require a showing of harm before courts could intervene. Chief Justice William H. Rehnquist and Justices Ruth Bader Ginsburg and Stephen G. Breyer joined O'Connor's opinion.

Justice David H. Souter, concurring in the judgment, said he would have upheld the Washington Supreme Court's decision that the state law was unconstitutional on its face, without regard to the specific facts in the case. In a separate concurring opinion, Justice Clarence Thomas called for applying the most stringent constitutional standard—"strict scrutiny"—before allowing courts to infringe on "fundamental parental rights." Under that test, a court would need a "compelling interest" to intervene. In this case, Thomas wrote, the court had no "legitimate governmental interest . . . in second-guessing a fit parent's decision."

The three dissenters took somewhat different approaches. In separate opinions Justices John Paul Stevens and Anthony M. Kennedy both faulted the Washington court for rejecting what Kennedy called the "well-recognized" best-interest-of-the-child standard. For his part, Justice Antonin Scalia directly challenged the whole notion of judicially enforced parental rights. He said the issues should be left to state legislatures and warned against "ushering in a new regime of judicially prescribed, and federally prescribed, family law."

In Washington state, Granville told reporters that she was "relieved" by the decision, but she called the case a "huge waste of time, money, and emotion." The Troxels voiced plaintive disappointment at having to accept only limited time with their granddaughters. "If one afternoon a month is what we get, we'll be happy with that," Jennifer Troxel said. "We miss them. They're still part of our family."

*Following are excerpts from the case,* Troxel v. Granville, *in which the Supreme Court ruled, by a 6–3 vote, on June 5, 2000, that parents have a fundamental right to rear their children. The document was obtained from the Internet at http://www.supremecourtus.gov/opinions/99pdf/99-138.pdf.*

No. 99-138

| Jenifer Troxel, et vir., Petitioners v. Tommie Granville | On writ of certiorari to the Supreme Court of Washington |

[June 5, 2000]

JUSTICE O'CONNOR announced the judgment of the Court and delivered an opinion, in which THE CHIEF JUSTICE, JUSTICE GINSBURG, and JUSTICE BREYER join. . . .

# I

Tommie Granville and Brad Troxel shared a relationship that ended in June 1991. The two never married, but they had two daughters, Isabelle and Natalie. Jenifer and Gary Troxel are Brad's parents, and thus the paternal grandparents of Isabelle and Natalie. After Tommie and Brad separated in 1991, Brad lived with his parents and regularly brought his daughters to his parents' home for weekend visitation. Brad committed suicide in May 1993. Although the Troxels at first continued to see Isabelle and Natalie on a regular basis after their son's death, Tommie Granville informed the Troxels in October 1993 that she wished to limit their visitation with her daughters to one short visit per month.

In December 1993, the Troxels commenced the present action by filing, in the Washington Superior Court for Skagit County, a petition to obtain visitation rights with Isabelle and Natalie. The Troxels filed their petition under . . . Washington statutes . . . §§26.09.240 and 26.10.160(3) [which] provides: "Any person may petition the court for visitation rights at any time including, but not limited to, custody proceedings. The court may order visitation rights for any person when visitation may serve the best interest of the child whether or not there has been any change of circumstances." At trial, the Troxels requested two weekends of overnight visitation per month and two weeks of visitation each summer. Granville did not oppose visitation altogether, but instead asked the court to order one day of visitation per month with no overnight stay. In 1995, the Superior Court issued an oral ruling and entered a visitation decree ordering visitation one weekend per month, one week during the summer, and four hours on both of the petitioning grandparents' birthdays.

Granville appealed, during which time she married Kelly Wynn. Before addressing the merits of Granville's appeal, the Washington Court of Appeals remanded the case to the Superior Court for entry of written findings of fact and conclusions of law. On remand, the Superior Court found that visitation was in Isabelle and Natalie's best interests. [Excerpt from opinion omitted.] Approximately nine months after the Superior Court entered its order on remand, Granville's husband formally adopted Isabelle and Natalie.

The Washington Court of Appeals reversed the lower court's visitation order and dismissed the Troxels' petition for visitation, holding that nonparents lack standing to seek visitation . . . unless a custody action is pending. . . .

The Washington Supreme Court granted the Troxels' petition for review and, after consolidating their case with two other visitation cases, affirmed. . . . The court rested its decision on the Federal Constitution, holding that §26.10.160(3) unconstitutionally infringes on the fundamental right of parents to rear their children. In the court's view, there were at least two problems with the nonparental visitation statute. First, according to the Washington Supreme Court, the Constitution permits a State to interfere with the right of parents to rear their children only to prevent harm or potential harm to a child. Section 26.10.160(3) fails that standard because it requires no threshold showing of harm. Second, by allowing " 'any person' to petition for forced visitation of a child at 'any time' with the only requirement being that the visitation serve the best interest of the child," the Washington visitation statute sweeps too broadly. . . .

We granted certiorari (1999), and now affirm the judgment.

## II

The demographic changes of the past century make it difficult to speak of an average American family. The composition of families varies greatly from household to household. While many children may have two married parents and grandparents who visit regularly, many other children are raised in single-parent households. In 1996, children living with only one parent accounted for 28 percent of all children under age 18 in the United States. Understandably, in these single-parent households, persons outside the nuclear family are called upon with increasing frequency to assist in the everyday tasks of child rearing. In many cases, grandparents play an important role. For example, in 1998, approximately 4 million children—or 5.6 percent of all children under age 18—lived in the household of their grandparents.

The nationwide enactment of nonparental visitation statutes is assuredly due, in some part, to the States' recognition of these changing realities of the American family. Because grandparents and other relatives undertake duties of a parental nature in many households, States have sought to ensure the welfare of the children therein by protecting the relationships those children form with such third parties. The States' nonparental visitation statutes are further supported by a recognition, which varies from State to State, that children should have the opportunity to benefit from relationships with statutorily specified persons—for example, their grandparents. The extension of statutory rights in this area to persons other than a child's parents, however, comes with an obvious cost. For example, the State's recognition of an independent third-party interest in a child can place a substantial burden on the traditional parent-child relationship. Contrary to JUSTICE STEVENS' accusation, our description of state nonparental visitation statutes in these terms, of course, is not meant to suggest that "children are so much chattel." Rather, our terminology is intended to highlight the fact that these statutes can present questions of constitutional import. In this case, we are presented with just such a question. Specifically, we are asked to decide whether §26.10.160(3), as applied to Tommie Granville and her family, violates the Federal Constitution.

The Fourteenth Amendment provides that no State shall "deprive any person of life, liberty, or property, without due process of law." We have long recognized that the Amendment's Due Process Clause, like its Fifth Amendment counterpart, "guarantees more than fair process." The Clause also includes a substantive component that "provides heightened protection against government interference with certain fundamental rights and liberty interests." [*Washington v. Glucksberg* (1997).]

The liberty interest at issue in this case—the interest of parents in the care, custody, and control of their children—is perhaps the oldest of the fundamental liberty interests recognized by this Court. More than 75 years ago, in *Meyer v. Nebraska* (1923), we held that the "liberty" protected by the Due Process Clause includes the right of parents to "establish a home and bring up children" and "to control the education of their own." Two years later, *in Pierce v. Society of Sisters* (1925), we again held that the "liberty of parents and guardians" includes the right "to direct the upbringing and education of children under their control." . . .

In subsequent cases also, we have recognized the fundamental right of parents to make decisions concerning the care, custody, and control of their children. [Citations omitted.] In light of this extensive precedent, it cannot now be doubted that the Due Process Clause of the Fourteenth Amendment protects the fundamental right of parents to make decisions concerning the care, custody, and control of their children.

Section 26.10.160(3), as applied to Granville and her family in this case, unconstitutionally infringes on that fundamental parental right. The Washington nonparental visitation statute is breathtakingly broad. According to the statute's text, "[a]ny person may petition the court for visitation rights at *any time*," and the court may grant such visitation rights whenever "visitation may serve *the best interest of the child*." §26.10.160(3) (emphases added). That language effectively permits any third party seeking visitation to subject any decision by a parent concerning visitation of the parent's children to state-court review. Once the visitation petition has been filed in court and the matter is placed before a judge, a parent's decision that visitation would not be in the child's best interest is accorded no deference. Section 26.10.160(3) contains no requirement that a court accord the parent's decision any presumption of validity or any weight whatsoever. Instead, the Washington statute places the best-interest determination solely in the hands of the judge. Should the judge disagree with the parent's estimation of the child's best interests, the judge's view necessarily prevails. Thus, in practical effect, in the State of Washington a court can disregard and overturn any decision by a fit custodial parent concerning visitation whenever a third party affected by the decision files a visitation petition, based solely on the judge's determination of the child's best interests. The Washington Supreme Court had the opportunity to give §26.10.160(3) a narrower reading, but it declined to do so. . . .

Turning to the facts of this case, the record reveals that the Superior Court's order was based on precisely the type of mere disagreement we have just described and nothing more. The Superior Court's order was not founded on any special factors that might justify the State's interference with Granville's fundamental right to make decisions concerning the rearing of her two daughters. To be sure, this case involves a visitation petition filed by grandparents soon after the death of their son—the father of Isabelle and Natalie—but the combination of several factors here compels our conclusion that §26.10.160(3), as applied, exceeded the bounds of the Due Process Clause.

First, the Troxels did not allege, and no court has found, that Granville was an unfit parent. That aspect of the case is important, for there is a presumption that fit parents act in the best interests of their children. . . . Accordingly, so long as a parent adequately cares for his or her children (i.e., is fit), there will normally be no reason for the State to inject itself into the private realm of the family to further question the ability of that parent to make the best decisions concerning the rearing of that parent's children.

The problem here is not that the Washington Superior Court intervened, but that when it did so, it gave no special weight at all to Granville's determination of her daughters' best interests. More importantly, it appears that the Superior Court applied exactly the opposite presumption. In reciting its oral ruling after the conclusion of closing arguments, the Superior Court judge explained:

> "The burden is to show that it is in the best interest of the children to have some visitation and some quality time with their grandparents. I think in most situations a commonsensical approach [is that] it is normally in the best interest of the children to spend quality time with the grandparent, unless the grandparent, [sic] there are some issues or problems involved wherein the grandparents, their lifestyles are going to impact adversely upon the children. That certainly isn't the case here from what I can tell."

The judge's comments suggest that he presumed the grandparents' request should be granted unless the children would be "impact[ed] adversely." In effect, the judge placed on Granville, the fit custodial parent, the burden of disproving that visitation would be in the best interest of her daughters. The judge reiterated moments later: "I think [visitation with the Troxels] would be in the best interest of the children and I haven't been shown it is not in [the] best interest of the children."

The decisional framework employed by the Superior Court directly contravened the traditional presumption that a fit parent will act in the best interest of his or her child. In that respect, the court's presumption failed to provide any protection for Granville's fundamental constitutional right to make decisions concerning the rearing of her own daughters. . . . In an ideal world, parents might always seek to cultivate the bonds between grandparents and their grandchildren. Needless to say, however, our world is far from perfect, and in it the decision whether such an intergenerational relationship would be beneficial in any specific case is for the parent to make in the first instance. And, if a fit parent's decision of the kind at issue here becomes subject to judicial review, the court must accord at least some special weight to the parent's own determination.

Finally, we note that there is no allegation that Granville ever sought to cut off visitation entirely. Rather, the present dispute originated when Granville informed the Troxels that she would prefer to restrict their visitation with Isabelle and Natalie to one short visit per month and special holidays. In the Superior Court proceedings Granville did not oppose visitation but instead asked that the duration of any visitation order be shorter than that requested by the Troxels. . . . The Superior Court gave no weight to Granville's having assented to visitation even before the filing of any visitation petition or subsequent court intervention. The court instead rejected Granville's proposal and settled on a middle ground, ordering one weekend of visitation per month, one week in the summer, and time on both of the petitioning grandparents' birth-days. Significantly, many other States expressly provide by statute that courts may not award visitation unless a parent has denied (or unreasonably denied) visitation to the concerned third party. [Citing Mississippi, Oregon, and Rhode Island statutes.]

Considered together with the Superior Court's reasons for awarding visita-tion to the Troxels, the combination of these factors demonstrates that the vis-itation order in this case was an unconstitutional infringement on Granville's fundamental right to make decisions concerning the care, custody, and con-trol of her two daughters. The Washington Superior Court failed to accord the determination of Granville, a fit custodial parent, any material weight. In fact, the Superior Court made only two formal findings in support of its visitation order. First, the Troxels "are part of a large, central, loving family, all located in this area, and the [Troxels] can provide opportunities for the children in the areas of cousins and music." Second, "[t]he children would be benefitted from spending quality time with the [Troxels], provided that that time is balanced with time with the childrens' [sic] nuclear family." These slender findings, in combination with the court's announced presumption in favor of grandparent visitation and its failure to accord significant weight to Granville's already hav-ing offered meaningful visitation to the Troxels, show that this case involves nothing more than a simple disagreement between the Washington Superior Court and Granville concerning her children's best interests. . . . As we have explained, the Due Process Clause does not permit a State to infringe on the fundamental right of parents to make childrearing decisions simply because a state judge believes a "better" decision could be made. Neither the Washing-ton nonparental visitation statute generally—which places no limits on either the persons who may petition for visitation or the circumstances in which such a petition may be granted—nor the Superior Court in this specific case required anything more. Accordingly, we hold that §26.10.160(3), as applied in this case, is unconstitutional.

Because we rest our decision on the sweeping breadth of §26.10.160(3) and the application of that broad, unlimited power in this case, we do not consider the primary constitutional question passed on by the Washington Supreme Court—whether the Due Process Clause requires all nonparental visitation statutes to include a showing of harm or potential harm to the child as a con-dition precedent to granting visitation. We do not, and need not, define today the precise scope of the parental due process right in the visitation context. In this respect, we agree with JUSTICE KENNEDY that the constitutionality of any standard for awarding visitation turns on the specific manner in which that standard is applied and that the constitutional protections in this area are best "elaborated with care." Because much state-court adjudication in this context occurs on a case-by-case basis, we would be hesitant to hold that specific nonparental visitation statutes violate the Due Process Clause as a *per se* matter. . . .

There is thus no reason to remand the case for further proceedings in the Washington Supreme Court. . . . As we have explained, it is apparent that the entry of the visitation order in this case violated the Constitution. We should say so now, without forcing the parties into additional litigation that would further burden Granville's parental right. We therefore hold that the application of §26.10.160(3) to Granville and her family violated her due process right to make decisions concerning the care, custody, and control of her daughters.

Accordingly, the judgment of the Washington Supreme Court is affirmed.

*It is so ordered.*

JUSTICE SOUTER, concurring in the judgment.

I concur in the judgment affirming the decision of the Supreme Court of Washington, whose facial invalidation of its own state statute is consistent with this Court's prior cases addressing the substantive interests at stake. . . .

The Supreme Court of Washington invalidated its state statute based on the text of the statute alone, not its application to any particular case. Its ruling rested on two independently sufficient grounds: the failure of the statute to require harm to the child to justify a disputed visitation order and the statute's authorization of "any person" at "any time" to petition and to receive visitation rights subject only to a free-ranging best-interests-of-the-child standard. I see no error in the second reason, that because the state statute authorizes any person at any time to request (and a judge to award) visitation rights, subject only to the State's particular best-interests standard, the state statute sweeps too broadly and is unconstitutional on its face. Consequently, there is no need to decide whether harm is required or to consider the precise scope of the parent's right or its necessary protections. . . .

JUSTICE THOMAS, concurring in the judgment.

. . . [N]either party has argued that our substantive due process cases were wrongly decided and that the original understanding of the Due Process Clause precludes judicial enforcement of unenumerated rights under that constitutional provision. As a result, I express no view on the merits of this matter. . . .

Consequently, I agree with the plurality that this Court's recognition of a fundamental right of parents to direct the upbringing of their children resolves this case. Our decision in *Pierce v. Society of Sisters* (1925) holds that parents have a fundamental constitutional right to rear their children, including the right to determine who shall educate and socialize them. The opinions of the plurality, JUSTICE KENNEDY, and JUSTICE SOUTER recognize such a right, but curiously none of them articulates the appropriate standard of review. I would apply strict scrutiny to infringements of fundamental rights. Here, the State of Washington lacks even a legitimate governmental interest—to say nothing of a compelling one—in second-guessing a fit parent's decision regarding visitation with third parties. On this basis, I would affirm the judgment below.

JUSTICE STEVENS, dissenting.

The Court today wisely declines to endorse either the holding or the reasoning of the Supreme Court of Washington. In my opinion, the Court would have been even wiser to deny certiorari. Given the problematic character of the trial court's decision and the uniqueness of the Washington statute, there was no pressing need to review a State Supreme Court decision that merely requires the state legislature to draft a better statute.

Having decided to address the merits, however, the Court should begin by recognizing that the State Supreme Court rendered a federal constitutional judgment holding a state law invalid on its face. In light of that judgment, I believe that we should confront the federal questions presented directly. For the Washington statute is not made facially invalid either because it may be invoked by too many hypothetical plaintiffs, or because it leaves open the possibility that someone may be permitted to sustain a relationship with a child without having to prove that serious harm to the child would otherwise result. . . .

Cases like this do not present a bipolar struggle between the parents and the State over who has final authority to determine what is in a child's best interests. There is at a minimum a third individual, whose interests are implicated in every case to which the statute applies—the child. . . .

A parent's rights with respect to her child have . . . never been regarded as absolute, but rather are limited by the existence of an actual, developed relationship with a child, and are tied to the presence or absence of some embodiment of family. These limitations have arisen, not simply out of the definition of parenthood itself, but because of this Court's assumption that a parent's interests in a child must be balanced against the State's long-recognized interests as parens patriae, and, critically, the child's own complementary interest in preserving relationships that serve her welfare and protection.

. . . [I]it seems to me extremely likely that, to the extent parents and families have fundamental liberty interests in preserving such intimate relationships, so, too, do children have these interests, and so, too, must their interests be balanced in the equation. . . . The constitutional protection against arbitrary state interference with parental rights should not be extended to prevent the States from protecting children against the arbitrary exercise of parental authority that is not in fact motivated by an interest in the welfare of the child.

. . . [W]e should recognize that there may be circumstances in which a child has a stronger interest at stake than mere protection from serious harm caused by the termination of visitation by a "person" other than a parent. The almost infinite variety of family relationships that pervade our ever-changing society strongly counsel against the creation by this Court of a constitutional rule that treats a biological parent's liberty interest in the care and supervision of her child as an isolated right that may be exercised arbitrarily. It is indisputably the business of the States, rather than a federal court employing a national standard, to assess in the first instance the relative importance of the conflicting interests that give rise to disputes such as this. Far from guaranteeing that parents' interests will be trammeled in the sweep of cases arising under the statute, the Washington law merely gives an individual—with whom a child may have an established relationship—the procedural right to ask the State to act as arbiter, through the entirely well-known best-interests standard, between the parent's protected interests and the child's. It seems clear to me that the Due Process Clause of the Fourteenth Amendment leaves room for States to consider the impact on a child of possibly arbitrary parental decisions that neither serve nor are motivated by the best interests of the child.

Accordingly, I respectfully dissent.

JUSTICE SCALIA, dissenting.

In my view, a right of parents to direct the upbringing of their children is among the "unalienable Rights" with which the Declaration of Independence proclaims "all Men . . . are endowed by their Creator." And in my view that right is also among the "othe[r] [rights] retained by the people" which the Ninth Amendment says the Constitution's enumeration of rights "shall not be construed to deny or disparage." The Declaration of Independence, however, is not a legal prescription conferring powers upon the courts; and the Constitution's refusal to "deny or disparage" other rights is far removed from affirming any one of them, and even farther removed from authorizing judges to identify what they might be, and to enforce the judges' list against laws duly enacted by the people. Consequently, while I would think it entirely compatible with the commitment to representative democracy set forth in the founding documents to argue, in legislative chambers or in electoral campaigns, that the state has no power to interfere with parents' authority over the rearing of their children, I do not believe that the power which the Constitution confers upon me as a judge entitles me to deny legal effect to laws that (in my view) infringe upon what is (in my view) that unenumerated right. . . .

Judicial vindication of "parental rights" under a Constitution that does not even mention them requires . . . not only a judicially crafted definition of parents, but also—unless, as no one believes, the parental rights are to be absolute—judicially approved assessments of "harm to the child" and judicially defined gradations of other persons (grandparents, extended family, adoptive family in an adoption later found to be invalid, long-term guardians, etc.) who may have some claim against the wishes of the parents. If we embrace this unenumerated right, I think it obvious . . . that we will be ushering in a new regime of judicially prescribed, and federally prescribed, family law. I have no reason to believe that federal judges will be better at this than state legislatures; and state legislatures have the great advantages of doing harm in a more circumscribed area, of being able to correct their mistakes in a flash, and of being removable by the people.

For these reasons, I would reverse the judgment below.

JUSTICE KENNEDY, dissenting. . . .

Given the error I see in the State Supreme Court's central conclusion. . . , that court should have the first opportunity to reconsider this case. I would remand the case to the state court for further proceedings. . . .

My principal concern is that the holding seems to proceed from the assumption that the parent or parents who resist visitation have always been the child's primary caregivers and that the third parties who seek visitation have no legitimate and established relationship with the child. That idea, in turn, appears influenced by the concept that the conventional nuclear family ought to establish the visitation standard for every domestic relations case. As we all know, this is simply not the structure or prevailing condition in many households. . . .

Cases are sure to arise—perhaps a substantial number of cases—in which a third party, by acting in a caregiving role over a significant period of time, has developed a relationship with a child which is not necessarily subject to absolute parental veto. . . . Some pre-existing relationships, then, serve to identify persons who have a strong attachment to the child with the concomitant motivation to act in a responsible way to ensure the child's welfare. . . . In the design and elaboration of their visitation laws, States may be entitled to consider that certain relationships are such that to avoid the risk of harm, a best interests standard can be employed by their domestic relations courts in some circumstances. . . .

. . . In my view, it would be more appropriate to conclude that the constitutionality of the application of the best interests standard depends on more specific factors. In short, a fit parent's right vis-à-vis a complete stranger is one thing; her right vis-à-vis another parent or a de facto parent may be another. The protection the Constitution requires, then, must be elaborated with care, using the discipline and instruction of the case law system. We must keep in mind that family courts in the 50 States confront these factual variations each day, and are best situated to consider the unpredictable, yet inevitable, issues that arise.

It must be recognized, of course, that a domestic relations proceeding in and of itself can constitute state intervention that is so disruptive of the parent-child relationship that the constitutional right of a custodial parent to make certain basic determinations for the child's welfare becomes implicated. . . . I do not discount the possibility that in some instances the best interests of the child standard may provide insufficient protection to the parent-child relationship. We owe it to the Nation's domestic relations legal structure, however, to proceed with caution. . . .

# U.S. COMMERCE DEPARTMENT ON A "DIGITAL ECONOMY"
## June 5, 2000

*Computers and related high-technology devices had transformed the American economy by 2000 into a "digital economy," according to a report released June 5, 2000, by the Commerce Department. The report was the department's third annual assessment of the impact of information technology (IT) on the overall marketplace. The first two reports, in 1998 and 1999, described the "emerging digital economy." To signify the extent of the impact, the 2000 report dropped the word* emerging. *Commerce Secretary William M. Daley said the many new forms of electronic business were "harbingers of a new economic era" similar to those resulting from the widespread introduction of the steam engine in the 1800s and electricity during the early 1900s.*

*Despite such enthusiasm, 2000 was a turning point of another sort for the high-technology industry. It was the year when high-flying technology stocks collapsed on Wall Street, and the "new economy" discovered that the laws of the old economy—most notably the desirability of turning a profit—applied to it as well. The NASDAQ stock index of the National Association of Security Dealers, the traditional trading place for many high-tech companies, fell 39.3 percent during 2000, a sharp contrast to its 85.6 percent gain in 1999. Shares of Internet-based companies plunged an average of about 65 percent, according to several major indexes. Dozens of high-tech companies cut back their operations and laid off employees for the first time, and some simply went out of business. Several major Internet-based firms also entered into mergers, most notably America Online, which moved on January 10, 2000, to buy Time Warner in what would be the biggest merger in history. (Mergers, p. 1034)*

### Maturing of the Digital Economy

*By 2000, the Commerce Department report said, investment in information technology had become the most important driving force in the nation's decade-long economic expansion. At the same time, prices of computer hard-*

*ware continued to fall, helping to keep inflation in check and contributing to a growth in business productivity, the report said.*

*Between 1995 and 1999 business investment in computer hardware and software more than doubled, from $243 billion to $510 billion annually. The latter figure represented about two-thirds of all U.S. business investment for 1999. In a broader measure of the impact of computerization, the report said that IT industries accounted for approximately 30 percent of U.S. economic growth between 1995 and 1999—a remarkable figure considering the fact that those industries represented only about 8 percent of the overall economy as of 2000.*

*Much of the credit for the expansion of high technology during the 1990s belonged to the continuing dramatic growth of the Internet, the report said. By 2000 an estimated 300 million people worldwide had access to the Internet—nearly double the number of just one year earlier. Because of the growing popularity of the Internet overseas, by 2000 the United States and Canada for the first time accounted for less than half of the world's population using it.*

## *Productivity Questions*

*It was obvious to just about anyone working in an office during the 1980s and 1990s that the introduction of computers did not necessarily improve efficiency. Technical glitches, computer down-time, training requirements, and the use of office computers for personal matters were among the factors that often made it seem that working with computers was no more productive than working with paper, pen, typewriters, and other old-fashioned devices. Economists even had a name for this phenomenon—the "productivity paradox"—and had statistics to bolster the general impression. Between 1973, when computers were beginning to enter the workplace, and 1995, when most U.S. businesses had computerized substantial portions of the operations, labor productivity (one of the two main productivity measures) increased by an annual average of just 1.4 percent—about half the average during the 1960s and early 1970s.*

*By 2000 most economists argued that the situation was changing and that computerization finally was improving the productivity of the U.S. economy. According to figures cited in the Commerce Department report, labor productivity jumped to about 2.8 percent annually between 1996 and 1999—double the weak average during the previous two decades. Several studies argued that most of that increase was due to the transformation of the economy by information technology. One of the most widely quoted studies, by Federal Reserve Bank economists Stephen D. Oliner and Daniel E. Sichel, also argued that productivity increases were likely to continue well into the twenty-first century.*

*The news media also cited statistics showing how computers had reduced the cost and complexity of work. For example, The Economist magazine noted on September 23 that the Ford Motor Company in 1985 spent $60,000 each time it crashed a car into a wall for an accident test. By 2000 the company could simulate the same accident on a computer for about $100.*

*Despite such reassuring evidence, some skeptics continued to argue that the "productivity paradox" remained in effect and that computers actually had done little to make the U.S. economy more efficient. One of the skeptics, Northwestern University economist Robert Gordon, offered evidence showing that nearly all the productivity increase in the latter half of the 1990s was due to overall improvements in the economy, not to the expanding penetration of computers into the workplace. E-commerce, he argued, simply replaced other economic activity (people buying music recordings or clothing over the Internet, rather than at retail stores) and was not necessarily more efficient. Gordon noted that "visits" to Internet sites offering retail sales tended to be concentrated during the daytime hours, an indication that many workers were shopping online at the office rather than tackling their assigned tasks.*

*Several economic studies released during the year found that productivity gains in most of the rest of the world during the late 1990s had failed to keep pace with that in the United States. The majority of the studies argued that the disparity resulted from the fact that the United States was much more heavily dependent on IT than any other nation. Again, the link between productivity gains and computerization was subject to dispute, in part because of the difficulty in drawing up-to-date comparisons among widely differing economies.*

### Questions Remain About E-Commerce

*Questions about productivity were not the only issues facing the IT industry at the turn of the century. Electronic commerce ("e-commerce," for short) was being heavily promoted in nearly all aspects of society, but its impact was far from being fully realized. Consumer sales over the Internet—the most visible aspect of e-commerce—continued to grow rapidly but still represented a minuscule portion of the market. The Bureau of the Census reported on May 31 that online retail sales totaled about $5.2 billion during the fourth quarter of 1999 and just under $5.3 billion for the first quarter of 2000. In each case, the figure represented less than 1 percent of all retail sales. Many of the best-known consumer Internet firms, such as Amazon.com and e-Bay, had yet to make a profit, as of 2000. Despite the rapid growth of the Internet, the medium was still not a universal presence, even in the United States. The National Association of Manufacturers, for example, found in a survey that more than two-thirds of manufacturing companies were still not conducting business electronically.*

*Of greater long-term importance than consumer sales, according to many experts, was the growth potential for electronic sales between businesses, known in the trade as "business-to-business," or "b2b" commerce. Industry promoters argued that doing business over the Internet would soon become the norm for nearly all sectors of the economy. Using the Internet, for example, a company that made refrigerators could order parts from suppliers and keep track of deliveries and sales much more efficiently than in the past. Perhaps the most dramatic development in this sector during the year was the announcement in February 2000 that three major automakers*

*(General Motors, Ford, and Daimler-Chrysler) would establish an Internet-based parts exchange involving some 60,000 suppliers. The companies said they expected the exchange eventually would do about $250 billion in business annually.*

*Washington took an important step during the year to make it easier for businesses and individuals to do business over the Internet. Congress passed, and President Bill Clinton on June 30 signed into law, a bill (PL 106–229) according full federal legal status to electronic transactions. In signing the bill, Clinton cited several advantages: "Companies will now be able to contract online to buy and sell products worth millions of dollars. Businesses will be able to collect and store transaction records that once filled up vast warehouses on servers the size of a laptop. And consumers will have the option of buying insurance, getting a mortgage, or opening a brokerage account online, without waiting for the paperwork to be mailed back and forth."*

## Wall Street's Skeptical Eye

*The year 2000 may have marked the point when the reality of the marketplace finally caught up with the high-technology industry. For several years, high-tech companies had operated in a "sky's-the-limit" environment. It often seemed that anyone knowledgeable about computers and with a business plan mentioning the Internet could secure millions of dollars in private financing for a "dot-com" startup company, whether or not it had a realistic chance of making a profit. Dozens of companies rocketed to the heights of Wall Street financing on the basis of hopes and expectations rather than historic business performance. Amazon.com, an Internet based retailer of books and other consumer goods that had never turned a profit, saw its stock value shoot over $100 early in the year. Priceline.com, which promoted discount air travel, at one point in 1999 had a stock market valuation greater than the combined worth of the airlines whose tickets it was selling.*

*At the same time, so-called old economy companies—including some of the country's best regarded manufacturers and retailers—saw their stocks tumble as investors shifted their hopes and money to the future of the Internet. Early in the year, one analysis showed that stocks of the thirty companies listed on the Dow Jones Industrial Average were valued an average of twenty-five times annual earnings, while stocks of major firms on the NASDAQ index, most of them in the high-tech sector, were valued at 150 times earnings.*

*High-tech stocks began a modest fall in mid-March, and two events in late March and early April signaled what turned out to be a general trend for the rest of the year. On March 28, Abby Joseph Cohen, an analyst for the Goldman Sachs brokerage firm who had helped stimulate the boom in high-tech stocks, warned that the sector was becoming overvalued. Four days later, on April 1, court-mediated talks aimed at settling the federal government's antitrust suit against Microsoft Corporation collapsed, setting in motion a train of events leading to an historic order intended to break the world's largest software company into two parts.* (Microsoft ruling, pp. 105, 308)

*The stock market tumbled in April, with Internet-based companies particularly hard hit. In general, analysts said, the managers of major mutual funds and pension fund portfolios were the first to pull out of the technology sector, while individual investors held onto their high-tech stocks well into the year, in some cases until it was too late. Stocks of many high-tech companies staged a modest recovery, or at least stopped falling so rapidly, during the middle months of the year. But a wave of bad news in third-quarter earnings reports, coupled with rising oil prices and the continuing impact of interest rate increases by the Federal Reserve Board, led to another Wall Street sell-off that began in October and continued for the rest of the year.*

*Dozens of Internet-based firms were facing the simple economic reality of expenses outrunning revenues, with little prospect of new cash infusions from investors who previously had been attracted by the chance to cash in on a booming trend. In an October 11 report the Seattle* Times *said seventeen publicly traded Internet firms in the Seattle area were losing money, including Amazon.com. Four of the seventeen companies were expected to run out of money within a year unless they sharply cut expenses or gained new cash infusions, the newspaper said. One of the four was drugstore.com, a well-known online pharmaceutical retailer.*

*At year's end every major sector of the high-tech industry had fallen sharply on Wall Street. According to the Bloomberg financial news service, stocks of Internet-based companies had fallen 66.3 percent, software firms 50.9 percent, telecommunications service companies 44.9 percent, telecommunications equipment companies 41.6 percent, and computer hardware firms 24.6 percent. Among the most dramatic falls were those of priceline.com, whose stock price peaked for the year at $104 but closed the year at $1.31, and of Yahoo, an Internet portal that was one of the few major Internet-based companies making a profit, whose stock price peaked at $251 but fell at years-end to $30.17—a drop of 86 percent.*

> *Following is the executive summary from the report, "Digital Economy 2000," released June 5, 2000, by the U.S. Department of Commerce and prepared by the department's economics and statistics administration. The document was obtained from the Internet at http://www.esa.doc.gov/de2000.pdf.*

The U.S. economic expansion is now in its tenth year, showing no signs of slowing down. The rate of labor productivity growth has doubled in recent years, instead of falling as the expansion matured as in previous postwar expansions. Moreover, core inflation remains low despite record employment and the lowest jobless rates in a generation. Our sustained economic strength with low inflation suggests that the U.S. economy may well have crossed into a new era of greater economic prosperity and possibility, much as it did after the development and spread of the electric dynamo and the internal combustion engine.

The advent of this new era has coincided with dramatic cost reductions in computers, computer components, and communications equipment. Declines in computer prices, which were already rapid—roughly 12 percent per year on average between 1987 and 1994—accelerated to 26 percent per year during 1995–1999. Between 1994 and 1998 (the last four years for which data are available), the price of telecommunications equipment declined by 2 percent a year.

Declining IT [information technology] prices and years of sustained economic growth have spurred massive investments not only in computer and communications equipment, but in new software that harnesses and enhances the productive capacity of that equipment. Real business investment in IT equipment and software more than doubled between 1995 and 1999, from $243 billion to $510 billion. The software component of these totals increased over the period from $82 billion to $149 billion.

The new economy is being shaped not only by the development and diffusion of hardware and software, but also by much cheaper and rapidly increasing electronic connectivity. The Internet in particular is helping to level the playing field among large and small firms in business-to-business e-commerce. In the past, larger companies had increasingly used private networks to carry out electronic commerce, but high costs kept the resulting efficiencies out of reach for most small businesses. The Internet has altered this equation by making it easier and cheaper for all businesses to transact business and exchange information.

There is growing evidence that firms are moving their supply networks and sales channels online, and participating in new online marketplaces. Firms are also expanding their use of networked systems to improve internal business processes—to coordinate product design, manage inventory, improve customer service, and reduce administrative and managerial costs. Nonetheless, the evolution of digital business is still in an early stage. A recent survey by the National Association of Manufacturers, for example, found that more than two-thirds of American manufacturers still do not conduct business electronically.

Advances in information technologies and the spread of the Internet are also providing significant benefits to individuals. In 2000, the number of people with Internet access will reach an estimated 304 million people world-wide, up almost 80 percent from 1999; and, for the first time, the United States and Canada account for less than 50 percent of the global online population. Further, according to Inktomi and the NEC Research Institute, the amount of information available online has increased ten-fold over the last three years, to more than a billion discrete pages.

As more people have moved online, so have many everyday activities. In March 2000, the Census Bureau released the first official measure of an important subset of business-to-consumer e-commerce, "e-retail." Census found that in the fourth quarter of 1999, online sales by retail establishments totaled

$5.3 billion, or 0.64 percent of all retail sales. People increasingly use the Internet not only to make purchases, but also to arrange financing, take delivery of digital products, and get follow-up service.

The vitality of the digital economy is grounded in IT-producing industries—the firms that supply the goods and services that support IT-enabled business processes, the Internet and e-commerce. Analysis of growth and investment patterns shows that the economic importance of these industries has increased sharply since the mid-1990s. Although IT industries still account for a relatively small share of the economy's total output—an estimated 8.3 percent in 2000—they contributed nearly a third of real U.S. economic growth between 1995 and 1999.

In addition, the falling prices of IT goods and services have reduced overall U.S. inflation—for the years 1994 to 1998, by an average of 0.5 percentage points a year, or from 2.3 percent to 1.8 percent. The rates of decline in IT prices accelerated through the 1990s—from about 1 percent in 1994, to nearly 5 percent in 1995, and an average of 8 percent for the years 1996 to 1998.

IT industries have also been a major source of new R&D [research and development] investment. Between 1994 and 1999, U.S. R&D investment increased at an average annual (inflation adjusted) rate of about 6 percent—up from roughly 0.3 percent during the previous five-year period. The lion's share of this growth—37 percent between 1995 and 1998—occurred in IT industries. In 1998, IT industries invested $44.8 billion in R&D, or nearly one-third of all company-funded R&D.

New investments in IT are helping to generate higher rates of U.S. labor productivity growth. Six major economic studies have recently concluded that the production and use of IT contributed half or more of the acceleration in U.S. productivity growth in the second half of the 1990s. This has occurred despite the fact that IT capital accounts for only 6 percent of private business income. Such remarkable leverage reflects in part the fact that businesses must earn immediate rates of return on investments in IT hardware high enough to compensate for the rapid obsolescence (i.e., depreciation) and falling market value of these assets. In short, IT investments must be extraordinarily productive during their short lives. Recent firm-level evidence indicates that IT investments are most effective when coupled with complementary investments in organizational change, and not very effective in the absence of such investments.

Although the official data show declining productivity for a number of major service industries that invest heavily in IT (e.g., health, business services), this probably reflects the inadequacy of official output measures for those industries. Until these measures are improved, the full effect of IT on service industry productivity will remain clouded.

In 1998, the number of workers in IT-producing industries, together with workers in IT occupations in other industries, totaled 7.4 million or 6.1 percent of all American workers. Growth in the IT workforce accelerated in the mid-1990s, with the most rapid increases coming in industries and job categories associated with the development and use of IT applications. Employment in the software and computer services industries nearly doubled, from

850,000 in 1992 to 1.6 million in 1998. Over the same period, employment in those IT job categories that require the most education and offer the highest compensation, such as computer scientists, computer engineers, systems analysts and computer programmers, increased by nearly 1 million positions or almost 80 percent.

At the same time, the rapid pace of technological change and increased competition have added an element of uncertainty to IT employment. The number of jobs has declined in some IT industries, such as computers and household audio and video equipment. Moreover, while IT-producing industries as a whole paid higher-than-average wages in 1998, some IT jobs remain low-skilled and low-paid.

Paradoxically, although America's IT-producing companies are clearly world-class, the United States regularly runs large trade deficits in IT goods—an estimated $66 billion in 1999. One reason is that American IT firms more often service foreign customers with sales from their overseas affiliates than by exports from their U.S. operations. In 1997, foreign sales by overseas affiliates of American IT companies totaled $196 billion, compared to U.S. exports by firms in comparable industries of $121 billion. In the same year, American affiliates of foreign-owned IT companies operating in the United States reported sales here of $110 billion. Therefore, while the U.S. balance of trade in IT products was negative, the "balance of sales" favored American companies by $86 billion.

IT has not only propelled faster growth during this expansion, but it will have a tendency to dampen the next business cycle downturn. Because IT investment is driven by competitive pressures to innovate and cut costs more than to expand capacity, it will be less affected by a slowdown in demand. In addition, by creating supply chain efficiencies that reduce inventories, IT should dampen the inventory effect that has worsened past recessions.

The strong performance of the U.S. economy since 1995 contrasts both with U.S. performance from 1973 to 1995 and with the rest of the industrial world in recent years. Historically, there have been long lags between fundamental technological breakthroughs, such as electricity and electric motors, and large economic effects from them. Although IT is generally available in world markets, the U.S. economy to date has achieved greater gains from IT than other countries at least partly because of favorable monetary and fiscal policies, a pro-competitive regime of regulation, and a financial system and business culture prepared to take risks.

Even in this country, however, the diffusion of IT has been uneven. Although the number of homes with computers and Internet connections has been rising rapidly, the majority of Americans do not have online connections at home. Those on the wrong side of the digital divide—disproportionately people with lower incomes, less education, and members of minority groups—are missing out on increasingly valuable opportunities for education, job search, and communication with their families and communities.

In conclusion, a growing body of evidence suggests that the U.S. economy has crossed into a new period of higher, sustainable economic growth and higher, sustainable productivity gains. These conditions are driven in part by a powerful combination of rapid technological innovation, sharply falling IT prices, and booming investment in IT goods and services across virtually all American industries. Analysis of the computer and communications industries in particular suggests that the pace of technological innovation and rapidly falling prices should continue well into the future. Moreover, businesses outside the IT sector almost daily announce IT-based organizational and operating changes that reflect their solid confidence in the benefit of further substantial investments in IT goods and services. The largest and clearest recent examples come from the automobile, aircraft, energy and retail industries, which all have announced new Internet-based forms of market integration that should generate large continuing investments in IT infrastructure. These examples mark only the beginning of the digital economy.

# U.S. DISTRICT COURT ON THE BREAKUP OF MICROSOFT
## June 7, 2000

*In one of the most sweeping rulings in one hundred years of U.S. antitrust law, a federal judge on June 7, 2000, ordered the Microsoft Corporation broken into two parts because of its predatory behavior as a monopoly controlling key aspects of the computer software market. District Court Judge Thomas Penfield Jackson, who had issued two previous rulings declaring Microsoft to be a monopoly that illegally thwarted competition, sided with the U.S. government and seventeen states in declaring that splitting the company in two parts would foster competition and stimulate technological innovation.* (Monopoly ruling, p. 105)

*The case was almost certain to go to the U.S. Supreme Court. Jackson's ruling, if upheld by the high court, had the potential to reshape much of the computer technology industry, which in the late twentieth century had become one of the pillars of the world economy. Microsoft dominated the computer software industry during the 1990s and used its power to influence technical and business decisions by scores of other companies.* (Growth of digital economy, p. 299)

*Some analysis said the Microsoft case was already having an impact on the computer software industry, which was noted for a no-holds-barred approach to business deals. By 2000, according to news reports, some software companies reportedly were beginning to drop restrictive licensing arrangements of the type that were central to the Microsoft case.*

*A breakup of Microsoft would be the largest single enforced dismantling of a corporation since the Standard Oil trust was split into thirty-four companies in 1911. AT&T, another of the country's dominant corporations, agreed in 1982 to settle an antitrust case by selling off its local telephone operations. In both of those cases, the smaller companies created by the courts went on to become industry giants, and some of them later remerged.* (AT&T case, Historic Documents of 1982, p. 17)

*Microsoft appealed Jackson's rulings and quickly scored two procedural victories. First, Jackson agreed on June 20 to delay implementation of his orders while the case went through the appeals process.*

On a second but related matter, Jackson sided with the government's desire to expedite the case by moving it straight to the U.S. Supreme Court, bypassing the U.S. Court of Appeals for the District of Columbia, which in the past had appeared receptive to Microsoft's arguments on antitrust matters. But the Supreme Court on September 26 ordered that the case proceed by regular channels through the appeals process. The Court's decision came in an 8–1 ruling, with Justice Stephen G. Breyer dissenting. The appellate court scheduled hearings on the case for February 2001. That schedule raised the possibility that a case centering on actions that took place in 1995 might not be concluded until 2002 or even 2003. Some analysts said the delay might ultimately save Microsoft from a breakup because changes in the technology industry were affecting many of the underlying factors in the case more quickly than federal judges could act.

Microsoft filed its opening brief with the appeals court on November 27, focusing largely on what it said was Jackson's mishandling of the case. The brief said the entire case "was infected with error" and charged that Jackson demonstrated a "profound misunderstanding of the antitrust laws." The brief also said that numerous comments Jackson made to the news media that were highly critical of Microsoft "would lead a reasonable observer to question his impartiality and—together with other procedural irregularities—the fairness of the entire proceeding."

Microsoft also took its case into the political arena, supporting political candidates at the state and national level who supported its point of view. The Washington Post reported on September 29 that Microsoft had donated more than $750,000 to trade groups, foundations, and other organizations that opposed the government's case. One group cited by the newspaper, Citizens for a Sound Economy, was said to have spent more than $100,000 in North Carolina to influence candidates for state attorney general to back out of the case. Several top Microsoft executives also supported the successful presidential candidacy of Republican George W. Bush, who was expected to take a more skeptical view of the antitrust case than the outgoing Clinton administration.

## Competing Proposals

The antitrust case against Microsoft was brought in 1998 by the U.S. Justice Department and the attorneys general of nineteen states and the District of Columbia. After a trial that ran from late 1998 to early 1999, Jackson ruled in November 1999 that Microsoft had monopoly control over the market for operating systems for personal computers and had used its power to attempt to gain a similar monopoly in the market for software to "browse" the Internet, or World Wide Web. Negotiations to settle the case collapsed on April 1, 2000, and Jackson ruled two days later that Microsoft's actions violated the Sherman Antitrust Act in three respects.

Immediately following Jackson's April 3 ruling, the government and Microsoft presented competing proposals for a "remedy." The Justice Department and seventeen states on April 28 submitted a proposal calling for severing Microsoft into two entities and imposing several restrictions on *the company's business operations. Justice Department officials said the proposal would increase competition, and therefore enhance innovation, in the computer software industry. Two of the original nineteen states in the case (Ohio and Illinois) refused to support the breakup proposal.*

*Microsoft on May 10 sent Jackson a counterproposal that rejected Jackson's findings and asked the judge to throw out the government's breakup plan. Even so, the company offered several restrictions on its business activities. All the proposed restrictions were substantially more limited than those demanded by the government. Microsoft said the breakup plan would destroy its business and cause "uncertainty and chaos" in the software industry.*

*Microsoft lawyers also demanded that Jackson allow a new round of testimony in the case so the company could offer more than a dozen witnesses who would explain why the company should not be dismantled. Jackson rejected that demand on May 24, saying the company already had plenty of opportunity to defend itself.*

*Jackson's breakup ruling June 7 came in two parts: a "final order" that spelled out the details of how the company should be split in two and what restrictions should be imposed on the business operations of the new entities, and a "memorandum and order" that castigated the company for its behavior during the case and explained his reasons for refusing the demand for another round of testimony. "Plaintiffs won the case," Jackson said, referring to the federal and state governments that sued Microsoft, and so they were entitled to the remedy of their choice.*

## *The Breakup Plan*

*In effect, Jackson endorsed the breakup proposal submitted by the government on April 28. That plan would create two separate companies, which would be barred from reuniting for ten years. One firm would continue to produce and develop the Windows family of personal computer operating systems, which as of late 2000 included Windows 2000, Windows Millennium Edition, Windows 98, Windows NT, and Windows CE. The other company would be responsible for Microsoft's software applications programs, including the Office suite of word processing, accounting, and business programs; consumer-oriented software; Internet Explorer and other Web-based operations, such as Microsoft Network (MSN); Microsoft's collaboration with the NBC television network (MSNBC); Windows Media Player; and Outlook and Outlook Express.*

*While it left intact Microsoft's monopoly over operating systems for personal computers, Jackson's plan imposed several important restrictions (known as "conduct remedies") on the future business practices of both successor companies. The restrictions were intended to make it difficult for Microsoft to engage in the types of monopolistic behavior that the judge had found objectionable. One of Jackson's most serious demands was that Microsoft disclose to the software industry important technical information about its Windows systems, including what were known as "application programming interfaces" (APIs)—the essential links between the*

Windows systems and software application programs, such as word processing. Disclosure of that information would make it easier for competitors to develop software that was not dependent on Windows.

Other restrictions included a ban on threats or retaliations against computer manufacturers that installed non-Microsoft products; a ban on exclusive contracts under which Microsoft required its business partners to accept conditions on how their own products were developed and distributed, or under which Microsoft required business partners to promote or distribute Microsoft products; a requirement that Microsoft produce a version of Windows that made it easy for consumers to remove "middleware" products, such as a Web browser; and creation of a uniform fee that computer manufacturers would pay Microsoft for installing Windows on their products.

Microsoft lawyers complained that some of the restrictions were "vague" or "ambiguous" in their wording. But Jackson said that was to Microsoft's benefit, because the company could propose the details of how those restrictions were to be implemented.

Both in his rulings and in news media interviews, Jackson portrayed his breakup plan as a modest remedy, especially when compared with alternatives he had considered. Some government lawyers had proposed breaking the company into three or even four parts. Jackson said he especially wanted to avoid establishing a complex mechanism under which the government would constantly monitor Microsoft's business practices. Jackson also said Microsoft probably could have secured a milder solution if it had been more forthcoming in negotiations.

As with Jackson's previous rulings, Microsoft officials blasted the breakup plan. "Today's ruling represents an unwarranted and unjustified intrusion into the software marketplace," Microsoft chairman William H. Gates said. "The idea that somebody would say that breakup is a reasonable thing comes as quite a surprise to us, and we are quite confident that it won't be something that ever comes into effect."

## Jackson's Handling of the Case

Microsoft's supporters—and even some of the company's critics—said the ultimate outcome could depend in large part on how the appeals court and Supreme Court viewed Jackson's handling of the case. Most legal analysts said Jackson clearly had mastered the enormous complexities of the case and had carefully drawn his findings to withstand scrutiny by higher courts. But critics, including Microsoft lawyers, argued that Jackson rushed the complex case, truncated the testimony of witnesses who supported company positions, and refused to give proper consideration to its legal filings.

After the government filed its breakup proposal on April 28, Jackson demanded a response from Microsoft within two weeks. The company's lead attorney, William Neukom, said: "Even the government will have to agree that an American company deserves more than twelve days to respond to a government proposal to tear apart a $400 billion company."

It was clear from the language in Jackson's final rulings that by

*June 2000 he had lost patience with what he viewed as Microsoft's obstructionist tactics. The tone of his "memorandum and order" stopped just short of mocking the company. Jackson took particular aim at Microsoft's claim that it was surprised by his May 24 rejection of the company's bid to, in effect, retry the case. "Microsoft's profession of surprise is not credible," he said, noting that the company had immediately submitted a thirty-page document summarizing the testimony of sixteen potential witnesses.*

*Jackson said he settled on the breakup plan "reluctantly" and only after giving Microsoft plenty of opportunity to negotiate a settlement. But in the end, he wrote, he concluded that splitting the company was "imperative" because "Microsoft as it is presently organized and led is unwilling to accept the notion that it broke the law or [to] accede to an order amending its conduct." Jackson also alleged that Microsoft had "proved untrustworthy" because of its actions in an early phase of the antitrust case.*

*In a September 28 speech to an antitrust seminar in Washington, Jackson directly blamed Microsoft for the failure of negotiations to settle the case before he issued his final rulings. "Judicial intervention—forcible application of law—became the last resort," Jackson said, according to a report in the* Washington Post. *"And in my judgment, Microsoft's intransigence was the reason."*

*Joel I. Klein, the U.S. assistant attorney general in charge of antitrust enforcement, agreed with Jackson's assessment, saying "Microsoft itself is responsible" for the outcome of the case. "Its repeated illegal actions were the result of decisions made at the highest levels of the company over a lengthy and sustained period of time," he said. "They reflected defiance of, not respect for, the rule of law."*

> *Following are excerpts from two rulings issued June 7, 2000, by U.S. District Court Judge Thomas Penfield Jackson in the case,* United States of America v. Microsoft Corporation. *The first document is Jackson's "Final Judgment" requiring that Microsoft be broken into two separate companies and imposing restrictions on the business activities of the two new firms. The second document is the "Memorandum and Order," in which Jackson reviewed procedural matters in the case and criticized Microsoft's behavior. The documents were obtained from the Internet at http:// usvms.gpo.gov.*

# FINAL JUDGMENT

Plaintiff, United States of America, having filed its complaint herein on May 18, 1998;

Plaintiff States, having filed their complaint herein on the same day;

Defendant Microsoft Corporation ("Microsoft") having appeared and filed its answer to such complaints;

The Court having jurisdiction of the parties hereto and of the subject matter hereof and having conducted a trial thereon and entered Findings of Fact on November 5, 1999, and Conclusions of Law on April 3, 2000;

The Court having entered judgment in accordance with the Findings of Fact and the Conclusions of Law on April 3, 2000, that Microsoft has violated Sections 1 and 2 of the Sherman Act, as well as the following state law provisions: [anti-trust laws of California, Connecticut, District of Columbia, Florida, Illinois, Iowa, Kansas, Kentucky, Louisiana, Maryland, Massachusetts, Michigan, Minnesota, New Mexico, New York, North Carolina, Ohio, Utah, West Virginia, and Wisconsin]; and

Upon the record at trial and all prior and subsequent proceedings herein, it is this seventh day of June, 2000, hereby:

ORDERED, ADJUDGED, AND DECREED as follows:

1. Divestiture
    a. Not later than four months after entry of this Final Judgment, Microsoft shall submit to the Court and the Plaintiffs a proposed plan of divestiture. The Plaintiffs shall submit any objections to the proposed plan of divestiture to the Court within 60 days of receipt of the plan, and Microsoft shall submit its response within 30 days of receipt of the plaintiffs' objections.
    b. Following approval of a final plan of divestiture by the Court (the "Plan") (1) (and the expiration of the stay pending appeal set forth in section 6.a), Microsoft shall implement such Plan.
    c. The Plan shall provide for the completion, within 12 months of the expiration of the stay pending appeal set forth in section 6.a., of the following steps:
        i. The separation of the Operating Systems Business from the Applications Business, and the transfer of the assets of one of them (the "Separated Business") to a separate entity along with (a) all personnel, systems, and other tangible and intangible assets (including Intellectual Property) used to develop, produce, distribute, market, promote, sell, license and support the products and services of the Separated Business, and (b) such other assets as are necessary to operate the Separated Business as an independent and economically viable entity.
        ii. Intellectual Property that is used both in a product developed, distributed, or sold by the Applications Business and in a product developed, distributed, or sold by the Operating Systems Business as of April 27, 2000, shall be assigned to the Applications Business, and the Operating Systems Business shall be granted a perpetual, royalty-free license to license and distribute such Intellectual Property in its products, and, except with respect to such Intellectual Property related to the Internet browser, to develop, license and distribute modified or derivative versions of such Intellectual Property, provided

313

that the Operating Systems Business does not grant rights to such versions to the Applications Business. In the case of such Intellectual Property that is related to the Internet browser, the license shall not grant the Operating Systems Business any right to develop, license, or distribute modified or derivative versions of the Internet browser.

iii. The transfer of ownership of the Separated Business by means of a distribution of stock of the Separated Business to Non-Covered Shareholders of Microsoft, or by other disposition that does not result in a Covered Shareholder owning stock in both the Separated Business and the Remaining Business.

d. Until Implementation of the Plan, Microsoft shall:

i. preserve, maintain, and operate the Operating Systems Business and the Applications Business as ongoing, economically viable businesses, with management, sales, products, and operations of each business held as separate, distinct and apart from one another as they were on April 27, 2000, except to provide the accounting, management, and information services or other necessary support functions provided by Microsoft prior to the entry of this Final Judgment;

ii. use all reasonable efforts to maintain and increase the sales and revenues of both the products produced or sold by the Operating Systems Business and those produced or sold by the Applications Business prior to the Implementation of the Plan and to support research and development and business development efforts of both the Operating Systems Business and the Applications Business;

iii. take no action that undermines, frustrates, interferes with, or makes more difficult the divestiture required by this Final Judgment without the prior approval of the Court; and

iv. file a report with the Court 90 days after entry of this Final Judgment on the steps Microsoft has taken to comply with the requirements of this section 1.d.

2. Provisions Implementing Divestiture

a. After Implementation of the Plan, and throughout the term of this Final Judgment, neither the Operating Systems Business nor the Applications Business, nor any member of their respective Boards of Directors, shall acquire any securities or assets of the other Business; no Covered Shareholder holding securities of either the Operating Systems Business or the Applications Business shall acquire any securities or assets of or shall be an officer, director, or employee of the other Business; and no person who is an officer, director, or employee of the Operating Systems Business or the Applications Business shall be an officer, director, or employee of the other Business.

b. After Implementation of the Plan and throughout the term of this Final Judgment, the Operating Systems Business and the Applications Business shall be prohibited from:

i. merging or otherwise recombining, or entering into any joint venture with one another;

    ii. entering into any Agreement with one another under which one of the Businesses develops, sells, licenses for sale or distribution, or distributes products or services (other than the technologies referred to in the following sentence) developed, sold, licensed, or distributed by the other Business;

    iii. providing to the other any APIs, [application programming interfaces] Technical Information, Communications Interfaces, or technical information that is not simultaneously published, disclosed, or made readily available to ISVs [Internet service providers], IHVs [independent hardware vendor], and OEMs [original equipment manufacturers]; and

    iv. licensing, selling or otherwise providing to the other Business any product or service on terms more favorable than those available to any similarly situated third party.

Section 2.b.ii shall not prohibit the Operating Systems Business and the Applications Business from licensing technologies (other than Middleware Products) to each other for use in each others' products or services provided that such technology (i) is not and has not been separately sold, licensed, or offered as a product, and (ii) is licensed on terms that are otherwise consistent with this Final Judgment.

  c. Three months after Implementation of the Plan and once every three months thereafter throughout the term of this Final Judgment, the Operating Systems Business and the Applications Business shall file with the Plaintiffs a copy of each Agreement (and a memorandum describing each oral Agreement) entered into between them.

  d. Throughout the term of this Final Judgment, Microsoft, the Operating Systems Business and the Applications Business shall be prohibited from taking adverse action against any person or entity in whole or in part because such person or entity provided evidence in this case.

  e. The obligations and restrictions set forth in sections 3 and 4 herein shall, after the Implementation of the Plan, apply only to the Operating Systems Business.

3. Provisions In Effect Until Full Implementation of the Plan of Divestiture. The provisions in this section 3 shall remain in effect until the earlier of three years after the Implementation of the Plan or the expiration of the term of this Final Judgment.

  a. OEM Relations.

    i. Ban on Adverse Actions for Supporting Competing Products. Microsoft shall not take or threaten any action adversely affecting any OEM (including but not limited to giving or withholding any consideration such as licensing terms; discounts; technical, marketing, and sales support; enabling programs; product information; technical information; information about future plans; developer tools or developer support; hardware certification; and permission to display trademarks or logos) based directly or indirectly, in whole or in part, on any actual or contemplated action by that OEM:

    (1) to use, distribute, promote, license, develop, produce or sell any
product or service that competes with any Microsoft product or
service; or

    (2) to exercise any of the options or alternatives provided under this
Final Judgment.

ii. Uniform Terms for Windows Operating System Products Licensed to
Covered OEMs. Microsoft shall license Windows Operating System
Products to Covered OEMs pursuant to uniform license agreements
with uniform terms and conditions and shall not employ market development allowances or discounts in connection with Windows Operating System Products. Without limiting the foregoing, Microsoft
shall charge each Covered OEM the applicable royalty for Windows
Operating System Products as set forth on a schedule, to be established by Microsoft and published on a web site accessible to plaintiffs and all Covered OEMs, that provides for uniform royalties for
Windows Operating System Products, except that—

    (1) the schedule may specify different royalties for different lan-
guage versions, and

    (2) the schedule may specify reasonable volume discounts based
upon actual volume of total shipments of Windows Operating
System Products.

Without limiting the foregoing, Microsoft shall afford Covered OEMs
equal access to licensing terms; discounts; technical, marketing, and
sales support; product information; technical information; information about future plans; developer tools or developer support; hardware certification; and permission to display trademarks or logos.
The foregoing requirement insofar as it relates to access to technical
information and information about future plans shall not apply to any
bona fide joint development effort by Microsoft and a Covered OEM
with respect to confidential matters within the scope of that effort.
Microsoft shall not terminate a Covered OEM's license for a Windows
Operating System Product without having first given the Covered
OEM written notice of the reason for the proposed termination and
not less than thirty days' opportunity to cure. Microsoft shall not enforce any provision in any Agreement with a Covered OEM that is inconsistent with this Final Judgment.

iii. OEM Flexibility in Product Configuration. Microsoft shall not restrict (by contract or otherwise, including but not limited to granting
or withholding consideration) an OEM from modifying the boot
sequence, startup folder, internet connection wizard, desktop, preferences, favorites, start page, first screen, or other aspect of a Windows Operating System Product to—

    (1) include a registration sequence to obtain subscription or other
information from the user;

    (2) display icons of or otherwise feature other products or services,
regardless of the size or shape of such icons or features, or to

      remove the icons, folders, start menu entries, or favorites of Microsoft products or services;

    (3) display any user interfaces, provided that an icon is also displayed that allows the user to access the Windows user interface; or

    (4) launch automatically any non-Microsoft Middleware, Operating System or application, offer its own Internet access provider or other start-up sequence, or offer an option to make non-Microsoft Middleware the Default Middleware and to remove the means of End-User Access for Microsoft's Middleware Product.

b. Disclosure of APIs, Communications Interfaces and Technical Information. Microsoft shall disclose to ISVs, IHVs, and OEMs in a Timely Manner, in whatever media Microsoft disseminates such information to its own personnel, all APIs, Technical Information and Communications Interfaces that Microsoft employs to enable—

    i. Microsoft applications to interoperate with Microsoft Platform Software installed on the same Personal Computer, or

    ii. a Microsoft Middleware Product to interoperate with Windows Operating System software (or Middleware distributed with such Operating System) installed on the same Personal Computer, or

    iii. any Microsoft software installed on one computer (including but not limited to server Operating Systems and operating systems for handheld devices) to interoperate with a Windows Operating System (or Middleware distributed with such Operating System) installed on a Personal Computer.

To facilitate compliance, and monitoring of compliance, with the foregoing, Microsoft shall create a secure facility where qualified representatives of OEMs, ISVs, and IHVs shall be permitted to study, interrogate and interact with relevant and necessary portions of the source code and any related documentation of Microsoft Platform Software for the sole purpose of enabling their products to interoperate effectively with Microsoft Platform Software (including exercising any of the options in section 3.a.iii).

c. Knowing Interference with Performance. Microsoft shall not take any action that it knows will interfere with or degrade the performance of any non-Microsoft Middleware when interoperating with any Windows Operating System Product without notifying the supplier of such non-Microsoft Middleware in writing that Microsoft intends to take such action, Microsoft's reasons for taking the action, and any ways known to Microsoft for the supplier to avoid or reduce interference with, or the degrading of, the performance of the supplier's Middleware.

d. Developer Relations. Microsoft shall not take or threaten any action affecting any ISV [independent software vendor] or IHV (including but not limited to giving or withholding any consideration such as licensing terms; discounts; technical, marketing, and sales support; enabling programs; product information; technical information; information about future plans; developer tools or developer support; hardware certification; and permission to display trademarks or logos) based directly or indirectly, in whole or in part, on any actual or contemplated action by that ISV or IHV to—

   i. use, distribute, promote or support any Microsoft product or service, or

   ii. develop, use, distribute, promote or support software that runs on non-Microsoft Middleware or a non-Microsoft Operating System or that competes with any Microsoft product or service, or

   iii. exercise any of the options or alternatives provided under this Final Judgment.

e. Ban on Exclusive Dealing. Microsoft shall not enter into or enforce any Agreement in which a third party agrees, or is offered or granted consideration, to—

   i. restrict its development, production, distribution, promotion or use of, or payment for, any non-Microsoft Platform Software,

   ii. distribute, promote or use any Microsoft Platform Software exclusively,

   iii. degrade the performance of any non-Microsoft Platform Software, or

   iv. in the case of an agreement with an Internet access provider or Internet content provider, distribute, promote or use Microsoft software in exchange for placement with respect to any aspect of a Windows Operating System Product.

f. Ban on Contractual Tying. Microsoft shall not condition the granting of a Windows Operating System Product license, or the terms or administration of such license, on an OEM or other licensee agreeing to license, promote, or distribute any other Microsoft software product that Microsoft distributes separately from the Windows Operating System Product in the retail channel or through Internet access providers, Internet content providers, ISVs or OEMs, whether or not for a separate or positive price.

g. Restriction on Binding Middleware Products to Operating System Products. Microsoft shall not, in any Operating System Product distributed six or more months after the effective date of this Final Judgment, Bind any Middleware Product to a Windows Operating System unless:

   i. Microsoft also offers an otherwise identical version of that Operating System Product in which all means of End-User Access to that Middleware Product can readily be removed (a) by OEMs as part of standard OEM preinstallation kits and (b) by end users using add-remove utilities readily accessible in the initial boot process and from the Windows desktop; and

   ii. when an OEM removes End-User Access to a Middleware Product from any Personal Computer on which Windows is preinstalled, the royalty paid by that OEM for that copy of Windows is reduced in an amount not less than the product of the otherwise applicable royalty and the ratio of the number of amount in bytes of binary code of

(a) the Middleware Product as distributed separately from a Windows Operating System Product to (b) the applicable version of Windows.

h. Agreements Limiting Competition. Microsoft shall not offer, agree to provide, or provide any consideration to any actual or potential Platform Software competitor in exchange for such competitor's agreeing to refrain or refraining in whole or in part from developing, licensing, promoting or distributing any Operating System Product or Middleware Product competitive with any Windows Operating System Product or Middleware Product.

i. Continued Licensing of Predecessor Version. Microsoft shall, when it makes a major Windows Operating System Product release (such as Windows 95, OSR 2.0, OSR 2.5, Windows 98, Windows 2000 Professional, Windows "Millennium," "Whistler," "Blackcomb," and successors to these), continue for three years after said release to license on the same terms and conditions the previous Windows Operating System Product to any OEM that desires such a license. The net royalty rate for the previous Windows Operating System Product shall be no more than the average royalty paid by the OEM for such Product prior to the release. The OEM shall be free to market Personal Computers in which it preinstalls such an Operating System Product in the same manner in which it markets Personal Computers preinstalled with other Windows Operating System Products.

4. Internal Antitrust Compliance. This section shall remain in effect throughout the term of this Final Judgment, provided that, consistent with section 2.e, this section shall not apply to the Applications Business after the Implementation of the Plan.

a. Within 90 days after the effective date of this Final Judgment, Microsoft shall establish a Compliance Committee of its corporate Board of Directors, consisting of not fewer than three members of the Board of Directors who are not present or former employees of Microsoft.

b. The Compliance Committee shall hire a Chief Compliance Officer, who shall report directly to the Compliance Committee and to the Chief Executive Officer of Microsoft.

c. The Chief Compliance Officer shall be responsible for development and supervision of Microsoft's internal programs to ensure compliance with the antitrust laws and this Final Judgment.

d. Microsoft shall give the Chief Compliance Officer sufficient authority and resources to discharge the responsibilities listed herein.

e. The Chief Compliance Officer shall:

i. within 90 days after entry of this Final Judgment, cause to be delivered to each Microsoft officer, director, and Manager, and each platform software developer and employee involved in relations with OEMs, ISVs, or IHVs, a copy of this Final Judgment together with additional informational materials describing the conduct prohibited and required by this Final Judgment;

ii. distribute in a timely manner a copy of this Final Judgment and such additional informational materials to any person who succeeds to a position of officer, director, or Manager, or platform software developer or employee involved in relations with OEMs, ISVs or IHVs;

iii. obtain from each officer, director, and Manager, and each platform software developer and employee involved in relations with OEMs, ISVs or IHVs, within 90 days of entry of this Final Judgment, and for each person thereafter succeeding to such a position within 5 days of such succession, a written certification that he or she:

(1) has read, understands, and agrees to abide by the terms of this Final Judgment; and

(2) has been advised and understands that his or her failure to comply with this Final Judgment may result in conviction for criminal contempt of court;

iv. maintain a record of persons to whom this Final Judgment has been distributed and from whom, pursuant to Section 4.e.iii, such certifications have been obtained;

v. establish and maintain a means by which employees can report potential violations of this Final Judgment or the antitrust laws on a confidential basis; and

vi. report immediately to Plaintiffs and the Court any violation of this Final Judgment.

f. The Chief Compliance Officer may be removed only by the Chief Executive Officer with the concurrence of the Compliance Committee.

g. Microsoft shall, with the supervision of the Chief Compliance Officer, maintain for a period of at least four years the e-mail of all Microsoft officers, directors and managers engaged in software development, marketing, sales and developer relations related to Platform Software.

5. Compliance Inspection. This section shall remain in effect throughout the term of this Final Judgment.

a. For purposes of determining or securing implementation of or compliance with this Final Judgment, including the provisions requiring a plan of divestiture, or determining whether this Final Judgment should be modified or vacated, and subject to any legally recognized privilege, from time to time:

i. Duly authorized representatives of a Plaintiff, upon the written request of the Assistant Attorney General in charge of the Antitrust Division of the United States Department of Justice, or the Attorney General of a Plaintiff State, as the case may be, and on reasonable notice to Microsoft made to its principal office, shall be permitted:

(1) Access during office hours to inspect and copy or, at Plaintiffs' option, demand Microsoft provide copies of all books, ledgers, accounts, correspondence, memoranda, source code, and other records and documents in the possession or under the control of Microsoft (which may have counsel present), relating to the matters contained in this Final Judgment; and

(2) Subject to the reasonable convenience of Microsoft and without restraint or interference from it, to interview, either informally or on the record, its officers, employees, and agents, who may have their individual counsel present, regarding any such matters.

ii. Upon the written request of the Assistant Attorney General in charge of the Antitrust Division of the United States Department of Justice, or the Attorney General of a Plaintiff State, as the case may be, made to Microsoft at its principal offices, Microsoft shall submit such written reports, under oath if requested, as may be requested with respect to any matter contained in this Final Judgment.

iii. No information or documents obtained by the means provided in this section shall be divulged by a representative of a Plaintiff to any person other than a duly authorized representative of a Plaintiff, except in the course of legal proceedings to which the Plaintiff is a party (including grand jury proceedings), or for the purpose of securing compliance with this Final Judgment, or as otherwise required by law.

iv. If at the time information or documents are furnished by Microsoft to a Plaintiff, Microsoft represents and identifies in writing the material in any such information or documents to which a claim of protection may be asserted under Rule 26(c)(7) of the Federal Rules of Civil Procedure, and Microsoft marks each pertinent page of such material, "Subject to claim of protection under Rule 26(c)(7) of the Federal Rules of Civil Procedure," then 10 calendar days notice shall be given by a Plaintiff to Microsoft prior to divulging such material in any legal proceeding (other than a grand jury proceeding) to which Microsoft is not a party.

6. Effective Date, Term, Retention of Jurisdiction, Modification.

a. This Final Judgment shall take effect 90 days after the date on which it is entered; provided, however that sections 1.b and 2 (except 2.d) shall be stayed pending completion of any appeals from this Final Judgment. [Judge Jackson on June 20, 2000 stayed implementation of all provisions of the Final Judgment pending completion of the appeals process].

b. Except as provided in section 2.e, the provisions of this Final Judgment apply to Microsoft as defined in section 7.o of this Final Judgment.

c. This Final Judgment shall expire at the end of ten years from the date on which it takes effect.

d. The Court may act *sua sponte* to issue orders or directions for the construction or carrying out of this Final Judgment, for the enforcement of compliance therewith, and for the punishment of any violation thereof.

e. Jurisdiction is retained by this Court for the purpose of enabling any of the parties to this Final Judgment to apply to this Court at any time for such further orders or directions as may be necessary or appropriate for the construction or carrying out of this Final Judgment, for the modification of any of the provisions hereof, for the enforcement of compliance herewith, and for the punishment of any violation hereof.

f. In accordance with the Court's Conclusions of Law, the plaintiff States shall submit a motion for costs and fees, with supporting documents as necessary, no later than 45 days after the entry of this Final Judgment. . . .

# MEMORANDUM AND ORDER

These cases are before the Court for disposition of the sole matter presently remaining for decision by the trial court, namely, entry of appropriate relief for the violations of the Sherman Act, Sections 1 and 2, and various state laws committed by the defendant Microsoft Corporation as found by Court in accordance with its Findings of Fact and Conclusions of Law. Final judgment will be entered contemporaneously herewith. No further proceedings will be required.

The Court has been presented by plaintiffs with a proposed form of final judgment that would mandate both conduct modification and structural reorganization by the defendant when fully implemented. Microsoft has responded with a motion for summary rejection of structural reorganization and a request for months of additional time to oppose the relief sought in all other respects. Microsoft claims, in effect, to have been surprised by the "draconian" and "unprecedented" remedy the plaintiffs recommend. What it proposes is yet another round of discovery, to be followed by a second trial—in essence an *ex post* and *de facto* bifurcation of the case already considered and rejected by the Court.

Microsoft's profession of surprise is not credible. From the inception of this case Microsoft knew, from well-established Supreme Court precedents dating from the beginning of the last century, that a mandated divestiture was a possibility, if not a probability, in the event of an adverse result at trial. At the conclusion of the trial the Court's Findings of Fact gave clear warning to Microsoft that the result would likely be adverse, yet the Court delayed entry of its Conclusions of Law for five months, and enlisted the services of a distinguished mediator, to assist Microsoft and the plaintiffs in reaching agreement on a remedy of some description that Microsoft knew was inevitable. Even assuming that Microsoft negotiated in utmost good faith in the course of mediation, it had to have in contemplation the prospect that, were mediation to fail, the prevailing plaintiffs would propose to the Court a remedy most to their liking and least likely to be acceptable to Microsoft. Its failure to anticipate and to prepare to meet such an eventuality gives no reason to afford it an opportunity to do so now.

These cases have been before the Court, and have occupied much of its attention, for the past two years, not counting the antecedent proceedings. Following a full trial Microsoft has been found guilty of antitrust violations, notwithstanding its protests to this day that it has committed none. The Court is convinced for several reasons that a final—and appealable—judgment should be entered quickly. It has also reluctantly come to the conclusion, for the same reasons, that a structural remedy has become imperative: Microsoft as it is presently organized and led is unwilling to accept the notion that it broke the law or accede to an order amending its conduct.

First, despite the Court's Findings of Fact and Conclusions of Law, Microsoft does not yet concede that any of its business practices violated the Sherman Act. Microsoft officials have recently been quoted publicly to the effect that the company has "done nothing wrong" and that it will be vindicated on appeal. The Court is well aware that there is a substantial body of public opinion, some of it rational, that holds to a similar view. It is time to put that assertion to the test. If true, then an appellate tribunal should be given early opportunity to confirm it as promptly as possible, and to abort any remedial measures before they have become irreversible as a practical matter.

Second, there is credible evidence in the record to suggest that Microsoft, convinced of its innocence, continues to do business as it has in the past, and may yet do to other markets what it has already done in the PC operating system and browser markets. Microsoft has shown no disposition to voluntarily alter its business protocol in any significant respect. Indeed, it has announced its intention to appeal even the imposition of the modest conduct remedies it has itself proposed as an alternative to the non-structural remedies sought by the plaintiffs.

Third, Microsoft has proved untrustworthy in the past. In earlier proceedings in which a preliminary injunction was entered, Microsoft's purported compliance with that injunction while it was on appeal was illusory and its explanation disingenuous. If it responds in similar fashion to an injunctive remedy in this case, the earlier the need for enforcement measures becomes apparent the more effective they are likely to be.

Finally, the Court believes that extended proceedings on the form a remedy should take are unlikely to give any significantly greater assurance that it will be able to identify what might be generally regarded as an optimum remedy. As has been the case with regard to Microsoft's culpability, opinion as to an appropriate remedy is sharply divided. There is little chance that those divergent opinions will be reconciled by anything short of actual experience. The declarations (and the "offers of proof") from numerous potential witnesses now before the Court provide some insight as to how its various provisions might operate, but for the most part they are merely the predictions of purportedly knowledgeable people as to effects which may or may not ensue if the proposed final judgment is entered. In its experience the Court has found testimonial predictions of future events generally less reliable even than testimony as to historical fact, and cross-examination to be of little use in enhancing or detracting from their accuracy.

In addition to its substantive objections, the proposed final judgment is also criticized by Microsoft as being vague and ambiguous. Plaintiffs respond that, to the extent it may be lacking in detail, it is purposely so to allow Microsoft itself to propose such detail as will be least disruptive of its business, failing which plaintiffs will ask the Court to supply it as the need appears.

Plaintiffs won the case, and for that reason alone have some entitlement to a remedy of their choice. Moreover, plaintiffs' proposed final judgment is the collective work product of senior antitrust law enforcement officials of the

United States Department of Justice and the Attorneys General of 19 states, in conjunction with multiple consultants. These officials are by reason of office obliged and expected to consider—and to act in—the public interest; Microsoft is not. The proposed final judgment is represented to the Court as incorporating provisions employed successfully in the past, and it appears to the Court to address all the principal objectives of relief in such cases, namely, to terminate the unlawful conduct, to prevent its repetition in the future, and to revive competition in the relevant markets. Microsoft's alternative decree is plainly inadequate in all three respects.

The final judgment proposed by plaintiffs is perhaps more radical than might have resulted had mediation been successful and terminated in a consent decree. It is less so than that advocated by four disinterested *amici curiae.* It is designed, moreover, to take force in stages, so that the effects can be gauged while the appeal progresses and before it has been fully implemented. And, of course, the Court will retain jurisdiction following appeal, and can modify the judgment as necessary in accordance with instructions from an appellate court or to accommodate conditions changed with the passage of time.

It is, therefore, this seventh day of June, 2000,

ORDERED, that the motion of defendant Microsoft Corporation for summary rejection of the plaintiffs' proposed structural reorganization is denied; and it is

FURTHER ORDERED, that defendant Microsoft Corporation's "position" as to future proceedings on the issue of remedy is rejected; and it is

FURTHER ORDERED, that plaintiffs' proposed final judgment, as revised in accordance with the proceedings of May 24, 2000 and Microsoft's comments thereon, be entered as a Final Judgment herein.

Thomas Penfield Jackson, U.S. District Judge

# UNITED NATIONS SPECIAL SESSION ON WOMEN'S RIGHTS
## June 10, 2000

*Delegates from more than 180 nations, meeting at a special session of the United Nations General Assembly, reaffirmed on June 10, 2000, a wide range of women's rights and freedoms that had first been delineated in Beijing in September 1995 at the UN's Fourth World Conference on Women. That conference had declared that governments should accord women "all human rights and fundamental freedoms," including the right to make their own decisions on matters relating to sexuality and childbearing "free of coercion, discrimination and violence."*

*Meeting in New York five years later, delegates to the Twenty-Third Special Session of the General Assembly fought off several attempts to weaken the Beijing document and added planks calling on governments to outlaw trafficking of women and girls and to make acts of domestic violence, including marital rape, a criminal offense. The final document also deplored violence resulting from cultural prejudice, racism, xenophobia, ethnic cleansing, religious and antireligious extremism, and terrorism. Such practices included dowry deaths, female infanticide, and acid attacks— crimes that were illegal in most countries but nonetheless condoned in some places by cultural mores.*

*"We were determined to get a strong document that did not in any way diminish the gains women had achieved in Beijing," said Angela King, the U.S. official in charge of the advancement of women. "We were also determined to go beyond Beijing, and we did, despite the efforts of countries that made the process such an arduous one." The document, entitled "Further Actions and Initiatives to Implement the Beijing Declaration and the Platform for Action," was negotiated behind closed doors. About 2,300 delegates participated in the conference, which was also attended by about 2,000 representatives from 1,200 nongovernmental organizations interested in women's issues.*

*In the United States the Supreme Court struck down a law that allowed victims of gender-based crimes such as rape to sue their attackers in federal court. Congress later reenacted the legislation to combat violence against women, but without the language granting the right to sue in federal court. Congress also cleared legislation making trafficking in persons a federal crime and creating a new nonimmigrant visa for as many as 5,000 victims of trafficking each year. The legislation was aimed at combating sex trafficking. "Fifty thousand innocent women and young children are forced, coerced, or fraudulently thrust into the sex trade industry with no way out," said Representative Christopher Smith (R-N.J.), the chief sponsor of the legislation in the House.*

## *Moving Beyond Beijing*

*The Beijing conference was the largest international gathering of women on record, and although the "Platform of Action" that came out of it did not have the force of law, it was a powerful tool in establishing an international standard for women's rights on a wide variety of economic, education, health, and social issues. The special session in 2000, known as "Beijing Plus Five," was intended to review the progress that had been made since the Beijing conference in 1995; to come up with concrete, practical ways to implement the planks contained in the 1995 plan of action; and to add new planks dealing with issues that had emerged or grown more important since the original conference.*

*In opening remarks, UN Secretary General Kofi Annan said that women had made significant progress since 1995, particularly in making more countries understand that "women's equality is a prerequisite for development." But he also noted that much remained to be done, particularly in education for girls. Education, Annan said, was the key to equality because it was "both the entry point into the global economy and the best defense against its pitfalls." Of the 110 million children of school age who did not attend school, two-thirds were girls. Annan's concerns were reflected in the final document produced by the delegates to the special session, in which they called on governments to close the gender gap in primary and secondary education by 2005; to ensure free, compulsory, and universal education by 2015; and to strengthen adult literacy programs. Leaders at the UN Millennium Summit in September included these same goals in their final statement.* (Millennium Summit story, p. 700)

*The final document also repeated calls for the world's governments to place priority on combating diseases that disproportionately affect women, including maternal mortality. Delegates also tied the lack of women's rights to the spread of acquired immunodeficiency syndrome (AIDS), and they called for affordable treatment and care for women and girls infected with the deadly disease and the virus that caused it, assistance for AIDS orphans, and support for women and other family members caring for AIDS victims. Nearly half of all people infected with the virus that causes AIDS were women, and an estimated 13 million children had been orphaned by the disease.* (AIDS report, p. 410)

*The most contentious issue at the conference, as it had been in Beijing, involved women's sexual and reproductive rights. Supported by the Vatican and some of the more conservative Roman Catholic and Islamic nations (such as Nicaragua, Libya, Sudan, and Iraq), antiabortion and religious groups charged that rich Western nations were pushing for "radical language" on abortion and sexual rights and were engaged in a "sexual colonialism" that was trying to spread "immorality" in the developing world. Although the 2,300 delegates did not backtrack on any of the positions adopted in Beijing regarding sexual rights, some activists said they were disappointed that the delegates did not set more specific goals for attaining women's rights. "We regret that there was not enough political will on the part of some governments and the UN system to agree on a stronger document with more concrete benchmarks, numerical goals, time-bound targets, indicators, and resources aimed at implementing the Beijing platform," read a statement issued by the Center for Women's Global Leadership at Rutgers University and the Women's Environment and Development Organization.*

## Violence Against Women

*Even before the UN special session, worldwide attention was beginning to focus on what some have called "culturally sanctioned" crimes against women and girls, including honor killings, female infanticide, acid attacks, and dowry deaths or bride burnings. Honor killing was an ancient practice in which men, to preserve the family "honor," killed female relatives who engaged in sexual activity outside marriage. Victims of honor killings included women who were only suspected of sexual activity outside marriage or even the victims of rape. Honor killings occurred primarily in the Middle East and South Asia. According to data compiled by United Nations International Children's Fund (UNICEF), in 1997 there were as many as 400 honor deaths in Yemen, 52 reported honor killings in Egypt, and as many as 300 in a single province of Pakistan.*

*Acid attacks and dowry deaths occurred in roughly the same geographic regions. It was estimated that more than 5,000 women were killed in India each year because their husbands' families considered their dowries to be inadequate. Women have been deliberately and painfully disfigured by acid for any number of reasons from rejecting a proposal of marriage to serving dinner late. According to the UNICEF compilation, the number of acid attacks in Bangladesh increased from 47 in 1996 to more than 200 in 1998.*

*Female infanticide occurred largely in societies that valued boys, economically and socially, more highly than girls. Although it still occurred, outright murder of female infants had declined in the face of world approbation. Nonetheless, medical testing for sex selection was common in China, India, and the Republic of Korea, despite laws making such testing illegal.*

*Overall, a report released on May 31 by UNICEF's Innocenti Research Centre in Florence, Italy, said that an estimated 60 million women were "missing from population statistics globally," the victims of domestic violence that cut across all cultures, classes, countries, and education and income levels. Although such violence was considered culturally sanctioned, by religious or social customs, some argued that holding a religion or cus-*

*tom responsible for acts of domestic violence simply masked the misuse of power by men. "This is not a religious phenomenon," said Adrienne Germain, president of the Women's Health Coalition. "It has to do with male dominance, patriarchy, and power."*

### Sex Trafficking Made a Federal Crime

*One form of violence against women and children—sex trafficking—was driven primarily by greed. Trafficking was the recruitment or abduction of men, women, and children who were then forced, coerced, or deceived into situations of slavery—either as sex workers or as forced laborers, often as domestics or in sweat shops. An estimated 2 million people, primarily women and young girls, fell victim every year to the international sex trafficking industry. According to one estimate, trafficking netted $7 billion annually. Some 45,000 to 50,000 of these women and children were brought into the United States, where they were forced into virtual slavery. Traditionally, the trafficking victims came from Southeast Asia and Latin America, but increasingly the victims were coming from Russia and countries in central and eastern Europe.*

*In October Congress cleared, and the president signed, a measure (PL 106–386) to make trafficking in persons a new federal crime. Current law already prohibited slavery and the sale of people into slavery, and the new measure extended that prohibition to a list of related activities defined as "trafficking." The maximum punishment for selling someone into slavery was twenty years. The bill also authorized nearly $94.5 million over two years to combat trafficking and to aid victims. The measure also created a nonimmigrant "T" visa, available for up to 5,000 trafficking victims annually. Victims who agreed to cooperate with law enforcement and who faced severe retribution in their home country would be eligible for the visas. Under certain circumstances, victims could apply for permanent residency.*

*The measure also authorized $3.3 billion over five years for a variety of grant programs aimed at curbing domestic violence, date rape, stalking, and other crimes directed largely at women. The bill also made it easier for women to get enforcement of protective orders and for battered immigrant women to call police and get help from government agencies without fear of deportation. The measure, however, excluded a provision of the original legislation, passed in 1994, that had allowed victims of gender-motivated attacks on women to sue for damages in federal court. The Supreme Court struck down that provision in a ruling issued May 15. By a 5–4 vote in the case of* United States v. Morrison, *the majority held that Congress did not have the authority under either the Commerce Clause or the Equal Protection Clause of the Fourteenth Amendment to regulate gender-motivated violent crime. The appropriate venue for seeking a remedy for such crimes was state court, the majority said, not the federal court system.*

*Following are excerpts from the third section of "Further Actions and Initiatives to Implement the Beijing Declaration and Plat-*

*form of Action," the final document issued June 10, 2000, by dele-*
*gates to the Twenty-Third Special Session of the United Nations*
*General Assembly, reaffirming a wide range of women's rights*
*and freedoms. The document was obtained from the Internet at*
*http://www.un.org/womenwatch/daw/followup/finaloutcome*
*.pdf.*

## III. Current challenges affecting the full implementation of the Beijing Declaration and the Platform for Action

28. The review and appraisal of the implementation of the Beijing Declaration and the Platform for Action occurred in a rapidly changing global context. Since 1995, a number of issues have gained prominence and acquired new dimensions which pose additional challenges to the full and accelerated implementation of the Platform in order to realize gender equality, development and peace by Governments, intergovernmental bodies, international organizations, the private sector, and non-governmental organizations [NGOs] as appropriate. Continued political commitment to gender equality, at all levels, is needed for the full implementation of the Platform for Action.

29. Globalization has presented new challenges for the fulfillment of the commitments made and the realization of the goals of the Beijing Conference. The globalization process has in some countries, resulted in policy shifts in favour of more open trade and financial flows, privatization of state-owned enterprises and in many cases lower public spending particularly on social services. This change has transformed patterns of production and accelerated technological advances in information and communication and affected the lives of women, both as workers and consumers. In a large number of countries, particularly in developing and least developed countries, these changes have also adversely impacted on the lives of women and have increased inequality. The gender impact of these changes has not been systematically evaluated. Globalization also has cultural, political, and social impacts affecting cultural values, lifestyles and forms of communication as well as implications for the achievement of sustainable development. Benefits of the growing global economy have been unevenly distributed leading to wider economic disparities, the feminization of poverty, increased gender inequality, including through often deteriorating work conditions and unsafe working environments especially in the informal economy and rural areas. While globalization has brought greater economic opportunities and autonomy to some women, many others have been marginalized, due to deepening inequalities among and within countries, by depriving them from the benefits of this process. Although in many countries the level of participation of women in the labour force has risen, in other cases, the application of certain economic policies have had a negative impact such that increases in women's employment often have not been matched by improvements in wages, promotions and working

conditions. In many cases, women continue to be employed in low paid, part-time, and contract jobs marked by insecurity and by safety and health hazards. In many countries women, especially new entrants into the labour market, continue to be among the first to lose jobs and the last to be rehired.

30. Increasing disparities in the economic situation among and within countries, coupled with a growing economic interdependence and dependence of States on external factors as well as the financial crises have, in recent years, altered prospects of growth and caused economic instability in many countries, with a heavy impact on the lives of women. These have affected the ability of States to provide social protection and social security as well as funding for the implementation of the Platform for Action. Such difficulties are also reflected in the shift of the cost of social protection, social security and other welfare provisions from the public sector to the household. The decreasing levels of funding available through international cooperation has contributed to further marginalization of a large number of developing countries and countries with economies in transition within which women are amongst the poorest. The agreed target of 0.7 per cent of the gross national product of developed countries for overall official development assistance has not been achieved. These factors have contributed to the increasing feminization of poverty, which has undermined efforts to achieve gender equality. Limited funding at the state-level makes it imperative that innovative approaches to the allocation of existing resources be employed, not only by Governments but also by NGOs and the private sector. One such innovation is the gender analysis of public budgets which is emerging as an important tool for determining the differential impact of expenditures on women and men to help ensure equitable use of existing resources. This analysis is crucial to promote gender equality.

30 bis. The impact of globalization and structural adjustment programmes, the high costs of external debt servicing and declining terms of international trade, in several developing countries, have worsened the existing obstacles to development, aggravating the feminization of poverty. Negative consequences of structural adjustment programmes, stemming from the inappropriate design and application, have continued to place a disproportionate burden on women, *inter-alia* through budget cuts in basic social services, including education and health.

30 ter. There is greater acceptance that the increasing debt burden faced by most indebted developing countries is unsustainable and constitutes one of the principle obstacles to achieving progress in people-centered sustainable development and poverty eradication. For many developing countries, as well as countries with economies in transition, excessive debt servicing has severely constrained their capacity to promote social development and provide basic services and has affected full implementation of the Platform for Action.

30 quinter. In countries with economies in transition women are bearing most of the hardships induced by the economic restructuring and being the first to lose jobs in times of recession. They are being squeezed out from fast growth sectors. Loss of childcare facilities due to elimination or privatization

of state work places, increased need for older care without the corresponding facilities, continuing inequality of access to training for finding re-employment and to productive assets for entering or expanding businesses are current challenges facing women in these countries.

31. Science and technology, as fundamental components of development, are transforming patterns of production, contributing to the creation of jobs and new job classifications, and ways of working, and contributing to the establishment of a knowledge-based society. Technological change can bring new opportunities for all women in all fields if they have equal access, and adequate training. Women should also be actively involved in the definition, design, development, implementation and gender impact evaluation of policies related to these changes. Many women world-wide are yet to effectively use these new communications technologies for networking, advocacy, exchange of information business, education, media consultation and e-commerce initiatives. For instance, millions of the world's poorest women and men still do not have access to and benefits from science and technologies and are currently excluded from this new field and the opportunities it presents.

32. The patterns of migratory flows of labour are changing. Women and girls are increasingly involved in internal, regional and international labour migration to pursue many occupations mainly in farm labour, domestic work and some forms of entertainment work. While this situation increases their earning opportunities and self-reliance, it also exposes them, particularly the poor, uneducated, unskilled and/or undocumented migrants to inadequate working conditions, increased health risk, the risk of trafficking, economic and sexual exploitation, racism, racial discrimination and xenophobia, and other forms of abuse, which impair their enjoyment of their human rights, and in some cases, constitute violations of human rights.

33. While recognizing that governments have the primary responsibility to develop and implement policies to promote gender equality, partnerships between governments and different actors of civil society are increasingly recognized as an important mechanism to achieve this goal. Additional innovative approaches can be further developed to foster this collaboration.

36. In some countries, current demographic trends, which show that lowered fertility rates, increased life expectancy and lower mortality rates, have contributed to ageing of the population, and increase in chronic health conditions and have implications for health care systems and spending, informal care systems and research. Given the gap between male and female life expectancy, the number of widows and older single women has increased considerably, often leading to their social isolation and other social challenges. Societies have much to gain from the knowledge and life experience of older women. On the other hand, the current generation of young people is the largest in history. Adolescent girls and young women have particular needs which will require increasing attention.

37. The rapid progression of the HIV/AIDS pandemic, particularly in the developing world, has had a devastating impact on women. Responsible behaviour and gender equality are among the important prerequisites for its

prevention. There is also the need for more effective strategies to empower women to have control over and decide freely and responsibly on matters related to their sexuality, to protect themselves from high risk and irresponsible behaviour leading to sexually transmitted infections including HIV/AIDS and to promote responsible, safe and respectful behaviour by men and to also promote gender equality. HIV/AIDS is an urgent public health issue, is outstripping efforts to contain it and, in many countries, is reversing hard [won] gains of development. The burden of care for people living with HIV/AIDS and for children orphaned by HIV/AIDS falls particularly on women, as infrastructures are inadequate to respond to the challenges being posed. Women with HIV/AIDS often suffer from discrimination and a stigma and are often victims of violence. Issues related to prevention, mother-to-child transmission of HIV/AIDS, breastfeeding, information and education in particular of youth, curbing high risks behaviour, intravenous drug users, support groups, counseling and voluntary testing, partner notification, and provision and high costs of essential drugs have not been sufficiently addressed. There are positive signs in the fight against HIV/AIDS in some countries that behavoural changes have occurred among young people and experience shows that educational programmes for young people can lead to a more positive view on gender relations and gender equality, delayed sexual initiation and reduced risks of sexually transmitted infections.

37 bis. Growing drug and substance abuse among young women and girls, both in developed and developing countries, has raised the need for increased efforts towards demand reduction and fight against illicit production, supply and trafficking of narcotic drugs, and psychotropic substances.

38. The increase in casualties and damage caused by natural disasters has raised awareness of the inefficiencies and inadequacies in the existing approaches and intervention methods in responding to such emergency situations, in which women, more often than men, are burdened with the responsibility of meeting the immediate daily needs of their families. This situation has raised awareness that a gender perspective must be incorporated whenever disaster prevention, mitigation and recovery strategies are being developed and implemented.

41. The changing context of gender relations, as well as the discussion on gender equality has led to increased reassessment of gender roles. This has further encouraged a discussion on the roles and responsibilities of women and men working together towards gender equality and the need for changing those stereotypical and traditional roles that limit women's full potential. There is a need for balanced participation between women and men in remunerated and unremunerated work. Failure to recognize and measure in quantitative terms unremunerated work of women which is often not valued in national accounts has meant that women's full contribution to social and economic development remains underestimated and undervalued. As long as there is insufficient sharing of tasks and responsibilities with men, the combination of remunerated work and care-giving will lead to the continued disproportionate burden for women in comparison to men.

## IV. Actions and initiatives to overcome obstacles and to achieve the full and accelerated implementation of the Beijing Platform for Action

42. In view of the evaluation of progress made five years since the Beijing Conference in implementing the Beijing Declaration and Platform for Action, contained in chapter II, as well as the current challenges affecting its full realization, outlined in chapter III, Governments now recommit themselves to the Beijing Declaration and Platform for Action and also commit to further actions and initiatives to overcome the obstacles and address the challenges. Governments, in taking continued and additional steps to achieve the goals of the Platform, recognize that the full enjoyment of all human rights -civil, cultural, economic, political and social, including the right to development -are universal, indivisible, interdependent and interrelated, and are essential for realizing gender equality, development and peace in the twenty-first century.

43. Organizations of the United Nations system and the Bretton Woods institutions, as well as the World Trade Organization, other international and regional intergovernmental bodies, parliaments, civil society, including the private sector and NGOs, trade unions and other stakeholders are called upon to support government efforts and, where appropriate, develop complementary programmes of their own to achieve full and effective implementation of the Platform for Action.

43 bis. Governments and intergovernmental organizations recognize the contribution and complementary role of NGOs, with full respect for their autonomy, in ensuring the effective implementation of the Platform for Action and should continue to strengthen partnerships with NGOs, particularly women's organizations in contributing to the effective implementation and follow-up of the Platform for Action.

43 ter. Experience has shown that the goal of gender equality can be fully achieved only in the context of renewed relations among different stakeholders at all levels. The full effective participation of women on the basis of equality in all spheres of society is necessary to contribute to this goal.

44. Achieving gender equality and empowerment of women requires redressing inequalities between women and men and girls and boys and ensuring their equal rights, responsibilities, opportunities, and possibilities. Gender equality implies that women's as well as men's needs, interests, concerns, experiences and priorities are an integral dimension of the design, implementation, national monitoring, and follow-up and evaluation, including at the international level, of all actions in all areas.

46. By adopting the Platform for Action governments and the international community agreed to a common development agenda with gender equality and women's empowerment as underlying principles. The efforts towards ensuring women's participation in development have expanded and need to combine a focus on women's conditions and basic needs with an holistic approach based on equal rights and partnerships, promotion and protection of all human rights and fundamental freedoms. Policies and programmes should be formulated to achieve the goal of people-centred sustainable development,

secure livelihoods and adequate social protection measures, including safety nets, strengthened support systems for families equal access to and control over financial and economic resources, and eliminate increasing and disproportionate poverty among women. All economic policies, institutions and resource allocation should adopt a gender perspective to ensure that development dividends are shared on equal grounds.

46 bis. Increased efforts are needed to provide equal access to education, health, and social services and to ensure women's and girls' rights to education and the enjoyment of the highest attainable standard of physical and mental health and well-being throughout the life cycle, as well as adequate, affordable and universally accessible health care and services including sexual and reproductive health, particularly in the face of the HIV/AIDS pandemic; they are also necessary with regard to the growing proportion of older women.

47. Given that a majority of the world's women are subsistence producers and users of environmental resources, there is a need to recognize and integrate women's knowledge and priorities in the conservation and management of such resources to ensure their sustainability. Programmes and infrastructures that are gender-sensitive are needed in order to effectively respond to disaster and emergency situations that threaten the environment, livelihood security, as well as the management of the basic requirements of daily life.

47 bis. Sustaining the livelihoods of populations in States with limited or scarce resources, including Small Island Developing States is critically dependent on the preservation and protection of the environment. Women's customary knowledge, management and sustainable use of biodiversity should be recognized. . . .

49. Political will and commitment at all levels are crucial to ensure mainstreaming of a gender perspective in the adoption and implementation of comprehensive and action oriented policies in all areas. Policy commitments are essential for further developing the necessary framework which ensures women's equal access to and control over economic and financial resources, training, services and institutions as well as their participation in decision making and management. Policy making processes require the partnership of women and men at all levels. Men and boys should also be actively involved and encouraged in all efforts to achieve the goals of the Platform for Action and its implementation.

51. Violence against women and girls is a major obstacle to the achievement of the objectives of gender equality, development and peace. Violence against women both violates and impairs or nullifies the enjoyment by women of their human rights and fundamental freedoms. Gender based violence, such as battering and other domestic violence, sexual abuse, sexual slavery and exploitation, and international trafficking in women and children, forced prostitution and sexual harassment, as well as violence against women, resulting from cultural prejudice, racism and racial discrimination, xenophobia, pornography, ethnic cleansing, armed conflict, foreign occupation, religious and anti-religious extremism and terrorism are incompatible with the dignity and worth of the human person and must be combated and eliminated.

51 ter. Women play a critical role in the family. The family is the basic unit of society and is a strong force for social cohesion and integration and as such should be strengthened. The inadequate support to women and insufficient protection and support to their respective families affect society as a whole and undermines efforts to achieve gender equality. In different cultural, political and social systems, various forms of the family exist and the rights, capabilities and responsibilities of family members must be respected. Women's social and economic contributions to the welfare of the family and the social significance of maternity and paternity continue to be inadequately addressed. Motherhood and fatherhood and the role of parents and legal guardians in the family and in the upbringing of children and the importance of all family members to the family's well-being is also acknowledged and must not be a basis for discrimination. Women also continue to bear a disproportionate share of the household responsibilities and the care of children, the sick and the elderly. Such imbalance needs to be consistently addressed through appropriate policies and programmes, in particular those geared towards education and through legislation where appropriate. In order to achieve full partnership, both in public and private spheres, both women and men must be enabled to reconcile and share equally work responsibilities and family responsibilities.

52. Strong national machineries for the advancement of women and promotion of gender equality require political commitment at the highest level and all necessary, human and financial resources to initiate, recommend and facilitate the development, adoption and monitoring of policies, legislation, programmes and capacity-building for the empowerment of women and to act as catalysts for open public dialogue on gender equality as a societal goal. This would enable them to promote the advancement of women and mainstreaming a gender perspective in policy and programmes in all areas, to play an advocacy role, and to ensure equal access to all institutions and resources, as well as enhanced capacity building for women in all sectors. Reforms to meet the challenges of the changing world are essential to ensure women's equal access to institutions and organizations. Institutional and conceptual changes are a strategic and important aspect of creating an enabling environment for the implementation of the Platform for Action.

53. Programme support to enhance women's opportunities, potentials and activities need to have a dual focus: one the one hand, programmes aimed at meeting the basic as well as the specific needs of women for capacity building, organizational development and empowerment; and on the other, gender mainstreaming in all programme formulation and implementation activities. It is particularly important to expand into new areas of programming to advance gender equality in response to current challenges.

53 bis. Girls and women of all ages with any form of disability are generally among the more vulnerable and marginalized of society. There is therefore need to take into account and to address their concerns in all policy making and programming. Special measures are needed at all levels to integrate them into the mainstream of development.

54. Effective and coordinated plans and programmes for the full implementation of the Platform for Action require a clear knowledge on the situation

of women and girls, a clear research-based knowledge and data disaggregated by sex, short and long-term time-bound targets and measurable goals and follow-up mechanisms to assess progress. Efforts are needed to ensure capacity building for all the actors involved in the achievement of these goals. Efforts are also needed at the national level, to increase transparency and accountability.

55. The realization of the goals of gender equality, development and peace at the national and international level needs to be supported by the allocation of necessary human and financial resources for specific and targeted activities to ensure gender equality at the local, national, regional and international level as well as by enhanced and increased international cooperation. The explicit attention to these goals in budgetary processes at the national, regional and international level is essential.

55 bis. Recognizing the persistent and increasing burden of poverty on women in many countries, particularly in developing countries, it is essential to continue from a gender perspective to review, modify and implement integrated macro-economic and social policies and programmes, including, *inter alia*, those related to structural adjustment and external debt problems, to ensure universal and equitable access to social services, in particular to education, and affordable quality health care services and equal access to and control over economic resources. . . .

# COMMITTEE OF SCIENTISTS ON THE IMPACT OF GLOBAL WARMING
## June 12, 2000

*Scientific evidence continued to mount confirming that the global climate was getting warmer and that human activity was contributing to climate change. But the latest round of international negotiations over ways of curtailing global warming fell short during the year, in large part because of conflicts over how to weigh the costs of action against the potential dangers of inaction.*

*For nearly two decades scientists had been producing evidence that the burning of fossil fuels—primarily oil, coal, and natural gas—was contributing to a perceived warming of the global climate. The burning of these fuels created carbon dioxide ($CO_2$), the most important of several gases said to cause a "greenhouse effect" by trapping heat in the Earth's atmosphere. Not all scientists accepted this theory; a minority of skeptics insisted that any warming of the global climate was due to natural causes rather than human activity.*

*In 1992 the United States joined 153 other nations in signing a United Nations-sponsored treaty—the Framework Convention on Climate Change—that called for industrialized countries to take voluntary steps to stabilize their emissions of greenhouse gases at the levels prevailing in 1990. Five years later the United States joined 150 other nations in negotiating a follow-up treaty, the Kyoto Protocol on Climate Change, that sought to toughen the provisions of the earlier accord. The Kyoto treaty committed nations to legally binding reductions in emissions of greenhouse gases; for the United States, that meant returning its greenhouse gas emissions to the 1990 level by 2012, in effect a 30 percent reduction. Most major U.S. industries staunchly opposed the Kyoto treaty, saying it would undermine the economy by forcing drastic changes in energy consumption. President Bill Clinton, who generally approved the treaty, never submitted it to the Senate for approval, but the Senate in 1998 put itself on record as opposing the treaty. Negotiations in November 2000 failed to produce agreement on technical details needed to implement the Kyoto treaty. (*Framework convention,

Historic Documents of 1992, p. 499; Kyoto treaty, Historic Documents of 1997, p. 859)

## *Climate Change in the United States*

*In 1990, when the global warming issue was just beginning to receive widespread international attention, Congress mandated a scientific study of how climate change might affect the United States during the twenty-first century. Scientific panels affiliated with the National Science Foundation worked on the study all during the 1990s. Their efforts became more serious toward the end of the decade, with the development of increasingly sophisticated computerized programs for modeling climate change. Finally, on June 12, 2000, scientists working on the project produced a report, "Climate Change Impacts on the United States," which they presented to President Clinton and Congress. The report was written by a thirteen-member National Assessment Synthesis Team and was based on the work of more than three hundred scientists, some of whom disagreed with many of the report's conclusions.*

*The National Assessment report was based on three fundamental assumptions: that global warming was occurring and was likely to accelerate during the twenty-first century, that man-made emissions of greenhouse gases were contributing to global warming, and that global warming was likely to have significant effects on the environment and on human society—some of which would be negative and some of which might be seen as positive from an economic or societal point of view. An additional assumption—one the report's authors clearly hoped would be proven wrong—was that world leaders would not take any significant action to reduce emissions of greenhouse gases, thereby failing to curtail the impact of global warming.*

*By 2000 the first assumption was no longer the subject of major controversy. Most of the scientists who in the past had voiced doubts about global warming had come to acknowledge that the weight of the evidence showed that the earth's atmosphere was in fact getting warmer. A report issued January 12 by the National Research Council of the National Academies of Science summarized what it called a "consensus" that average global temperatures had risen between 0.7 and 1.4°F over the past century. That temperature rise was considered significant because, according to most estimates, global temperatures in 2000 were only about 5–9°F higher than during the most recent ice age about 20,000 years ago.*

*The warming trend was expected to continue, and the National Assessment report said scientific evidence indicated that global warming "in the twenty-first century will be significantly larger than in the twentieth century." The report used various scenarios suggesting that average temperatures in the United States would rise by 5–9°F over the next century. That increase in temperature was likely to be accompanied by greater extremes of precipitation and faster evaporation of water—factors that would led to "greater frequency of both very wet and very dry conditions," depending on location, the report said.*

*The bulk of the report was devoted to describing the potential impact on the United States of global warming during the twenty-first century. The conclusions were based on long-term weather models developed by two major research centers: the Hadley Centre in the United Kingdom and the Canadian Centre for Climate Modeling and Analysis. Because the two models produced conflicting results on several key issues and because computer models inherently were general estimates based on available evidence rather than firm predictions, the National Assessment team included dozens of cautionary notes in its report. All estimates were rated according to their likelihood of occurring (ranging from "very unlikely" to "very probable").*

*In general, the report said that climate change during the twenty-first century probably would vary widely across the United States. Projections of regional differences were subject to great uncertainty, the report said, but the overall national trends would be higher temperatures and greater extremes of precipitation. Some areas, particularly the northeast and the southwest, could become much hotter and wetter than in the past, the report said, while much of the rest of the country might become hotter and drier. Alaska, the nation's coldest state, already was experiencing significantly higher temperatures and likely would see "more intense warming" than the lower forty-eight states, the report said. Both droughts and floods could become more common and more damaging across the country.*

*Rising temperatures and erratic precipitation could produce major changes in the national environment, the report said. Some of the most familiar elements of the American landscape—such as the northeastern sugar maples (responsible for maple syrup and New England's famed fall colors), wildflower-laden alpine meadows in the Rocky Mountains, low-lying wetlands and barrier islands along the Atlantic coast, winter snow-packs on the mountains of the Pacific Northwest, and Alaska's permafrost and glaciers—might decline dramatically or even disappear. Water levels in the Great Lakes might drop as much as five feet, and severe drought could become a semi-permanent condition in parts of the Great Plains. Rising temperatures and reduced snowfall might endanger the nation's ski industry, but producers and sellers of air conditioning systems could expect strong business for many decades.*

*Climate change "very likely" will magnify the impact of man-made stresses on the natural environment and human populations, the report said. Those factors included air and water pollution and the destruction of plant and wildlife habitat caused by development. Much of the nation's population growth projected for the twenty-first century would take place in coastal states such as Florida, Texas, and California, where a combination of development and climate change could wipe out remaining wetlands, thereby increasing such dangers as erosion and storm surges.*

*Some economic benefits could arise from a warmer climate, the report said, most notably an increase in agricultural production resulting from longer growing seasons and the higher concentrations of carbon dioxide, which plants need for photosynthesis. More food production probably would lead to falling prices, which would benefit consumers but would endanger small-scale farmers whose profits were already shrinking. Overall, the economic impact on the United States of global warming could be "modest," the report said, especially if Americans anticipated the effects of changes and took steps to adapt to them.*

*The report stressed the certainty of surprises: short-term or even long-term climactic events that simply could not be foreseen. As historical examples, the report noted the nation's widespread drought during the 1930s and the appearance during the 1980s of an ozone "hole" over the Antarctic.*

*The report made no recommendations for specific changes in governmental policies or private actions that could mitigate climate change or its effects. But a recurrent theme was that mankind needed to consider the potential impact of climate change when making plans for the future, whether building housing subdivisions in low-lying coastal areas or planting timber stands in areas that might experience increased drought.*

*Although the National Assessment report represented the consensus view of hundreds of scientists with a broad range of viewpoints, some dissenters rejected some or even all of its conclusions. In general, climate change "skeptics" disputed the report's conclusions that man-made greenhouse gases contributed to global warming and that climate change was likely to alter the environment. One skeptic, Anthony R. Lupo, professor of atmospheric science at the University of Missouri, wrote in the August 4 St. Louis* Post Dispatch *that the National Assessment presented "speculative science as the undeniable truth." Scientists still disagreed, he said, "whether or not humanity is, or could be, responsible for significantly altering the global climate." Robert E. Davis, associate professor of environmental science at the University of Virginia, said the unreliability of computerized climate models meant that "it's hardly worthwhile to even consider their projections for the future, which vary so much from projection to projection as to be irrelevant."*

## Another Warm Year

*Most Americans did not need elaborate computer models to tell them that 2000 was warmer than "normal"—even if that term was beginning to lose some of its traditional meaning. The National Oceanic and Atmospheric Administration (NOAA) reported on December 18 that the average temperature in the nation for the year was 54.1°F, which was significantly higher (in statistical terms) than the long-term average of 52.8°F. Depending on the standard used, that would make 2000 between the seventh and the twelfth warmest year since the advent of accurate weather records in 1895. The nation's record for warmth was set in 1998, with an average of 54.9°F. (Record* warmth, Historic Documents of 1998, p. 945)

*As was always the case, regional and seasonal variations in such a large country were extreme. Southern and western states experienced a severe, prolonged period of drought and high temperatures, contributing to one of the worst wildfire seasons in modern times. But much of the Midwest and Northeast saw cooler and wetter summers than normal, especially in July.*

*The months of November and December were exceptionally cool in much of the country, the major factor in preventing 2000 from breaking the 1998 record for warmth.* (Wildfires, p. 712)

*The year turned out to be warmer than normal in much of the rest of the world, as well. The World Meteorological Organization issued its annual report on December 19, noting that the mean surface temperature around the world was 0.32°C (about 0.58°F) above the long-term average. The report said 2000 was the twenty-second consecutive year in which the annual mean temperature was higher than the long-term normal.*

*Scientists reported several other empirical signs of global warming during the year. On August 19 the* New York Times *reported that ice had disappeared from much of the area around the North Pole during the summer. In the past the North Pole had been covered by a thick sheet of ice. Scientists at the National Aeronautics and Space Administration reported a similar loss of ice from the coastal regions of Greenland, the world's largest island, most of which is located within the Arctic Circle and is covered by ice. In addition, NOAA scientists reported in March that the world's three major oceans (the Atlantic, Indian, and Pacific) were becoming significantly warmer, both on the surface and at low depths. The Atlantic and Pacific oceans had been warming since the 1950s and the Indian ocean since the 1960s, NOAA scientists said in a study published in the March 23 edition of the journal* Science.

## Discord at The Hague

*Ever since the 1997 negotiations that produced the Kyoto protocol, government leaders, environmental organizations, and representatives of industry had been arguing about whether and how the goals of that treaty should be implemented. The United Nations, which had responsibility for the treaty, called a conference for November at The Hague, Netherlands. UN officials hoped that the major industrialized nations, most notably the United States and its political allies in Europe, could agree on methods to reduce their emissions of greenhouse gases to the levels demanded by the Kyoto treaty.*

*The United States produced about 24 percent of the world's greenhouse gas emissions, by far the largest share of any single country. To reach the Kyoto treaty targets, it was estimated in 2000 that the United States would have to decrease its greenhouse gas emissions by nearly one-third—an enormous reduction that would force sweeping changes in workplaces and the lifestyles of Americans.*

*In talks leading up to the conference, Clinton administration negotiators suggested that the United States should be given credit for the positive effect of its forests and agricultural fields, areas that absorbed a large portion of the nation's greenhouse gas emissions. Washington's negotiators also suggested a plan under which the United States could acquire "credits" for reducing greenhouse gases from Russia and Ukraine, two countries that were experiencing economic difficulties. Some European countries, which had moved more rapidly than the United States to reduce production of greenhouse gases, expressed a willingness to accept the U.S. plan, but others staunchly opposed it.*

*Two weeks of negotiations at The Hague produced strong disagreements over steps needed to implement the Kyoto treaty, and for many days it appeared unlikely that any agreement could be reached. In the early morning hours of November 25 representatives of U.S. and key European nations agreed on a compromise that would have given the United States some of the credits it sought in return for a strict commitment to reduce greenhouse gas emissions. That compromise lasted only a few hours, however, collapsing when diplomats from Germany and several other European countries refused to accept it. The chief U.S. delegate, Frank Loy, said he was disappointed that the conference failed to seize an opportunity to resolve one of the world's most contentious environmental issues: "Too many of our negotiating parties held fast to positions shaped more by political purity than by practicality, more by dogmatism than pragmatism."*

*Following are excerpts from the "Overview" of the report, "Climate Change Impacts on the United States: The Potential Consequences of Climate Variability and Change," released June 12, 2000, by the National Assessment Synthesis Team of the U.S. Global Change Research Program. The report was approved by the National Science and Technology Council, a cabinet-level body of federal agencies responsible for scientific research. The document was obtained from the Internet at http://www.gcrio.org/NationalAssessment.*

## Climate Change and Our Nation

Long-term observations confirm that our climate is now changing at a rapid rate. Over the 20th century, the average annual US temperature has risen by almost 1°F (0.6°C) and precipitation has increased nationally by 5 to 10%, mostly due to increases in heavy downpours. These trends are most apparent over the past few decades. The science indicates that the warming in the 21st century will be significantly larger than in the 20th century. Scenarios examined in this Assessment, which assume no major interventions to reduce continued growth of world greenhouse gas emissions, indicate that temperatures in the US will rise by about 5–9°F (3–5°C) on average in the next 100 years, which is more than the projected global increase. This rise is very likely to be associated with more extreme precipitation and faster evaporation of water, leading to greater frequency of both very wet and very dry conditions.

This Assessment reveals a number of national-level impacts of climate variability and change including impacts to natural ecosystems and water resources. Natural ecosystems appear to be the most vulnerable to the harmful effects of climate change, as there is often little that can be done to help them adapt to the projected speed and amount of change. Some ecosystems that are already constrained by climate, such as alpine meadows in the Rocky Mountains, are likely to face extreme stress, and disappear entirely in some places. It is likely that other more widespread ecosystems will also be vulnerable to climate change. One of the climate scenarios used in this Assessment suggests the potential for the forests of the Southeast to break up into a mosaic of forests, savannas, and grasslands. Climate scenarios suggest likely changes in the species composition of the Northeast forests, including the loss of sugar maples. Major alterations to natural ecosystems due to climate change could possibly have negative consequences for our economy, which depends in part on the sustained bounty of our nation's lands, waters, and native plant and animal communities.

A unique contribution of this first US Assessment is that it combines national-scale analysis with an examination of the potential impacts of climate change on different regions of the US. For example, sea-level rise will very likely cause further loss of coastal wetlands (ecosystems that provide vital nurseries and habitats for many fish species) and put coastal communities at greater risk of storm surges, especially in the Southeast. Reduction in snowpack will very likely alter the timing and amount of water supplies, potentially exacerbating water shortages and conflicts, particularly throughout the western US. The melting of glaciers in the high-elevation West and in Alaska represents the loss or diminishment of unique national treasures of the American landscape. Large increases in the heat index (which combines temperature and humidity) and increases in the frequency of heat waves are very likely. These changes will, at minimum, increase discomfort, particularly in cities. It is very probable that continued thawing of permafrost and melting of sea ice in Alaska will further damage forests, buildings, roads, and coastlines, and harm subsistence livelihoods. In various parts of the nation, cold-weather recreation such as skiing will very likely be reduced, and air conditioning usage will very likely increase.

Highly managed ecosystems appear more robust, and some potential benefits have been identified. Crop and forest productivity is likely to increase in some areas for the next few decades due to increased carbon dioxide in the atmosphere and an extended growing season. It is possible that some US food exports could increase, depending on impacts in other food-growing regions around the world. It is also possible that a rise in crop production in fertile areas could cause prices to fall, benefiting consumers. Other benefits that are possible include extended seasons for construction and warm weather recreation, reduced heating requirements, and reduced cold-weather mortality.

Climate variability and change will interact with other environmental stresses and socioeconomic changes. Air and water pollution, habitat fragmentation, wetland loss, coastal erosion, and reductions in fisheries are likely to be compounded by climate-related stresses. An aging populace nationally, and rapidly growing populations in cities, coastal areas, and across the South and West are social factors that interact with and alter sensitivity to climate variability and change.

There are also very likely to be unanticipated impacts of climate change

343

during the next century. Such "surprises" may stem from unforeseen changes in the physical climate system, such as major alterations in ocean circulation, cloud distribution, or storms; and unpredicted biological consequences of these physical climate changes, such as massive dislocations of species or pest outbreaks. In addition, unexpected social or economic change, including major shifts in wealth, technology, or political priorities, could affect our ability to respond to climate change.

Greenhouse gas emissions lower than those assumed in this Assessment would result in reduced impacts. The signatory nations of the Framework Convention on Climate Change are negotiating the path they will ultimately take. Even with such reductions, however, the planet and the nation are certain to experience more than a century of climate change, due to the long lifetimes of greenhouse gases already in the atmosphere and the momentum of the climate system. Adapting to a changed climate is consequently a necessary component of our response strategy.

Adaptation measures can, in many cases, reduce the magnitude of harmful impacts, or take advantage of beneficial impacts. For example, in agriculture, many farmers will probably be able to alter cropping and management practices. Roads, bridges, buildings, and other long-lived infrastructure can be designed taking projected climate change into account. Adaptations, however, can involve trade-offs, and do involve costs. For example, the benefits of building sea walls to prevent sea-level rise from disrupting human coastal communities will need to be weighed against the economic and ecological costs of seawall construction. The ecological costs could be high as seawalls prevent the inland shifting of coastal wetlands in response to sea-level rise, resulting in the loss of vital fish and bird habitat and other wetland functions, such as protecting shorelines from damage due to storm surges. Protecting against any increased risk of water-borne and insect-borne diseases will require diligent maintenance of our public health system. Many adaptations, notably those that seek to reduce other environmental stresses such as pollution and habitat fragmentation, will have beneficial effects beyond those related to climate change.

Vulnerability in the US is linked to the fates of other nations, and we cannot evaluate national consequences due to climate variability and change without also considering the consequences of changes elsewhere in the world. The US is linked to other nations in many ways, and both our vulnerabilities and our potential responses will likely depend in part on impacts and responses in other nations. For example, conflicts or mass migrations resulting from resource limits, health, and environmental stresses in more vulnerable nations could possibly pose challenges for global security and US policy. Effects of climate variability and change on US agriculture will depend critically on changes in agricultural productivity elsewhere, which can shift international patterns of food supply and demand. Climate-induced changes in water resources available for power generation, transportation, cities, and agriculture are likely to raise potentially delicate diplomatic issues with both Canada and Mexico.

This Assessment has identified many remaining uncertainties that limit our ability to fully understand the spectrum of potential consequences of climate change for our nation. To address these uncertainties, additional research is needed to improve understanding of ecological and social processes that are sensitive to climate, application of climate scenarios and reconstructions of past climates to impacts studies, and assessment strategies and methods. Results from these research efforts will inform future assessments that will continue the process of building our understanding of humanity's impacts on climate, and climate's impacts on us.

## Key Findings

1. **Increased warming.** Assuming continued growth in world greenhouse gas emissions, the primary climate models used in this Assessment project that temperatures in the US will rise 5–9°F (3–5°C) on average in the next 100 years. A wider range of outcomes is possible.

2. **Differing regional impacts.** Climate change will vary widely across the US. Temperature increases will vary somewhat from one region to the next. Heavy and extreme precipitation events are likely to become more frequent, yet some regions will get drier. The potential impacts of climate change will also vary widely across the nation.

3. **Vulnerable ecosystems.** Many ecosystems are highly vulnerable to the projected rate and magnitude of climate change. A few, such as alpine meadows in the Rocky Mountains and some barrier islands, are likely to disappear entirely in some areas. Others, such as forests of the Southeast, are likely to experience major species shifts or break up into a mosaic of grasslands, woodlands, and forests. The goods and services lost through the disappearance or fragmentation of certain ecosystems are likely to be costly or impossible to replace.

4. **Widespread water concerns.** Water is an issue in every region, but the nature of the vulnerabilities varies. Drought is an important concern in every region. Floods and water quality are concerns in many regions. Snowpack changes are especially important in the West, Pacific Northwest, and Alaska.

5. **Secure food supply.** At the national level, the agriculture sector is likely to be able to adapt to climate change. Overall, US crop productivity is very likely to increase over the next few decades, but the gains will not be uniform across the nation. Falling prices and competitive pressures are very likely to stress some farmers, while benefiting consumers.

6. **Near-term increase in forest growth.** Forest productivity is likely to increase over the next several decades in some areas as trees respond to higher carbon dioxide levels. Over the longer term, changes in larger-scale processes such as fire, insects, droughts, and disease will possibly decrease forest productivity. In addition, climate change is likely to cause long-term shifts in forest species, such as sugar maples moving north out of the US.

7. **Increased damage in coastal and permafrost areas.** Climate change and the resulting rise in sea level are likely to exacerbate threats to buildings, roads, powerlines, and other infrastructure in climatically sensitive places. For example, infrastructure damage is related to permafrost melting in Alaska, and to sea-level rise and storm surge in low-lying coastal areas.

8. **Adaptation determines health outcomes.** A range of negative health impacts is possible from climate change, but adaptation is likely to help protect much of the US population. Maintaining our nation's public health and community infrastructure, from water treatment systems to emergency shelters, will be important for minimizing the impacts of water-borne diseases, heat stress, air pollution, extreme weather events, and diseases transmitted by insects, ticks, and rodents.

9. **Other stresses magnified by climate change.** Climate change will very likely magnify the cumulative impacts of other stresses, such as air and water pollution and habitat destruction due to human development patterns. For some systems, such as coral reefs, the combined effects of climate change and other stresses are very likely to exceed a critical threshold, bringing large, possibly irreversible impacts.

10. **Uncertainties remain and surprises are expected.** Significant uncertainties remain in the science underlying regional climate changes and their impacts. Further research would improve understanding and our ability to project societal and ecosystem impacts, and provide the public with additional useful information about options for adaptation. However, it is likely that some aspects and impacts of climate change will be totally unanticipated as complex systems respond to ongoing climate change in unforeseeable ways.

## Our Changing Climate

### Climate and the Greenhouse Effect

Earth's climate is determined by complex interactions between the sun, oceans, atmosphere, land, and living things. The composition of the atmosphere is particularly important because certain gases (including water vapor, carbon dioxide, methane, halocarbons, ozone, and nitrous oxide) absorb heat radiated from the Earth's surface. As the atmosphere warms, it in turn radiates heat back to the surface, to create what is commonly called the "greenhouse effect." Changes in the composition of the atmosphere alter the intensity of the greenhouse effect. Such changes, which have occurred many times in the planet's history, have helped determine past climates and will affect the future climate as well.

### Human Activities Alter the Balance

Humans are exerting a major and growing influence on some of the key factors that govern climate by changing the composition of the atmosphere and by Modifying the land surface. The human impact on these factors is clear. The concentration of carbon dioxide ($CO_2$) has risen about 30% since the late 1800s. The concentration of $CO_2$ is now higher than it has been in at least the last 400,000 years. This increase has resulted from the burning of coal, oil, and natural gas, and the destruction of forests around the world to provide space for agriculture and other human activities. Rising concentrations of $CO_2$ and other greenhouse gases are intensifying Earth's natural greenhouse effect. Global projections of population growth and assumptions about energy use indicate that the $CO_2$ concentration will continue to rise, likely reaching between two and three times its late-19th-century level by 2100. This dramatic doubling or tripling will occur in the space of about 200 years, a brief moment in geological history.

## The Climate Is Changing

As we add more $CO_2$ and other heat-trapping gases to the atmosphere, the world is becoming warmer (which changes other aspects of climate as well). Historical records of temperature and precipitation have been extensively analyzed in many scientific studies. These studies demonstrate that the global average surface temperature has increased by over 1°F (0.6°C) during the 20th century. About half this rise has occurred since the late 1970s. Seventeen of the eighteen warmest years in the 20th century occurred since 1980. In 1998, the global temperature set a new record by a wide margin, exceeding that of the previous record year, 1997, by about 0.3°F (0.2°C). Higher latitudes have warmed more than equatorial regions, and nighttime temperatures have risen more than daytime temperatures.

As the Earth warms, more water evaporates from the oceans and lakes, eventually to fall as rain or snow. During the 20th century, annual precipitation has increased about 10% in the mid- and high-latitudes. The warming is also causing permafrost to thaw, and is melting sea ice, snow cover, and mountain glaciers. Global sea level rose 4 to 8 inches (10–20 cm) during the 20th century because ocean water expands as it warms and because melting glaciers are adding water to the oceans.

According to the Intergovernmental Panel on Climate Change (IPCC), scientific evidence confirms that human activities are a discernible cause of a substantial part of the warming experienced over the 20th century. New studies indicate that temperatures in recent decades are higher than at any time in at least the past 1,000 years. It is very unlikely that these unusually high temperatures can be explained solely by natural climate variations.

The intensity and pattern of temperature changes within the atmosphere implicates human activities as a cause.

The relevant question is not whether the increase in greenhouse gases is contributing to warming, but rather, what will be the amount and rate of future warming and associated climate changes, and what impacts will those changes have on human and natural systems. . . .

[Following sections discuss the use of historical records and computer models to develop information about the potential impacts of climate change on the United States. One section offers cautions concerning the use of various scenarios for possible climate change and notes the likelihood of "surprises."]

## Past and Future US Temperature Change

Observations from 1200 weather stations across the US show that temperatures have increased over the past century, on average by almost 1°F (0.6°C). The coastal Northeast, the upper Midwest, the Southwest, and parts of Alaska have experienced increases in the annual average temperature approaching 4°F (2°C) over the past 100 years. The rest of the nation has experienced less warming. The Southeast and southern Great Plains have actually experienced a slight cooling over the 20th century, but since the 1970s have had increasing temperatures as well. The largest observed warming across the nation has occurred in winter.

Average warming in the US is projected to be somewhat greater than for the world as a whole over the 21st century. In the Canadian model scenario, increases in annual average temperature of 10°F (5.5°C) by the year 2100 occur across the central US with changes about half this large along the east and west coasts. Seasonal patterns indicate that projected changes will be particularly large in winter, especially at night. Large increases in temperature are projected over much of the South in summer, dramatically raising the heat index (a measure of discomfort based on temperature and humidity).

In the Hadley model scenario [developed by the Hadley Centre in the United Kingdom], the eastern US has temperature increases of 3–5°F (2–3°C) by 2100 while the rest of the nation warms more, up to 7°F (4°C), depending on the region.

In both models, Alaska is projected to experience more intense warming than the lower 48, and in fact, this warming is already well underway. In contrast, Hawaii and the Caribbean islands are likely to experience less warming than the continental US, because they are at lower latitudes and are surrounded by ocean, which warms more slowly than land.

## Changes in Precipitation

Average US precipitation has increased by 5–10% over the last century with much of that due to an increase in the frequency and intensity of heavy rainfall. Precipitation increases have been especially noteworthy in the Midwest, southern Great Plains, and parts of the West and Pacific Northwest. Decreases have been observed in the northern Great Plains.

For the 21st century, the Canadian model projects that percentage increases in precipitation will be largest in the Southwest and California, while east of the Rocky Mountains, the southern half of the nation is projected to experience a decrease in precipitation. The percentage decreases are projected to be particularly large in eastern Colorado and western Kansas, and across an arc running from Louisiana to Virginia. Projected decreases in precipitation are most evident in the Great Plains during summer and in the East during both winter and summer. The increases in precipitation projected to occur in the West, and the smaller increases in the Northwest, are projected to occur mainly in winter.

In the Hadley model, the largest percentage increases in precipitation are projected to be in the Southwest and Southern California, but the increases are smaller than those projected by the Canadian model. In the Hadley model, the entire US is projected to have increases in precipitation, with the exception of small areas along the Gulf Coast and in the Pacific Northwest. Precipitation is projected to increase in the eastern half of the nation and in southern California and parts of Nevada and Arizona in summer, and in every region during the winter, except the Gulf States and northern Washington and Idaho.

In both the Hadley and Canadian models, most regions are projected to experience an increase in the frequency of heavy precipitation events. This is especially notable in the Hadley model, but the Canadian model shows the same characteristic.

While the actual amounts are modest, the large percentage increases in rainfall projected for the Southwest are related to increases in atmospheric moisture and storm paths. A warmer Pacific would pump moisture into the region and there would also be a southward shift in Pacific Coast storm activity. In the Sierra Nevada and Rocky Mountains, much of the increased precipitation is likely to fall as rain rather than snow, causing a reduction in mountain snow packs.

This would tend to increase winter-time river flows and decrease summer-time flows in the West. Across the Northwest, and the central and eastern US, the two model projections of precipitation change are in less agreement. These differences will be resolved only by improvements in climate modeling.

## Changes in Soil Moisture

Soil moisture is critical for both agriculture and natural ecosystems. Soil moisture levels are determined by an intricate interplay among precipitation, evaporation, run-off, and soil drainage. By itself, an increase in precipitation would increase soil moisture. However, higher air temperatures will increase the rate of evaporation and, in some areas, remove moisture from the soil faster than it can be added by precipitation. Under these conditions, some regions are likely to become drier even though their rainfall increases.

In fact, soil moisture has already decreased in portions of the Great Plains and Eastern Seaboard, where precipitation has increased but air temperature has risen. Since soil moisture projections reflect both changes in precipitation and in evaporation associated with warming, the differences between the two models are accentuated in the soil moisture projections. For example, in the Canadian model, soil moisture decreases of more than 50% are common in the Central Plains due to the combination of precipitation reductions exceeding 20% and temperature increases exceeding 10°F. In the Hadley model, this same region experiences more modest warming of about 5°F and precipitation increases of around 20%, generally resulting in soil moisture increases.

Increased drought becomes a national problem in the Canadian model. Intense drought tendencies occur in the region east of the Rocky Mountains and throughout the Mid-Atlantic-Southeastern states corridor. Increased tendencies toward drought are also projected in the Hadley model for regions immediately east of the Rockies. California and Arizona, plus a region from eastern

Nebraska to Virginia's coastal plain, experience decreases in drought tendency. The differences in soil moisture and drought tendencies will be significant for water supply, agriculture, forests, and lake levels.

## Ecosystems in the Future

The natural vegetation covering about 70% of the US land surface is strongly Influenced both by the climate and by the atmospheric carbon dioxide ($CO_2$) concentration. To provide a common base of information about potential changes in vegetation across the nation for use in the regional and sector studies, specialized ecosystem models were run using the two major climate model scenarios selected for this Assessment. A summary of the national level results follows. Agricultural and production forestry systems are the focus of separate sections of this Overview report.

### What are Ecosystems?

Ecosystems are communities of plants, animals, microbes, and the physical Environment in which they exist. They can be characterized by their biological richness, by the magnitude of flows of energy and materials between their constituent species and their physical environment, and by the interactions among the biological species themselves, that is, by which species are predators and prey, which are competitors, and which are symbiotic.

Ecologists often categorize ecosystems by their dominant vegetation—the Deciduous broad-leafed forest ecosystems of New England, the short-grass prairie ecosystems of the Great Plains, the desert ecosystems of the Southwest. The term "ecosystem" is used not only to describe natural systems (such as coral reefs, alpine meadows, old growth forests, or riparian habitats), but also for plantation forests and agricultural systems, although these ecosystems obviously differ in many important ways from the natural ecosystems they have replaced.

### Ecosystems Supply Vital Goods and Services

While we value natural ecosystems in their own right, ecosystems of all types, from the most natural to the most extensively managed, produce a variety of goods and services that benefit humans. Some of these enter the market and contribute directly to the economy. Thus, forests as sources of timber and pulpwood, and agro-ecosystems as sources of food are important to us. But ecosystems also provide a set of unpriced services that are valuable, but that typically are not traded in the marketplace. There is no current market, for example, for the services that forests and wetlands provide for improving water quality, regulating stream flow, and providing some measure of protection from floods. However, these services are very valuable to society.

Ecosystems are also valued for recreational, aesthetic, and ethical reasons. These are also difficult to value monetarily, but are nevertheless important. The bird life of the coastal marshes of the Southeast and the brilliant autumn colors of the New England forests are treasured components of our regional heritages, and important elements of our quality of life.

## Climate and Ecosystems

Climatic conditions determine where individual species of plants and animals can live, grow, and reproduce. Thus, the collections of species that we are familiar with—the southeastern mixed deciduous forest, the desert ecosystems of the arid Southwest, or the productive grasslands of the Great Plains—are influenced by climate as well as other factors such as land-use. The species in some ecosystems are so strongly influenced by the climate to which they are adapted that they are vulnerable even to modest climate changes. For example, alpine meadows at high elevations in the West exist where they do entirely because the plants that comprise them are adapted to the cold—conditions that would be too harsh for other species in the region. The desert vegetation of the Southwest is adapted to the high summer temperatures and aridity of the region. Forests in the east are adapted to relatively high rainfall and soil moisture; if drought conditions were to persist, grasses and shrubs could begin to out-compete tree seedlings, leading to completely different ecosystems.

There are also many freshwater and marine examples of sensitivities to climate variability and change. In aquatic ecosystems, for example, many fish can breed only in water that falls within a narrow range of temperatures. Thus, species of fish that are adapted to cool waters can quickly become unable to breed successfully if water temperatures rise. Wetland plant species can adjust to rising sea levels by dispersing to new locations, within limits. Too rapid sea-level rise can surpass the ability of the plants to disperse, making it impossible for coastal wetland ecosystems to re-establish themselves.

## Effects of Increased $CO_2$ Concentration on Plants

The ecosystem models used in this Assessment consider not only changes in climate, but also increases in atmospheric $CO_2$. The atmospheric concentration of $CO_2$ affects plant species in ecosystems since it has a direct physiological effect on photosynthesis, the process by which plants use $CO_2$ to create new biological material. Higher concentrations of $CO_2$ generally enhance plant growth if the plants also have sufficient water and nutrients, such as nitrogen, to sustain this enhanced growth. For this reason, the $CO_2$ levels in commercial greenhouses are sometimes boosted in order to stimulate plant growth. In addition, higher $CO_2$ levels can raise the efficiency with which plants use water. Different types of plants respond at different rates to increases in atmospheric $CO_2$, resulting in a divergence of growth rates due to $CO_2$ increase. Some species grow faster, but provide reduced nutritional value. The effects of increased $CO_2$ level off at some point; thus, continuing to increase $CO_2$ levels will not result in increased plant growth indefinitely. There is still much we do not understand about the $CO_2$ "fertilization" effect, its limits, and its direct and indirect implications.

## Species Responses to Changes in Climate and $CO_2$

The responses of ecosystems to changes in climate and $CO_2$ are made up of the individual responses of their constituent species and how they interact with each other. Species in current ecosystems can differ substantially in their tolerances of changes in temperature and precipitation, and in their responses to changes in $CO_2$; thus, new climate conditions are very likely to result in current ecosystems breaking apart, and new assemblages of species being created. Current ecosystem models have great difficulty in predicting these kinds of biological and ecological responses, thus leading to large uncertainties in projections.

## What the Models Project

Modeling results to date indicate that natural ecosystems on land are very likely to be highly sensitive to changes in surface temperature, precipitation patterns, other climate parameters, and atmospheric $CO_2$ concentrations. Two types of models utilized in this Assessment to examine the ecological effects of climate change are biogeochemistry models and biogeography models. Biogeochemistry models simulate changes in basic ecosystem processes such as the cycling of carbon, nutrients, and water (ecosystem function). Biogeography models simulate shifts in the geographic distribution of major plant species and communities (ecosystem structure).

The biogeochemistry models used in this analysis generally simulate increases in the amount of carbon in vegetation and soils over the next 30 years for the continental US as a whole. These probable increases are small—in the range of 10% or less, and are not uniform across the country. In fact, for some regions the models simulate carbon losses over the next 30 years. One of the biogeochemistry models, when operating with the Canadian climate scenario, simulates that by about 2030, parts of the Southeast will likely lose up to 20% of the carbon from their forests. A carbon loss by a forest is treated as an indication that it is in decline. The same biogeochemistry model, when operating with the Hadley climate scenario, simulates that forests in the same part of the Southeast will likely gain between 5 and 10% in carbon in trees over the next 30 years.

Why do the two climate scenarios result in opposite ecosystem responses in the Southeast? The Canadian climate scenario shows the Southeast as a hotter and drier place in the early decades of the 21st century than does the Hadley scenario. With the Canadian scenario, forests will be under stress due to insufficient moisture, which causes them to lose more carbon in respiration than they gain in photosynthesis. In contrast, the Hadley scenario simulates relatively plentiful soil moisture, robust tree growth, and forests that accumulate carbon.

## Ecosystems in the Future

Prolonged stress due to insufficient soil moisture can make trees more susceptible to insect attack, lead to plant death, and increase the probability of fire as dead plant material adds to an ecosystem's "fuel load." The biogeography models used in this analysis simulate at least part of this sequence of climate-triggered events in ecosystems as a prelude to shifts in the geographic distribution of major plant species. One of the biogeography models, when operating with the Canadian climate scenario, simulates that towards the end of the 21st century, a hot dry climate in the Southeast will result in the replacement of the current mixed evergreen and deciduous forests by savanna/ woodlands and grasslands, with much of the change involving fire. This change in habitat type in the Southeast would imply that the animal populations of the region would also change, although the biogeography models are not designed to simulate these changes. The same biogeography model, when operating with the Hadley scenario, simulates a slight northward expansion of the mixed evergreen and deciduous forests of the Southeast with no significant contraction along the southern boundary. Other biogeography models show similar results.

## Major Uncertainties

Major uncertainties exist in the biogeochemistry and biogeography models. For example, ecologists are uncertain about how increases in atmospheric $CO_2$ affect the carbon and water cycles in ecosystems. What they assume about these $CO_2$ effects can significantly influence model simulation results. One of these models was used to show the importance of testing these assumptions. Consideration of climate change alone results in a 10% decrease in plant productivity. Consideration of both climate and $CO_2$ effects results in an increase in plant productivity of 10%. This illustrates the importance of resolving uncertainties about the effects of $CO_2$ on ecosystems.

With respect to biogeography models, scientists are uncertain about the Frequency and size of disturbances produced by factors such as fire and pests that initiate changes in the distribution of major plant and animal species. Will disturbances caused by climate change be regular and small or will they be episodic and large? The latter category of disturbances is likely to have a negative impact on ecosystems services; the ability of ecosystems to cleanse the air and water, stabilize landscapes against erosion, and store carbon, for example, are very likely to be diminished.

## Our Changing Nation

Climate variability and change do not occur in isolation, but in an evolving, dynamic social and economic context. This context is very likely to affect the character and magnitude of climate impacts. Socioeconomic conditions are important drivers of climate change, and also influence the way society responds to change. The prosperity and structure of the economy, the echnologies available and in use, and the settlement patterns and demographic structure of the population, are all very likely to contribute to how and how much climate change will matter to Americans, and what they can and might wish to do about it.

Thinking explicitly about socioeconomic futures is speculative, but doing a coherent assessment of future climate impacts requires that potential future socioeconomic conditions be considered. Failing to explicitly consider these conditions risks making the assumption that the future will be largely like the present—an assumption that is virtually certain to be wrong. To see how wrong, one need only compare America's society and economy today to that of 100,50, or even 25 years ago.

To guide our thinking about socioeconomic futures, this Assessment developed three illustrative socioeconomic scenarios, which project high, medium, and low growth trends for the US population and economy through the 21st century. These scenarios necessarily involve uncertainties that grow large by the end of the century, as the figures show. Nevertheless, they represent a plausible range of socioeconomic conditions that could affect climate impacts and response capabilities. Using multiple scenarios avoids the errors of attempting specific predictions, or assuming no change at all. Region and sector teams were asked to use these scenarios when their analyses required demographic or economic inputs.

## Growing Prosperity

The US economy and population are growing. Barring major wars or other catastrophes, growth is likely to continue through the 21st century. If economic growth is higher, society is likely to be more able to take advantage of the opportunities a changing climate presents, and more able to cope with its negative impacts. Wealthier, industrialized societies derive less of their incomes from strongly climate-related activities than more traditional societies. With more technology and infrastructure, wealthy societies also have more resources to support adaptation, and can more easily endure climate-related losses. Within societies, some will very likely face greater burdens or greater opportunities than others. It is also possible that rapid economic growth can increase vulnerability, by increasing pollution (including greenhouse gas emissions), congestion, demand for land and resources, and stresses on natural ecosystems, and possibly their vulnerability to climate change.

## Changing Technology

Much of the recent US economic growth has been fueled by new technology. Although technological change can carry significant social and environmental costs, in aggregate it greatly increased Americans' material well being over the 20th century. For example, in the past decade, new information and communication technologies have transformed many activities, bringing increased productivity and new products and services.

Technology affects society's relationship to climate in many ways. It is very likely that technological change will strongly influence the success of any future efforts to control greenhouse gas emissions, and reduce vulnerability to climate change. For example, it is possible that information technology, combined with new cropping methods and advanced crop varieties, will increase farmers' ability to adapt to climate change or variability. Similarly, advances in medicine, public health, and information technology will likely strengthen our abilities in the early detection, prevention, and treatment of disease.

Technology can also increase society's vulnerability to unanticipated extremes of climate. This can happen because modern society is highly interdependent, relying in critical ways on electric power, transportation, and communications systems, all of which can be disrupted by extreme weather events if systems have not been adequately designed to deal with contingencies.

## A Growing, Aging, and Mobile Populace

The US population is projected to continue growing through the 21st century, but at a declining rate. The scenarios used in this Assessment project a US population in 2100 that ranges from 353 to 640 million (representing average annual growth rates of 0.31% to 0.86% over the 21st century), with 494 million in the middle scenario. Most of this uncertainty arises from alternative immigration assumptions.

The US population is aging. Over the 20th century, the fraction of Americans over age 65 increased from 1 in 25 to 1 in 8. Older people are physiologically more vulnerable to heat stress. Without adaptive measures, a warmer climate would likely bring an increase in heat-related illness and death, which society's aging would compound. There is also some chance that warming would reduce cold-related mortality, a trend that would also interact with the aging of the population, although the data suggest a weaker effect than for heat. Many older Americans prefer warmer climates, as the migration from northern regions to the Sunbelt demonstrates. Widespread use of one technology, air conditioning, powerfully advanced the growth of these southern regions. At the same time, rapid growth in arid regions has sharply increased these regions' vulnerability to water shortages.

America is becoming more urban. The fraction of Americans living in cities increased from 40% in 1900 to more than 75% today and this increase is projected to continue. Urbanization affects vulnerability to climate and the capacity to adapt in complex ways. City dwellers are less dependent on climate-sensitive activities for their livelihoods, and have more resources and social support systems close at hand. But dense concentrations of people and property in coastal or riverside metropolitan areas, dependent on extensive fixed infrastructure (including water, sewer, and energy utilities, roads, tunnels, and bridges) are likely to be vulnerable to extreme events such as floods, storms, storm surges, and heat waves. Combined with such other urban stresses as congestion, pollution, and the local heating that cities generate, it is possible that climate change could significantly harm urban quality of life and health.

Americans are also moving to the coasts. Some 53% of the population now live in the 17% of the land area that comprises the coastal zone, and the largest population growth for several decades is projected for coastal areas. Over the next 25 years, population growth of some 18 million is projected in the coastal states of Florida, California, Texas, and Washington. This trend is exacerbating wetland loss and coastal pollution. In addition, locating more people and property in low-lying coastal areas increases vulnerability to storms, storm surges, erosion, and sea-level rise—as several decades of damage trends, and extreme recent losses in Florida, Georgia, and the Carolinas, all confirm.

## Thinking about the Future: Coping with Complexity

A host of other factors are also likely to affect the ease with which society can adapt to, or take advantage of, climate variability and change. For particular regions or sectors, the factors likely to shape climate vulnerability include local zoning ordinances, housing styles, building codes, popular forms of recreation, the age and degree of specialization of capital in particular industries, world market conditions, and the distribution of income. To further complicate matters, many of these factors are likely to be influenced by climate variability and change, and to influence each other. Trying to project all such relevant factors, or to model their interactions, would be impossible.

Rather, this first Assessment took a highly simplified approach to projecting socioeconomic factors. When teams needed more detailed socioeconomic projections than the scenarios of population and economic growth provided, they were asked to follow a standard procedure to generate and document the projections they needed. They were asked to select one or two additional factors—such as development patterns, land use, technology, or market conditions—that they judged likely to have the most direct effect on the issue they were examining, and to vary these factors through an uncertainty range they judged plausible. This approach has clear limitations. In fact, teams found the complexity of even this simplified approach challenging, and made limited use of it beyond the basic scenarios. It has, however, allowed some preliminary investigations of the socioeconomic basis of impacts and vulnerability, which can be refined and extended as assessment methods and experience advance.

## Impacts, Adaptation, and Vulnerability

Climate impacts, vulnerability, and adaptation are distinct but related concepts. Given an assumed state of America's society and economy, the impacts of a specified climate scenario are the differences it yields relative to a continuation of the present climate. These impacts may be beneficial or harmful, with most climate scenarios bringing mixed effects: benefits to some people, places, and sectors, and harms to others. A system is more or less sensitive to climate depending on whether a specified change in climate brings large or small impacts.

People need not merely suffer the climate conditions they face, however, but can change their practices, institutions, or technology to take maximum advantage of the opportunities the climate presents and limit the harms they suffer from its variations. Through such adaptations, people and societies adjust to the average climate conditions and the variability of conditions they have experienced in the recent past. When habits, livelihoods, capital stock, and management practices are finely tuned to current climate conditions, the direct effect of many types of change in these conditions, particularly if the change occurs rapidly, is more likely to be harmful and disruptive than beneficial.

But just as societies adapt to the present climate, they can also adapt to changes in it. Adaptation can be intentional or not, and can be undertaken either in anticipation of projected changes or in reaction to observed changes. Society's capacity to adapt to future climate change is a crucial uncertainty in determining what the actual consequences of climate change will be. Societies and economies are vulnerable to climate change if they face substantial unfavorable impacts, and have limited ability to adapt. Socioeconomic conditions such as wealth, economic structure, settlement patterns, and technology play strong roles in determining vulnerability to specified climate conditions, as the history of US hurricane losses shows.

Human societies and economies have demonstrated great adaptability to wide-ranging environmental and climatic conditions found throughout the world, and to historical variability. Wealthy industrial societies like the US function quite similarly in such divergent climates as those of Fairbanks, Alaska and Orlando, Florida. While individual adaptability also contributes, it is principally social and economic adaptations in infrastructure, capital, technology, and institutions that make life in Orlando and Fairbanks so similar that individual Americans can move between them easily.

But adaptability has limits, for societies as for individuals, and individuals' ability to move through large climate differences tells us little about these limits. Moving between Orlando and Fairbanks may be easy for an individual, but rapidly imposing the climate of either place on the other would be very disruptive. The countless ways that particular local societies have adapted to current conditions and their history of variability can be changed, but not without cost, not all with equal ease, and not overnight. The speed of climate change, and its relationship to the speed at which skills, habits, resource-management practices, policies, and capital stock can change, is consequently a crucial contributor to vulnerability. Moreover, however wisely we may try to adjust long-lived decisions to anticipate coming climate changes, we will inevitability remain limited by our imperfect projections of the coming changes. Effective adaptation may depend as much on our ability to devise responses that are robust to various possible changes, and adjustable as we learn more, as on the quality of our projections at any particular moment. While societies shown substantial adaptability to climate variability, the challenge of adapting to a climate that is not stable, but evolving at an uncertain rate, has never been tested in an industrialized society.

Consequently, while adaptation measures can help Americans reduce harmful climate impacts and take advantage of associated opportunities, one cannot simply assume that adaptation will make the aggregate impacts of climate change negligible or beneficial. Nor can one assume that all available adaptation measures will necessarily be taken; even for such well-known hazards as fire, flood, and storms, people often fail to take inexpensive and easy risk-reduction measures in their choices of building sites, standards, and materials, sometimes with grave consequences. In this first Assessment, potential climate adaptation options were identified, but their feasibility, costs, effectiveness, or the likely extent of their actual implementation were not assessed. Careful assessment of these will needed.

## Multiple Stresses, Surprises, and Advancing Knowledge

Climate change will occur together with many other economic, technological, and environmental trends, which may stress the same ecological and social systems and interact with climatic stresses. Human society has imposed various stresses on the environment, at diverse scales, for centuries. Over the

21st century some non-climatic stresses will likely increase (such as loss of habitat) while others decrease (such as acidifying pollution); climate change is likely to compound some non-climatic stresses and mitigate others.

Systems that are already bearing multiple other stresses are likely to be more vulnerable to climatic stress. This applies to communities and managed ecosystems, such as marginal agriculture or resource-based communities suffering job loss and out-migration. It also applies to natural ecosystems, whose capacity for adaptation is, in general, likely to be much more limited than that of human communities. Although the central importance of considering interactions between multiple stresses is clear, present tools and methods for doing this are limited; this limitation points to an important set of research needs.

Many climate changes and their impacts will likely be extensions of trends that are already underway, and so are at least partly predictable, but some are not. We often expect natural and social systems to change and respond continuously: push the system a little, and it shifts a little. But complex climatic, ecological, and socioeconomic systems can sometimes respond in highly discontinuous ways: push the system a little more, and it might shift to a completely new state. Such discontinuities or surprises can be seen clearly after they happen, and attempting to explain them often generates important advances in our understanding, but they are extremely difficult to predict. Several possible surprises and discontinuities have been suggested for the Earth's atmosphere, oceans, and ecosystems. Still more potential for surprise arises from the intrinsic unpredictability of human responses to the challenges posed by climate change. Even if the probability of any particular surprise occurring is low (which might not be the case), potential surprises are so numerous and diverse that the likelihood of at least one occurring is much greater. We have been surprised by environmental and socioeconomic changes many times. Examples of past environmental surprises include the appearance of the 1930s drought, and the 1980s appearance of the Antarctic ozone hole. Potential large-consequence surprises present some of the more worrisome concerns raised by climate change, and pose the greatest challenges for policy and research.

Surprises are inherently unpredictable. But two broad approaches can help us prepare to live with a changing and uncertain climate, even considering the possibility of surprise. First, some of our assessment effort can be devoted to identifying and characterizing potential large-impact events, even if we presently judge their probability to be very small. Second, society can maintain a diverse and advancing portfolio of scientific and technical knowledge, and policies that encourage the creation and use of new knowledge and technology. This would provide a powerful foundation for adapting to whatever climate changes might come.

# JOINT STATEMENT BY LEADERS
# OF NORTH AND SOUTH KOREA
## June 15, 2000

*North Korea, one of the world's most secretive and repressive societies, suddenly began reaching out to the rest of the world during 2000. The reclusive North Korean leader, Kim Jong Il, in June held a historic summit meeting in Pyongyang with South Korean president Kim Dae-jung. The two leaders signed an agreement calling for reunification of their countries— a goal that had never seemed possible during a half-century of hostility on the Korean peninsula. The 1950–1953 Korean War had ended with an armistice, not a peace agreement, and the two countries were still technically at war. Reflecting on the significance of the summit, Japanese prime minister Yoshiro Mori compared it to "the collapse of the Berlin wall"—the dramatic 1989 event that led to the fall of the Soviet Union two years later. The South Korean leader was awarded the 2000 Nobel Peace Prize in recognition of his initiative in improving relations between the two countries and his decades-long struggle for democracy in his country.*

*Four months after the summit, the North Korean leader hosted U.S. secretary of state Madeleine K. Albright for yet another historic meeting that held promise for ending one of the last remnants of the cold war. Kim Jong Il also traveled to China and Russia, and his diplomats were busy around the world attempting to establish diplomatic relations with U.S. allies, including Australia, Canada, Great Britain, Germany, and Italy. Several dozen Koreans were reunited with relatives from opposite sides for the first time since the Korean War, and the two Koreas began work on a cross-border rail line that would reopen a direct transportation link between them. (Albright visit and U.S.-North Korean relations, p. 866)*

*These developments raised hopes that the day was approaching when the Korean peninsula would no longer be considered one of the most dangerous places in the world. But despite the breathtaking pace of diplomatic events during the year, most observers anticipated that reaching that goal would take many years of determined effort by the Koreans, with extensive aid from other countries and international agencies. Several modest efforts at reconciliation in previous years had foundered because of the intense level of distrust held over from the Korean War. In the months after the summit, hard-line factions in both countries made antagonistic statements that made it clear that unification would not be a smooth process.*

*North Korea's overtures were grounded in a depressing reality. Fifty years of rigid communism had failed to produce a successful economy there. The collapse of the Soviet Union in late 1991 had deprived North Korea of its primary patron and trading partner, exposing the country's inability to function without outside assistance. After more than five years of famine—partly relieved by massive aid from South Korea and the West— North Korea was desperate for more help. According to U.S. estimates, as many as 2 million North Koreans died of starvation during the most severe years of the famine, 1995–1997. Large sectors of the North Korean economy were idle, with factories unable to operate because they lacked raw materials, tools, and fuel. Most Western analysts suggested that Kim Jong Il was searching for a way to get more aid for his country without having to relax his communist regime's grip on power.*

## *Meeting of the Two Kims*

*Before it happened, virtually no one would have thought it possible that the leaders of the two heavily armed Koreas would spend three days together in Pyongyang discussing the difficult issues confronting their countries and treating each other to joyful celebrations. The two Koreas faced each other across the most heavily armed border in the world, and in the five decades since the Korean War they had developed conflicting economic and political systems. After decades of military rule, South Korea by the late 1990s was a functioning democracy with a dynamic capitalist economy. North Korea remained a Stalinist state, rigidly ruled by a communist party that devoted enormous resources to maintaining the fourth largest standing army in the world while allowing millions of citizens to live in desperate poverty.*

*Several attempts to promote reconciliation between the Koreas were tried between 1971 and 1990, most notably a meeting between the prime ministers of the two countries in September 1990. Each of those attempts produced limited results that were later set back by another round of bickering. In 1994 former U.S. president Jimmy Carter helped arrange a North-South Korean summit, but North Korean leader Kim Il Sung (father of Kim Jong Il) died before the meeting could take place. As late as 1999 the two Koreas narrowly avoided going to war after a brief naval clash over fishing rights in the Yellow Sea.*

*After taking office in February 1998, Kim Dae-jung launched a "Sunshine Policy" of encouraging better relations with the North. He took that policy to a new level during a speech in Berlin in March 2000, promising a major increase in aid to the North. A month later diplomats from the two Koreas met secretly in Beijing and began planning for a summit meeting between the two Kims. A key aspect of the agreement for the summit, according to press reports, was a promise by the South to provide fertilizer and other agricultural supplies to the North. The plans for the summit were announced simultaneously in Seoul and Pyongyang on April 10, just three days before parliamentary elections in South Korea—bringing complaints from the opposition Grand National Party that Kim Dae-jung was using diplomacy "for political gain."*

*Kim Dae-jung arrived at the Pyongyang airport on June 13 and got his first surprise of the visit: Kim Jong Il was there to greet him, a gesture that had not been included in the pre-summit planning. For the better part of three days, the two leaders and their aides held several meetings during which, they said, all major issues were discussed. The political and emotional high point of the summit came at a final lunch hosted by Kim Dae-jung on June 15; the leaders grasped hands and joined in singing a popular song, "Our Wish Is Unification." Later that day the leaders embraced as Kim Dae-jung prepared to board his airplane for the return trip to Seoul.*

*In their joint agreement signed June 15, the two leaders agreed to work toward unification, to deal with "humanitarian issues" such as allowing reunions of separated family members, and to promote cooperation in cultural, sports, public health, environmental, and other fields. The agreement set no specific timetables for future action, other than mentioning that Kim Dae-jung had invited Kim Jong Il to visit Seoul "at an appropriate time." The agreement also made no mention of South Korean economic aid to the North, apparently because Kim Jong Il did not want to be seen as linking aid and the improved relations.*

*The summit went a long way toward fulfilling the ambitions of both leaders. For South Korean president Kim Dae-jung, a successful trip to Pyongyang demonstrated that his dream of improving relations with the North was realistic and could produce tangible benefits for Koreans on both sides of the border. Before his election as president, Kim Dae-jung was a longtime South Korean opposition leader who in 1980 had narrowly escaped death at the hands of the military authorities in Seoul. His policy of reaching out to the North had been controversial at home, not least among military leaders who feared the North's treachery. But the summit proved to be enormously popular in South Korea, and the goodwill that it generated helped relieve domestic pressure on Kim Dae-jung caused by a series of political crises in his government.*

*For North Korean leader Kim Jong Il, the summit offered a measure of international acceptance that had long been denied to North Korea because of its bellicose behavior. The summit also appeared to demonstrate that Kim (who inherited power in 1994 upon the death of his father, the longtime North Korean leader Kim Il Sung), was confident enough of his standing at home to reach out to the rest of the world. Regardless of any possible impact on North-South Korean relations, the summit had the immediate effect of improving Kim Jong Il's public image outside his country. In previous years, a handful of sketchy reports from people who had met him had fostered an image of Kim as a reclusive, emotionally unstable playboy. But during the summit sessions that were televised, Kim appeared to be outgoing, relaxed, and fully aware of the significance of the events in which he was participating. Many news organizations went so far as to declare that*

*Kim Jong Il was the "star" of the summit—no mean feat, given the background and international stature of Kim Dae-jung.*

*Perhaps the most remarkable agreement between the two leaders concerned the role of the U.S. military. More than 37,000 U.S. troops had been stationed in South Korea since the end of the Korean War, a situation North Korea had repeatedly denounced as provocative. But at the summit, Kim Dae-jung later reported, the two leaders agreed that the U.S. military presence was important to maintaining the balance of power on the Korean peninsula. "The Korean people understand U.S. forces prevent another war on the Korean peninsula and contribute to regional stability," Kim told London's* Financial Times *newspaper in July. In August Kim told the* Washington Post *that the U.S. presence could prevent China, Japan, or Russia from becoming a dominant power in northeast Asia. If the United States were to withdraw, he told the* Post, *"that would create a huge vacuum that would draw these big countries into a fight over hegemony."*

## Post-Summit Developments

*Despite occasional outbursts of heated rhetoric from both sides, North and South Korea made limited progress during the second half of 2000 toward the lofty goals announced by the two Kims at the June summit. Senior diplomats and military officials from the two sides met in July, August, and September. After a senior North Korean intelligence official visited the South in mid-September, the two sides announced that Kim Jong Il would visit Seoul in the "near future," reportedly during the first half of 2001.*

*The first concrete sign of improved North-South relations following the summit was a mutual set of reunions of two hundred elderly Koreans who had been separated since the Korean War. For three days in mid-August, one hundred North Koreans visited with relatives in Seoul, while 100 South Koreans visited with relatives in Pyongyang. The two hundred people were among an estimated 10 million Koreans from either side of the border who had been separated from relatives since the Korean peninsula was divided in 1945.*

*Two other rounds of reunions were supposed to occur in early November and early December. But North Korea angrily postponed the November reunions after a South Korean Red Cross official made remarks that the North Korean Central News Agency called "slanderous." That dispute was resolved through diplomacy, and a second reunion took place for three days starting on November 30. Officials were hoping to schedule a third round of reunions early in 2001, and possibly others later. There was a sense of urgency because many of those separated from their families were quite elderly.*

*In another sign of improving relations, Kim Dae-jung on September 18 presided over the official opening of work to restore a rail link between the two countries. The rail line, replacing one that was dismantled shortly before the outbreak of the Korean War in 1950, would go through the heavily fortified border at the thirty-eighth parallel; it was scheduled to be completed in 2001.*

*On November 11 diplomats from the two Koreas signed economic treaties intended to encourage businesses from the South to invest in the North. Under the treaties, each country would offer legal protection to investments from the other side and would end double taxation. The two Koreas also agreed to appoint a committee to settle trade disputes and to open a direct electronic link for financial transactions.*

*Perhaps as much as anything else, the new era of inter-Korean relations was symbolized at the opening ceremony of the summer Olympics in Sidney, Australia. Athletes from the two Koreas marched together into the Olympic Stadium, wearing identical uniforms and following a neutral flag showing the Korean peninsula in blue against a white background. Athletes from the two countries competed separately during the Olympic games, however.*

*Following is the text of a joint statement issued June 15, 2000, in Pyongyang, North Korea, by Kim Dae-jung, president of South Korea, and North Korean leader Kim Jong Il (in his capacity as chairman of the country's National Defense Commission), in which the two leaders agreed to work toward unification of the two Koreas. The translation of the text was provided by the office of President Kim Dae-jung. The document was obtained from the Internet at http://www.cwd.go.kr/cgi-bin.*

## South-North Joint Declaration

In accordance with the noble will of the entire people who yearn for the peaceful reunification of the nation, President Kim Dae-jung of the Republic of Korea and National Defense Commission Chairman Kim Jong-il of the Democratic People's Republic of Korea held a historic meeting and summit talks in Pyongyang from June 13 to June 15, 2000.

The leaders of the South and the North, recognizing that the meeting and the summit talks, the first since the division of the country, were of great significance in promoting mutual understanding, developing South-North relations and realizing peaceful reunification, declared as follows:

1. The South and the North have agreed to resolve the question of reunification independently and through the joint efforts of the Korean people, who are the masters of the country.
2. Acknowledging that there is a common element in the South's proposal for a confederation and the North's proposal for a loose form of federation as the formulae for achieving reunification, the South and the North agreed to promote reunification in that direction.
3. The South and the North have agreed to promptly resolve humanitarian issues such as exchange visits by separated family members and relatives on the occasion of the August 15 National Liberation Day and the

       question of unswerving Communists who have been given long prison sentences in the South.

4. The South and the North have agreed to consolidate mutual trust by promoting balanced development of the national economy through economic cooperation and by stimulating cooperation and exchanges in civic, cultural, sports, public health, environmental and all other fields.

5. The South and the North have agreed to hold a dialogue between relevant authorities in the near future to implement the above agreement expeditiously. President Kim Dae-jung cordially invited National Defense Commission Chairman Kim Jong-il to visit Seoul, and Chairman Kim Jong-il decided to visit Seoul at an appropriate time.

(Signed)

Kim Dae-jung, President, The Republic of Korea National Defense Commission
Kim Jong-il, Chairman, National Defense Commission, the Democratic People's Republic of Korea

# SUPREME COURT ON
# PRAYER IN SCHOOL
## June 19, 2000

*The long-running controversy over prayer in public schools heated up again in 2000, when the Supreme Court ruled, 6–3, that a public school district's policy allowing an elected student representative to deliver a prayer before home football games was unconstitutional because it "has the improper effect of coercing those present to participate in an act of religious worship." When high school football games resumed in the fall, students and adults at many schools, primarily in the South, protested the ruling by leading Christian prayers in the stadium stands. In October a federal appeals court reinstated its earlier ruling upholding the right of students in an Alabama county to initiate prayer in classrooms and at public school events. The Supreme Court had asked the appeals court to reconsider its decision in light of the Court's ruling in the football case. Still pending before the same appeals court was a similar case from Florida that the Supreme Court had remanded for review. These decisions made it almost certain that the Supreme Court would be asked for further clarification on the circumstances under which students might pray aloud in public schools.*

*School prayer had been a divisive issue in the United States since 1962, when the Supreme Court first declared that officially sponsored prayer and religious observation in public school classrooms violated the First Amendment's prohibition on establishment of religion. Complaining that the Court was trying to make God unconstitutional, opponents of that decision tried unsuccessfully on several occasions to persuade Congress to adopt a constitutional amendment to permit public school prayer. Advocates of school prayer also searched for ways to circumvent the Court ruling, but to no avail. In 1963 the Court extended its prohibition to state-required daily recitations of the Lord's Prayer and Bible readings in public classrooms. Several states then replaced the daily prayer with a moment of silence, but in 1985 the Court ruled that moments of silence also violated the First Amendment if students were encouraged by the school or state to use that time for prayer.*

*In 1992 the Court ruled that a nonsectarian prayer delivered by a rabbi at a public school graduation violated the Establishment Clause because it had the effect of coercing youngsters to participate in a religious exercise. Afterward, Kenneth W. Starr, then the solicitor general who had argued for permitting such prayer, suggested that student-initiated prayers, unsupervised by school officials, might pass constitutional muster.* (Supreme Court on graduation prayer, Historic Documents of 1992, pp. 553)

## *Peanuts, Popcorn, and Prayer*

*The football prayer case,* Santa Fe Independent School District v. Doe, *was just such an attempt. It arose in the small community of Santa Fe, Texas, a predominantly Baptist town of about 8,500 people. Two families, one Mormon and one Catholic, filed a broad legal suit in 1995 claiming that their children's rights had been violated because school officials had encouraged students to attend revival meetings or to join religious clubs and that some students had been chastised for holding minority religious beliefs.*

*A federal district court judge in May 1995 issued an interim order that prohibited the school district from engaging in a variety of practices, such as using "blatantly religious denomination" lesson material in class. But the judge allowed students to select a speaker to deliver a nondenominational prayer at graduation. During the summer, the school board adopted a comparable policy for students to vote on whether to have invocations at football games and, if approved, then to elect one student to give the invocation for the entire season. As adopted, the policy made no specification about the content of the invocation. The policy, originally entitled "Prayer at Football Games," was amended in October to omit the word "prayer" and to refer to "messages" and "statements," as well as "invocations."*

*The students voted to have invocations at games and then elected a student to deliver them. But the federal district court barred the prayer at both graduation ceremonies and football games, arguing that it coerced student participation in religious events. Both the school district and the two families appealed to the Court of Appeals for the Fifth Circuit, which ruled that nonsectarian, nonproselytizing prayer approved by a vote of the students and delivered by a student was permissible at high school graduations, which were significant and solemn occasions. The Fifth Circuit barred similar prayer at football games, which, the appeals court said, were "hardly the sober type of annual event that can be appropriately solemnized with prayer." The Supreme Court agreed only to review the appeals court's ruling on student-led prayer at football games.*

## *An Improper Coercion*

*In its June 19 ruling, the Court's majority decisively rejected the school district's efforts to defend its policy as neutral toward religion and the invocation itself as a student's private expression of religion. "The delivery of such a message—over the school's public address system, by a speaker representing the student body, under the supervision of school faculty, and pursuant to a school policy that explicitly and implicitly encourages public prayer—is not properly characterized as 'private' speech," said Justice John Paul Stevens. Moreover, Stevens said, the "delivery of a pregame prayer has the improper effect of coercing those present to participate in an act of religious worship." Stevens's opinion was joined by Justices Sandra Day O'Connor, Anthony M. Kennedy, David H. Souter, Ruth Bader Ginsburg, and Stephen G. Breyer.*

*Stevens also rejected the school's contention that student attendance at football games was voluntary and therefore the invocation could not be considered "coercive." Stevens first observed that, in fact, many students— including the football players, cheerleaders, and band members—were required to attend, sometimes for class credit. For many others, he continued, high school home football games were "traditional gatherings" of students and faculty, family and friends, young and old, "to root for a common cause." A school may not constitutionally force a student to choose between "whether to attend these games or to risk facing a personally offensive religious ritual."*

*Stevens stressed—both in his written opinion and in his summary from the bench—that the Constitution did not bar all religious activity in public schools. Nothing prevented "any public school student from voluntarily praying at any time before, during, or after the school day," Stevens wrote. The dissenters were not mollified. The majority's opinion "bristles with hostility to all things religious in public life," wrote Chief Justice William H. Rehnquist for himself and Justices Antonin Scalia and Clarence Thomas.*

*The rest of Rehnquist's dissent, however, was short and narrow in scope. The school's policy had "plausible secular purposes" and could have been implemented in a neutral manner, he said. On that basis, Rehnquist said, the policy should have allowed to go into effect and blocked only if it was applied in an unconstitutional manner.*

*Republican presidential contender and Texas governor George W. Bush called the ruling "disappointing" and said he supported the "constitutionally guaranteed right of all students to express their faith freely and participate in voluntary, student-led prayer." According to an ABC News Poll conducted in March on the eve of arguments before the Supreme Court, two-thirds of the American public essentially agreed with Bush. His Democratic opponent, Vice President Al Gore, said through a spokesperson that he supported the decision. School board member John Couch II called the decision "disappointing, disturbing, and disillusioning." But the ruling elated a friend of the families who filed the suit. "This time it was football games, next it could have been a classroom," she said. "This school district knew what is was doing and kept pushing and pushing."*

## Continuing Challenge

*A week after ruling in the Santa Fe case, the Supreme Court on June 26 set aside a ruling from the Eleventh Circuit Court of Appeals that permitted public school students in DeKalb County, Alabama, to lead prayers over the student intercom and at graduations, student assemblies, and sports events. The justice asked the lower court to review the case in light of their ruling in the Santa Fe case. On October 2 the Supreme Court set aside a second decision by the Eleventh Circuit and asked the lower court to review that de-*

*cision, too, in light of the Santa Fe holding. That decision involved a public school policy in Duval County, Florida, in place since 1993, that allowed high school seniors to decide whether to choose a fellow student to give a "brief opening and/or closing message" at the graduation ceremony. The student would decide the message's content with no review by school officials.*

*Three weeks later, on October 19, the appeals court responded to the first remand by reinstating its original ruling in the Alabama case, saying it was consistent with the Santa Fe ruling. "Private speech endorsing religion is constitutionally protected—even in school," the appeals court said. "Such speech is not the school's speech even though it may occur in school. Such speech is not unconstitutionally coercive, even though it may occur before nonbeliever students." The Constitution, the court continued, "does not permit the state to confine religious speech to whispers or banish it to broom closets. If it did, the exercise of one's religion would not be free at all."*

*Opponents of school prayer said the appeals court was "thumbing its nose" at the Supreme Court. "When the nation's highest court vacates a ruling and says to write a new opinion according to what we are telling you is the law, you would expect the lower federal courts to take heed of that rather than defy the U.S. Supreme Court," said an attorney for the American Civil Liberties Union who had filed the original case. Alabama attorney general Bill Pryor, who argued for the reinstatement of the appeals court decision, disagreed that the reinstatement was in conflict with the Supreme Court holding. "This is the flip side of Santa Fe," he said. "For the same reason a school cannot sponsor a prayer or religious speech, it also cannot censor a prayer or religious speech. What the court does not want to see is the use of school machinery to choose who is leading the prayer or to set it up."*

*Following are excerpts from the majority opinion and dissent in the case of* Santa Fe Independent School District v. Doe, *in which the Supreme Court, by a 6–3 vote on June 19, held that a student-led, sudden-initiated prayer at public high school football games violated the First Amendment's Establishment Clause. The document was obtained from the Internet at http://www .supremecourtus.gov/opinions/99pdf/99-62.pdf.*

No. 99-62

| | |
|---|---|
| Santa Fe Independent School District, Petitioner <br> v. <br> Jane Doe, individually and as next friend for her minor children, Jane and John Doe et al. | On writ of certiorari to the United States Court of Appeals for the Fifth Circuit |

[June 19, 2000]

JUSTICE STEVENS delivered the opinion of the Court.

Prior to 1995, the Santa Fe High School student who occupied the school's elective office of student council chaplain delivered a prayer over the public address system before each varsity football game for the entire season. This practice, along with others, was challenged in District Court as a violation of the Establishment Clause of the First Amendment. While these proceedings were pending in the District Court, the school district adopted a different policy that permits, but does not require, prayer initiated and led by a student at all home games. The District Court entered an order modifying that policy to permit only nonsectarian, nonproselytizing prayer. The Court of Appeals held that, even as modified by the District Court, the football prayer policy was invalid. We granted the school district's petition for certiorari to review that holding.

# I

The Santa Fe Independent School District (District) is a political subdivision of the State of Texas, responsible for the education of more than 4,000 students in a small community in the southern part of the State. . . . Respondents are two sets of current or former students and their respective mothers. One family is Mormon and the other is Catholic. The District Court permitted respondents (Does) to litigate anonymously to protect them from intimidation or harassment.

Respondents commenced this action in April 1995 and moved for a temporary restraining order to prevent the District from violating the Establishment Clause at the imminent graduation exercises. In their complaint the Does alleged that the District had engaged in several proselytizing practices, such as promoting attendance at a Baptist revival meeting, encouraging membership in religious clubs, chastising children who held minority religious beliefs, and distributing Gideon Bibles on school premises. They also alleged that the District allowed students to read Christian invocations and benedictions from the stage at graduation ceremonies, and to deliver overtly Christian prayers over the public address system at home football games.

On May 10, 1995, the District Court entered an interim order addressing a number of different issues. With respect to the impending graduation, the order provided that "non-denominational prayer" consisting of "an invocation and/or benediction" could be presented by a senior student or students selected by members of the graduating class. The text of the prayer was to be determined by the students, without scrutiny or preapproval by school officials. References to particular religious figures "such as Mohammed, Jesus, Buddha, or the like" would be permitted "as long as the general thrust of the prayer is non-proselytizing."

In response to that portion of the order, the District adopted a series of policies over several months dealing with prayer at school functions. The policies enacted in May and July for graduation ceremonies provided the format for the August and October policies for football games. The May policy provided:

> "The board has chosen to permit the graduating senior class, with the advice and counsel of the senior class principal or designee, to elect by secret ballot to choose

whether an invocation and benediction shall be part of the graduation exercise. If so chosen the class shall elect by secret ballot, from a list of student volunteers, students to deliver nonsectarian, nonproselytizing invocations and benedictions for the purpose of solemnizing their graduation ceremonies."

The parties stipulated that after this policy was adopted, "the senior class held an election to determine whether to have an invocation and benediction at the commencement [and that the] class voted, by secret ballot, to include prayer at the high school graduation." In a second vote the class elected two seniors to deliver the invocation and benediction.

In July, the District enacted another policy eliminating the requirement that invocations and benedictions be "nonsectarian and nonproselytising," but also providing that if the District were to be enjoined from enforcing that policy, the May policy would automatically become effective.

The August policy, which was titled "Prayer at Football Games," was similar to the July policy for graduations. It also authorized two student elections, the first to determine whether "invocations" should be delivered, and the second to select the spokesperson to deliver them. Like the July policy, it contained two parts, an initial statement that omitted any requirement that the content of the invocation be "nonsectarian and nonproselytising," and a fallback provision that automatically added that limitation if the preferred policy should be enjoined. On August 31, 1995, according to the parties' stipulation, "the district's high school students voted to determine whether a student would deliver prayer at varsity football games. . . . The students chose to allow a student to say a prayer at football games." A week later, in a separate election, they selected a student "to deliver the prayer at varsity football games."

The final policy (October policy) is essentially the same as the August policy, though it omits the word "prayer" from its title, and refers to "messages" and "statements" as well as "invocations." It is the validity of that policy that is before us.

The District Court did enter an order precluding enforcement of the first, open-ended policy. Relying on our decision in *Lee v. Weisman* (1992), it held that the school's "action must not 'coerce anyone to support or participate in' a religious exercise." Applying that test, it concluded that the graduation prayers appealed "to distinctively Christian beliefs," and that delivering a prayer "over the school's public address system prior to each football and baseball game coerces student participation in religious events." Both parties appealed, the District contending that the enjoined portion of the October policy was permissible and the Does contending that both alternatives violated the Establishment Clause. The Court of Appeals majority agreed with the Does.

The decision of the Court of Appeals followed Fifth Circuit precedent that had announced two rules. In *Jones v. Clear Creek Independent School Dist.* (1992), that court held that student-led prayer that was approved by a vote of the students and was nonsectarian and nonproselytizing was permissible at high school graduation ceremonies. On the other hand, in later cases the Fifth Circuit made it clear that the Clear Creek rule applied only to high school graduations and that school-encouraged prayer was constitutionally impermissible at school-related sporting events. . . .

We granted the District's petition for certiorari, limited to the following question: "Whether petitioner's policy permitting student-led, student-initiated prayer at football games violates the Establishment Clause." (1999). We conclude, as did the Court of Appeals, that it does.

## II

The first Clause in the First Amendment to the Federal Constitution provides that "Congress shall make no law respecting an establishment of religion, or prohibiting the free exercise thereof." The Fourteenth Amendment imposes those substantive limitations on the legislative power of the States and their political subdivisions. In *Lee v. Weisman* (1992), we held that a prayer delivered by a rabbi at a middle school graduation ceremony violated that Clause. . . .

As we held in that case:

> "The principle that government may accommodate the free exercise of religion does not supersede the fundamental limitations imposed by the Establishment Clause. It is beyond dispute that, at a minimum, the Constitution guarantees that government may not coerce anyone to support or participate in religion or its exercise, or otherwise act in a way which 'establishes a [state] religion or religious faith, or tends to do so.'"

In this case the District first argues that this principle is inapplicable to its October policy because the messages are private student speech, not public speech. . . . [W]e are not persuaded that the pregame invocations should be regarded as "private speech."

These invocations are authorized by a government policy and take place on government property at government-sponsored school-related events. . . . [T]he school allows only one student, the same student for the entire season, to give the invocation. The statement or invocation, moreover, is subject to particular regulations that confine the content and topic of the student's message. . . .

Granting only one student access to the stage at a time does not, of course, necessarily preclude a finding that a school has created a limited public forum. Here, however, Santa Fe's student election system ensures that only those messages deemed "appropriate" under the District's policy may be delivered. That is, the majoritarian process implemented by the District guarantees, by definition, that minority candidates will never prevail and that their views will be effectively silenced. . . .

In *Lee*, the school district made the related argument that its policy of endorsing only "civic or nonsectarian" prayer was acceptable because it minimized the intrusion on the audience as a whole. We rejected that claim by explaining that such a majoritarian policy "does not lessen the offense or isolation to the objectors. At best it narrows their number, at worst increases their sense of isolation and affront." Similarly, while Santa Fe's majoritarian election might ensure that most of the students are represented, it does nothing to protect the minority; indeed, it likely serves to intensify their offense.

Moreover, the District has failed to divorce itself from the religious content in the invocations. . . . Contrary to the District's repeated assertions that it has adopted a "hands-off" approach to the pregame invocation, the realities of the situation plainly reveal that its policy involves both perceived and actual endorsement of religion. In this case, as we found in *Lee*, the "degree of school involvement" makes it clear that the pregame prayers bear "the imprint of the State and thus put school-age children who objected in an untenable position."

The District has attempted to disentangle itself from the religious messages by developing the two-step student election process. The text of the October policy, however, exposes the extent of the school's entanglement. . . . Even though the particular words used by the speaker are not determined by those votes, the policy mandates that the "statement or invocation" be "consistent with the goals and purposes of this policy," which are "to solemnize the event, to promote good sportsmanship and student safety, and to establish the appropriate environment for the competition."

In addition to involving the school in the selection of the speaker, the policy, by its terms, invites and encourages religious messages. The policy itself states that the purpose of the message is "to solemnize the event." A religious message is the most obvious method of solemnizing an event. Moreover, the requirements that the message "promote good citizenship" and "establish the appropriate environment for competition" further narrow the types of message deemed appropriate. . . . Thus, the expressed purposes of the policy encourage the selection of a religious message, and that is precisely how the students understand the policy. . . . We recognize the important role that public worship plays in many communities, as well as the sincere desire to include public prayer as a part of various occasions so as to mark those occasions' significance. But such religious activity in public schools, as elsewhere, must comport with the First Amendment.

The actual or perceived endorsement of the message, moreover, is established by factors beyond just the text of the policy. Once the student speaker is selected and the message composed, the invocation is then delivered to a large audience assembled as part of a regularly scheduled, school-sponsored function conducted on school property. The message is broadcast over the school's public address system, which remains subject to the control of school officials. It is fair to assume that the pregame ceremony is clothed in the traditional indicia of school sporting events, which generally include not just the team, but also cheerleaders and band members dressed in uniforms sporting the school name and mascot. The school's name is likely written in large print across the field and on banners and flags. The crowd will certainly include many who display the school colors and insignia on their school T-shirts, jackets, or hats and who may also be waving signs displaying the school name. It is in a setting such as this that "[t]he board has chosen to permit" the elected student to rise and give the "statement or invocation."

In this context the members of the listening audience must perceive the pregame message as a public expression of the views of the majority of the student body delivered with the approval of the school administration. . . . Regardless of the listener's support for, or objection to, the message, an objective Santa Fe High School student will unquestionably perceive the inevitable pregame prayer as stamped with her school's seal of approval.

The text and history of this policy, moreover, reinforce our objective student's perception that the prayer is, in actuality, encouraged by the school. . . .

According to the District, the secular purposes of the policy are to "foste[r] free expression of private persons . . . as well [as to] solemniz[e] sporting events, promot[e] good sportsmanship and student safety, and establis[h] an appropriate environment for competition." We note, however, that the District's approval of only one specific kind of message, an "invocation," is not necessary to further any of these purposes. Additionally, the fact that only one student is permitted to give a content-limited message suggests that this policy does little to "foste[r] free expression." Furthermore, regardless of whether one considers a sporting event an appropriate occasion for solemnity, the use of an invocation to foster such solemnity is impermissible when, in actuality, it constitutes prayer sponsored by the school. And it is unclear what type of message would be both appropriately "solemnizing" under the District's policy and yet non-religious.

Most striking to us is the evolution of the current policy from the long-sanctioned office of "Student Chaplain" to the candidly titled "Prayer at Football Games" regulation. This history indicates that the District intended to preserve the practice of prayer before football games. The conclusion that the District viewed the October policy simply as a continuation of the previous policies is dramatically illustrated by the fact that the school did not conduct a new election, pursuant to the current policy, to replace the results of the previous election, which occurred under the former policy. Given these observations, and in light of the school's history of regular delivery of a student-led prayer at athletic events, it is reasonable to infer that the specific purpose of the policy was to preserve a popular "state-sponsored religious practice."

School sponsorship of a religious message is impermissible because it sends the ancillary message to members of the audience who are nonadherents "that they are outsiders, not full members of the political community, and an accompanying message to adherents that they are insiders, favored members of the political community." The delivery of such a message—over the school's public address system, by a speaker representing the student body, under the supervision of school faculty, and pursuant to a school policy that explicitly and implicitly encourages public prayer—is not properly characterized as "private" speech.

## III

The District next argues that its football policy is distinguishable from the graduation prayer in *Lee* because it does not coerce students to participate in religious observances. Its argument has two parts: first, that there is no impermissible government coercion because the pregame messages are the product of student choices; and second, that there is really no coercion at all because attendance at an extracurricular event, unlike a graduation ceremony, is voluntary.

The reasons just discussed explaining why the alleged "circuit-breaker" mechanism of the dual elections and student speaker do not turn public speech into private speech also demonstrate why these mechanisms do not insulate the school from the coercive element of the final message. In fact, this aspect of the District's argument exposes anew the concerns that are created by the majoritarian election system. The parties' stipulation clearly states that the issue resolved in the first election was "whether a student would deliver prayer at varsity football games," and the controversy in this case demonstrates that the views of the students are not unanimous on that issue.

One of the purposes served by the Establishment Clause is to remove debate over this kind of issue from governmental supervision or control. . . . The two student elections authorized by the policy, coupled with the debates that presumably must precede each, impermissibly invade that private sphere. The election mechanism, when considered in light of the history in which the policy in question evolved, reflects a device the District put in place that determines whether religious messages will be delivered at home football games. The mechanism encourages divisiveness along religious lines in a public school setting, a result at odds with the Establishment Clause. Although it is true that the ultimate choice of student speaker is "attributable to the students," the District's decision to hold the constitutionally problematic election is clearly "a choice attributable to the State."

The District further argues that attendance at the commencement ceremonies at issue in *Lee* "differs dramatically" from attendance at high school football games, which it contends "are of no more than passing interest to many students" and are "decidedly extracurricular," thus dissipating any coercion. Attendance at a high school football game, unlike showing up for class, is certainly not required in order to receive a diploma. Moreover, we may assume that the District is correct in arguing that the informal pressure to attend an athletic event is not as strong as a senior's desire to attend her own graduation ceremony.

There are some students, however, such as cheerleaders, members of the band, and, of course, the team members themselves, for whom seasonal commitments mandate their attendance, sometimes for class credit. The District also minimizes the importance to many students of attending and participating in extracurricular activities as part of a complete educational experience. . . . High school home football games are traditional gatherings of a school community; they bring together students and faculty as well as friends and family from years present and past to root for a common cause. Undoubtedly, the games are not important to some students, and they voluntarily choose not to attend. For many others, however, the choice between whether to attend these games or to risk facing a personally offensive religious ritual is in no practical sense an easy one. The Constitution, moreover, demands that the school may not force this difficult choice upon these students. . . .

Even if we regard every high school student's decision to attend a home football game as purely voluntary, we are nevertheless persuaded that the delivery of a pregame prayer has the improper effect of coercing those present to participate in an act of religious worship. . . . As in *Lee*, "[w]hat to most believers may seem nothing more than a reasonable request that the nonbeliever respect their religious practices, in a school context may appear to the nonbeliever or dissenter to be an attempt to employ the machinery of the State to enforce a religious orthodoxy." The constitutional command will not permit the District "to exact religious conformity from a student as the price" of joining her classmates at a varsity football game.

The Religion Clauses of the First Amendment prevent the government from making any law respecting the establishment of religion or prohibiting the free exercise thereof. By no means do these commands impose a prohibition on all religious activity in our public schools. [Citation of cases omitted.] . . . [N]othing in the Constitution as interpreted by this Court prohibits any public school student from voluntarily praying at any time before, during, or after the schoolday. But the religious liberty protected by the Constitution is abridged when the State affirmatively sponsors the particular religious practice of prayer.

# IV

Finally, the District argues repeatedly that the Does have made a premature facial challenge to the October policy that necessarily must fail. The District emphasizes, quite correctly, that until a student actually delivers a solemnizing message under the latest version of the policy, there can be no certainty that any of the statements or invocations will be religious. Thus, it concludes, the October policy necessarily survives a facial challenge.

This argument, however, assumes that we are concerned only with the serious constitutional injury that occurs when a student is forced to participate in an act of religious worship because she chooses to attend a school event. But the Constitution also requires that we keep in mind "the myriad, subtle ways in which Establishment Clause values can be eroded," and that we guard against other different, yet equally important, constitutional injuries. One is the mere passage by the District of a policy that has the purpose and perception of government establishment of religion. Another is the implementation of a governmental electoral process that subjects the issue of prayer to a majoritarian vote.

. . . [T]he text of the October policy alone reveals that it has an unconstitutional purpose. The plain language of the policy clearly spells out the extent of school involvement in both the election of the speaker and the content of the message. Additionally, the text of the October policy specifies only one, clearly preferred message—that of Santa Fe's traditional religious "invocation." Finally, the extremely selective access of the policy and other content restrictions confirm that it is not a content-neutral regulation that creates a limited public forum for the expression of student speech.

. . . [T]he simple enactment of this policy, with the purpose and perception of school endorsement of student prayer, was a constitutional violation. We need not wait for the inevitable to confirm and magnify the constitutional injury. . . . [E]ven if no Santa Fe High School student were ever to offer a religious message, the October policy fails a facial challenge because the attempt by the District to encourage prayer is also at issue. Government efforts to endorse religion cannot evade constitutional reproach based solely on the remote possibility that those attempts may fail.

This policy likewise does not survive a facial challenge because it impermissibly imposes upon the student body a majoritarian election on the issue of prayer. Through its election scheme, the District has established a governmental electoral mechanism that turns the school into a forum for religious debate. It further empowers the student body majority with the authority to subject students of minority views to constitutionally improper messages. . . . Such a system encourages divisiveness along religious lines and threatens the imposition of coercion upon those students not desiring to participate in a religious exercise. Simply by establishing this school-related procedure, which entrusts the inherently nongovernmental subject of religion to a majoritarian vote, a constitutional violation has occurred. . . .

. . . [T]his policy does not provide the District with the constitutional safe harbor it sought. The policy is invalid on its face because it establishes an improper majoritarian election on religion, and unquestionably has the purpose and creates the perception of encouraging the delivery of prayer at a series of important school events.

The judgment of the Court of Appeals is, accordingly, affirmed.

*It is so ordered.*

CHIEF JUSTICE REHNQUIST, with whom JUSTICE SCALIA and JUSTICE THOMAS join, dissenting.

The Court distorts existing precedent to conclude that the school district's student-message program is invalid on its face under the Establishment Clause. But even more disturbing than its holding is the tone of the Court's opinion; it bristles with hostility to all things religious in public life. Neither the holding nor the tone of the opinion is faithful to the meaning of the Establishment Clause, when it is recalled that George Washington himself, at the request of the very Congress which passed the Bill of Rights, proclaimed a day of "public thanksgiving and prayer, to be observed by acknowledging with grateful hearts the many and signal favors of Almighty God."

We do not learn until late in the Court's opinion that respondents in this case challenged the district's student-message program at football games before it had been put into practice. . . . No speech will be "chilled" by the existence of a government policy that might unconstitutionally endorse religion over nonreligion.

Therefore, the question is not whether the district's policy may be applied in violation of the Establishment Clause, but whether it inevitably will be.

The Court, venturing into the realm of prophesy, decides that it "need not wait for the inevitable" and invalidates the district's policy on its face. . . .

. . . The Court applies *Lemon* and holds that the "policy is invalid on its face because it establishes an improper majoritarian election on religion, and unquestionably has the purpose and creates the perception of encouraging the delivery of prayer at a series of important school events." The Court's reliance on each of these conclusions misses the mark.

First, the Court misconstrues the nature of the "majoritarian election" permitted by the policy as being an election on "prayer" and "religion." To the contrary, the election permitted by the policy is a two-fold process whereby students vote first on whether to have a student speaker before football games at all, and second, if the students vote to have such a speaker, on who that speaker will be. It is conceivable that the election could become one in which student candidates campaign on platforms that focus on whether or not they will pray if elected. It is also conceivable that the election could lead to a Christian prayer before 90 percent of the football games. If, upon implementation, the policy operated in this fashion, we would have a record before us to review whether the policy, as applied, violated the Establishment Clause or unduly suppressed minority viewpoints. But it is possible that the students might vote not to have a pregame speaker, in which case there would be no threat of a constitutional violation. It is also possible that the election would not focus on prayer, but on public speaking ability or social popularity. And if student campaigning did begin to focus on prayer, the school might decide to implement reasonable campaign restrictions.

But the Court ignores these possibilities by holding that merely granting the student body the power to elect a speaker that may choose to pray, "regardless of the students' ultimate use of it, is not acceptable." The Court so holds despite that any speech that may occur as a result of the election process here would be private, not government, speech. The elected student, not the government, would choose what to say. Support for the Court's holding cannot be found in any of our cases. And it essentially invalidates all student elections. A newly elected student body president, or even a newly elected prom king or queen, could use opportunities for public speaking to say prayers. Under the Court's view, the mere grant of power to the students to vote for such offices, in light of the fear that those elected might publicly pray, violates the Establishment Clause.

Second . . . the Court holds that "the simple enactment of this policy, with the purpose and perception of school endorsement of student prayer, was a constitutional violation." But the policy itself has plausible secular purposes: "[T]o solemnize the event, to promote good sportsmanship and student safety, and to establish the appropriate environment for the competition." . . . The Court grants no deference to—and appears openly hostile toward—the policy's stated purposes, and wastes no time in concluding that they are a sham.

For example, the Court dismisses the secular purpose of solemnization by claiming that it "invites and encourages religious messages." . . . The Court so concludes based on its rather strange view that a "religious message is the most obvious means of solemnizing an event." But it is easy to think of solemn messages that are not religious in nature, for example urging that a game be fought fairly. And sporting events often begin with a solemn rendition of our national anthem, with its concluding verse "And this be our motto: 'In God is our trust.' " Under the Court's logic, a public school that sponsors the singing of the national anthem before football games violates the Establishment

Clause. Although the Court apparently believes that solemnizing football games is an illegitimate purpose, the voters in the school district seem to disagree. Nothing in the Establishment Clause prevents them from making this choice.

The Court bases its conclusion that the true purpose of the policy is to endorse student prayer on its view of the school district's history of Establishment Clause violations and the context in which the policy was written, that is, as "the latest step in developing litigation brought as a challenge to institutional practices that unquestionably violated the Establishment Clause." But the context—attempted compliance with a District Court order—actually demonstrates that the school district was acting diligently to come within the governing constitutional law. The District Court ordered the school district to formulate a policy consistent with Fifth Circuit precedent, which permitted a school district to have a prayer-only policy. But the school district went further than required by the District Court order and eventually settled on a policy that gave the student speaker a choice to deliver either an invocation or a message. In so doing, the school district exhibited a willingness to comply with, and exceed, Establishment Clause restrictions. Thus, the policy cannot be viewed as having a sectarian purpose.

The Court also relies on our decision in *Lee v. Weisman* to support its conclusion. In *Lee*, we concluded that the content of the speech at issue, a graduation prayer given by a rabbi, was "directed and controlled" by a school official. In other words, at issue in *Lee* was *government* speech. Here, by contrast, the potential speech at issue, if the policy had been allowed to proceed, would be a message or invocation selected or created by a student. That is, if there were speech at issue here, it would be *private* speech. . . .

Had the policy been put into practice, the students may have chosen a speaker according to wholly secular criteria—like good public speaking skills or social popularity—and the student speaker may have chosen, on her own accord, to deliver a religious message. Such an application of the policy would likely pass constitutional muster. . . .

The policy at issue here may be applied in an unconstitutional manner, but it will be time enough to invalidate it if that is found to be the case. I would reverse the judgment of the Court of Appeals.

# NASA REPORT ON THE POSSIBILITY OF WATER ON MARS
## June 22, 2000

*Nearly three decades after the first Earth-based explorations found Mars to be a cold and dry planet hostile to any conceivable forms of life, findings announced in 2000 fostered renewed speculation that the red planet might have some of the conditions necessary for life, after all. Scientists analyzing data sent back to Earth by the* Mars Global Surveyor *concluded that large quantities of frozen water might lie just beneath the Martian surface. They based that conclusion on images appearing to show the consequences of sudden water flows that likely occurred in relatively recent times.*

*The findings contributed to a decision by the National Aeronautics and Space Administration (NASA) to plan two missions to Mars in 2003, each carrying a roving robot that would analyze surface soil and rocks. The rovers would cover much more Martian territory than the successful* Sojourner *robot, which covered only a few hundred feet of surface during eighty-three days of operation in 1997.*

*In addition, NASA planned to launch a new orbiting spacecraft,* 2001 Mars Odyssey, *early in 2001. Once in orbit around Mars, starting in late October 2001, that craft was assigned to study physical features indicating the presence of underground water and ice and to measure radiation in the atmosphere. NASA officials hoped the new missions would put the agency's Mars exploration program back on track, followed embarrassing failures late in 1999.* (Mars program failures, p. 88)

### *Looking for Water on Mars*

*Mars had long been considered the one planet in the solar system most likely to harbor a form of life recognizable to those on Earth. The increasing sophistication of telescopes in the 1800s led to the conclusion that Mars had polar ice caps that expanded and contracted with the seasons; later observations showed that the ice caps were composed primarily of dry ice, not frozen water. Speculation about Mars reached a fever pitch in the late 1880s after an Italian astronomer claimed to have found* canali *("channels" in Ital-*

*ian) on the surface—a word that, when mistranslated into English, implied the existence of artificially made "canals."*

*The development of increasingly more powerful telescopes gradually showed that Mars had no canals, not to mention rivers, swamps, or cities. The* Mariner 4 *spacecraft, which circled Mars in 1965, and then the* Viking 1 *and* Viking 2 *spacecraft, which landed on Mars in 1976, sent back images and other data showing a dry and rocky Martian landscape apparently inhospitable to any form of life known on Earth.*

*Then in 1996 NASA announced that a meteor, presumed to have originated on Mars, contained molecules that appeared to represent a very crude form of life. Some scientists expressed deep skepticism that the finding implied the existence of life on Mars. Studies of the potato-size rock were continuing in 2000. Other scientific teams reported evidence from* Global Surveyor *in 1999 and 2000 indicating that volcanic activity on Mars might have continued until much more recently than previous studies had assumed. A still-warm interior would increase the prospects that life existed on Mars.* Global Surveyor's *close-up images also confirmed speculation that vast oceans existed on Mars billions of years ago, when the planet was young and had a denser atmosphere than in modern times.* (Life on Mars, Historic Documents of 1996, p. 471; first reports from *Global Surveyor*, Historic Documents of 1999, p. 175).

## *Global Surveyor* Images

Global Surveyor, *an orbiting satellite, reached Mars in 1997 and, after technical adjustments to its equipment, began sending images and other findings back to Earth in 1998. Beginning in mid-1999, a camera developed for* Global Surveyor *by Malin Space Science Systems, a San Diego research company, snapped images that appeared to show gullies on Mars, similar to gullies on Earth caused by rapid surges of water down hills or mountains. In general, the Martian gully formations appeared to start as triangle-shaped alcoves high on the slopes of craters and hills. V-shaped channels ran downhill from these alcoves and ended in what geologist called an "apron" or delta-like formation of rocks and other debris.*

*Scientists Michael C. Malin and Kenneth S. Edgett said at a NASA-sponsored news conference on June 22 that they at first were reluctant to believe the Martian gullies could have been caused by water, simply because there was no evidence of liquid water on Mars. In addition, they noted that most of the gullies appeared on the coldest parts of Mars, where water was least likely to exist in liquid form—toward the two Martian poles and on slopes facing away from the Sun.*

*But as more images arrived from* Global Surveyor *showing the gully-type features, the two researchers intensified their search for possible explanations. Edgett said he ultimately was "dragged kicking and screaming" to the conclusion that the gullies were caused by water. The two developed a theory that water existed in porous layers of rocks within a few hundred meters of the Martian surface, and that pressure from the rocky layers kept the water from freezing. Gradually, some of the water would seep through the layers of rock, freezing into an ice dam once it reached the surface. But water would continue to seep toward the surface, with the pressure eventually blowing away the ice dam and causing a sudden surge of water downhill, which would create the gullies. The water would then vaporize in the thin Martian atmosphere.*

*Malin and Edgett said they believed the Martian gullies were of relatively recent vintage because none showed the pockmarks of craters and some swept through sand dunes, which were in a constant state of change on a planet frequently swept by massive, prolonged dust storms. Malin said the gullies could have formed as long ago as a million years or as recently as the day before. But it was unlikely that the gullies dated from Mars' youth as a planet, many billions of years ago, he said.*

*Edward J. Weiler, the NASA associate administrator for science, said the release of Malin and Edgett's findings was "the first step in the science process" of evaluating the evidence. If further research and exploration showed the current existence of water near the surface of Mars, "it has profound implications for the possibilities of life on Mars," he said.*

*Weiler cautioned against reading too much into the finding that water might exist on Mars. "They have not found lakes or rivers flowing on Mars," he told reporters. "They have not found hot springs. They certainly have not found hot tubs with Martians in them."*

*Despite his caution, Weiler acknowledged that the findings might build pressure for eventual human exploration of Mars. In addition to the lure of searching for life there, humans might be able to tap the water for drinking or conversion to oxygen for breathing and hydrogen for rocket fuel.*

## Reaction and Skepticism

*Immediately after the public release of the Mars "gully" images, some scientists expressed deep skepticism about the theory propounded by Malin and Edgett. Michael H. Carr, a planetary geologist with the U.S. Geological Survey in Menlo Park, California, told the* New York Times *that he believed any water near the frigid Martian surface would have to be frozen and could not possibly be in liquid form, as Malin and Edgett had surmised. "Either this interpretation is wrong or there is some mechanism we don't know of to keep water liquid under these conditions," Carr told the newspaper.*

*Another planetary geologist for the U.S. Geological Survey, Kenneth L. Tanaka, warned against applying Earth-based explanations to observations of a place as distant as Mars. "We shouldn't forget that this is another planet," he said. "We haven't set foot on it."*

*Yet another potential challenge to the thesis posed by Malin and Edgett came from the work of another NASA scientist, Pascal Lee, a geologist at the agency's Ames Research Center. According to an October 31 report by the* Boston Globe, *Lee for four years had been conducting research on Canada's Devon Island, in the Arctic Ocean—a location said to be remarkably similar to the surface of Mars. The newspaper said Lee had photographed geological formations on the island that appeared to be identical to those found by Malin and Edgett on Mars. The formations on Devon Island were not caused by the seepage of water, Lee said, but by the melting of patches of snow. As a result, Lee surmised that the Martian formations might have developed more than 100,000 years ago, the most recent time that scientists believed snow could have fallen on that planet.*

### *Martian Lakes?*

*In a follow-up announcement on December 4 NASA reported that Malin and Edgett had photographed numerous examples of what appeared to be sedimentary rock on Mars. The photographs presented "irrefutable evidence" that sedimentary rocks are widespread on Mars, Malin said, and those rocks "may have formed in lakes and shallow seas" during the distant past.*

*Photographs released by NASA showed terraced hills and craters that appeared to be layers of sedimentary rock, such as those on Earth at the bottom of ancient lakes and oceans. Malin and Edgett speculated that the sedimentary layers might be 3.5 million to 4.5 million years old. "These images tell us that early Mars was very dynamic and may have been a lot more like Earth than many of us have been thinking," Malin said.*

*Scientists who studied the latest photographs noted that any fossils of early life forms on Mars—if they existed at all—were most likely preserved in sedimentary layers such as those photographed by* Global Surveyor. *On Earth the beds of prehistoric lakes and oceans yielded fossils of thousands of creatures and plants, many of which are now extinct.*

*Malin and Edgett said it was possible that wind or volcanic eruptions on Mars created the newly photographed landforms. But they said it was much more likely that the Martian terraces were the work of ancient bodies of water that evaporated when the planet's atmosphere became too thin to sustain surface water.*

> *Following is the text of an announcement, released by the National Aeronautics and Space Administration on June 22, 2000, reporting findings from the* Mars Global Surveyor *indicating that liquid water might have caused the gully-type formations on Mars. The document was obtained from the Internet at ftp://ftp.hq .nasa.gov/pub/pao/pressrel/2000/00-099.txt.*

## New Images Suggest Present-Day Sources of Liquid Water on Mars

In what could turn out to be a landmark discovery in the history of Mars exploration, imaging scientists using data from NASA's *Mars Global Surveyor* spacecraft have recently observed features that suggest there may be current sources of liquid water at or near the surface of the red planet.

The new images, available at http://www.jpl.nasa.gov/pictures/mars or http://www.msss.com/mars_images/moc/june2000/, show the smallest fea-

tures ever observed from Martian orbit—about the size of a sport-utility vehicle. NASA scientists compare the features to those left by flash floods on
Earth.

"We see features that look like gullies formed by flowing water and the de-
posits of soil and rocks transported by these flows. The features appear to be
so young that they might be forming today. We think we are seeing evidence
of a groundwater supply, similar to an aquifer," said Dr. Michael Malin, principal investigator for the Mars Orbiter Camera on the *Mars Global Surveyor*
spacecraft at Malin Space Science Systems, San Diego, Calif. "These are new
landforms that have never been seen before on Mars."

The findings will be published in the June 30 issue of *Science* magazine.

"Twenty-eight years ago the Mariner 9 spacecraft found evidence—in the
form of channels and valleys—that billions of years ago the planet had water
flowing across its surface," said Dr. Ken Edgett, staff scientist at Malin Space
Science Systems and co-author of the paper in Science. "Ever since that time,
Mars science has focused on the question, 'Where did the water go?' The new
pictures from *Global Surveyor* tell us part of the answer—some of that water
went under ground, and quite possibly it's still there."

"For two decades scientists have debated whether liquid water might have
existed on the surface of Mars just a few billion years ago," said Dr. Ed Weiler,
associate administrator for space science at NASA Headquarters. "With today's discovery, we're no longer talking about a distant time. The debate has
moved to present-day Mars. The presence of liquid water on Mars has profound implications for the question of life not only in the past, but perhaps
even today. If life ever did develop there, and if it survives to the present time,
then these landforms would be great places to look."

The gullies observed in the images are on cliffs, usually in crater or valley
walls, and are made up of a deep channel with a collapsed region at its upper
end (an "alcove") and at the other end an area of accumulated debris (an
"apron") that appears to have been transported down the slope. Relative to the
rest of the martian surface, the gullies appear to be extremely young, meaning
they may have formed in the recent past.

"They could be a few million years old, but we cannot rule out that some of
them are so recent as to have formed yesterday," Malin said.

Because the atmospheric pressure at the surface of Mars is about 100 times
less than it is at sea level on Earth, liquid water would immediately begin to
boil when exposed at the martian surface. Investigators believe that this boiling would be violent and explosive. So how can these gullies form? Malin explained that the process must involve repeated outbursts of water and debris,
similar to flash floods on Earth.

"We've come up with a model to explain these features and why the water
would flow down the gullies instead of just boiling off the surface. When water evaporates it cools the ground—that would cause the water behind the initial seepage site to freeze. This would result in pressure building up behind an
'ice dam.' Ultimately, the dam would break and send a flood down the gully,"
said Edgett.

The occurrence of gullies is quite rare: only a few hundred locations have been seen in the many tens of thousands of places surveyed by the orbiter camera. Most are in the martian southern hemisphere, but a few are in the north.

"What is odd about these gullies is that they occur where you might not expect them—in some of the coldest places on the planet," Malin indicated. "Nearly all occur between latitudes 30 degrees and 70 degrees, and usually on slopes that get the least amount of sunlight during each Martian day."

If these gullies were on Earth they would be at latitudes roughly between New Orleans, Louisiana, and Point Barrow, Alaska, in the northern hemisphere; and Sydney, Australia, to much of the Antarctic coast in the south.

The water supply is believed to be about 100 to 400 meters (300 to 1,300 feet) below the surface, and limited to specific regions across the planet. Each flow that came down each gully may have had a volume of water of, roughly, 2,500 cubic meters (about 90,000 cubic feet)—about enough water to sustain 100 average households for a month or fill seven community-size swimming pools. The process that starts the water flowing remains a mystery, but the team believes it is not the result of volcanic heating.

"I think one of the most interesting and significant aspects of this discovery is what it could mean if human explorers ever go to Mars," said Malin. "If water is available in substantial volumes in areas other than the poles, it would make it easier for human crews to access and use it—for drinking, to create breathable air, and to extract oxygen and hydrogen for rocket fuel or to be stored for use in portable energy sources."

"This latest discovery by the *Mars Global Surveyor* is a true 'watershed'—that is, a revolution that pushes the history of water on Mars into the present," said Dr. Jim Garvin, Mars Program Scientist, NASA Headquarters. "To follow up on this discovery we will continue the search with *Mars Global Surveyor* and its rich array of remote sensing instruments, and in 2001, NASA will launch a scientific orbiter with a high spatial resolution middle-infrared imaging system that will examine the seepage sites in search of evidence of water-related minerals.

"Furthermore, NASA is in the process of evaluating two options for a 2003 mission to Mars, both of which could provide independent information concerning the remarkable sites identified by Malin and Edgett."

NASA's Jet Propulsion Laboratory (JPL), Pasadena, Calif., manages the *Mars Global Surveyor* mission for NASA's Office of Space Science, Washington, D.C. JPL is a division of the California Institute of Technology in Pasadena. Malin Space Science Systems built and operates the camera system.

JPL's industrial partner is Lockheed Martin Astronautics, Denver, Colo., which developed and operates the spacecraft.

# SUPREME COURT ON
# THE MIRANDA RULING
## June 26, 2000

*By a surprisingly strong 7–2 vote, the Supreme Court declined to over-
turn its thirty-four-year-old decision in* Miranda v. Arizona, *which held that
confessions from criminal suspects who had not been warned of their rights
before being interrogated could not be used as evidence against them. In
reaffirming the constitutional validity of a criminal suspect's rights to remain silent, to have an attorney, and to have an attorney present during
questioning, the Court held unconstitutional a law Congress enacted in
1968 to overturn the* Miranda *ruling. "We hold that* Miranda, *being a constitutional decision of this Court, may not be in effect overruled by an act
of Congress, and we decline to overrule* Miranda *ourselves," Chief Justice
William H. Rehnquist wrote for the majority in the case of* Dickerson v.
United States.*

*One of the most important—and controversial—decisions made by the
liberal Court under Chief Justice Earl Warren, the* Miranda *decision was an
effort to bring some rationality to determinations of whether confessions
obtained during police interrogations were given voluntarily. Under the
Fifth Amendment, no one could be compelled to incriminate himself, and
courts had routinely held that coerced confessions were not admissible as
evidence. But there was no single test a court could use to determine whether
a suspect's testimony had been freely given or was instead the result of some
overt or covert coercion. As Solicitor General Seth Waxman said during oral
arguments in the* Dickerson *case, in nearly three dozen cases it heard in the
middle 1900s the Supreme Court "was simply unable to articulate manageable rules for the lower courts to apply."*

*Then, in 1966, the Court laid out the set of procedural safeguards that
would become known as the* Miranda *warning: "Prior to any questioning
the person must be warned that he has the right to remain silent, that any
statement he does make may be used as evidence against him, and that he
has a right to the presence of an attorney, either retained or appointed. The
defendant may waive effectuation of these rights, provided the waiver is*

*made voluntarily, knowingly and intelligently. If, however, he indicates in any manner and at any stage of the process, that he wishes to consult with an attorney before speaking there can be no questioning." Incriminating statements made by any defendant in custody who had not been warned of these rights were inadmissible as evidence under the Fifth Amendment, the Court said.*

*Police, prosecutors, and public officials at all levels of government cried out against the decision, warning that it meant guilty suspects would go free. In 1968 Congress included a provision in a massive anticrime bill that would in effect overturn the* Miranda *ruling by allowing "voluntary" confessions to be admitted in court even if the defendant had not been warned of his rights. No administration, from Richard M. Nixon's to Bill Clinton's, ever tried to implement the legislation, which applied only to federal courts. In the meantime, the* Miranda *warning, heard regularly on law-and-order television programs, became as familiar in people's living rooms as in police stations. In his opinion, Rehnquist said one reason not to overrule* Miranda *was the depth of the public's acceptance of it. "Miranda has become embedded in routine police practice to the point where the warning have become part of our national culture," Rehnquist wrote.*

*The reaffirmation of* Miranda *surprised many observers because several of the justices joining the majority had expressed doubt about its validity in the past. Rehnquist himself in 1974 wrote that the rights were "not themselves rights protected by the Constitution." Others noted, however, that in upholding* Miranda *the Court was also extending its recent line of rulings curbing the reach of Congress. "It's power, pure power," Leon Friedman, a constitutional law professor at Hofstra Law School, told the* New York Times. *"The court is telling Congress: 'You can't overturn our good decisions, and you can't overturn our bad decisions. You can't overturn our decisions—period.'" Since it ruled in 1995 that Congress had exceeded its authority when it made carrying a gun within 1,000 feet of a school a federal crime, the Rehnquist Court had invalidated all or part of more than twenty federal statutes primarily on the ground that they infringed on state powers or breached the separation of powers between the three branches of the federal government.* (Gun safety zone, Historic Documents of 1995, p. 183)

*Most reaction to the ruling centered on its immediate implications for law enforcement. "It is a sad day for victims of crime and law-abiding Americans," said Paul G. Cassell, a professor at the University of Utah College of Law, who argued the case against the* Miranda *ruling before the Court. "The tragic result will be that thousands of confessed dangerous criminals will go free just because police officers have made a mistake in following the highly technical Miranda rules." Others disagreed, noting that 80 to 90 percent of all criminal suspects waived their* Miranda *rights and that only rarely did criminals go free because their rights under* Miranda *were violated. The* Miranda *warnings "have worked for law enforcement by providing clear standards for our officers," President Clinton said, "and they have worked to protect the rights of our citizens."*

## *Unusual Route to the Supreme Court*

*The* Dickerson *case challenging* Miranda *came to the Supreme Court by a highly unusual route. The issue before the Supreme Court in* Dickerson *was the constitutional status of the procedural safeguards embodied in the* Miranda *decision. If they were a rule of constitutional law under the Fifth Amendment, Congress could overturn them only through a constitutional amendment. If the safeguards were simply procedures to govern the admissibility of evidence, Congress could supersede them with legislation.*

*The issue had been laid as soon as the Omnibus Crime Control Act of 1968 became law. In that legislation Congress provided that a voluntary confession could be entered into evidence in federal criminal cases, even if the defendant had not been warned of his rights. It would be up to the presiding judge to determine if the confession was given voluntarily "under all the circumstances." This provision, also known as Section 3501, did not apply to state criminal cases because Congress did not have jurisdiction over criminal rules of evidence in state courts.*

*The constitutionality of Section 3501 might have been tested sooner except that no administration, Republican or Democratic, ever sought to use the provision to admit a confession into evidence. Then in 1997 Charles T. Dickerson of Takoma Park, Maryland, was charged with robbing a bank in Alexandria, Virginia. Under questioning by FBI agents, but before he was warned of his rights, Dickerson made statements effectively confessing to the robbery. Dickerson then challenged the use of those statements against him in court because he had not been read his Miranda rights. The federal district court agreed and suppressed the statements. The federal government appealed to U.S. Court of Appeals for the Fourth Circuit, arguing that the statements should have been admissible because Dickerson had waived his rights at an earlier stage of the questioning. Continuing the decades-old Justice Department policy, however, federal prosecutors refused to invoke Section 3501.*

*At that point, the Fourth Circuit, widely noted as being one of the most conservative and activist of the U.S. appeals courts, invited the Washington Legal Foundation, a conservative policy group, to enter the case. Attorneys for the foundation made the argument that Section 3501 effectively overturned* Miranda *in federal courts. By a 2–1 vote, the appeals court agreed. The presumption implicit in the* Miranda *ruling—that a confession made in the absence of the Miranda warning was not a voluntary confession— was not required by the Fifth Amendment, the court said. Congress was therefore free to overrule it, as it had by adopting section 3501. The full appeals court, by a vote of 8–5, refused to reconsider the three-judge panel's decision. Dickerson appealed the decision to the Supreme Court in July 1999.*

*After months of internal debate, the Justice Department filed a brief asking the Court to hear the case and to use it as an opportunity to affirm the* Miranda *decision as one that "has come to play a unique and important role in the nation's conception of our criminal justice system." Attorney General Janet Reno took the unusual step of signing her name on the brief to reinforce the seriousness of the administration's commitment to its position.*

*Because the prosecution and the defense were both arguing in favor of the* Miranda *ruling, the Supreme Court appointed Paul Cassell to argue the Fourth Circuit's position. Cassell, a former law clerk first to Justice Antonin Scalia when he was an appeals court judge and then to Chief Justice Warren E. Burger, had frequently argued, in and out of court, that* Miranda *should be overturned.*

*The Fourth Circuit's opinion was backed by several law enforcement organizations and victims' rights groups, which filed briefs with the Supreme Court asking that* Miranda *be overturned or at least loosened. The included the Fraternal Order of Police (the largest police union), the National Association of Police Organizations, the Federal Bureau of Investigation Agents Association, and the National District Attorneys Association.*

*The Justice Department argued that the* Miranda *warnings offered workable guidelines to police and instilled public confidence in law enforcement. Civil rights organizations also supported the original* Miranda *decision. "Police manuals and reported cases continue to detail the sometimes illegal lengths to which law enforcement officials will go, even with the protections of* Miranda *to get a confession from a suspect," the American Civil Liberties Union said in a brief. "These sources provide a disturbing glimpse of what police practices could become in a world without* Miranda*—where police need not tell citizens of the right to remain silent, and need not respect that right once invoked." The attorney for Dickerson said* Miranda *was "an easy rule to follow, and when police do, they can rest fairly assured that they will be able to use the confession."*

## The Court's Opinion

*The Court's opinion reversing the Fourth Circuit decision was short and straightforward. "Congress may not legislatively supersede our decisions interpreting and applying the Constitution," Rehnquist wrote, and* Miranda *clearly "announced a constitutional rule. "The Warren court in the* Miranda *decision said it was giving "concrete constitutional guidelines for law enforcement agencies and courts to follow," Rehnquist noted. Moreover, the Court applied the* Miranda *ruling to proceedings in a state court, something it was barred from doing if the decision had not been based in the Constitution.*

*Although the Supreme Court had the authority to overturn its earlier decisions, Rehnquist said the Court declined to do so in this case. "Whether or not we agree with* Miranda's *reasoning and its resulting rule, were we addressing the issue in the first instance, the principles of stare decisis weigh heavily against overruling it now." (Stare decisis, Latin for "let the decision stand," meant accepting the principles of law established in earlier cases as authoritative in similar later cases.) Acknowledging that later Courts had made exceptions to* Miranda, *Rehnquist said that these changes had not "undermined"* Miranda's *"doctrinal underpinnings. . . . If anything, our subsequent cases have reduced the impact of the Miranda rule on legitimate law enforcement while reaffirming the decision's core ruling that unwarned statements may not be used as evidence in the prosecution's case. . . ."*

*Finally, Rehnquist rejected the contention that Section 3501 was an adequate substitute for* Miranda. *"The disadvantage of the Miranda rule is that statements which may be by no means involuntary, made by a defendant who is aware of his 'rights,' may nonetheless be excluded and a guilty defendant go free as a result," Rehnquist wrote. "But experience suggest that the totality-of-the-circumstances test which Section 3501 seeks to revive is more difficult than Miranda for law enforcement officers to conform to, and for courts to apply in a consistent manner."*

*Rehnquist's opinion was joined by Justices John Paul Stevens, Sandra Day O'Connor, Anthony M. Kennedy, David H. Souter, Ruth Bader Ginsburg, and Stephen G. Breyer. In a scathing dissent joined by Justice Clarence Thomas, Justice Scalia wrote that the Constitution did not require a specific warning to ensure that a confession was not coerced and that Congress was therefore within its powers to enact legislation that superceded the Miranda rule. "By disregarding congressional action that concededly does not violate the Constitution, the court flagrantly offends fundamental principles of separation of powers and arrogates to itself prerogatives reserved to the representatives of the people," Scalia wrote. "Today's judgment converts* Miranda *from a milestone of judicial overreaching into the very Cheop's Pyramid . . . of judicial arrogance."*

> *Following are excerpts from the majority opinion, written by Chief Justice William H. Rehnquist, and the dissent, written by Justice Antonin Scalia, in the case of* Dickerson v. United States, *in which the Supreme Court reaffirmed by a vote of 7–2 its opinion in* Miranda v. Arizona *(1966), holding that confessions could not be admitted into evidence against criminal defendants who had not been warned of their rights to remain silent and to have an attorney present during questioning. The document was obtained from the Internet at http://www.supremecourtus.gov/ opinions/99pdf/99-5525.pdf.*

No. 99-5525

| | |
|---|---|
| Charles Thomas Dickerson, Petitioner <br> v. <br> United States | On writ of certiorari to the <br> United States Court of Appeals <br> for the Fourth Circuit |

[June 26, 2000]

CHIEF JUSTICE REHNQUIST delivered the opinion of the Court.

In *Miranda v. Arizona* (1966), we held that certain warnings must be given before a suspect's statement made during custodial interrogation could be admitted in evidence. In the wake of that decision, Congress enacted 18 U.S.C. §3501, which in essence laid down a rule that the admissibility of such statements should turn only on whether or not they were voluntarily made. We hold that *Miranda*, being a constitutional decision of this Court, may not be in effect overruled by an Act of Congress, and we decline to overrule *Miranda* ourselves. We therefore hold that *Miranda* and its progeny in this Court govern the admissibility of statements made during custodial interrogation in both state and federal courts.

Petitioner Dickerson was indicted for bank robbery, conspiracy to commit bank robbery, and using a firearm in the course of committing a crime of violence, all in violation of the applicable provisions of Title 18 of the United States Code. Before trial, Dickerson moved to suppress a statement he had made at a Federal Bureau of Investigation field office, on the grounds that he had not received "*Miranda* warnings" before being interrogated. The District Court granted his motion to suppress, and the Government took an interlocutory appeal to the United States Court of Appeals for the Fourth Circuit. That court, by a divided vote, reversed the District Court's suppression order. It agreed with the District Court's conclusion that petitioner had not received *Miranda* warnings before making his statement. But it went on to hold that §3501, which in effect makes the admissibility of statements such as Dickerson's turn solely on whether they were made voluntarily, was satisfied in this case. It then concluded that our decision in *Miranda* was not a constitutional holding, and that therefore Congress could by statute have the final say on the question of admissibility. (1999).

Because of the importance of the questions raised by the Court of Appeals' decision, we granted certiorari (1999), and now reverse.

We begin with a brief historical account of the law governing the admission of confessions. Prior to *Miranda*, we evaluated the admissibility of a suspect's confession under a voluntariness test. The roots of this test developed in the common law, as the courts of England and then the United States recognized that coerced confessions are inherently untrustworthy. [Citation of cases omitted.] Over time, our cases recognized two constitutional bases for the requirement that a confession be voluntary to be admitted into evidence: the Fifth Amendment right against self-incrimination and the Due Process Clause of the Fourteenth Amendment. . . .

We have never abandoned this due process jurisprudence, and thus continue to exclude confessions that were obtained involuntarily. But our decisions in *Malloy v. Hogan* (1964) and *Miranda* changed the focus of much of the inquiry in determining the admissibility of suspects' incriminating statements. In *Malloy*, we held that the Fifth Amendment's Self-Incrimination Clause is incorporated in the Due Process Clause of the Fourteenth Amendment and thus applies to the States. We decided *Miranda* on the heels of *Malloy*.

In *Miranda*, we noted that the advent of modern custodial police interrogation brought with it an increased concern about confessions obtained by coercion. Because custodial police interrogation, by its very nature, isolates and pressures the individual, we stated that "[e]ven without employing brutality, the 'third degree' or [other] specific stratagems, . . . custodial interrogation exacts a heavy toll on individual liberty and trades on the weakness of individuals." We concluded that the coercion inherent in custodial interrogation blurs the line between voluntary and involuntary statements, and thus heightens the risk that an individual will not be "accorded his privilege under the Fifth Amendment . . . not to be compelled to incriminate himself." Accordingly, we laid down "concrete constitutional guidelines for law enforcement agencies and courts to follow." Those guidelines established that the admissibility in evidence of any statement given during custodial interrogation of a suspect would depend on whether the police provided the suspect with four warnings. These warnings (which have come to be known colloquially as "*Miranda* rights") are: a suspect "has the right to remain silent, that anything he says can be used against him in a court of law, that he has the right to the presence of an attorney, and that if he cannot afford an attorney one will be appointed for him prior to any questioning if he so desires."

Two years after *Miranda* was decided, Congress enacted §3501. That section provides, in relevant part:

> "(a) In any criminal prosecution brought by the United States or by the District of Columbia, a confession . . . shall be admissible in evidence if it is voluntarily given. Before such confession is received in evidence, the trial judge shall, out of the presence of the jury, determine any issue as to voluntariness. If the trial judge determines that the confession was voluntarily made it shall be admitted in evidence and the trial judge shall permit the jury to hear relevant evidence on the issue of voluntariness and shall instruct the jury to give such weight to the confession as the jury feels it deserves under all the circumstances.

> "(b) The trial judge in determining the issue of voluntariness shall take into consideration all the circumstances surrounding the giving of the confession, including (1) the time elapsing between arrest and arraignment of the defendant making the confession, if it was made after arrest and before arraignment, (2) whether such defendant knew the nature of the offense with which he was charged or of which he was suspected at the time of making the confession, (3) whether or not such defendant was advised or knew that he was not required to make any statement and that any such statement could be used against him, (4) whether or not such defendant had been advised prior to questioning of his right to the assistance of counsel; and (5) whether or not such defendant was without the assistance of counsel when questioned and when giving such confession.

> "The presence or absence of any of the above-mentioned factors to be taken into consideration by the judge need not be conclusive on the issue of voluntariness of the confession."

Given §3501's express designation of voluntariness as the touchstone of admissibility, its omission of any warning requirement, and the instruction for trial courts to consider a nonexclusive list of factors relevant to the circumstances of a confession, we agree with the Court of Appeals that Congress intended by its enactment to overrule *Miranda*. . . . Because of the obvious conflict between our decision in *Miranda* and §3501, we must address whether Congress has constitutional authority to thus supersede *Miranda*. If Congress has such authority, §3501's totality-of-the-circumstances approach must prevail over *Miranda*'s requirement of warnings; if not, that section must yield to *Miranda*'s more specific requirements.

The law in this area is clear. This Court has supervisory authority over the federal courts, and we may use that authority to prescribe rules of evidence and procedure that are binding in those tribunals. However, the power to judicially create and enforce nonconstitutional "rules of procedure and evidence for the federal courts exists only in the absence of a relevant Act of Congress." [Citations omitted.] Congress retains the ultimate authority to modify or set aside any judicially created rules of evidence and procedure that are not required by the Constitution.

But Congress may not legislatively supersede our decisions interpreting and applying the Constitution. This case therefore turns on whether the *Miranda* Court announced a constitutional rule or merely exercised its supervisory authority to regulate evidence in the absence of congressional direction. Recognizing this point, the Court of Appeals surveyed *Miranda* and its progeny to determine the constitutional status of the *Miranda* decision. Relying on the fact that we have created several exceptions to *Miranda*'s warnings requirement and that we have repeatedly referred to the *Miranda* warnings as "prophylactic," *New York v. Quarles* (1984), and "not themselves rights protected by the Constitution," *Michigan v. Tucker* (1974), the Court of Appeals concluded that the protections announced in *Miranda* are not constitutionally required.

We disagree with the Court of Appeals' conclusion, although we concede that there is language in some of our opinions that supports the view taken by that court. But first and foremost of the factors on the other side—that *Miranda* is a constitutional decision—is that both *Miranda* and two of its companion cases applied the rule to proceedings in state courts—to wit, Arizona, California, and New York. Since that time, we have consistently applied *Miranda*'s rule to prosecutions arising in state courts. It is beyond dispute that we do not hold a supervisory power over the courts of the several States. . . . With respect to proceedings in state courts, our "authority is limited to enforcing the commands of the United States Constitution." . . .

The *Miranda* opinion itself begins by stating that the Court granted certiorari "to explore some facets of the problems . . . of applying the privilege against self-incrimination to in-custody interrogation, *and to give concrete constitutional guidelines for law enforcement agencies and courts to follow*" (emphasis added). In fact, the majority opinion is replete with statements indicating that the majority thought it was announcing a constitutional rule. Indeed, the Court's ultimate conclusion was that the unwarned confessions obtained in the four cases before the Court in *Miranda* "were obtained from the defendant under circumstances that did not meet constitutional standards for protection of the privilege."

Additional support for our conclusion that *Miranda* is constitutionally based is found in the *Miranda* Court's invitation for legislative action to protect the constitutional right against coerced self-incrimination. After discussing the "compelling pressures" inherent in custodial police interrogation, the

*Miranda* Court concluded that, "[i]n order to combat these pressures and to permit a full opportunity to exercise the privilege against self-incrimination, the accused must be adequately and effectively appraised of his rights and the exercise of those rights must be fully honored." However, the Court emphasized that it could not foresee "the potential alternatives for protecting the privilege which might be devised by Congress or the States," and it accordingly opined that the Constitution would not preclude legislative solutions that differed from the prescribed *Miranda* warnings but which were "at least as effective in apprising accused persons of their right of silence and in assuring a continuous opportunity to exercise it."

The Court of Appeals also relied on the fact that we have, after our *Miranda* decision, made exceptions from its rule in cases such as *New York v. Quarles* and *Harris v. New York* (1971). But we have also broadened the application of the *Miranda* doctrine in cases such as *Doyle v. Ohio* (1976) and *Arizona v. Roberson* (1988). These decisions illustrate the principle—not that *Miranda* is not a constitutional rule—but that no constitutional rule is immutable. No court laying down a general rule can possibly foresee the various circumstances in which counsel will seek to apply it, and the sort of modifications represented by these cases are as much a normal part of constitutional law as the original decision. . . .

As an alternative argument for sustaining the Court of Appeals' decision, the court-invited *amicus curiae* contends that the section complies with the requirement that a legislative alternative to *Miranda* be equally as effective in preventing coerced confessions. We agree with the *amicus'* contention that there are more remedies available for abusive police conduct than there were at the time *Miranda* was decided. . . . But we do not agree that these additional measures supplement §3501's protections sufficiently to meet the constitutional minimum. *Miranda* requires procedures that will warn a suspect in custody of his right to remain silent and which will assure the suspect that the exercise of that right will be honored. As discussed above, §3501 explicitly eschews a requirement of pre-interrogation warnings in favor of an approach that looks to the administration of such warnings as only one factor in determining the voluntariness of a suspect's confession. The additional remedies cited by *amicus* do not, in our view, render them, together with §3501 an adequate substitute for the warnings required by *Miranda*.

The dissent argues that it is judicial overreaching for this Court to hold §3501 unconstitutional unless we hold that the *Miranda* warnings are required by the Constitution, in the sense that nothing else will suffice to satisfy constitutional requirements. But we need not go farther than *Miranda* to decide this case. In *Miranda*, the Court noted that reliance on the traditional totality-of-the-circumstances test raised a risk of overlooking an involuntary custodial confession, a risk that the Court found unacceptably great when the confession is offered in the case in chief to prove guilt. The Court therefore concluded that something more than the totality test was necessary. As discussed above, §3501 reinstates the totality test as sufficient. Section 3501 therefore cannot be sustained if *Miranda* is to remain the law.

Whether or not we would agree with *Miranda*'s reasoning and its resulting rule, were we addressing the issue in the first instance, the principles of *stare decisis* weigh heavily against overruling it now. . . . While "'stare decisis is not an inexorable command'" [citation omitted], particularly when we are interpreting the Constitution, "even in constitutional cases, the doctrine carries such persuasive force that we have always required a departure from precedent to be supported by some 'special justification.'" [Citation omitted.]

We do not think there is such justification for overruling *Miranda*. *Miranda* has become embedded in routine police practice to the point where the warnings have become part of our national culture. . . . While we have overruled our precedents when subsequent cases have undermined their doctrinal underpinnings, we do not believe that this has happened to the *Miranda* decision. If anything, our subsequent cases have reduced the impact of the *Miranda* rule on legitimate law enforcement while reaffirming the decision's core ruling that unwarned statements may not be used as evidence in the prosecution's case in chief.

The disadvantage of the *Miranda* rule is that statements which may be by no means involuntary, made by a defendant who is aware of his "rights," may nonetheless be excluded and a guilty defendant go free as a result. But experience suggests that the totality-of-the-circumstances test which §3501 seeks to revive is more difficult than *Miranda* for law enforcement officers to conform to, and for courts to apply in a consistent manner. . . . The requirement that *Miranda* warnings be given does not, of course, dispense with the voluntariness inquiry. But as we said in *Berkemer v. McCarty* (1984), "[c]ases in which a defendant can make a colorable argument that a self-incriminating statement was 'compelled' despite the fact that the law enforcement authorities adhered to the dictates of *Miranda* are rare."

In sum, we conclude that *Miranda* announced a constitutional rule that Congress may not supersede legislatively. Following the rule of *stare decisis*, we decline to overrule *Miranda* ourselves. The judgment of the Court of Appeals is therefore

*Reversed.*

JUSTICE SCALIA, with whom JUSTICE THOMAS joins, dissenting.

. . . [A]n Act of Congress will not be enforced by the courts if what it prescribes violates the Constitution of the United States. That was the basis on which *Miranda* [*v. Arizona* (1966)] was decided. One will search today's opinion in vain, however, for a statement . . . that what 18 U.S.C. §3501 prescribes—the use at trial of a voluntary confession, even when a *Miranda* warning or its equivalent has failed to be given—violates the Constitution. The reason the statement does not appear is not only (and perhaps not so much) that it would be absurd, inasmuch as §3501 excludes from trial precisely what the Constitution excludes from trial, viz., compelled confessions; but also that Justices whose votes are needed to compose today's majority are on record as believing that a violation of *Miranda* is not a violation of the Constitution. . . . And so, to justify today's agreed-upon result, the Court must adopt a significant new, if not entirely comprehensible, principle of constitutional law. As the Court chooses to describe that principle, statutes of Congress can be disregarded, not only when what they prescribe violates the Constitution, but when what they prescribe contradicts a decision of this Court that "announced a constitutional rule." . . . [T]he only thing that can possibly mean in the context of this case is that this Court has the power, not merely to apply the Constitution but to expand it, imposing what it regards as useful "prophylactic" restrictions upon Congress and the States. That is an immense and frightening antidemocratic power, and it does not exist. . . .

## [I omitted]

## II

As the Court today acknowledges, since *Miranda* we have explicitly, and repeatedly, interpreted that decision as having announced, not the circumstances in which custodial interrogation runs afoul of the Fifth or Fourteenth Amendment, but rather only "prophylactic" rules that go beyond the right against compelled self-incrimination. Of course the seeds of this "prophylactic" interpretation of *Miranda* were present in the decision itself. [Excerpts from *Miranda* omitted.] In subsequent cases, the seeds have sprouted and borne fruit: The Court has squarely concluded that it is possible—indeed not uncommon—for the police to violate *Miranda* without also violating the Constitution. . . .

[Description of several cases narrowing the application of *Miranda* omitted.]

In light of these cases, and our statements to the same effect in others, it is simply no longer possible for the Court to conclude . . . that a violation of *Miranda*'s rules is a violation of the Constitution. But . . . that is what is required before the Court may disregard a law of Congress governing the admissibility of evidence in federal court. . . . By disregarding congressional action that concededly does not violate the Constitution, the Court flagrantly offends fundamental principles of separation of powers, and arrogates to itself prerogatives reserved to the representatives of the people. . . .

## [III, IV omitted]

Today's judgment converts *Miranda* from a milestone of judicial overreaching into the very Cheops' Pyramid (or perhaps the Sphinx would be a better analogue) of judicial arrogance. In imposing its Court-made code upon the States, the original opinion at least asserted that it was demanded by the Constitution. Today's decision does not pretend that it is—and yet still asserts the right to impose it against the will of the people's representatives in Congress. Far from believing that *stare decisis* compels this result, I believe we cannot allow to remain on the books even a celebrated decision—especially a celebrated decision—that has come to stand for the proposition that the Supreme Court has power to impose extraconstitutional constraints upon Congress and the States. This is not the system that was established by the

Framers, or that would be established by any sane supporter of government by the people.

I dissent from today's decision, and, until §3501 is repealed, will continue to apply it in all cases where there has been a sustainable finding that the defendant's confession was voluntary.

# CLINTON ON SEQUENCING THE HUMAN GENOME
## June 26, 2000

*In a White House ceremony more like a celebration than a news confer-*
*ence, President Bill Clinton announced on June 26, 2000, that scientists*
*had largely succeeded in mapping the human genome—the genetic code*
*that defines each individual human being. "Today, we are learning the lan-*
*guage in which God created life. We are gaining ever more awe for the com-*
*plexity, the beauty, the wonder of God's most divine and sacred gift," the*
*proud and beaming American president said before the two competing*
*teams of scientists that used two different methods to arrive at roughly the*
*same place at the same time.*

*Scientists had long predicted that once they understood how the human*
*genome functioned, they would be able to use that knowledge to revolution-*
*ize the diagnosis, prevention, and treatment of disease. The first step in that*
*process was sequencing the genome—determining the order and arrange-*
*ment of the roughly 3 billion bits of deoxyribonucleic acid (DNA) contained*
*in every ordinary human cell. Some of those bits—no one yet knew for sure*
*how many—were linked together into genes that directed the development*
*of individual human beings, determining everything from physical ap-*
*pearance to predilection to specific disease.*

*The celebration at the White House may have minimized the difficulties*
*still to be faced. While applauding the feat, many scientists cautioned that*
*it could be years before the promise of the genome project was realized. Still*
*others worried about the ethical and moral implications resulting from un-*
*derstanding the functioning of the basic components of human life. The an-*
*nouncement also masked the bitter rivalry between the two teams—one a*
*public international consortium, the Human Genome Project, and the other*
*a private company, Celera Genomics Corporation, which hoped to profit*
*financially from its discoveries.*

*Clinton was joined in the announcement by Britain's prime minister*
*Tony Blair via satellite hookup. The Wellcome Trust in England and the Na-*
*tional Institutes of Health (NIH) in the United States were the two primary*

*supporters of the public project, which involved more than a thousand sci-
entists working at sixteen institutions in France, Germany, Japan, and
China as well as the United States. Also speaking at the White House were
Francis S. Collins, director of the National Human Genome Research Institute at the NIH who coordinated the international Human Genome Project,
and J. Craig Ventner, president of Celera. Among the many scientists who
attended the ceremony was James Watson, an American who, with his British colleague Francis Crick, discovered in 1953 the double helix structure
of DNA.*

*Neither the public project nor Celera had fully completed work on decod-
ing the human genome; Celera was about 90 percent finished at the time of
the announcement, while the Human Genome Project had completed about
85 percent of its work. Neither side had completed the work by the end of the
year. According to NIH, the public project spent about $300 million on its
working draft of the human genome. Total costs for the program were estimated at $3 billion, which included work on a number of related projects,
including study of ethical, legal, and social issues related to genetics. Celera
was thought to have spent about $250 million on its working draft.*

## The Book of Life

*The road to sequencing the human genome began nearly one hundred
years earlier in 1866, when Gregor Mendel, an Austrian monk, hypothesized the existence of specific hereditary "factors" that determined recognizable traits. Research over the next century found that each human cell
had a nucleus containing twenty-three pairs of chromosomes, one set from
each parent. Each chromosome was composed of long strands of DNA coiled
into a double helix that measured about five feet long but only twenty microns wide (a human hair was about fifty microns wide). DNA in turn was
divided into some 3.1 billion units, or bases, that were made up of four types
of chemicals called nucleotides—adenine, thymine, cytosine, and guanine,
or A, T, C, and G, the "letters" of genetic code that composed the "book of life."
These bases were weakly paired together—A with T and C with G—to link
the sides of the DNA double helix in a structure that resembled rungs of a
coiled stair or ladder. Most of the base pairs had no known functions and
were referred to as "junk" DNA. The others were arranged into genes, the
units responsible for directing the formation or expression of proteins that
a cell used to function, repair or defend itself, and divide. Sequencing the
human genome entailed determining the order of all the bases along
the strands of DNA and distinguishing the genes from the junk DNA.*

*Even with a large percentage of the genome mapping completed, no one
was sure how many genes were contained in the human body; estimates
ranged from about 38,000 to more than 120,000. Whatever the number,
every person has the same set of genes; yet only in identical twins was the
gene structure the same. In everyone else, most genetic variation was
caused by single nucleotide polymorphisms (SNPs), sites on the DNA where
one unit has changed to another. The Human Genome Project said it had al-*

*ready found more than 300,000 SNPs and expected to find 1 million by the end of the year. These tiny variations in genetic code made each individual unique and were likely to prove invaluable in studying human disease and evolution.*

## *The Race*

*The race between the public consortium and the private corporation to finish the human genome sequencing first turned on competing methodologies for producing the sequence. The public project began in 1990 and initially set 2005 as the target for completing the sequencing of the human genome using a method it called the "hierarchical shotgun" approach. Under this approach, scientists broke the genome into large segments of about 150,000 DNA letters, after "mapping" the genome to show where each of the large segments belonged on the parent chromosome. The large segments were then broken down into much tinier segments no more than 500 DNA letters long, which were then sequenced by computer and reassembled into the larger segment. The Celera method, called the "whole shotgun" approach, skipped the time-consuming mapping stage and broke the whole genome into segments that were no more than 50,000 DNA letters in length, each of which was analyzed, and then all were reassembled in one computer run.*

*Ventner, a geneticist, began to develop Celera's sequencing approach in 1990 while he was a researcher at NIH. Finding little support for his ideas among the academic establishment inside the government, Ventner left NIH in 1992 to set up a nonprofit private research company called the Institute for Genomic Research, supported by the for-profit company Human Genome Sciences. In 1995 Ventner used his method to sequence the bacteria* Hemophilus influenzae, *a major cause of childhood ear infections and meningitis. By some accounts the feud between Ventner and the government project intensified during this period when an expert committee at NIH concluded that Ventner's methods would not work and denied his application for grant money.*

*In May 1998 Ventner became president of a new company, later called Celera, owned by PE Biosystems, which made leading brand of DNA sequencing machines (including those used by the public project) and which had developed technology that permitted large-scale, accelerated sequencing. The new company announced that it would complete the sequencing of the human genome by the end of 2000. Celera reckoned that by finishing its genome well before the 2005 target set by the public project, it could command a top price for its genetic data from drug companies and other subscribers.*

*Several scientists working with the public project continued to deride Ventner's approach, arguing that Celera would not be able to overcome several problems associated with reassembling the sequenced fragments of the genome. Nonetheless, Francis Collins, who had succeeded James Watson as director of National Human Genome Research Institute in 1992, advanced the public consortium's timetable for completing 90 percent of the sequenc-*

*ing. The government's main reason for wanting to beat Celera to the finish line was to prevent Celera and other private companies from patenting the data and making it unavailable to outside researchers. The public project made its sequencing available to the public daily. "Every piece we get, it's like saving another block from speculators," Collins told* Newsweek *magazine in late 1999.*

*The public project's confidence grew in December 1998, when it announced that it had decoded the first complete genome for an animal, the roundworm* Caenorhabditis elegans. *At about the same time, the project resolved some problems it had been having with its work on the human genome and began producing large quantities of sequenced material on schedule. Then in March 2000 Celera announced that it used its whole shotgun approach and the biggest civilian supercomputer in the world to fully decode the fruit fly* Drosophila melanogaster. *Celera's success with the fruit fly, a far more complex animal than the roundworm, demonstrated that the naysayers might have been wrong and that Celera would in fact be able to decode the human genome. A month later Celera announced that it had completed the first phase of the human genome.*

*With it now clear that both teams would reach the same point at about the same time, the two sides began to adopt a more conciliatory attitude toward each other. Ventner said the continued feud was bad for science and for the investors. By the time of the White House announcement both sides were acknowledging that the two approaches were complementary, with the Celera approach being faster but also dependent on the genome map produced by the public project to reassemble the sequenced fragments of DNA. In a separate statement on June 26, Collins said the public consortium planned to use a hybrid version of the two approaches in its project to sequence the mouse genome.*

## Ethical Implications

*The race between the public consortium and the private company highlighted one of the ethical dilemmas involved in human genetics, the question of patenting gene discoveries. Celera, for example, had already filed some 6,500 provisional patent applications, although the company said it was likely to request only a few hundred. Another genomics company, Incyte, hoped to file a full-length patent on every drug target in the human genome. Some argued that patenting was the only way that drug and bioengineering companies would undertake the costly research needed to develop drugs aimed at specific gene targets. Others worried that a company might file patents that it did not then pursue but that still would prevent other researchers from working in the area covered by the patent.*

*Another worrisome ethical question involved the potential misuse of genetic testing by insurance companies or employers to discriminate against job seekers or insurance applicants. President Clinton had issued an executive order barring discrimination against federal employees because of their genetic makeup, and on December 20 he issued sweeping new rules to protect the privacy of medical records. But there was no federal legislation barring workplace discrimination for other employees or requiring a person's consent before genetic testing, and the medical privacy rules came under immediate challenge.* (Medical records privacy, p. 1063)

*Still others feared that advances in genetic testing and engineering could lead some on a quest for "perfection." Embryonic testing for some gene mutations that cause disease and deformity, including cystic fibrosis, was already available and used by some parents for making decisions about continuing or aborting a pregnancy. Apart from the already controversial issue of abortion, the implications of the potential to test or engineer for characteristics unrelated to health, such as intelligence, physical ability, or appearance, were worrisome to many. "The further science goes, the further the worst case scenario goes," Steven Jenkins, a spokesman for the Church of England, told Reuters after the White House-Downing Street announcement. "It's the difference between using genetics to correct something that has gone wrong and using them to create something considered perfect. The idea of designing humans from scratch along with the prospect of an enormous increased in abortion is not the world we want."*

*Another potential misuse was that people might blame their genes for all sorts of misbehavior, including criminal behavior. "This whole emphasis on the genome is leading people to what some are calling* genetic determinism—*the idea that genes are determinant of everything—and that's clearly not true," one geneticist said. "There's much more to a human being and to illness and health than genes. Genes are really important, but so is the environment and the interaction between genes and environment."*

> *Following are excerpts from the June 26, 2000, announcement by President Bill Clinton that two working maps of the human genome had been completed. Also speaking were British prime minister Tony Blair (via satellite); Francis S. Collins, director of the National Human Genome Research Institute and leader of the public Human Genome Project; and J. Craig Ventner, president of Celera Genomics Corporation. The document was obtained from the Internet at http://www.whitehouse.gov/WH/New/html/ genome-20000626.html.*

**President Bill Clinton:** Good morning. . . .

Nearly two centuries ago, in this room, on this floor, Thomas Jefferson and a trusted aide spread out a magnificent map—a map Jefferson had long prayed he would get to see in his lifetime. The aide was Meriwether Lewis and the map was the product of his courageous expedition across the American frontier, all the way to the Pacific. It was a map that defined the contours and forever expanded the frontiers of our continent and our imagination.

Today, the world is joining us here in the East Room to behold a map of even greater significance. We are here to celebrate the completion of the first survey of the entire human genome. Without a doubt, this is the most important, most wondrous map ever produced by humankind.

The moment we are here to witness was brought about through brilliant and painstaking work of scientists all over the world, including many men and women here today. It was not even 50 years ago that a young Englishman named Crick and a brash even younger American named Watson, first discovered the elegant structure of our genetic code. "Dr. Watson, the way you announced your discovery in the journal *Nature*, was one of the great understatements of all time. This structure has novel features, which are of considerable biological interest." Thank you, sir.

How far we have come since that day. In the intervening years, we have pooled the combined wisdom of biology, chemistry, physics, engineering, mathematics and computer science; tapped the great strengths and insights of the public and private sectors. More than 1,000 researchers across six nations have revealed nearly all 3 billion letters of our miraculous genetic code. I congratulate all of you on this stunning and humbling achievement.

Today's announcement represents more than just an epic-making triumph of science and reason. After all, when Galileo discovered he could use the tools of mathematics and mechanics to understand the motion of celestial bodies, he felt, in the words of one eminent researcher, "that he had learned the language in which God created the universe."

Today, we are learning the language in which God created life. We are gaining ever more awe for the complexity, the beauty, the wonder of God's most divine and sacred gift. With this profound new knowledge, humankind is on the verge of gaining immense, new power to heal. Genome science will have a real impact on all our lives—and even more, on the lives of our children. It will revolutionize the diagnosis, prevention and treatment of most, if not all, human diseases.

In coming years, doctors increasingly will be able to cure diseases like Alzheimer's, Parkinson's, diabetes and cancer by attacking their genetic roots. Just to offer one example, patients with some forms of leukemia and breast cancer already are being treated in clinical trials with sophisticated new drugs that precisely target the faulty genes and cancer cells, with little or no risk to healthy cells. In fact, it is now conceivable that our children's children will know the term cancer only as a constellation of stars.

But today's historic achievement is only a starting point. There is much hard work yet to be done. That is why I'm so pleased to announce that from this moment forward, the robust and healthy competition that has led us to this day and that always is essential to the progress of science, will be coupled with enhanced public-private cooperation.

Public and private research teams are committed to publishing their genomic data simultaneously later this year, for the benefit of researchers in every corner of the globe. And after publication, both sets of teams will join together for an historic sequence analysis conference. Together, they will examine what scientific insights have been gleaned from both efforts, and how we can most judiciously proceed toward the next majestic horizons.

What are those next horizons? Well, first, we will complete a virtually error-free final draft of the human genome before the 50th anniversary of the discovery of the double helix, less than three years from now. Second, through sustained and vigorous support for public and private research, we must sort through this trove of genomic data to identify every human gene. We must discover the function of these genes and their protein products, and then we must rapidly convert that knowledge into treatments that can lengthen and enrich lives.

I want to emphasize that biotechnology companies are absolutely essential in this endeavor. For it is they who will bring to the market the life-enhancing applications of the information from the human genome. And for that reason, this administration is committed to helping them to make the kind of long-term investments that will change the face of medicine forever.

The third horizon that lies before us is one that science cannot approach alone. It is the horizon that represents the ethical, moral and spiritual dimension of the power we now possess. We must not shrink from exploring that far frontier of science. But as we consider how to use new discovery, we must also not retreat from our oldest and most cherished human values. We must ensure that new genome science and its benefits will be directed toward making life better for all citizens of the world, never just a privileged few.

As we unlock the secrets of the human genome, we must work simultaneously to ensure that new discoveries never pry open the doors of privacy. And we must guarantee that genetic information cannot be used to stigmatize or discriminate against any individual or group.

Increasing knowledge of the human genome must never change the basic belief on which our ethics, our government, our society are founded. All of us are created equal, entitled to equal treatment under the law. After all, I believe one of the great truths to emerge from this triumphant expedition inside the human genome is that in genetic terms, all human beings, regardless of race, are more than 99.9 percent the same.

What that means is that modern science has confirmed what we first learned from ancient fates. The most important fact of life on this Earth is our common humanity. My greatest wish on this day for the ages is that this incandescent truth will always guide our actions as we continue to march forth in this, the greatest age of discovery ever known.

Now, it is my great pleasure to turn to my friend, Prime Minister Tony Blair, who is joined in the State Dining Room at 10 Downing Street by Dr. Fred Sanger and other world-renowned scientists. With the generous support of the Wellcome Trust, British scientists have played an invaluable role in reaching this milestone.

On behalf of the American people, I would like to thank the Prime Minister, the scientists, and the British nation for the brilliant work you have brought to this international effort. . . .

**Prime Minister Tony Blair:** Well, thank you very much, President Clinton. . . .

I would also like to pay tribute to President Clinton's support for the Human Genome Project, and for the huge role the United States has played in it. . . .

Scientists from Japan and Germany, France, China, and around the world have been involved, as well as the U.K. and the U.S. And this undertaking, therefore, has brought together the public, private and non-profit sectors in an unprecedented international partnership. In particular, I would like to single out the Wellcome Trust, without whose vision and foresight, Britain's 30-percent contribution to the overall result would not have been possible. And I would like, too, to mention the imaginative work of Celera and Dr. Craig Venter, who in the best spirit of scientific competition, has helped accelerate today's achievement.

For let us be in no doubt about what we are witnessing today—a revolution in medical science whose implications far surpass even the discovery of antibiotics, the first great technological triumph of the 21st century. And every so often in the history of human endeavor there comes a breakthrough that takes humankind across a frontier and into a new era. And like President Clinton, I believe that today's announcement is such a breakthrough—a breakthrough that opens the way for massive advances in the treatment of cancer and hereditary diseases, and that is only the beginning.

Ever since Francis Crick and Jim Watson . . . made their historic discovery in the middle of the last century, we've known that DNA was the code to life on Earth. And yet, I guess for Crick and Watson, the process of identifying the billions of units of DNA and piecing them together to form a working blueprint of the human race must have seemed almost a superhuman task, beyond the reach of their generation. And yet, today, it is all but complete.

Nothing better demonstrates the way technology and science are driving us, fast-forwarding us all into the future. But with the power of this discovery comes, of course, the responsibility to use it wisely. As with the greatest scientific achievements, the ethical and the moral questions raised by this astonishing breakthrough are profound. We, all of us, share a duty to ensure that the common property of the human genome is used freely for the common good of the whole human race; to ensure that the powerful information now at our disposal is used to transform medicine, not abused, to make man his own creator or invade individual privacy.

For most of us, today's developments are almost too awesome fully to comprehend. They underline the extraordinary scale of economic, technological, scientific change that sweeps across the modern world. I'm proud that Britain has played, with others, a pioneering role in that. But I believe it says something very important about the process of change. We cannot resist change, but our job, indeed our duty, is to make sense of change, to help people through it, to seize the massive opportunities for better health and a better quality of life; and then, with equal vigor, to minimize the threats such developments pose. . . .

And the decision for us really as humanity is whether we are going to engage in the right cooperation across national frontiers so that we shape our destiny in a way that genuinely does benefit all our people, that makes the most of the possibilities, and faces up to the challenges and the dangers that it poses. And in a way, I think that the scientists that have been involved in this great undertaking have shown the spirit of cooperation that should now motivate the governments in taking this forward another step. They have given us this opportunity that we, all of us, are going to have a common responsibility in using it in the right way. . . .

**President Clinton:** . . . Now, in a few moments, we'll hear from Celera President, Dr. Craig Venter, who shares in the glory of this day, and deservedly so because of his truly visionary pursuit of innovative strategies to sequence the human genome as rapidly as possible. And I thank you, Craig, for what you have done to make this day possible.

And now I'd like to invite Dr. Francis Collins to the lectern. I also want to congratulate him. From his development of some of the central methods for finding human disease genes, to his successful application of those methods, to the discovery of the cystic fibrosis gene in 1989, to his current leadership for the International Human Genome Project, he has combined the talents of rigorous science and a profound sensitivity to ethical, legal and social issues. He is a physician scientist of great faith, compassion, energy and integrity. And he has truly helped us, more than anyone else, to understand how the marvels of genome science will actually improve human health.

So Dr. Collins, please come up to the lectern.

**Dr. Francis Collins:** Mr. President, distinguished Ambassadors, ladies and gentlemen. It is truly a humble—humbling and profound experience to be asked to speak here this morning. . . .

Science is a voyage of exploration into the unknown. We are here today to celebrate a milestone along a truly unprecedented voyage, this one into ourselves. Alexander Pope wrote, "Know then thyself. Presume not God to scan. The proper study of mankind is man." What more powerful form of study of mankind could there be than to read our own instruction book?

I've been privileged over the last seven years to lead an international team of more than a thousand of some of the best and brightest scientists of our current generation, some of them here in this room, who have been truly dedicated to this goal. Today, we celebrate the revelation of the first draft of the human book of life.

Now, this milestone could only have come about with the happy combination of vision, determination, creative innovation and teamwork, and we stand on many shoulders here today. Beginning 15 years ago, leaders in the Department of Energy, the National Academy of Sciences and the National Institutes of Health, began to dream this dream.

At first, many thought it unrealistic and unattainable; yet, inspired by visionaries such as James Watson, who is here with us this morning, creative geniuses, such as Waterston, Sulston, Lander, Branscomb, Gibbs and many others here with us this morning, entered the fray. The vigorous involvement of talented colleagues in other countries, now including China, France, Germany, Japan and the United Kingdom, have made this project particularly gratifying to me. I would also like to recognize, publicly, the dedicated leadership of my friend and colleague, Ari Patrinos, of the Department of Energy, in moving this project forward so effectively here in the U.S.

Surely, the human genome is our shared inheritance, and it is fitting and proper that we are all working on it together. Now, thus far, every milestone set by the International Human Genome Project has been met—on schedule or in some cases, ahead of schedule.

Today, we deliver, ahead of schedule again, the most visible and spectacular milestone of all. Most of the sequencing of the human genome by this international consortium has been done in just the last 15 months. During that time, this consortium has developed the capacity to sequence 1,000 letters of the DNA code per second, seven days a week, 24 hours a day. We have developed a map of overlapping fragments that includes 97 percent of the human genome, and we have sequenced 85 percent of this.

The sequence data is of higher quality than expected with half of it in finished or near-finished form. And all of this information has been placed in public databases every 24 hours, where any scientist with an Internet connection can use it to help unravel the mysteries of human biology. Already, more than a dozen genes, responsible for diseases from deafness to kidney disease to cancer, have been identified using this resource just in the last year. . . .

I think I speak for all of us in this room, and for the millions of others who have come to believe in the remarkable promise of biomedical research, that we must redouble our efforts to speed the application of these profound and fundamental observations about the human genome to the cure of disease. That most desirable of all outcomes will only come about with a continued powerful and dedicated partnership between basic science investigators and academia, and their colleagues in the biotechnology and pharmaceutical industries.

As the President has said, we still have much to do. Many tasks lie ahead if we are to learn how to speak the language of the genome fluently. Today is most certainly not the end of genomics, but perhaps it's the end of the beginning. Together we must develop the advances in medicine that are the real reason for doing this work. And with just as much vigor, we must provide the protections against potential misuses of genetic information. If there is anyone within the sound of my voice who has not seen that as a priority, I hope today's announcement is the necessary wake-up call.

It's a happy day for the world. It is humbling for me and awe-inspiring to realize that we have caught the first glimpse of our own instruction book, previously known only to God. What a profound responsibility it is to do this work. Historians will consider this a turning point. Researchers in a few years will have trouble imagining how we studied human biology without the genome sequence in front of us. I particularly welcome the opportunity to celebrate this moment jointly with our scientific colleagues at Celera Genomics, and I wish to express my personal gratitude to Dr. Craig Venter for his openness in the cooperative planning process that led to this joint announcement. I congratulate him and his team on the work done at Celera, which uses an elegant and innovative strategy that is highly complementary to the approach taken by the public project. Much will be learned from a comparison of the two.

I'm happy that today, the only race we are talking about is the human race.

It is now my distinct pleasure to introduce to you Dr. J. Craig Venter, the President of Celera Genomics. Inspired by a life-changing experience as a medical corpsman in Vietnam, Craig charged into the field of human biology with remarkable energy and determination. Never satisfied with the status quo, always seeking new technology, inventing new approaches when the old ones wouldn't do, he has made profound contributions to the field of genomics.

His development of the expressed sequence tag, or EST, approach for sampling the expressed part of the genome, reduced to practice the notion of considering the human genome as a bounded, but ascertainable set of information. Just a few years later, he electrified the scientific community by publishing, with his colleague, Hamilton Smith, the complete sequence of a free-living organism, the bacterium *hemophilus influenzae*. And just three months ago, using the innovative whole genome shotgun approach he developed, and working with Gerry Rubin of the University of California at Berkeley, he and his colleagues published a sequence of the fruit fly, drosophila, another remarkable milestone in biology.

Articulate, provocative, and never complacent, he has ushered in a new way of thinking about biology. Now under his leadership, Celera Genomics has accomplished a remarkable goal, their own first assembly of the human genome sequence.

It is an honor and a pleasure the invite him to tell you about this landmark achievement.

**Dr. J. Craig Venter:** . . . Mr. President, Mr. Prime Minister, members of the Cabinet, honorable members of Congress, ambassadors and distinguished guests. Today, June 26, in the year 2000, marks an historic point in the 100,000-year record of humanity. We're announcing today, for the first time our species can read the chemical letters of its genetic code.

At 12:30 p.m. today, at a joint press conference with the public genome effort, Celera Genomics will describe the first assembly of the human genetic code from the whole genome shotgun method. Starting only nine months ago, on September 8, 1999, 18 miles from the White House, a small team of scientists headed by myself, Hamilton Smith, Mark Adams, Gene Myers, and Granger Sutton, began sequencing the DNA of the human genome using a novel method pioneered by essentially the same team five years earlier at the Institute for Genomic Research.

The method used by Celera has determined the genetic code of five individuals. We have sequenced the genome of three females and two males, who have identified themselves has Hispanic, Asian, Caucasian, or African-American. We did this sampling not in an exclusionary way, but out of respect for the diversity that is America, and to help illustrate that the concept of race has no genetic or scientific basis.

In the five Celera genomes, there is no way to tell one ethnicity from another. Society and medicine treats us all as members of populations, where as individuals we are all unique, and population statistics do not apply.

I would like to acknowledge and congratulate Francis Collins and our colleagues in the public genome effort in the U.S., Europe and Asia, for their tremendous effort in generating a working draft of the human genome. I'd also like to personally thank Francis for his direct actions in working with me to foster cooperation in the genome community, and to shift our collective focus to this historic moment and its future impact on humanity. I would also like to thank the President for his commitment to public-private cooperation, and for making this day even more an historic event. . . .

I would like to particularly acknowledge Charles DeLisi from the Department of Energy, and Jim Watson from Cold Spring Harbor, both here, for their vision in helping to initiate the Genome Project. The completion of the human genetic blueprint would not have possible without the continued investment of the U.S. Government and basic research. I applaud the President's efforts and the work of Congress during the last several years in producing the largest funding increases to fuel the engines of basic science.

At the same time, we could not overlook the investment of the private sector in research in America. There would be no announcement today if it were not for the more than $1 billion that P.E. Biosystems invested in Celera, and into the development of the automated DNA sequencer that both Celera and the public effort used to sequence the genome. In turn, some of the investment was driven by the public investment in science.

Thirty-three years ago, as a young man serving in the medical corps in Vietnam, I learned firsthand how tenuous our hold on life can be. That experience inspired my interest in learning how the trillions of cells in our bodies interact to create and sustain life. When I witnessed firsthand that some men live through devastating trauma to their bodies, while others died after giving up from seemingly small wounds, I realized that the human spirit was at least as important as our physiology.

We're clearly much, much more than the sum total of our genes, just as our society is greater than the sum total of each of us. Our physiology is based on complex and seemingly infinite interactions amongst all our genes and the environment, just as our civilization is based on the interactions amongst all of us.

One of the wonderful discoveries that my colleagues and I have made while decoding the DNA of over two dozen species, from viruses to bacteria to plants to insects, and now human beings, is that we're all connected to the commonality of the genetic code in evolution. When life is reduced to its very essence, we find that we have many genes in common with every species on Earth, and that we're not so different from one another.

You may be surprised to learn that your sequencers are greater than 90 percent identical to proteins in other animals. It's my belief that the basic knowledge that we're providing the world will have a profound impact on the human condition and the treatments for disease, and our view on our place in the biological continuum.

The genome sequence represents a new starting point for science and medicine, with potential impact on every disease. Taking the example, cancer, each day approximately 2,000 die in America from cancer. As a consequence of the genome efforts that you've heard described by Dr. Collins and myself this morning, and the research that will be catalyzed by this information, there's at least the potential to reduce the number of cancer deaths to zero during our lifetimes. The development of new therapeutics will require continued public investment in basic science, and the translations of discoveries into new medicine by the biotechs and pharmaceutical industry.

However, I am concerned, as many of you are, that there are some who will want to use this new knowledge as a basis of discrimination. A CNN-Time poll this morning reported that 46 percent of Americans polled believe that the impact of the Human Genome Project will be negative. We must work together toward higher science literacy and the wise use of our common heritage.

I know from personal discussions with the President over the past several years, and his comments here this morning, that genetic discrimination has been one of his major concerns about the impact of the genomic revolution. While those who will base social decisions on genetic reductionism will be ultimately defeated by science, new laws to protect us from genetic discrimination are critical in order to maximize the medical benefits from genome discoveries.

Some have said to me that sequencing the human genome will diminish humanity by taking the mystery out of life. Poets have argued that genome sequencing is an example of sterilizing reductionism that will rob them of their inspiration. Nothing could be further from the truth. The complexities and wonder of how the inanimate chemicals that are our genetic code give rise to the imponderables of the human spirit should keep poets and philosophers inspired for the millenniums.

Thank you.

**President Clinton:** Well, thank you both for those remarkable statements. I suppose, in closing, the most important thing I could do is to associate myself with Dr. Venter's last statement. When we get this all worked out and we're all living to be 150—young people will still fall in love, old people will still fight about things that should have been resolved 50 years ago—we will all, on occasion, do stupid things, and we will all see the unbelievable capacity of humanity to be noble. This is a great day.

Thank you very much.

# UNAIDS REPORT ON THE GLOBAL AIDS EPIDEMIC
## June 27, 2000

*Acquired immunodeficiency syndrome, commonly known as AIDS, continued to devastate populations around the world in 2000, but perhaps for the first time in many years international health experts were cautiously optimistic that they might yet be able to slow its spread. Two significant events contributed to this tentative optimism: the number of new infections by human immunodeficiency virus (HIV), the virus that caused AIDS, declined slightly in sub-Saharan Africa, the region with the highest prevalence of AIDS/ HIV; and for the first time since the epidemic broke out, international organizations and individual countries markedly stepped up their commitments to help eradicate the incurable disease. The United Nations, the World Bank, and the United States all declared that the epidemic was a threat to development and national security and increased their financial support of efforts to prevent and treat the disease. Meeting at UN headquarters in September, 150 heads of state and government set the year 2015 as the target for halting the spread of AIDS and called for a major summit in 2001 to address the complex health, social, and economic issues raised by the epidemic.*

*Yet even as leaders in the Western world were committing new resources to the fight against the epidemic, South African president Thabo Mbeki sparked an international controversy when he publicly questioned whether HIV actually caused AIDS and suggested the real causes were poverty and malnutrition. AIDS experts, health officials, and policymakers were outraged by Mbeki's comments, saying that they would only contribute to the ignorance and misinformation about AIDS and lead to even more deaths. With an estimated 4.2 million cases, South Africa had the highest number of HIV infections in the world; the rate of infection there had increased from nearly 13 percent of the population to nearly 20 percent in just two years.*

### Grim Statistics Around the World

*In its annual report updating the scope of the AIDS epidemic, the Joint United Nations Program on HIV/AIDS (UNAIDS) said an estimated 3 million people would die of AIDS in 2000, while 5.3 million would become*

410

*newly infected with HIV. Altogether an estimated 36.1 million people were living with HIV or AIDS, many millions of them were unaware that they were infected. Some 19 million people had died since the epidemic began in the early 1970s. More than 13 million children under age fifteen, 95 percent of them African, had lost their mothers or both parents to AIDS.*

*The number of new infections and deaths remained relatively stable in Europe and North America. About 45,000 people were newly infected and about 20,000 people were expected to die in the United States during 2000. Peter Piot, the executive director of UNAIDS, criticized the stability as a sign of complacency, saying there was "no excuse" for having the same number of new infections in 2000 as there were in 1990. He also noted a decline in investment in AIDS prevention education programs. "The availability of treatment has resulted in a complacency which is becoming really dangerous," Piot said.*

*Although the absolute numbers remained relatively small, the fastest spread of AIDS in the world in 2000 was in eastern Europe and the former Soviet Union. Piot characterized the rapid increase as "alarming." The number of cases in Russia more than doubled, from 130,000 in 1999 to 300,000 in 2000, and AIDS was appearing in cities across the country. Intravenous drug use was thought to be the primary mode of transmission in that area.*

*Africa remained the hardest hit area by far. In sub-Saharan Africa, an estimated 25.3 million people were infected—about 70 percent of all infection worldwide—and 2.4 million were expected to die in 2000. One hopeful sign was that the number of new infections in the region dropped in 2000 to 3.8 million, from 4 million in 1999. UNAIDS and other health experts cautioned against reading too much into the numbers. For one thing, the decline was nearly within the estimation's margin of error for all new infections. Paul DeLay of the U.S. Agency for International Development said he felt "fairly safe in saying that it is leveling off, it is plateauing." Others said they wanted to see how the epidemic affected Nigeria, the most populous country in sub-Saharan Africa, where the infection rate was low for the region.*

*Even if the rate of HIV infection were to begin to decline throughout sub-Saharan Africa, the region would still face years of devastation as a result of the disease. Sixteen African countries had adult HIV infection rates above 10 percent: Botswana (35.8 percent), Swaziland (25.3), Zimbabwe (25.1), Lesotho (23.6), Zambia (20.0), South Africa (19.9), Namibia (19.5), Malawi (16.0), Kenya (14.0), Central Africa Republic (13.8), Mozambique (13.2), Djibouti (11.8), Burundi (11.3), Rwanda (11.2), Ivory Coast (10.8), and Ethiopia (10.6).*

*More unsettling, even if these rates were to begin to decline, UNAIDS predicted that in the worst-hit countries (those where 20 percent of the population was already infected with HIV), about 50 percent of all fifteen-year-olds would die. If the infection rates remained high, perhaps 70 percent of the fifteen-year-olds would die. "The world has never before experienced death rates of this magnitude among young adults of both sexes across all social strata," Piot said June 27. "We are going into societies where there are more people in their sixties and seventies than in their forties and thirties."*

*Piot's remarks came at a press conference where UNAIDS released its second comprehensive report on the AIDS epidemic. The release was timed to coordinate with the thirteenth international AIDS conference, which was held July 9–14 in Durban, South Africa.*

*Unlike the rest of the world, where AIDS was transmitted largely through unprotected homosexual sex and intravenous drug use, the disease in Africa was spread through heterosexual contact, and more women than men were infected with HIV. Teenage girls were at especially high risk, in part because male-to-female transmission was easier than female-to-male, and in part because young women often had sexual contact with older men, who tended to be more experienced sexually and thus more likely to be infected. In some areas of Africa, men actively sought out young female sexual partners in the belief that intercourse with a virgin would cure AIDS.*

*In many areas of Africa so many farmers, teachers, managers, and other workers had succumbed to the disease that businesses and schools were closing and farm production was down. In a rapidly worsening economic crisis, extended families could not always take in orphans, many of whom ended up in overcrowded orphanages or on the streets, where they suffered from malnutrition, illness, abuse, and sexual exploitation. Health care systems and national budgets were overwhelmed.*

*Despite the bleak picture, UNAIDS found some glimmers of light. More young people were delaying sex, decreasing their numbers of sexual partners, and using condoms more often. UNAIDS also emphasized that a "nationally driven agenda" enlisting "the persistent engagement of the highest levels of government" could turn the epidemic around. As examples, Piot pointed to Uganda and Senegal. Uganda's government was the first to recognize the danger of AIDS for national development and mounted a broad-based nationwide program to educate the population on preventive measures. As a result Uganda's infection rate dropped from 14 percent in the early 1990s to about 8 percent. Senegal also took early action to avert a crisis, mounting an aggressive education campaign and setting up free clinics to treat sexually transmitted diseases, including HIV. Senegal's infection rate was under 2 percent.*

*The UNAIDS report stressed that in addition to political will and leadership, an effective national response to the AIDS epidemic required governments "to make HIV visible and the factors leading to its spread, discussible." Only by breaking the silence surrounding the disease would governments begin to reduce the fear and denial that contributed to the spread of the disease and ease the stigma associated with it. The UN agency recommended that nations begin with a single comprehensive plan for combating the disease that involved participation from government at all levels, civil society, the private sector, and international donors. Community-based responses were crucial to the success of any program, the UNAIDS report said, and it urged that people with HIV/AIDS be encouraged to play a prominent role both in planning and implementing community prevention and treatment programs. "We are not powerless against this epidemic," Piot wrote in a preface to the report, "but our response it still at a fraction of what it needs to be."*

## *International Response to Perceived Security Threat*

*The realization that the AIDS epidemic had already reversed economic growth in some parts of Africa and threatened development in other parts of the world appeared to mobilize the international community to greater action in 2000. The United Nations Security Council began the year with its first session ever on a health issue. On July 17 the Security Council passed a resolution to step up AIDS prevention education among UN peacekeepers and to encourage voluntary testing for the disease so that military and civilian personnel did not contract or spread the disease. Studies showed that during peacetime the rate of sexually transmitted diseases, including HIV, was two to five times higher among military personnel than among civilians, and that it increased in times of conflict. At its September meetings the UN General Assembly set a goal of stopping the spread of AIDS by 2015 and passed a resolution calling for a special session of the United Nations on AIDS, similar to past special sessions on women, the environment, and global warming. That session was scheduled for June 25–27, 2001, in New York. (UN Summit, p. 700)*

*The World Bank pledged on April 17 to make AIDS-related programs its top lending priority. The bank did not administer health programs itself but had been lending money to finance AIDS prevention and treatment programs in Africa, India, eastern Europe, and elsewhere. In September the bank announced creation of a $500 million loan fund to support HIV-education programs, condom distribution, and training of health care workers in sub-Saharan African countries. The new commitments were seen as part of the bank's response to protests that international organizations were promoting economic globalization at the expense of the poor nations. Bank officials also promised to step up pressure on rich countries to forgive developing country debt. Piot among others complained that poor countries could spend more on AIDS prevention if they did not have to use such a high proportion of their budgets to pay interest on their debt. In late October Congress agreed to appropriate $425 million toward a debt relief program intended to help at least two dozen countries, most in Africa. (Debt relief, p. 475)*

*The Clinton administration also began to talk of the epidemic in terms of national security. In February the White House created an interagency group "to develop a series of expanded initiatives" to deal with international ramifications of the epidemic, and it proposed doubling the amount of money the United States spent to combat AIDS overseas. The new initiatives were in part a political response in an election year to prominent African-American political leaders who had made AIDS in Africa a cause. The initiatives were also driven by a National Intelligence Estimate report, prepared in January, which said that the sort of "demographic catastrophe" being experienced in some parts of Africa were a strong risk factor for "revolutionary wars, ethnic wars, genocides and disruptive regime transitions" in the developing world. The report expressed particular concern about the potential for instability in Asia, which appeared poised on the edge of a full-blown epidemic. Although infection rates in Asia were about the same level or less than those in North America, epidemiologists feared that accelerating international trade and travel were combining with underlying conditions favorable to the disease to push many Asian countries toward "a dramatic increase" in the incidence of HIV/AIDS, the report said. A few countries such as Thailand had mounted effective campaigns against the disease, but in the world's two most populous countries, China and India, AIDS prevention efforts were minimal, and the HIV infection rate appeared to be rising swiftly in both countries.*

*Some politicians dismissed the administration's concerns. Senate Majority Leader Trent Lott (R-Miss.) said he did not see AIDS in Africa as a threat to U.S. security. "I guess this is just the president trying to make an appeal to, you know, certain groups," Lott said on a national television talk show April 30. Nonetheless, in addition to agreeing to debt relief, Congress doubled the amount of money the U.S. government spent on AIDS prevention overseas and backed a plan for an AIDS trust fund, to be administered by the World Bank.*

*Under intense pressure from AIDS activists, the United Nations, and the World Bank, five major pharmaceutical companies promised to work with "committed countries" to make AIDS drugs available at substantially reduced rates. One German company, Boehringer-Ingelheim, said it would donate the drug nevirapine for five years to help developing countries prevent mother-to-child transmission of the disease. Some critics continued to question whether the drugs would be affordable in countries where the annual average amount spent per capita on health care was in the $10–$20 range. Even if the drugs were free, health officials warned, there would still be difficulties because as many as 90 percent of those carrying HIV were unaware that they had the disease. Moreover, health care systems, already devastated by the disease, did not have the personnel or the training to administer the complex drugs. UNAIDS and the World Health Organization said that greater availability of common and affordable drugs such as cotrimoxazole and isoniazid could be extremely helpful in warding off the secondary infections, such as malaria, diarrhea, and tuberculosis (TB), that killed thousands of people already weakened by HIV/AIDS. TB was the immediate cause of death in one-third of all AIDS cases worldwide.*

## Controversy over Cause of AIDS

*A simmering international controversy over statements by South African president Thabo Mbeki on the root cause of AIDS broke into the open during the thirteenth International AIDS Conference, which Mbeki hosted in Durban, South Africa. For some months, and in the face of overwhelming evidence to the contrary, Mbeki had repeatedly said that there was no proven link between HIV and AIDS and that HIV was just one of several factors, including poverty and malnutrition, that caused the disease. Mbeki also questioned the efficacy and safety of the anti-HIV drugs, such as AZT and nevirapine. Until late 2000, his administration refused to distribute the drugs even to pregnant women, even though they had been shown to cut the transmission of HIV to newborns. Mbeki sought to portray his question-*

*ing of the accepted cause of and solutions to AIDS as part of a search to find an "African solution" to the epidemic.*

*Health professionals, churches leaders, AIDS activists, and others were outraged by Mbeki's statements. Most said Mbeki's position would undermine prevention and education programs and could even mislead people into believing what many of them want to believe—that the disease does not exist. "We don't have the luxury for this debate," an AIDS specialist at Pretoria University told the* Washington Post. *Another AIDS worker recalled a South African proverb: "If you meet a snake, you don't ask him 'Mr. Snake, where do you come from?' No, you kill the snake."*

*In the weeks leading up to the Durban conference, 5,000 AIDS researchers and physicians signed an open letter affirming that the scientific evidence linking HIV to AIDS was "clear cut, exhaustive and unambiguous." The statement, known as the Durban Declaration, appeared in the July 6 issue of the science journal* Nature.

*The declaration seemed to have little persuasive effect on Mbeki. In opening remarks to the convention, Mbeki refused to acknowledge that HIV caused AIDS. He said he had begun to look into the causes of AIDS in an effort to understand how his country could be swept by one of the worst epidemics in history just as it had broken free from white majority rule, known as apartheid. "As I listened and heard the whole story told about our own country, it seemed to me that we could not blame everything on a single virus," Mbeki said. Hundreds of people stormed out of the convention in protest.*

*Addressing the conference on its closing day, Mbeki's predecessor, Nelson Mandela, sought to reduce tensions by urging AIDS workers to focus on the strategies that had been proven effective, were inexpensive, and could be implemented quickly. "Promoting abstinence, safe sex and the use of condoms and ensuring the early treatment of sexually transmitted diseases are some of the steps needed and about which there can be no dispute," Mandela said.*

*Following are excerpts from two sections of the "Report on the Global HIV/AIDS Epidemic," released June 27, 2000, by the Joint United Nations Program on HIV/AIDS; the first section discusses the social and economic impacts of the disease, and the second details the common features of effective national strategies for combating the disease. The document was obtained from the Internet at http://www.unaids.org/epidemic_update/report/index.html.*

## AIDS in a New Millennium: A Grim Picture with Glimmers of Hope

When AIDS emerged from the shadows two decades ago, few people could predict how the epidemic would evolve, and fewer still could describe with any certainty the best ways of combating it. Now, at the start of a new millennium, we are past the stage of conjecture. We know from experience that AIDS can devastate whole regions, knock decades off national development, widen the gulf between rich and poor nations and push already-stigmatized groups closer to the margins of society.

Just as clearly, experience shows that the right approaches, applied quickly enough with courage and resolve, can and do result in lower HIV infection rates and less suffering for those affected by the epidemic. An ever-growing AIDS epidemic is not inevitable; yet, unless action against the epidemic is scaled up drastically, the damage already done will seem minor compared with what lies ahead. This may sound dramatic, but it is hard to play down the effects of a disease that stands to kill more than half of the young adults in the countries where it has its firmest hold—most of them before they finish the work of caring for their children or providing for their elderly parents. Already, 18.8 million people around the world have died of AIDS, 3.8 million of them children. Nearly twice that many—34.3 million—are now living with HIV, the virus. The most recent UNAIDS/WHO estimates show that, in 1999 alone, 5.4 million people were newly infected with HIV. . . .

## Social and Economic Impacts

The premature death of half of the adult population, typically at ages when they have already started to form their own families and have become economically productive, can be expected to have a radical effect on virtually every aspect of social and economic life. While it is difficult to measure the precise impact of HIV at a national level in most hard-hit countries, a great deal of information does exist about how the epidemic is affecting everything from households to the public and private sector of the economy.

## Household Impacts

The few surveys of the impact of having a family member with AIDS show that households suffer a dramatic decrease in income. Decreased income inevitably means fewer purchases and diminishing savings.

In a study in Thailand, one-third of rural families affected by AIDS experienced a halving of their agriculture output, which threatened their food security. Another 15% had to take their children out of school, and over half of the elderly people were left to take care of themselves. In urban areas in Côte d'Ivoire, the outlay on school education was halved, food consumption went down 41% per capita, and expenditure on health care more than quadrupled. When family members in urban areas fall ill, they often return to their villages to be cared for by their families, thus adding to the call on scarce resources and increasing the probability that a spouse or others in the rural community will be infected.

Families make great sacrifices to provide treatment, relief and comfort for a sick breadwinner. In the Thai study, the families spent on average US$ 1000 during the last year of an AIDS patient's life—the equivalent of an average annual income. A common strategy in AIDS-affected households is to send one or more children away to extended family members to ensure that they are fed and cared for. Such extended family structures have been able to absorb some of the stress of increasing numbers of orphans, particularly in Africa. However, urbanization and migration for labour, often across borders, are destroying those structures. As the number of orphans grows . . . and the number of potential caregivers shrinks, traditional coping mechanisms are stretched to breaking point. Households headed by orphans are becoming common in high-prevalence countries. Studies in Uganda have shown that following the death of one or both parents, the chance of orphans going to school is halved and those who do go to school spend less time there than they did formerly. Other work from Uganda has suggested that orphans face an increased risk of stunting and malnourishment.

There is a consensus that help for orphans should be targeted at supporting families and improving their capacity to cope, rather than setting up institutions for the children. Orphanages may not be relevant to a long-term solution. Moreover, in a subsistence economy, children sent away from their village may lose their rights to their parents' land and other property as well as their sense of belonging to a family.

## The Toll on Teaching

Education is an essential building block in a country's development. In areas where HIV infection is common, HIV-related illness is taking its toll on education in a number of ways. First, it is eroding the supply of teachers and thus increasing class sizes, which is likely to dent the quality of education. Secondly, it is eating into family budgets, reducing the money available for school fees and increasing the pressure on children to drop out of school and marry or enter the workforce. Thirdly, it is adding to the pool of children who are growing up without the support of their parents, which may affect their ability to stay in school.

Skilled teachers are a precious commodity in all countries, but in some parts of the world, they are becoming too sick to work or dying of HIV-related illness long before retirement. The Central African Republic, where around one in every seven adults is estimated to be infected with HIV, already has a third fewer primary school teachers than it needs. A recent study of the impact of HIV on the educational sector showed that almost as many teachers died as retired between 1996 and 1998. Of those who died, some 85% were HIV-positive, and they died an average of 10 years before reaching the minimum retirement age of 52. The study recorded that 107 schools had closed owing to staff shortages, and only 66 remained open. With the teacher short-age expected to worsen, researchers calculate that over 71 000 children aged 6–11 will be deprived of a primary education by the year 2005. A similarly dramatic impact has been found in Côte d'Ivoire, where teachers with HIV miss up to six months of classes before dying (compared with 10 days missed by teachers dying of other causes) and where confirmed cases of HIV/AIDS account for 7 out of 10 deaths among teachers.

In Zambia, deaths among teachers are very high and still rising rapidly. In the first 10 months of 1998, Zambia lost 1300 teachers—the equivalent of around two-thirds of all new teachers trained annually. AIDS may aggravate the existing disparity in educational access between town and countryside. In a national survey of 6–15-year-olds in 1996, over 70% of those living in cities were enrolled in school, compared with just over half of those in rural areas. Rural postings are already unpopular among teachers in many countries, and the Zambian study suggested that the need to be close to a source of health care—a town or city—acted as an extra disincentive to teachers to go to rural areas.

## The Toll on Learning

It is commonly assumed that children drop out of school when their parents die, whether of AIDS or another cause. While there has been little rigorous research, a few studies can point to AIDS in the family as a direct cause of school drop-out. For example, in a study of commercial farms in Zimbabwe, where most farmworker deaths are attributed to AIDS, 48% of the orphans of primary-school age who were interviewed had dropped out of school, usually at the time of their parent's illness or death, and not one orphan of secondary-school age was still in school.

Information collected in large household surveys representative of the general population confirms the general assumption that children whose parents have both died are less likely to be in school than children who are living with one or both parents. . . .

The impact of parental AIDS is not necessarily a direct one or seen only in children who have already been orphaned. A child's schooling may be temporarily interrupted by a shortage of cash occasioned by spending on a parent's ill-health or by periods of work in the home to help sick parents. By the time children are actually orphaned, they are likely to be over-age for their class, even if they are still in school. This was the case in both the Zimbabwean and Kenyan studies cited here. Being older than their classmates was in turn associated with a higher rate of dropping out of school for a number of other reasons, including pregnancy and the need to take paying work. Many of the marriages that led to drop-out were arranged, so it is quite possible that relatives or sick parents themselves saw marrying a girl off as a relatively painless way of ensuring that she would be cared for after their death. In at least one study of orphans in Kenya, boys tended to give economic reasons for dropping out of primary school (64% said they could not afford fees or needed to earn cash from fishing) while 28% of girls said that they had become pregnant and 41% had left to get married.

## Health Sector under Stress

Since the start of the epidemic, 18.8 million children and adults have fallen sick and died and almost twice that number are now living with HIV, with some 5.4 million newly infected people joining their ranks in 1999. As a consequence, the epidemic's impact on the health sector over the coming decade will be predictably greater than in the past two decades combined.

Already, however, the increased demand for health care from people with HIV-related illnesses is heavily taxing the overstretched public health services of many developing countries. In the mid-1990s, it was estimated that treatment for people with HIV consumed 66% of public health spending in Rwanda and over a quarter of health expenditures in Zimbabwe. A recent study estimates that in 1997, public health spending for AIDS alone already exceeded 2% of gross domestic product (GDP) in 7 of 16 African countries sampled—a staggering figure in countries where total health spending accounts for 3–5% of GDP. In recent years, HIV-positive patients have occupied half of the beds in the Provincial Hospital in Chiang Mai, Thailand, 39% of the beds in Kenyatta National Hospital in Nairobi, Kenya, and 70% of the beds in the Prince Regent Hospital in Bujumbura, Burundi. A related impact of the epidemic is that patients suffering from other conditions are being crowded out. The hospital sector in Kenya has seen increased mortality among HIV-negative patients, who are being admitted at later stages of illness.

The shifting and growing demand on health care systems is underscored by the exploding tuberculosis epidemic in the countries most heavily affected by HIV. As noted elsewhere in this report, as HIV weakens people's immune systems it makes them far more vulnerable to developing active tuberculosis. . . .

Tuberculosis has become the leading cause of death among people with HIV infection, accounting for about a third of AIDS deaths worldwide. Hospital data from Africa show that up to 40% of HIV-infected patients have active tuberculosis. With a greater number of HIV-positive people developing active tuberculosis, there is also a greater risk that the tubercle bacillus will pass to others in the community. The World Bank has estimated that 25% of HIV-negative persons dying of tuberculosis in the coming years would not have been infected with the bacillus in the absence of the HIV epidemic. Each of these new tuberculosis infections represents a further cost to the health sector.

The development of new therapies for HIV-infected persons and of vaccines will further raise health sector costs in infrastructure, drugs, training, and personnel expenditures. At the same time, HIV-related illness and premature death among health care workers themselves will continue to create costs of another kind for the health sector. Sickness and death due to AIDS is growing rapidly among health care personnel, but few countries have as yet fully understood the epidemic's impact on human resources in their health sector. A study in Zambia showed that in one hospital, deaths in health care workers increased 13-fold over the 10-year period from 1980 to 1990, largely because of HIV. As in other sectors of the economy, rising rates of HIV infection in health care workers will increase rates of absenteeism, reduce productivity, and lead to higher levels of spending for treatment, death benefits, additional staff recruitment and training of new health personnel.

## Impact on Agriculture

Agriculture is one of the most important sectors in many developing countries, particularly when measured by the percentage of people dependent on it for their living.

Although the sector may produce only 20% of a country's wealth (measured as a percentage of the gross national product), it might provide a living or survival for as much as 80% of the country's population. Indirectly, it provides a livelihood for still other parts of the population, such as processing workers on sugar estates. . . .

The effect of AIDS is devastating at family level. As an infected farmer becomes increasingly ill, he and the family members looking after him spend less and less time working on his family's crops. The family begins to lose income from unmarketed or incompletely tended cash crops, has to buy food it normally grows for itself, and may even have to sell off farm equipment or household goods to survive.

The vicious circle is compounded by the high costs of health care, whether the sick person turns to a traditional healer or to the health services. A 1997 study by the Food and Agriculture Organization of the United Nations (FAO) showed that in the mid-west of Côte d'Ivoire, care for male AIDS patients cost on average about US$ 300 a year, representing a quarter to a half of the net annual income of most small-scale farms.

The time lost by family members must also be taken into account. For instance, the repeated absence of another member of the farm to accompany the patient to a healer also reduces the farm's production. And when the most debilitating phases of AIDS coincide with key farming periods such as sowing or clearing, the time spent nursing a sick person and lost to farm labour is sorely missed. A recent survey in the rural Bukoba district of the United Republic of Tanzania found a radical shift in the allocation of labour time: a woman with a sick husband spent 60% less time on agricultural activities than she would normally do.

Altogether, the effects on production can be serious. In West Africa, many cases have been reported of reduced cultivation of cash crops or food products. These include market gardening in the provinces of Sanguié and Boulkiemdé in Burkina Faso and cotton, coffee and cocoa plantations in parts of Côte d'Ivoire. A recent study in Namibia by the FAO concluded that the impact on livestock is considerable, with a heavy gender bias: households headed by women and children generally lose their cattle, thus jeopardizing the food security of the surviving members.

But even the poorer male-headed households experience a decrease in livestock when a wife dies. In Zimbabwe, the output of communal agriculture (much of it subsistence farming) has fallen by 50% over the past five years owing largely, though not solely, to the AIDS epidemic, according to a report published in 1998. Maize production has seen a decline of 54% of harvested quantity and a further drop of 61% in marketed output. The number of hectares under cotton has decreased by about 34% and marketed output by a further 47%, and the production of ground-nuts and sunflowers has fallen by 40%. The Southern Africa AIDS Information Dissemination Service (SAfAIDS), an AIDS-related nongovernmental organization in Zimbabwe, warned that a food crisis could erupt in Zimbabwe within the next 20 years as the group of people of productive age shrinks and the areas under cultivation diminish as a result.

## The Bottom Line: HIV Is Hurting Business

Given the proportion of adults infected with HIV and dying from associated diseases in Africa, it is inevitable that the business sector, as well as families, schools and other sectors, will feel the cost. Yet many companies (in common with many governments) have ignored the early warning signs and have not acted against HIV until sickness and deaths become too common to ignore. While experience suggests that HIV prevention is most effective when it is introduced very early on, before the virus gets a grip and the population of infected people becomes uncontrollably large, business people have taken some persuading. Interviews conducted in engineering and construction companies in Gaborone, Botswana, found resistance to the idea of implementing HIV prevention and planning measures even though 39% of people of working age in the city were estimated to be infected in 1998.

Some companies in Africa have already felt the impact of HIV on their bottom line. Managers at one sugar estate in Kenya said they could count the cost of HIV infection in a number of ways: absenteeism (8000 days of labour lost due to sickness between 1995 and 1997 alone), lower productivity (a 50% drop in the ratio of processed sugar recovered from raw cane between 1993 and 1997) and higher overtime costs for workers obliged to work longer hours to fill in for sick colleagues. Direct cash costs related to HIV infection have risen dramatically in this same company: spending on funerals rose fivefold between 1989 and 1997, while health costs rocketed up by more than 10-fold over the same period, reaching KSh 19.4 million (US$ 325 000) in 1997. The company estimated that at least three-quarters of all illness is related to HIV infection. Indeed, illness and death have jumped from last to first place in the list of reasons for people leaving a company, while old-age retirement slipped from the leading cause of employee drop-out in the 1980s to just 2% by 1997. . . .

Experience has shown that there are effective measures that businesses can take to respond to the epidemic. . . . A study in 40 Zimbabwean factories demonstrated that strengthened prevention efforts in the workplace can reduce HIV transmission (and the future costs associated with it) when compared with workplaces that have weaker prevention programmes. In all 40 factories, workers were given information about preventing HIV and were offered voluntary counselling and HIV testing. In half the factories, workers could also choose to speak privately with one of the peer educators—workers who had been specially trained to discuss HIV prevention with their colleagues, make condoms available, and provide information about sexually transmitted infections and where they could be treated.

Discouragingly, the number of new HIV infections actually rose over the two-year period of the study in both groups of factories and in all age groups. But the good news for the managers of factories with peer educators was that the rise was 34% less in these factories than in the others. This substantial reduction was achieved at a cost of around US$ 6 per employee—less than the cost of one set of protective overalls.

Since untreated syphilis, gonorrhoea and other sexually transmitted infections increase the risk of acquiring and passing on HIV . . . companies seeking to prevent HIV in the workforce have a clear interest in making sure that these infections are treated quickly and effectively. Many companies have their own clinics at which workers can be treated for free. Companies that consider this option too expensive might reflect on the findings of a company survey in Botswana, which showed that workers lost several hours waiting at government clinics where free external treatment was available. The associated lost productivity probably cost the company much more than providing private treatment would have done.

In fact, some studies suggest that providing services to the wider community can have as much of an effect on the health of the workforce as providing them to the workers alone. In a study in South Africa, a mine-sponsored service for treating sexually transmitted infections in sex workers in the surrounding community led to a significant reduction in the number of infections among the miners themselves. Over the same period, in another mining community where there was no special prevention effort, sexually transmitted infections among miners increased.

Government policy can encourage companies in the private sector to invest in HIV prevention in the workforce, for example by providing tax breaks for those with active prevention programmes. Some development agencies now require an assessment of the impact of AIDS in every development project, and a few governments, for example that of Botswana, are considering including AIDS prevention in the workplace as a requirement for any large tender. . . .

## National Responses to the Epidemic:
## Factors that Make a Difference

This report demonstrates that the AIDS epidemic is a true development crisis that threatens the social and economic fabric, and the political stability, of whole nations.

Yet this report also shows that the epidemic is not out of control everywhere; some countries and communities have managed to stabilize HIV rates or achieve a turnaround, and some have maintained very low prevalence rates, due to a range of factors that are not yet fully understood. Other communities have made significant progress on care and support for people both infected and affected. A closer look at individual country responses, and at the corresponding achievements and failures, helps pinpoint some of the factors behind these successes.

Looking back over past efforts against the epidemic the initial reaction of many countries was to try to persuade individuals and selected groups to change their behaviour by providing information about HIV/AIDS. Gradually, however, behaviour change was understood to require more than mere information; the importance of decision-making and negotiation skills, accessibility of commodities and services, and supportive peer norms became increasingly apparent.

By the mid-1980s, it was well appreciated that individuals do not always control their own risk situations. This led to the development of prevention programmes aimed at enabling particular groups or communities such as sex workers and men who have sex with men to adopt safer behaviour. At the same time, as individuals infected with HIV earlier in the epidemic gradually fell ill and died, challenging family and community structures alike, the need to provide health care and cushion the epidemic's impact became increasingly obvious. Simultaneously, the importance of work on non-discrimination, protection and promotion of human rights, and against the stigmatization brought by HIV/AIDS, was more widely recognized, including the importance of involving different sectors of society.

With the mid-1990s, and deepening epidemics in many countries, came a growing realization that HIV/AIDS is also a development challenge. To the extent that people's vulnerability to infection has social and economic roots, often including marginalization, poverty and women's subordinate status, these conditions need to be tackled as a way of making society as a whole less vulnerable to HIV over the long term.

Advancing other social goals such as education, empowerment of women and human rights protection are important for reducing overall societal vulnerability to infection, as well as critical in their own right. At the same time, planners need to bear in mind that development projects such as the construction of a major highway or the creation of free-trade zones may exacerbate the epidemic by promoting rapid urbanization, splitting families and depriving individuals of familiar social support systems. These negative effects need to be anticipated and actively countered.

## Common Features of Effective National Responses

Analysis of effective programmes shows that a number of features characterize the responses of communities and countries which have already managed to stabilize or reverse their epidemic trends. This is not to say that there is one ideal expanded response or universal blueprint, but some basic, common principles of effective response can be identified. It is important for each country to find locally relevant pathways to a response that are likely to include most, if not all, of the elements summarized below.

Successful national responses have generally comprised the following features:

### 1. Political will and leadership

Political will expresses the national commitment and provides overall leadership to the nation in response to AIDS. Effective responses are characterized by political commitment from community leadership up to a country's highest political level.

Such commitment leads to high-profile advocacy and helps bring in all the sectors and players, along with the necessary human and financial resources. It is also critical for making the hard political choices often involved in adopting intervention methods that really work—such as making sex work safer—and can lead to helpful policy changes and supportive legislation.

Ultimately, the success of a programme is determined by the dedication and efforts of the change agents who are closest to its level of impact. They, however, need to be constantly motivated, supervised and supported by the political leadership.

### 2. Societal Openness and Determination to Fight Against Stigma

To be effective, programmes need to make HIV visible and the factors leading to its spread, discussible. Programmes need to make people aware of the existence of HIV and how it is spread, without stigmatizing the behaviours that lead to its transmission. They also need to facilitate discussion about an individual or community's own vulnerability, and how to reduce it. This involves dissipating fear and prejudice against people who are already living with HIV or AIDS.

Successful programmes impart knowledge, counter stigma and discrimination, create social consensus on safer behaviour, and boost AIDS prevention and care skills. These can be accomplished cost-effectively through mass media campaigns, and through peer/outreach education and life-skills programmes in schools and workplaces. Programmes such as TASO in Uganda have demonstrated the enormously positive impact of openness and honesty in facing HIV. Ensuring that counselling and voluntary HIV testing are available, so that an individual can find out her or his HIV status, is a further critical ingredient in counteracting denial.

## 3. A Strategic Response

A single, powerful national AIDS plan involving a wide range of actors—government, civil society, the private sector and (where appropriate) donors—is a highly valuable starting point. The development of a country strategy begins with an analysis of the national HIV/AIDS situation, risk behaviours and vulnerability factors, with the resulting data serving to prioritize and focus initial action. It is essential to find out where people in the country are already infected, where they are most vulnerable, and why. Effective strategy development then involves drawing on evidence-based methods of HIV/AIDS prevention, care and impact alleviation—"best practices"—recognizing that some of these may be culturally sensitive (e.g. sex education in schools) or require hard political choices (e.g. needle exchange for injecting drug users). At the same time, attention needs to be given to ensuring that the relevant services and commodities such as condoms or STD services are acceptable, affordable and available. Given the resource constraints facing many countries, the development of a strategy will also involve some prioritization.

Effective strategies offer both prevention and care. As illness mounts in the epidemic, so does the need for health care and social support. Care services have benefits that extend beyond caring for sick individuals. They help convince others that the threat of HIV is real and they therefore make prevention messages more credible. Messages and programmes that build compassion and skills in health care settings, communities and families are needed right from the start, and combined training for prevention and care helps reduce costs.

An important point about programme elements is that they tend to work in synergy. Individual features of effective action can be found in most programmes. The tragedy is that in many countries, action remains sporadic and patchy rather than comprehensive. "Boutique" projects may provide services for one or two communities, while large areas of the countryside have nothing. Many programmes have yet to become comprehensive in either geographical coverage or content. The national response may focus solely on sex workers, for example; elsewhere, efforts may go into AIDS and life skills education among the young in schools and out of schools, but the risks and vulnerability of men who have sex with men are ignored. While human and other resource constraints may hamper efforts to scale up, a sound strategic plan based on epidemiological evidence and best practices will at least ensure basic coverage.

Strategic planning of national responses is neither easy nor quick. But as the experience of a number of countries has proved—for example, Botswana, Cambodia, China, Côte d'Ivoire, Dominican Republic, Guatemala, Honduras, Malawi, Mozambique, Papua New Guinea, Romania and the United Republic of Tanzania—it can be done effectively, and the process itself is critical in bringing on board a wide range of actors whose commitment is key to successful outcomes.

## 4. Multisectoral and Multilevel Action

Successful programmes involve multisectoral and multilevel partnerships between government departments and between government and civil society, with AIDS being routinely factored into individual and joint agendas. Only a combined effort will "mainstream" AIDS and establish it firmly on the development agenda.

Multisectoral and multilevel partnerships make sense for all stakeholders. Government sectors and businesses are affected in multiple ways by a serious epidemic and hence have an important stake in participating in AIDS prevention, care and support at all levels, but especially in ensuring sustained, large-scale programmes. Ministries of Labour for example can mandate workplace prevention programmes in the private sector. Ministries of Defence can use their budgets to implement programmes for the military, and Ministries of Education for teachers, schoolchildren and their parents. Private firms can contribute in cash and in kind. While Ministries of Health undoubtedly have a critical role to play in responding to the epidemic, leaving the management of the overall national response to them is unlikely to prove effective in the longer term. NGOs, who are trusted by vulnerable populations, are best positioned to support prevention programmes in collaboration with these communities themselves. The mass media can promote safer behaviour and tolerance through their own channels.

## 5. Community-Based Responses

The eventual outcome of the AIDS epidemic is decided within the community. People, not institutions, ultimately decide whether to adapt their sexual, economic and social behaviour to the threat of HIV infection. They are the subjects of the response to AIDS, not merely the objects of outside interventions. Therefore, responses to HIV are in the first instance local: they imply the involvement of people where they live—in their homes, their neighbourhoods and their workplaces.

Community members are also indispensable for mobilizing local commitment and resources for effective action. In particular, people living with HIV/AIDS must play a prominent role and bring their unique experience and perspective into programmes, starting from the planning stage.

Community mobilization against HIV/AIDS is taking place successfully all over the world. The activities carried out in community projects are as diverse as the peoples and cultures that make up these communities. Some are entirely "home-grown" and self-sufficient, while others have benefited from external advice and funding. Some are based in religious centres, others in medical institutions, and still others in neighbourhood meeting places. Many concentrate on public education, others on providing care, and still others on prevention and other goals.

## 6. Social Policy Reform to Reduce Vulnerability

HIV transmission is associated with specific risk-taking behaviours. These behaviours are influenced by personal and societal factors that determine people's vulnerability to infection. To be effective, risk-reduction programmes must be designed and implemented in synergy with other programmes, which, in the short and long term, increase the capacity and autonomy of those people particularly vulnerable to HIV infection. Therefore, the question is how to address directly the societal forces which determine, more than anything else, vulnerability to HIV/AIDS. Issues such as gender imbalance and the inability of women to negotiate when, how and with whom they have sex is a social policy issue. The chronic and acute poverty of urban households that leads to their eventual breakdown and the migration of children to the street is not an issue that can be easily addressed at a household or community level alone.

Addressing the societal forces which determine vulnerability to HIV requires engagement at the policy level and political will and resources. Effective social policy reform is a long-term agenda, but even small-scale and incremental steps can send important messages about political commitment to reducing the vulnerability of individuals and communities to infection.

## 7. Longer-Term and Sustained Response

Even a comprehensive response to HIV/AIDS does not yield immediate results. Measurable impact may take four to five years to develop. Therefore, a long-term approach must be taken, which involves building societal resistance to HIV. Beginning with the youngest generation, the reinforcement of safer attitudes and behaviour will gradually fortify a generation against the spread of AIDS, and in time have a significant impact on incidence.

Effective programmes are characterized by focused action and steadily expanding coverage. To begin with, using existing resources, it makes strategic sense to focus on important vulnerable populations and geographic areas where rapid HIV spread takes on the characteristics of an emergency. Planners must nevertheless take into account the need to reach many different populations, including those who will become exposed tomorrow: individual risk and vulnerability change over the life cycle as children mature into adolescence and adulthood.

There is also evidence that continued vigilance is critical even when behaviour change appears to have become established. The use of condoms among a newly sexually active generation of men who have sex with men for example cannot be assumed, just because an older generation changed its behaviour.

Gradually, without losing focus, action must expand steadily until complete country coverage is achieved.

## 8. Learning from Experience

The last 15 years of HIV prevention and care have led to the development of a rich body of experience and expertise. While it is essential that individual countries "own" their response there is a great deal of evidence that some policies, strategies and technologies are particularly effective: that which UNAIDS calls "best practice." Drawing on best practice and adapting it to local circumstances is valuable both at the outset, and as the response matures. Learning within a national context is also important.

District bureaucracies provide the critical link between local and national activities.

The district level is well placed in many countries to analyse, document and disseminate what they learn from the local responses. They can then press for, and negotiate with, the national authorities the changes and reforms needed in key sectors to sustain local responses. There are multiple examples of good HIV "projects"—successful interventions that have identified the recipe for success in a given environment. They can provide valuable insights to national programmes.

Similarly, national programmes are in a strong position to scale up local responses to the national level by incorporating local lessons into their strategic planning and reform processes. For example, governments can effectively adopt policy changes and programme approaches that have "passed the test" at the local level.

## 9. Adequate Resources

The reassignment of national priorities must be reflected in a reallocation of budgets. There are success stories in developing countries where government budgets for AIDS have been increased significantly; for example in Brazil, China, India and Thailand. At the same time, however, it is a fallacy to assume that because designated AIDS funding is limited, so must AIDS action be. Effective programmes identify opportunities to involve partners with similar goals and objectives, and capitalize on synergies between AIDS and other programmes. If the action needed for risk-reduction and vulnerability-reduction becomes part of the mainstream of national life, direct costs will be less, the benefits will have many spin-offs, and programmes are more likely to be sustainable. For example, including information on HIV/STDs and life skills in a school curriculum has only marginal costs, but the resulting decision-making and negotiation skills may bring about extra benefits such as declines in STDs, unwanted pregnancies and drug use. Similarly, boosting the educational and economic opportunities of young girls in rural areas not only reduces HIV transmission by providing alternatives to commercial sex, but also contributes to sustainable rural development and an improvement in the status of women.

Redirecting to AIDS existing project resources already programmed for social funds, education and health projects, infrastructure and rural development is fully justified, as the AIDS epidemic is undermining the very goals of these other investments.

Even though international financial assistance is not always necessary, international assistance is crucial in many poor countries with limited public budgets.

## Conclusion

Two decades of action against the epidemic have generated important insights into an effective response. While international political, financial and technical support are important, lowering incidence and mitigating the epidemic's impacts must be a nationally driven agenda. To be effective and credible, national responses require the persistent engagement of the highest levels of government. Countries that have adopted forward-looking strategies to fight the epidemic are reaping the rewards in falling incidence. Other countries are yet to see the fruits of their efforts, and in the absence of rapid and visible results, sustaining a response becomes more difficult.

However, evidence shows that the combination of approaches described in this chapter have brought about a lowering of incidence in some countries. At present, and until the arrival of a vaccine, these approaches are the strongest weapons in our fight back against HIV/AIDS.

# SUPREME COURT ON PARTIAL BIRTH ABORTION
## June 28, 2000

*In one of the most anxiously awaited decisions of the 1999–2001 term, the Supreme Court, by a 5–4 decision, on June 28, 2000, struck down a state law banning a procedure opponents referred to as "partial birth" abortion. The ruling was a defeat for antiabortion activists who throughout the 1990s had used graphic descriptions of the grisly late-term procedure to undermine public support for abortion. Thirty states had passed laws prohibiting use of the method, and Congress had twice passed similar legislation but was unable both times to override President Bill Clinton's veto.*

*Abortion rights advocates had what one called a "champagne and shivers" reaction to the ruling. On the one hand, they were pleased with the ruling, which went beyond the appeals court ruling to hold not only that the language of the prohibition was unconstitutionally broad, but also that the law was fatally flawed because it did not contain an exception to protect the health of the mother. On the other hand, abortion rights advocates were surprised, as were many other observers, by Justice Anthony M. Kennedy's dissent. In 1992, the last time an abortion case had reached the Supreme Court docket, Kennedy had voted to reaffirm a woman's constitutional right to an abortion. His dissent in 2000 made it abundantly clear that the future of abortion in the United States could well rest on future appointments to the Supreme Court by the next president. The eventual winner of the presidential election, Republican George W. Bush, was opposed to abortion.*

*Abortion foes said they would rework state laws to meet the Court's objections, but in September they were handed a new challenge, when the Food and Drug Administration approved the controversial abortion pill, known as RU–486.* (Story, p. 781)

### *Abortion: A Right under Siege*

*The Supreme Court first recognized a woman's right to an abortion in the case of* Roe v. Wade, *decided in 1973 by a 7–2 vote. The ruling guaranteed women an unfettered right to an abortion during the first three months of pregnancy. In the second trimester, a state could impose regulations to protect a woman's health or safety; in the third trimester—when the fetus was usually capable of living on its own—a state could ban abortion altogether so long as the law permitted exceptions to protect the woman's life or health. Most states acted to prohibit abortions in the third trimester, and abortion foes won enactment of numerous state laws regulating abortions in the second trimester.*

*The Court upheld some of these state laws and ruled against others. In a 1989 case four justices signaled their willingness to reconsider or overrule* Roe v. Wade. *With the appointment of conservative Justice Clarence Thomas in 1991, many "right-to-life" advocates thought their position might now have a majority on the Court. But, in a 5–4 vote in the case of* Planned Parenthood v. Casey, *the Court in 1992 reaffirmed* Roe *and said a state could not impose an "undue burden" on a woman's right to an abortion by placing a "substantial obstacle in her path." (*Casey *case, Historic Documents of 1992, p. 589)*

*During the next few years the Court passed up several opportunities to elaborate what it meant by "undue burden." One of the cases that it declined to take up for full consideration involved the first state law in the nation to ban partial birth abortions. A federal appeals court struck down the Ohio law, and the justices rejected the state's petition to review the decision.*

*The term "partial birth abortion" usually referred to a procedure described in the medical terminology as "dilation and extraction," or D&X. In this procedure, the woman's cervix was dilated and the fetus brought feet first from the uterus into the vagina. Then, because the head was too large to pass through the cervix, the doctor pierced the fetal skull, suctioned out the contents, and crushed or collapsed the skull to complete removal of the fetus. The American College of Obstetrics and Gynecology viewed the procedure as a variant of the more common "dilation and evacuation," or D&E, procedure, in which the fetus was dismembered as it was brought through the cervical opening into the vagina. But the antiabortion forces disagreed, and in 1995 the National Right to Life Committee coined a new term for the D&X procedure: "partial birth abortion." Using graphic pictures of nearly intact fetuses with their brains spilling out of collapsed skulls, antiabortion organizations likened the procedure to infanticide and mounted lobbying campaigns asking state legislatures and the U.S. Congress to ban the operation.*

## Challenge to the Nebraska Law

*Nebraska adopted its partial birth abortion prohibition in 1997 with only one dissenting vote in the state's unicameral legislature. The law defined partial birth abortion as "partially deliver[ing] vaginally a living unborn child before killing the unborn child and completing the delivery." The law prohibited "deliberately and intentionally delivering into the vagina a living unborn child or a substantial portion thereof, for the purpose of performing a procedure that the person performing such procedure knows will*

*kill the unborn child and does kill the unborn child." The procedure was pro-
hibited except when "necessary to save the life of the mother." Doctors convicted of violating the ban faced up to twenty years in prison, a fine of up to
$25,000, and the loss of their medical license.*

*The Nebraska law was challenged by LeRoy Carhart, one of three Ne-
braska physicians who performed abortions and the only one in the state to
perform the operation on women more than sixteen weeks pregnant. Carhart used the D&X procedure in twenty cases or so a year. In his suit,
Carhart claimed that by its terms the provision covered not only the D&X
procedure but also the D&E procedure. In both procedures, Carhart told
the trial court, the doctor brought a "substantial portion" of the fetus into the
vaginal canal while it was still alive. Carhart's lawyers emphasized that
the Nebraska legislature had rejected an amendment to the bill to refer
specifically to "dilation and extraction" instead of "partial birth abortion."*

*The state's attorneys countered that the language of the statute as well as
the legislature's intent clearly established that the statute applied only to the
D&X procedure. In a D&E procedure, the state argued, the doctor did not intend to deliver an "unborn child." As for the "substantial portions" phrase,
the state argued it was used only to prevent abortion doctors from creating
a loophole in the law.*

*Carhart and the state argued one other issue: the law's failure to include
an exception to permit the procedure to protect the health of the mother. Carhart's attorneys argued that Roe clearly mandated a health exception, but
the state's lawyers argued that no health exception was needed. A partial
birth abortion was never medically necessary, they claimed, because safe
alternative methods were available. Carhart disagreed, insisting that the
D&X procedure was the only safe procedure in some cases.*

*A federal district court in Omaha agreed with Carhart that the law was
unconstitutional on both issues. On appeal the Eighth Circuit Court of Appeals also ruled the law unconstitutional but only on the ground that the
statute imposed an "undue burden" on a woman's right to abortion by prohibiting D&E and D&X procedures. The ruling coincided with most other
court decisions on partial birth abortions. But a month later the Seventh
Circuit Court of Appeals upheld partial birth abortion bans enacted in Illinois and Wisconsin. The conflict between the two circuit courts, along with
the continuing controversy over the issue, made it harder for the Supreme
Court justices to ignore the dispute, and in January 2000 the Court agreed
to take up the Nebraska case.*

## The Court's Decision

*The Supreme Court's decision in* Stenberg v. Carhart *was handed down on
June 28, the final day of the Court's 1999–2000 term. The majority and minority opinions in* Stenberg *relied on opposing interpretation of the Court's
1992 decision in* Casey. *Justice Stephen G. Breyer, writing for the majority,
began by acknowledging "the controversial nature of the problem" and the
"virtually irreconcilable points of view" on the issue. In the remainder of
his opinion, Breyer proceeded unemotionally through medical and legal de-*

*tails in concluding that the law was unconstitutional both because it was too broad and therefore imposed an "undue burden" on the right to abortion and because it did not include a health exception.*

*Starting with the health exception issue, Breyer detailed eight arguments the state had made for omitting the exception and rejected them one by one. A state law "that altogether forbids D&X creates a significant health risk," he concluded. "The statute must consequently contain a health exception." Breyer also detailed and then rejected the state's interpretation of the statute as applying only to D&X procedures. "[U]sing this law, some present prosecutors and future Attorneys General may choose to pursue physicians who use D&E procedures," he said. "All those who perform abortion procedures using that method must fear prosecution, conviction, and punishment. The result is an undue burden on a woman's right to make an abortion decision."*

*Four justices joined with Breyer: John Paul Stevens, Sandra Day O'Connor, David H. Souter, and Ruth Bader Ginsburg. In a concurring opinion, O'Connor briefly recapped the reasons for holding Nebraska's law unconstitutional and then indicated her willingness to accept a more carefully drafted statute that clearly applied solely to the D&X procedure and that included a health exception. In separate concurrences, Stevens and Ginsburg both said they saw no legal distinction between the two procedures. "[T]he notion that either of these two equally gruesome procedures performed at this late stage of gestation is more akin to infanticide than the other, or that the State furthers any legitimate interest by banning one but not the other, is simply irrational," Stevens wrote.*

*Justice Thomas, who called the majority opinion "indefensible," wrote the longest of the four dissenting opinions. Thomas insisted that the majority was misreading "the plain language of the statute" when it applied it to D&E procedures and, in any event, was wrong to substitute its interpretation for the state attorney general's. As for the health exception, Thomas said the majority was wrong to require an exception merely because a woman or doctor preferred one procedure to the other. "The exception entirely swallows the rule," he wrote. "[T]here will always be some support for a procedure and there will always be some doctors who conclude that the procedure is preferable." Thomas's opinion was joined by Chief Justice William H. Rehnquist and Justice Antonin Scalia, who each wrote short separate dissents. Justice Kennedy, in a separate dissent, said the Carhart ruling "repudiates" the "understanding" that states could enact laws "to promote the life of the unborn and to ensure respect for all human life and its potential."*

## Restriction Upheld on Demonstrations Outside Clinics

*In another decision handed down June 28, the Court, by a 6–3 majority, upheld a Colorado law restricting antiabortion demonstrations outside health clinics. The law, which was challenged as a violation of free speech guarantees, barred people from counseling, distributing leaflets, or displaying signs within eight feet of others, without their consent, whenever they were within one hundred feet of a health clinic entrance. "This statute sim-*

*ply empowers private citizens entering a health care facility with the ability to prevent a speaker, who is within eight feet and advancing, from communicating a message they do not wish to hear," Justice Stevens wrote for the majority in the case of* Hill v. Colorado. *"The right to free speech . . . includes the right to attempt to persuade others to change their views, and may not be curtailed simply because the speaker's message may be offensive to his audience," Stevens wrote. "But the protection afforded to offensive messages does not always embrace offensive speech that is so intrusive that the unwilling audience cannot avoid it." Stevens was joined by Rehnquist, O'Connor, Souter, Ginsburg, and Breyer. Scalia, Kennedy, and Thomas dissented. Reading portions of his opinion from the bench, Scalia said the decision was "one of many aggressively pro-abortion novelties announced by the Court in recent years." Kennedy said the decision was "an unprecedented departure" from the Court's previous holdings on unpopular speech in public places.*

*The Colorado law was enacted in 1993 after abortion patients complained of being spat upon, kicked, and otherwise harassed as they entered abortion clinics. Abortion rights activists claimed that the incidence of violence outside abortion clinics was increasing. According to a survey by the Feminist Majority Foundation, one-fifth of 360 clinics surveyed in 1999 reported that they had experienced blockades, invasions, bomb threats, or actual bombings in the previous year. The challenge to the Colorado law was supported by several liberal groups, including the American Civil Liberties Union and the AFL-CIO, which argued that its language was general enough to apply, for example, to striking health workers picketing outside hospitals.*

> *Following are excerpts from the opinion, concurring opinions, and dissents in the case of* Stenberg v. Carhart, *in which the Supreme Court on June 28, 2000, by a 5–4 vote, struck down a state law seeking to ban partial birth abortions because the statute imposed an "undue burden" on the right of a woman to obtain an abortion and because it did not contain an exception to protect the health of the mother. The document was obtained from the Internet at http://www.supremecourtus.gov/opinions/99pdf/998-1856.pdf.*

No. 99-830

| Don Stenberg, Attorney General of Nebraska, et al., Petitioners<br>v.<br>Leroy Carhart | } | On writ of certiorari to the United States Court of Appeals for the Eighth Circuit |

[June 28, 2000]

JUSTICE BREYER delivered the opinion of the Court.

We again consider the right to an abortion. We understand the controversial nature of the problem. Millions of Americans believe that life begins at conception and consequently that an abortion is akin to causing the death of an innocent child; they recoil at the thought of a law that would permit it. Other millions fear that a law that forbids abortion would condemn many American women to lives that lack dignity, depriving them of equal liberty and leading those with least resources to undergo illegal abortions with the attendant risks of death and suffering. Taking account of these virtually irreconcilable points of view, aware that constitutional law must govern a society whose different members sincerely hold directly opposing views, and considering the matter in light of the Constitution's guarantees of fundamental individual liberty, this Court, in the course of a generation, has determined and then redetermined that the Constitution offers basic protection to the woman's right to choose. *Roe v. Wade* (1973); *Planned Parenthood of Southeastern Pa. v. Casey* (1992). We shall not revisit those legal principles. Rather, we apply them to the circumstances of this case.

Three established principles determine the issue before us. We shall set them forth in the language of the joint opinion in *Casey*. [Joint opinion of O'CONNOR, KENNEDY, and SOUTER, JJ.] First, before "viability ... the woman has a right to choose to terminate her pregnancy."

Second, "a law designed to further the State's interest in fetal life which imposes an undue burden on the woman's decision before fetal viability" is unconstitutional. An "undue burden is ... shorthand for the conclusion that a state regulation has the purpose or effect of placing a substantial obstacle in the path of a woman seeking an abortion of a nonviable fetus."

Third, "'subsequent to viability, the State in promoting its interest in the potentiality of human life may, if it chooses, regulate, and even proscribe, abortion except where it is necessary, in appropriate medical judgment, for the preservation of the life or health of the mother.'" [Quoting *Roe v. Wade*.]

We apply these principles to a Nebraska law banning "partial birth abortion." The statute reads as follows:

"No partial birth abortion shall be performed in this state, unless such procedure is necessary to save the life of the mother whose life is endangered by a physical disorder, physical illness, or physical injury, including a life-endangering physical condition caused by or arising from the pregnancy itself." Neb. Rev. Stat. Ann. §28-328(1)

The statute defines "partial birth abortion" as:

"an abortion procedure in which the person performing the abortion partially delivers vaginally a living unborn child before killing the unborn child and completing the delivery." §28-326(9).

It further defines "partially delivers vaginally a living unborn child before killing the unborn child" to mean "deliberately and intentionally delivering into the vagina a living unborn child, or a substantial portion thereof, for the purpose of performing a procedure that the person performing such procedure knows will kill the unborn child and does kill the unborn child."

. . . We hold that this statute violates the Constitution.

# I

## A

Dr. Leroy Carhart is a Nebraska physician who performs abortions in a clinical setting. He brought this lawsuit in Federal District Court seeking a declaration that the Nebraska statute violates the Federal Constitution, and asking for an injunction forbidding its enforcement. After a trial on the merits, during which both sides presented several expert witnesses, the District Court held the statute unconstitutional (1998). On appeal, the Eighth Circuit affirmed (1999). . . . We granted certiorari to consider the matter.

## B

Because Nebraska law seeks to ban one method of aborting a pregnancy, we must describe and then discuss several different abortion procedures. Considering the fact that those procedures seek to terminate a potential human life, our discussion may seem clinically cold or callous to some, perhaps horrifying to others. There is no alternative way, however, to acquaint the reader with the technical distinctions among different abortion methods and related factual matters, upon which the outcome of this case depends. . . .

1. About 90% of all abortions performed in the United States take place during the first trimester of pregnancy, before 12 weeks of gestational age. During the first trimester, the predominant abortion method is "vacuum aspiration," which involves insertion of a vacuum tube (cannula) into the uterus to evacuate the contents. Such an abortion is typically performed on an outpatient basis under local anesthesia. Vacuum aspiration is considered particularly safe. . . . As the fetus grows in size, however, the vacuum aspiration method becomes increasingly difficult to use.

2. Approximately 10% of all abortions are performed during the second trimester of pregnancy (12 to 24 weeks). In the early 1970's, inducing labor through the injection of saline into the uterus was the predominant method of second trimester abortion. Today, however, the medical profession has switched from medical induction of labor to surgical procedures for most second trimester abortions. The most commonly used procedure is called "dilation and evacuation" (D&E). That procedure (together with a modified form of vacuum aspiration used in the early second trimester) accounts for about 95% of all abortions performed from 12 to 20 weeks of gestational age.

3. D&E "refers generically to transcervical procedures performed at 13 weeks gestation or later." [Detailed description of procedure as performed at 13-15 weeks of gestation, after 15 weeks, and after 20 weeks omitted.]

There are variations in D&E operative strategy. . . . However, the common points are that D&E involves (1) dilation of the cervix; (2) removal of at least some fetal tissue using nonvacuum instruments; and (3) (after the 15th week) the potential need for instrumental disarticulation or dismemberment of the fetus or the collapse of fetal parts to facilitate evacuation from the uterus.

4. When instrumental disarticulation incident to D&E is necessary, it typically occurs as the doctor pulls a portion of the fetus through the cervix into the birth canal. . . .

5. The D&E procedure carries certain risks. The use of instruments within the uterus creates a danger of accidental perforation and damage to neighboring organs. Sharp fetal bone fragments create similar dangers. And fetal tissue accidentally left behind can cause infection and various other complications. Nonetheless, studies show that the risks of mortality and complication that accompany the D&E procedure between the 12th and 20th weeks of gestation are significantly lower than those accompanying induced labor procedures. . . .

6. At trial, Dr. Carhart and Dr. [Philip] Stubblefield described a variation of the D&E procedure, which they referred to as an "intact D&E." Like other versions of the D&E technique, it begins with induced dilation of the cervix. The procedure then involves removing the fetus from the uterus through the cervix "intact," *i.e.*, in one pass, rather than in several passes. It is used after 16 weeks at the earliest, as vacuum aspiration becomes ineffective and the fetal skull becomes too large to pass through the cervix. The intact D&E proceeds in one of two ways, depending on the presentation of the fetus. If the fetus presents head first (a vertex presentation), the doctor collapses the skull; and the doctor then extracts the entire fetus through the cervix. If the fetus presents feet first (a breech presentation), the doctor pulls the fetal body through the cervix, collapses the skull, and extracts the fetus through the cervix. The breech extraction version of the intact D&E is also known commonly as "dilation and extraction," or D&X. In the late second trimester, vertex, breech, and traverse/compound (sideways) presentations occur in roughly similar proportions.

7. The intact D&E procedure can also be found described in certain obstetric and abortion clinical textbooks, where two variations are recognized. The first, as just described, calls for the physician to adapt his method for extracting the intact fetus depending on fetal presentation. This is the method used by Dr. Carhart. A slightly different version of the intact D&E procedure, associated with Dr. Martin Haskell, calls for conversion to a breech presentation in all cases.

8. The American College of Obstetricians and Gynecologists describes the D&X procedure in a manner corresponding to a breech-conversion intact D&E, including the following steps:

"1. deliberate dilatation of the cervix, usually over a sequence of days;

"2. instrumental conversion of the fetus to a footling breech;

"3. breech extraction of the body excepting the head; and

"4. partial evacuation of the intracranial contents of a living fetus to effect vaginal delivery of a dead but otherwise intact fetus." American College of Obstetricians and Gynecologists Executive Board, Statement on Intact Dilation and Extraction (Jan. 12, 1997) (hereinafter ACOG Statement).

Despite the technical differences we have just described, intact D&E and D&X are sufficiently similar for us to use the terms interchangeably.

9. Dr. Carhart testified he attempts to use the intact D&E procedure during weeks 16 to 20 because (1) it reduces the dangers from sharp bone fragments passing through the cervix, (2) minimizes the number of instrument passes needed for extraction and lessens the likelihood of uterine perforations caused by those instruments, (3) reduces the likelihood of leaving infection-causing fetal and placental tissue in the uterus, and (4) could help to prevent potentially fatal absorption of fetal tissue into the maternal circulation. The District Court made no findings about the D&X procedure's overall safety. The District Court concluded, however, that "the evidence is both clear and convincing that Carhart's D&X procedure is superior to, and safer than, the . . . other abortion procedures used during the relevant gestational period in the 10 to 20 cases a year that present to Dr. Carhart."

10. The materials presented at trial referred to the potential benefits of the D&X procedure in circumstances involving nonviable fetuses, such as fetuses with abnormal fluid accumulation in the brain (hydrocephaly). . . . Others have emphasized its potential for women with prior uterine scars, or for women for whom induction of labor would be particularly dangerous. . . .

11. There are no reliable data on the number of D&X abortions performed annually. Estimates have ranged between 640 and 5,000 per year. . . .

## II

The question before us is whether Nebraska's statute, making criminal the performance of a "partial birth abortion," violates the Federal Constitution, as interpreted in *Planned Parenthood of Southeastern Pa. v. Casey* (1992) and *Roe v. Wade* (1973). We conclude that it does for at least two independent reasons. First, the law lacks any exception "for the preservation of the . . . health of the mother." Second, it "imposes an undue burden on a woman's ability" to choose a D&E abortion, thereby unduly burdening the right to choose abortion itself. . . .

## A

The *Casey* joint opinion reiterated what the Court held in Roe; that "subsequent to viability, the State in promoting its interest in the potentiality of human life may, if it chooses, regulate, and even proscribe, abortion *except where it is necessary, in appropriate medical judgment, for the preservation of the life or health of the mother*" (emphasis added).

The fact that Nebraska's law applies both pre- and postviability aggravates the constitutional problem presented. The State's interest in regulating abortion previability is considerably weaker than postviability. Since the law requires a health exception in order to validate even a postviability abortion regulation, it at a minimum requires the same in respect to previability regulation. . . .

The quoted standard also depends on the state regulations "promoting [the State's] interest in the potentiality of human life." The Nebraska law, of course, does not directly further an interest "in the potentiality of human life" by saving the fetus in question from destruction, as it regulates only a method of performing abortion. Nebraska describes its interests differently. It says the law "show[s] concern for the life of the unborn," "prevent[s] cruelty to partially born children," and "preserve[s] the integrity of the medical profession." But we cannot see how the interest-related differences could make any difference to the question at hand, namely, the application of the "health" requirement.

Consequently, the governing standard requires an exception "where it is necessary, in appropriate medical judgment for the preservation of the life or health of the mother," *Casey*, for this Court has made clear that a State may promote but not endanger a woman's health when it regulates the methods of abortion. [Citations to four previous cases omitted.]

JUSTICE THOMAS says that the cases just cited limit this principle to situations where the pregnancy itself creates a threat to health. He is wrong. The cited cases, reaffirmed in *Casey*, recognize that a State cannot subject women's health to significant risks both in that context, and also where state regulations force women to use riskier methods of abortion. Our cases have repeatedly invalidated statutes that in the process of regulating the methods of abortion, imposed significant health risks. They make clear that a risk to a woman's health is the same whether it happens to arise from regulating a particular method of abortion, or from barring abortion entirely. . . .

## 1

Nebraska responds that the law does not require a health exception unless there is a need for such an exception. And here there is no such need, it says. It argues that "safe alternatives remain available" and "a ban on partial-birth abortion/D&X would create no risk to the health of women." The problem for Nebraska is that the parties strongly contested this factual question in the trial court below; and the findings and evidence support Dr. Carhart. The State fails to demonstrate that banning D&X without a health exception may not create significant health risks for women, because the record shows that significant medical authority supports the proposition that in some circumstances, D&X would be the safest procedure. [Summary of district court's findings omitted.]

[Section 2, listing the state's arguments for not needing a health exception, and Section 3, stating why the majority found these arguments "insufficient," omitted.]

## 4

The upshot is a District Court finding that D&X significantly obviates health risks in certain circumstances, a highly plausible record-based explanation of why that might be so, a division of opinion among some medical experts over whether D&X is generally safer, and an absence of controlled medical studies that would help answer these medical questions. Given these medically related evidentiary circumstances, we believe the law requires a health exception.

The word "necessary" in *Casey*'s phrase "necessary, in appropriate medical judgment, for the preservation of the life or health of the mother" cannot refer to an absolute necessity or to absolute proof. Medical treatments and procedures are often considered appropriate (or inappropriate) in light of estimated comparative health risks (and health benefits) in particular cases. Neither can that phrase require unanimity of medical opinion. Doctors often differ in their estimation of comparative health risks and appropriate treatment. And *Casey*'s words "appropriate medical judgment" must embody the judicial need to tolerate responsible differences of medical opinion. . . .

For another thing, the division of medical opinion about the matter at most means uncertainty, a factor that signals the presence of risk, not its absence. . . . [T]he uncertainty means a significant likelihood that those who believe that D&X is a safer abortion method in certain circumstances may turn out to be right. If so, then the absence of a health exception will place women at an unnecessary risk of tragic health consequences. If they are wrong, the exception will simply turn out to have been unnecessary.

In sum, Nebraska has not convinced us that a health exception is "never necessary to preserve the health of women." Rather, a statute that altogether forbids D&X creates a significant health risk. The statute consequently must contain a health exception. This is not to say, as JUSTICE THOMAS and JUSTICE KENNEDY claim, that a State is prohibited from proscribing an abortion procedure whenever a particular physician deems the procedure preferable. . . . [W]here substantial medical authority supports the proposition that banning a particular abortion procedure could endanger women's health, *Casey* requires the statute to include a health exception. . . .

## B

The Eighth Circuit found the Nebraska statute unconstitutional because, in *Casey*'s words, it has the "effect of placing a substantial obstacle in the path of a woman seeking an abortion of a nonviable fetus." It thereby places an "undue burden" upon a woman's right to terminate her pregnancy before viability. Nebraska does not deny that the statute imposes an "undue burden" if it applies to the more commonly used D&E procedure as well as to D&X. And we agree with the Eighth Circuit that it does so apply.

Our earlier discussion of the D&E procedure shows that it falls within the statutory prohibition. The statute forbids "deliberately and intentionally delivering into the vagina a living unborn child, or a substantial portion thereof, for the purpose of performing a procedure that the person performing such procedure knows will kill the unborn child." We do not understand how one could distinguish, using this language, between D&E (where a foot or arm is drawn through the cervix) and D&X (where the body up to the head is drawn through the cervix). . . .

Even if the statute's basic aim is to ban D&X, its language makes clear that it also covers a much broader category of procedures. The language does not track the medical differences between D&E and D&X—though it would have been a simple matter, for example, to provide an exception for the performance of D&E and other abortion procedures. [Citing Kansas statute.] Nor does the statute anywhere suggest that its application turns on whether a portion of the fetus' body is drawn into the vagina as part of a process to extract an intact fetus after collapsing the head as opposed to a process that would dismember the fetus. Thus, the dissenters' argument that the law was generally intended to bar D&X can be both correct and irrelevant. The relevant question is not whether the legislature wanted to ban D&X; it is whether the law was intended to apply only to D The plain language covers both procedures. . . .

The Nebraska State Attorney General argues that the statute does differentiate between the two procedures. He says that the statutory words "substantial portion" mean "the child up to the head." He consequently denies the statute's application where the physician introduces into the birth canal a fetal arm or leg or anything less than the entire fetal body. He argues further that we must defer to his views about the meaning of the state statute.

We cannot accept the Attorney General's narrowing interpretation of the Nebraska statute. This Court's case law makes clear that we are not to give the Attorney General's interpretative views controlling weight. For one thing, this Court normally follows lower federal-court interpretations of state law. . . . In this case, the two lower courts have both rejected the Attorney General's narrowing interpretation.

For another, our precedent warns against accepting as "authoritative" an Attorney General's interpretation of state law when "the Attorney General does not bind the state courts or local law enforcement authorities." . . .

Nor can we say that the lower courts used the wrong legal standard in assessing the Attorney General's interpretation.

Regardless, even were we to grant the Attorney General's views "substantial weight," we still have to reject his interpretation, for it conflicts with the statutory language. . . .

We are aware that adopting the Attorney General's interpretation might avoid the constitutional problem discussed in this section. But we are "without power to adopt a narrowing construction of a state statute unless such a construction is reasonable and readily apparent." [Citation omitted.] For the reasons stated, it is not reasonable to replace the term "substantial portion" with the Attorney General's phrase "body up to the head." . . .

In sum, using this law some present prosecutors and future Attorneys General may choose to pursue physicians who use D procedures, the most commonly used method for performing previability second trimester abortions. All those who perform abortion procedures using that method must fear prosecution, conviction, and imprisonment. The result is an undue burden upon a woman's right to make an abortion decision. We must consequently find the statute unconstitutional.

The judgment of the Court of Appeals is

*Affirmed.*

JUSTICE STEVENS, with whom JUSTICE GINSBURG joins, concurring.

Although much ink is spilled today describing the gruesome nature of late-term abortion procedures, that rhetoric does not provide me a reason to believe that the procedure Nebraska here claims it seeks to ban is more brutal, more gruesome, or less respectful of "potential life" than the equally gruesome procedure Nebraska claims it still allows. . . . [T]he notion that either of these two equally gruesome procedures performed at this late stage of gestation is more akin to infanticide than the other, or that the State furthers any legitimate interest by banning the one but not the other, is simply irrational.

JUSTICE O'CONNOR, concurring.
. . . I agree that Nebraska's statute cannot be reconciled with our decision in *Planned Parenthood of Southeastern Pa. v. Casey* (1992) and is therefore unconstitutional. . . .
. . . [U]nlike Nebraska, some other States have enacted statutes more narrowly tailored to proscribing the D&X procedure alone. Some of those statutes have done so by specifically excluding from their coverage the most common methods of abortion, such as the D&E and vacuum aspiration procedures. [Citing Kansas, Utah, and Montana statutes.]
If Nebraska's statute limited its application to the D&X procedure and included an exception for the life and health of the mother, the question presented would be quite different than the one we face today. . . . [A] ban on partial-birth abortion that only proscribed the D&X method of abortion and that included an exception to preserve the life and health of the mother would be constitutional in my view. . . .

JUSTICE GINSBURG, with whom JUSTICE STEVENS joins, concurring.
I write separately only to stress that amidst all the emotional uproar caused by an abortion case, we should not lose sight of the character of Nebraska's "partial birth abortion" law. As the Court observes, this law does not save any fetus from destruction, for it targets only "a method of performing abortion." Nor does the statute seek to protect the lives or health of pregnant women. Moreover, as JUSTICE STEVENS points out, the most common method of performing previability second trimester abortions is no less distressing or susceptible to gruesome description. . . .

CHIEF JUSTICE REHNQUIST, dissenting.
I did not join the joint opinion in *Planned Parenthood of Southeastern Pa. v. Casey* (1992) and continue to believe that case is wrongly decided. Despite my disagreement with the opinion, . . . the *Casey* joint opinion represents the holding of the Court in that case. I believe JUSTICE KENNEDY and JUSTICE THOMAS have correctly applied *Casey*'s principles and join their dissenting opinions.

JUSTICE SCALIA, dissenting.
I am optimistic enough to believe that, one day, *Stenberg v. Carhart* will be assigned its rightful place in the history of this Court's jurisprudence beside *Korematsu* and *Dred Scott*. The method of killing a human child—one cannot even accurately say an entirely unborn human child—proscribed by this statute is so horrible that the most clinical description of it evokes a shudder

of revulsion. And the Court must know (as most state legislatures banning this procedure have concluded) that demanding a "health exception"—which requires the abortionist to assure himself that, in his expert medical judgment, this method is, in the case at hand, marginally safer than others (how can one prove the contrary beyond a reasonable doubt?)—is to give live-birth abortion free rein. . . .

[In the remainder of his opinion, Scalia sharply criticized the *Casey* decision and its "undue burden" standard, which he had described in dissent in that case as "unprincipled in origin" and "hopelessly unworkable in practice." He concluded: "*Casey* must be overruled."]

JUSTICE KENNEDY, with whom THE CHIEF JUSTICE joins, dissenting.

. . . When the Court reaffirmed the essential holding of *Roe* [*v. Wade* (1973)], a central premise was that the States retain a critical and legitimate role in legislating on the subject of abortion, as limited by the woman's right the Court restated and again guaranteed. *Planned Parenthood of Southeastern Pa. v. Casey* (1992). The political processes of the State are not to be foreclosed from enacting laws to promote the life of the unborn and to ensure respect for all human life and its potential. [Citing joint opinion of O'CONNOR, KENNEDY, and SOUTER, JJ.] . . .

The Court's decision today, in my submission, repudiates this understanding by invalidating a statute advancing critical state interests, even though the law denies no woman the right to choose an abortion and places no undue burden upon the right. The legislation is well within the State's competence to enact. Having concluded Nebraska's law survives the scrutiny dictated by a proper understanding of *Casey*, I dissent from the judgment invalidating it.

# I

The Court's failure to accord any weight to Nebraska's interest in prohibiting partial-birth abortion is erroneous and undermines its discussion and holding. . . . The majority views the procedures from the perspective of the abortionist, rather than from the perspective of a society shocked when confronted with a new method of ending human life. . . .

. . . The State's brief describes its interests as including concern for the life of the unborn and "for the partially-born," in preserving the integrity of the medical profession, and in "erecting a barrier to infanticide." A review of *Casey* demonstrates the legitimacy of these policies. The Court should say so.

States may take sides in the abortion debate and come down on the side of life, even life in the unborn. . . .

States also have an interest in forbidding medical procedures which, in the State's reasonable determination, might cause the medical profession or society as a whole to become insensitive, even disdainful, to life, including life in the human fetus. . . .

A State may take measures to ensure the medical profession and its members are viewed as healers, sustained by a compassionate and rigorous ethic and cognizant of the dignity and value of human life, even life which cannot survive without the assistance of others.

... It is argued, however, that a ban on the D&X does not further these interests. This is because, the reasoning continues, the D&E method, which Nebraska claims to be beyond its intent to regulate, can still be used to abort a fetus and is no less dehumanizing than the D&X method.... The issue is not whether members of the judiciary can see a difference between the two procedures. It is whether Nebraska can. The Court's refusal to recognize Nebraska's right to declare a moral difference between the procedure is a dispiriting disclosure of the illogic and illegitimacy of the Court's approach to the entire case....

## II

Demonstrating a further and basic misunderstanding of *Casey*, the Court holds the ban on the D&X procedure fails because it does not include an exception permitting an abortionist to perform a D&X whenever he believes it will best preserve the health of the woman. Casting aside the views of distinguished physicians and the statements of leading medical organizations, the Court awards each physician a veto power over the State's judgment that the procedures should not be performed. Dr. Carhart has made the medical judgment to use the D&X procedure in every case, regardless of indications, after 15 weeks gestation. Requiring Nebraska to defer to Dr. Carhart's judgment is no different than forbidding Nebraska from enacting a ban at all; for it is now Dr. Leroy Carhart who sets abortion policy for the State of Nebraska, not the legislature or the people. *Casey* does not give precedence to the views of a single physician or a group of physicians regarding the relative safety of a particular procedure. [Remainder of section omitted.]

## III

The Court's next holding is that Nebraska's ban forbids both the D&X procedure and the more common D&E procedure. In so ruling the Court misapplies settled doctrines of statutory construction and contradicts *Casey*'s premise that the States have a vital constitutional position in the abortion debate.... Like the ruling requiring a physician veto, requiring a State to meet unattainable standards of statutory draftsmanship in order to have its voice heard on this grave and difficult subject is no different from foreclosing state participation altogether. [Remainder of section omitted.]

## IV

Ignoring substantial medical and ethical opinion, the Court substitutes its own judgment for the judgment of Nebraska and some 30 other States and sweeps the law away. The Court's holding stems from misunderstanding the record, misinterpretation of *Casey*, outright refusal to respect the law of a State, and statutory construction in conflict with settled rules. The decision nullifies a law expressing the will of the people of Nebraska that medical procedures must be governed by moral principles having their foundation in the intrinsic value of human life, including life of the unborn. Through their law the people of Nebraska were forthright in confronting an issue of immense moral consequence. The State chose to forbid a procedure many decent and civilized people find so abhorrent as to be among the most serious of crimes against human life, while the State still protected the woman's autonomous right of choice as reaffirmed in *Casey*. The Court closes its eyes to these profound concerns.

From the decision, the reasoning, and the judgment, I dissent.

JUSTICE THOMAS, with whom THE CHIEF JUSTICE and JUSTICE SCALIA join, dissenting. . . .

Today, the Court inexplicably holds that the States cannot constitutionally prohibit a method of abortion that millions find hard to distinguish from infanticide and that the Court hesitates even to describe. This holding cannot be reconciled with *Casey*'s undue-burden standard, as that standard was explained to us by the authors of the joint opinion, and the majority hardly pretends otherwise. In striking down this statute—which expresses a profound and legitimate respect for fetal life and which leaves unimpeded several other safe forms of abortion—the majority opinion gives the lie to the promise of *Casey* that regulations that do no more than "express profound respect for the life of the unborn are permitted, if they are not a substantial obstacle to the woman's exercise of the right to choose" whether or not to have an abortion. Today's decision is so obviously irreconcilable with *Casey*'s explication of what its undue-burden standard requires, let alone the Constitution, that it should be seen for what it is, a reinstitution of the pre-*Webster* abortion-on-demand era in which the mere invocation of "abortion rights" trumps any contrary societal interest. If this statute is unconstitutional under *Casey*, then *Casey* meant nothing at all, and the Court should candidly admit it.

To reach its decision, the majority must take a series of indefensible steps. The majority must first disregard the principles that this Court follows in every context but abortion: We interpret statutes according to their plain meaning and we do not strike down statutes susceptible of a narrowing construction. The majority also must disregard the very constitutional standard it purports to employ, and then displace the considered judgment of the people of Nebraska and 29 other States. The majority's decision is lamentable, because of the result the majority reaches, the illogical steps the majority takes to reach it, and because it portends a return to an era I had thought we had at last abandoned.

## [I–III omitted.]

## IV

Having resolved that Nebraska's partial birth abortion statute permits doctors to perform D&E abortions, the question remains whether a State can constitutionally prohibit the partial birth abortion procedure without a health exception. Although the majority and JUSTICE O'CONNOR purport to rely on the standard articulated in the *Casey* joint opinion in concluding that a State may not, they in fact disregard it entirely.

## [A omitted.]

## B

There is no question that the State of Nebraska has a valid interest—one not designed to strike at the right itself—in prohibiting partial birth abortion. *Casey* itself noted that States may "express profound respect for the life of the unborn." States may, without a doubt, express this profound respect by prohibiting a procedure that approaches infanticide, and thereby dehumanizes the fetus and trivializes human life. The [American Medical Association] has recognized that this procedure is "ethically different from other destructive abortion techniques because the fetus, normally twenty weeks or longer in gestation, is killed outside the womb. The 'partial birth' gives the fetus an autonomy which separates it from the right of the woman to choose treatments for her own body." AMA Board of Trustees Factsheet on H. R. 1122 (June 1997). Thirty States have concurred with this view....

## C

The next question, therefore, is whether the Nebraska statute is unconstitutional because it does not contain an exception that would allow use of the procedure whenever "necessary in appropriate medical judgment, for the preservation of the ... health of the mother."...

The majority and JUSTICE O'CONNOR suggest that their rule is dictated by a straightforward application of *Roe* and *Casey*. But that is simply not true.... These cases addressed only the situation in which a woman must obtain an abortion because of some threat to her health from continued pregnancy. But *Roe* and *Casey* say nothing at all about cases in which a physician considers one prohibited method of abortion to be preferable to permissible methods....

... [T]he majority expands the health exception rule ... in one additional and equally pernicious way. Although *Roe* and *Casey* mandated a health exception for cases in which abortion is "necessary" for a woman's health, the majority concludes that a procedure is "necessary" if it has any comparative health benefits.... But such a health exception requirement eviscerates *Casey*'s undue burden standard and imposes unfettered abortion-on-demand. The exception entirely swallows the rule. In effect, no regulation of abortion procedures is permitted because there will always be some support for a procedure and there will always be some doctors who conclude that the procedure is preferable.... JUSTICE O'CONNOR's assurance that the constitutional failings of Nebraska's statute can be easily fixed is illusory. The majority's insistence on a health exception is a fig leaf barely covering its hostility to any abortion regulation by the States....

## D

The majority assiduously avoids addressing the actual standard articulated in *Casey*—whether prohibiting partial birth abortion without a health exception poses a substantial obstacle to obtaining an abortion. And for good reason: Such an obstacle does not exist. There are two essential reasons why the Court cannot identify a substantial obstacle. First, the Court cannot identify any real, much less substantial, barrier to any woman's ability to obtain an abortion. And second, the Court cannot demonstrate that any such obstacle would affect a sufficient number of women to justify invalidating the statute on its face. [Remainder of section omitted.]

We were reassured repeatedly in *Casey* that not all regulations of abortion are unwarranted and that the States may express profound respect for fetal life. Under *Casey*, the regulation before us today should easily pass constitutional muster. But the Court's abortion jurisprudence is a particularly virulent strain of constitutional exegesis. And so today we are told that 30 States are prohibited from banning one rarely used form of abortion that they believe to border on infanticide. It is clear that the Constitution does not compel this result.

I respectfully dissent.

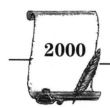
# July

# ORGANIZATION OF AFRICAN UNITY REPORT ON RWANDAN GENOCIDE
## July 7, 2000

*Six years after at least 500,000 Rwandans were slaughtered in a brutal genocide, world leaders were still trying to come to grips with the question of why it was allowed to happen. An international panel appointed by the Organization of African Unity (OAU) reported in July that the 1994 genocide in Rwanda could have been prevented, or at least minimized, if the United Nations and key countries—most notably France and the United States—had been willing to take more assertive action. The panel said Rwanda was owed "reparations" by the international community.*

*The OAU panel was the second major international body to issue a report condemning the world's failure to take more action at the time of the Rwandan tragedy. In 1999 an investigating committee appointed by United Nations Secretary General Kofi Annan concluded that the UN did not meet its responsibilities in part because of a lack of "political will" on the part of UN Security Council member nations. That report did not name individual nations but did condemn the Security Council's unwillingness to bolster a UN peacekeeping force in Rwanda that lacked the resources or the mandate to halt the genocide. The OAU and UN reports closely paralleled the findings of important nongovernmental organizations that had probed the Rwanda genocide, including Human Rights Watch and Amnesty International.* (Rwanda genocide, Historic Documents of 1994, p. 541; UN report, Historic Documents of 1999, p. 860)

*Six weeks after the OAU issued its report, another UN panel, also appointed by Annan, issued broader findings on the state of the world body's peacekeeping efforts. The UN's failure in Rwanda was a key stimulus for that report.* (Peacekeeping report, p. 642)

*Earlier in the year, on April 14, the UN Security Council held a session at which representatives of various nations acknowledged the world's failure to act in Rwanda. Canadian foreign minister Lloyd Axworthy, who chaired the session, said: "I doubt any in this chamber can look back at that time without remorse and a great deal of sadness at the failure to help the people of Rwanda in their time of need." The full Security Council did not issue a formal statement at that session.*

*Despite the renewed attention to the Rwandan genocide, there appeared to be no concerted effort made by world leaders during the year to ease the continuing suffering in that country. The OAU panel's call for reparations was met with silence in key world capitals, and the UN did not act on the issue. The World Bank and the International Monetary Fund agreed late in the year to forgive about $500 million in Rwandan government debt under an international debt-relief program. In Rwanda itself, the Tutsi-led government launched its first full campaign to document exactly how many people had died in the genocide; the campaign was still under way at year's end.* (Debt relief, p. 475)

*The underlying questions attending the Rwandan genocide were of more than historical interest. The brutal killings in Rwanda caused massive flows of refugees throughout the Great Lakes region of Africa, leading to the 1997 overthrow of neighboring Zaire's longtime leader, Mobutu Sese Seko, and then a bloody war against Mobutu's successor that involved seven African nations, including Rwanda. The UN Security Council—often blamed for its failure to support a UN peacekeeping mission stationed in Rwanda at the time of the genocide—struggled during 2000 with questions of how to manage peacekeeping missions in Congo and Sierra Leone.* (Congo war, p. 978; Sierra Leone war, p. 1072)

*Lingering uncertainties about what the United States should have done in Rwanda in 1994 also came into play during the 2000 presidential election campaign. During their televised debate on October 11, Democrat Al Gore and Republican George W. Bush were asked about the lessons of the genocide. Bush said the Clinton administration acted correctly when it did not send U.S. troops to try to stop the killing. Bush also argued that the genocide did not directly involve U.S. national or strategic interests. Gore said that "in retrospect, we were too late getting in" to Rwanda and that "we could have saved more lives if we had acted earlier."*

## Background to the Genocide

*The OAU appointed the seven-member panel in 1998. Panel members were Q. K. J. Masire, former president of Botswana; Amadou Toumani Roure, former president of Mali; Lisbet Palme, a child psychologist from Sweden; Ellen Johnson-Sirleaf, former finance minister of Liberia; P. N. Bhagwati, former chief justice of the Supreme Court of India; Hocine Djoudi, an Algerian judge and diplomat; and Stephen Lewis, of Canada, former deputy executive director of United Nations International Children's Emergency Fund.*

*The panel was given a broad mandate to investigate the causes and consequences of the Rwandan genocide. Apparently taking that mandate seriously, the panel delved into the history of Rwanda, beginning with its status as a German colony in the late 1800s. The underlying theme of the panel's report was that outside forces—starting in the colonial era and continuing to the present day—helped shape the essential character of Rwanda as a nation divided into two distinct ethnic groups, the Hutu and the Tutsi. Throughout the century before the genocide, the OAU report said, these groups alternated in power. A "culture of impunity" gradually evolved in which the group in power felt free to engage in ruthless domination of the other. Genocide, in which extremist leaders of the Hutu majority orchestrated mass killings of Tutsi and even Hutu moderates, was the eventual consequence.*

*Exploring Rwanda's colonial history, the OAU panel argued that German, and later Belgian, rulers sharpened already existing ethnic cleavages in the country by elevating the Tutsi minority to a privileged status, at the expense of the Hutu majority. Starting in 1959 a Hutu revolt against the Belgian-sanctioned Tutsi monarchy led to a series of clashes throughout the 1960s that resulted in the death of some 20,000 Tutsi. Another 200,000 Tutsi fled to neighboring countries, the panel said, setting the stage for the regional crisis of the 1990s. Neighboring Burundi, which also had a Hutu majority and Tutsi minority, likewise experienced ethnic conflicts in the years before and after the two countries gained independence in 1962.*

*Tension heightened dramatically in Rwanda in 1990, when a Tutsi-led rebel army, based in Uganda, invaded Rwanda and attacked forces of the Hutu-dominated government, led by President Juvenal Habyarimana. Many of the Tutsi rebels were the children of refugees from the battles during the 1960s, and most had never before set foot in Rwanda. The two sides fought for three years before reaching a peace agreement, signed at Arusha, Tanzania, in August 1993. The accord, which was never fully implemented, called for power sharing in Rwanda and established procedures for the return of hundreds of thousands of Tutsi refugees. Also as part of the agreement, the UN was to send a peacekeeping force to Rwanda. The UN's lightly armed force of 2,500 soldiers, with no mandate to enforce the peace, took up positions in the country early in 1994. The OAU panel said this UN force was totally inadequate for the task.*

*Intended to resolve the conflict between Hutu and Tutsi in Rwanda, the 1993 Arusha agreement instead heightened the conflict, the OAU panel said, by fostering fears among Hutu extremists that the Tutsi rebel army was bent on assuming power. During late 1993 and early 1994, these Hutu extremists—calling themselves "Hutu Power"—hatched plans for anti-Tutsi attacks that would later develop into genocide.*

*The OAU panel detailed several incidents during this period that should have alerted the international community that an immense tragedy was looming in Rwanda. By far the best documented event was a fax sent to UN headquarters on January 11, 1994, by General Romeo Dallaire, the Canadian commander of the UN peacekeeping force in Rwanda. The fax reported that a Rwandan military source had revealed plans for massive attacks on Tutsi in the capital, Kigali. Dallaire asked for permission to seize a cache of weapons that the source said had been assembled for the attacks. UN headquarters denied that request, as well as all of Dallaire's subsequent requests for permission to take forceful action to head off killings. The OAU report also cited numerous news reports and diplomatic cables early in 1994 that should have alerted world capitals to the deteriorating situation in Rwanda.*

*"There were a thousand early warnings that something appalling was about to occur in Rwanda," the OAU report said. "If not a genocide, it was at least a catastrophe of so great a magnitude that it should command international intervention."*

*The incident that sparked the genocide was the shooting down, near the Kigali airport on April 6, 1994, of an airplane carrying Rwandan president Habyarimana and his Burundian counterpart, Cyprien Ntaryamira, killing all aboard. The identity of those responsible for downing the plane was never established, and the OAU panel called for further investigation into the matter.*

*Within hours of the plane crash, Hutu extremists had seized power in Kigali, killed moderate Hutu leaders (including the prime minister, who was hunted down and shot at a UN office, where she had sought refuge), and launched sweeping attacks on Tutsi throughout the country.*

*On April 7, the first full day of the genocide, Hutu Power forces captured and killed ten Belgian members of the UN peacekeeping force, setting off alarms in world capitals about the fate of the peacekeepers. The Belgian government decided to withdraw its contingent of the UN force, and leading Western governments took steps to evacuate their nationals living in Rwanda.*

*Within the first two weeks of the genocide, an estimated 200,000 people had been killed, the vast majority of them Tutsi. Hutu extremists rounded up Tutsi by the dozen, often forcing them into schools, churches, and other public spaces where they were systematically slaughtered with guns, machetes, clubs—any lethal tools at hand. Thousands of Hutu civilians who had no personal grudge against the Tutsi were coerced to cooperate with the genocide. The OAU panel and other investigators documented cases in which husbands killed wives and children, priests killed parishioners, and teachers killed students during a national frenzy of hatred and revenge.*

*After the outbreak of the killings, the Tutsi-led rebel army—the Rwandan Popular Front, or RPF—launched counterattacks that by mid-July drove the Hutu extremists and hundreds of thousands of Hutu civilians from Rwanda, ending the genocide. The most conservative estimates were that more than 500,000 people had died during the genocide. The OAU panel said it was more likely that the death toll was close to 800,000, the "vast majority" of them Tutsi.*

## An International Failure to Act

*The OAU panel harshly denounced world leaders for failing to take actions that it said might have prevented the genocide or at least saved thousands of lives. The panel's three chief targets were the United Nations and the governments of France and the United States.*

*Key UN officials—including then-secretary general Boutros Boutros-Ghali and Annan, who at the time headed the UN's peacekeeping depart-*

*ment—ignored or played down indications that a genocide was possible and refused to allow the UN peacekeepers to take action against the Hutu extremists, the panel said. "From beginning to end, the UN record on Rwanda was appalling beyond belief," the panel said.*

*An understandable—but not excusable—reason for inaction by UN officials, the panel said, was that key nations represented on the Security Council had no appetite for deeper involvement in Rwanda. The panel noted in particular the roles of the United States and France, two of the five permanent members of the Security Council. U.S. leaders, the panel said, were still haunted by the killing in October 1993 of eighteen soldiers stationed in Somalia as part of an unsuccessful UN peacekeeping mission. The highly publicized deaths of those soldiers quickly undermined public support in the United States for UN peacekeeping missions, and led to a decision by the Clinton administration to oppose any further missions that did not have a high probability of success. The panel said the French government was even more directly implicated than Washington was in the genocide because of its longstanding financial, political, and military support for Rwanda's Hutu government.*

*In large part because of the U.S. and French positions, the UN Security Council in 1994 refused to authorize an expanded UN military presence in Rwanda. In fact, the Security Council on April 12 voted unanimously to reduce the existing force to a token presence of only 270 personnel. General Dallaire, the unit's commander, managed to hold onto a force of about 450 men, the OAU report said, but he had neither the mandate nor the resources to take any serious action against the genocide.*

*Using passionate language, the OAU panel denounced the U.S., French, Belgian, and Italian governments for sending military units to evacuate their citizens in Rwanda within days of the beginning of the genocide, while refusing to use armed force to blunt the terror against Rwandans. "Millions of views around the world have seen the television documentaries showing Western soldiers escorting white people to safety through crowds of Rwandans who would soon be slaughtered," the panel said. "We condemn those countries and those UN bureaucrats who were guilty of this flagrant double standard."*

*In releasing the report, one panel member, Canadian diplomat Stephen Lewis, sought to focus particular attention on the role of U.S. Secretary of State Madeleine K. Albright, who in 1994 was ambassador to the United Nations. It had been widely reported that Albright had lobbied behind the scenes to block a forceful UN intervention in Rwanda. "I don't know how Madeleine Albright lives with it," Lewis told reporters. Asked to respond, Albright defended her actions, telling an interviewer on ABC's* This Week *program on July 9 that she had "screamed about the instructions that I got" on the Rwanda issue from her superiors in Washington. Albright said the Rwandan massacre was "horrendous" but insisted that "it is wrong to place the blame on the United States." She noted that the United States "has done a great deal for Rwanda since then in terms of assistance."*

*In a statement released July 13, the Rwandan government said the OAU panel had "reached the conclusion that we, in Rwanda, have always known, and have been trying to tell the world with varying levels of success. Starkly put, one million Rwandans did not need to die in the genocide that ended the last century."*

## Rwanda since the Genocide

*The OAU panel painted a complex and troubling portrait of Rwanda in the years following the genocide. On one hand, the panel said, the new Tutsi-led government and the Rwandan people were struggling against enormous odds to rebuild a society devastated by years of war and the genocide. Foreign governments and international agencies had provided millions of dollars worth of aid, but not nearly enough to meet the country's needs, the panel said.*

*At the same time, the panel faulted outsiders for pressuring Rwanda to stop "dwelling on" the genocide and to focus solely on the need to rebuild society. The panel said the Rwandan government was misleading itself, and its people, with a campaign of pretending that ethnic distinctions between Tutsi and Hutu no longer mattered. "They do [matter], and they will," the panel said. "But they need not be divisive categories."*

*Rwanda's de facto leader since the end of the genocide, Paul Kagame, emerged in April 2000 as the country's first Tutsi president. Kagame led the RPF forces that ousted the Hutu regime in 1994 and then took the positions of vice president and defense minister. In those posts he ran the country for nearly six years, while a Hutu, Pasteur Bizimungu, held the presidency under a power-sharing arrangement intended to demonstrate a new era of ethnic unity in Rwanda. That arrangement was never a comfortable one. Early in 2000 the government fell into turmoil when Bizimungu resigned, along with several other leading officials including the prime minister (a Hutu) and the parliament speaker (a Tutsi). The defections stripped away the appearance of ethnic diversity at the highest level of governments and left Kagame as the undisputed leader. The parliament named him president on April 17. Kagame took office on April 22, promising that "unity is the foundation of everything."*

## Genocide Trials Under Way

*While the rest of the world still argued about who was responsible for allowing the genocide to happen, the slow process of bringing those accused of committing the murders to justice continued. The UN-sponsored International Criminal Tribunal of Rwanda continued its work of trying leaders charged with directing or fomenting the killings. The chief development in that arena during 2000 was the affirmation, by an appellate court, of the conviction of Jean Kambanda, a Hutu who took over as the Rwandan prime minister during the early stages of the genocide. Kambanda in 1998 had pled guilty to genocide charges and was sentenced to life in prison—thus becoming the first head of government ever convicted under the terms of the post-World War II Genocide Convention. Kambanda later retracted his con-*

*fession and asked for a retrial, alleging that he had not received proper legal advice. In rejecting that request on October 19, the appeals court said Kambanda "was capable of understanding the consequences of the crimes he had admitted to."*

*Inside Rwanda, courts established by the government were processing the cases of an estimated 125,000 persons charged with various genocide crimes. As of July 2000 a Rwandan-based human rights group, LIPROD-HOR, said 3,000 suspects had been tried. Of those, 400 had been sentenced to death (and 22 had been executed), 500 had been acquitted, and the remainder had been sentenced to prison.*

*Following are the executive summary and recommendations from the report, "Rwanda: The Preventable Genocide," released July 7, 2000, by the International Panel of Eminent Personalities to Investigate the 1994 Genocide in Rwanda and the Surround Events, appointed by the Assembly of Heads of State and Government of the Organization of African Unity. The document was obtained from the Internet at http://www.oau-oua.org/Document/ipep/ipep.htm.*

# Executive Summary

## Mandate

E.S.1. The International Panel of Eminent Personalities to Investigate the 1994 Genocide in Rwanda and the Surrounding Events was created in 1998 by the Organization of African Unity (OAU) with a mandate "to investigate the 1994 genocide in Rwanda and the surrounding events in the Great Lakes Region . . . as part of efforts aimed at averting and preventing further wide-scale conflicts in the . . . Region." The OAU asked the panel "to establish the facts about how such a grievous crime was conceived, planned, and executed, to look at the failure to enforce the [United Nations] Genocide Convention in Rwanda and in the Great Lakes Region, and to recommend measures aimed at redressing the consequences of the genocide and at preventing any possible recurrence of such a crime."

E.S.2. The Panel was asked specifically to investigate the 1993 Arusha Peace Agreement, the 1994 killing of Rwandan President Juvenal Habyarimana and the genocide that followed, and the subsequent refugee crisis that culminated in the overthrow of the Mobutu regime in Zaire. It was also directed to investigate the role, before, during, and after the genocide, of the UN and its agencies, the OAU, "internal and external forces," and non-governmental organizations. The Panel was also mandated to investigate "what African and non-African leaders and governments individually or collectively could have done to avert the genocide."

## Before independence

E.S.3. It is possible to identify the key steps that led from the late pre-colonial period to the genocide a full century later. There was nothing inexorable about this process. At its heart was the deliberate choice of successive elites to deepen the cleavages between Rwanda's two main ethnic groups, to dehumanize the group out of power, and to legitimate the use of violence against that group. In the process, a culture of impunity gradually became entrenched.

E.S.4. It was under Mwami ("King") Kigeri IV Rwabugiri, a Tutsi who ruled during the late 1800s, that the chief characteristics of modern Rwanda were fixed for the next 100 years. A powerful head of a centralized state, dominated first by Tutsi until 1960 and then by Hutu until the 1994 genocide, provided firm direction to an elaborate series of subordinate structures. In the colonial era, under German and then Belgian rule, Roman Catholic missionaries, inspired by the overtly racist theories of 19th century Europe, concocted a destructive ideology of ethnic cleavage and racial ranking that attributed superior qualities to the country's Tutsi minority. These 15 per cent were approaching, however gradually, the exalted level of white people, as contrasted with the declared brutishness and innate inferiority of the "Bantu" (Hutu) majority. Since the missionaries ran the colonial-era schools, these pernicious values were systematically transmitted to several generations of Rwandans, along with more conventional Catholic teachings.

E.S.5. The alleged differences between ethnic groups were arbitrary and baseless, yet they soon took on a life of their own. The Belgians made the Mwami's complex structures more rigid and ethnically inflexible. They institutionalized the cleavage between the two groups, culminating in the issuance to every Rwandan of an ethnic identity card. This card system was maintained for more than 60 years until in a tragic irony it became the instrument that enabled Hutu killers during the genocide to identify the Tutsi, who were its original beneficiaries.

E.S.6. While it served them, the Tutsi elite was only too pleased to believe in their own natural superiority and to run the country for its Belgian patrons. The Hutu majority was treated with a harshness appropriate to a lower "caste." Soon many Hutu came to agree that the two ethnic groups, distinguished mostly by vocation in prior centuries, were indeed fundamentally dissimilar in nature and irreconcilable in practice. Tutsi came to be demonized by the Hutu as a foreign invading power with no entitlements in Rwanda.

E.S.7. As the colonial era drew to its close during the 1950s, democracy throughout Europe's former colonies in Africa became synonymous with majority rule. The tragedy of Rwanda is that the majority came to be defined by ethnicity alone. A national independence movement, an umbrella under which all citizens could unite to oppose colonial rule, failed to thrive in Rwanda. Voices of moderation and inclusiveness were drowned out by extremists advocating ethnic exclusivity.

E.S.8. Yet there had been little open violence before the independence period. Hutu were unquestionably considered the "serfs," but only some Tutsi benefited from colonialism. In fact, many Tutsi led lives no better than the Hutu peasantry. Then, as always, the notion of ethnic homogeneity was contradicted by the divisions within both Hutu and Tutsi communities.

E.S.9. While Hutu resented their status and treatment, some intermarriage took place between the two groups which, after all, shared a common language, religion, geography and, often as not, appearance. Tutsi cattle herders and Hutu farmers complemented each other. Hatred between the two groups needed careful nurturing. Until political parties formed on the basis of ethnic origins, there were no massacres of either ethnic group by the other.

E.S.10. Instead of an independence struggle directed against their colonial masters, the Hutu party targeted their masters' surrogates: the Tutsi. Surprisingly enough, Hutu politicians now found themselves supported by the Belgians and the Catholic church, both reversing their original stance once they realized Hutu rule was inevitable. This support continued even when violence broke out. Between 1959 and 1967, 20,000 Tutsi were killed, and 300,000 fled in terror to neighbouring countries.

## The first Rwandan governments

E.S.11. The newly independent government of Grégoire Kayibanda made its colours apparent from the start. As early as 1961, the United Nations reported that, "The developments of these last 18 months have brought about the racial dictatorship of one party. . . . An oppressive system has been replaced by another one." The government pleased no one, not even the large majority of its fellow Hutu. Life for the peasantry remained precarious, while a small Hutu elite from the north and northwest grew increasingly dissatisfied with its marginal role in the government.

E.S.12. As pressure grew on Kayibanda, he unleashed ethnic terror once again, hoping to save his regime by uniting the Hutu against a common Tutsi "enemy." At the same moment, ethnic cleavages were reinforced, neither for the first nor last time, by events south of the border in Burundi. After an appalling massacre in 1972 of the Hutu majority by the Tutsi government, terrorized Burundian Hutu flooded into Rwanda, where they inflamed ethnic tensions and joined in anti-Tutsi attacks. While relatively few Tutsi were killed, many thousands joined their ethnic kin in exile.

E.S.13. But Kayibanda's exploitation of ethnic fears failed to save his regime. He was replaced in 1973 by Juvenal Habyarimana, head of the Rwandan army. For about the next 15 years, Rwanda enjoyed good times, with little ethnic violence. Habyarimana opened the country to the world, and efficient, stable little Rwanda soon became the darling of the West's burgeoning development industry. As for the Tutsi, first and foremost, they were now safe for the first time since ethnic violence had broken out in the late 1950s. While it is true they were allowed to play only a marginal role in politics, were shut out of the military, and were limited by quota to 10 per cent of education placements, they thrived in the public sector and were successful in the liberal professions as well as some public service institutions.

E.S.14. More than 60 per cent of Rwandans were Catholics, and the church remained a trusted ally and reliable bulwark of the Habyarimana regime, giving it legitimacy and comfort until the end. In common with the foreign governments and aid agencies that were involved with Rwanda, church leaders rarely challenged the ethnic basis of public life or Habyarimana's one-party military dictatorship.

E.S.15. By the late 1980s, however, all economic progress ended. Rwanda's economic integration with the international economy had been briefly advantageous; now the inherent risks of excessive dependence were felt. Government revenues declined as coffee and tea prices dropped. International financial institutions imposed programs that exacerbated inflation, unemployment, land scarcity, and unemployment. Young men were hit particularly hard. The mood of the country was raw.

E.S.16. It was at this vulnerable moment, on October 1, 1990, that Rwanda was invaded. The children of the Tutsi refugees who had earlier fled from the Kabiyanda pogroms into Uganda now emerged as a rebel army, the Rwandan Patriotic Front (RPF). Often scapegoated and persecuted while in exile in Uganda, Rwandan Tutsi also remained unwelcome back in Rwanda. According to Habyarimana, his country was too poor and had too little land to accommodate the exiled community. If their right to return home peacefully were thus denied, the rebels had decided, it was time to use more forceful means.

E.S.17. The October 1990 RPF invasion of Rwanda and the Government's response constituted a giant step on the road to genocide. Habyarimana at that moment had a choice. Contrary to RPF expectations, few Rwandans of any background welcomed these unknown "Ugandan" soldiers. A united front among all Rwandans against outside invaders would have been possible, but an opportunistic and threatened Habyarimana government chose the opposite course. With great deliberation, it awakened the sleeping dogs of ethnic division. The Tutsi were portrayed as alien invaders. Any question of class or regional divisions among Hutu was to be submerged in a common front against the intruders. All Tutsi were denounced as fifth columnists, secret supporters of the RPF. Anti-Tutsi propaganda, largely muted for the previous 17 years, was unleashed anew.

E.S.18. At the same time, Habyarimana called on his foreign friends for military help. Rwanda was a French-speaking country, and the response from France was the most positive. Its forces prevented a swift RPF victory over the inept Rwandan army, and French soldiers and advisers remained in the country counselling Habyarimana's people politically and militarily on keeping these "anglo-saxon" interlopers from English-speaking Uganda at bay. The Habyarimana government learned it could always count on the unconditional public and private support of the French President and government.

E.S.19. Immediately after the RPF raid, the OAU threw itself into peacemaking and attempts to resolve the conflict. For the OAU in Rwanda and then in the Great Lakes Region, the 1990s were a time of well-meant initiatives, incessant meetings, commitments made, and commitments broken. In the end, however, the OAU as such had the resources and the power to do nothing more than bring adversaries together, hope first that they would agree, and then hope they did not violate their agreements.

E.S.20. The impact of the RPF raid was devastating in every way. RPF advances, together with the government's anti-Tutsi propaganda drove terrified Hutu into internal settlement camps. In a short time, close to 300,000 Rwandans had been driven from or had fled their land either to become "internally displaced persons" or refugees abroad. In early 1993, another large-scale RPF attack led to a further million, mostly Hutu, internally displaced persons. The country was in turmoil. The ailing economy had little chance to recover. Anti-Tutsi violence, organized by the government or its allies, spread like wildfire, while RPF insurgents similarly showed little restraint, dealing brutally with Hutu civilians in the areas they "liberated."

E.S.21. Within the Habyarimana government, real power increasingly resided with a small faction of insiders from the northwest called the Akazu ("the little house"). It was also widely known as "le Clan de Madame," since its core was the President's wife and family and close associates, who were the chief beneficiaries of the corruption that characterized the regime. As the economic collapse significantly reduced the available spoils of power and called into question the very legitimacy of the regime, the Akazu began playing on ethnic cleavages to divert attention from serious divisions among the Hutu; the main division was between those from the northwest and everyone else.

E.S.22. This should not be taken to mean that planning the genocide was initiated at a precise, documented moment. It is true that a campaign of both physical and rhetorical violence against the Tutsi continued to escalate from the 1990 RPF raid until the genocide started in April 1994. It is true this campaign was organized and promoted. It is also true that at some point in this period these anti-Tutsi activities turned into a strategy for genocide. But that exact point is unknown.

E.S.23. What is known, however, is that from October 1, 1990, Rwanda endured three and a half years of violent anti-Tutsi incidents, each of which in retrospect can be interpreted as a deliberate step in a vast conspiracy culminating in the shooting down, on April 6, 1994, of President Habyarimana's plane and the subsequent unleashing of the genocide. But all such interpretations remain speculative. There is no generally accepted version of the plane crash, nor can it be demonstrated that the countless manifestations of anti-Tutsi sentiment in these years were all part of a diabolical master plan. The evidence most plausibly suggests that the idea of genocide could have emerged only gradually, beginning after the 1990 RPF invasion, continuing possibly through 1991 and 1992, and accelerating in determination through 1993 and into 1994.

E.S.24. Later, when it was finally over, a major international argument broke out over who knew what about the events unfolding in Rwanda. There can be no debate on this question: The facts speak for themselves. The world that mattered to Rwanda—its Great Lakes Region neighbours, the UN, all the major western powers—knew exactly what was happening and that it was being masterminded at the highest levels of the Rwandan government. These observers knew this was no senseless case of "Hutu killing Tutsi and Tutsi killing Hutu," as the genocide was sometimes dismissively described. They knew that a terrible fate had befallen Rwanda. They even knew that some individuals in Rwanda were talking openly of eliminating all Tutsi, although few observers could then contemplate that an actual genocide was even conceivable.

E.S.25. Anti-Tutsi violence, it was widely known, was revived immediately after the RPF invasion, when some organized anti-Tutsi massacres began (and ended only when the genocide itself ended). Massacres of Tutsi were carried out in October 1990, January 1991, February 1991, March 1992, August 1992, January 1993, March 1993, and February 1994. On each occasion, scores of Tutsi were killed by mobs and militiamen associated with different political parties, sometimes with the involvement of the police and army, incited by the media, directed by local government officials, and encouraged by some national politicians.

E.S.26. As the terror heightened, the organizers learned that they could not only massacre large numbers of people quickly and efficiently, they could get away with it. A culture of impunity developed as the conspirators grew bolder. Extremist army officers conspired with the circles surrounding Habyarimana and the Akazu to form secret societies and Latin American-style death squads known as "Amasasu" (bullets) and the "Zero Network." They did not long remain secret; in 1992, their existence and connections were publicly exposed.

E.S.27. But contrary forces were at work at the same time. Pressure for democratization from both within and outside the country forced Habyarimana to accept multiparty politics. A host of new parties emerged, most of them Hutu, wanting to participate in the process. However, one of these new parties, the Coalition Pour la Défense de la République (CDR), represented Hutu radicals and had links to the death squads. Worse, parties organized their own youth militia, the most notorious being the "Interahamwe" formed by Habyarimana's own Mouvement Républicain National pour la Démocratie et Développement (MRND). At the same time, new hate-propagating media sprang up, most infamously a radio station calling itself Radio-Télévision libre des mille collines, sponsored by the Akazu faction. While his militia terrorized opponents and beat up Tutsi and his radio station incited ethnic hatred and violence, Habyarimana nonetheless, and with great reluctance, agreed to accept a coalition government.

E.S.28. Immediately the new ministers joined with the OAU and western powers to pressure Habyarimana to agree to negotiations with the RPF in Arusha, Tanzania. In August 1993, after long, drawn-out sessions, agreements were reached on a series of key issues, including power sharing within the government and military and the future of refugees. But these were never implemented. Ultimately, the Arusha process backfired. The more it appeared that power and the limited spoils of office would have to be shared, not only with other Hutu parties but also with the RPF, the more determined became Akazu insiders to share nothing with anyone.

E.S.29. At the same moment, a deadly new weapon was unexpectedly delivered into the hands of the Rwandan Hutu. The assassination in October 1993 of Burundi's democratically elected Hutu President Melchior Ndadaye and the appalling massacres that followed were taken by many Hutu as final proof that power-sharing between Tutsi and Hutu was forever doomed: The Tutsi could never be trusted. "Hutu Power" as an explicit and public organizing concept, was the immediate consequence of the Burundi upheaval. Large Hutu Power rallies attracted members of all parties attesting to the new reality that ethnic solidarity trumped party allegiances. Political life, in these last turbulent months before the genocide, was re-organized strictly around the two opposing ethnic poles.

E.S.30. As the conspiracy thus widened and deepened, so did knowledge of the conspirators' intentions. Virtually everyone in Rwanda associated with the UN, the diplomatic community, or human rights groups, knew about death lists, accelerating massacres, and threats to opposition politicians. International arms traders worked overtime behind the scenes. Rwanda's capital, Kigali, resembled an arms bazaar, with modern weaponry easily available in the city's markets. The UN military mission uncovered a high-level Interahamwe informant, whose revelations led UN commander General Romeo Dallaire to send his famous fax of January 11, 1994 to the UN's headquarters in New York. In his fax Dallaire reported that "Jean-Pierre [the Interahamwe informer] has been ordered to register all Tutsi in Kigali. He suspects it is for their extermination. Example he gave was that in 20 minutes his personnel could kill up to 1,000 Tutsi."

E.S.31. When it was finally unleashed, only three months later, the violence was organized and co-ordinated. Its goal was explicit: genocide. A clique of Rwandan Hutu supremacists planned to mobilize the Hutu people with the express intention of exterminating all Tutsi in the country, including women and children. The rest of the world knew that a great disaster loomed for Rwanda but did not envisage the possibility that the radicals would resort to genocide. They were soon proved wrong.

## The external actors before the genocide

E.S.32. At the same time, several outside actors carry a heavy responsibility for the events now unfolding. Within Rwanda itself, those with the heaviest responsibility were the Catholic and Anglican hierarchies and the French government, all supporters of the Habyarimana government. Church leaders failed to use their unique moral position among the overwhelmingly Christian population to denounce ethnic hatred and human rights abuse. The French government was guilty of the same failure at the elite level. Its unconditional public backing of the Habyarimana government constituted a major disincentive for the radicals to make concessions or to think in terms of compromise. Though some French officials knew that many of their clients at the highest echelons of the Rwandan regime were guilty of human rights violations, they failed to use their influence to demand that such violations stop. The radicals drew the obvious encouraging lesson: They could get away with anything.

E.S.33. At the UN, the Security Council, led unremittingly by the United States, simply did not care enough about Rwanda to intervene appropriately. What makes the Security Council's betrayal of its responsibility even more intolerable is that the genocide was in no way inevitable. First, it could have been prevented entirely. Then, even once it was allowed to begin, the destruction could have been significantly mitigated. All that was required was a reasonable-sized international military force with a strong mandate to enforce the Arusha agreements. Nothing of the kind was ever authorized by the Security Council either before or during the genocide.

E.S.34. The U.S. has formally apologized for its failure to prevent the genocide. President Clinton insists that his failure was a function of ignorance. The facts show, however, that the American government knew precisely what was happening, not least during the months of the genocide. But domestic politics took priority over the lives of helpless Africans. After losing 18 soldiers in Somalia in October 1993, the US was unwilling to participate in any further peacekeeping missions, and was largely opposed to the Security Council's authorizing any new serious missions at all, with or without American participation.

E.S.35. In October 1993, the first UN mission to Rwanda (UNAMIR), was set up, notable mostly for its weak mandate and minimal capacity. No amount of credible early warnings could persuade either the members of the Security Council to treat the mission seriously or the UN Secretariat to authorize the mission to interpret its mandate flexibly. The single occasion in the life of UNAMIR when it was authorized to go beyond its passive observer mandate was at the very outbreak of the genocide, when several European nations evacuated their nationals. UNAMIR was in this case authorized not only to assist the evacuation, but also to go beyond its mandate, if that were required to assure the safety of foreign nationals. Never was such permission granted for the protection of Rwandans.

E.S.36. The significance of the Security Council's action should not be underestimated: Its refusal to sanction a serious mission made the genocide more likely. The feeble UN effort helped persuade the Hutu radicals that they had nothing to fear from the outside world, regardless of their deeds. This assessment proved only too accurate, as will be described later.

## The genocide

E.S.37. The rockets that brought down President Habyarimana's plane on April 6, 1994, became the catalyst for one of the great calamities of our age. After the chaos of the first hours following the plane crash ended, the government military structure built since the 1990 RPF invasion of Rwanda was used by the interim Hutu Power government and the Rwandan military leaders to execute the genocide, as well as to fight a civil war. It could now be seen clearly that the instigators of genocide had an overall strategy they implemented with scrupulous planning and organization. They had at their disposal control of the levers of government, highly motivated soldiers and militia, the means to kill vast numbers of people, the capacity to identify and kill the victims, and tight control of the media to disseminate the right messages both inside and outside the country.

E.S.38. When the genocide ended, little more than 100 days later, between a half-million and 800,000 women, children and men—the vast majority of them Tutsi—lay dead. Thousands more were raped, tortured, and maimed for life. Victims were treated with sadistic cruelty and suffered unimaginable agony.

E.S.39. The attacks had many targets. The priority list for elimination included government and opposition members; Hutu moderates, thousands of whom were slaughtered without mercy in the first days; critics such as journalists and human rights activists; any Tutsi seen as a community leader, including professionals, political activists, lawyers, and teachers; priests, nuns, and other clergy who were Tutsi or who sheltered intended victims.

E.S.40. Together, military leaders and the new interim government of Hutu Power supporters sworn in after the crash made the overall decisions, while Rwanda's elaborate governing structure implemented the genocide with gruesome efficiency. All received indispensable support from the Hutu leadership of the Catholic and Anglican churches. With some heroic exceptions, church leaders played a conspicuously scandalous role in these months, at best remaining silent or explicitly neutral. This stance was easily interpreted by ordinary Christians as an implicit endorsement of the killings, as was the close association of church leaders with the leaders of the genocide. Perhaps this helps explain the greatest mystery about the genocide: the terrible success of Hutu Power in making so many ordinary people accomplices in genocide. In no other way could so many human beings have been killed so swiftly.

E.S.41. Because of the nature of the event, it has always been difficult to establish the numbers killed in the genocide. The highest persuasive figure for Tutsi killed seems to be 800,000, the lowest, 500,000. Even if the most conservative figure is used, it still means that over three-quarters of the entire population registered as Tutsi were systematically killed in just over 100 days. As well, millions of Rwandan Hutu became internally displaced within the country or fled to become refugees in neighbouring countries.

## The world during the genocide

E.S.42. Until the day the genocide ended with the RPF's military victory in the civil war, the UN, the governments of the US, France, and Belgium, African governments, and the OAU, all failed to define the massacres as a full-blown genocide. All continued to recognize members of the genocidaire government as legitimate official representatives of Rwanda. All except the French government retained a neutral public stance between a government practising genocide and that government's sole adversary, the RPF. In practice, however, neutrality allowed the genocide to happen. Once the genocide began, the US repeatedly and deliberately undermined all attempts to strengthen the UN military presence in Rwanda. Belgium became an unexpected ally in this goal. On Day Two of the crisis, the day after the April 6, 1994, plane crash that killed President Habyarimana, 10 Belgian soldiers were murdered by Rwandan soldiers. As the radicals had anticipated, Belgium immediately decided to pull out all its troops, leaving the 2,000 Tutsi they were protecting at a school site to be slaughtered within hours. The Belgian government decided that its shameful retreat would be at least tempered if it were shared by others and strenuously lobbied to disband UNAMIR entirely. Although the US supported the idea, it was too outrageous to pursue. Instead, with the genocide taking tens of thousands of lives daily, the Security Council, ignoring the vigorous opposition of the OAU and African governments, chose to cut the UN forces in half at the exact moment they needed massive reinforcement. As the horrors accelerated, the Council did authorize a stronger mission, UNAMIR II, but once again the US did all in its power to undermine its effectiveness. In the end, not one single additional soldier or piece of military hardware reached the country before the genocide ended.

E.S.43. The French government, for its part, remained openly hostile to the RPF throughout the genocide. In June, after two months of conflict that started with the fatal plane crash, the French government, with the surprising concurrence of the Security Council, sent a force to Rwanda. Called Opération Turquoise, it soon created a safe zone in the southwest of the country. As the RPF advanced, frightened Hutu peasants escaped to the protection and safety of this zone, but so too did a significant number of government and military leaders involved in the genocide as well as many Rwandan soldiers and militia. All the genocide leaders, soldiers, and militia who succeeded in reaching the French safe zone were then permitted to cross the border into eastern Zaire, joining there with fellow genocidaires who had escaped through other routes. All were ready to resume their war against the new government in Kilgali that had replaced Hutu Power. The French troops pulled out in August 1994, a month after the new government was sworn in.

E.S.44. The facts are not in question: A small number of major actors could directly have prevented, halted, or reduced the slaughter. They include France in Rwanda itself; the US at the Security Council; Belgium, whose soldiers knew they could save countless lives if they were allowed to remain in the country; and Rwanda's church leaders. In the bitter words of the commanders of the UN's military mission, the "international community has blood on its hands."

E.S.45. In the years since, the leaders of the UN, the US, Belgium, and the Anglican church have all apologized for their failures to stop the genocide. No apology has yet come from the French government or the Catholic church. Nor has any responsible government or institution suggested that Rwanda is owed restitution for these failures, and in no single case has any responsible individual resigned in protest or been held to account for his or her actions during this period.

## Rwanda after the genocide

E.S.46. When the war and the genocide ended on July 18, 1994, the situation in Rwanda was almost indescribably grim. Rarely had a people anywhere had to face so many seemingly insuperable obstacles with so few resources. Their physical and psychological scars are likely to linger for decades.

E.S.47. The country was wrecked, a wasteland. Three-quarters of Rwanda's original population of seven million inhabitants had been killed, displaced, or had fled. Of these victims, as many as 15 per cent were dead, two million were internally displaced, and another two million had become refugees. Many of those who remained had suffered greatly. Large numbers had been tortured and wounded. Many women had been raped and humiliated, some becoming infected with HIV/AIDS. Ninety per cent of the children who survived had at the least witnessed bloodshed. An entire nation was both brutalized and traumatized. They were, in their own phrase, "the walking dead."

E.S.48. This was the situation a new, inexperienced government had to face. Its challenges were monumental and its strategies not always convincing. While it called itself a Government of National Unity, most observers have always been convinced that real power in the land, political and military, has been exercised by a small group of the original "RPF Tutsi." Some saw a government not trusted by its people and a people not trusted by their government.

E.S.49. Nor, for very compelling reasons, did the new government trust the international community. Yet it immediately found itself overwhelmingly dependent on western nations, international agencies, and financial institutions to begin reconstruction. Given its past record, the world's response to Rwanda's needs ranged from modest to disappointing to downright scandalous.

E.S.50. To make matters worse, only months after the genocide ended, many of the foreigners who had returned to help with re-building began to argue that Rwandans ought to get on with the task of rebuilding their society. "Quit dwelling on the past and concentrate on rebuilding for the future," Rwandans were earnestly advised. Within six months of the end of the genocide, relief workers were already saying, "Yes, the genocide happened, but it's time to get over it and move on."

E.S.51. It was not so easy then, nor is it now. Among an endless host of problems, highly complex questions and dilemmas of justice, guilt, and reconciliation haunt Rwanda to this day. The UN set up an International Criminal Tribunal in Arusha, Tanzania, and Rwanda has its own courts. In both cases, the process of trying accused genocidaires is long, laborious, and frustrating. Only seven convictions have been handed down in Arusha after five years of work, while in Rwanda only some 2,000 cases have been disposed of. At least 120,000 Hutu rot in prison in appalling circumstances, often without proper charges. At the present rate it is estimated it will take anywhere between two and four centuries to try all those in detention. The Rwandan government has developed a new procedure called "gacaca," lower-level tribunals that attempt to blend traditional and contemporary mechanisms to expedite the justice process in a way that promotes reconciliation. The impact of gacaca remains to be seen, and as a process it certainly needs substantial external resources to function properly.

E.S.52. In the meantime, questions of justice and reconciliation, perplexing in any post-conflict situation let alone a genocide, will remain to bedevil government decisions and popular expectations. Reconciliation is not just a matter to be assigned to the justice system. All governmental institutions and policies must foster a culture of reconciliation, and all opposition to government must function in the same manner. This is no easy task, given the reality of a badly polarized country. In the words of one scholar, "The Tutsi want justice above all else and the Hutu want democracy above all else. The minority fears democracy. The majority fears justice. The minority fears the demand for democracy is a mask for finishing an unfinished genocide. The majority fears the demand for justice is a minority ploy to usurp power forever." Somehow, justice and democracy must both prevail, and ethnicity must stop being the sole element in determining a Rwandan's interests and identity.

## The regional consequences

E.S.53. While these questions absorbed Rwandans internally, beyond its borders the genocide had created another monumental crisis. Two million citizens fled the conflict in every direction: more than a half-million east to Tanzania, more than a quarter-million south to Burundi, and most dramatically, at least 1.2 million west to the eastern Kivu region of Zaire. At the same time, much of the leadership and many of the troops and militia of the genocide had escaped from Rwanda into eastern Zairian refugee camps, where they had unlimited access to weapons. This was a sure-fire formula for disaster.

E.S.54. The international media, which had first ignored and then largely misinterpreted the genocide as nothing more than tribes fighting tribes, now made the Kivu refugee camps a universal cause célébre. Foreign aid and foreign aid workers flooded in. Unfortunately, the Ex-FAR (the former Rwandan army) and the militia had almost completely taken over the camps and were benefitting from the work of the humanitarian community. Genuine refugee needs could be met only when the non-governmental agencies finished serving the demands of the military controlling the camps.

E.S.55. The goals of Hutu Power were transparent and well known to everyone involved in dealing with the Kivu crisis. Hutu Power was determined to overthrow the Kigali government. Almost immediately after their leaders resettled in the Zairian refugee camps, Hutu Power supremacists started to raid back into Rwanda, adding yet another major emergency for the Kigali government to deal with. Widespread demands for the international community to disarm the killers went unheeded. Once again, the leaders of the Security Council badly failed Rwanda. In some ways they actually added, once again, to Rwanda's woes. The French government, with tacit American approval, supported Zaire's President Mobutu as the only person who could help with the refugee crisis in his country. In fact, important groups in the Zairian government became the primary supplier of arms to the Ex-FAR and militia, although many other countries and groups were involved in weapons trading as well.

E.S.56. The consequences for Africa of these international decisions were largely foreseeable and wholly disastrous. The post-genocide Rwandan government had long made it abundantly clear that it would not forever tolerate the camps of eastern Zaire being used as launching pads for the genocidaires' return. By late 1996, the Kigali government had had enough. Hostility among Zairians to the many former Rwandan Tutsi lived in Zaire's Kivu region had increased ominously, and the Rwandan government secretly began training young Tutsi men in the region. Under the flag of an alliance of anti-Mobutu Zairians, and with the active support of Uganda, the Rwandan army launched a vicious attack on the entire complex of Hutu refugee camps in the Kivu region in October and November, 1996. A flood of refugees fled back into Rwanda, but the cost in human life was enormous. Large numbers of other camp dwellers fled west, deeper into Zaire. Some of these were genuine refugees, while some were EX-FAR and Interahamwe. Led by the Rwandan army, the anti-Mobutu alliance pursued them ruthlessly, killing many. In the process, they perpetrated atrocious human rights abuses.

E.S.57. But the military action soon spread far beyond eastern Zaire. The anti-Mobutu alliance, led still by the Rwandan army and bolstered by the forces of Uganda, Angola and Burundi, now set its sites on Mobutu, launching what proved to be the first Congo war. In May 1997, only months later, Mobutu fled, and the government in Kinshasa fell. But there was to be no happy ending to the saga. The new head of Zaire (renamed the Democratic Republic of the Congo [DRC]) Laurent Kabila, soon clashed with his Rwandan advisers. In July 1998, little more than a year after the Rwandans had helped him become president, the Rwandan and Ugandan military were thrown out of the DRC by Kabila.

E.S.58. Within days they returned as an enemy force. The second Congo war in two years now began; it almost immediately escalated to continental dimensions. Directly or indirectly, some one-fifth of African governments and armies from across the continent are involved, as well as perhaps a dozen or more armed groups. The alliances between and among these groups, with their varied and conflicting interests, has been bewildering. The situation is further endlessly complicated by the DRC's enormous mineral resources—an irresistible lure for governments, rogue gangs and powerful corporations alike—and by the continuing problem of arms proliferation sponsored by governments throughout the world as well as a multitude of unscrupulous private hustlers. In July 1999, one year after the second Congo war began, the Lusaka agreement on a cease-fire and peace process was signed. Although the cease-fire has been repeatedly violated since, attempts to implement a genuine peace continue.

E.S.59. The original Rwanda catastrophe shows that what is now required in the DRC is a very large UN military mission with a mandate to enforce the Lusaka agreement. Yet what has been authorized by the Security Council is a modest monitoring mission, and even it is not to be deployed unless peace and co-operation among conflicting forces break out. The consequence, as OAU officials point out, is that the international community is only willing to intervene when it is not needed, a reflection of Africa's marginalized status within the international community. If, however, the governments now at war with each other in central Africa were prepared to turn their forces over to a UN mission, the moral pressure on the rest of the world to offer logistic support would be considerably increased.

## Rwanda and the region today

E.S.60. The dilemma for the region is clear. Rwanda will not retreat from DRC so long as Ex-FAR and Interahamwe are free to continue destabilizing the present regime. But so long as the conflict continues, reconciliation and reconstruction in Rwanda will be significantly retarded. The Rwandan government can hardly be expected to let its guard down against its mortal enemies. But in the government's determination to be vigilant, innocent Hutu are killed, and abuses of human right occur. Tutsi-Hutu tensions are inexorably heightened. Scarce funds are diverted to non-productive functions. Without peace, the chances of success for the government's ambitious initiatives for national reconciliation are seriously threatened.

E.S.61. This reality is equally true for Burundi and the DRC. While Rwanda, Burundi, and the DRC each has its own multiple challenges to meet, their interconnectedness can hardly be overestimated. Without peace, their futures are all jeopardized, with incalculable consequences not only for their own citizens but also for the entire continent. Beyond domestic solutions to domestic problems, therefore, must be found regional solutions to regional problems.

E.S.62. Predicting the future is not easy. Looking at Rwanda itself, it is possible to be either relatively optimistic or quite pessimistic. In many ways, the progress the country has made since the 1994 genocide is remarkable. The ubiquitous devastation is no longer apparent. The country is beginning to think in terms of future development instead of emergency assistance. To the superficial observer, Rwanda has returned to normality.

E.S.63. At best, however, that status simply makes Rwanda a desperately poor, underdeveloped country, now eleventh from the bottom in the United Nations Development Programme's human development rankings. But in reality, the legacy of the genocide can be found in every aspect of society and governance. Just as there is no statute of limitations for genocidaires, so is there none for their victims.

E.S.64. Old ethnic tensions simmer beneath the surface. Political machinations are invariably dissected for their ethnic implications, whether they exist or not. The hold on real power by the "Ugandans," as the RPF is also still known, alienates Hutu moderates who courageously want to work with them. Tutsi who have returned home from elsewhere in the diaspora feel themselves underrepresented and neglected by the present government. This view is shared, surprisingly enough, by genocide survivors. There is also much regional antagonism to the government's insistence on its right to chase alleged genocidaires across any border it chooses. These "soldiers without frontiers" reinforce a widening conspiracy theory (grounded ironically in the same 19th century European racism that originally rigidified ethnic differences in Rwanda) positing a so-called pan-Tutsi plot to impose domination over the authentic "Bantus" of Africa (such as the Hutu). The present Rwandan government appears to be caught up in a militaristic logic likely to lead Rwanda and the region into deeper conflict. It is necessary to change this logic in order to strengthen the peace process.

E.S.65. Rwanda's situation goes well beyond the usual litany of deep-rooted social and economic challenges faced by any poor country with scarce land and a booming population. It must never be forgotten that we are dealing here with the extraordinary circumstances of a post-genocidal society. The burden of the onerous Rwandan government debt is exacerbated by the knowledge that it was largely incurred by the previous Habyarimana and interim governments for weapons that were ultimately used against the moderate Hutu and Tutsi in the genocide. There are, as well, enormous funding needs that spring directly from the genocide: for assistance to survivors; for orphans, traumatized children, street children, and child-headed households; for violated women; for the great burdens of the justice system; for programs to inculcate national reconciliation and human rights; for resettling the millions of refugees and internally displaced persons; for the army, for the battered education system. The list is virtually limitless, a burden that is the consequence of a tragedy that could have been prevented or mitigated. Yet Rwanda today is dependent on foreign sources for a third of its meagre budget, while almost all initiatives crucial to rehabilitation, reconciliation, and a culture of rights depend for their viability on outside funding sources.

E.S.66. Views on Rwanda are remarkably diverse. Some conflicting opinions can be discarded. Hutu Power advocates, still thriving, continue to deny the genocide. If a genocide took place, they insist, it consisted of the RPF's attacks on Hutu within Rwanda and in the DRC. But it is more difficult to dismiss the accusations of former supporters of the government who now accuse it of being controlled by an RPF-Tutsi version of the old Akazu, a small clique that controls real power and is guilty of corruption and gross human rights violations. The cancellation last year—for a further four years—of scheduled national elections adds weight to some of these criticisms of the "transition government."

E.S.67. But there are those who are hopeful for the future. As a lengthy Hutu Power insurgency in the northwest has finally been beaten back, so human rights abuses have decreased. A sense of the end of impunity for such abuses may be taking hold. Some voices continue to remind the world that Rwanda is, after all, not just another poor country, but one just beginning to recover from a vicious genocide. New programs for healing the wounds, for coming to grips with the past and its consequences, are just being put into place.

E.S.68. Of course the regional conflict must be settled. More genocidaire leaders must be brought to trial swiftly. The 120,000 Hutu held in prison in squalid conditions must be dealt with justly, fairly, and soon. The international community must be made to understand the need for reparations for its complicity in the calamities of the past decade. National elections must be held, under conditions that honour the majority's right to govern while guaranteeing the security of the minority.

E.S.69. For Rwanda to recover properly, it is essential that majorities and minorities will be perceived in non-ethnic terms. Governments, like civil society, must be based on interests and convictions beyond mere ethnicity. But there should be no pretense that ethnic identities do not matter in Rwanda. They do, and they will. But they need not be divisive categories. Diversity, properly appreciated, strengthens a society. Unity in diversity has the potential to be a great strength. People are far more complicated than their ethnic heritage makes them. In fact, the modern history of Rwanda has repeatedly demonstrated that members of the same ethnic group often have different interests, a phenomenon never more tragically played out than when Hutu Power slaughtered thousands of Hutu moderates in the early days of the genocide.

E.S.70. Putting these ideas, principles and concepts into practice is not a chore to be underestimated. But it is hard to see how anything less can create the new Rwanda in which the nightmares of the past can never again recur.

# Recommendations

. . . .

## A. Rwanda

### I. Nation building

1. The Rwandan people and government fully understand the tragic and destructive nature of divisive ethnicity. At the same time, we urge Rwandans to acknowledge the ethnic realities that characterize their society. This central fact of Rwandan life must be faced squarely. Pretending that ethnic groups do not exist is a doomed strategy. But the destructive and divisive ethnicity of the past must be replaced with a new inclusive ethnicity. We urge all Rwandans, both in government and civil society, to work together to forge a united society based on the inherent strength and rich heritage of Rwanda's diverse ethnic communities.

2. Long-term strategies and policies are necessary to promote a climate in which these values predominate. Large-scale public involvement in all such strategies is essential. We believe it is essential that all government initiatives, from the justice system to foreign policy, be conceived with their impact on the concept of inclusive ethnicity consistently in mind.

3. All institutions of Rwandan society share the obligation to inculcate in all citizens the values of unity in diversity, solidarity, human rights, equity, tolerance, mutual respect, and appreciation of the common history of the country. Responsibility for this task should include all levels of the formal education system, public agencies, civil society, and churches.

4. We urge that the school curriculum be directed towards fostering a climate of mutual understanding among all peoples, as well as instilling in young Rwandans the capacity for critical evaluation. Active participation in open discussions is an essential element in such a process.

5. A vigorous program of political education must be developed to change the present equation of ethnic with political identities. Majorities and minorities should not be seen simply in ethnic terms. The Rwandan people, like all others, have interests and identities based on many aspects of life beyond ethnicity. Ethnic differences are real and should be recognized as such, but all ethnic groups must be considered as social and moral equals.

### II. The political framework

6. Before the general election scheduled for the year 2003, the Rwandan government should establish an independent African or international commission to devise a democratic political system based on the following principles: the rule of the political majority must be respected while the rights of minorities must be protected; governance should be seen as a matter of partnership among the people of Rwanda; and the political framework should take into account such variables as gender, region, and ethnicity.

7. Other public institutions such as the military, the police, and the justice system should be organized on the basis of merit, taking into account where appropriate these same principles.

## III. Justice

8. All leaders of the genocide must be brought to trial with the utmost speed. We call on all countries either to extradite accused genocide leaders they are harbouring or to try them in exile, on the basis of obligations imposed by the Genocide Convention.

9. We encourage the introduction of the planned new gacaca tribunal system. In order to ensure that the proposed system works with fairness and efficiency, and that it observes the requirements of due process, we urge that external resources be generously provided to assist with capacity building and logistics.

10. The International Criminal Tribunal for Rwanda in Arusha, Tanzania, should be transferred to Rwanda within a reasonable period of time. In turn, we call on the government of Rwanda to guarantee the free operation of the tribunal according to international standards.

11. To create confidence among the population that justice is being done, a culture where all human rights abuses are punished must replace a culture where impunity for such abuses flourishes.

## IV. Economic and social reconstruction

12. Apologies alone are not adequate. In the name of both justice and accountability, reparations are owed to Rwanda by actors in the international community for their roles before, during, and since the genocide. The case of Germany after World War Two is pertinent here. We call on the UN secretary-general to establish a commission to determine a formula for reparations and to identify which countries should be obligated to pay, based on the principles set out in the report, titled The Right to Restitution, Compensation and Rehabilitation for Victims of Gross Violations of Human Rights and Fundamental Freedoms, submitted January 18, 2000, to the UN Economic and Social Council.

13. The funds paid as reparations should be devoted to urgently needed infrastructure developments and social service improvements on behalf of all Rwandans.

14. Given the enormous number of families of genocide survivors supported by the Rwandan government, the international community, including NGOs [nongovernmental organizations], should contribute generously to the government's Survivor's Fund, built up out of the five per cent of the national budget that is allocated annually to survivors. Among survivors, the special needs of women should take priority.

15. Rwanda's onerous debt, much of it accumulated by the governments that planned and executed the genocide, should immediately be canceled in full.

16. In their special programs for post-conflict societies, the International Monetary Fund, the World Bank and the African Development Bank should

significantly increase the amount of funds available to Rwanda in the form of grants. Such funds should target such serious problems as youth unemployment, land scarcity, and high population growth.

## V. The media

17. The Rwandan Parliament should introduce legislation prohibiting hate propaganda and incitement to violence, and should establish an independent media authority to develop an appropriate code of conduct for media in a free and democratic society.

## B. The Great Lakes Region and the Continent

## I. Education

18. A common human rights curriculum with special reference to the genocide and its lessons should be introduced in all schools in the Great Lakes Region. Such a curriculum should include peace education, conflict resolution, human rights, children's rights, and humanitarian law.

## II. Refugees

19. The OAU should establish a monitoring function to ensure that all states adhere rigorously to African and international laws and conventions which establish clear standards of acceptable treatment for refugees.

20. International financial support should be increased for African states bearing a disproportionate burden of caring for refugees from the conflicts of others.

## III. Regional integration

21. In order to reduce conflict and take advantage of their individual economic strengths, we urge the states of the Great Lakes Region to implement polices for economic integration as proposed by Abuja Treaty and other OAU conventions as well as by the UN Economic Commission for Africa.

## C. Organization of African Unity

22. Since Africa recognizes its own primary responsibility to protect the lives of its citizens, we call on: a) the OAU to establish appropriate structures to enable it to respond effectively to enforce the peace in conflict situations; and b) the international community to assist such endeavours by the OAU through financial, logistic, and capacity support.

23. The capacity of the OAU Mechanism for the Prevention, Management and Resolution of Conflicts needs to develop:

- an early warning system for all conflicts based on continuous and indepth country political analyses
- negotiation/mediation skills
- peacekeeping capacity, as recommended by the chiefs of staff of the continent's military forces

- research and data-gathering capacity on continental and global issues, particularly economic and political trends
- stronger links with sub-regional organizations
- increased participation of women and civil society in conflict resolution
- stronger links with the UN and its agencies

24. Monitoring of human rights violations should be undertaken by the African Human Rights Commission, which should be made an independent body of the OAU, with increased capacity to carry out its independent activities.

25. The OAU should strengthen its information mechanisms and its links with the African media. Initiatives should also be taken to interest the international media in developing an African perspective on events on the continent.

26. The OAU should ask the International Commission of Jurists to initiate an independent investigation to determine who was responsible for shooting down plane carrying Rwanda President Juvenal Habyarimana and Burundi President Cyprien Ntaryamira.

## D. The International Community

26 [sic]. We concur with the recent report of the Independent Inquiry into the Actions of the UN During the 1994 Genocide in Rwanda that the UN secretary-general should play "a strong and independent role" in promoting an early resolution to conflict. We call on the Secretary-General to actively exercise his right under Article 99 of the UN Charter to bring to the attention of the Security Council any matter that might threaten international peace and security.

27. We urge all those parties that have apologized for their role in the genocide, and those who have yet to apologize, to support strongly our call for the secretary-general to appoint a commission to determine reparations owed by the international community to Rwanda.

28. We support the Security Council resolution of February 2000 calling for a special international conference on security, peace and development for the Great Lakes Region.

29. We call on international NGOs to co-ordinate their efforts better when working in the same country or region, and to be more respectful to the legitimate concerns of the host country.

## E. The Genocide Convention

30. We call for a substantial re-examination of the 1948 Geneva Convention on Genocide. Among the areas that should be pursued are the following:

- the definition of genocide
- a mechanism to prevent genocide
- the absence of political groups and of gender as genocidal categories
- determining the intention of perpetrators
- the legal obligation of states when genocide is declared
- the process for determining when a genocide is occurring
- a mechanism to ensure reparations to the victims of genocide
- expansion of the Convention to NGO actors

- the concept of "universal jurisdiction," that is, the right of any government to arrest and try a person for the crime of genocide wherever it was committed

31. At the same time as the Convention is being re-assessed, we urge that mechanisms be strengthened within the UN for collecting and analyzing information concerning situations that are at risk for genocide. One possible step is to create a post—a Special Rapporteur for the Genocide Convention—within the office of the UN High Commissioner for Human Rights and responsible for referring pertinent information to the secretary-general and the Security Council.

# G-8 SUMMIT LEADERS ON
# REDUCING WORLD POVERTY
## July 23, 2000

*Attempting to counter growing worldwide protests against the negative effects of globalization, world economic and political leaders pledged during 2000 to step up efforts to relieve poverty and promote economic development in poor countries. In July the Group of Eight (G-8) summit of the world's leading industrialized countries, plus Russia, launched an ambitious series of promises, including cutting in half the share of the world's people living in poverty by 2015. Two months later the World Bank issued its annual policy guide, the "World Development Report," with a new emphasis on combating poverty.*

*By year's end few of the pledges had been followed with concrete action. At their summit, the G-8 leaders rejected a Canadian proposal that each of the industrialized nations increase its development aid by 5 to 10 percent. It remained unclear just how far the G-8 leaders would carry through a plan they had announced in 1999, and reaffirmed in 2000, to ease the debt burdens of some of the world's poorest countries. The G-8 leaders had pledged to forgive about $100 billion worth of debt owed by three dozen countries, but by late 2000 only twenty-two countries had become eligible for the program. In Washington, President Bill Clinton managed to win congressional approval for the U.S. share of the debt-relief plan, as well as legislation offering limited trade concessions for African countries. (African trade program, p. 63)*

*The G-8 summit was the last for Clinton, who for years had dominated the annual sessions, both because of his force of personality and because he represented the world's wealthiest nation. At the time of the summit, Clinton was hosting peace talks at the presidential retreat in Camp David, Maryland, between Israeli prime minister Ehud Barak and Palestinian leader Yasir Arafat. Clinton arrived late at the summit and left a day early so he could return to the Camp David negotiations. (Middle East negotiations, p. 494)*

## A New Emphasis

*The new emphasis on confronting world poverty differed both in tone and substance from the pronouncements of many world leaders and main-*

*stream economists during the previous decade. For many years there had been a general consensus among most of the world's economic leaders that allowing free international trade and eliminating governmental restraints on markets inevitably would lead to economic growth and thus to a broader sharing of economic wealth. This consensus even had an informal name—the "Washington consensus,"—stemming from a 1990 book advocating free markets and economic reform. In practice, this economic theory became the central component of globalization: the growing interconnectedness of the world's economy as a result of free trade and the role of multinational corporations.*

*During the 1990s Clinton was perhaps the leading advocate of this point of view. He preached the gospel of market liberalization to dozens of audiences around the world, ranging from political leaders in eastern Europe to impoverished farmers in Africa. The World Bank, the International Monetary Fund (IMF), and other international organizations put financial muscle behind the free market philosophy, conditioning billions of dollars in loans on pledges that poor countries open their economies to international trade.*

*Starting in the late 1990s the leaders of many developing countries expressed increasing frustration that globalization had not led to improved living standards for their people. They also argued that multinational corporations, based in New York, Tokyo, and other financial capitals, were becoming the dominant economic players in the developing world. Even some of the strongest advocates for globalization, including Clinton, acknowledged that the benefits of free trade were concentrated in some areas (such as East Asia), while much of the world was left out. The Asian financial crisis of 1997 made it obvious that those countries whose economies had surged because of global trade were increasingly vulnerable to the turbulence of world financial markets. South Korea, Thailand, and other Asian countries that had boomed all through the 1980s and 1990s experienced sudden recessions—with millions of people thrown out of work—when world currency traders withdrew billions of dollars from their economies.* (Asian crisis, Historic Documents of 1997, p. 832; Historic Documents of 1998, p. 722)

*At the same time, environmental groups, labor unions, and advocates for the poor argued that negative side effects of globalization—such as pollution and exploitation of workers—were being ignored by the economic superpowers. Some of these groups staged protests at the November 1999 World Trade Organization meeting in Seattle and the joint World Bank-IMF meeting in Washington in April 2000.* (Seattle protest, Historic Documents of 1999, p. 797)

## G-8 Summit

*The Group of Eight consisted of the world's leading industrialized countries (the United States, Japan, Germany, Britain, France, Canada, and Italy), plus the president of the European Commission. Russia president Vladimir Putin participated in discussions of political issues but had no formal role in the group's original core function—increasing cooperation on world economic matters. The G-8 leaders held their 2000 meeting July 21–23 on the island of Okinawa, Japan.*

*The 2000 summit was the first, since the annual meetings began in 1975, to focus primarily on economic development in the world's poorest countries. Leaders reviewed several reports from their finance ministers that described the progress of globalization but also outlined how and why billions of people still lived in poverty. The G-8 leaders on July 23 approved a lengthy communiqué devoted in large part to stimulating economic development in hopes of improving the lives of the impoverished.*

*The leaders' central commitment was to endorse a series of pledges, collectively referred to as International Development Goals, intended to cut in half the number of people living in extreme poverty by 2015. Specific goals included enrolling all the world's children in primary school by 2015, eliminating gender disparities between the enrollment of boys and girls in primary and secondary schools by 2005, reducing infant and child mortality rates by 75 percent by 2015, reducing maternal mortality by ensuring that at least 75 percent of all births were attended by skill health personnel by 2015, providing universal access to contraception services by 2015, and implementing national strategies throughout the world by 2005 for "sustainable development" (economic development that could be sustained indefinitely without undue damage to the environment). These same goals were endorsed by the leaders of 181 nations attending the United Nations Millennium Summit in September. (Millennium summit, p. 700)*

*Despite those lofty goals, the G-8 leaders offered little in the way of new help for the developing countries where poverty was concentrated. Canadian prime minister Jean Chretien proposed that each of the seven wealthiest countries pledge to increase its development aid (known as "official development assistance") by 5 to 10 percent, but the other leaders rejected that plan. French president Jacques Chirac discounted the importance of that refusal, noting that the overall level of aid to developing countries was on the rise. In their communiqué, the leaders said they were committed to "strengthening the effectiveness" of development aid by focusing it on the poverty reduction goals. Clinton offered one of the few specific promises by any of the leaders: a plan to use $300 million worth of surplus U.S. agricultural goods to provide school lunches in poor countries. Clinton and other leaders also said they would work to narrow the "digital divide" between countries with broad public access to computer technology and those without it.*

*Representatives of several organizations that lobbied for increased aid to the developing world said they were pleased that the G-8 leaders talked about reducing poverty, but they expressed disappointment that the summit produced few concrete plans to do anything about it. Jubilee 2000, a coalition of religious groups that pushed for debt forgiveness, said the summit's focus on information technology was misplaced because most of the world's poor people needed electricity, access to clean water, and adequate nutrition more than they needed computers.*

*Clinton on December 14 devoted one of his last major speeches as presi-*

*dent to the subject of making globalization work for all the world's people. Speaking at the University of Warwick in England, Clinton said that helping to reduce poverty "is not only the right thing to do, it is plainly in our interest to do so. We have seen how abject poverty accelerates turmoil and conflict, how it creates recruits for terrorists and those who incite ethnic and religious hatred, how it fuels a violent rejection of the open economic and social order upon which our future depends. Global poverty is a powder keg, ignitable by our indifference." Again, Clinton offered no specific new proposals but said the richest countries needed to expand efforts to open their economies to imports from the developing world and to forgive the debts of countries that had policies of helping their people. "Every penny we spend on reducing worldwide poverty, improving literacy, wiping out disease will come back to us and our children a hundredfold," Clinton said.*

## World Bank Report

*The basic premise of the World Bank's report, issued September 13, was that too many people remained impoverished in a world with conspicuous wealth. Nearly half of the world's 6 billion people—2.8 billion people—lived on less than $2 a day, and of those 1.2 billion scraped by on less than $1 a day. At the same time, the bank said, the distribution of wealth around the world was becoming more, rather than less, unequal. The average income in the richest twenty countries was thirty-seven times the average in the poorest twenty countries, and the size of the gap had doubled over the previous forty years, the report said. More than anything else, the report said, the place of one's birth determined one's economic fate. Poverty was on the rise in Latin America, South Asia, sub-Saharan Africa, and in many former communist countries. The report made only an indirect reference to the fact that even in the United States—by far the world's wealthiest country—the gap between the richest and poorest citizens had grown during the 1980s and 1990s.*

*Implicitly acknowledging some of the criticisms of globalization, the World Bank's report said it was clear that promoting economic growth would not, by itself, eliminate poverty or broaden economic opportunity. The "pattern or quality" of economic growth was crucial, as well, the report said, noting that enriching only a small segment of society, while the mass of the population remained impoverished, was a prescription for instability. Moreover, the report said too little attention had been paid to the fact that narrowing the gap between rich and poor helped promote economic growth.*

*As a practical matter, the report said it could not offer a worldwide "cookie cutter" approach to eliminating poverty, since the economic, social, cultural, and political factors of each country were unique. But key aspects of broad economic development, according to the report, included eliminating corruption, making governmental institutions more accountable to the people, improving the delivery of public services, and establishing "safety net" programs to reduce the vulnerability of poor people to the effects of nat-*

*ural disasters, economic recessions, and other setbacks. All these steps were more complex and difficult than simply eliminating tariffs or allowing multinational corporations to establish plants in a developing country, but the report said all were necessary as part of a "comprehensive approach to attacking poverty."*

## Debt Relief Passed in Congress

*Thanks in large part to lobbying by religious leaders and entertainment figures, Congress approved funding for U.S. participation in the international drive to forgive billions of dollars worth of debts owed by low-income countries in Africa and other regions. Under the program, known as the Heavily Indebted Poor Country Initiative, international lenders would forgive 90 percent of the debt owed by developing countries, provided that those nations were making political and economic reforms and pledged to build up their education, health, and other social systems with the money that would have gone into debt payments. Most of the debt was held by international financial institutions, such as the World Bank, the IMF, and regional banks for Africa, Asia, and Latin America. The United States held $5.7 billion in debt, all of which was to be forgiven if developing countries met the necessary conditions.*

*In a February 17 speech on Africa, Clinton said he wanted to expand the program because "struggling democratic governments should not have to choose between feeding and educating their children and paying interest on a debt." Clinton asked Congress for $435 million for U.S. contributions during fiscal years 2000 and 2001 to the G-8 program. Congress took little action on the request for most of the year, until a coalition of groups supporting the debt-forgiveness plan launched a broad lobbying campaign. Appeals came from Pope John Paul II, other religious leaders, and figures such as the Irish pop singer Bono. Also among those supporting the legislation were several conservative Republicans in Congress, including House Budget Committee Chairman John Kasich of Ohio. Congress approved the debt-relief money as part of the fiscal 2001 foreign operations appropriations bill (PL 106–429), which Clinton signed into law November 6. (Clinton speech on Africa, p. 63)*

*On December 22 the World Bank and IMF announced that twenty-two countries had qualified for a total of $34 billion worth of debt relief. On average, those countries would see their annual foreign debt payments reduced by one-half. The qualifying nations were Benin, Bolivia, Burkina Faso, Cameroon, Gambia, Guinea, Guinea-Bissau, Guyana, Honduras, Malawi, Mali, Mauritania, Mozambique, Nicaragua, Niger, Rwanda, Sao tome and Principe, Senegal, Tanzania, Uganda, and Zambia. Leaders of some of the poorest countries complained that the G-8 program was moving too slowly, largely because the conditions for forgiving debt were too strict.*

*Following are excerpts from the final communiqué, issued July 23, 2000, of the summit meeting of the Group of Eight in-*

*dustrialized nations. The document was obtained from the Internet at http://www.g8kyushu-okinawa.go.jp/e/documents/commu .html.*

# Preamble

1. We, the Leaders of eight major industrialised democracies and the President of the European Commission, met together here in Okinawa for the 26th Summit in the year which heralds a new millennium. We reflected upon the challenges faced and progress made since the First Summit in Rambouillet in working toward peace and prosperity throughout the world, and we discussed the role the G8 should play as it evolves in the 21st century.

2. During the last quarter of the 20th century, the world economy has achieved unprecedented levels of prosperity, the Cold War has come to an end, and globalisation has led to an emerging common sense of community. Driving these developments has been the global propagation of those basic principles and values consistently advocated by the Summiteers—democracy, the market economy, social progress, sustainable development and respect for human rights. Yet we are keenly aware that even now in many parts of the world poverty and injustice undermine human dignity, and conflict brings human suffering.

3. As we make the transition into the new century, we will continue to exercise leadership and responsibility in addressing these persistent problems and squarely face new challenges as they arise. We must tackle the root causes of conflict and poverty. We must bravely seize the opportunities created by new technologies in such areas as information and communications technology (IT) and life sciences. We must acknowledge the concerns associated with globalisation, while continuing to be innovative in order to maximise the benefits of globalisation for all. In all our endeavours we must build on our basic principles and values as the foundations for a brighter world in the 21st century.

4. In a world of ever-intensifying globalisation, whose challenges are becoming increasingly complex, the G8 must reach out. We must engage in a new partnership with non-G8 countries, particularly developing countries, international organisations and civil society, including the private sector and non-governmental organisations (NGOs). This partnership will bring the opportunities of the new century within reach of all.

5. We hope that our discussions in Okinawa provide a positive contribution to the United Nations Millennium Summit, which we expect to articulate, in the spirit of the Secretary-General's report "We the Peoples," a vision that will guide the United Nations as it rises to the challenges of the new century. To that end, we will continue to work for a strengthened, effective and efficient United Nations and remain convinced that reforms of the United Nations, including the Security Council, are indispensable.

6. A new era dawns. Let us move forward together, with hope, toward a 21st century of greater prosperity, deeper peace of mind and greater stability.

## Toward a 21st century of greater prosperity

### World Economy

7. The 20th century has achieved unprecedented economic progress. Yet the financial and economic crises of the past few years have presented enormous challenges for the world economy. Together with many of our partners around the world, we have devoted ourselves to alleviating the adverse effects of the crisis, stimulating economic recovery, and identifying ways to help prevent future upheavals, including measures to strengthen the international financial architecture. The world economy will grow strongly this year, and we are particularly encouraged by the strength of recovery in most crisis-affected countries.

8. While the pace of recovery varies across Asia, trade is expanding and indeed some countries have achieved dynamic growth. Reform efforts must now focus on maintaining the momentum behind financial and corporate sector reforms, improving public and private sector governance and transparency, and strengthening social safety nets to ensure strong, sustainable growth and avoid future instability.

9. Despite recent positive developments in the world economy, we recognise that there is no time for complacency as globalisation intensifies and the rapid diffusion of IT brings about fundamental structural changes to our economies. There are encouraging signs of a new reality in the improvement of productivity in the United States and, to a lesser extent, in other G8 economies. But to capitalise on the opportunities before us, we must renew our unwavering commitment to structural change in our own economies, including greater competition and more adaptable labour markets, underpinned by appropriate macro-economic policies.

### Information and Communications Technology (IT)

10. IT empowers, benefits and links people the world over, allows global citizens to express themselves and know and respect one another. It also has immense potential for enabling economies to expand further, countries to enhance public welfare and promote stronger social cohesion and thus democracy to flourish. Access to the digital opportunities must, therefore, be open to all.

11. We clearly recognise that the process of globalisation and the fast pace at which IT is advancing have engendered various concerns. We need to address such concerns so that we can contribute to greater peace of mind for all. Acting in concert, we will maximise the benefits of IT and ensure that they are spread to those at present with limited access. In this regard, we welcome contributions from the private sector, such as those of the Global Digital Divide Initiative of the World Economic Forum and Global Business Dialogue on Electronic Commerce (GBDe).

12. In support of these goals, we commit ourselves to pursuing the aims and ambitions set out in the Okinawa Charter on the Global Information Society. We will set up a Digital Opportunities Task Force (dot force), which will be asked to report to our next meeting its findings and recommendations on global action to bridge the international information and knowledge divide.

## Development

13. The 21st century must be a century of prosperity for all, and we commit ourselves to the agreed international development goals, including the overarching objective of reducing the share of the world's population living in extreme poverty to half its 1990 level by 2015. 13. We welcome the Report on Poverty Reduction by Multilateral Development Banks (MDBs) and the International Monetary Fund (IMF) which we requested in Cologne, and we look forward to receiving an annual poverty report as we review progress each year in reducing poverty across the globe. This report shows that progress is possible where the right conditions are created for growth and social development. But it reminds us of the vast challenges that remain. While the percentage of poor in developing countries declined from 29% in 1990 to 24% in 1998, there are still 1.2 billion people living on less than one dollar a day and there are marked differences both within and between regions. In particular, many developing countries, notably in Africa, are growing too slowly. The HIV/AIDS pandemic aggravates the situation.

14. As the report indicates, many countries have made significant progress in overcoming poverty in the past quarter century, and their example is a beacon of hope for others. From their success, we have learned that poverty can best be overcome in resilient, peaceful, and democratic societies with freedom and opportunity for all, growing and open economies and dynamic private sectors, and strong and accountable leaders and institutions.

15. Robust, broad-based and equitable economic growth is needed to fight poverty and rests on expanding people's capabilities and choices. Government must, in co-operation with the private sector and broader civil society, establish economic and social foundations for broad-based, private sector growth. Small and medium sized enterprises, together with the opportunities presented by IT can be powerful tools for development. We will work with developing countries to put in place policies, programmes and institutions that offer people a fair chance to better their lives. We therefore welcome the constructive discussions of the Tenth Meeting of the United Nations Conference on Trade and Development (UNCTAD X) in Bangkok, and will work in the United Nations and other fora to further reduce poverty, especially in the Least Developed Countries (LDCs).

16. We also welcome the increasing co-operation between the International Labour Organisation (ILO) and the International Financial Institutions (IFIs) in promoting adequate social protection and core labour standards. We urge the IFIs to incorporate these standards into their policy dialogue with member countries. In addition, we stress the importance of effective co-operation between the World Trade Organisation (WTO) and the ILO on the social dimensions of globalisation and trade liberalisation.

17. Trade and investment are critical to promoting sustainable economic growth and reducing poverty. We commit ourselves to put a higher priority on trade-related capacity-building activities. We are also concerned that certain regions remain marginalised as regards foreign direct investment, and that the 48 LDCs attract less than 1% of total foreign direct investment flows to the developing countries. We urge multilateral development organisations and financial institutions to support developing countries' efforts to create a favourable trade and investment climate, including through the Poverty Reduction Strategy Papers (PRSPs) and the Integrated Framework (IF).

18. We are particularly concerned about the severity of the challenges facing the LDCs, particularly those in Africa, which are held back from sharing in the fruits of globalisation by a debilitating and self-reinforcing combination of conflict, poverty and weak governance.

19. We are committed to mobilising the instruments and resources of the international community to support and reinforce the efforts of these countries to combat and overcome these challenges, with particular priority on promoting equitable distribution of the benefits of growth through sound social policies, including regarding health and education. To this end, as we set out in detail below, we have agreed to:

- Push forward the Heavily Indebted Poor Countries (HIPC) debt initiative;
- Provide significantly improved access to our markets;
- Strengthen the effectiveness of our official development assistance (ODA);
- Implement an ambitious plan on infectious diseases, notably HIV/AIDS, malaria and tuberculosis (TB);
- Follow up vigorously the conclusions of the recent Dakar Conference on Education by ensuring that additional resources are made available for basic education;
- Address the widening digital divide;
- Implement measures to prevent conflict, including by addressing the issue of illicit trade in diamonds.

20. ODA is essential in the fight against poverty. We commit ourselves to strengthening the effectiveness of our ODA in support of countries' own efforts to tackle poverty, including through national strategies for poverty reduction. We will take a long-term approach favouring those countries where governments have demonstrated a commitment to improve the well-being of their people through accountable and transparent management of resources devoted to development. To achieve increased effectiveness of ODA, we resolve to untie our aid to the Least Developed Countries on the basis of progress made in the Organisation for Economic Co-operation and Development (OECD) to date and a fair burden-sharing mechanism that we will agree with our OECD partners. We believe that this agreement should come into effect on 1 January 2002. In the meantime, we urge those countries which maintain low levels of untying of ODA to improve their performance. We will also seek to demonstrate to the public that well-targeted ODA gets results, and on that ba-

sis will strive to give increased priority to such assistance. Well co-ordinated assistance is helpful for developing countries and we will consider how best to improve such co-ordination.

21. We also agree to give special attention to three issues—debt, health, and education, as a spur to growth.

## Debt

22. Last year in Cologne, we agreed to launch the Enhanced HIPC Initiative to deliver faster, broader and deeper debt relief, releasing funds for investment in national poverty reduction strategies. We welcome endorsement of this initiative by the international community last autumn.

23. Since then, while further efforts are required, progress has been made in implementing the Enhanced HIPC Initiative. Nine countries (Benin, Bolivia, Burkina Faso, Honduras, Mauritania, Mozambique, Senegal, Tanzania and Uganda) have already reached their Decision Points and are seeing the benefits of the Initiative. Total debt relief under the HIPC Initiative for these countries should amount to more than US$15 billion in nominal terms (US$8.6 billion in Net Present Value).

24. We welcome the efforts being made by HIPCs to develop comprehensive and country-owned poverty reduction strategies through a participatory process involving civil society. IFIs [international financial institutions, such as the World Bank] should, along with other donors, help HIPCs prepare PRSPs and assist their financial resource management by providing technical assistance. We are concerned by the fact that a number of HIPCs are currently affected by military conflicts which prevent poverty reduction and delay debt relief. We call upon these countries to end their involvement in conflicts and to embark quickly upon the HIPC process. We agree to strengthen our efforts to help them prepare and come forward for debt relief, by asking our Ministers to make early contact with the countries in conflict to encourage them to create the right conditions to participate in the HIPC Initiative. We will work together to ensure that as many countries as possible reach their Decision Points, in line with the targets set in Cologne, giving due consideration to the progress of economic reforms and the need to ensure that the benefits of debt relief are targeted to assist the poor and most vulnerable. We will work expeditiously together with HIPCs and the IFIs to realise the expectation that 20 countries will reach the Decision Point within the framework of the Enhanced HIPC Initiative by the end of this year. In this regard, we welcome the establishment of the Joint Implementation Committee by the World Bank and the IMF. We for our part will promote more responsible lending and borrowing practices to ensure that HIPCs will not again be burdened by unsupportable debt.

25. We note the progress made in securing the required financing of the IFIs for effective implementation of the Enhanced HIPC Initiative, and welcome pledges including those to the HIPC Trust Fund. We reaffirm our commitment to make available as quickly as possible the resources we have pledged in the spirit of fair burden sharing.

## Health

26. Health is key to prosperity. Good health contributes directly to economic growth whilst poor health drives poverty. Infectious and parasitic diseases, most notably HIV/AIDS, TB and malaria, as well as childhood diseases and common infections, threaten to reverse decades of development and to rob an entire generation of hope for a better future. Only through sustained action and coherent international co-operation to fully mobilise new and existing medical, technical and financial resources, can we strengthen health delivery systems and reach beyond traditional approaches to break the vicious cycle of disease and poverty.

27. We have committed substantial resources to fighting infectious and parasitic diseases. As a result, together with the international community, we have successfully arrived at the final stage of polio and guinea worm eradication, and have begun to control onchocerciasis.

28. But we must go much further and we believe that the conditions are right for a step change in international health outcomes. We have widespread agreement on what the priority diseases are and basic technologies to tackle much of the health burden are in place. In addition there is growing political leadership and recognition in the most afflicted countries that health is central to economic development. We particularly welcome the success of the recent HIV/AIDS conference held in Durban and the importance attached to tackling HIV/AIDS by African leaders, donors, international financial institutions and the private sector.

29. We therefore commit ourselves to working in strengthened partnership with governments, the World Health Organisation (WHO) and other international organisations, industry (notably pharmaceutical companies), academic institutions, NGOs and other relevant actors in civil society to deliver three critical UN targets:

- Reduce the number of HIV/AIDS-infected young people by 25% by 2010 (UN Secretary-General Report to the General Assembly on 27/3/2000);
- Reduce TB deaths and prevalence of the disease by 50% by 2010 (WHO Stop TB Initiative);
- Reduce the burden of disease associated with malaria by 50% by 2010 (WHO Roll Back Malaria).

30. In order to achieve this ambitious agenda our partnership must aim to cover:

- Mobilising additional resources ourselves, and calling on the MDBs to expand their own assistance to the maximum extent possible;
- Giving priority to the development of equitable and effective health systems, expanded immunisation, nutrition and micro-nutrients and the prevention and treatment of infectious diseases;
- Promoting political leadership through enhanced high-level dialogue designed to raise public awareness in the affected countries;
- Committing to support innovative partnerships, including with the NGOs, the private sector and multilateral organisations;

- Working to make existing cost-effective interventions, including key drugs, vaccines, treatments and preventive measures more universally available and affordable in developing countries;
- Addressing the complex issue of access to medicines in developing countries, and assessing obstacles being faced by developing countries in that regard;
- Strengthening co-operation in the area of basic research and development on new drugs, vaccines and other international public health goods.

31. We note with encouragement new commitments in these areas. We strongly welcome the World Bank's commitment to triple International Development Association (IDA) financing for HIV/AIDS, malaria, and TB. We also welcome the announcements to expand assistance in this area made by bilateral donors.

32. In addition, we will convene a conference in the autumn this year in Japan to deliver agreement on a new strategy to harness our commitments. The conference should look to define the operations of this new partnership, the areas of priority and the timetable for action. Participation of developing country partners and other stakeholders will be essential. We will take stock of progress at the Genoa Summit next year and will also work with the UN to organise a conference in 2001 focusing on strategies to facilitate access to AIDS treatment and care.

## Education

33. Every child deserves a good education. But in some developing countries access to education is limited, particular for females and the socially vulnerable. Basic education not only has intrinsic value, but is also key to addressing a wide range of problems faced by developing countries. Without accelerated progress in this area, poverty reduction will not be achieved and inequalities between countries and within societies will widen. Building on the Cologne Education Charter, we therefore support the Dakar Framework for Action as well as the recommendations of the recently concluded follow-up to the Fourth World Conference on Women, and welcome the efforts of developing countries to implement strong national action plans. We reaffirm our commitment that no government seriously committed to achieving education for all will be thwarted in this achievement by lack of resources.

34. We therefore commit ourselves to strengthen efforts bilaterally and together with international organisations and private sector donors to achieve the goals of universal primary education by 2015 and gender equality in schooling by 2005. We call on IFIs, in partnership with developing countries, to focus on education in their poverty reduction strategies and provide greater assistance for countries with sound education strategies. These strategies should maximise the potential benefits of IT in this area through distance learning wherever possible and other effective means.

## Trade

35. The multilateral trading system embodied by the WTO, which represents the achievements of half a century of untiring efforts on the part of

the international community to realise rule-based free trade, has provided its Members, developed and developing countries alike, with enormous trade opportunities, spurring economic growth and promoting social progress. In order to extend these benefits to a greater number of countries in a more tangible manner, the system needs to better address legitimate concerns of its developing country members, particularly the LDCs. The adoption of the short-term package in Geneva, regarding implementation of Uruguay Round undertakings, increased market access for the LDCs, technical assistance for enhanced capacity building as well as improvement in WTO transparency, was an important first step in this direction and must be pursued expeditiously. We recognise the need to go further with greater urgency in this area. And we will do so. In particular, in view of critical importance of trade for the development of developing countries, trade-related capacity building should be substantially expanded, which would be conducive to the more effective participation of developing countries in the system, and especially to fuller utilisation of improved market access in their favour. We also commend bilateral and regional initiatives in this regard. We commit ourselves to playing a leading role by strengthening our support to developing country members for capacity building in line with their individual needs. We also call on international organisations including the WTO, the World Bank, the IMF, the United Nations Development Programme (UNDP), and UNCTAD, to join with us in working collectively toward this objective.

36. We must ensure that the multilateral trading system is strengthened and continues to play its vital role in the world economy. Recognising this responsibility, we are firmly committed to a new round of WTO trade negotiations with an ambitious, balanced and inclusive agenda, reflecting the interests of all WTO members. We agree that the objective of such negotiations should be to enhance market access, develop and strengthen WTO rules and disciplines, support developing countries in achieving economic growth and integration into the global trading system, and ensure that trade and social policies, and trade and environmental policies are compatible and mutually supportive. We agree to intensify our close and fruitful co-operation in order to try together with other WTO members to launch such a round during the course of this year.

37. We recognise that more comprehensive partnership must be developed to help address the challenges of globalisation. In this regard, international and domestic policy coherence should be enhanced, and co-operation between the international institutions should be improved. We also underline the importance of our engagement with our publics to establish a constructive dialogue on the benefits and challenges of trade liberalisation.

38. It is in our common interest to integrate all economies into the multilateral trading system. We therefore welcome the progress made on China's accession to the WTO and support the efforts of other applicants toward early accession. . . .

# AIR FRANCE STATEMENT ON CRASH OF THE CONCORDE PLANE
## July 25, 2000

*A supersonic Concorde airplane—long considered the safest passenger jet in the world—crashed in a fireball shortly after takeoff from Charles de Gaulle Airport near Paris on July 25, 2000, killing all 109 passengers and crew on board, plus 4 people on the ground. Preliminary results of an investigation appeared to indicate that the crash of Air France flight 4590 resulted from a chain reaction of events that started when the plane ran over a small metal strip on the runway.*

*Authorities in France and Great Britain grounded the remaining twelve Concorde planes owned by Air France and British Airways, pending the result of investigations to determine whether any characteristics of the plane contributed to the crash. None of the planes had ever crashed since the first flight of a Concorde in 1969. The planes crossed the Atlantic in three and one-half hours, about half the time of conventional jets. Passengers paid premium prices for the service, with fares occasionally reaching as much as $10,000 for a one-way trip.*

### A Chain Reaction?

*Air France flight 4590—a charter flight filled mostly with German tourists—headed down a runway at Charles de Gaulle airport at 4:44 P.M. local time, on July 25, bound for New York. Even before the plane became airborne, controllers at the airport tower frantically radioed the crew that the rear of the plane was on fire. But it was too late to abort the takeoff, and the pilot reported that one engine had lost power and he could not retract the landing gear. The other engine also failed, the plane lost altitude, rolled to its left, and crashed in a fiery explosion into a small hotel in the town of Gonesse, a few miles west of the airport. All 100 passengers and 9 crew members died instantly, as did 4 persons at the hotel, named the Hotelissimo. Of the passengers, 96 were German, 2 Danish, 1 Austrian, and 1 American.*

*In the days immediately following the crash, speculation centered on two possible causes: an explosion of one of the plane's tires or perhaps faulty repairs to one of the engines. Numerous reports emerged implicating ex-*

ploding tires in several previous incidents involving Concordes in the late 1970s and early 1980s—none of which resulted in serious accidents. In each of those incidents, a tire exploded on takeoff or landing and threw chunks of rubber into the plane's engines or wings.

Just one day before the crash, Air France and British Airways had announced that microscopic cracks had been found in the wings of several Concorde planes (although not on the one that crashed). Air France said the cracks were so small that they posed no danger to the planes.

The French Accident Investigation Bureau on August 31 released a preliminary report that focused on the role of a small metal strip, about 17 inches long, that may have fallen onto the airport runway. French investigators said the Concorde apparently ran over the metal strip, which caused a gash in a tire on the plane's left landing gear. The tire exploded, sending large chunks of rubber at high speed toward a fuel tank in the plane's left wing. The rubber punctured the fuel tank, which leaked fuel and caused a fire that ultimately shut down one or both of the plane's engines. As of year's end French investigators were working to reconstruct the wreckage of the plane to determine the exact sequence of events. A separate French judicial inquiry was under way to determine legal issues involving the crash.

One of the major questions still unanswered at year's end was whether the metal strip had fallen from a Continental Airlines DC-10 plane that used the runway just a few minutes before the Concorde. French and U.S. investigators examined the DC-10 on September 2 and concluded that a metal strip was missing from the plane, and Continental Airlines acknowledged that the metal strip found after the Concorde accident appeared to match the DC-10's missing part. But investigators had not concluded by year's end whether the two parts were one and the same. Continental spokesman David Messing told the Associated Press on October 24 that it was not possible to conclude, on the basis of available evidence, that the metal strip caused the Concorde crash. Air France in September filed suit against Continental in French courts alleging that the U.S. carrier was responsible for the metal strip.

A London-based aviation magazine, Flight International, reported in late October that the strip found on the airport runway was made of titanium, a very hard metal, and could have caused the gash in the Concorde tire. The magazine also reported that the strip appeared not to have been original DC-10 equipment and instead was part of a "poorly executed" repair.

The July 25 crash left Air France and British Airways with a host of questions about the future of the twelve remaining Concordes. The airlines pulled all twelve from service, and the British Civil Aviation Authority in mid-August withdrew the certificate of airworthiness for the Concorde. One Air France plane, which had been in New York at the time of the crash, was allowed to return to Paris on September 25.

London newspapers reported in November that the Civil Aviation Authority investigation into the airworthiness of the Concorde was nearly complete, and that British Airways was hoping to resume flying its seven Concordes on the London-New York route by mid-2001. In the meantime,

*British Airways was keeping its Concorde pilots certified through the use of flight simulators. The airline reportedly had planned to continue flying the planes—all of which were built during the 1970s—into the second decade of the twenty-first century, but news reports indicated that plan might no longer be realistic. Many observers said the final report of French investigators might play a significant role in determining whether the Concorde would ever fly again, and for how long.*

## *Other Major Air Accidents*

*Three other major air crashes occurred worldwide during 2000, each with a different apparent cause. On January 31 Alaska Airlines flight 261, en route from Puerto Vallarta, Mexico, to San Francisco, crashed off the coast of California at about 4:21 P.M. local time. All 83 passengers and 5 crew members on board were killed. News reports indicated that the pilot lost control of the MD-83 plane while attempting to make an emergency landing at Los Angeles airport after discovering an equipment problem.*

*The Federal Aviation Administration (FAA) on February 10 ordered U.S. airlines to inspect a unit of the tail sections on more than one thousand planes with a design similar to the MD-83. Inspections of two similar planes, right after the crash, had turned up signs of wear on the tail section's horizontal stabilizer unit, which helps keep the plane level. The pilot of Air Alaska flight 261 had reported a problem with his plane's stabilizer just before the crash.*

*The FAA on June 29 faulted Air Alaska for a series of maintenance lapses, not specifically involving flight 261. Among other things, the airline failed to tell pilots about inoperable equipment on planes and allowed mechanics to work on equipment for which they were not certified, the agency said. Air Alaska promised to hire additional mechanics, engineers, and maintenance supervisors.*

*The NTSB conducted a three-day hearing on the crash in mid-December. Most of the testimony focused on maintenance issues, particularly a change of grease used on a jackscrew in the tail section's horizontal stabilizer. Safety board investigators had focused their attention on the jackscrew, which was recovered after the crash—its threads stripped, possibly from lack of lubrication.*

*On August 23, at about 7:30 P.M. local time, Gulf Air flight 072, en route from Cairo, Egypt, to Bahrain, crashed upon its approach to the Bahrain airport. All 135 passengers and 8 crew members were killed. The cause of the crash had not been formally determined as of year's end. Preliminary data released by investigators early in September indicated there was considerable confusion in the cockpit just before the crash. The plane's mechanical systems appeared to be in good working order, according to the preliminary findings.*

*Finally, on October 31, Singapore Airlines flight 006, bound for Los Angeles, crashed on takeoff at the Taipei, Taiwan, airport, killing 83 of 179 passengers. The Boeing 747/400 plane struck construction equipment* on a runway that was closed for repairs. Singapore Airlines accepted responsibility for the crash and said the plane's pilot used the wrong runway. An investigation was under way.

The National Transportation Safety Board (NTSB) on August 23 concluded its probe of Trans World Airlines flight 800, which crashed July 17, 1996, shortly after takeoff from New York's Kennedy airport, killing all 230 people on board. Investigations of the crash by the NTSB and the FBI had been among the most intense of any air accident in history, in part because of theories that the plane had been the target of terrorism. The FBI said in 1997 that it could find no evidence that a terrorist bomb or missile had downed the plane. The safety board said it concluded that the plane's center fuel tank had exploded, most likely because of a short-circuit of faulty wiring. The NTSB made numerous recommendations for fuel tank safety and wiring improvements, particularly for older-model planes such as the twenty-five-year-old 747 involved in the TWA flight 800 crash. (FBI investigation, Historic Documents of 1997, p. 780)

## *Airport Near Misses*

Two federal agencies sparred during the year on the issue of how to prevent near misses (cases in which a plane or ground vehicle intrudes onto a runway where a plane is landing or taking off). The NTSB on June 13 issued a report alleging that its sister agency, the FAA, was not moving quickly enough on various programs to head off collisions involving airplanes and other vehicles on airport runways and taxiways. The safety board said the number of near misses was on the rise. More than three hundred such incidents were reported in both 1998 and 1999, the agency said, well above the annual average for other years during the 1980s and 1990s. One of the most widely publicized near misses occurred in April 1999, when a Korean Air 747 taking off from Chicago's O'Hare airport narrowly avoided crashing into an Air China 747 that pulled onto the runway. The two planes held 387 people.

The FAA had been working on a computerized program to alert airport personnel and pilots to possible collisions. The system was supposed to have been ready for installation at major airports in 1992, but by 2000 the scope of the system had been scaled back and initial installations were scheduled for 2002. In the meantime, the FAA established new procedures to avoid runway near misses and held several hundred seminars for pilots and other personnel.

In its June 13 report, the NTSB said the FAA's scaled-back computer warning system would not give pilots and airport personnel enough time to head off some runway collisions. The board noted, for example, that a simulation showed the system "would not have prevented" the 1999 incident at O'Hare airport.

The safety board called for two steps: the installation of "direct warnings" at airports, such as runway edge lights and automated stop bars at runway and taxiway intersections, and a requirement that pilots stop at all run-

*way and taxiway crossings. Under that proposed regulation, a pilot could proceed through a crossing only after receiving an explicit instruction from the control tower.*

*The FAA said it was studying the safety board recommendations. The New York Times, in a June 14 report, quoted aviation experts as noting that requiring pilots to stop at all crossings might lead to flight delays. Air traffic controllers might be hard-pressed to handle the additional volume of radio contacts with pilots, some experts said.*

> *Following is the text of a statement issued July 25, 2000, by Christopher Korenke, vice president and general manager of Air France USA, announcing details of the crash earlier that day of Air France flight 4590 near Paris, killing all 109 passengers and crew on board and 4 people on the ground. The document was obtained from the Internet at http://www.airfrance.com/double6/ US/infolocale.nsf/(LookupPublishedWeb)/en-NLPRL-NewsView? OpenDocument.*

First, let me express my deepest and most profound sympathy to the families, friends and colleagues of our passengers and crew on this chartered Concorde flight. As you can imagine, this is a very emotional and sad time for all of us at Air France, and there are no words to express adequately the pain and grief we share with the families of the victims on this tragic flight. We pledge to the families as our first priority our assistance during this most difficult time.

In addition, I want to express my sincere thanks on behalf of all of us at Air France to the people—both in Europe and here in the U.S.—who responded with offers of assistance when news of this accident was reported. I met with New York Mayor [Rudy] Giuliani a few minutes ago and want to thank him for offering help from the City, including grief counsellors and other resources that may be needed here.

The fullest resources of Air France are devoted to this accident—both to attending to the needs of the family members, and to working with aviation authorities seeking the cause of this tragedy.

Now, let me review what we know about this tragic charter flight accident at this time:

- Charter flight 4590 operating from Paris (CDG) to New York (Kennedy)
- 100 passengers, 9 crew
- Involved in accident on takeoff at 4:44 p.m. local time in Paris
- All onboard as well as 4 persons on the ground were killed
- The nationalities of the passengers are as follows: 96 German citizens, two Danish citizens, one American citizen, and one Austrian citizen
- In accordance with laws in Europe, next-of-kin in Europe are expected to be notified by government officials in their country of residence

- Transportation is being provided for family members to Paris or to the victims' homes
- An Air France management team is on site at the accident, focused as I said on assisting families and on working with aviation investigating authorities

We at Air France want desperately to know—just as you do, and as the families of the victims do—why this tragedy happened. After so many years of great, reliable, and safe service from this aircraft, we all need to know what happened so we can help ensure it never happens again.

Until such time as the proper investigating authorities have determined a cause, we will not enter into any speculation. That would be unfair to the families of the victims of the accident, to the investigating authorities, to the travelling public, and to the people of Air France.

In the meantime, our thoughts and prayers join with those of people all over the world for the families of the 113 people killed so tragically today.

# CLINTON, MIDDLE EAST LEADERS ON CAMP DAVID SUMMIT
## July 25, 2000

*President Bill Clinton in July took a bold gamble on negotiating a historic peace agreement between Israel and the Palestinians. But his gamble failed and the age-old conflict between the two bitter enemies exploded into extended violence that threatened to undo nearly a decade's worth of peacemaking. At year's end the president was working diligently to repair the damage in the few weeks remaining before he left office in January 2001.*

*Despite warnings that Palestinian leader Yasir Arafat was not yet ready for compromise, Clinton on July 11, 2000, convened a summit meeting at his Camp David, Maryland, presidential retreat, between Arafat and Israeli prime minister Ehud Barak. During two weeks of meetings, Barak agreed to significant concessions leading to a comprehensive peace agreement with the Palestinians. But Arafat hesitated to accept the offered compromises, and the Camp David summit collapsed without an agreement.*

*Arafat later backed down from his previously stated determination to declare a Palestinian state by mid-September—an action that would have provoked a harsh reaction from Israel. Despite that restraint, violence broke out at the end of September after right-wing Israeli leader Ariel Sharon made a provocative visit to a site in East Jerusalem considered holy by both Jews and Muslims. Outraged Palestinians responded with violent protests that quickly escalated into the worst street violence in Israel and the occupied West Bank in more than a decade.*

*The diplomatic failure at Camp David and the subsequent violence came in a year of significant change in the Middle East. In May Israel withdrew from a "security zone" it had occupied in southern Lebanon since 1978. The withdrawal left the area under the control of the radical Hezbollah ("Party of God") Islamic guerrillas but removed Lebanon—at least for the moment—as a point of contention between Israel and its Arab neighbors.*

*Lebanon remained under the effective control of Syria, which itself underwent its most important political transformation in a generation. In March Syrian president Hafez al-Assad rebuffed a personal plea by Clinton to begin substantive peace negotiations with Israel, under terms outlined during tentative talks in December 1999 and January 2000 between Barak and Syrian foreign minister Farouk al-Shara. Three months later, on June 10, Assad died of a heart attack, leaving Syria in the hands of his son, Bashar Assad, an ophthalmologist. Hafez al-Assad, who had ruled Syria with an iron hand since taking power in a coup in 1971, also had been the leader of hard-line Arab forces opposed to any concessions to Israel.* (Israel-Syria talks, Historic Documents of 1999, p. 890)

## *Pre-Summit Maneuvering*

*A convergence of events and deadlines had made it seem possible that 2000 would be the year when Israel and the Palestinians finally reached a long-term peace deal. The two sides had been negotiating on and off since 1993, when Norwegian-sponsored meetings in Oslo created a process intended to resolve all their outstanding disputes. At the end of that process, the Palestinians were to have their own independent state, based in what had been Israeli-occupied territory in the Gaza Strip and the West Bank of the Jordan River. In turn, Israel was to have the assurance of peace with the people whose hostility could at any moment plunge the Middle East into its fourth war since 1948.* (Oslo accords, Historic Documents of 1993, p. 747)

*In 2000 Israel had a prime minister, Barak, who was committed to peace and whose military background (he was the country's most decorated army officer) offered him a measure of political protection against hard-liners who opposed any concessions to the Palestinians. Barak had won election in 1999 on a pro-peace platform, and he clearly needed a success to preserve his shaky majority in parliament.* (Barak election, Historic Documents of 1999, p. 359)

*Two looming deadlines also served to focus attention on the need for some kind of peace agreement. The first was September 13, the seventh anniversary of the Oslo accords and the deadline for a final peace agreement between Israel and the Palestinians. Arafat had pledged to declare an independent state on that date if a peace agreement had not yet been reached. The second deadline was the January 20, 2001, expiration of Clinton's second and final term as president. An avid proponent of personal diplomacy, Clinton had devoted an unprecedented amount of time and prestige to Middle East negotiations. It was widely assumed that if he could not broker a deal, his successor would be unable to do so for months or even years.*

*Israel's withdrawal from Lebanon in May enabled Barak to turn his undivided attention to negotiations with the Palestinians. During June the Clinton administration launched preparatory talks with Israeli and Palestinian officials, and Clinton formally invited Barak and Arafat to Camp David. Signs of trouble emerged even before the leaders gathered at the retreat July 11. Arafat made it clear early in July that he was not ready for high-level peace talks. Three right-leaning parties bolted from Barak's coalition just before he left for the United States, leaving him without a working majority in parliament.*

## *Negotiations Fail*

*Despite the warning signs, Clinton held several days of one-on-one talks with Barak and Arafat before leaving Camp David for the previously scheduled G-8 summit in Japan. During his absence Secretary of State Madeleine K. Albright and her top aides continued the discussions with Barak and Arafat, gradually narrowing points of disagreement. Clinton returned to Camp David on July 23 for what he hoped would be a final push toward an agreement.*

*By all accounts Clinton managed to win significant concessions from both sides on outstanding issues, most notably the boundaries of a Palestinian state within the West Bank. Israel had captured the West Bank— including all of Jerusalem—from Jordan during the 1967 Arab-Israeli war and during the subsequent three decades had allowed construction of hundreds of Jewish settlements in the area. At Camp David Barak agreed to turn nearly 95 percent of the West Bank over to Palestinian jurisdiction, in exchange for protection of existing Jewish settlements. Israel would annex the remaining 5 percent—the land where about 75 percent of the 170,000 Jewish settlers on the West Bank lived. Barak also agreed to close down Jewish settlements in the Gaza Strip, most of which had been turned over to the Palestinians in earlier negotiations.*

*The breakdown came over the two most difficult issues: the fate of some 3 million Palestinian refugees in the Middle East, and control of East Jerusalem as well as historic sites that were considered sacred by Jews, Christians, and Muslims.*

*The refugee issue was difficult because of the numbers involved. Hundreds of thousands of Arabs fled Palestine after 1948, when Jews declared the Israeli state there and then fought a war with its Arab neighbors. In the subsequent decades many of the Palestinians lived in United Nations-sponsored refugee camps in Lebanon, Jordan, and Syria—states that never wanted them and did little to support them. Israel had refused to accept a large contingent of refugees, fearing they would destabilize the country and that this would lead, ultimately, to Jews becoming a minority in the Jewish state.*

*The U.S. plan on the table at the close of the Camp David talks provided for Israel to accept about 100,000 Palestinian refugees in an internationally financed and supervised "family reunification" program. In addition to funding most of that program, the United States, along with other countries, would provide money for the permanent settlement of Palestinian refugees in the Palestinian state and the neighboring Arab countries. Clinton said he offered a "significant contribution" by the United States toward the cost of resettling the refugees, but he declined to specify an amount. Barak reportedly accepted this plan, but Arafat refused, apparently because it left the fate of most Palestinian refugees uncertain.*

*The status of Jerusalem was even more complex because it involved historical, religious, and emotional questions at the heart of the dispute between Arabs and Jews. After capturing the West Bank in 1967 Israel declared Jerusalem as its capital and asserted sovereignty over the entire city, in-*

*cluding the section called East Jerusalem, which was occupied almost exclusively by Palestinians. The "old city," with its ancient religious sites, was located at the edge of Jewish West Jerusalem and Arab East Jerusalem. Palestinians had long planned on basing their new state in East Jerusalem.*

*Clinton on July 24 put forward an American-drafted proposal for a complex solution to the Jerusalem puzzle. According to news reports and later statements by those involved in the talks, the proposal involved shared control of East Jerusalem. The Palestinians would have sovereignty over much of East Jerusalem, and Israel would annex several Jewish settlements adjacent to the old city, as well as the Jewish quarter of the old city itself. Barak reportedly gave his tentative approval to this plan at Camp David, despite the fact that it represented a significant retreat from Israel's insistence on total sovereignty over all of Jerusalem.*

*During a late night session on July 24 Arafat balked at the plan and spurned Clinton's emotional appeals for compromise. Arafat also rejected a fall-back plan, offered by Clinton, under which the two sides would settle all issues except for the status of Jerusalem, which would be postponed until later negotiations.*

*With Arafat adamant in his rejection, Clinton reluctantly called a halt to the negotiations on July 25. He had to settle for a five-point "trilateral statement" in which Barak and Arafat agreed only to continue seeking a peace agreement and to avoid "unilateral actions that prejudge the outcome of negotiations." Clinton made that statement public at a White House news conference on July 25 during which he lavishly praised Barak for his "courage" and "vision" and said "the people of Israel should be very proud of him." By contrast, Clinton said of Arafat only that he "remains committed to the path of peace." Clinton expressed disappointment at the failure of his high-stakes gamble for peace but insisted that the two sides had made "significant" progress on issues—particularly Jerusalem—that they had never fully discussed before.*

*Barak insisted he had been ready for a historic deal but Arafat had not. "We were ready to end the conflict, we looked for an equilibrium point that will provide a peace for generations, but unfortunately Arafat somehow hesitated to take the historic decisions that were needed in order to put an end to it," he said.*

## What Went Wrong?

*In the days and weeks following the summit, there appeared to be general agreement among most observers that Clinton had tried to push Arafat into positions he was not yet ready to adopt. Arafat had said repeatedly, before the summit, that the time was not yet right for a major push toward peace. Clinton brushed aside Arafat's hesitations, only to discover that the Palestinian leader had meant what he said.*

*Some observers also said Clinton made a tactical mistake in putting Arafat into the hothouse atmosphere of a summit, where he would be under pressure to make momentous decisions surrounded only by a handful of close aides. Throughout his long career, the Palestinian leader had preferred* more collegial settings in which he could consult with fellow Arab leaders before taking important steps. Arafat had survived the tumult of Middle East politics in large part because of his caution. As a leader who could never count on the unswerving support of his people, Arafat instinctively wanted to make sure that any actions he took would be endorsed by other Arab leaders who could bolster his position. Confronted at Camp David with significant proposals that had never been widely discussed in the Middle East, Arafat reacted with his customary hesitation and then retreated into a rejectionist posture when Clinton implored him to take the necessary risks for peace.

Moreover, Arafat faced pressure from fellow Arab leaders not to accept any compromise that involved recognizing Israeli sovereignty over Jerusalem. Egyptian president Hosni Mubarak and Saudi Arabian Crown Prince Abdullah—normally among the closest U.S. allies in the Arab world—were among those who had warned Arafat that he could not act on behalf of Arabs on the Jerusalem issue.

After the summit Clinton and his aides discounted criticism that the timing was not right for a major push. "I think, on balance, it was very much the right thing to do, and it increases the chance of a successful agreement, and it increases the chance of avoiding a disaster," he said at the close of the summit. Despite the failure to reach a final agreement, he said, "We made progress on all the core issues. We made really significant progress on many of them."

Clinton said the fundamental importance of the Camp David talks was that the two sides had opened discussion on issues that previously had never been on the table for negotiation, especially those concerning Jerusalem. "I want to give credit to both sides in the sense that they were really coming to grips with things they had never seriously come to grips with before," he said. A final solution would only come, Clinton said, when the leaders could reach an agreement "in which everybody is a little disappointed and nobody is defeated, in which neither side requires the other to say they have lost everything, and they find a way to a shared result."

## Events after Camp David

The collapse of the Camp David talks left Barak in a weakened political position at home, where critics accused him of making too many concessions on issues of fundamental importance to Israel. His foreign minister, David Levy, resigned August 2, capping a series of cabinet defections that left Barak with only a tenuous hold on power in parliament. Fortunately for Barak, the parliament went on its annual recess on August 3, offering him a two-month period during which the opposition could voice its complaints but could not throw his government out of office. Barak had himself been elected independently of parliament, but he could not govern effectively without a working legislative majority.

Arafat, by contrast, returned to the Middle East from Camp David claiming to be a hero for refusing to give into Clinton's pressure for compromise. Arafat went on a tour of Arab capitals to explain his position and to shore *up his support. Fellow Arab leaders supported his position, but several of them—along with key Western leaders—urged him to back down from his stated determination to declare an independent Palestinian state on September 13.*

*On September 6, at the United Nations "Millennium Summit" in New York, Clinton met separately with Arafat and Barak in another unsuccessful attempt to break the deadlock. But Clinton apparently did succeed in persuading Arafat to withhold his statehood declaration. Four days later, the Palestinian parliament agreed to delay statehood indefinitely to allow time for further negotiations.*

*The September 13 deadline for a final peace agreement, agreed to by Arafat and then Israeli prime minister Yitzhak Rabin in 1993, passed without major incident. On September 26–27, high-level Israeli and Palestinian negotiators met in Washington for one more effort to narrow the gaps between the two sides. Dennis Ross, who had been Clinton's special Middle East envoy for eight years, later said those sessions came very close to producing a final agreement. But on September 28—as the negotiators left Washington—Sharon paid his controversial visit to Jerusalem's Temple Mount, setting off clashes between Israelis and Palestinians that would last the rest of the year and end, at least temporarily, any further efforts at peacemaking. By year's end, nearly 400 people, most of them Palestinians, had died.* (Middle East violence, p. 930)

*Despite his lame-duck status after the November election, Clinton continued his efforts right through the end of the year to broker a peace agreement. On December 29 he said he would meet with Arafat early in January, and he called on the Palestinian leader to accept proposals based on the outline presented at Camp David. Clinton attempted to convey a sense of urgency, noting that he would soon leave office. "I don't think the circumstances [for an agreement] are going to get better," he told reporters. "I think that, in all probability, they'll get more difficult. This is by far the closest we have ever been."*

> *Following is the text of a "trilateral statement" issued July 25, 2000, by President Bill Clinton after negotiations with Israeli prime minister Ehud Barak and Palestinian leader Yasir Arafat, followed by excerpts from a White House news conference with Clinton. The documents were obtained from the Internet at http: www.pub.whitehouse.gov/uri-res/l2R?urn:pdi://oma.eop.gov.us/ 2000/7/25/9.text.1.*

# TRILATERAL STATEMENT

Between July 11 and 24, under the auspices of President Clinton, Prime Minister Barak and Chairman Arafat met at Camp David in an effort to reach an agreement on permanent status. While they were not able to bridge the gaps and reach an agreement, their negotiations were unprecedented in both scope and detail. Building on the progress achieved at Camp David, the two leaders agreed on the following principles to guide their negotiations:

1. The two sides agreed that the aim of their negotiations is to put an end to decades of conflict and achieve a just and lasting peace.
2. The two sides commit themselves to continue their efforts to conclude an agreement on all permanent status issues as soon as possible.
3. Both sides agree that negotiations based on UN Security Council Resolutions 242 and 338 are the only way to achieve such an agreement and they undertake to create an environment for negotiations free from pressure, intimidation and threats of violence.
4. The two sides understand the importance of avoiding unilateral actions that prejudge the outcome of negotiations and that their differences will be resolved only by good faith negotiations.
5. Both sides agree that the United States remains a vital partner in the search for peace and will continue to consult closely with President Clinton and Secretary Albright in the period ahead.

## PRESIDENT CLINTON'S NEWS CONFERENCE

**President Clinton:** After 14 days of intensive negotiations between Israelis and Palestinians, I have concluded with regret that they will not be able to reach an agreement at this time. As I explained on the eve of the summit, success was far from guaranteed—given the historical, religious, political and emotional dimensions of the conflict.

Still, because the parties were not making progress on their own and the September deadline they set for themselves was fast approaching, I thought we had no choice. We can't afford to leave a single stone unturned in the search for a just, lasting and comprehensive peace.

Now, at Camp David, both sides engaged in comprehensive discussions that were really unprecedented because they dealt with the most sensitive issues dividing them; profound and complex questions that long had been considered off limits.

Under the operating rules that nothing is agreed until everything is agreed, they are, of course, not bound by any proposal discussed at the summit. However, while we did not get an agreement here, significant progress was made on the core issues. I want to express my appreciation to Prime Minister Barak, Chairman Arafat and their delegations for the efforts they undertook to reach an agreement.

Prime Minister Barak showed particular courage vision, and an understanding of the historical importance of this moment. Chairman Arafat made it clear that he, too, remains committed to the path of peace. The trilateral statement we issued affirms both leaders' commitment to avoid violence or unilateral actions which will make peace more difficult and to keep the peace process going until it reaches a successful conclusion.

At the end of this summit, I am fully aware of the deep disappointment that will be felt on both sides. But it was essential for Israelis and Palestinians, finally, to begin to deal with the toughest decisions in the peace process. Only they can make those decisions, and they both pledged to make them, I say again, by mid-September.

Now, it's essential that they not lose hope, that they keep working for peace, they avoid any unilateral actions that would only make the hard task ahead more difficult. The statement the leaders have made today is encouraging in that regard.

Israelis and Palestinians are destined to live side by side, destined to have a common future. They have to decide what kind of future it will be. Though the differences that remain are deep, they have come a long way in the last seven years, and, notwithstanding the failure to reach an agreement, they made real headway in the last two weeks.

Now, the two parties must go home and reflect, both on what happened at Camp David and on what did not happen. For the sake of their children, they must rededicate themselves to the path of peace and find a way to resume their negotiations in the next few weeks. They've asked us to continue to help, and as always, we'll do our best. But the parties themselves, both of them, must be prepared to resolve profound questions of history, identity and national faith—as well as the future of sites that are holy to religious people all over the world who are part of the Islamic, Christian and Judaic traditions.

The children of Abraham, the descendants of Isaac and Ishmael can only be reconciled through courageous compromise. In the spirit of those who have already given their lives for peace and all Israelis, Palestinians, friends of peace in the Middle East and across the world, we long for peace and deserve a Holy Land that lives for the values of Judaism, Islam and Christianity.

Thank you.

**Q:** Was Jerusalem—Mr. President, was Jerusalem the main stumbling block? And where do you go from here?

**Clinton:** It was the most difficult problem. And I must tell you that we tried a lot of different approaches to it, and we have not yet found a solution. But the good news is that there is not a great deal of disagreement—and I want to emphasize this—it seemed to me, anyway, there was not a great deal of disagreement in many of these areas about what the facts on the ground would be after an agreement were made—that is, how people would live. For example, everyone conceded that Jerusalem is a place that required everyone to have access to the holy sites and the kinds of things you've heard, and lot of other things in terms of how, operationally, the Israelis and the Palestinians have worked together; there was actually more agreement than I had thought there would be.

But obviously, the questions around Jerusalem go to the core identity of both the Palestinians and the Israelis. There were some very, as I said—it has been reported Prime Minister Barak took some very bold decisions, but we were in the end unable to bridge the gaps.

I think there will be a bridge, because I think the alternative is unthinkable.

**Q:** There is a striking contrast between the way you described Prime Minister Barak's courageous and visionary approach to this, and Mr. Arafat seemed to be still committed to the path of peace. It sounds like that at the end of the day, Prime Minister Barak was ready to really step up to something that President Arafat wasn't yet ready to step up to.

**Clinton:** Let me be more explicit. I will say again: We made progress on all of the core issues. We made really significant progress on many of them. The Palestinian teams worked hard on a lot of these areas. But I think it is fair to say that at this moment in time, maybe because they had been preparing for it longer, maybe because they had thought through it more, that the Prime Minister moved forward more from his initial position than Chairman Arafat, on—particularly surrounding the questions of Jerusalem.

Now, these are hard questions. And as I said to both of them, none of us, no outsider can judge for another person what is at the core of his being, at the core of his sense of national essence. But we cannot make an agreement here without a continuing effort of both sides to compromise.

I do believe that—let me say this—and you will appreciate this, Tom, because you've been covering this a long time—but I want to give credit to both sides in the sense that they were really coming to grips with things they had never seriously come to grips with before.

Oh, yes, there were always side papers—even going back to 1993—about how these final issues would be solved. There were always speculation, there were always the odd conversation between Palestinians and Israelis who were friends and part of the various—the different government operations. But these folks really never had to come together before, and in an official setting put themselves on the line. And it is profoundly difficult.

So I said what I said, and my remarks should stand for themselves, because not so much as a criticism of Chairman Arafat, because this is really hard and never been done before, but in praise of Barak. He came there knowing that he was going to have to take bold steps, and he did it. And I think you should look at it more as a positive toward him than as a condemnation of the Palestinian side.

This is agonizing for them—both of them. And unless you have lived there and lived with them and talked to them, or lived with this problem a long time, it is hard to appreciate it. But I do think—I stand by the statement as written. I think they both remain committed to peace, I think they will both find a way to get there if they don't let time run away with them so that external events rob them of their options. And that's why I decided to call the summit in the first place.

I got worried that—this is like going to the dentist without having your gums deadened, you know. I mean, this is not easy. And I got worried that if we didn't do the summit and we didn't force a process to begin, which would require people to come to grips with this in a disciplined, organized way, as well as to face—look themselves in the mirror and look into the abyss and think: What can I do and what can't I do, that we would never get there. Now, I believe because of the work that was done within both teams and what they did with each other, we can still do it. Let me just make one other observation and then I'll answer your question.

You know, when we worked, I remember when we went to Dayton over Bosnia; when we went to Paris over Bosnia. After the Kosovo conflict—and I went there and met with all the people who were going to have to work on Kosovo's future—even when we first started the Irish peace talks, we were dealing with people who would hardly speak to each other. We were dealing with people who still often wouldn't shake hands. We were dealing with people who thought they were from another planet from one another, whose wounds were open.

Let me give you some good news. Of all the peace groups I ever worked with, these people know each other, they know the names of each other's children, they know how many grandchildren the grandparents have, they know their life stories, they have a genuine respect and understanding for each other. It is truly extraordinary and unique in my experience in almost eight years of dealing with it.

So I'm not trying to put a funny gloss on this; they couldn't get there. That's the truth. They couldn't get there. But this was the first time in an organized, disciplined way they had to work through, both for themselves and then with each other how they were going to come to grips with issues that go to the core of their identity.

And I think on balance, it was very much the right thing to do, and it increases the chance of a successful agreement, and it increases the chances of avoiding a disaster.

**Q:** What is your assessment of whether Arafat's going to go through with the threat to declare statehood unilaterally? Did you get any sort of sense on whether he's going to go through with that? Did you have any—

**Clinton:** Well, let me say this. One of the reasons that I wanted to have this summit is that they're both under—will be under conflicting pressures as we go forward. One of the things that often happens in a very difficult peace process is that people, if they're not careful, will gravitate to the intense position rather than the position that will make peace. And it's very often that people know that a superficially safe position is to say no, that you won't get in trouble with whoever is dominating the debate back home wherever your home is, as long as you say no.

One of the reasons I called this summit is so that we could set in motion a process that would give the Palestinians the confidence that all of us—and most of all, the Israelis—really didn't want to make peace, so that it would offset the pressure that will be increasingly on Chairman Arafat as we approach the September 13th deadline.

**Q:** Are you implying that he should give up his claim to East Jerusalem—the Palestinians should?

**Clinton:** No, I didn't say that.

**Q:** Or any kind of a foothold?

**Clinton:** I didn't say that. I didn't say that. I didn't say that. And let me say, I presume, I am bound—I'm going to honor my promise not to leak about what they talked about, but I presume it will come out. No, I didn't say that. I said only this: I said "I will say again—the Palestinians changed their position; they moved forward. The Israelis moved more from the position they had. I said what I said; I will say again: I was not condemning Arafat, I was praising Barak. But I would be making a mistake not to praise Barak because I think he took a big risk. And I think it sparked, already, in Israel a real debate, which is moving Israeli public opinion toward the conditions that will make peace. So I thought that was important, and I think it deserves to be acknowledged.

But the overriding thing you need to know is that progress was made on all fronts, that significant progress was made on some of the core issues, that Jerusalem, as you all knew it would be, remains the biggest problem for the reasons you know.

But what we have to find here, if there is going to be an agreement—by definition, an agreement is one in which everybody is a little disappointed and nobody is defeated, in which neither side requires the other to say they have lost everything and they find a way to—a shared result.

And there's no place in the world like Jerusalem. There is no other place in the world like Jerusalem, which is basically at the core of the identity of all three monotheistic religions in the world, at the core of the identity of what it means to be a Palestinian, at the core of the identity of what it means to be an Israeli. There is no other place like this in the world. So they have to find a way to work through this.

And it shouldn't surprise you that when they first come to grips with this in an official, disciplined way where somebody has to actually say something instead of sort of be off in a corner having a conversation over a cup of coffee that no one ever—that has no—it just vanishes into air, that it's hard for them to do.

**Q:** But did they make enough progress, sir, to now go back home, check with their people, and possibly come back during your administration—next month or in September—to come back to Camp David and try again?

**Clinton:** I don't know if they need to come back to Camp David. I think that it rained up there so much, I'm not sure I'll ever get them back there. But I think if you asked me did they make enough progress to get this done? Yes. But they've got to go home and check; they've got to feel around. And what I want to say to you is, the reason I tried to keep them there so long—and I feel much better about this than I did when we almost lost it before—and you remember, and I got them and we all agreed to stay—I didn't feel that night like I feel today.

Today, I feel that we have the elements here to keep this process going. But it's important that the people whose—both leaders represent, support their continuing involvement in this and stick with them, and understand that this is a script that's never been written before. They have to write a script and they've got to keep working at it.

But, yes, I think it can happen—

**Q:** During your administration?

**Clinton:** Yes. Not because it's my administration, that's irrelevant. They're operating on their timetable, not mine. It has nothing to do with the fact that it's my administration. I think it can happen because they set for themselves a September 13th deadline. And if they go past it, every day they go past it will put more pressure on the Palestinians to declare a Palestinian state unilaterally and more pressure on the Israelis to have some greater edge in conflict in their relations as a result of that.

Neither one of them want that; so I think they will find a way to keep this going. And the only relevance of my being here is that I've been working with them for eight years, and I think they both trust us and believe that Secretary Albright and Dennis [Ross] and Sandy [Berger] and our whole team, that we will heave to, to make peace.

**Q:** But, Mr. President, the Prime Minister came here in quite a precarious position to begin with back home. And some of the things you call bold and courageous, his critics back home have called treason. Can he go home, and do you believe he will have the political stability to come back at this, and did he voice any concerns to you about that?

**Clinton:** First of all, this is not a weak man. It's not for nothing that he's the most decorated soldier in the history of Israel. He didn't come over here to play safe with his political future; he came over here to do what he thought was right for the people of Israel, and I think that he—he knows that he would never do anything to put the security of Israel at risk, and that the only long-term guarantee of Israel's security is a constructive peace that's fair with her neighbors—all of them—starting with the Palestinians.

So I think the people of Israel should be very proud of him. He did nothing to compromise Israel's security, and he did everything he possibly could within the limits that he thought he had, all the kinds of constraints that operate on people in these circumstances to reach a just peace. So I would hope the people of Israel will support him, and let this thing percolate, not overreact, and say keep trying.

I want the people on both sides to tell their leaders to keep trying—to keep trying. You know, that's the only real answer here is just to bear down and go on.

**Q:** Mr. President, couldn't you have gotten a partial agreement and left Jerusalem for later? Was that a possibility at all?

**Clinton:** That possibility was explored and rejected.

**Q:** Why?

**Clinton:** I can't talk about it. If they want to talk about it, that's their business; but I can't.

**Q:** Have you done all you can do, sir, or would you be making more proposals?

**Clinton:** Oh, I think—well, first of all, we all agreed to reassess here. So the first thing we're going do to is, we're going to let each side go home and try to get a little sleep. I mean, we've all been sort of—we're kind of—nobody knows what time it is, I don't think, on either team.

Last night, we quit at 3:00 A.M.; the night before, we went all night long. And so, we've been working very hard at this. So what I'm going to do is let them take a deep breath and then our side, Madeleine [Albright] and Sandy and all of our team and I—Dennis, we'll try to think what we think we ought to do, then we'll ask them what they want to do, and then we'll figure out what we're going to do.

We don't have a lot of time, and I wouldn't rule out the possibility that all of us will be coming up with new ideas here. I wouldn't rule anything out. The clock is still working against us. The bad news is, we don't have a deal. The good news is, they are fully and completely and comprehensively engaged in an official way for the first time on these fundamental issues.

Keep in mind: When the Oslo Agreement was drafted, these things were put down as final status issues because the people that drafted them knew it would be hard. And they took a gamble. And their gamble was that if the Israelis and the Palestinians worked together over a seven-year period and they began to share security cooperation, for example, they began to—we had some land transfers and we saw how they would work in a different geographical way, and if they kept making other specific agreements, that by the time we got to the end of the road, there would be enough knowledge and trust and understanding of each other's positions that these huge, epochal issues could be resolved.

Now, we started the process and we've got to finish. And so, and again, I say, the thing I hope most of all is that the people in the Middle East will appreciate the fact that a lot was done here and we'll support their leaders in coming back and finishing the job. The venue is not important; the mechanisms aren't important. But we know what the state of play is now and if we'll keep at it, I still think we can get it done.

**Q:** Can you describe what type of U.S. role was discussed in sealing the agreement financially and otherwise?

**Clinton:** Let me say, first of all, anything that would require our participation, other than financial, was not finalized. But there were a lot of ideas floated around. None of it amounted to large numbers of people. But they were potentially significant in terms of the psychology of the situation. But there was no decision made about that.

On the money, basically, you know, I think that the United States should be prepared to make a significant contribution to resolving the refugee problem. You've got refugees that have to be resettled, you've got some compensation which has to be given, and there are lots of issues in that refugee pot that cost money, and then there's the whole question of working out the economic future of the Palestinians and the whole question of working out what the security

relationships will be and the security needs will be for Israel and in this new partnership that they will have—the Palestinians. How is that going to work and what should we do.

I also, when I went to the G-8, I gave a briefing to the G-8, and I asked the people who were there to help pay, too. I said, you know, this is going to have to be a worldwide financial responsibility, but because of the United States' historic involvement, which goes back many decades in the Middle East, we were the first country under President Truman to recognize Israel, we've had Republicans and Democrats alike up to their ears in the Middle East peace process for a long time, and because we have such a lot of strategic interest over there, if there could be an agreement, I think we ought to lead the way in financial contributions, but the others who are able to do so should play their part as well.

Thank you.

# REPUBLICAN
# PARTY PLATFORM
## July 31, 2000

*Setting aside its ideological differences, at least momentarily, the Republican Party used its national convention to present the American public with an image of an inclusive, centrist political party solidly united behind its standard-bearer, Texas governor George W. Bush. Absent from the carefully scripted four-day extravaganza in Philadelphia were any blatant signs of the disagreements that had split the moderate and conservative wings of the party at the previous two conventions. Also absent was much of the strident rhetoric of the religious right castigating anyone who did not agree with its uncompromising stances on abortion, affirmative action, and other politically charged social issues. In its place, Bush and other party dignitaries portrayed the party as one that offered "compassionate conservatism" and Bush as a leader with new ideas who was above the bitterly partisan fray that had marked Washington politics for the eight years of Bill Clinton's presidency.*

*Overall, few speakers at the July 31–August 3 convention launched direct attacks on the Democratic Party, its controversial president, or Bush's presumptive Democratic opponent, Vice President Al Gore. Instead, with Bush's nomination assured and his forces firmly in control of the proceedings, Bush used the convention to reposition the party to appeal to undecided voters in the political middle—the voters that both parties calculated they needed to win the election. Bush made a direct appeal to this audience in his August 3 acceptance speech, promising to use the nation's prosperity "for great goals" including reforming Social Security, improving the nation's schools, strengthening the national defense, and extending "the promise of prosperity to every forgotten corner of this country." The Bush forces were also able to ease the party platform toward the political center by incorporating the candidate's policy proposals on key issues such as education, immigration, tax cuts, and health care. Bush also backed away from some of the more controversial planks in the 1996 Republican platform, such as a call to abolish several Cabinet departments. The result was a document less strident in tone than its immediate forebears were, and it was quickly adopted on the convention floor.* (Bush acceptance speech, p. 519)

*Bush's success in sidelining the more vocal right-wing conservatives in the party stood in sharp contrast to the 1992 convention, which nominated his father, President George Bush, for a second term. That convention was dominated by Christian conservatives who blamed Democratic policies and programs for breakdowns in traditional family unity and rising problems with homelessness, AIDS, teen pregnancies, crime, and a host of other ills plaguing modern society. In November 1992 Bush lost the election to Democrats Bill Clinton and Al Gore in a three-way race with Dallas billionaire Ross Perot. Most analysts thought that Perot's candidacy helped Clinton by splitting the anti-Democratic vote, but voters also held Bush accountable for the badly faltering economy and were noticeably appreciative of Clinton's mainstream policy views and forward-looking campaign.*

*The conservative wing of the GOP was even more visible in 1996. Not only did it control much of the Republican Party machinery, but under the leadership of House Majority Leader Newt Gingrich the conservatives controlled Congress, where their demands to reverse forty years of Democratic programs went too far for many voters. The Republican presidential nominee, Bob Dole, a moderate, was unable to overcome Clinton's attacks on the Republicans as being against Medicare, Medicaid, education, and the environment.*

## Party Platform: Inching Toward the Middle

*Delegates to the Republican National Convention adopted the party platform by voice vote without dissent on July 31, 2000. In large measure the document wrapped the agenda of the conservative wing of the party in the Bush campaign's rhetoric of compassion and inclusiveness. Governor Tommy Thompson of Wisconsin, chairman of the platform committee and a Bush ally, said he hoped the platform reflected "a more uplifting view of the Republican Party, one that's more inclusive, that attempts to build a winning team, that people can rally around." Overall, however, the document continued to emphasize conservative themes put in place during the "Reagan Revolution" of the 1980s—a limited role for the federal government, adherence to traditional notions of family and religious values, and a reliance on private enterprise and initiative to drive economic growth.*

*The 2000 platform was far less combative in tone than the 1996 version and was produced with far less duress. A potentially divisive battle over abortion was avoided early in the process, when the Bush forces said they would accept the language in the 1996 platform. Although Bush had said that he supported abortion in the case of rape or incest or to save the life of the mother, the decision to accept already established language opposing abortion under any circumstances eliminated a large source of potential trouble for the presidential candidate. In 1996 Republican presidential choice Bob Dole tried unsuccessfully to add the so-called tolerance plank, acknowledging that some Republicans had deeply held but differing views on the matter. Conservative opposition was not only a public rebuff of the party's standard-bearer, but also helped to underline the depth of power wielded by the conservative wing of the party.* (Republican Party platform of 1996, Historic Documents of 1996, p. 496)

*At the prodding of Bush supporters, the 107-member platform committee dropped the 1996 call for abolition of the Education Department, but conservatives insisted on language stating that the role of the federal government in education "must be progressively limited as we return control to parents, teachers, and local school boards." Also at Bush's behest, the committee included language welcoming all legal immigrants and dropped a provision of the 1996 platform that would deny automatic citizenship to children born to illegal immigrants. (Under the Constitution anyone born on American soil is an American citizen by right.)*

*On other issues of particular interest to the religious conservative wing of the party, Bush supported the death penalty, opposed gun controls, and favored allowing faith-based organizations to receive federal funding for providing welfare and other social services. The platform committee reaffirmed the party's opposition to gays in the military, rejecting Bush's support of the existing "don't ask, don't tell policy," in which gays could serve if they did not make their sexual preferences known.* (Military homosexual ban, Historic Documents of 1993, p. 153)

*Like the convention itself, the 2000 platform was notable for its restraint in directly attacking the Democratic contender. Only in one paragraph of the lengthy document was Gore mentioned by name, and that was reportedly an error—Gore's name was supposed to have been deleted in the final draft. Unlike the 1996 document, which mentioned President Clinton by name 153 times, the 2000 document did not name the president once, and only one oblique reference was made to his impeachment in 1998 by the Republican-led House of Representatives. Nonetheless, the platform took every opportunity to blame the country's shortcomings on the Clinton administration and to credit the country's successes to past Republican administrations and the current Republican Congress. For example, the document attributed the nation's unprecedented economic growth wholly to the groundwork laid by the Reagan and Bush administration and continued by the Republican-led Congress, without mentioning that the nation's largest budget deficits occurred under the Reagan and Bush administrations and that the economic recession that began during the senior Bush's administration was a key factor leading to Clinton's election in 1992.*

## *Convention: Orchestrated Harmony*

*With no real decisions to be made, the 2000 convention held little drama for either the delegates or television viewers. Many delegates unabashedly told reporters that the proceedings were "boring," an opinion confirmed by the prime-time television audience, only a small portion of which bothered to tune into the proceedings. Much of the action took place off the convention floor, where politicians, lobbyists, and delegates were entertained at lavish fund-raisers and corporate-sponsored receptions, golf outings, and shop-ping excursions. According to one official count, there were more than 900 separate events; one Republican official described it as "the biggest orgy of hedonism in the history of politics." In an interview with the* National Jour-nal, *Bush acknowledged that conventions had become an anachronism in the nominating process but said they still served an important purpose. "The convention provides a system of rewards for hardworking, grass-roots people who end up being delegates," he said. "I view it as an opportunity for these people to go back home, energized to help me get elected."*

*Bush's control of the convention proceedings was apparent in the nightly parade of party officials and dignitaries who trooped before the television cameras presenting upbeat but generally brief messages on a range of top-ics. The intent was to leave voters an image of a vibrant, racially and eth-nically diverse Republican Party unified on the issues and solidly behind the GOP ticket. As they had in 1996, convention planners carefully chose convention speakers and gave them guidelines on what and what not to say. Every speech—with the exception of the presidential and vice presidential acceptance speeches—had to be submitted for review, although most speak-ers reported that the planners were more concerned about the length, rather than the content, of the speeches. Even Bush's key rival in the primaries, Arizona senator John McCain, had his speech vetted; Bush's people report-edly made no changes in it.*

*The opening night of the convention was focused on unity and inclusion. Highlights included an address by General Colin L. Powell, the former head of the Joint Chiefs of Staff, and a testimonial speech from Laura Bush em-phasizing her husband's family values. Powell, the most prominent African American in the Republican Party, called on Republicans to follow Bush's lead "and reach out to minority communities and particularly the African-American community—and not just during an election-year campaign." Powell said the party had to overcome the "cynicism in the black community that is created when . . . some in our party miss no opportunity to roundly and loudly condemn affirmative action that helped a few thousand blacks kids get an education, but hardly a whimper is heard from them over af-firmative action for lobbyists who load our federal tax codes with prefer-ences for special interests." Powell, who had considered running for the presidency himself but decided against it, had made a similar speech at the 1996 convention.*

*The second night of the convention, August 1, showcased several Repub-lican dignitaries, many of whom spoke on issues of national security. Gen-eral H. Norman Schwarzkopf, who directed Operation Desert Storm against Iraq under former president George Bush, spoke via satellite on military readiness, while McCain, a former prisoner of war in Vietnam, spoke on the need for military strength. Former senator Bob Dole, the party's standard-bearer in 1996 and a veteran of World War II, led a tribute to American veterans, while his wife, Elizabeth Dole, spoke about strength through com-passion. Elizabeth Dole had run a brief campaign for the presidency earlier in the year. The third and fourth nights of the convention were taken up with the balloting and the acceptance speeches by Bush and Cheney. (Story, p. 519)*

*Behind the scenes, some delegates lamented that convention speakers missed an opportunity to condemn the Clinton-Gore administration more forcefully or to advocate more conservative views. A small group of Texas delegates protested in silent prayer when an openly gay House member, Jim Kolbe of Arizona, addressed the convention on trade issues. But most seemed willing to go along with the Reverend Jerry Falwell and other conservative leaders who said helping Bush win the presidential election should be the conservatives' first priority. "Our crowd needs to get into this battle, keep their mouths shut, and help this man win," Falwell told the* New York Times.

*Following are excerpts from the Republican Party platform adopted July 31, 2000, by voice vote at the Republican National Convention in Philadelphia. The document was obtained from the Internet at http://www.rnc.org/2000/2000platform1.*

**Taxes and Budget.** . . . When the average American family has to work more than four months out of every year to fund all levels of government, it's time to change the tax system, to make it simpler, flatter, and fairer for everyone. It's time for an economics of inclusion that will let people keep more of what they earn and accelerate movement up the opportunity ladder.

We therefore enthusiastically endorse the principles of Governor Bush's Tax Cut with a Purpose:

- Replace the five current tax brackets with four lower ones, ensuring all taxpayers significant tax relief while targeting it especially toward low-income workers.
- Help families by doubling the child tax credit to $1,000, making it available to more families, and eliminating the marriage penalty.
- Encourage entrepreneurship and growth by capping the top marginal rate, ending the death tax, and making permanent the Research and Development credit.
- Promote charitable giving and education. Foster capital investment and savings to boost today's dangerously low personal savings rate. . . .

**Family Matters.** We support the traditional definition of "marriage" as the legal union of one man and one woman, and we believe that federal judges and bureaucrats should not force states to recognize other living arrangements as marriages. . . . We do not believe sexual preference should be given special legal protection or standing in law.

**Education.** . . . Raise academic standards through increased local control and accountability to parents, shrinking a multitude of federal programs into five flexible grants in exchange for real, measured progress in student achievement.

Assist states in closing the achievement gap and empower needy families to escape persistently failing schools by allowing federal dollars to follow their children to the school of their choice.

. . . We recognize that . . . the role of the federal government must be progressively limited as we return control to parents, teachers, and local school boards. . . . The Republican Congress rightly opposed attempts by the Department of Education to establish federal testing that would set the stage for a national curriculum. We believe it's time to test the Department, and each of its programs, instead. . . .

**Abortion.** . . . The Supreme Court's recent decision, prohibiting states from banning partial-birth abortions—a procedure denounced by a committee of the American Medical Association and rightly branded as four-fifths infanticide—shocks the conscience of the nation. As a country, we must keep our pledge to the first guarantee of the Declaration of Independence. That is why we say the unborn child has a fundamental individual right to life which cannot be infringed. We support a human life amendment to the Constitution and we endorse legislation to make clear that the Fourteenth Amendment's protections apply to unborn children. . . .

**Gun Laws.** . . . We defend the constitutional right to keep and bear arms, and we affirm the individual responsibility to safely use and store firearms.

Because self-defense is a basic human right, we will promote training in their safe usage, especially in federal programs for women and the elderly. A Republican administration will vigorously enforce current gun laws, neglected by the Democrats, especially by prosecuting dangerous offenders identified as felons in instant background checks. Although we support background checks to ensure that guns do not fall into the hands of criminals, we oppose federal licensing of law-abiding gun owners and national gun registration as a violation of the Second Amendment and an invasion of privacy of honest citizens. . . .

**New Americans.** . . . Our country's ethnic diversity within a shared national culture is unique in all the world. We benefit from our differences, but we must also strengthen the ties that bind us to one another. Foremost among those is the flag. Its deliberate desecration is not "free speech" but an assault against both our proud history and our greatest hopes. We therefore support a constitutional amendment that will restore to the people, through their elected representatives, their right to safeguard Old Glory.

Another sign of our unity is the role of English as our common language. . . . For newcomers, it has always been the fastest route to the mainstream of American life. English empowers. That is why fluency in English must be the goal of bilingual education programs. We support the recognition of English as the nation's common language. At the same time, mastery of other languages is important for America's competitiveness in the world market. . . .

As a nation of immigrants, we welcome all new Americans who have entered lawfully and are prepared to follow our laws and provide for themselves and their families. In their search for a better life, they strengthen our economy, enrich our culture, and defend the nation in war and in peace. To ensure fairness for those wishing to reside in this country, and to meet the manpower needs of our expanding economy, a total overhaul of the immigration system is sorely needed. . . .

**Saving Social Security.** . . . Anyone currently receiving Social Security, or close to being eligible for it, will not be impacted by any changes. Key changes should merit bipartisan agreement so any reforms will be a win for the American people rather than a political victory for any one party.

Real reform does not require, and will not include, tax increases.

Personal savings accounts must be the cornerstone of restructuring. Each of today's workers should be free to direct a portion of their payroll taxes to personal investments for their retirement future. . . . Today's financial markets offer a variety of investment options, including some that guarantee a rate of return higher than the current Social Security system with no risk to the investor. Choice is the key. Any new options for retirement security should be voluntary, so workers can choose to remain in the current system or opt for something different. . . .

**Health Care.** . . . Medicare, at age 35, needs a new lease on life. It's time to bring this program, so critical for 39 million seniors and individuals with disabilities, into the Twenty-first Century. It's time to modernize the benefit package to match current medical science, improve the program's financial stability, and cut back the bureaucratic jungle that is smothering it. It's time to give older Americans access to the same health insurance plan the Congress has created for itself, so that seniors will have the same choices and security as Members of Congress, including elimination of all current limitations and restrictions that prevent the establishment of medical savings accounts. . . .

Medicare, the bedrock of care for our elderly, is suffocating under more than 130,000 pages of federal rules, three times the size of the entire IRS code. It pays for only 53 percent of seniors' care, provides no outpatient prescription drugs, and does not cover real long-term care, and it is still headed for bankruptcy in the near future. The doctor-patient relationship has been eroded, and in some instances replaced, by external decision-making and managed care bureaucracy.

We intend to save this beleaguered system with a vision of health care adapted to the changing demands of a new century. It is as simple, and yet as profound, as this: All Americans should have access to high-quality and affordable health care. . . . In achieving that goal, we will promote a health care system that supports, not supplants, the private sector; that promotes personal responsibility in health care decision-making; and that ensures the least intrusive role for the federal government. . . .

**Women's Health.** . . . Across this country, and at all levels of government, Republicans are at the forefront in aggressively developing health care initiatives targeted specifically at the needs of women. The enormous increases in the NIH [National Institutes of Health] budget brought about by the Republican Congress will make possible aggressive new research and clinical trials into diseases and health issues that disproportionately affect women as well as into conditions that affect the elderly, the majority of whom are women. And we are leading efforts to reach out to underserved and minority female populations, where disparities persist in life expectancy, infant mortality and death rates from cancer, heart disease, and diabetes. . . .

**Energy.** . . . By any reasonable standard, the Department of Energy has utterly failed in its mission to safeguard America's energy security. The Federal Energy Regulatory Commission has been no better, and the Environmental Protection Agency (EPA) has been shutting off America's energy pipeline with a regulatory blitz that has only just begun. In fact, 36 oil refineries have closed in just the last eight years, while not a single new refinery has been built in this country in the last quarter-century. EPA's patchwork of regulations has driven fuel prices higher in some areas than in others. . . .

**A Military for the Twenty-first Century.** . . . Over the past seven years, a shrunken American military has been run ragged by a deployment tempo that has eroded its military readiness. Many units have seen their operational requirements increased four-fold, wearing out both people and equipment. Only last fall the Army certified two of its premier combat divisions as unready for war because of underfunding, mismanagement, and over commitment to peacekeeping missions around the globe. More Army units and the other armed services report similar problems. It is a national scandal that almost one quarter of our Army's active combat strength is unfit for wartime duty. . . .

The new Republican government will renew the bond of trust between the Commander-in-Chief, the American military, and the American people. The military is not a civilian police force or a political referee. We believe the military must no longer be the object of social experiments. We affirm traditional military culture. We affirm that homosexuality is incompatible with military service. . . .

**The Middle East and Persian Gulf.** . . . It is important for the United States to support and honor Israel, the only true democracy in the Middle East. We will ensure that Israel maintains a qualitative edge in defensive technology over any potential adversaries. We will not pick sides in Israeli elections. The United States has a moral and legal obligation to maintain its Embassy and Ambassador in Jerusalem. Immediately upon taking office, the next Republican president will begin the process of moving the U.S. Embassy from Tel Aviv to Israel's capital, Jerusalem. . . .

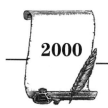
# August

# REPUBLICAN NATIONAL CONVENTION AND SPEECHES
## August 2–3, 2000

*Delegates to the Republican National Convention in Philadelphia tapped George W. Bush, the governor of Texas and son of the former president, to be the party's standard-bearer in the November 2000 elections. The only previous son of a president to be nominated by either major party was John Quincy Adams, in 1824. Robert Todd Lincoln and Robert A. Taft both sought to follow their fathers into office, but neither won the nomination. By comparison, the younger Bush won the nomination with ease, clinching the nomination with victories in the early caucuses and primaries. That left him free at the convention to concentrate on projecting himself as a leader who could unite the country and "renew America's purpose."*

*Bush's nomination was a remarkable political achievement for a man who had only entered politics six years earlier and who had a reputation for being intellectually shallow and uninterested in the details of policy. Not since World War II hero General Dwight D. Eisenhower was elected in 1952 had a presidential nominee of either major party had so little political experience. Detractors said that Bush would never have won the nomination had he not been his father's son.*

*Yet Bush, at age fifty-four, was a younger and more affable spokesperson for the party than it had had in many years. Although he did not have the communications skills of a Ronald Reagan or Bill Clinton, he was able to establish a rapport with voters, and he was a formidable fund-raiser. He was not identified with the bitter partisan politics that had embroiled Washington throughout the eight years of Clinton's presidency, and Bush used that point effectively to compare himself with his presumptive Democratic opponent Al Gore, who had spent a lengthy political career in the House and Senate before becoming vice president. In short, many influential Republicans saw Bush as offering their best chance to regain the White House that his father had lost to Clinton and Gore in 1992.*

*In retrospect, Bush's nomination may have been the last unalloyed victory he had during the campaign. In one of the most unusual elections in American history, Bush won the White House by winning the vote in the electoral college after the Supreme Court stopped a vote recount in Florida that might have awarded the state's electoral votes, and thus the election, to Vice President Al Gore and his running mate, Senator Joe Lieberman. The certified vote count in Florida showed Bush ahead by 537 votes, out of more than 6 million votes cast statewide. The Democratic ticket won the national popular vote by nearly 540,000 votes.* (Presidential election contest, p. 999, 1025)

## *The Path to Philadelphia*

*Although his father had devoted much of his life to public service, culminating in eight years as vice president under Ronald Reagan and then a single term as president in his own right, the younger Bush demonstrated little interest in politics during much of his adult life. A graduate of Yale, with an MBA from Harvard Business School in 1975, Bush spent the late 1970s and 1980s in his hometown of Midland, Texas, where he worked in the oil business with only moderate success. In 1978 he ran unsuccessfully for a seat in the U.S. House; some said his run was motivated more by the trappings of the office than any deep desire to serve the public.*

*Bush's tendency to "drift through life," as at least one reporter put it, began to change in 1988, when he served as a paid worker in his father's presidential campaign. In 1989 he put together a consortium that bought a major share of the Texas Rangers baseball team and in the next few years made a name for himself around the state as the team improved its standing and its ability to draw fans. Bush, who had invested about $600,000 of his own money in the venture, eventually sold his share for $15 million, solidifying his financial future. Bush considered and decided against running for governor of Texas in 1990, but he took the plunge in 1994 and scored something of an upset when he defeated incumbent Democrat Ann Richards. He won reelection in 1998 with 69 percent of the vote and soon thereafter mounted his campaign for the presidency.*

*Working with many of the policy advisers and political operatives from his father's days in the White House and armed with a substantial war chest, Bush took a commanding lead in the early public opinion polls against other Republicans contenders as well as against Vice President Gore. His campaign was momentarily shocked by the popularity of Arizona senator John McCain, whose antiestablishment message and pointed calls for campaign finance reform resonated well with voters in the middle of the political spectrum. In New Hampshire, where Democrats and Independents could vote in the Republican primary, McCain defeated Bush by eighteen percentage points. But in the next few weeks the Bush campaign spent more than $60 million attacking McCain as a closet liberal. McCain dropped out of the race after Bush won decisive victories in several key states, including California and Ohio on March 7, Super Tuesday. By March 21 Bush had won enough delegates to lock up the nomination.* (Republican platform, p. 508)

## *Selection of the Vice Presidential Nominee*

*Bush did not name his choice for running mate until July 25, just days before the convention, and the selection of Richard B. Cheney came as some-*

*thing of a surprise. Cheney was heading the campaign's search for a vice presidential choice when Bush tapped him for the position. A long-time Bush family friend, Cheney had served as chief of staff to President Gerald R. Ford, represented Wyoming in the House from 1979 to 1989, and been secretary of defense under President Bush. Cheney thus had the political and policy experience that Bush lacked. Cheney also had credibility with the military establishment; Bush had avoided going to Vietnam by joining the Texas National Guard. In the corporate-style organization that Bush envisioned for the White House, Cheney was likely to fill the position of chief operating officer, handling many of the day-to-day operations.*

*Cheney was not without some negatives. Although adept at explaining policy programs in small settings, he was not a dynamic stump speaker. He had a very conservative voting record in the House, which may have helped to solidify Bush's position with the Republican right. But Cheney's past positions did little to advance his cause among undecided voters in the political center that the ticket was actively courting. Critics also said Cheney's selection made it easier for Democrats to claim that Bush was not really the centrist candidate he portrayed himself to be. Some observers, including some Republicans, questioned why Bush, who said he wanted to put a fresh face on the Republican Party, would choose someone with strong ties to the Republican establishment. They also questioned why a man who professed to want to emerge from the shadow of his father would choose one of the more visible members of his father's Cabinet as a running mate.*

*Cheney also had a history of heart trouble. He suffered his first attack in 1978 at the age of thirty-seven; he also had heart attacks in 1984 and 1988, when he underwent quadruple bypass surgery. Although his doctors declared him to be in excellent health at the time of his nomination, Cheney had a fourth, mild heart attack in November in the midst of the Florida election controversy. Doctors placed a stent in a clogged artery, and Cheney returned to work as head of the Bush transition team within days of the incident.*

## *Accepting the Nominations*

*Like virtually every other speech and event at the convention, Bush and Cheney's acceptance speeches were carefully crafted to deliver a focused message. Cheney's speech, on August 2, shortly after delegates nominated both men by acclamation, attested to Bush's qualities as a leader and attacked the Clinton-Gore campaign for squandering opportunities. In his speech August 3, Bush outlined his policy program and offered his vision of an innovative and idealistic Republican Party that would extend the nations' economic prosperity to all Americans.*

*Cheney attacked Gore largely by attacking Clinton. In a not-so-subtle jab at Clinton's personal misbehavior, Cheney called Bush a man of principle and honor who "on the first hour of the first day" in office would "restore decency and integrity to the Oval Office." Gore, Cheney said, was trying to get out from under Clinton's shadow, "but somehow we will never see one without thinking of the other. Does anyone—Republican or Democrat—*

*seriously believe that under Mr. Gore the next four years will be any differ-
ent from the last eight?"*

*Politics during the Clinton-Gore years was "an endless onslaught of ac-
cusations, a constant setting of groups one against another," Cheney said,
all of it designed to mask the fact that the Democratic administration failed
to improve education, reform Social Security, or maintain the nation's
military readiness. "We are all a little weary of the Clinton-Gore routine,"
Cheney concluded, and then he repeated the mantra that Gore used so
successfully in the 1992 campaign against Bush's father, "it is time for
them to go!"*

*Bush's acceptance speech marked the first time that the Texas governor
had addressed a national audience, and he used the opportunity to assure
the American public that he was capable of leading the country. In a move
reminiscent of Clinton's campaign in 1992, Bush also staked a claim to several issues normally thought of as belonging to the Democrats and reached
out to voters the Republican Party had often ignored in the recent past. Bush
began by making the case for turning the Democrats out of office. He accused
the Clinton-Gore administration of squandering great opportunities. "Our
current president embodied the potential of a generation. So many talents.
So much charm. Such great skill. But, in the end, to what end? So much
promise, to no great purpose." He acknowledged that his own "background
may lack the polish of Washington," but "then again, I don't have a lot of the
things that come with Washington. I don't have enemies to fight. And I have
no stake in the bitter arguments of the last few years. I want to change the
tone of Washington to one of civility and respect."*

*Bush then outlined his policy program, which in some respects—an
across-the-board tax cut, a stronger military, and a new missile defense
system, for example—repeated traditional Republican themes. But Bush
also took on the Democrats on their own turf. He called for standards and
accountability in education and for expanding Head Start into an early
learning program for all children. He promised to put Medicare on a solid
financial footing and provide prescription drug benefits for "every senior
who needs them." He promised to strengthen Social Security by letting workers invest a portion of their payroll taxes in individual accounts, but he
assured seniors that their benefits would not be touched.*

*Bush called for tearing down the wall between "wealth and technology,
education and ambition" on one side and "poverty and prison, addiction
and despair" on the other. "Big government is not the answer," he said. "But
the alternative to bureaucracy is not indifference. It is to put conservative
values and conservative ideas into the thick of the fight for justice and opportunity. This is what I mean by compassionate conservatism. And on
this ground we will govern the nation."*

*Not surprisingly, most Republicans gave Bush high marks for his per-
formance. "I'm very encouraged by the evolution of the Republican Party
from an angry, naysaying outfit challenging the American people to do it
our way or else . . . into one offering fresh solutions to real problems," New*

*York governor George E. Pataki, a close friend to Bush, told the* Washington
Post. *Even some Democrats conceded that Bush had done a good job of
obscuring the differences between the two parties. "The Republicans have
succeeded in projecting an image that is not only at total variance with
their record but in contradiction of their own platform," Senator Robert G.
Torricelli of New Jersey said after the speech.*

> *Following are texts of speeches at the Republican National Con-
> vention in Philadelphia, as delivered by Richard B. Cheney on
> August 2, 2000, and George W. Bush on August 3, 2000, accept-
> ing their party's nomination for vice president and president,
> respectively. The documents were obtained from the Internet at
> http://www.georgewbush.com/News.asp?FormMode=SP&ID=49
> &Search=1 and http://www.georgewbush.com/News.asp?Form
> Model=SP.*

# CHENEY ACCEPTANCE SPEECH

Mr. Chairman, delegates, and fellow citizens:

I am honored by your nomination, and I accept it.

I thank you for giving such a warm welcome to Lynne and me and our family. And, my friends in the Wyoming delegation, I especially want to thank you
for your support.

The first campaign stop that Lynne and I were privileged to make with Governor and Laura Bush was in Casper, Wyoming . . . our home town, where
Lynne and I graduated from high school 41 years ago. The love and support
and enthusiasm of the people of our home state, have buoyed our spirits and
strengthened our resolve.

We are going to win this election. We will prevail.

I have to tell you that I never expected to be in this position. Eight years
ago, when I completed my years as secretary of defense, I loaded a U-Haul
truck and drove home to Wyoming.

I didn't plan on a return to public office. Lynne and I settled into a new private life. There was time for fishing and grandchildren, and we were content.

But now I am glad to be back in the arena, and let me tell you why. I have
been given an opportunity to serve beside a man who has the courage, and the
vision, and the goodness, to be a great president: Governor George W. Bush.

I have been in the company of leaders. I was there on August 9, 1974, when
Gerald Ford assumed the presidency during our gravest constitutional crisis
since the Civil War. I saw how character and decency can dignify a great office
and unite a great nation.

I was a congressman when another man of integrity lived in the White
House. I saw a president restore America's confidence, and prepare the foun-

dation for victory in the cold war. I saw how one man's will can set the nation on a new course.

I learned the meaning of leadership from President Ronald Reagan. I left Congress to join the cabinet of President Reagan's successor. And I'm proud to say that I'm not the only man on this ticket who has learned from the example of President George Bush.

I saw resolve in times of crisis . . . the steady hand that shaped an alliance and threw back a tyrant. He earned the respect and confidence of the men and women of America's armed forces.

I have been in the company of leaders. I know what it takes. And I see in our nominee the qualities of mind and spirit our nation needs, and our history demands.

Big changes are coming to Washington. To serve with this man, in this cause, is a chance I would not miss.

This country has given me so much opportunity. When Lynne and I were growing up, we had so many blessings. We went to good public schools, where we had fine, dedicated teachers.

Our mothers, like our fathers, worked outside the home so that we could go to college. We lived in a caring community, where parents were confident that their children's lives could be even better than their own. And that is as it should be, and as it can be again.

We can make our public schools better. We can reform the tax code, so that families can keep more of what they earn . . . more dollars that they can spend on what they value, rather than on what the government thinks is important.

We can restore the ideals of honesty and honor that must be a part of our national life, if our children are to thrive.

When I look at the administration now in Washington, I am dismayed by opportunities squandered. Saddened by what might have been, but never was. These have been years of prosperity in our land, but little purpose in the White House. Bill Clinton vowed not long ago to hold onto power "until the last hour of the last day." That is his right. But, my friends, that last hour is coming. That last day is near.

The wheel has turned . . . and it is time . . . it is time for them to go.

George W. Bush will repair what has been damaged. He is a man without pretense and without cynicism. A man of principle, a man of honor.

On the first hour of the first day . . . he will restore decency and integrity to the oval office. He will show us that national leaders can be true to their word . . . and that they can get things done by reaching across the partisan aisle, and working with political opponents in good faith and common purpose.

I know he'll do these things, because for the last five years I've watched him do them in Texas.

George W. Bush came to the Governor's office with a clear view of what he wanted to achieve. He said he would bring higher standards to public schools, and he has. Walk into those schools today, and you will see children with better scores . . . classrooms with better discipline . . . and teachers with better pay.

He pledged to reduce taxes, and he has. He did it twice, with the biggest tax reduction in state history. And not only is the budget in balance, it's running a surplus of more than a billion dollars.

He promised to reform the legal system . . . to get rid of junk lawsuits . . . and he has. Today the legal system serves all the people, not just the trial lawyers.

None of these reforms came easily. When he took office, both houses of the Legislature were controlled by Democrats, and the House of Representatives still is.

But Governor Bush doesn't accept old lines of argument and division. He brings people together . . . reaching across party lines to do the people's business. He leads by conviction, not calculation.

You will never see him pointing the finger of blame for failure . . . you will only see him sharing the credit for success. That is exactly the spirit that is missing from Washington. In the last eight years, that city has often become a scene of bitterness, and ill will, and partisan strife. American politics has always been a tough business . . . even in 1787 here in Philadelphia, when George Washington himself wondered if delegates could ever agree on a constitution.

They did agree, as Americans always have when it mattered most . . . guided by the public interest and a decent regard for one another. But in Washington today, politics has become war by other means . . . an endless onslaught of accusation . . . a constant setting of groups one against the other.

This is what Bill Bradley was up against, and others before him. The Gore campaign, Senator Bradley said, is "a thousand promises, a thousand attacks."

We are all a little weary of the Clinton-Gore routine. But the wheel has turned. And it is time . . . it is time for them to go.

In this election, they will speak endlessly of risk . . . we will speak of progress.

They will make accusations . . . we will make proposals.

They will feed fear . . . we will appeal to hope.

They will offer more lectures, and legalisms, and carefully worded denials. We offer another way . . . a better way . . . and a stiff dose of truth.

For eight years, the achievement gap in our schools has grown worse . . . poor and disadvantaged children falling further and further behind.

For all of their sentimental talk about children, Clinton and Gore have done nothing to help children oppressed by bureaucracy, monopoly, and mediocrity. But those days are ending.

When George W. Bush is President and I am Vice President, tests will be taken, results will be measured, and schools will answer to parents . . . and no child will be left behind.

For eight years, Clinton and Gore have talked about Social Security reform . . . never acting, never once offering a serious plan to save the system. In the time left to them, I have every confidence they'll go right on talking about it.

Those days are passing, too.

There will be no more spreading of fear and panic . . . no more dividing of generations against one another . . . no more delaying and excuse making and shirking of our duties to the elderly.

George W. Bush and I, with the united Congress, will save Social Security.

For eight years, Clinton and Gore have extended our military commitments while depleting our military power. Rarely has so much been demanded of our armed forces, and so little given to them in return. George W. Bush and I are going to change that, too.

I have seen our military at its finest . . . with the best equipment, the best training, and the best leadership.

I'm proud of them. I have had the responsibility for their wellbeing. And I can promise them now . . . help is on the way.

Soon, our men and women in uniform will once again have a commander-in-chief they can respect—one who understands their mission and restores their morale.

And now, as the man from Hope goes home to New York . . . Mr. Gore tries to separate himself from his leader's shadow. But somehow we will never see one without thinking of the other. Does anyone—Republican or Democrat—seriously believe that under Mr. Gore, the next four years would be any different from the last eight?

If the goal is to unite our country—to make a fresh start in Washington, to change the tone of our politics—can anyone say with conviction that the man for the job is Al Gore?

They came in together. Now let us see them off together.

Ladies and gentlemen, the wheel has turned, and it is time . . . it is time for them to go.

This campaign will not be easy. Governor Bush and I face a real fight.

We're ready for it. We know the territory, we know the opposition, and we know what's at stake.

We will give all we have to this cause. And in the end, with your help, George W. Bush will defeat this vice president, and I will replace him.

Ladies and gentlemen, we are so privileged to be citizens of this great republic. I was reminded of that time and again when I was in my former job, as Secretary of Defense.

I traveled a lot . . . and when I came home, my plane would land at Andrews Air Force Base, and I'd return to the Pentagon by helicopter. When you make that trip from Andrews to the Pentagon, and you look down on the city of Washington, one of the first things you see is the Capitol, where all the great debates that have shaped 200 years of American history have taken place.

You fly down along the Mall and see the monument to George Washington, a structure as grand as the man himself. To the north is the White House, where John Adams once prayed "that none but honest and wise men [may] ever rule under this roof."

Next you see the memorial to Thomas Jefferson, the third president and the author of our Declaration of Independence. And then you fly over the memorial to Abraham Lincoln . . . this greatest of presidents, the man who saved the union.

Then you cross the Potomac, on approach to the Pentagon. But just before you settle down on the landing pad, you look upon Arlington National Cemetery . . . its gentle slopes and crosses row on row.

I never once made that trip without being reminded how enormously fortunate we all are to be Americans, and what a terrible price thousands have paid so that all of us—and millions more around the world—might live in freedom.

This is a great country, ladies and gentlemen, and it deserves great leadership. Let us go forth from this hall in confidence and courage, committed to restoring decency and honor to our republic.

Let us go forth, knowing that our cause is just, and elect George W. Bush the forty third president of the United States.

Thank you.

# BUSH ACCEPTANCE SPEECH

Mr. Chairman, delegates, and my fellow citizens. . . . I accept your nomination.

Thank you for this honor. Together, we will renew America's purpose.

Our founders first defined that purpose here in Philadelphia. Ben Franklin was here. Thomas Jefferson. And, of course, George Washington—or, as his friends called him, "George W."

I am proud to have Dick Cheney at my side. He is a man of integrity and sound judgment, who has proven that public service can be noble service. America will be proud to have a leader of such character to succeed Al Gore as Vice President of the United States.

I am grateful for John McCain and the other candidates who sought this nomination. Their convictions strengthen our party.

I am especially grateful tonight to my family. No matter what else I do in life, asking Laura to marry me was the best decision I ever made.

To our daughters, Barbara and Jenna, we love you, we're proud of you, and as you head off to college this fall. . . . Don't stay out too late, and e-mail your old dad once in a while, will you?

And mother, everyone loves you and so do I.

Growing up, she gave me love and lots of advice. I gave her white hair. And I want to thank my father—the most decent man I have ever known. All my life I have been amazed that a gentle soul could be so strong. And Dad, I want you to know how proud I am to be your son.

My father was the last president of a great generation. A generation of Americans who stormed beaches, liberated concentration camps and delivered us from evil. Some never came home.

Those who did put their medals in drawers, went to work, and built on a heroic Scale—highways and universities, suburbs and factories, great cities and grand alliances—the strong foundations of an American Century. Now the question comes to the sons and daughters of this achievement. . . . What is asked of us?

This is a remarkable moment in the life of our nation. Never has the promise of prosperity been so vivid. But times of plenty, like times of crisis, are tests of American character.

Prosperity can be a tool in our hands—used to build and better our country. Or it can be a drug in our system—dulling our sense of urgency, of empathy, of duty.

Our opportunities are too great, our lives too short, to waste this moment. So tonight we vow to our nation: We will seize this moment of American promise. We will use these good times for great goals. We will confront the hard issues—threats to our national security, threats to our health and retirement security—before the challenges of our time become crises for our children.

And we will extend the promise of prosperity to every forgotten corner of this country.

To every man and woman, a chance to succeed. To every child, a chance to learn. To every family, a chance to live with dignity and hope.

For eight years, the Clinton/Gore administration has coasted through prosperity. And the path of least resistance is always downhill.

But America's way is the rising road.

This nation is daring and decent and ready for change.

Our current president embodied the potential of a generation. So many talents. So much charm. Such great skill. But, in the end, to what end? So much promise, to no great purpose.

Little more than a decade ago, the Cold War thawed and, with the leadership of Presidents Reagan and Bush, that wall came down. But instead of seizing this moment, the Clinton/Gore administration has squandered it. We have seen a steady erosion of American power and an unsteady exercise of American influence.

Our military is low on parts, pay and morale. If called on by the commander-in-chief today, two entire divisions of the Army would have to report "Not ready for duty, sir."

This administration had its moment. They had their chance. They have not led. We will.

This generation was given the gift of the best education in American history. Yet we do not share that gift with everyone. Seven of ten fourth-graders in our highest poverty schools cannot read a simple children's book.

And still this administration continues on the same old path with the same old programs—while millions are trapped in schools where violence is common and learning is rare.

This administration had its chance. They have not led. We will.

America has a strong economy and a surplus. We have the public resources and the public will—even the bipartisan opportunities—to strengthen Social Security and repair Medicare.

But this administration—during eight years of increasing need—did nothing.

They had their moment. They have not led. We will.

Our generation has a chance to reclaim some essential values—to show we have grown up before we grow old. But when the moment for leadership came, this administration did not teach our children, it disillusioned them.

They had their chance. They have not led. We will.

And now they come asking for another chance, another shot.

Our answer? "Not this time. Not this year."

This is not a time for third chances, it is a time for new beginnings. The rising generations of this country have our own appointment with greatness. It does not rise or fall with the stock market. It cannot be bought with our wealth.

Greatness is found when American character and American courage overcome American challenges. When Lewis Morris of New York was about to sign the Declaration of Independence, his brother advised against it, warning he would lose all his property.

Morris, a plain-spoken Founder, responded, "Damn the consequences, give me the pen." That is the eloquence of American action.

We heard it during World War II, when General Eisenhower told paratroopers on D-Day morning not to worry—and one replied, "We're not worried, General. . . . It's Hitler's turn to worry now."

We heard it in the civil rights movement, when brave men and women did not say "We shall cope" or "We shall see." They said, "We shall overcome."

An American president must call upon that character. Tonight, in this hall, we resolve to be, not the party of repose, but the party of reform.

We will write, not footnotes, but chapters in the American story. We will add the work of our hands to the inheritance of our fathers and mothers—and leave this nation greater than we found it.

We know the tests of leadership. The issues are joined.

We will strengthen Social Security and Medicare for the greatest generation, and for generations to come. Medicare does more than meet the needs of our elderly, it reflects the values of our society. We will set it on firm financial ground, and make prescription drugs available and affordable for every senior who needs them.

Social Security has been called the "third rail of American politics"—the one you're not supposed to touch because it shocks you. But, if you don't touch it, you can't fix it. And I intend to fix it.

To seniors in this country. . . . You earned your benefits, you made your plans, and President George W. Bush will keep the promise of Social Security— no changes, no reductions, no way.

Our opponents will say otherwise. This is their last, parting ploy, and don't believe a word of it.

Now is the time for Republicans and Democrats to end the politics of fear and save Social Security, together.

For younger workers, we will give you the option—your choice—to put a part of your payroll taxes into sound, responsible investments. This will mean a higher return on your money, and, over 30 or 40 years, a nest egg to help your retirement, or pass along to your children.

When this money is in your name, in your account, it's not just a program, it's your property. Now is the time to give American workers security and independence that no politician can ever take away.

On education. . . . Too many American children are segregated into schools without standards, shuffled from grade-to-grade because of their age, regardless of their knowledge. This is discrimination, pure and simple—the soft bigotry of low expectations. And our nation should treat it like other forms of discrimination. We should end it.

One size does not fit all when it comes to educating our children, so local people should control local schools. And those who spend your tax dollars must be held accountable.

When a school district receives federal funds to teach poor children, we expect them to learn. And if they don't, parents should get the money to make a different choice.

Now is the time to make Head Start an early learning program, teach all our children to read, and renew the promise of America's public schools.

Another test of leadership is tax relief. The last time taxes were this high as a percentage of our economy, there was a good reason. . . . We were fighting World War II.

Today, our high taxes fund a surplus. Some say that growing federal surplus means Washington has more money to spend. But they've got it backwards.

The surplus is not the government's money. The surplus is the people's money.

I will use this moment of opportunity to bring common sense and fairness to the tax code. And I will act on principle. On principle. . . . every family, every farmer and small businessperson, should be free to pass on their life's work to those they love. So we will abolish the death tax.

On principle. . . . No one in America should have to pay more than a third of their income to the federal government. So we will reduce tax rates for everyone, in every bracket.

On principle. . . . Those in the greatest need should receive the greatest help. So we will lower the bottom rate from 15 percent to 10 percent and double the child tax credit. Now is the time to reform the tax code and share some of the surplus with the people who pay the bills.

The world needs America's strength and leadership, and America's armed forces need better equipment, better training, and better pay. We will give our military the means to keep the peace, and we will give it one thing more—a commander-in-chief who respects our men and women in uniform, and a commander-in-chief who earns their respect.

A generation shaped by Vietnam must remember the lessons of Vietnam. When America uses force in the world, the cause must be just, the goal must be clear, and the victory must be overwhelming.

I will work to reduce nuclear weapons and nuclear tension in the world—to turn these years of influence into decades of peace.

And, at the earliest possible date, my administration will deploy missile defenses to guard against attack and blackmail. Now is the time, not to defend outdated treaties, but to defend the American people.

A time of prosperity is a test of vision. And our nation today needs vision. That is a fact—or as my opponent might call it, a "risky truth scheme."

Every one of the proposals I've talked about tonight, he has called a "risky scheme," over and over again. It is the sum of his message—the politics of the roadblock, the philosophy of the stop sign.

If my opponent had been there at the moon launch, it would have been a "risky rocket scheme."

If he'd been there when Edison was testing the light bulb, it would have been a "risky anti-candle scheme."

And if he'd been there when the Internet was invented well . . . I understand he actually was there for that.

He now leads the party of Franklin Delano Roosevelt. But the only thing he has to offer is fear itself.

That outlook is typical of many in Washington—always seeing the tunnel at the end of the light. But I come from a different place, and it has made me a different leader. In Midland, Texas, where I grew up, the town motto was "the sky is the limit," and we believed it.

There was a restless energy, a basic conviction that, with hard work, anybody could succeed, and everybody deserved a chance.

Our sense of community was just as strong as that sense of promise. Neighbors helped each other. There were dry wells and sandstorms to keep you humble, and lifelong friends to take your side, and churches to remind us that every soul is equal in value and equal in need.

This background leaves more than an accent, it leaves an outlook. Optimistic. Impatient with pretense. Confident that people can chart their own course.

That background may lack the polish of Washington. Then again, I don't have a lot of things that come with Washington.

I don't have enemies to fight. And I have no stake in the bitter arguments of the last few years. I want to change the tone of Washington to one of civility and respect.

The largest lesson I learned in Midland still guides me as governor. . . . Everyone, from immigrant to entrepreneur, has an equal claim on this country's promise.

So we improved our schools, dramatically, for children of every accent, of every background.

We moved people from welfare to work.

We strengthened our juvenile justice laws.

Our budgets have been balanced, with surpluses, and we cut taxes not only once, but twice.

We accomplished a lot. I don't deserve all the credit, and don't attempt to take it. I worked with Republicans and Democrats to get things done.

A bittersweet part of tonight is that someone is missing, the late Lt. Governor of Texas Bob Bullock. Bob was a Democrat, a crusty veteran of Texas politics, and my great friend. He worked by my side, endorsed my re-election, and I know he is with me in spirit in saying to those who would malign our state for political gain, "Don't mess with Texas."

As governor, I've made difficult decisions, and stood by them under pressure.

I've been where the buck stops—in business and in government. I've been a chief executive who sets an agenda, sets big goals, and rallies people to believe and achieve them.

I am proud of this record, and I'm prepared for the work ahead. If you give me your trust, I will honor it. Grant me a mandate, and I will use it. Give me the opportunity to lead this nation, and I will lead.

And we need a leader to seize the opportunities of this new century—the new cures of medicine, the amazing technologies that will drive our economy and keep the peace.

But our new economy must never forget the old, unfinished struggle for human dignity. And here we face a challenge to the very heart and founding premise of our nation.

A couple of years ago, I visited a juvenile jail in Marlin, Texas, and talked with a group of young inmates. They were angry, wary kids. All had committed grownup crimes.

Yet when I looked in their eyes, I realized some of them were still little boys.

Toward the end of conversation, one young man, about 15, raised his hand and asked a haunting question: "What do you think of me?"

He seemed to be asking, like many Americans who struggle, "Is there hope for me? Do I have a chance?" And, frankly, "Do you, a white man in a suit, really care what happens to me?"

A small voice, but it speaks for so many. Single moms struggling to feed the kids and pay the rent. Immigrants starting a hard life in a new world. Children without fathers in neighborhoods where gangs seem like friendship, where drugs promise peace, and where sex, sadly, seems like the closest thing to belonging. We are their country, too.

And each of us must share in its promise, or that promise is diminished for all. If that boy in Marlin believes he is trapped and worthless and hopeless— if he believes his life has no value, then other lives have no value to him—and we are ALL diminished.

When these problems aren't confronted, it builds a wall within our nation. On one side are wealth and technology, education and ambition.

On the other side of the wall are poverty and prison, addiction and despair. And, my fellow Americans, we must tear down that wall.

Big government is not the answer. But the alternative to bureaucracy is not indifference. It is to put conservative values and conservative ideas into the thick of the fight for justice and opportunity.

This is what I mean by compassionate conservatism. And on this ground we will govern our nation.

We will give low-income Americans tax credits to buy the private health insurance they need and deserve. We will transform today's housing rental program to help hundreds of thousands of low-income families find stability and dignity in a home of their own.

And, in the next bold step of welfare reform, we will support the heroic work of homeless shelters and hospices, food pantries and crisis pregnancy centers—people reclaiming their communities block-by-block and heart-by-heart.

I think of Mary Jo Copeland, whose ministry called "Sharing and Caring Hands" serves 1,000 meals a week in Minneapolis, Minnesota. Each day, Mary Jo washes the feet of the homeless, then sends them off with new socks and shoes.

"Look after your feet," she tells them. "They must carry you a long way in this world, and then all the way to God."

Government cannot do this work. It can feed the body, but it cannot reach the soul. Yet government can take the side of these groups, helping the helper, encouraging the inspired.

My administration will give taxpayers new incentives to donate to charity, encourage after-school programs that build character, and support mentoring groups that shape and save young lives.

We must give our children a spirit of moral courage, because their character is our destiny. We must tell them, with clarity and confidence, that drugs and alcohol can destroy you, and bigotry disfigures the heart.

Our schools must support the ideals of parents, elevating character and abstinence from afterthoughts to urgent goals. We must help protect our children, in our schools and streets, by finally and strictly enforcing our nation's gun laws.

Most of all, we must teach our children the values that defeat violence. I will lead our nation toward a culture that values life—the life of the elderly and the sick, the life of the young, and the life of the unborn. I know good people disagree on this issue, but surely we can agree on ways to value life by promoting adoption and parental notification, and when Congress sends me a bill against partial-birth abortion, I will sign it into law.

Behind every goal I have talked about tonight is a great hope for our country. A hundred years from now, this must not be remembered as an age rich in possessions and poor in ideals.

Instead, we must usher in an era of responsibility. My generation tested limits—and our country, in some ways, is better for it. Women are now treated more equally. Racial progress has been steady, if still too slow. We are learning to protect the natural world around us. We will continue this progress, and we will not turn back.

At times, we lost our way. But we are coming home.

So many of us held our first child, and saw a better self reflected in her eyes. And in that family love, many have found the sign and symbol of an even greater love, and have been touched by faith.

We have discovered that who we are is more important than what we have. And we know we must renew our values to restore our country.

This is the vision of America's founders. They never saw our nation's greatness in rising wealth or advancing armies, but in small, unnumbered acts of caring and courage and self-denial. Their highest hope, as Robert Frost described it, was "to occupy the land with character."

And that, 13 generations later, is still our goal—to occupy the land with character.

In a responsibility era, each of us has important tasks—work that only we can do.

Each of us is responsible—to love and guide our children, and help a neighbor in need.

Synagogues, churches and mosques are responsible—not only to worship but to serve.

Corporations are responsible—to treat their workers fairly, and leave the air and waters clean.

Our nation's leaders are responsible—to confront problems, not pass them on to others.

And to lead this nation to a responsibility era, a president himself must be responsible. And so, when I put my hand on the Bible, I will swear to not only uphold the laws of our land, I will swear to uphold the honor and dignity of the office to which I have been elected, so help me God.

I believe the presidency—the final point of decision in the American government—was made for great purposes. It is the office of Lincoln's conscience and Teddy Roosevelt's energy and Harry Truman's integrity and Ronald Reagan's optimism.

For me, gaining this office is not the ambition of a lifetime, but it IS the opportunity of a lifetime. And I will make the most of it.

I believe great decisions are made with care, made with conviction, not made with polls. I do not need to take your pulse before I know my own mind. I do not reinvent myself at every turn. I am not running in borrowed clothes.

When I act, you will know my reasons. When I speak, you will know my heart.

I believe in tolerance, not in spite of my faith, but because of it.

I believe in a God who calls us, not to judge our neighbors, but to love them.

I believe in grace, because I have seen it. In peace, because I have felt it. In forgiveness, because I have needed it.

I believe true leadership is a process of addition, not an act of division. I will not attack a part of this country, because I want to lead the whole of it.

And I believe this will be a tough race, down to the wire. Their war room is up and running—but we are ready. Their attacks will be Relentless—but they will be answered. We are facing something familiar, but they are facing something new.

We are now the party of ideas and innovation. The party of idealism and inclusion. The party of a simple and powerful hope. . . .

My fellow citizens, we can begin again. After all of the shouting, and all of the scandal. After all of the bitterness and broken faith. We can begin again. The wait has been long, but it won't be long now.

A prosperous nation is ready to renew its purpose and unite behind great goals . . . and it won't be long now.

Our nation must renew the hopes of that boy I talked with in jail, and so many like him . . . and it won't be long now.

Our country is ready for high standards and new leaders . . . and it won't be long now.

An era of tarnished ideals is giving way to a responsibility era . . . and it won't be long now.

I know how serious the task is before me. I know the presidency is an office that turns pride into prayer. But I am eager to start on the work ahead. And I believe America is ready for a new beginning.

My friend, the artist Tom Lea of El Paso, captured the way I feel about our great land. He and his wife, he said, "live on the east side of the mountain. It is the sunrise side, not the sunset side. It is the side to see the day that is coming, not the side to see the day that is gone."

Americans live on the sunrise side of mountain. The night is passing. And we are ready for the day to come.

Thank you. And God bless you.

# WORLD HEALTH ORGANIZATION ON THE TOBACCO CONSPIRACY
## August 2, 2000

*Stepping up its campaign to eradicate smoking worldwide, the World Health Organization (WHO), an agency of the United Nations, released a special report on August 2, 2000, showing that leading American tobacco companies had engaged in a secret campaign to discredit WHO and undermine its antismoking campaign. In October WHO convened a conference in Geneva with delegates from 150 countries to begin negotiations on a worldwide treaty to regulate tobacco. The meetings drew a remarkable amount of unanimity on the goals, but delegates cautioned that the devil was in the details and that a great many contentious issues had to be resolved before a treaty could be finalized. Nonetheless, Matt Myers, president of the Campaign for Tobacco-Free Kids, and a prominent leader of the antismoking forces in the United States, said the meeting "was the single most significant action ever proposed to reduce tobacco use worldwide." WHO hoped to have negotiations on the treaty completed by 2003.*

*The WHO special report noted that American tobacco companies sought to turn other United Nations agencies against WHO and to persuade developing countries that tobacco control would come at their expense. Many of the internal company documents on which the WHO report was based had first come to light through lawsuits in the United States against the tobacco companies in the 1990s. Revelations that the tobacco companies had long known of the health hazards of smoking despite their public denials had helped to make the American public more receptive to regulation of tobacco and tobacco advertising, and it seemed clear that WHO hoped its report would have a similar effect.*

*Worldwide, an estimated 1.1 billion people smoked, and smoking-related illnesses, such as lung cancer, heart disease, and emphysema, killed about 4 million people a year—as many as died from acquired immunodeficiency syndrome (AIDS) and tuberculosis combined. WHO predicted that if current trends continued, by 2030 as many as 10 million people a year would die from smoking-related illness. (AIDS epidemic, p. 410)*

*The problem was particularly acute in the developing world, where smok-*

*ing rates were high and on the rise. About 80 percent of the world's smokers lived in developing countries, particularly in Asia. One-third of the world's smokers lived in China. Two-thirds or more of all adult men in China, Indonesia, the Philippines, and Vietnam smoked. Rates of smoking were much lower among Asian women, averaging about 8 percent, but public health officials were warning that the incidence of smoking among young women was rising rapidly.*

*Public health officials were also worried that as smoking declined and regulations tightened in the industrialized world, tobacco companies were focusing their attentions on the potential markets in the developing world. Philip Morris, for example, recently built a $300 million cigarette manufacturing plant in the Philippines, while Japan Tobacco recently bought the RJR Tobacco International Division, which had cigarette sales in seventy countries. Tobacco companies in several Asian countries were still owned in whole or in part by the governments of those countries, a situation that created conflicts between public agencies wanting to protect public health and those wanting to hold on to the revenues brought in by tobacco sales.*

### *Framework Convention on Tobacco Control*

*The negotiations on a tobacco control treaty represented the first time that WHO had sought to deal with a public health issue through an international treaty. It was given the green light to proceed in 1999 by health ministers of 191 nations meeting at the World Health Assembly, which authorized WHO to set up working groups to draw up possible planks, or "draft elements," of a treaty that could then be negotiated. At a minimum WHO said the treaty should ban multinational tobacco companies from advertising their products and sponsoring sports events, increase taxes to make cigarettes prohibitively expensive, stop cigarette smuggling, and take steps to discourage teens and children from starting to smoke. A report prepared by WHO and the World Bank found that a complete ban on advertising and promotion of tobacco products could cut tobacco use by 7 percent; a 10 percent increase in the cost of a pack of cigarettes would slow demand in developing countries by 8 percent—twice as much as in industrialized countries.*

*Nations attending the opening negotiating sessions in Geneva October 16–21 were nearly unanimous in their support of a ban on tobacco advertising and sponsorship. The United States was one influential country that stopped short of supporting a complete advertising ban, citing issues of free speech. It also appeared likely that a total ban could run afoul of free trade agreements. On October 5 the European Court of Justice in Luxembourg overturned a European Union directive banning tobacco advertising on the grounds that the ban interfered with the free movement of goods and services. Some smaller countries were dependent on tobacco sponsorship; in Papua New Guinea tobacco support was used to finance their highly popular rugby teams.*

*Another controversial issue was whether tobacco-producing countries such as Malawi, Turkey, and Zimbabwe would receive any aid to help them abandon tobacco production in favor of some other crop. Canada and the*

*United States suggested that such assistance be voluntary and bilateral, whereas several of the developing countries called for a global fund with mandatory assessments. Other controversial issues were likely to involve curbs on cigarette smuggling, restrictions on exports of tobacco products, and bans on smoking in public places, especially places frequented by children. "It will be very tough negotiating," said one American observer. "There will be over 100 countries involved, and the tobacco industry has longstanding ties with many of the people in government."*

*During two days of public hearings that preceded the negotiations, the industry indicated that it was willing to accept some "sensible" regulation. Antismoking advocates remained skeptical, suggesting that the companies would say they favored some regulation but would then raise objections to key provisions, such as marketing and advertising restrictions. Others suggested that the companies wanted to preserve their ability to advertise and market new smoking products that might be less harmful. R. J. Reynolds Tobacco Co. was already aggressively marketing an experimental cigarette in the United States. The company was claiming that the cigarette, which heated the tobacco rather than burning it, might pose less risk of lung cancer than regular cigarettes.*

## WHO Report on Tobacco Company Interventions

*WHO's release of its report on the American tobacco industry's attempts to undermine the agency's antismoking efforts on August 2 was part of the agency's stated strategy to hold the industry accountable for the harm caused by tobacco use. "Nobody who is working in the area of tobacco control is surprised that tobacco companies are trying to limit our influence," Dr. Thomas Zeltner told the* New York Times. *"But the surprise is how elaborate and well financed this whole activity was." Zeltner, a Swiss public health official, was chairman of the committee of experts that prepared the report after reviewing hundreds of internal company documents that had been made public as a result of lawsuits and other investigations in the United States. Another prominent member of the committee was David Kessler, dean of the medical school at Yale University and the former head of the U.S. Food and Drug Administration, whose efforts to regulate tobacco as a drug were overturned by a Supreme Court decision in March. (Smoking and FDA regulations, p. 555)*

*The strategies the companies used to undermine and discredit WHO ranged from "dirty trick" tactics, such as staging media events to distract attention from tobacco-related WHO events, to using front groups to influence WHO decision making, to putting pressure on WHO budgets. Perhaps the most serious misdeed along these lines, according to the report, was the companies' attempt to influence WHO's tobacco-control activities by developing close relationships with current and former WHO staff members. In some cases, the companies succeeded in having their own paid consultants placed in positions of influence within the agency. The report also detailed efforts by tobacco company representatives to sour developing countries on antismoking campaigns by stressing the economic damage that would occur in poor tobacco-producing countries if the demand for cigarettes and other tobacco products declined.*

*"That top executives of tobacco companies sat together to design and set in motion elaborate strategies to subvert a public health organization is unacceptable and must be condemned," the Committee of Experts on Tobacco Industry Documents concluded. "To many in the international community, tobacco prevention may be seen today as a struggle against chemical addiction, cancers, cardiovascular diseases and other health consequences of smoking. This inquiry adds to the mounting evidence that it is also a struggle against an active, organized and calculating industry."*

*In a statement, David Davies, a vice president of Philip Morris International, did not deny that report's contents as they related to his company but said that the documents were at least ten years old and no longer represented company practices. "Our goal today is to create a different environment, one of less rancor, where there can be real progress in resolving important issues relating to the regulation of tobacco." A spokesman for British-American Tobacco, another company cited in the report, took a similar if harsher tack: "It is very sad that the WHO of all people have succumbed to the plaintiffs' obsession with old documents rather than how we might work together constructively to move things forward."*

*Following are excerpts from the foreword and the executive summary of the report, "Tobacco Company Strategies to Undermine Tobacco Control Activities at the World Health Organization," prepared by a committee of experts in behalf of the organization and released August 2, 2000. The document was obtained from the Internet at http://filestore.who.int/<who/home/tobacco/tobacco.pdf.*

## Foreword

Evidence from tobacco industry documents reveals that tobacco companies have operated for many years with the deliberate purpose of subverting the efforts of the World Health Organization (WHO) to control tobacco use. The attempted subversion has been elaborate, well financed, sophisticated, and usually invisible.

The release of millions of pages of confidential tobacco company documents as a result of lawsuits against the tobacco industry in the United States has exposed the activities of tobacco companies in resisting tobacco control efforts. That tobacco companies resist proposals for tobacco control comes as no surprise. What is now clear is the scale and intensity of their often-deceptive strategies and tactics.

The tobacco companies' own documents show that they viewed WHO, an international public health agency, as one of their foremost enemies. The documents show further that the tobacco companies instigated global strategies to discredit and impede WHO's ability to carry out its mission. The tobacco companies' campaign against WHO was rarely directed at the merits of the public health issues raised by tobacco use. Instead, the documents show that tobacco companies sought to divert attention from the public health issues, to reduce budgets for the scientific and policy activities carried out by WHO, to pit other UN agencies against WHO, to convince developing countries that WHO's tobacco control program was a "First World" agenda carried out at the expense of the developing world, to distort the results of important scientific studies on tobacco, and to discredit WHO as an institution.

Although these strategies and tactics were frequently devised at the highest levels of tobacco companies, the role of tobacco industry officials in carrying out these strategies was often concealed. In their campaign against WHO, the documents show that tobacco companies hid behind a variety of ostensibly independent quasi-academic, public policy, and business organizations whose tobacco industry funding was not disclosed. The documents also show that tobacco company strategies to undermine WHO relied heavily on international and scientific experts with hidden financial ties to the industry. Perhaps most disturbing, the documents show that tobacco companies quietly influenced other UN agencies and representatives of developing countries to resist WHO's tobacco control initiatives.

That top executives of tobacco companies sat together to design and set in motion elaborate strategies to subvert a public health organization is unacceptable and must be condemned. The committee of experts believes that the tobacco companies' activities slowed and undermined effective tobacco control programs around the world. Given the magnitude of the devastation wrought by tobacco use, the committee of experts is convinced that, on the basis of the volume of attempted and successful acts of subversion identified in its limited search, it is reasonable to believe that the tobacco companies' subversion of WHO's tobacco control activities has resulted in significant harm. Although the number of lives damaged or lost as a result of the tobacco companies' subversion of WHO may never be quantified, the importance of condemning the tobacco companies' conduct, and taking appropriate corrective action, is overriding.

The committee of experts urges WHO and member countries to take a strong position against the tobacco companies' conduct as described in this report. This report contains a number of recommendations aimed at protecting against the strategies employed by tobacco companies. Among the most important of these recommendations are that: (1) member countries carry out similar investigations into tobacco company influence on those countries' tobacco control efforts, (2) WHO monitor the future conduct of the tobacco industry to determine whether the strategies identified in this report are continuing, and (3) WHO assist member countries to determine what steps are appropriate to remedy tobacco companies' past misconduct.

Some tobacco companies in the US have made public claims that they have reformed their behavior and therefore need not be penalized for past misconduct. Such promises, even if true, must not be limited to the industry's conduct in a single country. It is not enough for tobacco companies to now begin acting "responsibly" in the US, if they continue to use unacceptable strategies and tactics in the rest of the world. If the strategies and tactics identified in this report continue to be used internationally by tobacco companies, WHO must bring this behavior into the world's view. Member countries must also carefully assess the impact of past influence of tobacco companies on the health and welfare of their citizens and consider appropriate actions both to correct past misconduct and to deter future abuses.

[signed]

Thomas Zeltner, M.D.

David A. Kessler, M.D.

Anke Martiny, Ph.D.

Fazel Randera, M.D.

## Executive Summary

### A. Introduction

In the summer of 1999, an internal report to the Director-General of the World Health Organization (WHO) suggested that there was evidence in formerly confidential tobacco company documents that tobacco companies had made "efforts to prevent implementation of healthy public policy and efforts to reduce funding of tobacco control within UN organizations." In response to this report, Director-General Gro Harlem Brundtland assembled a committee of experts to research the once confidential, now publicly available, tobacco company documents.

The documents reveal that tobacco companies viewed WHO as one of their leading enemies, and that they saw themselves in a battle against WHO. According to one major company's master plan to fight threats to the industry, "WHO's impact and influence is indisputable," and the company must "contain, neutralize, [and] reorient" WHO's tobacco control initiatives. The documents show that tobacco companies fought WHO's tobacco control agenda by, among other things, staging events to divert attention from the public health issues raised by tobacco use, attempting to reduce budgets for the scientific and policy activities carried out by WHO, pitting other UN agencies against WHO, seeking to convince developing countries that WHO's tobacco control program was a "First World" agenda carried out at the expense of the developing world, distorting the results of important scientific studies on tobacco, and discrediting WHO as an institution.

Tobacco company strategy documents reveal the companies' goals and tactics:

"Attack W.H.O."

"[U]ndertake a long-term initiative to counteract the WHO's aggressive global anti-smoking campaign and to introduce a public debate with respect to a redefinition of the WHO's mandate."

"[B]lunt [WHO's] programme initiatives."

"[Try] to stop the development towards a Third World commitment against tobacco."

"[A]llocate the resources to stop [WHO] in their tracks."

"Discredit key individuals."

"[Contain WHO's] funding from private sources."

"Work with journalists to question WHO priorities, budget, role in social engineering, etc."

"[Reorient]/reprioritiz[e] IARC [International Agency for Research on Cancer] priorities/budget allocations."

"[Try] to change the very nature and tone of the [WHO-sponsored] conference."

"[Establish] ITGA [International Tobacco Growers Association] [as a] front for our third world lobby activities at WHO."

"[P]ersuade PAHO [Pan American Health Organization] to take tobacco off their list of priorities for this year."

"[I]nhibit incorporation of ILO [UN's International Labor Organization] into WHO Anti-Smoking Program."

"Split F.A.O. [U.N. Food and Agriculture Organization]/W.H.O."

This report serves as the final product of the committee of experts' research, to be submitted to the Director-General for review.

## B. Methodology

The investigation focused on the collection and review of tobacco company documents made publicly available as a result of US lawsuits against the tobacco industry. The available documents come from Philip Morris Companies, Inc. (Philip Morris), R. J. Reynolds Tobacco Company (RJR), Brown & Williamson Tobacco Company (B&W), American Tobacco Company (ATC), Lorillard Tobacco Company (Lorillard), the Tobacco Institute (TI), the Council for Tobacco Research (CTR) and the British American Tobacco Company (BAT). Unless specifically noted otherwise, where the report refers to "tobacco companies," it is a reference to two or more of these companies. The phrase "tobacco companies" is not intended to refer to any other companies not listed here.

In addition, a limited number of individuals were interviewed, following consultation with the Director-General. The information provided by these individuals served to clarify information already found in the tobacco company documents.

## C. Strategies and Tactics Used by Tobacco Companies to Influence WHO Tobacco Control

The tobacco company documents reviewed by the committee of experts reveal that tobacco companies have focused significant resources on undermining WHO tobacco control activities and have used a wide range of tactics to achieve their goal. Evidence before the committee of experts suggests that some of these strategies were successful in influencing WHO activities, while others were not. In some cases, the committee of experts was not able to determine the success of certain strategies based on available information. . . .

- ## Establishing inappropriate relationships with WHO staff to influence policy

In one of their most significant strategies for influencing WHO's tobacco control activities, tobacco companies developed and maintained relationships with current or former WHO staff, consultants and advisors. In some cases, tobacco companies hired or offered future employment to former WHO or UN officials in order to indirectly gain valuable contacts within these organizations that might assist in its goal of influencing WHO activities. Of greatest concern, tobacco companies have, in some cases, had their own consultants in positions at WHO, paying them to serve the goals of tobacco companies while working for WHO. Some of these cases raise serious questions about whether the integrity of WHO decision making has been compromised. All of them illustrate the need for rules requiring that current and prospective WHO employees, including consultants, advisors, and members of expert committees, disclose any ties to the tobacco industry.

- ## Wielding financial power to influence WHO policy

In several cases, tobacco companies have attempted to undermine WHO tobacco control activities by putting pressure on relevant WHO budgets. Tobacco companies have also used their resources to gain favor or particular outcomes by making well-placed contributions.

- ## Using other UN agencies to influence or resist WHO tobacco control

The committee of experts' research reveals that tobacco companies attempted to use other UN agencies to acquire information about WHO's tobacco control activities and to interfere with or resist WHO's tobacco related policies. Most of the tobacco companies' efforts appear to have focused on the Food and Agricultural Organization (FAO), but the documents also reveal that tobacco companies targeted other UN agencies, including the World Bank, the United Nations Conference on Trade and Development (UNCTAD), the United Nations Economic and Social Council (ECOSOC) and the International Labor Organization (ILO), either directly or through surrogates. Tobacco company lobbying was aimed at influencing the FAO to take a stance against WHO's tobacco control policies and to promote the economic importance of tobacco as more significant than the health consequences of tobacco use.

- ## Discrediting WHO or WHO officials to undermine WHO's effectiveness

Tobacco companies used "independent" individuals and institutions to attack WHO's competence and priorities in published articles, and presentations to the media and to politicians, while concealing its own role in promoting these attacks.

- ## Influencing WHO decision making through surrogates

Documents in this study illustrate that tobacco companies utilized a number of outside organizations to lobby against and influence tobacco control activities at WHO including trade unions, tobacco company-created front groups and tobacco companies' own affiliated food companies.

Additionally, delegates of member states from developing countries were lobbied by tobacco companies. The documents indicate that tobacco companies believe that as a result, an increasing number of delegates from these countries have resisted WHO tobacco control resolutions.

- ## Distorting WHO research

Tobacco company strategies and tactics included manipulating the scientific and public debate about the health effects of tobacco. Tobacco companies secretly funded "independent" experts to conduct research, publish papers, appear at conferences and lobby WHO's scientific investigators with the intention of influencing, discrediting or distorting study results. Their own agenda was promoted through tobacco company-funded symposia, counter-research and scientific coalitions developed specifically to criticize studies used to support anti-tobacco legislation. The most notable result of this tobacco company strategy is the misrepresentation of the 1998 study on environmental tobacco smoke (ETS) by the International Agency for Research on Cancer (IARC). The tobacco company distortion of these study results continues today to shape public opinion and policies surrounding the health effects of ETS.

- ## Media events

The documents show that tobacco companies staged media events to distract attention from tobacco-related WHO events such as the World Conference on Tobacco OR Health.

- ## Surveillance of WHO activities

Finally, the documents show that tobacco companies have carried out intensive monitoring of WHO and its Regional Offices to gather intelligence about its tobacco control programs. In some cases, tobacco companies have secretly monitored WHO meetings and conferences, had confidential WHO contacts, and obtained confidential documents and information.

## D. Case Studies

The following case studies offer specific examples of many of tobacco company strategies discussed in this chapter. These case studies show that:

- One tobacco company targeted WHO as part of a massive and far-reaching campaign to subvert tobacco control activities around the world.
- Tobacco companies have conducted an ongoing, global campaign to convince developing and tobacco-producing countries to resist WHO tobacco control policies.

- One tobacco company consultant attacked WHO in the media and in presentations to regulatory authorities, without revealing his ties to tobacco companies. This consultant was also named to a WHO committee where he attempted to use a WHO Regional Office in tobacco company plans to distract attention from a WHO-sponsored conference.
- Tobacco companies attempted to stage elaborate diversions from, and disruptions of, a WHO-sponsored conference on tobacco.
- Tobacco companies secretly funded a temporary adviser to a WHO committee, raising questions about whether WHO's international standard-setting activities related to pesticide safety were affected.
- Tobacco companies carried out a multi-million dollar campaign to halt or influence the results of an important IARC study on the relationship between passive smoking and lung cancer, relying on consultants to conceal their role.

Some of these cases raise serious concerns about whether the integrity of WHO decision making has been compromised. Each case study includes specific recommendations for WHO to consider in preventing future tobacco company influence.

## 1. The Boca Raton Action Plan

In November 1988, under the direction of Geoffrey Bible, then President of Philip Morris International (now Chief Executive Officer of Philip Morris Companies Inc.), top executives from Philip Morris' regional offices and its New York headquarters convened in Boca Raton, Florida, to plan for the succeeding year. The resulting Action Plan—one of the publicly available tobacco company documents—is a master plan for, among many goals, attacking WHO's tobacco control programs, influencing the priorities of WHO Regional Offices, and targeting the structure, management and resources of WHO. The Plan identified 26 global threats to the tobacco industry and multiple strategies for countering each. First among these threats was the World Health Organization's tobacco control program, addressed under the heading, "WHO/UICC/IOCU Redirection/ containment strategies."

### • Tobacco company surrogates to "redirect WHO"

Tobacco company documents reveal that in order to "redirect" WHO, Philip Morris used its powerful food companies and other non-tobacco subsidiaries, as well as tobacco industry organizations, business organizations, and front groups and other ostensibly independent surrogates. These organizations were used to influence WHO directly and indirectly through the press, national governments and international organizations.

### • Creation and use of ostensibly independent organizations to gain access to WHO

Much of the Boca Raton Action Plan involved the creation or manipulation of seemingly independent organizations with strong tobacco company ties. The documents show that some of these organizations such as LIBERTAD, the

New York Society for International Affairs, the America-European Community Association and the Institute for International Health and Development, were used successfully to gain access to dozens of national and world leaders, health ministers, WHO and other United Nations agency delegates.

### • Mobilization of INFOTAB and CORESTA against WHO

Another key element of the Boca Raton plan was Philip Morris' decision to transform the industry organizations INFOTAB (International Tobacco Information Center) and CORESTA (Cooperation Centre for Scientific Research Relative to Tobacco) into political instruments and to mobilize them to lobby against WHO health advocacy programs. The documents also illustrate that Philip Morris used its regional offices and non-tobacco subsidiaries to press business groups like the International Chamber of Commerce (ICC) to lobby the World Health Assembly (WHA), WHO's governing body, and ILO. Additionally, Philip Morris attempted to use FAO, ILO, and other United Nations agencies, WHO Regional Offices and Coordinating Centers, and the governments of developing countries to influence WHO tobacco policies and WHA resolutions.

### • Boca Raton status report

Details of the Plan's implementation were outlined in status reports prepared every two months from January 31, 1989 through September 30, 1989. A final summary followed on October 30th, 1989. Under each of the 26 issues addressed in the Plan was a list of accomplishments for each. The reports refer to numerous detailed appendices, which were originally attached to the reports, but which are rarely included in the electronic versions of the reports available at the Minnesota Document Depository or posted on Philip Morris' document website. With considerable effort, the committee of experts was able to locate many of the attachments but several crucial documents could not be located. Other tobacco company documents were used to fill in these gaps when possible.

The Boca Raton Action Plan appears to have lasted for one year. It is unclear whether similar master plans were adopted in subsequent years, as the committee of experts was unable to locate any such plans in the public documents. There is, however, evidence that elements of the Plan continued well into the 1990s. The Plan itself provides insight into the magnitude and sophistication of the ongoing opposition to WHO's work.

The impact of the Boca Raton Action Plan must be judged within the context of its entire set of goals and strategies. The Plan was remarkable in its scope, encompassing 26 wide-ranging and ambitious goals, to which Philip Morris dedicated its top executives, scientists, attorneys and consultants. It was organized internationally, coordinating all of the company's regional offices and using both tobacco industry organizations and front groups to accomplish an impressive list of achievements.

As one of the world's largest multinational corporations, Philip Morris had the advantage of an international structure which is, in many ways, parallel to that of WHO, with regional offices in several of the same countries or areas of the world, including Philip Morris' research and development center in Neuchatel, Switzerland, near WHO headquarters. These local offices allowed Philip Morris personnel to develop relationships with WHO and UN contacts, especially in Geneva. Through at least one of these contacts, Philip Morris was able to aid in the adoption of a pro-tobacco amendment to a WHA smoking and health resolution. . . .

Philip Morris' business interests and ties to other tobacco companies enabled it to use organizations such as the International Chamber of Commerce (ICC) and the International Tobacco Growers Association (ITGA) to influence international agencies that, in turn, have influence on WHO. Through surrogates, Philip Morris was able to meet with numerous senior officials of both national governments and international organizations, including current and former Director Generals of the ILO and FAO.

Perhaps more significant than any specific policy achievement of the Boca Raton Action Plan, however, was its erection of elaborate and well-concealed mechanisms for sustained opposition to WHO. Today, a decade after these mechanisms were set in place, it is likely that they will soon be mobilized for action against WHO's Tobacco Free Initiative and the proposed Framework Convention on Tobacco Control. If these predictions are correct, the Boca Raton Plan may offer more than insight into the past: it may offer a preview of what lies ahead.

## 2. The "Third World Issue"

As the 1970s drew to a close, tobacco industry officials worried that WHO and the anti-tobacco movement would use criticism of tobacco industry activities in the developing world to fuel a global campaign against smoking. Quickly, tobacco companies launched a massive campaign to win developing countries' attention and assistance within the UN. Tobacco company lobbyists attempted to foster the concerns of officials from developing countries, as well as economically oriented UN agencies, about the economic importance of tobacco to these countries. Tobacco company representatives attempted to convince developing countries that the loss of tobacco as a cash crop would result in economic destabilization in tobacco-growing countries, significantly increasing the burden of poverty and malnutrition in tobacco-growing countries. According to tobacco company documents, the companies fostered the view that tobacco control was a "First World" concern and that the damage to health in the Third World from tobacco control activities might exceed the toll from tobacco use itself.

When tobacco industry officials first became aware of international criticism of its activities in developing countries, they perceived a serious threat to long-term profitability. At a tobacco company conference in July 1980, a workshop taught participants that "third world issues can't be 'left for tomorrow to deal with' since they affect the very basis of raw material supply." An anti-tobacco effort by developing countries might limit tobacco growing in such countries as Brazil, Zimbabwe, and Malawi. Even more worrisome was the possibility that the countries of the United Nations might find common purpose in attacking tobacco companies, creating a universally appealing enemy.

Faced with such a threat, industry officials recognized the need to develop a developing country strategy of its own. An industry consultant proposed the following goals:

> *"We must try to stop the development towards a Third World commitment against tobacco.*
>
> *We must try to get all or at least a substantial part of Third World countries committed to our cause.*
>
> *We must try to influence official FAO and UNCTAD [United Nations Conference on Trade and Development] policy to take a pro tobacco stand.*
>
> *We must try to mitigate the impact of WHO by pushing them [sic] into a more objective and neutral position."* [Emphasis in original.]

Throughout the 1980s and well into the 1990s, tobacco companies sought to mobilize officials from developing countries to advance a pro-tobacco agenda on the world stage. The goal was for representatives from UN member states in the developing world—and not tobacco companies themselves—to make tobacco's case within the FAO, WHO and other UN bodies. This developing country strategy was coordinated by an international consortium of tobacco industry officials that was first called ICOSI (International Council on Smoking Issues) and later renamed INFOTAB. Individual companies, most notably Philip Morris and British American Tobacco Company, also made important contributions.

Although the documents reveal only a part of the tobacco companies' activities, their strategy involved research, concerted lobbying of diplomats from developing countries, and extensive public relations. Industry representatives contacted government officials and UN delegates from around the world. At meetings that followed a common pattern, tobacco company officials would provide presentations on the economic importance of tobacco to developing countries, providing research on such topics as the "social and economic benefit" of tobacco and the lack of sustainable alternatives. Tobacco company lobbyists also tried to build resentment against the developed world, stressing that tobacco-related illnesses were a concern of rich countries, and that the developed countries were unconcerned about the economic realities or real health issues of the developing world.

In this campaign, tobacco companies made prominent use of the International Tobacco Growers' Association (ITGA). ITGA claims to represent the interests of local farmers. The documents indicate, however, that tobacco companies have funded the organization and directed its work. Through their persistent outreach to officials from developing countries, tobacco companies gradually built a base of support within UN agencies and structures, most notably the WHA and the FAO. Tobacco companies then worked to turn this support into action. Through contacts and influence with numerous officials from developing countries, the tobacco companies aimed to promote their agenda within multiple UN agencies and structures.

## • Food and Agriculture Organization

Because FAO's agricultural activities supported tobacco growing for many years, by the late 1970s and early 1980s, tobacco companies considered FAO a "natural ally" and a "pressure point for dealing with WHO." In the 1980s and 1990s, by appealing to delegates from developing countries, tobacco companies sought to keep FAO's support and use the agency to make the case for the economic importance of tobacco within the United Nations. As a result of lobbying FAO delegates from developing countries, as well as FAO's Permanent Representatives, industry officials believed they were successful in gaining FAO's support at the UN in resisting tobacco control efforts by WHO. During this period the FAO issued several reports and statements that industry representatives used to support their position on the economic importance of tobacco for developing countries.

## • World Health Assembly

Documents demonstrate that tobacco companies sought to influence the outcome of several WHA sessions. Tobacco company representatives lobbied delegates from developing countries to propose amendments and resolutions aimed at limiting the scope of the WHO tobacco control program. The case study focuses on the 39th, 41st, and 45th World Health Assemblies, held in 1986, 1988, and 1992, respectively. These sessions were characterized by a massive tobacco company lobbying effort to get delegates from developing countries to oppose new tobacco control resolutions. In 1992, tobacco companies celebrated the adoption at WHA of a resolution—dubbed the "Malawi Resolution"—that led to the creation of a so-called UN "focal point" for tobacco issues in the UN Economic and Social Council (ECOSOC). Industry representatives viewed this event as a victory that would open new doors at the UN to tobacco company arguments about the economic importance of tobacco.

## • UN Economic and Social Council

The "focal point" was directed to coordinate a UN collaboration on tobacco issues, including several UN agencies that would be more receptive to tobacco companies' economic arguments. Taking advantage of this opportunity, tobacco companies continued the successful pattern that they had long used as part of their developing country strategy. Industry representatives lobbied government officials, UN delegates, and UN officials about the economic importance of tobacco. Although the focal point in ECOSOC was closed down before producing any notable achievements, industry officials believed that they were successful in their attempts to get FAO, once again, to take a pro-tobacco position with ECOSOC.

Tobacco companies' developing country strategy involved extensive outreach to government officials and UN delegates of these countries. By pressing the economic importance of tobacco and stirring resentment against the developed world, industry officials believed that they had influenced delegates to alter WHO and FAO policy on tobacco. Rather than face world condemnation for its actions in developing countries, the tobacco industry benefited from these countries' representation of tobacco's interests at the international level.

By the mid-1990s, tobacco company documents show that industry representatives believed their developing country strategy had successfully led the FAO to release pro-industry reports on the economic importance of tobacco, had inspired delegates from developing countries to make pro-tobacco objections, amendments and resolutions at the WHA, and had countered anti-tobacco efforts at the UN "focal point" on tobacco.

The publicly available tobacco company documents, which largely end in the mid-1990s, do not reveal what further activities industry representatives pursued to resist tobacco control efforts through their developing world allies. However, all indications are that the developing country strategy is still active and may play a role in the tobacco company campaign against the Framework Convention on Tobacco Control. . . .

### 3. An "Independent" Critic of WHO

A key part of tobacco companies' strategy to undermine tobacco control activities at WHO in the 1980s and 1990s was to redefine the mandate of WHO, or at least redirect its priorities away from tobacco. To this end, tobacco companies used "independent" academic institutions, consultants, and journalists to undermine the organization's credibility, to question its "mission and mandate," and to divert its priorities from tobacco control to other health needs. These individuals and institutions were, in fact, secretly paid by tobacco companies to promote pro-tobacco or anti-WHO opinions.

Many tobacco company documents suggest that Paul Dietrich, an American lawyer with long-term ties to tobacco companies, played a significant role in this element of the tobacco company strategy. Dietrich wrote articles and editorials attacking WHO's priorities, which were published in major media outlets and widely disseminated by tobacco company officials. He also traveled around the world for tobacco companies, giving presentations to journalists and government officials on WHO's inappropriate spending and priorities. No mention was ever made in his articles and presentations that he received significant tobacco company funding.

In 1990, Dietrich, while still working with tobacco companies, was appointed to the Development Committee of the Pan American Health Organization (PAHO), an organization that also serves as WHO's regional office for the Americas. While there, the documents indicate that Dietrich attempted to redirect PAHO's priorities away from tobacco. According to the documents, he also played a role in getting PAHO to produce and sponsor an important media event that was used by tobacco companies to divert attention from the WHO-sponsored 8th World Conference on Tobacco OR Health. Dietrich denies that he ever knowingly participated in any tobacco industry event or project, or that he was ever paid by the tobacco industry for his work. . . .

### • Relationship with and financial ties to tobacco companies

Tobacco company documents provide evidence of Paul Dietrich's long association with and financial links to tobacco companies. According to the documents, Dietrich and the institutions he operated were at different times associated with the Tobacco Institute, Philip Morris, and, most significantly, BAT. Many documents show that Dietrich and the organizations he operated received significant funding from tobacco companies. Indeed, tobacco company documents include bills from Dietrich to BAT. Another document refers to Dietrich's "expensive consultancy" with BAT.

The case study illustrates one of the ways that tobacco companies, whose public credibility is low, have their positions publicly advocated by ostensibly independent "third parties." Although Dietrich denies that his long-standing campaign against WHO was funded by tobacco companies or that he worked with the industry on any of the projects described in this case study, the documents paint a different picture. The documents strongly suggest that Dietrich had a long relationship with members of the tobacco industry and that tobacco companies used this relationship to promote their anti-WHO agenda.

The fact that Dietrich had such a relationship with tobacco companies raises concerns about his appointment to a committee at PAHO. The committee of experts believes that there are significant conflict of interest issues raised by holding a position on a PAHO committee while simultaneously working for the tobacco industry, and has made a series of recommendations to help ensure that such conflicts do not arise.

### 4. 8th World Conference on Tobacco OR Health

A review of internal tobacco company documents relating to the 8th World Conference on Tobacco OR Health (WCToH), held in Buenos Aires in 1992, shows that BAT and Philip Morris, the two largest private tobacco companies, initiated a campaign to undermine the Conference, using an extraordinary range of tactics, some of which might be termed "dirty tricks." These included staging elaborate diversions from the Conference, and training journalists to both hound a conference participant and take over a WCToH press conference. Tobacco companies' planned use of the media in this context deserves special mention. In this campaign, journalists were to play a central and, in some cases, a knowing role in the manipulation of public opinion. Like so many of the other tobacco company campaigns described in this report, this case study exemplifies tobacco companies' consistent intent to conceal its role in carrying out plans to undermine WHO tobacco control initiatives.

The documents also suggest that tobacco companies made use of PAHO, an organization that also serves as WHO's Regional Office for the Americas, in its campaign. Through the offices of Paul Dietrich, identified in the documents as a tobacco company consultant who also sat on PAHO's Development Committee, the documents suggest that tobacco companies were able to guide the development of, and then exploit, a PAHO-sponsored media program, for the purpose of undermining the 8th WCToH. However, Dietrich claims that the industry was not involved in his media program, and PAHO officials dispute that Dietrich had any role in the media program. . . .

[Case studies on tobacco company influence in UN standard-setting for tobacco pesticides and on a epidemiological study of the relationship between lung cancer and environmental tobacco smoke omitted.]

## E. Recommendations

In the course of this inquiry, the committee of experts has identified many reasons for concern about the integrity of the process for international decision-making about tobacco. The evidence shows that tobacco companies have operated for many years with the deliberate purpose of subverting the efforts of WHO to address tobacco issues. The attempted subversion has been elaborate, well financed, sophisticated and usually invisible. That tobacco companies resist proposals for tobacco control comes as no surprise, but what is now clear is the scale, intensity and, importantly, the tactics, of their campaigns. To many in the international community, tobacco prevention may be seen today as a struggle against chemical addiction, cancers, cardiovascular diseases and other health consequences of smoking. This inquiry adds to the mounting evidence that it is also a struggle against an active, organized and calculating industry.

This has implications for WHO, and perhaps for other international bodies, in terms of both program activities and internal procedures. The committee of experts hopes this report will contribute to a broad discussion of those implications within the international community, and will lead to the necessary changes in practices and programs to ensure that the integrity of international decision-making is protected.

### • Increasing public awareness of tobacco company influence

The committee of experts recommends that WHO increase public awareness of tobacco company influence on international tobacco control policies. Specifically, WHO should release and publish this report for discussion at public hearings on the Framework Convention on Tobacco Control in October 2000, in addition to a broader public distribution.

### • Further investigation by other UN agencies and member countries

In the course of its review, the committee of experts has seen statements suggesting possible tobacco company influence on the policies of other UN agencies and member countries. The committee of experts therefore recommends that WHO urge other UN organizations and member countries to conduct investigations similar to this one to uncover possible tobacco company influence.

### • The Framework Convention on Tobacco Control

It is likely that tobacco companies will attempt to defeat the proposed Framework Convention on Tobacco Control, or to transform the proposal into a vehicle for weakening national tobacco control initiatives. Such a campaign is likely to be sophisticated and sustained, and to use tactics similar to those described in this report. The committee of experts recommends that WHO develop a sophisticated communications campaign to support the Framework Convention on Tobacco Control and counter any campaign of opposition by tobacco companies.

## • Protecting the integrity of WHO's decision making process

In the course of this inquiry, the committee of experts identified several areas in which it felt the process and rules currently in place at WHO to guard against potential conflicts of interest involving the tobacco industry should be clarified, strengthened or expanded. These recommendations are intended for application throughout WHO, including within its Collaborating Centers.

The existing conflict of interest requirements for WHO employees are contained in one page of staff regulations promulgated by the WHA and one page of staff rules established by the Director-General. As a general observation, the committee of experts notes that these ethical rules have been clarified significantly in recent years, and that internal review of the rules is continuing.

Based on its review, the committee of experts identified specific opportunities for improving this regulatory regime. Taken together, the committee of experts hopes that the specific recommendations set forth in this report will help protect the integrity of WHO's decision making. They include suggestions for screening prospective employees, consultants, advisors, and committee members for conflicts of interest, and clarifying the consequences of violations of ethical rules.

The recommendations also urge WHO to place before the WHA, for discussion by member countries, questions related to disclosure of affiliations between WHA delegates and tobacco companies, and between Non-Governmental Organizations (NGOs) and tobacco companies.

## • Protecting scientific integrity

As demonstrated by this report's case studies of the IARC ETS study and the review of dithiocarbamate pesticides, additional safeguards are needed to protect against tobacco company attempts to distort scientific research sponsored by, or associated with, WHO and affiliated organizations. To this end, the committee of experts has offered: (1) recommendations for educating scientific investigators about tobacco companies' efforts to undermine research; (2) guidelines for contact with industry representatives and disclosure of information and funding sources; and (3) suggestions for interagency communication standards among UN bodies. The committee of experts also recommends that WHO and IARC develop affirmative communications plans to anticipate and counter tobacco company misrepresentation of important new research findings.

## • Addressing tobacco companies' developing country strategy

Tobacco companies' successful efforts to reach out to developing countries based on the economic importance of tobacco suggest that WHO must address these countries' concerns to achieve a global consensus on tobacco control. WHO should develop a strategy to counter the tactics employed by tobacco companies to gain opposition to tobacco control in the developing world. This strategy must address the legitimate economic issues raised by the loss of tobacco as a cash crop.

- **Correcting past tobacco company misconduct
  and protecting the public from future misconduct**

This report details a pattern of influence and misconduct by tobacco companies aimed at thwarting global tobacco control initiatives. The committee of experts believes that the harm caused by the tobacco companies' conduct was significant and far-reaching. The report recommends that WHO take two important steps to correct the results of past misconduct and guard against future tobacco company misconduct.

First, WHO should assist member states in determining whether they have a legal and factual basis to seek restitution from tobacco companies for past misconduct.

Second, WHO should monitor tobacco company activities to determine whether the pattern of behavior described in this report has ceased or is continuing. To ensure that tobacco company misconduct does not remain hidden, as it has in the past, WHO should make regular public reports on its findings.

## F. Conclusion

This inquiry demonstrates the magnitude of tobacco companies' opposition to WHO tobacco programs, and offers insight into their activities, strategies and attitudes. Moreover, it demonstrates that tobacco is unlike other threats to health. Reversing the epidemic of tobacco use will be about more than fighting addiction and disease; it will be about overcoming a determined and powerful industry, many of whose most important counter-strategies are carried out in secret. If this inquiry contributes to that understanding, the committee of experts will have succeeded in its work.

# SURGEON GENERAL ON
# REDUCING TOBACCO USE
## August 9, 2000

*The war against tobacco and the tobacco industry continued unabated in 2000, with U.S. cigarette manufacturers sustaining some significant losses in both the courts of law and the court of public opinion. The year began with a major victory for the manufacturers, when the Supreme Court ruled in March that the Food and Drug Administration (FDA) did not have authority to regulate tobacco products. That ruling nullified proposed federal rules that would have severely restricted advertising directed at adolescents. But in the next few months, a Florida jury ordered the tobacco industry to pay nearly $145 billion in punitive damages to an estimated 500,000 Florida smokers, and the federal government issued a major report setting out dozens of effective strategies to help smokers quit and to deter others from ever starting. On the international stage, and the World Health Organization (WHO) convened delegates from 150 nations to begin negotiations on a treaty to control tobacco products worldwide. (Story, p. 536)*

*The tobacco industry had been on the defensive in the United States since the early 1990s, when the disclosure of previously secret documents revealed that the cigarette makers had long known about the health hazards of smoking, including the addictive nature of nicotine, despite their repeated public denials that tobacco products were directly linked to such illnesses as lung cancer, heart disease, and emphysema. The documents also strongly suggested that the companies directed their marketing and advertising to teenagers to ensure a continuing market for their products.*

*These revelations sparked two tracks of attack on the tobacco industry. Claiming that it had authority to regulate nicotine as an addictive drug and cigarettes as drug-delivery devices, the FDA in 1996 issued a set of regulations curbing tobacco sales and advertising aimed at minors. At about the same time, the states began to sue the tobacco companies to recover the money that they had spent under Medicaid to treat thousands of sick smokers. After one settlement agreement fell apart in the spring of 1997, a second settlement was finally reached in 1998. Under this arrangement, the companies did not have to pay as much as they did under the first agreement—*

*$246 billion in the 1998 accord, as opposed to $368.5 billion in the first agreement—but they were still liable to class-action and individual lawsuits as well as to suit from the federal government. They agreed to a set of restrictions on promotion and advertising of tobacco products to teenagers that were similar to but not as stringent as the regulations issued by the FDA.* (FDA regulations, Historic Documents of 1996, p. 589; initial tobacco settlement, Historic Documents of 1997, p. 331; multistate settlement, Historic Documents of 1998, p. 842)

*In 1999 the Justice Department filed a civil suit charging the tobacco company with conspiracy to commit fraud and seeking the recovery of Medicare and other funds it had spent and would spend on smoking-related health care costs for the elderly, veterans, and federal employees. On September 28, 2000, a federal district judge threw out the government's claim for recovery but allowed the Justice Department to pursue its civil claim that the tobacco industry violated federal racketeering laws.* (Justice Department's civil suit, Historic Documents of 1999, p. 536)

## Supreme Court on FDA Regulatory Authority

*For decades the FDA had resisted pressure from public health groups to regulate cigarettes, saying it did not have the authority under the Food, Drug and Cosmetic Act, which created the agency in 1906. Agency officials under Democratic and Republican presidents alike said that cigarettes did not fall within the law's definition of "drugs" because manufacturers make no claims for health benefits from smoking. The FDA changed its stance under the direction of David Kessler. Armed with the formerly secret tobacco company documents indicating that cigarette manufacturers had not only known that nicotine was addictive but had also manipulated nicotine levels in cigarettes to keep smokers hooked, Kessler—with strong backing from the Clinton administration—let it be known that he would act to regulate tobacco as a drug if Congress did not. When Congress took no action, Kessler in August 1995 unveiled proposed regulations, which restricted access to tobacco products by anyone under eighteen, regulated the appearance and content of cigarette advertisements in publications that appealed to teenagers, and barred brand-name advertisement of tobacco products at sports and entertainment events.*

*The regulations became final in August 1996 and were immediately challenged by the tobacco industry. A federal district court judge ruled in 1997 that the FDA had authority to regulate tobacco products but not to control advertising or marketing practices. Both the industry and the government appealed that decision, and in 1998 the Fourth U.S. Circuit Court of Appeals overturned the regulations. The Justice Department immediately appealed to the Supreme Court, which on March 21, 2000, agreed, 5–4, that the FDA had exceeded its authority and would have to receive explicit authority from Congress if it wanted to regulate tobacco products. Writing for the majority, Justice Sandra Day O'Connor said that "Congress, for better or for worse, has created a distinct regulatory scheme for tobacco products, squarely rejected proposals to give the FDA jurisdiction over tobacco, and repeatedly acted to preclude any agency from exercising significant policy-making authority in the area."*

*Although Congress did not take any action on legislation to give the FDA authority to regulate tobacco, some industry observers thought passage of such legislation was only a matter of time. Not only had Vice President Al Gore and Texas governor George W. Bush, the presumptive presidential nominees of the Democratic and Republican parties, both called on Congress to enact stricter regulations, but so too did some tobacco company officials. Stephen Parrish, senior vice president of Philip Morris Co., the largest cigarette manufacturer, said the ruling was "an opportunity . . . to come up with a tough, sensible . . . approach" to cigarette regulation. "The bottom line is that the industry wants peace—they want their stocks to be stable," Mary Aronson, a tobacco industry analyst told the* Washington Post. *"The only way they see to an end of the litigation threat is if Congress is reinvolved. So I think that industry is positioning itself so it can go to Congress and ask for some kind of protection from tobacco litigation in exchange for regulation."*

### *Florida Class-Action Case*

*Four months later, on July 14, a six-member jury in Miami, Florida, handed down the largest damage award in the nation's history, ordering the tobacco industry to pay $144.8 billion in punitive damages to an estimated 500,000 Florida smokers or their survivors. A year earlier, the same jury had found that the tobacco companies had conspired to hide the health risks of smoking. The Florida case was the first class-action suit brought on behalf of individual smokers to reach a verdict. The decision was a major blow to the tobacco companies that had until recent years won most lawsuits brought by individual smokers on the ground that smokers chose to smoke despite knowing of the health hazards involved.*

*After the award was announced, the jury foreman told the* New York Times *that the point of the award was not whether people chose to smoke but that the tobacco companies knew that they were selling a hazardous product and denied that it was hazardous. "They belittled or denied causation of the health effects of smoking and addiction, and had the gall to challenge public health authorities," the foreman said. "We thought [the award] was fair," he continued. "It would bring to the forefront, for the first time in the history of this country, the issues surrounding this product and the millions of lives that have been affected by this. And it would put the companies on notice—not just the tobacco companies, all companies—concerning fraud or misrepresentation. . . ."*

*The amount each of the five tobacco companies was ordered to pay was based on its market share, along with other financial information, the jurors said. Philip Morris was ordered to pay $73.96 billion; R. J. Reynolds $36.28 billion; Brown & Williamson, $17.59 billion; Lorillard Tobacco, $26.25 billion, and Liggett Group Incorporated, $790 million. The remainder was to be paid by two, now-defunct research arms of the tobacco industry that had been found to falsify data on the hazards of smoking.*

*The tobacco companies vowed to fight the verdict. "There is no industry in America . . . that could withstand a verdict of this size," said an attorney for one of the companies. Although appeals of the case were expected to last for years, the tobacco companies lost two of the earliest proceedings. On November 3 a federal district judge rejected the company's bid to move the class-action case into the federal court system, and on November 6 the state court judge who had presided over the trial denied the companies' motion to scale back the verdict and reduce the award.*

## Surgeon General on Reducing Tobacco Use

*Declaring tobacco use to be the "most challenging and tenacious health issue facing the country," Surgeon General David Satcher on August 9 released a report that detailed dozens of concrete steps to help smokers kick the habit and to persuade nonsmokers never to start. About 70 percent of smokers said they wanted to quit, Satcher said, but in any given year only 2.5 percent succeeded. Full implementation of existing, effective antismoking strategies could cut the number of smokers in the United States in half by the year 2010, Satcher said. Such strategies ranged from encouraging doctors to talk to their patients about the dangers of smoking, to increased tobacco taxes, to greater use of drugs to fight nicotine addiction, to cracking down on tobacco advertising, especially ads aimed at adolescents and teenagers.*

*Although the percentage of the population that smoked had declined significantly since the mid-1960s when the government first declared smoking to be a health hazard, about 48 million adults and 4 million adolescents smoked—roughly about one-quarter of all adults and one-third of all adolescents. Nearly 3,000 teenagers began smoking every day. About 400,000 Americans died prematurely each year due to smoking-relating illnesses, such as lung cancer, heart disease, and emphysema. The federal Centers for Disease Control and Prevention estimated that treating smoking-related illness cost the nation about $100 billion a year—more than $50 billion in health care costs and another $47 billion in lost earnings and lost productivity. "During the past four decades we have made unprecedented gains in preventing and controlling tobacco use. But the sobering reality is that it remains the leading cause of preventable death and disease in our country," Satcher said during a news conference at the Eleventh World Conference on Tobacco or Health, held in Chicago.*

*Satcher described the tobacco-control programs set out in the report as a blueprint to prevent people from starting to smoke, help smokers stop, decrease the exposure of nonsmokers to tobacco smoke in the environment, and decrease the future health burden from tobacco-related disease and death. Satcher was careful to say that the report was a summary of antismoking strategies that were known to work and not formal policy recommendations. Yet many of the strategies—from greater regulation of the advertising, marketing, and sales of cigarettes to sharply increased taxes to increased smoking bans—would require action by policymakers at the national and state levels.*

*The report also warned that a comprehensive antismoking campaign would also have to contend with the "pervasive, countervailing influence" of tobacco marketing by the tobacco industry. Despite overwhelming evidence of the adverse health effects of cigarettes and major legal challenges to cigarette manufacturers, the tobacco industry persisted in promoting the use of tobacco, the report said. In 1998 the industry spent $6.7 billion—or more than $18 million a day—to market cigarettes. "We need fair but aggressive measures to regulate these marketing activities," declared Satcher, "especially those that influence young people."*

*The surgeon general's office had published twenty-eight reports dealing with the health effects of smoking since 1964, when the first "Surgeon General's Report on Smoking and Health" concluded that smoking caused lung cancer in men. Satcher's report was the first time the surgeon general's office had drawn together an in-depth analysis of a wide variety of methods found effective in reducing tobacco use. The 460-page report divided these strategies into five broad categories: educational, clinical, regulatory, economic, and comprehensive. Some individual strategies were relatively simple, such as making all public schools smoke- and tobacco-free. Others were more complicated, such as combining behavioral counseling with use of the nicotine patch to help smokers quit smoking. No one strategy was going to work for everyone, the report said, and often a combination of strategies could produce a better result than a single strategy used alone. For example, the report said that effective school-based programs combined with community and media-based antismoking campaigns could prevent 20–40 percent of adolescents from smoking or postpone the time that they began to smoke. Among the key strategies that could reduce or prevent the use of tobacco were the following:*

- *Full implementation of the CDC's national guidelines for schools that offered a wide array of curricula, protocols, and recommendations for effectively controlling tobacco in schools. By one count only 5 percent of the nation's schools were implementing the programs. While more than 60 percent of all schools reported having smoke-free building policies in 1994, only 30 percent said such policies extended to the entire school environment, including faculty and staff and all school grounds and school events.*

- *Nicotine replacement therapies, such as the nicotine patch, and other pharmacological treatment when combined with behavioral counseling could produce 20–25 percent quit rates at one year for those who received the treatment. Less intensive interventions, such as a physician's advice to stop smoking, could produce quit rates of 5–10 percent a year. Such clinical interventions, the report said, were more cost effective than other common clinical preventive services such as mammograms, Pap tests, colon cancer screening, and treatment of high cholesterol levels.*

- *A 10 percent increase in the price of cigarettes could reduce overall cigarette consumption by 3–5 percent. Moreover, youth, minority,*

*and low-income smokers were two to three times more likely to quit
or smoke less in response to a price increase than were other smokers.*

*Following are excerpts from the executive summary of "Reducing
Tobacco Use," a report issued August 9, 2000, by Surgeon General
David Satcher, providing a blueprint of effective strategies for
deterring people from starting to smoke and helping smokers
quit the habit. The document was obtained from the Internet at
http://www.cdc.gov/tobacco/sgr_tobacco_pdf/execsumm.pdf.*

This report of the Surgeon General on smoking and health, *Reducing Tobacco Use,* appears at a time of considerable upheaval in the arena of tobacco
use control and prevention. Legal and legislative efforts to protect children
from tobacco initiation and to diminish the prevalence of smoking among
adults are in a state of flux, with some important gains and some sobering setbacks. Major changes in the public stance of the tobacco industry have evoked
a reevaluation of strategies for controlling and preventing tobacco uptake.
Enormous monetary settlements have provided the resources to fuel major
new comprehensive antitobacco efforts, but the ultimate cost and benefit of
these resources are still to be determined. Into this changing landscape, the
report introduces an assessment of information about the value approaches
that have been used—educational, clinical, regulatory, economic, and comprehensive—to reduce tobacco use. The report evaluates the scientific evidence for each approach, attempts to place the approaches in the larger
context of tobacco control, and provides a vision of the trajectory for tobacco
use prevention and control based on these available tools. Thus, *although
our knowledge about tobacco control remains imperfect, we know more than
enough to act now.* Widespread dissemination of the approaches and methods
shown to be effective in each modality and especially in combination would
substantially reduce the number of young people who will become addicted to
tobacco, increase the success rate of young people and adults trying to quit
using tobacco, decrease the level of exposure of nonsmokers to environmental tobacco smoke, reduce the disparities related to tobacco use and its health
effects among different population groups, and decrease the future health burden of tobacco-related disease and death in this country. These achievable improvements parallel the health objectives set forth in *Healthy People 2010,*
the national action plan for improving the health of all people living in the
United States for the first decade of the 21st century. Twenty-one specific
national health objectives related to tobacco use are listed in *Healthy People
2010,* including reducing the rates among young people and adults to less than
half of the current rate of use. Attaining all of these tobacco-related objectives
will almost certainly require significant national commitment to the various
successful approaches described in this report.

The major conclusions of this report are not formal policy recommendations. Rather, they offer a summary of the scientific literature about what works. In short, this report is intended to offer policymakers, public health professionals, professional and advocacy organizations, researchers, and, most importantly, the American people guidance on how to ensure that efforts to prevent and control tobacco use are commensurate with the harm it causes.

## Major Conclusions

1. Efforts to prevent the onset or continuance of tobacco use face the pervasive, countervailing influence of tobacco promotion by the tobacco industry, a promotion that takes place despite overwhelming evidence of adverse health effects from tobacco use.

2. The available approaches to reducing tobacco use—educational, clinical, regulatory, economic, and comprehensive—differ substantially in their techniques and in the metric by which success can be measured. A hierarchy of effectiveness is difficult to construct.

3. Approaches with the largest span of impact (economic, regulatory, and comprehensive) are likely to have the greatest long-term population impact. Those with a smaller span of impact (educational and clinical) are of greater importance in helping individuals resist or abandon the use of tobacco.

4. Each of the modalities reviewed provides evidence of effectiveness:
   - Educational strategies, conducted in conjunction with community- and media-based activities, can postpone or prevent smoking onset in 20 to 40 percent of adolescents.
   - Pharmacologic treatment of nicotine addiction, combined with behavioral support, will enable 20 to 25 percent of users to remain abstinent at one year posttreatment. Even less intense measures, such as physicians advising their patients to quit smoking, can produce cessation proportions of 5 to 10 percent.
   - Regulation of advertising and promotion, particularly that directed at young people, is very likely to reduce both prevalence and uptake of smoking.
   - Clean air regulations and restriction of minors' access to tobacco products contribute to a changing social norm with regard to smoking and may influence prevalence directly.
   - An optimal level of excise taxation on tobacco products will reduce the prevalence of smoking, the consumption of tobacco, and the long-term health consequences of tobacco use.

5. The impact of these various efforts, as measured with a variety of techniques, is likely to be underestimated because of the synergistic effect of these modalities. The potential for combined effects underscores the need for comprehensive approaches.

6. State tobacco control programs, funded by excise taxes on tobacco products and settlements with the tobacco industry, have produced early, encouraging evidence of the efficacy of the comprehensive approach to reducing tobacco use.

# Chapter Conclusions

Following are the specific conclusions for each chapter of the report. Note that Chapters 1 and 8 have no conclusions.

## Chapter 2. Historical Review

1. In the years preceding the development of the modern cigarette, and for some time thereafter, antismoking activity was largely motivated by moralistic and hygienic concerns. Health concerns played a lesser role.
2. In contrast, in the second half of the 20th century, the impetus for reducing tobacco use was largely medical and social. The resulting platform has been a more secure one for efforts to reduce smoking.
3. Despite the growing scientific evidence for adverse health effects, smoking norms and habits have yielded slowly and incompletely. The reasons are complex but attributable in part to the industry's continuing stimulus to consumption.

## Chapter 3. Educational Strategies

1. Educational strategies, conducted in conjunction with community- and media-based activities, can postpone or prevent smoking onset in 20 to 40 percent of adolescents.
2. Although most U.S. schools have tobacco use prevention policies and programs in place, current practice is not optimal.
3. More consistent implementation of effective educational strategies to prevent tobacco use will require continuing efforts to build strong, multi-year prevention units into school health education curricula and expanded efforts to make use of the influence of parents, the mass media, and other community resources.

## Chapter 4. Management of Nicotine Addiction

1. Tobacco dependence is best viewed as a chronic disease with remission and relapse. Even though both minimal and intensive interventions increase smoking cessation, most people who quit smoking with the aid of such interventions will eventually relapse and may require repeated attempts before achieving long-term abstinence. Moreover, there is little understanding of how such treatments produce their therapeutic effects.
2. There is mixed evidence that self-help manuals are an efficacious aid to smoking cessation. Because these materials can be widely distributed, such strategies may have a significant public health impact and warrant further investigation.
3. Programs using advice and counseling—whether minimal or more intensive—have helped a substantial proportion of people quit smoking.
4. The success of counseling and advice increases with the intensity of the program and may be improved by increasing the frequency and duration of contact.
5. The evidence is strong and consistent that pharmacologic treatments for smoking cessation (nicotine replacement therapies and bupropion,

in particular) can help people quit smoking. Clonidine and nortriptylene may have some utility as second-line treatments for smoking cessation, although they have not been approved by the Food and Drug Administration (FDA) for this indication.

## Chapter 5. Regulatory Efforts

### Advertising and Promotion

1. Since 1964, numerous attempts to regulate advertising and promotion of tobacco products have had only modest success in restricting such activity.
2. Current regulation in the United States is considerably less restrictive than that in several other countries, notably Canada and New Zealand.
3. Current case law supports the contention that advertising does not receive the protections of free speech under the First Amendment to the Constitution that noncommercial speech does.

### Product Regulation

1. Warning labels on cigarette packages in the United States are weaker and less conspicuous than those of other countries.
2. Smokers receive very little information regarding chemical constituents when they purchase a tobacco product. Without information about toxic constituents in tobacco smoke, the use of terms such as "light" and "ultra light" on packaging and in advertising may be misleading to smokers.
3. Because cigarettes with low tar and nicotine contents are not substantially less hazardous than higher-yield brands, consumers may be misled by the implied promise of reduced toxicity underlying the marketing of such brands.
4. Additives to tobacco products are of uncertain safety when used in tobacco. Knowledge about the impact of additives is negligible and will remain so as long as brand-specific information on the identity and quantity of additives is unavailable.
5. Regulation of tobacco product sale and promotion is required to protect young people from influences to take up smoking.

### Clean Indoor Air Regulation

1. Although population-based data show declining environmental tobacco smoke (ETS) exposure in the workplace over time, ETS exposure remains a common public health hazard that is entirely preventable.
2. Most state and local laws for clean indoor air reduce but do not eliminate nonsmokers' exposure to ETS; smoking bans are the most effective method for reducing ETS exposure.
3. Beyond eliminating ETS exposure among nonsmokers, smoking bans have additional benefits, including reduced smoking intensity and potential cost savings to employers. Optimal protection of nonsmokers and smokers requires a smoke-free environment.

## Minors' Access to Tobacco

1. Measures that have had some success in reducing minors' access include restricting distribution, regulating the mechanisms of sale, enforcing minimum age laws, and providing merchant education and training. Requiring licensure of tobacco retailers provides both a funding source for enforcement and an incentive to obey the law when revocation of the license is a provision of the law.

2. The effect of reducing minors' access to tobacco products on smoking prevalence requires further evaluation.

## Litigation Approaches

1. Two historic waves of tobacco litigation were initiated by private citizens, were based largely on theories of negligence and implied warranty, and were unsuccessful.

2. A third wave has brought in new types of claimants, making statutory as well as common-law claims and using more efficient judicial procedures. Although several cases have been settled for substantial money and have yielded public health provisions, many other cases remain unresolved.

3. Private law initiative is a diffuse, uncentralized activity, and the sum of such efforts is unlikely to produce optimal results for a larger policy to reduce tobacco use. On the other hand, the actions of individuals are likely to be a valuable component in some larger context of strategies to make tobacco use less prevalent.

## Chapter 6. Economic Approaches

1. The price of tobacco has an important influence on the demand for tobacco products, particularly among young people.

2. Substantial increases in the excise taxes on cigarettes would have considerable impact on the prevalence of smoking and, in the long-term, reduce the adverse health effects caused by tobacco.

3. Policies that influence the supply of tobacco, particularly those that regulate international commerce, can have important effects on tobacco use.

4. Although employment in the tobacco sector is substantial, the importance of tobacco to the U.S. economy has been overstated. Judicious policies can be joined to higher tobacco taxes and stronger prevention policies to ease economic diversification in tobacco-producing areas.

## Chapter 7. Comprehensive Programs

1. The large-scale interventions conducted in community trials have not demonstrated a conclusive impact on preventing and reducing tobacco use.

2. Statewide programs have emerged as the new laboratory for developing and evaluating comprehensive plans to reduce tobacco use.

3. Initial results from the statewide tobacco control programs are favorable, especially regarding declines in per capita consumption of tobacco products.

4. Results of statewide tobacco control programs suggest that youth behaviors regarding tobacco use are more difficult to change than adult ones, but initial results of these programs are generally favorable.

## Background

What works?

It would be a boon if the answer were as easy to state as the question. Programs to reduce the use of tobacco have a long history in the United States and in other countries, and the accumulated experience has provided considerable empirical understanding of the prospects and pitfalls of such efforts. Rigorous answers to formal evaluation questions are difficult to obtain, however, in part because of the wide variety of influences that are brought to bear on the use of tobacco. Researchers have little control over many of these influences and are only beginning to learn how to measure some of them.

Nonetheless, a substantial body of literature exists on attempts to reduce the use of tobacco. This report provides an overview of the major modalities that have been studied and used intensively, and it attempts, where possible, to differentiate their techniques and outcomes. The report also attempts a more difficult task: to provide some qualitative observations about how these efforts interact. The report is thus a prologue to the development of a coherent, long-term policy that would permit these modalities to be used as effectively as possible.

This report of the Surgeon General was prepared by the Office on Smoking and Health, National Center for Chronic Disease Prevention and Health Promotion, Centers for Disease Control and Prevention (CDC), U.S. Department of Health and Human Services, to report current information on the health effects of cigarette smoking and smokeless tobacco use. Previous reports have dealt with some of the issues included in this report, but a composite assessment of efforts to reduce tobacco use is a new topic for this series. However, the current report must acknowledge the considerable contributions of two prior monographs: *Growing Up Tobacco Free*, a report of the Institute of Medicine, and *Healthy People 2000: National Health Promotion and Disease Prevention Objectives*, an ongoing work of the Office of Health Promotion and Disease Prevention. . . .

Several concerns guided preparation of the report. First, it was clear that the primary countervailing influence against reducing tobacco use is the effort of the tobacco industry to promote the use of tobacco products. Although this report was not conceived as a documentation of such industry efforts, repeated reference to them is necessary to underscore the difficulties both in achieving desired outcomes and in evaluating the effectiveness of efforts to reduce the use of the industry's products. Second, the report has attempted to present the wide variety of techniques and methods used for tobacco control, but the disparate methods make comparisons difficult. The result is more a menu than a cookbook—a set of activities . . . whose combination depends on specific circumstances and the context in which they are undertaken. Third, a result of this methodological diversity is that rigorous evaluation of the ways in which tobacco reduction efforts interact remains part of the unfinished research agenda. Although interaction of interventive efforts is noted several places in the report . . . such demonstration of synergy has been elusive.

Finally, during the report's preparation, a cascade of legal and legislative events substantially changed the landscape where the diverse efforts to reduce tobacco use take place. Several legal rulings, still under adjudication, and the Master Settlement Agreement between states and the tobacco industry to recover costs of government programs have altered prospects for reducing tobacco use through large-scale social maneuvers. Many of these issues are still unresolved, and they are likely to influence activities in the coming years. . . .

## Findings

Each of the approaches described in this report shows evidence of effectiveness. In some instances, the synergism that might be expected through interaction among these various efforts has been documented, and the implications for future tobacco control and prevention activities are noted.

### Historical Review (Chapter 2)

The forces that have shaped the movement to reduce tobacco use over the past 100 years are complex and intertwined. In the early years (1880–1920), antitobacco activity—some of it quite successful—was motivated by moral and hygienic principles. After important medical and epidemiologic observations of the midcentury linked smoking to lung cancer and other diseases, and after the subsequent appearance of the 1964 report of the advisory committee to the Surgeon General on smoking and health (U.S. Department of Health, Education, and Welfare 1964), the movement to reduce tobacco use was fueled by knowledge of the health risks that tobacco use poses and by reaction against the continued promotion of tobacco in the face of such known risks. Despite overwhelming evidence of adverse health consequences of smoking, the stubborn norm of smoking in the United States has receded slowly, in part because of such continued promotion that works synergistically with tobacco addiction. Although strategies have varied, health advocates have focused in recent years on the prevention of harm to nonsmokers and on the concept of smoking as a pediatric disease, with the consequent need for protecting young persons from forces influencing them to smoke.

### Educational Strategies (Chapter 3)

The design of educational programs for tobacco use prevention and the methods used to evaluate them have become increasingly refined over the past two decades. . . .

To summarize the major findings, school-based social influences programs have significant and substantial short-term impacts on smoking behavior.

Those programs with more frequent educational contacts during the critical years for smoking adoption are more likely to be effective, as are programs that address a broad range of educational needs. These effects have been demonstrated in a range of implementation models and student populations. The smoking prevention effects of strong school programs can be extended through the end of high school or longer when combined with relatively intensive efforts directed through other powerful channels, such as strategies that vigorously engage the influences of parents, the mass media, and other community resources. These conclusions have been codified in national guidelines for school programs to prevent tobacco use.

Thus, an extensive body of research findings document the most effective educational programs for preventing tobacco use. This research has produced a wide array of curricula, protocols, and recommendations that have been codified into national guidelines for schools. Implementing guidelines could postpone or prevent smoking onset in 20 to 40 percent of U.S. adolescents. Unfortunately, existing data suggest that evidence-based curricula and national guidelines have not been widely adopted. By one set of criteria, less than 5 percent of schools nationwide are implementing the major components of CDC's *Guidelines for School Health Programs to Prevent Tobacco Use and Addiction.* . . . Almost two-thirds of schools (62.8 percent) had smoke-free building policies in 1994, but significantly fewer (36.5 percent) reported such policies that included the entire school environment.

Schools, however, should not bear the sole responsibility for implementing educational strategies to prevent tobacco use. Research findings, as noted, indicate that school-based programs are more effective when combined with mass media programs and with community-based efforts involving parents and other community resources. In addition, CDC's school health guidelines and numerous *Healthy People 2010* objectives recognize the critical role of implementing tobacco-free policies involving faculty, staff, and students and relating to all school facilities, property, vehicles, and events. Although significant progress is still required, the current evaluation base provides clear direction for the amalgamation of school-based programs with other modalities for reducing tobacco use.

## Management of Nicotine Addiction (Chapter 4)

The management of nicotine addiction is a complex field that continues to broaden its understanding of the determinants of smoking cessation. Current literature suggests that several modalities are effective in helping smokers quit. Although the overall effect of such intervention is modest if measured by each attempt to quit, the process of overcoming addiction is a cyclic one, and many who wish to quit are eventually able to do so. The available approaches to management of addiction differ in their results.

### Self-Help Manuals and Minimal Clinical Interventions

Although self-help manuals have had only modest and inconsistent success at helping smokers quit, manuals can be easily distributed to the vast population of smokers who try to quit on their own each year. Adjuvant behavioral interventions, particularly proactive telephone counseling, may significantly increase the effect of self-help materials. . . .

Substantial evidence suggests that minimal clinical interventions (e.g., a health care provider's repeated advice to quit) foster smoking cessation and that the more multifactorial or intensive interventions produce the best outcomes. These findings highlight the importance of cessation assistance from clinicians, who have access to more than 70 percent of smokers each year. Moreover, minimal clinical interventions have been found to be effective in increasing smokers' motivation to quit and are cost-effective. . . . However, research has not fully clarified the specific elements of minimal interventions that are most important to clinical success or the specific changes they produce in smokers that lead to abstinence.

## Intensive Clinical Interventions

Intensive programs—more formally, systematic services to help people quit smoking—serve an important function in the nation's efforts to reduce smoking, despite the resources the programs demand and the relatively small population of smokers who use them. Such programs may be particularly useful in treating those smokers who find it most difficult to quit. Because intensive smoking cessation programs differ in structure and content, evaluation is often hampered by variation in methodology and by a lack of research addressing specific treatment techniques. . . .

## Pharmacologic Interventions

Abundant evidence confirms that nicotine gum and the nicotine patch are effective aids to smoking cessation. The efficacy of nicotine gum may depend on the amount of behavioral counseling with which it is paired. The 4-mg dose (rather than the 2-mg dose) may be the better pharmacologic treatment for heavy smokers or for those highly dependent on nicotine. The nicotine patch appears to exert an effect independent of behavioral support, but absolute abstinence rates increase as more counseling is added to patch therapy. Nicotine inhalers and nicotine nasal spray are effective aids for smoking cessation, although their mechanisms of action are not entirely clear. All nicotine replacement therapies produce side effects, but these are rarely so severe that patients must discontinue use. Nicotine nasal spray appears to have greater potential for inappropriate use than other nicotine replacement therapies. Nicotine replacement therapies, especially the gum and the patch, have been shown to delay but not prevent weight gain following smoking cessation. All nicotine replacement therapies are thought to work in part by reducing withdrawal severity. The available evidence suggests that they do ameliorate some elements of withdrawal, but the relationship between withdrawal suppression and clinical outcome is inconsistent.

Bupropion is the first nonnicotine pharmacotherapy for smoking cessation to be studied in large-scale clinical trials. Results suggest that bupropion is an effective aid to smoking cessation. In addition, bupropion has been demonstrated to be safe when used jointly with nicotine replacement therapy. In the only direct comparison with a nicotine replacement product, bupropion achieved quit rates about double those achieved with the nicotine patch. Bupropion appears to delay but not prevent postcessation weight gain. The available literature contains inconsistent evidence regarding bupropion-mediated withdrawal relief. Bupropion does not appear to work by reducing postcessation symptoms of depression, but its mechanism of action in smoking cessation remains unknown.

Evidence has suggested that clonidine is capable of improving smoking cessation rates. Clonidine is hypothesized to work by alleviating withdrawal symptoms. Although clonidine may reduce craving for cigarettes after cessation, it does not consistently ameliorate other withdrawal symptoms, and its effects with weight gain are unknown. Unpleasant side effects are common with clonidine use.

Antidepressants and anxiolytics are potentially useful agents for smoking cessation. At present only nortriptylene appears to have consistent empirical evidence of smoking cessation efficacy. However, tricyclic antidepressants produce a number of side effects, including sedation and various anticholinergic effects, such as dry mouth.

In summary, research on methods to treat nicotine addiction has documented the efficacy of a wide array of strategies. The broad implementation of these effective treatment methods could produce a more rapid and probably larger short-term impact on tobacco-related health statistics than any other component of a comprehensive tobacco control effort. It has been estimated that smoking cessation is more cost-effective than other commonly provided clinical preventive services, including Pap tests, mammography, colon cancer screening, treatment of mild to moderate hypertension, and treatment of high levels of serum cholesterol.

Contemporaneously with the appearance of this report, research advances in managing nicotine addiction have been summarized in evidence-based clinical practice guidelines by the Centers for Disease Control and Prevention (CDC). That document confirms that less intensive interventions, such as brief physician advice to quit smoking, could produce cessation rates of 5 to 10 percent per year. More intensive interventions, combining behavioral counseling and pharmacologic treatment of nicotine addiction, can produce 20 to 25 percent quit rates at one year. Thus, the universal provision of even less intensive interventions to smokers at all clinical encounters could each year help millions of U.S. smokers quit.

Progress has been made in recent years in disseminating clinical practice guidelines on smoking cessation. *Healthy People 2010* Objective 27-8 calls for universal insurance coverage of evidence-based treatment for nicotine dependency by both public and private payers. Similarly, CDC's *Best Practices for Comprehensive Tobacco Control Programs* advises states that tobacco-use treatment initiatives should include:

- Establishing population-based counseling and treatment programs, such as cessation help lines.

- Making the system changes recommended by the CDC-sponsored cessation guidelines.
- Covering treatment for tobacco use under both public and private insurance.
- Eliminating cost barriers to treatment for underserved populations, particularly the uninsured. . . .

## Regulatory Efforts (Chapter 5)

### Advertising and Promotion

Attempts to regulate advertising and promotion of tobacco products were initiated in the United States almost immediately after the appearance of the 1964 report to the Surgeon General on the health consequences of smoking. . . . Underlying these attempts is the hypothesis that advertising and promotion recruit new smokers and retain current ones, thereby perpetuating a great risk to public health. The tobacco industry asserts that the purpose of marketing is to maintain brand loyalty. Considerable evidence has accumulated showing that advertising and promotion are perhaps the main motivators for adopting and maintaining tobacco use. Attempts to regulate tobacco marketing continue to take place in a markedly adversarial and litigious atmosphere.

The initial regulatory action, promulgated in 1965, provided for a general health warning on cigarette packages but effectively preempted any further federal, state, or local requirements for health messages. In 1969, a successful court action invoked the Fairness Doctrine (not previously applied to advertising) to require broadcast media to air antitobacco advertising to counter the paid tobacco advertising then running on television and radio. Indirect evidence suggests that such counteradvertising had considerable impact on the public's perception of smoking. Not surprisingly, the tobacco industry supported new legislation (adopted in 1971) prohibiting the advertising of tobacco products on broadcast media, because such legislation also removed the no-cost broadcasting of antitobacco advertising. A decade later, a Federal Trade Commission (FTC) staff report asserted that the dominant themes of remaining (nonbroadcast) cigarette advertising associated smoking with "youthful vigor, good health, good looks and personal, social and professional acceptance and success." A nonpublic version of the report detailed some of the alleged marketing strategy employed by the industry; the industry denied the allegation that the source material for the report represented industry policy. Nonetheless, some of these concerns led to the enactment of the Comprehensive Smoking Education Act of 1984 (Public Law 98-474), which required a set of four rotating warnings on cigarette packages. The law did not, however, adopt other FTC recommendations that product packages should bear information about associated risks of addiction and miscarriage, as well as information on toxic components of cigarettes. In fact, many FTC-recommended requirements for packaging information that have been enacted in other industrialized nations have not been enacted in the United States.

The role of advertising is perhaps best epitomized by R. J. Reynolds Tobacco Company's Camel brand campaign (initiated in 1988) using the cartoon character "Joe Camel." Considerable research has demonstrated the appeal of this character to young people and the influence that the advertising campaign has had on minors' understanding of tobacco use and on their decision to smoke. In 1997, the FTC brought a complaint asserting that by inducing minors to smoke, R. J. Reynolds' advertising practices violated the Federal Trade Commission Act (Public Law 96-252). The tobacco company subsequently agreed to cease using the Joe Camel campaign. Although the FTC's act grants no private right of enforcement, a private lawsuit in California resulted in a settlement whereby the tobacco company agreed to cease its Joe Camel campaign; notably, the Supreme Court of California rejected R. J. Reynolds' argument that the Comprehensive Smoking Education Act of 1984 preempted the suit's attempt to further regulate tobacco advertising.

## Product Regulation

Current tobacco product regulation requires that cigarette advertising disclose levels of "tar" (an all-purpose term for particulate-phase constituents of tobacco smoke, many of which are carcinogenic or otherwise toxic) and nicotine (the psychoactive drug in tobacco products that causes addiction) in the smoke of manufactured cigarettes and that warning labels appear on packages and on some (but not all) advertising for manufactured cigarettes and smokeless tobacco. The current federal laws preempt, in part, states and localities from imposing other labeling regulations on cigarettes and smokeless tobacco. Federal law (the Comprehensive Smokeless Tobacco Health Education Act of 1986 and the Comprehensive Smoking Education Act of 1984) requires cigarette and smokeless tobacco product manufacturers to submit a list of additives to the Secretary of Health and Human Services; attorneys for the manufacturers released such lists in 1994 to the general public. Smokeless tobacco manufacturers are required to report the total nicotine content of their products, but these data may not be released to the public. Tobacco products are explicitly protected from regulation in various federal consumer safety laws. No federal public health laws or regulations apply to cigars, pipe tobaccos, or fine-cut cigarette tobaccos (for "roll-your-own" cigarettes).

Although much effort has been devoted to considering the need for regulating nicotine delivery, tar content, and the use of additives, until recently no regulation had directly broached the issue of whether tobacco should be subject to federal regulation as an addictive product. Responding in part to several petitions filed by the Coalition on Smoking OR Health in 1988 and 1992, the FDA began serious consideration of the need for product regulation. Motivated by the notion that the cigarette is a nicotine delivery system, by allegations of product manipulation of nicotine levels, and by the concept that smoking is a pediatric disease and that young people are especially susceptible to cigarette advertising and promotion, in August 1995 the FDA issued in the *Federal Register* (1) a proposed rule of regulations restricting the sale and distribution of cigarettes and smokeless tobacco products to protect children and adolescents and (2) an analysis of the FDA's jurisdiction over cigarettes and smokeless tobacco. The final regulations published by the FDA on August 28, 1996, differed only slightly from the proposed regulation. The announcement prompted immediate legal action on the part of the tobacco industry, advertising interests, and the convenience store industry, which challenged the FDA's jurisdiction over tobacco products. In April 1997, a federal district court upheld the FDA's jurisdiction over tobacco products, but held that it lacked authority under the statutory provision relied on to regulate tobacco product advertising.

Although many of the FDA's regulations on tobacco sales and distribution were incorporated, to some extent, in the June 20, 1997, proposed settlement of lawsuits between 41 state attorneys general and the tobacco industry, the settlement presupposed congressional legislation that would uphold the FDA's asserted jurisdiction. After considerable congressional negotiation, no such legislation emerged. In August 1998, a three-judge panel of the United States Court of Appeals for the Fourth Circuit held that the FDA lacked jurisdiction to regulate tobacco products. In November 1998, the full court of appeals rejected the government's request for rehearing by the entire court. On March 21, 2000, in a 5 to 4 decision, the United States Supreme Court affirmed the decision of the United States Court of Appeals for the Fourth Circuit and held that the FDA lacks jurisdiction under the Federal Food, Drug, and Cosmetic Act to regulate tobacco products as customarily marketed. As a result of this decision, the FDA's August 1996 assertion of jurisdiction over cigarettes and smokeless tobacco and regulations restricting the sale and distribution of cigarettes and smokeless tobacco to protect children and adolescents (principally codified at 21 Code of Federal Regulations Part 897) are invalid.

## Clean Indoor Air Regulation

Unlike the regulation of tobacco products per se and of their advertising and promotion, regulation of exposure to ETS has encountered less resistance. This course is probably the result of (1) long-standing grassroots efforts to diminish exposure to ambient tobacco smoke and (2) consistent epidemiologic evidence of adverse health effects of ETS. Since 1971, a series of rules, regulations, and laws have created smoke-free environments in an increasing number of settings: government offices, public places, eating establishments, worksites, military establishments, and domestic airline flights. As of December 31, 1999, smoking was restricted in public places in 45 states and the District of Columbia. Currently, some 820 local ordinances, encompassing a variety of enforcement mechanisms, are in place.

The effectiveness of clean indoor air restrictions is under intensive study. Most studies have concluded that even among smokers, support for smoking restrictions and smoke-free environments is high. Research has also verified that the institution of smoke-free workplaces effectively reduces nonsmokers' exposure to ETS. Although smoke-free environments have not reduced smoking prevalence in most studies, such environments have been shown to decrease daily tobacco consumption among smokers and to increase smoking cessation.

## Minors' Access to Tobacco

There is widespread approval for restricting the access of minors to tobacco products. Recent research, however, has demonstrated that a substantial proportion of teenagers who smoke purchase their own tobacco, and the proportion varies with age, social class, amount smoked, and factors related to local availability. In addition, research has shown that most minors can easily purchase tobacco from a variety of retail outlets. It has been suggested that a reduction in commercial availability may result in a reduced prevalence of tobacco use among minors.

Several approaches have been taken to limiting minors' access to tobacco. All states prohibit sale or distribution of tobacco to minors. More than two-thirds of states regulate the means of sale through restrictions on minors' use of vending machines, but many of these restrictions are weak, and only two states have total bans on vending machines. Restrictions on vending machines are a subclass of the larger category of regulation of self-service cigarette sales; in general, such regulation requires that cigarettes be obtained from a salesperson and not be directly accessible to customers. Such policies can reduce shoplifting as well, an important source of cigarettes for some minors.

Regulations directed at the seller include the specification of a minimum age for sale (18, in all but two states and Puerto Rico), a minimum age for the seller, and the prominent in-store announcement of such policy. Providing merchant education and training is an important component of comprehensive minors' access programs. Penalties for sales to minors vary considerably; in general, civil penalties have been found to be more effective than criminal ones. Requiring licensure of tobacco retailers has been found to provide a funding source for compliance checks and to serve as an incentive to obey the law when revocation of the license is a provision of the law. Applying penalties to business owners, instead of to clerks only, is considered essential to preventing sales to minors. Tobacco retail outlets and the tobacco industry have vigorously opposed this policy. An increasing number of states and local jurisdictions are imposing sanctions against minors who purchase, possess, or use tobacco products. Sanctions against both buyers and sellers are enforced by a variety of agencies and mechanisms. Because regulations in general may be more effective if generated and enforced at the local level, considerable energy is devoted to the issue of opposing or repealing preemption of local authority by states. Public health analyses have resulted in strong recommendations that state laws not preempt local action to curb minors' access to tobacco.

## Litigation Approaches

Private litigation shifts enforcement of public health remedies from the enterprise or the government to the private individual—typically, victims or their surrogates. In the tort system, the coalescence of instances in which injurers are forced to compensate the injured can create a force that generates preventive effects. Though relatively inefficient as a system for compensating specific classes of injuries, the tort system is justified by its generation of preventive actions and by its flexibility. Tobacco represents an atypical pattern of litigation and product modification, because private law remedies have not yet succeeded in institutionalizing recovery for tobacco injuries or have not yet generated significant preventive effects. In the case of tobacco, regulation has been the predominant control, and such regulation has been distinctive in relying primarily on notification requirements rather than safety requirements.

Private litigation against tobacco has occurred in several distinct waves. The first wave was launched in 1954 and typically used one or both of two legal theories: negligence and implied warranty. Courts proved unreceptive to both these arguments, and this approach had receded by the mid-1970s. In many of these and subsequent cases, legal devices and exhaustion of plaintiff resources figured prominently in the defendants' strategy. A second wave began in 1983 and ended in 1992. In these cases, the legal theory shifted from warranty to strict liability. The tobacco industry based its defense on smokers' awareness of risks and so-called freedom of choice. For example, plaintiffs argued that the addictive nature of nicotine limited free choice; defense counsel rebutted by pointing to the large number of former smokers who successfully quit. Taking freedom-of-choice defense even further, counsel argued that the claimant's lifestyle was overly risky by choice or was in some way immoral. The case that symbolized the second-wave litigation was that filed by Rose Cipollone, a dying smoker, in 1983. The Supreme Court accepted the tobacco industry's defense that federal law requiring warning labels on product packages had preempted claims under state law that imposed liability for failure to warn. The United States Supreme Court left open several other approaches, but the likelihood of recovery seemed small, and counsel for the Cipollone estate withdrew.

In the third wave, begun soon after the Cipollone decision and still ongoing, diverse legal arguments have been invoked. This third wave of litigation differs from its predecessors by enlarging the field of plaintiffs, focusing on a range of legal issues, using the class action device, and making greater attempts to use private law for public policy purposes. These new claims have been based on theories of intentional misrepresentation, concealment, and failure to disclose, and such arguments have been joined to a new emphasis on addiction. For example, in one case that ended as a mistrial, plaintiffs were barred from presenting evidence that the tobacco companies may have manipulated nicotine levels. The class action device has figured prominently in these new cases, which have included claims of smokers as well as claims of those who asserted that they have been injured by ETS. Arguably the most notable series of third-wave claims brought against tobacco companies is the proposed 1997 settlement of suits brought by 41 state attorneys general attempting to recover the states' Medicaid expenditures for treating tobacco-related illnesses. In the absence of congressional legislation needed to give that settlement the force of law, four states made independent settlements with the tobacco industry. Notably, each state obtained a concession guaranteeing that it would benefit from any more favorable agreement that another state might later obtain from the tobacco industry. Subsequently, a multistate

Master Settlement Agreement was negotiated in November 1998 covering the remaining 46 states, the District of Columbia, and five commonwealths and territories. Another notable recent development is the filing of large claims by other third-party payers, such as large health care plans.

Perhaps in partial response, the level of litigation initiated by the tobacco industry itself has increased in recent years and has included a number of well-publicized cases, including a threatened suit against the media to prevent airing of a program that accused a tobacco company of manipulating nicotine levels. The company was successful in making the network withdraw the program, even though similar information was later made public in other contexts. Although the industry continues aggressive legal pursuit of its interests on a number of fronts, litigation against the industry has had undoubted impact on tobacco regulation and is likely to continue to play a key role in efforts to reduce tobacco use.

## Overview and Implications

Tobacco products are far less regulated in the United States than they are in many other developed countries. This level of regulation applies to the manufactured tobacco product; to the advertising, promotion, and sales of these products; and to the protection of nonsmokers from the involuntary exposure to ETS from the use of these products. As with all other consumer products, adult users of tobacco should be fully informed of the products' ingredients and additives and of any known toxicity when used as intended. Additionally, as with other consumer products, the manufactured tobacco product should be no more harmful than necessary given available technology. The sale, distribution, and promotion of tobacco products need to be sufficiently regulated to protect underage youth from influences to take up smoking. Finally, involuntary exposure to ETS remains a common public health hazard that is entirely preventable by appropriate regulatory policies.

Such are the basic, reasonable regulatory issues related to tobacco products. Yet these issues remain unresolved as the new millennium begins. When consumers purchase a tobacco product, they receive little information regarding the ingredients, additives, or chemical composition in the product. Although public knowledge about the potential toxicity of most of these constituents is negligible, findings in this report conclude that the warning labels on cigarette packages in this country are weaker and less conspicuous than in other countries. Further, the popularity of "low tar and nicotine" brands of cigarettes has shown that consumers may be misled by another, carefully crafted kind of information—that is, by the implied promise of reduced toxicity underlying the marketing of these products.

Current regulation of the advertising and promotion of tobacco products in this country is considerably less restrictive than in several other countries, notably Canada and New Zealand. The review of current case law in this report supports the contention that greater restrictions of tobacco product advertising and promotion could be legally justified. In fact, the report concludes that regulation of the sale and promotion of tobacco products is needed to protect young people from smoking initiation.

ETS contains more than 4,000 chemicals; of these, at least 43 are known carcinogens. Exposure to ETS has serious health effects. . . . Despite this documented risk, research has demonstrated that more than 88 percent of nonsmokers in this country aged 4 years and older had detectable levels of serum cotinine, a marker for exposure to ETS. The research reviewed in this report indicates that smoking bans are the most effective method for reducing ETS exposure. Four *Healthy People 2010* objectives address this issue and seek optimal protection of nonsmokers through policies, regulations, and laws requiring smoke-free environments in all schools, worksites, and public places.

Despite the widespread support among the general public, policymakers, and the tobacco industry for restricting the access of minors to tobacco products, a high proportion of underage youth smokers across this country continue to be able to purchase their own tobacco. National efforts by the Substance Abuse and Mental Health Services Administration to increase the enforcement of state laws to comply with the Synar Amendment and by the FDA to implement the access restrictions defined in their 1996 rule have reduced the percentage of retailers in many states who sell to minors. Unfortunately, nine states failed to attain their Synar Amendment targets in 1999. Additionally, the March 2000 Supreme Court ruling that the FDA lacks jurisdiction to regulate tobacco products has suspended all enforcement of the agency's 1996 regulations. Although several states have increased emphasis on this issue as part of their state-funded program efforts, the loss of the FDA's program removes a major infrastructure in support of these state efforts. The current regulatory environment poses considerable challenges for the interweaving of regulation into a comprehensive, multicomponent approach to tobacco use control and prevention.

### Economic Approaches (Chapter 6)

The argument for using economic policy for reducing tobacco use requires considerable technical and analytic understanding of economic theory and data. Because experiments and controlled trials—in the usual sense—are not available to the economist, judgment and forecasting depend on the results of complex analysis of administrative and survey data. Such analyses have led to a number of conclusions regarding the importance of the tobacco industry in the U.S. economy and regarding the role of policies that might affect the supply of tobacco, affect the demand for tobacco, and use different forms of taxation as a possible mechanism for reducing tobacco use.

### Supply

The tobacco support program has successfully limited the supply of tobacco and raised the price of tobacco and tobacco products. However, the principal beneficiaries of this program are not only the farmers whose income is supported but also the owners of the tobacco allotments. If policies were initiated to ameliorate some short-run effects, the tobacco support program could be removed without imposing substantial losses for many tobacco farmers. Eliminating the tobacco support program would lead to a small reduction in the prices of cigarettes and other tobacco products, which would lead to slight increases in the use of these products. However, because the support program has created a strong political constituency that has successfully impeded stronger legislation to reduce tobacco use, removing the support program could make it easier to enact stronger policies that would more than offset the impact that the resulting small reductions in price would have on demand.

Throughout the 1980s and 1990s, competition within the tobacco industry appeared to have decreased as a result of the favorable deregulatory business climate and an apparent increase in collusive behavior. This reduction in competition, coupled with the addictive nature of cigarette smoking, has magnified the impact that higher cigarette taxes and stronger smoking reduction policies would have on demand.

The recent expansion of U.S. trade in tobacco and tobacco products through multinational agreements, together with the U.S. threat of retaliatory trade sanctions were other countries to impede this expansion, is nearly certain to have increased the use of tobacco products worldwide. Such an increase would result in a consequent global rise in morbidity and mortality related to cigarette smoking and other tobacco use. These international trade policy efforts conflict with current domestic policies (and the support of comparable international efforts) that aim to reduce the use of tobacco products because of their harmful effects on health.

## Industry Importance

Although employment in the tobacco industry is substantial, the industry greatly overstates the importance of tobacco to the U.S. economy. Indeed, most regions would likely benefit—for example, through redistribution of spending and changes in types of job—from the elimination of revenues derived from tobacco products. Moreover, as the economies of tobacco-growing regions have become more diversified, the economic importance of tobacco in these areas has fallen. Higher tobacco taxes and stronger prevention policies could be joined to other efforts to further ease the transition from tobacco in major tobacco-producing regions. Finally, trading lives for jobs is an ill-considered strategy, particularly with the availability of stronger policies for reducing tobacco use.

## Demand

Increases in the price of cigarettes will lead to reductions in both smoking prevalence and cigarette consumption among smokers; relatively large reductions are likely to occur among adolescents and young adults. Limited research indicates that increases in smokeless tobacco prices will similarly reduce the use of these products. More research is needed to clarify the impact of cigarette and other tobacco prices on the use of these products in specific sociodemographic groups, particularly adolescents and young adults. Additional research also is needed to address the potential substitution among cigarettes and other tobacco products as their relative prices change.

## Taxation

After the effects of inflation are accounted for, federal and average state excise taxes on cigarettes are well below their past levels. Similarly, average cigarette excise taxes in the United States are well below those imposed in most other industrialized countries. Moreover, U.S. taxes on smokeless tobacco products are well below cigarette taxes. Studies of the economic costs of smoking report a wide range of estimates for the optimal tax on cigarettes. However, when recent estimates of the costs of ETS (including the long-term costs of fetal and perinatal exposure to ETS) are considered, and when the premature death of smokers is not considered an economic benefit, a tax that would generate sufficient revenues to cover the external costs of smoking is almost certainly well above current cigarette taxes. The health benefits of higher cigarette taxes are substantial. By reducing smoking, particularly among youth and young adults, past tax increases have significantly reduced smoking-related morbidity and mortality. Further increases in taxes, indexed to account for the effects of inflation, would lead to substantial long-run improvements in health.

The revenue potential of higher cigarette and other tobacco taxes—obviously not in itself a goal—is considerable; significant increases in these taxes would lead to sizable increases in revenues for many years. However, because of the greater price responsiveness of adolescents and young adults and the addictive nature of tobacco use, the long-run increase in revenues is likely to be less than the short-run gain. Nevertheless, current federal and most state tobacco taxes are well below their long-run revenue-maximizing levels.

In short, the research reviewed in this report supports the position that raising tobacco prices is good public health policy. Further, raising tobacco excise taxes is widely regarded as one of the most effective tobacco prevention and control strategies. Research indicates that increasing the price of tobacco products would decrease the prevalence of tobacco use, particularly among minors and young adults. As noted, however, this report finds that both the average price of cigarettes and the average cigarette excise tax in this country are well below those in most other industrialized countries and that the taxes on smokeless tobacco products are well below those on cigarettes. Making optimal use of economic strategies in a comprehensive program poses special problems because of the complexity of government and private controls over tobacco economics and the need for a concerted, multilevel, political approach.

## Comprehensive Programs (Chapter 7)

Community-based interventions were originally developed as research projects that tested the efficacy of a communitywide approach to risk reduction. A number of national and international efforts to control cardiovascular disease (in the United States, notably the Minnesota, Stanford, and Pawtucket studies) used controlled designs. The results from these and other studies were largely disappointing, particularly regarding prevention and control of tobacco use. Other large-scale research efforts, such as the Community Intervention Trial (COMMIT) for Smoking Cessation, also failed to meet their primary goals for smoking reduction and cessation. Similarly, the results to date from numerous worksite-based cessation projects suggest either no impact or a small net effect. . . .

As these studies were under way in the 1970s and 1980s, health promotion—an organized approach to changing social, economic, and regulatory environments—emerged as a more effective mechanism for population behavior change than traditional health education. Although the aforementioned community-based research projects used a health promotion perspective, they lacked the reach and penetration required for effective social change. In any event, the results made clear the distinction between a specific program (even one using multiple modalities) and a comprehensive [multimessage], multichannel approach. . . .

On a broader scale, other social initiatives can also serve some of these same purposes through means that are not directly related to changing population behavior. For example, direct advocacy—the presentation of information to decision makers to encourage their support for nonsmoking policies—has been pursued vigorously by health advocates since the organization of grassroots movements for nonsmokers' rights in the early 1970s. Much of the clean air legislation now in place may be attributed in part to such direct advocacy. An interesting observation that supports the logic behind comprehensive programs is that initial short-comings in direct advocacy activity may have been related to a failure of coordination among grassroots groups and professional organizations. In recent years, in part as the result of electronic networking and mediating by the Advocacy Institute, a more unified approach to reducing tobacco use has been achieved among the participating organizations.

Media advocacy—the use of mass media to advance public policy initiatives—has also been effective in placing smoking issues in the public eye and maintaining a continued impetus for reducing tobacco use. . . .

Countermarketing activities can promote smoking cessation and decrease the likelihood of initiation. Countermarketing campaigns also can have a powerful influence on public support for tobacco control activities and provide an educational climate that can enhance the efficacy of school- and community-based efforts. For youth, the CDC has estimated that the average 14-year-old has been exposed to more than $20 billion in imagery advertising and promotions since age 6, creating a "friendly familiarity" for tobacco products. The recent increase in movie depictions of tobacco use further enhances the image of tobacco use as glamorous, socially acceptable, and normal. In light of the ubiquitous and sustained protobacco messages, countermarketing campaigns need to be of comparable intensity and duration to alter the general social and environmental atmosphere supporting tobacco use.

Perhaps the most important aspect of comprehensive programs has been the emergence of statewide tobacco control efforts as a laboratory for their development and evaluation. The number of states with such programs grew slowly in the early and mid-1990s, but in recent years there has been a surge in funding for such efforts fueled by the state settlements with the tobacco industry. Although the data on the impact of these programs on per capita consumption, adult prevalence, and youth prevalence are generally favorable, the uniform data systems needed to conduct more controlled evaluations of these efforts are still emerging. Nevertheless, the Institute of Medicine has concluded that these "multifaceted state tobacco control programs are effective in reducing tobacco use." The challenge for the new millennium will be to ensure that these ever-increasing comprehensive statewide tobacco control programs are as efficient and effective as possible.

The review of statewide tobacco control programs indicates that reducing the broad cultural acceptability of tobacco use necessitates changing many facets of the social environment. In addition, this report stresses—as does the *Best Practices* document—that these individual components must work together to produce the synergistic effects of a comprehensive program. However, both of these findings highlight the complexity involved in evaluating these types of programs. Within the current statewide tobacco control programs, each of these various modalities discussed in this report is represented with varying degrees of intensity. As noted above, some of the recommendations for actions within these modalities could most effectively be done at the national rather than the state level. Thus, the overall efficacy of these emerging statewide programs will depend in some ways on public health advances at the national level. Again, this synergy between the statewide and national efforts adds greater complexity to the evaluation issue.

Finally, this report concludes that the span of impact of these educational, clinical, regulatory, economic, and social approaches indicates the importance of their sustained and long-term implementation. Program evaluation and research efforts are needed to improve our understanding of how these various elements work. Although knowledge about the efficacy of comprehensive programs is imperfect, evidence points to early optimism for their continuance. With the expansion of tobacco control surveillance and evaluation systems and increases in the number and diversity of statewide tobacco control programs, critical questions can be answered about how to make these efforts more efficient and effective. . . .

## Tobacco Control in the New Millennium

Tobacco use will remain the leading cause of preventable illness and death in this nation and a growing number of other countries until tobacco prevention and control efforts are commensurate with the harm caused by tobacco use. This report provides the composite review of the major methods—educational, clinical, regulatory, economic, and social—that can guide the development of this expanded national effort. This report is, therefore, a prologue to the development of a coherent, long-term tobacco policy for this nation.

# UNITED NATIONS MONITOR
# ON HUMAN RIGHTS IN IRAQ
## August 14, 2000

*Ten years after Iraq invaded Kuwait, Iraqi leader Saddam Hussein remained locked in confrontation with his Western antagonists, principally the United States and Great Britain. Hussein, who was forced by a U.S.-led coalition to retreat from Kuwait during the 1991 Persian Gulf War, appeared by late 2000 to be gaining ground in a campaign to free himself of the tough economic sanctions imposed by the United Nations Security Council. Under UN resolutions, the sanctions were to remain in place until Iraq had cooperated fully with UN inspections to uncover ballistic missiles and chemical, biological, and nuclear weapons it had developed before the war. But Saddam had refused since December 1998 to allow the UN inspectors into Iraq. Even so, support for the sanctions was weakening among UN Security Council members, key U.S. allies were moving to restore diplomatic relations with Iraq, and several countries were undermining the effect of the sanctions. The incoming administration of President George W. Bush faced a daunting task of maintaining a hard-line policy that was rapidly losing international support.*

*The international discord over Iraq developed in large part because of growing anxiety about the impact of sanctions on the Iraqi public. By 2000 it was clear that tens of thousands of Iraqis—some reports put the figure in the range of 500,000 to 1 million—had died during the previous decade from malnutrition and disease resulting from the country's postwar economic collapse. The Iraqi government claimed all the deaths were caused by the sanctions, which prevented normal economic activity in the country. The United States blamed Saddam for the deaths, charging that he spent millions of dollars to rebuild his army and more than a dozen palaces while his citizens starved. Some U.S. allies, along with representatives of international humanitarian and human rights organizations, said there was some truth in both of the competing arguments. They noted that, either way, Iraqi civilians were the ones to suffer.* (Persian Gulf War and Iraqi sanctions, Historic Documents of 1991, pp. 165, 191; UN weapons inspection, Historic Documents of 1998, p. 482)

## Human Rights in Iraq

*Ever since he gained power in 1979, Saddam Hussein had run one of the world's most authoritarian regimes. He suppressed all internal dissent by imprisoning or murdering opposition figures and by controlling the media and all institutions of public life. Saddam stepped up his repression after the war, launching brutal attacks on the Kurds, most of whom lived in northern Iraq, and the Islamic Shiite majority, many of whom lived in the south (Saddam and his inner circle were members of the Sunni branch of Islam, which was a minority in Iraq).*

*Throughout the decade after the war, the UN and human rights organizations called on Saddam to ease his repression and abide by international standards of human rights. Iraq responded to such calls either with silence or with strident denunciations of international "interference" in the country's affairs.*

*Some of the most pointed criticisms of Saddam's regime during the 1990s came from Max van der Stoel, a former foreign minister of the Netherlands who beginning in 1991 had served as the UN's "special rapporteur" to investigate the human rights situation in Iraq. In his first report, issued in 1992, van der Stoel called the Iraqi government one of the most repressive anywhere since World War II. That report so angered Saddam's government that van der Stoel was never allowed to visit Iraq again. Van der Stoel resigned his post in November 1999 after issuing two final reports saying the human rights situation in Iraq was worsening.* (Human rights in Iraq, Historic Documents of 1999, p. 144)

*Van der Stoel's successor was Andreas Mavrommatis, a former Cypriot ambassador to the United Nations who had served for twenty years on the UN Human Rights Committee. Mavrommatis had even less success than Van der Stoel did in gaining access to Iraq. In his first report submitted August 14, 2000, Mavrommatis said the Iraqi government did not reply to his request for permission to visit the country. Instead, Mavrommatis visited Kuwait, where he reviewed claims that Iraq was still holding Kuwaiti troops from the war, and met in London and Geneva with Iraqi émigrés and representatives of the Baghdad government. Mavrommatis said he also reviewed numerous reports and documents concerning human rights in Iraq.*

*In general, Mavrommatis gave a picture of Iraq similar to the one presented by his predecessor—but without van der Stoel's provocative language. Mavrommatis recounted, and appeared to give credence to, numerous examples of human rights abuses, including mass executions of prisoners (among whom were political prisoners), murderous attacks on peaceful demonstrators, the arbitrary arrest and torture of dissidents, harassment of family members of exiled opposition leaders, the suppression of all political rights, and mass expulsions of non-Arabs (primarily Kurds) from their homelands. Mavrommatis called on the Iraqi government to respect international standards of human rights and ended his report by declaring that "nothing can justify serious violations of human rights and fundamental freedoms." That observation was a clear rebuttal of the Iraqi government's claim that its actions were a justified response to U.S.-led "aggression."*

*By year's end the fate of the Kurds in northern Iraq was attracting renewed international attention. Saddam's regime had killed 50,000 to 200,000 Kurds, reportedly with chemical weapons, in 1987–1988. At the end of the Persian Gulf War in 1991, the Kurds rebelled against the Iraqi government, but a massive counterattack by Saddam's Republican Guards pushed more than 1 million Kurds into neighboring Turkey and Iran. To protect the Kurds, the United States and its allies in April 1991 established a "no-fly zone" barring Iraqi air traffic north of the thirty-sixth parallel, essentially converting the northern portion of the country into a Kurdish enclave under international protection. Another no-fly zone, covering the southern half of Iraq, was intended to curb Iraqi attacks against Shiites and other opposition groups.*

*In the late 1990s the Iraqi military began a new series of attacks against Kurds and other non-Arab minorities (including the Turkomen) who were still living in territory controlled by the Iraqi government, primarily in the oil-producing region around Kirkuk, a city about 200 miles north of Baghdad. In a November 29 report to the Security Council on the overall situation in Iraq, Secretary General Kofi Annan cited estimates that Iraq had forced more than 800,000 Kurds and minorities from their homes; most took refuge in the no-fly zone. Annan said there was "an urgent requirement" for tents, blankets, and other supplies for those refugees.*

## Sanctions under Pressure

*A convergence of events in the last half of 2000 enabled Saddam to gain ground in his long-running battle with the United States over the sanctions issue. The first development was a gradual rise in oil prices, which caused fears of international economic instability and gave Iraq—the third largest oil producer in the Middle East—a new source of political and economic leverage. Next was the outbreak in late September of violence between Palestinians and Israelis following the failure of U.S.-led peace negotiations. Many Arab leaders, including Washington's closest allies in the region, blamed the United States for allowing Israel to use heavy-handed tactics to attempt to quell Palestinian protests. Partly as a way of distancing themselves from U.S. policy, Arab leaders moved to establish better relations with Iraq.* (Middle East violence, p. 930)

*In late November and early December—just as the United States was focused on a controversy over its close presidential election—Saddam successfully maneuvered at the United Nations to ease some of the restrictions on a program that enabled Iraq to sell oil on the world market and use some of the proceeds to buy food and other supplies. Initiated in 1996, the "oil-for-food" program was intended to alleviate the worst effects of the economic sanctions imposed after the Persian Gulf War, while maintaining restraints against the reconstruction of Saddam's army. Under the program, UN inspectors carefully monitored Iraqi oil sales. Proceeds from the sales went* *into UN accounts, where about one-half was deducted for administrative expenses and for a fund to reimburse Kuwait for damages caused by the Iraqi occupation. Iraq then applied to the UN for purchases of food, medicine, and other supplies, which were financed by the balance of the oil revenue. In 1998 the UN Security Council agreed to allow Iraq to use some of the money to rebuild its oil industry infrastructure, which had been damaged during the war and through years of neglect. As of December 2000, according to UN figures, Iraq had sold $38.6 billion worth of oil under the program. Of that total, $10.3 billion had been spent on various goods and services for Iraq, including $6.4 billion for food and $1.1 billion for medicines and health services.*

*U.S. officials and other observers repeatedly charged that Iraq was misusing the oil-for-food program by stockpiling medicines rather than giving them to civilians, by using a food rationing system for political purposes to reward friends and punish dissenters, and by diverting goods and supplies to the military and government supporters. Always suspicious that Iraq was attempting to use the oil money to buy parts and equipment for its military, U.S. diplomats routinely held up dozens of Iraq's purchase orders when they arrived at UN headquarters. Annan complained in December 2000 that these "holds" were endangering important humanitarian efforts in Iraq, including the reconstruction of water and sewage treatment plants. By late 2000 Iraq was able to circumvent some restrictions on its oil sales by reopening a long-abandoned pipeline to Syria, which was not under UN control.*

*The Security Council had routinely renewed the oil-for-food program for six-month periods, and the latest renewal period was to expire December 5—just as criticism of the UN sanctions was becoming more intense, both internationally and within the United States. The French and Russian governments, both of which had long pressed for an easing of the sanctions, made it clear they would demand greater freedom for Iraq to spend its oil money (France and Russia were two of the five permanent members of the Security Council, with veto power). In a report to the Security Council on November 29, Annan made his most critical remarks to date about the "unintended consequence" of the sanctions. "I deeply regret the continuing suffering of the Iraqi people and hope that the sanctions imposed on Iraq can be lifted sooner rather than later," he said.*

*The issue of the Iraqi sanctions received only modest attention in the United States, but criticism of longstanding U.S. policy was beginning to emerge from a broad range of opinion. On August 4 representatives of six human rights and economic development organizations based in the United States and Great Britain wrote the Security Council, asking for "recognition that the sanctions have contributed in a major way to persistent life-threatening conditions" in Iraq. The* Chicago Tribune, *a newspaper with a generally conservative editorial policy, said in a September 25 editorial that the U.S. policy toward Iraq was "increasingly a humanitarian and diplomatic disaster."*

*The Clinton administration defended its policy against such attacks and insisted that Saddam bore responsibility for the fate of his people because of his refusal to cooperate with UN-mandated weapons inspections. Even so, the administration faced difficult negotiations in advance of the December 5 renewal date for the oil-for-food program. Attempting to put additional pressure on the UN, Iraq announced on December 1 that it was stopping its oil exports and would require oil companies to pay a 50 cents a barrel "surcharge" directly to an Iraqi bank account, outside of UN control. This move followed by several weeks Iraq's demand that payments for its oil exports be made in euros (the new European currency) rather than in U.S. dollars; that demand, which the Security Council accepted, was generally seen as an attempt to garner favor with European nations and annoy the United States.*

*The Security Council approved a new extension of the oil-for-food program on December 5, adopting a French-sponsored provision giving Iraq more flexibility to use its oil earnings. Most importantly, the council agreed to allow Iraq to spend 600 million euros (about $525 million) locally on repairing and maintaining its oil industry.*

## No Arms Inspections Yet

*UN weapons inspectors had not been in Iraq since December 16, 1998, when they were pulled out as a result of the Iraqi government's latest refusal to allow full access to weapons facilities. Hours after the inspectors left, President Bill Clinton ordered missile and bombing attacks on Iraqi military targets.* (Bombings, Historic Documents of 1998, p. 934)

*Despite Saddam's insistence that UN weapons inspectors would never be allowed back into Iraq, the Security Council in December 1999 approved a new inspections mission, called the UN Monitoring, Verification, and Inspection Commission. Annan appointed Hans Blix, a former director general of the UN International Atomic Energy Agency, to chair the commission and called on Iraq to allow new inspections. Blix recruited and trained an international team of nearly four dozen inspectors and was prepared by late August 2000 to resume the inspection. But Iraq held firm to its refusal to accept new inspections, and Blix was forced to send team members back to their home countries, where they remained on call. Blix told reporters in Washington on December 6 that he was optimistic that arrangements could be made to resume the inspections during 2001.*

*Following are excerpts from the report, "Situation of Human Rights in Iraq," submitted to the United Nations by Andreas Mavrommatis, a "special rapporteur" appointed by the UN Commission on Human Rights to investigate the human rights situation in Iraq. The document was obtained from the Internet at http://www.unhchr.ch/Huridocda/Huridoca.nsf/(Symbol)/A.55 .294.EN?Opendocument.*

# III. Findings

## A. Right to life

12. It appears that executions continued unabated during the period covered by the report. The Special Rapporteur received information that on 3 February 2000, 21 male prisoners were executed at Abu Gharib prison. Allegedly, 43 other male prisoners were executed at the same location on 12 February 2000, of whom 30 were accused of theft, 2 of drug trafficking and 11 of affiliation with the political opposition. Allegedly, the remains of the executed political offenders were buried at an unknown location in Baghdad. According to the same source, on 9 March 2000, 58 male prisoners who had been held in solitary confinement at Abu Gharib prison were executed. The bodies of 44 prisoners who had been charged with "criminal offences" were handed over to their families, while the bodies of 14 political prisoners were buried during the night. Reportedly, many of these prisoners were originally detained for opposition to the ruling party, but were later convicted of criminal charges and sentenced to death.

13. Unfortunately, the information supplied to the Special Rapporteur was not always detailed enough to enable him to draw conclusions as to whether the reported executions violated Iraq's international obligations under articles 6 and 14 of the International Covenant on Civil and Political Rights, which provide respectively for the limitation of the death sentence to the most serious crimes and for the right to a fair and public hearing by a competent, independent and impartial tribunal established by law.

14. The names of the prisoners allegedly executed, the date of the alleged execution and a general description of the crimes, were submitted to the Government on 22 May 2000 with a request for clarification and details, including the relevant part of the record of the legal proceedings and whether convictions and sentences were reviewed on appeal. Furthermore, the Special Rapporteur asked for information on the whereabouts of the mortal remains of those whose bodies allegedly were not handed over to the families. The Government of Iraq has not as yet provided replies to these cases, explaining that the task was complicated and time consuming and insufficient time was given to respond in writing.

15. During the last meeting with the Permanent Representative of Iraq, the Special Rapporteur requested the Government of Iraq to supply him with the text of the criminal code, as well as any other law or regulation that provides for the death penalty, and the text of the criminal procedure law. The request was made with a view to engaging the Government in a dialogue on the possibility of at least reducing the numbers of crimes that carry the death penalty and ensuring the fairness of criminal trials.

16. It appears from information received by several sources that during the reporting period the Government of Iraq was allegedly involved in staged car accidents resulting in the deaths of prominent religious or other local leaders and/or members of their families, as well as of members of the regime and individuals suspected of belonging to the opposition. Some of these incidents

led to riots resulting in further loss of life. Many of these incidents followed threats and intimidation of the victims in connection with their political or religious activities. It appears that these allegations were not properly or at all investigated by the Government, whose reply to these allegations is still pending.

17. One such case was the case of the killing of Ayatollah Sadeq al-Sadr and his two sons on 19 February 1999. According to information received, during a peaceful demonstration that followed the events described above, security forces fired into the crowd of protesters allegedly killing hundreds civilians, including women and children. This allegation was brought to the attention of the Government which promised to provide the Special Rapporteur with a detailed reply in the very near future. More recent information, not as yet transmitted to the Government, referred to 30 theology students arrested following the events having been very recently executed. No names were given, however.

18. The Special Rapporteur also received information that government forces were involved in sometimes lethal attacks against the lives of men and women suspected of belonging to the opposition or against members of their families. Such attacks were blamed by the authorities on criminal gangs. The Special Rapporteur met with an Iraqi citizen who testified on condition of anonymity that he had been shot at 12 times by the security forces without any warning and left for dead in the street. In another instance the mother of a prominent member of the opposition living outside Iraq was found shot dead following threats and after being arrested and obliged to call her son and ask him to stop his political activities abroad.

19. The Government of Iraq does not deny that numerous executions were carried out in the reporting period, but alleges that these were necessitated by the extraordinarily dangerous situation, the upsurge of crime and the considerable number of subversive acts.

20. The Special Rapporteur did receive certain information from several sources regarding continued attacks against Iraqi security forces and government officials, sometimes resulting in the deaths of the targeted individuals. However, the Special Rapporteur is of the opinion that Iraq continues to be in violation of its obligations under the International Covenant on Civil and Political Rights, if only because of the sheer number of executions that are taking place and what appear to be extrajudicial executions on political grounds and in the absence of a due process of law.

21. Also connected with the right to life are cases of disappearances. Although the Special Rapporteur did not receive specific allegations regarding recent disappearances, there have not yet been replies in respect of past cases. The Special Rapporteur related to the Government the case of 106 students of religion in al-Najaf who were detained for a short period of time after the arrest of Ayatollah Abu al-Quassem al-Kho'i on 20 March 1991 and whose whereabouts are still unknown. Another case of disappearance which was brought to the attention of the Special Rapporteur was that of two brothers who were arrested in 1982 during a campaign of expulsion of Iraqi citizens of Iranian origin to the Islamic Republic of Iran. The two brothers were last seen in prison in 1985.

22. With regard to both the above-mentioned cases, the Special Rapporteur requested the Government to make inquiries into the whereabouts of the disappeared and, in case they are detained, to communicate the charges against them and the current status of the legal proceedings, if any.

23. The Special Rapporteur awaits the detailed replies of the Government on these allegations and shall revert to them, as well as to other violations in respect of which replies are pending, in his next report to the Commission on Human Rights.

## B. Arbitrary arrest and detention and due process of law

24. From testimonies and accounts related to the Special Rapporteur, it appears that the Government of Iraq continues not to respect its obligations under articles 9 and 14 of the International Covenant on Civil and Political Rights. Men, women and minors continue to be arrested and detained on suspicion of political or religious activities, or simply because of family ties with members of the opposition. Allegedly, men and women continue to be detained for long periods of time without charges being brought against them and without having access to a lawyer. The families of the arrested are not always informed of their whereabouts and of the status of legal proceedings against them. Young children are allegedly detained with their mothers.

25. There is also information to the effect that trials are not public and defence attorneys are either not present or are nominated pro forma but do not take any effective action during the proceedings. The Special Rapporteur was told of a case where the defendant was told that if he remained silent during the trial he would be acquitted; this individual was tried after being released from six months' detention, on charges that had nothing to do with the matters about which he had been repeatedly questioned. In another instance the defendant was allegedly sentenced to death in absentia. Sentences pronounced by Revolutionary Courts appear not to be subject to appeal or review.

26. The Special Rapporteur intends to study this subject further, including by reviewing the criminal and civil procedure codes and other laws that the Government promised to make available and by continuing to interview victims and witnesses. The Special Rapporteur shall revert to this issue in the next report to the Commission on Human Rights.

## C. Torture and ill-treatment

27. It appears that torture and ill-treatment of men and women continue to occur in Iraq. The Special Rapporteur received information to the effect that suspects, including members of the opposition and their collaborators and/or relatives, are subjected to ill-treatment and torture during questioning and in detention by members of the Iraqi forces and intelligence service. Means of torture allegedly include electric shocks, suspension by the hands, beatings, rape and sexual abuse of both men and women, threats and psychological pressure.

28. Prison conditions appear to be grave. Allegedly private houses as well as public building are used as detention facilities. Prisons, especially in Bagh-

dad, are seriously overcrowded and prisoners are reportedly regularly beaten and, in the case of female detainees, raped. Juvenile offenders are kept together with adults. The Special Rapporteur was informed that in two different detention facilities in Baghdad prisoners are kept locked in metal boxes as big as coffins which are opened only 30 minutes a day.

29. None of the individuals who were victims of such treatment and who were interviewed by the Special Rapporteur agreed to have their names and cases related to the Government for investigation and clarification because of fear of retaliation. The Special Rapporteur shall seek more information on the above and revert to this issue in the next report to the Commission on Human Rights. It is also to be hoped that by visiting Iraq, and also by receiving complete and reasoned replies from its Government on each case, the Special Rapporteur would be able to arrive at appropriate conclusions, which the Special Rapporteur may have to do even in the absence of such full cooperation.

## D. The fate of Kuwaitis unaccounted for since Iraq's occupation of Kuwait

30. The Special Rapporteur, accompanied by a staff member from the Office of the High Commissioner for Human Rights and an interpreter, visited Kuwait from 29 June to 3 July 2000. The visit followed a series of meetings held in Geneva with the Permanent Representative of Kuwait and other Kuwaiti government officials, as well as with officers of the International Committee of the Red Cross, that had as their main objective the examination of the situation of Kuwaiti prisoners of war and detainees still unaccounted for, in accordance with the terms of Commission resolution 1992/71 and subsequent relevant resolutions.

31. The Government of Kuwait extended to the Special Rapporteur and his team its full cooperation, including absolute freedom to visit any prisons and/or detention centres they might wish to have access to.

32. The Special Rapporteur met with the families of some of the Kuwaiti prisoners of war and detainees still unaccounted for, the Chairman of the National Assembly, the First Deputy Prime Minister and Minister for Foreign Affairs, the Deputy Prime Minister and Minister of Defence, the Minister of the Interior, members of the Parliamentary Human Rights Committee, members of the National Committee for the Missing and Prisoners of War Affairs, the Director and other members of the Centre for Research and Studies of Kuwait, the Director and members of the Kuwait Martyrs Bureau, the President of the Kuwaiti Red Crescent Society, and others.

33. During the above-mentioned meetings it was repeatedly stressed that the Tripartite Commission and its Technical Subcommittee were the most effective mechanism to deal with the issue of Kuwaiti prisoners of war still unaccounted for, provided that there existed the necessary political will on the part of all parties concerned. The Special Rapporteur believes that his task is to do everything possible to assist these bodies in discharging their mandate and he made this clear to all concerned. It should be recalled that the Tripartite Commission was created in March 1991, pursuant to Security Council resolutions 686 (1991) and 687 (1991).

34. The Special Rapporteur, together with members of the National Committee for the Missing and Prisoners of War Affairs, went through some of the 605 individual files compiled by the Committee. A wrap-up session was later held in Geneva. This exercise was undertaken with a view to drawing conclusions as to whether sufficient data are included in the files to permit deductions or call for further investigations.

35. It is worth noting that the Government of Kuwait has devoted extraordinary efforts and resources to the cause of its prisoners of war and detainees still unaccounted for and has done everything in its power to alleviate the suffering of their families by relentlessly pursuing the investigation of their fate and/or whereabouts and by fully cooperating with its counterparts, within the international framework and on a bilateral basis.

36. It is the opinion of the Special Rapporteur that enough material was produced to support the Kuwaiti claim that the Government of Iraq is in a position to clarify the fate and/or whereabouts of Kuwaitis unaccounted for.

37. The Special Rapporteur related his views and findings to the Government of Iraq during the meeting held on 16 July. It was stressed that the Government of Iraq, as a consequence of the bombing, does not intend to participate in the meetings of the mechanisms chaired by ICRC as long as the United Kingdom of Great Britain and Northern Ireland and the United States of America also take part. However, it was also stated that Iraq is willing to extend its cooperation to ICRC and to have bilateral meetings with representatives of Kuwait.

38. During the meeting, the Special Rapporteur expressed the view that an unjustifiably long time had elapsed since the files were submitted to the Government of Iraq and that general replies, which ended normally with the claim that the Kuwaiti prisoners of war had last been seen in south Iraq at the time of the uprising, could not be considered satisfactory and that an effort should be made to investigate the events during and immediately after the end of the uprising and to give more complete answers. The Special Rapporteur also stressed that the testimonies alleging that Kuwaiti prisoners of war had been seen after the uprising in places other than the south should not be dismissed with sweeping statements that the witnesses are lying, but investigations of the records of the alleged places of detentions, as well as interviews with personnel of the detention centres at the time when the prisoners of war were allegedly seen, should be carried out and the results made available.

39. The Special Rapporteur is of the opinion that the question of the missing Kuwaitis and Kuwaiti prisoners of war and detainees is a purely humanitarian question and that no reason, political or other, could justify delaying or obstructing the task of the Tripartite Commission and its Technical Subcommittee. What appears to be lacking is the necessary political will on the part of the Iraqi authorities to participate in the work and to examine speedily and effectively each and every case before the Commission.

40. It should be noted that the Security Council, in its resolution 1284 (1999), reiterated the obligation of Iraq, in furtherance of its commitment to facilitate the repatriation of all Kuwaiti and third country nationals referred to in paragraph 30 of resolution 687 (1991), to extend all necessary cooperation

to the International Committee of the Red Cross, and called upon the Government of Iraq to resume cooperation with the Tripartite Commission and Technical Subcommittee established to facilitate work on this issue.

## E. The fate of the Iraqis unaccounted for since Iraq's invasion of Kuwait

41. The Government of Iraq alleges that there are 1,250 missing Iraqi citizens in respect of whom there exists evidence to the effect that they were seen alive in Kuwait after the war had ended. The Government of Kuwait dismissed these allegations as "mere afterthoughts."

42. The Special Rapporteur asked the representatives of Iraq to provide him with more detailed information and evidence supporting this claim. The Special Rapporteur proposes to make such information available to the Government of Kuwait, which stressed that the Special Rapporteur would be guaranteed access to any place of detention in the country at any time without any restrictions.

43. It appears that the Government of Kuwait has officially received, through ICRC, a total of 660 files, 592 of which were to be considered under the second stage.

## F. Harassment and threats against Iraqi opposition members and members of their families

44. The most disturbing of the recent complaints related to the Special Rapporteur concerns harassment, intimidation and threats against the families of Iraqi opposition members residing abroad to induce them to stop their activities. Although this practice existed in the past, as previous reports indicated, it allegedly has become much more prevalent. Allegations include the rounding-up and arrest of family members, as well as attempts by officials of the security forces to extort money from the families in exchange for putting an end to harassment and helping them to flee the country.

45. A case that illustrates the above-mentioned allegations is that of General Njeeb Alsalhi, a senior officer in the Iraqi Army who left the country in 1995 and now resides in Jordan where he is an active member of the Iraqi opposition. Since he left Iraq, his male and female relatives in Iraq have been subjected to arrests, questioning and other forms of harassment. His brother was forced to travel twice to Jordan to try and persuade him to return to Iraq. General Alsalhi reported that on 7 June 2000 he received a telephone call from Baghdad and was told to go and collect a "gift" from a store in Amman. This consisted of a video tape showing the rape of a female family member. Ten days later he reportedly received a call from the Iraqi Intelligence Service. He was asked if he had received the gift and was told that one of his female family members was in the hands of Iraqi Intelligence. He was then again urged to stop his activities. General Alsalhi, during an interview with the Special Rapporteur, stated that he is willing to surrender the video tape only at the trial of a top Iraqi government official. The case was brought to the attention of the Government which denied the allegations and promised a formal reply later.

46. During the visit to London the Special Rapporteur was told of other

cases of a similar nature where the video taped rape of a female family member was used to take advantage of the stigma which is attached to sexual molestation in Iraqi traditional society to silence members of the opposition. This means of intimidation is reportedly very effective as such incidents are normally not reported for fear of negative repercussions on the victim and her family. Rape is considered a dishonour affecting the whole family and, in extreme cases, the victim might be killed by the family itself in order to wipe out the stigma.

47. The Special Rapporteur is also very concerned about what appears to be a practice of targeting the families of those opposing or suspected of opposing the regime. The Special Rapporteur interviewed Iraqi women who reported that after their husbands or male relatives were arrested, or executed, or went into hiding out of fear of persecution, they experienced several forms of abuse and intimidation, ranging from the withdrawal of the ration card through which medicines and food are made available to the population, to cuts in electric power supplies, to expropriation of property, frequent house searches and questioning, arrest and threats. Women and children are affected the most by these practices.

48. These allegations were brought for the first time to the attention of the Government of Iraq on 16 July, immediately after the Special Rapporteur's visit to London. The seriousness of the allegations was stressed as well as the necessity for complete and well-documented replies and thorough investigation of the claims. Again, pending the Government's reaction, the Special Rapporteur cannot but express his concern and reiterate his call to the Government to take stern measures to put an end to such occurrences which violate not only the freedom of expression and opinion as established in article 19 of the International Covenant on Civil and Political Rights, but also often entail the most serious forms of the universal crime of torture.

## G. Mass relocations and relocation of non-Arabs and Arabization of areas from which they are expelled

49. The former Special Rapporteur, Max van der Stoel, reported in detail on instances of forced relocations of non-Arabs and Arabization of certain areas of Iraq. Therefore, the task of the Special Rapporteur was to see whether and to what extent such practice continued. During the Special Rapporteur's mission to London such allegations were made by leaders of all political groups of the northern Kurdish governorates, which are not under the control of the Government of Iraq, as well as by a variety of other sources.

50. Allegations refer to the fact that non-Arab residents of the Kirkuk area—especially Kurds, Turkomen and Assyrians—are driven from their homes by the Government through the use of different means. On the one hand, the policy of "Arabization" is reported to be continuing and the Government reportedly maintains in force measures to that effect, such as the provision of grants and other incentives to Arabs to move to the Kirkuk area and legal impediments to the possession and transfer of property by non-Arabs. On the other hand, forced deportations of non-Arab families living in the Kirkuk area and confiscation of their property are also reported to continue on a large scale.

Allegedly, those who refused to comply with the order to leave their homes are subjected to intimidation, arrest, economic hardship through the revocation of ration cards and, eventually, forced expulsion. Allegedly, no compensation is provided for the loss of property. The allegations are serious and the following figures were provided in respect of the number of families forced to leave the area: 13,367 families from 1991 to 1993; 112 in 1994; 395 in 1995; 282 in 1996; 710 in 1997; 394 in 1998; 449 in 1999; and 155 in 2000 (as of 4 June). The total number of individuals who were forced to leave Kirkuk since 1991 reportedly amounts to 94,026.

51. The Special Rapporteur asked those alleging the above to supply him with a list of the families who left the Kirkuk area, containing names, addresses, circumstances and date of departure from Kirkuk, copy or mention of any legal documents invoked or served on them, and information on circumstances connected with their relocation, as well as information as to who moved into their abandoned residences.

52. The above allegations were related to the representative of the Government of Iraq during the of 16 July meeting. The seriousness of the allegations was stressed. The representative of the Government of Iraq denied the allegations and pointed to the huge number of Kurds and non-Arabs remaining in Government-controlled areas. The representative of Iraq asked for details so as to be able to reply in respect of each case. The Special Rapporteur will forward such details as soon as they are received.

## H. Political rights

53. Allegations and information regarding violations related under the preceding sections of the report also cover serious allegations of violations of political rights through systematic repression taking the form of intimidation, arrest, torture and even death. The Special Rapporteur shall deal more extensively with political rights and shall also deal with the need to introduce such constitutional and other changes as would be consistent with Iraq's obligations under the International Covenant on Civil and Political Rights.

54. It should be noted that Iraq did attempt to deal with this issue by establishing the necessary processes before the Gulf war. It is now high time they deal seriously with this problem again.

## I. Humanitarian issues

55. The Special Rapporteur has felt from the beginning that, although humanitarian issues are not strictu sensu within his mandate, they could not be brushed aside or ignored when dealing with violations of not only the right to life, but also of rights under the International Covenant on Economic, Social and Cultural Rights. The Special Rapporteur also wishes to stress that the relevant Security Council resolutions are binding on the Government of Iraq, as well as on all other countries, and should be implemented.

56. As a result, the Special Rapporteur held a series of meetings in New York with members of the Security Council, as well as with the Executive Director of the Iraq Programme, the Secretary-General of the United Nations, and heads of departments dealing with humanitarian issues. The contacts

with the members of the Security Council and other Governments were continued, in particular with the representatives of the Governments of Iraq, France, Kuwait, the United States of America and the United Kingdom.

57. The Special Rapporteur has also been closely following developments in this field through the periodic reports of the Secretary-General to the Security Council, as well as through reports of United Nations bodies and specialized agencies such as the United Nations Children's Fund (UNICEF) and the World Health Organization (WHO) and information provided by, inter alia, the above-mentioned Governments.

58. It appears that although the humanitarian situation remains serious, as a result of resolution 1284 (1999) and the increased price of oil, more money is now available under the oil-for-food programme and a marked improvement has been observed in respect of food and medicines. It also appears that there were improvements in respect of purchases connected with infrastructure, such as water, electricity, sewerage and the repair of the oil production plants. The Special Rapporteur was also informed that the number of contracts on hold has dropped since his last report to the Commission.

59. With respect to the availability of medicaments, the Special Rapporteur received information that the Government of Iraq is directing more medicines to hospitals for the privileged officials and stockpiling medicaments for use in a war emergency. As reported above, the Special Rapporteur was also informed that the ration card system is used by the Government as a means of pressure and intimidation. There is also information to the effect that the Government of Iraq can today afford to spend more money out of its budget on food and medicines rather than on other non-essential projects.

60. These allegations were brought to the attention of the Government during the 16 July meeting, together with the observation that, in respect of medications and food supplies, the situation appeared to be much better in the northern governorates. Another allegation which was received by the Special Rapporteur and related to the Government was that infant and maternal mortality rates were exaggerated by the Government for propaganda purposes.

61. The representatives of Iraq vehemently denied those allegations and referred to mortality and morbidity rates reported by United Nations specialized agencies as well as by the Secretary-General. On the question of the situation in the northern governorates, it was stressed by the Government representative that for political and other reasons that area received considerable international assistance and that imported as well as smuggled goods were available all the time in huge quantities. The Permanent Representative of Iraq also made extensive reference to the long-term effects of the embargo, particularly on health and education.

62. The Special Rapporteur is of the opinion that although the situation has improved, the humanitarian concerns should be kept under constant review and necessary adjustments should continue to be made. In this respect the Special Rapporteur believes that an increase in the number of monitors under the oil-for-food programme would help ensure that the positive effects of the above-mentioned developments reach the totality of the population of Iraq and that imports of goods are used exclusively for approved purposes.

63. The Special Rapporteur is also of the opinion that the Government of Iraq should, in accordance with its obligation under article 2, paragraph 1, of the International Covenant on Economic, Social and Cultural Rights, take more steps to the maximum of its available resources, with a view to achieving progressively the full realization of the rights recognized by that Covenant.

## IV. Recommendations

64. Pending further consultation with the Government and verification of the allegations received, as well as further analysis of specific issues, the Special Rapporteur reserves the right to make fuller recommendations in the report to be submitted to the Commission on Human Rights.

65. The Special Rapporteur urges the Government of Iraq to review and revise laws permitting the imposition of the death sentence and, pending the conclusion of such process, to consider a moratorium on executions.

66. The Special Rapporteur, in view of the humanitarian nature of the question of the missing and prisoners of war, calls upon the Government to rejoin the work of the Tripartite Commission and the Technical Subcommittee and to conduct thorough examinations of the individual files submitted by the Government of Kuwait.

67. The Special Rapporteur urges the Government of Iraq to put an end to the harassment of families of people engaged in opposition activities abroad as well as to practices against the families of wanted or arrested Iraqi citizens and the widows and children of those executed.

68. The Special Rapporteur calls upon the Government of Iraq to ensure that no forced relocations of any citizens takes place and that all submitted allegations to the contrary be investigated and the results presented to the Special Rapporteur.

69. The Special Rapporteur urges the Government of Iraq to put an end to unlawful practices of arrest and torture and to consider becoming a party to the Convention against Torture and Other Cruel, Inhuman or Degrading Treatment or Punishment.

70. The Special Rapporteur invites the Government of Iraq to begin introducing democratic and political freedoms in accordance with its obligations under the International Covenant on Civil and Political Rights.

71. The Special Rapporteur urges the Government of Iraq to accept and comply with the terms of all Security Council resolutions and in particular resolution 1284 (1999), in order that it might alleviate the suffering of the Iraqi people.

72. The Special Rapporteur wishes to reiterate what he stated at the last session of the Commission on Human Rights: nothing can justify serious violations of human rights and fundamental freedoms.

# CLINTON'S SPEECH TO THE DEMOCRATIC CONVENTION
## August 14, 2000

*Bill Clinton took the first formal step toward leaving the presidency by handing over the leadership of the Democratic Party to his vice president and would-be successor Al Gore on August 14, 2000. In a valedictory speech to wildly cheering delegates on the opening night of the Democratic National Convention in Los Angeles, the president commended Gore to the voters, calling him "a profoundly good man" who was "thoughtful and hard-working" and "one strong leader."*

*Clinton's legacy as the nation's forty-second president was certain to be debated by historians and others for some time to come. In his two terms in office, Clinton presided over the longest economic expansion in the history of the country, promoted free trade and the expansion of the global economy, signed into law the most sweeping welfare reform bill ever enacted, and helped Israel and the Palestinians move closer to a peace settlement than they had ever been. Yet Clinton suffered some humiliating legislative defeats—most notably, his national health care reform proposal, lost his Democratic majorities in the House and Senate, and saw his presidency nearly collapse under the weight of personal misconduct that led to his impeachment by the House and a trial in the Senate. Although his personal popularity faltered, Clinton's job approval ratings stayed remarkably steady and impressively high. On the eve of the convention, 61 percent of the people approved of Clinton's job performance. At the same point in his presidency, Republican Ronald Reagan, the last president to hold office a full two terms, had a job approval rating of 54 percent.*

*Historians would also ponder how much Clinton's personal misconduct might have affected the outcome of the 2000 presidential elections. In 1998 the House impeached Clinton for perjury and obstruction of justice in connection with an affair he had with a White House intern. In an extraordinary public apology, Clinton admitted that he had misled his family and the nation about his relationship with Monica S. Lewinsky, but he insisted that he had not lied under oath about it. Even though most observers thought the president was splitting legal hairs, the Senate acquitted Clinton on the im-*

*peachment charges. In addition, the president and his wife, Hillary Rodham Clinton, were the targets of a six-year investigation into their involvement with an Arkansas land deal known as Whitewater. The Justice Department also looked into allegations that both Clinton and Vice President Al Gore had violated campaign financing laws. In September the independent prosecutor closed the Whitewater investigation without bringing charges against the Clintons. The Justice Department had declined to name an independent prosecutor to look into the campaign financing allegations.* (Clinton impeachment, Historic Documents of 1998, p. 958; impeachment trial, Historic Documents of 1999, p. 15; campaign financing inquiry, Historic Documents of 1998, p. 890; final Whitewater report, p. 762)

*Clinton's legacy left Gore with more immediate problems—how to run on the administration's record of economic prosperity without also being tarnished by the president's admitted and alleged misconduct and how to emerge from the shadow of a man whose force of personality often made him seem larger than life. Any hopes that Clinton might have helped defuse the situation at the convention, however, soon faded. Although Clinton made no mention of his personal trials during his convention speech, on August 10, on his way to Los Angeles, Clinton made a public appearance before several thousand evangelical ministers in South Barrington, Illinois, where he gave a remarkably personal and candid assessment about his "terrible mistake" as well as his feelings about the presidency. Clinton told the ministers that "surely no fair-minded person would blame [Gore] for any mistake I made."*

*The following day, however, Gore's Republican opponent, George W. Bush, took the opportunity to say that there was "no question" that the president's ethical lapses had "embarrassed the nation" and that "Americans want to be assured that the next administration will bring honor and dignity to the White House." Bush stopped short of accusing Gore of condoning Clinton's behavior, but he challenged Gore to make his views known. "If Al Gore has differences with the president, he ought to say . . . loud and clear what they are," Bush said.*

*Clinton spent the weekend before the convention in Los Angeles, and was feted at one round of parties and receptions after another—to the disappointment of some Gore aides, who had hoped to keep the convention spotlight focused on the vice president. Clinton and his wife also used the time to do some fund raising for her New York Senate campaign and his presidential library.* (Democratic convention and platform, pp. 609, 617; Hillary Clinton's senate race, p. 906)

## *"A Matter of Choice"*

*Clinton's convention appearance was clearly an emotional high for the president, who used the speech not only to praise Gore but to review the accomplishments of his administration. The president did not mention Bush by name, but he sharply defended his record against Bush's accusation at the Republican National Convention two weeks earlier that Clinton and Gore had "coasted" through good economic times. "To those who say the progress of the last eight years was an accident, that we just coasted along, let's be clear: America's success was not a matter of chance. It was a matter of choice."* (Bush acceptance speech, p. 519)

*Clinton reminded the Democratic delegates that in 1993 every single Republican in Congress voted against his plan to reduce the deficit and turn the economy around. "Remember, our Republican friends said then they would absolutely not be held responsible for our economic policies," Clinton said, pausing briefly and then continuing. "I hope the American people take them at their word." He then reviewed his administration's economic record—the longest economic expansion in history, the lowest unemployment in thirty years, the creation of 22 million new jobs, the highest home-ownership in history, and the largest government surpluses in history.*

*Clinton also detailed numerous other achievements, including more teachers and more accountability in the nation's public schools, more funding for the Head Start program, a big expansion of college aid, reduced crime, better health care, better insurance coverage for children, and a cleaner environment. He credited Republicans for working with Democrats on welfare reform but said Democrats were the ones who insisted on additional health, food, and training support for families moving from welfare to work. He also lauded his administration's role in peace negotiations between Israel and the Palestinians and in Northern Ireland, in ending ethnic cleansing in Bosnia and Kosovo, and in building stronger ties with Africa, Asia, Latin America, and the Caribbean. Clinton also added that the American military was the best trained, best equipped, and most effective armed force in the world.*

*Clinton then warned that the economic prosperity he had worked so hard to achieve was in danger of being lost. The Republican ticket, he said, would spend "every dime" of the projected surplus and "then some" on tax cuts, leaving nothing for education, Social Security, or Medicare reform. In contrast, he said, the Democratic ticket "will keep the prosperity going by paying down the debt, investing in education and health care, . . . and providing family tax cuts we can afford."*

## *"A Terrible Mistake"*

*Clinton's appearance before the evangelical ministers was a decidedly more personal tour of his presidency. About 4,500 pastors and church leaders listened in the Willow Creek Community Church and via satellite as Clinton was interviewed by Bill Hybels, the senior pastor of the church. Hybels had counseled Clinton on personal and spiritual matters regularly since 1992, and Clinton said he had promised to appear at one of Hybels's leadership conferences before he left office. The interview, which was marked by humor as well as reflection, was perhaps the most intimate public exchange ever undertaken by a sitting president.*

*Clinton seemed almost eager to discuss the state of his spiritual life in the aftermath of his public apology about his relationship with Monica Lewinsky. The president said that he felt "much more at peace" than he used to and that he was "now in the second year of a process of trying to totally rebuild my life from a terrible mistake I made. And I now see . . . that it's always a work in progress and you just have to hope you're getting better every day. But if you're not getting better, chances are you're getting worse. That this has to be a dynamic, ongoing effect." Clinton also said that the public admission of his affair was cathartic: "In a funny way, when you realize there is nothing left to hide, then it sort of frees you up to do what you ought to be doing anyway. I don't know if that makes any sense, but to me, I feel this overwhelming sense of gratitude."*

*Asked by Hybels to respond to charges that he had never fully apologized for his actions, Clinton said he thought he "gave a clear, unambiguous, brutally frank, and frankly personally painful statement. . . . I stood up there and said what I did and said it was wrong and apologized for it." Clinton first publicly acknowledged and apologized for his misconduct with Lewinsky in a nationally televised address on August 17, 1998, and he repeated that apology on several subsequent occasions. But he never acknowledged making misleading statements about his conduct in a sworn deposition in a related lawsuit, even though he paid a $90,000 fine as punishment for that testimony. (Clinton scandal, Historic Documents of 1998, pp. 564, 632)*

*The discussion touched on a range of other issues. Clinton said that according to the public opinion polls, the "most unpopular decision" he ever made as president "at the moment I made it, was to give financial aid to Mexico when they were going broke." If he could have only one wish for America, he said, "it would be that we would find a way to live together as one America." Among the toughest decisions he made were to send troops into the Kosovo conflict and to take military action against Saddam Hussein in 1993 after learning that the Iraqi president had authorized an assassination attempt on former president George Bush. (Kosovo war, Historic Documents of 1999, p. 134)*

*Clinton also said it was hard to ask Democrats to stick with him in 1993 and support his plan to reduce massive federal budget deficits through a combination of increased taxes and reduced spending. The plan passed in the House by two votes; Gore broke a 50–50 tie in the Senate. "When the Republicans announced that they would give no votes to it . . . I knew what I was asking [Democratic legislators] to do. But . . . I also believed very strongly it would work, and I thought if we didn't do something about the deficit and the accumulating debt that we would never turn the country around. And so I did it. But it was very hard for me, because I knew that the Congress would pay the price because there was no way the economy could be that much better by '94 in the elections. And that if I was right and it worked, that I would be reelected in '96 and they would have, in effect, sacrificed for a decision that I made and got them to support." In the 1994 elections, Democrats lost sixty-three seats in the House and Senate, and Republicans gained control of Congress for the first time in forty years. (Clinton deficit reduction plan, Historic Documents of 1993, p. 181; 1994 election results, Historic Documents of 1994, p. 513)*

*In addition to winning the 1993 fight on his deficit reduction plan, Clin-*

*ton said the other bright moments in his presidency were the signing of the Israeli-Palestinian peace accords at the White House in September 1993, his November 1995 trip to Northern Ireland to promote peace efforts there, and his 1998 visit with South African president Nelson Mandela to the cell on Robben Island where Mandela had been incarcerated for eighteen of the twenty-seven years he was held as a political prisoner. Besides his personal crisis, Clinton said the lowest moments were the loss of eighteen U.S. soldiers in a firefight in Somalia in 1993 and the bombing of the federal building in Oklahoma City in 1995.* (Israeli-Palestinian peace accords, Historic Documents of 1993, p. 747; Clinton's trip to Northern Ireland, Historic Documents of 1995, p. 727; Oklahoma City bombing, Historic Documents of 1995, p. 176; Clinton's South African visit, Historic Documents of 1998, p. 161)

*Clinton said he would like to be remembered as "the president that led America from the industrial era into the information age, into a new global society that reaffirmed the importance of our mutual responsibility to one another and the importance of guaranteeing an opportunity to everybody; and that I was a force for peace and freedom and decency in the world, that tried to bring people together instead of drive people apart, tried to empower poor people so that they could have a chance like everybody else. . . . That's how I'd like to be remembered."*

*On the presidency itself, Clinton said, "believe it or not, it's a job like other jobs. . . . Sometimes I think it assumes proportions . . . that are both too mythical and too trivial, as if it's all just positioning and politics. Not true. . . . It matters what you think you're supposed to do. It matters whether you've got a strategy to get there. It matters whether you've got a good team. And it matters how hard you work. . . . And it's just been a joy. I can't even— I don't even have the words to describe how much I love the work."*

*Following are excerpts from the text of a speech delivered August 14, 2000, by President Bill Clinton to the Democratic National Convention in Los Angeles. The document was obtained from the Internet at http://www.whitehouse.gov/library/hot_ releases/August_14_2000_1.html.*

**President Clinton:** Thank you, ladies and gentlemen. Isn't it great to be here in California together?

Forty years ago the great city of Los Angeles launched John Kennedy and the New Frontier. Now Los Angeles is launching the first president of the new century, Al Gore.

I come here tonight above all to say a heartfelt thank you.

Thank you for giving me the chance to serve, thank you for being so good to Hillary and Chelsea. I am so proud of them. Didn't she give a good talk? I thought it was great.

I thank you for supporting the new Democratic agenda that has taken our country to new heights of prosperity, peace and progress. As always, of course, the lion's share of the credit goes to the American people who do the work, raise the kids, and dream the dreams.

Now, at this moment of unprecedented good fortune, our people face a fundamental choice. Are we going to keep this progress and prosperity going?

**Audience:** Yes!

**Clinton:** Yes, we are. But, my friends, we can't take our future for granted. We cannot take it for granted. So let's just remember how we got here.

Eight years ago, when our party met in New York it was in a far different time for America. Our economy was in trouble, our society was divided, our political system was paralyzed. Ten million of our fellow citizens were out of work, interest rates were high, the deficit was $290 billion and rising.

After 12 years of Republican rule, the federal debt had quadrupled, imposing a crushing burden on our economy and on our children. Welfare rolls, crime, teen pregnancy, income and equality; all had been skyrocketing, and our government was part of the problem, not part of the solution.

I saw all this in a very personal way in 1992. Out there in the real America with many of you. I remember a child telling me her father broke down at the dinner table because he lost his job.

I remember an older couple crying in front of me because they had to choose between filling their shopping carts and filling their prescriptions.

I remember a hard working immigrant in a hotel kitchen who said his son was not really free because it wasn't safe for him to play in the neighborhood park.

I ran for president to change the future for those people. And I asked you to embrace new ideas, rooted in enduring values; opportunity for all, responsibility from all, and a community of all Americans.

You gave me the chance to turn those ideas and values into action after I made one of the very best decisions of my entire life, asking Al Gore to be my partner.

Now, first we proposed a new economic strategy—get rid of the deficit to reduce interest rates, invest more in our people, sell more American products abroad.

We sent our plan to Congress. It passed by a single vote in both Houses. In a deadlocked Senate, Al Gore cast the tie-breaking vote.

Now, not a single Republican supported it. Here's what their leaders said.

Their leaders said our plan would increase the deficit, kill jobs, and give us a one-way ticket to a recession.

Time has not been kind to their predictions. Now, remember, our Republican friends said then they would absolutely not be held responsible for our economic policies.

I hope the American people take them at their word.

Now, today after seven-and-a-half years of hard effort, we're in the midst of the longest economic expansion in history. More than 22 million new jobs, the lowest unemployment in 30 years, the lowest female unemployment in 40 years, the lowest Hispanic and African-American unemployment rate ever recorded, and the highest home ownership in history.

Now, along the way in 1995 we turned back the largest cuts in history in

Medicare, Medicaid, education, and the environment. And just two years later we proved that we could find a way to balance the budget and protect our values.

Today we have gone from the largest deficit in history to the largest surpluses in history. And if—but only if we stay on course, we can make America debt free for the first time since Andy Jackson was president in 1835.

For the first time in decades, wages are rising at all income levels, we have the lowest child poverty in 20 years, the lowest poverty rate for single mothers ever recorded.

The average family's income has gone up more than $5,000, and for African-American families, even more.

The number of families who own stock in our country has grown by 40 percent.

You know, Harry Truman's old saying has never been more true. "If you want to live like a Republican, you better vote for the Democrats."

But our progress is about far more than economics. America is also more hopeful, more secure, and more free. We're more hopeful because we're turning our schools around with higher standards, more accountability, more investment.

We have doubled funding for Head Start and provided after school and mentoring to more than a million more young people.

We're putting 100,000 well-trained teachers in the early grades to lower class size. Ninety-five percent of our schools are already connected to the Internet.

Reading, math, and SAT scores are up and more students than ever are going on to college thanks to the biggest expansion of college aid since the G.I. Bill fifty years ago.

Now, don't let anybody tell you that all children can't learn or that our public schools can't make the grade. Yes, they can. Yes, they can.

Now, we're also more hopeful because we ended welfare as we knew it. Now those who can work must work.

On that we and the Republicans agree. But we Democrats also insisted on support for good parenting. So that poor children don't go hungry or lose their health care, unmarried teens stay in school, and people get the job training, child care, and transportation they need.

It has worked.

Today there are more than $7\frac{1}{2}$ million people who have moved from welfare to work, and the welfare rolls in our administration have been cut in half.

Because of the way we cut taxes, to help Americans meet the challenges of working and child rearing, this year alone our Hope scholarship and Life-Long Learning tax credits will help ten million families pay for college.

Our Earned Income tax credit will help 15 million families work their way into the middle class. Twenty-five million families will get a $500 child tax credit.

Our Empowerment tax zone credits are bringing new businesses and new jobs to our hardest pressed communities from the inner cities to Appalachia to the Mississippi delta to our native American reservations.

And the typical American family today is paying a lower share of its income in federal income taxes than at anytime during the past 35 years.

We are more hopeful because of the Family and Medical Leave Act. A bill that the previous administration vetoed. They said it would cost jobs.

It's the first bill I signed.

And we now have a test. Twenty-two million new jobs later, over twenty million Americans have been able to take a little time off to care for a newborn child or a sick relative.

That's what it means. That's what it really means to be pro-family.

We are a more secure country because we cut crime with tougher enforcement, more than 100,000 new community police officers, a ban on assault weapons, and the Brady law, which has kept guns out of the hands of half a million felons, fugitives and stalkers.

Today, crime in America is at a twenty-five year low. And we're more secure because of advances in health care.

We've extended the life of the Medicare trust fund by 26 years, added coverage for cancer screening, and cutting edge clinical trials.

We're coming closer to cures for dreaded diseases.

We made sure that people with disabilities could go to work without losing their health care, and that people could switch jobs without losing their coverage.

We dramatically improved diabetes care, we provided health coverage under the Children's Health Insurance Program to two million previously uninsured children, and for the first time in our history, more than 90 percent of our kids have been immunized against serious childhood diseases.

You can be proud of that Democratic record. We are more secure because our environment is cleaner.

We have set aside more land in the lower 48 states than any administration since Teddy Roosevelt. Saving national treasures like Yellowstone, the great California Redwoods, the Florida Everglades.

Moreover, our air is cleaner, our water is cleaner, our food is safer, and our economy is stronger.

You can grow the economy and protect the environment at the same time.

Now, we are more free because we are closer today to the one America of our dreams. Celebrating our diversity, affirming our common humanity, opposing all forms of bigotry from church burnings to racial profiling to murderous hate crimes.

We are fighting for the employment nondiscrimination legislation and for equal pay for women.

We have found ways to mend, not end affirmative action.

We have given America the most diverse administration in history. It really looks like America.

You know, if I could just get my administration up here, it would be just as good a picture as anything you saw a couple of weeks ago in Philadelphia, the real people running it.

And, and we created Americorps, which already has given more than

150,000 of our young people a chance to earn some money for college by serving in our communities.

We are more secure and we are more free because of our leadership in the world for peace, freedom and prosperity, helping to end a generation of conflict in northern Ireland, stopping a brutal ethnic cleansing in Bosnia and Kosovo and bringing the Middle East closer than ever to a comprehensive peace.

We have built stronger ties to Africa, Asia and our, Latin American and Caribbean neighbors, we brought Poland, Hungary and the Czech Republic into NATO. We're working with Russia to destroy nuclear weapons and materials.

We are fighting head on the new threats and injustices of the global age, terrorism, narcotrafficking, biological and chemical warfare. The trafficking of women and young girls and the deadly spread of aids and in the great tradition of President Jimmy Carter, who is here tonight, we are still the world's leading force for human rights around the world.

Thank you, President Carter.

Now, the American military is the best trained, best equipped, most effective fighting force in the world. Our men and women have shown that time and again in Bosnia, in Kosovo, in Haiti, in Iraq.

I can tell you that their strength, their spirit, their courage and their commitment to freedom have never been greater.

Any adversary who believes those who say otherwise is making a grave mistake. Now, now, my fellow Americans, that is the record.

Or as that very famous Los Angeles detective, Sergeant Joe Friday used to say, "Just the facts, ma'am."

Let's remember, I ask you, let's remember the standard our Republican friends used to have for whether a party should continue in office.

My fellow Americans, are we better off today than we were eight years ago? You bet we are. You bet we are.

But, but—yes, we are, but we are not just better off. We are also a better country.

We are today more tolerant, more decent, more humane and more united. Now, that's the purpose of prosperity.

Since 1992, America has grown not just economically, but as a community.

Yes, jobs are up, but so are adoptions.

Yes, the debt is down, but so is teen pregnancy.

We are becoming both more diverse and more united.

My fellow Americans, tonight we can say with gratitude and humility, we built our bridge to the 21st century. We crossed that bridge together, and we are not going back. . . .

For those who say, and I'm sure you heard this somewhere in the last few days, to those who say the progress of these last eight years was just some sort of accident that we just kind of coasted along, let me be clear.

America's success was not a matter of chance. It was a matter of choice.

And today, today America faces another choice. It is every bit as momentous as the one we faced eight years ago. For what a nation does with its good fortune is just as stern a test of its character, values and judgment as how it deals with adversity.

My fellow Americans, this is a big election. With great consequences for every American because the differences, the honest differences between our candidates and their visions are so profound.

We can have a good old-fashioned election here. We should posit that our opponents are good, honorable, patriotic people and that we have honest differences, but the differences are there.

Consider this, just this. We in America would already have this year a real patient's bill of rights, a minimum wage increase, stronger equal pay laws for women and middle class tax cuts for college tuition and long-term care if the Democratic party win the majority in Congress with Dick Gephardt as Speaker and Tom Daschle as majority leader.

And come November, they will be.

Now, that has to be clear to people, and that is why every House and every Senate seat is important.

But if you will give me one moment of personal privilege, I'd like to say a word about Hillary.

When I first met her 30 years ago, she already had an abiding passion to help children, and she has pursued it ever since. Her very first job out of law school was with the Children's Defense Fund.

Every year I was governor, she took lots of time away from her law practice to work for better schools or better children's health or jobs for parents who live in poor areas.

Then when I became president, she became a full-time advocate for her lifetime cause, and what a job she has done.

She championed at family leave law, children's health insurance, increased support for foster children and adoptions. She wrote a best selling book about caring for our children, and then she took care of them by giving all the profits to children's charities.

For 30 years, 30 years from the first day I met her, she has always been there for all our kids.

She has been a great First Lady.

She has always been there for our family, and she will always be there for the families of New York and America.

Now, of course, we all know, we all know that the biggest choice that the American people have to make this year is in the presidential race.

Now, you all know how I feel. But it is not my decision to make. That belongs to the American people.

I just want to tell all of you here in this great arena and all the folks watching and listening at home a few things that I know about Al Gore.

We have worked closely together for eight years now in the most challenging moments when we faced the most difficult issues of war and peace, of whether to take on some powerful interest, he was always there. And he always told me exactly what he thought was right.

Everybody knows he is thoughtful and hard working, but I can tell you personally he is one strong leader.

In 1993, in 1993, there was nobody around the table more willing to make the tough choices to balance the budget the right way and take this tough

605

stance against balancing the budget on the backs of the poor and working people of America.

I have seen this kind of positioning and this kind of strength time and time again, whether it was, in how we reform welfare or in protecting the environment or in closing the digital divide or bringing jobs to rural and urban America through the Empowerment Zone program, the greatest champion of ordinary Americans has always been Al Gore.

I'll tell you something else about him.

More than anybody else I have known in public life, Al Gore understands the future, and how sweeping change and scientific breakthroughs will affect ordinary Americans lives and I think we need somebody in the White House at the dawn of the 21st century who really understands the future.

Finally, I want to say something more personal. Virtually every week for the last seven-and-a-half years, until he became occupied with more important matters, Al Gore and I had lunch, and we talked about the business between us and the business of America, but we would often talk about our families, what our kids were doing, how school was going, what was going on in their lives.

I know him. He is a profoundly good man.

He loves his children more than life, and he has a perfectly wonderful wife who has fought against homelessness and who has done something for me and all Americans in bringing the cause of mental health into the broad sunlight of our national public life.

We owe Tipper Gore our thanks.

Al has picked a great partner in Joe Lieberman. . . .

Hillary and I have known Joe for 30 years, since we were in Connecticut in law school. I supported him in his first race for public office in 1970 when I learned he had been a freedom rider, going into danger to register black voters in the then segregated South.

It should not be a surprise to anyone that Al Gore picked the leader of the new Democrats to be his Vice President because Joe Lieberman has supported all our efforts to reform welfare, reduce crime, protect the environment, protect civil rights and a woman's right to choose, and to keep this economy going.

All of them.

And he has shown time and time again that he will work with President Gore to keep putting people and progress over partisanship.

Now, it's up, frankly, to the Presidential nominee and the Vice Presidential nominee to engage in this debate and to point out the differences, but there are two issues I care a lot about, and I want to make brief comments on them, and I hope I've earned the right to make comments on them.

One is the economy. I know a little something about that.

And the other is our efforts to build one America.

First, on the economy. Al Gore and Joe Lieberman will keep our prosperity going by paying down the debt, investing in education and health care, moving more people from welfare to work, and providing family tax cuts we can afford.

Now, that stands in stark contrast to the position of our Republican friends. Here is their position. They say we have a big projected ten-year surplus, and they want to spend every dime of it and then some on tax cuts right now.

That would leave nothing for education or Medicare, prescription drugs, nothing to extend the life of Medicare and Social Security for the baby boomers, nothing in case the projected surpluses don't come in.

Now, think about your own family's budget for a minute. Or your own business budget.

Would you sign a binding contract today to spend all your projected income for a decade, leaving nothing for your family's basic needs?

**Audience:** No!

**Clinton:** Nothing for emergencies?

**Audience:** No!

**Clinton:** Nothing for a cushion in case you didn't get the raise you thought you were going to get. Of course you wouldn't do that and America shouldn't do it, either.

We should stick with what works.

Now, let me say something to you that's even more important than the economy to me.

When Al Gore picked Joe Lieberman, the first Jewish American to join a national ticket to be his partner, and he joined with our Presidential nominee who has, along with his great mother and late father, a lifetime commitment to civil rights and equal opportunity for all, even when it was not popular down home in the South.

When they did that, we had a ticket that embodies the Democratic commitment to one America. They believe in civil rights and equal opportunity for everybody. They believe in a woman's right to choose, and this may be the most important of all.

They believe the folks that you're buying your soft drinks and popcorn from here at the Staples Center should have the exact same chance that they do to send their kids to college and give them a good life and a good future.

My fellow Americans, I am very proud of our leaders, and I want you to know that the opportunity I have had to serve as President at the dawn of a new era in human history has been an honor, a privilege, and a joy.

I have done everything I knew how to do to empower the American people, to unleash their amazing optimism and imagination and hard work, to turn our country around from where it was in 1992 and to get us moving forward together.

Now, what I want you to understand tonight is that the best is still out there. The best is yet to come if we make the right choices in this election year.

The choices will make all the difference.

In February the American people achieved the longest economic expansion in our history. When that happened, I asked our folks at the White House when the previous longest economic expansion was.

You know when it was? It was from 1961 through 1969.

Now, I want the young people especially to listen to this. I remember this well.

I graduated from high school in 1964. Our country was still very sad because of President Kennedy's death, but full of hope under the leadership of President Johnson.

And I assumed then like most Americans that our economy was absolutely on automatic, that nothing could derail it. I also believed then that our civil rights problems would all be solved in Congress and the courts, and in 1964 when we were enjoying the longest economic expansion in history, we never dreamed that Vietnam would so divide and wound America. So we took it for granted.

And then before we knew it, there were riots in the streets, even here.

The leaders that I adored as a young man—Martin Luther King and Robert Kennedy—were killed.

Lyndon Johnson, a president from my part of the country, I admired so much for all he did for civil rights, for the elderly and the poor, said he would not run again because our nation was so divided.

And then we had an election in 1968 that took America on a far different and more divisive course, and you know within months after that election the last longest economic expansion in history was itself history.

Why am I telling you this tonight? Not to take you down, but to keep you looking up.

I have waited, not as President, but as your fellow citizen for over 30 years to see my country once again in the position to build a future of our dreams for our children.

We are a great and good people, and we have an even better chance this time than we did then, with no great internal crisis and no great external threat.

Still, I have lived long enough to know that opportunities must be seized or they will be lost.

My friends, fifty-four years ago this week I was born in a summer storm to a young widow in a small Southern town. America gave me the chance to live my dreams. And I have tried as hard as I knew how to give you a better chance to live yours.

Now my hair's a little grayer, my wrinkles are a little deeper, but with the same optimism and hope I brought to the work I loved so eight years ago, I want you to know my heart is filled with gratitude.

My fellow Americans, the future of our country is now in your hands. You must think hard, feel deeply, and choose wisely.

And remember, whenever you think about me, keep putting people first. Keep building those bridges.

And don't stop thinking about tomorrow.

# DEMOCRATIC PARTY PLATFORM
## August 15, 2000

*Democrats convened August 14–17, 2000, in Los Angeles to bid an emotional farewell to their president of the last eight years, Bill Clinton, and to rally support behind the party's new standard-bearer, Vice President Al Gore, and his running mate, Senator Joseph I. Lieberman. The party that had been known for its fractiousness in the past was remarkably unified going into the convention. One sign of that was the adoption of the party platform on August 15 by voice vote without dissent. It was the third convention in a row that Democrats had adopted a platform turning the party away from its liberal New Deal roots to a more centrist philosophy that called for economic growth, personal responsibility, family vitality, law and order, and military readiness.*

*Some party officials speculated that the unity resulted in part from Clinton's legislative successes on deficit reduction and welfare reform; others suggested that the party recognized that a unified front was crucial to holding on to the White House and regaining control of the House and Senate. Whatever the reasons, there were grumblings among some traditional Democratic supporters that the party might be moving too far from its roots. Union officials were still upset about the free trade agreement with China that the Clinton administration had pushed through Congress. Some black Democrats also voiced concerns about the strength of the party's commitment to issues such as affirmative action. Lieberman spent some time at the convention assuring the leaders of the National Education Association that, despite his previous support for an experimental school voucher program, he would now join Gore in opposition to vouchers. For months later, after Gore's loss to Texas governor George W. Bush in one of the closest elections in American history, it seemed likely that the Democratic Party would once again be debating its position on these and a host of other concerns. (China trade deal, p. 213; presidential election, pp. 999, 1025)*

*Few of those concerns surfaced publicly during the four days of the convention. The most visible tension at the convention was not over the substance of the platform or party philosophy, but over when Clinton would leave Los Angeles and turn the spotlight over to Gore. Like most vice presidents seeking to replace a sitting president, Gore had experienced trouble throughout his campaign emerging from Clinton's shadows, in large part because he did not have the easy and instant rapport with the public that Clinton did. But Gore had the added problem of figuring out how to take credit for the achievements of the administration—many of which he had helped bring to fruition—without also being tarred by the personal scandal that had led to Clinton's impeachment in 1998.*

*Gore campaign officials had hoped that Clinton would spend only a day or so in Los Angeles before delivering his valedictory speech on August 14, the opening day of the convention. He would then travel to Michigan for a campaign rally with Gore, who would then proceed to Los Angeles as the new head of the Democratic Party. Instead, the president spent the weekend in Los Angeles, attending a round of parties and raising money for his presidential library and his wife's campaign for the New York Senate seat. Any hopes in the Gore camp that reminders of Clinton's affair with White House intern Monica Lewinsky would not emerge during the convention were dashed when, en route to Los Angeles, Clinton stopped in Illinois to give a personal and public assessment of his presidency, including his relationship with Lewinsky, to a group of evangelical ministers. (Clinton convention speech, p. 596)*

## *Holding to a Centrist Position*

*One clear legacy of the Clinton presidency was the party platform, which Clinton had pushed into the political center from its liberal posture of the New Deal-Great Society eras. During the drafting process, the Gore campaign turned aside liberal attempts to pull the platform back toward the left to develop a document that largely endorsed the vice president's centrist position on fiscal, trade, environmental, education, and military policy. In so doing, the Gore camp also turned away from its own move to the left to combat a challenge from former senator Bill Bradley during the primary season.*

*The platform called for a $500 billion tax cut spread across ten years, promised to eliminate the national debt by 2012, and set aside part of the surplus to strengthen the Social Security and Medicare programs. It endorsed "fair and free" trade and "fast track" authority, which allowed the president to negotiate trade agreements that were not subject to congressional approval. The platform supported several of Gore's environmental campaign promises, including prohibiting logging and drilling in the wilderness areas of national forests, restrictions on oil drilling off the coasts of Florida and California, and restoration of the Florida Everglades.*

*On education the platform called for federal funding to increase teachers' pay, hire more teachers, and reduce class size. It also called for more accountability, some testing of students, and testing of all new teachers. It also called for periodic evaluations of all teachers to help make it easier for schools to get rid of bad teachers. The platform also endorsed women's right to abortion, an end to racial profiling, and the adoption of a strong campaign finance bill and federal hate crimes legislation. A move by some lib-*

*erals to call a moratorium on the use of the death penalty failed, but the platform called for thorough postconviction reviews, DNA testing, and "effective legal representation" in all death-row cases.*

*In addition to a death penalty moratorium, liberals also sought planks that would punish corporations for paying low wages, provide better health care for prisoners, and impose tougher labor and environmental rules for international trade. All these were either voted down overwhelmingly or withdrawn during a final drafting session in Cleveland on July 29. Liberals also sought to excise a plank that called for a limited missile defense system, arguing that the program was untested and likely to start a new arms race. Gore supporters argued that, without the plank, Republicans could argue that Democrats were soft on defense. Republican nominee George W. Bush supported a massive missile defense system based on land, sea, and possibly space.*

*Some of the liberals attending the Cleveland meeting spoke out against the control over the platform the Gore campaign exercised. "They talk about a big tent," Rep. Dennis J. Kucinich of Ohio said of the Gore camp. "But this tent just got a bit smaller." Others, such as Tom Hayden, a California state senator, said the platform did nothing to address the challenge from the Green Party, whose presidential candidate was consumer activist Ralph Nader. During the fall campaign, the Green Party's progressive stance on labor and environmental issues drew enough support away from the liberal end of the political spectrum that the Democrats began to worry that Nader might cost Gore the election in key states.* (Nader candidacy, p. 895)

*Still, several organizations that in the past would have opposed the centrist positions outlined in the platform decided not put up much of a fight in 2000. Organized labor, for example, had for decades opposed free trade, most recently in the fight to normalize trade relations with China, but the AFL-CIO quietly accepted the plank calling for "free and fair trade." Teachers unions chose not to fight the language calling for testing teachers and firing those who did not measure up. In part that was because many of these issues had already been fought and settled (even if the settlement was an agreement to disagree) during Clinton's presidency. But the Democrats' unity also stemmed from their perception that the centrist policies of the Gore campaign were far preferable to the policies outlined by Bush. "There are sections of this platform that I am not wild about," said Senator Richard Durbin of Illinois, a co-chair of the platform committee. "But the bottom line is, we know how much different and how much better this is than the Republican alternative." Amy Issacs, national director of the liberal Americans for Democratic Action, agreed. She added that, although "liberals in this country are very uneasy" with the centrist direction of the Democratic Party, when the Democratic platform is put "up against what is being offered by the Bush campaign, there is no contest."*

## The Convention: A Sendoff and a Welcome

*Like the Republican convention in Philadelphia two weeks earlier, the Democrats had virtually no decisions to make at their convention, and so events were designed to showcase the Democratic Party to the viewing public. Like the Republicans, Democrats spread their nomination roll call vote across the first three nights, interspersing it with many short speeches delivered by party officials who either delivered a specific policy message or testified to Gore's record in government. One difference from the Republicans was that the Democrats could not keep to their schedule, so their convention had a feeling of spontaneity that was lacking in Philadelphia. Another difference was the abundance of high-tech gadgetry on the convention floor, a not-so-subtle hint that Democrats wanted viewers to see them as the party of the future. Each convention delegate was given a card that could be used at any of one hundred computer kiosks scattered around the convention floor and in hotels to get the latest information from party officials and to talk with other delegates. Convention speakers were asked to participate in online discussions on the Internet immediately after speaking.*

*The opening night ceremonies not only paid tribute to Clinton but also focused attention on Democratic women seeking election to the Senate— most prominently, Clinton's wife Hillary Rodham Clinton, who was running for a Senate seat in New York. Massachusetts senator Edward M. Kennedy, the Rev. Jesse L. Jackson, and speakers representing traditional liberal Democratic causes such as labor, gay rights, and women's right took center stage on Tuesday night August 15. Also stepping to the podium to endorse the Gore-Lieberman ticket was Bill Bradley, the former senator from New Jersey who had challenged Gore unsuccessfully for the nomination.*

*On Wednesday night, August 16, delegates and the viewing public were introduced to Gore's running mate, Joe Lieberman, a senator from Connecticut and the first Jew to run on a major party ticket. Lieberman, who was formally nominated the following evening, still seemed a little stunned by his selection. "Is America a great country or what?" he asked rhetorically in his acceptance speech.*

*Gore was also formally declared to be the Democratic presidential nominee on August 16. He was nominated by his college roommate, the actor Tommy Lee Jones, and was seconded by his oldest daughter, Karena Gore Schiff. Gore appeared unannounced on stage after his daughter's speech, waved to the crowd, and then left the stage as the rolling ballot continued. Ironically, Florida's delegation gave Gore the votes he needed for the nomination—2,170. The honor was intended to signal that the Gore campaign would fight for Florida's vote; little did anyone suspect at the time just what that fight would entail. It was in Florida that Gore's battle to win a majority in the electoral college came to an end.*

*On the final evening of the convention Gore strode on stage at the convention hall, gave his wife Tipper a long kiss, and turned to the wildly cheering delegates. "I stand here tonight as my own man," he declared, and then ticked off the planks in his campaign platform. "If you entrust me with the presidency," he concluded, "I know I won't always be the most exciting politician. But I pledge to you tonight: I will work for you every day and I will never let you down."* (Gore, Lieberman acceptance speeches, p. 617)

*Like the Republican convention, much of the Democratic convention re-*

*volved around star-studded parties and fund-raisers. About an hour after delivering his acceptance speech, in which he promised to make campaign finance reform his first legislative priority, Gore attended a traditional end-of-convention concert that raised $5.2 million for his campaign. As they had in Philadelphia, corporations and lobbying associations that had business before Congress sponsored many of the receptions and dinners in Los Angeles. The most controversial event might have been a corporate-sponsored, invitation-only party hosted by Representative Loretta Sanchez of California, the chair of the political action committee Hispanic Unity USA. Sanchez had planned to stage the event at the home of* Playboy *magazine founder Hugh Hefner. Fearing that an event at the Playboy Mansion would send the wrong signals to voters, even though Gore himself had accepted campaign contributions from Hefner, Democratic officials pressured Sanchez to move the party to B.B. King's Blues Club at Universal Studios. Sanchez eventually agreed to the move but canceled her scheduled speech at the convention. By then, the story was attracting more media attention than many of the convention events purposefully staged for that purpose.*

*Following are excerpts from the Democratic Party platform, adopted August 15, 2000, by voice vote at the Democratic National Convention in Los Angeles. The document was obtained from the Internet at http://www.dems2000.com/AboutTheConvention/03a_introduction.html.*

**Fiscal Discipline.** . . . Today, for most families, the federal tax burden is the lowest it has been in twenty years. The Bush tax slash takes a different course. It is bigger than any cut Newt Gingrich ever dreamed of. It would let the richest one percent of Americans afford a new sports car and middle class Americans afford a warm soda. It is so out-of-step with reality that the Republican Congress refused to enact it. It would undermine the American economy and undercut our prosperity. . . . Democrats seek the right kind of tax relief—tax cuts that are specifically targeted to help those who need them the most.

These tax cuts would let families live their values by helping them save for college, invest in their job skills and lifelong learning, pay for health insurance, afford child care, eliminate the marriage penalty for working families, care for elderly or disabled loved ones, invest in clean cars and clean homes, and build additional security for their retirement.

**Retirement Security.** . . . The choice for Americans on this vital part of our national heritage has never been more clear: Democrats believe in using our prosperity to save Social Security; the Republicans' tax cut would prevent America from ensuring our senior citizens have a secure retirement. We owe it to America's children and their children to make the strength and solvency of Social Security a major national priority.

That's why Al Gore is committed to making Social Security safe and secure for more than half a century by using the savings from our current unprecedented prosperity to strengthen the Social Security Trust Fund in preparation for the retirement of the Baby Boom generation. . . .

To build on the success of Social Security, Al Gore has proposed the creation of Retirement Savings Plus—voluntary, tax-free, personally-controlled, privately-managed savings accounts with a government match that would help couples build a nest egg of up to $400,000. . . .

**Education.** . . . George W. Bush and the Republican Party offer neither real accountability nor reasonable investment [in education]. . . . Their version of accountability relies on private school vouchers that would offer too few dollars to too few children to escape their failing schools. These vouchers would pass the buck on accountability while pulling bucks out of the schools that need them most. . . .

By the end of the next presidential term, we should have a fully qualified, well trained teacher in every classroom in every school in every part of this country and every teacher should pass a rigorous test to get there.

By the end of the next presidential term, every failing school in America should be turned around—or shut down and reopened under new public leadership.

By the end of the next presidential term, we should ensure that no high school student graduates unless they have mastered the basics of reading and math—so that the diploma they receive really means something.

By the end of the next presidential term, parents across the nation ought to be able to choose the best public school for their children. . . .

We should make a college education as universal as high school is today. Al Gore has proposed a new National Tuition Savings program to tie together state tuition savings programs in more than 30 states so that parents can save for college tax-free and inflation-free. We propose a tax cut for tuition and fees for post-high school education and training that allows families to choose either a $10,000 a year tax deduction or a $2,800 tax credit. . . .

**Fighting Crime.** . . . Strong and Sensible Gun Laws. . . . Democrats believe that we should fight gun crime on all fronts—with stronger laws and stronger enforcement. That's why Democrats fought and passed the Brady Law and the Assault Weapons Ban. We increased federal, state, and local gun crime prosecution by 22 percent since 1992. Now gun crime is down by 35 percent.

Now we must do even more. We need mandatory child safety locks, to protect our children. We should require a photo license I.D., a full background check, and a gun safety test to buy a new handgun in America. We support more federal gun prosecutors, ATF agents and inspectors, and giving states and communities another 10,000 prosecutors to fight gun crime.

**Hate Crimes.** . . . Hate crimes are more than assaults on people, they are assaults on the very idea of America. They should be punished with extra force. Protections should include hate violence based on gender, disability or sexual orientation. And the Republican Congress should stop standing in the way of this pro-civil rights, anti-crime legislation. . . .

**Valuing Families.** . . . Responsible Entertainment. . . . Parents and the entertainment industry must accept more responsibility. Many parents are not aware of the resources available to them, such as the V-chip technology in television sets and Internet filtering devices, that can help them shield children from violent entertainment. The entertainment industry must accept more responsibility and exercise more self-restraint, by strictly enforcing movie ratings, by taking a close look at violence in its own advertising, and by determining whether the ratings systems are allowing too many children to be exposed to too much violence and cruelty.

**Health Care.** Universal Health Coverage. There is much more left to do. We must redouble our efforts to bring the uninsured into coverage step-by-step and as soon as possible. We should guarantee access to affordable health care for every child in America. We should expand coverage to working families, including more Medicaid assistance to help with the transition from welfare to work. . . . In addition, Americans aged 55 to 65—the fastest growing group of uninsured—should be allowed to buy into the Medicare program to get the coverage they need. By taking these steps, we can move our nation closer to the goal of providing universal health coverage for all Americans.

. . . A Real Patients' Bill of Rights. Medical decisions should be made by patients and their doctors and nurses, not accountants and bureaucrats at the end of a phone line a thousand miles away. . . . Americans need a real, enforceable Patients' Bill of Rights with the right to see a specialist, the right to appeal decisions to an outside board, guaranteed coverage of emergency room care, and the right to sue when they are unfairly denied coverage. . . .

**Protecting and Strengthening Medicare.** It is time we ended the tragedy of elderly Americans being forced to choose between meals and medication. It is time we modernized Medicare with a new prescription drug benefit. This is an essential step in making sure that the best new cures and therapies are available to our seniors and disabled Americans. We cannot afford to permit our seniors to receive only part of the medical care they need. . . .

**Abortion.** Choice. The Democratic Party stands behind the right of every woman to choose, consistent with *Roe v. Wade*, and regardless of ability to pay. We believe it is a fundamental constitutional liberty that individual Americans—not government—can best take responsibility for making the most difficult and intensely personal decisions regarding reproduction. This year's Supreme Court rulings show to us all that eliminating a woman's right to choose is only one justice away. That's why the stakes in this election are as high as ever. . . .

**Campaign Finance Reform.** . . . The big-time lobbyists and special interest were so eager [in 2000] to invest in George W. Bush and deliver campaign cash to him hand-over-fist that he became the first major party nominee to pull out of the primary election financing structure and refuse to abide by campaign spending limits.

In this year's presidential primaries it became clear that the Republican establishment is violently opposed to John McCain's call for reforming our democracy. Al Gore supports John McCain's campaign for political reform. In fact, the McCain-Feingold bill is the very first piece of legislation that a President Al Gore will submit to Congress—and he will fight for it until it becomes the law of the land.

Then he will go even further—much further. He will insist on tough new lobbying reform, publicly-guaranteed TV time for debates and advocacy by candidates, and a crackdown on special interest issue ads. . . .

**Transforming the Military.** . . . The Democratic Party understands that, good as they are, the armed forces must continue to evolve. They must not only remain prepared for conventional military action, but must sharpen their ability to deal with new missions and new kinds of threats. They must become more agile, more versatile, and must more completely incorporate the revolutionary implications and advantages of American supremacy in information technology.

. . . A high-tech fighting force must recruit, train, and retain a professional all-volunteer force of the highest caliber. . . . While the number of soldiers and families on food stamps is down by two-thirds over the past decade, it is unacceptable that any member of our armed forces should have to rely on food stamps. Al Gore is committed to equal treatment of all service members and believes all patriotic Americans be allowed to serve their country without discrimination, persecution, and violence. . . .

**Middle East.** . . . Jerusalem is the capital of Israel and should remain an undivided city accessible to people of all faiths. In view of the government of Israel's courageous decision to withdraw from Lebanon, we believe special responsibility now resides with Syria to make a contribution toward peace. The recently-held Camp David summit, while failing to bridge all the gaps between Israel and the Palestinians, demonstrated President Clinton's resolve to do all the United States could do to bring an end to that long conflict. Al Gore, as president, will demonstrate the same resolve. . . .

# DEMOCRATIC NATIONAL
# CONVENTION AND SPEECHES
## August 16, 17, 2000

*In one of the most important performances of his political life, Vice President Al Gore used his August 17 speech accepting the Democratic Party's presidential nomination to allay many of the concerns that had been troubling his candidacy. In a deft speech that he reportedly largely drafted himself, Gore asserted his independence from President Bill Clinton, promising to fight "for the people" and never let them down. He acknowledged his own shortcomings as a campaigner—"I know I won't always be the most exciting politician," he said, as he tried to shift the presidential campaign from a personality contest to one focused on the issues.*

*Gore faced a formidable array of problems—some of his own making, some largely out of his control. He had to show, for example, that he had played a key role in the Clinton administration's accomplishments of the last eight years but not in its personal scandals. Only hours before Gore addressed the Democratic National Convention in Los Angeles, news leaked out in Washington that a grand jury had been convened to determine whether President Clinton should be indicted after he left office for lying under oath about his relationship with a White House intern. Gore also had to face repeated allegations about the propriety of his own campaign fundraising activities. A week after the convention, Attorney General Janet Reno for the third time said there was not enough evidence to warrant naming a special prosecutor to investigate those allegations.*

*Gore, whose policy platform sat firmly in the center of the political spectrum, also had to stem defections from the liberal wing of the party, many of whom were threatening to sit out the election or to vote for the third-party candidacy of Ralph Nader. Running under the banner of the Green Party, the consumer activist contended that there were no real differences between the two major parties and that both were equally beholden to the special interests in Washington.*

*The vice president also had to contend with his inability to forge an emotional tie with the voters. A serious and intelligent man with a mastery of policy detail, Gore in private was said to be charming and persuasive. In campaign appearances, however, he often came across as wooden, his speeches delivered in a dull monotone with little of the spark that energized crowds. Occasionally Gore could be overbearing or patronizing. In contrast, his Republican opponent, Texas governor George W. Bush, projected amiability and in general seemed more comfortable than Gore when working a crowd, often speaking in the generalities and campaign platitudes that voters seemed to find reassuring.*

*In his acceptance speech Gore addressed the issues forcefully and confidently. Declaring his independence from Clinton, Gore told the wildly cheering delegates that he was his own man. Aligning himself with the progressive tradition of the Democratic Party, he promised to fight "for the people" against the "powerful interests" that "stand in your way." Seeking to deflect criticism that he did not have the same rapport with the voters as Bush, Gore said the presidency "is more than a popularity contest" and that he was there to "talk seriously about the issues" because the voters "deserve to know specifically what a candidate proposes to do."*

*At the heart of the vice president's speech, however, was an effort to shed his image as a politician who wanted so much to be president that he paid too much attention to the opinion polls and was too willing to tailor his positions to his audience. "I want you to know me for who I truly am," Gore told the convention as he spoke about the values instilled in him by his parents—"faith and family, duty and honor, and trying to make the world a better place."*

*The speech buoyed Democratic delegates in the convention center and struck a responsive chord among some voters. Gore had arrived in Los Angeles trailing Bush in the national opinion polls. When he departed barely forty-eight hours later to begin a campaign swing down the Mississippi River with his running mate, Connecticut senator Joseph I. Lieberman, opinion polls were showing that the Democratic ticket had pulled even with or a few points ahead of the Republican ticket. In one of the many ironies of the election, it was Gore who in the end won the popular vote, although Bush won the disputed contest in Florida that ultimately gave him the presidency.*

## A Lifelong Dream

*Born March 31, 1948, Al Gore was the son of a senator from Tennessee who always expected his son to take up a career in politics—and to some day be president. The young Gore attended the elite St. Alban's prep school in Washington and spent summers on the family farm near Carthage, Tennessee. Gore graduated from Harvard in 1969, enlisted in the army, and spent five months in Vietnam as an army reporter. He returned to Nashville in 1970, where he married his high school sweetheart, went to work as a reporter for the* Nashville Tennessean, *and was crushed when his father lost his bid for reelection in 1970. The senior Gore, who supported civil rights and opposed the Vietnam War, was considered too aloof and too out of step with the voters of Tennessee. In 1976 Gore, at age twenty-eight, ran successfully for an open U.S. House seat, which he held until his election to a*

*U.S. Senate seat in 1984. Four years later, in 1988, Gore, who was just turning forty, made his first attempt at the presidency, in some measure to please his father, who said he wanted to see his son elected president before he died. Gore lost the nomination to Massachusetts governor Michael Dukakis, but his campaign earned him name recognition outside Washington and Tennessee. In 1992 and again in 1996 Bill Clinton tapped him to be his running mate.*

*As vice president Gore may have enjoyed unprecedented authority. Unlike previous vice presidents who had limited access to the president, Gore lunched weekly with Clinton and had full responsibility for a range of interests, including environmental and high-tech policy. He was also in charge of the "reinventing government" project, finding ways for the federal government to improve delivery of services with fewer people and at less cost. The project pared some 377,000 federal jobs, making it the smallest federal government since Dwight D. Eisenhower was president. It also eliminated some two hundred outdated or unnecessary federal programs.*

*As the 2000 campaign season approached, Gore's claim on the democratic presidential nomination seemed unassailable. Former New Jersey senator Bill Bradley challenged Gore in some of the early primaries but dropped out after failing to win, or even come close, in any. Like Bush, that left Gore free to concentrate on shoring up his support, finding his opponent's vulnerabilities, and selecting a running mate.*

## *Lieberman Chosen*

*On August 7, Gore announced that he had selected Joseph Lieberman as his running mate. Lieberman was the first Jew ever to run on a major party ticket, and his selection was said to illustrate not only Gore's commitment to tolerance but also his willingness to take political risk. Lieberman was an Orthodox Jew, who observed the Sabbath from sundown on Friday to sundown on Saturday. As a result Lieberman said he would not campaign on Saturdays, although he quickly assured voters that, as a sitting vice president, he would break the Sabbath if, for example, he were needed to break a tie vote in the Senate. Unlike 1960, when John F. Kennedy became the first Roman Catholic presidential nominee, Lieberman's selection seemed more a celebration of religious diversity in the country rather than a cause for concern, although some Jewish leaders said they feared a possible anti-Semitic backlash.*

*Lieberman's selection was seen as beneficial to the Gore campaign in at least two others ways. He was the first Democrat in the Senate to denounce Clinton publicly for his affair with Monica S. Lewinsky. At the time, Lieberman spoke of his "deep disappointment and personal anger" with the president, and called his behavior "immoral" and "harmful." Lieberman was also a political moderate who had worked across party lines in the Senate, notably with Republican senator John McCain on campaign finance reform.*

*At the same time, Lieberman had also taken some positions that Gore had opposed. Lieberman, for example, had supported a pilot school voucher program and had expressed interest in allowing workers to invest part of their*

*Social Security payroll taxes in the stock market. The Bush camp wasted no time in suggesting the Lieberman was closer to the Republican nominee than to Gore on these issues, but Lieberman denied it. "With all due respect," he said, "I think that's like saying that the veterinarian and the taxidermist are in the same business because either way you get your dog back." Nonetheless, Lieberman and the Gore campaign took pains to reassure Democrats that the senator would support Gore on the issues. In addition to meeting privately with leaders of various labor unions and other organizations that generally backed Democrats, Lieberman appeared on five news shows the Sunday before the convention in an effort to minimize his differences with Gore.*

*Although he was not formally nominated as vice president until August 17, Lieberman delivered his acceptance speech on August 16. The speech was largely a testimony to Gore both as a man and as a leader and an attack on the Republican ticket, which Lieberman accused of using a lot of new rhetoric to cover up same old policies. Pointing to "very real differences" between the two parties, Lieberman said that even though the Republican camp talked about saving the environment, improving schools, and expanding health insurance coverage, they had done little to achieve those ends.*

## Gore's Acceptance Speech

*On the evening of August 17, Gore was introduced to the cheering convention delegates by his wife, Tipper, who showed a video album of family photos displaying "the man I love in a way you may not have seen him before." Coming on stage at the end of the video, Gore swept his wife into his arms and gave her a lengthy kiss that was the subject of television talk shows and newspaper op-ed columns for several days.*

*In his speech Gore mentioned Clinton by name only once, saying that "millions of Americans will live better lives for a long time to come because of the job that's been done by President Bill Clinton." He mentioned Bush not at all but drew pointed comparisons between the two men's credentials to be president and the differences in their programs. Drawing an implicit contrast with Bush, who joined the National Guard to avoid going to Vietnam, Gore spoke of his army service in Vietnam, although he acknowledged that he "didn't do the most, or run the gravest danger."*

*Gore promised that he would stand up to "the powerful forces and powerful interests" and stand up for "the working families." He then ran through a long list of policy promises, starting with making campaign finance reform the first piece of legislation he would send to Congress. He pledged to save and strengthen Social Security and Medicare, enact affordable health care for all, and move toward universal health insurance coverage, starting with children. He said he would set higher standards and more accountability in schools, test all new teachers and give then training and better salaries. He promised to uphold abortion rights, civil rights, affirmative action, and rights for the disabled and to defend the environment.*

*"I know that sometimes people say I'm too serious, that I talk too much*

*substance and policy. Maybe I've done that tonight," Gore said to laughter and shouts of "No!" from the audience. "But the Presidency is more than a popularity contest. It's a day-by-day fight for people. . . . If you entrust me with the Presidency, I know I won't always be the most exciting politician. But I pledge to you tonight: I will work for you every day and I will never let you down."*

> *Following are the text of a speech at the Democratic National Convention in Los Angeles, as delivered by Connecticut senator Joseph I. Lieberman on August 16, 2000, and excerpts of the speech delivered August 17, 2000, by Vice President Al Gore, accepting their party's nomination for vice president and president, respectively. The documents were obtained from the Internet at http://www.algore.com/speeches/sp_08172000_dnc.html and http://www.dems2000.com/eMersion/eCoverage/03_lieberman_j_speech.html.*

# LIEBERMAN ACCEPTANCE SPEECH

Is America a great country, or what?

Ten days ago, with courage and friendship, Al Gore asked me to be his running mate. This has been an extraordinary week for my family and me.

There's an old saying that behind every successful man . . . there is a surprised mother-in-law. I am here tonight to tell you: it's true.

I want to thank the daughter of my mother-in-law, the woman who just introduced me. Hadassah—even before Al Gore made me his running mate, you made me the luckiest guy in the world. I am fortunate to have you by my side on this journey and I thank you sweetheart.

That miraculous journey begins here and now. Tonight, I am so proud to stand as your candidate for Vice President of the United States. Only in America.

I am humbled by this nomination and so grateful to Al Gore for choosing me. And I want you to know, I will work my heart out to make sure Al Gore is the next President of the United States.

We have become the America that so many of our parents dreamed for us. But the great question this year is what will we dream for our country . . . and how will we make it come true?

We who gather here tonight believe, as Al Gore has said, that it's not just the size of our national feast that is important, but the number of people we can fit around the table. There must be room for everybody.

As every faith teaches us—and as Presidents from Lincoln to Roosevelt to Reagan to Clinton have reminded us—we must, as Americans, try to see our nation not just through our own eyes, but through the eyes of others.

In my life, I have seen the goodness of this country through many sets of eyes. I have seen it through the eyes of my grandmother. She was raised in Central Europe, in a village where she was often harassed because of the way she worshiped God.

Then, she immigrated to America. On Saturdays, she used to walk to synagogue, and often, her Christian neighbors would pass her and say, "Good Sabbath, Mrs. Manger." It was a source of endless delight and gratitude for her that here in this country, she was accepted for who she was.

I have seen America through the eyes of my parents, Henry and Marcia Lieberman. My father lived in an orphanage when he was a child. He went on to drive a bakery truck and own a package store in Stamford, Connecticut. He taught my sisters and me the importance of work and responsibility. With my mother by his side, he saw me become the first person in my family to graduate from college.

My mom is here tonight. She's 85 years old, and never felt younger than she does today. Mom—thank you, I love you—and you and I know how proud dad would be tonight.

And I have tried to see America through the eyes of people I have been privileged to know. In the early 1960s, when I was a college student, I walked with Martin Luther King in the March on Washington. Later that fall, I went to Mississippi, where we worked to register African-Americans to vote.

The people I met never forgot that in America, every time a barrier is broken the doors of opportunity open wider for everyone.

And I have tried to see America through the eyes of families who had the deck stacked against them, but fought back. As Connecticut's Attorney General, I worked to be the people's lawyer. I went after polluters who were spoiling our water and our air. I stood with single moms to go after deadbeat dads. We even sued big oil companies who were trying to gouge consumers at the pump.

And I have seen America through the eyes of my wife and her parents. By now, most of you know Hadassah's story. Her family was literally saved by American GI's who liberated the concentration camps. Then her parents escaped Communism and were welcomed as immigrants to America and given a new life.

The fact that a half century later, their daughter would be standing on this stage is a testament to the power of the American Dream. In my life I have tried to see this world through the eyes of those who have suffered discrimination. And that's why I believe that the time has come to tear down the remaining walls of discrimination in this nation based on race, gender, nationality or sexual orientation. And that's why I continue to say, when it comes to affirmative action: mend it, don't end it.

When you try to see the world through other people's eyes, you understand that the smallest changes can make the biggest differences in all of our lives. That's something I'm sorry to say I don't think our Republican friends really understand.

They're fond of dismissing the achievements of the past eight years. But at the end of the day the people I talk with tell me that their lives are better than they were eight years ago.

Our opponents are decent and likable men. I am proud to call many in their party my friends. But America must understand: there are very real differences between us in this election.

Two weeks ago, our Republican friends tried to walk and talk a lot like us. But let's be honest. We may be near Hollywood, but not since Tom Hanks won an Oscar has there been that much acting in Philadelphia.

I am glad the GOP has changed their rhetoric, but I wish they would also change their policies. As my friend John McCain might say, and let me say that John is in our thoughts and prayers tonight—let me now do some straight talking.

I think it's a good thing that our opponent talks about the environment. But I'm sad to say that in Texas, the quality of the air and water is some of the worst in America.

We see the environment through a different set of eyes. For more than 20 years Al Gore has been a leader on the environment. He and I will continue the work we have done together to keep our air, water and land clean. We are going to continue to work to make sure that a child can drink a glass of water, or a father can fish in a stream, or a family can go to a park, without having to worry that their health and safety is at risk.

And it's a good thing that our opponent is talking about health care. But I'm sad to say that Texas is also falling behind on that. Texas led the nation in the percentage of residents who were uninsured. Today, it ranks next to last for health insurance for both women and kids.

We see health care through a different set of eyes. We know that health care is one of the most important problems facing families today. We believe that medical decisions should be made by doctors, not bureaucrats. We believe that senior citizens shouldn't be stopped from filling a prescription because they can't afford to pay for it. And Al Gore and I are the only candidates in this race who will extend access to health care coverage to every single child in America.

And, I think it's a good thing that our opponent talks about education. Schools need to be held to the highest standards of performance and accountability. But I'm sad to say their plan doesn't provide the resources our schools need to meet those high standards. Sometimes it seems to me like their idea of school modernization means buying a new calendar for every building.

We see education through a different set of eyes. We're committed to making America's public schools the best in the world. We are going to target more education funding to the schools that need it most . . . to rebuild and modernize our crumbling classrooms and to provide all children with the skills they need to succeed in the 21st Century. And we're going to do one other thing that our Republican friends will not: We are going to treat the people who teach our children like the professionals that they are.

This is a question of priorities. Our opponents want to use America's hard-earned surplus to give a tax break to those who need it least, at the expense of all our other needs.

Under their plan, the middle class gets a little . . . and the wealthy get a lot. Their tax plan operates under that old theory that the best way to feed the birds is to give more oats to the horse.

We see the surplus through a different set of eyes—the eyes of working middle-class families. We want to use America's hard-earned success to preserve the future of Social Security and Medicare, to pay off our national debt, and cut the taxes of middle class families. We want to make the investments that will keep our economy moving forward.

It's this simple—we Democrats will expand the prosperity; they will squander it.

And this party will reform campaign finance, because it is only Al Gore and not George W. Bush who will send the McCain-Feingold bill to Congress and sign it when it's passed.

For those of you at home who haven't made up your mind if you want to build on our prosperity . . . if you want progress not partisanship in Washington . . . if you want to reform the system and not retreat from the problems, then your choice is clear: Al Gore is the best man for the job.

I have known Al for 15 years. I know his record and I know his heart. I know him as a public servant and I know what it is like to sit with him around the dining room table.

We have discussed—sometimes even debated—policy issues, and we have shared private moments of prayer. I can tell you that Al Gore is a man of family and faith—a father, and now a grandfather.

When my daughter was six, after spending time with Al, she looked at me and said, "He must be a daddy."

Al Gore is a man of courage and conviction. He believes in service to America. He volunteered for Vietnam.

Together, we crossed party lines to support the Gulf War. I was there in the room when he forcefully argued that America's principles and interests were at stake in Bosnia and Kosovo.

Two weeks ago, our opponent claimed that America has a hollow military. I must tell you, that made me angry.

America, we know better than that. Our fighting men and women are the best-trained, best-equipped, most potent fighting force in the history of the world, and they will stay that way when Al Gore and I are elected.

And Al Gore is also a man of vision and values. Long before it became popular, Al and Tipper led a crusade to renew the moral center of this nation, to call America to live by its highest ideals.

He knows that in many Americans, there is a swelling sense that our standards of decency and civility have eroded. No parent should be forced to compete with popular culture to raise their children.

For his entire career, Al Gore's values have guided the way he meets the challenges that lie ahead. That's why I hope you will conclude—as I have—that for his honesty, for his strength, for his integrity, and for his character, Al Gore must become the next President of the United States.

Forty years ago, we came to this city and crossed a new frontier with a leader who inspired me, and so many in my generation, into public service. Today, we return with prosperity at home and freedom throughout the world that John F. Kennedy could have only dreamed about.

We may wonder where the next frontier really is. Tonight I believe that the next frontier isn't just in front of us . . . but inside of us, to overcome the differences that are still between us, to break down the barriers that remain, and to help every American claim the limitless possibilities of their own lives.

Sometimes, I try to see this world as my dad saw it from his bakery truck. About this time, he'd be getting ready for the all-night run. And I know that somewhere in America right now, there is another father loading a bakery truck, or a young woman programming a computer, or a parent dreaming of a better future for their daughter or their son.

If we keep the faith, then 40 years from now, one of their children will stand before a gathering like this, with a chance to serve and lead this country that we love. So, let them look back to this time, and this place, and this stage and say of us: They kept the faith.

Let them say that we helped them realize their hopes and their dreams. And let them look around at this great and good nation that we are all so blessed to share, and say: Only in America.

## GORE ACCEPTANCE SPEECH

I speak tonight of gratitude, achievement, and high hopes for our country. Tonight, I think first of those who helped get me here—starting with the people of Tennessee. Then, those who braved the first snows of Iowa and New Hampshire—and all of you here, from all over this country, who have come with me into the warm sunlight of this great city.

While I can't thank each of you individually in words, I do so in my heart. And I know you won't mind if I single out someone who has just spoken so eloquently, someone I've loved with my whole heart since the night of my high school senior prom—my wife, Tipper. We've been lucky enough to find each other all over again at each new stage of our lives—and we just celebrated our 30th wedding anniversary.

I want to acknowledge with great pride our four children: Kristin, Sarah, and Albert; our oldest daughter Karenna and her husband Drew; and the youngest member of our family, who a little over a year ago was born on the Fourth of July—our grandson Wyatt.

I'm honored tonight by the support of a leader of high ideals and fundamental decency, who will be an important part of our country's future—Senator Bill Bradley.

There's someone else who will shape that future—a leader of character and courage. A defender of the environment, and working families—the next Vice President of the United States, Joe Lieberman.

I picked him for one simple reason: he's the best person for the job.

For almost eight years now, I've been the partner of a leader who moved us out of the valley of recession and into the longest period of prosperity in American history. I say to you tonight: millions of Americans will live better lives for a long time to come because of the job that's been done by President Bill Clinton.

Instead of the biggest deficits in history, we now have the biggest surpluses. The highest home ownership ever. The lowest inflation in a generation. Instead of losing jobs, we have 22 million new jobs.

Above all, our success comes from you, the people who have worked hard for your families. Let's not forget that a few years ago, you were also working hard. But your hard work was undone by a government that didn't work, didn't put people first, and wasn't on your side.

Together, we changed things, to help unleash your potential, and innovation and investment in the private sector, the engine that drives our economic growth. And our progress on the economy is a good chapter in our history. But now we turn the page and write a new chapter. And that's what I want to speak about tonight.

This election is not an award for past performance. I'm not asking you to vote for me on the basis of the economy we have. Tonight, I ask for your support on the basis of the better, fairer, more prosperous America we can build together.

Together, let's make sure that our prosperity enriches not just the few, but all working families. Let's invest in health care, education, a secure retirement, and middle class tax cuts.

I'm happy that the stock market has boomed and so many businesses and new enterprises have done well. This country is richer and stronger. But my focus is on working families—people trying to make house payments and car payments, working overtime to save for college and do right by their kids.

Whether you're in a suburb, or an inner-city. Whether you raise crops or drive hogs and cattle on a farm, drive a big rig on the Interstate, or drive e-commerce on the Internet. Whether you're starting out to raise your own family, or getting ready to retire after a lifetime of hard work.

So often, powerful forces and powerful interests stand in your way, and the odds seemed stacked against you—even as you do what's right for you and your family. How and what we do for all of you—the people who pay the taxes, bear the burdens, and live the American dream—that is the standard by which we should be judged.

And for all of our good times, I am not satisfied.

To all the families in America who have to struggle to afford the right education and the skyrocketing cost of prescription drugs. I want you to know this: I've taken on the powerful forces. And as President, I'll stand up to them, and I'll stand up for you.

To all the families who are struggling with things that money can't measure—like trying to find a little more time to spend with your children, or protecting your children from entertainment that you think glorifies violence and indecency—I want you to know: I believe we must challenge a culture with too much meanness, and not enough meaning. And as President, I will stand with you for a goal that we share: to give more power back to the parents, to choose what your own children are exposed to, so you can pass on your family's basic lessons of responsibility and decency.

The power should be in your hands. The future should belong to everyone in this land. We could squander this moment—but our country would be the poorer for it. Instead, let's lift our eyes, and see how wide the American horizon has become. We're entering a new time. We're electing a new President. And I stand here tonight as my own man, and I want you to know me for who I truly am.

I grew up in a wonderful family. I have a lot to be thankful for. And the greatest gift my parents gave me was love. When I was a child, it never once occurred to me that the foundation upon which my security depended would ever shake.

And of all the lessons my parents taught me, the most powerful one was unspoken—the way they loved one another. My father respected my mother as an equal, if not more. She was his best friend, and in many ways, his conscience. And I learned from them the value of a true, loving partnership that lasts for life. They simply couldn't imagine being without each other. And for 61 years, they were by each other's side.

My parents taught me that the real values in life aren't material but spiritual. They include faith and family, duty and honor, and trying to make the world a better place.

I finished college at a time when all that seemed to be in doubt, and our nation's spirit was being depleted. We saw the assassination of our best leaders. Appeals to racial backlash. And the first warning signs of Watergate. I remember the conversations I had with Tipper back then—and the doubts we had about the Vietnam War.

But I enlisted in the Army because I knew if I didn't go, someone else in the small town of Carthage, Tennessee, would have to go in my place. I was an Army reporter in Vietnam. When I was there, I didn't do the most, or run the gravest danger. But I was proud to wear my country's uniform.

When I came home, running for office was the very last thing I ever thought I would do. I studied religion at Vanderbilt, and worked nights as a police reporter at the *Nashville Tennessean*. And I saw more of what could go wrong in America—not only on the police beat, but as an investigative reporter covering local government.

I also saw so much of what could go right—citizens lifting up local communities, family by family, block by block, neighborhood by neighborhood, in churches and charities, on school boards and City Councils.

And then, Tipper and I started our own family. And when our first daughter Karenna was born, I began to see the future through a fresh set of eyes. I know a lot of you have had that feeling, too. And I decided that I could not turn away from service at home—any more than I could have turned away from service in Vietnam.

That's why I ran for Congress. In my first term, a family in Hardeman County, Tennessee, wrote a letter and told how worried they were about toxic waste that had been dumped near their home. I held some of the first hearings on the issue.

And ever since, I've been there in the fight against the big polluters. Our children should not have to draw the breath of life in cities awash in pollution. When they come in from playing on a hot summer afternoon, every child in America, anywhere in America, ought to be able to turn on the faucet and get a glass of safe, clean drinking water.

On the issue of the environment, I've never given up, I've never backed down, and I never will.

And I say it again tonight: we must reverse the silent, rising tide of global warming.

In the Senate and as Vice President, I fought for welfare reform. Over and over again, I talked to folks who told me how they were trapped in the old welfare system. I saw what it did to families. So I fought to end welfare as we then knew it—to help those in trouble, but to insist on work and responsibility. Others talked about welfare reform. We actually reformed welfare and set time limits. Instead of hand-outs, we gave people training to go from welfare to work. And we have cut the welfare rolls in half and moved millions into good jobs.

For almost 25 years now, I've been fighting for people. And for all that time, I've been listening to people—holding open meetings, in the places where they live and work.

And you know what? I've learned a lot. And if I'm your President, I'm going to keep on having open meetings all over this country. I'm going to go out to you, the people, because I want to stay in touch with your hopes; with the quiet, every-day heroism of hard-working Americans. . . .

So this is not just an election between my opponent and me. It's about our people, our families, and our future—and whether forces standing in your way will keep you from having a better life. . . .

It's about millions of Americans whose names we may never know—but whose needs and dreams must always be our calling. And so here tonight, in the name of all the working families who are the strength and soul of America—I accept your nomination for President of the United States.

I'm here to talk seriously about the issues. I believe people deserve to know specifically what a candidate proposes to do. I intend to tell you tonight. You ought to be able to know, and then judge for yourself. If you entrust me with the Presidency, I will put our democracy back in your hands, and get all the special-interest money—all of it—out of our democracy, by enacting campaign finance reform. I feel so strongly about this, I promise you that campaign finance reform will be the very first bill that Joe Lieberman and I send to Congress.

Let others try to restore the old guard. We come to this convention as the change we wish to see in America.

And what are those changes? At a time when most Americans will live to know even their great-grandchildren, we will save and strengthen Social Security and Medicare—not only for this generation, but for generations to come.

At a time of almost unimaginable medical breakthroughs, we will fight for affordable health care for all—so patients and ordinary people are not left powerless and broke. We will move toward universal health coverage, step by step, starting with all children. Let's get all children covered by the year 2004.

And let's move to the day when we end the stigma of mental illness, and treat it like every other illness, everywhere in this nation. Within the next few years, scientists will identify the genes that cause every type of cancer. We need a national commitment equal to the promise of this unequalled moment. So we will double the federal investment in medical research. We will find new medicines and new cures—not just for cancer, but for everything from diabetes to HIV/AIDS.

At a time when there is more computer power in a Palm Pilot than in the spaceship that took Neil Armstrong to the moon, we will offer all our people lifelong learning and new skills for the higher-paying jobs of the future.

At a time when the amount of human knowledge is doubling every five years, we will do bold things to make our schools the best in the world. I will fight for the single greatest commitment to education since the G.I. Bill. For revolutionary improvements in our schools. For higher standards and more accountability. To put a fully-qualified teacher in every classroom, test all new teachers, and give teachers the training and professional development they deserve. It's time to treat and reward teachers like the professionals they are.

It's not just about more money. It's about higher standards, accountability—new ideas. But we can't do it without new resources. And that's why I will invest far more in our schools—in the long-run, a second-class education always costs more than a first-class education.

And I will not go along with any plan that would drain taxpayer money away from our public schools and give it to private schools in the form of vouchers. This nation was a pioneer of universal public education. Now let's set a specific new goal for the first decade of the 21st Century: high-quality universal pre-school—available to every child, in every family, all across this country.

We also have to give middle-class families help in paying for college with tax-free college savings, and by making most college tuition tax-deductible. Open the doors of learning to all.

And all of this—all of this—is the change we wish to see in America. Not so long ago, a balanced budget seemed impossible. Now our budget surpluses make it possible to give a full range of targeted tax cuts to working families. Not just to help you save for college, but to pay for health insurance or child care. To reform the estate tax, so people can pass on a small business or a family farm. And to end the marriage penalty—the right way, the fair way— because we shouldn't force couples to pay more in income taxes just because they're married.

But let me say it plainly: I will not go along with a huge tax cut for the wealthy at the expense of everyone else and wreck our good economy in the process.

Under the tax plan the other side has proposed, for every ten dollars that goes to the wealthiest one percent, middle class families would get one dime. And lower-income families would get one penny.

In fact, if you add it up, the average family would get about enough money to buy one extra Diet Coke a day. About 62 cents in change. Let me tell you: that's not the kind of change I'm working for.

I'll fight for tax cuts that go to the right people—to the working families who have the toughest time paying taxes and saving for the future.

I'll fight for a new, tax-free way to help you save and build a bigger nest egg for your retirement. I'm talking about something extra that you can save and invest for yourself. Something that will supplement Social Security, not be subtracted from it.

But I will not go along with any proposal to strip one out of every six dollars from the Social Security trust fund and privatize the Social Security that you're counting on. That's Social Security minus. Our plan is Social Security plus.

We will balance the budget every year, and dedicate the budget surplus first to saving Social Security. In the next four years, we will pay off all the national debt this nation accumulated in our first 200 years. This will put us on the path to completely eliminating the debt by 2012, keeping America prosperous far into the future. But there's something at stake in this election that's even more important than economic progress. Simply put, it's our values; it's our responsibility to our loved ones, to our families.

And to me, family values means honoring our fathers and mothers, teaching our children well, caring for the sick, respecting one another—giving people the power to achieve what they want for their families.

Putting both Social Security and Medicare in an iron-clad lock box where the politicians can't touch them—to me, that kind of common sense is a family value.

Getting cigarettes out of the hands of kids before they get hooked is a family value. I will crack down on the marketing of tobacco to our children, no matter how hard the tobacco companies lobby, no matter how much they spend.

A new prescription drug benefit under Medicare for all our seniors—that's a family value. And let me tell you: I will fight for it, and the other side will not. They give in to the big drug companies. Their plan tells seniors to beg the HMO's and insurance companies for prescription drug coverage.

And that's the difference in this election. They're for the powerful, and we're for the people. Big tobacco, big oil, the big polluters, the pharmaceutical companies, the HMOs. Sometimes you have to be willing to stand up and say no—so families can have a better life.

I know one thing about the job of the President. It is the only job in the Constitution that is charged with the responsibility of fighting for all the people. Not just the people of one state, or one district; not just the wealthy or the powerful—all the people. Especially those who need a voice; those who need a champion; those who need to be lifted up, so they are never left behind. So I say to you tonight: if you entrust me with the Presidency, I will fight for you.

There's one other word we've heard a lot of in this campaign, and that word is *honor*. To me, honor is not just a word, but an obligation.

And you have my word: we will honor hard work by raising the minimum wage so that work always pays more than welfare.

We will honor families by expanding child care, and after-school care, and family and medical leave—so working parents have the help they need to care for their children—because one of the most important jobs of all is raising our children. And we'll support the right of parents to decide that one of them will stay home longer with their babies if that's what they believe is best for their families.

We will honor the ideal of equality by standing up for civil rights and defending affirmative action.

We will honor equal rights and fight for an equal day's pay for an equal day's work.

And let there be no doubt: I will protect and defend a woman's right to choose. The last thing this country needs is a Supreme Court that overturns *Roe v. Wade.*

We will remove all the old barriers—so that those who are called disabled can develop all their abilities.

And we will also widen the circle of opportunity for all Americans, and enforce all our civil rights laws.

We will pass the Employment Non-Discrimination Act.

And we will honor the memory of Matthew Shepard, Joseph Ileto, and James Byrd, whose families all joined us this week—by passing a law against hate crimes.

We will honor the hard work of raising a family—by doing all we can to help parents protect their children. Parents deserve the simple security of knowing that their children are safe whether they're walking down the street, surfing the World Wide Web, or sitting behind a desk in school.

To make families safer, we passed the toughest crime bill in history, and we're putting 100,000 new community police on our streets. Crime has fallen in every major category for seven years in a row. But there's still too much danger and there's still too much fear.

So tonight I want to set another new, specific goal: to cut the crime rate year after year—every single year throughout this decade. That's why I'll fight to add another 50,000 new police—community police who help prevent crime by establishing real relationships between law enforcement and neighborhood residents—which, incidentally, is the opposite of racial profiling, which must be brought to an end.

I will fight for a crime victims' bill of rights, including a Constitutional amendment to make sure that victims, and not just criminals, are guaranteed rights in our justice system.

I'll fight to toughen penalties on those who misuse the Internet to prey on our children and violate our privacy. And I'll fight to make every school in this nation drug-free and gun-free.

I believe in the right of sportsmen and hunters and law-abiding citizens to own firearms. But I want mandatory background checks to keep guns away from criminals, and mandatory child safety locks to protect our children.

Tipper and I went out to Columbine High School after the tragedy there, and we embraced the families of the children who were lost. And I will never forget the words of the father who whispered into my ear, "Promise me that these children will not have died in vain."

All of us must join together to make that promise come true. Laws and programs by themselves will never be enough. All of us, and especially all parents need to take more responsibility. We need to change our hearts—and make a commitment to our children and to one another.

I'm excited about America's prospects and full of hope for America's future. Our country has come a long way, and I've come a long way since that long ago time when I went to Vietnam.

I've never forgotten what I saw there—and the bravery of so many young Americans. The price of freedom is sometimes high, but I never believed that America should turn inward.

As a Senator, I broke with many in our party and voted to support the Gulf War when Saddam Hussein invaded Kuwait—because I believed America's vital interests were at stake.

Early in my public service, I took up the issue of nuclear arms control and nuclear weapons—because nothing is more fundamental than protecting our national security.

Now I want to lead America because I love America. I will keep America's defenses strong. I will make sure our armed forces continue to be the best-equipped, best-trained, and best-led in the entire world. In the last century, this nation more than any other freed the world from fascism and communism. But a newly free world still has dangers and challenges, both old and new. We must always have the will to defend our enduring interests—from Europe, to the Middle East, to Japan and Korea. We must strengthen our partnerships with Africa, Latin America, and the rest of the developing world.

We must welcome and promote truly free trade. But I say to you: it must be fair trade. We must set standards to end child labor, to prevent the exploitation of workers and the poisoning of the environment. Free trade can and must be—and if I'm President, will be—a way to lift everyone up, not bring anyone down to the lowest common denominator.

So those are the issues, and that's where I stand. But I also want to tell you just a little more about two of my greatest heroes, my father and my mother. They did give me a good life. But like so many in America, they started out with almost nothing.

My father grew up in a small community named Possum Hollow in Middle Tennessee. When he was just eighteen, he went to work as a teacher in a one-room school. Then the Great Depression came along and taught him a lesson that couldn't be found in any classroom. He told me and my sister often how he watched grown men, with wives and children they could neither feed nor clothe, on farms they could no longer pay for.

My father didn't know whether he could help those families—but he believed he had to try. And never in the years to come—in Congress, and in the

United States Senate—did he lose sight of the reason he entered public service: to fight for the people, not the powerful.

My mother grew up in a poor farming community in northwest Tennessee. Her family ran a small country store in Cold Corner. A store that went bust during the Great Depression. She worked her way through college, then got a room in Nashville at the YWCA and waited tables at an all-night coffee shop for 25-cent tips. She then went on to become one of the first women in history to graduate from Vanderbilt Law School.

As Tipper told you tonight, we lost my dad a year and a half ago. But we're so lucky that my mother Pauline continues to be part of our lives, every single day. She's here tonight.

Sometimes in this campaign, when I visit a school and see a hard-working teacher trying to change the world one child at a time—I see the face of my father.

And I know that teaching our children well is not just the teacher's job; it's everyone's job. And it has to be our national mission.

I've shaken hands in diners and coffee shops all across this country. And sometimes, when I see a waitress working hard and thanking someone for a tip, I see the face of my mother. And I know: for that waitress carrying trays, or a construction worker in the winter cold, I will never agree to raise the retirement age to 70, or threaten the promise of Social Security.

I say to you tonight: we've got to win this election—because every hard-working American family deserves to open the door to their dream.

In our democracy, the future is not something that just happens to us; it is something we make for ourselves—together.

So to the young people watching tonight, I say: this is your time to make new the life of our world. We need your help to rekindle the spirit of America.

And I ask all of you, my fellow citizens: from this city that marked both the end of America's journey westward and the beginning of the New Frontier, let us set out on a new journey to the best America.

A new journey on which we advance not by the turning of wheels, but by the turning of our minds; the reach of our vision; the daring grace of the human spirit.

Yes, we have our problems. But the United States of America is the best country ever created—and still, as ever, the hope of humankind.

Yes, we're all imperfect. But as Americans we all share in the privilege and challenge of building a more perfect union.

I know my own imperfections. I know that sometimes people say I'm too serious, that I talk too much substance and policy. Maybe I've done that tonight.

But the Presidency is more than a popularity contest. It's a day-by-day fight for people. Sometimes, you have to choose to do what's difficult or unpopular. Sometimes, you have to be willing to spend your popularity in order to pick the hard right over the easy wrong.

There are big choices ahead, and our whole future is at stake. And I do have strong beliefs about it.

If you entrust me with the Presidency, I know I won't always be the most exciting politician. But I pledge to you tonight: I will work for you every day and I will never let you down.

If we allow ourselves to believe, without reservation, that we can do what's right and be the better for it—then the best America will become our America. In this City of Angels, we can summon the better angels of our nature. Do not rest where we are, or retreat. Do all we can to make America all it can become.

Thank you—God bless you—and God bless America.

# DEFENSE SECRETARY COHEN ON RUSSIAN SUBMARINE DISASTER
## August 18, 2000

*A giant Russian submarine, the* Kursk, *sank in the frigid waters of the Barents Sea during a naval exercise on August 12, 2000, killing all 118 crewmen and visitors aboard. The exact cause of the submarine disaster was still under investigation at year's end. Senior Russian military officials insisted that a "foreign" (presumably American) submarine had rammed the boat. But most international naval experts said it was likely that one or more torpedoes aboard* Kursk *exploded, setting off a massive explosion that tore a large hole in the hull of the 505-foot-long boat.*

*The sinking of the submarine—one of the newest boats in Russia's dwindling naval fleet—set off a wave of recriminations and soul-searching in Russia, forcing citizens of the once-swaggering superpower to face troubling questions about the country's attempts to maintain a semblance of its military might from the cold war era. Russians accused the military of delaying, and then bungling, the effort to rescue the sailors aboard the crippled submarine. The government's hesitant, often contradictory explanations of events served as a reminder that a newly democratic Russia was still struggling to escape the reflexive secrecy and denial of its communist past. A frustrated defense minister, Igor D. Sergeyev, said the military had been "robbed and stripped" of needed resources. President Vladimir Putin, elected to office just five months earlier, acknowledged "responsibility and guilt" for the disaster.* (Putin election, p. 171)

### *The Sinking of the* Kursk

*The Northern Fleet, once the jewel of Russia's navy, on August 10 began a large-scale exercise in the Barents Sea, which lies inside the Arctic Circle just north of northwestern Russia and the Scandinavian peninsula. According to Russian and Western news reports, Russian admirals had hoped the exercise would demonstrate the importance of the country's navy and help convince leaders in Moscow of the urgent need for increased funding of the military. Ever since the collapse of the Soviet Union at the end of 1991—and the resultant economic upheaval during the transformation from commu-*

*nism to capitalism—the country's once-mighty military had faced deep cutbacks and was struggling just to pay its soldiers, sailors, and airmen.*

*The nuclear-powered Kursk, commissioned in 1995, was one of the newest of what the Russians called the Antey class of attack submarines. When fully armed, it carried two dozen cruise missiles (fitted with either nuclear or conventional warheads) with a range of several hundred miles and two dozen conventional torpedoes. As an economy measure, the torpedoes aboard the Kursk were powered by a low-grade fuel that some experts said was more combustible and difficult to handle than traditional fuel.*

*On August 12 the Kursk was scheduled to play its part in the naval exercise with a series of torpedo attacks. At 11:28 A.M. local time, Norwegian, Russian, and U.S. sensing devices in the area detected an explosion. U.S. ships then detected what appeared to be engine noise—what U.S. officials assumed was a frantic attempt by the Kursk to reach the surface. A second, much larger, explosion came about two minutes after the first blast. A minute or so later, according to U.S. reports, a large metal object, presumed to be the Kursk, could be heard hitting the bottom of the sea, about 350 feet below the surface.*

*The cause of the explosions was the subject of much speculation in the coming weeks and months. Some Russian admirals and military officials insisted that the Kursk had been hit by a "foreign" submarine or surface ship, which somehow managed to escape. Alternatively, they speculated that the Kursk hit a mine left over from World War II. But other Russian officials, and most international experts quoted in news reports, offered other explanations. In general, those theories held that the first explosion most likely was the misfiring of one of the Kursk's torpedoes. That explosion, in turn, could have triggered the second, larger, explosion—possibly involving some or all of the conventional warheads stored aboard the submarine.*

*According to the official Russian military account of events, the navy was unable to locate the stricken Kursk until early in the morning of August 13, nearly sixteen hours after it sank. Another fifteen hours went by before a Russian diving bell reached the Kursk, but divers were unable to enter the sub. Divers reported hearing sounds that Russian officials later said were distress signals—possibly sailors tapping on the submarine's hull.*

*The news of the Kursk's sinking was made public on August 14—two days after the event—and the United States and Great Britain immediately offered to help with the rescue effort. Russian officials at first declined any international assistance, but then agreed on August 16, four days after the sinking, to ask for help from Great Britain and Norway. Defense Secretary William S. Cohen repeated the U.S. offer on August 18, saying the Defense Department "remains ready, willing, and able to provide whatever assistance we can to the Russian authorities that they would find helpful." Meanwhile, Russian divers made frantic efforts to enter the Kursk, all of them unsuccessful.*

*British and Norwegian rescue vessels finally arrived on the scene during the evening of August 19. Early on August 21—nine days after the acci-*

dent—Norwegian divers opened an emergency hatch and found that the air lock and at least one compartment at the aft (rear) of the sub were flooded. Based on that information, the commanders of the Northern Fleet concluded later that day that all 118 persons aboard the Kursk had died.

The Norwegian and British rescuers then left the scene, and the Russian government contracted with the Norwegian affiliate of Haliburton, the U.S. oil exploration firm, to retrieve as many bodies as possible from the Kursk. Beginning on October 21, Norwegian and Russian divers worked to cut openings in the hull. Russian divers entered the Kursk on October 25 and retrieved four bodies. The next day, October 26, divers recovered the body of Lt. Captain Dimitri Kolesnikov, the commander of a turbine room toward the boat's aft. In his uniform, wrapped in plastic, was a message Kolesnikov had dated at 1:15 P.M. the day of the accident.

"All the crew of the sixth, seventh, and eighth compartments moved to the ninth," the message read. "There are twenty-three of us here. We have made this decision as a result of the accident. None of us can get out." On the reverse side of the paper, Kolesnikov wrote another message, dated at 3:45 P.M.: "It is dark here, but I will try to write by feel. It looks that there are no chances." Kolesnikov included a personal message for his family—which Russian officials did not make public—and ended his note: "Greetings to all. Don't despair."

The publication of Kolesnikov's message on October 26 caused a sensation in Russia because it confirmed that some members of the Kursk's crew survived the August 12 explosions—at least for a few hours. Russian news organizations reported that a second note, dated August 15 (three days after the sinking), was found on Kolesnikov's body. But that note, if it existed, was not made public.

During the closing days of October and the first week of November, divers examined several other compartments of the Kursk. But with the weather rapidly worsening, and with divers unable to gain access to most of the boat, officials decided on November 7 to suspend the operation. By that time, only twelve bodies had been recovered from the Kursk, all of them from the aft sections. The Russian navy said it would try to raise the remains of the Kursk during the summer of 2001.

## Recriminations in Russia

The sinking of the Kursk and the prolonged efforts to rescue its crew were generally regarded as a national calamity in Russia, which was forced to confront the painful reality that its military was no longer the seemingly invulnerable force of the Soviet era. Civilian and military leaders, from Putin on down, suddenly faced a barrage of hostility from citizens who had endured nearly a decade of economic and social turmoil.

Putin, a former secret service officer who had been in the public eye for just a year, quickly discovered the hazard of appearing to be indifferent in times of crisis. At the time of the accident, Putin was on vacation at a Black Sea resort. He stayed put for nearly a week, saying he would only be in the *way if he traveled to the scene of the disaster. Finally, on August 22, Putin traveled to the Kursk's home base near Murmansk and met with families of the submarine's crew, some of whom bitterly denounced the government's rescue efforts. Opinion polls taken in subsequent weeks showed that Putin's popularity had fallen, but a strong majority of Russians still voiced general approval of the way he was handling his job.*

*Russian news organizations heatedly denounced failures by the Russian military, including the contradictory explanations of what had happened and the delays in locating the Kursk and in asking for international help for the rescue effort. Critics were especially scathing in noting that Russian divers failed, during a week of work, to open the Kursk's hatches, but British and Norwegian divers were able to gain entry to the Kursk within a day of arriving on the scene. Such criticisms became more intense after the Norwegian admiral heading that country's role in the rescue publicly complained about Russian incompetence. "At times there were so many wrong details and disinformation from Russia that it was close to endangering the divers," Admiral Einar Skorgen said in an interview with the Norwegian newspaper Nordlandposten. "We couldn't rely on the information we were getting."*

*In a nationally televised interview on August 23, Putin sought to dampen criticism of the government's handling of the affair. Putin said he felt "the full sense of guilt and responsibility for this crisis," even though he had only recently become president. Putin dismissed criticism of the Russian military, and he refused to accept resignations from his defense minister and two top navy commanders. Putin also defended the delays in asking for international assistance, citing undefined "technical parameters" and arguing that the sailors aboard the Kursk almost certainly died before any rescuers could possibly have arrived.*

*On November 9, nearly three months after the Kursk sank, the Kremlin announced plans for a deep reduction in Russian military spending. The main impact would be to reduce the number of uniformed and civilian military personnel by about 600,000, representing about one-fifth of the total force of 3 million. Kremlin officials portrayed the budget cut as part of an effort to reform and streamline the country's military.*

> *Following are excerpts from an August 18, 2000, news conference during which Secretary of Defense William S. Cohen reiterated a United States offer of assistance to Russia in its effort to rescue the stranded submarine Kursk. The document was obtained from the Internet at http://www.defenselink.mil/news/Aug2000/ t08182000_t818subm.html.*

**Secretary William S. Cohen:** First, let me thank you for coming down here today. I'd like to take a few moments to share some of my thoughts with you on this accident involving the *Kursk*. I've been following this very closely, ever since the Russian authorities announced this tragic event over the weekend, and I'd like to take this opportunity to express my concern for the sailors on the *Kursk*.

There is an inherent sense of camaraderie that is felt by military people that transcends nationality and political differences, and I know from my conversations here in the Pentagon over the past few days that our military men and women are not looking at this accident as something that has happened to the Russians, but as something that has happened to fellow uniformed professionals. It's personal and it's very deep.

I want to express my concern for the sailors' families. It must be a very terrible time of fear and doubt for them right now, and we can only imagine the agony that they are suffering as they await the information on their loved ones. And so, on behalf of everyone in the department, I want to express our concern and hope during this most difficult time.

And finally, I'd like to make it clear that the Defense Department remains ready, willing and able to provide whatever assistance we can to the Russian authorities that they would find helpful. And I think most of you know that on Tuesday I wrote a letter to Minister of Defense Sergeyev offering our assistance, and then I received a response last evening. He expressed appreciation for our offer of assistance and he asked that we work through NATO channels to coordinate, and this we are glad to do.

We are hopeful that our British and Norwegian friends, working closely with their Russian counterparts, can be successful in effecting a rescue of the sailors of the *Kursk*, reuniting them with their families.

I'd be happy to take a few questions, but I should forewarn you that I have very little information beyond that which you already know. . . .

**Question:** Mr. Secretary, how would you work through NATO channels? Does that mean you are, in fact, going to provide help? And are you disappointed that you didn't hear earlier? And could the United States have provided better help had it been requested earlier?

**Cohen:** Well, there are a lot of questions that certainly will have to be asked and answered in the coming days and weeks. I think right now the focus has to be on what assistance can be provided and how quickly it can be provided. We have offered to work through NATO channels. In fact, yesterday, last evening, we had a video- teleconference with Russians participating, laying out certain things that we would be in a position to do. There will be another VTC tomorrow morning. And we stand ready to provide whatever assistance would be required and called for.

There were basically three courses of action that have been laid out to the Russian authorities. We have proposed having teams of experts who have a so-called reach-back capability to provide well-organized, mission-specific expertise that will be made up of engineers, divers, medical support, to provide whatever technical assistance would be necessary.

There's a second course of action, which would be an international coordination cell so that we could provide a core of international coordination people to facilitate the international rescue efforts. And then we have a third course of action, which would be a so-called fly-away diving capability, to provide atmospheric suits and diving capability to support Russia in this.

So we're waiting to explore this further with them, and we will take, again, every measure that we can consistent with their request.

**Q:** By "we," are you talking about the United States or are you talking about allies?

**Cohen:** In the three courses of action, there would be allied participation, but we certainly have a team of experts here that we're prepared to send to work on site if requested.

**Q:** You're assembling that team now?

**Cohen:** The team is being assembled for potential use, yes.

**Q:** And are they being sent anywhere? Will they go to Brussels [NATO headquarters] or—

**Cohen:** No. They will remain here until such time as there is a request made for their assistance. They'll be on the ready. They could be deployed within a period of 24 hours to the site itself if it's requested.

**Q:** Mr. Secretary, could you clarify a couple things on that? Now, this team that's being assembled, is it for all of the options you laid out or one particular course of action, such as the reach-back or—

**Cohen:** The reach-back capability, that's the team that's being assembled here that could, in fact, be deployed to the region. The second course of action would be an international coordination cell. And the third would be to prove the atmospheric suits. That coordination cell would be assembled, we assume, in Brussels in the NATO organization.

**Q:** So the team that you have just said is being assembled is basically the engineers, divers, medical, that sort of thing?

**Cohen:** Right. Right.

**Q:** And the VTC that was held last night—was that bilateral, U.S. and Russia?

**Cohen:** It was in NATO headquarters, and the VTC will be held similarly through NATO headquarters. . . .

**Q:** What reason have the Russians given you to believe that there are still people alive on the submarine?

**Cohen:** Well, I haven't had specific discussions with the Russian authorities. But to the extent that they are in fact agreeable and willing to have NATO assistance, should it be necessary, in their judgment, then that is some indication that they still feel that there are sailors alive. And so we are prepared to offer whatever we can to help them.

**Q:** Mr. Secretary, have you offered or provided any information that might help the Russians understand what happened to the submarine, the cause of the accident?

**Cohen:** No, at this point we will have to wait until all of the facts are in. But I can only assure you and the American people that there were no American ships involved in this matter. . . .

**Q:** One more on the submarine, sir. Did I just understand you also correctly, you are not ruling out the possibility of U.S. Navy personnel in the water in the Barents Sea helping on this mission?

**Cohen:** We've never ruled that out. As a matter of fact, what I indicated in my initial letter to Marshal Sergeyev, is that we are prepared to do whatever we can to help in this rescue effort, and we would be more than willing to contribute our resources to doing that, to help provide for that rescue.

**Q:** At what point does it become too late?

**Cohen:** I think that's a determination that the Russian authorities will have to make. They are the ones who are on the scene trying to organize the rescue effort. We hope that the British and Norwegian participation will be productive and produce a happy result. And there are great questions as to whether or not that will be the result, but we're hopeful.

Thank you.

# UNITED NATIONS PANEL ON PEACEKEEPING REFORM
## August 21, 2000

*The United Nations in 2000 acknowledged fundamental flaws in its peacekeeping operations and launched a series of reforms intended to correct them. A high-level panel of experts reported in August that UN peacekeeping forces were consistently sent into the field without enough manpower, equipment, or authority to accomplish their missions. The UN's inability to support its peacekeepers contributed to several disasters in the mid-1990s, notably the 1994 genocide in Rwanda and the 1995 slaughter of Muslims in Bosnia, the panel said. The panel laid most of the blame on UN member nations, which were responsible for providing the necessary troops and money for peacekeeping.*

*UN Secretary General Kofi Annan, who appointed the panel, accepted nearly all its recommendations and won general endorsement of them from the Security Council. The General Assembly in late December approved increased spending for peacekeeping operations—in effect endorsing much of the panel's recommendations.*

*By the end of the twentieth century, peacekeeping had become one of the UN's most important and controversial missions. Peacekeeping was the biggest single item in the UN budget—costing nearly $3 billion in the 2000–2001 fiscal year—and debates over how to respond to various situations frequently bedeviled the Security Council. Moreover, the UN's spectacular failures in Rwanda and Bosnia had severely undermined its reputation.*

*Even as the panel was preparing its report, a UN peacekeeping mission in Sierra Leone represented a microcosm of nearly all the problems the panel discovered. In January rebels seized hundreds of rifles and three armored vehicles from Guinean troops that were en route to join the UN force. Another 500 lightly armed peacekeepers were held captive for more than a month by rebels, and rebels trapped 230 peacekeepers and observers at a base in the eastern part of the country until mid-July, when they were rescued by British commandos. (Sierra Leone, p. 1072)*

*Two new UN peacekeeping missions in Africa got under way during 2000, one with a reasonable hope of success and the other facing enormous*

*obstacles. On November 16 the first units of a 4,200-strong UN military mission begin monitoring a June cease-fire agreement between Ethiopia and Eritrea, which had elevated a border dispute into one of the bloodiest wars of the late twentieth century. Annan told the Security Council on November 17 that the mission held "great promise" of success because both countries appeared committed to peace. Much less promising was a proposed peacekeeping mission in the Democratic Republic of the Congo (formerly Zaire), where guerrillas backed by Rwanda and Uganda were battling the regime of President Laurent Kabila, who had support from Angola and Zimbabwe. The signing of a peace agreement in 1999 led the Security Council to establish a peacekeeping mission for the Congo, with a total military strength of 5,537. But fighting continued sporadically throughout 2000, and Annan delayed sending the full mission into Congo. As of late 2000, 264 UN military observers were on the scene, waiting for a definitive end to the war.*
(Congo war, p. 978)

## *Background on UN Peacekeeping*

*For many years UN peacekeeping missions generally had been limited to separating warring parties once a conflict had been ended by a peace agreement. Prominent examples were the UN mission in Cyprus, which since 1974 had patrolled a cease-fire line separating Greeks and Turks following Turkey's invasion of the island, and a UN mission that since 1978 had monitored a truce subsequent to Israel's invasion of southern Lebanon.*

*The fundamental nature of UN peacekeeping changed dramatically following the end of the cold war. After the fall of the Berlin Wall in 1989 and the collapse of the Soviet Union two years later, ethnic tensions that had long been masked or suppressed during the cold war suddenly emerged into full-scale conflicts in the Balkans, central Africa, and other regions. Several of those conflicts were halted, at least temporarily, with cease-fires or peace agreements that failed to resolve the underlying issues in dispute. Confronted with almost impossible situations, UN peacekeeping forces failed in Somalia in 1993, in Rwanda in 1994, and in Bosnia in 1995. By far the greatest tragedy occurred in Rwanda when a weak, undermanned international force was unable to prevent a genocide that eventually killed an estimated 500,000 to 800,000 people. In Bosnia, a tiny Dutch peacekeeping force stood by helplessly in 1995 as Serbian military forces systematically murdered an estimated 7,000 civilians around the town of Srebrenica.*
(Rwanda genocide, Historic Documents of 1994, p. 541; Srebrenica killings, Historic Documents of 1999, p. 735; OAU report on the Rwanda massacre, p. 449)

*Two reports issued in 1999 condemned the UN failures in Bosnia and Rwanda and spurred Annan to appoint a ten-member panel of international experts to examine the UN's peacekeeping operations and make recommendations for improvements. The panel was chaired by Lakhdar Brahimi, a former Algerian foreign minister who had conducted numerous trouble-shooting missions for the United Nations. The other panel members were J. Brian Atwood, president of Citizens International and former administrator of the U.S. Agency for International Development; Colin Granderson, of Trinidad and Tobago, executive director of the Organization of American States; Dame Ann Hercus, former ambassador to the United Nations from New Zealand; Richard Monk, former member of the United Kingdom's Inspectorate of Constabulary; Klaus Naumann, former German defense chief; Hisako Shimura, president of Tsuda College in Tokyo and former senior UN official; Vladimir Shustov, Russian ambassador-at-large; General Philip Sibanda, chief of staff for operations and training in the Zimbabwe Army; and Cornelio Sommaruga, former president of the International Committee of the Red Cross.*

## Brahimi Panel Findings and Recommendations

*The underlying premise of the Brahimi panel's report was that the UN could not possibly attempt to police every conflict in the world, and so it should launch peacekeeping operations only if member states were prepared to support them with enough personnel, materiel, and diplomacy to succeed. The panel found fault with UN peacekeeping operations both at the New York headquarters and in the field, and it generally identified the immediate cause of the problem as the lack of adequate resources for the task.*

*Too often, the panel said, the UN had sent peacekeeping missions into situations where some or all of the combatants were not yet ready to give up the struggle. With few exceptions, the panel said, the UN simply lacked the political and military muscle to create peace when local forces were not yet ready for it. The panel offered no specific examples, but the failure of the UN peacekeeping mission in Bosnia during 1995 clearly fell into this category. In other cases, such as in Rwanda, UN peacekeepers were not given the military muscle and political support to accomplish their mission. These were examples, the panel said, in which a secretary general had gone to the Security Council with a peacekeeping proposal based not on what was needed in the field but on what he presumed "to be acceptable to the Council politically."*

*Without a reasonable chance of success, it would be better not to send a peacekeeping mission, the panel said. In particular, the panel suggested that the secretary general should refrain from asking the Security Council for authority to send a peacekeeping mission until he had obtained "solid commitments" from member nations for the necessary forces. "To deploy a partial force incapable of solidifying a fragile peace would first raise and then dash the hopes of a population engulfed in conflict or recovering from war, and damage the credibility of the United Nations as a whole," the panel said.*

*The panel offered several dozen proposals for improving the effectiveness of UN peacekeeping missions. Many recommendations dealt with administrative details (for example, improved cooperation and information-sharing among various UN agencies). The most important, and potentially most controversial, proposals were that member states give the UN the re-*

sources to deploy "robust" military units with specific mandates and the ability to exert "credible force" when challenged.

The panel rejected an often-discussed proposal for the UN to have a standing army for peacekeeping missions. Instead, the panel called for creation of five brigade-size units (of about 5,000 members each) that would be available for rapid deployment once the Security Council authorized a new peacekeeping mission. Officers and soldiers assigned to those units would remain on duty with their national forces until called to action by the UN. In addition, the UN should create a pool of about one hundred senior military officers on call for top command positions in future peacekeeping missions, the panel said. With the proper standby arrangements, coupled with an improved capacity to analyze conflict situations, the United Nations should be able to deploy traditional peacekeeping missions within thirty days of approval by the Security Council and more complex missions within ninety days, the panel said.

Similarly, the panel said the UN needed a standby reserve of police commanders and officers who could be sent to help with peacekeeping missions. In numerous cases during the 1990, UN missions were desperately short of policemen to enforce the law and protect the rights of civilians in post-conflict situations. The Brahimi panel noted that police officers recruited for UN missions typically served for just six months to a year, leading to high turnover and excessive training requirements. The panel made several suggestions for improving coordination among police forces from different nations and cultures, including the creation of a standard set of procedures for handling human rights violations.

The UN's chronic shortage of military and police personnel was the direct responsibility of member nations—especially the advanced, industrialized nations that had become increasingly reluctant to provide manpower for peacekeeping missions, the panel said. During the 1990s nearly all UN missions were staffed primarily by developing countries, while the United States and other major powers provided the bulk of the money. As of June 2000, the panel said, 77 percent of the troops in UN peacekeeping missions came from developing countries. Moreover, no developed country had contributed troops to "the most difficult" UN missions, those in Sierra Leone and Congo.

The United States stopped providing military personnel for UN missions in 1994, a year after eighteen U.S. servicemen were killed while on duty with a peacekeeping mission in Somalia. However, the United States continued to provide thousands of military personnel for peacekeeping missions led by NATO in Bosnia (after a 1995 peace agreement) and in Kosovo (following the NATO air war that forced Yugoslavia out of that province). At the same time, Congress repeatedly cut and delayed U.S. contributions to the UN for peacekeeping missions.

One consequence of the UN's increasing reliance on developing countries for peacekeeping manpower was that many military units lacked adequate equipment or supplies. Often, the panel said, companies or brigades would arrive on the scene of a peacekeeping mission without such basic items as

*rifles, helmets, or flak jackets. Poorly equipped units could not possibly con-
tribute effectively to a peacekeeping mission, especially in circumstances
where one or more of the parties to the conflict seemed ready to challenge the
authority of the mission. At the very least, the panel said, a nation unable
to equip its own soldiers for a peacekeeping mission should alert the UN
ahead of time.*

*Peacekeeping forces needed not just manpower and equipment, the panel
said, but adequate authority—known in UN language as a "mandate"—
to deal with the situations they confronted. In the Rwanda case, UN headquarters officials, including Annan (then head of the UN peacekeeping department), expressly forbade peacekeepers from taking military action to
protect civilians because the Security Council mandate did not authorize it.*

*In the future, the panel said, Security Council mandates should be ex-
plicitly tailored to the situations that peacekeepers were expected to confront. In particular, peacekeepers who witness violence against civilians
should have automatic authority to intervene. But the panel expressed concern that extending a "blanket mandate" for civilian protection would raise
expectations that the UN might not be able to meet. At any given time there
would be hundreds of thousands of civilians living in postconflict areas
where UN missions operated. Any UN peacekeeping force mandated to
guard civilians should be given the "specific resources" for the job of protecting victims from aggressors, the panel said.*

*At least half of the panel's recommendations concerned UN headquarters
in New York, where peacekeeping missions were planned and managed. In
blunt language, the panel said that UN offices, including the Department of
Peacekeeping Operations, had neither the personnel nor the administrative
capability to manage complex peacekeeping missions. The peacekeeping department had just thirty-two military officers to support 27,000 troops in
the field, nine civilian police officers to oversee 8,600 police in the field, and
fifteen political desk officers for sixteen existing and newly planned peace
operations. No member nation would attempt to manage operations of the
size and complexity of UN peacekeeping forces with such limited numbers
of support personnel, the panel said.*

*Moreover, the panel said the UN over the years had grown accustomed to
awarding staff positions on the basis of such factors as the political prefer-
ences of member nations, rather than competence. The most qualified workers were given "unreasonable workloads" to compensate for the less capable,
the panel said, creating resentment and bad morale. "Put simply, the United
Nations is far from being a meritocracy today, and unless it takes steps to
become one it will not be able to reverse the alarming trend of qualified personnel, the young among them in particular, leaving the organization," the
panel said.*

*Despite its detailed analysis of problems plaguing peacekeeping mis-
sions, the panel was unable to propose a definitive solution to what many
observers considered the fundamental problem facing the UN: a lack of political will on the part of member nations to make the difficult decisions
needed to promote the success of UN missions. Most failures of UN peace-*

keeping missions occurred because "the Security Council and the member states crafted and supported ambiguous, inconsistent and under-funded mandates and then stood back and watched as they failed, sometimes even adding critical public commentary as the credibility of the United Nations underwent its severest tests," the panel said. The panel called on member states to meet their responsibilities, but it could offer no guaranteed means of forcing them to do so.

In particular, the panel was unable to offer concrete suggestions for preventing a recurrence of the underlying cause of the Rwanda experience. In that case, according to numerous studies, key nations (notably the United States and France) prevented the Security Council from giving the UN mission on the scene enough manpower, equipment, and authority to prevent the genocide.

Annan took note of this broader issue in his formal response to the panel's recommendations, dated October 20. The UN's peacekeeping performance "will not improve unless member states, and particularly those possessing the greatest capacity and means to do so, are ready to participate with soldiers, police officers, and civilian experts, to support cooperation between countries of the South and of the North, including with equipment and training, and to pay their fair share of the costs in full and on time," he wrote. In various statements during the year, Annan also said the UN and other world bodies needed to place more emphasis on eliminating the root causes of conflict. He noted that most wars under way at the turn of the century involved the world's poorest nations, in many cases because those countries were unable to meet the needs of their people.

## UN Endorses Recommendations

In contrast to the work of many special commissions, the report of the peacekeeping panel received almost immediate action at the highest levels of the UN. Annan immediately appointed Deputy Secretary General Louise Frechette to oversee implementation of the recommendations. Annan also appointed a new under-secretary general for peacekeeping operations, Jean-Marie Guehenno, of France. Guehenno assumed his post on October 1, taking the place of Bernard Miyet, who had been widely criticized for his resistance to change.

Annan presented major items from the report to the UN's Millennium Summit in New York. On September 7 the heads of state and heads of government from the nations represented on the Security Council adopted a statement endorsing the general thrust of the report and pledging to put its recommendations into action. (Millennium summit, p. 700)

On October 20 Annan sent the Security Council a detailed response to the report. Annan accepted nearly all the recommendations and promised to implement those that fell within his own power as secretary general. Annan also said he would submit to the General Assembly and Security Council the proposals requiring action by those bodies.

Acting on Annan's recommendation, the Security Council on November 13 adopted Resolution 1327 endorsing major components of the Brahimi *panel report. Most notably, the council pledged to give future peacekeeping operations "clear, credible, and achievable mandates," along with a "credible deterrent capability." However, representatives of the United States and the four other permanent council members rejected a proposal by Bangladesh that would have obligated each of the five nations to contribute at least 5 percent of the troops assigned to every peacekeeping mission.*

*Some aspects of the Brahimi panel's report encountered more resistance among members of the General Assembly, particularly developing nations. During debates in General Assembly committees in mid-November, representatives of India, Jordan, Zambia, and other countries said the Brahimi panel failed to target the major powers—especially the United States—as being primarily responsible for past failures in UN peacekeeping missions. At a committee meeting on November 8, for example, Mwelwa Musambachime of Zambia said the major powers would only send troops into situations where they saw a "national interest" involved. Meanwhile, he said, developing countries were shouldering the burden of providing troops for peacekeeping missions. Representatives of several developing countries also expressed concern that the UN would put more money into peacekeeping at the expense of programs intended to relieve poverty.*

*Annan on October 27 submitted to the General Assembly a revised budget for fiscal years 2000–2001 based on the recommendations of the Brahimi report. It called for $22 million in additional spending on peacekeeping to implement key recommendations of the peacekeeping panel. The General Assembly on December 23 approved a budget including about $9.5 million in additional funding to allow Annan to begin implementing the panel's recommendations.*

> *Following are three excerpts—the "Executive Summary," "Challenges to Implementation," and "Summary of Recommendations"—from the* Report of the Panel on United Nations Peace Operations, *released August 23, 2000, in which the panel called for sweeping changes in UN peacekeeping operations. The document was obtained from the Internet at http://www.un.org/peace/reports/peace_operations.*

## Executive Summary

The United Nations was founded, in the words of its Charter, in order "to save succeeding generations from the scourge of war."

Meeting this challenge is the most important function of the Organization, and to a very significant degree it is the yardstick with which the Organization is judged by the peoples it exists to serve. Over the last decade, the United Nations has repeatedly failed to meet the challenge, and it can do no better today. Without renewed commitment on the part of Member States, significant institutional change and increased financial support, the United Nations will not be capable of executing the critical peacekeeping and peace-building tasks that the Member States assign to it in coming months and years. There are many tasks which United Nations peacekeeping forces should not be asked to undertake and many places they should not go. But when the United Nations does send its forces to uphold the peace, they must be prepared to confront the lingering forces of war and violence, with the ability and determination to defeat them.

The Secretary-General has asked the Panel on United Nations Peace Operations, composed of individuals experienced in various aspects of conflict prevention, peacekeeping and peace-building, to assess the shortcomings of the existing system and to make frank, specific and realistic recommendations for change. Our recommendations focus not only on politics and strategy but also and perhaps even more so on operational and organizational areas of need.

For preventive initiatives to succeed in reducing tension and averting conflict, the Secretary-General needs clear, strong and sustained political support from Member States. Furthermore, as the United Nations has bitterly and repeatedly discovered over the last decade, no amount of good intentions can substitute for the fundamental ability to project credible force if complex peacekeeping, in particular, is to succeed. But force alone cannot create peace; it can only create the space in which peace may be built. Moreover, the changes that the Panel recommends will have no lasting impact unless Member States summon the political will to support the United Nations politically, financially and operationally to enable the United Nations to be truly credible as a force for peace.

Each of the recommendations contained in the present report is designed to remedy a serious problem in strategic direction, decision-making, rapid deployment, operational planning and support, and the use of modern information technology. Key assessments and recommendations are highlighted below, largely in the order in which they appear in the body of the text (the numbers of the relevant paragraphs in the main text are provided in parentheses). In addition, a summary of recommendations is contained in the annex.

## Experience of the past

It should have come as no surprise to anyone that some of the missions of the past decade would be particularly hard to accomplish: they tended to deploy where conflict had not resulted in victory for any side, where a military stalemate or international pressure or both had brought fighting to a halt but at least some of the parties to the conflict were not seriously committed to ending the confrontation. United Nations operations thus did not *deploy into* post-conflict situations but tried to create them. In such complex operations, peacekeepers work to maintain a secure local environment while peacebuilders work to make that environment self-sustaining. Only such an environment offers a ready exit to peacekeeping forces, making peacekeepers and peacebuilders inseparable partners.

## Implications for preventive action and peace-building: The need for strategy and support

The United Nations and its members face a pressing need to establish more effective strategies for conflict prevention, in both the long and short terms. In this context, the Panel endorses the recommendations of the Secretary-General with respect to conflict prevention contained in the Millennium Report and in his remarks before the Security Council's second open meeting on conflict prevention in July 2000. It also encourages the Secretary-General's more frequent use of fact-finding missions to areas of tension in support of short-term crisis-preventive action.

Furthermore, the Security Council and the General Assembly's Special Committee on Peacekeeping Operations, conscious that the United Nations will continue to face the prospect of having to assist communities and nations in making the transition from war to peace, have each recognized and acknowledged the key role of peace-building in complex peace operations. This will require that the United Nations system address what has hitherto been a fundamental deficiency in the way it has conceived of, funded and implemented peace-building strategies and activities. Thus, the Panel recommends that the Executive Committee on Peace and Security (ECPS) present to the Secretary-General a plan to strengthen the permanent capacity of the United Nations to develop peace-building strategies and to implement programmes in support of those strategies.

Among the changes that the Panel supports are: a doctrinal shift in the use of civilian police and related rule of law elements in peace operations that emphasizes a team approach to upholding the rule of law and respect for human rights and helping communities coming out of a conflict to achieve national reconciliation; consolidation of disarmament, demobilization, and reintegration programmes into the assessed budgets of complex peace operations in their first phase; flexibility for heads of United Nations peace operations to fund "quick impact projects" that make a real difference in the lives of people in the mission area; and better integration of electoral assistance into a broader strategy for the support of governance institutions.

## Implications for peacekeeping: the need for robust doctrine and realistic mandates

The Panel concurs that consent of the local parties, impartiality and the use of force only in self-defence should remain the bedrock principles of peacekeeping. Experience shows, however, that in the context of intra-State/transnational conflicts, consent may be manipulated in many ways. Impartiality for United Nations operations must therefore mean adherence to the principles of the Charter: where one party to a peace agreement clearly and incontrovertibly is violating its terms, continued equal treatment of all parties by the United Nations can in the best case result in ineffectiveness and in the worst may amount to complicity with evil. No failure did more to damage the standing and credibility of United Nations peacekeeping in the 1990s than its reluctance to distinguish victim from aggressor. In the past, the United Nations has often found itself unable to respond effectively to such challenges. It is a fundamental premise of the present report, however, that it must be able to do so. Once deployed, United Nations peacekeepers must be able to carry out their mandate professionally and successfully. This means that United Nations military units must be capable of defending themselves, other mission components and the mission's mandate. Rules of engagement should be sufficiently robust and not force United Nations contingents to cede the initiative to their attackers.

This means, in turn, that the Secretariat must not apply best-case planning assumptions to situations where the local actors have historically exhibited worst-case behaviour. It means that mandates should specify an operation's authority to use force. It means bigger forces, better equipped and more costly but able to be a credible deterrent. In particular, United Nations forces for complex operations should be afforded the field intelligence and other capabilities needed to mount an effective defence against violent challengers.

Moreover, United Nations peacekeepers—troops or police—who witness violence against civilians should be presumed to be authorized to stop it, within their means, in support of basic United Nations principles. However, operations given a broad and explicit mandate for civilian protection must be given the specific resources needed to carry out that mandate.

The Secretariat must tell the Security Council what it needs to know, not what it wants to hear, when recommending force and other resource levels for a new mission, and it must set those levels according to realistic scenarios that take into account likely challenges to implementation. Security Council mandates, in turn, should reflect the clarity that peacekeeping operations require for unity of effort when they deploy into potentially dangerous situations.

The current practice is for the Secretary-General to be given a Security Council resolution specifying troop levels on paper, not knowing whether he will be given the troops and other personnel that the mission needs to function effectively, or whether they will be properly equipped. The Panel is of the view that, once realistic mission requirements have been set and agreed to, the Council should leave its authorizing resolution in draft form until the Secretary-General confirms that he has received troop and other commitments from Member States sufficient to meet those requirements.

Member States that do commit formed military units to an operation should be invited to consult with the members of the Security Council during mandate formulation; such advice might usefully be institutionalized via the establishment of ad hoc subsidiary organs of the Council, as provided for in Article 29 of the Charter. Troop contributors should also be invited to attend Secretariat briefings of the Security Council pertaining to crises that affect the safety and security of mission personnel or to a change or reinterpretation of the mandate regarding the use of force.

## New headquarters capacity for information management and strategic analysis

The Panel recommends that a new information-gathering and analysis entity be created to support the informational and analytical needs of the Secretary-General and the members of the Executive Committee on Peace and Security (ECPS). Without such capacity, the Secretariat will remain a reactive institution, unable to get ahead of daily events, and the ECPS will not be able to fulfil the role for which it was created.

The Panel's proposed ECPS Information and Strategic Analysis Secretariat (EISAS) would create and maintain integrated databases on peace and security issues, distribute that knowledge efficiently within the United Nations system, generate policy analyses, formulate long-term strategies for ECPS and bring budding crises to the attention of the ECPS leadership. It could also propose and manage the agenda of ECPS itself, helping to transform it into the decision-making body anticipated in the Secretary-General's initial reforms.

The Panel proposes that EISAS be created by consolidating the existing Situation Centre of the Department of Peacekeeping Operations (DPKO) with a number of small, scattered policy planning offices, and adding a small team of military analysts, experts in international criminal networks and information systems specialists. EISAS should serve the needs of all members of ECPS.

### Improved mission guidance and leadership

The Panel believes it is essential to assemble the leadership of a new mission as early as possible at United Nations Headquarters, to participate in shaping a mission's concept of operations, support plan, budget, staffing and Headquarters mission guidance. To that end, the Panel recommends that the Secretary-General compile, in a systematic fashion and with input from Member States, a comprehensive list of potential special representatives of the Secretary-General (SRSGs), force commanders, civilian police commissioners, their potential deputies and potential heads of other components of a mission, representing a broad geographic and equitable gender distribution.

### Rapid deployment standards and "on-call" expertise

The first 6 to 12 weeks following a ceasefire or peace accord are often the most critical ones for establishing both a stable peace and the credibility of a new operation. Opportunities lost during that period are hard to regain.

The Panel recommends that the United Nations define "rapid and effective deployment capacity" as the ability to fully deploy traditional peacekeeping operations within 30 days of the adoption of a Security Council resolution establishing such an operation, and within 90 days in the case of complex peacekeeping operations.

The Panel recommends that the United Nations standby arrangements system (UNSAS) be developed further to include several coherent, multinational, brigade-size forces and the necessary enabling forces, created by Member States working in partnership, in order to better meet the need for the robust peacekeeping forces that the Panel has advocated. The Panel also recommends that the Secretariat send a team to confirm the readiness of each potential troop contributor to meet the requisite United Nations training and equipment requirements for peacekeeping operations, prior to deployment. Units that do not meet the requirements must not be deployed. To support such rapid and effective deployment, the Panel recommends that a revolving "on-call list" of about 100 experienced, well qualified military officers, carefully vetted and accepted by DPKO, be created within UNSAS. Teams drawn from this list and available for duty on seven days' notice would translate broad, strategic-level mission concepts developed at Headquarters into concrete operational and tactical plans in advance of the deployment of troop contingents, and would augment a core element from DPKO to serve as part of a mission start-up team.

Parallel on-call lists of civilian police, international judicial experts, penal experts and human rights specialists must be available in sufficient numbers to strengthen rule of law institutions, as needed, and should also be part of UNSAS. Pre-trained teams could then be drawn from this list to precede the main body of civilian police and related specialists into a new mission area, facilitating the rapid and effective deployment of the law and order component into the mission.

The Panel also calls upon Member States to establish enhanced national "pools" of police officers and related experts, earmarked for deployment to United Nations peace operations, to help meet the high demand for civilian police and related criminal justice/rule of law expertise in peace operations dealing with intra-State conflict. The Panel also urges Member States to consider forming joint regional partnerships and programmes for the purpose of training members of the respective national pools to United Nations civilian police doctrine and standards.

The Secretariat should also address, on an urgent basis, the needs: to put in place a transparent and decentralized recruitment mechanism for civilian field personnel; to improve the retention of the civilian specialists that are needed in every complex peace operation; and to create standby arrangements for their rapid deployment.

Finally, the Panel recommends that the Secretariat radically alter the systems and procedures in place for peacekeeping procurement in order to facilitate rapid deployment. It recommends that responsibilities for peacekeeping budgeting and procurement be moved out of the Department of Management and placed in DPKO. The Panel proposes the creation of a new and distinct body of streamlined field procurement policies and procedures; increased delegation of procurement authority to the field; and greater flexibility for field missions in the management of their budgets. The Panel also urges that the Secretary-General formulate and submit to the General Assembly, for its approval, a global logistics support strategy governing the stockpiling of equipment reserves and standing contracts with the private sector for common goods and services. In the interim, the Panel recommends that additional "start-up kits" of essential equipment be maintained at the United Nations Logistics Base (UNLB) in Brindisi, Italy.

The Panel also recommends that the Secretary-General be given authority, with the approval of the Advisory Committee on Administrative and Budgetary Questions (ACABQ) to commit up to $50 million well in advance of the adoption of a Security Council resolution establishing a new operation once it becomes clear that an operation is likely to be established.

## Enhance Headquarters capacity to plan
## and support peace operations

The Panel recommends that Headquarters support for peacekeeping be treated as a core activity of the United Nations, and as such the majority of its resource requirements should be funded through the regular budget of the Organization. DPKO and other offices that plan and support peacekeeping are currently primarily funded by the Support Account, which is renewed each year and funds only temporary posts. That approach to funding and staff seems to confuse the temporary nature of specific operations with the evident permanence of peacekeeping and other peace operations activities as core functions of the United Nations, which is obviously an untenable state of affairs.

The total cost of DPKO and related Headquarters support offices for peacekeeping does not exceed $50 million per annum, or roughly 2 per cent of total peacekeeping costs. Additional resources for those offices are urgently needed to ensure that more than $2 billion spent on peacekeeping in 2001 are well spent. The Panel therefore recommends that the Secretary-General submit a proposal to the General Assembly outlining the Organization's requirements in full.

The Panel believes that a methodical management review of DPKO should be conducted but also believes that staff shortages in certain areas are plainly obvious. For example, it is clearly not enough to have 32 officers providing military planning and guidance to 27,000 troops in the field, nine civilian police staff to identify, vet and provide guidance for up to 8,600 police, and 15 political desk officers for 14 current operations and two new ones, or to allocate just 1.25 per cent of the total costs of peacekeeping to Headquarters administrative and logistics support.

## Establish Integrated Mission Task Forces for mission
## planning and support

The Panel recommends that Integrated Mission Task Forces (IMTFs) be created, with staff from throughout the United Nations system seconded to them, to plan new missions and help them reach full deployment, significantly enhancing the support that Headquarters provides to the field. There is currently no integrated planning or support cell in the Secretariat that brings together those responsible for political analysis, military operations, civilian police, electoral assistance, human rights, development, humanitarian assistance, refugees and displaced persons, public information, logistics, finance and recruitment.

Structural adjustments are also required in other elements of DPKO, in particular to the Military and Civilian Police Division, which should be reorganized into two separate divisions, and the Field Administration and Logistics Division (FALD), which should be split into two divisions. The Lessons Learned Unit should be strengthened and moved into the DPKO Office of Operations. Public information planning and support at Headquarters also needs strengthening, as do elements in the Department of Political Affairs (DPA), particularly the electoral unit. Outside the Secretariat, the ability of the Office of the United Nations High Commissioner for Human Rights to plan and support the human rights components of peace operations needs to be reinforced.

Consideration should be given to allocating a third Assistant Secretary-General to DPKO and designating one of them as "Principal Assistant Secretary-General," functioning as the deputy to the Under-Secretary-General.

## Adapting peace operations to the information age

Modern, well utilized information technology (IT) is a key enabler of many of the above-mentioned objectives, but gaps in strategy, policy and practice impede its effective use. In particular, Headquarters lacks a sufficiently strong responsibility centre for user-level IT strategy and policy in peace operations. A senior official with such responsibility in the peace and security arena should be appointed and located within EISAS, with counterparts in the offices of the SRSG in every United Nations peace operation.

Headquarters and the field missions alike also need a substantive, global, Peace Operations Extranet (POE), through which missions would have access to, among other things, EISAS databases and analyses and lessons learned.

## Challenges to Implementation

The Panel believes that the above recommendations fall well within the bounds of what can be reasonably demanded of the Organization's Member States. Implementing some of them will require additional resources for the Organization, but we do not mean to suggest that the best way to solve the problems of the United Nations is merely to throw additional resources at them. Indeed, no amount of money or resources can substitute for the significant changes that are urgently needed in the culture of the Organization.

The Panel calls on the Secretariat to heed the Secretary-General's initiatives to reach out to the institutions of civil society; to constantly keep in mind that the United Nations they serve is *the* universal organization. People everywhere are fully entitled to consider that it is *their* organization, and as such to pass judgement on its activities and the people who serve in it.

Furthermore, wide disparities in staff quality exist and those in the system are the first to acknowledge it; better performers are given unreasonable workloads to compensate for those who are less capable. Unless the United Nations takes steps to become a true meritocracy, it will not be able to reverse the alarming trend of qualified personnel, the young among them in particular, leaving the Organization. Moreover, qualified people will have no incentive to join it. Unless managers at all levels, beginning with the Secretary-General and his senior staff, seriously address this problem on a priority basis, reward excellence and remove incompetence, additional resources will be wasted and lasting reform will become impossible.

Member States also acknowledge that they need to reflect on their working culture and methods. It is incumbent upon Security Council members, for example, and the membership at large to breathe life into the words that they produce, as did, for instance, the Security Council delegation that flew to

Jakarta and Dili in the wake of the East Timor crisis in 1999, an example of effective Council *action* at its best: *res, non verba.*

We—the members of the Panel on United Nations Peace Operations—call on the leaders of the world assembled at the Millennium Summit, as they renew their commitment to the ideals of the United Nations, to commit as well to strengthen the capacity of the United Nations to fully accomplish the mission which is, indeed, its very *raison d'être:* to help communities engulfed in strife and to maintain or restore peace.

While building consensus for the recommendations in the present report, we have also come to a shared vision of a *United* Nations, extending a strong helping hand to a community, country or region to avert conflict or to end violence. We see an SRSG ending a mission well accomplished, having given the people of a country the opportunity to do for themselves what they could not do before: to build and hold onto peace, to find reconciliation, to strengthen democracy, to secure human rights. We see, above all, a United Nations that has not only the will but also the ability to fulfil its great promise, and to justify the confidence and trust placed in it by the overwhelming majority of humankind. . . .

## VI. Challenges to Implementation

265. The present report targets two groups in presenting its recommendations for reform: the Member States and the Secretariat. We recognize that reform will not occur unless Member States genuinely pursue it. At the same time, we believe that the changes we recommend for the Secretariat must be actively advanced by the Secretary-General and implemented by his senior staff.

266. Member States must recognize that the United Nations is the sum of its parts and accept that the primary responsibility for reform lies with them. The failures of the United Nations are not those of the Secretariat alone, or troop commanders or the leaders of field missions. Most occurred because the Security Council and the Member States crafted and supported ambiguous, inconsistent and under-funded mandates and then stood back and watched as they failed, sometimes even adding critical public commentary as the credibility of the United Nations underwent its severest tests.

267. The problems of command and control that recently arose in Sierra Leone are the most recent illustration of what cannot be tolerated any longer. Troop contributors must ensure that the troops they provide fully understand the importance of an integrated chain of command, the operational control of the Secretary-General and the standard operating procedures and rules of engagement of the mission. It is essential that the chain of command in an operation be understood and respected, and the onus is on national capitals to refrain from instructing their contingent commanders on operational matters.

268. We are aware that the Secretary-General is implementing a comprehensive reform programme and realize that our recommendations may need to be adjusted to fit within this bigger picture. Furthermore, the reforms we have recommended for the Secretariat and the United Nations system in general will not be accomplished overnight, though some require urgent action.

We recognize that there is a normal resistance to change in any bureaucracy, and are encouraged that some of the changes we have embraced as recommendations originate from within the system. We are also encouraged by the commitment of the Secretary-General to lead the Secretariat toward reform even if it means that long-standing organizational and procedural lines will have to be breached, and that aspects of the Secretariat's priorities and culture will need to be challenged and changed. In this connection, we urge the Secretary-General to appoint a senior official with responsibility for overseeing the implementation of the recommendations contained in the present report.

269. The Secretary-General has consistently emphasized the need for the United Nations to reach out to civil society and to strengthen relations with non-governmental organizations, academic institutions and the media, who can be useful partners in the promotion of peace and security for all. We call on the Secretariat to take heed of the Secretary-General's approach and implement it in its work in peace and security. We call on them to constantly keep in mind that the United Nations they serve is *the* universal organization. People everywhere are fully entitled to consider that it is *their* organization, and as such to pass judgement on its activities and the people who serve in it.

270. There is wide variation in quality among Secretariat staff supporting the peace and security functions in DPKO, DPA and the other departments concerned. This observation applies to the civilians recruited by the Secretariat as well as to the military and civilian police personnel proposed by Member States. These disparities are widely recognized by those in the system. Better performers are given unreasonable workloads to compensate for those who are less capable. Naturally, this can be bad for morale and can create resentment, particularly among those who rightly point out that the United Nations has not dedicated enough attention over the years to career development, training and mentoring or the institution of modern management practices. Put simply, the United Nations is far from being a meritocracy today, and unless it takes steps to become one it will not be able to reverse the alarming trend of qualified personnel, the young among them in particular, leaving the Organization. If the hiring, promotion and delegation of responsibility rely heavily on seniority or personal or political connections, qualified people will have no incentive to join the Organization or stay with it. Unless managers at all levels, beginning with the Secretary-General and his senior staff, seriously address this problem on a priority basis, reward excellence and remove incompetent staff, additional resources will be wasted and lasting reform will become impossible.

271. The same level of scrutiny should apply to United Nations personnel in the field missions. The majority of them embody the spirit of what it means to be an international civil servant, traveling to war-torn lands and dangerous environments to help improve the lives of the world's most vulnerable communities. They do so with considerable personal sacrifice, and at times with great risks to their own physical safety and mental health. They deserve the world's recognition and appreciation. Over the years, many of them have given their lives in the service of peace and we take this opportunity to honour their memory.

272. United Nations personnel in the field, perhaps more than any others, are obliged to respect local norms, culture and practices. They must go out of their way to demonstrate that respect, as a start, by getting to know their host environment and trying to learn as much of the local culture and language as they can. They must behave with the understanding that they are guests in someone else's home, however destroyed that home might be, particularly when the United Nations takes on a transitional administration role. And they must also treat one another with respect and dignity, with particular sensitivity towards gender and cultural differences.

273. In short, we believe that a very high standard should be maintained for the selection and conduct of personnel at Headquarters and in the field. When United Nations personnel fail to meet such standards, they should be held accountable. In the past, the Secretariat has had difficulty in holding senior officials in the field accountable for their performance because those officials could point to insufficient resources, unclear instructions or lack of appropriate command and control arrangements as the main impediments to successful implementation of a mission's mandate. These deficiencies should be addressed but should not be allowed to offer cover to poor performers. The future of nations, the lives of those whom the United Nations has come to help and protect, the success of a mission and the credibility of the Organization can all hinge on what a few individuals do or fail to do. Anyone who turns out to be unsuited to the task that he or she has agreed to perform must be removed from a mission, no matter how high or how low they may be on the ladder.

274. Member States themselves acknowledge that they, too, need to reflect on their working culture and methods, at least as concerns the conduct of United Nations peace and security activities. The tradition of the recitation of statements, followed by a painstaking process of achieving consensus, places considerable emphasis on the diplomatic process over operational product. While one of the United Nations main virtues is that it provides a forum for 189 Member States to exchange views on pressing global issues, sometimes dialogue alone is not enough to ensure that billion- dollar peacekeeping operations, vital conflict prevention measures or critical peacemaking efforts succeed in the face of great odds. Expressions of general support in the form of statements and resolutions must be followed up with tangible action.

275. Moreover, Member States may send conflicting messages regarding the actions they advocate, with their representatives voicing political support in one body but denying financial support in another. Such inconsistencies have appeared between the Fifth Committee on Administrative and Budgetary Matters on the one hand, and the Security Council and the Special Committee on Peacekeeping Operations on the other.

276. On the political level, many of the local parties with whom peacekeepers and peacemakers are dealing on a daily basis may neither respect nor fear verbal condemnation by the Security Council. It is therefore incumbent that Council members and the membership at large breathe life into the words that they produce, as did the Security Council delegation that flew to

Jakarta and Dili in the wake of the East Timor crisis last year, an example of effective Council *action* at its best: *res, non verba.*

277. Meanwhile, the financial constraints under which the United Nations labours continue to cause serious damage to its ability to conduct peace operations in a credible and professional manner. We therefore urge that Member States uphold their treaty obligations and pay their dues in full, on time and without condition.

278. We are also aware that there are other issues which, directly or indirectly, hamper effective United Nations action in the field of peace and security, including two unresolved issues that are beyond the scope of the Panel's mandate but critical to peace operations and that only the Member States can address. They are the disagreements about how assessments in support of peacekeeping operations are apportioned and about equitable representation on the Security Council. We can only hope that the Member States will find a way to resolve their differences on these issues in the interests of upholding their collective international responsibility as prescribed in the Charter.

279. We call on the leaders of the world assembled at the Millennium Summit, as they renew their commitment to the ideals of the United Nations, to commit as well to strengthen the capacity of the United Nations to fully accomplish the mission which is, indeed, its very *raison d'être:* to help communities engulfed in strife and to maintain or restore peace.

280. While building consensus for the recommendations in the present report, we—the members of the Panel on United Nations Peace Operations— have also come to a shared vision of a *United* Nations, extending a strong helping hand to a community, country or region to avert conflict or to end violence. We see an SRSG ending a mission well accomplished, having given the people of a country the opportunity to do for themselves what they could not do before: to build and hold onto peace, to find reconciliation, to strengthen democracy, to secure human rights. We see, above all, a United Nations that has not only the will but also the ability to fulfil its great promise and to justify the confidence and trust placed in it by the overwhelming majority of humankind. . . .

## Summary of Recommendations

### 1. Preventive action:

(a) The Panel endorses the recommendations of the Secretary-General with respect to conflict prevention contained in the Millennium Report and in his remarks before the Security Council's second open meeting on conflict prevention in July 2000, in particular his appeal to "all who are engaged in conflict prevention and development—the United Nations, the Bretton Woods institutions, Governments and civil society organizations—[to] address these challenges in a more integrated fashion";

(b) The Panel supports the Secretary-General's more frequent use of fact-finding missions to areas of tension, and stresses Member States' obligations, under Article 2(5) of the Charter, to give "every assistance" to such activities of the United Nations.

## 2. Peace-building strategy:

(a) A small percentage of a mission's first-year budget should be made available to the representative or special representative of the Secretary-General leading the mission to fund quick impact projects in its area of operations, with the advice of the United Nations country team's resident coordinator;

(b) The Panel recommends a doctrinal shift in the use of civilian police, other rule of law elements and human rights experts in complex peace operations to reflect an increased focus on strengthening rule of law institutions and improving respect for human rights in post-conflict environments;

(c) The Panel recommends that the legislative bodies consider bringing demobilization and reintegration programmes into the assessed budgets of complex peace operations for the first phase of an operation in order to facilitate the rapid disassembly of fighting factions and reduce the likelihood of resumed conflict;

(d) The Panel recommends that the Executive Committee on Peace and Security (ECPS) discuss and recommend to the Secretary-General a plan to strengthen the permanent capacity of the United Nations to develop peace-building strategies and to implement programmes in support of those strategies.

## 3. Peacekeeping doctrine and strategy:

Once deployed, United Nations peacekeepers must be able to carry out their mandates professionally and successfully and be capable of defending themselves, other mission components and the mission's mandate, with robust rules of engagement, against those who renege on their commitments to a peace accord or otherwise seek to undermine it by violence.

## 4. Clear, credible and achievable mandates:

(a) The Panel recommends that, before the Security Council agrees to implement a ceasefire or peace agreement with a United Nations-led peacekeeping operation, the Council assure itself that the agreement meets threshold conditions, such as consistency with international human rights standards and practicability of specified tasks and timelines;

(b) The Security Council should leave in draft form resolutions authorizing missions with sizeable troop levels until such time as the Secretary-General has firm commitments of troops and other critical mission support elements, including peace-building elements, from Member States;

(c) Security Council resolutions should meet the requirements of peacekeeping operations when they deploy into potentially dangerous situations, especially the need for a clear chain of command and unity of effort;

(d) The Secretariat must tell the Security Council what it needs to know, not what it wants to hear, when formulating or changing mission mandates, and countries that have committed military units to an operation should have access to Secretariat briefings to the Council on matters affecting the safety and security of their personnel, especially those meetings with implications for a mission's use of force.

## 5. Information and strategic analysis:

The Secretary-General should establish an entity, referred to here as the ECPS Information and Strategic Analysis Secretariat (EISAS), which would support the information and analysis needs of all members of ECPS; for management purposes, it should be administered by and report jointly to the heads of the Department of Political Affairs (DPA) and the Department of Peacekeeping Operations (DPKO).

## 6. Transitional civil administration:

The Panel recommends that the Secretary-General invite a panel of international legal experts, including individuals with experience in United Nations operations that have transitional administration mandates, to evaluate the feasibility and utility of developing an interim criminal code, including any regional adaptations potentially required, for use by such operations pending the re-establishment of local rule of law and local law enforcement capacity.

## 7. Determining deployment timelines:

The United Nations should define "rapid and effective deployment capacities" as the ability, from an operational perspective, to fully deploy traditional peacekeeping operations within 30 days after the adoption of a Security Council resolution, and within90 days in the case of complex peacekeeping operations.

## 8. Mission leadership:

(a) The Secretary-General should systematize the method of selecting mission leaders, beginning with the compilation of a comprehensive list of potential representatives or special representatives of the Secretary-General, force commanders, civilian police commissioners, and their deputies and other heads of substantive and administrative components, within a fair geographic and gender distribution and with input from Member States;

(b) The entire leadership of a mission should be selected and assembled at Headquarters as early as possible in order to enable their participation in key aspects of the mission planning process, for briefings on the situation in the mission area and to meet and work with their colleagues in mission leadership;

(c) The Secretariat should routinely provide the mission leadership with strategic guidance and plans for anticipating and overcoming challenges to mandate implementation, and whenever possible should formulate such guidance and plans together with the mission leadership.

## 9. Military personnel:

(a) Member States should be encouraged, where appropriate, to enter into partnerships with one another, within the context of the United Nations Standby Arrangements System (UNSAS), to form several coherent brigade-size forces, with necessary enabling forces, ready for effective deployment within 30 days of the adoption of a Security Council resolution establishing a traditional peacekeeping operation and within 90 days for complex peace-keeping operations;

(b) The Secretary-General should be given the authority to formally can-vass Member States participating in UNSAS regarding their willingness to contribute troops to a potential operation, once it appeared likely that a cease-fire accord or agreement envisaging an implementing role for the United Na-tions, might be reached;

(c) The Secretariat should, as a standard practice, send a team to confirm the preparedness of each potential troop contributor to meet the provisions of the memoranda of understanding on the requisite training and equipment requirements, prior to deployment; those that do not meet the requirements must not deploy;

(d) The Panel recommends that a revolving "on-call list" of about 100 mili-tary officers be created in UNSAS to be available on seven days' notice to augment nuclei of DPKO planners with teams trained to create a mission head-quarters for a new peacekeeping operation.

## 10. Civilian police personnel:

(a) Member States are encouraged to each establish a national pool of civil-ian police officers that would be ready for deployment to United Nations peace operations on short notice, within the context of the United Nations Standby Arrangements System;

(b) Member States are encouraged to enter into regional training partner-ships for civilian police in the respective national pools, to promote a common level of preparedness in accordance with guidelines, standard operating pro-cedures and performance standards to be

promulgated by the United Nations;

(c) Members States are encouraged to designate a single point of contact within their governmental structures for the provision of civilian police to United Nations peace operations;

(d) The Panel recommends that a revolving on-call list of about 100 police officers and related experts be created in UNSAS to be available on seven days' notice with teams trained to create the civilian police component of a new peacekeeping operation, train incoming personnel and give the compo-nent greater coherence at an early date;

(e) The Panel recommends that parallel arrangements to recommendations (a), (b) and (c) above be established for judicial, penal, human rights and other relevant specialists, who with specialist civilian police will make up collegial "rule of law" teams.

## 11. Civilian specialists:

(a) The Secretariat should establish a central Internet/Intranet-based ros-ter of pre-selected civilian candidates available to deploy to peace operations on short notice. The field missions should be granted access to and delegated authority to recruit candidates from it, in accordance with guidelines on fair geographic and gender distribution to be promulgated by the Secretariat;

(b) The Field Service category of personnel should be reformed to mirror the recurrent demands faced by all peace operations, especially at the mid- to senior-levels in the administrative and logistics areas;

(c) Conditions of service for externally recruited civilian staff should be revised to enable the United Nations to attract the most highly qualified candidates, and to then offer those who have served with distinction greater career prospects;

(d) DPKO should formulate a comprehensive staffing strategy for peace operations, outlining, among other issues, the use of United Nations Volunteers, standby arrangements for the provision of civilian personnel on 72 hours' notice to facilitate mission start-up, and the divisions of responsibility among the members of the Executive Committee on Peace and Security for implementing that strategy.

## 12. Rapidly deployable capacity for public information:

Additional resources should be devoted in mission budgets to public information and the associated personnel and information technology required to get an operation's message out and build effective internal communications links.

## 13. Logistics support and expenditure management:

(a) The Secretariat should prepare a global logistics support strategy to enable rapid and effective mission deployment within the timelines proposed and corresponding to planning assumptions established by the substantive offices of DPKO;

(b) The General Assembly should authorize and approve a one-time expenditure to maintain at least five mission start-up kits in Brindisi, which should include rapidly deployable communications equipment. These start-up kits should then be routinely replenished with funding from the assessed contributions to the operations that drew on them;

(c) The Secretary-General should be given authority to draw up to US$50 million from the Peacekeeping Reserve Fund, once it became clear that an operation was likely to be established, with the approval of the Advisory Committee on Administrative and Budgetary Questions (ACABQ) but prior to the adoption of a Security Council resolution;

(d) The Secretariat should undertake a review of the entire procurement policies and procedures (with proposals to the General Assembly for amendments to the Financial Rules and Regulations, as required), to facilitate in particular the rapid and full deployment of an operation within the proposed timelines;

(e) The Secretariat should conduct a review of the policies and procedures governing the management of financial resources in the field missions with a view to providing field missions with much greater flexibility in the management of their budgets;

(f) The Secretariat should increase the level of procurement authority delegated to the field missions (from $200,000 to as high as $1 million, depending on mission size and needs) for all goods and services that are available locally and are not covered under systems contracts or standing commercial services contracts.

## 14. Funding Headquarters support for peacekeeping operations:

(a) The Panel recommends a substantial increase in resources for Headquarters support of peacekeeping operations, and urges the Secretary-General to submit a proposal to the General Assembly outlining his requirements in full;

(b) Headquarters support for peacekeeping should be treated as a core activity of the United Nations, and as such the majority of its resource requirements for this purpose should be funded through the mechanism of the regular biennial programme budget of the Organization;

(c) Pending the preparation of the next regular budget submission, the Panel recommends that the Secretary-General approach the General Assembly with a request for an emergency supplemental increase to the Support Account to allow immediate recruitment of additional personnel, particularly in DPKO.

## 15. Integrated mission planning and support:

Integrated Mission Task Forces (IMTFs), with members seconded from throughout the United Nations system, as necessary, should be the standard vehicle for mission-specific planning and support. IMTFs should serve as the first point of contact for all such support, and IMTF leaders should have temporary line authority over seconded personnel, in accordance with agreements between DPKO, DPA and other contributing departments, programmes, funds and agencies.

## 16. Other structural adjustments in DPKO:

(a) The current Military and Civilian Police Division should be restructured, moving the Civilian Police Unit out of the military reporting chain. Consideration should be given to upgrading the rank and level of the Civilian Police Adviser;

(b) The Military Adviser's Office in DPKO should be restructured to correspond more closely to the way in which the military field headquarters in United Nations peacekeeping operations are structured;

(c) A new unit should be established in DPKO and staffed with the relevant expertise for the provision of advice on criminal law issues that are critical to the effective use of civilian police in the United Nations peace operations;

(d) The Under-Secretary-General for Management should delegate authority and responsibility for peacekeeping-related budgeting and procurement functions to the Under-Secretary-General for Peacekeeping Operations for a two-year trial period;

(e) The Lessons Learned Unit should be substantially enhanced and moved into a revamped DPKO Office of Operations;

(f) Consideration should be given to increasing the number of Assistant Secretaries-General in DPKO from two to three, with one of the three designated as the "Principal Assistant Secretary-General" and functioning as the deputy to the Under-Secretary-General.

### 17. Operational support for public information:

A unit for operational planning and support of public information in peace operations should be established, either within DPKO or within a new Peace and Security Information Service in the Department of Public Information (DPI) reporting directly to the Under-Secretary-General for Communication and Public Information.

### 18. Peace-building support in the Department of Political Affairs:

(a) The Panel supports the Secretariat's effort to create a pilot Peace-building Unit within DPA, in cooperation with other integral United Nations elements, and suggests that regular budgetary support for this unit be revisited by the membership if the pilot programme works well. . . .

(b) The Panel recommends that regular budget resources for Electoral Assistance Division programmatic expenses be substantially increased to meet the rapidly growing demand for its services, in lieu of voluntary contributions;

(c) To relieve demand on the Field Administration and Logistics Division (FALD) and the executive office of DPA, and to improve support services rendered to smaller political and peace-building field offices, the Panel recommends that procurement, logistics, staff recruitment and other support services for all such smaller, non-military field missions be provided by the United Nations Office for Project Services (UNOPS).

### 19. Peace operations support in the Office of the United Nations High Commissioner for Human Rights:

The Panel recommends substantially enhancing the field mission planning and preparation capacity of the Office of the United Nations High Commissioner for Human Rights, with funding partly from the regular budget and partly from peace operations mission budgets.

### 20. Peace operations and the information age:

(a) Headquarters peace and security departments need a responsibility centre to devise and oversee the implementation of common information technology strategy and training for peace operations, residing in EISAS. Mission counterparts to the responsibility centre should also be appointed to serve in the offices of the special representatives of the Secretary-General in complex peace operations to oversee the implementation of that strategy;

(b) EISAS, in cooperation with the Information Technology Services Division (ITSD), should implement an enhanced peace operations element on the current United Nations Intranet and link it to the missions through a Peace Operations Extranet (POE);

(c) Peace operations could benefit greatly from more extensive use of geographic information systems (GIS) technology, which quickly integrates operational information with electronic maps of the mission area, for applications as diverse as demobilization, civilian policing, voter registration, human rights monitoring and reconstruction;

(d) The IT needs of mission components with unique information technology needs, such as civilian police and human rights, should be anticipated and met more consistently in mission planning and implementation;

(e) The Panel encourages the development of web site co-management by Headquarters and the field missions, in which Headquarters would maintain oversight but individual missions would have staff authorized to produce and post web content that conforms to basic presentational standards and policy.

# FEDERAL GUIDELINES ON
# STEM CELL RESEARCH
## August 23, 2000

*The federal government on August 23, 2000, announced new guidelines under which it would fund research using stem cells from human embryos. Scientists were hopeful that the research could lead to cures for a variety of devastating and debilitating diseases, including Parkinson's, diabetes, some cancers, heart disease, and nerve damage. But antiabortion advocates and religious leaders, among others, objected to the research, arguing that it destroyed human embryos, which theoretically had the potential to become human beings. The National Institutes of Health (NIH) had imposed a moratorium on research on human embryo stem cells in January 1999 while it wrote guidelines addressing the scientific and ethical questions involved in the research.*

*In announcing the guidelines the NIH said the "potential medical benefits" of human stem cell research "are compelling and worthy of pursuit in accordance with appropriate ethical standards." In an impromptu news conference, President Bill Clinton endorsed the guidelines. "I think we cannot walk away from the potential to save lives and improve lives, to help people literally get up and walk, to do all kinds of things we never could have imagined as long as we meet rigorous, ethical standards," the president said. The guidelines took several steps to prevent anyone from donating embryos for profit or for the medical benefit of relatives and to prohibit researchers from creating embryos specifically to harvest stem cells. The guidelines also applied to stem cells derived from fetal tissue.*

*The guidelines closely followed the draft version that NIH had made available for public comment in December 1999, so the content did not come as a surprise to anyone who had been following the controversy. Nonetheless, they were immediately criticized by some members of Congress, who said that the guidelines violated a congressional ban on federal funding of embryo research and that scientists could achieve similar results by using adult stem cells. They found a powerful ally in Republican presidential nominee George W. Bush, who said, through a spokesman, that he opposed federal funding for research "that involves destroying a living human em-*

667

*bryo." Bush and other opponents of the research also scoffed at the provision
in the guidelines that barred federal funding to researchers who destroyed
human embryos directly but permitted those researchers to obtain stem cells
taken from embryos by privately funded researchers. Such a distinction
was meaningless, they said.*

## A Promising Area of Medical Research . . .

*Pluripotent human stem cells were the source of most of the various spe-
cialized tissues that made up the body—blood, bone, muscle, brain, and so
forth. Pluripotent stem cells began to form about four days after a human
egg was fertilized and quickly differentiated into specialized cells. For some
time scientists had postulated that these cells, which were self-renewing and
capable of endless division in the laboratory, might be coaxed into growing
replacement tissues and organs for the human body. Often-cited examples
include healthy, insulin-producing pancreatic cells that could be implanted
in diabetes sufferers or new nerve cells for people suffering from spinal cord
injuries. Scientists also said that stem cell research offered the best glimpse
yet into the earliest stages of human development, which could help reveal
the causes of birth defects and certain kinds of cancers and could improve the way drugs were tested for safety and efficacy. Those hopes were
reinforced with the announcement in June that working drafts of the human genome had been completed several years ahead of schedule.* (Human
genome, p. 397)

*Stem cell research took a significant step forward in late 1998 when two
teams of scientists, working separately, became the first researchers to isolate human stem cells. A team from the University of Wisconsin extracted
stem cells from discarded embryos donated by fertility clinics, while a team
from Johns Hopkins University extracted stem cells from the gonads of
aborted fetuses. Unsure about whether their work might violate the ban on
federal funding of embryo research, first enacted in 1995, both teams were
careful to use only private money. The key source of the private funding was
Geron Corporation, a biotechnology firm in Menlo Park, California. The
University of Wisconsin subsequently set up a nonprofit research institute
to sell embryonic stem cells for research purposes.*

## . . . and a Tangle of Ethical Issues

*In an effort to settle at least some of the ethical issues surrounding stem
cell research, the NIH guidelines stipulated that only cells from frozen human embryos that otherwise would have been discarded by fertility clinics
could qualify for federal funding. Embryo donors could not be paid and
could not specify the person to receive stem cells from the embryo. Moreover,
the doctor involved in the fertility treatment could not be the same person
who was using the embryos to derive stem cells. Those stipulations were intended to discourage abortions as well as a "black market" in human embryos and to prevent women from creating embryos solely to aid a sick
relative.*

*The guidelines also set out several areas of research that were out of bounds for federal funding. These included research using human embryo stem cells to create or contribute to a human embryo, using human stem cells in combination with animal embryos, and using human embryos created specifically for research purposes. The guidelines also prohibited researchers from using the nucleus of a human somatic cell (an ordinary body cell) to create stem cells or from performing research on stem cells created with human somatic cells. In theory the nucleus of a somatic cell from a patient could be inserted into a human egg cell and directed in the laboratory to grow the type of tissue that the patient needed to have replaced. Researchers were also barred from inserting somatic cell nuclei into human egg cells to reproductively clone humans. This was the process researchers in Scotland used to clone Dolly the sheep.* (Dolly, Historic Documents of 1997, p. 212)

*The guidelines did little to satisfy those who believed that life begins at conception and who were thus opposed to destroying human embryos to obtain the stem cells. "We're talking about dismembering a living being, according to our interpretation," Representative Jay Dickey (R-Ark.), told the* New York Times. *Dickey was the author of the 1995 ban that barred federal funding of research on human embryos.*

*Senator Sam Brownback (R-Kan.) called the NIH rules "illegal, immoral, and unnecessary" in an August 23 statement and said scientists could achieve the same goals by using stem cells extracted from adults. Most adult organs had stem cells that generated new cells, and scientists had shown that some of these, such as the stem cells that make red and white blood cells, might be forced in the laboratory to make muscle or nerve cells. Using adult stem cells from a patient to grow replacement tissue for that patient not only would avoid the ethical problems associated with the use of stem cells from embryos but also would reduce the potential that the patient's body would reject the transplanted tissue. It was not clear, however, whether there was an adult stem cell for every type of cell in the body and, even if there were, whether they could be isolated and extracted. More important, evidence showed that adult stem cells might be more limited than those extracted from embryos and more vulnerable to disease. According to a press release accompanying the guidelines, NIH concluded it was "vitally important" to study human stem cells taken from all three sources—embryos, fetal tissue, and adult cells—to determine which worked best under what circumstances.*

*Many scientists and patients' rights organizations argued that research on both embryonic and adult stem cells was necessary to realize the full medical potential of the science. They also argued that without federal funding and the NIH guidelines, some research might lead to the very behavior that opponents of federal funding were trying to prevent. "The best way" to ensure responsible research with public accountability "is to have the federal government get behind an advance such as the culture of human stem cells and to allow the broadest number of scientists to participate," Daniel Perry, chairman of the Patient's Coalition for Urgent Research, told the*

*Associated Press. "It would be bad public policy to wall off by congressional action any avenue that science might find to cure the patient's needs." Perry's group was created specifically to advocate federal support of stem cell research.*

> *Following is the text of a fact sheet on the guidelines for federal funding of human stem cell research, issued August 23, 2000, by the National Institutes of Health. The document was obtained from the Internet at http://www.nih.gov/news/stemcell/index .htm.*

## The Promise of Stem Cell Research

Human pluripotent stem cells are a unique scientific and medical resource. They can develop into most of the specialized cells and tissues of the body, such as muscle cells, nerve cells, liver cells, and blood cells and they can divide for indefinite periods in the laboratory, making them readily available for research, and potentially, treatment purposes. Scientists derived these unique cells from human embryos and from non-living fetuses.

The establishment of human pluripotent stem cell lines represents a major step forward in the understanding of human biology. These unique cells have captured the interest of scientists and the public, particularly patients and their advocates. Although such research promises new treatments and, possibly even cures for many debilitating diseases and injuries, including Parkinson's disease, diabetes, heart disease, multiple sclerosis, burns and spinal cord injuries, the NIH acknowledges that the ethical issues related to this research need due consideration.

## The Need for *Guidelines* to Govern Research Using Pluripotent Stem Cells

Federal law currently restricts the use of Department of Health and Human Services (DHHS) funds for human embryo research. DHHS funds cannot be used for the derivation of stem cells from human embryos. The Congressional restriction, however, does not prohibit funding for research utilizing human pluripotent stem cells because such cells are not embryos.

The purpose of the NIH *Guidelines* is to prescribe procedures to help ensure that NIH-funded research in this area is conducted in an ethical and legal manner. By issuing these *Guidelines*, the NIH aims to enhance both the scientific and ethical oversight of this important arena of research and the pace at which scientists can explore its many promises. These *Guidelines* will encourage openness, help make certain that researchers can make use of these critical research tools, and help assure public access to the practical medical benefits of research using these cells.

In an effort to help ensure that any research utilizing human pluripotent stem cells is appropriately and carefully conducted, the NIH sought the advice of scientists, patients and patient advocates, ethicists, clinicians, lawyers, the National Bioethics Advisory Commission (NBAC), members of Congress, among others in drafting these *Guidelines*. The draft *Guidelines* were published for public comment in the *Federal Register* and after reviewing and considering all comments, the NIH will publish the final NIH *Guidelines* in the *Federal Register* on August 25, 2000.

## Specifics of the *Guidelines*

The *Guidelines* prescribe the documentation and assurances that must accompany requests for NIH funding for research using human pluripotent stem cells derived from human embryos or fetal tissue.

- For studies using cells derived from human embryos, NIH funds may be used only if the cells were derived from frozen embryos that were created for the purposes of fertility treatment and were in excess of clinical need.
- The *Guidelines* prohibit the use of inducements, monetary or otherwise, for the donation of the embryo. There must also have been a clear separation between the fertility treatment and the decision to donate embryos for this research.
- Investigators who propose to use human pluripotent stem cells from fetal tissue will be expected to follow both the *Guidelines* and all laws and regulations governing human fetal tissue and human fetal tissue transplantation research.
- The *Guidelines* require that the informed consent specify whether or not information that could identify the donor(s) will be retained.
- They require that the donation of human embryos or fetal tissue be made without any restriction regarding the individual(s) who may be the recipient of the cells derived from the human pluripotent stem cells for transplantation.
- They also require review and approval of the derivation protocol by an Institutional Review Board.
- The informed consent should include statements that the embryos or fetal tissue will be used to derive human pluripotent stem cells for research, that may include human transplantation research; that derived cells may be kept for many years; that the research is not intended to provide direct medical benefit to the donor; and, for cells derived from embryos, that embryos donated will not be transferred to a woman's uterus and will not survive the stem cell derivation process.
- The informed consent must also state the possibility that the results of the research may have commercial potential, and that the donor will not receive any benefits from any such future commercial development.

## Areas of Research Ineligible for NIH Funding

As required by law, NIH funds cannot be used for the derivation of pluripotent stem cells from human embryos. The *Guidelines* also set forth several other areas of research that are ineligible for NIH funding, including: 1) research in which human pluripotent stem cells are utilized to create or contribute to a human embryo; 2) research utilizing pluripotent stem cells that were derived from human embryos created for research purposes; 3) research in which human pluripotent stem cells are derived using somatic cell nuclear transfer; 4) research utilizing human pluripotent stem cells that were derived using somatic cell nuclear transfer; 5) research in which human pluripotent stem cells are combined with an animal embryo; and 6) research in which human pluripotent stem cells are derived using somatic cell nuclear transfer for the purposes of reproductive cloning of a human.

## Requirements for Investigators Applying for Funds

A request for NIH funds for research using these cells must include a signed assurance that the cells were derived from human embryos in accordance with the *Guidelines* and that the institution will maintain documentation in support of the assurance.

This assurance must also affirm that:

- The human pluripotent stem cells to be used in the research were, or will be, obtained through a donation or through a payment that does not exceed the reasonable costs associated with the quality control, processing, transportation, preservation, and storage of the stem cells.
- The proposed research is not a class of research that is ineligible for NIH funding.

Investigators must also submit:

- A sample informed consent document, with patient identifier information removed, and a description of the informed consent process along with documentation of IRB approval of the derivation protocol.
- An abstract of the scientific protocol used to derive human pluripotent stem cells along with a title of the research proposal that proposes the use of human pluripotent stem cells.

## Ensuring Compliance with the *Guidelines*

Investigators requesting NIH funds for research using pluripotent stem cells will need to provide documentation that they are in compliance with the *Guidelines* prior to receiving NIH funds for this class of research. Submitted documentation will be reviewed by a newly-created NIH working group called the Human Pluripotent Stem Cell Review Group (HPSCRG).

Members of the working group will:

- Review documentation of compliance with the *Guidelines* for funding requests that propose the use of human pluripotent stem cells.
- Advise the NIH Center for Scientific Review Advisory Committee (CSRAC) of the outcome of their review, which, if appropriate, will be approved by the CSRAC. This decision will be forwarded to the funding Institute or Center.

- Hold public meetings when a request proposes the use of a line of human pluripotent stem cells that has not been previously reviewed by the HPSCRG.

In no event will NIH fund research or allow existing funds to be used for research using human pluripotent stem cells derived from human embryos or human fetal tissue until the derivation protocol has received HPSCRG review and CSRAC approval. Continued compliance with the *Guidelines* is a term and condition of the NIH award. . . .

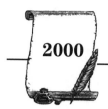

# September

# CLINTON ON THE NATIONAL MISSILE DEFENSE SYSTEM
## September 1, 2000

*President Bill Clinton on September 1, 2000, postponed a decision on one of the most controversial policy issues facing him: whether to proceed with plans to build a high-technology system to protect the United States against attack by ballistic missiles. Clinton's action effectively left the matter to his successor, who turned out to be Republican George W. Bush. Bush had advocated a much more extensive, and expensive, system than Clinton had been considering.*

*Clinton's decision not to make a decision won general praise, although some Republicans, including Bush, took the opportunity to blast Clinton— and Vice President Al Gore, who was running against Bush in the 2000 presidential race—for failing to move more aggressively to protect the country against potential missile attacks. Leaders of most other countries, including Russia, China, and key U.S. allies in Europe, had opposed an American missile defense system. They said such a system could lead to a renewed nuclear arms race and destabilize world security.*

### Expensive Ideas and Failures

*Suggestions for a defense against attacks by nuclear-armed ballistic missiles first arose during the 1950s, when the Eisenhower administration considered ways of countering the rapid buildup of nuclear weapons by the Soviet Union. The Johnson and Nixon administrations in the late 1960s and early 1970s developed a system to protect U.S. nuclear missiles in North Dakota against a Soviet attack. That system, called "Safeguard," cost $25 billion to build but was abandoned just four months after it was finished in October 1975. The Soviet Union built a limited system to protect its capital, Moscow, against a potential U.S. attack; that system reportedly remained in operation as of late 2000.*

*In the meantime, the United States and the Soviet Union in 1972 signed the Anti-Ballistic Missile (ABM) treaty that, as eventually modified, allowed each nuclear superpower to build only one limited system to protect part of its territory against missile attacks. The theory behind the treaty was that neither nation would choose to begin a nuclear war if its territory was unprotected against retaliation by the other.*

*In 1983 President Ronald Reagan revived the idea of a missile shield, proposing a massive system of land- and space-based radars, lasers, and missiles that would prevent any ballistic missiles from reaching U.S. territory. Reagan called his proposal the Strategic Defense Initiative. Critics, scoffing that Reagan, a former movie actor, had gotten his ideas from Hollywood, called it "Star Wars" after a popular series of space-age movies.*

*The Reagan administration spent tens of billions of dollars on that proposal, which President George Bush jettisoned in 1989 in favor of a less ambitious plan called Global Protection Against Limited Strikes. Under that plan, also known as "Brilliant Pebbles," the United States was to be protected from missile attacks by one thousand space-based interceptors, along with a comparable number of interceptors based on the ground.*

*The collapse of the Soviet Union at the end of 1991 undermined political support for Bush's proposal, and Clinton, upon taking office in 1993, renounced the concept of a space-based missile defense system. Clinton suggested he might support a much more limited missile defense system—but only if it did not violate the terms of the ABM treaty. Under his interpretation, the treaty allowed only a fixed, land-based missile defense system and prohibited systems that were based in space or on submarines at sea, as well as mobile systems based on land. Clinton authorized research on a limited system to protect the United States against a small-scale attack, perhaps by a "rogue" state such as North Korea, or an accidental launch of missiles by China or Russia.*

*Republicans in Congress, with the active support of defense contractors hoping to revive their business in the wake of Pentagon cutbacks, lobbied all through the 1990s for a more extensive missile defense system. The proponents got a major boost in 1998 when a presidential commission headed by former defense secretary Donald H. Rumsfeld issued a report estimating that Iran and North Korea would be able to launch ballistic missiles against the United States by 2003—about seven years earlier than previous intelligence estimates. Six weeks after that report was issued, North Korea test-fired a three-stage ballistic missile over Japan and the Pacific Ocean—an act that appeared to confirm the commission's assessment. George W. Bush in December 2000 named Rumsfeld as his defense secretary, effectively ensuring a new push for a missile defense system.* (Rumsfeld commission report, Historic Documents of 1998, p. 481)

*Early in 1999 the Clinton administration began a series of efforts, all ultimately unsuccessful, to persuade Russia to agree to changes in the ABM treaty that would allow the United States to build a limited missile defense system then being tested. Congress, galvanized by the Rumsfeld commission report and the North Korean test-firing, passed legislation in 1999 committing the United States to a national missile defense system "as soon as it is technologically feasible." Clinton signed that legislation on July 27, 1999, and said he would determine in 2000 whether to deploy such a system.*

*In the meantime the Pentagon had carried out a series of tests of the system Clinton had agreed to consider. If fully deployed, that system was to have one hundred interceptor missiles and a radar station based in Alaska. In the event of a missile attack against the United States, the interceptors would be launched and guided by radar and satellites toward the attacking missiles. Each interceptor would destroy one incoming missile by slamming into it at about 15,000 miles an hour.*

*During 1997 and 1998 the Pentagon conducted three tests on the system's ability to track incoming missiles. Only one of tests was an unqualified success. In October 1999 the Pentagon began a series of three tests in which an interceptor missile was to track and collide with an "enemy" missile. The Pentagon called the first test, in October 1999, a success, but later admitted that the interceptor missile had collided with a decoy, not with the "enemy" missile it was supposed to attack. Two more tests in January and July 2000 also failed because of mechanical flaws. The Pentagon had planned to conduct sixteen additional tests before actually deploying the system.*

*According to a White House statement, the Clinton administration had spent approximately $5.7 billion on the system as of September 1, 2000, and had budgeted an additional $10.4 billion for the following five fiscal years, through deployment in 2005 or later. The total cost of the system, from fiscal years 1991 through 2009, was estimated at about $25 billion, the White House said. A report issued April 25 by the Congressional Budget Office had put a much higher estimate of $60 billion on the total cost of the program.*

*Clinton had said the July test was to be the last before he made a decision on whether to begin work leading to full deployment of the missile defense system by 2005. The failure of the three tests in less than a year made it likely that he either would postpone a decision or call for more testing. Critics claimed the system was so flawed that it would never work. One of the most vocal critics was Theodore A. Postol, a professor of science, technology, and national security at the Massachusetts Institute of Technology, who produced several reports claiming that the Pentagon had covered up data proving the inherent flaws of the system.*

*Adding to the technological problems were new questions in 2000 about one threat that had been a primary justification for building a missile defense system. Throughout the last half of the 1990s the Clinton administration argued that North Korea posed the most likely threat because it was working on a long-range ballistic missile and its communist regime was implacably hostile to U.S. interests. But in 2000 North Korean leader Kim Jong Il opened a diplomatic offensive to improve his relations with the United States and its allies. He held a historic summit meeting in June with South Korean president Kim Dae-Jung, established diplomatic relations with several key U.S. allies, and hosted Secretary of State Madeleine K. Albright for talks in Pyongyang in October. Albright said Kim informally offered to shelve his ballistic missile program in exchange for U.S. help in launching North Korean satellites. In the meantime, Kim said he had im-posed a moratorium on further missile tests.* (Korean summit meeting, p. 359; Albright trip to North Korea, p. 866)

## *Postponing a Decision*

*Clinton went to his alma mater—Georgetown University in Washington, D.C.—to announce his decision on September 1 before an audience of students, faculty, diplomats, and national security experts. Clinton said the United States faced a potential threat of missile attack, and he said a missile defense was a justified response to such a threat. A missile defense, "if it worked properly, could give us an extra dimension of insurance in a world where proliferation has complicated the task of preserving peace," he said.*

*Clinton said the Pentagon had made "substantial progress" in developing the system he had approved, which "could be deployed sooner than any of the proposed alternatives." But the system "as a whole is not yet proven," he said, and "I simply cannot conclude, with the information I have today, that we have enough confidence in the technology, and the operational effectiveness of the entire NMD [national missile defense] system, to move forward to deployment."*

*The immediate effect of Clinton's announcement was to halt the Pentagon's plans to request bids for construction on Shemya Island in Alaska of a ground-based radar station that was to provide the tracking capability for the interceptor missiles. Pentagon officials had hoped to begin work on the radar station in 2001 so that the entire system would be operational by 2005. But the test failures and other technical difficulties had led many analysts to conclude that the system probably would not be ready until 2006 or 2007.*

*Construction of the radar was important for reasons other than the timing of the system. Clinton administration lawyers had concluded that work on the radar would violate the ABM treaty, as it was written. As of late 2000, Clinton had been unable to convince Russian president Vladimir Putin to accept a treaty amendment that would permit development of the U.S. missile defense system, and Clinton was reluctant to violate the treaty, which he had called a "cornerstone" of strategic stability.*

*Clinton's decision to postpone action on the missile defense system won widespread praise from international leaders, including Putin, who called it a "well thought-out and responsible step." The Chinese Foreign Ministry called the decision "rational," and leaders of Great Britain, France, Germany, Canada, and other U.S. allies also expressed relief. The allies in western Europe had been particularly concerned about the deployment of a system that defended only the United States, fearing that it would lead to what they called the "decoupling" of U.S.-European security arrangements through the NATO alliance.*

*For the most part, reaction among U.S. politicians fell predictably along partisan lines. Most Democrats, including Gore, praised the postponement, while most Republicans used the opportunity to attack Clinton for his past actions on the issue. Bush, for example, hardened his own position. In May, Bush had called for Clinton to postpone a decision, saying "no decision" would be better than a "flawed" one that "ties the hands of the next presi-*

*dent." But in September, with the election getting nearer, Bush charged that Clinton and Gore had "failed to lead" on a program "to protect all fifty states and our friends and allies." Without providing specific details, Bush had advocated a much broader defense system that included antimissile interceptors based in space and at sea. Despite that criticism, Clinton received support from two key Republican members of the Senate Foreign Relations Committee, Gordon H. Smith of Oregon and Chuck Hagel of Nebraska, both of whom praised his willingness to leave a decision on the matter to his successor.*

*Retired general Colin L. Powell, named by Bush on December 16 to be secretary of state, said, "We're going to go forward" with a national missile defense system after taking office. Powell acknowledged that the new Bush administration would have to engage in "tough negotiations" with its allies and Russia on the issue. But he said those nations "will have to come to the understanding that we feel this is in the best interests of the American people—and not only the American people, the people of the world" to establish such a system.*

> *Following are excerpts from a September 1, 2000, speech by President Bill Clinton to an audience at Georgetown University in Washington, D.C., in which he announced his decision to postpone key work on a defense system to protect the United States against ballistic missile attacks. The document was obtained from the Internet at http://www.pub.whitehouse.gov/uri-res/l2R ?urn:pdi://oma.eop.gov.us/2000/0/1/9.text.1.*

. . . I came today to talk about a subject that is not fraught with applause lines, but one that is very, very important to your future: the defense of our nation. At this moment of unprecedented peace and prosperity, with no immediate threat to our security or our existence, with our democratic values ascendant and our alliances strong, with the great forces of our time, globalization and the revolution in information technology so clearly beneficial to a society like ours, with our diversity and our openness, and our entrepreneurial spirit.

At a time like this it is tempting, but wrong, to believe there are no serious long-term challenges to our security. The rapid spread of technology across increasingly porous borders, raises the specter that more and more states, terrorists and criminal syndicates could gain access to chemical, biological or even nuclear weapons, and to the means of delivering them—whether in small units deployed by terrorists within our midst, or ballistic missiles capable of hurtling those weapons halfway around the world.

Today I want to discuss these threats with you, because you will live with them a lot longer than I will. Especially, I want to talk about the ballistic missile threat. It is real and growing, and has given new urgency to the debate about national missile defenses, known in the popular jargon as NMD.

When I became President, I put our effort to stop the proliferation of weapons of mass destruction at the very top of our national security agenda. Since then, we have carried out a comprehensive strategy to reduce and secure nuclear arsenals, to strengthen the international regime against biological and chemical weapons and nuclear testing, and to stop the flow of dangerous technology to nations that might wish us harm.

At the same time, we have pursued new technologies that could strengthen our defenses against a possible attack, including a terrorist attack here at home.

None of these elements of our national security strategy can be pursued in isolation. Each is important, and we have made progress in each area. For example, Russia and the United States already have destroyed about 25,000 nuclear weapons in the last decade. And we have agreed that in a START III treaty, we will go 80 percent below the level of a decade ago.

In 1994, we persuaded Ukraine, Kazakhstan and Belarus, three of the former Soviet Republics, to give up their nuclear weapons entirely. We have worked with Russia and its neighbors to dispose of hundreds of tons of dangerous nuclear materials, to strengthen controls on a list of exports, and to keep weapon scientists from selling their services to the highest bidder.

We extended the nuclear non-proliferation treaty indefinitely. We were the very first nation to sign the comprehensive test ban treaty, an idea first embraced by Presidents Kennedy and Eisenhower. Sixty nations now have ratified the test ban treaty. I believe the United States Senate made a serious error in failing to ratify it last year, and I hope it will do so next year.

We also negotiated and ratified the international convention to ban chemical weapons, and strengthened the convention against biological weapons. We've used our export controls to deny terrorists and potential adversaries access to materials and equipment needed to build these kinds of weapons.

We've imposed sanctions on those who contribute to foreign chemical and biological weapons programs, we've invested in new equipment and medical countermeasures to protect people from exposure. And we're working with state and local medical units all over our country to strengthen our preparedness in case of a chemical or biological terrorist attack, which many people believe is the most likely new security threat of the 21st century.

We have also acted to reduce the threat posed by states that have sought weapons of mass destruction and ballistic missiles, while pursuing activities that are clearly hostile to our long-term interests. For over a decade—for almost a decade, excuse me—we have diverted about 90 percent of Iraq's oil revenues from the production of weapons to the purchase of food and medicine.

This is an important statistic for those who believe that our sanctions are only a negative for the people, and particularly the children, of Iraq. In 1989, Iraq earned $15 billion from oil exports, and spent $13 billion of that money on its military. This year, Iraq is projected to earn $19 billion from its legal oil-for-food exports that can spend none of those revenues on the military.

We worked to counter Iran's efforts to develop nuclear weapons and missile technology, convincing China to provide no new assistance to Iran's nuclear program, and pressing Russia to strengthen its controls on the export of sensitive technologies.

In 1994, six years after the United States first learned that North Korea had a nuclear weapons program, we negotiated the agreement that verifiably has frozen its production of plutonium for nuclear weapons. Now, in the context of the United States negotiations with the North, the diplomatic efforts by former Defense Secretary Bill Perry and, most lately, the summit between the leaders of North and South Korea, North Korea has refrained from flight testing a new missile that could pose a threat to America.

We should be clear: North Korea's capability remains a serious issue and its intentions remain unclear. But its missile testing moratorium is a good development worth pursuing.

These diplomatic efforts to meet the threat of proliferation are backed by the strong and global reach of our armed forces. Today, the United States enjoys overwhelming military superiority over any potential adversary. For example, in 1985, we spent about as much on defense as Russia, China and North Korea combined. Today, we spend nearly three times as much, nearly $300 billion a year. And our military technology clearly is well ahead of the rest of the world.

The principle of deterrence served us very well in the Cold War, and deterrence remains imperative. The threat of overwhelming retaliation deterred Saddam Hussein from using weapons of mass destruction during the Gulf War. Our forces in South Korea have deterred North Korea in aggression for 47 years.

The question is, can deterrence protect us against all those who might wish us harm in the future? Can we make America even more secure? The effort to answer these questions is the impetus behind the search for NMD. The issue is whether we can do more, not to meet today's threat, but to meet tomorrow's threat to our security.

For example, there is the possibility that a hostile state with nuclear weapons and long range missiles may simply disintegrate, with command over missiles falling into unstable hands; or that in a moment of desperation, such a country might miscalculate, believing it could use nuclear weapons to intimidate us from defending our vital interests, or from coming to the aid of our allies, or others who are defenseless and clearly in need.

In the future, we cannot rule out that terrorist groups could gain the capability to strike us with nuclear weapons if they seized even temporary control of a state with an existing nuclear weapons establishment.

Now, no one suggests that NMD would ever substitute for diplomacy or for deterrence. But such a system, if it worked properly, could give us an extra dimension of insurance in a world where proliferation has complicated the task of preserving the peace. Therefore, I believe we have an obligation to determine the feasibility, the effectiveness, and the impact of a national missile defense on the overall security of the United States.

The system now under development is designed to work as follows. In the event of an attack, American satellites would protect the launch of missiles.

Our radar would track the enemy warhead and highly accurate, high-speed, ground-based interceptors would destroy them before they could reach their target in the United States.

We have made substantial progress on a system that would be based in Alaska and that, when operational, could protect all 50 states from the near-term missile threats we face, those emanating from North Korea and the Middle East. The system could be deployed sooner than any of the proposed alternatives.

Since last fall, we've been conducting flight tests to see if this NMD system actually can reliably intercept a ballistic missile. We've begun to show that the different parts of this system can work together.

Our Defense Department has overcome daunting technical obstacles in a remarkably short period of time, and I'm proud of the work that Secretary Cohen, General Shelton and their teams have done.

One test proved that it is, in fact, possible to hit a bullet with a bullet. Still, though the technology for NMD is promising, the system as a whole is not yet proven. After the initial test succeeded, our two most recent tests failed, for different reasons, to achieve an intercept. Several more tests are planned. They will tell us whether NMD can work reliably under realistic conditions. Critical elements of the program, such as the booster rocket for the missile interceptor, have yet to be tested.

There are also questions to be resolved about the ability of the system to deal with countermeasures. In other words, measures by those firing the missiles to confuse the missile defense into thinking it is hitting a target when it is not.

There is a reasonable chance that all these challenges can be met in time. But I simply cannot conclude with the information I have today that we have enough confidence in the technology, and the operational effectiveness of the entire NMD system, to move forward to deployment.

Therefore, I have decided not to authorize deployment of a national missile defense at this time. Instead, I have asked Secretary Cohen to continue a robust program of development and testing. That effort still is at an early stage. Only three of the 19 planned intercept tests have been held so far. We need more tests against more challenging targets, and more simulations before we can responsibly commit our nation's resources to deployment.

We should use this time to ensure that NMD, if deployed, would actually enhance our overall national security. And I want to talk about that in a few moments.

I want you to know that I have reached this decision about not deploying the NMD after careful deliberation. My decision will not have a significant impact on the date the overall system could be deployed in the next administration, if the next President decides to go forward.

The best judgment of the experts who have examined this question is that if we were to commit today to construct the system, it most likely would be operational about 2006 or 2007. If the next President decides to move forward next year, the system still could be ready in the same time frame.

In the meantime, we will continue to work with our allies and with Russia to strengthen their understanding and support for our efforts to meet the emerging ballistic missile threat, and to explore creative ways that we can cooperate to enhance their security against this threat, as well.

An effective NMD could play an important part of our national security strategy, but it could not be the sum total of that strategy. It can never be the sum total of that strategy for dealing with nuclear and missile threats.

Moreover, ballistic missiles, armed with nuclear weapons, as I said earlier, do not represent the sum total of the threats we face. Those include chemical and biological weapons, and a range of deadly technologies for deploying them. So it would be folly to base the defense of our nation solely on a strategy of waiting until missiles are in the air, and then trying to shoot them down.

We must work with our allies, and with Russia, to prevent potential adversaries from ever threatening us with nuclear, chemical and biological weapons of mass destruction in the first place, and to make sure they know the devastating consequences of doing so.

The elements of our strategy cannot be allowed to undermine one another. They must reinforce one another, and contribute to our national defense in all its dimensions. That includes the profoundly important dimension of arms control.

Over the past 30 years, Republican and Democratic presidents alike have negotiated an array of arms control treaties with Russia. We and our allies have relied on these treaties to ensure strategic stability and predictability with Russia, to get on with the job of dismantling the legacy of the Cold War, and to further the transition from confrontation to cooperation with our former adversary in the most important arena, nuclear weapons.

A key part of the international security structure we have built with Russia and, therefore, a key part of our national security, is the anti-ballistic missile treaty signed by President Nixon in 1972. The ABM treaty limits anti-missile defenses according to a simple principle: neither side should deploy defenses that would undermine the other side's nuclear deterrent, and thus tempt the other side to strike first in a crisis or to take countermeasures that would make both our countries less secure.

Strategic stability, based on mutual deterrence, is still important, despite the end of the Cold War. Why? Because the United States and Russia still have nuclear arsenals that can devastate each other. And this is still a period of transition in our relationship.

We have worked together in many ways. Signed an agreement of cooperation between Russia and NATO. Served with Russian troops in Bosnia and Kosovo. But while we are no longer adversaries, we are not yet real allies. Therefore, for them as well as for us, maintaining strategic stability increases trust and confidence on both sides. It reduces the risk of confrontation. It makes it possible to build an even better partnership and an even safer world.

Now, here's the issue: NMD, if deployed, would require us either to adjust the treaty or to withdraw from it—not because NMD poses a challenge to the strategic stability I just discussed, but because by its very words, NMD prohibits any national missile defense.

What we should want is to both explore the most effective defenses possible, not only for ourselves, but for all other law-abiding states, and to maintain our strategic stability with Russia. Thus far, Russia has been reluctant to agree, fearing I think, frankly, that in some sense, this system or some future incarnation of it could threaten the reliability of its deterrence and, therefore, strategic stability.

Nevertheless, at our summit in Moscow in June, President Putin and I did agree that the world has changed since the ABM treaty was signed 28 years ago, and that the proliferation of missile technology has resulted in new threats that may require amending that treaty. And again, I say, these threats are not threats to the United States alone.

Russia agrees that there is an emerging missile threat. In fact, given its place on the map, it is particularly vulnerable to this emerging threat. In time, I hope the United States can narrow our differences with Russia on this issue. The course I have chosen today gives the United States more time to pursue that, and we will use it.

President Putin and I have agreed to intensify our work on strategic defense, while pursuing, in parallel, deeper arms reductions in START III. He and I have instructed our experts to develop further cooperative initiatives in areas such as theater missile defense, early warning and missile threat discussions for our meeting just next week in New York.

Apart from the Russians, another critical diplomatic consideration in the NMD decision is the view of our NATO allies. They have all made clear that they hope the United States will pursue strategic defense in a way that preserves, not abrogates, the ABM treaty. If we decide to proceed with NMD deployment we must have their support, because key components of NMD would be based on their territories.

The decision I have made also gives the United States time to answer our allies' questions and consult further on the path ahead.

Finally, we must consider the impact of a decision to deploy on security in Asia. As the next President makes a deployment decision, he will need to avoid stimulating an already dangerous regional nuclear capability from China to South Asia. Now, let me be clear: no nation can ever have a veto over American security, even if the United States and Russia cannot reach agreement; even if we cannot secure the support of our allies at first; even if we conclude that the Chinese will respond to NMD by increasing their arsenal of nuclear weapons substantially with a corollary, inevitable impact in India and then in Pakistan.

The next President may nevertheless decide that our interest in security in 21st century dictates that we go forward with deployment of NMD. But we can never afford to overlook the fact that the actions and reactions of others in this increasingly interdependent world do bear on our security.

Clearly, therefore, it would be far better to move forward in the context of the ABM treaty and allied support. Our efforts to make that possible have not been completed. For me, the bottom line on this decision is this: because the emerging missile threat is real, we have an obligation to pursue a missile defense system that could enhance our security.

We have made progress, but we should not move forward until we have absolute confidence that the system will work, and until we have made every reasonable diplomatic effort to minimize the cost of deployment, and maximize the benefit, as I said, not only to America's security, but to the security of law abiding nations everywhere subject to the same threat.

I am convinced that America and the world will be better off if we explore the frontiers of strategic defenses, while continuing to pursue arms control, to stand with our allies and to work with Russia and others to stop the spread of deadly weapons.

I strongly believe this is the best course for the United States, and therefore the decision I have reached today, is in the best security interest of the United States. In short, we need to move forward with realism, with steadiness, and with prudence, not dismissing the threat we face, or assuming we can meet it, while ignoring our overall strategic environment, including the interests and concerns of our allies, friends and other nations. A national missile defense, if deployed, should be part of a larger strategy to preserve and enhance the peace, strength and security we now enjoy, and to build an even safer world.

I have tried to maximize the ability of the next President to pursue that strategy. In so doing, I have tried to maximize the chance that all you young students will live in a safer, more humane, more positively interdependent world. I hope I have done so. I believe I have.

Thank you very much.

# FEDERAL AND COMPANY OFFICIALS
# ON FIRESTONE TIRE RECALL
## September 6, 2000

*Two of the biggest names in American manufacturing history—Firestone and Ford—were involved in one of the country's most highly publicized product liability cases in history. The Bridgestone/Firestone Corp. on August 9, 2000, issued a recall of an estimated 6.5 million tires that had been installed on sport utility vehicles (SUVs). Firestone issued the recall after media reports indicated an unusually high rate of tread separation on the tires, most often in cases involving Ford Explorers driven at high speed in hot weather. By year's end the National Highway Traffic Safety Administration had linked the tires to 148 fatalities and more than 500 injuries in hundreds of accidents. In a significant portion of the cases, Explorers rolled over when the tires failed.*

*Congress quickly responded by passing a bill requiring new safety standards, many of which the auto industry had successfully blocked for years. The bill's most controversial provision, which was vigorously opposed by the auto industry, established criminal penalties for industry officials who withheld information about safety defects.*

*The faulty tire issue also was being played out in the courts. Firestone settled several product liability lawsuits involving its tires, but several dozen other cases were pending at year's end. In addition to legal and public relations difficulties, the recall caused financial setbacks for both companies, especially Firestone. Citing lagging sales and built-up inventory, Firestone on October 17 laid off 450 workers at the Decatur, Illinois, plant where most of the faulty tires had been manufactured and temporarily closed that plant and two others. A month later, Firestone broadened the layoffs, announcing that about 1,100 additional workers at two plants would be idled for at least five months. Sales of Ford Explorers, which for years had been the company's profit leader, softened in the months after the recall issue hit the headlines.*

## The Tire Recall

*Lawyers handling product liability cases had for several years claimed that Firestone tires mounted on Ford Explorers were responsible for a sus-*

piciously high rate of accidents leading to personal injuries, deaths, and property damage. In most cases, treads separated from the main body of the tires when the vehicle was traveling at high speeds. Although they had gathered evidence implicating the tires, few lawyers had filed complaints with the highway safety agency—apparently because they feared the agency might side with the tire maker, an action that would have made winning their cases extremely difficult.

The issue received little official attention until a February 7 report by Houston television station KHOU prompted dozens of consumer complaints and spurred the National Highway Traffic Safety Administration into opening a preliminary inquiry on May 2. The announcements of those inquiries brought hundreds more complaints and heightened public concern about the safety of both the Firestone tires and the Explorer.

By early August the safety agency had received 193 complaints about faulty Firestone tires; 21 of the cases reported at that point involved fatal accidents. The safety agency on August 4 suggested to Bridgestone/Firestone that it consider recalling the tires. Five days later, on August 9, Firestone and Ford jointly announced that Firestone was recalling 14.4 million 15-inch ATX, ATX II, and Wilderness AT tires made after 1991 for use on Explorers and other light trucks and SUVs. The company estimated that about 6.5 million of the tires were still in use. By year's end nearly 6 million tires had been replaced. It was the second largest tire recall in history. In 1978 Firestone was forced to recall 14.5 million tires because of corrosion of the steel belts. The earlier recall put the company under severe financial stress, which led to Firestone's acquisition in 1988 by Bridgestone, the largest Japanese tire maker.

On August 30 the highway safety agency asked Firestone to recall another 1.4 million fifteen-inch tires, most of which had been sold as replacements for models on Ford, Chevy, Nissan, and other SUVs. The agency said those models could pose just as much danger as those already recalled. The company refused that request, and on September 1 the safety agency took the highly unusual step of issuing a public advisory recommending that owners "consider replacing the tires in question." Firestone disputed the agency's contention that the tires were unsafe but said it would replace them free of charge—but only when consumers specifically asked for replacements.

Until its August 9 recall, Firestone routinely denied that its tires were at fault for any accidents. Instead, the company blamed consumers for underinflating the tires or overloading their vehicles. During congressional hearings in mid-September, company officials began shifting the blame by accepting some responsibility but pointing the finger at Ford, as well. At a hearing held September 6 by two subcommittees of the House Commerce Committee, Bridgestone/Firestone chief executive officer Masatoshi Ono apologized for the tire problems and said he accepted "full and personal responsibility on behalf of Bridgestone/Firestone for the events that led to this hearing." However, Ono said the company was still investigating to determine the "root causes" of the tire failures.

*Less than a week later, on September 12, Firestone officials said at a Senate hearing that the company believed that design flaws and variations in manufacturing at its tire plant in Decatur, Illinois, were mainly to blame. The plant had experienced a ten-month strike in 1994–1995 (a period when many of the faulty tires were produced), and several newspaper reports quoted plant workers as saying the facility had experienced heavy production demands and lax quality control.*

*While acknowledging problems at its Decatur plant, Firestone officials insisted during the congressional hearings that Ford shared in the blame. Company executives noted that Ford for years had told owners of Explorers to inflate vehicle tires to twenty-six pounds per square inch, compared to a thirty-pound standard that Firestone recommended. The reduced tire pressure helped to give Explorers a softer, more comfortable ride. Moreover, Firestone officials said the design of the Explorer encouraged users to overload the vehicle.*

*Ford executives rejected the Firestone contention, noting that similar tires made by Goodyear had a much lower failure rate, even when inflated at the lower pressure. In their congressional testimony, Ford officials repeatedly insisted the accidents and deaths were due to a "tire problem"—not a vehicle problem.*

*On December 19, Firestone issued a statement detailing what it said were the results of an internal four-month investigation into the tire failures. The statement listed four major causes for the tendency of the recalled tires to separate:*

- *Manufacturing processes at the Decatur plant had led to variations in the use of rubber components and adhesive compounds that led to the production of tires that were less stable than those made at other company plants. In particular, the company found that the Decatur plant had used too much lubricant in rubber compounds, a factor that reduced the adhesion of the steel and rubber layers that made up the tires.*

- *Flaws in the design of the tire could cause "cracking" of the tire, something the statement said "could become the starting point of a failure. . . ." As an example, Firestone said the "shoulder pockets" (indentations in the tread that gave traction in snow and mud) were too deep on the ATX tires, leaving a too-thin layer of rubber covering the underlying steel belts.*

- *Ford's design of the Explorer caused the vehicle to be heavier—and to be used to carry much heavier loads of passengers and cargo—than had originally been specified for the tires. Firestone also repeated its contention that Ford was incorrect in suggesting that Explorer owners keep their tires inflated to only twenty-six pounds per square inch; this "under-inflation" could cause the tires to overheat and separate, Firestone said. Ford again rejected this claim, saying on December 19 that it had concluded that "the vehicle is not a significant contributor to tread separation."*

- *Some tires failed because they were abused by customers (generally by "severe impacts," such as running into curbs at high speed) or had not been properly repaired.*

*At year's end perhaps the most important unanswered question was why officials at both Firestone and Ford failed to act on information that indicated possible safety problems with their products. According to news reports, Firestone officials had known of problems with some of its tires for at least two years, and possibly for as long as four years. Ford's top executives had been told in September 1999 of cases in Venezuela and three Persian Gulf countries of failures of Firestone tires on Explorers. In both cases, the companies said the information that might have indicated problems did not reach the appropriate officials. As an example, Firestone said that its safety experts had not seen reports on warranty claims, which were under the jurisdiction of the company's sales staff.*

## Congress Toughens Auto Safety Law

*Acting with unaccustomed speed, both houses of Congress on October 11 passed and sent to President Bill Clinton a bill (PL 106–414) that significantly strengthened national auto safety laws. Some of the bill's provisions had been blocked for years by industry lobbyists and their allies in Congress—but the tire recall controversy gave consumers a temporary advantage over economic interests on Capitol Hill. Even so, Congress adopted the milder of two major proposals before it. An unidentified senator prevented Senate action on the stronger measure, sponsored by Sen. John McCain (R-Ariz.).*

*The enacted measure, which had been sponsored by Rep. Fred Upton (R-Mich.), required the National Highway Traffic Safety Administration to begin, within two years, driving tests of rollover risks and to make test results public; required automakers and their suppliers to notify the safety agency about safety defects discovered in foreign countries and to report personal injury claims and other information that might help identify safety defects; increased the maximum penalty for civil violations of auto safety laws to $15 million, from $925,000; and established a maximum fifteen-year prison term for automotive industry officials found guilty of withholding information from the safety agency on auto safety defects.*

*The measure's two most controversial provisions were those establishing jail terms for industry officials who withheld safety data and requiring testing for vehicle rollovers. The auto industry had fought rollover standards for years, and early in 2000 it appeared that the industry would be successful in blocking plans by the safety agency to rate the rollover danger of all vehicles. But the tire recall controversy undermined the industry position and swept aside congressional reluctance to act on the issue.*

## Ford Explorer Problems

*The problem with tread separation on Firestone tires might not have been so serious had it not been combined with the tendency of Ford Explorers and other SUVs to roll over. The vehicles essentially were metal and glass boxes fitted onto chasses originally designed for pickup trucks—a feature that enabled automakers to avoid complying with gas mileage and other regulations that applied only to passenger cars.*

*Because they were higher off the ground than passenger cars and therefore had higher centers of gravity, SUVs were less stable than passenger cars and more likely to roll over in accidents. An additional factor was a psychological one. Ford and other automakers marketed SUVs as adventure vehicles, capable of racing through mountainous terrain or splashing through muddy streams. Moreover, SUVs appeared to be safer than passenger cars, if only because they were bigger. The vehicles thus appealed to drivers who wanted to be free of the constraints of regular cars and who therefore tended to be less cautious. A survey by Ford in 1993 found that owners of SUVs said they drove faster than drivers of passenger cars and were more likely to use their vehicles in bad weather—the two factors that led to a majority of serious accidents, whether or not faulty tires were involved.*

*The* New York Times *reported on December 7 that more than 1,200 people had died in rollover accidents involving the Explorer since 1991. In an analysis of federal crash statistics, the newspaper said occupants of Explorers "have been 2.3 times as likely to die in rollovers—tire-related or not—as people in traditional cars." Moreover, the* Times *said, Explorer passengers were nearly twice as likely to die in rollovers as were occupants of Jeep Cherokees and Grand Cherokees, which for years had been built on car chasses.*

*Compounding the public relations problem of being linked to the Firestone recall, Ford issued several recalls for its vehicles during 2000, including two major recalls in December for Explorers and other SUVs. The company recalled more than 800,000 1995–1997 Explorers and Mercury Mountaineers to correct a problem with components of their suspension systems and also recalled about 100,000 Explorers to correct a computer module that was supposed to prevent the vehicle from going faster than the 112 mile-per-hour maximum speed rating for the Firestone tires.*

*During the late 1990s, even before the Firestone tire recall, Ford and other automakers began to change the design of SUVs to make them safer, as well as less damaging to smaller passenger cars in accidents. The model 2002 Explorer was to be wider and with a lower frame than earlier models; in addition, its tires were to be larger than the 15-inch models involved in the recall.*

> *Following are excerpts from statements given September 6, 2000, at a joint hearing of the House Commerce Subcommittee on Telecommunications Trade and Consumer Protection and the Subcommittee on Oversight and Investigation, by Sue Bailey, administrator of the National Highway Traffic Safety Administration; Masatoshi Ono, chief executive officer of Bridgestone/ Firestone Inc.; and Jac Nasser, president and chief executive officer of the Ford Motor Company. The document was obtained*

*from the Internet at http://com-notes.house.gov/cchear/hearings*
*106.nsf/HearingExpand?OpenView&StartKey=55AB126A91AF*
*2617852569510051B526.*

**Sue Bailey:** I am pleased to appear before you this morning to address the investigation and recall of Firestone ATX, ATX II and Wilderness AT tires. This is the first subject on which I have appeared before Congress as Administrator of the National Highway Traffic Safety Administration (NHTSA), and I welcome the opportunity to address this important issue.

The agency's mission is to prevent deaths and injuries in motor vehicle crashes. Our program to investigate safety defects is a key part of that mission. I will give you a quick overview of the agency's authority to investigate safety defects, describe the procedures that the agency follows in its investigations, outline the Firestone investigation in that context, and share with you some of my observations about the investigative process.

## Overview

First, our authority: Congress passed the basic motor vehicle safety law 34 years ago, in 1966, and amended the law in 1974 to establish the current notification and remedy provisions. In brief, the law provides that if a manufacturer decides that one of its products contains a defect that relates to motor vehicle safety, the manufacturer must notify the agency and owners and provide a remedy at no cost to the owners. When the defect is in a tire sold as original equipment on a new vehicle, the tire manufacturer is the responsible manufacturer, as opposed to the vehicle manufacturer, and the remedy may either be to repair or replace the tire.

The law gives us authority to investigate possible defects, to decide whether a defect exists, and to order a manufacturer to provide a remedy for any defect. If a manufacturer refuses to provide a remedy, the law authorizes us to go to court to compel it to do so. This is seldom necessary. In all but very rare cases, manufacturers agree to remedy the defect without our having to reach a final decision. In a typical year, we open between 80 and 100 defect investigations, of which more than half result in recalls. In addition, manufacturers conduct an average of 200 defect recalls each year that are not influenced by NHTSA investigations.

## Investigative Procedures

We receive complaints from a wide variety of sources about possible defects in motor vehicles and motor vehicle equipment. The sources include our toll-free consumer hotline, our web page, e-mail, phone calls, and letters. We enter all complaints into a database which is continuously screened by a team of five investigators in the agency's Office of Defects Investigation (ODI) to identify potential defect trends. In an average year, we receive between 40,000 and 50,000 complaints from these sources.

When the screening process identifies a potential problem, ODI takes steps to open an investigation as a "Preliminary Evaluation" (PE). We inform the manufacturer and the public at this time, and begin the process of gathering information from the manufacturer and other appropriate sources. We give the manufacturer an opportunity to present its views. Preliminary Evaluations are generally resolved within four months from the date of their opening. They may be closed if we determine that further information is not warranted, or if the manufacturer decides to conduct a recall.

If our review of information at the end of a PE suggests that further investigation is warranted, we move the investigation to a second stage, the Engineering Analysis (EA), in which we conduct a more detailed and complete analysis of the character and scope of the alleged defect. The EA supplements the information collected during the preliminary evaluation with appropriate inspections, tests, surveys, and additional information from the manufacturer. ODI attempts to resolve all EAs within one year from the date they are opened.

At the conclusion of the EA, we may close an investigation because the additional information does not support a finding that a defect exists or because the manufacturer decides to conduct a recall. If ODI continues to believe that the data indicate a defect, the Associate Administrator for Safety Assurance may convene a panel of experts from the agency to review the information. The manufacturer is notified that a panel is being convened and of the panel's result, and is given an opportunity to present new analysis or new data.

If the panel concurs with ODI, the next step is to send a "recall request letter" to the manufacturer. If the manufacturer declines to conduct a recall in response to this letter, the Associate Administrator may issue an "Initial Decision" that a safety-related defect exists. An Initial Decision is followed by a public meeting, at which the manufacturer and interested members of the public can present information and arguments on the issue, as well as written materials. The entire investigative record is then presented to the NHTSA Administrator, who may issue a "Final Decision" that a safety defect exists and order the manufacturer to conduct a recall. If necessary, the agency will then go to court to enforce such an order.

## The Firestone ATX/Wilderness Recall

With this description of our investigative procedures as context, I will turn now to the Firestone investigation.

Firestone originally began producing the tires under investigation in 1991. By the end of 1999, approximately 47 million had been produced. By that time, NHTSA had received 46 reports scattered over 9 years about incidents involving these tires. The tires were on a variety of vehicles, primarily on Ford Explorer sport utility vehicles. In view of the large number of tires that had been produced, the variety of possible causes of tire failure (road hazards, excessive wear, etc.), and the fact that all types of tires can fail in use, the reports that we received did not indicate a problem that would warrant opening a defect investigation regarding these tires. The informal submission by State Farm in 1998 of 21 claims over an eight-year period also did not provide such an indication.

The situation changed rapidly following the airing of a news story by KHOU in Houston on February 7, 2000, that dramatized the question of the tires' safety. In addition to highlighting two fatalities, the KHOU story alluded to a number of other crashes and fatalities.

Upon learning of the KHOU story, we contacted the station to obtain more details about the incidents. They have not given us the information we requested, but the growing publicity generated other reports to us, including several provided by other media outlets and by plaintiffs' attorneys. Over the next few weeks, we were able to verify many of these reports. We opened a Preliminary Evaluation on May 2. At that time, the agency was aware of 90 complaints, including reports of 33 crashes, and 4 fatalities. On May 8 and 10, we sent Ford and Firestone extensive Information Requests asking for information about the tires. At that point NHTSA began a constant communication with both companies, which continues today.

Information accumulated rapidly as a result of the investigation and attendant publicity. By August 1, we had 193 complaints alleging tread separations on these tires, with 21 reported fatalities. In a meeting on August 4, we suggested that Firestone consider recalling the tires. By August 9, when Firestone announced that it was recalling the ATX and ATX II tires, and Wilderness AT tires produced at its Decatur, Illinois, plant, we had over 300 complaints, with 46 reported fatalities. The number has continued to grow. As of August 31, we have 1400 complaints with reports of 88 fatalities and 250 injuries.

Firestone has recalled all of the ATX and ATX II tires of the P235/75R15 size manufactured since 1991. It has also recalled Wilderness AT tires of that size made at its Decatur, Illinois, plant, for a total of 14.4 million tires out of the 47 million tires covered by our investigation. Firestone estimates that approximately 6.5 million of the 14.4 million tires included in the recall are still on the road. Ford and Firestone are taking a number of measures to provide replacement tires.

NHTSA is continuing its investigation to ensure that the scope of the recall is proper and that all unsafe tires are recalled. At our request, Firestone and Ford have given us voluminous information about the tires, and we have sent follow-up requests for additional information to both companies and to Goodyear Tire and Rubber Company, for a peer comparison. We are continuing to monitor the recall to ensure that all defective tires are replaced promptly.

Our review of data from Firestone has already disclosed that other tire models and sizes of the tires under investigation have rates of tread separation as high or higher than the tires that Firestone is recalling. On August 30, we recommended to Firestone that it expand its recall to include these tires. When Firestone declined to expand the recall, we issued a consumer advisory on September 1 to advise owners of these tires to take actions to assure their safety.

## Observations

We now know that in September 1999 Ford conducted a campaign (referred to by Ford as an "Owner Notification Program") to replace Wilderness tires mounted on Ford Explorers that had been sold in the states around the Arabian Gulf (primarily Saudi Arabia). Similar actions were taken in Venezuela in May 2000 and in Columbia, Ecuador, Malaysia, and Thailand. Ford would have been required to notify NHTSA of such an owner notification program if it had occurred in the United States, but our regulations do not apply to actions taken outside the United States. Ford thus had no obligation to advise NHTSA when it took these actions. If we find that we need additional legislative authority to require manufacturers to provide such information, we will seek to obtain it.

A number of claims, and several lawsuits, had been filed against Ford and Firestone before we became aware of any trend that would indicate a potential defect. We received no information about those events from the companies or from the plaintiffs' attorneys. Our current regulations do not require the manufacturers to give us information about claims or litigation. The existing law gives us broad authority to seek information from vehicle and equipment manufacturers during the course of an investigation. We are exploring measures that would allow us to track claims and litigation information routinely.

Mr. Chairman, I want to assure you that this investigation is the highest priority in NHTSA. We will remain focused on the investigation, closely monitor the current recall campaign, and seek any expansion of the campaign that may be necessary. . . .

**Masatoshi Ono:** . . . As chief executive officer, I come before you to apologize to you, the American people and especially to the families who have lost loved ones in these terrible rollover accidents. I also come to accept full and personal responsibility on behalf of Bridgestone/Firestone for the events that led to this hearing. Whenever people are hurt or fatally injured in automobile accidents, it is tragic. Whenever people are injured while riding on Firestone tires, it is cause for great concern among Bridgestone/Firestone management and our 35,000 American employees.

On August 8, we met with the National Highway Traffic Safety Administration. We reviewed what we knew—at that time—about the performance of the tires which are associated with tread separations and accidents primarily on the ford explorer vehicle. On the following day, August 9, Bridgestone/Firestone announced a voluntary safety recall of 6.5 million tires.

Since that time, our highest priorities have been to complete the recall as quickly as possible and to determine the root cause of the tire failures. At this time we have replaced nearly two million of the recalled tires. We have maximized worldwide production of replacements for tires that have been recalled. To speed up the process, we are using our competitors' tires and air lifting additional replacement tires and these shipments will continue as long as necessary.

We have a team working around the clock using all our available resources to try and determine the root causes for the tire problem. We are reviewing every aspect of our manufacturing and quality control processes. This includes microscopic examination of many recalled tires. In addition, we are working with Ford Motor Company and experts to thoroughly examine every possible cause.

Unfortunately, I am not able to give you a conclusive cause at this time. However, you have my word that we will continue until we find the cause.

While we search for the root cause, we are also undertaking the following actions.

First, we will appoint an outside independent investigator to assist in tire analysis and determine the root cause of the tire problem we have experienced. We are taking this action to help assure you and the public that Firestone tires are reliable now and in the future.

Second, we will fully cooperate with this committee about the safety as well as problems that have occurred with our tires. We will release data and information in order to assure consumer safety with our products.

Third, we are accelerating the rollout of a nationwide consumer education program. The program will be run through more than 7,000 company stores and Firestone dealers. It will provide consumers with information on proper tire maintenance through the use of in-store videos, showroom displays, brochures, windshield tags and tire pressure gauges.

Fourth, we pledge to continue working with NHTSA toward developing early understandings and complete reporting of accidents and developing approaches that make it easier for drivers to determine tire pressure.

In closing, this year Firestone is observing its 100th anniversary. It is a proud history. Henry Ford used Firestone tires on the original model-t. For 100 years, millions of families have placed their trust and faith in the good people of Firestone. We feel a heavy responsibility to make certain that we are worthy still of your continued trust and confidence. . . .

**Jac Nasser:** . . . . I have been with Ford Motor Company for more than 30 years in a variety of positions around the world. I am proud of the great contributions Ford Motor Company has made to improve the standard of living of millions of people around the world. I am driven to make sure that everything we do serves all customers, and clearly their safety is uppermost on our minds. For that reason, I am deeply troubled by the fact that there are defective tires on some of our vehicles.

As you know, Firestone manufactured and warranted these tires. However, because so many of these tires were used as original equipment on Ford products, we have taken extraordinary steps to support this recall and ensure the safety of our customers. Ford Motor Company is absolutely committed to doing the right thing to protect our customers and to maintain their trust.

Throughout this period, we have been guided by three principles. First, we will do whatever we can to guarantee our customers' safety. We are committed not only to their physical safety, but also their feelings of security when driving our vehicles. Second, we are working hard to find and replace bad tires with good tires. That includes making sure that we understand the scope of the problem and finding the cause of the problem. Third, we will continue to be open about any data, statistics or information that we have, and will share anything new as soon as we know it.

Because I don't want there to be any question about our openness, I wanted to personally discuss Ford's actions with you at this hearing.

## Actions We Have Taken

Now, lets talk about the actions Ford has taken to support the recall and why we believe these are the right actions.

First, this is a tire issue, not a vehicle issue. We have millions of Goodyear tires on 1995 through 1997 Explorers—the same specification tire operating under the same conditions—and they haven't experienced these problems.

Furthermore, the Explorer is one of the safest SUVs on the road. Proof of this is our exemplary safety record over the last decade. The most recent data from the Department of Transportation show that the Explorer has a lower fatality rate than both the average passenger car and competitive SUV. . . . Additionally, Explorer's fatality rate in rollover accidents is 26 percent lower than other compact SUVs.

Second, we strongly support Firestone's decision to recall 15″ ATX and Decatur-built Wilderness AT tires. Based on the Firestone data we have, we've determined that these tires are problem tires. . . .

What we still don't know is why these tires fail. We are working hard on that.

## Customer Focus

As I said, our top priority is to replace faulty tires as fast as possible. I'd like to highlight a few of the many things we have done to support Firestone's recall and speed replacement. As of September 1, about 1.5 million tires have been replaced—about 23 percent of the total population of affected tires. We worked with the tire industry to increase production of 15inch tires by more than 250,000 tires per month by the end of September. We have suspended production at three assembly plants, adding approximately 70,000 tires to the replacement population. We have engaged 3,100 Ford and Lincoln-Mercury dealers to perform tire replacements.

We've also made a major effort to communicate information about the Firestone recall to our customers. For example, we have opened an additional call center to deal specifically with inquiries on the tire recall. We are using our website to provide detailed information on the recall action. And we are running national and local newspaper and television ads to alert customers to the recall and show them how to tell if their vehicles are affected.

## Overseas Actions

I would also like to comment on our actions overseas. When reports of tread separation in the Middle East came to our attention, we asked Firestone to investigate. They concluded that the tire failures were due to external causes, such as poor repairs, road hazard damage, and extreme operating conditions. But given the problems our customers were having, we decided to replace the tires with a more puncture resistant tire.

Another market where we have experienced tire problems is Venezuela. The situation in Venezuela is complicated by the fact that about three-quarters of the tires were locally produced. Again, Firestone concluded that the tread separations were caused by poor repairs, road hazard damage, and extreme operating conditions. In May, we began replacing all the Firestone tires on Ford Explorers and certain light trucks in Venezuela.

Concern about the safety of all of our customers, including our U.S. customers, drove us to look aggressively for evidence of a defect in the U.S. at the same time we were taking actions overseas. I share this with you, not to finger point at Firestone, but simply to tell you what we did. As early as April of 1999, we were searching all available data bases — our own and the government's. We asked Firestone to check its records. And we had new tires tested under three separate, severe test conditions to try to cause tread separation to happen. Last Fall, we kicked off a tire inspection test program in the Southwest of the U.S. No defect trend was found.

When NHTSA opened their investigation, and required Firestone to assemble and provide data on property damage, personal injury, and lawsuits, Ford insisted on obtaining the data as well. When we received the data late in July, we quickly analyzed it and identified the problem tires that were recalled August 9.

It has been standard practice in the automotive industry that tires are the only part of the vehicle not warranted by the vehicle manufacturer. They are the only part for which vehicle manufacturers do not receive field performance data. At Ford, this will change.

Through all this, we were always open and sought only to find the facts and do the right thing for our customers.

## Conclusion

Our mission remains to replace bad tires with good tires as quickly as possible. The safety, trust and peace of mind of our consumers are paramount to Ford Motor Company.

# UN DECLARATION AT THE MILLENNIUM SUMMIT
## September 8, 2000

*For three days in early September 2000 more than one hundred fifty world leaders gathered for the largest summit meeting ever at the United Nations. Despite prominent disagreements on many issues facing the world, they managed to agree on dozens of points contained in the "United Nations Millennium Declaration," which was intended to serve as an agenda for the world body at the start of the twenty-first century. The heart of the declaration was a series of pledges for action to reduce world poverty—most notably a call to cut in half, by 2015, the proportions of the world's people whose income was less than one dollar a day, who suffered from hunger, and who lacked access to safe drinking water.*

*The General Assembly in mid-December endorsed the declaration as a primary basis for the UN's work and established committees to implement the promises contained in the document. General Assembly president Harri Holkeri, of Finland, told reporters on December 21 that the summit declaration was "one of the most important documents of our time" and pledged to work to implement its provisions.*

### Annan Report

*Most of the pledges made by the summit leaders originated in a "state of the world" report issued on April 3 by Secretary General Kofi Annan. Called "We the Peoples: The Role of the United Nations in the 21st Century," the report offered a detailed analysis of the principal problems facing the world on a broad range of issues, along with recommendations for action by the UN and its agencies, individual nations, and private organizations.*

*In many ways the heart of Annan's eighty-page report was a twenty-one page chapter, "Freedom from Want," highlighting the plight of the world's poorest people, most of whom lived in sub-Saharan Africa and South Asia. Annan marshaled dozens of statistics to bolster his point that about one-half of the world's 6 billion people lived in poverty, with consequences for everyone else. "Extreme poverty is an affront to our common humanity," he said. "It also makes other problems worse. For example, poor counties—*

*especially those with significant inequality between ethnic and religious communities—are far more likely to be embroiled in conflicts than rich ones. Most of these conflicts are internal, but they almost invariably create problems for neighbors or generate a need for humanitarian assistance."*

*Annan outlined a series of suggestions for action by the Millennium Summit, many of them containing bold pledges, such as ensuring that by 2015 all children in the world complete a full course of primary education. Most of these suggestions were incorporated in the "Millennium Declaration."*

*Annan devoted one chapter of the report to the subject of "globalization," the catch-all term that became popular during the 1990s as a summary of the growing importance of global commerce. Globalization had produced many benefits for the world, Annan said, but it also had heightened awareness of the economic disparities among the world's peoples. The benefits of global trade "remain highly concentrated among a relatively small number of countries and are spread unevenly within them," he said. Citing the Asian financial crisis of 1997, he also noted that globalization had made millions of people increasingly vulnerable to "unfamiliar and unpredictable forces that can bring on economic instability and social dislocation, sometimes with lightening speed."* (Asian financial crisis, Historic Documents of 1997, p. 832, Historic Documents of 1998, p. 722)

*Annan offered an impassioned defense of his statement, delivered to the General Assembly in September 1999, that the world had a moral obligation to act against mass murder and egregious human rights violations—even if that meant intervening in the internal affairs of member states. Several governments denounced that proposition; some said the UN had an equal obligation to honor the sovereignty of member states, and others said the UN had neither the resources nor the political clout to be the world's policeman.* (Annan statement on human rights violations, Historic Documents of 1999, p. 860)

*In his April 2000 report, Annan acknowledged the criticisms but said the UN could not ignore the lessons of massive human right violations during the 1990s, most notably the 1994 genocide in Rwanda and the 1995 massacre of Muslims in Srebrenica, Bosnia. There were no easy answers, he said, "but surely no legal principle—not even sovereignty—can ever shield crimes against humanity. Where such crimes occur and peaceful attempts to halt them have been exhausted, the Security Council has a moral duty to act on behalf of the international community. The fact that we cannot protect people everywhere is no reason for doing nothing when we can. Armed intervention must always remain the option of last resort, but in the fact of mass murder, it is an option that cannot be relinquished."*

## *Millennium Summit*

*For three days in early September, New York City was truly the capital of the world, as a strong majority of the leaders of the 189 nations belonging to the UN attended the biggest summit meeting in world history. One hundred forty-nine of the leaders—kings, princes, presidents, prime ministers, and other senior officials—had lunch together on September 6, an event the* New York Times *called "the ultimate power lunch."*

*Each leader was given five minutes to address the UN General Assembly. U.S. president Bill Clinton, representing the host nation, led off those speeches on September 6 with a call for action to protect innocent people endangered by internal conflicts around the world. Some leaders joined Clinton in urging help for the world's disadvantaged. Among then, Irish prime minister Bertie Ahern warned that globalization could lead to "an ever more lopsided world" unless leaders recognized that "we live in a society, not a marketplace." Many other leaders used their brief moment on the world's stage to voice concerns particular to their own nations. One leader, Maumoon Abdul Gayoom, president of the Maldives (a nation of islands in the Indian Ocean, south of India), raised an alarm about global warming, which some scientists had said might cause the oceans to rise, thus flooding many coastal areas and islands. "When the UN meets to usher in yet another century, will the Maldives and other low-lying island nations be represented here?" he said. "Not only a sobering thought, but an alarming one."*

*As with most summits, much of the important business—or attempted important business—was conducted behind the scenes in private meetings. President Clinton met privately with Israeli prime minister Ehud Barak and Palestinian leader Yasir Arafat in an unsuccessful attempt to make progress on peace negotiations, which had faltered since the collapse of talks at Camp David in July. Clinton also met individually with the leaders of China, Russia, and several other countries. In an unscheduled encounter, Cuban President Fidel Castro marched up to Clinton and offered a friendly greeting and handshake—the first one-to-one meeting ever between Castro and a U.S. president.* (Mideast peace talks, p. 494)

*A tragic incident on the opposite side of the world offered a sobering moment for the leaders as their summit got under way. Early on September 6 a violent mob attacked a UN compound in West Timor, Indonesia, and killed three UN relief workers, along with three other local civilians. The UN workers had been stationed in West Timor to help refugees who had fled neighboring East Timor during a massive rampage of violence following a referendum on independence from Indonesia in September 1999. Members of the UN Security Council sat stunned as Sadako Ogata, the UN High Commissioner for Refugees, read an e-mail message from Carlos Caceres-Collazo, one of those killed in the September 6 attack. As the mob approached the UN office, he wrote: "We are waiting for this enemy. We sit here like bait, unarmed, waiting for [the] wave to hit." At the UN summit, Annan confronted Indonesian president Abdurraham Wahid and demanded improved security for UN workers. Wahid, who appeared to have little control over his nation's military forces, promised to send two battalions of troops to bolster the security situation in West Timor.* (East Timor independence, Historic Documents of 1999, p. 511)

*On September 7 the fifteen presidents and prime ministers whose nations comprised the Security Council met in a special session to review the report of a special commission that investigated the UN's peacekeeping operations.*

*The leaders endorsed the report and its recommendations in general terms, but at that point they shied away from a formal pledge to carry out the sweeping changes the commission demanded. However, the leaders did pass a resolution pledging to "address the root causes of conflicts, including their economic and social dimensions." Despite its innocuous-sounding tone, that resolution was the subject of some debate, with Chinese president Jiang Zemin expressing concern about UN interference in the internal affairs of member states. Later in the year, the Security Council and the General Assembly agreed to implement most of the peacekeeping recommendations.* (Peacekeeping report, p. 642)

*The leaders closed their summit on September 8 by approving, by acclamation, the thirty-two point "United Nations Millennium Declaration." Much of the declaration consisted of formulaic restatements of longstanding UN principles, such as a commitment to "a just and lasting peace in the world" and adherence to the UN's founding Charter and Declaration on Human Rights. But the summit declaration also featured numerous ambitious pledges, including the goals stated in Annan's earlier report, such as ensuring that all the world's children have at least an elementary school education and cutting in half the proportion of the world's population living on less than $1 a day. The declaration offered no specifics on how those goals would be met, however.*

*A key section of the declaration dealt with meeting "the special needs of Africa," one of the themes Annan—a Ghanian and the first secretary general from sub-Saharan Africa—had been promoting during his tenure. In that section, the leaders promised to support efforts in Africa to build democracy, reduce poverty, end wars, and combat the spread of AIDS.* (AIDS in Africa, p. 410; wars in Africa, pp. 449, 978, 1072)

*Following is the text of the "United Nations Millennium Declaration," agreed to on September 8, 2000, by more than 150 world leaders attending a Millennium Summit at the United Nations. The document was obtained from the Internet at http://www.un .org/documents/ga/res/55/a55r002.pdf.*

# United Nations Millennium Declaration

## I. Values and principles

1. We, heads of State and Government, have gathered at United Nations Headquarters in New York from 6 to 8 September 2000, at the dawn of a new millennium, to reaffirm our faith in the Organization and its Charter as indispensable foundations of a more peaceful, prosperous and just world.

2. We recognize that, in addition to our separate responsibilities to our individual societies, we have a collective responsibility to uphold the prin-

ciples of human dignity, equality and equity at the global level. As leaders we have a duty therefore to all the world's people, especially the most vulnerable and, in particular, the children of the world, to whom the future belongs.

3. We reaffirm our commitment to the purposes and principles of the Charter of the United Nations, which have proved timeless and universal. Indeed, their relevance and capacity to inspire have increased, as nations and peoples have become increasingly interconnected and interdependent.

4. We are determined to establish a just and lasting peace all over the world in accordance with the purposes and principles of the Charter. We rededicate ourselves to support all efforts to uphold the sovereign equality of all States, respect for their territorial integrity and political independence, resolution of disputes by peaceful means and in conformity with the principles of justice and international law, the right to self-determination of peoples which remain under colonial domination and foreign occupation, non-interference in the internal affairs of States, respect for human rights and fundamental freedoms, respect for the equal rights of all without distinction as to race, sex, language or religion and international cooperation in solving international problems of an economic, social, cultural or humanitarian character.

5. We believe that the central challenge we face today is to ensure that globalization becomes a positive force for all the world's people. For while globalization offers great opportunities, at present its benefits are very unevenly shared, while its costs are unevenly distributed. We recognize that developing countries and countries with economies in transition face special difficulties in responding to this central challenge. Thus, only through broad and sustained efforts to create a shared future, based upon our common humanity in all its diversity, can globalization be made fully inclusive and equitable. These efforts must include policies and measures, at the global level, which correspond to the needs of developing countries and economies in transition and are formulated and implemented with their effective participation.

6. We consider certain fundamental values to be essential to international relations in the twenty-first century. These include:

- **Freedom.** Men and women have the right to live their lives and raise their children in dignity, free from hunger and from the fear of violence, oppression or injustice. Democratic and participatory governance based on the will of the people best assures these rights.

- **Equality.** No individual and no nation must be denied the opportunity to benefit from development. The equal rights and opportunities of women and men must be assured.

- **Solidarity.** Global challenges must be managed in a way that distributes the costs and burdens fairly in accordance with basic principles of equity and social justice. Those who suffer or who benefit least deserve help from those who benefit most.

- **Tolerance.** Human beings must respect one other, in all their diversity of belief, culture and language. Differences within and between societies should be neither feared nor repressed, but cherished as a precious asset of humanity. A culture of peace and dialogue among all civilizations should be actively promoted.
- **Respect for nature.** Prudence must be shown in the management of all living species and natural resources, in accordance with the precepts of sustainable development. Only in this way can the immeasurable riches provided to us by nature be preserved and passed on to our descendants. The current unsustainable patterns of production and consumption must be changed in the interest of our future welfare and that of our descendants.
- **Shared responsibility.** Responsibility for managing worldwide economic and social development, as well as threats to international peace and security, must be shared among the nations of the world and should be exercised multilaterally. As the most universal and most representative organization in the world, the United Nations must play the central role.

7. In order to translate these shared values into actions, we have identified key objectives to which we assign special significance.

## II. Peace, Security and Disarmament

8. We will spare no effort to free our peoples from the scourge of war, whether within or between States, which has claimed more than 5 million lives in the past decade. We will also seek to eliminate the dangers posed by weapons of mass destruction.

9. We resolve therefore:
   - To strengthen respect for the rule of law in international as in national affairs and, in particular, to ensure compliance by Member States with the decisions of the International Court of Justice, in compliance with the Charter of the United Nations, in cases to which they are parties.
   - To make the United Nations more effective in maintaining peace and security by giving it the resources and tools it needs for conflict prevention, peaceful resolution of disputes, peacekeeping, post-conflict peace-building and reconstruction. In this context, we take note of the report of the Panel on United Nations Peace Operations and request the General Assembly to consider its recommendations expeditiously.
   - To strengthen cooperation between the United Nations and regional organizations, in accordance with the provisions of Chapter VIII of the Charter.
   - To ensure the implementation, by States Parties, of treaties in areas such as arms control and disarmament and of international humanitarian law and human rights law, and call upon all States to consider signing and ratifying the Rome Statute of the International Criminal Court.
   - To take concerted action against international terrorism, and to accede as soon as possible to all the relevant international conventions.

- To redouble our efforts to implement our commitment to counter the world drug problem.
- To intensify our efforts to fight transnational crime in all its dimensions, including trafficking as well as smuggling in human beings and money laundering.
- To minimize the adverse effects of United Nations economic sanctions on innocent populations, to subject such sanctions regimes to regular reviews and to eliminate the adverse effects of sanctions on third parties.
- To strive for the elimination of weapons of mass destruction, particularly nuclear weapons, and to keep all options open for achieving this aim, including the possibility of convening an international conference to identify ways of eliminating nuclear dangers.
- To take concerted action to end illicit traffic in small arms and light weapons, especially by making arms transfers more transparent and supporting regional disarmament measures, taking account of all the recommendations of the forthcoming United Nations Conference on Illicit Trade in Small Arms and Light Weapons.
- To call on all States to consider acceding to the Convention on the Prohibition of the Use, Stockpiling, Production and Transfer of Anti-personnel Mines and on Their Destruction, as well as the amended mines protocol to the Convention on conventional weapons.

10. We urge Member States to observe the Olympic Truce, individually and collectively, now and in the future, and to support the International Olympic Committee in its efforts to promote peace and human understanding through sport and the Olympic Ideal.

## III. Development and poverty eradication

11. We will spare no effort to free our fellow men, women and children from the abject and dehumanizing conditions of extreme poverty, to which more than a billion of them are currently subjected. We are committed to making the right to development a reality for everyone and to freeing the entire human race from want.

12. We resolve therefore to create an environment—at the national and global levels alike—which is conducive to development and to the elimination of poverty.

13. Success in meeting these objectives depends, inter alia, on good governance within each country. It also depends on good governance at the international level and on transparency in the financial, monetary and trading systems. We are committed to an open, equitable, rule-based, predictable and non-discriminatory multilateral trading and financial system.

14. We are concerned about the obstacles developing countries face in mobilizing the resources needed to finance their sustained development. We will therefore make every effort to ensure the success of the High-level International and Intergovernmental Event on Financing for Development, to be held in 2001.

15. We also undertake to address the special needs of the least developed countries. In this context, we welcome the Third United Nations Conference on the Least Developed Countries to be held in May 2001 and will endeavour to ensure its success. We call on the industrialized countries:
    - to adopt, preferably by the time of that Conference, a policy of duty- and quota-free access for essentially all exports from the least developed countries;
    - To implement the enhanced programme of debt relief for the heavily indebted poor countries without further delay and to agree to cancel all official bilateral debts of those countries in return for their making demonstrable commitments to poverty reduction; and
    - To grant more generous development assistance, especially to countries that are genuinely making an effort to apply their resources to poverty reduction.

16. We are also determined to deal comprehensively and effectively with the debt problems of low- and middle-income developing countries, through various national and international measures designed to make their debt sustainable in the long term.

17. We also resolve to address the special needs of small island developing States, by implementing the Barbados Programme of Action and the outcome of the twenty-second special session of the General Assembly rapidly and in full. We urge the international community to ensure that, in the development of a vulnerability index, the special needs of small island developing States are taken into account.

18. We recognize the special needs and problems of the landlocked developing countries, and urge both bilateral and multilateral donors to increase financial and technical assistance to this group of countries to meet their special development needs and to help them overcome the impediments of geography by improving their transit transport systems.

19. We resolve further:
    - To halve, by the year 2015, the proportion of the world's people whose income is less than one dollar a day and the proportion of people who suffer from hunger and, by the same date, to halve the proportion of people who are unable to reach or to afford safe drinking water.
    - To ensure that, by the same date, children everywhere, boys and girls alike, will be able to complete a full course of primary schooling and that girls and boys will have equal access to all levels of education.
    - By the same date, to have reduced maternal mortality by three quarters, and under-five child mortality by two thirds, of their current rates.
    - To have, by then, halted, and begun to reverse, the spread of HIV/AIDS, the scourge of malaria and other major diseases that afflict humanity.
    - To provide special assistance to children orphaned by HIV/AIDS.
    - By 2020, to have achieved a significant improvement in the lives of at least 100 million slum dwellers as proposed in the "Cities Without Slums" initiative.

20. We also resolve:
    - To promote gender equality and the empowerment of women as effec-

tive ways to combat poverty, hunger and disease and to stimulate development that is truly sustainable.

- To develop and implement strategies that give young people everywhere a real chance to find decent and productive work.
- To encourage the pharmaceutical industry to make essential drugs more widely available and affordable by all who need them in developing countries.
- To develop strong partnerships with the private sector and with civil society organizations in pursuit of development and poverty eradication.
- To ensure that the benefits of new technologies, especially information and communication technologies, in conformity with recommendations contained in the ECOSOC 2000 Ministerial Declaration, are available to all.

## IV. Protecting Our Common Environment

21. We must spare no effort to free all of humanity, and above all our children and grandchildren, from the threat of living on a planet irredeemably spoilt by human activities, and whose resources would no longer be sufficient for their needs.

22. We reaffirm our support for the principles of sustainable development, including those set out in Agenda 21, agreed upon at the United Nations Conference on Environment and Development.

23. We resolve therefore to adopt in all our environmental actions a new ethic of conservation and stewardship and, as first steps, we resolve:
    - To make every effort to ensure the entry into force of the Kyoto Protocol, preferably by the tenth anniversary of the United Nations Conference on Environment and Development in 2002, and to embark on the required reduction in emissions of greenhouse gases.
    - To intensify our collective efforts for the management, conservation and sustainable development of all types of forests.
    - To press for the full implementation of the Convention on Biological Diversity and the Convention to Combat Desertification in those Countries Experiencing Serious Drought and/or Desertification, particularly in Africa.
    - To stop the unsustainable exploitation of water resources by developing water management strategies at the regional, national and local levels, which promote both equitable access and adequate supplies.
    - To intensify cooperation to reduce the number and effects of natural and man-made disasters.
    - To ensure free access to information on the human genome sequence.

## V. Human rights, democracy and good governance

24. We will spare no effort to promote democracy and strengthen the rule of law, as well as respect for all internationally recognized human rights and fundamental freedoms, including the right to development.

25. We resolve therefore:
    - To respect fully and uphold the Universal Declaration of Human Rights.

- To strive for the full protection and promotion in all our countries of civil, political, economic, social and cultural rights for all.
- To strengthen the capacity of all our countries to implement the principles and practices of democracy and respect for human rights, including minority rights.
- To combat all forms of violence against women and to implement the Convention on the Elimination of All Forms of Discrimination against Women.
- To take measures to ensure respect for and protection of the human rights of migrants, migrant workers and their families, to eliminate the increasing acts of racism and xenophobia in many societies and to promote greater harmony and tolerance in all societies.
- To work collectively for more inclusive political processes, allowing genuine participation by all citizens in all our countries.
- To ensure the freedom of the media to perform their essential role and the right of the public to have access to information.

## VI. Protecting the Vulnerable

26. We will spare no effort to ensure that children and all civilian populations that suffer disproportionately the consequences of natural disasters, genocide, armed conflicts and other humanitarian emergencies are given every assistance and protection so that they can resume normal life as soon as possible.

    We resolve therefore:

    - To expand and strengthen the protection of civilians in complex emergencies, in conformity with international humanitarian law.
    - To strengthen international cooperation, including burden sharing in, and the coordination of humanitarian assistance to, countries hosting refugees and to help all refugees and displaced persons to return voluntarily to their homes, in safety and dignity and to be smoothly reintegrated into their societies.
    - To encourage the ratification and full implementation of the Convention on the Rights of the Child and its optional protocols on the involvement of children in armed conflict and on the sale of children, child prostitution and child pornography.

## VII. Meeting the Special Needs of Africa

27. We will support the consolidation of democracy in Africa and assist Africans in their struggle for lasting peace, poverty eradication and sustainable development, thereby bringing Africa into the mainstream of the world economy.

28. We resolve therefore:
    - To give full support to the political and institutional structures of emerging democracies in Africa.
    - To encourage and sustain regional and subregional mechanisms for preventing conflict and promoting political stability, and to ensure a reliable flow of resources for peacekeeping operations on the continent.

- To take special measures to address the challenges of poverty eradication and sustainable development in Africa, including debt cancellation, improved market access, enhanced Official Development Assistance and increased flows of Foreign Direct Investment, as well as transfers of technology.
- To help Africa build up its capacity to tackle the spread of the HIV/AIDS pandemic and other infectious diseases.

## VIII. Strengthening the United Nations

29. We will spare no effort to make the United Nations a more effective instrument for pursuing all of these priorities: the fight for development for all the peoples of the world, the fight against poverty, ignorance and disease; the fight against injustice; the fight against violence, terror and crime; and the fight against the degradation and destruction of our common home.

30. We resolve therefore:
   - To reaffirm the central position of the General Assembly as the chief deliberative, policy-making and representative organ of the United Nations, and to enable it to play that role effectively.
   - To intensify our efforts to achieve a comprehensive reform of the Security Council in all its aspects.
   - To strengthen further the Economic and Social Council, building on its recent achievements, to help it fulfil the role ascribed to it in the Charter.
   - To strengthen the International Court of Justice, in order to ensure justice and the rule of law in international affairs.
   - To encourage regular consultations and coordination among the principal organs of the United Nations in pursuit of their functions.
   - To ensure that the Organization is provided on a timely and predictable basis with the resources it needs to carry out its mandates.
   - To urge the Secretariat to make the best use of those resources, in accordance with clear rules and procedures agreed by the General Assembly, in the interests of all Member States, by adopting the best management practices and technologies available and by concentrating on those tasks that reflect the agreed priorities of Member States.
   - To promote adherence to the Convention on the Safety of United Nations and Associated Personnel.
   - To ensure greater policy coherence and better cooperation between the United Nations, its agencies, the Bretton Woods Institutions and the World Trade Organization, as well as other multilateral bodies, with a view to achieving a fully coordinated approach to the problems of peace and development.
   - To strengthen further cooperation between the United Nations and national parliaments through their world organization, the Inter-Parliamentary Union, in various fields, including peace and security, economic and social development, international law and human rights and democracy and gender issues.

- To give greater opportunities to the private sector, non-governmental organizations and civil society, in general, to contribute to the realization of the Organization's goals and programmes.

31. We request the General Assembly to review on a regular basis the progress made in implementing the provisions of this Declaration, and ask the Secretary-General to issue periodic reports for consideration by the General Assembly and as a basis for further action.

32. We solemnly reaffirm, on this historic occasion, that the United Nations is the indispensable common house of the entire human family, through which we will seek to realize our universal aspirations for peace, cooperation and development. We therefore pledge our unstinting support for these common objectives and our determination to achieve them.

# AGRICULTURE AND INTERIOR SECRETARIES ON U.S. WILDFIRES
## September 8, 2000

*One of the most devastating wildfire seasons in decades may have brought about an unusual degree of consensus among U.S. political leaders for a significant expansion of efforts to prevent major forest fires. More than 92,000 wildfires burned about 7.4 million acres—most in the arid West— during 2000's prolonged and intense fire season. In terms of acreage, fires caused more damage in 2000 than in any year in the previous four decades, except for 1988, when massive fires raged through Yellowstone National Park and many other sections of the West. Even so, the destruction was well below the tens of millions of acres consumed by fire each year until the 1950s.*

*In response to the year's fires, the Clinton administration developed a long-term plan for blunting the danger of fire in the nearly 200 million acres of forest land owned by the federal government. A key component of the plan involved an expanded program of "thinning" the forests to remove small trees and undergrowth that provided much of the fuel for fires. The plan won support from western governors who had been highly critical of the administration's federal land-management programs, from many environmental groups, and from Congress, which voted an additional $1.6 billion Clinton had requested for dealing with wildfires.*

### The 2000 Fire Season

*A combination of factors led to a fire season that was unusual both in its duration and intensity, according to federal and local fire officials and scientists. One short-term factor was the lingering impact, early in the year, of the periodic "La Nina" weather pattern, which produced an abnormally wet winter in the Pacific Northwest but exceptionally dry conditions along the southern half of the United States, ranging from California to Florida. For most of the West, the summer of 2000 was one of the hottest on record and featured a seemingly endless succession of thunderstorms, providing perfect conditions for fires.*

712

*In addition, there was a general consensus by the late 1990s that American forests—especially those on public lands—were tinder boxes ready to explode. The reason was that fire suppression efforts all through the twentieth century had prevented many natural fires that would have cleared underbrush from the forests while leaving most big trees intact. As a result, the forests were loaded with dry fuel. In 1995 the Clinton administration launched efforts to clear the underbrush from some of the forests, but these efforts were limited in scope and could not possibly make up for nearly a century's worth of fuel buildup.*

*The 2000 fire season got under way early, in February, with large grass fires in New Mexico, followed by forest and grass fires through much of the South. By April major fires had caused extensive damage in national forests in California and Arizona.*

*One of the earliest big fires turned into a massive embarrassment for the Clinton administration. On May 4 National Park Service personnel set a "prescribed fire" in the Bandelier National Monument, near Los Alamos, New Mexico, to remove thick brush. Unexpectedly strong winds quickly blew the fire out of control and toward the city of Los Alamos. The fire destroyed 235 homes in the city, forced a two-week closing of the U.S. Energy Department's Los Alamos National Laboratory, and eventually burned 47,650 acres. In response, Interior Secretary Bruce Babbitt imposed a moratorium on prescribed fires in the West and ordered the development of new procedures for any such fires in the future. Babbitt in August approved the new guidelines, which required extensive analysis of the risks and benefits before the deliberate setting of fires.*

*By July much of the West was facing a severe drought, and a series of dry thunderstorms (bearing lightening but little rain) began setting off hundreds of wildfires. By July 25, according to the U.S. Forest Service's National Fire Information Center, large fires were blazing in nine of eleven geographic regions designated by the Forest Service. Only the New England states and Alaska were spared.*

*At the end of July more than 20,000 firefighters were deployed, most of them in the West, and the Forest Service called on the Pentagon for help. More than 2,000 troops from the army and the marines—along with state and local personnel, National Guard units, and volunteers from Australia, Canada, Mexico, and New Zealand—brought the total number of firefighters to more than 30,000, according to the Forest Service. The fire-fighting effort cost the federal, state, and local governments more than $2 billion, the Forest Service said.*

*By late August the country was facing nearly ninety major forest fires in the West and South, along with thousands of smaller fires in those areas and elsewhere. The four states hardest hit by the fires were Idaho, Montana, Nevada, and Utah, with Idaho and Montana facing the most severe range of fires and experiencing the two largest fires of the season. By the end of the year, fires had burned nearly 1.4 million acres in Idaho and 950,000 acres in Montana.*

*The fires also destroyed hundreds of homes, most of them in recently built developments in mountain areas throughout the West. Fire officials said many homeowners had failed to take precautions against fires, such as clearing brush near their homes. The increased population of rural areas also meant a greater risk of fires, since nearly 90 percent of all wildfires during the 1990s were started by people, according to Forest Service statistics.*

*Cooler temperatures and rain showers in September gradually helped bring the fires under control. By mid-October the Fire Service said it was battling only one major fire. Final figures from the Forest Service showed 92,250 wildfires in the United States consumed 7,393,493 acres during 2000. The number of fires was below the annual average of 106,306 for the 1990s, but the acreage burned was about twice the yearly average of 3.6 million for the decade. In descending order of the number of acres burned, other major fire seasons since 1960 were 1988, with 7.4 million acres; 1963, with 7.1 million acres; and 1996 and 1969, both with 6.7 million acres.*

*In addition to being an extraordinary year for fires, 2000 was a presidential election year, and so it was perhaps natural that the two elements would become mixed. By mid-August, Republican governors in the West, Republican members of Congress, and the Republican candidate for president, George W. Bush, were charging that Clinton administration policies had contributed to the severity of the fires. "The Clinton administration didn't cause these fires, but their policies have left the Forest Service under funded and under prepared for this crisis," Montana governor Marc Racicot told the* New York Times. *"I don't think it's a conspiracy, but it's a philosophy they have that leads to explosive fires that destroy everything."*

*In particular, Racicot and other Republicans—along with representatives of the timber industry—argued that the administration had gone too far in curtailing timber cutting in the national forests. Reduced timber cutting was a major reason the forests were so loaded with excessive wood ready to burn, they said.*

*Babbitt rejected the charges as "politically motivated," and several independent experts said weather, not reduced timber cutting, was the primary cause of the severity of the year's fires. A study conducted by the Congressional Research Service and released on September 1 by Senator Ron Wyden (D-Ore.) found little relationship in previous years between the amount of timber cut in the forests and the number of acres burned by fires.*

## A New National Fire Plan

*On August 8, while the fires were at their height, Clinton visited the scene of a major fire in Idaho's Payette National Forest and asked his agriculture and interior secretaries to develop plans for responding to the year's fires and for reducing the danger of future fires. The Agriculture Department was the parent organization of the Forest Service, and the Interior Department oversaw the National Park Service, the Bureau of Land Management, and other agencies responsible for federally owned public lands.*

*Agriculture Secretary Dan Glickman and Interior Secretary Babbitt pre-*

*sented their report to Clinton on September 8, and the president endorsed it the following day during his weekly nationally broadcast radio address. The report recommended $1.6 billion in additional expenditures for federal fire programs, more than doubling the $1.2 billion that Clinton earlier had requested from Congress for fiscal 2001. Nearly half of the additional money—$770 million—was needed to replenish emergency funds that were depleted in fighting the 2000 fires. Most of the rest was to expand the scope of existing wildfire programs, including training and financial support for state and local fire departments. Glickman and Babbitt placed a top priority on preventing fires in what experts called the "wildland-urban interface": rural communities located in or at the edge of wild forests and grasslands. The plan included $10 million for training and equipment for rural, volunteer fire departments.*

*The report recommended no radical changes in federal policy but suggested a major intensification of ongoing efforts to prevent future fires by eliminating small trees and underbrush from national forests and parks—a process the departments called "fuel reduction." Many experts said these techniques would help restore the forests to the more natural—and thus more fire-resistant—condition first encountered by white settlers. Before the heavy emphasis on fighting fires during the twentieth century, these experts said, most American forests were relatively open spaces featuring broad grasslands and a few dozen trees on each acre of land. A century of fire-suppression had created much more crowded forests, often with hundreds of trees, both large and small, on each acre.*

*Babbitt and Glickman asked for an additional $257 million for techniques such as prescribed fires and mechanical removal of small trees and brush, putting the year's total for these programs at $385 million. They acknowledged that thinning the forests was an expensive proposition that would take decades to complete. But they rejected the contention of Republican governors and the timber industry that increased logging of the national forests would be necessary. Elimination of small diameter trees and brush "can successful reduce fire risk without relying on increased commercial logging," they said. Even so, they included money in their plan for research on ways to make commercial use of the small trees and shrubs to be taken from the forests; in the past those plants were burned or shredded.*

*In a politically important nod to the sentiments of local and state governments in the West, many of which deeply resented Washington's control over public lands, Babbitt and Glickman said local officials should be directly involved in determining where and how this work was to take place.*

*Ten days after delivering their report to Clinton, Babbitt and Glickman traveled to Salt Lake City, Utah, where they met with six western governors, five of them Republicans who had been critical of the administration's antifire efforts. The governors endorsed the new administration plan, praising in particular its large-scale financial support for state and local communities and its expanded emphasis on local decision making. "History may show this to be one of the more significant meetings to occur relating to fire management in the West," Utah governor Michael O. Leavitt, a Republican, said at a news conference. "These changes will have lots of implications down the line."*

*Representatives of most major environmental groups also supported the plan, especially the increased emphasis on eliminating the heavy underbrush in the forests. But they warned that the "thinning" of the forests for fire prevention should not be used to justify expanded logging.*

*The broad support from western governors helped ensure exceptionally swift and unanimous congressional approval of the funding requested in the plan. The fiscal 2001 appropriations bills for the agriculture and interior departments, given final approval by Congress in October, approved nearly all the $2.8 billion for wildfire programs that Clinton had requested, including $1.6 billion in additional funds.*

*Following are the "Key Points and Recommendations" of the report, "Managing the Impact of Wildfires on Communities and the Environment," submitted to President Bill Clinton on September 8, 2000, by Secretary of Agriculture Dan Glickman and Secretary of the Interior Bruce Babbitt, in which they recommended increased funding and new programs for combating wildfires on public lands. The document was obtained from the Internet at http://www.whitehouse.gov/CEQ/firereport.html.*

## V. Key Points and Recommendations

### 1. Continue to Make All Necessary Firefighting Resources Available.

**As a first priority, the Departments will continue to provide all necessary resources to ensure that fire suppression efforts are at maximum efficiency in order to protect life and property. The United States' wildland firefighting organization is the finest in the world and deserves our strong support. To ensure continued readiness of the firefighting force, the Departments recommend providing additional resources for firefighting activities.**

Wildland firefighting is a difficult and dangerous job, and it is essential that our firefighters continue to be well trained, with the appropriate equipment and resources they need to do their job. Safety of our firefighters and members of the public is, and always will be, the Administration's number one priority. We will continue to provide all necessary resources that our firefighting force need to continue the battle against this year's fires in as safe a manner as possible.

To fully fund the fire management preparedness programs, the Departments recommend additional resources in FY 2001 of about $337 million, including

$204 million for the Forest Service and $133 million for the Department of the Interior over the President's request. This continuing funding would provide the Departments' fire management organizations with the capability to prevent, detect, and take prompt, effective action to control wildfires. These funds also would support the personnel, equipment, and technology necessary to conduct proper planning, prevention, detection, information, education, and training.

## 2. Restore Damaged Landscapes and Rebuild Communities.

**After ensuring that suppression resources are sufficient, invest in the restoration of communities and landscapes impacted by the year 2000 fires. The Departments also recommend that investments in the treatment of landscapes through thinning and the restoration of fire be continued and expanded to help reduce the risk of catastrophic fires.**

## Providing Economic Assistance to Hard-Hit Communities

As discussed above, the year 2000 fires have hit many communities hard. Both the Federal Emergency Management Agency (FEMA) and the Small Business Administration (SBA) are responding to the immediate need for assistance. FEMA anticipates that more than 10,000 citizens from Idaho and Montana may qualify for disaster unemployment assistance, and it is anticipated that the SBA may offer more than $50 million in small business loans to assist affected businessmen. The USDA's Forest Service and rural development program also are preparing to provide immediate economic assistance, using existing resources. In receiving grant or loan applications under these programs, the Department of Agriculture will fully consider the impact of the season's wildfires on communities seeking assistance, giving such communities a competitive advantage in the USDA grant-making and loan-making.

In addition to these short-term actions, the Departments recommend that stabilization and restoration investments be made in areas that have been damaged by fire and which are at risk of erosion, invasive species germination or water supply contamination. These investments should be made in a manner that provides maximum benefit to hard-hit communities with local contractors and the local workforce being utilized to maximum extent possible.

In a similar vein, the Departments also are recommending below that forest treatment activities be stepped up in intensity. These activities can be labor intensive and, once again, the Departments intend to involve local communities and the local workforce in implementing these activities.

Key aspects of these programs are set forth below.

## Burned Area Stabilization and Restoration

*Stabilization*

Stabilization activities include short-term actions to remove hazards and stabilize soils and slopes. Examples of specific actions or "treatments" might include the removal of hazards; seeding by helicopter, plane, or by hand; constructing dams or other structures to hold soil on the slope; placing bundles of straw on the ground, parallel to the slope to slow the movement of soil down hill; contour furrowing or trenching (ditches cut into the mountain or hillsides to catch soil moving down hill); correcting road drainage by realigning poorly designed roads and culvert replacement to manage water and soil movement after the fire; and temporarily fencing cattle and people out of burned areas.

Priorities for stabilization activities include protecting human life and property; protecting public health and safety; stabilizing municipal watersheds; stabilizing steep slopes and unstable terrain; protecting archeological resources; and replacing culverts.

### Restoration

Restoration activities include longer-term actions to repair or improve lands that are unlikely to recover naturally from severe fire damage. Examples of specific actions or "treatments" might include planting or seeding native species; reforesting desired tree species; chemical or mechanical treatment to reduce competition; and other efforts to limit the spread of invasive species.

Priorities for restoration activities include preventing introduction of non-native invasive species; promoting restoration of ecosystem structure and composition; rehabilitating threatened and endangered species habitat; and improving water quality.

Because of the large amount of acreage affected by this Year's fires, the Departments propose to develop a stabilization and restoration plan that is coordinated with all affected agencies, including appropriate state and local agencies.

Responsibility for implementation of individual projects lies at the field-level. Projects covering multiple jurisdictions will be planned and implemented on an interagency basis. The Departments recognize that the scope of this effort will require additional resources. Three specific aspects of the program may require special support:

(1) Native plant/seed sources: Availability of native seeds and plant materials is limited. Significant effort will be needed to encourage the production of seeds and plant materials by the private sector and develop agency seed storage capabilities to support restoration activities.

(2) Science and research: Significant information collection, research, and data analysis is required to assess the effectiveness of restoration techniques and develop improved techniques. Current technologies and techniques are largely based on experiences from agricultural practices in the early part of the 20th Century. Special attention will be focused on techniques applicable to non-agricultural lands and to treatments using native seeds and plants.

(3) Capital equipment: The current post-fire program relies on a limited amount of capital equipment (e.g., drill-seeders), much of which is not dedicated to this program. Additional equipment will be needed to support the expanded requirements, especially in the application of native seeds.

## 3. Investments in Projects to Reduce Fire Risk

As discussed above, the Departments have been implementing new approaches to address the long-term buildup of hazardous fuels in our forests and rangelands. The fires of 2000 have underscored the importance of pursuing an aggressive program to address the fuels problem with the help of local communities, particularly those in wildland-urban interface areas, where threats to lives and property are greater and the complexity and costs of treatments higher.

The Departments recommend continuing current fuel reduction strategies and seeking additional budgetary resources to treat additional acreage. The Departments are requesting $257 million for fuels reduction activities in FY 2001, over the President's request including $115 million for the Forest Service and $142 million for the Department of the Interior. These funds will cover accelerated treatments, especially in the wildland-urban interface area and will work to support additional research and eradication of invasive species. Funding will be available to support Endangered Species Act consultation work by the U.S. Fish and Wildlife Service and the National Marine Fisheries Service.

## Implementation of Fuels Reduction Program

The most significant implementation challenge for the Departments is to substantially increase the number of acres of forestlands that receive fuels treatment. Both Departments are utilizing one aspect of fuels treatments, prescribed fires, increasingly. That program will continue to play a key role, although the lessons from the Cerro Grande fire demand that this strategy be implemented with great care. In that regard, the Departments will implement recommendations from the independent review of the Cerro Grande fire.

In addition to prescribed burns, the physical removal of undergrowth and other fuels needs to be stepped up in intensity in order to have a more significant impact on dangerous fuels buildup. Because of the importance of this activity, the Departments recommend that experienced personnel be dedicated full time to this activity, with direct chains of command to the Secretaries of Agriculture and the Interior. The Secretaries, in turn, should meet periodically to assess the progress of these efforts.

### Markets for Removed Materials

Because much of the hazardous fuels in forests are excessive levels of forest-based biomass—dead, diseased and down trees—and small diameter trees, there are several benefits of finding economical uses for this material, including helping offset forest restoration cost; providing economic opportunities for rural, forest-dependent communities; reducing the risks from catastrophic wildfires; protecting watersheds; helping restore forest resiliency, and protecting the environment.

USDA Forest Service research teams are working to develop new uses for small tress and new ways to process them. A need exists to transfer and commercialize new technology as it comes on line and to develop and expand local markets for these products. Both Departments propose to partner with communities, universities, and businesses to conduct additional research on the stimulation of small diameter and other vegetative products industries.

Small diameter logs, for example, can be used for housing material such as trim, siding, and sub-flooring. Recent technology now makes it possible for wood composites—fibers, flakes and strands—from lower quality species of trees such as juniper, pinyon pine, and insect-killed white fir to be used successfully for particleboard and replacement filler for thermoplastic composites that make up a wide range of consumer products such as highway signs. Similar uses are being expanded for pulp chips. The woody residues that make up a forest's undergrowth has historically been burned or allowed to accumulate in huge piles on the forest floor. This material could potentially be economically used as compost and mulch material.

### Research Needs

Given the severity of this Year's fires and the additional fuels management and restoration activities recommended by this report, the Departments have a number of additional research needs. They recommend research on the relationship between invasive species and fires and the effectiveness of various treatment efforts. They also recommend research based on recent fire seasons regarding relationships between land management practices and the occurrence and intensity of fires.

### Budget

The two Departments request additional resources of $130 million in FY 2001 over the President's request to fully fund a burned area restoration program as described above, including $45 million for the Forest Service and $85 million for the Department of the Interior.

## 4. Work Directly with Local Communities.

Working with local communities is a critical element in restoring damaged landscapes and reducing fire hazards proximate to homes and communities. To accomplish this, the Departments recommend:

   a. **Expanding the participation of local communities in efforts to reduce fire hazards and the use of local labor for fuels treatment and restoration work.**
   b. **Improving local fire protection capabilities through financial and technical assistance to state, local, and volunteer firefighting efforts.**
   c. **Assisting in the development of markets for traditionally underutilized small diameter wood as a value added outlet for removed fuels.**
   d. **Encouraging a dialogue within and among communities regarding opportunities for reducing wildfire risk and expanding outreach and education to homeowners and communities about fire prevention through use of programs such as Firewise.**

As discussed above, the Departments have been working with communities on fire-related activities through a variety of programs. On the operational side, the National Interagency Fire Center provides training opportunities for local firefighters, and the Fire Center has developed cooperative arrangements with many local and state entities to facilitate coordinated firefighting efforts. The Departments also work with local communities to assist in fire protection activities through the Firewise program and other outreach efforts. In addition, the Departments currently work with local communities on fuels treatment and post-fire restoration projects.

Although Federal agencies are engaged in these activities on an on-going basis, the Departments recommend that a significant new initiative be undertaken to coordinate appropriate investments and outreach activities with affected communities. The proposed initiative would focus on three major arenas: (1) improving community-based firefighting capabilities and coordination with state and Federal firefighting efforts; (2) working closely with communities-at-risk in implementing post-fire restoration activities and fuels reduction activities; and (3) expanding joint education and outreach efforts regarding fire prevention and mitigation in the wildlife-urban interface.

Rural and volunteer fire departments provide the front line of defense, or initial attack, on up to 90 percent of the communities. Volunteer fire departments are the backbone of fire protection in America. County, State, and Federal agencies provide immediate backup to local fire departments when a wildland-urban interface fire gets out of control. Strong readiness capability at the state and local levels go hand-in-hand with optimal efficiency at the Federal level. The level of funding being proposed will provide a more optimum efficiency level for the states and local fire departments in the impacted areas.

### Budget

To support this initiative for community involvement and participation, additional funding of $88 million in FY 2001 is required. The USDA Forest Service proposes increases of $53.8 million for state and volunteer fire assistance, as well as an additional $12.5 million for economic action programs and $12 million for forest health activity. The Department of the Interior proposes a new program to support rural fire districts, particularly those intermingled with Bureau of Land Management lands. Funding of $10 million is proposed for FY 2001.

## 5. Be Accountable

**A Cabinet-level management structure should be established to ensure that the actions recommended by the Departments receive the highest priority. The Secretaries of Agriculture and the Interior should co-chair this effort. Regional integrated management teams should be accountable for fuels treatment, restoration, and fire preparedness. Local teams, working closely with communities and other agency partners, would manage projects on the ground.**

Wildland fires know no jurisdictional boundaries. It is for that reason that the five primary Federal agencies that have operational responsibility for preparing for, and responding to, wildfires, formed the National Interagency Fire Center. The Fire Center is a model of cross-agency cooperation and accountability, and it provides a key focal point for coordination with state and local firefighting efforts.

As with fighting fires, Federal, State and local governments will have to cooperate to restore damaged lands, invest in protecting affected communities, and reduce hazardous fuel loads.

A number of existing, regional integrated management teams are in place to assist in the setting of regional priorities for land restoration, fuels treatment, and community cooperation and outreach. The Departments recommend that these regional structures be utilized and/or retooled, as appropriate, to provide a focal point for these initiatives.

The Departments would also establish locally led teams with the Department of Commerce and other appropriate agencies. These integrated teams would identify specific land restoration, fuels treatment, and preparedness projects; coordinate environmental reviews and consultations; facilitate and encourage public participation; and monitor and evaluate project implementation.

Because of the critical importance of these matters, the Departments recommend Cabinet-level oversight of the implementation of these initiatives, cochaired by the Secretaries of Agriculture and the Interior. Among other things, the new management team would be responsible for ensuring that appropriate performance objectives are established and met, ensuring that adequate financial and other resources are made available, establishing a system for identifying and addressing implementation issues promptly, and ensuring that the environmental reviews required by the National Environmental Policy Act, and all other environmental requirements, are undertaken and completed on a timely basis.

The Departments recommend that the Cabinet-level group assess the progress towards implementing these tasks, and provide periodic reports to the President.

# APOLOGY TO INDIANS BY DIRECTOR OF THE BUREAU OF INDIAN AFFAIRS
## September 8, 2000

*The director of the U.S. Bureau of Indian Affairs (BIA) apologized, on September 8, 2000, for the bureau's long history of actions that he said were intended to "destroy all things Indian." Kevin Gover, the assistant secretary of Indian affairs of the Department of the Interior and himself a Pawnee Indian, reportedly became the highest U.S. official ever to apologize for the government's systematic maltreatment of Indians.*

*"We accept this inheritance, this legacy of racism and inhumanity," Gover said of himself and the bureau's 10,000 employees, most of them Indians. "And by accepting this legacy, we also accept the moral responsibility of putting things right."*

*Gover stressed that he was not speaking for the entire U.S. government, but only for the agency with primary responsibility for dealing with the country's estimated 2.5 million people of Indian descent. However, White House officials reviewed and approved Gover's apology in advance. An attorney from New Mexico, Gover had headed the Bureau of Indian Affairs for three years.*

*The Canadian government in 1998 apologized for key elements of that country's persecution of Indians, including forcing Indian children to attend Christian boarding schools and banning the use of Indian languages and customs. By 2000 the legacy of the boarding schools had become a major problem for several churches, which acknowledged that many Indian children had suffered psychological and sexual abuse in the schools they had run. Tribes filed lawsuits demanding hundreds of millions of dollars in compensation. The Anglican Church in Canada said it might be forced into bankruptcy as a result of the demands.*

### Acknowledging "Sorrowful Truths"

*Gover offered his apology at a ceremony in Washington, D.C., commemorating the 175th anniversary of the establishment in 1824 of the first Office of Indian Affairs within the War Department. Originally intended for 1999, the ceremony was pushed back a year so it would not be overshadowed by the 150th anniversary in 1999 of the creation of the Interior Department. The Indian Affairs office was moved from the War Department to the Interior Department in 1849. During the last quarter of the twentieth century, people of Indian descent generally ran the bureau.*

*Gover offered an unvarnished appraisal of what he called the "sorrowful truths" of the bureau's actions toward Indians. Those actions began with the bureau's first major mission in 1838: evicting members of the Eastern Cherokee and other tribes from their homelands in Georgia and forcing them to march about one thousand miles westward into the Indian Territory, in what is now Oklahoma. Gover said thousands of Indians died along what came to be known as the "Trail of Tears."*

*Later in the nineteenth century, as white settlement expanded relentlessly into the western territories, "this agency participated in the ethnic cleansing that befell the western tribes," Gover said, using a term developed in the Balkans in the late twentieth century for the removal of unwanted ethnic groups. "It must be acknowledged that the deliberate spread of disease, the decimation of the might bison herds, the use of the poison alcohol to destroy mind and body, and the cowardly killing of women and children made for tragedy on a scale so ghastly that it cannot be dismissed merely as the inevitable consequence of the clash of competing ways of life," he said.*

*Once the western Indians were forced from their homelands on the Great Plains and moved into government-sponsored reservations, the Bureau of Indian Affairs "set out to destroy all things Indian," Gover said. The bureau tried to stamp out Indian culture by prohibiting Indian languages and traditional religious ceremonies and generally making "Indian people ashamed of who they were," he said.*

*The bureau's worst action, he said, was the establishment, starting in 1879, of boarding schools where thousands of Indian children were sent for training free of influence from their parents and Indian culture. In those schools, he said, the bureau brutalized the children "emotionally, physically, and spiritually." The legacy of those schools was still alive, Gover said in the "trauma of shame, fear and anger" that passed from generation to generation of Indians. "Many of our people live lives of unrelenting tragedy as Indian families suffer the ruin of lives by alcoholism, suicides made of shame and despair, and violent death at the hands of one another," he said. "So many of the maladies suffered today in Indian country result from failures of this agency. Poverty, ignorance, and disease have been the product of this agency's work." Gover said he offered a "formal apology to Indian people for the historical conduct of this agency."*

*Gover acknowledged that the government could not undo all the wrongs of the past, but he pledged "a new commitment to the people and communities" the bureau was supposed to serve. "Never again will we attack your religions, your languages, your rituals, or any of your tribal ways," he said. "Never again will we seize your children, nor teach them to be ashamed of who they are. Never again."*

## *Reaction to the Apology*

*About three hundred Indian leaders, bureau employees, and Interior Department officials—including Secretary Bruce Babbitt—attended the September 8 anniversary ceremony and gave Gover a standing ovation as he concluded his speech in tears. Most of the Indian leaders in attendance praised the speech and said Gover demonstrated courage in offering the apology.*

*"I thought it was a very heroic and historic moment," Susan Masten, president of the National Congress of American Indians told the Associated Press. "For us, there was a lot of emotion in that apology. It's important for us to begin to heal from what has been done. . . ." Masten also was chairwoman of the Yurok tribe in California.*

*Ben Nighthorse Campbell, a Colorado Republican and the only American Indian serving in the U.S. Senate, also praised Gover's speech. "These are brutal things to say and nobody likes to hear them but Kevin was right on. It came from an Indian because a non-Indian wouldn't say these things."*

*Several other Indian leaders said the apology was too little, too late, and some charged that the federal government was still depriving Indians of their heritage by refusing to hand over several billion dollars in trust funds generated by the sale of Indian-held lands since the mid-nineteenth century. At the time of Gover's speech the Bureau of Indian Affairs was battling a lawsuit, brought by several western tribal leaders on behalf of an estimated 300,000 Indians, that sought to transfer control of the trust funds from the government to a federal judge. Eloise Cobell, a member of the Blackfeet tribe in Montana and the lead plaintiff in the lawsuit, told the* Denver Post: *"When I read it [the apology], I asked why hasn't he apologized to the trust beneficiaries?" The wrongs Gover described were in "the past," she said, "but what about what's happening today?"*

*Several Indian leaders expressed disappointment that the apology came from an Indian, not from a representative of the dominant white society that ultimately was responsible for persecution of the Indians. "I think that the apology, given by Gover, is still not acceptable," said Claudia Vigil-Muniz, president of the Jicarilla Apache Nation in northern New Mexico. "He, too, is Native American. They were one man's words. Along with that apology, much more has to come from the years of destruction."*

*Gover said he received numerous messages in response to his apology. Most were positive, he said, but many were filled with hate—apparently from whites offended by his characterization of a key aspect of American history.*

*On November 14 Gover stood before the annual meeting of the National Congress of American Indians and acknowledged the irony "of an Indian person apologizing on behalf of an Indian agency" for actions against the Indian people. But he said his point "was to make clear that this is now a different BIA, a BIA run by Indian people for Indian people." In that speech, Gover said directly that the bureau had committed "crimes against the Indian people." He had not used the word* crime *in the September 8 apology.*

*Following is the text of a speech delivered September 8, 2000, by Kevin Gover, assistant secretary of Indian affairs in the Department of the Interior, in which he apologized for past mistreatment of American Indians by the Bureau of Indian Affairs. The document was obtained from the Internet at http://www.doi.gov/ bia/as-ia/175gover.htm.*

In March of 1824, President James Monroe established the Office of Indian Affairs in the Department of War. Its mission was to conduct the nation's business with regard to Indian affairs. We have come together today to mark the first 175 years of the institution now known as the Bureau of Indian Affairs.

It is appropriate that we do so in the first year of a new century and a new millennium, a time when our leaders are reflecting on what lies ahead and preparing for those challenges. Before looking ahead, though, this institution must first look back and reflect on what it has wrought and, by doing so, come to know that this is no occasion for celebration; rather it is time for reflection and contemplation, a time for sorrowful truths to be spoken, a time for contrition.

We must first reconcile ourselves to the fact that the works of this agency have at various times profoundly harmed the communities it was meant to serve. From the very beginning, the Office of Indian Affairs was an instrument by which the United States enforced its ambition against the Indian nations and Indian people who stood in its path. And so, the first mission of this institution was to execute the removal of the southeastern tribal nations. By threat, deceit, and force, these great tribal nations were made to march 1,000 miles to the west, leaving thousands of their old, their young and their infirm in hasty graves along the Trail of Tears.

As the nation looked to the West for more land, this agency participated in the ethnic cleansing that befell the western tribes. War necessarily begets tragedy; the war for the West was no exception. Yet in these more enlightened times, it must be acknowledged that the deliberate spread of disease, the decimation of the mighty bison herds, the use of the poison alcohol to destroy mind and body, and the cowardly killing of women and children made for tragedy on a scale so ghastly that it cannot be dismissed as merely the inevitable consequence of the clash of competing ways of life. This agency and the good people in it failed in the mission to prevent the devastation. And so great nations of patriot warriors fell. We will never push aside the memory of unnecessary and violent death at places such as Sand Creek, the banks of the Washita River, and Wounded Knee.

Nor did the consequences of war have to include the futile and destructive efforts to annihilate Indian cultures. After the devastation of tribal economies and the deliberate creation of tribal dependence on the services provided by this agency, this agency set out to destroy all things Indian.

This agency forbade the speaking of Indian languages, prohibited the conduct of traditional religious activities, outlawed traditional government, and

726

made Indian people ashamed of who they were. Worst of all, the Bureau of Indian Affairs committed these acts against the children entrusted to its boarding schools, brutalizing them emotionally, psychologically, physically, and spiritually. Even in this era of self-determination, when the Bureau of Indian Affairs is at long last serving as an advocate for Indian people in an atmosphere of mutual respect, the legacy of these misdeeds haunts us. The trauma of shame, fear and anger has passed from one generation to the next, and manifests itself in the rampant alcoholism, drug abuse, and domestic violence that plague Indian country .Many of our people live lives of unrelenting tragedy as Indian families suffer the ruin of lives by alcoholism, suicides made of shame and despair, and violent death at the hands of one another. So many of the maladies suffered today in Indian country result from the failures of this agency. Poverty, ignorance, and disease have been the product of this agency's work.

And so today I stand before you as the leader of an institution that in the past has committed acts so terrible that they infect, diminish, and destroy the lives of Indian people decades later, generations later. These things occurred despite the efforts of many good people with good hearts who sought to prevent them. These wrongs must be acknowledged if the healing is to begin.

I do not speak today for the United States. That is the province of the nation's elected leaders, and I would not presume to speak on their behalf. I am empowered, however, to speak on behalf of this agency, the Bureau of Indian Affairs, and I am quite certain that the words that follow reflect the hearts of its 10,000 employees.

Let us begin by expressing our profound sorrow for what this agency has done in the past. Just like you, when we think of these misdeeds and their tragic consequences, our hearts break and our grief is as pure and complete as yours. We desperately wish that we could change this history, but of course we cannot. On behalf of the Bureau of Indian Affairs, I extend this formal apology to Indian people for the historical conduct of this agency.

And while the BIA employees of today did not commit these wrongs, we acknowledge that the institution we serve did. We accept this inheritance, this legacy of racism and inhumanity. And by accepting this legacy, we accept also the moral responsibility of putting things right.

We therefore begin this important work anew, and make a new commitment to the people and communities that we serve, a commitment born of the dedication we share with you to the cause of renewed hope and prosperity for Indian country. Never again will this agency stand silent when hate and violence are committed against Indians. Never again will we allow policy to proceed from the assumption that Indians possess less human genius than the other races. Never again will we be complicit in the theft of Indian property. Never again will we appoint false leaders who serve purposes other than those of the tribes. Never again will we allow unflattering and stereotypical images of Indian people to deface the halls of government or lead the American people to shallow and ignorant beliefs about Indians. Never again will we attack your religions, your languages, your rituals, or any of your tribal ways. Never again will we seize your children, nor teach them to be ashamed of who they are. Never again.

We cannot yet ask your forgiveness, not while the burdens of this agency's history weigh so heavily on tribal communities. What we do ask is that, together, we allow the healing to begin: As you return to your homes, and as you talk with your people, please tell them that time of dying is at its end. Tell your children that the time of shame and fear is over. Tell your young men and women to replace their anger with hope and love for their people.

Together, we must wipe the tears of seven generations. Together, we must allow our broken hearts to mend. Together, we will face a challenging world with confidence and trust. Together, let us resolve that when our future leaders gather to discuss the history of this institution, it will be time to celebrate the rebirth of joy, freedom, and progress for the Indian Nations. The Bureau of Indian Affairs was born in 1824 in a time of war on Indian people. May it live in the year 2000 and beyond as an instrument of their prosperity.

# FTC ON MARKETING VIOLENT ENTERTAINMENT TO CHILDREN
## September 11, 2000

*A hard-hitting government report concluded that the entertainment industry violated its own codes by deliberately marketing movies, music recordings, and computer games containing violence to children. The report, issued September 11, 2000, by the Federal Trade Commission (FTC), clearly embarrassed many leaders of the entertainment industry, who later agreed to take some steps to limit the marketing of violent products to children.*

*The FTC report also helped make entertainment violence an issue in the presidential campaign. One day before the report was released, Al Gore, the Democratic candidate for president, and his running mate, Joseph Lieberman, said they would propose legislation on the issue if the entertainment industry failed to halt its sales of violent material to children. Republicans accused Gore of hypocrisy on the matter, noting that his campaign had accepted millions of dollars in political contributions from Hollywood executives.*

### The FTC Report

*President Bill Clinton and several congressional leaders asked the FTC to study the marketing of violent entertainment products to children in the wake of a violent attack on students and teachers at Columbine High School, in Littleton, Colorado, in April 1999. Two teenagers had killed thirteen fellow students and teachers before killing themselves. The killers left behind tapes and diaries showing their rage at being taunted by classmates and others for refusing to dress and act like other teenagers. The FTC noted that numerous news reports had suggested that "the boys involved in the Columbine killings were immersed in a violent entertainment culture"—thus focusing public attention on violence in the media.* (Columbine shootings, Historic Documents of 1999, p. 179; school crime study, p. 873)

*In its study the FTC analyzed the marketing of movies, musical recordings, and electronic games that contained violent material. In each case the industry had adopted a standard that gave parents some guidance about the content of the products. The commission said it studied two questions Clinton had asked: Did those industries advertise products "they themselves acknowledge warrant parental caution in venues where children make up a substantial percentage of the audience?" and are those advertisements "intended to attract children and teenagers?" The answer to both questions, the commission report said, was yes.*

*The commission examined the marketing of 44 movies that carried the movie industry's "R" rating, meaning that they contained violent material suitable only for audiences aged seventeen or above. Of those films, the FTC said, 35 were directly marketed to children under seventeen. In fact, the industry marketing plans for 28 of the films contained what the FTC called "express statements" that the target audience was children under seventeen. In some cases, the movie industry included children as young as ten to twelve in "test audiences" that were used routinely to help develop marketing plans. In most cases, the R-rated films were advertised during television shows aimed at young audiences or in youth-oriented magazines. Some movie studios even advertised their R-rated films in newspapers and magazines that were circulated exclusively in schools and targeted youth groups such as the Boy Scouts and Girl Scouts, the report said.*

*Similarly, the FTC found that the music recording and electronic games industries consistently violated their own standards when marketing material that carried a parental advisory warning of "explicit content," such as graphic language about sex, drugs, or violence. The commission examined marketing materials for 55 music recordings that carried the explicit content warning and found that every one had been targeted to children under seventeen. Of the 118 electronic games carrying a "mature" rating for violence, 83 were directly targeted to children under seventeen, the commission said. Some games, the commission said, contained "astonishing levels of violence."*

*The producers of entertainment media were not the only ones who failed to adhere to age-based standards, the commission said. In a survey of movie theaters, the FTC said it found that "just under half" of them allowed youths aged thirteen to sixteen to attend moves with "R" ratings even though they were not accompanied by a parent or guardian. Young teenagers also were routinely able to purchase "explicit" music recordings and electronic games rated for mature users only.*

*The FTC said it did not conduct an independent study of the controversial question of whether entertainment violence influenced youth to engage in violent behavior. A survey of scholarly literature, the commission said, found general agreement that "exposure to violent materials alone does not cause a child to commit a violent act" and may not even be the most important factor. Even so, the commission said, the widespread availability of violent entertainment to children "is a valid cause for concern" because youngsters could develop a flawed perspective of the consequences of violence in society.*

## Senate Hearings

The FTC report was the subject of two hearings held on September 13 and September 27 by the Senate Commerce Committee, whose chairman, Arizona Republican John McCain, had been a vocal critic of the entertainment industry. At the September 13 hearing, some industry executives acknowledged that they had been too aggressive in marketing violent material to children. Jack Valenti, president of the Motion Picture Association of America, said, "some marketing people had stepped over the line" by promoting R-rated films to young teenagers.

That hearing also became a forum for the two presidential campaigns. Connecticut senator Lieberman, the Democratic vice presidential candidate, testified that the entertainment industry had engaged in "deceptive" and "outrageous" marketing programs. He said he and Gore would push for new regulations if the marketing of violent entertainment to youth did not stop in six months. Lynne V. Cheney, a former chairman of the National Endowment for the Humanities and the wife of Republican vice presidential candidate Richard B. Cheney, also condemned the marketing to youth of explicit material. Cheney said she was even more upset about the content of the material than about the marketing of it—but she acknowledged that attempting to regulate the content of entertainment could "threaten the First Amendment."

At a second hearing on September 27, some movie industry executives again acknowledged that their companies had not followed their own standards. "We have not been as careful as we could have been," said Rob Friedman, vice chairman of Paramount Pictures. Stacy Snider, chairman of Universal Pictures, told the committee that some details of the FTC report "shock me and dismay me." But other executives said parents, not the entertainment industry, were to blame when children gained access to material that was inappropriate for them. "I reject any allegation that we are systematically or deliberately trying to circumvent our own rating system and the authority of parents," Warner Brothers chairman Alan Horn said. "I'm neither embarrassed nor do I apologize for anything in the report as far as Warner Brothers practices are concerned." The FTC report did not name individual entertainment companies.

## Industry Actions in Response to the Report

In response to the FTC report, sectors of the entertainment industry took limited steps to curtail the marketing of violent media to children. The first to act was the recording industry, which attempted to preempt some of the impact of the FTC report by announcing changes in late August intended to give greater prominence, in advertisements and other marketing materials, to the parental advisories that accompanied recordings with explicit lyrics.

One day before the second hearing by McCain's committee, the Motion Picture Association of America announced a twelve-point plan that was labeled as a response to the FTC report. Among other things, the movie industry pledged to exclude children under seventeen years of age from so-

*called focus groups that helped develop marketing plans for R-rated movies. Industry executives also promised to provide more information about why films received their ratings and said they would encourage theater owners not to run promotional material (called "trailers") for R-rated movies when the audience was about to view a film rated "G" for "general audiences."*

*McCain was one of several senators who suggested that the movie industry plan did not go far enough. He was especially critical of a section saying the industry would not "inappropriately, specifically" target children in the marketing of R-rated films. "I don't understand this language; it's filled with loopholes," McCain said.*

*Then, in early November, the National Association of Theater Owners announced a new voluntary standard under which audiences waiting to see films rated "G" and "PG" (for "parental guidance advised") would not be shown previews for R-rated movies. The theater owners also pledged to be more careful in preventing children not accompanied by a parent or guardian from attending R-rated movies. Among other things, the owners promised to hire additional security staff to check the ages of youth attempting to attend moves with exceptionally violent scenes.*

*Later in November several news organizations reported that the movie industry was considering changing its rating system to provide better guidance to parents about the content of movies. One proposal reportedly under consideration called for a two-tier "R" rating: one for films containing substantial amounts of violence and/or sex, and another for films with no violence and a limited degree of sex. None of the proposed changes had been announced by year's end. The Directors Guild of America, representing more than 10,000 movie and television directors, had called on September 14 for a broad revamping of the rating system and a new code of conduct governing the marketing of movies.*

### Legal Action Unlikely

*Two months after issuing its report, the FTC acknowledged that the government had few options for taking legal action against the entertainment industry. In a letter to Senator McCain, commission chairman Robert Pitofsky noted that the First Amendment to the Constitution effectively prohibited the government from regulating the content of movies and other entertainment products.*

*Pitofsky's letter was in response to a question McCain had asked during the September 13 Commerce Committee hearing on whether the marketing of violent media material to children violated the Federal Trade Commission Act. Pitofsky said commission lawyers reviewed various arguments about whether the entertainment industry practices could be considered to fall under the legal prohibitions against "deceptive" or "unfair" advertising. The commission staff—and then the commission itself—ultimately concluded that it would be difficult, if not impossible, to use existing law against the entertainment industry, he said.*

*Furthermore, Pitofsky warned against an attempt by the government to force the entertainment industry to abide by its own voluntary standards that supposedly curtailed the marketing of violent products to children. Legal action attempting to enforce self-regulation standards might backfire, he said, because it "might create a disincentive for improved industry self-regulation."*

    *Following are excerpts from the "executive summary" and "conclusion" of the report, "Marketing Violent Entertainment to Children: A Review of Self-Regulation and Industry Practices in the Motion Picture, Music Recording and Electronic Games Industries," released September 11, 2000, by the Federal Trade Commission. The document was obtained from the Internet at http:// www.ftc.gov/reports/violence/vioreport.pdf.*

## Executive Summary

On June 1, 1999, President Clinton asked the Federal Trade Commission and the Department of Justice to undertake a study of whether the movie, music recording, and computer and video game industries market and advertise products with violent content to youngsters. The President's request paralleled Congressional calls for such a study. The President raised two specific questions: Do the industries promote products they themselves acknowledge warrant parental caution in venues where children make up a substantial percentage of the audience?

And are these advertisements intended to attract children and teenagers?

For all three segments of the entertainment industry, the answers are plainly "yes."

Although the motion picture, music recording and electronic game industries have taken steps to identify content that may not be appropriate for children, companies in those industries routinely target children under 17 as the audience for movies, music and games that their own rating or labeling systems say are inappropriate for children or warrant parental caution due to their violent content. Moreover, children under 17 frequently are able to buy tickets to R-rated movies without being accompanied by an adult and can easily purchase music recordings and electronic games that have a parental advisory label or are restricted to an older audience. The practice of pervasive and aggressive marketing of violent movies, music and electronic games to children undermines the credibility of the industries' ratings and labels. Such marketing also frustrates parents' attempts to make informed decisions about their children's exposure to violent content.

For years—over backyard fences and water coolers, on talk radio and in academic journals—parents, social scientists, criminologists, educators, policymakers, health care providers, journalists and others have struggled to understand how and why some children turn to violence.

The dialogues took on new urgency with the horrifying school shooting on April 20, 1999, in Littleton, Colorado.

Scholars and observers generally have agreed that exposure to violence in entertainment media alone does not cause a child to commit a violent act and that it is not the sole, or even necessarily the most important, factor contributing to youth aggression, anti-social attitudes and violence.

Nonetheless, there is widespread agreement that it is a cause for concern. The Commission's literature review reveals that a majority of the investigations into the impact of media violence on children find that there is a high correlation between exposure to media violence and aggressive, and at times violent, behavior. In addition, a number of research efforts report that exposure to media violence is correlated with increased acceptance of violent behavior in others, as well as an exaggerated perception of the amount of violence in society.

For their part, the entertainment industries have recognized these concerns and taken steps to alert parents to violent or explicit content through self-regulatory product rating or labeling programs. Self-regulation by these industries is especially important considering the First Amendment protections that prohibit government regulation of content in most instances.

The self-regulatory programs of the motion picture, music recording and electronic game industries each address violence, as well as sexual content, language, drug use and other explicit content that may be of concern to parents. In keeping with the President's request, the Commission focused on the marketing of entertainment products designated as violent under these systems. In its analysis, the Commission accepted each industry's determination of whether a particular motion picture, music recording or electronic game contains violent content; the Commission did not examine the content itself.

The motion picture industry uses a rating board to rate virtually all movies released in the United States, requires the age-related rating to appear in advertising and makes some effort to review ads for rated movies to ensure that their content is suitable for general audiences. The music recording industry recommends the use of a general parental advisory label on music with "explicit content." The decision to place a parental advisory label on a recording is made by the artist and the music publishing company and involves no independent third-party review; nor does the industry provide for any review of marketing and advertising. In late August 2000, the recording industry trade association recommended that recording companies not advertise explicit-content labeled recordings in media outlets with a majority under-17 audience. The electronic game industry requires games to be labeled with age- and content-based rating information and requires that the rating information appear in advertising. Only the electronic game industry has adopted a rule prohibiting its marketers from targeting advertising for games to children below the age designations indicated by the rating.

The Commission carefully examined the structure of these rating and labeling systems, and studied how these self-regulatory systems work in practice. The Commission found that despite the variations in the three industries' systems, the outcome is consistent: individual companies in each industry routinely market to children the very products that have the industries' own parental warnings or ratings with age restrictions due to their violent content.

Indeed, for many of these products, the Commission found evidence of marketing and media plans that expressly target children under 17. In addition, the companies' marketing and media plans showed strategies to promote and advertise their products in the media outlets most likely to reach children under 17, including those television programs ranked as the "most popular" with the under-17 age group, such as *Xena: Warrior Princess*, *South Park* and *Buffy the Vampire Slayer*; magazines and Internet sites with a majority or substantial (i.e., over 35 percent) under-17 audience, such as *Game Pro*, *Seventeen* and *Right On!*, as well as *mtv.com*, *ubl.com* and *happypuppy.com*; and teen hangouts, such as game rooms, pizza parlors and sporting apparel stores.

**Movies.** Of the 44 movies rated R for violence the Commission selected for its study, the Commission found that 35, or 80 percent, were targeted to children under 17. Marketing plans for 28 of those 44, or 64 percent, contained express statements that the film's target audience included children under 17. For example, one plan for a violent R-rated film stated, "Our goal was to find the elusive teen target audience and make sure everyone between the ages of 12–18 was exposed to the film." Though the marketing plans for the remaining seven R-rated films did not expressly identify an under-17 target audience, they led the Commission to conclude that children under 17 were targeted nonetheless. That is, the plans were either extremely similar to the plans of the films that did identify an under-17 target audience, or they detailed actions synonymous with targeting that age group, such as promoting the film in high schools or in publications with majority under-17 audiences.

**Music.** Of the 55 music recordings with explicit content labels the Commission selected for its study, marketing plans for 15, or 27 percent, expressly identified teenagers as part of their target audience. One such plan, for instance, stated that its "Target audience" was "Alternative/urban, rock, pop, hardcore—12–34." The marketing documents for the remaining 40 explicit-content labeled recordings examined did not expressly state the age of the target audience, but they detailed the same methods of marketing as the plans that specifically identified teens as part of their target audience, including placing advertising in media that would reach a majority or substantial percentage of children under 17.

**Games.** Of the 118 electronic games with a Mature rating for violence the Commission selected for its study, 83, or 70 percent, targeted children under 17. The marketing plans for 60 of these, or 51 percent, expressly included children under 17 in their target audience. For example, one plan for a game rated Mature for its violent content described its "target audience" as "Males 12–17—Primary Males 18–34—Secondary." Another plan referred to the target market as "Males 17–34 due to M rating (the true target is males 12–34)." Documents for the remaining 23 games showed plans to advertise in magazines or on television shows with a majority or substantial under-17 audience. Most of the plans that targeted an under-17 audience set age 12 as the younger end of the spectrum, but a few plans for violent Mature-rated games targeted children as young as six.

Further, most retailers make little effort to restrict children's access to products with violent content. Surveys conducted for the Commission in May through July 2000 found that just over half the movie theaters admitted children ages 13 to 16 to R-rated films even when not accompanied by an adult. The Commission's surveys also indicate that unaccompanied children have various strategies to see R-rated movies when theaters refuse to sell them tickets.

Additionally, the Commission's surveys showed that unaccompanied children ages 13 to 16 were able to buy both explicit content recordings and Mature-rated electronic games 85 percent of the time.

Although consumer surveys show that parents value the existing rating and labeling systems, they also show that parents' use and understanding of the systems vary. The surveys also consistently reveal high levels of parental concern about violence in the movies, music and video games their children see, listen to and play. These concerns can only be heightened by the extraordinary degree to which young people today are immersed in entertainment media, as well as by recent technological advances such as realistic and interactive video games. The survey responses indicate that parents want and welcome help in identifying which entertainment products might not be suitable for their children.

Since the President requested this study over a year ago, each of the industries reviewed has taken positive steps to address these concerns. Nevertheless, the Commission believes that all three industries should take additional action to enhance their self-regulatory efforts. The industries should:

1. *Establish or expand codes that prohibit target marketing to children and impose sanctions for violations.* All three industries should improve the usefulness of their ratings and labels by establishing codes that prohibit marketing R-rated/M-rated/explicit-labeled products in media or venues with a substantial under-17 audience. In addition, the Commission suggests that each industry's trade associations monitor and encourage their members' compliance with these policies and impose meaningful sanctions for non-compliance.

2. *Increase compliance at the retail level.* Restricting children's retail access to entertainment containing violent content is an essential complement to restricting the placement of advertising. This can be done by checking identification or requiring parental permission before selling tickets to R movies, and by not selling or renting products labeled "Explicit" or rated R or M, to children.

3. *Increase parental understanding of the ratings and labels.* For parents to make informed choices about their children's entertainment, they must understand the ratings and the labels, as well as the reasons for them. That means the industries should all include the reasons for the rating or the label in advertising and product packaging and continue their efforts to educate parents—and children—about the meanings of the ratings and descriptors. Industry should also take steps to better educate parents about the ratings and labels.

The Commission emphasizes that its review and publication of this Report, and its proposals to improve self-regulation, are not designed to regulate or even influence the content of movies, music lyrics or electronic games. The First Amendment generally requires that creative decisions about content be left to artists and their distributors. Rather, the Commission believes the industries can do a better job of helping parents choose appropriate entertainment for their children by providing clear and conspicuous notification of violent content. Industry self-regulation also should support parents' decisions by prohibiting the direct sale and marketing to children of products labeled as inappropriate or warranting parental guidance due to their violent content.

Implementation of the specific suggestions outlined above would significantly improve the present self-regulatory regimes. The Report demonstrates, however, that mere publication of codes is not sufficient. Self-regulatory programs can work only if the concerned industry associations actively monitor compliance and ensure that violations have consequences. The Commission believes that continuous public oversight is also required and that Congress should continue to monitor the progress of self-regulation in this area. . . .

## VIII. Conclusion

Members of the motion picture, music recording, and electronic game industries routinely target children under 17 as the audience for movies, music, and games that they themselves acknowledge are inappropriate for children or warrant parental caution due to their level of violent content. The motion picture industry and, until late August, the music recording industry take the position that targeting children is consistent with their rating and labeling programs; the game industry does make targeting children a violation of its self-regulatory code, but violations are widespread. The Commission believes that by targeting children when marketing these products, the entertainment industries undermine their own programs and limit the effectiveness of the parental review upon which these programs are based. Moreover, most retailers make little effort to restrict children's access to these products with violent content.

For the motion picture, music recording, and electronic game industries, a self-regulatory program in which the public can have confidence should include: comprehensive ratings or labels that provide parents with meaningful information about the nature, intensity, and appropriateness for children of depictions of violence; an accurate and consistent rating or labeling process with clear standards; clear and conspicuous disclosures of the rating or label—with related age and content information—on packaging and in advertising; sales and marketing policies that are consistent with the ratings or labels; industry-wide participation; and mechanisms to ensure compliance.

The motion picture, music recording, and electronic game industries should stop targeting children under 17 in their marketing of products with violent content. All three industries should increase consumer outreach, both to educate parents about the meaning of the ratings and to alert them to the critical part the industries assume parents play in mediating their children's exposure to these products. Because of First Amendment protections afforded to these products, industry is in the best position to provide parents with the information they need. Finally, parents must become familiar with the ratings and labels, and with the movies, music, and games their children enjoy, so they can make informed choices about their children's exposure to entertainment with violent content.

The body of the Report describes the result of the Commission's survey of marketing practices. The empirical inquiry, however, inevitably suggests certain conclusions about ways in which the present system of self-regulation could be improved.

### Industry should establish or expand codes that prohibit target marketing and impose sanctions for violations.

The target marketing of R-rated films, explicit-labeled music, and M-rated games to children under 17 is pervasive, and the target marketing of PG–13-rated films and T-rated games to children under 12 is common. The Commission believes that these marketing efforts send children the message that these are movies they should see, music recordings they should listen to, and games they should play. At the same time, the message inherent in the rating or label—that the product's content is inappropriate for children or that it requires a strong warning to parents—is not adequately conveyed. Marketing directly to children essentially is an end-run around the parental review role underlying the ratings and advisory labels.

While it comes up short on compliance, the electronic game industry at least acknowledges that targeting children undermines its rating system; it has crafted a code of conduct to address this issue. In late August 2000, the music recording industry trade association recommended that recording companies not advertise explicit-labeled recordings in outlets where a majority of the audience is under 17. The motion picture industry has no similar code or guideline. All three industries should institute codes of conduct that:

- Prohibit placing advertising for R-rated/M-rated/explicit-labeled products in media or venues with a substantial under-17 audience.
- Prohibit licensees from marketing action figures, toys, and other products associated with R movies and M games to under-age audiences and require a disclosure that the product is based on an entertainment product rated R or M.
- Provide for no-buy lists of media outlets popular with under-17 audiences (including school venues, youth-oriented comic books, top teen TV shows, and younger teen magazines).
- Encourage the auditing of ad placement to verify that advertisements are not reaching a substantial under-17 audience.
- Encourage media screening of ads for consistency with these principles.
- Provide for the associations to monitor and encourage member compliance with these policies, and to impose meaningful sanctions for non-compliance.

## Industry should improve self-regulatory system compliance at the retail level.

Restricting children's access to R-rated movies, explicit-labeled music recordings, and M-rated games is an essential complement to all the rating and labeling programs. The industries should encourage their members, as well as third-party retailers, to:

- Check age or require parental permission before selling or renting R-rated/M-rated/advisory-labeled products.
- Clearly and conspicuously display the ratings and advisories on packaging and in advertising, and avoid covering or obscuring them.
- Avoid sales of R-rated/M-rated/advisory-labeled products on retail Internet sites unless they use a reliable system of age verification.
- Develop guidelines for the electronic transfer of movies, music, and games. Without action to address electronic access to these products, the ratings and advisory label may be of limited value to parents in the future.

## Industry should increase parental awareness of the ratings and labels.

The industries should expand their outreach programs to parents to facilitate informed choice and raise awareness and understanding of the ratings, content descriptors, and advisory labels. They have begun to move in that direction with www.parentalguide.org, which provides links to the various association sites that have information about each rating or label. In addition, the industries should:

- Clearly and conspicuously display the rating or advisory label and the descriptors in all advertising and product packaging.
- Encourage the media to include rating and labeling information in reviews. This information often is included in movie reviews, but less frequently is included in game or music reviews.
- Take additional steps to inform parents, especially by including rating and labeling information in retail stores and on Web sites, where products can be sampled, downloaded, or purchased.

Implementation of these specific suggestions would significantly improve the present regimes of self-regulation. The Report demonstrates, however, that mere publication of codes is not sufficient. Self-regulatory programs can work only if the concerned industry associations actively monitor compliance and ensure that violations have consequences. The Commission believes that continuous public oversight also is required, and that Congress should continue to monitor the progress of self-regulation is this area.

# FEDERAL JUDGE AND U.S. ATTORNEY GENERAL ON WEN HO LEE SPY CASE
## September 13, 2000

*What had appeared to be the most sensational case in decades involving the alleged theft of nuclear weapons secrets collapsed in September 2000, causing a deep embarrassment for the Clinton administration. Wen Ho Lee, a Taiwanese-American scientist who had been employed at the Los Alamos National Laboratory in New Mexico, entered into a plea bargain with the federal government, thus ending a high-profile investigation into allegations that he might have provided weapons secrets to China. Lee on September 13 pleaded guilty to one count of mishandling classified weapons secrets; in return the government dropped fifty-eight other charges against him.*

*The government's handling of the case was widely criticized. The federal judge who oversaw the case apologized to Lee, saying government prosecutors had misled him into forcing Lee to spending nearly nine months in solitary confinement. Even more unusual, President Bill Clinton said he was "deeply troubled" by some of his own administration's decisions in the case.*

### Background of the Lee Case

*Lee was a native of Taiwan who moved to the United States in 1964 and went to work at the Los Alamos laboratory in 1978 as a research scientist specializing in hydrodynamics. That lab was one of three national research centers responsible for developing the nation's nuclear weapons and monitoring their continued safety.*

*Lee had been suspected of security violations in 1982 and 1994, in both cases because of his allegedly inappropriate contacts with Chinese officials. In 1996 the government launched a broad investigation to determine whether China had secretly obtained classified information about some of the most advanced U.S. nuclear weapons. Lee reportedly emerged as a prime target of that investigation in part because of his past contacts with Chinese officials and because he had traveled to China twice in the 1980s. In December 1998 Los Alamos officials revoked Lee's high-level security clearances, but the government's probe reportedly turned up no specific evidence that Lee, or any other scientist at Los Alamos, had given secret data to China.*

*With the investigation proceeding fitfully, the* New York Times *on March 6, 1999, published an article alleging that an unidentified computer scientist at Los Alamos was under investigation as the possible source of nuclear weapons information obtained by China. The publication of that article came in the midst of an uproar in Congress caused by a politically charged report from a special committee of the House of Representatives that alleged widespread Chinese espionage into U.S. strategic weapons systems.*

*Two days after the* Times *story appeared, Energy Secretary Bill Richardson ordered the University of California—which ran the Los Alamos laboratory for the government—to fire Lee. The grounds of the dismissal were that Lee had mishandled information and had failed to tell superiors, as required, about his contacts with a visiting Chinese nuclear weapons scientist. Richardson later acknowledged that he was under political pressure to take action in the case and chose to make "an example" of Lee.*

*On December 10, 1999, a federal grand jury in Albuquerque indicted Lee on fifty-nine charges of violating the Atomic Energy Act and the Foreign Espionage Act. All the counts dealt with his alleged illegal copying and removal of computer data at the Los Alamos laboratory. Lee was not charged with espionage or turning secrets over to a foreign government. Lee pleaded not guilty to all the charges.*

*The indictment charged that, starting in 1993, Lee had copied 1.4 gigabytes of information—the equivalent of about 400,000 pages—about nuclear weapons programs. About half of the total, 806 megabytes, was classified but much of the remainder was publicly available. The government said Lee had copied the information onto ten computer tapes. Investigators found three of the tapes when they searched Lee's office and home. The other seven were missing, and federal investigators said Lee refused to say what he had done with them.*

*At the end of December 1999, prosecutors claimed that Lee posed a serious danger to national security and urged U.S. District Judge James A. Parker to order Lee's incarceration without the possibility of being freed on bail. John Kelly, the U.S. attorney for New Mexico at the time, told Parker that the decision to request that Lee be held without bail was made at the "highest levels" of the U.S. government in Washington. Parker agreed to the request, although he later urged prosecutors to loosen the harsh conditions of Lee's confinement. A federal appeals court on February 29, 2000, upheld Parker's decision to deny Lee's request for bail.*

*Lee was held in solitary confinement at the Santa Fe County Detention Center, a privately run jail, in a cell measuring less than one hundred square feet. Lee was allowed to see his family for just one hour each week, with every word monitored by FBI agents. However, he was allowed extensive meetings with his attorneys. For nearly five months the government denied him any reading material and forced him to wear leg irons during his daily exercise period. Prosecutors said Lee needed to be kept in solitary confinement so he could not pass nuclear secrets to any outsiders.*

*With Lee in jail, the investigation continued through the first half of 2000 but with no visible sign of substantial progress. Lee, according to investigators, refused to talk, and the government had little direct evidence against him aside from his copying of the computer tapes. Lee's children and many supporters insisted he had been singled out for prosecution because he was a Chinese-American—a charge that government officials strenuously denied.*

*News reports quoted several of Lee's former Los Alamos colleagues as saying Lee's actions were inappropriate and foolish but probably did not constitute a major security threat. Some colleagues suggested that Lee was trying to assemble a private library for scientific work and writing on his own if he lost his job at Los Alamos; he had received a notice that he might be laid off in 1993, the year he began copying the computer data.*

*Federal investigators portrayed Lee's actions in a much more sinister light, however, noting that Lee had copied, and stored in insecure computer files, millions of lines of computer code describing some of the nation's most sensitive nuclear weapons secrets. That information, the investigators said, could be of enormous help to scientists in China or another country with a program to build such weapons.*

*A key break in the case came at an August 17 court hearing on Lee's request to be freed on bail. At that hearing, several of Lee's Los Alamos colleagues testified that much of the information allegedly copied by Lee was already available to the public or carried only low levels of security classification. More dramatically, Lee's attorneys forced Robert Messemer, the lead FBI agent in the case, to recant previous testimony that had put some of Lee's actions in the worst possible light. In particular, Messemer acknowledged that he had been wrong to claim that Lee had deceived a colleague to gain access to his computer, which Lee allegedly used for some of the copying. Messemer also admitted that he had misled the court by saying Lee had sent letters to several foreign research institutes looking for a job; Messemer admitted that the government was not certain that Lee had ever sent any of the letters. Messemer said his early testimony had been an "honest mistake," but the development helped create the impression that the government's case against Lee was unraveling. More important, Messemer's admission helped convince Judge Parker to grant Lee's request for freedom; he ruled on August 24 that Lee should be freed on $1 million bail.*

*The government appealed Parker's ruling, but twelve days later Attorney General Janet Reno, FBI director Louis J. Freeh, and other top Justice Department officials met in Washington to review the case. They reluctantly agreed to drop the bulk of the case against Lee in return for his admission of wrongdoing and his promise to give sworn testimony about what he had done with the computer tapes. According to news reports and their own statements, the officials concluded that, to win their case against Lee in court, they would have to disclose too much secret information—including details of the investigation in the case and some of the weapons secrets Lee had copied. Moreover, even a conviction of Lee might not give the govern-*

ment the information it wanted: why Lee copied the secret information and what he had done with it.

Early in September, prosecutors negotiated a deal with Lee's lawyers under which Lee would plead guilty to one felony count of mishandling classified information in return for a dropping of the other fifty-eight counts in the indictment against him. As part of the plea agreement, Lee agreed to answer detailed questions, under oath, about his handling of the computer data. If his answers were truthful, he was to be given immunity from further prosecution.

## *Judge Parker's Statement*

At the climactic September 13 hearing in Judge Parker's courtroom, Lee pleaded guilty to one charge of violating the Atomic Energy Act, and government attorneys moved to dismiss the remaining counts against him. Parker accepted the plea bargain and sentenced Lee to the 278 days he had already spent in jail. Parker told Lee that he had committed a "serious crime," a felony offense. "There was never really any dispute" about having improperly copied classified information, Parker told Lee, adding that the scientist "faced some risk of conviction" if the case had gone to trial.

Parker then delivered an extraordinary denunciation of the government's handling of the case, in particular the demand by prosecutors that Lee be jailed under what Parker called "demeaning, unnecessarily punitive conditions." Parker reviewed the history of the government's demands for keeping Lee in prison without bail and noted that key government decisions were made in Washington.

"I am truly sorry that I was led by our executive branch of government to order your detention last December, Dr. Lee," Parker said. "I tell you with great sadness that I feel I was led astray last December by the executive branch of our government. . . . I am sad for you and your family because of the way in which you were kept in custody while you were presumed under the law to be innocent of the charges the executive branch brought against you."

Parker said he did not know "the real reasons" why prosecutors had insisted on Lee's detention, adding that "we will not learn why" because the plea agreement relieved the government of the need to submit key documents in the case. Those documents, he said, "might have supplied the answer."

Attorney General Reno and FBI director Freeh both issued statements defending the government's handling of the case and portraying Lee's plea bargain agreement as a victory for prosecutors. Reno said the plea agreement presented "the best chance to find out where those [computer] tapes are, where they have been, and who else had access to them, if anyone." In his statement, Freeh said the government's highest priority was determining "what happened to the tapes."

Local prosecutors strongly disagreed with Parker's comments, arguing that Lee had posed a threat to national security. "When you steal our nuclear secrets, we're not going to let you communicate with anyone, and no American can expect us to do it," George A. Stamboulidis, the chief federal prosecutor in the case, told reporters.

*Lee himself offered no immediate public comment on his ordeal. "For the next few days I'm going fishing," he told reporters outside the federal courthouse in Albuquerque.*

*President Clinton echoed Judge Parker's comments the next day, telling reporters he had been "deeply troubled" by his own government's demands that Lee be held without bail. "I think it's very difficult to reconcile the two positions that one day he's a terrible risk to the national security and the next day they're making a plea agreement for an offense far more modest than what had been alleged," he said. "I don't think you can justify in retrospect keeping a person in jail without bail when you're prepared to make that kind of [plea] agreement."*

*On September 26, during testimony before the Senate Judiciary Committee, Reno and Freeh defended the government's handling of the case, saying in a joint statement that "we remain convinced that we made the right decisions, for the right reasons, at the right time." Facing harsh criticism from some senators, Reno admitted that the government had made some mistakes but said the end result was that Lee had admitted to committing a serious crime. "Dr. Lee is no hero," she told the committee. "He is not an absent-minded professor. He is a felon. He committed a very serious, calculated crime, and he pleaded guilty to it."*

## FBI Interviews of Lee

*Under the terms of the September 13 plea agreement, federal investigators questioned Lee under oath for ten days during the fall of 2000. News reports late in the year indicated that Lee had not fully answered the government's central questions: why he had copied the secret weapons information at Los Alamos and what he had done with the computer tapes.*

*The Washington Post reported on December 15 that Lee had told FBI agents that he had copied the computer files as a safeguard against computer failures and that he had never removed the copied computer tapes from the Los Alamos laboratory or given them to anyone else. The newspaper also said Lee told agents he had thrown the seven missing tapes into a trash container outside the laboratory, but the FBI was unable to find the tapes at the county landfill.*

*On December 24 the Post reported that Lee had not informed his superiors at Los Alamos about several trips to Taiwan, where he was born. During the late 1980s and early 1990s, the Post reported, Lee said he had served as a paid consultant to a Taiwanese businessman who helped arrange for him to spend four weeks during the spring of 1998 at Taiwan's military research center, the Chung Shan Institute of Science and Technology. Lee's attorney, Mark Holscher, told the newspaper that his client's visits to Taiwan were appropriate and legal.*

## Missing Hard Drives

*In the midst of the controversy over Lee, the Los Alamos laboratory suffered another major embarrassment concerning inadequate security for computerized information. In May, as preparations were under way for a temporary evacuation of the laboratory because of a dangerous wildfire, security officials discovered that two highly classified computer hard drives were missing. The hard drives contained specifications for nuclear weapons in arsenals of the United States and several allied nations.* (Wildfires, p. 712)

Senior laboratory officials were not told about the problem for nearly three weeks, and an intensive search of the facility failed to locate the missing hard drives. On June 16 the hard drives mysteriously reappeared behind a photocopier in the laboratory's top-secret weapons division. The FBI was still investigating the matter at year's end.

### Sagging Morale at Los Alamos

In a September report on security lapses at Los Alamos, two respected former members of Congress told Energy Secretary Richardson that morale at the laboratory had plummeted dangerously, largely because of the controversies generated by the investigations of Lee and the missing hard drives. The report was written by Howard H. Baker Jr., who was Senate Republican leader during the 1980s, and Lee H. Hamilton, a former Democratic chairman of the House Intelligence Committee and the House Foreign Affairs Committee. They recommended that the Energy Department relax some of the security regulations that had been tightened during the Wen Ho Lee case.

"Once issues of management oversight give way to criminal investigation, and lab employees fear that committing a security error may expose them not just to management discipline but to prosecution and imprisonment, any hope that individuals will volunteer information that could reflect security lapses is annihilated," Baker and Hamilton wrote. "The employees we met with expressed fear and deep concern over the influx of FBI agents and yellow crime-scene tape in their work space, the interrogation of their colleagues by the FBI and federal prosecutors before a federal grand jury, and the resort of some of their colleagues to taking a second mortgage on their homes to pay for attorney fees."

Several news reports during the year also focused on sagging morale at Los Alamos. On August 27, the Washington Post *reported that fourteen top computer scientists, representing nearly half the staff of the laboratory's Advanced Computing section, had quit during the year. Several Los Alamos scientists were lured away by higher salaries and better working conditions at private high technology companies, and the laboratory was having trouble recruiting qualified scientists for crucial positions, the newspaper said. The* Post *also quoted senior officials as saying the exodus of scientists could jeopardize one of the laboratory's most important duties: conducting computer simulations to determine the viability of the nation's nuclear weapons.*

Another report, prepared in June for the House Permanent Select Intelligence Committee, said the Energy Department had failed to "sell" employees at its three weapons laboratories—including Los Alamos—on the need for increased security. "No organization, governmental or private, can have effective counterintelligence without active, visible, and sustained support

*from management and active 'buy-in' by the employees," the report said. The
report was prepared by a committee headed by Paul Redmond, a former
chief of counterintelligence at the Central Intelligence Agency. Most importantly, the report said the Energy Department had failed to explain to
employees at the weapons labs the necessity for regular polygraph examinations. As a result, employee attitudes about the exams were overwhelmingly negative, the report said.*

> *Following is the text of remarks by U.S. District Court Judge
> James A. Parker at a September 13, 2000, hearing of Wen Ho Lee,
> a former nuclear scientist at Los Alamos National Laboratory
> who pleaded guilty to one felony count of mishandling national
> security information, followed by a statement on the case issued
> the same day by Attorney General Janet Reno. The documents
> were obtained from the Internet at http://www.aslanam.org/
> judge_parker.htm.*

# REMARKS OF JUDGE PARKER

Dr. Lee, you have pled guilty to a serious crime. It's a felony offense. For
that, you deserved to be punished. In my opinion, you have been punished
harshly, both by the severe conditions of pretrial confinement and by the fact
that you have lost valuable rights as a citizen.

Under the laws of our country, a person charged in federal court with commission of a crime normally is entitled to be released from jail until that person is tried and convicted. Congress expressed in the Bail Reform Act its
distinct preference for pretrial release from jail and prescribed that release on
conditions be denied to a person charged with a crime only in exceptional circumstances.

The Executive Branch of the United States Government has until today actually, or just recently, vigorously opposed your release from jail, even under
what I had previously described as Draconian conditions of release. During
December 1999, the then-United States Attorney, who has since resigned, and
his Assistants presented me, during the three-day hearing between Christmas
and New Year's Day, with information that was so extreme it convinced me
that releasing you, even under the most stringent of conditions, would be a
danger to the safety of this nation.

The then-United States Attorney personally argued vehemently against
your release and ultimately persuaded me not to release you. In my opinion
and order that was entered Dec. 30, 1999, I stated the following: "With a great
deal of concern about the conditions under which Dr. Lee is presently being
held in custody, which is in solitary confinement all but one hour of the week,
when he is permitted to visited his family, the Court finds, based on the record

before it, that the government has shown by clear and convincing evidence that there is no combination of conditions of release that would reasonably assure the safety of any other person and the community or the nation."

After stating that in the opinion, I made this request in the opinion right at the end: "Although the Court concludes that Dr. Lee must remain in custody, the Court urges the government attorneys to explore ways to lessen the severe restrictions currently imposed upon Dr. Lee while preserving the security of sensitive information."

I was very disappointed that my request was not promptly heeded by the government attorneys.

After December, your lawyers developed information that was not available to you or them during December. And I ordered the Executive Branch of the government to provide additional information that I reviewed, a lot of which you and your attorneys have not seen.

With more complete, balanced information before me, I felt the picture had changed significantly from that painted by the government during the December hearing. Hence, after the August hearing, I ordered your release despite the continued argument by the Executive Branch, through its government attorneys, that your release still presented an unacceptable extreme danger.

I find it most perplexing, although appropriate, that the Executive Branch today has suddenly agreed to your release without any significant conditions or restrictions whatsoever on your activities. I note that this has occurred shortly before the Executive Branch was to have produced, for my review in camera, a large volume of information that I previously ordered it to produce.

From the beginning, the focus of this case was on your motive or intent in taking the information from the secure computers and eventually downloading it on to tapes. There was never really any dispute about your having done that, only about why you did it.

What I believe remains unanswered is the question: What was the government's motive in insisting on your being jailed pretrial under extraordinarily onerous conditions of confinement until today, when the Executive Branch agrees that you may be set free essentially unrestricted? This makes no sense to me.

A corollary question I guess is: Why were you charged with the many Atomic Energy Act counts for which the penalty is life imprisonment, all of which the Executive Branch has now moved to dismiss and which I just dismissed?

During the proceedings in this case, I was told two things: first, the decision to prosecute you was made at the highest levels of the Executive Branch of the United States government in Washington, D.C.

With respect to that, I quote from a transcript of the August 15, 2000, hearing, where I asked this question. This was asked of Dr. Lee's lawyers. "Who do you contend made the decision to prosecute?" Mr. (Mark) Holscher responded, "We know that the decision was made at the highest levels in Washington. We know that there was a meeting at the White House the Saturday before the indictment, which was attended by the heads of a number of agencies. I believe the number two and number three persons in the Department of Justice were present. I don't know if the Attorney General herself was present. "It was actually held at the White House rather than the Department of Justice, which is, in our view, unusual circumstances for a meeting." That statement by Mr. Holscher was not challenged.

The second thing that I was told was that the decision to prosecute you on the 39 Atomic Energy Act, each of which had life imprisonment as a penalty, was made personally by the President's Attorney General. In that respect, I will quote one of the Assistant U.S. Attorneys, a very fine attorney in this case—this was also at the August 15 hearing. This is talking about materials that I ordered to be produced in connection with Dr. Lee's motion relating to selective prosecution.

The first category of materials involved the January 2000 report by the Department of Energy Task Force on racial profiling. "How would that in any way disclose prosecutorial strategy?" Miss (Laura) Fashing responded, "That I think falls more into the category of being burdensome on the government. I mean if the government—if we step back for just a second—I mean the prosecution decision and the investigation in this case, the investigation was conducted by the FBI, referred to the United States Attorney's Office, and then the United States Attorney's Office, in conjunction with—well, actually the Attorney General, Janet Reno, made the ultimate decision on the Atomic Energy Act counts."

Dr. Lee, you're a citizen of the United States and so am I, but there is a difference between us. You had to study the Constitution of the United States to become a citizen. Most of us are citizens by reason of the simple serendipitous fact of our birth here. So what I am now about to explain to you, you probably already know from having studied it, but I will explain it anyway.

Under the Constitution of the United States, there are three branches of government. There is the Executive Branch, of which the President of the United States is the head. Next to him is the Vice-president of the United States. The President operates the Executive Branch with his cabinet, which is composed of secretaries or heads of the different departments of the Executive Branch. The Vice-president participates in cabinet meetings.

In this prosecution, the more important members of the President's cabinet were the Attorney General and the Secretary of the Department of Energy, both of whom were appointed to their positions by the President. The Attorney General is the head of the United States Department of Justice, which despite its title, is a part of the Executive Branch, not a part of the Judicial Branch of our government. The United States Marshal Service, which was charged with overseeing your pretrial detention, also is a part of the Executive Branch, not the Judicial Branch. The Executive Branch has enormous power, the abuse of which can be devastating to our citizens.

The second branch of our national government is the Legislative Branch, our Congress. Congress promulgated the laws under which you were prosecuted, the criminal statutes. And it also promulgated the Bail Reform Act, under which in hindsight you should not have been held in custody.

The Judicial Branch of government, of which I am a member, is called the Third Branch of government because it's described in Article III of our Constitution. Judges must interpret the laws and must preside over criminal prosecutions brought by the Executive Branch.

Since I am not a member of the Executive Branch, I cannot speak on behalf of the President of the United States, the Vice-president of the United States, their Attorney General, their Secretary of the Department of Energy or their former United States Attorney in this District, who vigorously insisted that you had to be kept in jail under extreme restrictions because your release pretrial would pose a grave threat to our nation's security.

I want everyone to know that I agree, based on the information that so far has been made available to me, that you, Dr. Lee, faced some risk of conviction by a jury if you were to have proceeded to trial. Because of that, I decided to accept the agreement you made with the United States Executive Branch under Rule 11(e) (1) (C) of the Federal Rules of Criminal Procedure.

Further, I feel that the 278 days of confinement for your offense is not unjust; however, I believe you were terribly wronged by being held in custody pretrial in the Santa Fe County Detention Center under demeaning, unnecessarily punitive conditions.

I am truly sorry that I was led by our Executive Branch of government to order your detention last December. Dr. Lee, I tell you with great sadness that I feel I was led astray last December by the Executive Branch of our government through its Department of Justice, by its Federal Bureau of Investigation and by its United States Attorney for the District of New Mexico, who held the office at that time.

I am sad for you and your family because of the way in which you were kept in custody while you were presumed under the law to be innocent of the charges the Executive Branch brought against you.

I am sad that I was induced in December to order your detention, since by the terms of the plea agreement that frees you today without conditions, it becomes clear that the Executive Branch now concedes, or should concede, that it was not necessary to confine you last December or at any time before your trial.

I am sad because the resolution of this case drug on unnecessarily long. Before the Executive Branch obtained your indictment on the 59 charges last December, your attorney, Mr. Holscher, made a written offer to the Office of the United States Attorney to have you explain the missing tapes under polygraph examination.

I'll read from that letter of December 10, 1999. I quote from that letter: "Dear United States Attorney Kelly and First Assistant Gorence, "I write to accept Mr. Kelly's request that we provide them with additional credible and verifiable information which will prove that Dr. Lee is innocent.

"On the afternoon of Wednesday, December 8th, Mr. Kelly informed me that it was very likely that Dr. Lee will be indicted within the next three to four business days. In our phone conversation, Mr. Kelly told me that the only way that we could prevent this indictment would be to provide a credible and verifiable explanation of what he described as missing tapes.

"We will immediately provide this credible and verifiable explanation. Specifically we are prepared to make Dr. Lee immediately available to a mutually agreeable polygraph examiner to verify our repeated written representations that at no time did he mishandle those tapes in question and to confirm that he did not provide the tapes to any third party.

"As a sign of our good faith, we will agree to submit Dr. Lee to the type of polygraph examination procedure that has recently been instituted at the Los Alamos Laboratory to question scientists. It is our understanding that the government has reaffirmed that this new polygraph procedure is the best and most accurate way to verify that scientists are properly handling classified information."

At the inception of the December hearing, I asked the parties to pursue that offer made by Mr. Holscher on behalf of Dr. Lee, but that was to no avail.

**Mr. [George] Stamboulidis (assistant U.S. attorney):** Your Honor, most respectfully I take issue with that. There has been a full record of letters that were sent back and forth to you, and Mr. Holscher withdrew that offer.

**The Court:** Nothing came of it, and I was saddened by the fact that nothing came of it. I did read the letters that were sent and exchanged. I think I commented one time that I think both sides prepared their letters primarily for use by the media and not by me. Notwithstanding that, I thought my request was not taken seriously into consideration.

Let me turn for the moment to something else. Although I have indicated that I am sorry that I was led by the Executive Branch to order your detention last December, I want to make a clarification here.

In fairness, I must note that virtually all of the lawyers who work for the Department of Justice are honest, honorable, dedicated people, who exemplify the best of those who represent our federal government.

Your attorney, Mr. Holscher, formerly was an Assistant United States Attorney. The new United States Attorney for the District of New Mexico, Mr. Norman Bay, and the many Assistant United States Attorneys here in New Mexico—and I include in this Mr. Stamboulidis and Mr. Liebman, who are present here today—have toiled long hours on this case in opposition to you. They are all outstanding members of the Bar, and I have the highest regard for all of them.

It is only the top decision makers in the Executive Branch, especially the Department of Justice and the Department of Energy and locally, during December, who have caused embarrassment by the way this case began and was handled. They did not embarrass me alone. They have embarrassed our entire nation and each of us who is a citizen of it.

I might say that I am also sad and troubled because I do not know the real reasons why the Executive Branch has done all of this. We will not learn why because the plea agreement shields the Executive Branch from disclosing a lot of information that it was under order to produce that might have supplied the answer.

Although, as I indicated, I have no authority to speak on behalf of the Executive Branch, the President, the Vice-president, the Attorney General, or the Secretary of the Department of Energy, as a member of the Third Branch of the United States Government, the Judiciary, the United States Courts, I sincerely apologize to you, Dr. Lee, for the unfair manner you were held in custody by the Executive Branch.

Court will be in recess.

# STATEMENT BY ATTORNEY GENERAL RENO

[FBI] Director [Louis] Freeh and I shoulder the awesome responsibility of protecting the national security. It is a responsibility that both of us take very seriously.

Last year, we charged Dr. Wen Ho Lee with downloading classified information about our nuclear arsenal from a secured computer onto 10 unsecured computer tapes. Despite repeated efforts by law enforcement, including repeated requests to Dr. Lee to tell us what he did with the tapes, the fate of 7 of those tapes has never been determined.

Today, after denying any wrongdoing for months, Dr. Lee pleaded guilty to the indictment's charge of unlawfully collecting and keeping classified information related to the national defense—a felony offense. Specifically, he admits to deliberately downloading and willfully retaining information related to the national defense. This is contrary to his longstanding claim that he only acted negligently.

In accepting the plea offer, we now, for the first time, have an opportunity to determine what Dr. Lee did with the tapes—something he has repeatedly refused to tell us since April 1999. And he will provide the information necessary to allow us to verify his explanation. That is an extremely important development because, in these types of cases, the need to find out what happened may require that the government forgo seeking the maximum punishment possible.

We saw this plea agreement as the best chance to find out where those tapes are, where they have been, and who else has had access to them, if anyone. Had the case proceeded to trial, and we prevailed, Dr. Lee would have faced many years in prison. But we might never have learned what happened to the tapes. Of equal importance, the trial court's recent rulings regarding classified evidence suggested that a trial of Dr. Lee might have required the government to divulge nuclear secrets at trial. The plea agreement avoids that harm to our national security.

Under the plea, Dr. Lee will be subjected to extensive questioning over the course of the next year about the whereabouts of the tape, as well as his other activities and contacts with foreign officials over the years. Furthermore, the government will have the means to test his veracity. He will be under oath and subject to a polygraph exam. If at any time we believe he is not being truthful, we can seek to void the agreement and prosecute the case to the full extent of the law.

I want to extend my appreciation to the lead prosecutor George A. Stamboulidis, the U.S. Attorney Norman Bay, their team of attorneys and all the agents and government scientists who have worked on this case.

This is an agreement that is in the best interest of our national security in that it gives us our best chance to find out what happened to the tapes."

# UN SECRETARY GENERAL ON ERITREA-ETHIOPIA WAR
## September 18, 2000

*A two-year war between two of the world's poorest countries came to an end in 2000—but not before it had killed upwards of 100,000 people and left hundreds of thousands homeless and impoverished. In the end, the war between Eritrea and Ethiopia resolved a longstanding border dispute.*

*The two countries were equal in only one respect: the economies of both had been devastated by years of war and famine. In other respects it was a lopsided contest between Ethiopia, with a population of more than 60 million, and Eritrea, with only 4 million. The size disparity eventually made the difference. Eritrea, which had fought a thirty-year guerrilla war for independence from Ethiopia, ultimately was unable to withstand the weight of military pressure from its much bigger neighbor. In the end, the Eritrean foreign minister called the fighting "senseless."*

### Background to the Conflict

*As with many wars in Africa, the conflict between Eritrea and Ethiopia had its origins in colonial days. Ethiopia was an independent country for at least two thousand years, making it one of the oldest nation-states in the world. But in 1936, Italy—which had been trying for more than forty years to occupy Ethiopia—invaded the country and ousted its ruler, Haile Selassie. British forces, aided by Ethiopian exiles, drove the Italians out of Ethiopia in 1941, during World War II, and Haile Selassie returned to power.*

*A major question after the war involved the status of Eritrea, which had been an Italian colony since 1890 and had served as a base for several Italian invasions of Ethiopia. In 1952 the United Nations declared Eritrea to be an autonomous zone in a loose federation with Ethiopia; the rationale was that landlocked Ethiopia needed access to the Red Sea. But Haile Selassie resisted that plan and in 1962 proclaimed Eritrea to be a province within the Ethiopian empire. A coalition of Eritrean forces, dominated by the Marxist Eritrean People's Liberation Front, immediately launched a guerilla war against Ethiopia, which continued for three decades. During that period Ethiopia and the entire Horn of Africa region underwent one upheaval and tragedy after another: the overthrow of Haile Selassie by communist forces in 1974, a large-scale war between Ethiopia and neighboring Somalia over the Ogaden region between 1977 and 1988, a massive famine in 1984–1985 that killed an estimated 1 million people, and the ousting of Ethiopia's communist government in 1991 during a guerrilla war for the independence of Tigre, a northern province between Ethiopia and Eritrea.*

*The new government in Ethiopia acknowledged Eritrean independence in 1991, in exchange for continued access to the Red Sea, and two years later the Eritreans voted overwhelmingly in favor of formal independence. By that point, wars, famine, and incompetent (or nonexistent) governments had destroyed the economies of Eritrea, Ethiopia, and Somalia and made millions of people in the Horn of Africa totally dependent for their survival on international aid. A UN survey in 1994 showed that three-fourths of Eritrea's 4 million people had no source of food other than foreign aid. Despite the difficulties, the leaders of both countries won praise and aid from Western countries for their efforts to revive their economies. During his historic trip to Africa in 1998, President Bill Clinton cited Ethiopian prime minister Meles Zenawi and Eritrean president Isaias Afewerki as being among a small number of African leaders committed to improving the lives of their people. (Clinton Africa trip, Historic Documents of 1998, p. 159)*

*The resolution of the Eritrean independence war had left one major issue unsettled: the exact border between Eritrea and Ethiopia. The 620-mile boundary had never been formalized in the colonial era, and during the 1990s the two countries fell into dispute over control of specific areas and Ethiopian access to the Red Sea.*

*On May 6, 1998, the Eritrean army invaded the Badme region along the western part of the border—territory claimed by Ethiopia. Within a month the conflict had developed into a full-scale war. The opposing armies dug extensive trenches and periodically flung massive assaults, involving tens of thousands of soldiers, against each other. Military observers called it the largest example of trench warfare anywhere since World War I. By some estimates, the two impoverished governments spent a combined total of more than $1 billion to buy planes, helicopters, tanks, and other weapons on the international arms market.*

## Negotiating a Settlement

*Shortly after the war broke out in May 1998, the UN and the Organization of African Unity (OAU) launched efforts to try to broker a settlement. Those efforts produced a "framework agreement" in July 1999 setting out the broad terms for a peace, most importantly the withdrawal by each country to positions held before the war started. International mediation efforts continued through the rest of 1999 and into 2000. President Clinton engaged in personal diplomacy at several points and dispatched Anthony Lake, his former national security adviser, to help with the negotiations.*

*On May 8–9, 2000—after Western intelligence services detected Ethiopian preparations for a major offensive—a seven-member committee representing the UN Security Council met in the region with the leaders of both countries to urge a settlement. But that high-level effort failed, and on May 12 Ethiopia sent thousands of troops deep into uncontested territory in western Eritrea. Within a week Ethiopia had captured several towns, including the western regional capital of Barentu, and had driven more than 300,000 Eritreans from their homes.*

*The UN Security Council immediately condemned the fighting as a "threat to regional peace and security" and on May 17 voted to impose an arms embargo against both countries. The embargo was a step that had been considered during the earlier phases of the war, but the Clinton administration had opposed it as ineffective. China and Russia, which also were Security Council members, had been among the largest providers of arms to the warring countries.*

*The rapid success of Ethiopia's offensive pushed Eritrea into a no-win position and made possible a final diplomatic drive toward ending the war. Lake and other diplomats representing the OAU, the UN, and the European Union shuttled back and forth between the Eritrean and Ethiopian capitals. Meeting in Algiers on June 18, the foreign ministers of the warring countries signed a cease-fire agreement, under which they pledged to stop the war, to negotiate a final peace agreement, and to accept a UN peacekeeping force that would patrol an agreed-upon border.*

*Of the two countries, Eritrea made the bigger concession by agreeing to pull its troops from a fifteen mile-wide "buffer zone" on its side of the disputed border. Speaking at the signing ceremony, Eritrean foreign minister Haile Woldensae gave this blunt assessment of the situation: "We are now certain after two years of senseless fighting that there can be no military solution to this conflict."*

*The UN Security Council agreed on July 31 to establish the United Nations Mission in Ethiopia and Eritrea, with an initial force of up to one hundred military observers and support personnel. Secretary General Kofi Annan on August 9 sent the Security Council a proposal for a peacekeeping mission of 4,200 military personnel, to be deployed in three phases before and after Ethiopia and Eritrea signed a formal peace agreement. The council approved Annan's proposal on September 15, authorizing the UN mission until March 15, 2001, at which time the council would review progress and determine whether to prolong the mandate. The main body of the UN force began deploying to the border region in November. The Eritrea-Ethiopia force was one of three major UN peacekeeping operations that were under way or in the planning stages for Africa in 2000; others were in the Congo and Sierra Leone.* (Reform of UN peacekeeping, p. 642; Congo, p. 978; Sierra Leone, p. 1072)

*In the meantime, Lake and other diplomats continued their shuttle diplomacy between the two countries and produced a final agreement that was signed in Algiers on December 12 by Ethiopian prime minister Zenawi and Eritrean president Afewerki. The agreement established a neutral UN-sponsored Boundary Commission to determine a final border and called for the establishment of a commission to process claims for financial losses on both sides and an independent commission to investigate the origins of the conflict. Annan, who attended the signing ceremony, called the agreement "a victory for the voice of reason, for the power of diplomacy and for the recognition that neither one of these countries—not the continent as a whole—can afford another decade, another year, another day of conflict."*

## *A Humanitarian Disaster*

*Estimates of casualties and damage caused by the war ranged widely. In general, the intelligence agencies of the United States and other Western countries estimated that 50,000 to 100,000 soldiers and civilians had died as a direct result of the fighting. In March 2000, before the final Ethiopian offensive, UN humanitarian agencies estimated that about 370,000 Eritreans and 350,000 Ethiopians had been forced from their homes or had suffered other direct consequences of the war. The May 2000 offensive shifted the balance significantly by driving more than 1 million people in western and central Eritrea from their homes at least temporarily. Moreover, the millions of dollars spent on the war meant that both countries fell behind on plans to modernize their economies and promote economic development.*

*A war between two countries as poor as Eritrea and Ethiopia would have been damaging under any circumstances. The impact of this war was worsened by a drought throughout much of eastern Africa, beginning in 1998. In December 2000 the UN Food and Agriculture Organization estimated that more than 20,000,000 people—including 10,000,000 Ethiopians and at least 300,000 Eritreans—faced "serious food shortages" in the region. Other affected countries were Djibouti, Kenya, Somalia, the Sudan, Tanzania, and Uganda.*

*Following are excerpts from a report to the UN Security Council, dated September 18, 2000, in which Secretary General Kofi Annan reviewed the status of peace negotiations between Eritrea and Ethiopia and the humanitarian situation in both countries. The document was obtained from the Internet at http://www.un .org/Docs/sc/reports/2000/879e.pdf.*

## II. Political Developments

3. According to the communiqué issued on 12 June 2000 by the Organization of African Unity (OAU), the proximity talks between Ethiopia and Eritrea that resumed in Algiers on 30 May 2000, and subsequently led to the signing of the Agreement on Cessation of Hostilities between the two countries on 18 June 2000, had been intended to resolve the practical aspects of the implementation of the peace plan. The plan was to begin with the withdrawal of Ethiopian forces from positions taken by them since 6 February 1999 and end with the settlement of the border dispute through delimitation and demarcation and, if necessary, through arbitration. However, at Ethiopia's request and with Eritrea's consent, it had been agreed to first finalize a cessation of hos-

tilities agreement and then negotiate and finalize a second agreement on the other outstanding issues.

4. In accordance with the decision taken by OAU at its recent summit in Lomé, the President of Algeria, Abdelaziz Bouteflika, is assessing the best timing for the resumption of the proximity talks under the auspices of OAU, with due consideration to progress in the deployment of UNMEE [the United Nations Mission in Ethiopia and Eritrea].

5. The Committee established pursuant to resolution 1298 (2000) to monitor the implementation of the measures imposed against Ethiopia and Eritrea in paragraph 6 of the resolution agreed to elect Ambassador Hasmy Agam (Malaysia) as Chairman and Argentina and Tunisia as Vice-Chairmen of the Committee until 31 December 2000. Currently, the Committee is in the process of finalizing the guidelines for the conduct of its work. In paragraph 11 of resolution 1298 (2000), States were requested to report in detail to the Secretary-General within 30 days of its adoption on the specific steps they had taken to give effect to the measures imposed against Ethiopia and Eritrea. As at 15 September 2000, 36 States had submitted their reports, which had been issued as documents of the Committee.

## III. Humanitarian Developments

### Ethiopia

6. In January 2000, the Government of Ethiopia and the United Nations country team estimated that 349,837 people had been displaced as a result of the conflict in the northern regions of Tigray and Afar. While most of those internally displaced persons were accommodated in host communities, local basic infrastructure was insufficient to support their presence. Since the signing of the Agreement on Cessation of Hostilities, the situation has changed significantly for those persons, and many of them have had the opportunity to return to their places of origin. According to the Government of Ethiopia, approximately 30 per cent of them have started rebuilding their lives in their hometowns since last August.

7. The returning internally displaced persons need assistance in practically all sectors, as most of them lost their possessions in the conflict. Their return is a cause for major concern because a number of areas of return are located in former war zones and are, in many cases, heavily mined. The presence of mines also negatively affects the implementation of development assistance programmes.

8. The complex emergency situation in Ethiopia is further exacerbated by the drought, which has left over 10 million people in need of emergency food assistance, including over 1.4 million children under 5 years of age. While the situation in the Somali region continues to be a source of concern, the overall donor response for both food and non-food needs has helped to prevent the crisis from degenerating into a famine. However, people are still dying of drought-related illnesses, and it is therefore imperative to deliver non-food items such as medicine, water and sanitation.

9. In support of the Government's appeal released in January 2000, the

United Nations country team in Ethiopia issued a relief action plan for internally displaced persons requesting $27.5 million in combined food and non-food assistance. As of June 2000, donor response to this request amounted to $19.7 million. Eighty per cent of the food requirements were met, but only 22 per cent of the non-food items were funded. The non-food activities include construction and rehabilitation of water points, emergency education assistance, provision of medical supplies, distribution of shelter materials and mine risk education.

## Eritrea

10. Since the signing of the Agreement on Cessation of Hostilities on 18 June 2000, a number of important changes have occurred in the humanitarian situation in Eritrea. With the improvement of security conditions, the past three months have witnessed the return of some 400,000 internally displaced persons to their areas of origin located in accessible and relatively safe parts of the administrative zones bordering Ethiopia. Furthermore, the repatriation of Eritrean refugees from the Sudan, organized by the Office of the United Nations High Commissioner for Refugees (UNHCR) and the Governments of Eritrea and the Sudan, has continued on a weekly basis. Of 94,000 refugees, a total of 23,881 have returned under this repatriation operation, while an estimated 25, 000 have returned spontaneously.

11. While the return of internally displaced persons and refugees to their places of origin constitutes a positive development, many of the returnees will continue to need humanitarian assistance. Food aid on an ongoing basis will be required since much of the planting season has been missed and normal economic activities in war-affected areas have been severely disrupted. Furthermore, shelter materials and household items are needed in view of the destruction of homes and household assets in certain areas. There is also a need to re-establish basic infrastructure and social services in these areas of return. It is equally essential to support income-generating and productive capacities through the provision of agricultural implements to farmers and of microcredit to small entrepreneurs.

12. At present, there are still over 200,000 internally displaced persons accommodated in camps and other settlements in the northern Red Sea, Gash Barka and Debub zones. These persons cannot currently return to their original homes because of security concerns or the lack of resources to re-establish their lives. As long as they remain in camps, they will continue to require a wide array of vital humanitarian services, including the delivery of emergency food assistance, health, shelter and household items, and water and sanitation.

13. In addition, a substantial number of internally displaced persons continue to be accommodated in host communities. The plight of these persons and their host families, who have been sharing their meagre resources with an additional number of people for the past few months, requires continued attention from the humanitarian community. The situation is further exacerbated by the fact that the most fertile agricultural areas have been affected by both war and drought.

14. Over the past few months, an increasing number of humanitarian agencies have arrived in Eritrea to assist the Government in providing emergency relief assistance to populations in need. On 10 June 2000, the Government of Eritrea issued a new appeal for $183 million for emergency humanitarian assistance to some 1.6 million people affected by the war and drought, as well as to the urban poor and affected host communities. The appeal is to cover the period until the end of the year. In response to the Government appeal, the United Nations country team in Eritrea issued a revised United Nations appeal last July. The appeal has a total value of $87.3 million and addresses the priority humanitarian needs among over 1 million war-affected Eritreans. The donor response to the food aid component of the revised United Nations country team appeal has been very positive so far. Regrettably, the donor pledges and contributions have been less than expected for other critical interventions in sectors such as health, nutrition, water and sanitation, social services and agriculture.

## IV. Status of the United Nations Mission in Ethiopia and Eritrea

15. Since the adoption of Security Council resolution 1312 (2000) establishing the United Nations Mission in Ethiopia and Eritrea, active preparations have continued for the deployment of both the first group of 100 military observers and the necessary civilian support staff to Ethiopia and Eritrea.

16. The United Nations military liaison officers, who were dispatched to Addis Ababa [capital of Ethiopia] and Asmara [capital of Eritrea] (five in each capital) at the outset of the Mission, have undertaken, in close cooperation with the parties, field visits to military positions of Ethiopia and Eritrea, and established contacts with key civilian and military authorities.

17. Accompanied by the Mission logistics team, United Nations liaison officers have also completed a survey of potential deployment areas in both countries. As a result, locations for liaison functions with Ethiopian and Eritrean military headquarters at the front positions have been identified and a deployment timetable for military observers has been prepared. According to the timetable, a total of 46 military observers (23 at Addis Ababa and 23 at Asmara) will assemble for comprehensive four-day training sessions, to be followed by deployment to operational positions in both countries later this month. The induction of the military personnel began on 13 September. The second group of military observers are to be dispatched to the Mission area around mid-October 2000.

18. In anticipation of the adoption by the Security Council on 15 September 2000 of resolution 1320 (2000), authorizing the deployment of phase III of the Mission, the draft status-of-forces agreements to be concluded between the United Nations and Ethiopia and Eritrea, respectively, were transmitted to the two Governments.

### Logistics

19. In the meantime, logistical build-up for the new mission has also continued, with the arrival of supplies and equipment from the United Nations

Logistics Base at Brindisi, Italy. The opening of direct air and road corridors between the two countries for the use of United Nations flights and convoys will be of critical importance to Mission operations, and the United Nations is actively pursuing this issue. The Organization has also started dispatching the necessary civilian support staff, as envisaged in Security Council resolution 1312 (2000). To date, a total of 37 civilian support personnel have arrived in the Mission area. As a result of these efforts, UNMEE has already established functioning offices at Addis Ababa and Asmara.

20. Both parties have extended their cooperation in this regard. The United Nations Liaison Office to OAU and the representatives of the United Nations Development Programme (UNDP) have also played an invaluable role in setting up the new mission. At the same time, the United Nations has continued to maintain close contact with OAU, in particular regarding issues related to logistical support for the military liaison officers to be designated by OAU.

## Mine action

21. Pursuant to the Agreement on Cessation of Hostilities and Security Council resolution 1312 (2000), the United Nations is launching a multi-component mine action programme to assist the Governments of Ethiopia and Eritrea. To this end, a Mine Action Coordination Office is being established within the UNMEE structure. The purpose of the Office is to record and process information related to mines and unexploded ordnance, set priorities for mine action, assign tasks to operators, and supervise their activities. To accurately ascertain the extent of the landmine problem, a rapid landmine/ unexploded ordnance survey will be conducted by a United Kingdom non-governmental organization, the Halo Trust, and coordinated by the Department of Peacekeeping Operations. Survey teams from the Halo Trust have already arrived in the Mission area and will start assessing relevant areas, with the aim of completing the survey by mid-December 2000. In the meantime, mine awareness for the returning population is provided by the United Nations Children's Fund and UNHCR.

22. The overall requirements for mine clearance in the temporary security zone will be determined on the basis of the survey described above. Both the Agreement on Cessation of Hostilities and Security Council resolution 1312 (2000) envisage a crucial role for the parties' armed forces in mine clearance. This requires that the two countries proceed with mine lifting as soon as possible and carry out this exercise in a coordinated manner, and comply with international standards for humanitarian mine clearance. Any postponement in mine clearance would affect the deployment of United Nations military observers and troops and the early establishment of the temporary security zone.

23. Local capacity-building through training and assistance provided by the international community will be required to reach the objectives set out above. The overreaching aim of the United Nations is to assist the parties in accomplishing these important goals, in line with its policy on mine action, which confers on UNDP the leading role in assisting Member States in na-

tional mine action capacity-building. These efforts will be funded by voluntary contributions; and I appeal to the donor community to strongly support this vital area of United Nations activities.

## V. Observations

24. To date, the Governments of Ethiopia and Eritrea have shown commitment to ensuring the implementation of the Agreement on Cessation of Hostilities signed at Algiers on 18 June 2000 and I should like to commend them for that.

25. Since the establishment of UNMEE pursuant to Security Council resolution 1312 (2000), the United Nations has pursued every effort to expedite the deployment of the first group of military observers and the necessary civilian support staff to Ethiopia and Eritrea, in anticipation of the peacekeeping operation authorized by the Council in its resolution 1320 (2000). Pursuant to that resolution, I intend to nominate a Special Representative and a Force Commander in the very near future.

26. The cooperation extended to the United Nations by both Governments has facilitated the establishment of the UNMEE offices, as well as the conduct of field surveys and other preparations for the Mission's deployment. I count on the parties to continue to cooperate closely with the Mission in the implementation of its mandate, in particular in the expeditious establishment of the temporary security zone, and the earliest possible start of mine-clearance, which is essential for UNMEE to commence its work in the relevant zones. I also call on all Member States which have the capacity to do so to provide this important Mission with all the military personnel, equipment and other resources necessary for the fulfilment of its mandate

27. While the security conditions in the contested zones have improved, the humanitarian situation remains a cause for major concern. The donor pledges and contributions for critical interventions in key sectors have fallen short of expectations thus far. I therefore urge the international donor community to respond generously to the United Nations country team requests for humanitarian assistance in the two countries. I count on both Governments to continue to exercise every restraint in order to prevent any further deterioration of the humanitarian and human rights situation.

28. I am concerned by the continuing mutual accusations of human rights abuses by the two countries even after the signing of the Agreement on Cessation of Hostilities. In this regard, I have written to the President of Eritrea, Isaias Afwerki, and the Prime Minister of Ethiopia, Meles Zenawi, and indicated that I had asked the United Nations High Commissioner for Human Rights to provide me with recommendations on how the United Nations might be of assistance in addressing pressing human rights issues. After discussing this matter with both parties, I intend to establish a small component within UNMEE to follow human rights issues. I also called on both leaders to exercise restraint in sustaining the momentum for peace created by the signing of the Agreement on Cessation of Hostilities.

# INDEPENDENT COUNSEL ON CLOSING THE WHITEWATER INVESTIGATION
## September 20, 2000

*The six-year Whitewater investigation came to a formal close on September 20, 2000, when independent counsel Robert W. Ray announced that the evidence gathered was insufficient to bring criminal charges against either President Bill Clinton or his wife, Hillary Rodham Clinton, in connection with their involvement in a failed Arkansas land deal. Earlier in the year Ray had also closed related investigations into allegations of misconduct in connection with the firing of several White House travel office employees and acquisition by the Clinton White House of confidential FBI files.*

*Still pending, however, was a grand jury investigation into whether President Clinton had lied under oath to cover up his relationship with White House intern Monica Lewinsky. Clinton had been impeached by the House in 1998 but acquitted in the Senate in 1999 on similar charges. Ray was not expected to make a decision on a possible indictment of Clinton until after the president left office on January 20, 2001. Also pending was an investigation into whether the White House aides illegally withheld thousands of e-mails from congressional and Justice Department investigators; that investigation was not expected to involve either of the Clintons directly.*

*Ray's conclusions in the Whitewater case were not unexpected. A year earlier, his predecessor as independent counsel, Kenneth W. Starr, had suggested that no new indictments would be forthcoming. But Ray's wording was not the exoneration that the Clintons might have hoped for. On the questions of whether either of the Clintons had engaged in criminal misconduct in connection with the Whitewater-related financial and legal transactions, or had concealed evidence or obstructed justice in connection with the Whitewater investigation, Ray said only that "the evidence was insufficient to prove to a jury beyond a reasonable doubt" that they had committed the crime.*

*For Hillary Clinton, who was running for a New York Senate seat, Ray's announcement was a two-edged sword, absolving her of criminal conduct at the same time that it reminded voters that she was under investigation.*

*Clinton faced a similar situation in the closing weeks of her campaign, after Ray's full report on the travel office investigation was made public on October 19. In that case Ray concluded that the investigation had not turned up sufficient evidence to prove beyond a reasonable doubt that Hillary Clinton had either lied or obstructed justice during the investigation, but he said that she had made "factually inaccurate" statements. The innuendo did not appear to have much effect on New York voters, who elected the first lady to the Senate by a substantial margin.* (Clinton Senate election, p. 906)

*The timing of Ray's announcements was also an unwelcome reminder for Vice President Al Gore, who had struggled throughout his presidential campaign to disassociate himself from President Clinton's personal scandals. The lowest point for Gore might have come on August 17, when news that a grand jury was considering indicting Clinton for perjury was leaked to the press just hours before Gore was scheduled to make his speech accepting the Democratic presidential nomination. "The timing of this leak reeks to high heaven," White House spokesman Jake Siewert said. Gore also had been dogged by allegations of wrongdoing in connection with some fund-raising activities in 1996. Attorney General Janet Reno on August 23 declined for the third time to appoint a special prosecutor to investigate the matter.* (Fund-raising controversy, Historic Documents of 1998, p. 890; Gore acceptance speech, p. 617)

*The sprawling set of investigations that fell under the Whitewater umbrella arose during the 1992 presidential campaign with allegations that the Clintons had received preferential treatment for their 1978 investment in a real estate development deal because he was governor of Arkansas. Mrs. Clinton also came under suspicion for her possible role, while she was an Arkansas attorney, of working to prop up a failing savings and loan association, Madison Guaranty, which was used to keep the failing land development going. Madison Guaranty was owned by James B. McDougal, who together with his wife Susan were investors with the Clintons in the Whitewater deal. The failure of Madison Guaranty eventually cost taxpayers $73 million.*

*Once Clinton was in office, congressional pressure on Reno to name an independent counsel to investigate the charges became overwhelming; the investigation's first special prosecutor, Robert B. Fiske, began work in January 1994. In August 1994 Fiske was replaced by Kenneth W. Starr, who successfully expanded the investigation to cover the FBI files and the travel office firings. Starr got involved in the Lewinsky case late in 1997 and early 1998, when his office was given evidence that Clinton had asked Lewinsky to lie about their relationship in a deposition she was asked to give in the sexual harassment case brought against the president by Paula Corbin Jones. In his own deposition in that case and in public comments, Clinton denied that he had had a sexual relation with Lewinsky or that he had asked her to lie about it. Starr's investigation of the Lewinsky case led directly to Clinton's impeachment by the House in December 1998 on charges of perjury and obstruction of justice. The Senate acquitted him of those charges early in 1999, and Starr indicated that he was unlikely to pursue the matter further.* (Investigations and impeachment, Historic Documents of 1998, pp. 564, 632, 695, 958; Senate acquittal, Historic Documents of 1999, p. 15)

*Meanwhile, Starr's investigation created nearly as much controversy as the revelations about the president's affair. The Clintons and their supporters said that the special prosecutor was allied with right-wing interests who wanted to drive the president out of office and were willing to use almost any means to do so. Starr's seemingly limitless pursuit of Clinton led to growing public and congressional dissatisfaction with the law that authorized the Office of Independent Counsel, and Congress did not renew it when it expired on June 30, 1999. Starr resigned as special prosecutor in October 1999, when Ray, whose job was to wrap up the loose ends of all the investigations still pending, replaced him.* (Independent counsel law, Historic Documents of 1998, p. 905; Historic Documents of 1999, p. 165)

*The investigation was also expensive. The Office of Independent Counsel had spent at least $56 million on the Whitewater investigations, and that did not count more than $11 million in legal fees incurred by the Clintons.*

## Ray's Conclusions in the Whitewater Investigation

*In his announcement, Ray said his office determined that "the evidence was insufficient" to prove beyond a reasonable doubt that either of the Clintons "knowingly participated in," knew of, or tried to cover up any criminal conduct involving Madison Guaranty, the Whitewater Development Corporation, or Capital Management Services (CMS), an entity that had dealings with Madison Guaranty. The McDougals and Jim Guy Tucker, who succeeded Clinton as governor of Arkansas, were convicted of fraud in the case in 1996.*

*The statement said that the independent counsel had specifically investigated whether Clinton had knowingly given false testimony when he testified that he had never received a loan from Madison Guaranty; that he did not know about a $300,000 loan from CMS to Susan McDougal, $50,000 of which was used to benefit Whitewater; and that he did not know how Madison Guaranty had come to retain the services of the Rose Law Firm, where Hillary Clinton was a partner. The independent counsel also investigated whether Hillary Clinton had lied about the relationship between the savings and loan and her law firm and about her work for Madison Guaranty. Ray also said that the circumstances surrounding her delay in turning her billing records over to investigators "could not be established."*

*Finally, the statement said that Ray's office had investigated whether consulting fees paid to Webster L. Hubbell by Clinton supporters after Hubbell left his position as associate attorney general in 1994 amounted to a "criminal quid pro quo" for his keeping silent about Whitewater matters. Hubbell, a former law partner in the Rose Law Firm, was one of twelve people convicted of various crimes resulting from the Whitewater investigation.*

## FBI Files and "Travelgate" Investigations

The first report Ray filed, on March 16, exonerated the White House of any criminal wrongdoing in connection with several hundred confidential FBI files found in the White House. The report itself was not made public, but lawyers familiar with the investigation said Ray's office had concluded that the files were inadvertently collected when a mid-level security officer requisitioned them from the FBI using an outdated list compiled by the Secret Service of people who had passes to the White House. Among the mistakenly collected files were those of several prominent Republicans, including Brent Scowcroft, who was President George Bush's national security adviser, and Marlin Fitzwater, who had served as press secretary to presidents Bush and Ronald Reagan. The report also cleared Bernard W. Nussbaum, Clinton's first White House counsel, of allegations that he had lied in sworn testimony to a congressional committee.

In a statement filed with the report, Ray said: "In the FBI files matter, the independent counsel determined there was no evidence that any senior White House official, or First Lady Hillary Rodham Clinton, was involved in seeking confidential Federal Bureau of Investigation background reports of former White House staff from the administrations of President Bush and President Reagan."

The report on the travel office firings was filed June 23 and made public October 19. The case involved charges that Hillary Clinton had lied or obstructed justice to cover up her role in the May 1993 firing of seven employees of the White House travel office. At the time the White House said evidence of financial mismanagement had been found in the office, but when then employees were replaced with Clinton friends and relatives, congressional opponents accused the Clintons of cronyism.

Ray concluded that the seven fired employees were all political employees who could be fired without cause and that the concerns about financial irregularities were legitimate. But he said that the first lady had made "factually false" statements when she said in a sworn deposition that she had played no role in the firings. In fact, Ray said, the evidence showed that she had had eight separate conversations with three White House aides about the matter, although he was unable to show that Clinton had "knowingly intended to influence the Travel Office decision or was aware that she had such influence at this early stage of the Administration."

In a written response to Ray's findings, Mrs. Clinton's attorney, David E. Kendall, said characterizing the first lady's statements as factually false was "highly unfair and misleading." White House spokesman Jake Siewert said Ray's conclusions confirmed what the White House had said from the beginning: "There were financial improprieties in the travel office, the firings were lawful, and the decision to remove the travel office employees was made by White House staff, not the first lady." In June and again in October, Mrs. Clinton said that "after all these years and millions of dollars," she was just glad the investigation was over.

## *Clinton Disbarment*

*In a related development, a Committee on Professional Conduct, appointed by the Arkansas Supreme Court, on July 1 sued Bill Clinton in an effort to revoke his law license for lying under oath in the Paula Jones case. The committee accused Clinton of "serious misconduct" involving "dishonesty, deceit, fraud and misrepresentation." It also said that the president's conduct on that case "damages the legal profession and demonstrates a lack of overall fitness to hold a license to practice law." The judge in the Jones case had already found that Clinton had testified falsely and fined him $90,000 for civil contempt of court.*

*Clinton was first given a law license in 1973, although he had not practiced since the early 1980s. Clinton was fighting the disbarment through his attorneys, but the case was unlikely to be resolved before he left office in January 2001. He was the first sitting president to be sued for disbarment. The state of New York stripped Richard Nixon of his license to practice after he resigned the presidency on August 9, 1974.*

> *Following is the text of a statement issued September 20, 2000, by independent counsel Robert W. Ray, announcing that he had found "insufficient evidence" to charge President Bill Clinton or his wife, Hillary Rodham Clinton, with criminal wrongdoing in connection with their involvement in the failed Whitewater land deal. The document was obtained from the Internet at http://www .oicstarr.com/press/000920.htm.*

This Office has now concluded, with certain limited exceptions, its investigation of the matters commonly referred to as "Madison Guaranty/Whitewater." At this time, it is appropriate, in the public interest, and consistent with the law to inform the public of the findings and conclusions regarding the core matters within this Office's Madison Guaranty/Whitewater jurisdiction. Except for limited pending matters, the Madison Guaranty/Whitewater investigation is now closed.

Following enactment of the Independent Counsel Reauthorization Act of 1994, this Office was established on August 5, 1994 to continue the work of regulatory Independent Counsel Robert B. Fiske Jr. to investigate the relationship of James B. McDougal and President and Mrs. Clinton to Madison Guaranty Savings & Loan Association ("Madison Guaranty"), Capital Management Services, Inc. ("CMS"), and the Whitewater Development Corporation ("Whitewater Development"). Eleven months ago, on October 18, 1999, the judges of the United States Court of Appeals for the District of Columbia Circuit's Division for Appointing Independent Counsels appointed me as Independent Counsel with respect to all matters within the previously ordered jurisdiction of this Office, including the Madison Guaranty/Whitewater investigation. Since my appointment, this Office has concluded two matters within our jurisdiction—matters commonly referred to as the "FBI Files" matter and the "Travel Office" matter.

The Madison Guaranty/Whitewater investigation resulted in the conviction of 12 defendants, including former Arkansas Governor Jim Guy Tucker, Jim and Susan McDougal, and former Associate Attorney General Webster L. Hubbell. This Office investigated whether Jim and Susan McDougal committed any crimes in connection with Madison Guaranty, CMS, or Whitewater Development by using control of two financial institutions—Madison Guaranty and Madison Bank & Trust—to lend money to or for the benefit of Whitewater Development and to pay Whitewater Development financial obligations at a time when the McDougals and the Clintons jointly owned Whitewater Development. In May 1996, Jim and Susan McDougal were convicted in federal court in Arkansas of various crimes involving Madison Guaranty, CMS, and Whitewater Development. According to one federal bank regulatory agency, the failure of Madison Guaranty cost the taxpayers $73 million.

This Office investigated whether President and Mrs. Clinton knowingly participated in any criminal conduct related to Madison Guaranty, CMS, or Whitewater Development or had any knowledge of such conduct. This Office determined that the evidence was insufficient to prove to a jury beyond a reasonable doubt that either President or Mrs. Clinton knowingly participated in any criminal conduct involving Madison Guaranty, CMS, or Whitewater Development or knew of such conduct. The evidence relating to their testimony and conduct, in connection with this investigation and other investigations involving the same entities, was also, in the judgment of this Office, insufficient to prove to a jury beyond a reasonable doubt that either of them committed any criminal offense, including perjury (18 U.S.C. § 1621) or obstruction of justice (18 U.S.C. § 1503).

The following findings and conclusions relate to publicly disclosed matters investigated by this Office. Information obtained through grand jury proceedings or other confidential methods is not included in this statement. Upon conclusion of pending matters, this Office intends to submit to the Court a final report "setting forth fully and completely a description of the work" of the Office. 28 U.S.C. § 594(h).

The investigation made the following findings and conclusions:

- **This Office investigated whether President Clinton gave knowingly false testimony when he testified in the 1996 trial of Mr. McDougal, Ms. McDougal, and Governor Tucker that he "never borrowed any money from Madison Guaranty," "[n]ever caused anybody to borrow any money for [his] benefit," and "[n]ever ha[d] any personal loan with Madison Guaranty at any time."**
  - At Susan McDougal's 1999 trial for criminal contempt (18 U.S.C. § 402) and obstruction of justice (18 U.S.C. § 1503) for her refusal to testify about matters that included an alleged $27,600 Madison Guaranty loan to President Clinton, the government introduced two checks as evidence of the alleged loan. The first check was an actual Madison Guaranty cashier's check, dated November 15, 1982, made out to "Bill

Clinton" in the amount of $27,600 that was found, by happenstance, among other Madison Guaranty records in the trunk of a car in July 1997 following a tornado. The second check was a microfilm copy, dated August 1, 1983, from the James B. McDougal Trustee account in the amount of $5,081.82 made out to Madison Guaranty. The latter check was signed by Susan McDougal, and the government presented testimony at trial that the amount of the check was precisely equal to the amount of principal and interest remaining due on the alleged loan at the time. The memo line of the check contained the words "Payoff Clinton."

- ○ Neither check reflected a signature or endorsement by Bill Clinton. The backs of both checks contained bank stamps, indicating that they had been deposited and processed. The government presented evidence at trial that both checks were used to the benefit of Whitewater Development. A government agent testified at trial that the fingerprints on the $27,600 check were not sufficiently clear to permit a comparison to any known fingerprints.

- ○ This Office determined that the evidence regarding this alleged loan was insufficient to prove beyond a reasonable doubt that President Clinton borrowed money from Madison Guaranty, caused anyone to borrow money for his benefit from Madison Guaranty, or had any personal loan at any time from Madison Guaranty. Consequently, the evidence was, in the judgment of this Office, insufficient to prove beyond a reasonable doubt that his testimony regarding the alleged loan was knowingly false.

- **This Office also investigated whether President Clinton gave knowingly false testimony when he testified at the same trial that he did not know of a $300,000 loan made by CMS to Susan McDougal in April 1986 that benefitted Whitewater Development and that was the subject of Susan McDougal's 1996 convictions for fraud.**

  - ○ This Office determined that the evidence was insufficient to prove beyond a reasonable doubt that President Clinton knew of the loan or that his testimony regarding the loan was knowingly false.

- **This Office investigated whether President Clinton gave knowingly false testimony at the same trial regarding the circumstances of Madison Guaranty's retention of the Rose Law Firm.**

  - ○ This Office determined that the evidence was insufficient to prove beyond a reasonable doubt that President Clinton's testimony regarding these matters was knowingly false.

- **This Office also investigated whether Mrs. Clinton made knowingly false statements to the Resolution Trust Corporation regarding the relationship between Madison Guaranty and the Rose Law Firm, as well as her own work related to Madison Guaranty.**

  - ○ This Office determined that the evidence, including evidence reflected in the billing records of the Rose Law Firm, was insufficient to prove beyond a reasonable doubt that her statements to the RTC regarding these matters were knowingly false.

- **This Office investigated whether Mrs. Clinton was involved in any effort to obstruct this or other investigations by withholding relevant evidence or information in connection with Rose Law Firm billing records.**
  - On January 5, 1996, some 18 months after Mrs. Clinton received a subpoena for all records in her possession involving Madison Guaranty and related entities, a copy of the Rose Law Firm billing records reflecting the Firm's and Mrs. Clinton's representation of Madison Guaranty and related entities were produced by counsel for Mrs. Clinton.
  - The circumstances surrounding the 18-month delay in producing the billing records could not be established. Mr. Hubbell testified in the Senate that he and former Deputy Counsel to the President Vincent W. Foster Jr. had the billing records in February/March 1992. Carolyn Huber, an assistant to President Clinton, testified in the Senate that she found certain documents in the White House residence in August 1995 and placed them in an office where they remained until January 1996. She also testified in the Senate that in January 1996, she found them again and realized that those same documents were the billing records. At that time, they were produced to this Office.
  - This Office determined that the evidence of the circumstances surrounding the handling of the records between March 1992 and August 1995 and January 1996 was inconclusive and thus was insufficient to prove beyond a reasonable doubt that any person, including Mrs. Clinton, knowingly and willfully possessed the billing records with the intent to obstruct justice or that any person, including Mrs. Clinton, gave knowingly false testimony regarding the handling of the billing records.
- **This Office investigated whether the employment of Webster L. Hubbell by supporters of the President following Mr. Hubbell's resignation from the Department of Justice constituted a criminal quid pro quo to obstruct this investigation's access to truthful testimony from Mr. Hubbell.**
  - This Office determined that the evidence was insufficient to prove beyond a reasonable doubt that the employment of Mr. Hubbell constituted a criminal quid pro quo and, consequently, the evidence was also insufficient, in the judgment of this Office, to prove beyond a reasonable doubt that President or Mrs. Clinton was involved in any effort to provide such a quid pro quo to Mr. Hubbell.
- **This Office also investigated whether contacts between White House and Treasury Department officials regarding the Resolution Trust Corporation's criminal referrals involving Madison Guaranty and President and Mrs. Clinton constituted an effort to obstruct justice by corruptly influencing the handling of the referrals.**

○ This Office determined that the evidence was insufficient to prove beyond a reasonable doubt that any White House official, or President
or Mrs. Clinton, was involved in any effort to obstruct justice in this
matter.

* * * * *

As in the Travel Office investigation, this Office experienced delay caused
by the White House and others involving both the production of relevant evidence and the filing of legal claims that were ultimately rejected by the courts.
Delays in obtaining relevant evidence included Susan McDougal's refusal to
testify, despite a court order compelling her testimony, and the failure of the
White House to produce the Rose Law Firm billing records until January 1996.
Unmeritorious litigation by the White House included its claim to an attor-
ney/client privilege between an individual involved in a federal criminal investigation and a government lawyer. *In re: Grand Jury Subpoena Duces
Tecum*, 112 F.3d 910 (8th Cir. 1997).

Finally, the remaining matters within this Office's Madison/Whitewater jurisdiction include pending appeals and the continuing investigation of the
White House's failure to search and produce relevant records, including electronic mail, to this and other investigations. Former Arkansas Governor Jim
Guy Tucker's second appeal of his conviction for conspiracy and mail fraud
has been pending before the Eighth Circuit since oral argument on September 13, 1999. Governor Tucker's sentence of restitution for one million dollars
on his tax fraud conspiracy conviction was remanded to the Eastern District
of Arkansas for resentencing, which is scheduled for October 27, 2000. Once
these matters are concluded, this Office intends to file a final report promptly.

Accordingly, the Madison Guaranty/Whitewater investigation, with the exception of these matters, is now closed. The investigation of other remaining
matters within the jurisdiction of this Office continues.

# CLINTON ADMINISTRATION ON RACISM IN AMERICA
## September 21, 2000

*The United States had been more successful than most other nations in confronting racism, but American society still fell far short of achieving racial harmony, a study submitted to the United Nations by the Clinton administration concluded. The study, written by the State and Justice departments, said the United States had eliminated "the scourge of officially sanctioned segregation." But, it acknowledged, "de facto segregation and persistent racial discrimination" continued to be significant problems.*

*That study came on the heels of numerous reports by civil rights groups and news organizations focusing new attention on disparities in the treatment of blacks and whites in the country's criminal justice system. "Racial profiling"—the targeting of minorities by police officers and others in authority—became an issue in the election campaign, with both major party candidates for president promising to take steps to end the practice.*

### Reporting to the UN

*The report on racism was submitted to the UN in compliance with a UN treaty, the Convention on the Elimination of All Forms of Racial Discrimination, which the United States ratified in 1994. The UN planned to hold a conference on racism in South Africa in 2001, and in preparation for the conference every nation was expected to report on its compliance with the treaty's terms. Each nation's report was to be examined by the United Nations Committee on the Elimination of Racial Discrimination.*

*The U.S. report was a detailed examination of the nation's history of racial discrimination—beginning with the attacks on Native Americans by white settlers and continuing through the slavery of blacks and discriminatory laws and actions against blacks, Asian Americans, and others. The United States began dealing with the consequences of that history in the wake of the Civil War, the study said, with the passage of the Thirteenth, Fourteenth, and Fifteenth amendments to the Constitution, which were all aimed at guaranteeing the rights of blacks and other minorities. Further progress was made with the 1954 Supreme Court decision* Brown v. Board of Education of Topeka, *barring racial segregation in public schools, and with the passage of the Civil Rights Act, the Voting Rights Act, and other civil rights legislation starting in the 1960s. The sum total of those laws and court decisions, the study said, was to build "strong and effective protections against discrimination on the basis of race, color, ethnicity, or national origin" in the United States.*

*The report also noted that President Bill Clinton had signed eight executive orders barring various forms of racial discrimination or promoting affirmative action programs, and that Clinton had sponsored a "race initiative" that led to a 1998 advisory panel report suggesting numerous steps for improving race relations in America.* (Advisory board report, Historic Documents of 1998, p. 665)

*Despite these actions and legal protections, the United States had not succeeded in eliminating either segregation or racial discrimination, the study said. "The forms of discriminatory practices have changed and adapted over time, but racial and ethnic discrimination continues to exist and limit equal opportunity in the United States. For many, the true extent of contemporary racism remains clouded by ignorance as well as differences of perception. Recent surveys indicate that, while most whites do not believe there is much discrimination today in American society, most minorities see the opposite in their life experiences."*

*Two senior Clinton administration officials who were sons of immigrants from Asian countries released the study. Harold Hongju Koh, the assistant secretary of state for democracy, human rights, and labor, was the son of a South Korean diplomat. Bill Lann Lee, the assistant attorney general for civil rights, was the son of Chinese immigrants. Both men told reporters they believed the United States had made more progress in combating racism than nearly any other country in the world. "There may be other countries who have fewer problems of racial discrimination, but they may have less diversity to begin with, or more homogeneity," Koh said. In the United States, he added, "you have a country of 273 million representing every racial, ethnic, linguistic, and cultural tradition, and a more sustained political struggle to address those questions and a more sustained constitutional and legal response by all branches of government than I've seen in any other country in the world."*

*One dissent to that view came from Morton Sklar, the executive director of the World Organization Against Torture USA, which issued its own report charging that the United States was violating the UN racism treaty with such practices as racial profiling and the death penalty. "I don't think it's fair to say we're far ahead of other nations," Sklar told the Associated Press. "It's totally unfair to downplay these problems by saying we're doing better than other nations."*

## Minorities and the Criminal Justice System

*Several reports and news events during the year focused public attention on continuing racism within the criminal justice system in the United States. One issue that received an increasing amount of attention was the practice of "racial profiling" by police. Reports emerged during 1999 that state police in New Jersey for years had systematically targeted black and Hispanic drivers for interrogations and searches as part of an aggressive antinarcotics program. One investigation showed that three-fourths of the motorists stopped on the roadways in one part of the state were members of racial minorities. The U.S. Justice Department and the state of New Jersey had signed an agreement in 1999 barring racial or ethnic profiles as the basis for stopping motorists. It was the first time the federal government had forced a state to agree to such a ban. On November 27 New Jersey attorney general John J. Farmer Jr. released 91,000 pages of state documents detailing the use of racial profiling. He said the policy had been effective in helping curb crime, but he acknowledged that "the social consequences of pursuing this policy was a disaster."*

*One potentially important court decision on the racial profiling issue came on April 11, when the U.S. Court of Appeals for the Ninth Circuit, in San Francisco, ruled that law enforcement officers could not, as a general rule, use ethnic appearance as a basic for deciding when to stop a person as a potential criminal suspect. The case (U.S. v German Espinoza Montero Camargo) involved the 1996 arrest, by the U.S. Border Patrol, of two Mexicans who were found to be carrying marijuana and a pistol; the Mexicans were subsequently convicted on narcotics and weapons charges, imprisoned, and deported back to Mexico. In a 7–4 ruling, the appellate court said the Border Patrol was justified in stopping the Mexicans because they had engaged in suspicious behavior—but ethnic appearance, by itself, was not a valid reason for stopping them. Noting that the area where the Mexicans had been arrested was nearly three-fourths Hispanic in population, the court ruled that "Hispanic appearance is of little or no use in determining which particular individuals among the vast Hispanic populace should be stopped by law enforcement officials on the lookout for illegal aliens." Legal observers said the court's ruling appeared to challenge a 1975 Supreme Court opinion that had said law enforcement officers could use racial appearance as one of several factors in deciding whether to stop a potential suspect.*

*Democratic presidential candidate Al Gore made racial profiling an issue in the election campaign, promising to take aggressive steps at the federal level to halt the practice. In response, Gore's Republican opponent and eventual winner of the presidential race, George W. Bush, said he, too, opposed racial profiling.*

*Several studies released during the year examined the broader relationship between the criminal justice system and racial minorities. One study, issued May 4 by the Leadership Conference on Civil Rights, charged that blacks and other minorities experienced "separate and unequal justice" in the courts and prisons. The report, "Justice on Trial," pulled together numerous statistical studies showing that blacks and Hispanics tended to receive less favorable treatment by courts and law enforcement authorities than did whites. For example, the report cited one study showing that blacks who killed whites were sentenced to death twenty-two times more frequently than were blacks who killed blacks, and seven times more frequently than whites who killed blacks. Another study, by the Youth Law Center, reported that when a black youth and a white youth were charged with a similar crime, and neither had a prior arrest record, the black was six times more likely to be imprisoned than the white. (Death penalty issues, p. 988)*

*Human Rights Watch, an international watchdog group, turned its attention on the United States and reported on June 7 that blacks were the primary targets of the nation's war on drugs—even though whites were more likely to use drugs than were blacks. The report said that blacks made up 62 percent of those sent to state prisons in 1996 for drug offenses; blacks represented only 12 percent of the overall national population. "Black and white drug offenders get radically different treatment in the American justice system," Human Rights Watch executive director Kenneth Roth said. "This is not only profoundly unfair to blacks, it also corrodes the American ideal of equal justice for all."*

*During June and July, the* New York Times *ran a series of fourteen stories detailing racial problems in the United States. The newspaper said its series "portrayed a stubbornly enduring racial divide." The series concluded with a July 11 report on a national public opinion survey, commissioned by the newspaper, which showed that "even as the rawest forms of bigotry have receded they have been replaced by remoteness and distrust in places of work, learning, and worship." A majority of both blacks and whites said they believed race relations were improving in the United States, the newspaper said. But about 40 percent of the blacks surveyed said they did not believe there had been any real progress in eliminating racial discrimination since the 1960s. On many questions in the survey, the* Times *reported, "blacks and whites seemed to be living on different planets." For example, the survey found that blacks were about four times more likely than whites to say that blacks were treated less fairly at work and in shops, restaurants, and other public places. Similarly, two-thirds of blacks expressed the belief that blacks were treated unfairly by police, while only one-fourth of whites held that view.*

*Following are excerpts from the "Introduction" of the "Initial Report of the United States of America to the United Nations Committee on the Elimination of Racial Discrimination," released September 21, 2000, in compliance with the United Nation's Convention on the Elimination of All Forms of Racial Discrimination. This document was obtained from the Internet at http://www.state.gov/www/global/human_rights/cerd_report/cerd_toc.html.*

# Introduction

The Government of the United States of America welcomes the opportunity to report to the Committee on the Elimination of Racial Discrimination on the legislative, judicial, administrative and other measures giving effect to its undertakings under the Convention on the Elimination of All Forms of Racial Discrimination, in accordance with Article 9 thereof. The form and content of this Report follow the General Guidelines adopted by the Committee in July 1993.

This Report has been prepared by the U.S. Department of State with extensive assistance from the White House, the Civil Rights Division of the U.S. Department of Justice, the Equal Employment Opportunity Commission, and other departments, agencies and entities of the United States Government most closely concerned with the issues addressed by the Convention. Contributions were also solicited and received from interested members of the many non-governmental organizations and other public interest groups active in the area of civil rights, civil liberties and human rights in the United States. The Report covers the situation in the United States through August 2000 and constitutes the initial report to the Committee.

The United States ratified the Convention on the Elimination of All Forms of Racial Discrimination in October 1994, and the Convention entered into force for the United States on November 20, 1994. In its instrument of ratification, which was deposited with the Secretary General of the United Nations pursuant to Article 17(2) of the Convention, the United States conditioned its ratification upon several reservations, understandings and declarations. These are set forth at Annex I and discussed at the relevant portions of this Report.

Since June 17, 1997, the federal government has been engaged in a major review of domestic race issues. On that date, the President established an "Initiative on Race" and authorized creation of a seven-member Advisory Board to examine issues of race, racism and racial reconciliation and to make recommendations on how to build a more united America for the 21st Century. . . . The Advisory Board submitted its report to the President on September 18, 1998. Based on its recommendations, the Administration is proceeding to formulate specific proposals and plans for action. A copy of the Initiative's final report and a chart-book prepared for the President's Initiative by the Council of Economic Advisers entitled "Changing America: Indicators of Social and Economic Well Being by Race and Hispanic Origin" (September 1998) are available at the White House web site: http://www.whitehouse.gov.

Since 1992, the United States has also been a party to the International Covenant on Civil and Political Rights, some provisions of which have wider application than those of the Convention on the Elimination of All Forms of Racial Discrimination. The initial U.S. Report under the Covenant, which provides general information, was submitted to the Human Rights Committee in July 1994 (http://www.state.gov). The United States also ratified the Convention Against Torture and Other Cruel, Inhuman or Degrading Treatment or Punishment at the same time as it ratified the Convention on the Elimination of All Forms of Racial Discrimination. The Initial U.S. Report under the Convention Against Torture was submitted to the Committee Against Torture in September 1999 and is available on the Department of State web site, http://www.state.gov/www/global/human_rights/torture_index.html.

Prior to ratifying the Convention on the Elimination of All Forms of Racial Discrimination, the United States Government undertook a careful study of the requirements of the Convention in light of existing domestic law and policy. That study concluded that U.S. laws, policies and government institutions are fully consistent with the provisions of the Convention accepted by the United States. Racial discrimination by public authorities is prohibited throughout the United States, and the principle of non-discrimination is central to governmental policy throughout the country. The legal system provides strong protections against and remedies for discrimination on the basis of race, color, ethnicity or national origin by both public and private actors. These laws and policies have the genuine support of the overwhelming majority of the people of the United States, who share a common commitment to the values of justice, equality, and respect for the individual.

The United States has struggled to overcome the legacies of racism, ethnic intolerance and destructive Native American policies, and has made much progress in the past half century. Nonetheless, issues relating to race, ethnicity and national origin continue to play a negative role in American society. Racial discrimination persists against various groups, despite the progress made through the enactment of major civil rights legislation beginning in the 1860s and 1960s. The path towards true racial equality has been uneven, and substantial barriers must still be overcome.

Therefore, even though U.S. law is in conformity with the obligations assumed by the United States under the treaty, American society has not yet fully achieved the Convention's goals. Additional steps must be taken to promote the important principles embodied in its text. In this vein, the United States welcomed the visit of the UN Special Rapporteur on Contemporary Forms of Racism, Racial Discrimination, Xenophobia and Related Intolerance during the fall of 1994 and took note of the report of his findings. . . . In November 1997, the White House convened an unprecedented Hate Crimes Conference to formulate effective responses to the increasing number of violent crimes motivated by racial and ethnic sentiments. The President's Initiative on Race, the establishment of the White House Office on the President's Initiative for One America, and the preparation of this report constitute important parts of that effort. Indeed, in confronting issues of race every day, the American public is engaged in an ongoing dialogue to determine how best to resolve racial and ethnic tensions that persist in U.S. society.

Reflecting the multi-ethnic, multi-racial and multi-cultural nature of America today, the private sector plays an important role in combating racism in the United States, through activities and programs conducted by such non-governmental groups ("NGOs") as the American-Arab Anti-Discrimination Committee, the American Civil Liberties Union (ACLU), Amnesty International, the Anti-Defamation League, the Asian American Legal Defense and Education Fund, B'nai Brith, the Cuban-American National Council, Human Rights Watch, Indigenous Environmental Network, the Japanese American Citizens League, the Lawyers Committee for Human Rights, the Lawyers' Committee on Employment Rights, the League of United Latin-American Citizens, the Mexican-American Legal Defense and Education Fund (MALDEF), the National Asian Pacific American Legal Consortium, the National Association for the Advancement of Colored People (NAACP), the NAACP Legal Defense and Education Fund, the National Conference for Community and Justice, the National Council of La Raza, the National Congress of American Indians, the National Urban League, the Native American Rights Foundation, Na Koa Ikaika, the Organization of Chinese Americans, the Southern Organizing Committee, the Southern Poverty Law Center, and the Southwest Network for Economic and Environmental Justice, among many others. NGOs played a vital role in the Civil Rights Movement, have been actively involved in the President's Initiative on Race, and continue to be instrumental in working towards full achievement of the purposes of this Convention. Information about the activities of these and many other civil rights NGOs can be obtained through the Leadership Conference on Civil Rights, a coalition of organizations dedicated to promoting civil and human rights in the United States http://www .civilrights.org.

As a functioning, multi-racial democracy, the United States seeks to enforce the established rights of individuals to protection against discrimination based upon race, color, national origin, religion, gender, age, disability status, and citizenship status in virtually every aspect of social and economic life. Federal law prohibits discrimination in the areas of education, employment, public accommodation, transportation, voting, and housing and mortgage credit access, as well as in the military and in programs receiving federal financial assistance. The federal government has established a wide-ranging set of enforcement procedures to administer these laws, with the U.S. Department of Justice exercising a major coordination and leadership role on most critical enforcement issues. State and local governments have complementary legislation and enforcement mechanisms to further these goals.

At both the federal and state levels, the United States has developed a broad range of legal and regulatory provisions and administrative systems to protect and to promote respect for civil rights. Enforcement agencies have worked diligently over the last three decades to improve enforcement of these rights and to promote education, training and technical assistance. In addition, over the years, the U.S. Congress has significantly strengthened the enforcement provisions of some of the civil rights statutes. The federal government remains committed to providing full, prompt, and effective administration of these laws.

This commitment to eliminating racial discrimination began with the Emancipation Proclamation (effective on January 1, 1863), which freed the slaves in the Confederacy (the region comprised of the southern states which attempted to secede from the Union), and with the end of the American Civil War (1861–65). Since that time, American society has sought to create ever more effective means to address and resolve racial and ethnic differences without violence. Indeed, the amendments to the United States Constitution enacted at the war's conclusion, the Thirteenth Amendment (ending slavery), the Fourteenth Amendment (guaranteeing equal protection of the laws and due process of law), and the Fifteenth Amendment (guaranteeing Black citizens the right to vote), directly addressed questions of racial discrimination.

The laws enacted in the Reconstruction Era, immediately following the Civil War, also addressed the rights of minorities. Unfortunately, however, these laws did not succeed in changing attitudes born of generations of discrimination, and through restrictive interpretation and non-application, they were largely ineffective. Moreover, the U.S. Supreme Court invalidated federal authority to protect Blacks and others from state-sponsored discrimination. As a result, through the first half of the 20th Century, racial discrimination and segregation was required by law (*de jure*) in many of our country's southern states in such key areas as education, housing, employment, transportation, and public accommodations. Discrimination and segregation was a common practice (*de facto*) in most other portions of the country. In addition, though the Fifteenth Amendment guaranteed that the "right of citizens of the United States to vote shall not be abridged by the United States or by any state on account of race, color, or previous condition of servitude," many southern states enacted laws that were seemingly neutral, but were designed and implemented in a way to deny Black citizens the opportunity to participate in elections.

Prior to the middle of the 20th Century, there were no laws to address other forms of racial discrimination, such as discriminatory provisions in U.S. immigration law and policy. After the U.S. acquisition of California in 1848, there arose a need for cheap labor, and Chinese immigrants flocked to the western United States to work on the rapidly developing railroads. Anti-Asian prejudice and the competition that Chinese immigrants provided to American workers led to anti-Chinese riots in San Francisco in 1877, and then to the Chinese Exclusion Act of 1882. The Act banned all Chinese immigration for ten years, and it was extended until 1924 when a new immigration law prohibited all Asian immigration to the United States. Several years later, law and policy toward Asian immigrants was again changed, extending citizenship rights to those already in the United States and establishing a quota for immigrants from various countries. The quota was abolished in 1965. With regard to Native Americans, the United States has historically recognized Native American tribes as self-governing political communities that pre-date the U.S. Constitution. From 1778 until 1871, the United States entered into numerous treaties with Indian tribes, which recognized tribal self-government, reserved tribal lands as "permanent homes" for Indian tribes, and pledged Federal protection for the tribes. Yet, the United States engaged in a series of Indian wars in the 19th Century, which resulted in significant loss of life and lands among Indian tribes. In the 1880s, over the protests of Indian leaders, including Sitting Bull and Lone Wolf, the United States embarked on a policy of distributing tribal community lands to individual Indians in an attempt to "assimilate" Indians into the agrarian culture of our Nation. This "Allotment Policy" resulted in a loss of almost 100 million acres of Indian lands from the 1880s until 1934, when President Franklin D. Roosevelt ended the policy with the enactment of the Indian Reorganization Act in 1934. This Act was intended to encourage Indian tribes to revitalize tribal self-government, so that Indian tribes might use their own lands and resources to provide a sustainable economy for their people. This policy of respect for Native American and Alaska

Native tribes and cultures acknowledges tribal self-government and promotes tribal economic self-sufficiency.

In 1941, Franklin D. Roosevelt issued an Executive Order prohibiting discrimination on the basis of race, color, creed or national origin in the war industries or federal government. However, the U.S. armed forces continued to operate racially segregated combat units until 1948. During World War II, persons of Japanese, German, and Italian ancestry suffered blatant forms of discrimination, justified on grounds of military necessity. Thousands of U.S. citizens, the majority of whom were ethnically Japanese, were "relocated" to internment camps throughout the western United States. This policy was held lawful by the U.S. Supreme Court in *Korematsu v. United States*, 321 U.S. 760 (1944). In recent years, however, the United States has recognized the wrongfulness of this policy and made lump sum payments to Japanese Americans who were detained in accordance with this policy, or to their survivors.

Following World War II, a combination of grass roots civic action and critical decisions by the Executive and Judicial branches of the federal government set the stage for strategies for overcoming the legacy of slavery. In 1948, the U.S. Supreme Court banned the use of racially restrictive covenants that limited the sale of housing to members of racial or religious minorities. *Shelly v. Kramer*, 334 U.S. 1 (1948). In the same year, President Truman issued an Executive Order requiring equality of treatment for all persons in the U.S. Armed Forces. In 1954, the Supreme Court rendered its landmark decision in *Brown v. Board of Education of Topeka*, 347 U.S. 483 (1954), banning state-sponsored racial segregation in public education and creating the foundation for the emergence of the contemporary civil rights movements.

During the past forty years there has been a steady stream of legislation at the federal, state and local levels creating remedies for individuals affected by racial discrimination. Some of the most significant pieces of federal civil rights legislation include: the Civil Rights Act of 1964, which outlawed discrimination in public accommodations, employment, and education; the Voting Rights Act of 1965, which prohibited voting discrimination and thus brought Blacks from southern states into the political process, and which continues to protect all racial and language minorities throughout the nation from discrimination in the political process; and the 1968 Fair Housing Act which eliminated discrimination in housing and mortgage lending. Executive Orders issued by Presidents through the years have supplemented this catalog of protections by specifically requiring non-discrimination in a vast range of public programs. Similarly, the Immigration Act of 1965 repealed restrictions on the permanent entry of Asians and made family reunification, not race or national origin, the cornerstone of U.S. immigration policy.

In each of the areas covered by this Convention, the American people can point with pride at the great strides towards equality made over the past half-century. However, despite these enormous accomplishments, much remains to be done to eliminate racial discrimination altogether. While the scourge of officially-sanctioned segregation has been eliminated, de facto segregation and persistent racial discrimination continue to exist. The forms of discriminatory practices have changed and adapted over time, but racial and ethnic discrimination continues to restrict and limit equal opportunity in the United States. For many, the true extent of contemporary racism remains clouded by ignorance as well as differences of perception. Recent surveys indicate that, while most Whites do not believe there is much discrimination today in American society, most minorities see the opposite in their life experiences.

Indeed, in recent years the national conscience has been sharply reminded of the challenges to eradicating racism by such notorious incidents as the 1991 beating of Rodney King by two Los Angeles police officers; the death of Amadou Diallo in New York; the burning of Black churches, synagogues and mosques; the brutal murder of James Byrd, Jr., in Texas; the shootings at a Jewish cultural center in Los Angeles, and the pattern of discrimination revealed in civil rights litigation against the Denny's Restaurant chain and the Adams Mark Hotel. Further, heightened awareness and discussion of racial issues have led some to call on Americans to reexamine our history and to consider making reparations in some form to Blacks for past slavery. These and other issues have prompted vigorous debate in schools, media and government over issues of race.

No country or society is completely free of racism, discrimination or ethnocentrism. None can claim to have achieved complete success in the protection and promotion of human rights, and, therefore, all should welcome open dialogue and constructive criticism. As a society, the United States continues to search for the best means to eliminate all forms of racial, ethnic and religious discrimination through the mechanisms available within a pluralistic, federal system of government.

The United States has long been a vigorous supporter of the international campaign against racism and racial discrimination. Indeed, the United States will play an active role in the upcoming World Conference Against Racism, Racial Discrimination, Xenophobia and Related Intolerance in 2001. Toward that end, the United States is engaged in a domestic preparatory process that will invite the involvement of state and local government officials as well as academia and civil society.

The last half century of progress has provided the United States with a useful perspective from which to offer insights to other countries with diverse and growing minority populations. By the same token, the people and government of the United States can learn from the experiences of others. The United States looks forward to a constructive dialogue with the members of the Committee.

# FOOD AND DRUG ADMINISTRATION ON THE ABORTION PILL
## September 28, 2000

*Sixteen years after it was first tested in the United States, a controversial abortion pill gained final approval from the Food and Drug Administration (FDA) on September 28, 2000. The agency's approval of the drug, RU-486, or mifepristone, was a milestone event in the always contentious debate over abortion in the United States. Supporters of abortion rights hailed the decision as a victory for their cause because it offered women the option of having an abortion in the privacy of their own homes without having to undergo surgery or visit abortion clinics, which were often picketed. Abortion opponents bitterly complained that the drug would make having an abortion too easy and thereby increase the number of abortions in the United States.*

*At least in the early weeks after the FDA's decision, both supporters and opponents of abortion seemed to be wrong about their assumptions. Thousands of women called their doctors and abortion clinics asking about the drug. But doctors said many of those women were discouraged by what they heard: that ending a pregnancy with the drug required at least three trips to a doctor's office and could lead to side-effects, such as bleeding, cramping, and headaches. Moreover, the drug could be used only during the first seven weeks of pregnancy. Because of the complicated procedures involved with using drug, many doctors seemed to be shying away from it. Most of the early use of the drug appeared to be taking place in abortion clinics, such as those run by the Planned Parenthood Federation of America and other organizations.*

*It was unclear at year's end what position the incoming administration of George W. Bush would take on the abortion pill. The FDA had banned the pill in 1989, when Bush's father was president, and the younger Bush opposed abortions except when necessary to spare the life of the mother. Bush called the FDA's decision "wrong," but during a debate the week after the FDA acted Bush said he did not believe he would have the authority, as president, to overrule the agency. Antiabortion activists later said they would press Bush to try to overturn the approval of the drug.* (Abortion protests, Historic Documents of 1998, p. 809)

## Long Road to Approval

*The RU-486 drug was developed in France in 1980 and found, in tests two years later, to be effective in preventing pregnancy and inducing abortion. French authorities approved use of the drug in 1988; by 2000 the drug also had been approved for use in Britain, China, Germany, Spain, Russia, and several other countries.*

*The FDA in 1983 allowed testing of the drug in the United States; clinical trials began the next year at the University of Southern California. Facing protest threats from antiabortion forces, the French pharmaceutical firm that made the drug—Roussel-Uclaf SA—decided not to attempt to market it in the United States. In 1989 the FDA banned the importation of the drug for personal use. Four years later the political situation had changed; just two days after his inauguration in January 1993 President Bill Clinton directed the Department of Health and Human Services to investigate procedures for renewed testing of the drug. New clinical trials began in October 1994, and in September 1996 the FDA reversed course and gave conditional approval for the drug, pending receipt of additional information about how it was to be manufactured and labeled. In the meantime, more than 100,000 women had used mifepristone in the clinical tests, and a group of investors had formed a company, Danco Laboratories LLC, in New York City, to distribute the drug under the trade name Mifeprex. The Population Council, a nonprofit research group that advocated the availability of birth control and abortion, held the U.S. patent rights to the drug. It took Danco several years to locate a company to manufacture the drug. As of late 2000 the company refused to name the manufacturer, although the FDA had inspected it.*

*During its review leading up to final approval of the drug, the FDA reportedly considered attaching a number of tight restrictions on the circumstances under which doctors could prescribe it. Among other things, according to news reports during 2000, the FDA considered restricting use of the drug to doctors who were licensed to perform surgical abortions. At one point, the FDA reportedly also considered establishing a registry of doctors authorized to use the drug. Abortion supporters said those requirements almost certainly would have curtailed availability and use of the drug, since few family doctors also performed abortions and many doctors feared having their names published as abortion providers, because of possible retaliation by antiabortion activists.*

*In its final approval, issued September 28, the FDA included several restrictions on how mifepristone would be used but did not impose the tight restrictions that supporters of abortion had feared. Under one apparent compromise, the FDA ruled that the drug could be prescribed only by doctors who were licensed to perform abortions—or who had made arrangements with another doctor for a surgical abortion should one become necessary. The FDA allowed use of the drug only during the first seven weeks of a pregnancy, in effect requiring that a doctor be able to determine when a pregnancy began. Upon receiving the drug, women would have to be given written instructions on its use and a description of potential side-effects. In addition, women using the drug would have to agree to undergo a surgical abortion if the drug did not work as intended.*

*Because the drug was so controversial, the FDA did not publish the names of medical experts who had conducted scientific reviews of it for the agency. The agency agreed not to disclose the name of the manufacturer. According to news reports, it was widely believed that the manufacturer was located overseas.*

*To use the drug, a woman would have to visit a doctor at least three times. On the first visit, after receiving counseling on the drug, she would take three pills of mifepristone, which stopped the effect of progesterone, a hormone essential to pregnancy. Within two to three days, the woman would return to the doctor's office to take two pills of misoprostol, a separate drug that would contract her uterus, causing the fetus to be expelled; misoprostol was a previously approved drug, normally used for treatment of ulcers. About two weeks after taking the mifepristone pills, the woman would return to the doctor for a final checkup to make sure the abortion had succeeded. Clinical studies had found that use of the mifepristone and misoprostol resulted in completely successful abortions about 95 percent of the time; in the remaining cases, a surgical abortion was necessary to remove remaining fetal material from the uterus. In announcing the FDA's approval of the drug, Commissioner Jane Henney said: "For those who choose to have an early termination of their pregnancy, this is a reasonable medical alternative" to surgical abortion.*

## Reaction to the FDA Decision

*Reaction to the FDA's approval of mifepristone for abortions fell along predictable lines, with supporters of abortion praising the decision and abortion opponents condemning it. Gloria Feldt, president of the Planned Parenthood Federation of America, noted that the drug had been approved only after going through an "arduous political process," as well as the customary scientific reviews. She said mifepristone was "the most significant technological advance in women's reproductive health care since the birth control pill." Planned Parenthood began offering the drug in its clinics in late November. "American women want this option; they have been asking us for it, and not just since September, when it was approved in the U.S.," Feldt said in a statement issued on November 16. "They have been asking us for it during the entire twelve years that have passed since it first became available in Europe. We are thrilled we can finally say 'yes, it's here.'"*

*President Clinton praised the FDA's decision and insisted that politics had not played a role in the approval process. "This administration treated that issue as purely one of science and medicine," he said. "And the decision to be made under our law is whether the drug should be approved by the FDA on the grounds of safety."*

*Abortion opponents, who for years had lobbied intensively against approval of the drug, were furious, and they vowed a new campaign to have the decision reversed. Among them, Jodie Brown, of the American Life League, said: "We will not tolerate the FDA's decision to approve the destruction of innocent human persons through chemical abortion." Representatives of several radical antiabortion groups that routinely mounted protests at abortion clinics said they would try to pressure doctors not to use mifepristone. Troy Newman, an official with Operation Rescue West, said his organization would call doctors' offices to find out which ones were willing to prescribe the drug. "Then we will treat them the exact same way we treat an abortion provider," Newman told the* Washington Post.

*In addition to the fundamental question of the morality of abortions, one important disagreement between supporters and opponents of abortion was whether the general availability of mifepristone would lead to more abortions in the United States. Supporters argued that the drug would not significantly affect the overall number of abortions, which had averaged about 1.3 million annually during the late 1990s. Because the drug could be used only during the first seven weeks of a pregnancy, it likely would be only a substitute for surgical abortions, they said. Abortion opponents painted exactly the opposite picture, including Bush, who in his initial reaction to the FDA's decision said he feared availability of the drug would make abortions "more and more common rather than more and more rare."*

*In the early weeks after the FDA's decision, news organizations reported that the drug was not being as widely used as either side in the abortion debate had assumed. Many of the women who called their doctors inquiring about the pill decided not to use it once they were told about the possible side effects and the restrictions on its use. Moreover, many doctors said they were reluctant to prescribe the drug. Some doctors who performed abortions said they preferred surgical procedures. Others said they feared being targeted by antiabortion protesters, and many doctors did not have the necessary equipment in their own offices to determine whether a woman's pregnancy fit the necessary criteria for use of the drug. In effect, the abortion drug turned out to be more difficult to use than supporters had hoped for or opponents had claimed. "There's a very common misconception in the lay public, and even way too common among physicians, that this is a nice, easy way to get rid of a pregnancy," Dr. William Ramos, head of an abortion clinic in Las Vegas, Nevada, told the* New York Times.

> *Following is the text of a statement issued September 28, 2000, by the U.S. Food and Drug Administration announcing that it had given final approval for the use in the United States of the drug mifepristone for abortions. The document was obtained from the Internet at http://www.fda.gov/bbs/topics/news/NEW00737 .html.*

The Food and Drug Administration today approved mifepristone (trade name Mifeprex) for the termination of early pregnancy, defined as 49 days or less, counting from the beginning of the last menstrual period.

Under the approved treatment regimen, a woman first takes 600 milligrams of mifepristone (three 200 milligram pills) by mouth. Two days later, she takes 400 micrograms (two 200-microgram pills) of misoprostol, a prostaglandin. Women will return for a follow-up visit approximately 14 days after taking mifepristone to determine whether the pregnancy has been terminated.

Because of the importance of adhering to this treatment regimen, each woman receiving mifepristone will be given a Medication Guide that clearly explains how to take the drug, who should avoid taking it, and what side effects can occur.

"The approval of mifepristone is the result of the FDA's careful evaluation of the scientific evidence related to the safe and effective use of this drug," said Jane E. Henney, M.D., Commissioner of Food and Drugs. "The FDA's review and approval of this drug has adhered strictly to our legal mandate and mission as a science-based public health regulatory agency."

FDA based its approval of mifepristone on data from clinical trials in the United States and France.

The labeling for mifepristone emphasizes that most women using the product will experience some side effects, primarily cramping and bleeding. Bleeding and spotting typically last for between 9 and 16 days. In about one of 100 women, bleeding can be so heavy that a surgical procedure will be required to stop the bleeding.

The drug's labeling also warns that it should not be used in women with the following conditions:

- Confirmed or suspected ectopic ("tubal") pregnancies
- Intrauterine device (IUD) in place
- Chronic failure of the adrenal glands
- Current long-term therapy with corticosteroids
- History of allergy to mifepristone, misoprostol or other prostaglandins
- Bleeding disorders or current anticoagulant (blood-thinning) therapy.

Under the terms of the approval, mifepristone will be distributed to physicians who can accurately determine the duration of a patient's pregnancy and detect an ectopic (or tubal) pregnancy. Physicians who prescribe mifepristone must also be able to provide surgical intervention in cases of incomplete abortion or severe bleeding—or they must have made plans in advance to provide such care through others.

To gather additional data about the use of mifepristone, the Population Council (sponsor of the product) has made a commitment to conduct post-marketing studies. These include a study comparing patient outcomes among physicians who refer their patients needing surgical intervention, compared to those who perform surgical procedures themselves; an audit of prescribers that will examine whether patients and their physicians are signing the patient agreement and placing it in the patient's medical record, as required; and a system for surveillance, reporting and tracking rare ongoing pregnancies after treatment with mifepristone in the U.S.

Mifepristone, which was developed by a French pharmaceutical firm, was first approved for use in France in 1988. Since then, more than 620,000 European women have taken mifepristone in combination with a prostaglandin to terminate pregnancy. The drug has also been approved in the United Kingdom, Sweden, and other countries.

Mifepristone will be distributed in the U.S. by Danco Laboratories, LLC, New York, N.Y.

More detailed information about this product is available on FDA's website at www.fda.gov/cder/drug/infopage/mifepristone/.

# U.S. CENSUS BUREAU ON
# HEALTH INSURANCE COVERAGE
## September 28, 2000

*The nation's strong economy helped lead to a drop, during 1999, in the portion of the American population lacking health insurance. The decline, of about 1.7 million people, was the first recorded by the Census Bureau in the annual studies it had conducted since 1987 of health insurance coverage. Analysts said the major reason for the slight improvement appeared to be that more employers were offering health insurance to attract workers in a tight labor market.*

*Despite the decline, some 42.6 million Americans were without health insurance in 1999, and a sharp rise in premiums raised questions about whether the trend could continue. A study by the Kaiser Family Foundation found that employer-based health insurance premiums rose an average of 8.3 percent between 1999 and 2000—about three times the overall rate of inflation and twice the rate of the previous year's increase. Higher costs for prescription drugs accounted for most of the increase, the study said.*

### The Uninsured

*Ever since Democratic presidential candidate Michael Dukakis first made it a major political issue in 1988, the number of Americans lacking health insurance had been seen by many observers as a key indicator of the nation's social welfare. Dukakis used figures from the Census Bureau's first study of the issue, which showed that 31 million Americans were not covered by health insurance in 1987; that figure represented 12.9 percent of the population.*

*The increased attention paid to the inability of many Americans to obtain health insurance did not, in itself, make the situation any better. From 1988 through 1998, the percentage of Americans lacking health insurance rose every year, reaching 14.1 percent in 1991, 15 percent in 1992 (at the end of a recession), and 16.3 percent in 1998—representing 44.3 million people. On average, the number of people without health insurance grew by about 1 million a year during the 1987–1998 period.* (Previous reports, Historic Documents of 1999, p. 561)

*The Census Bureau found that the number of uninsured Americans had dropped to 42.6 million in 1999, or 15.5 percent of the total population. The difference was considered to be statistically significant in the bureau's survey of 50,000 households nationwide. "I would never call one year a trend, but the fact that it's never happened since we've been measuring it, including in some pretty strong economic years, makes me consider it a pretty significant finding," Charles Nelson, a bureau analyst told the* Washington Post.

*The most important factor accounting for the increase, Census Bureau officials and independent observers said, was the booming economy. For 1999, the bureau's study said, 62.8 percent of Americans were covered by a health insurance plan at work; that was an increase of 0.8 percent over 1998. Faced with a tight labor market during the late 1990s, employers were using incentives such as health insurance to attract workers.*

*An additional explanation for the drop in the number of uninsured was the introduction of the Children's Health Insurance Program, funded by the federal and state governments to help low-income families with children. Enacted by Congress in 1997, the program took effect in most states only in 1999. According to the Census Bureau study, the number of children eighteen and younger not covered by health insurance dropped from 11.1 million (15.4 percent of the total) in 1998 to 10 million (13.9 percent of the total) in 1999.*

*As could be expected, most of the 42.6 million Americans not covered by health insurance were at the lower end of the economic spectrum. Nearly one-quarter (24.1 percent) of people in households with incomes of less than $25,000 lacked health insurance. The study showed that Medicaid did not provide health insurance for all poor people: 12.9 million poor people were covered under Medicaid but 10.4 million were not (most of them were nonelderly low-income adults).*

*As in the past, the study found that having a job did not guarantee access to health insurance: about three-fourths of the uninsured were in families where at least one person was working full time. Ron Pollack, executive director of the consumer advocacy group Families USA, noted that the enactment of welfare reform during the late 1990s had contributed to the increased number of low-income people without health insurance. "Many people lost health coverage when they moved from welfare into entry-level jobs that have no health benefits," he said.* (Welfare reform, Historic Documents of 1999, p. 257)

*About one in three Hispanics lacked health insurance, by far the highest rate of any ethnic group. About one in five blacks and Asian-Pacific Islanders were uninsured, and the rate for non-Hispanic whites was only one in nine.*

*Despite the relatively good news in the report, representatives of groups that advocated health insurance reform said the figures showed that millions of Americans still lacked adequate access to health care. "We still have a pretty significant problem we have to address," David Helms, president of the Academy for Health Services Research and Health Policy told the* Washington Post. *"With this much wealth in our society, to still have 43 million*

*people without basic health insurance coverage is not a reason to celebrate."*
*Helms and others said they worried that the improvement shown in 1999*
*could be reversed quickly if the economy faltered.*

## Rising Costs of Health Insurance

Other reports during the year showed that health insurance was becoming increasingly expensive—raising the question of whether the 1999 drop in the number of uninsured would be repeated. One of the most sobering reports came on September 25 from the Kaiser Family Foundation, which surveyed 3,402 employers nationwide. That survey found that monthly premiums for health insurance rose an average of 8.3 percent between the spring of 1999 and the spring of 2000; the increase for the previous twelve-month period had been 4.8 percent. The increase was even greater, 10.3 percent, in small firms with fewer than 200 workers.

In its study, the foundation said one factor in the increase could have been "catch-up pricing"—a move by health insurers to boost their profits after several years of "intense price competition." Another factor was the rapidly rising cost of prescription drugs, which were covered at least in part by most employer-based health insurance plans. Other studies released during the year showed that prescription drug costs for Americans rose by more than 17 percent in 1999. (Drug prices, p. 131)

News organizations quoted employers, at both large and small firms, as expressing frustration at their rapidly rising health insurance costs. In a survey of employers in the northeast, the Boston Globe said several companies reported health insurance premium increases of 20 to 30 percent in the coming year. The Washington Post said some small firms might stop offering health insurance for their workers if the rate increases continued. The New York Times reported on September 6 that employers who had turned to "managed care" programs (such as health maintenance organizations, or HMOs) during the 1990s in an effort to reduce their costs were now finding that those plans were becoming prohibitively expensive as well. Many firms were switching from HMOs to preferred-provider organizations (PPOs—networks of doctors and hospitals) because their administrative costs were lower, the Times reported.

Both chambers of Congress passed legislation giving consumers some new rights in dealing with their "managed care" health insurers, principally HMOs. The chambers took sharply different approaches to the issue, with the House bill allowing patients to sue their health plans for damages in state courts—a step the Senate refused to take. When the two chambers were unable to resolve their differences, the issue died in a conference committee. The House also passed narrowly focused legislation encouraging health insurance companies to provide prescription drug coverage to senior citizens, but the Senate took no action. The issue of financing prescription drugs for seniors became a major issue in the presidential campaign. Democratic candidate Al Gore proposed adding prescription drug coverage to the Medicare program, while Republican George W. Bush favored allowing private insurance companies to handle such insurance.

*Following are excerpts from the report, "Health Insurance Cover-*
*age: 1999," issued September 28, 2000, by the U.S. Bureau of the*
*Census. The document was obtained from the Internet at http://*
*www.census.gov/hhes/www/hlthin99.html.*

Reversing a 12-year trend, the share of the population without health insurance declined in 1999, the first decline since 1987 when comparable health
insurance statistics were first available. In 1999, 15.5 percent of the population
were without health insurance coverage during the entire year, down from
16.3 percent in 1998. From 1987 to 1998, this rate either increased or was unchanged from one year to the next. Similarly, the number of people without
health insurance coverage declined for the first time in 1999, to 42.6 million
people, down 1.7 million from the previous year.

The estimates in this report are based on the March 2000 Current Population Survey (CPS), conducted by the U.S. Census Bureau. Respondents provide answers to the survey questions to the best of their ability, but as with all
surveys, the estimates may differ from the actual values.

Other highlights:

- The number and percent of people covered by employment-based health
  insurance rose significantly in 1999, driving the overall increase in
  health insurance coverage.
- Mirroring what happened for the total population, the proportion of uninsured children declined in 1999—to 13.9 percent of children—the
  lowest rate since 1995. The number of uninsured children declined to
  10.0 million.
- Although medicaid insured 12.9 million poor people, 10.4 million poor
  people still had no health insurance in 1999, representing about one-third
  of the poor (32.4 percent), which was not significantly different from 1998.
- Compared with the previous year, health insurance coverage rates increased for those with household incomes of less than $50,000, but were
  unchanged for those with $50,000 and higher household incomes.
- Hispanics (66.6 percent) were less likely than White non-Hispanics
  (89.0 percent) to be covered by health insurance. The coverage rate for
  Blacks in 1999 (78.8 percent) did not differ statistically from the coverage rate for Asians and Pacific Islanders (79.2 percent).
- American Indians and Alaska Natives were less likely to have health
  insurance than other racial groups, based on a 3-year average (1997–
  1999)—72.9 percent, compared with 78.4 percent of Blacks, 79.1 percent
  of Asians and Pacific Islanders, and 88.4 percent of White non-Hispanics.
  However, they were more likely to have insurance than were Hispanics
  (65.7 percent).
- Among the entire population 18 to 64 years old, workers (both full- and
  part-time) were more likely to have health insurance (82.6 percent) than
  nonworkers (73.5 percent), but among the poor, workers were less likely

to be covered. Just over one-half, 52.5 percent, of poor workers were insured in 1999, while the rate for poor nonworkers in 1999 was 59.2 percent.

- The foreign-born population was less likely than the native population to be insured—66.6 percent compared with 86.5 percent in 1999.
- Young adults (18 to 24 years old) were less likely than other age groups to have health insurance coverage—71.0 percent in 1999 compared with 82.9 percent of those 25 to 64 and, reflecting widespread medicare coverage, 98.7 percent of those 65 years and over.

**Employment-based insurance, the leading source of health insurance coverage, drove the increase in insurance coverage rates.**

Most people (62.8 percent) were covered by a health insurance plan related to employment for some or all of 1999, an increase of 0.8 percentage points over the previous year. The increase in private health insurance coverage reflects the increase in employment-based insurance; it also increased 0.8 percentage points to 71.0 percent in 1999.

The government also provides health insurance coverage, but there was no change between 1998 and 1999 in the overall government- provided health insurance coverage rate. Among the entire population, 24.1 percent had government insurance, including medicare (13.2 percent), medicaid (10.2 percent), and military health care (3.1 percent). Many people carried coverage from more than one plan during the year; for example, 7.5 percent of people were covered by both private health insurance and medicare.

**The poor and near poor are less likely to have health insurance than the total population.**

Despite the medicaid program, 32.4 percent of the poor (10.4 million people) had no health insurance of any kind during 1999. This percentage— double the rate for the total population—did not change statistically from the previous year. The uninsured poor comprised 24.5 percent of all uninsured people.

Medicaid was the most widespread type of health insurance among the poor, with 39.9 percent (12.9 million) of those in poverty covered by medicaid for some or all of 1999. This percentage did not change statistically from the previous year.

Among the near poor (those with a family income greater than the poverty level but less than 125 percent of the poverty level), 25.7 percent (3.1 million people) lacked health insurance in 1999. This percentage decreased significantly from 1998, however, when 29.9 percent of the near poor lacked health insurance. The percentage of the near poor who had private health insurance rose from 38.3 percent in 1998 to 41.7 percent in 1999. Government health insurance coverage among the near poor also increased, from 42.3 percent in 1998 to 43.9 percent in 1999.

**Key demographic factors affect health insurance coverage.**

*Age*—People 18 to 24 years old were less likely than other age groups to have health insurance coverage during 1999. Their coverage rate (71.0 percent) rose by 1.0 percentage point from 1998. Because of medicare, most people 65 years and over (98.7 percent) had health insurance in 1999. For other age groups, health insurance coverage ranged from 76.8 percent to 86.2 percent.

Among the poor, adults ages 18 to 64 had a markedly lower health insurance coverage rate (55.8 percent) in 1999 than either children (76.7 percent) or the elderly (96.6 percent).

*Race and Hispanic origin*—The uninsured rate declined significantly in 1999 for Hispanics and White non-Hispanics—for Hispanics, from 35.3 percent to 33.4 percent and for White non-Hispanics, from 11.9 percent to 11.0 percent. Among Blacks, the uninsured rate dropped by 1 percentage point from 22.2 percent in 1998 to 21.2 percent in 1999. The uninsured rate among Asians and Pacific Islanders did not change significantly from 1998—20.8 percent of Asians and Pacific Islanders were without health coverage in 1999.

The Current Population Survey, the source of these data, samples 50,000 households nationwide and is not large enough to produce reliable annual estimates for American Indians and Alaska Natives. . . .

*Nativity*—In 1999, the proportion of the foreign-born population without health insurance (33.4 percent) was more than double that of the native population (13.5 percent). Among the foreign born, noncitizens were more than twice as likely as naturalized citizens to lack coverage—42.6 percent compared with 17.9 percent.

Health insurance coverage rates among the foreign born increase with length of residence and citizenship. For example, while about half (53.0 percent) of non-citizen immigrants living in the United States less than 10 years had health insurance coverage, the rate rises to 91.1 percent for non-citizen immigrants living in the U.S. for 40 years or more. Among naturalized citizens, the comparable rates were 69.5 percent and 96.4 percent.

*Educational attainment*—Among adults, the likelihood of being insured increased as the level of education rose. Among those who were poor in 1999, there were no differences in health insurance coverage rates across the education groups.

**Economic status affects health insurance coverage.**

*Income*—The likelihood of being covered by health insurance rises with income. Among households with annual incomes of less than $25,000, the percentage with health insurance was 75.9 percent; the level rises to 91.7 percent for those with incomes of $75,000 or more.

Compared with the previous year, coverage rates increased for those with household incomes of less than $50,000, but were unchanged for those with $50,000 or higher household incomes. For those with household incomes of less than $25,000, the coverage rate increased 1.1 percentage points to 75.9 percent, whereas for those with incomes between $25,000 and $50,000, it increased 0.6 percentage points to 81.9 percent in 1999.

*Work experience*—Of those 18 to 64 years old in 1999, full-time workers were more likely to be covered by health insurance (83.6 percent) than part-time workers (77.6 percent), and part-time workers were more likely to be insured than nonworkers (73.8 percent). However, among the poor, nonworkers (59.2 percent) were more likely to be insured than workers (52.5 percent).

Poor full-time workers did not fare better than poor part-time workers—52.5 percent and 52.7 percent, respectively.

*Firm size*—Of the 139.2 million workers in the United States (18–64 years old), 55.5 percent had employment-based health insurance policies in their own name. The proportion generally increased with the size of the employing firm—30.6 percent of workers employed by firms with fewer than 25 employees and 68.3 percent for workers employed by firms with 1000 or more employees, for example. (These estimates do not reflect the fact that some workers were covered by another family member's employment-based policy).

**The uninsured rate for children decreased between 1998 and 1999.**

The percentage of children (people under 18 years old) without health insurance in the United States dropped from 15.4 percent in 1998 to 13.9 percent in 1999. The increase in employment-based insurance accounted for most of the change; no change occurred in government health insurance coverage.

Among poor children, the uninsured rate also fell, from 25.2 percent in 1998 to 23.3 percent in 1999. An increase in government health insurance coverage accounted for most of this drop; no change occurred in employment-based coverage. Poor children made up 28.2 percent of all uninsured children in 1999.

Among near-poor children (children in families with incomes greater than the poverty level but less than 125 percent of the poverty level), the proportion without health insurance fell substantially from 27.2 percent in 1998 to 19.7 percent in 1999. Increases in both government health insurance coverage (from 40.6 percent to 43.8 percent) and private health insurance coverage (from 38.3 percent to 44.8 percent) accounted for the change. The State Children's Health Insurance Program, which expanded access to health coverage for low-income children under age 19, likely contributed substantially to the increase in government coverage.

**Children's characteristics affect their likelihood of health insurance coverage.**

- Children 12 to 17 years of age were more likely to be uninsured than those under 12—14.4 percent compared with 13.6 percent.
- For Hispanic children and for White non-Hispanic children, the uninsured rate declined significantly in 1999—from 30.0 percent to 27.2 percent for Hispanic children and from10.6 percent to 8.9 percent for White non-Hispanic children. For Black children, the uninsured rate declined from 19.7 percent to 17.9 percent, whereas 16.7 percent of Asian and Pacific Islander children were uninsured in 1999, statistically unchanged from 1998.
- While most children (68.9 percent) were covered by an employment-based or privately purchased health insurance plan in 1999, one in five (20.0 percent) were covered by medicaid.
- Black children had a higher rate of medicaid coverage in1999 than children of any other racial or ethnic group—36.2 percent, compared with 30.8 percent of Hispanic children, 16.7 percent of Asian and Pacific Islander children, and 13.2 percent of White non-Hispanic children.

- Children living in single-parent families in 1999 were less likely to be in-sured than children living in married-couple families—81.8 percent com-pared to 88.4 percent.

**Some states had higher uninsured rates than others.**

The proportion of people without health insurance ranged from 8.8 percent in Minnesota to 24.1 percent in Texas, based on 3-year averages for 1997, 1998, and 1999. The Census Bureau does not recommend that these esti-mates be used to rank the states, however. For example, the uninsured rate for Texas was not statistically different from that in Arizona, while the rate for Minnesota was not statistically different from Rhode Island or Hawaii. . . .

Comparisons of 2-year moving averages (1997–1998 and 1998–1999) show that the proportion of people without coverage fell in 15 states: Arizona, Arkansas, California, Connecticut, Iowa, Maine, Massachusetts, Missis-sippi, Missouri, New Jersey, New York, North Dakota, Rhode Island, Ten-nessee, and Texas. Meanwhile, the proportion of people without coverage rose in eight states: Hawaii, Illinois, Louisiana, Nevada, New Mexico, Ver-mont, Washington, and Wisconsin.

## Accuracy of the Estimates

Statistics from surveys are subject to sampling and nonsampling error. All comparisons presented in this report take sampling error into account and meet the Census Bureau's standards for statistical significance. Nonsampling errors in surveys may be attributed to a variety of sources, such as how the survey was designed, how respondents interpret questions, how able and will-ing respondents are to provide correct answers, and how accurately answers are coded and classified. The Census Bureau employs quality control proce-dures throughout the production process including the overall design of sur-veys, the wording of questions, review of the work of interviewers and coders, and statistical review of reports.

The Current Population Survey employs ratio estimation, whereby sample estimates are adjusted to independent estimates of the national population by age, race, sex, and Hispanic origin. This weighting partially corrects for bias due to undercoverage, but how it affects different variables in the survey is not precisely known. Moreover, biases may also be present when people who are missed in the survey differ from those interviewed in ways other than the cate-gories used in weighting (age, race, sex, and Hispanic origin). All of these con-siderations affect comparisons across different surveys or data sources. . . .

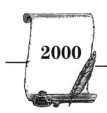

# October

# PRESIDENTIAL AND VICE PRESIDENTIAL DEBATES
## October 3, 5, 11, and 17, 2000

*Three debates between presidential nominees Al Gore, Democratic vice president, and George W. Bush, Republican governor of Texas, may have clarified policy and personality differences between the two men in the minds of some voters. Overall, Bush probably came out the "winner" by demonstrating that he had more skill as a debater and more facility with the issues than many had believed. By contrast, Gore, a master of policy detail and a skilled debater, may have damaged himself by being overly aggressive, particularly in the first meeting between the two men. According to most public opinion polls, the presidential tickets were in a statistical dead heat when the debates began October 3, 2000. When they ended on October 17, the polls showed that the two tickets were still statistically even, although Bush seemed to have gained some momentum in the polls.*

*The vice presidential nominees, Richard B. Cheney, the former secretary of defense under President George Bush, and Joseph I. Lieberman, the Democratic senator from Connecticut, met in a debate October 5 that was notable for its civility but that broke no new ground.*

*The three nationally televised presidential debates highlighted clear differences between Bush and Gore on both substance and approach. Bush repeatedly tried to paint Gore as a big spender beholden to special interests in Washington and mired in the partisan wrangling that infected the nation's capital. Gore repeatedly attacked Bush as favoring the wealthy and big business at the expense of the poor and vulnerable.*

*The real debate, however, lay not so much in the positions the two men set forward as in the images that each sought to project. Bush, who had comparatively little governing experience and virtually no foreign policy experience, took every opportunity to show that he was in command of the wide range of domestic and foreign policy issues that a president of the United States might encounter. Gore, noted for his encyclopedic knowledge but also for his tendency to show off how much he knew, tried to present a less patronizing and aggressive image. Neither man was totally successful. Bush often retreated to policy generalities and statements of intent, such as as-*

*serting that he would be a good leader. Gore rarely was able to convey a totally relaxed demeanor. Particularly in the first debate, his exasperated sighs as Bush answered questions, his quickness to jump in with an answer, and his tendency to talk over his time allotment all made Gore appear overbearing.*

*In the second debate both Bush and Gore were more restrained in their approaches, often noting points where they were in agreement. At several points the debate moderator, Jim Lehrer of the PBS* News Hour, *had to ask them to point out how their policy on a particular issue differed from one or another. By the third debate, which took the form of a town hall meeting, both Gore and Bush seemed to have hit their stride, engaging in spirited, often pointed exchanges in response to questions from members of the audience.*

### Establishing the Debate Formats

*The private, bipartisan Commission on Presidential Debates, which had overseen every presidential election since 1988, organized the debates. As finally agreed by the commission and the two campaigns, each of the three presidential debates was ninety minutes long and was moderated by Lehrer. The first debate, on October 3 at the University of Massachusetts in Boston, was the most formal of the three, with each candidate standing at a lectern. In the second, on October 11 at Wake Forest University in Winston-Salem, North Carolina, the setting was more informal, with the candidates sitting at a table. The third debate, on October 17 at Washington University in St. Louis, used the town hall format, with the candidates answering questions from the audience. The vice presidential debate, at Centre College in Danville, Kentucky, on October 5, was moderated by Bernard Shaw of CNN; the candidates sat at a semicircular-shaped table.*

*As the fall campaign kicked off, the Bush camp proposed an alternative series of debates that would have included sixty-minute debates on CNN's* Larry King Live *and NBC's* Meet the Press, *hosted by Tim Russert, as well as the commission-sponsored debate scheduled for St. Louis. Bush communications director Karen P. Hughes said the governor thought the more casual atmosphere of the television studios would better serve the public than the "canned and stilted formats that have been the case in past presidential debates." When the Gore forces refused to go along with this proposal, preferring to stick with the commission plan that Gore had agreed to months earlier, the Bush campaign ran a television commercial taunting the vice president as a reluctant campaigner. But when people in Bush's own party suggested that Bush looked like he was trying to avoid the debates, the governor gave in and agreed to the commission debates. The Bush camp continued to object to some aspects of the plan however. They argued, for example, that the Boston venue gave an unfair advantage to Gore because the university campus was located near the John F. Kennedy Library.*

*Third-party candidates Ralph Nader of the Green Party and Pat Buchanan of the Reform Party sought to participate in the debates, but the commission held firm to its decision, made earlier in the year, to allow participation by only those candidates who had reached at least 15 percent in the national opinion polls. Under that ruling, neither Nader nor Buchanan qualified. Nader was subsequently given a hard-to-come-by ticket to the Boston debate by one of his supporters, but he was turned away at the door by commission officials. "It's already been decided that whether or not you have a ticket, you are not welcome in the debate," a commission official told the consumer advocate. Nader threatened to file a civil lawsuit against the commission. "I just think I have to do that because of possible future misbehavior by the debate commission," Nader told the* New York Times. *"They are obviously drunk with their own power." (Nader's candidacy, p. 895)*

## Taxes and Texas

*Although the debates were remarkably free of personal attacks, both Bush and Gore attacked the other's policy proposals. As he had at the Democratic National Convention, Gore said Bush's tax cut plan favored the wealthiest 1 percent of taxpayers, that his prescription drug benefit plan would leave many of the elderly uncovered, and that his Social Security reform proposals offered little assurance that benefits would actually be available upon retirement. Accusing Gore of using "fuzzy math" and "running on Medi-scare," Bush charged that Gore's smaller, targeted tax plan was overly complicated and would provide no tax relief at all to 50 million taxpayers. Bush also said Gore would be unable to foster the kind of bipartisanship that would be needed to enact Medicare and Social Security reforms.*

*The two men also differed significantly in their approach to those reforms. In very broad terms, Bush preferred programs that relied on the competition of the marketplace to resolve a problem, such as providing education vouchers, and opposed federal programs that would place restrictions on the free operation of markets. He said, for example, that he was opposed to government-imposed price controls on prescription drugs and to proposed federal legislation that would allow patients to sue their health maintenance organizations under some circumstances. Gore did not endorse outright price controls on drugs, but said he favored streamlining the approval of generic drugs to spur lower prices through competition.*

*On other domestic issues, both men said they opposed racial profiling and gay marriage, although Gore seemed more willing to recognize some sort of civil union for gay couples. Gore also endorsed hate crimes legislation pending in Congress that would extend to acts against gays and charged Bush with helping to keep similar legislation from coming to the floor of the Texas legislature. The two also had differing approaches on environmental problems. For example, Bush supported and Gore opposed opening the Arctic National Wildlife Refuge in Alaska to drilling. Gore believed that the causes of global warming were well understood and should be addressed; Bush said it was a serious issue, but that there was still doubt in some quarters about the causes and that decisions about how to resolve the problem should not be made until all the facts were known.*

*On foreign policy issues, the two candidates were clearest in their differing approaches to military engagements overseas. Bush said he would restrict such engagements to matters where the nation's security interests were clearly threatened and would not support what he called "nation-building" exercises. Gore said he would be judicious in committing troops but indicated that his view of national security interests was broader than Bush's. The two also disagreed on the current state of military readiness and on the extent of a missile defense system. Gore favored a limited land-based defense, while Bush favored a global deployment on land and sea and in space.*

### *Vice Presidential Debate*

*The vice presidential debate between Cheney and Lieberman might have served as a model for a class in civil discussion. The two men were cordial and polite even when they disagreed, and both kept their answers focused on the issues under discussion rather than questioning the character or credibility of the opposing ticket. Several viewers, noting the contrast between the vice presidential debate and the more combative exchanges between Bush and Gore in the first presidential debate two days earlier, said they wished that Cheney and Lieberman were the presidential nominees. "They were seasoned pros," one said, "above all the mudslinging."*

> *Following are excerpts from the first presidential debate, held October 3, 2000, at the University of Massachusetts in Boston, between Vice President Al Gore and Texas governor George W. Bush; the vice presidential debate, held October 5, 2000, at Center College in Danville, Kentucky, between Connecticut senator Joseph I. Lieberman and former defense secretary Richard B. Cheney; the second presidential debate, held October 11, 2000, at Wake Forest University in Winston-Salem, North Carolina; and the third presidential debate, held October 17, 2000, at Washington University in St. Louis. The documents were obtained from the Internet at http://www.debates.org/transcripts/textfiles/ CPD_Debate_1_Final_Transcript_(English).txt, http://www .debates.org/transcripts/textfiles/CPD_Debate_2_Final_ Transcript_(English).txt, http://www.debates.org/transcripts/ textfiles/CPD_Debate_3_Final_Transcript_(English).txt, and http://www.debates.org/transcripts/textfiles/CPD_Debate_4_ Final_Transcript_(English).txt.*

# FIRST PRESIDENTIAL DEBATE

**Moderator:** . . . Vice President Gore, you have questioned whether Governor Bush has the experience to be President of the United States. What exactly do you mean?

**Gore:** . . . I have actually not questioned Governor Bush's experience. I have questioned his proposals. And here is why. I think this is a very important moment for our country. We have achieved extraordinary prosperity. And in this election, America has to make an important choice. Will we use our prosperity to enrich not just the few, but all of our families? I believe we have to make the right and responsible choices.

If I'm entrusted with the presidency, here are the choices that I will make. I will balance the budget every year. I will pay down the national debt. I will put Medicare and Social Security in a lockbox and protect them. And I will cut taxes for middle-class families. I believe it's important to resist the temptation to squander our surplus. If we make the right choices, we can have a prosperity that endures and enriches all of our people.

If I'm entrusted with the presidency, I will help parents and strengthen families because, you know, if we have prosperity that grows and grows, we still won't be successful unless we strengthen families by, for example, ensuring that children can always go to schools that are safe. By giving parents the tools to protect their children against cultural pollution. I will make sure that we invest in our country and our families. And I mean investing in education, health care, the environment, and middle-class tax cuts and retirement security. That is my agenda and that is why I think that it's not just a question of experience.

**Moderator:** Governor Bush, one minute rebuttal.

**Bush:** Well, we do come from different places. I come from being a West Texan. The governor is the chief executive officer. We know how to set agendas as a governor. I think you'll find the difference reflected in our budgets. I want to take one-half of the surplus and dedicate it to Social Security. One-quarter of the surplus for important projects, and I want to send one-quarter of the surplus back to the people who pay the bills.

I want everybody who pays taxes to have their tax rates cut. And that stands in contrast to my worthy opponent's plan, which will increase the size of government dramatically. His plan is three times larger than President Clinton's proposed plan eight years ago. It is a plan that will have 200 new programs—expanded programs and creates 20,000 new bureaucrats. It empowers Washington. My vision is to empower Americans to be able to make decisions for themselves in their own lives.

**Moderator:** So I take it by your answer, then, Mr. Vice President, in an interview recently with the "New York Times" when you said that you questioned whether or not Governor Bush has experience enough to be president, you were talking about strictly policy differences.

**Gore:** Yes, Jim. I said that his tax cut plan, for example, raises the question of whether it's the right choice for the country. And let me give you an example of what I mean. Under Governor Bush's tax cut proposal, he would spend more money on tax cuts for the wealthiest 1% than all of the new spending that he proposes for education, health care, prescription drug and national defense all combined. Now, I think those are the wrong priorities.

Now, under my proposal, for every dollar that I propose in spending for things like education and health care, I will put another dollar into middle class tax cuts. And for every dollar that I spend in those two categories, I'll put $2 toward paying down the national debt. I think it's very important to keep the debt going down and completely eliminate it. And I also think it's very important to go to the next stage of welfare reform.

Our country has cut the welfare rolls in half. I fought hard from my days in the Senate and as vice president to cut the welfare rolls and we've moved millions of people in America into good jobs. But it's now time for the next stage of welfare reform, and include fathers and not only mothers. . . .

Let me just say that obviously tonight we're going to hear some phony numbers about what I think and what we ought to do. People need to know that over the next ten years it is going to be $25 trillion of revenue that comes into our treasury and we anticipate spending $21 trillion. And my plan say why don't we pass 1.3 trillion of that back to the people who pay the bills? Surely we can afford 5% of the $25 trillion that are coming into the treasury to the hard working people that pay the bills. There is a difference of opinion. My opponent thinks the government—the surplus is the government's money. That's not what I think. I think it's the hard-working people of America's money and I want to share some of that money with you so you have more money to build and save and dream for your families. It's a difference of opinion. It's a difference between government making decisions for you and you getting more of your money to make decisions for yourself.

**Moderator:** Let me just follow up one quick question. When you hear Vice President Gore question your experience, do you read it the same way, that he's talking about policy differences only?

**Bush:** Yes. I take him for his word. Look, I fully recognize I'm not of Washington. I'm from Texas. And he's got a lot of experience, but so do I. And I've been the chief executive officer of the second biggest state in the union. I have a proud record of working with both Republicans and Democrats, which is what our nation needs. Somebody that can come to Washington and say let's forget all the finger pointing and get positive things done on Medicare, prescription drugs, Social Security, and so I take him for his word.

**Gore:** Jim, if I could just respond. I know that. The governor used the phrase phony numbers, but if you look at the plan and add the numbers up, these numbers are correct. He spends more money for tax cuts for the wealthiest 1% than all of his new spending proposals for health care, prescription drug, education and national defense all combined. I agree that the surplus is the American people's money, it's your money. That's why I don't think we should give nearly half of it to the wealthiest 1%, because the other 99% have had an awful lot to do with building the surplus in our prosperity.

**Moderator:** Three-and-a-half minutes is up. New question. Governor Bush, you have a question. This is a companion question to the question I asked Vice President Gore. You have questioned whether Vice President Gore has demonstrated the leadership qualities necessary to be President of the United States. What do you mean by that?

**Bush:** Actually what I've said, Jim. I've said that eight years ago they campaigned on prescription drugs for seniors. And four years ago they campaigned on getting prescription drugs for seniors. And now they're campaigning on getting prescription drugs for seniors. It seems like they can't get it done. Now, they may blame other folks, but it's time to get somebody in Washington who is going to work with both Republicans and Democrats to get some positive things done when it comes to our seniors. And so what I've said is that there's been some missed opportunities.

They've had a chance. They've had a chance to form consensus. I've go a plan on Medicare, for example, that's a two-stage plan that says we'll have immediate help for seniors and what I call immediately Helping Hand, a $48 billion program. But I also want to say to seniors, if you're happy with Medicare the way it is, fine, you can stay in the program. But we're going to give you additional choices like they give federal employees in the federal employee health plan. They have a variety of choices to choose, so should seniors. And my point has been, as opposed to politicizing an issue like Medicare, in other words, holding it up hoping somebody bites it and try to clobber them over the head for political purposes, this year it's time to get it done once and for all. That's what I've been critical about the administration for.

Same with Social Security. I think there was a good opportunity to bring Republicans and Democrats together to reform the Social Security system so seniors will never go without. Those on Social Security today will have their promise made, but also to give younger workers the option at their choice of being able to manage some of their own money in the private sector to make sure there's a Social Security system around tomorrow. There are a lot of young workers at our rallies we go to that when they hear I'll trust them at their option to be able to manage, under certain guidelines, some of their own money to get a better rate of return so that they'll have a retirement plan in the future, they begin to nod their heads and they want a different attitude in Washington.

**Moderator:** One minute rebuttal.

**Gore:** Well, Jim, under my plan all seniors will get prescription drugs under Medicare. The governor has described Medicare as a government HMO. It's not, and let me explain the difference. Under the Medicare prescription drug proposal I'm making, here is how it works, you go to your own doctor. Your doctor chooses your prescription. No HMO or insurance company can take those choices away from you. Then you go to your own pharmacy. You fill the prescription and Medicare pays half the cost. If you're in a very poor family or if you have very high costs, Medicare will pay all the costs, a $25 premium, and much better benefits than you can possibly find in the private sector. Now here is the contrast. 95% of all seniors would get no help whatsoever under my opponent's plan for the first four or five years. Now, one thing I don't understand, Jim, is why is it that the wealthiest 1% get their tax cuts the first year, but 95% of seniors have to wait four to five years before they get a single penny?

**Bush:** I guess my answer to that is the man is running on Medi-scare. Trying to frighten people into the voting booth. It's not what I think and it's not my intentions and not my plan. I want all seniors to have prescription drugs in Medicare. We need to reform Medicare. This administration has failed to do it. Seniors will have not only a Medicare plan where the poor seniors will have prescription drugs paid for, but there will be a variety of options. . . .

You've had your chance, Vice President, you've been there for eight years and nothing has been done. My point is, is that my plan not only trusts seniors with options, my plan sets aside $3.4 trillion for Medicare over the next ten years. My plan also says it requires a new approach in Washington, D.C. It's going to require somebody who can work across the partisan divide. . . .

**Moderator:** Let me ask you both this and we'll move on on the subject. As a practical matter, both of you want to bring prescription drugs to seniors, correct? . . .

**Gore:** The difference is I want to bring it to 100% and he wants to bring it to 5%.

**Bush:** That's totally false for him to stand up here and say that. Let me make sure the seniors hear me loud and clear. They have had their chance to get something done. I'm going to work with Democrats and Republicans to reform the system. All seniors will be covered, all seniors will have their prescription drugs paid for, and in the meantime, we'll have a plan to help poor seniors and in the meantime it could be one year or two years. GORE: Let me call your attention to the key word there. He said all poor seniors.

**Bush:** Wait a minute. All seniors are covered under prescription drugs in my plan.

**Gore:** In the first year?

**Bush:** If we can get it done in the first year, you bet.

**Gore:** It's a two-phase plan. For the first four years—it takes a year to pass it and for the first four years only the poor are covered. Middle class seniors like George McKinney and his wife are not covered for four to five years. . . .

**Moderator:** New question, new subject. Governor Bush. If elected president, would you try to overturn the FDA's approval last week of the abortion pill RU-486?

**Bush:** I don't think a president can do that. I was disappointed in the ruling because I think abortions ought to be more rare in America, and I'm worried that that pill will create more abortions and cause more people to have abortions. This is a very important topic and it's a very sensitive topic, because a lot of good people disagree on the issue. I think what the next president ought to do is to promote a culture of life in America. Life of the elderly and life of those women all across the country. Life of the unborn.

As a matter of fact, I think a noble goal for this country is that every child, born or unborn, need to be protected by law and welcomed to life. I know we need to change a lot of minds before we get there in America. What I do believe is that we can find good, common ground on issues of parental consent or parental notification. I know we need to ban partial birth abortions. This is a place where my opponent and I have strong disagreement. I believe banning partial birth abortions would be a positive step to reducing the number of abortions in America. . . .

Surely we can find common ground to reduce the number of abortions in America. As to the drug itself, I mentioned I was disappointed. I hope the FDA took its time to make sure that American women will be safe who use this drug. . . .

**Gore:** Well, Jim, the FDA took 12 years, and I do support that decision. They determined it was medically safe for the women who use that drug. This is indeed a very important issue. First of all on the issue of partial birth or so-called late-term abortion, I would sign a law banning that procedure, provided that doctors have the ability to save a woman's life or to act if her health is severely at risk. That's not the main issue.

The main issue is whether or not the *Roe v. Wade* decision is going to be overturned. I support a woman's right to choose. My opponent does not. It is important because the next president is going to appoint three and maybe even four justices of the Supreme Court. And Governor Bush has declared to the anti-choice group that he will appoint justices in the mold of Scalia and Clarence Thomas, who are known for being the most vigorous opponents of a woman's right to choose. Here is the difference. He trusts the government to order a woman to do what it thinks she ought to do. I trust women to make the decisions that affect their lives, their destinies and their bodies. And I think a woman's right to choose ought to be protected and defended. . . .

**Moderator:** On the Supreme Court question. Should a voter assume—you're pro-life.

**Bush:** I am pro-life.

**Moderator:** Should a voter assume that all judicial appointments you make to the supreme court or any other court, federal court, will also be pro-life?

**Bush:** The voters should assume I have no litmus test on that issue or any other issue. Voters will know I'll put competent judges on the bench. People who will strictly interpret the Constitution and not use the bench for writing social policy. That is going to be a big difference between my opponent and me. I believe that the judges ought not to take the place of the legislative branch of government. That they're appointed for life and that they ought to look at the Constitution as sacred. They shouldn't misuse their bench. I don't believe in liberal activist judges. I believe in strict constructionists. Those are the kind of judges I will appoint. . . .

**Moderator:** What kind of appointments should they expect from you?

**Gore:** We both use similar language to reach an exactly opposite outcome. I don't favor a litmus test, but I know that there are ways to assess how a potential justice interprets the Constitution. And in my view, the Constitution ought to be interpreted as a document that grows with our country and our history. And I believe, for example, that there is a right of privacy in the Fourth Amendment. And when the phrase *a strict constructionist* is used and when the names of Scalia and Thomas are used as the benchmarks for who would be appointed, those are code words, and nobody should mistake this, for saying the governor would appoint people who would overturn *Roe v. Wade*. It's very clear to me. I would appoint people that have a philosophy that I think will be quite likely would uphold *Roe v. Wade*.

**Moderator:** Is the vice president right?

**Bush:** It sounds like he's not very right tonight. I just told you the criteria on which I'll appoint judges. I have a record of appointing judges in the State of Texas. That's what a governor gets to do. A governor gets to name Supreme Court judges. He also reads all kinds of things into my tax plan and into my Medicare plan. I want the viewers out there to listen to what I have to say about it.

**Moderator:** Reverse the question. What code phrases should we read by what you said about what kind of people you would appoint?

**Gore:** It would be likely that they would uphold *Roe v. Wade.* I do believe it's wrong to use a litmus test. If you look at the history of a lower court judge's rulings, you can get a pretty good idea of how they'll interpret questions. A lot of questions are first impression, and these questions that have been seen many times come up in a new context and so—but, you know, this is a very important issue. Because a lot of young women in this country take this right for granted and it could be lost. It is on the ballot in this election, make no mistake about it.

**Bush:** I'll tell you what kind of judges he'll put on. He'll put liberal activists justices who will use their bench to subvert the legislature, that's what he'll do.

**Moderator:** New question. How would you go about as president deciding when it was in the national interest to use U.S. force, generally?

**Bush:** Well, if it's in our vital national interest, and that means whether our territory is threatened or people could be harmed, whether or not the alliances are—our defense alliances are threatened, whether or not our friends in the Middle East are threatened. That would be a time to seriously consider the use of force. Secondly, whether or not the mission was clear. Whether or not it was a clear understanding as to what the mission would be. Thirdly, whether or not we were prepared and trained to win. Whether or not our forces were of high morale and high standing and well-equipped. And finally, whether or not there was an exit strategy. I would take the use of force very seriously. I would be guarded in my approach.

I don't think we can be all things to all people in the world. I think we've got to be very careful when we commit our troops. The vice president and I have a disagreement about the use of troops. He believes in nation building. I would be very careful about using our troops as nation builders. I believe the role of the military is to fight and win war and therefore prevent war from happening in the first place. So I would take my responsibility seriously. And it starts with making sure we rebuild our military power. Morale in today's military is too low. We're having trouble meeting recruiting goals. We met the goals this year, but in the previous years we have not met recruiting goals. Some of our troops are not well-equipped. I believe we're overextended in too many places. And therefore I want to rebuild the military power. It starts with a billion dollar pay raise for the men and women who wear the uniform. A billion dollars more than the president recently signed into law. It's to make sure our troops are well-housed and well-equipped. Bonus plans to keep some of our high-skilled folks in the services and a commander in chief that sets the mission to fight and win war and prevent war from happening in the first place.

**Moderator:** Vice President Gore, one minute.

**Gore:** I want to make it clear, our military is the strongest, best-trained, best-equipped, best-led fighting force in the world and in the history of the world. Nobody should have any doubt about that, least of all our adversaries or potential adversaries. If you entrust me with the presidency, I will do whatever is necessary in order to make sure our forces stay the strongest in the world. In fact, in my ten-year budget proposal I've set aside more than twice as much for this purpose as Governor Bush has in his proposal.

Now, I think we should be reluctant to get involved in someplace in a foreign country. But if our national security is at stake, if we have allies, if we've tried every other course, if we're sure military action will succeed, and if the costs are proportionate to the benefits, we should get involved. Now, just because we don't want to get involved everywhere doesn't mean we should back off anywhere it comes up. I disagree with the proposal that maybe only when oil supplies are at stake that our national security is at risk. I think that there are situations like in Bosnia or Kosovo where there's a genocide, where our national security is at stake there.. . .

**Moderator:** New subject. New question. Should the voters of this election, Vice President Gore, see this in the domestic area as a major choice between competing political philosophies?

**Gore:** Oh, absolutely. This is a very important moment in the history of our country. Look, we've got the biggest surpluses in all of American history. The key question that has to be answered in this election is will we use that prosperity wisely in a way that benefits all of our people and doesn't go just to the few. Almost half of all the tax cut benefits, as I said under Governor Bush's plan, go to the wealthiest 1%.

I think we have to make the right and responsible choices. I think we have to invest in education, protecting the environment, health care, a prescription drug benefit that goes to all seniors, not just to the poor, under Medicare, not relying on HMOs and insurance companies. I think that we have to help parents and strengthen families by dealing with the kind of inappropriate entertainment material that families are just heart sick that their children are exposed to. I think we've got to have welfare reform taken to the next stage. I think that we have got to balance the budget every single year, pay down the national debt and, in fact, under my proposal the national debt will be completely eliminated by the year 2012.

I think we need to put Medicare and Social Security in a lockbox. The governor will not put Medicare in a lockbox. I don't think it should be used as a piggy bank for other programs. I think it needs to be moved out of the budget and protected. I'll veto anything that takes money out of Social Security or Medicare for anything other than Social Security or Medicare. Now, the priorities are just very different. I'll give you a couple of examples.

For every new dollar that I propose for spending on health care, Governor Bush spends $3 for a tax cut for the wealthiest 1%. Now, for every dollar that I propose to spend on education, he spends $5 on a tax cut for the wealthiest 1%. Those are very clear differences. . . .

**Bush:** The man is practicing fuzzy math again. There's differences. Under Vice President Gore's plan, he is going to grow the federal government in the largest increase since Lyndon Baines Johnson in 1965. We're talking about a massive government, folks. We're talking about adding to or increasing 200 programs, 20,000 new bureaucrats. Imagine how many IRS agents it is going to take to be able to figure out his targeted tax cut for the middle class that excludes 50 million Americans. There is a huge difference in this campaign. He says he's going to give you tax cuts. 50 million of you won't receive it.

He said in his speech he wants to make sure the right people get tax relief. That's not the role of a president to decide right and wrong. Everybody who pays taxes ought to get tax relief. After my plan is in place, the wealthiest Americans will pay more tax, the poorest of Americans, six million families, won't pay any tax at all. It's a huge difference. A difference between big exploding federal government that wants to think on your behalf and a plan that meets priorities and liberates working people to be able to make decisions on your own. . . .

**Moderator:** . . . Education. Governor Bush. Both of you have promised dramatically to change—to change dramatically public education in this country. Of the public money spent on education, only 6% of that is federal money. You want to change 100% of the public education on 6% of the money, is it possible to change it?

**Bush:** We can make a huge difference by saying if you receive federal money we expect you to show results. . . . Here is the role of the federal government. One is to change Head Start to a reading program. Two is to say if you want to access reading money, you can do so. The goal is for every single child to learn to Read. There must by K-2 diagnostic teaching tools available. We have to consolidate the system to free the schools and encourage innovators. Let them reach out beyond the confines of the current structure to recruit teach-for-the-children type teachers. Four, we're going to say if you receive federal money, measure third, fourth, fifth, sixth, seventh and eighth grade. Show us if they are learning to read, write, add and subtract there will be bonus plans. If not, instead of continuing to subsidize failure, the money will go to—the federal money will go to the parents for public school or charter school or tutorial or Catholic school. What I care about is children. . . .

**Gore:** We agree on a couple of things on education. I strongly support new accountability, so does Governor Bush. I strongly support local control, so does Governor Bush. I'm in favor of testing as a way of measuring performance. Every school and every school district, have every state test the children. I've also proposed a voluntary national test in the fourth grade and eighth grade, and a form of testing the governor has not endorsed. I think that all new teachers ought to be tested, including in the subjects that they teach. We've got to recruit 100,000 new teachers. And I have budgeted for that. We've got to reduce the class size so that the student who walks in has more one-on-one time with the teacher. We ought to have universal pre-school and we ought to make college tuition tax deductible, up to $10,000 a year. . . .

**Moderator:** New question. Are there issues of character that distinguish you from Vice President Gore?

**Bush:** The man loves his wife and I appreciate that a lot. And I love mine. The man loves his family a lot, and I appreciate that, because I love my family. I think the thing that discouraged me about the vice president was uttering those famous words, "No controlling legal authority." I felt like there needed to be a better sense of responsibility of what was going on in the White House. I believe that—I believe they've moved that sign, "The buck stops here" from the Oval Office desk to "The buck stops here" on the Lincoln bedroom. It's not good for the country and it's not right.

We need to have a new look about how we conduct ourselves in office. There's a huge trust. I see it all the time when people come up to me and say, I don't want you to let me down again. And we can do better than the past administration has done. It's time for a fresh start. It's time for a new look. It's time for a fresh start after a season of cynicism. And so I don't know the man well, but I've been disappointed about how he and his administration have conducted the fundraising affairs. You know, going to a Buddhist temple and then claiming it wasn't a fundraiser isn't my view of responsibility.

**Moderator:** Vice President Gore?

**Gore:** I think we ought to attack our country's problems, not attack each other. I want to spend my time making this country even better than it is, not trying to make you out to be a bad person. You may want to focus on scandal. I want to focus on results. As I said a couple of months ago, I stand here as my own man and I want you to see me for who I really am. Tipper and I have been married for 30 years. We became grandparents a year-and-a-half ago. We've got four children. I have devoted 24 years of my life to public service and I've said this before and I'll say it again, if you entrust me with the presidency, I may not be the most exciting politician, but I will work hard for you every day. I will fight for middle-class families and working men and women and I will never let you down.

**Moderator:** So, Governor, what are you saying when you mention the fundraising scandals or the fundraising charges that involve Vice President Gore? What are you saying that the voters should take from that that's relevant to this election?

**Bush:** They ought to factor in it when they go to the voting booth.

**Moderator:** In what way?

**Bush:** I think people need to be held responsible for the actions they take in life. I think that—well, I think that's part of the need for a cultural change. We need to say we each need to be responsible for what we do. People in the highest office of the land must be responsible for decisions they make in life. And that's the way I've conducted myself as Governor of Texas and that's the way I'll conduct myself as President of the United States, should I be fortunate enough to earn your vote.

**Moderator:** Are you saying all this is irrelevant, Vice President Gore?

**Gore:** No. I think the American people should take into account who we are as individuals, what our experience is, what our positions are on the issues and proposals are. I'm asking you to see me for who I really am. I'm offering you my own vision, my own experience, my own proposals. And incidentally, one of them is this. This current campaign financing system has not reflected credit on anybody in either party. And that's one of the reasons I've said before, and I'll pledge here tonight, if I'm president, the very first bill that Joe Lieberman and I will send to the United States Congress is the McCain-Feingold campaign finance reform bill. . . . And I wish Governor Bush would join me this evening in endorsing the McCain-Feingold Campaign Finance Reform Bill.

**Bush:** You know, this man has no credibility on the issue. . . . [W]hat you need to know about me is I will uphold the law, I'm going to have an attorney general that enforces the law. The time for campaign funding reform is after the election. This man has outspent me and the special interests are out-spending me. And I am not going to lay down my arms in the middle of the campaign for somebody who has got no credibility on the issue. . . .

# VICE PRESIDENTIAL DEBATE

**Cheney:** . . . If you look, for example, at our opponent's tax proposal, they discriminate between stay-at-home moms with children that they take care of themselves and those who go to work or who, in fact, have their kids taken care of outside the home. You, in effect, as a stay-at-home mom get no tax advantage under the Gore tax plan. As contrasted with the Bush proposal, which, in fact, provides tax relief for absolutely everybody who pays taxes.

And it's important to understand the things we're trying to change and the things we're trying to address in the course of the campaign and what our agenda is for the future, or plans are for the future, focus very much about giving as much control as we can to individual Americans, be they men or women, be they single or married, as much control as possible over their own lives, especially in the area of taxation. We want to make certain that the American people have the ability to keep more of what they earn and then they can get to decide how to spend it.

The proposal we have from Al Gore, basically, doesn't do that. It in effect lays out some 29 separate tax credits. And if you live your life the way they want you to live your life, if you do, in fact, behave in a certain way, then you qualify for a tax credit, and at that point you get some relief. Bottom line, though, is 50 million American taxpayers out there get no advantages at all out of the Gore tax proposal, whereas under the Bush plan everybody who pays taxes will, in fact, get tax relief. . . .

**Lieberman:** Right. This is an important difference between us, and I want to try to clarify it briefly, if I can. The first thing is that, in fact, the tax relief program that Al Gore and I have proposed, one of those many tax credits for the middle class that Dick just referred to, includes a $500 tax credit for stay-at-home moms just as a way of saying we understand that you are performing a service for our society. We want you to have that tax credit.

Second, the number of 50 million Americans not benefiting from our tax cut program is absolutely wrong. It's an estimate done on an earlier form of our tax cut program and it's just plain wrong. And secondly, although Governor Bush says that his tax cut program, large as it is, gives a tax cut to everybody, as the newspapers indicated earlier this week, the Joint Committee on Taxation, again a nonpartisan group in Congress, has said that 27 million Americans don't get what the Governor said they would in their tax program.

Again, Al Gore and I want to live within our means. We're not going to give it all away in one big tax cut, and certainly not to the top 1% of the public that doesn't need it now. So we're focusing our tax cuts on the middle class in the areas where they tell us they need it. Tax credits for better and more expensive child care. Tax credits for middle-class families that don't have health insurance from their employers. The tax deduction I talked about earlier. Very exciting deduction for up to $10,000 a year in the cost of a college tuition. A $3,000 tax credit for the cost—well, actually for a family member who stays home with a parent or grandparent who is ill.

And a very exciting tax credit program that I hope I'll have a chance to talk about later, Bernie, that encourages savings by people early in life and any time in life by having the federal government match savings for the 75 million Americans who make $100,000 or less, up to $2,000 a year. So very briefly, if a young couple making $50,000 a year saves $1,000, the government will put another $1,000 in that account. By the time they retire, they'll not only have guaranteed Social Security, but more than $200,000 in that retirement fund. . . .

**Moderator:** Your question, Mr. Secretary. You and Governor Bush charge that the Clinton-Gore administration have presided over the deterioration and overextension of America's armed forces. Should U.S. military personnel be deployed as warriors or peacekeepers?

**Cheney:** My preference is to deploy them as warriors. There may be occasion when it's appropriate to use them in a peacekeeping role, but I think that role ought to be limited, I think there ought to be a time limit on it. The reason we have a military is to be able to fight and win wars. And to maintain with sufficient strength so that would-be adversaries are deterred from ever launching a war in the first place. I think that the administration has, in fact, in this area failed in a major responsibility. We've seen a reduction in our forces far beyond anything that was justified by the end of the Cold War. At the same time we've seen a rapid expansion of our commitments around the world as troops have been sent hither and yon. There was testimony just last week by the Joint Chiefs of Staff before the House Armed Services Committee that pointed out a lot of these problems. . . .

So we're overcommitted and we're underresourced. This has had some other unfortunate effects. I saw a letter, for example, the other day from a young captain stationed out at Fort Bragg, a graduate of West Point in '95, getting ready to get out of the service because he's only allowed to train with his troops when fuel is available for the vehicles and only allowed to fire their weapons twice a year. He's concerned that if he had to ever send them into combat that it would mean lives lost. That is a legitimate concern. And this is a very important area, and the fact the U.S. military is worse off today than it was eight years ago. Major responsibility for us in the future, and a high priority for myself and Governor Bush, will be to rebuild the U.S. military and to give them the resources they need to do the job we ask them to do for us and to give them good leadership.

**Moderator:** Senator, you're shaking your head in disagreement.

**Lieberman:** Well, I am, Bernie, and most important I want to assure the American people that the American military is the best-trained, best-equipped, most powerful force in the world. And that Al Gore and I will do whatever it takes to keep them that way. It's not right, and it's not good for our military, to run them down essentially in the midst of a partisan political debate.

The fact is that you've got to judge the military by what the military leaders say. And Secretary Bill Cohen, a good Republican, and General Shelton, chairman of the Joint Chiefs of Staff, both will tell you that the American military is ready to meet any threat we may face in the world today. And the fact is, judging by its results from Desert Storm to the Balkans, Bosnia and Kosovo, to the operations that are still being conducted to keep Saddam Hussein in a box in Iraq, the American military has performed brilliantly.

In fact, this administration has turned around the drop in spending on the military that began in the mid-'80's and went right through the Bush-Cheney administration, and the early years of the Clinton administration, but now that's stopped. In fact, we passed the largest pay increase in a generation for our military. And the interesting fact here, in spite of the rhetoric that my opponent has just spoken, is that the reality is if you look at our projected budgets for the next ten years, Al Gore and I actually commit more than twice as much, $100 billion in additional funding for our military than Governor Bush does. And their budget allows nothing additional for acquisition of new weapons systems. That's something that . . . all the . . . chiefs of the services will not be happy about because they need the new equipment, the new systems that Al Gore and I are committed to giving them.

**Cheney:** Bernie, this is a special interest of mine. I would like a chance to elaborate further, if I might. The facts are dramatically different. I'm not attacking the military, Joe. I have enormous regard for the men and women of the U.S. military. I had the great privilege of working with them for the four years I was Secretary of Defense. No one has a higher regard than I do for them. But it's irresponsible to suggest that we should not have this debate in a presidential campaign, that we should somehow ignore what is a major, major concern. And if you have friends or relatives serving in the U.S. military, you know there's a problem.

If you look at the data that's available, 40% of our Army helicopters that are not combat ready. The combat readiness level in the Air Force that's dropped from 85% to 65%. Significant problems of retention. The important thing for us to remember is that we're a democracy and we're defended by volunteers. Everybody out there tonight wearing the uniform standing on guard to protect the United States is there because they volunteered to put on a uniform. And when we don't give them the spare parts they need to maintain their equipment, when we don't give our pilots the flying hours they need to maintain their proficiency, when we don't give them the kind of leadership that spells out what their mission is and lets them know why they're there and what they're doing, why they're putting their lives at risk, then we undermine that morale. That is an extraordinarily valuable trust.

There is no more important responsibility for a President of the United States than his role as Commander in Chief. The obligation that he undertakes on behalf of all of us to decide when to send our young men and women to war. When we send them without the right kind of training, when we send them poorly equipped or with equipment that's old and broken down, we put their lives at risk. We will suffer more casualties in the next conflict if we don't look to those basic fundamental problems now. And with all due respect, Joe, this administration has a bad track record in this regard, and it's available for anybody who wants to look at the record and wants to talk to our men and women in uniform, and wants to spend time with the members of the Joint Chiefs, wants to look at readiness levels and other—other indicators. Final point, the issue of procurement is very important because we're running now off the buildup of the investment we made during the Reagan years. As that equipment gets old, it has to be replaced. We've taken money out of the procurement budget to support other ventures. We have not been investing in the future of the U.S. military.

**Lieberman:** Bernie, I think it's very important to respond to this. Yes, of course it's an important debate to have as part of this campaign, but I don't want either the military to feel uneasy or the American people to feel insecure. And what I'm saying now I'm basing on service on the Senate Armed Services Committee talking to exactly the people Dick Cheney has mentioned, the Secretary of Defense, the Chiefs of Staff.

I've visited our fighting forces around the world. And I'm telling you that we are ready to meet any contingency that might arise. The good news here, and the interesting news, is that we have met our recruitment targets in each of the services this year. In fact, in the areas where our opponents have said we are overextended, such as the Balkans, the soldiers there have a higher rate of re-enlistment than anywhere else in the service because they feel a sense of purpose, a sense of mission. In fact, this administration has begun to transform the American military to take it away from being a Cold War force to prepare it to meet the threats of the new generation of tomorrow, of weapons of mass destruction, of ballistic missiles, of terrorism, even of cyber warfare. And the fact is that Governor Bush recommended in his major policy statement on the military earlier this year that we skip the next generation of military equipment; helicopters, submarines, tactical air fighters, all the rest. That would really cripple our readiness. Exactly the readiness that Dick Cheney is talking about.

Al Gore and I are committed to continuing this acquisition program, transforming the military. There's fewer people in uniform today, but person-to-person, person-by-person, unit-by-unit, this is the most powerful and effective military, not only in the world today, but in the history of the world. And again, Al Gore and I will do whatever is necessary to keep it that way.

**Moderator:** Senator Lieberman, this question to you. Once again in the Middle East, peace talks on the one hand, deadly confrontations on the other, and the flashpoint, Jerusalem, and then there's Syria. Is United States policy what it should be?

**Lieberman:** Yes, it is. It has truly pained me in the last week, Bernie, to watch the unrest and the death occurring in the Middle East between the Israelis and the Palestinians. So much work has been done by the people there with the support of this administration. So much progress has been made in the original Oslo agreements between the Israelis and the Palestinians, adopted in 1993, in the peace between Israel and Jordan thereafter. And America has a national strategic interest and a principled interest in peace in the Middle East, and Al Gore has played a critical role in advancing that process over the last eight years.

What pains me as I watched the unrest in recent days between the Israelis and the Palestinians is that these two peoples have come in some senses, generations forward, centuries forward, in the last seven years. They are so close to a final peace agreement, I hope and pray that the death and unrest in the last week will not create the kinds of scars that make it hard for them to go back to the peace table with American assistance and achieve what I'm convinced the great majority of the Israeli and Palestinian people want, and these people throughout the Middle East, which is peace. Secretary Albright has been in Paris meeting with the Prime Minister Barak and Chairman Arafat. I hope and pray that her mission is successful, that there is a cease fire, and the parties return to the peace table.

Now, we've been on a very constructive course in the Middle East, played an unusual, unique role. And I'm convinced that Al Gore and I—I commit that Al Gore and I will continue to do that. I hope I might, through my friendships in Israel and throughout the Arab world, play a unique role in bringing peace to this sacred region of the world.

**Cheney:** Bernie, it has been a very, very difficult area to work in for a long time. Numerous administrations going back certainly to World War II have had to wrestle with the problem of what should happen in the Middle East. We made significant breakthroughs, I think, at the end of the Bush administration because of the Gulf War. In effect, we had joined together with Arab allies and done enormous damage to the Iraqi armed forces. And Iraq at the time was the biggest military threat to Israel.

By virtue of the end of the Cold War, the Soviets were no longer a factor. They used to fish in troubled waters whenever they had the opportunity in the Middle East. But with the end of the Soviet Union, the implosion, if you will, of the empire, that created a vacuum, if you will, and made it easier for us to operate there. We were able to, I think, reassure both Arabs and Israelis that the United States would play a major role there. That we had the ability and the will to deploy forces to the region if we had to, to engage in military operations to support our friends and oppose our foes. And, of course, we were able to convene a conference that in effect the first time Arab and Israelis sat down face-to-face and began this process of trying to move the peace process forward. . . .

I hope that we can get this resolved as soon as possible. My guess is that the next administration is going to be the one that is going to have to come to grips with the current state of affairs there. I think it's very important that we have an administration where we have a president with firm leadership who has the kind of track record of dealing straight with people, of keeping his word so that friends and allies both respect us and our adversaries fear us. . . .

**Moderator:** Senator Lieberman, this question is to you. Many experts are forecasting continuing chaotic oil prices in the world market. Wholesale natural gas prices here in our country are leaping. Then there are coal and electricity. Have previous Republican and Democratic Congresses and administrations, including this one, done their job to protect the American people?

**Lieberman:** Not enough. But this administration and Vice President Gore and I have had both a long-term strategy to develop energy independence and a short-term strategy. In fact, if the—this administration had been given the amount of funding that it had requested from the Republican Congress, we would be further along in the implementation of that long-term strategy, which is aimed at developing alternative cleaner sources of energy. Aimed at giving tax credits to individuals and businesses to conserve and use energy more efficiently. Aimed at a partnership for a new generation of vehicles with the American automobile industry, which is making great progress and can produce a vehicle that can get 80 miles per gallon.

We also have a short-term strategy, to deal with exactly the kind of ups and downs of energy prices. And I know it was controversial, but Al Gore and I believed that it was important in the short-term to reach into the strategic petroleum reserve. Take some of that oil that we have, put it in the market, show the big oil companies and the OPEC oil-producing countries that we've got some resources with which we can fight back. We not just going to lay back and let them roll over our economy. And we did it also because gasoline prices were rising and home heating oil inventories were real low. And both of our tickets agree on LIHAP, the low income housing assistance program, but our opponents really offer no assistance to middle-class families who are hit by rising gas prices and a shortage of home heating oil. The fact is that since the reserve was opened, the price of oil on world markets has dropped $6 a barrel. Now that's a good result and I'm proud of it.

**Moderator:** Mr. Secretary.

**Cheney:** Bernie, this is an area where again I think Joe and I have fairly significant disagreements. My assessment is that there is no comprehensive energy policy today. That as a nation, we are in trouble because the administration has not addressed these issues. We have the prospects of brownouts in California. We have a potential home heating oil crisis in the northeast. We've had gasoline price rises in various other places. For years now the administration has talked about reducing our dependence on foreign sources of oil, but they haven't done it.

In fact, we've gone exactly in the opposite direction. We've got the lowest rate of domestic production of oil now in 46 years. You have to go back to 1954 to find a time when we produced as little oil as we do today. Our imports are at an all-time record high. In the month of June we imported almost 12 million barrels a day. That means we're more subject to the wide fluctuations and swings in price. We have other problems. We don't have refinery capacity. We haven't built a new refinery in this country for over ten years. And the refineries are now operating at 96% or 97% of capacity, which means that even with more crude available, they're probably not going to be able to do very much by way of producing additional home heating oil for this winter.

We have a serious, long-term problem of our growing dependence on foreign sources of energy. That will always be the case. But we ought to be able to shift the trend and begin to move it in the right direction. We need to do a lot more about generating the capacity for power here at home. We need to get on with the business and we think we can do it very safely in an environmentally sound manner. We don't think that we ought to buy into this false choice that somehow we cannot develop energy resources without being cautious with the environment. We can. We've got the technology to do it and we ought to do it. We do support the low income energy assistance program. We think that's very important so that senior citizens, for example, don't suffer this winter. But we need to get on with the business of having a plan to develop our domestic energy resources in producing more supplies, and this administration hasn't produced them. . . .

**Moderator:** . . . Secretary Cheney. Have you noticed a contradiction or hypocritical shift by your opponent on positions and issues since he was nominated?

**Cheney:** Boy, we've been trying very hard to keep this on a high plane, Bernie.

**Lieberman:** Thanks, Bernie.

**Cheney:** I do have a couple of concerns where I liked the old Joe Lieberman better than I do the new Joe Lieberman. Let me see if I can put it in those terms. Joe established, I thought, an outstanding record in his work on this whole question of violence in the media and the kinds of materials that were being peddled to our children. And many of us on the Republican side admired him for that. There is, I must say, the view now that having joined with Al Gore on the ticket on the other side, that that depth of conviction that we had admired before isn't quite as strong as it was, perhaps, in the past.

The temptation on the one hand to criticize the activities of the industry, as was pointed out recently in the Federal Trade Commission where they're taking clearly material meant for adults and selling it to our children, while at the same time they are participating in fundraising events with some of the people responsible for that activity has been a source of concern for many of us. We were especially disturbed, Joe, at a recent fundraiser you attended where there was a comedian who got up and criticized George Bush's religion. I know you're not responsible for having uttered any words of criticism of his religion, but to some extent my concern would be, frankly, that you haven't been as— as consistent as you had been in the past. That a lot of your good friends like Bill Bennett and others of us who had admired your firmness of purpose over the years, have felt that you're not quite the crusader for that cause that you once were.

**Lieberman:** Well, Bernie, you'll not be surprised to hear that I disagree. First let me talk about that joke about religion, which I found very distasteful. And believe me, if anybody has devoted his life to respecting the role of religion in American life and understands that Americans from the beginning of our history have turned to God for strength and purpose, it's me. And any offense that was done, I apologize for. I thought that humor was unacceptable. Let me come to the question of Hollywood and then answer the general question.

Al Gore and I have felt for a long time, first as parents and then only second as public officials, that we cannot let America's parents stand alone in this competition that they feel they're in with Hollywood to raise their own kids and give their kids the faith and the values that they want to give them. I've been a consistent crusader on that behalf. John McCain and I actually requested the Federal Trade Commission report that came out three or four weeks ago, which proved conclusively that the entertainment industry was marketing adult-rated products to our children. Now, that is just not acceptable. And one finding was that they were actually using 10 to 12-year-olds to test screen adult-rated products. When that report came out, Al Gore and I said to the entertainment industry, stop it. And if you don't stop it in six months, we're going to ask the Federal Trade Commission to take action against you. There was no similar strong response from our opponents. We repeated that message when we went to Los Angeles. I repeat it today. We will not stop until the entertainment industry stops marketing its products to our children. . . .

Al Gore and I agree on most everything, but we disagree on some things. And he said to me from the beginning, be yourself, that's why I chose you. Don't change a single position you have. And I have not changed a single position since Al Gore nominated me to be his vice president. . . .

## SECOND PRESIDENTIAL DEBATE

**Moderator:** . . . What do you think the United States should do right now to resolve that conflict over there?

**Gore:** The first priority has to be on ending the violence, dampening down the tensions that have arisen there. We need to call upon Syria to release the three Israeli soldiers who have been captured. We need to insist that Arafat send out instructions to halt some of the provocative acts of violence that have been going on. I think that we also have to keep a weather eye toward Saddam Hussein because he is taking advantage of this situation to once again make threats, and he needs to understand that he's not only dealing with Israel, he is dealing—he's dealing with us if he is making the kind of threats that he's talking about there. The use of diplomacy in this situation has already, well, it goes hour-by-hour and day-by-day now. It's a very tense situation there. But in the last 24 hours there has been some subsiding of the violence there. It's too much to hope that this is going to continue, but I do hope that it will continue. Our country has been very active with regular conversations with the leaders there. And we just have to take it day-to-day right now. But one thing I would say where diplomacy is concerned, Israel should feel absolutely secure about one thing. Our bonds with Israel are larger than agreements or disagreements on some details of diplomatic initiatives. They are historic, they are strong, and they are enduring. And our ability to serve as an honest broker is something that we need to shepherd. . . .

**Bush:** Well, I think during the campaign, particularly now during this difficult period, we ought to be speaking with one voice, and I appreciate the way the administration has worked hard to calm the tensions. Like the vice president, I call on Chairman Arafat to have his people pull back to make the peace.

I think credibility is going to be very important in the future in the Middle East. I want everybody to know should I be the president Israel's going to be our friend. I'm going to stand by Israel. Secondly, that I think it's important to reach out to moderate Arab nations, like Jordan and Egypt, Saudi Arabia and Kuwait. It's important to be friends with people when you don't need each other so that when you do there's a strong bond of friendship. And that's going to be particularly important in dealing not only with situations such as now occurring in Israel, but with Saddam Hussein. The coalition against Saddam has fallen apart or it's unraveling, let's put it that way. The sanctions are being violated. We don't know whether he's developing weapons of mass destruction. He better not be or there's going to be a consequence should I be the president. But it's important to have credibility and credibility is formed by being strong with your friends and resoluting your determination. One of the reasons why I think it's important for this nation to develop an anti-ballistic missile system that we can share with our allies in the Middle East if need be to keep the peace is to be able to say to the Saddam Husseins of the world or the Iranians, don't dare threaten our friends. It's also important to keep strong ties in the Middle East, credible ties, because of the energy crisis we're now in. After all, a lot of the energy is produced from the Middle East, and so I appreciate what the administration is doing. I hope to get a sense of should I be fortunate to be the president how my administration will react to the Middle East.

**Moderator:** So you don't believe, Vice President Gore, that we should take sides and resolve this right now? A lot of people pushing hey, the United States should declare itself and not be so neutral in this particular situation.

**Gore:** Well, we stand with Israel, but we have maintained the ability to serve as an honest broker. And one of the reasons that's important is that Israel cannot have direct dialogue with some of the people on the other side of conflicts, especially during times of tension, unless that dialogue comes through us. And if we throw away that ability to serve as an honest broker, then we have thrown—we will have thrown away a strategic asset that's important not only to us but also to Israel.

**Moderator:** You agree with that, Governor?

**Bush:** I do. I do think this, though. When it comes to timetables it can't be the United States timetable as to how discussions take place. It's got to be a timetable that all parties can agree to, like the Palestinians and Israelis. Secondly, any lasting peace is going to have to be a peace that's good for both sides. And therefore, the term honest broker makes sense. This current administration's worked hard to keep the parties at the table. I will try to do the same thing. But it won't be on my timetable, it will be on the timetable that people are comfortable with in the Middle East. . . .

**Moderator:** . . . Vice President Gore, would you support or sign, as president, a federal law banning racial profiling by police and other authorities at all levels of government?

**Gore:** Yes, I would. The only thing an executive order can accomplish is to ban it in federal law enforcement agencies, but I would also support a law in the Congress that would have the effect of doing the same thing. I just—I think that racial profiling is a serious problem. . . . And I think we've now got so many examples around the country that we really have to find ways to end this. Imagine what it—what it is like for someone to be singled out unfairly, unjustly, and feel the unfair force of law simply because of race or ethnicity. Now, that runs counter to what the United States of America is all about at our core. And it's not an easy problem to solve. But if I am entrusted with the presidency, it will be the first Civil Rights Act of the 21st century.

**Bush:** Yeah, I can't imagine what it would be like to be singled out because of race and stopped and harassed. That's just flat wrong, and that's not what America is all about. And so we ought to do everything we can to end racial profiling. One of my concerns, though, is I don't want to federalize the local police forces. I want to—obviously in the egregious cases we need to enforce civil rights law, but we need to make sure that internal affairs decisions at the local level do their job and be given a chance to do their job. . . .

[M]ost police officers are good, dedicated, honorable citizens who are doing their job, putting their lives at risk who aren't bigoted or aren't prejudiced. . . . But I do think we need to find out where racial profiling occurs and do something about it and say to the local folks, get it done. And if you can't, there will be a federal consequence. . . .

**Gore:** . . . And I think that racial profiling is part of a larger issue of how we deal with race in America. And as for singling people out because of race, you know, James Byrd was singled out because of his race in Texas. And other Americans have been singled out because of their race or ethnicity. And that's why I think we can embody our values by passing a hate crimes law. I think these crimes are different. I think they're different because they're based on prejudice and hatred, which gives rise to crimes that have not just a single victim, but they're intended to stigmatize and dehumanize a whole group of people.

**Moderator:** You have a different view of that.

**Bush:** No, I don't, really.

**Moderator:** On hate crimes laws?

**Bush:** No. We've got one in Texas. And guess what? The three men who murdered James Byrd, guess what's going to happen to them? They're going to be put to death. A jury found them guilty. It's going to be hard to punish them any worse after they get put to death. And it's the right cause. It's the right decision. Secondly, there is other forms of racial profiling that goes on in America. Arab-Americans are racially profiled in what is called secret evidence. People are stopped, and we have to do something about that. My friend, Senator Spencer Abraham of Michigan, is pushing a law to make sure that Arab-Americans are treated with respect. So racial profiling isn't just an issue at local police forces. It's an issue throughout our society. And as we become a diverse society, we're going to have to deal with it more and more. I believe, though—I believe, as sure as I'm sitting here, that most Americans really care. They're tolerant people. They're good, tolerant people. It's the very few that create most of the crises, and we just have to find them and deal with them. . . .

**Moderator:** Vice President Gore, what would be on your racial discrimination elimination list as president?

**Gore:** Well, I think we need tough enforcement of the civil rights laws. I think we still need affirmative action. I would pass a hate crimes law, as I said, and I guess I had misunderstood the governor's previous position. The Byrd family may have a misunderstanding of it in Texas also. But I would like to shift, if I could, to the big issue of education.

**Moderator:** Hold on one second. What is the misunderstanding? Let's clear this up.

**Gore:** Well, I had thought that there was a controversy at the end of the legislative session where the hate crimes law in Texas was—failed, and that the Byrd family, among others, asked you to support it, Governor, and it died in committee for lack of support. Am I wrong about that?

**Bush:** Well, you don't realize we have a hate crimes statute? We do.

**Gore:** I'm talking about the one that was proposed to deal—

**Bush:** No—well, what the Vice President must not understand is we've got a hate crimes bill in Texas. And secondly, the people that murdered Mr. Byrd got the ultimate punishment. The death penalty.

**Moderator:** They were prosecuted under the murder laws, were they not, in Texas?

**Bush:** In this case when you murder somebody it's hate, Jim. The crime is hate. And they got the ultimate punishment. I'm not exactly sure how you enhance the penalty any more than the death penalty. We happen to have a statute on the books that's a hate crimes statute in Texas. . . .

**Gore:** I don't want to jump in. I may have been misled by all the news reports about this matter, because the law that was proposed in Texas that had the support of the Byrd family and a whole lot of people in Texas did, in fact, die in committee. There may be some other statute that was already on the books, but certainly the advocates of the hate crimes law felt that a tough new law was needed. And it's important, Jim, not only—not just because of Texas, but because this mirrors the national controversy. There is pending now in the Congress a national hate crimes law because of James Byrd, because of Matthew Shepard, who was crucified on a split rail fence by bigots, and because of others. And that law has died in committee also because of the same kind of opposition.

**Moderator:** And you would support that bill.

**Gore:** Absolutely.

**Moderator:** Would you support a national hate crimes law?

**Bush:** I would support the Orrin Hatch version of it, not the Senator Kennedy version. But let me say to you, Mr. Vice President, we're happy with our laws on our books. That bill did—there was another bill that did die in committee. But I want to repeat, if you have a state that fully supports the law like we do in Texas, we're going to go after all crime. And we're going to make sure people get punished for the crime. And in this case we can't enhance the penalty any more than putting those three thugs to deaths. And that's what's gonna happen in the State of Texas.

**Moderator:** New subject, new question. Another vice presidential debate follow-up. Governor, both Senator Lieberman and Secretary Cheney said they were sympathetically rethinking their views on same sex relationships. What's your position on that?

**Bush:** I'm not for gay marriage. I think marriage is a sacred institution between a man and a woman. And I appreciated the way the administration signed the Defense of Marriage Act. I presume the Vice President supported it when the President signed that bill and supports it now. But I think marriage is a sacred institution. I'm going to be respectful for people who may disagree with me. I've had a record of doing so in the State of Texas. I've been a person that had been called a uniter, not a divider, because I accept other people's points of view. But I feel strongly that marriage should be between a man and a woman. . . .

**Gore:** I agree with that, and I did support that law. But I think that we should find a way to allow some kind of civic unions, and I basically agree with Dick Cheney and Joe Lieberman. And I think the three of us have one view and the Governor has another view. . . .

**Bush:** I'm not sure what kind of view he's describing to me. I can just tell you, I'm a person who respects other people. I respect their—I respect—on the one hand he says he agrees with me and then he says he doesn't. I'm not sure where he's coming from. But I will be a tolerant person. I've been a tolerant person all my life. I just happen to believe strongly that marriage is between a man and a woman.

**Moderator:** Do you believe in general terms that gays and lesbians should have the same rights as other Americans?

**Bush:** Yes. I don't think they ought to have special rights, but I think they ought to have the same rights.

**Gore:** Well, there's a law pending called the Employment Non-Discrimination Act. I strongly support it. What it says is that gays and lesbians can't be fired from their job because they're gay or lesbian. And it would be a federal law preventing that. Now, I wonder if the—it's been blocked by the opponents in the majority in the Congress. I wonder if the Governor who lend his support to that law.

**Bush:** Well, I have no idea. I mean, he can throw out all kinds—I don't know the particulars of this law. I will tell you I'm the kind of person, I don't hire or fire somebody based upon their sexual orientation. As a matter of fact, I would like to take the issue a little further. I don't really think it's any of my—you know, any of my concerns what—how you conduct your sex life. And I think that's a private matter. And I think that's the way it ought to be. But I'm going to be respectful for people, I'll tolerate people, and I support equal rights but not special rights for people.

**Moderator:** Special rights, how does that affect gays and lesbians?

**Bush:** Well, it would be if they're given special protective status. That doesn't mean we shouldn't fully enforce laws and fully protect people and fully honor people, which I will do as the President of the United States. . . .

**Moderator:** New question, new subject. Vice President Gore, on the environment. In your 1992 book you said, quote, "We must make the rescue of our environment the central organizing principle for civilization and there must be a wrenching transformation to save the planet." Do you still feel that way?

**Gore:** I do. I think that in this 21st century we will soon see the consequences of what's called global warming. There was a study just a few weeks ago suggesting that in summertime the north polar ice cap will be completely gone in 50 years. Already people see the strange weather conditions that the old timers say they've never seen before in their lifetimes. And what's happening is the level of pollution is increasing significantly. Now, here is the good news, Jim. If we take the leadership role and build the new technologies, like the new kinds of cars and trucks that Detroit is itching to build, then we can create millions of good new jobs by being first into the market with these new kinds of cars and trucks and other kinds of technologies. You know the Japanese are breathing down our necks on this. They're moving very rapidly because they know that it is a fast-growing world market. Some of these other countries, particularly in the developing world, their pollution is much worse than anywhere else and their people want higher standards of living. And so they're looking for ways to satisfy their desire for a better life and still reduce pollution at the same time. I think that holding onto the old ways and the old argument that the environment and the economy are in conflict is really outdated. We have to be bold. We have to provide leadership. Now it's true that we disagree on this. The governor said that he doesn't think this problem is necessarily caused by people. He's for letting the oil companies into the Arctic National Wildlife Refuge. Houston has just become the smoggiest city in the country. And Texas is number one in industrial pollution. We have a very different outlook. And I'll tell you this, I will fight for a clean environment in ways that strengthen our economy. . . .

**Bush:** Well, let me start with Texas. We are a big industrial state. We reduced our industrial waste by 11%. We cleaned up more brown fields than any other administration in my state's history, 450 of them. Our water is cleaner now. . . .

**Moderator:** Where do you see the basic difference in very simple terms in two or three sentences between you and the governor on the environment? If a voter wants to make a choice, what is it?

**Gore:** I'm really strongly committed to clean water and clean air, and cleaning up the new kinds of challenges like global warming. He is right that I'm not in favor of energy taxes. I am in favor of tax cuts to encourage and give incentives for the quicker development of these new kinds of technologies. And let me say again, Detroit is rearing to go on that. We differ on the Arctic National Wildlife Refuge, as I have said. We differ on whether or not pollution controls ought to be voluntary. I don't think you can—I don't think you can get results that way. We differ on the kinds of appointments that we would make.

**Moderator:** Would you say it's a fundamental difference?

**Gore:** I think it's a fundamental difference. . . .

**Moderator:** . . . [H]ow would you draw the differences, Governor?

**Bush:** Well, I don't believe in command and control out of Washington, D.C. I believe Washington ought to set standards, but again I think we ought to be collaborative at the local levels and I think we ought to work with people at the local levels. And by the way, I just want to make sure—I can't let him just say something and not correct it. The electric decontrol bill that I fought for and signed in Texas has mandatory emission standards, Mr. Vice President. That's what we ought to do at the federal level when it comes to grandfathered plants for utilities. I think there's a difference. I think, for example, take— when they took 40 million acres of land out of circulation without consulting local officials, I thought that was—

**Moderator:** That was out in the west?

**Bush:** Out in the west, yeah. And so—on the logging issue. That's not the way I would have done it. Perhaps some of that land needs to be set aside. But I certainly would have consulted with governors and elected officials before I would have acted unilaterally.

**Moderator:** Would you believe the federal government still has some new rules and new regulations and new laws to pass in the environmental area or do you think—

**Bush:** Sure, absolutely, so long as they're based upon science and they're reasonable. So long as people have input.

**Moderator:** What about global warming?

**Bush:** I think it's an issue that we need to take very seriously. But I don't think we know the solution to global warming yet. And I don't think we've got all the facts before we make decisions. I tell you one thing I'm not going to do is I'm not going to let the United States carry the burden for cleaning up the world's air. . . .

**Gore:** . . . I disagree that we don't know the cause of global warming. I think that we do. It's pollution, carbon dioxide, and other chemicals that are even more potent, but in smaller quantities, that cause this. Look, the world's temperature is going up, weather patterns are changing, storms are getting more violent and unpredictable. What are we going to tell our children? I'm a grandfather now. I want to be able to tell my grandson when I'm in my later years that I didn't turn away from the evidence that showed that we were doing some serious harm. In my faith tradition, it is—it's written in the book of Matthew, "Where your heart is, there is your treasure also." And I believe that—that we ought to recognize the value to our children and grandchildren of taking steps that preserve the environment in a way that's good for them.

**Bush:** Yeah, I agree. I just—I think there has been—some of the scientists, I believe, Mr. Vice President, haven't they been changing their opinion a little bit on global warming? . . . I—of course there's a lot—look, global warming needs to be taken very seriously, and I take it seriously. But science, there's a lot—there's differing opinions. And before we react, I think it's best to have the full accounting, full understanding of what's taking place. And I think to answer your question, I think both of us care a lot about the environment. We may have different approaches. We may have different approaches in terms of how we deal with local folks. . . .

**Moderator:** New question. Last question. For you, Governor. And this flows somewhat out of the Boston debate. You, your running mate, your campaign officials have charged that Vice President Gore exaggerates, embellishes and stretches the facts, etc. Are you—do you believe these are serious issues? . . .

**Bush:** Well, we all make mistakes. I've been known to mangle a syllable [pronounced sy-LAB-al] or two myself, you know, if you know what I mean. I think credibility is important. It is going to be important for the president to be credible with Congress, important for the president to be credible with foreign nations. And yes, I think it's something that people need to consider. This isn't something new. I read a report, or a memo, from somebody in his 1988 campaign—I forgot the fellow's name—warning then Senator Gore to be careful about exaggerating claims. . . .

And so I think this is an issue. I found it to be an issue in trying to defend my tax relief package. I thought there was some exaggerations about the numbers. But the people are going to have to make up their mind on this issue. And I am going to continue to defend my record and defend my propositions against what I think are exaggerations. Exaggerations like, for example, only 5% of seniors receive benefits under my Medicare reform package. That's what he said the other day, and that's simply not the case. And I have every right in the world to defend my record and positions. That's what debates are about and that's what campaigns are about.

**Moderator:** Vice President Gore?

**Gore:** I got some of the details wrong last week in some of the examples that I used, Jim, and I'm sorry about that. And I'm going to try to do better. One of the reasons I regret it is that getting a detail wrong interfered several times with the point that I was trying to make. . . . I can't promise that I will never get another detail wrong. I can promise you that I will try not to, and hard. But I will promise you this with all the confidence in my heart and in the world, that I will do my best if I'm elected president, I'll work my heart out to get the big things right for the American people. . . .

# THIRD PRESIDENTIAL DEBATE

**Member of Audience:** How do you feel about HMOs and insurance companies making the critical decisions that affect people's lives instead of the medical professionals, and why are the HMOs and insurance companies not held accountable for their decisions?

**Gore:** Mr. Hankins, I don't feel good about it, and I think we ought to have a patient's bill of rights to take the medical decisions away from the HMOs and give them back to the doctors and nurses. . . .

Doctors are giving prescriptions, they're recommending treatments, and then their recommendations are being overruled by HMOs and insurance companies. That is unacceptable. I support a strong national patient's bill of rights. It is actually a disagreement between us, a national law that is pending on this, the Dingle-Norwood bill, a bipartisan bill, is one that I support and that the governor does not. . . .

**Bush:** . . . Actually, Mr. Vice President, it's not true. I do support a national patient's bill of rights. As a matter of fact, I brought Republicans and Democrats together to do just that in the State of Texas to get a patient's bill of rights through. It requires a different kind of leadership style to do it, though. You see, in order to get something done on behalf of the people, you have to put partisanship aside, and that's what we did in my state. We have one of the most advanced patient's bill of rights. . . .

We're one of the first states that said you can sue an HMO for denying you proper coverage. Now there's what's called an Independent Review Organization that you have to go through first. It says you have a complaint with your insurance company, you can take your complaint to an objective body. If the objective body rules on your behalf, the insurance company must follow those rules. However, if the insurance company doesn't follow the findings of the IRO, then that becomes a cause of action in a court of law. It's time for our nation to come together and do what's right for the people, and I think this is right for the people. You know, I support a national patient's bill of rights, Mr. Vice President, and I want all people covered. I don't want the law to supersede good law like we've got in Texas. . . .

**Moderator:** Just a minute, Mr. Vice President. . . . [W]ould you agree that you two agree on a national patient's bill of rights?

**Gore:** Absolutely not. I referred to the Dingle-Norwood bill. It is the bipartisan bill that is now pending in the Congress. The HMOs and the insurance companies support the other bill that's pending, the one that the Republican majority has put forward. They like it because it doesn't accomplish what I think really needs to be accomplished to give the decisions back to the doctors and nurses and give you a right of appeal to somebody other than the HMO or insurance company, let you go to the nearest emergency room without having to call an HMO before you call 911, to let you see a specialist if you need to, and it has strong bipartisan support. It is being blocked by the Republican leadership in the Congress. . . . And I specifically would like to know whether Governor Bush will support the Dingle-Norwood bill, which is the main one pending.

**Moderator:** Governor Bush, you may answer that if you'd like. But also I'd like to know how you see the differences between the two of you, and we need to move on.

**Bush:** Well, the difference is is that I can get it done. That I can get something positive done on behalf of the people. That's what the question in this campaign is about. It's not only what's your philosophy and what's your position on issues, but can you get things done? And I believe I can.

**Gore:** What about the Dingle-Norwood bill? . . .

**Bush:** I'm not quite through. Let me finish. I talked about the principles and the issues that I think are important in a patient's bill of rights. It's kind of Washington, D.C. focus. Well, it's in this committee or it's got this sponsor. If I'm the president, we're going to have emergency room care, we're going have gag orders, we're going to have direct access to OB/GYN. People will be able to take their HMO insurance company to court. That's what I've done in Texas and that's the kind of leadership style I'll bring to Washington. . . .

**Member of Audience:** Are either of you concerned with—are either of you concerned with finding some feasible way to lower the price of pharmaceutical drugs such as education on minimizing intake, revamp of the FDA process or streamlining the drug companies' procedures instead of just finding more money to pay for them?

**Bush:** Well, that's a great question. I think one of the problems we have, particularly for seniors, is there is no prescription drug coverage in Medicare. And therefore, when they have to try to purchase drugs they do so on their own, there's no kind of collective bargaining, no power of purchasing among seniors. So I think step one to make sure prescription drugs is more affordable for seniors, and those are the folks who really rely upon prescription drugs a lot these days, is to reform the Medicare system, is to have precipitation drugs as an integral part of Medicare once and for all.

The problem we have today is like the patient's bill of rights, particularly with health care, there's a lot of bickering in Washington, D.C. It's kind of like a political issue as opposed to a people issue. So what I want to do is I want to call upon Republicans and Democrats to forget all the arguing and finger pointing, and come together and take care of our seniors' prescription drug program, that says we'll pay for the poor seniors, we'll help all seniors with prescription drugs. In the meantime, I think it's important to have what's called Immediate Helping Hand, which is direct money to states so that seniors, poor seniors, don't have to choose between food and medicine. That's part of an overall overhaul. The purchasing powers. And I'm against price controls. I think price controls would hurt our ability to continue important research and development. Drug therapies are replacing a lot of medicines as we used to know it. One of the most important things is to continue the research and development component. And so I'm against price controls. Expediting drugs through the FDA makes sense, of course. Allowing the new bill that was passed in the Congress made sense to allow for, you know, drugs that were sold overseas to come back and other countries to come back into the United States. That makes sense. But the best thing to do is to reform Medicare.

**Moderator:** Vice President Gore, two minutes.

**Gore:** All right, here we go again. Now look, if you want someone who will spend a lot of words describing a whole convoluted process and then end up supporting legislation that is supported by the big drug companies, this is your man. If you want someone who will fight for you and who will fight for the middle-class families and working men and women, who are sick and tired of having their parents and grandparents pay higher prices for prescription drugs than anybody else, then I want to fight them. And you asked a great question because it's not only seniors.

Listen, for 24 years I have never been afraid to take on the big drug companies. They do some great things. They discover great new cures and that's great. We want them to continue that. But they are now spending more money on advertising and promotion. You see all these ads? Than they are on research and development. And they are trying artificially extend the monopoly patent protection so they can keep charging these very high prices. I want to streamline the approval of the competing generic drugs and the new kinds of treatments that can compete with them so we bring the price down for everybody. Now, briefly, let me tell you how my prescription drug plan works. The governor talked about Medicare. I propose a real prescription drug benefit under Medicare for all seniors, all seniors, and here's how it works. You pick your own doctor, and nobody can take that away from you. The doctor chooses the prescription that you need and nobody can overrule your doctor. You go to your own pharmacy and then Medicare pays half the price. If you're poor, they pay all of it. If you have extraordinarily high cost, then they pay all over $4,000 out-of-pocket. And I'll bring new competition to bring the price down. And if you pass the big drug companies' bill, nothing will happen. . . .

**Member of Audience:** . . . Would you be open to the idea of a national health care plan for everybody? And if not, why? If so, is this something you would try to implement if you are elected into office and what would you do to implement this plan?

**Gore:** I think that we should move step-by-step toward universal health coverage, but I am not in favor of government doing it all. We've spent 65 years now on the development of a hybrid system, partly private, partly public, and 85% of our people have health insurance, 15% don't. That adds up to 44 million people.

That is a national outrage. We have got to get health coverage for those who do not have it and we've got to improve the quality for those who do with a patient's bill of rights that's real and that works, the Dingle-Norwood bill, and we have got to fill in the gaps in coverage by finally bringing parity for the treatment of mental illness, because that's been left out. We have got to deal with long-term care. Now, here are the steps that I would take, first of all. I will make a commitment to bring health care coverage of high quality that is affordable to every single child in America within four years. And then we'll fill other gaps by covering the parents of those children when the family is poor or up to two and a half times the poverty rate.

I want to give a tax credit for the purchase of individual health insurance plans. I want to give small business employers a tax credit, 25%, to encourage the providing of health insurance for the employees in small businesses. I want to give seniors who are, well, the near elderly, I don't like that term because I am just about in that category, but those 55 to 65 ought to be able to buy into Medicare for premiums that are reasonable and fair and significantly below what they have to get now. Now, we have a big difference on this. And you need to know the record here. Under Governor Bush, Texas has sunk to be 50th out of 50 in health care—in health insurance for their citizens. Last week he said that they were spending 3.7 billion dollars, or 4.7 billion dollars on this. . . .

**Bush:** I'm absolutely opposed to a national health care plan. I don't want the federal government making decisions for consumers or for providers. I remember what the administration tried to do in 1993. They tried to have a national health care plan. And fortunately, it failed. I trust people, I don't trust the federal government. It's going to be one of the themes you hear tonight. I don't want the federal government making decisions on behalf of everybody. There is an issue with the uninsured, there sure is. And we have uninsured people in my state. Ours is a big state, a fast-growing state. We share a common border with another nation. But we're providing health care for our people.

One thing about insurance, that's a Washington term. The question is, are people getting health care, and we have a strong safety net, and there needs to be a safety net in America. There needs to be more community health clinics where the poor can go get health care. We need a program for the uninsured. They've been talking about it in Washington, D.C. The number of uninsured has now gone up for the past seven years. We need a $2,000 credit, rebate for people, working people that don't have insurance, they can get in the market-place and start purchasing insurance. We need to have—allow small businesses to write insurance across jurisdictional lines so small business can afford health care, small restaurants can afford health care. So health care needs to be affordable and available. We have to trust people to make decisions with their lives. . . .

**Moderator:** Vice President Gore, is the governor right when he says that you're proposing the largest federal spending in years?

**Gore:** Absolutely not. Absolutely not. I'm so glad that I have the chance to knock that down. Look, the problem is that under Governor Bush's plan, $1.6 trillion tax cut, mostly to the wealthy, under his own budget numbers, he proposes spending more money for a tax cut just for the wealthiest 1% than all the new money he budgets for education, health care and national defense combined.

Now under my plan we'll balance the budget every year. I'm not just saying this. I'm not just talking. I have helped to balance the budget for the first time in 30 years, paid down the debt. And under my plan, in four years, as the percentage of our gross domestic product, federal spending will be the smallest that it has been in 50 years. One reason is, you know, the third biggest spending item in our budget is interest on the national debt? We get nothing for it. We keep the good faith and credit of the United States.

I will pay down the debt every single year until it is eliminated early in the next decade. That gets rid of the third biggest intrusion of the federal government in our economy. Now, because the governor has all this money for a tax cut mostly to the wealthy, there is no money left over, so schools get testing and lawsuit reform and not much else.

**Moderator:** Governor, the vice president says you're wrong.

**Bush:** Well, he's wrong. Just add up all the numbers. It's three times bigger than what President Clinton proposed. The Senate Budget Committee—

**Moderator:** Three times—excuse me, three times bigger than what President Clinton proposed?

**Gore:** That was in an ad, Jim, that was knocked down by the journalists who analyzed the ad and said it was misleading.

**Bush:** My turn?

**Moderator:** Yes, sir.

**Bush:** Forget the journalists. He proposed more than Walter Mondale and Michael Dukakis combined. This is a big spender. And you ought to be proud of it, it's part of his record. We just have a different philosophy. Let me talk about tax relief. If you pay taxes, you ought to get tax relief. The Vice President believes only the right people ought to get tax relief. I don't think that's the role of the president to pick you're right and you're not right. I think if you're going to have tax relief, everybody ought to get it. And therefore, wealthy people are going to get it. But the top 1% will end up paying one-third of the taxes in America and they get one-fifth of the benefits. And that's because we structured the plan so that six million additional American families pay no taxes. If you're a family of four making $50,000 in Missouri, you get a 50% cut in your federal income taxes. What I've done is set priorities and funded them. And there's extra money. And I believe the people who pay the bills ought to get some money back. It's a difference of opinion. He wants to grow the government and I trust you with your own money. I wish we could spend an hour talking about trusting people. It's just the right position to take. . . .

**Member of Audience:** . . . I'm very concerned about the morality of our country now. TV, movies, the music that our children are, you know, barraged with every day. And I want to know if there's anything that can be worked out with the—Hollywood, or whoever, to help get rid of some of this bad language and whatever, you know. It's just bringing the country down. And our children are very important to us and we're concerned about their education at school. We should be concerned about their education at home, also. Thank you.

**Bush:** Appreciate that question. Laura and I are proud parents of teenage girls, twin daughters, and I know what you're saying. Government ought to stand on the side of parents. Parents are teaching their children right from wrong, and the message oftentimes gets undermined by the popular culture. You bet there's things that government can do. We can work with the entertainment industry to provide family hour. We can have filters on Internets where public money is spent. There ought to be filters in public libraries and filters in public schools so if kids get on the Internet, there is not going to be pornography or violence coming in. I think we ought to have character education in our schools. I know that doesn't directly talk about Hollywood, but it does reinforce the values you're teaching. Greatly expand character education funding so that public schools will teach children values, values which have stood the test of time. There's afterschool money available. I think that afterschool money ought to be available for faith-based programs and charitable programs that exist because somebody has heard the call to love a neighbor like you would like to be loved yourself. That will help reinforce the values that parents teach at home as well. Ours is a great land, and one of the reasons why is because we're free. And so I don't support censorship. But I do believe that we ought to talk plainly to the Hollywood moguls and people who produce this stuff and explain the consequences. I think we need to have rating systems that are clear. I happen to like the idea of having technology for the TV, easy for parents to use so you can tune out these programs you don't want in your house. I'll remind mothers and dads the best weapon is the off/on button, and paying attention to your children, and eating dinner with them and . . .

**Gore:** My turn.

**Moderator:** Vice President Gore.

**Gore:** I care a lot about this. It's not just movies; television, video games, music, the Internet. Parents now feel like you have to compete with the mass culture in order to raise your kids with the values that you want them to have. Tipper and I have four children. And God bless them, every one of them decided on their own to come here this evening. I don't want to embarrass our oldest daughter. She and her husband made us grandparents almost a year-and-a-half ago, and yet if she'll forgive me, when she was little, she brought a record home that had some awful lyrics in it and Tipper hit the ceiling. And that launched a campaign to try to get the record companies to put ratings that—warning labels for parents. And I'm so proud of what she accomplished in getting them on there.

I've been involved myself in negotiating and helping to move along the negotiations with the Internet service providers to get a parents' protection page every time 95% of the pages come up. And a feature that allows parents to automatically check with one click what sites your kids have visited lately. You know, some parents are worried about those filters, that you will have to ask your kids how to put them on there. But if you can check up on them, that's real power. And recently the Federal Trade Commission pointed out that some of these entertainment companies have warned parents that the material is inappropriate for children, and then they've turned around behind the backs of the parents and advertised that same adult material directly to children. That is an outrage. Joe Lieberman and I gave them six months to clean up their act. And if they don't do it, we're gonna ask for tougher authority in the hands of the FTC on the false and deceptive advertising. I'll tell you this, I want to do something about this. Respect the First Amendment, but I will do something to help you raise your kids without that garbage. . . .

**Member of Audience:** In one of the last debates held, the subject of capital punishment came up, and in your response to the question, you seemed overly joyed and as a matter of fact proud that Texas led the nation in the execution of prisoners. Sir, did I misread your response and are you really, really proud of the fact that Texas is number one in executions?

**Bush:** No, I'm not proud of that. The death penalty is a very serious business, Leo. It's an issue that good people obviously disagree on. I take my job seriously. And if you think I was proud of it, I think you misread me, I do. I was sworn to uphold the laws of my state. During the course of the campaign in 1994 I was asked do you support the death penalty. I said I did if administered fairly and justly. Because I believe it saves lives, Leo, I do. If it's administered swiftly, justly and fairly, it saves lives. One of the things that happens when you're a governor, at least oftentimes you have to make tough decisions. You can't let public persuasion sway you, because the job is to enforce the law. And that's what I did, sir. There have been some tough cases come across my desk. Some of the hardest moments since I've been the governor of the State of Texas is to deal with those cases. But my job is to ask two questions, sir. Is the person guilty of the crime? And did the person have full access to the courts of law? And I can tell you looking at you right now, in all cases those answers were affirmative. I'm not proud of any record. I'm proud of the fact that violent crime is down in the State of Texas. I'm proud of the fact that we hold people accountable. But I'm not proud of any record, sir, I'm not. . . .

**Gore:** I support the death penalty. I think that it has to be administered not only fairly with attention to things like DNA evidence, which I think should be used in all capital cases, but also with very careful attention. If, for example, somebody confesses to the crime and somebody is waiting on death row, there has to be alertness to say wait a minute, have we got the wrong guy? If the wrong guy is put to death, then that's a double tragedy. Not only has an innocent person been executed, but the real perpetrator of the crime has not been held accountable for it. And in some cases may be still at large. But I support the death penalty in the most heinous cases.

**Moderator:** Do both of you believe the death penalty actually deters crime? Governor?

**Bush:** I do. It's the only reason to be for it. Let me finish, sir. I don't think you should support the death penalty to seek revenge. I don't think that's right. I think the reason to support the death penalty is because it saves other people's lives.

**Gore:** I think it is a deterrent. I know that's a controversial view, but I do believe it's a deterrent. . . .

**Moderator:** All right. Now we're going to go to closing statements. Vice President Gore, you're first.

**Gore:** Thank you very much, Jim, and I'll begin by answering your questions—your last question. I believe that a lot of people are skeptical about people in politics today because we have seen a time of great challenge for our country. Since the assassination of our best leaders in the '60's, since the Vietnam War, since Watergate, and because we need campaign finance reform.

I would like to tell you something about me. I keep my word. I have kept the faith. I've kept the faith with my country. I volunteered for the Army. I served in Vietnam. I kept the faith with my family. Tipper and I have been married for 30 years. We have devoted ourselves to our children and now our nearly one-and-a-half-year-old grandson.

I have kept the faith with our country. Nine times I have raised my hand to take an oath to the Constitution, and I have never violated that oath. I have not spent the last quarter century in pursuit of personal wealth. I have spent the last quarter century fighting for middle-class working men and women in the United States of America. I believe very deeply that you have to be willing to stand up and fight no matter what powerful forces might be on the other side.

If you want somebody who is willing to fight for you, I am asking for your support and your vote and, yes, your confidence and your willingness to believe that we can do the right thing in America, and be the better for it. We've made some progress during the last eight years. We have seen the strongest economy in the history of the United States. Lower crime rates for eight years in a row. Highest private home ownership ever, but I'll make you one promise here. You ain't seen nothing yet. And I will keep that promise.

**Moderator:** Governor Bush, two minutes.

**Bush:** Well, Jim, I want to thank you and thank the folks here at Washington University and the vice president. Appreciate the chance to have a good, honest dialogue about our differences of opinion. I think after three debates the good people of this country understand there is a difference of opinion. There is a difference between big federal government and somebody who is coming from outside of Washington who will trust individuals.

I've got an agenda that I want to get done for the country. It's an agenda that says we're going to reform Medicare to make sure seniors have got prescription drugs and to give seniors different options from which they can choose. It's an agenda that says we're listen to the young voices in Social Security and say we're going to think differently about making sure we have a system, but also fulfill the promise to the seniors in America. A promise made will be a promise kept should I be fortunate enough to become your president. I want to have the military keeping the peace. I want to make sure the public school system in America keeps its promise so not one child is left behind.

After setting priorities, I want to give some of your money back. I don't think the surplus is the government's money. I think it's the people's money. I don't think it exists because of the ingenuity and hard work of the federal government, I think in exists because of the ingenuity and hard work of the American people. And you ought to have some of this surplus so you can save and dream and build. I look forward to the final weeks of this campaign. I'm asking for your vote. For those of you for me, thanks for your help. For those of you for my opponent, please only vote once. But for those who have not made up their mind, I would like to conclude by this promise. Should I be fortunate enough to become your president, when I put my hand on the Bible, I will swear to not only uphold the laws of the land, but I will also swear to uphold the honor and the dignity of the office to which I have been elected, so help me God. Thank you very much. . . .

# KOSTUNICA ON INAUGURATION AS PRESIDENT OF YUGOSLAVIA
## October 7, 2000

*Slobodan Milosevic, Europe's last holdover communist leader from the cold war era, was pushed from office in the fall of 2000 by the voters of Yugoslavia, who refused to accept his final attempt to cling to power. The ouster of Milosevic meant that for the first time in history all major European governments were in the hands of democratically elected leaders. On a more practical level, Yugoslavia's democratic revolution appeared to offer the opportunity for an end to the bloody ethnic wars that had brutalized the Balkans since Yugoslavia split apart in 1991.*

*Milosevic was defeated in a September 24, 2000, presidential election by Voislav Kostunica, a constitutional lawyer who represented a coalition of opposition parties united primarily by their desire to force Milosevic from power. Milosevic at first refused to accept his defeat, but ten days later, on October 5, massive demonstrations in Belgrade and other cities undercut his support among the military and security forces. Kostunica declared victory and was sworn in as president on October 7.*

*Kostunica's anti-Milosevic forces maintained their unity through late December when they swept the last remnants of the old regime from power in the Serbian republic, one of two national units (along with Montenegro) that constituted what remained of the Federal Republic of Yugoslavia. Despite their political victories, Kostunica and his allies faced many hurdles, starting with the country's economy, which had been savaged by years of corruption and the effect of international sanctions imposed during the 1999 war in Kosovo. Western governments, including the United States, promised tens of millions of dollars worth of aid, and they lifted the sanctions. The United Nations, which had expelled Yugoslavia in 1992 following the breakup of the country, on November 1 accepted Kostunica's application for readmission.*

### Background to the Fall of Milosevic

*Milosevic, a Communist Party functionary, in 1987 rose to power in Serbia—the dominant republic in what was then the multirepublic Federal*

833

*Peoples' Republic of Yugoslavia. He fostered a revival of Serbian national-
ism in 1989, the six hundredth anniversary of the Turkish Ottoman empire's defeat of Serbia at the Battle of Kosovo, an event that remained central
to Serbian national identity. After the fall of the Berlin Wall in 1989 and the
collapse of the Soviet Union two years later, Yugoslavia split apart, with
only Serbia and Montenegro remaining in the federation, which Milosevic
controlled. Slovenia, Croatia, and Bosnia-Herzegovina declared their independence, provoking brutal ethnic wars in Croatia in 1991–1992 and in
Bosnia in 1992–1995. In both cases, Milosevic supported efforts by Serbian
minorities to carve out separate Serbian enclaves.* (Bosnian war, Historic
Documents of 1995, p. 717)

*In November 1996, a year after he accepted a negotiated end to the Bos-
nian war, Milosevic and his ruling Socialist Party faced their first serious
political challenge from Serbian opposition forces, which won elections in
more than a dozen cities, including Belgrade. A government attempt to an-
nul the results of those elections provoked widespread protests for nearly
three months. In a tactical retreat, Milosevic ceded control of the cities to the
opposition parties. But he proved shrewder than his opponents, who could
not agree on a long-range program and thus lost the momentum generated
by the protests.*

*In 1998 Milosevic fired two of his most influential advisors, the head of
the Serbian Secret Service and the director of the Serbian radio-television
service. Observers said he then retreated into an even more isolated core of
supporters, headed by his wife, Mirjana Markovic, who headed her own political party.*

*A drive for independence by Albanian Muslims, who were the majority
population in the southern Serbian province of Kosovo, provoked a harsh
reaction from Milosevic in late 1998 and early 1999. European and American efforts to negotiate a solution to the crisis failed, leading to a U.S.-led
NATO bombing campaign against Yugoslavia that forced Milosevic to pull
Serbian military forces out of Kosovo in June 1999. Polls showed that the
vast majority of Serbs blamed Milosevic for the destruction—even while denouncing the United States and its allies.* (Kosovo war, Historic Documents
of 1999, pp. 134, 285, 802)

*NATO's bombs, a series of international sanctions imposed during
the 1990s, and government mismanagement and corruption devastated the
Serbian economy and created broad public unrest. Early in 2000 a series of
gangland-type killings among hard-line Serbian factions helped create an
impression that Milosevic might be losing some of the tight control he had
exercised over security forces and other levers of power. Among those killed
was Zeljko Raznatovic, known as Arkan, the head of a Serbian militia infamous for its killings of Muslims and Croats in Bosnia.*

*Over the years Milosevic had become a master tactician, famous for his
ability to declare victory from defeat and then dodge and weave to keep his
opponents off balance. On July 6 he announced a constitutional change providing for direct popular election of the president, rather than by parliament, as in the past. Three weeks later he called presidential elections for*

*September 24, despite the fact that he still had a year to serve in his current term.*

*Milosevic's surprise move forced opposition groups, who were united only in their hatred of him, into an unprecedented level of unity. Eighteen parties formed a loose coalition called the Democratic Opposition of Serbia, with a reluctant Kostunica emerging as the candidate for president. Most importantly, Zoran Djindjic, head of the larger Democratic Party, agreed to step aside in favor of Kostunica.*

*The government-dominated media effectively shut out Kostunica, forcing him literally to take to the streets to get his message across. With a small number of aides, Kostunica traveled all over Serbia in August and September to meet constituents in homes, shops, and factories. He campaigned on the themes of democracy, Serb patriotism, anticommunism, and, most of all, the need for Milosevic to give up power.*

*The United States and European Union (EU) nations provided money and logistical support for opposition forces during the election, although not directly to the Kostunica campaign. One of the most visible aspects of that support was a series of public opinion polls financed by the National Democratic Institute, a U.S. government-funded agency that promoted elections overseas. Through groups based in Budapest, the United States also provided backing for unions and student groups that would play an important role in organizing the protests that drove Milosevic from power.*

*By mid-September polls showed Kostunica with a significant lead over Milosevic. But even the most optimistic opposition leaders said they believed Milosevic would manipulate the election results to ensure his reelection.*

*Kostunica claimed victory the day after the election, saying that returns monitored by the opposition showed that he had received more than 52 percent of the vote. He declared himself the "peoples' president." The response from the government came a day later, when the Federal Election Commission insisted that Kostunica had won only 49 percent of the vote—short of the majority needed for outright victory—and Milosevic had won 38.6 percent. The commission said a second round of voting would be necessary, and it set an October 8 date. Officials later acknowledged that the commission had simply deducted several hundred thousand votes from Kostunica's total.*

## Ten Days of Turmoil

*At least initially, Milosevic's gambit of demanding another vote produced the desired result: discord among the opposition. Thousands of protesters gathered in Belgrade and other cities on September 27, but for several days opposition leaders appeared unsure about what to do next.*

*Kostunica insisted he would not participate in a second round, and the opposition laid plans for a strike. A turning point came September 29, when more than 7,000 miners walked off their jobs at the Kolubara coal mine complex near the town of Lazarevac, an area just south of Belgrade that long had been a base of support for Milosevic. The strike threatened electrical power to the capital and, more importantly, provided a focal point around which the opposition could rally. A general strike began October 2, with schools and many businesses closed. Kostunica visited the striking miners to thank them for their support, vowing that "we will finish this struggle together." Milosevic responded with defiance, insisting during a nationally televised speech that opposition forces were traitors controlled by NATO. On October 4, several hundred riot police tried to take control of one of the mines, but they retreated when protesters arrived to support the striking miners.*

*Emboldened by this victory, opposition leaders called for a mass protest in Belgrade the following day, October 5, and set a 3 P.M. deadline for Milosevic to concede the election to Kostunica. More than a half-million protesters—blue-collar workers, students, business people, and other representatives of the shrinking middle class—gathered in Belgrade's streets that morning and listened to speeches by opposition figures.*

*Perhaps the most important development was something that did not happen. The military and security forces did not launch a massive attack against the protesters. Instead, they remained in their barracks—a silent but effective protest by officers and troops against the bloody role they had been forced to play in Milosevic's wars.*

*Shortly after noon protesters clashed briefly with police, who fired tear gas and rounds of live ammunition into the air. Another clash came about the time of the 3 P.M. deadline, when hundreds of protesters broke through barricades in front of the federal parliament building. Police fired tear gas, but a determined band of protesters broke into the building; some police fled, but many joined the protest. Protesters trashed offices, hurled pictures and furniture out windows, and set several fires. In the building they found thousands of ballots marked for Milosevic.*

*The focus of the protest then shifted to the headquarters of the state-run radio-television service. After a brief gun battle, protesters seized control in the early evening and began broadcasting under the name "New Radio Television Serbia."*

*At about 6:30 P.M., Kostunica emerged on the balcony of the Belgrade City Hall, near the parliament building, and shouted: "Good evening, dear liberated Serbia." That set off a massive all-night celebration, with tens of thousands of people singing patriotic songs and dancing in the streets.*

*News reports indicated that Milosevic still was not prepared to give up power, but in the following two days the last remaining elements of his support melted away. Russian foreign minister Igor Ivanov flew to Belgrade on October 6, declared that Moscow recognized Kostunica as the new Yugoslav president, and met with Milosevic to urge him to step aside. Later that day, Army Chief of Staff Nebojsa Pavkovic met with Kostunica to declare the army's support for his presidency. Pavkovic and Kostunica then drove together to a presidential palace on the outskirts of Belgrade and met with Milosevic, who reportedly agreed to acknowledge Kostunica's victory in the election. Late that night Milosevic appeared on television, announced that he had just learned that he had lost the election, and conceded that Kostunica was the new president.*

*Kostunica took the oath of office on October 7 during a low-key ceremony held at a conference center in Belgrade because of damage to the parliament building. He gave a brief acceptance speech, saying that "after all the hard-ships and suffering, the peoples of Yugoslavia are desperate for peace and tranquility, in the most simple meaning of those words. I hope that that time is just ahead for us, and that we will be able to come to terms with all the problems which await us, and which aren't at all simple."*

## Yugoslavia's New Leader

*Kostunica, fifty-six at the time of his election, was a constitutional lawyer who had taught at Belgrade University law school until 1974, when he was fired for supporting a critic of longtime Yugoslavian leader Joseph Broz Tito. He described himself as a liberal democrat and a Serbian nationalist—but one who rejected the more extreme nationalism of some other opposition leaders.*

*A member of the Serbian parliament from 1990 to 1997, he had supported the Serbian wars in Croatia and Bosnia during the early 1990s, although associates said he condemned the Serbian "ethnic cleansing" that killed and displaced tens of thousands of Croats and Muslims. Even so, several news re-ports said he had good relations with Bosnian Serb leader Radovan Karadzic, who had been indicted by the UN war crimes tribunal for atrocities during the war in Bosnia. In a September 28 report, the* Washington Post *said sev-eral representatives of Serbian liberal democratic parties expressed dis-comfort with Kostunica's past positions but supported him because he was not corrupt and he might be able to defeat Milosevic in an open election.*

*In his statements and actions both before and after the election, Kostu-nica sought to affirm his independence from the Western powers, especially the United States. During the height of the struggle to oust Milosevic, he was especially critical of Washington's demands that Milosevic be turned over to a UN tribunal in the Hague to face war crimes charges from the 1999 war in Kosovo. The United States, he said on October 2, appeared to believe that the indictment of Milosevic "is more important at this moment than the fu-ture of the whole country, its people and stability in the region." Moreover, Kostunica said the U.S. position was reinforcing Milosevic's resistance by reminding him that the election was "a question of life and death for him." Kostunica also said U.S. support for opposition forces, including aid to the groups that helped his rise to power, constituted "meddling" in Yugoslavia's internal affairs.*

## Postelection Challenges

*Despite his desire to remain independent of outside influence, Kostunica quickly agreed to reestablish diplomatic relations with, and accept economic aid from, the United States and major European nations. President Bill Clin-ton announced on November 17 that he was restoring diplomatic ties with Yugoslavia, about twenty months after relations had been severed in the buildup to the war in Kosovo.*

*Clinton also said the United States would provide $45 million in emer-gency food aid to help Serbia get through the coming winter; that was in ad-dition to $100 million that Congress had appropriated for general aid to*

*Serbia and $89 million for aid to Montenegro in response to the defeat of Milosevic. The EU in November approved $165 million worth of aid for energy supplies, food, medicine, and other supplies.*

*Battered by years of war and economic sanctions imposed in 1999, the Yugoslav economy by late 2000 was in shambles. Even in Belgrade the government was able to provide electricity for only a few hours each day. Food supplies were short, and many workers and pensioners had not received checks from a government that had no cash. Tens of thousands of Serbian refugees from Bosnia and Kosovo placed an added burden on the country.*

*In addition to providing for the needs of the people, Kostunica and his allies faced an enormous task of reorganizing a government that had been under the dictatorial control of Milosevic for more than a decade. Throughout October and November Kostunica worked to replace Milosevic supporters in key government ministries. A major obstacle was that Milosevic's Socialist Party still controlled the parliament and agencies of the Serbian government, which was the real center of power in Yugoslavia.*

*After a series of negotiations, the government called Serbian elections for December 23. Even so, Milosevic tried to maintain his presence on the public stage, maneuvering his reelection on November 25 as leader of the Socialist Party. However, Milosevic did not stand as a candidate in the Serbian parliamentary elections.*

*Kostunica's coalition—still known as the Democratic Opposition of Serbia despite its new status in the federal government—won an overwhelming victory in the December 23 voting, capturing 65 percent of the vote and 176 of the 250 seats in the Serbian parliament. Milosevic's Socialist Party won 13.5 percent of the vote, making it the major opposition party in parliament. Djindjic, the Democratic Party leader who had supported Kostunica for the Yugoslav presidency, was named Serbian prime minister.*

*Notwithstanding its victory, the democratic coalition faced enormous obstacles in governing both the Yugoslav federation and the Serbian republic. Montenegro was threatening to leave the federation, and Kosovo's Albanians wanted independence from Serbia. The Serbian government faced the difficult task of persuading its people to be patient during what was certain to be a painful and lengthy process of putting the country back together again. Moreover, the government needed to convince foreign businesses that it now was not only safe, but wise, to invest in the Yugoslav economy.*

*At year's end the government also was considering what to do about Milosevic. Djindjic said he wanted to prosecute the former leader on charges of corruption and abuse of power. But there seemed little support in the post-Milosevic Yugoslavia for meeting Western demands for his extradition to face international war crimes charges at the Hague.*

> *Following is a statement released by the office of the Yugoslav presidency summarizing the address of Voislav Kostunica upon his inauguration as the president of the Federal Republic of Yugoslavia on October 7, 2000. The document was obtained from the Internet at www.gov.yu/1024/institutions/speech.html.*

At a historical moment for the country in which we live, for our people, for Serbia and Montenegro, the new president of the Federal Republic of Yugoslavia held a speech in front of members of both Chambers of the Federal Assembly. He expressed hope that peace lies ahead for Serbia and the Federal Republic of Yugoslavia, stating that he hoped that the union of Serbia and Montenegro would become more solid than ever before.

"After all the hardships and suffering, the peoples of Yugoslavia are desperate for peace and tranquility, in the most simple meaning of those words. I hope that that time is just ahead for us, and that we will be able to come to terms with all the problems which await us, and which aren't at all simple. I am certain that we are entering a new era in which peace will prevail among us, among us and other peoples in the world. I hope that we will succeed in overcoming all problems in our union, and that the union of Serbia and Montenegro will become more solid than ever before; that Kosovo will be even more under our sovereignty, and that we will once again become a part of the international community, but with our heads held high, proudly respecting and defending our national interests and our dignity. For a long period of time, many years and decades, we lived in a system where democracy, from the most simple to the real meaning of that word, did not exist."

President [Voislav] Kostunica went on to say that on today's day. the Federal Republic of Yugoslavia "has entered into a line of democratic peoples, democratic communities of peoples," and has "demonstrated to the world, that along with all the differences which exist among us, when the interest of the country and the people is put above all else, we can work and debate in the Federal Assembly."

President Kostunica called all political sides and subjects in society to express tolerance, underlining that the road to democracy is not possible without that.

"This whole time, I always imagined how we would one day, with all our differences, be able to communicate in a civilized manner, that we would, even when we donut agree the most, be able to still be together, without the use of harsh words, without initiating violence among us. That is the order given by the people. That order and request made by the people was forwarded to all deputies of the Federal Assembly, no matter what their party or political beliefs are. This is a moment when we are reaching that point, when after something that is the basic criterion of every democratic system, that is a change of rule, has taken place, and yet in this Parliament are gathered people with different beliefs, but what must exist above all else, is the welfare of this country, our beautiful and big Federal Republic of Yugoslavia."

President Kostunica said that he will, in his new role, work the hardest, first and foremost, in the interest, and for the welfare, of the country.

His speech ended with the following words: "I truly love this country, the Federal Republic of Yugoslavia and Serbia."

# GENERAL ACCOUNTING OFFICE
# ON COLOMBIA AID PROGRAM
## October 12, 2000

*The United States dramatically escalated its involvement in the narcotics wars of Colombia, agreeing to provide nearly $1 billion in military aid over two years to help that country's beleaguered government battle drug traffickers. President Bill Clinton and congressional leaders said the aid was the U.S. contribution to a $7.5 billion multiyear program launched in 1999 by Colombian president Andres Pastrana. The aid program made Colombia the third largest recipient in the world of U.S. military assistance, behind Israel and Egypt.*

*U.S. intelligence agencies estimated that Colombia produced about 90 percent of the world's supply of cocaine and about two-thirds of the world trade in heroin. Colombia's cocaine production was growing at a rapid rate, more than doubling in the last five years of the twentieth century. In large part, the growth in Colombian production reflected the success of antinarcotic efforts in Peru and Bolivia. As coca fields were eliminated in those countries, tens of thousands of acres in Colombia were converted from forest and other agricultural crops to coca.*

*Perhaps the fundamental problem facing the United States was its attempt to help Colombia battle narcotics traffickers without getting drawn into the four-decade battle between the Bogota government and two leftist guerrilla groups, neither of which had much popular support but were richly financed with proceeds from the drug trade. The larger of the two groups, the Revolutionary Armed Forces of Colombia (FARC), was reported to have about 15,000 fighters in 2000, most of them located in the south of the country. The smaller National Liberation Army reportedly had fewer than 5,000 fighters concentrated in the northeast.*

*The Clinton administration insisted that Washington could help fight the antinarcotics battle while avoiding Colombia's counterinsurgency war. Critics called that contention dangerously naive, given the links between the guerrillas and the drug traffickers, and they warned that the United States could be sucked into a quagmire, just as it had been in Vietnam in the 1960s. In a tough assessment of the obstacles facing the antinarcotics war* in Colombia, the General Accounting Office gave Congress a report on October 12 saying that both the Colombian and the U.S. government had failed to develop the detailed plans needed for the effort.

## Colombia's Troubles

A nation of 40 million people, Colombia in 2000 was a society with little more than the trappings of a functioning government. The federal government had no control over large sections of national territory. Guerrilla groups, drug traffickers, and right-wing militias dominated even most major cities, including the capital, Bogota. Corruption was entrenched at all levels of government, including in the national congress, the court system, and the executive branch. The military, an institution that often provided the backbone for many Latin American governments, was undermanned, ill-trained, and ill-equipped in Colombia.

After the outbreak of the guerilla war in the 1960s, wealthy landowners and military leaders jointly set up right-wing militias, which quickly became powerful forces outside civilian government control and by the late 1990s were themselves deeply involved in the drug trade. Carlos Castano, leader of the largest militia group, the United Self-Defense Forces of Colombia, openly bragged about his drug funding. International human rights groups called the militias "death squads" and accused them of killings hundreds of people each year, most of them civilians. U.S. organizations estimated that the militias had 5,000 to 7,000 fighters.

Colombia for many decades had been a major link in the international drug trade, serving primarily as the administrative and processing center for cocaine that was grown in neighboring Bolivia and Peru. Two major cartels, one headquartered in Cali and the other in Medellin, dominated the drug trade and were among the largest criminal enterprises in the world. The Medellin cartel collapsed in the late 1980s, but the Cali cartel survived until the mid-1990s when the government arrested its key leaders and most of its functions were taken over by dozens of smaller operations.

Ironically, the success of U.S.-funded antinarcotics efforts in Bolivia and Peru contributed to Colombia's worsening troubles in the late 1990s. With drug production in those countries cut in half, many drug traffickers simply moved to rural areas of Colombia, including the southwestern provinces of Putumayo and Caqueta, where the FARC already was well-established. By 2000 U.S. officials estimated that more than 100,000 acres in those provinces were being cultivated with coca, some of it directly controlled by FARC and the rest under the protection of the guerrillas, who received a share of the drug producers' profits.

While drug traffickers, the guerrillas, and paramilitary units grew rich from the narcotics trade, most Colombians were stuck in deep poverty. Unemployment was estimated at more than 20 percent, and the country's economy shrank by about 5 percent in 1999.

The war between the government and the guerrillas was a bloody one, resulting in the deaths of an estimated 35,000 people during the 1990s. International agencies estimated that more than 1.5 million Colombians had *been forced from their homes because of the fighting, giving Colombia the third-largest population of "internally displaced persons" in the world, behind the Sudan and Angola. An estimated 800,000 Colombians—a large proportion of the country's educated middle class—fled the country in the last half of the decade, most of them heading for the United States.*

*Andres Pastrana was elected president of Colombia in 1998 on a platform of negotiating an end to the war with the guerrillas. Shortly after entering office, he took a bold gamble by designating an enormous section of southern Colombia, which the FARC essentially controlled, as a "demilitarized zone," in effect conceding that area to the guerrillas. The tactic backfired, as the FARC quickly developed increased coca production in the area, giving the guerrillas a huge new income source. Freed of the need to battle the government, and with hundreds of millions of dollars in new income, the guerrillas had no incentive to negotiate with the government, and so the peace talks Pastrana had promised went nowhere. The guerrillas launched a major offensive in 1999 that brought them uncomfortably close to Bogota. That action captured the attention of the Clinton administration, which had given only limited support to Pastrana's predecessor, Ernesto Samper, whose commitment to battling the drug trade was called into question by revelations that he had accepted $6 million in campaign contributions from the Cali cartel.*

*Pastrana started negotiations with FARC in May 1999 but the talks had made little progress by the end of 2000. FARC commander Manuel Marulanda proved to be adept at wringing concessions from Pastrana, who appeared to be much more anxious for the negotiations to continue.*

## Plan Colombia

*With significant U.S. help, Pastrana's government developed its antinarcotics plan in the summer of 1999. Known as Plan Colombia, it called for billions of dollars worth of military and economic aid from the United States, Europe, Japan, and other countries for a multifaceted approach to solving Colombia's problems. The nation's armed forces and antinarcotics police units would receive training and sophisticated equipment to battle the drug traffickers, the nation's judicial system would be reformed, peasants in narcotics-producing areas would be encouraged to plant alternative crops, and education and other social programs would be developed to help pull the economy out of a deep recession. Overall, Pastrana said his plan was aimed at ending his country's dependence on the drug trade by cutting the cultivation and production of narcotics in half during a six-year period.*

*Pastrana estimated that his plan would cost $7.5 billion over three years, and he asked the United States to provide nearly half that total, $3.5 billion. Pastrana also asked European nations to contribute about $1 billion for social and economic programs, but by the end of 2000 the European Union had pledged only $280 million.*

*Despite its role in helping develop the plan, the Clinton administration at first balked at supporting major U.S. participation beyond the $330 million already budgeted for fiscal years 2000 and 2001. Pastrana's failure to* *win U.S. support quickly undermined Pastrana's domestic credibility and political support. Later in 1999 Republicans in Congress launched a drive for U.S. backing of Pastrana's plan, introducing their own proposal for $1.6 billion in military-related aid over three years. That move put new pressure on Clinton, who in December 1999 said he would soon propose a "substantial, effective" aid program for Colombia.*

*Clinton unveiled his proposal on January 11. It called for spending $1.3 billion over two years, $905 million of which was to be included in an "emergency" supplemental appropriation for the current fiscal year, 2000. Colombia was to receive $860 million of the total, most of it for a fleet of sixty-three attack helicopters: thirty-three Bell UH-1N "Huey" helicopters and thirty Sikorsky UH-60L "Blackhawks." These heavily armed helicopters would be used to track down and destroy cocaine crops in remote areas of Colombia. Congress later switched the mix of helicopters, approving funding for forty-two Hueys and nineteen Blackhawks. Clinton's plan also included $127 million over two years for "alternative development" programs, such as helping peasants plant cash crops other than cocaine. Clinton said U.S. military personnel would train Colombian forces in the use of military equipment and antinarcotics tactics but would not engage in actual combat. In addition to the aid for Colombia, Clinton's proposal included $440 million for aid to other countries in the Andean region and for U.S. law enforcement agencies.*

*Clinton's proposal already had broad backing from Republican leaders in Congress. Many Democrats, traditionally reluctant to provide military aid to unstable regimes in Latin America, set aside their qualms when the administration produced reports of skyrocketing drug production in Colombia. White House drug policy director Barry R. McCaffrey on February 14 released estimates that cultivation of coca in Colombia had increased 140 percent over five years and that production of cocaine had risen 126 percent in the same period. "We have a drug emergency in Colombia," McCaffrey said.*

*The House approved a modified version of Clinton's request on June 29. The Senate approved it the next day, and Clinton signed it into law (PL 106–246) on July 13. In both chambers, a majority of Republicans and Democrats supported the measure, but a higher proportion of Democrats was opposed. Opponents said the administration had no clear strategy for its program in Colombia, and they warned that it would impossible to combat drug traffickers without tackling the guerrillas and right-wing militias that profited from the narcotics trade.*

*A key element of the congressional aid package was a series of amendments conditioning the aid on presidential certification that the Colombian government and military were taking seven distinct steps to respect human rights . However, the bill gave the president the right to waive those conditions if he found the U.S. national security interest required doing so.*

*Clinton took advantage of the waiver provision on August 22, signing a document that allowed the aid package to go forward even through the human rights conditions demanded by Congress had not been met. Clinton's action was strongly condemned by human rights organizations. A coalition of Amnesty International, Human Rights Watch, and the Washington Office on Latin America said Clinton had ignored "overwhelming evidence" that Colombia had not met the conditions laid down by Congress.*

*On August 30 Clinton traveled to Colombia for a one-day visit to signify U.S. support for Pastrana's antinarcotics campaign. It was the first trip to Colombia by a U.S. president in ten years. Visiting the resort town of Cartagena on the Caribbean coast, Clinton disputed assertions by some critics that a stepped-up antinarcotics campaign in Colombia would force thousands of refugees to flee to other countries, including the United States. "If you really say Colombia can't attack this in an aggressive way because there will be some negative consequences on our border, the logical conclusion is that all the cancer of narco-trafficking and lawless violence in this entire vast continent should rest on the shoulders and burden the children of this one nation," he said. "And that's not right."*

*At the end of 2000, one troubling question concerned the extent to which Colombia's wars would spill over into neighboring countries, especially Ecuador to the southwest and Venezuela to the east. Thousands of Colombians fleeing guerrillas or paramilitary units had taken refuge in both countries, which were struggling with their own economic difficulties. Clinton administration officials began talking late in the year about the need for a regional strategy that would provide aid to countries from Panama to Peru in hopes of preventing widespread instability. The incoming U.S. president, George W. Bush, had strongly supported Clinton's aid program for Colombia during the 2000 election campaign. But neither Bush nor his senior foreign policy aides had clearly stated any long-term vision for U.S. relations with troubled Latin American countries.*

> *Following are excerpts from the report, "Drug Control: Challenges in Implementing Plan Colombia," submitted by the General Accounting Office on October 12, 2000, to the Subcommittee on Criminal Justice, Drug Policy, and Human Resources of the House Committee on Government Reform. The document was obtained from the Internet at http://www.gao.gov/new.items/d0176t.pdf.*

## Background

For more than two decades, the United States has supported Colombia's efforts to reduce drug-trafficking activities and to stem the flow of illegal drugs entering the United States. [A table listed U.S. aid for antinarcotics programs in Colombia for fiscal years 1996 through 2000. The total for the five-year period was $765.2 million.]

The Colombian government's $7.5 billion, 6-year Plan Colombia represents a significant change from prior efforts. The government recognizes that the program must address the conditions that foster the growth in illegal drug activities. Central to the program is the Colombian government's effort to regain control of the drug-producing regions of the country from insurgent and paramilitary groups, increase drug interdiction efforts, provide coca farmers alternative ways to earn a living, and enhance the protection of human rights. All key Colombian ministries, including the Justice and Defense ministries, are assigned roles and specific tasks in the plan.

In July 2000, Congress appropriated over $860 million in additional funding for fiscal years 2000–01 to directly support activities in Plan Colombia. The activities include providing equipment, such as helicopters and fixed-wing aircraft, and training to support counternarcotics operations of the Colombian military and National Police; alternative development projects in drug producing areas; judicial reform and rule of law initiatives; strengthening Colombian human rights organizations; assisting displaced persons; and supporting the peace process.

## The Changing Nature of the Drug Threat in Colombia

Historically, Colombia has been the world's largest producer of cocaine. However, starting in 1997, Colombia surpassed Bolivia and Peru as the world's largest cultivator of coca. Since 1995, the area under coca cultivation in Colombia expanded by over 140 percent to over 300,000 acres in 1999. Most of this increased cultivation took place in the areas of southern Colombia that are controlled by insurgents and paramilitary groups. Moreover, the amount of cocaine produced in Colombia has increased by 126 percent since 1995, from 230 metric tons to 520 metric tons in 1999. Finally, according to the Drug Enforcement Administration (DEA), Colombia has become a major source of the heroin consumed in the United States, producing about 6 metric tons annually.

Despite U.S. and Colombian efforts to disrupt drug-trafficking activities, the U.S. Embassy in Colombia has not reported any net reduction in the processing or export of refined cocaine to the United States. Moreover, according to DEA, while two major groups (the Medellin and Cali cartels) dominated drug-trafficking activities during the late 1980s and early 1990s, hundreds of smaller and more decentralized organizations are now involved in all aspects of the drug trade. According to DEA, several billion dollars flow into Colombia each year from the cocaine trade alone. This vast amount of drug money has made it possible for these organizations to gain unprecedented economic, political, and social power and influence.

To further complicate matters, the two largest insurgent groups—the Revolutionary Armed Forces of Colombia and the National Liberation Army—and paramilitary groups have expanded their involvement in drug-trafficking. The insurgents exercise some degree of control over 40 percent of Colombia's territory east and south of the Andes, an area equal in size to Texas.

According to DOD [U.S. Department of Defense], two-thirds of the Revolutionary Armed Forces of Colombia's units and one-third of the National Liberation Army units are involved in some form of drug-trafficking activity. U.S. Embassy officials stated that information over the past 2 years indicates that units of the Revolutionary Armed Forces of Colombia have become more heavily involved in growing coca, establishing coca prices, and transporting cocaine in Colombia.

Moreover, in 1998, DEA reported that certain leaders of some paramilitary groups that emerged as self-defense forces in response to the insurgents' violence had become major drug traffickers.

## Problems in Managing U.S. Assistance to Colombia

The United States has had long-standing problems in providing counternarcotics assistance to Colombian law enforcement and military agencies involved in counternarcotics activities. In 1998, we reported that planning and management problems hampered U.S. counternarcotics efforts in Colombia. For example, we reported that limited planning and coordination between U.S. agencies hampered the delivery of some counternarcotics equipment, such as fixed-wing aircraft, helicopters, and boats, to the National Police and the Colombian military. We reported that this equipment required substantial funding to make it operational.

Between October 1998 and August 1999, State [U.S. State Department] provided the National Police with six additional Bell 212 helicopters and six UH-II helicopters. Neither set of helicopters was provided with adequate spare parts or the funds to ensure adequate logistics support because of budget constraints. Recognizing that the National Police could not operate and maintain the helicopters, the Narcotics Affairs Section budgeted $1.25 million in fiscal year 2000 to replenish the low supply of spare parts. However, according to a U.S. Embassy official, the funding was not available until March 2000 because of delays in submitting State's plan for the funds to the Congress. Further aggravating the situation, the Embassy requested spare parts for some of these helicopters from DOD stocks. While DOD agreed to provide $3.1 million worth of helicopter spare parts, only $378,000 worth had been delivered as of September 1, 2000. Although DOD intends to deliver the remaining parts, a DOD official did not know when.

Furthermore, in September 1999, State and DOD initiated a plan to provide the Colombian Army with 33 UH-1N helicopters State had purchased from Canada to support Colombia's three counternarcotics battalions. Between November 1999 and February 2000, 18 of the helicopters were delivered to Colombia, and a U.S. contractor trained 24 pilots and 28 Colombian Army copilots to operate them. The original plan called for using these helicopters beginning in May 2000 to support the first U.S.-trained counternarcotics battalion, which was ready to begin operations on January 1, 2000. The helicopters were to move troops into insurgent-controlled areas so they could secure the areas and enable the National Police to conduct eradication or interdiction missions.

At the time State agreed to purchase the helicopters, it had not included the funds necessary to procure, refurbish, and support them in its fiscal year 1999 and 2000 budgets. As a result, the helicopters could not be used for conducting counternarcotics operations and 17 of the 24 contractor pilots trained to fly the 18 UH-1Ns were laid off beginning in May 2000.

In August 2000, after the U.S. assistance for Plan Colombia was approved, State reprogrammed $2.2 million from the U.S. counternarcotics program for Mexico to rehire and retrain additional personnel. According to State and U.S. Embassy officials, it will take about 3 months for the counternarcotics battalion to commence operations with the helicopters—nearly a year after the original date to begin operations.

During fiscal years 1996 through 1999, the United States agreed to provide Colombia almost $148 million worth of equipment and services from DOD inventories to support counternarcotics efforts. As of September 1, 2000, it had provided only about $58.5 million. According to DOD officials, the difference between the amount of assistance requested and the amount delivered is the result of a combination of factors—from overvaluing the items when the request was initially developed to the unavailability of some items in DOD inventories and the length of time to obtain and the ship articles. For example, in 1996, DOD agreed to provide the Colombian military and National Police with 90 secure radios and supporting communications equipment from its inventories. However, according to DOD records, this equipment was not available.

Beginning in 1998, U.S. Embassy officials became concerned over the increased U.S. presence in Colombia and associated costs with an aerial eradication program. At the time, the Embassy began developing a plan to phase out U.S. contractor support of aerial eradication by having the National Police assume increased operational control over this program. This would be accomplished by providing the National Police with training, aircraft, and other support needed to develop an infrastructure to enhance their overall abilities to eradicate coca leaf and opium poppy. According to Embassy personnel, the National Police have not formally approved the plan, and State has not approved the funding needed to begin the phaseout. Now, according to State officials, implementing Plan Colombia is a higher priority, and they do not know when the phaseout program will be approved.

According to U.S. Embassy officials, despite extensive training and other efforts to have the National Police develop a management program that would ensure a more effective aerial eradication program, little progress has been made. For example, the National Police continue to emphasize training high-ranking officers, even though the Narcotics Affairs Section has informed the National Police that training should be given to junior officers in areas such as logistics, operations, flight instructors, maintenance, and administration. Moreover, the July 2000 State Inspector General report stated that the National Police rotate more experienced mechanics into other areas for developmental purposes. The Police are therefore constantly training new personnel, making it difficult to maintain a skilled workforce that is needed to repair the aerial eradication aircraft. According to the Inspector General report, it will take 3 to 4 years before entry-level mechanics will become productive journeymen.

Department of State policy requires that Narcotics Affairs Sections adequately oversee U.S. counternarcotics assistance to ensure that it is being used as intended and that it can be adequately accounted for. However, U.S. Embassy officials stated that the National Police have not always provided necessary documents, such as budgetary and planning documents, to determine if the National Police are using the resources in accordance with eradication and interdiction plans. In two instances, U.S. Embassy officials said they observed the National Police using U.S.-provided helicopters for purposes other than counternarcotics, but the Police did not cooperate in their attempts to clarify how the helicopters were being used.

Also, until recently, neither the U.S. Embassy nor the Colombian National Police had conducted program reviews, as required in annual bilateral agreements. Recognizing it may have a problem, the Narcotics Affairs Section requested in early 2000 that the State Inspector General audit the major National Police accounts for the first time in 15 years. In May 2000, the State auditors reported to the Narcotics Affairs Section that the National Police could not account for 469,000 of the 2.76 million gallons of fuel provided for counternarcotics missions in 1999. The auditors concluded that the fuel may have been misused.

### Financial, Management, and Social Challenges Will Complicate Efforts to Meet Goals of Plan Colombia

The governments of the United States and Colombia face a number of challenges in implementing Colombia's strategy to reduce the cultivation, processing, and distribution of narcotics by 50 percent in 6 years. Although both governments are taking steps to identify funding and complete implementation plans, at this point, the total cost of U.S.-supported activities required to meet the plan's goals remains unknown. In addition, Colombia must deal with the political and economic instability fostered by Colombia's long-standing insurgency and human rights problems.

As in the past, State and DOD will have to request additional funding to support U.S.-provided equipment. Officials from State and DOD recently testified that they do not know if sufficient funding is available to procure the number of helicopters mandated by the Congress because they have not determined how the helicopters will be equipped and configured. According to State, the funding proposed by the administration and approved by the Congress was not intended to support the equipment scheduled to be provided through the 6-year life of Plan Colombia. State officials noted that they are still developing cost estimates for fiscal year 2002 and beyond but that funding just to sustain the equipment included in the current assistance for Colombia would be substantial.

During our recent visit to Colombia, government defense and budgeting officials said that with their already tight defense budget they cannot afford to operate and sustain the new U.S. helicopters by themselves. Colombian and U.S. Embassy officials agreed that Colombia will need to establish a new logistical and support system, including maintenance and repair, for the Huey IIs that are not currently in the Colombian's inventory and that this will likely require continuing U.S. support.

Most of the assistance provided under Plan Colombia is targeted for the Colombian military, but U.S. Southern Command officials said their original input on Colombia's needs was based on the information they had and intuitive assessments of the Colombian military's basic requirements. At the time the administration was developing its assistance package, Colombia did not have a military plan on which to base its needs. Moreover, the Southern Command had not expected large increases in the levels of assistance for the military, and the daily management of the current assistance program precluded military officials in the U.S. Embassy from assessing Colombian overall needs.

To better define the Colombian military's requirements, DOD recently undertook two studies. The first specifically targeted the deployment of the helicopters included in the assistance package and addressed issues such as support for mission requirements and the organization, personnel, and logistical support needed. The second addressed how the Colombian military should structure and modernize itself to address the internal threats of narcotics and insurgents. DOD officials said that these two studies provide sufficient information to develop the operational doctrine, structure, and systems necessary to use U.S. assistance and meet counternarcotics goals effectively.

State is also drafting an implementation plan for U.S. assistance that is necessary to better synchronize all U.S. programs and activities involved in supporting Plan Colombia. State officials presented their draft to the Colombian government to help them develop their strategy for the use of U.S. funds. State officials stated that they expect the U.S. implementation plan to be approved by U.S. agencies in October 2000.

State anticipates that it can obligate some funds for Plan Colombia activities by the end of September 2000. However, DOD and the Colombian Army have not finalized specifications for the Blackhawk helicopters and State officials testified in September 2000 that the first Blackhawk may not arrive in Colombia until October 2002. Similarly, State testified that the first Huey IIs may not be delivered until mid-2001. In addition, although State expects to initiate pilot projects such as alternative and economic development and judicial reform in September or October 2000, State and the U.S. Embassy cautioned that it will take years to show measurable results.

U.S. Embassy officials said that the ability to begin implementing and overseeing programs will hinge on obtaining additional staff to manage programs. The Narcotics Affairs Section estimated it might need up to 24 additional staff, and USAID estimated it might need 40 more staff to implement programs envisioned under Plan Colombia. As of September 2000, State and other agencies involved were still determining the number of additional personnel needed and ways to address security and other issues, such as the lack of secure office space in the U.S. Embassy.

Although the Colombian government has pledged $4 billion for Plan Colombia, State and Colombian government officials were pessimistic about Colombia's ability to obtain much new money without cutting other government programs. They expect that Colombia will try to raise $1 billion from bonds and loans. As of August 2000, it had collected $325 million from domestic bonds and planned to collect an additional $325 million from bonds by the end of 2001. Colombian government officials indicated that, at best, most of the funds that will be available are already included in the national budget. However, according to an official with the Planning Ministry, it is difficult to document the purposes of funding in Colombian budgets because Colombian ministries' budget preparation and coordination among ministries vary.

The Colombian government is also seeking donations of more than $2 billion from donors other than the United States to fund the social, economic, and good governance development portions of Plan Colombia. As of July 2000, other donors had pledged about $621 million, and State officials were optimistic that the remainder could be obtained. They said that many donors responded favorably to Plan Colombia and made plans for meetings in the fall 2000 to revisit the issue.

The Colombian government has not yet developed the detailed implementation plans necessary for funding, sequencing, and managing activities included in Plan Colombia. In early 2000, State officials began asking the Colombian government for plans showing, step-by-step, how Colombian agencies would combat illicit crop cultivation in southern Colombia, institute alternative means of making a livelihood, and strengthen the Colombian government's presence in the area. In May 2000, State officials provided Colombia extracts from the U.S. draft implementation plan with the expectation that the Colombian government would develop a similarly detailed plan. However, Colombia's product, provided in June 2000, essentially restated Plan Colombia's broad goals without detailing how Colombia would achieve them. A U.S. interagency task force went to Colombia in July 2000 to help the Colombians prepare the required plan. The Government of Colombia provided their action plan in September 2000 which addressed some of the earlier concerns.

The Colombian government agrees that ending the civil conflict is central to solving Colombia's problems. State reports have noted that a peace agreement would stabilize the nation, speed economic recovery, help ensure the protection of human rights, and restore the authority and control of the Colombian government in the coca-growing regions.

However, unless such an agreement is reached, the continuing violence would limit the government's ability to institute its planned economic, social, and political improvements.

The U.S. Embassy has already reported that initial Plan Colombia activities have been affected because of security concerns. Specifically, the lack of security on the roads in southern Colombia prevented the Justice Ministry from establishing a justice center there. Moreover, indications are that the insurgents have warned farmers in one area not to participate in alternative crop development projects unless they are part of an overall peace plan. The Embassy has reported that these security impediments are probably a small indication of future security problems if peace is not achieved.

Regarding human rights, the Colombian government has stated that it is committed to protecting the human rights of its citizens. State and DOD officials said they will apply the strictest human rights standards before approving assistance under Plan Colombia. For example, State did not approve training for the second counternarcotics battalion until an individual officer suspected of a violation was removed from the unit, even though the Colombian government had cleared the person of wrongdoing. Nevertheless, human rights organizations continue to allege that individuals in the Colombian armed forces have been involved with or condoned human rights violations and that they do so with impunity. As such, Colombia's failure to adhere to U.S. to human rights policies could delay or derail planned counternarcotics activities.

Although the Congress required the President to certify that Colombia had met certain human rights standards prior to disbursing assistance for Plan Colombia, 9 the President waived the certification as permitted by the act. According to State officials, the waiver was issued because it was too soon to determine the extent to which Colombia was complying with the legislation's requirements. . . .

# FEDERAL BUREAU OF INVESTIGATION REPORT ON CRIME
## October 15, 2000

*Serious crime in the United States fell sharply again during 1999, cap-*
*ping an eight-year trend that coincided with the longest economic expan-*
*sion in the nation's history. But the downward trend may have leveled off in*
*2000. Preliminary figures showed only a marginal decline in serious crime*
*during the first half of 2000, with some categories on the rise for the first*
*time in years.*

*"The 1990s crime drop has ended with the 1990s," said James Allan*
*Fox, a professor of criminal justice at Northeastern University. "This is*
*the criminal justice limbo stick, we just can't go any lower. We've had eight*
*straight wonderful years of declining crime rates, and at a certain point*
*you just can't push those numbers further down, and we've hit that point."*
(Previous reports, Historic Documents of 1999, p. 614)

### Continuing Drop in Crime for 1999

*In its annual report,* Crime in the United States, *released October 15, the*
*Federal Bureau of Investigation (FBI) said that the rate of serious crime*
*had declined 7.6 percent in 1999 from the previous year—the eighth con-*
*secutive annual decline. Overall, the crime rate for 1999 was 19 percent be-*
*low the 1995 level and 27 percent below the 1990 level, the FBI reported.*

*The bureau had reported declining levels of crime for every year since*
*1992, by far the longest trend since it began collecting national statistics in*
*1960. The previous record was a three-year drop in crime rates from 1982*
*through 1984.*

*Experts cited numerous factors for the decline in crime, including the ag-*
*ing of the "baby boom" population born after World War II, concerted efforts*
*by police in urban areas to reduce the use of crack cocaine and to keep guns*
*out of the hands of criminals, and the long-term economic expansion, which*
*began in 1992 after a brief recession. Taking advantage of the fact that 2000*
*was an election year, Republicans and Democrats in Washington each sought*
*to claim credit, as well. President Bill Clinton, a Democrat, issued a state-*

*ment on October 15 noting that crime "rose steadily through much of the 1980s"—a period when Republicans controlled the White House. But during his tenure in office, he said, "our nation has come together to reverse those trends," primarily through federal programs aiding local law enforcement agencies. Republican congressional leaders insisted their policies deserved the credit, most importantly legislation that provided federal subsidies for construction of prisons in states that imposed longer prison terms.*

*Whatever the causes, the FBI report said that the rate of violent crime for 1999 was at the lowest level since 1978—525 offenses per 100,000 people. That represented a 7 percent decline from 1998, the report said. All categories of violent crime fell, both in the numbers of crimes and the rate per 100,000 people. Murder declined 8 percent to the lowest level since 1966, rape dropped 5 percent to the lowest level since 1985, robbery was down 8 percent, and aggravated assault was down 6 percent. All categories of serious property crimes also declined during 1999. Auto theft was down 8 percent to the lowest level since 1985, burglary dropped 10 percent, and larceny-theft dropped 6 percent.*

*As in previous years, crime rates varied markedly by region. In general, southern states were the most crime-ridden and violent in the country, the FBI reported. With 35 percent of the nation's population, the South accounted for 41 percent of the total reported crime. Comparable figures for other regions were: the West, 22 percent of the population and 23 percent of the crime; the Midwest, 23 percent of the population and 22 percent of the crime; and the Northeast, 19 percent of the population and 14 percent of the crime. The murder rate was substantially higher in the South than in any other region: 6.9 murders per 100,000 people, compared with rates of 5.5 in the West, 5.3 in the Midwest, and 4.1 in the Northeast.*

*Despite the generally good news contained in the report for 1999, some of the specifics indicated that the overall downward trend for crime might be coming to an end. The most important indicator, according to some criminal justice experts, was the murder rate in the nation's eight biggest cities—those with populations of 1 million or more. The decline in the murder rate for those cities was just 1.8 percent, compared with the national average decline of 8 percent. The number of murders in New York City rose for the first time in several years, from 633 in 1998 to 671 in 1999. "The big cities were the first to go up [in crime] in the 1980s, the first to come down in the 1990s," said Alfred Blumstein, a professor at Carnegie-Mellon University who directed the National Consortium on Violence Research. "Now, having the lowest murder rate decline suggests they'll be the first to stabilize. Murders and crime can't go down forever."*

*Initial reports for 2000 appeared to indicate that Blumstein's hunch was correct. The FBI's preliminary figures for the first six months of 2000 showed that serious crime fell just 0.3 percent compared to the same period in 1999. Several categories of crime rose in the first half of 2000, although by very small margins: auto theft was up 1.2 percent, rape and aggravated assault both rose by 0.7 percent, and larceny-theft was up by 0.1 percent.*

## Other Reports on Crime

*The Department of Justice and other organizations released several other reports during 2000 dealing with criminal statistics. Among these were the following:*

**Domestic violence.** *Social programs, emergency hotlines, and legal efforts had contributed to a long-term decline in domestic violence, according to a study issued on May 17 by the Bureau of Justice Statistics. The study, "Intimate Partner Violence," said there had been a general decline since the mid-1970s in most forms of violence between husbands and wives and among unmarried couples. In general, violence against males by their female partners had declined at a more rapid rate than had male violence against females. In 1976, the study said, more than 3,000 men and women were killed by their intimate partners, a slight majority of the victims were women. By 1998, the overall figure had fallen to 1,830, but the proportion of female victims was much higher: 1,320 of the victims were women and 510 were men. When the figures were broken down by race, the study showed that the number of "intimate" murders of black men had fallen by 74 percent between 1976 and 1998 for black men, of black women by 45 percent, and of white men by 44 percent. But the murders of white women by their partners had risen by 3 percent. Experts said the relatively greater decline in the murder of men might have resulted from the establishment of numerous programs, such as shelters, for abused women. "We've given wives alternatives to feeling like they have to pick up a loaded gun to kill their loaded husbands," Professor Fox said. "Divorce is easier."*

**Incarceration rates.** *The number of people held in the nation's jails and prisons rose again in 1999, continuing a long-term trend. Just more than 2 million people were in jail or prison at the end of 1999, an increase of nearly 200,000 over the previous year, a study released August 9 by the Bureau of Justice Statistics showed. Of the total, just under 1.3 million were in state and federal prisons, and just under 700,000 were in local jails. A total of 6.3 million were on probation, in jail or prison, or on parole, representing 3.1 percent of all adult U.S. residents. The overall incarceration rate had more than tripled since 1980, the study said. During 1999 federal prisons experienced a 9.9 percent increase in inmate population, the greatest single year gain ever, the bureau said. Analysts said two explanations accounted for most of the growth in prison populations: increasing prison terms (the average term went from twenty months in 1990 to twenty-eight months in 1999) and a rapidly rising rate of parolees being returned to prison because of parole violations, such as failing drug tests.*

**Likelihood of going to prison.** *Another study by the Bureau of Justice Statistics, "Homicide Trends in the United States," said that if recent incarceration rates remained unchanged, an estimated one of every twenty people in the United States, or 5.1%, would serve some time in jail or prison during their lifetime. Broken down by various groups, the lifetime chances were shown as 9 percent for men, 1.1 percent for women, 16.2 percent for blacks, 9.4 percent for Hispanics, and 2.5 percent for whites. Based on cur-*

*rent rates of first incarceration, the study said, an estimated 28 percent of black men would enter state or federal prison during their lifetimes, compared to 16 percent of Hispanic men and 4.4 percent of white men.*

***Juveniles in adult prisons.** States were increasingly prosecuting juveniles as adults and sending them to prison for violent crimes, the Justice Department reported on February 27. In 1997, the study said, 7,400 youths aged seventeen or younger were sent to adult prisons after having been convicted in either juvenile or adult courts—more than twice as many as in 1985. Seventy percent of those juvenile offenders had been convicted of violent crimes, such as robbery, murder, and aggravated assault. Largely in response to numerous high-profile cases of violent crimes by juveniles, thirty states had passed laws since 1992 allowing juveniles to be tried in adult criminal court under certain circumstances.*

*California became the most recent state to toughen its laws against juvenile crime. On March 7 California voters approved a referendum known as Proposition 21 that allowed prosecutors—rather than judges—to decide whether to try juveniles as adults for serious crimes such as murder. Juveniles could be subject to mandatory minimum sentences, and authorities could disclose names of juvenile suspects even before they were charged. In addition, the new law limited the authority of judges to sentence convicted juveniles to probation or to treatment facilities, rather than prison. Ironically, voters approved the changes overwhelmingly (by a margin of 62 percent of 38 percent) despite the fact that juvenile crime had been declining in California since 1995.*

***Drug use among jail inmates.** A nationwide study reported by the Bureau of Justice Statistics on May 10 found that 70 percent of inmates in local jails had committed a drug-related offense or had used drugs regularly before their arrests. Moreover, of those inmates who were tested for drugs in June 1998, 10.5 percent were found to be positive.*

*Following is the text of a news release issued October 15, 2000, by the Federal Bureau of Investigation summarizing the findings of its annual report,* Crime in the United States, 1999. *The document was obtained from the Internet at http://www.fbi.gov/ucr .htm.*

The Federal Bureau of Investigation today announced the eighth consecutive annual decrease in serious crime. The final 1999 statistics released by the Uniform Crime Reporting (UCR) Program in the annual publication *Crime in the United States, 1999* indicate that reported serious crime was down 7 percent from the 1998 figure and 16 percent from the 1995 figure.

Compared to totals for 1998, both violent and property crime totals declined by 7 percent according to publication figures.

Decreases of 8 percent from 1998 to 1999 were recorded for the violent crimes of both murder and robbery. Aggravated assault figures fell by 6 percent, and forcible rape statistics fell by 4 percent. In 1999, the number of violent crimes was 20 percent below the 1995 figure and 21 percent below the 1990 figure.

The property crimes of burglary, motor vehicle theft, and larceny-theft demonstrated decreases of 10, 8, and 6 percent, respectively. The number of property crimes reported in 1999 was 15 percent below the 1995 level and 19 percent below the 1990 level.

The 8-percent decline in reported serious crime in suburban counties was only slightly higher than the 7-percent decline reported in rural areas and in the Nation's cities overall.

Crime in the United States, 1999, based on reports submitted by approximately 17,000 city, county, and state law enforcement agencies across the country, contains the most current national crime data available. Estimates are included for nonreporting areas.

Highlights from the 1999 edition include:

## Crime Volume

- Crime Index total of approximately 11.6 million offenses in 1999 represents a 7-percent decline from the 1998 total. National totals have declined 16 percent since 1995 and 20 percent since 1990.
- Representing 35 percent of the country's population, the South accounted for 41 percent of the reported crime total. The West, with 22 percent of the population, accounted for 23 percent; the Midwest, with 23 percent of the population, accounted for 22 percent; and the Northeast, comprising 19 percent of the population, accounted for 14 percent. Overall Crime Index total decreases of 10 percent in the West, 7 percent in both the Northeast and the Midwest, and 5 percent in the South were recorded.

## Crime Rate

- The 1999 Crime Index rate, 4,267 offenses per 100,000 population, was 8 percent lower than in 1998. For 5- and 10-year trend increments, the 1999 rate was 19 percent below the 1995 rate and 27 percent lower than the 1990 rate.
- By region, the South registered a Crime Index rate of 4,932 offenses per 100,000 population. The West registered a rate of 4,328; the Midwest, a rate of 4,041; and the Northeast, a rate of 3,233. Declines from the previous year's rates were reported in all four regions.
- A Crime Index rate of 4,600 offenses per 100, 000 inhabitants was recorded in Metropolitan Statistical Areas. A rate of 4,561 per 100,000 was registered in cities outside the Nation's metropolitan areas, and a rate of 1,901 was recorded in rural counties.

## Violent Crime

- Marking the lowest violent crime rate since 1978_525 offenses per 100,000 inhabitants—an estimated 1.4 million violent crimes were reported in 1999.

- Compared to the 1998 figures, declines in both volume and rate were recorded in all the violent crime categories: murder, forcible rape, robbery, and aggravated assault.
- Aggravated assaults accounted for 64 percent and robberies for 29 percent of all violent crimes reported to law enforcement in 1999. Murder accounted for 1 percent of the total.
- In 1999 personal weapons (hands, fists, feet, etc.) were used in slightly more than 32 percent of the murder, robbery, and aggravated assault offenses, collectively. Firearms were used in 25 percent of those crimes. Knives or cutting instruments were used in 15 percent, and other dangerous weapons accounted for the remaining 27 percent.

## Property Crime

- The 1999 volume and rate figures fell in all property crime categories. Totaling an estimated 10.2 million offenses, the property crime total was 7 percent lower than the 1998 figure.
- At 3,742 offenses per 100,000 population, the property crime rate was 8 percent lower than the 1998 figure.
- Estimated at a total loss of nearly $14.8 billion for 1999, the value of property stolen in connection with property crime offenses averaged $1,449.

## Hate Crime

- In 1999, of the total 7,876 hate crime incidents reported, 4,295 were motivated by racial bias, 1,411 by religious bias, 1,317 by sexual orientation bias, 829 by ethnic bias, and 19 by disability bias. Five of the incidents were motivated by multiple bias.
- Nearly 233 million of the Nation's populace was represented by the 12,122 agencies participating in hate crime data collection for 1999.
- Sixty-seven percent of the 9,301 offenses reported were recorded as crimes against persons. Of these crimes, intimidation accounted for 53 percent of the total. Simple and aggravated assault accounted for 29 and 18 percent, respectively. Murder and rape each accounted for less than 1 percent.

## Crime Clearances

- A Crime Index clearance rate of 21 percent was recorded by law enforcement agencies across the Nation. The clearance rate for violent crimes was 50 percent; for property crimes, 18 percent.
- Recorded at 69 percent, the national clearance rate was highest for murder. The lowest clearance rate, 14 percent, was recorded for burglary.
- Offenses involving only offenders under 18 years of age accounted for 19 percent of the overall Crime Index clearances, 12 percent of the violent crime clearances, and 22 percent of the property crime clearances.

## Arrests

- The estimated 14 million arrests made for all criminal infractions (excluding traffic violations) during the year represents a decrease of 5 percent over the 1998 figure. Violations for drug abuse and driving under the influence registered the highest number of estimated arrests, over 1.5 million each. There were an estimated 1.2 million arrests for larceny-theft and 1.3 million for simple assault. In 1999 there were 5,317 arrests per 100,000 population.

- Compared to figures from 1998, juvenile arrests decreased 8 percent in 1999. Adult arrests fell 4 percent. Arrests of both juveniles and adults for violent crime fell 8 and 6 percent, respectively.
- Forty-five percent of all persons arrested in 1999 were under the age of 25, and 17 percent were under the age of 18. Juveniles and females were most frequently arrested for larceny-theft. Adults and males were most often arrested for drug abuse violations and driving under the influence. Males comprised 78 percent of persons arrested, and whites accounted for 69 percent.
- Thirty-one percent of all arrests were for drug abuse violations and alcohol-related offenses.

## Murder

- The murder count for 1999 was estimated at 15,533, a total 8 percent lower than the 1998 estimate and 28 percent lower than the 1995 estimate. The recorded rate of 6 per 100,000 inhabitants was the lowest figure since 1966.
- Supplemental data were submitted for 12,658 murders, demonstrating that 88 percent of murder victims in 1999 were aged 18 years or older and 76 percent were male. Fifty percent of victims were white, 47 percent were black, and the remaining were persons of other races.
- Data based on a total of 14,112 murder offenders showed that 90 percent of the assailants were male, and 90 percent were 18 years of age or older. Fifty percent of the offenders were black, 45 percent were white, and the remaining were persons of other races.
- Murder victims were slain by people they knew in 48 percent of the incidents. Husbands or boyfriends were the offenders in 32 percent of the murders in which females were victims. Wives or girlfriends were the offenders in 3 percent of the incidents in which males were killed.
- By circumstance, 30 percent of the murders resulted from arguments and 17 percent from felonious activities such as robbery, arson, etc.
- Data indicate that murder is most often intraracial. Ninety-four percent of black murder victims were slain by black offenders in 1999. Eighty-five percent of white victims were slain by white offenders.
- Firearm use in murder incidents increased from 6 out of every 10 in 1998 to 7 out of 10 in 1999.

## Forcible Rape

- Representing the seventh year of decline, the estimated total of 89,107 forcible rapes reported to law enforcement during 1999 was the lowest total since 1985.

- The 1999 rape rate—64 out of every 100,000 females—was 5 percent lower that the previous year's rate.

## Robbery

- In 1999, law enforcement agencies recorded an estimated 409,670 robberies, a rate of 150 robberies per 100,000 population nationwide. The volume of robbery was down 8 percent from the 1998 total.
- Monetary loss attributed to property stolen in connection with this offense was estimated at over $463 million. Bank robberies resulted in the highest average losses, $4,552 per offense; convenience store robberies in the lowest, $620.
- Slightly less than half of all robberies took place on streets or highways.
- Robberies committed through the use of strong-arm tactics accounted for 42 percent of all robberies perpetrated in 1999. Those committed with firearms accounted for 40 percent of the total. Knives or cutting instruments were involved in 8 percent of the total, and other weapons were used in the remainder.

## Aggravated Assault

- Dropping 6 percent from the 1998 figure, 1999 aggravated assaults totaled an estimated 916,383 offenses.
- Aggravated assaults accounted for 64 percent of the violent crimes in 1999.
- Thirty-five percent of the aggravated assaults in 1999 were committed with blunt objects or other dangerous weapons. Personal weapons were used in 29 percent of the incidents, and firearms and knives or cutting instruments each accounted for 18 percent.

## Burglary

- Representing a decline of 10 percent from the 1998 figure, an estimated 2.1 million burglaries were reported in 1999. Residences were targeted in 2 of every 3 burglaries.
- Property stolen during burglaries was valued at an estimated $3.1 billion.
- Forcible entry was involved in 64 percent of all reported burglaries. Fifty-three percent of burglaries were committed during daylight hours. Monetary loss associated with residential burglaries averaged $1,441 and with nonresidential burglaries, $1,490.

## Larceny-theft

- An estimated total of 7 million larceny-thefts were reported in 1999. This offense comprised 68 percent of the property crime total and 60 percent of the Crime Index total.
- The total dollar loss to victims nationwide was over $4.7 billion. The average value of property stolen was $678 per incident.
- Thefts of motor vehicle parts, accessories, and contents made up the largest portion of reported larceny-thefts, 36 percent.

## Motor Vehicle Theft

- The estimated 1.1 million motor vehicle thefts in 1999 was the lowest reported since 1985. The 1999 total represents an 8-percent drop in motor vehicle thefts from the 1998 figure.
- The estimated value of motor vehicles stolen nationwide was over $7 billion. The estimated average value of stolen motor vehicles was $6,104.
- Automobiles, comprising 75 percent of all motor vehicle theft offenses, were the vehicles most frequently reported stolen. Trucks and buses accounted for 19 percent, and the remainder included other types of vehicles.

## Arson

- A total of 76,045 arson offenses was reported in 1999, a 4-percent decline from the previous year's total.
- For 45 percent of reported arson offenses, structures were the most frequent targets. Sixty-one percent of the structural arson incidents during the year targeted residential property, and 43 percent of these structural arsons were directed at single-family dwellings.
- Property damaged due to arson was valued at an average $10,882 per offense.
- Persons under the age of 18 were involved in 48 percent of arson incidents cleared in 1999. Of the 8 Crime Index offenses, arson had the highest percentage of juvenile involvement.

## Law Enforcement Employees

- A total of 13,313 city, county, and state law enforcement agencies submitted law enforcement employee data to the national UCR Program. Collectively, these agencies employed 637,551 officers and 261,567 civilians and provided law enforcement services to nearly 253 million inhabitants across the country in 1999.
- The 1999 average rate of 2.5 full-time officers for every 1,000 inhabitants remained the same as in 1998.
- The Nation's cities collectively employed 2.5 officers per 1,000 inhabitants, rural law enforcement 2.6 officers per 1,000, and suburban law enforcement 2.7 officers per 1,000.
- Geographically, the highest rate of officers to population was recorded in the Northeastern States with 2.9 officers per 1,000 inhabitants.
- Twenty-nine percent of the total law enforcement employees were comprised of civilians.

# CLINTON ON THE BOMBING
# OF THE USS *COLE*
## October 18, 2000

*The USS* Cole, *a warship docked at the port of Aden, Yemen, was bombed on October 12, 2000, by a small boat carrying heavy explosives. Seventeen U.S. sailors aboard the* Cole—*as well as two terrorists aboard the attack boat—were killed in the blast, and thirty-nine other sailors were injured on the* Cole. *The Yemeni government, aided by a large task force of U.S. investigators, detained at least six men suspected of helping plan the bombing.*

*U.S. officials said ultimate responsibility for the attack rested with Osama bin Laden, a wealthy Saudi Arabian businessman who had also been accused of plotting the bombing in September 1998 of U.S. embassies in Kenya and Tanzania in August 1998; those attacks killed twelve Americans and more than two hundred Africans. Prior to the* Cole *bombing, the most recent successful terrorist attack against a U.S. military target was the 1996 bombing of the Khobar Towers apartment complex in Saudi Arabia, killing nineteen American air force personnel and injuring more than five hundred Americans and Saudis.* (Khobar Tower bombings, Historic Documents of 1996, p. 672; Embassy bombings, Historic Documents of 1998, p. 555)

*U.S. officials said late in the year that they had uncovered evidence that the bombing of the* Cole *was part of a broader plan for terrorist attacks against the United States—several of which were supposed to have taken place at the beginning of the year. According to this evidence, the attack on the* Cole *originally had been planned instead against another ship, the USS* The Sullivans, *which had been at the Aden port for a refueling stop on January 3. A boat that was supposed to attack* The Sullivans *reportedly sank before it could carry out its mission. Terrorist attacks might also have been planned against targets in the United States but were foiled by the arrest in December 1999 of Ahmed Ressem, who was stopped while allegedly trying to smuggle bomb-making equipment from Canada to Washington State.* (Ressem arrest, Historic Documents of 1999, p. 499)

*Two U.S. military investigations were under way to determine whether security lapses could have made the* Cole *vulnerable to the terrorist bombing. One probe, by the navy, reportedly found no grounds for punishing the ship's captain and crew, even though they had failed to take some precautionary measures. A broader Defense Department review was looking into possible shortcomings in U.S. policy or intelligence gathering. Several other panels issued reports during the year warning that the United States was becoming increasingly vulnerable to a broad range of terrorist threats.* (Terrorism reports, p. 277)

*Speaking at a memorial service for the dead sailors, held in Norfolk, Virginia, on October 18, President Bill Clinton pledged to take action against those responsible for the bombing. "To those who attacked them, we say, 'You will not find a safe harbor. We will find you and justice will prevail.'" Clinton and other senior administration officials said the attack on the* Cole *would not deter the United States from its military and diplomatic roles in the Middle East. "We're not leaving," Defense Secretary William S. Cohen said during a visit to Bahrain on November 16.*

## What Went Wrong

*On October 12 the* Cole—*a destroyer of the Arleigh Burke class—was at the port of Aden for a routine refueling stop on its way to join a U.S. naval task force in the Persian Gulf. Shortly before noon, local time, a small boat, with two men aboard, approached the port side, about mid-ship, of the 505-foot-long warship. Suddenly, a massive explosion erupted, blowing a 40' × 40' hole in the* Cole *at the waterline and demolishing the attack boat. The blast flooded several compartments of the* Cole *and killed seventeen sailors, most in their late teens or early twenties. Most of the bodies remained in flooded areas below deck for several days after the attack as sailors worked frantically to keep the damaged ship from sinking.*

*In the first hours and days after the attack, navy officials issued conflicting and confusing reports about what had happened. At first, the navy said the attack boat was one of several small vessels that were helping the* Cole *tie up to the refueling station—a situation that raised the possibility that the attackers were employed by or associated with the local port authority. A week later, the navy revealed that the* Cole *already had moored and was in the refueling process when it was attacked. Armed guards patrolling the* Cole's *decks took no action to head off the boat. Several sailors later said they assumed the boat was a "scow" that was preparing to help remove some of the tons of garbage aboard the* Cole.

*The* Washington Post *reported on December 9 that an internal investigation by the U.S. Navy had found that the* Cole's *captain, Commander Kirk S. Lippold, had not fully implemented a security plan he had filed with superiors before his ship entered the port of Aden. The newspaper said details of the plan, and the exact extent of Lippold's compliance with it, had not been revealed. But navy officials told the* Post *that the attack against the* Cole *probably would have been successful even if the security plan had been in full effect. Navy officials said it was also unclear whether Lippold had received intelligence information from higher authorities that would have given him adequate warning of the terrorist threat his ship faced.*

*A broader question facing Pentagon investigators was why senior U.S.*

*military commanders had listed the port of Aden at a relatively low-risk level—known as "Threat Condition Bravo"—despite a high level of turmoil in the Middle East at the time and the fact that Yemen was known to be home to numerous terrorists. The attack against the* Cole *came just two weeks after the eruption of violence between Israelis and Palestinians following the failure of U.S.-led peace talks. Many Arabs condemned the United States for its support of Israel.* (Middle East violence, p. 930)

*The* Cole *was shipped back to the United States aboard a massive Norwegian transport ship, the* M/V Blue Marlin. *At year's end the* Cole *was undergoing repairs at the Ingalls Shipyard in Pascagoula, Mississippi, where it had been built in 1995. The navy said the repairs were expected to take about one year and cost about $240 million.*

## *Searching for the Terrorists*

*News reports on December 12 listed six suspects, who were said to have been detained by Yemeni authorities in connection with the bombing. According to the reports, the most important of the six suspects was Jamal al-Badawi, who was said to have been in charge of arranging some details of the bombing, including obtaining the boat that carried the explosives.*

*A seventh suspect—the man who might have supervised the bombing on bin Laden's behalf—was still at large as the year ended. He was Mohammed Omar al-Harazi, a Saudi citizen born in the Haraz mountains of Yemen, an area said to have produced numerous terrorists. News reports said Al-Badawi had identified al-Harazi as the man who gave him instructions, by telephone, for the bombing of the* Cole. *Al-Badawi reportedly said he and al-Harazi had first met in Afghanistan during the decade-long war against the Soviet occupation of that country. Also according to the news reports, Al-Badawi told investigators that he assumed that al-Harazi's involvement meant that bin Laden was ultimately responsible for planning and financing the operation.*

> *Following is the text of a speech delivered October 18, 2000, by President Bill Clinton during a memorial service at the Norfolk Naval Shipyard, Virginia, for seventeen sailors killed when the USS* Cole *was bombed in Aden, Yemen, on October 12. The document was obtained from the Internet at http://www.pub .whitehouse.gov/uri-res/l2R?urn:pdi://oma.eop.gov.us/2000/10/ 18/9.text.1.*

. . . Today, we honor our finest young people; fallen soldiers who rose to freedom's challenge. We mourn their loss, celebrate their lives, offer the love and prayers of a grateful nation to their families.

For those of us who have to speak here, we are all mindful of the limits of our poor words to lift your spirits or warm your hearts. We know that God has given us the gift of reaching our middle years. And we now have to pray for your children, your husbands, your wives, your brothers, your sisters, who were taken so young. We know we will never know them as you did or remember them as you will; the first time you saw them in uniform, or the last time you said goodbye.

They all had their own stories and their own dreams. We Americans have learned something about each and every one of them over these last difficult days as their profiles, their lives, their loves, their service, have been given to us. For me, I learned a little more when I met with all the families this morning.

Some follow the family tradition of Navy service; others hoped to use their service to earn a college degree. One of them had even worked for me in the White House. Richard Costelow was a technology wizard who helped to update the White House communications system for this new century.

All these very different Americans, all with their different stories, their lifelines and love ties, answered the same call of service and found themselves on the USS *Cole*, headed for the Persian Gulf, where our forces are working to keep peace and stability in a region that could explode and disrupt the entire world.

Their tragic loss reminds us that even when America is not at war, the men and women of our military still risk their lives for peace. I am quite sure history will record in great detail our triumphs in battle, but I regret that no one will ever be able to write a full account of the wars we never fought, the losses we never suffered, the tears we never shed because men and women like those who were on the USS *Cole* were standing guard for peace. We should never, ever forget that.

Today, I ask all Americans just to take a moment to thank the men and women of our Armed Forces for a debt we can never repay, whose character and courage, more than even modern weapons, makes our military the strongest in the world. And in particular, I ask us to thank God today for the lives, the character and courage of the crew of the USS *Cole*, including the wounded and especially those we lost or are missing: Hull Maintenance Technician Third Class Kenneth Eugene Clodfelter; Electronics Technician Chief Petty Officer First Class Richard Costelow; Mess Management Specialist Seaman Lakeina Monique Francis; Information Systems Technician Seaman Timothy Lee Gauna; Signalman Seaman Apprentice Cheron Louis Gunn; Seaman James Rodrick McDaniels; Engineman Second Class Mark Ian Nieto; Electronics Warfare Technician Third Class Ronald Scott Owens; Seaman Apprentice Lakiba Nicole Palmer. Engine Fireman Joshua Langdon Parlett; Fireman Apprentice Patrick Howard Roy; Electronics Warfare Technician Second Class Kevin Shawn Rux; Mess Management Specialist Third Class Ronchester Managan Santiago; Operations Specialist Second Class Timothy Lamont Saunders; Fireman Gary Graham Swenchonis, Jr.; Ensign Andrew Triplett; Seaman Apprentice Craig Bryan Wibberley.

In the names and faces of those we lost and mourn, the world sees our nation's greatest strength. People in uniform rooted in every race, creed and region on the face of the earth; yet, bound together by a common commitment to freedom and a common pride in being American. That same spirit is living today as the crew of the USS *Cole* pulls together in a determined struggle to keep the determined warrior afloat.

The idea of common humanity and unity amidst diversity, so purely embodied by those we mourn today, must surely confound the minds of the hate-filled terrorists who killed them. They envy our strength without understanding the values that give us strength. For, for them, it is their way or no way. Their interpretation, twisted though it may be, of a beautiful religious tradition. Their political views, their racial and ethnic views. Their way or no way.

Such people can take innocent life. They have caused your tears and anguish, but they can never heal, or build harmony, or bring people together. That is work only free, law-abiding people can do. People like the sailors of the USS *Cole*.

To those who attacked them, we say: you will not find a safe harbor. We will find you, and justice will prevail. America will not stop standing guard for peace or freedom or stability in the Middle East and around the world.

But some way, someday, people must learn the lesson of the lives of those we mourn today, of how they worked together, of how they lived together, of how they reached across all the lines that divided them and embraced their common humanity and the common values of freedom and service.

Not far from here, there is a quiet place that honors those who gave their lives in service to our country. Adorning its entrance are words from a poem by Archibald Macleish; not only a tribute to the young we lost, but a summons to those of us left behind. Listen to them.

The young no longer speak, but:

They have a silence that speaks for them at night.

They say: we were young, remember us.

They say: we have done what we could, but until it is finished, it is not done.

They say: our deaths are not ours; they are yours; they will mean what you make them.

They say: whether our lives and our deaths were for peace and a new hope, we cannot say; it is you who must say this.

They say: we leave you our deaths. Give them their meaning.

The lives of the men and women we lost on the USS *Cole* meant so much to those who loved them, to all Americans, to the cause of freedom. They have given us their deaths. Let us give them their meaning. Their meaning of peace and freedom, of reconciliation and love, of service, endurance and hope. After all they have given us, we must give them their meaning.

I ask now that you join me in a moment of silence and prayer for the lost, the missing, and their grieving families.

(A moment of silence is observed.)

Amen. Thank you, and may God bless you all.

# SECRETARY OF STATE ALBRIGHT ON HER VISIT TO NORTH KOREA
## October 24, 2000

*One of the most important—and dangerous—remaining vestiges of the cold war began to crumble during 2000 as the communist regime of North Korea began to emerge from a half-century of diplomatic isolation. North Korean leader Kim Jong Il met in Pyongyang in June with his South Korean counterpart, President Kim Dae-jung, and four months later hosted U.S. Secretary of State Madeleine K. Albright for the highest-level talks ever held between the two countries. North Korea also established diplomatic relations with more than a half-dozen U.S. allies, including Great Britain.* (North-South Korean summit, p. 359)

*Until the last days of the year, it appeared possible that President Bill Clinton might visit North Korea before he left office in January 2001. But Clinton resisted the temptation to become the first U.S. president to visit Pyongyang and said on December 29 that "there is not enough time" for the two countries to negotiate agreements that he considered to be a necessary prelude to such a trip. Most important, U.S. and North Korean diplomats had been unable to conclude an agreement to halt North Korea's development and export of ballistic missiles.*

### Background to U.S.-North Korean Talks

*The United States and North Korea had been hostile enemies ever since the beginning of the Korean War in 1950, when Pyongyang sent hundreds of thousands of troops across the border into South Korea. The United States came to South Korea's aid and after a three-year war managed to push North Korea and its communist Chinese allies back across the border. The war ended in 1953 with an armistice. Ever since, the United States had stationed nearly 40,000 troops in South Korea.*

*The first serious diplomatic discussions between the United States and North Korea came in 1994, when the Clinton administration moved to head off that country's production of plutonium that could be used to in nuclear weapons. Under an "Agreed Framework" signed in 1994, North Korea pledged to stop producing plutonium (and to place its existing plutonium under international supervision) in return for a U.S.- and Japanese-led international program to help the country with its energy production, including building two nuclear power reactors.*

*Complying with that agreement, North Korea placed enough plutonium to make five or six nuclear weapons under the control of the International Atomic Energy Agency. In 1999 North Korea also allowed U.S. officials to inspect an underground site that intelligence specialists had suspected was a secret nuclear weapons facility; the officials said they uncovered no evidence to justify those suspicions. Despite these steps, some U.S. experts said they believed North Korea still might have a significant quantity of nuclear weapons-grade plutonium.*

*A second issue arose in 1998 when North Korea launched a medium-range ballistic missile, reportedly in a failed attempt to put a small communications satellite into orbit. That step generated widespread fears that Pyongyang ultimately could develop the capabilities to produce nuclear weapons and to deliver them long distances, reaching even the United States and western Europe. At Clinton's request, former secretary of defense William J. Perry traveled to Pyongyang in 1999 and developed a long-term plan to address U.S. concerns about North Korea's actions. At Perry's request, North Korea agreed to a moratorium on further missile tests; in return, Clinton in September 1999 announced plans to ease some U.S. economic sanctions against North Korea.* (Perry report, Historic Documents of 1999, p. 568)

*In parallel with these developments on security issues, the United States joined most other Western countries in responding with huge quantities of food and humanitarian supplies to alleviate a prolonged famine in North Korea, which began during a drought in 1995. In 1999–2000 the United States provided more than 550,000 tons of food for North Korea, according to the State Department.*

*The continuing effects of the famine, coupled with the near-collapse of his country's economy as the consequence of a half-century of communist mismanagement, led North Korean leader Kim Jong Il to respond favorably to Kim Dae-jung's overtures for improved relations. In June the two leaders met in Pyongyang and signed an agreement calling for eventual unification of their countries. Acknowledging that unification probably would take years, the two Kims initiated several preliminary steps, including reunions of family members who had been separated ever since the Korean War. Kim Dae-jung in December was awarded the Nobel Peace Prize in recognition of his leadership in improving relations between the two Koreas.*

## Albright in Pyongyang

*A direct consequence of the inter-Korean summit was a new push for high-level diplomatic discussions between the United States and North Korea. Most of the action took place during a two-week period in October. First, on October 10–11, Jo Myong Rok—generally considered to be Kim Jong Il's second-in-command—visited Washington and met with Clinton, Albright, Defense Secretary William S. Cohen, and other senior administration offi-*

*cials. Jo thus became the highest ranking North Korean official ever to visit Washington and meet with a U.S. president.*

*On October 23 Albright arrived in Pyongyang, becoming the highest-ranking U.S. official ever to visit North Korea. On the evening of her first day in the capital, Albright was treated to an astonishing spectacle at the city's sports stadium: an estimated 100,000 performers celebrating the history of the North Korean Workers Party in song, dance, and synchronized movements. During a news conference the next day, Albright said that during the performance, when an image of North Korea's new medium-range missile was displayed, Kim "turned to me and quipped this was the first satellite launch and it would be the last." Albright and other U.S. officials said that remark appeared to be a deliberate attempt by Kim to assure the United States that he was willing to consider ending his country's ballistic missile program.*

*Albright said she had found Kim to be a "very good listener, a good interlocutor," in contrast to a widespread perception of him as a playboy who was addicted to movies and uninterested in matters of serious policy. Kim became North Korea's leader in 1994 after the death of his father, Kim Il-Sung, who had dominated the country for nearly a half-century.*

*News reporters who accompanied Albright found Pyongyang to be a clean but drab city with little automobile traffic and few consumer goods for sale in stores. Reporters were not allowed to travel outside the city, and all encounters with citizens and government officials were strictly choreographed to convey an impression of well-being.*

*In the days after her trip, Albright came under sharp criticism for some of her actions in Pyongyang, including her reported failure to make North Korea's poor human rights record a major topic of discussions. Several commentators also criticized Albright's attendance at the Workers Party celebration. Among them, the* Washington Post *said in an editorial: "We were amazed that the secretary of state would allow herself to be photographed, smiling, as 100,000 essentially enslaved laborers performed for her and one of the world's most repressive dictators. Secretary Albright clinked champagne glasses with Mr. Kim; she found him to be 'very decisive and practical and serious.' But about the nation's 150,000 political prisoners, she had no public comment."*

*In response to such criticisms, Albright said: "I have been a student of communist affairs all my life and so one knows perfectly well how these performances are put together. I just can assure you that these glasses that I have on are not rose-colored."*

### Planning a Presidential Visit

*During Albright's visit, Kim Jong Il invited President Clinton to visit Pyongyang, and for two months U.S. and North Korean diplomats discussed the preliminary steps that were necessary for such a historic event to take place. The key item on the agenda was the Clinton administration's insistence that North Korea end all aspects of its ballistic missile program, including exports of missile systems and components to other countries.*

*In a Washington news conference held November 2, Albright said she had returned from her trip to Pyongyang "convinced that the possibilities for mutually acceptable agreements on missiles are real." The administration was not necessarily rushing to reach an agreement before the end of Clinton's term, she said, but added: "We would be irresponsible if we didn't take advantage of a historic opportunity to move beyond fifty years of cold war divisions and reduce the dangers of North Korean missiles, that the North Korean missiles pose around the globe."*

*One day after Albright spoke, senior U.S. and North Korean diplomats concluded a series of meetings in Kuala Lumpur, Malaysia, without reaching an agreement on the missile issue. Robert Einhorn, an assistant secretary of state who led the U.S. delegation, said "significant issues remain to be explored and resolved," but he offered no details on the substance of the talks. As a result, other administration officials said it appeared unlikely that Clinton would be traveling to Pyongyang. Even so, throughout the rest of November and into December administration officials held out some hope that it would be possible to reach an agreement setting the stage for such a trip. On December 29 Clinton issued a statement saying he had concluded that he did not have enough time to conclude the necessary agreement. The United States has "a clear national interest in seeing it through," he said, offering the prediction that "the next administration will be able to consummate this agreement."*

*The next administration was to be headed by George W. Bush, who, along with his top foreign policy aides, had expressed deep reservations about the wisdom of the Clinton administration's overtures to North Korea. Bush had cited North Korea's missile program as the primary justification for his proposal for an extensive national missile defense system.* (Missile defense, p. 677)

> *Following is the text of a news conference conducted October 24, 2000, by Secretary of State Madeleine K. Albright during her visit to Pyongyang, the capital of the Democratic People's Republic of Korea (North Korea). The document was obtained from the Internet at http://secretary.state.gov/www/statements/2000/001024b .html.*

**Secretary Albright:** I came to Pyongyang to convey directly to Chairman Kim Jong Il the views of President Clinton and to prepare for a possible visit by the President to the DPRK [Democratic People's Republic of Korea]. During my visit, I have held six hours of serious and constructive talks with Chairman Kim, and also had an opportunity to meet with him more informally over dinners and at cultural events.

I also met with Vice Marshall Jo Myong Rok, Presidium President Kim Yong Nam, and Foreign Minister Paek Nam Sun.

I want to thank Chairman Kim, Vice Marshall Jo, and the North Korean people for the exceptional hospitality they have shown me and our delegation during this first ever visit by an American Cabinet Officer to the DPRK. I was struck by the beauty of Pyongyang, and by the genuine sweetness of the children.

I explained to Chairman Kim America's vision for relations between our countries free from past hostility, relations which contribute to peace and stability throughout the region, and which support the process of reconciliation between the North and the South.

It is important that we work to overcome the enmities of the past and focus on the prospect for a brighter future for our peoples.

Chairman Kim and I had serious, constructive, and in-depth discussions of proposals on diplomatic relations, missile restraint, and security issues.

Chairman Kim and I discussed the full range of our concerns on missiles, including both the DPRK's indigenous missile programs and exports. We also discussed Chairman Kim's idea of exchanging DPRK restraint in missiles for launches of DPRK satellites. Chairman Kim was quite clear in explaining his understanding of U.S. concerns.

Indeed, during the October 23 mass performance we attended together, an image of the DPRK Taepodong missile appeared. He immediately turned to me and quipped that this was the first satellite launch and it would be the last.

While here, I also raised with our DPRK hosts the full range of our concerns, including global issues and compliance with international norms, terrorism, human rights, the need to obtain the fullest possible accounting of missing persons, humanitarian issues, and the need for concrete steps at tension reduction on the Peninsula.

We made important progress, but much work remains to be done, and I am pleased to announce that our missile experts will reconvene next week.

I also had an opportunity to visit a World Food Program distribution center and see with my own eyes some of the very talented and hopeful children to whom our food aid is directed, and I hope my visit here will be a step in helping them and all children on the Peninsula to build a better future.

I will be reporting back to President Clinton on these talks and consulting in Seoul with our Republic of Korea and Japanese allies.

Thank you and I am ready for your questions.

**Question:** Madame Secretary, the quip you eluded to at the event last night: Do you take that as an unqualified pledge on Chairman Kim's part not to test missiles anymore?

**Albright:** Well, as you well know, we have a moratorium on testing of all long-range missiles, and we obviously are continuing these very serious missile discussions. I take what he said on these issues as serious in terms of his desire and ours to move forward to resolve the various questions that continue to exist on the whole range of missile issues.

**Question:** Madame Secretary, what steps do you think are necessary before a presidential trip would be warranted? What benefits would such a trip produce in terms of improving this relationship?

**Albright:** First of all, I think it's very important to understand how long discussions have been going on in an attempt to have the North-South relationship improve and to also have a change in terms of our own relationship. This has been going on for at least a year and a half in a variety of venues and on a variety of subjects—the whole range of subjects. And we are taking this on a very step-by-step approach and doing everything that we are doing in terms of U.S. national interests.

I will report to the President the results of this trip and the results of what I have described, characterized as constructive talks and the value, frankly, of face-to-face discussions. I believe that the six hours of serious talks that I had with the Chairman are a very good way, I think, to learn more about his intentions and those of his country. It's always useful to have these kinds of discussions, but I will be reporting to the President and he will make the decisions about future steps.

**Question:** Madame Secretary, I'm curious a little bit about your personal impressions of this country. It's one that has been closed to Americans for many years. It's not easy for Americans to travel here. Your personal impressions of President Kim Jong Il and also of the performance last night—given your background as a refugee from certain kinds of absolutist regimes, what your reflections are on that?

**Albright:** First of all, I think we have to keep things in perspective. We haven't exactly seen a lot of this country. We have seen Pyongyang, and I must say even though I had seen some photographs that I found that it is an impressive city. Quite beautiful, I think, with its landscaping and heroic monuments, and I was obviously interested in seeing that. I found the performance last night—first of all I wasn't born yesterday, and I have been a student of communist affairs all my life, and so one knows perfectly well how these performances are put together. I must say that I thought it was, of that kind of a performance, it was quite spectacular and amazing. And I just can assure you that these glasses that I have on are not rose-colored.

As far as the Chairman himself, I was obviously very glad to meet him. He is somewhat of a mystery to the world and to Americans. I spent, as I said, not only the six hours at meetings, but our inner last night and the performance. And we're going to be having dinner tonight. So there have been informal times, too. I think I would describe him as a very good listener and a good interlocutor.

He strikes me as very decisive and practical and serious. We had serious discussions.

**Question:** Madame Secretary, after two days of talks in Pyongyang, what is your suggestion to Japan? Do you, are you now hoping that Japan would go as quickly as the United States in improving its relations with the DPRK, or do you think that they should take their time and address their own concern about the Japanese Red Army terrorists and kidnapping incidents and so on? And have you got any indication whatsoever from the North Korean leaders that they would expel the Japanese Red Army terrorists sometime in the near future?

**Albright:** I spoke with Foreign Minister Kono before I got to Pyongyang, and I'm looking forward to seeing him tomorrow in Seoul. I believe that it's very important for each country to determine its own pace. I do think there's value in our trilateral cooperation, which is unique, I think, in this circumstance. But everybody, each of the countries, we build on—at least from the American perspective—our relationship is being built on what President Kim Dae Jung was able to do. The Japanese have to make their own assessment, and it's very hard for me to judge what the North Korean reaction is to the Japanese conditions. We discussed it, but I think that it's difficult for me to make an assessment of what they will do.

**Question:** Several of our European allies have announced intentions to resume relations. Did the Chairman indicate to you whether he would be interested in seeing in an American liaison or a diplomatic facility open here? And secondly, on the missile issue, in the talks next week, does this indicate that there was enough progress made that you're trying to get closer to some kind of formal agreement, or does it indicate that we didn't make enough progress on this round of talks—that other talks are needed?

**Albright:** On representation, that's also been a subject that has been under discussion for some time and obviously the Chairman was interested in having just generally across the board, I think, more informal and formal relations with the United States.

I think that the fact that talks are resuming on the expert level is an important step forward, because there are numbers of issues that are discussed in a general way but that need to be discussed by experts specifically. So I would not take it as not enough work having been done. On the contrary, that we are in a very systematic way progressing in discussing what are clearly the most important issues.

**Question:** You told us that you had lengthy discussions with our Chairman Kim Jong Il. I'd like to know what are your impressions of the Chairman, and also what kind of discussions did you have?

**Albright:** I have to say that I was very gratified by the length of our discussions, by the fact that we took up all the subjects of importance to our side and presumably to his, and I found him a very practical and decisive listener and interlocutor.

**Question:** Madame Secretary, by the State Department's own report, North Korea has one of the most repressive human rights records. How did you bring up this subject with the Chairman, what examples did you cite, and how did he respond?

**Albright:** The issue of human rights was raised, the first time that we have raised it, obviously, by a Cabinet-level person. I think that it's obviously a subject of concern, but we have just begun our discussions on the subject. They, obviously, will continue.

# FEDERAL REPORT ON SCHOOL CRIME AND SAFETY
## October 26, 2000

*A series of government reports issued during the year shed new light on the phenomenon of violence in American schools—an issue that had attracted widespread public attention during the 1980s and 1990s. The 1999–2000 school year saw a drop in fatal shootings in the nation's schools, and other indicators pointed to an overall declining level of criminal behavior during the latter part of the decade. But parents, teachers, and students remained deeply concerned about school violence just one year after the April 1999 tragedy at Columbine High School in Littleton, Colorado, in which two teenage boys shot and killed thirteen students and teachers before turning their guns on themselves. The repercussions of the Columbine shootings extended to the nation's entertainment industry, which came under government criticism for its marketing of violent movies, recordings, and electronic games to children. (Columbine shootings, Historic Documents of 1999, p 179; marketing violent entertainment, p. 729)*

*Thirteen school-age children were murdered in the nation's schools during the 1999–2000 school year, a drop of ten from the year before (when the Columbine incident occurred) and the lowest number for any year during the 1990s. The worst year of the decade was 1992–1993, when fifty-two children died in school violence. For the first time in several years, there were no mass killings in U.S. schools during the 1999–2000 academic year.*

## Declining Violence in the Schools

*For the third straight year, the federal education and justice departments jointly issued studies indicating that crime in general was declining in elementary and secondary schools. Released on October 26, 2000, the studies countered public perceptions, as demonstrated in opinion polls and media coverage, that the schools were becoming more dangerous places. One study, "Indicators of School Crime and Safety: 2000," provided a detailed analysis of crime and violent incidents in the nation's schools during the years 1993 through 1998. The other report, the third "Annual Report on School Safety," gave a broader overview of trends in the field, including suggestions for making schools safer for students, teachers, and staff.* (Previous reports, Historic Documents of 1998, p. 735)

*The general thrust of the "Indicators" study was that crime and violence remained serious problems in schools but appeared to be on a downward trend. By nearly every measure used in the report, school crime had declined during the 1990s or, at worst, held steady. Between 1992 and 1998, the study said, the "violent victimization rate" at schools (the number of students subjected to violent attacks) dropped from 48 crimes per 1,000 students to 43 crimes per 1,000 students. That reduction was considered statistically significant. The report also included several measures by which students, teachers, and staff reported their own perceptions of crime and safety and school, including surveys in which they were asked whether they had been victimized by criminal behavior. According to these surveys, for example, the percentage of students who said they were the victims of crime while at school (such as theft or violent crime) declined from 10 percent in 1995 to 8 percent in 1998. However, there was little change during the same period when students were asked if they had been injured or threatened with a weapon on school property; surveys in 1993, 1995, and 1997 all showed about 7 to 8 percent of students in grades nine through twelve said they had experienced an injury or threat in the previous year.*

*Overall, the report found, children were less likely to be hurt by violence while in school than during the rest of the day. In 1998, according to one measure, 253,000 children aged twelve to eighteen were the victims of serious violent crimes (such as sexual assault or robbery) while at school—compared to some 550,000 children of the same age who were victimized by similar crimes away from school. In making this comparison, the study noted that children spend considerably more time away from school than at school. Another study, by the Centers for Disease Control, noted that during a five-year period ending in 1999 fewer than 1 percent of all student homicides took place in the schools.*

## Staying Alert to School Violence

*Two other studies conducted by the country's premier law enforcement agencies attempted to offer parents and school professionals guidance on how to recognize warning signs of possible student violence. One study, "The School Shooter: A Threat Assessment Perspective," was issued September 6 by the Federal Bureau of Investigation. Based on an analysis of school shooting cases and a symposium held in July 1999 (three months after the Columbine shootings), the study offered examples of aberrant behaviors that could indicate that a young person might be considering engaging in violent activity. Alienation from others (including parents and fellow students), excessive fascination with violence, and admiration of "negative role models," such as Hitler or Satan, were among the more than forty examples offered.*

*The study cautioned that there was no "profile" of a typical school shooter or a "checklist of danger signs." Attorney General Janet Reno, in an introduction, warned of the need to avoid "the risk of unfairly labeling and stig-*

*matizing children." Even so, the report said parents and educators needed to pay attention to threats or possible threats—especially when a student had exhibited some signs of aberrant behavior—and develop effective strategies for dealing with them. Despite the FBI's cautions, some educators and specialists expressed concerns that school authorities might use the list of personality traits contained in the study to target troubled students for inappropriate discipline or surveillance.*

*Similar findings came from a study of thirty-seven school shootings since 1974. The study was conducted by the Secret Service in cooperation with the Education Department. Contrary to popular perceptions, the study found, most students who engaged in violent behavior did not act impulsively or "snap" in reaction to a provocation. In 75 percent of the cases studied, violent students had planned their attacks and had told one or more of their peers (often a sibling) about their plans beforehand. For example, the study cited one case in which a student told two dozen friends and fellow students that he wanted to kill others.*

*Like the FBI report, the Secret Service study found that violent students did not fit into a neat profile. Their backgrounds, academic achievement levels, social skills, and behavior patterns varied markedly, the study found. Moreover, the study found that most of the students did not exhibit changed behavior just before engaging in violence—at least so far as educators and parents could tell.*

*Commenting on the study, Education Secretary Richard Riley said: "Young people who need help do not keep it a secret." The problem, he added, was that adults, who could offer the necessary help, "are often the last ones to know." One of the study's coauthors, Education Department official Bill Modzeleski, said it demonstrated the importance of "listening to kids, developing better connections between kids and adults, and developing a culture within the school that allows kids to talk freely and openly about things that are bothering them."*

## *Columbine Report*

*Nearly thirteen months after the Columbine shootings, the Jefferson County, Colorado, Sheriff's Office on May 15 released a detailed account of the event, including a minute-by-minute chronology complete with sound and video recordings. The authors said the report was based on more than 4,000 interviews and more than 10,000 pieces of evidence.*

*The report offered no major disclosures but provided a wealth of details, including the fact that all thirteen people killed had been shot within the first sixteen minutes of the violence. According to the report's chronology, the student killers—Eric Harris and Dylan Klebold—placed two propane bombs in the school cafeteria at 11:14 A.M. When the bombs failed to detonate as planned at 11:15 A.M., the two ran back into the school at 11:19 A.M., first killing two students outside, and then headed to the school library, where they killed the rest of their victims by 11:35 A.M. Harris and Klebold then roamed the hallways, firing their weapons and exploding bombs. The first law enforcement officer, Sheriff's Deputy Neil Gardner, arrived at the school parking lot at 11:23 A.M., and the first police SWAT team entered the school at 12:06 P.M. Two minutes later, Harris and Klebold returned to the library, where they shot themselves in the head. SWAT team members did not reach the library until 3:22 P.M., four hours after the killing began. The shooting rampage left twelve students and one teacher dead. Another twenty-three students were injured.*

> *Following is the executive summary of the report, "Indicators of School Crime and Safety: 2000," issued October 26, 2000, by the National Center of Education Statistics of the U.S. Department of Education and the Bureau of Justice Statistics of the U.S. Department of Justice. The document was obtained from the Internet at http://www.ojp.usdoj.gov/bjs/abstract/iscs00.htm.*

Schools should be safe and secure places for all students, teachers, and staff members. Without a safe learning environment, teachers cannot teach and students cannot learn. In fact, as the data in this report show, more victimizations happen away from school than at school. In 1998, students were about two times as likely to be victims of serious violent crime away from school as at school.

In 1998, students ages 12 through 18 were victims of more than 2.7 million total crimes at school. In that same year, these students were victims of about 253,000 serious violent crimes at school (that is, rape, sexual assault, robbery, and aggravated assault). There were also 60 school-associated violent deaths in the United States between July 1, 1997 and June 30, 1998—including 47 homicides.

The total nonfatal victimization rate for young people declined between 1993 and 1998. The percentage of students being victimized at school also declined over the last few years. Between 1995 and 1999, the percentage of students who reported being victims of crime at school decreased from 10 percent to 8 percent. This decline was due in part to a decline for students in grades 7 through 9. Between 1995 and 1999, the prevalence of reported victimization dropped from 11 percent to 8 percent for 7th graders, from 11 percent to 8 percent for 8th graders, and from 12 percent to 9 percent for 9th graders.

However, for some types of crimes at school, rates have not changed. For example, between 1993 and 1997, the percentage of students in grades 9 through 12 who were threatened or injured with a weapon on school property in the past 12 months remained constant—at about 7 or 8 percent. The percentage of students in grades 9 through 12 who reported being in a physical fight on school property in the past 12 months also remained unchanged between 1993 and 1997—at about 15 percent.

As the rate of victimization in schools has declined or remained constant, students also seem to feel more secure at school now than just a few years ago. The percentage of students ages 12 through 18 who reported avoiding one or more places at school for their own safety decreased between 1995 and 1999—from 9 to 5 percent. Furthermore, the percentage of students who reported that street gangs were present at their schools decreased from 1995 to 1999. In 1999, 17 percent of students ages 12 through 18 reported that they had street gangs at their schools compared with 29 percent in 1995.

There was an increase in the use of marijuana among students between 1993 and 1995, but no change between 1995 and 1997. In 1997, about 26 percent of these students had used marijuana in the last 30 days. Furthermore, almost one-third of all students in grades 9 through 12 (32 percent) reported that someone had offered, sold, or given them an illegal drug on school property—an increase from 24 percent in 1993.

Therefore, the data shown in this report present a mixed picture of school safety. While overall school crime rates have declined, violence, gangs, and drugs are still evident in some schools, indicating that more work needs to be done. . . .

## Key Findings

Some of the key findings from the various sections of this report are as follows:

### Violent Deaths at School

From July 1, 1997 through June 30, 1998, there were 60 school-associated violent deaths in the United States. Forty-seven of these violent deaths were homicides, 12 were suicides, and one was a teenager killed by a law enforcement officer in the line of duty. Thirty-five of the 47 school-associated homicides were of school age children. By comparison, a total of 2,752 children ages 5 through 19 were victims of homicide in the United States from July 1, 1997 through June 30, 1998. Seven of the 12 school-associated suicides occurring from July 1, 1997 through June 30, 1998 were of school age children. A total of 2,061 children ages 5 through 19 committed suicide that year.

### Nonfatal Student Victimization—Student Reports

Students ages 12 through 18 were more likely to be victims of nonfatal serious violent crime—including rape, sexual assault, robbery, and aggravated assault—away from school than when they were at school. In 1998, students in this age range were victims of about 550,000 serious violent crimes away from schools, compared with about 253,000 at school.

- The percentage of students in grades 9 through 12 who have been threatened or injured with a weapon on school property has not changed significantly in recent years. In 1993, 1995, and 1997, about 7 to 8 percent of students reported being threatened or injured with a weapon such as a gun, knife, or club on school property in the past 12 months.
- In 1998, 12- through 18-year-old students living in urban, suburban, and rural locales were equally vulnerable to serious violent crime and theft at school. Away from school, however, urban and suburban students

were more vulnerable to serious violent crime and theft than were rural students.

- Younger students (ages 12 through 14) were more likely than older students (ages 15 through 18) to be victims of crime at school. However, older students were more likely than younger students to be victimized away from school.

## Violence and Crime at School—Public School Principal/Disciplinarian Reports

In 1996–97, 10 percent of all public schools reported at least one serious violent crime to the police or a law enforcement representative. Principals' reports of serious violent crimes included murder, rape or other type of sexual battery, suicide, physical attack or fight with a weapon, or robbery. Another 47 percent of public schools reported a less serious violent or nonviolent crime (but not a serious violent one). Crimes in this category include physical attack or fight without a weapon, theft/larceny, and vandalism. The remaining 43 percent of public schools did not report any of these crimes to the police.

- Elementary schools were much less likely than either middle or high schools to report any type of crime in 1996–97. They were much more likely to report vandalism (31 percent) than any other crime (19 percent or less).
- At the middle and high school levels, physical attack or fight without a weapon was generally the most commonly reported crime in 1996–97 (9 and 8 per 1,000 students, respectively). Theft or larceny was more common at the high school than at the middle school level (6 versus 4 per 1,000 students).

## Nonfatal Teacher Victimization at School—Teacher Reports

Over the 5-year period from 1994 through 1998, teachers were victims of 1,755,000 nonfatal crimes at school, including 1,087,000 thefts and 668,000 violent crimes (rape or sexual assault, robbery, and aggravated and simple assault). This translates into 83 crimes per 1,000 teachers per year.

- In the period from 1994 through 1998, senior high school and middle/junior high school teachers were more likely to be victims of violent crimes (most of which were simple assaults) than elementary school teachers (38 and 60, respectively, versus 18 crimes per 1,000 teachers).
- In the 1993–94 school year, 12 percent of all elementary and secondary school teachers were threatened with injury by a student, and 4 percent were physically attacked by a student. This represented about 341,000 teachers who were victims of threats of injury by students that year, and 119,000 teachers who were victims of attacks by students.

## School Environment

Between 1995 and 1999, the percentages of students who felt unsafe while they were at school and while they were going to and from school decreased. In 1995, 9 percent of students ages 12 through 18 sometimes or most of the time feared they were going to be attacked or harmed at school. In 1999, this percentage had fallen to 5 percent. During the same period, the percentage of students fearing they would be attacked while traveling to and from school fell from 7 percent to 4 percent.

- Between 1993 and 1997, the percentage of students in grades 9 through 12 who reported carrying a weapon on school property within the previous 30 days fell from 12 percent to 9 percent (a 25 percent reduction).
- Between 1995 and 1999, the percentage of students ages 12 through 18 who avoided one or more places at school for fear of their own safety decreased, from 9 to 5 percent. In 1999, this percentage represented 1.1 million students.
- Between 1995 and 1999, the percentage of students who reported that street gangs were present at their schools decreased. In 1995, 29 percent of students reported gangs being present in their schools. By 1999, this percentage had fallen to 17 percent.
- In 1997, about 51 percent of students in grades 9 through 12 had at least one drink of alcohol in the previous 30 days. A much smaller percentage (about 6 percent) had at least one drink on school property during the same period.
- There was an increase in the use of marijuana among students between 1993 and 1995, but no change between 1995 and 1997. About one quarter (26 percent) of ninth graders reported using marijuana in the last 30 days in 1997. However, marijuana use on school property did not increase significantly between 1993 and 1995, nor between 1995 and 1997.
- In 1995 and 1997, almost one-third of all students in grades 9 through 12 (32 percent) reported that someone had offered, sold, or given them an illegal drug on school property. This was an increase from 1993 when 24 percent of such students reported that illegal drugs were available to them on school property.
- In 1999, about 13 percent of students ages 12 through 18 reported that someone at school had used hate-related words against them. That is, in the prior 6 months someone at school called them a derogatory word having to do with race/ethnicity, religion, disability, gender, or sexual orientation. In addition, about 36 percent of students saw hate-related graffiti at school.

# BRITISH INQUIRY REPORT ON "MAD COW" DISEASE
## October 26, 2000

*An outbreak of bovine spongiform encephalopathy (BSE), commonly known as "mad cow" disease, in several European countries late in 2000 led to widespread consumer panic, forcing the European Union (EU) to adopt strict rules in hopes of halting the spread of the disease. Consumption of some beef products infected with BSE could cause Creutzfeld-Jacob disease (CJD), a related disease in humans that was invariably fatal. Fewer than one hundred people were known to have died of the disease since it was first reported in Great Britain in 1986, but the European public's reaction to the latest outbreak of the disease was so strong that sales of beef products quickly fell by about 50 percent in several countries. Governments and farmers warned that the future of the continent's economically important beef industry was at risk. Moreover, the scare put strains on Europe's ongoing moves toward political and economic unity. Seeking to protect their own citizens, individual countries prohibited imports of beef from neighboring countries.*

*The European uproar came just one month after a British investigating commission lambasted that country's handling of the original outbreak of mad cow disease. The commission found that, over a ten-year period beginning in late 1986, the British government misled the public by discounting the danger of humans contracting the disease.*

### The Origin and Transmission of Mad Cow

*Fourteen years after it was first identified, BSE still held mysteries for scientists, the most important of which were its origin and exact means of transmission. According to a "fact sheet" published in December by the World Health Organization (WHO), scientists were still working on theories about the origin of the disease. One theory held that the disease occurred spontaneously in cattle and then spread through the carcasses of infected animals; another theory was that the disease originated from a similar disease, scrapie, common in sheep. In its report, the British inquiry board said the ultimate cause "will probably never be known with certainty."*

Likewise, WHO said, scientists remained uncertain about the exact nature of the agent that transmitted the disease. According to one widely held theory, the agent was an aberrant protein, known as a "prion." But some evidence also supported a competing theory that the disease was transmitted by a virus-like agent, the WHO said. Whatever the makeup of the agent, scientists were nearly certain that the disease was spread through the use of feed that contained ground meat and bone products from infected cattle. Using animal products in livestock feed had been a common practice since World War II.

The disease attacked the nervous system of infected cattle, ultimately destroying the brain and causing death. After the disease was first uncovered in Britain, televised images of infected cows stumbling around their fields, seemingly deranged, led to the "mad cow" nickname.

Humans could contract the disease by consuming meat products or pharmaceutical products that contained material from the brains, spinal columns, or bone marrow of infected cattle. According to the WHO fact sheet, there had been no reports of humans contracting the disease by consuming beef muscle tissue or milk and milk products. In humans, mad cow disease was a variant of a rare illness known as Creutzfeld-Jacob disease, which could have a gestation period of ten to twenty-five years. Between October 1996 and December 2000, eighty-seven people had been infected in Great Britain, three in France, and one in the Republic of Ireland. Most of the infected humans were under thirty years of age. The WHO said it did not have enough information to make valid predictions about the future number of cases. As of late 2000 no cases of mad cow disease, or the human variant, had been reported in the United States. Canadian authorities had reported several cases of the disease in cows imported from Britain.

## The BSE Inquiry Report

The BSE Inquiry commission reviewed the government's handling of the mad cow controversy between the discovery of the disease in November 1986 and the acknowledgment, on March 20, 1996, that the disease probably had been transmitted to humans. The commission traced a series of government failings, including lack of communication among government agencies, bureaucratic delays, a widespread obsession with secrecy, and a conflict between the twin missions of the government's agriculture ministry to ensure the safety of food and to promote the interests of the farming industry.

Much of the report was devoted to an examination of the government's staunch assurances to the public, over a period of nearly ten years, that humans could not contract mad cow disease. Government brochures and advertising campaigns proclaimed: "Beef Is Safe." As late as 1995 Prime Minister John Major assured the House of Commons that "there is no scientific evidence that BSE can be transmitted to humans or that eating beef causes it in humans."

Reflecting on such statements, the commission said it concluded that "the government did not lie to the public" about mad cow disease. "The government was preoccupied with preventing an alarmist over-reaction to BSE *because it believed that the risk was remote." Once the government finally acknowledged the danger to humans, the commission said, "the public felt that they had been betrayed" and confidence in government pronouncements about safety became "a further casualty of BSE."*

*Publication of the commission report brought a series of admissions from top officials who had been in office at the time. Former prime minister Major said that "all of us must accept our responsibilities for short-comings." Tim Yeo, spokesman on agricultural issues for Major's Conservative Party, said in parliament: "I am truly sorry for what happened, and I apologize."*

*Although it gave faulty assurances to the public about human suscepti-bility to mad cow disease, the British government did act relatively quickly to stem the spread of the disease in cattle. The government ordered the de-struction of all cattle over thirty months old, because the disease had never been detected in younger cattle. In 1998 the government banned the use of animal byproducts in cattle feed, and over the next several years it took sev-eral steps to prohibit the use of "offal" (waste matter, such as intestines) from cattle in the food chain. The EU prohibited the export of British beef products to other countries in 1996; that ban was lifted in 1999 for products that met certain criteria that reduced the risk of mad cow disease. Mad cow disease reached its peak in Britain in 1992 and declined rapidly through the rest of the decade. Between 1987 and 2000 slightly more than 180,000 British cattle had been diagnosed with the disease; all were destroyed, along with more than 4 million cattle over thirty months of age.*

## Europe-Wide Scare

*During the years that Britain was attempting to contain the disease, European nations declared the safety of products from their own beef in-dustries. But in 2000 more aggressive testing for mad cow disease began turning up an increasing number of cases in France, reaching a total of more than 120 infected cattle by late December. Three people in France, two of whom had died by the end of the year, were diagnosed with CJD, the human variant of the disease. The government ordered thousands of cattle destroyed, and French consumers reacted by curtailing their consumption of beef products. Butchers reported that sales were off by 20 to 50 percent; some butchers said consumers were turning to alternative products, even horse meat.*

*In late November a cow in Germany was found to be infected with the dis-ease. Other diseased German cows were found in December, along with a handful of infected cattle in the Netherlands, Portugal, Spain, and Switzer-land. Suddenly, consumers all over Europe were shunning beef, and govern-ments were scrambling to protect their livestock industries. Greece, Italy, and Poland banned beef imports from France. Austria banned beef from Germany. Several countries where the disease had not been reported began marketing their own beef as being "safe."*

*Worried about the widespread panic, the European Commission acted quickly, approving a series of measures on December 4 that mirrored the* steps Britain had taken in the late 1980s and early 1990s to eradicate the disease. The commission ordered a six-month ban, starting January 2, 2001, on the use of meat and bone meal in feed for all farm animals and the destruction of all cattle over thirty months of age unless they had been tested and found to be free of mad cow disease. The commission ordered "spot checks" to ensure that its plan was "properly applied and controlled" in all member nations. Even so, some health experts warned that many farmers would continue using the banned feed.

These measures were expected to be expensive. The commission estimated that buying and destroying existing stocks of feed would cost about 4.5 billion euros, or about $4 billion. The EU was to pay 70 percent of the $800 million estimated cost of reimbursing farmers for the market value of cattle that had to be destroyed; the remaining 30 percent was to be paid by national governments. European Agriculture Commissioner Franz Fischler said the actions, and their costs, were necessary "to prevent a breakdown of the beef market and enormous costs for public intervention."

## U.S. Food Inspections

As of late 2000 mad cow disease had not become a major issue in the United States, which claimed to have to have the safest food-production system in the world. But the U.S. Agriculture Department—responsible for ensuring the safety of meat and poultry products—faced new challenges to a system it had implemented in 1996 to modernize its testing procedures. Under the new system, called Hazard Analysis Critical Control Points (HACCP), meat and poultry producers were required to identify potential hazards for foodborne pathogens at their slaughterhouses and packing plants and then establish controls to reduce them. Agriculture Department inspectors then inspected the plants and conducted limited laboratory testing to make sure the controls were being followed. This system replaced the ninety-year-old program in which inspectors poked and smelled animal carcasses. (HACCP system, Historic Documents of 1996, p. 414)

In May the U.S. District Court for Northern Texas handed the Agriculture Department a defeat in the first major legal challenge to the new testing. The court ruled that the department could not shut down a Dallas hamburger processing plant, owned by the Supreme Beef Processors Inc., after it failed three tests for salmonella contamination. The court said it was unfair for the department to declare that the entire plant failed to meet certain standards on the basis of tests for a limited number of products. The department planned to appeal the ruling and later noted that the Supreme Beef plant had failed a fourth inspection.

On June 21 the department's own inspector general issued a report saying that inspectors were not conducting enough tests under the new HACCP system. The system itself was effective, the inspector general said, but in implementing changes the Agriculture Department "reduced its oversight beyond what was prudent and necessary for the protection of the consumer." Among specific findings, the inspector general said the department had failed in some cases to require plants to establish the required HACCP pro-

*cedures. Inspectors also were not conducting enough tests for major micro-*
*bial hazards, such as E. coli and salmonella, the inspector general said.*

*Despite that finding, the Centers for Disease Control and Prevention re-*
*leased a report on March 16 saying the new inspection system had helped*
*reduce the risk of food poisoning in the United States. The report said the*
*number of Americans sickened by the most common foodborne illnesses had*
*fallen in both 1998 and 1999. Investigators attributed at least some of the*
*decline to improved procedures in the food processing industry—including*
*changes mandated by the Agriculture Department's HACCP system.*

*Following are excerpts from the executive summary of "The BSE*
*Inquiry: Report on the 'Mad Cow Disease' Epidemic in the U.K.,"*
*issued October 26, 2000. The document was obtained from the*
*Internet at http://www.bseinquiry.gov.uk/report/index.htm.*

## 1. Key conclusions

- BSE [Bovine Spongiform Encephalopathy] has caused a harrowing fatal disease for humans. As we sign this Report the number of people dead and thought to be dying stands at over 80, most of them young. They and their families have suffered terribly. Families all over the UK have been left wondering whether the same fate awaits them.
- A vital industry has been dealt a body blow, inflicting misery on tens of thousands for whom livestock farming is their way of life. They have seen over 170,000 of their animals dying or having to be destroyed, and the precautionary slaughter and destruction within the United Kingdom of very many more.
- BSE developed into an epidemic as a consequence of an intensive farm-ing practice—the recycling of animal protein in ruminant feed. This practice, unchallenged over decades, proved a recipe for disaster.
- In the years up to March 1996 most of those responsible for responding to the challenge posed by BSE emerge with credit. However, there were a number of shortcomings in the way things were done.
- At the heart of the BSE story lie questions of how to handle hazard—a known hazard to cattle and an unknown hazard to humans. The Govern-ment took measures to address both hazards. They were sensible mea-sures, but they were not always timely nor adequately implemented and enforced.
- The rigour with which policy measures were implemented for the pro-tection of human health was affected by the belief of many prior to early 1996 that BSE was not a potential threat to human life.
- The Government was anxious to act in the best interests of human and animal health. To this end it sought and followed the advice of inde-pendent scientific experts sometimes when decisions could have been reached more swiftly and satisfactorily within government.

- In dealing with BSE, it was not MAFF's [Ministry of Agriculture, Fisheries, and Food] policy to lean in favour of the agricultural producers to the detriment of the consumer.
- At times officials showed a lack of rigour in considering how policy should be turned into practice, to the detriment of the efficacy of the measures taken.
- At times bureaucratic processes resulted in unacceptable delay in giving effect to policy.
- The Government introduced measures to guard against the risk that BSE might be a matter of life and death not merely for cattle but also for humans, but the possibility of a risk to humans was not communicated to the public or to those whose job it was to implement and enforce the precautionary measures.
- The Government did not lie to the public about BSE. It believed that the risks posed by BSE to humans were remote. The Government was preoccupied with preventing an alarmist over-reaction to BSE because it believed that the risk was remote. It is now clear that this campaign of reassurance was a mistake. When on 20 March 1996 the Government announced that BSE had probably been transmitted to humans, the public felt that they had been betrayed. Confidence in government pronouncements about risk was a further casualty of BSE.
- Cases of a new variant of CJD (vCJD) [Creutzfeldt-Jacob disease] were identified by the CJD Surveillance Unit and the conclusion that they were probably linked to BSE was reached as early as was reasonably possible. The link between BSE and vCJD is now clearly established, though the manner of infection is not clear.

## 2. The identification of the emergence of BSE

- Individual cattle were probably first infected by BSE in the 1970s. If some lived long enough to develop signs of disease, these were not reported to or subject to investigation by the Central Veterinary Laboratory (CVL) of the State Veterinary Service (SVS).
- The Pathology Department of the CVL first investigated the death of a cow that had succumbed to BSE in September 1985, but the nature of the disease that had caused its death was masked by other factors and was not recognised at the time. This is not a matter for criticism.
- The Pathology Department considered two further cases of BSE at the end of 1986 and identified these as being likely to be a Transmissible Spongiform Encephalopathy (TSE) in cattle. This identification was commendable.
- This part of the story demonstrates both the benefits and the limitations of the passive surveillance system operated by the SVS.

## 3. The cause of BSE

- Gathering of data about the extent of the spread of BSE was impeded in the first half of 1987 by an embargo within the SVS on making information about the new disease public. This should not have occurred.

- By the end of 1987 Mr John Wilesmith, the Head of the CVL Epidemiology Department, had concluded that the cause of the reported cases of BSE was the consumption of meat and bone meal (MBM), which was made from animal carcasses and incorporated in cattle feed. This conclusion was correct. It had been reached with commendable speed.
- The following provisional conclusions of Mr Wilesmith, which were generally accepted at the time as a basis for action, were reasonable but fallacious:
  —the cases identified between 1986 and 1988 were index (ie, first generation) cases of BSE;
  —the source of infection in the MBM was tissues derived from sheep in-·fected with conventional scrapie;
  —the MBM had become infectious because rendering methods which had previously inactivated the conventional scrapie agent had been changed.
- The cases of BSE identified between 1986 and 1988 were not index cases, nor were they the result of the transmission of scrapie. They were the consequences of recycling of cattle infected with BSE itself. The BSE agent was spread in MBM.
- BSE probably originated from a novel source early in the 1970s, possibly a cow or other animal that developed disease as a consequence of a gene mutation. The origin of the disease will probably never be known with certainty.
- The theory that BSE resulted from changes in rendering methods has no validity. Rendering methods have never been capable of completely inactivating TSEs.
- The theory that BSE is caused by the application to cattle of organophosphorus pesticides is not viable, although there is a possibility that these can increase the susceptibility of cattle to BSE.
- The theory that BSE is caused by an autoimmune reaction is not viable.

## 4. Assessment of risk posed by BSE to humans

- One of the most significant features of BSE and other TSEs is the fact that they are diseases with very long incubation periods. Thus the question whether BSE was transmissible to humans was unlikely to be answered with any certainty for many years, and scientific experiments were bound to take a long time. The Government had to deal with BSE against this background of uncertainty as to the transmissibility of the disease.
- MAFF officials appreciated from the outset the possibility that BSE might have implications for human health.
- By the end of 1987 MAFF officials had become concerned as to whether it was acceptable for cattle showing signs of BSE to be slaughtered for human consumption. However, the Department of Health (DH) was not asked to collaborate with MAFF in considering the implications that BSE had for human health. It should have been.
- Only in March 1988, by which time MAFF officials had advised their Minister that animals showing signs of BSE should be destroyed and com-

pensation paid, did MAFF advise the Chief Medical Officer (CMO) Sir Donald Acheson of the emergence of BSE and ask him for his view of the possible human health implications.

- On Sir Donald's advice, an expert working party, chaired by Sir Richard Southwood, was set up to advise on the implications of BSE. After their first meeting in June 1988, the Southwood Working Party advised that cattle showing signs of BSE should be slaughtered and destroyed. This advice was of crucial importance in safeguarding human health. The Working Party had concerns about some occupational health risks in relation to BSE and some risks posed by medicinal products. They notified the responsible authorities of these concerns. On 9 February 1989 they submitted a Report to the Government in the knowledge that it would be published. The report concluded that the risk of transmission of BSE to humans appeared remote and that 'it was most unlikely that BSE would have any implications for human health'.
- This assessment of risk was made on the following basis:
  —BSE was probably derived from scrapie and could be expected to behave like scrapie. Scrapie had not been transmitted to humans in over 200 years and so BSE was not likely to transmit either.
  —So far as occupational and medicinal risks were concerned, the authorities which had been notified about these could be relied upon to take appropriate measures to address them.
- The Report did not, as it should have done, make clear the basis for its assessment of risk. It did comment that if the assessment was incorrect the implications would be extremely serious. This warning was lost from sight. The Southwood Report was, in years to come, repeatedly cited as constituting a scientific appraisal that the risks posed by BSE to humans were remote and that no precautionary measures were needed other than those recommended by the Working Party.
- Precautionary measures were nonetheless put in place that went beyond those recommended by the Working Party. The wisdom of those measures was demonstrated as the years went by and facts were learned about BSE which threw doubt on the theory both that it was derived from scrapie and that it would behave like scrapie.
- In May 1990 a domestic cat was diagnosed as suffering from a 'scrapie-like' spongiform encephalopathy. This generated widespread public and media concern that BSE had been transmitted to the cat and might also be transmissible to humans. Subsequently, more domestic cats were similarly diagnosed. These events shifted the perception of some scientists of the likelihood that BSE might be transmissible to humans. By 1994 the Spongiform Encephalopathy Advisory Committee (SEAC) evaluated the risk of transmissibility to humans as remote only because precautionary measures had been put in place.

## 5. Communication of the risk posed by BSE to humans

- The increasing knowledge about BSE over the years, which threw doubt on the theory that it would behave like scrapie, was not concealed from the public. However, the public was not informed of any change in the perceived likelihood that BSE might be transmissible to humans.

- The public was repeatedly reassured that it was safe to eat beef. Some statements failed to explain that the views expressed were subject to proper observance of the precautionary measures which had been introduced to protect human health against the possibility that BSE might be transmissible. These statements conveyed the message not merely that beef was safe but that BSE was not transmissible.

- The impression thus given to the public that BSE was not transmissible to humans was a significant factor leading to the public feeling of betrayal when it was announced on 20 March 1996 that BSE was likely to have been transmitted to people.

## 6. Measures to eradicate the disease in cattle

- Once Mr Wilesmith had identified MBM as the probable vector of BSE, the Government introduced the appropriate measure to prevent further infection and to stop the spread of the BSE agent—a ban on incorporating ruminant protein in ruminant feed. This had a dramatic effect in reducing to a fraction what had been an escalating rate of infection. It did not, however, bring infection to an end.

- The manner in which the Government introduced the ruminant feed ban was influenced by misconceptions as to:
  —the scale of the infection;
  —the amount of infective material needed to transmit the disease.

- Ignorant of the fact that the rate of infection had escalated to thousands of cases a week, the Government gave the animal feed trade a 'period of grace' of some five weeks to clear existing stocks of feed before the ban took effect. Some members of the feed trade, being given an inch, felt free to take a yard and continued to clear stocks after the ban came into force. Farmers in their turn used up the stocks that they had purchased. This led to thousands of animals being infected after the ruminant feed ban came into force on 18 July 1988.

- More serious was a failure to give rigorous consideration to the amount of infective material that was proving capable of transmitting the disease. The false assumption was made that any cross-contamination of cattle feed in feedmills from pig or poultry feed containing ruminant protein would be on too small a scale to matter.

- In fact, as subsequent experiments were to demonstrate, a cow can become infected with BSE as a result of eating an amount of infectious tissue as small as a peppercorn. Cross-contamination in feedmills resulted in the continued infection of thousands of cattle. Because it takes, on average, five years after initial infection for the clinical signs of BSE to become apparent, this was not appreciated until 1994.

- From September 1990 contamination of cattle feed with pig and poultry feed should not have resulted in infection. This was because, following the experimental transmission of BSE to a pig, MAFF on the advice of

SEAC introduced a measure in September 1990 aimed at protecting pigs and poultry from BSE. This was a ban on the inclusion in pig and poultry feed of MBM derived from the parts of the cow that might be expected to carry high infectivity if an animal were incubating or suffering from the disease—'Specified Bovine Offal' or SBO.

- However, there was a failure to give proper thought to the terms of this measure when it was introduced. The animal SBO ban was unenforceable and widely disregarded. Infectious bovine offal continued to find its way into pig and poultry feed and then, by cross-contamination, into cattle feed.

- Only in 1994 did the fact of the continuing infection and the reasons for it become appreciated. Regulations were revised and a rigorous enforcement campaign launched to coincide with the takeover in 1995 by a new national Meat Hygiene Service (MHS) of the enforcement duties in slaughterhouses, previously carried out by local authorities. The success of these measures is now becoming apparent. They were replaced after 20 March 1996 by the radical step of banning the incorporation of all animal protein in animal feed.

## 7. Measures to address the risks posed by BSE to humans

*Slaughter and compensation*

- Compulsory slaughter and destruction of all animals showing signs of BSE was a crucial measure to protect human health and, incidentally, animal health. It prevented the use, for any purposes, of sick animals, which could otherwise have been sent to the slaughterhouse for human consumption.

- A compulsory slaughter and compensation scheme was introduced in August 1988, following the commendable interim advice of the Southwood Working Party. Had there been prompt and adequate collaboration between MAFF and DH, this measure could and should have been introduced months earlier.

- Levels of compensation to farmers were adjusted on two occasions, but at no time did they lead to any significant failure to comply with the duty to notify the SVS of animals showing signs of BSE.

*Food risks*

- The Southwood Working Party considered that all reasonably practicable precautions should be taken to reduce the risks that would exist should BSE prove to be transmissible to humans. However, they did not make this plain in their Report and did not recommend that the possible risks from eating animals incubating BSE but not yet showing signs of the disease ('subclinical cases') called for any precautions, other than a recommendation that manufacturers should not include ruminant offal and thymus in baby food. This was a shortcoming in their Report.

- Because of a failure to subject the Southwood Report to an adequate review, MAFF and DH failed to identify this shortcoming. Concern about the food risks posed by subclinical cases was, however, expressed by some scientists, by the media and by the public. With the agreement of DH, MAFF reacted by announcing in June 1989 that those categories of offal of cattle most likely to be infectious (SBO) were to be banned from use in human food. The introduction of this vital precautionary measure was commendable. However, this ban was presented to the public in terms that underplayed its importance as a public health measure.

- Careful consideration was given by MAFF and DH in 1989 to the terms of the human SBO ban, with one important exception. During the consultation process, concerns were raised about the practicality of ensuring the removal of all of the spinal cord during abattoir processes, and about the practice of mechanical recovery of scraps left attached to the vertebral column for use in human food ('mechanically recovered meat' or MRM). However, MAFF officials discounted these concerns without subjecting them to rigorous consideration—in particular no advice was sought as to the minimum quantity of spinal cord that might transmit the disease in food.

- MAFF gave detailed consideration to spinal cord and MRM in 1990. A lengthy paper was submitted to SEAC, the Government's new expert advisory committee on TSEs. Unhappily, as a result of a breakdown of communications, MAFF officials understood that the members of SEAC were not concerned about the inclusion in human food of an occasional scrap of spinal cord, so that no action was called for. In fact the advice of some, at least, of the members of SEAC was premised on the false assumption that spinal cord could readily be removed from the carcass in its entirety, and would be so removed.

- This was one of a number of occasions that has given rise to lessons for the future about the proper use of expert committees by the Government.

- Not until 1995 was action taken in relation to MRM. Following the takeover by the Meat Hygiene Service of the enforcement of Regulations in slaughterhouses, occasional instances were discovered of failure to remove all spinal cord from the carcass. Strenuous and successful steps were taken to improve standards of compliance with the Regulations in slaughterhouses. Eventually, in December 1995, on SEAC's advice the extraction of MRM from the spinal column of cattle was banned.

- Up to 1995, MRM was a potential pathway to the infection of humans with BSE, not merely because of the risk of inclusion of the occasional portion of spinal cord, but because the material recovered by the MRM process included dorsal root ganglia. These were peripheral nervous tissues which were not thought to be infectious at the time, but which have since been demonstrated to be infectious in the late stages of incubation. . . .

[Sections 8 through 11 reviewed the government's handling of questions about whether BSE could be contracted through medicines and cosmetics containing animal products and by workers coming into contact with diseased animals. Section 12 reviewed the MAFF's handling of pollution and waste control issues arising from the BSE disease.]

## 13. The identification of vCJD

- The Southwood Working Party noted that if BSE were to be transmitted to humans it would be likely to resemble CJD and suggested that surveillance be put in place to identify atypical cases or changing patterns of the disease.
- The task of detecting any variation in the characteristics of cases of CJD which might indicate infection with BSE was entrusted to the CJD Surveillance Unit (CJDSU), a research team of dedicated medical scientists headed by Dr Robert Will, a neurologist with extensive experience of CJD.
- No role in this was given to the Public Health Laboratory Service (PHLS), an established service for the surveillance of new and existing disease, among other things.
- The decision to establish a new team specifically for this purpose was vindicated by the prompt detection of the emergence of vCJD by the CJDSU.
- The conclusion reached by SEAC on 16 March 1996 that the most likely explanation for the cases of a new variant of CJD in young people was exposure to BSE has since been compellingly supported by scientific evidence.
- It should have been apparent to both MAFF and DH by early February 1996 at the latest that there was a serious possibility that the scientists would conclude that it was likely that BSE had been transmitted to humans. The two Departments should have worked together, in consultation with SEAC, to explore the possible policy options that would be available should this occur.
- There was no interdepartmental discussion or consideration of policy options within either Department until the middle of March 1996. The views of SEAC were awaited, both as to whether the cases of vCJD were linked with BSE, and as to what action should be taken if they were. This was an inadequate response.
- Under intense pressure from the Government, on 20 March 1996 SEAC advised among other things that the appropriate course was that carcasses from cattle over 30 months old should be deboned in licensed plants supervised by the Meat Hygiene Service and the trimmings classified as SBO.
- The Government immediately announced that it was accepting this advice. In doing so it was wrong-footed, for this course proved neither practicable nor acceptable to the public. A policy of banning consumption of cattle over 30 months had to be introduced instead.

## 14. Victims and their families

- The unusual problems of the diagnosis, treatment and care of the early cases of vCJD meant that for some of the victims and their families the tragic horror of the disease was made the more difficult to bear by lack of the appropriate treatment, assistance and support.

- Victims of vCJD and their families have special needs which should be addressed. . . .

[Section 15 reviewed various efforts to conduct research on BSE.]

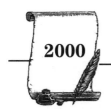
# November

# REMARKS BY PRESIDENTIAL CANDIDATE NADER
## November 5, 2000

*A third-party presidential ticket headed by consumer advocate Ralph Nader may have had a far greater impact on the outcome of the 2000 election than its vote total of 3 percent might indicate. Throughout his campaign for president on the progressive Green Party ticket, Nader argued that a viable third party was the only way to break the hold of special interests on the two major political parties and to help restore political power to the people, where it rightfully belonged. Nader ran as a consumer and environmental advocate and as a friend of labor and the poor, issues that had long resonated with many in the Democratic Party. Although he never rose to more than about 7 percent support in public opinion polls, in the final weeks of the campaign Democrats began to worry that he might draw enough Democratic votes from their candidate, Vice President Al Gore, to give the presidency to Republican George W. Bush. Nader spurned all suggestions that he withdraw from the race, and after the election angry Democrats accused him of costing Gore the presidency.*

*Even with the presidential race still hanging in the balance the day after the election, some Democrats were already calling Nader a spoiler and warning that he had damaged his own reputation beyond repair. Nader brushed aside the complaints. "You can't spoil a system spoiled to the core," he told supporters at the National Press Club on election night. Nader also vowed to carry on his populist political movement, which among other things called for universal health care, an increased minimum wage, and better protections for the environment. "We're in it for the long run," he declared, although his failure to capture 5 percent of the total vote meant that the Green Party would not qualify for public campaign financing in the 2004 presidential election campaign.*

*Nader and his running mate, Winona LaDuke, an author and activist, were officially nominees of the Association of State Green Parties, although Nader was not a registered member. In the 1990s the association had broken away from the older and more radical Green Party USA, which among other things advocated abolition of the Senate and the breaking up of the 500 largest corporations. In addition to running the presidential campaign, the Green Party fielded some 270 candidates in forty-five states for offices ranging from the U.S. Senate to town council.*

*The last time a third-party candidate influenced the outcome of a presidential election was in 1992, when Dallas billionaire Ross Perot and his Reform Party called for a balanced budget, campaign finance reform, and free trade. Perot won 19 percent of the popular vote that year and was widely thought to have hurt the Republican incumbent, George Bush, more than the Democratic challenger, Bill Clinton, who won the election with 43 percent of the vote to Bush's 37 percent. A badly faltering economy and the widespread perception that Bush was doing little about it suggested to many, however, that Bush would have lost even in a two-way race.* (1992 elections, Historic Documents of 1992, pp. 717, 1019)

*Both Perot on the right and Nader on the left ran independent presidential campaigns in 1996, but neither man's candidacy had much, if any, effect on the outcome of that race. Clinton solidly defeated former Senate majority leader Bob Dole to become the first Democrat since Franklin Delano Roosevelt to win a second term in the White House. Perot won 8 percent of the vote, giving the Reform Party $12.6 million in public financing for the 2000 elections, but he then dropped out of politics. With Perot gone, Patrick J. Buchanan, a conservative commentator who had twice run unsuccessfully for the Republican presidential nomination, set his sights on the Reform Party. He won the party's presidential nomination—and control of the public financing funds—but only after a bitter argument that left the party split in two. Unpopular with much of the Reform Party and viewed as negative by half of the voters, Buchanan was unable to advance his candidacy. He won fewer than 500,000 votes on election day.*

### The Nader Campaign

*Nader, who first came to national attention in the 1960s when he mounted a campaign to force the auto industry to design safer cars, had made a career of supporting consumers, workers, and the environment against what he considered the abuses of corporate power. As the presidential nominee of the Green Party, Nader blamed much of the nation's ills on giant corporations that he said pursued profit and power at the expense of ordinary taxpayers, the poor, and the environment. He called for full public financing of elections, universal health care, an increase in the minimum wage to $10 an hour, an end to restrictions on the rights of unions to organize, an end to the death penalty, more affordable housing, and a revitalization of the nation's inner cities. To restore and preserve the environment, Nader supported increased use of renewable energy such as solar and wind power, diminished use of fossil fuels to combat global warming, an end to commercial logging and road building in all national forests, and improved air quality standards. He opposed continued U.S. membership in the World Trade Organization and the North American Free Trade Agreement, citing his belief that they hurt American workers and the environment.*

*Nader's chief targets were the two major political parties, which he said* had "indentured themselves" to corporate interests by taking millions of dollars in campaign financing in return for supporting policies and programs that favored corporate interests. "The two parties have morphed into a corporate party representing the same business interests at the same dinners, at the same hotels, day after day after day," he said in most of his campaign speeches. Nader said the Democratic Party had strayed so far from its progressive roots, that there were no real differences left between the two parties. He described Bush as "a big corporation running for president disguised as a person." Some of his most scathing comments were reserved for the vice president, particularly after Democrats began to suggest that Nader drop out of the race. "Al Gore thinks he's entitled to your votes," Nader said at campaign rallies. "Al Gore thinks we are supposed to be helping him get elected. I've got news for Al Gore. If he can't beat that bumbling Texan with the terrible record, he shouldn't be running."

Nader's message found small enthusiastic audiences, composed primarily of college students, disaffected Democrats, and others who said that the two major parties either ignored their interests or no longer represented them. Nader had hoped to gain national attention for his campaign by forcing the two major parties into including him in the presidential debates held in October. However, the private organization that sponsored the debates refused to allow him (or any other independent candidate) to participate on stage and actually barred him from attending the October 3 debate in Boston, even though he had been given a ticket by a supporter. (Presidential debates, p. 797)

## Pleas to Bow Out of the Race

Although Nader actually lost ground in national public opinion polls after Gore began to promise that he would fight for the people and against the special interests, Democrats began to worry that Nader might draw enough votes in a few key states, such as Oregon and Washington, to swing the election to Bush. Claiming that "a vote for Nader is a vote for Bush," Democrats and even some defectors from the Green Party tried to discourage votes for Nader. Several online websites were set up to match Democratic voters in states that were solidly in the Gore column with Nader voters in toss-up states. The voters were encouraged to "swap" votes, thus ensuring that Nader would get a vote counting toward his immediate goal of winning 5 percent of the vote, thereby qualifying for public financing in 2004; Gore would get a vote in a state where it could make a difference. (Several of these sites were shut down when their operators were warned that they might be violating state election laws.)

Nader spurned all calls to step aside, saying that he "did not run for president to help elect one or the other of the two major party candidates" and reasserting his contention that there were no real differences between the two major parties or between Bush and Gore—or "Tweedledee and Tweedledum," as he repeatedly called them. He remained defiant even after the election, when some Democrats angrily called him a spoiler. "His standing has been severely diminished by his actions," said Amy Issacs, the national di-

897

*rector of the liberal Americans for Democratic Action, on November 8. "People basically view him as having been on a narcissistic, self-serving, Sancho Panza, windmill-tilting excursion." Kate Michelman, president of the National Abortion and Reproductive Rights Action League, said many women were enraged that Nader might have effectively helped put an antiabortion president in the White House. "He may pay a price," she said. "He has damaged his own credibility by so willfully dismissing, so cavalierly dismissing, this major concern of many, many voters."*

*Ironically, Nader's presence in the race did not hurt Gore in four states that Democrats had been most concerned about; the vice president won Michigan, Oregon, Washington, and Wisconsin. If Nader made a difference, it was in the crucial state of Florida, where he won 97,488 votes. After the Supreme Court stopped a recount of contested ballots in several counties, Bush was certified the winner with a 537-vote margin over Gore. That gave Bush Florida's twenty-five electoral votes and the presidency. Exit polls in states closely contested by Gore and Bush showed that about one-half of those who voted for Nader would have voted for Gore in a two-way race, and that about one-third would not have voted at all.* (Contested Florida election results, pp. 999, 1025)

> *Following are excerpts of remarks delivered November 5, 2000, by consumer advocate Ralph Nader, the presidential nominee of the Green Party, at a campaign rally in Washington, D.C. This document was not available on the Internet at the time of publication.*

. . . This week, on Tuesday, Election Day, millions of independent-minded voters will invest their conscience, their hopes, their dreams, their interests and the interests of their descendants in making the Green Party a party of, by, and for the people so that it can move to make our government a government of, by, and for the people in reality.

For this effort, a deliberative democracy is required, a democracy where people spend more time, every week, every month, every year, on their civic responsibilities and their political duties as they see them. People must spend more time on democracy to make it work. They must spend more time if they are going to allow themselves to apply their talents and their skills and their vision and their foresight. The only place where democracy comes before work, one might add, is in the dictionary.

A few weeks ago, *Business Week* magazine had a wonderful cover on too much corporate power over all aspects of our lives, and they detailed it in page after page. And then, in an editorial, they said something extraordinary. This is a major magazine with full ads by big corporations; think of the courage it took. They concluded that corporations have so much power that, quote, "Corporations should get out of politics," end quote, is what *Business Week* magazine said. Corporations should get out of politics.

I found *Business Week* magazine more courageous, more forthright, and more progressive than the Democratic Party, not to mention the Republican Party.

Corporations are not people. And in the words of our forebears, who established the laws that chartered corporations as artificial persons, in their words, "corporations were designed to be our servants, not our masters," and we must reassert the vision of our forebears in that respect.

Elections are for real people, not artificial entities like corporations full of massive power and massive money, driven overwhelmingly by their own commercial motives.

Our campaign has striven to move the political agenda into the areas where too much concentration of wealth and power damage or destroy the legitimate interests and rights of the American people and, I might add, too many oppressed people all over the world.

We stand for strong civil rights and civil liberties. Both of these are the pillars of our democracy. And both of them have been weakened by the current administration that uses florid oratory to camouflage a dismal dashing of expectations in these two areas of civil rights and civil liberties.

Civil rights and civil liberties apply to all people, but they are necessary to apply more intensively to the first Native Americans, to African-Americans, to Hispanics, to women, to gay-lesbians, and to the latest immigrants to our country who, by the newest, often are excoriated and discriminated against the most.

And one group of immigrants is being subjected to recurrent ethnic profiling. And just like the Irish who came to America and were discriminated against, and then it was the Jews who were discriminated against when they came, then it was the Italians, now it's the turn of the Muslim people who come to this country. And this must also be subject to strong civil rights enforcement. . . .

We have brought a focus, the Green Party and their candidates, on the very lax enforcement regarding waves of systemic corporate crime, fraud and abuse that is taking hundreds of billions of dollars from consumers, investors, taxpayers each year, and endangering so many people's health and safety. These violations and deceptions reduce family incomes as if they were subjected to pay cuts at work. And when not stopped, these corporate criminal practices help drive out honest business practices through this unfair, unlawful competition that escapes law and order. . . .

All this is happening around the country. You travel around the country and so many of our precious natural resources have been turned into corporate sewers, toxic sewers, producing respiratory ailments and cancer and genetic damage. This is corporate crime. This is the silent corporate criminal violence that needs 100,000 prosecutors for corporate crime prosecution.

We urge a fundamental redirection of public taxpayer budgets, turning governments away from misusing tax dollars for corporate welfare, such as subsidies to giant agro-businesses that are starving small farmer incomes and creating incredible distress in rural America.

Companies like ADM and Cargill and others who have had their hand in the trough here in Washington for all too long.

We want a redirection of subsidies that now go to the giant drug companies in the form of taxpayer-funded drug research leading to the discovery and testing of Taxol and AZT and all kinds of other significant pharmaceutical products that, under our government's policy, is given away free to a drug company under a monopoly marketing agreement that turns around and charges thousands and thousands of dollars per patient for a set of treatments, like $14,000 to a woman with ovarian cancer for the drug Taxol by Bristol-Myers Squibb that didn't spend a cent discovering and testing it. You[r] tax dollars did.

This must be ended.

Corporate welfare subsidies that involve giveaways of our precious natural resources around the country on public lands. You know, we're the only country in the world that gives away its gold, its silver, its copper and other hard rock metals like molybdenum, the only country in the world that gives it away because of an 1872 mining act. . . .

The Green Party stands for an end to selling our great trees in the national forests for a pittance. No more commercial logging on our national forests.

We want our children and grandchildren, their descendants, to enjoy our pristine national forests, not to inherit a bunch of tree stumps. And by the way, spending $1 billion now that goes to the timber corporations—that's how much you subsidize them, $1.2 billion, you build the roads for them, you subsidize them—we put that money into restoring and preserving the national forest, it will create more jobs, provide more recreational and eco-tourism, and proudly pass these forests onto future generations.

It is outrageous that you go to work every day and you pay your taxes every two weeks, withheld, and it comes to Washington and some of these taxes go to bail out bankers who are running their banks into the ground because of mismanagement and speculation. They go to defense contractors who set new records for cost overruns, as the Pentagon calls them, waste, waste, waste. The golden handcuffs pumping up these weapon systems to fantastic levels, weapons systems now in the pipeline costing us hundreds of billions of dollars that retired admirals and generals who don't go to work for the military contract business have said are unnecessary, wasteful, no strategic need. There is no more Soviet Union, there is no major enemy in the world. . . .

It is now the year 2000 A.D., poor people of color and other poor people still pay more, suffer more, are excluded discriminately in many, many ways, are imprisoned at hugely disproportionate rates, are racially profiled more and more, and die earlier than other people. And that is what discrimination and class distinctions do to tens of millions of hard-working Americans. . . .

By the way, you know what the biggest public housing project in America has been in the last years? Building prison cells, largely in corporate prisons.

The Green Party says that our country should prohibit all corporate-owned prisons. It's not a profit enterprise, it's a public responsibility.

And the same is true to universal health care. I mean, how long are we going to wait on that one? . . .

Oh, how long are we going to wait? Only as long as the Republican and Democratic Parties remain in charge. Is that how long we're going to wait?

Let's not wait for that long. It's time to say once and forever that health care is a right in America, a human right for everyone.

And people should not have to go to Canada to buy drugs at half the price, made by the same U.S. drug companies who overcharge Americans for drugs, higher than any other country in the world. . . .

A national Marshall plan for our cities is needed, learning from past mistakes and enlisting new political and civic energies. This must become a central part of our political discourse. This must include a living wage for the 47 million full-time workers, one out of every three workers, who today do not earn a living wage.

The federal minimum wage is at $5.15, which is over $2 lower in real purchasing power than the federal minimum wage was in 1968, when the economic output per capita was half what it is today, and when the productivity was 60 percent less. Who's getting the gains? We know, it's the top 10 percent and more the top 5 percent and more the top 1 percent. The top 1 percent of the wealthiest people in this country have wealth equal to the combined wealth of the bottom 95 percent. And you take the poorest 120 million Americans and their combined net wealth is equal to the wealth of Bill Gates a year ago, one man—one man. . . .

Allowing workers to form trade unions is a pretty good idea that escapes the Republicans and Democrats. Democrats talk a good game, of course, but are they willing to repeal the notorious Taft-Hartley Act of 1947, which is a choke-hold on tens of millions of workers who cannot form unions without huge obstructions, getting fired for just trying to form a trade union in order to lift their standard of living? I have yet to see the Democratic Party take a stand on that.

At the Platform Committee in Los Angeles, the Democratic Party not only turned down a platform saying that they were for universal health care, they turned down a platform that asked them to expand aid to the poor. Can you imagine what they would do if they were offered a repeal of Taft-Hartley? They'd probably swoon by the very prospect of it.

This is not the old Democratic Party. This is a hollow party; a party that engages in tens of millions of dollars of fund-raising, like its counterpart Republican Party, and campaigns with 30-second television ads and doesn't have any more roots back home, and tells labor unions and minority groups, "You can't go to the Republican, you got no where to go, because we're not as bad as the Republican Party." What a great choice: a choice between the bad and the worse.

This country deserves the best. It deserves a broad choice for the people. . . .

Now, both parties endorsed and support the WTO and NAFTA, which subordinate . . . to the imperatives of international commerce, health/safety considerations in the workplace, environment, marketplace, even existing regulations, as well as improved standards in these areas. That reverses the way we progressed in our country. Whenever we progressed, environment, worker safety, consumer protection, motor vehicle safety, abolishing child labor, we basically said to corporations, "Your profit imperative's got to take second seat. You're going to have to adjust your commerce to these improvements in the health, safety and economic rights of Americans."

And WTO, NAFTA reverses that completely. It's trade *uber alles*, in a system of autocratic, secretive governance that shuts out the press from the courts in Geneva, Switzerland, and has secret harmonization committees to bring our higher standards downward in harmony with lower standards overseas, because that's what the corporations want: lower standards, lower costs, no matter what the price is paid by the people who suffer.

The Green Party stands for the following: that the United States initiate the provide-for six-month notice to withdraw from GATT, WTO, and NAFTA and renegotiate trade agreements to pull standards up, not pull standards down, and to do it in a full, open, democratic manner. . . .

Both parties do not address the rampant corporate commercialism that is moving in every nook and cranny of our society, commercialism sweeping everything away in its path, making us feel like everything's for sale. It's like everything's for sale under a commercially dominated society. Our government is for sale. Our democracy is for sale. Our childhood is for sale to these corporate commercial exploiters of young children. Our human genes are for sale. Our personal privacies are for sale. Our right to choose a doctor or hospital of our own choosing, that's for sale. Our environment is for sale.

But there's one thing that is not for sale, and that's the Green Party of the United States.

Commercialism is sweeping over our schools and our universities, blocking the establishment of civic curriculums where students can learn citizen skills, learn how to practice democracy, connect classroom with the community, concentrate on the reality of life instead of memorization and phony standardized tests that are absurd.

Commercialism that distorts university research priorities to bend to the corporate imperative. Commercialism that compromises the independence of our faculty and the free exchange of scientific and other research findings. Commercialism that denigrates the humanities and the social scientist in favor of a massively trade school dominated higher education curriculum.

The Green Party pledges to enforce the antitrust laws of our land. Both Republican and Democratic Parties have abetted the massive merger wave in the last 10 years among HMOs and hospital chains and agro-business giants and telecommunication, cable goliaths, drug company goliaths, aerospace corporations, military contractors, oil companies and massive media consolidation.

All of these massive mergers would be unheard of 20, 30 years ago. The Democratic Party would have stopped them in a heartbeat. But now, the Democratic Party and the Republican Party are taking money from all of these companies and they are giving value received back. Most of them have never seen a merger they didn't like.

The Green Party is serious about enforcing the antitrust laws, reducing concentration of corporate power in our country, reducing the pressures on valiant small businesses who are trying to give us better products, more organic food, more recycled products, more arts, more crafts, better service, and they've got these corporations on their back. We've got to free small business in this country.

And, of course, both parties support the utterly failed war on drugs, where two-thirds of the tens of billions of dollars do not go to rehabilitation of drug addicts, they go to militarizing and criminalizing addiction. We do not send alcoholics to jail, we do not send nicotine addicts to jail, and we should not send drug addicts to jail, we should have them rehabilitated as human beings in need. . . .

The Green Party believes that the thin slice of life around our globe that sustains life on our globe, that few miles of air, water and soil called the biosphere, must be given priority protection. We must do this by sustainable. . . .

We must do this for the rest of the world by setting an example, not being the biggest coal-burning company—country, the biggest nuclear power generating country.

We want to set an example, the Green Party does, by setting examples, becoming the leading user of solar energy in the world.

By setting zero-pollution goals for motor vehicles and industrial activity. . . .

The Green Party favors more U.S. Department of Agriculture support for organic farming; one of the few ways farmers can make any money anymore.

Much more regulatory scrutiny on the most tumultuous, brazen technology in the history of the world, the biotechnology industry that wants to convert the genetic inheritance of the world into their own 17-year monopoly past.

Imagine, this technology—this biotechnology industry has essentially no regulation, no ethical, no legal framework, and they basically want to control the genetic inheritance of the globe. . . . We need to reassert civilized values over this industry. We also need to let our farmers, at long last—after George Washington, Thomas Jefferson and others grew this product—to at long last allow them to grow industrial hemp.

Yes, our country can legally important industrial hemp from France, Canada and China, but it cannot grow it here, because Mr. Clinton and Mr. Gore and General McCaffrey somehow believe that a plant that can give us food, fiber, fuel, paper without chlorine, lubricants, medicines and 5,000 other uses that have been developed over 5,000 years, that somehow that is a stalking horse for marijuana.

Well, I have news for you, Mr. Clinton, Mr. Gore, and Mr. McCaffrey: At 0.3 percent THC, even President Clinton . . . even President Clinton smoking a bushel of industrial hemp, even if he inhaled it, he'd get no more than a stomach ache. . . .

The Green Party supports a foreign policy that sides with the workers and the peasants in very concrete ways, supporting democratic movements, land reform, credit facilities, cooperatives, free independent trade unions. It's really important to redefine national security in a post-Soviet Union/Cold War era. It's important to move while we have such a great opportunity, as the dominant power in the world, to move more aggressively for global arms reduction, the abolition of nuclear weapons and to address the serious environmental degradation of our planet—the forests, the oceans, the land erosion, the contaminated water; to launch a massive program against malaria, tuberculosis, AIDS and other infectious diseases that are spreading all over the world, often in drug-resistance fashion. That is a national security matter, and that's what we should define national security: environmentally and health-wise.

And the abolition of poverty. Poverty and repression are national security priorities in a Green Party administration.

How many opportunities our country has had and has foregone to lift the spirit and the vision and the stature and the status of people around the world who look to us for this kind of leadership, who saw the Statue of Liberty as a symbol.

We have to recover that spirit. We have to think much more highly of our own significance as a nation. We have so much to offer to this world, to this tormented world, to the repressed and the damned and the disadvantaged and the starving, to the people who want a decent life. We have so much more to offer to this world, so much more for your young generation to offer to this world than land mines and napalm and jet planes and tanks and other weapons of mass destruction which make up the global weapons trade.

Supporting democratic movements around the world helps liberate the manifold genius of Third World peoples, the genius that will be able to come forward, be able to find the solutions, be able to address the injustices. We know that we don't have all the answers, and certainly the IMF and the World Bank do not have very many answers either. . . .

The Green Party recognizes that every major social justice movement in our history was made possible by a gift of more power to the people, away from the power that the few control. And it's way past time for a shift of power today from big business to the people. . . .

Shift of power is an essential contention of politics. That's what it's all about. If we don't have a more equitable distribution of power, there is no equitable distribution of wealth or income, and people who work hard will not get their just rewards.

And the main way to shift power—if you had to have one reform—that's public funding of public elections. Public funding of public elections.

Clean money. Clean money, clean elections. Clean money and clean elections to stop the nullification of your votes by special interest money.

Just think about it. You go down to vote, you expect it to count. Millions go down to vote, they expect it to count. And the votes are cut off at the past by fancy fund-raising dinners all over the country where fat cats pay off politicians for present and future favors, and the politicians shake down the fat cats in a kind of combined symbiosis of legalized bribery and legalized extortion.

And Senator John McCain condemned this again and again last year, along with Senator Russ Feingold, again and again.

This campaign—our campaign has been conducted in an honorable and exemplary manner, because we believe if you advocate reforms, you have to practice what you preach in order to preach what you practice.

. . . [W]e do not take PAC money, soft money, corporate interest money, only individual contributions from all over the country, either by mail, by fund-raisers that are really political house party dinners, and by transmission by generous donors, individuals, no ax to grind, over our web site: votenader.com or votenader.org. . . .

It's not easy challenging the entrenched two-party system. They command the statutory barriers to get on the ballot for third parties, they command the money, they command the media, they command the phony debate commission that excludes significant third-party candidates from being on the debate. . . .

I remember a time when citizen groups could get something done in Washington, because they had Democratic Senate and House committee chair people, they had people in the White House who were interested in change. I got the motor vehicle industry regulated so that cars and other motor vehicles are much safer and the death rate went down like this. You couldn't do that today.

This couldn't be done today. . . .

I hope that those of you who are talking with others who are wavering on the least-of-the-worst or lesser-of-two-evils syndrome will remind them of what Franklin Delano Roosevelt once said, when he said, "Each citizen is equal to each other citizen in the ballot booth, where privacy reigns and they can only answer to their conscience."

And a vote for conscience, a vote for your hopes, a vote for your dreams, a vote for a higher expectation level of what our country can become and what it can mean to the world, those are the votes that you need to register, not a lesser of two evils where at the end of the day you're still left with evil. . . .

I want to end with a quote by Mahatma Gandhi. And I want to have you think about this very closely, and here's what he said decades ago. He listed seven blunders of the world that lead to violence and injustice. First, wealth without work. Second, pleasure without conscience. Third, knowledge without character. Fourth, commerce without morality. Fifth, science without humanity. Sixth, worship without sacrifice. And lastly, politics without principle.

# HILLARY CLINTON ON HER
# ELECTION TO THE U.S. SENATE
## November 7, 2000

*Overcoming widespread concerns about her character, integrity, and in-tentions, Hillary Rodham Clinton became the only first lady ever to win elec-tion to public office. Clinton soundly defeated Representative Rick A. Lazio on November 7, 2000, to win the New York Senate seat being vacated by retiring Democrat Daniel Patrick Moynihan. Clinton won the race with 55 percent of the vote to Lazio's 43 percent, a notable feat for someone who had never held public office before, who had not lived in the state when she began her campaign, and who evoked nearly as much controversy as her husband, President Bill Clinton. "Thank you for opening up your minds and your hearts, for seeing the possibility of what we could do together for our children and for our future, here in this state and in this nation," Clin-ton said in her victory speech, her husband and daughter at her side.*

*No other first lady had ever even run for public office. The only former first lady to hold an official government position was Eleanor Roosevelt, who was named as a delegate to the new United Nations in 1946, where she was in-strumental in writing the Universal Declaration of Human Rights. Clinton was also the first woman to be independently elected to statewide office in New York. Former House member Geraldine Ferraro, who was the Demo-cratic vice presidential nominee in 1984, unsuccessfully sought the New York Democratic Senate nomination in 1992 and 1998.*

*Clinton denied widespread rumors that she was using the New York Sen-ate seat simply as a platform to run for president in 2004. In her first news conference after her election, Clinton said she was "going to serve my six years as the junior senator from New York."*

### Women in Congress

*Hillary Clinton would be one of fifty Democrats in a Senate that was evenly divided between the two parties. Republicans lost a net of four seats in the Senate but retained their control because of the Republican takeover of the White House. Because the vice president acted as president of the Senate, Richard B. Cheney, the Republican vice president-elect, would break any tie* votes. Republicans also held onto their control of the House of Representatives, albeit by only a nine-vote margin. The last year that the Republicans won control of the White House and both chambers of Congress was in 1952.

Clinton would also be one of seventy-two women in Congress—the most ever elected. A total of thirteen women, ten Democrats and three Republicans, would sit in the Senate when the 107th Congress convened in January 2001—an increase of four from the 106th Congress. One of the new women was Jean Carnahan, Democrat of Missouri and widow of Governor Mel Carnahan, who was elected to the seat even though he had died in a plane crash on October 16, three weeks before the election. Jean Carnahan was appointed by her husband's gubernatorial successor to fill the first two years of what would have been her husband's term; a special election would be held to fill the other four years. Fifty-nine women—eighteen Republicans and forty-one Democrats—were elected to the House.

## The First Lady's Senate Race

Not since Eleanor Roosevelt had a first lady been as controversial as Hillary Clinton. Both first ladies were strong-willed, highly opinionated, and outspoken—traits that did not always fit well with the traditional role of supportive wife and hostess played by most other first ladies. Both women were also political liberals, which exacerbated tensions with at least some conservatives who thought the first ladies were overstepping their bounds.

A lawyer by profession, who practiced in Little Rock, Hillary Clinton came to Washington expecting to play a key policy role in her husband's administration. But her first effort, as head of the President's Task Force on National Health Care Reform, was a disaster, and she was assigned a large share of the blame for mishandling the health care reform legislation that contributed to a Republican takeover of the House and Senate in 1995. At about the same time, a special prosecutor began a criminal investigation into the Clintons' roles in a failed Arkansas land deal, and the first lady also came under investigation for her role in the firing of the White House travel office. When the president's affair with a White House intern first came to light in January 1998, Hillary Clinton was first vilified for covering up for him. Then, when it became apparent that he had deceived her as well, she became an object of public sympathy as well as criticism from those who said she was staying in her marriage simply to hold on to power. (Closing the Whitewater investigation, p. 762)

Although Clinton had been mentioned as a possible New York Senate candidate since Senator Moynihan announced that he would not seek reelection, she made few public statements until July 1999, when she traveled throughout the state on a "listening tour." Her candidacy seemed assured when it was announced in September 1999 that the Clintons purchased a home in the wealthy New York suburb of Chappaqua in Westchester County, but Clinton did not formally announce her candidacy until February 6, 2000. "I may be new to your neighborhood," Clinton said, "but I'm not new to your concerns."

Clinton expected to be in a tight race with Republican New York City *mayor Rudolph W. Giuliani, the combative former prosecutor who seemed to have a love-hate relationship with the voters. Although she did not mention Giuliani by name, Clinton made pointed references to his prickly personality and to his unsympathetic response to outcries from New York's African Americans in the wake of two high-profile incidents of misuse of force by the police. In her announcement Clinton promised to fight against "the politics of revenge and retribution. . . . If you put me to work for you, I'll work to lift people up, not push them down." The two antagonists were soon trading barbed jabs. Clinton called Giuliani harsh and temperamentally unsuited to work in the Senate; Giuliani called Clinton an opportunist and untrustworthy.*

*On May 19 Giuliani abruptly withdrew from the race to grapple with prostate cancer. Although he denied it had anything to do with his decision to withdraw, Giuliani's recent announcement that he was separating from his wife, Donna Hanover, and that he was seeing a "very good" friend, Judith Nathan, had also left his campaign in turmoil. The New York Republican Party quickly turned to Lazio, a member of the U.S. House from Long Island, to replace Giuliani.*

*Like Giuliani, Lazio tried to capitalize on those aspects of the first lady's career that roused the most negative feelings among the voters. He continually questioned her trustworthiness, scoffed at her stated concern for the people of New York, and hammered away at her lack of experience. Clinton tried to identify Lazio with the conservative policies of Newt Gingrich, the former Republican House majority leader whose unbridled pursuit to drive President Clinton out of the White House backfired, causing him to resign his seat in Congress. She also noted that she had been fighting for education and health issues for years and that she had played an instrumental role behind the scenes in the 1997 passage of the federal-state child health insurance program, known as CHIP; in developing the Corporation for National Services; and in earmarking foreign aid money for micro-credit for poor women overseas to start small businesses, among other things.*

*The turning point in the campaign may well have been the nationally televised debate on September 13, in which Lazio went on the attack, describing Clinton as "beyond shameless" and asking her to sign a pledge, which he put in front of her, not to use soft money during the campaign. The most striking moment may have been when Tim Russert, the moderator of the debate and the host of NBC's* Meet the Press *played a videotape from the* Today *program of January 27, 1998, just days after allegations of the president's affair with Monica Lewinsky became public, in which Clinton defended her husband and denied that he had the affair. Russert than asked Clinton if she regretted "misleading the American people." With her head bowed, Clinton responded: "Well, you know, Tim, that was a very, a very painful time for me, for my family, and for our country. It is something I regret deeply that anyone had to go through. I've tried to be as forthcoming as I could, given the circumstances that I faced. Obviously, I didn't mislead anyone. I didn't know the truth. And there's a great deal of pain associated with that and my husband has clearly acknowledged that and made it clear that he did mislead the country as well as his family."*

*Shortly after the debate, state polls began to show a decided upswing in support for Clinton among women, who found Lazio's debate performance overbearing and rude. Lazio's campaign also made several other tactical errors. The most damaging may have been a telephone campaign organized by the state Republican chairman to attempt to link Clinton to the terrorist attack on the USS Cole in Yemen. The "link" was a campaign donation from a Muslim group that Clinton had received and later returned. Lazio did not denounce the telephone campaign for nearly four days.*

*On election day, Clinton was helped not only by Lazio's inept campaign but also by Vice President Al Gore's large margin in the state over Republican George W. Bush, an increase in the number of registered Democratic voters in the state, and a well-organized get-out-the-vote drive by labor unions. But it was Clinton's campaigning in upstate New York—virtually everything outside metropolitan New York City—that tipped the state in her favor. Beginning with her listening tour in the summer of 1999 and continuing throughout the campaign, she devoted a great deal of attention to the needs and concerns of upstate voters. Generally Republicans needed to win upstate New York by ten percentage points to compensate for the heavy Democratic majorities in New York City. On November 7 Clinton won 47 percent of the vote in upstate New York to Lazio's 50 percent. In her victory speech Clinton promised that her first bill would be a package of measures to help the upstate economy and similarly afflicted areas elsewhere in the country by improving the technological infrastructure and high-tech work skills. She also pledged to help enact tax cuts for small businesses in communities that had lost population.*

*Giuliani pledged to work with her, "for the good of the city and the state," and he congratulated her on her winning campaign. "She is entitled, as I told her, to a great deal of credit," he said. "She ran a very, very strong, tough campaign; she worked very hard, and when you're in this business you can admire even people who are . . . adversaries, when they have a very, very strong work ethic as she does."*

*The race was the most expensive in the state's history. Together the three campaigns spent more than $83 million, much of it raised from contributors outside the state. Clinton raised much of her money among the entertainment and celebrity crowd that had supported her husband throughout his presidency, while Giuliani and Lazio appealed to contributors who wanted to see both Clintons out of office and out of Washington. In one fundraising letter, Lazio said he could sum up why people should support his candidacy in just six words: "I'm running against Hillary Rodham Clinton."*

*Clinton was likely to receive a similar mixed reception into what has been called the "world's most exclusive club." Senate minority leader Tom Daschle said she would be effective because, after working with members on various pieces of legislation over the years, "she knows the Senate and the*

*people." Clinton herself seemed sensitive to the fact that her celebrity status
as first lady might not count for much in her new career. "You have to be
willing to work hard to learn the ropes and the rules, build relationships
with people, all of which I intend to do," she said. Some Republicans, however, not only disagreed with Clinton's political philosophy but also appeared concerned that she might upstage more senior members of the
Senate. "I tell you one thing," Republican leader Trent Lott of Mississippi
said shortly after the election, "when this Hillary gets to the Senate, if she
does—maybe lightening will strike and she won't—she will be one of 100
and we won't let her forget it."*

*Even before she was sworn in, Clinton sparked yet another controversy
when she signed a deal with Simon & Schuster on December 15 that would
give her an $8 million advance for a memoir about her years in the White
House. Republicans and others immediately questioned the propriety of the
advance, which was only slightly smaller than the record $8.5 million ad-
vance paid to Pope John Paul. After the 1994 House majority leader Gingrich eventually was forced to forgo a $4.5 million advance for a book deal
when Democrats persisted in questioning the ethics of that deal. Under Senate rules, book advances were permissible so long as they were "usual and
customary." Clinton had donated to charity the profits from her four other
books, all published by Simon & Schuster.*

*Following are excerpts of Hillary Rodham Clinton's victory speech
in New York City on November 7, 2000, upon her election to the U.S.
Senate from New York. The document was obtained from the Internet at http://www.hillary2000.org/issues/speeches/001107.html.*

Thank you. Thank you so much. I mean, wow, this is amazing. Thank
you all.

You know, we started this great effort on a sunny July morning in Pinders
Corner on Pat and Liz Moynihan's beautiful farm and 62 counties, 16 months,
three debates, two opponents, and six black pantsuits later, because of you,
here we are.

You came out and said that issues and ideals matter. Jobs matter, downstate
and upstate. Health care matters, education matters, the environment matters,
Social Security matters, a woman's right to choose matters. It all matters and
I just want to say from the bottom of my heart, thank you, New York.

Thank you for opening up your minds and your hearts, for seeing the possibility of what we could do together for our children and for our future here
in this state and in our nation. I am proudly grateful to all of you for giving
me the chance to serve you. I will do everything I can to be worthy of your
faith and trust and to honor the powerful example of Senator Daniel Patrick
Moynihan.

I would like all of you and the countless New Yorkers and Americans watching to join me in honoring him for his incredible half century of service to New

York and our nation. Senator Moynihan, on behalf of New York and America, thank you.

And I thank [New York senator] Chuck Schumer for his generous support and friendship. He has been and will be a great champion for the people of New York and I very much look forward to fighting by his side in the United States Senate.

I want to thank both of my opponents, Mayor [Rudolph W.] Giuliani and Congressman [Rick A.] Lazio. Congressman Lazio and I just spoke. I congratulate him on a hard-fought race and I thank him for his service to the people of New York and Long Island and I wish him, Pat, and their two beautiful daughters well.

I promise you tonight that I will reach across party lines to bring progress for all of New York's families. Today we voted as Democrats and Republicans. Tomorrow we begin again as New Yorkers.

And how fortunate we are indeed to live in the most diverse, dynamic and beautiful state in the entire union.

You know, from the South Bronx to the Southern Tier, from Brooklyn to Buffalo, from Montauk to Massena, from the world's tallest skyscrapers to breathtaking mountain ranges, I've met people whose faces and stories I will never forget. Thousands of New Yorkers from all 62 counties welcomed me into your schools, your local diners, your factory floors, your living rooms and front porches. You taught me, you tested me and you shared with me your challenges and concerns—about overcrowded or crumbling schools, about the struggle to care for growing children and aging parents, about the continuing challenge of providing equal opportunity for all and about children moving away from their home towns because good jobs are so hard to find in upstate New York.

Now I've worked on issues like these for a long time, some of them for 30 years, and I am determined to make a difference for all of you. You see, I believe our nation owes every responsible citizen and every responsible family the tools that they need to make the most of their own lives.

That's the basic bargain I'll do my best to honor in the United States Senate. And to those of you who did not support me, I want you to know that I will work in the Senate for you and for all New Yorkers. And to those of you who worked so hard and never lost faith even in the toughest times, I offer you my undying gratitude. I will work my heart out for you for the next six years.

And I wouldn't be here if it weren't for the steady support of so many people. I want to thank . . . the entire New York Democratic Congressional delegation, my future colleagues. I'm very grateful for the support of our Democratic statewide elected officials. . . .

I want to thank . . . all the Democratic assembly members and all the Democratic members of the state Senate.

I want to thank all of my upstate friends who couldn't be here tonight, . . . all the county chairs and other elected officials. And thank you to all of my downstate friends. . . . And particularly my friends right here in New York City, the citywide officials, the borough presidents, the city council members and two great friends: former mayors, Ed Koch and David Dinkins.

And somebody just yelled, "Don't forget Long Island, we got beat up out there!"

And I am grateful to everybody from Long Island. And I want to thank all my friends in the state Democratic party leadership, . . . all the hardworking labor leaders who really helped turn out the vote today, . . . and the other local, state and national labor leaders whose support was so crucial.

And I want to thank all of the people who started volunteering with me from the very beginning. You knocked on doors, you raised funds, you built rallies, you did everything necessary to bring us to this point and today I want to thank the 25,000 volunteers from all across the state who started phone banking, knocking on doors, giving out palm cards the minute the polls opened at 6 a.m. and didn't stop until the last voter left. You made a difference in this race and I'm very grateful to you.

And I want to thank Harold Ickes, my campaign chairman, Bill DiBlasio, my campaign manager, and Gigi George, the coordinated campaign director, and I want to thank the best, hardest working campaign staff any candidate has ever had.

And finally, I want to echo Chuck Schumer in saying that I know I would not be here without my family. And I want to thank my mother and my brothers, and I want to thank my husband and my daughter.

You know, because this campaign was about ideas and issues, we have a lot of work to do and I am looking forward to doing that work with all of you from one end of the state to the other. I tonight am just overwhelmed by the kindness and support that I've been given and I will work my heart out for the next six years for all of you.

Thank you, thank you, thank you and God bless you all.

# CLINTON ON HIS VISIT
# TO VIETNAM
## November 17, 2000

*A quarter century after the end of the Vietnam War, the United States and Vietnam took two major steps to move beyond their shared history in that conflict. In July the two former enemies signed a comprehensive trade agreement that had the potential to ease the grip of communism on Vietnam's economy—and possibly even its political system. Then in November Bill Clinton became the first U.S. president to visit Vietnam since the end of the war, and therefore the first to set foot in a Vietnam that was united under the control of the side that defeated the United States and its South Vietnamese ally during that war.*

*The twin events of 2000 represented the culmination of a reconciliation process that began in earnest in 1994 when the Clinton administration lifted economic sanctions against Vietnam, thus allowing limited trade between the two nations. In 1995—twenty years after the end of the war— the United States and Vietnam established formal diplomatic relations. Douglas "Pete" Peterson, a former American prisoner-of-war in Vietnam, returned as the U.S. ambassador in 1997. In 1999 Secretary of State Madeline K. Albright dedicated a new U.S. consulate built near the site of the old U.S. embassy in Saigon, now known as Ho Chi Minh City.* (Sanctions lifted, Historic Documents of 1994, p. 95; establishment of diplomatic relations, Historic Documents of 1995, p. 472; dedication of U.S. consulate, Historic Documents of 1999, 475)

## *Trade Agreement*

*After the war, the United States and Vietnam remained enemies, at least as far as economic relations were concerned. Even after the lifting of economic sanctions in 1994, Vietnam remained one of only six countries that did not have normal trade relations with the United States. U.S. and Vietnamese diplomats in 1996 began negotiations toward an agreement intended to promote trade, starting by reducing tariffs on each other's imports and opening Vietnam's economy to U.S. investments. The diplomats reached an agreement in July 1999, but in subsequent months senior Vietnamese government officials and representatives of the nation's state-run factories objected to numerous details. Despite the repeated urging of Albright and other U.S. officials, Vietnam refused to sign that agreement.*

*Negotiations resumed in 2000, but with a considerable change in the diplomatic climate. In May the U.S. House of Representatives approved a historic trade agreement between the United States and China, all but ensuring the normalizing of trade relations between those two countries. Vietnam's leaders, whose economy was dwarfed by China's, apparently feared being left behind in the race for closer ties with the massive U.S. economy. The Chinese and Vietnamese governments had similar goals: modernizing their economies by attracting American investments and increasing their exports to the United States of textiles and other low-cost consumer goods, while maintaining rigid political systems that would guarantee continued dominance by the ruling Communist Party. By mid-2000, Vietnam's leaders also faced the prospect that China would soon gain membership in the World Trade Organization (which set the rules of international trade), but Vietnam would still be knocking on the door. Moreover, economic growth in Vietnam lagged behind much of the rest of Asia, partly because Vietnam's bureaucrats made doing business difficult there and partly because Vietnam remained vulnerable to the effects of a regional financial crisis in 1997–1998.* (Asian financial crisis, Historic Documents of 1997, p. 832; China trade agreement, p. 213)

*U.S. and Vietnamese trade negotiators met in Washington for a renewed push in July and quickly came to an agreement, which they signed on July 13. Clinton praised the agreement during a White House ceremony. "From the bitter past we plant the seeds of a better future," he said. "This agreement is one more reminder that former adversaries can come together to find common ground."*

*Under the agreement the United States was required to reduce its tariffs (import taxes) on Vietnamese goods from an average of about 40 percent of value to about 3 percent of value. That provision was expected to make Vietnam a more attractive place for large corporations to build plants where the nation's industrious but low-paid workers could produce consumer goods for the U.S. market. In return Vietnam agreed to open its economy to U.S. investors and traders—a development that inevitably would weaken the grip of communist bureaucrats. But Vietnam insisted that several elements of that economic opening be phased in. For example, U.S. companies would have to wait three years to enter into joint ventures with Vietnamese telecommunications firms and would be limited to minority positions; that restriction apparently was aimed at enabling the Communist Party to retain control over institutions they considered vital to their hold on political power.*

*Despite the signing of the agreement in 2000, neither nation was expected to ratify it until 2001. In the United States, approval by Congress was necessary for ratification. Most observers predicted Congress would give its approval. Labor unions, which had opposed the China trade agreement because of that country's lack of worker protection laws, were considered likely to oppose the Vietnam agreement on similar grounds.*

## Clinton's Visit

*President Clinton arrived in Hanoi on November 16 for a three-day visit to Vietnam. He spent his first two full days, November 17–18, in Hanoi and the region of what used to be North Vietnam. On November 19 he visited Ho Chi Minh City.*

*In addition to its historic symbolism, Clinton's visit to Vietnam was full of ironies. From the American point of view, one was the fact that Clinton had actively opposed the Vietnam War and had avoided being drafted to fight in it. As a president in his early fifties, he represented one side of an American generation that had been deeply divided by the war: the opponents, many of them college students whose protest marches helped undermine public support for U.S. intervention in Vietnam, versus an estimated 3 million men—most of them draftees—who fought in the war. Of the latter group, many left Vietnam with ambivalent feelings about the war, and 52,000 of them died in Vietnam or neighboring countries during the unsuccessful struggle to "save" Southeast Asia from communism.*

*From the Vietnamese point of view, Clinton's visit served as a reminder both of how much things had changed in a quarter century and how much they had stayed the same. Vietnam was a united nation, proud of having defeated the world's most powerful nation. Saigon, the capital of U.S.-backed South Vietnam, was now named after Ho Chi Minh, the North Vietnamese leader whose guerrilla strategy won the war. But the United States remained the world's most powerful nation, both militarily and economically, and Vietnam was still struggling to reach its economic potential. With a population of 78 million people, Vietnam in 1999 had a per capita gross national product of slightly above $1 a day, ranking it 167th out of 206 nations, according to the World Bank.*

*Although the Vietnamese government played down Clinton's visit, the president received an enthusiastic welcome on November 17, his first full day in Hanoi. Tens of thousands of people gathered on the streets to watch his motorcade as it passed through the city; they waved, yelled "Hello" to him, and pressed around him as he visited the sites on his itinerary. After a brief visit to one museum, the Temple of Literature, Clinton headed straight for the crowd, shaking hands—ever the politician he had been all his adult life.*

*In his major public speech of the trip, delivered on that first day to an audience of students and teachers at the Vietnam National University and then broadcast twice over nationwide television, Clinton talked of the legacy of the Vietnam War—a conflict he acknowledged the Vietnamese knew as the "American war." After years of bitterness resulting from the war, he said, the two countries were beginning to work together, first on such projects as helping to locate the remains of soldiers from both sides still missing from the war, and later on economic cooperation. "Finally, America is coming to see Vietnam as your people have asked for years—as a country, not a war," he said.*

*Clinton talked of the benefits of global trade. He acknowledged that many people feared the affects of globalization but told his young audience that Vietnam's new openness to the world "is a great opportunity for you." An estimated 1.4 million Vietnamese entered the work force each year—more people than the government and state-run enterprises could employ, he said. The answer for Vietnam would come through global trade in the high technology industries that needed young, educated workers.*

*Clinton also stressed the importance of freedoms, such as freedom of religion and freedom of the press. But he added: "We do not seek to impose these ideas, nor could we. . . . Only you can decide if you will continue to open your markets, open your society, and strengthen the rule of law. Only you can decide how to weave individual liberties and human rights into the rich and strong fabric of Vietnamese national identity."*

*Despite Clinton's assertions that he was offering advice, not instructions, the country's senior Communist Party leader later lectured the president on Vietnam's view of the world, especially its view of what the United States had done during the war. In a meeting at party headquarters in Hanoi, Le Kha Phieu said U.S. "imperialism" was the cause of the war and the root cause of Vietnam's continuing problems.*

*On November 18 Clinton paid an emotion-packed visit to a site near Hanoi where workers were trying to recover the remains of an American pilot, Lt. Col. Lawrence G. Evert, whose plane was shot down in 1967. Clinton was accompanied by the pilot's two sons, who joined in searching through the mud of rice paddies for evidence of Evert's plane. Evert was one of an estimated 1,400 U.S. servicemen still missing from the war; Vietnam said at least 30,000 of its fighters were still missing.*

*Clinton wound up his trip with a visit to Ho Chi Minh City on November 19. The president was again greeted by large, admiring crowds composed both of young people for whom the war was an event in history and of older Vietnamese who had survived the war. Clinton met with a youth group for a free-wheeling roundtable discussion, paid a visit to the city's Roman Catholic archbishop, and spoke to a business group at a shipping terminal. Throughout the day he spoke of the virtues of freedom, even if always in a nonconfrontational way. Like every other country, he said, Vietnam had a choice of how to develop its own economic and political systems. But he left no doubt that he believed the right choice for Vietnam was for more freedom.*

*Following are excerpts from an address delivered November 17, 2000, by President Bill Clinton to an audience at Vietnam National University in Hanoi, Vietnam. The document was obtained from the Internet at http://www.whitehouse.gov/WH/New/november2000/speeches11_17.html.*

Thank you very much, and good afternoon. I can think of no more fitting place to begin my visit at this hopeful moment in our common history than here at Hanoi National University. I was given a Vietnamese phrase; I am going to try to say it. If I mess it up, feel free to laugh at me. *Xin chao cac ban.* ["Hello, everybody."]

So much of the promise of this youthful nation is embodied with you. I learned that you have exchanges here with students from nearly 100 universities, from Canada to France to Korea—and that you are now hosting more than a dozen full-time students from your partner school in the United States, the University of California.

I salute your vigorous efforts to engage the world. Of course, like students everywhere, I know you have things to think about other than your studies. For example, in September, you had to study for your classes and watch the Olympic accomplishments of Tran Hieu Ngan in Sydney. And this week you have to study and cheer Le Huynh Duc and Nguyen Hong Son in Bangkok at the football matches.

I am honored to be the first American President to see Hanoi, and to visit this university. But I do so conscious that the histories of our two nations are deeply intertwined in ways that are both a source of pain for generations that came before, and a source of promise for generations yet to come.

Two centuries ago, during the early days of the United States, we reached across the seas for partners in trade and one of the first nations we encountered was Vietnam. In fact, one of our founding fathers, Thomas Jefferson, tried to obtain rice seed from Vietnam to grow on his farm in Virginia 200 years ago. By the time World War II arrived, the United States had become a significant consumer of export from Vietnam. In 1945, at the moment of your country's birth, the words of Thomas Jefferson were chosen to be echoed in your own Declaration of Independence: "All men are created equal. The Creator has given us certain inviolable rights—the right to life, the right to be free, the right to achieve happiness."

Of course, all of this common history, 200 years of it, has been obscured in the last few decades by the conflict we call the Vietnam War and you call the American War. You may know that in Washington, D.C., on our National Mall, there is a stark black granite wall engraved with the name of every single American who died in Vietnam. At this solemn memorial, some American veterans also refer to the "other side of the wall," the staggering sacrifice of the Vietnamese people on both sides of that conflict—more than three million brave soldiers and civilians.

This shared suffering has given our countries a relationship unlike any other. Because of the conflict, America is now home to one million Americans of Vietnamese ancestry. Because of the conflict, three million Americans veterans served in Vietnam, as did many journalists, embassy personnel, aid workers and others who are forever connected to your country.

Almost 20 years ago now, a group of American servicemen took the first step to reestablish contacts between the United States and Vietnam. They traveled back to Vietnam for the first time since the war, and as they walked

917

through the streets of Hanoi, they were approached by Vietnamese citizens who had heard of their visit: Are you the American soldiers, they asked? Not sure what to expect, our veterans answered, yes, we are. And to their immense relief, their hosts simply said, welcome to Vietnam.

More veterans followed, including distinguished American veterans and heroes who serve now in the United States Congress: Senator John McCain (R-Ariz.), Senator Bob Kerrey (D-Neb.), Senator Chuck Robb (R-Va.), and Senator John Kerry (D-Mass.) from Massachusetts, who is here with me today, along with a number of representatives from our Congress, some of whom are veterans of the Vietnam conflict. When they came here, they were determined to honor those who fought without refighting the battles; to remember our history, but not to perpetuate it; to give young people like you in both our countries the chance to live in your tomorrows, not in our yesterdays. As Ambassador Pete Peterson has said so eloquently, "We cannot change the past. What we can change is the future."

Our new relationship gained strength as American veterans launched nonprofit organizations to work on behalf of the Vietnamese people, such as providing devices to people with war injuries to help them lead more normal lives. Vietnam's willingness to help us return the remains of our fallen servicemen to their families has been the biggest boost to improve ties. And there are many Americans here who have worked in that endeavor for many years now, including our Secretary of Veterans Affairs, Hershel Gober.

The desire to be reunited with a lost family member is something we all understand. It touches the hearts of Americans to know that every Sunday in Vietnam one of your most-watched television shows features families seeking viewers' help in finding loved ones they lost in the war so long ago now. And we are grateful for the Vietnamese villagers who have helped us to find our missing and, therefore, to give their families the peace of mind that comes with knowing what actually happened to their loved ones.

No two nations have ever before done the things we are doing together to find the missing from the Vietnam conflict. Teams of Americans and Vietnamese work together, sometimes in tight and dangerous places. The Vietnamese government has offered us access to files and government information to assist our search. And, in turn, we have been able to give Vietnam almost 400,000 pages of documents that could assist in your search. On this trip, I have brought with me another 350,000 pages of documents that I hope will help Vietnamese families find out what happened to their missing loved ones.

Today, I was honored to present these to your President, Tran Duc Luong. And I told him before the year is over, America will provide another million pages of documents. We will continue to offer our help and to ask for your help as we both honor our commitment to do whatever we can for as long as it takes to achieve the fullest possible accounting of our loved ones.

Your cooperation in that mission over these last eight years has made it possible for America to support international lending to Vietnam, to resume trade between our countries, to establish formal diplomatic relations and, this year, to sign a pivotal trade agreement.

Finally, America is coming to see Vietnam as your people have asked for years—as a country, not a war. A country with the highest literacy rate in Southeast Asia; a country whose young people just won three Gold Medals at the International Math Olympiad in Seoul; a country of gifted, hardworking entrepreneurs emerging from years of conflict and uncertainty to shape a bright future.

Today, the United States and Vietnam open a new chapter in our relationship, at a time when people all across the world trade more, travel more, know more about and talk more with each other than ever before. Even as people take pride in their national independence, we know we are becoming more and more interdependent. The movement of people, money and ideas across borders, frankly, breeds suspicion among many good people in every country. They are worried about globalization because of its unsettling and unpredictable consequences.

Yet, globalization is not something we can hold off or turn off. It is the economic equivalent of a force of nature—like wind or water. We can harness wind to fill a sail. We can use water to generate energy. We can work hard to protect people and property from storms and floods. But there is no point in denying the existence of wind or water, or trying to make them go away. The same is true for globalization. We can work to maximize its benefits and minimize its risks, but we cannot ignore it—and it is not going away.

In the last decade, as the volume of world trade has doubled, investment flows from wealthy nations to developing ones have increased by six times, from $25 billion in 1990 to more than $150 billion in 1998. Nations that have opened their economies to the international trading system have grown at least twice as fast as nations with closed economies. Your next job may well depend on foreign trade and investment. Come to think of it, since I have to leave office in about eight weeks, my next job may depend on foreign trade and investment.

Over the last 15 years, Vietnam launched its policy of Doi Moi, joined APEC and ASEAN, normalized relations with the European Union and the United States, and disbanded collective farming, freeing farmers to grow what they want and earn the fruits of their own labor. The results were impressive proof of the power of your markets and the abilities of your people. You not only conquered malnutrition, you became the world's second largest exporter of rice and achieved stronger overall economic growth.

Of course, in recent years the rate of growth has slowed and foreign investment has declined here, showing that any attempt to remain isolated from the risks of a global economy also guarantees isolation from its rewards, as well.

General Secretary Le Kha Phieu said this summer, and I quote, "We have yet to achieve the level of development commensurate with the possibilities of our country. And there is only one way to further open up the economy." So this summer, in what I believe will be seen as a pivotal step toward your future prosperity, Vietnam joined the United States in signing an historic bilateral trade agreement, building a foundation for Vietnam's entry eventually into the World Trade Organization.

Under the agreement, Vietnam will grant to its citizens, and over time to citizens of other countries, rights to import, export and distribute goods, giving the Vietnamese people expanding rights to determine their own economic destiny. Vietnam has agreed it will subject important decisions to the rule of law and the international trading system, increase the flow of information to its people, and accelerate the rise of a free economy and the private sector.

Of course, this will be good for Vietnam's foreign partners, like the United States. But it will be even better for Vietnam's own entrepreneurs, who are working hard to build businesses of their own. Under this agreement, Vietnam could be earning, according to the World Bank, another $1.5 billion each and every year from exports alone.

Both our nations were born with a Declaration of Independence. This trade agreement is a form of declaration of interdependence, a clear, unequivocal statement that prosperity in the 21st century depends upon a nation's economic engagement in the rest of the world.

This new openness is a great opportunity for you. But it does not guarantee success. What else should be done? Vietnam is such a young country, with 60 percent of your population under the age of 30, and 1.4 million new people entering your work force every year. Your leaders realize that government and state-owned businesses cannot generate 1.4 million new jobs every year. They know that the industries driving the global economy today—computers, telecommunications, biotechnology—these are all based on knowledge. That is why economies all over the world grow faster when young people stay in school longer, when women have the same educational opportunities that men have, when young people like you have every opportunity to explore new ideas and then to turn those ideas into your own business opportunities.

You can be—indeed, those of you in this hall today must be—the engine of Vietnam's future prosperity. As President Tran Duc Luong has said, the internal strength of the country is the intellect and capacity of its people.

The United States has great respect for your intellect and capacity. One of our government's largest educational exchange programs is with Vietnam. And we want to do more. Senator Kerry is right there, and I mentioned him earlier—is leading an effort in our United States Congress, along with Senator John McCain and other veterans of the conflict here, to establish a new Vietnam Education Foundation. Once enacted, the foundation would support 100 fellowships every year, either here or in the United States, for people to study or teach science, math, technology and medicine.

We're ready to put more funding in our exchange programs now so this effort can get underway immediately. I hope some of you in this room will have a chance to take part. And I want to thank Senator Kerry for this great idea. Thank you, sir, for what you have done.

Let me say, as important as knowledge is, the benefits of knowledge are necessarily limited by undue restrictions on its use. We Americans believe the freedom to explore, to travel, to think, to speak, to shape decisions that affect our lives enrich the lives of individuals and nations in ways that go far beyond economics.

Now, America's record is not perfect in this area. After all, it took us almost a century to banish slavery. It took us even longer to give women the right to vote. And we are still seeking to live up to the more perfect union of our founders' dreams and the words of our Declaration of Independence and Constitution. But along the way over these 226 years—224 years—we've learned some lessons. For example, we have seen that economies work better where newspapers are free to expose corruption, and independent courts can ensure that contracts are honored, that competition is robust and fair, that public officials honor the rule of law.

In our experience, guaranteeing the right to religious worship and the right to political dissent does not threaten the stability of a society. Instead, it builds people's confidence in the fairness of our institutions, and enables us to take it when a decision goes in a way we don't agree with. All this makes our country stronger in good times and bad. In our experience, young people are much more likely to have confidence in their future if they have a say in shaping it, in choosing their governmental leaders and having a government that is accountable to those it serves.

Now, let me say emphatically, we do not seek to impose these ideals, nor could we. Vietnam is an ancient and enduring country. You have proved to the world that you will make your own decisions. Only you can decide, for example, if you will continue to share Vietnam's talents and ideas with the world; if you will continue to open Vietnam so that you can enrich it with the insights of others. Only you can decide if you will continue to open your markets, open your society and strengthen the rule of law. Only you can decide how to weave individual liberties and human rights into the rich and strong fabric of Vietnamese national identity.

Your future should be in your hands, the hands of the Vietnam people. But your future is important to the rest of us, as well. For as Vietnam succeeds, it will benefit this region and your trading partners and your friends throughout the world.

We are eager to increase our cooperation with you across the board. We want to continue our work to clear land mines and unexploded ordnance. We want to strengthen our common efforts to protect the environment by phasing out leaded gasoline in Vietnam, maintaining a clean water supply, saving coral reefs and tropical forests. We want to bolster our efforts on disaster relief and prevention, including our efforts to help those suffering from the floods in the Mekong Delta. Yesterday, we presented to your government satellite imagery from our Global Disaster Information Network—images that show in great detail the latest flood levels on the Delta that can help Vietnam to rebuild.

We want to accelerate our cooperation in science, cooperation focused this month on our meeting in Singapore to study together the health and ecological effects of dioxin on the people of Vietnam and the Americans who were in Vietnam; and cooperation that we are advancing further with the Science and Technology Agreement our two countries signed just today.

We want to be your ally in the fight against killer diseases like AIDS, tuberculosis and malaria. I am glad to announce that we will nearly double our support of Vietnam's efforts to contain the AIDS crisis through education, prevention, care and treatment. We want to work with you to make Vietnam a safer place by giving you help to reduce preventable injuries—on the streets, at home and in the workplace. We want to work with you to make the most of this trade agreement, by providing technical assistance to assure its full and smooth implementation, in finding ways to encourage greater United States investment in your country.

We are, in short, eager to build our partnership with Vietnam. We believe it's good for both our nations. We believe the Vietnamese people have the talent to succeed in this new global age as they have in the past.

We know it because we've seen the progress you have made in this last decade. We have seen the talent and ingenuity of the Vietnamese who have come to settle in America. Vietnamese-Americans have become elected officials, judges, leaders in science and in our high-tech industry. Last year, a Vietnamese-American achieved a mathematical breakthrough that will make it easier to conduct high-quality video-conferencing. And all America took notice when Hoang Nhu Tran graduated number one in his class at the United States Air Force Academy.

Vietnamese-Americans have flourished not just because of their unique abilities and their good values, but also because they have had the opportunity to make the most of their abilities and their values. As your opportunities grow to live, to learn, to express your creativity, there will be no stopping the people of Vietnam. And you will find, I am certain, that the American people will be by your side. For in this interdependent world, we truly do have a stake in your success.

Almost 200 years ago, at the beginning of the relations between the United States and Vietnam, our two nations made many attempts to negotiate a treaty of commerce, sort of like the trade agreement that we signed today. But 200 years ago, they all failed, and no treaty was concluded. Listen to what one historian said about what happened 200 years ago, and think how many times it could have been said in the two centuries since. He said, "These efforts failed because two distant cultures were talking past each other, and the importance of each to the other was insufficient to overcome these barriers."

Let the days when we talk past each other be gone for good. Let us acknowledge our importance to one another. Let us continue to help each other heal the wounds of war, not by forgetting the bravery shown and the tragedy suffered by all sides, but by embracing the spirit of reconciliation and the courage to build better tomorrows for our children.

May our children learn from us that good people, through respectful dialogue, can discover and rediscover their common humanity, and that a painful, painful past can be redeemed in a peaceful and prosperous future.

Thank you for welcoming me and my family and our American delegation to Vietnam. Thank you for your faith in the future. *Chuc cac ban suc khoe va thanh cong.* ["May you have health and success."]

Thank you very much.

# PANIAGUA ON HIS INAUGURATION AS PRESIDENT OF PERU
## November 22, 2000

*Alberto Fujimori, who during ten years as president of Peru became one of Latin America's most successful authoritarian leaders in recent decades, suffered an astonishingly rapid fall from power in 2000. Fujimori engineered his reelection to a third five-year term in late May, brushing aside widespread protests about fraud in the electoral process. Four months later his most powerful supporter—intelligence chief Vladimiro Montesinos— was shown on television bribing an opposition legislator. A storm of public protest forced Fujimori to announce that he would leave office at an unspecified time. When Fujimori tried to delay his departure, another round of protests forced him to flee to Japan, the land of his parents. The Peruvian congress elected a transition government headed by centrist politician Valentin Paniagua. New elections were scheduled for early in 2001.*

*The peaceful ouster of Fujimori ended one of the most remarkable careers in modern Latin American history. The son of Japanese immigrants, Fujimori had been a university official before he was elected president in 1990, defeating novelist Mario Vargas Llosa. Fujimori temporarily dismissed the national congress and wielded authoritarian powers in 1992, saying strong measures were needed to defeat a violent leftist insurgency and drug traffickers. Fujimori's success against both of those foes, along with his use of social welfare programs to help the millions of landless peasants who were the base of his political support, enabled him to defeat former United Nations Secretary General Javier Perez de Cuellar and win reelection in 1995. But his overreaching attempt to win a third term in 2000 set the stage for the crisis that led to his downfall.*

*The Clinton administration—along with much of the U.S. foreign policy establishment—had decidedly mixed views about Fujimori. On the one hand, he had been a close ally in the U.S. antinarcotics campaign in the Andean region and had largely succeeded in curtailing the influence of drug traffickers in Peru. Fujimori also had decisively defeated the violent "Shining Path" Maoist guerrilla movement, had put his nation's economy on a relatively stable footing, and had built schools, health clinics, and other so-cial services for Peru's impoverished majority. Balanced against these vir-tues, in Washington's perception, was the fact that Fujimori acted in an authoritarian manner and derived much of his political power from the military and intelligence services. In the latter sense, Fujimori seemed to be a throwback to the old style of Latin American dictators that Washington policymakers liked to portray as having gone out of fashion.*

## *Rigging an Election*

*The year's drama began in April with the first round of the presidential election, which was surprisingly close. Prohibited by the constitution from running for a third term, Fujimori had successfully appealed to the coun-try's weak judiciary for a legal opinion allowing his candidacy. Fujimori faced an unexpectedly strong opponent in Alejandro Toledo, a U.S.-educated business school professor who mounted an aggressive campaign and won broad support from the nation's besieged middle class. As the April 9 voting approached, the government went through its customary procedures of at-tempting to ensure Fujimori's victory, provoking an international outcry. An observer team sent by the Organization of American States (OAS) re-leased a report shortly before the voting warning that actions by Fujimori's supporters had "impeded the citizenry from having the confidence that suf-ficient conditions exist for the exercise of effective democracy."*

*After the voting, the government announced that Fujimori was very close to having the bare majority necessary to avoid a runoff. For three days, the nation and international observers watched as the government counted votes and as Fujimori weighed the consequences of declaring outright vic-tory. Toledo mounted street demonstrations to demand a runoff, while the OAS observer mission issued reports denouncing election fraud and threat-ening economic and political sanctions if Fujimori blocked another vote. Faced with those pressures, Fujimori allowed the elections commission to announce on April 12 that he had fallen just 0.2 percent short of a majority. Toledo declared the announcement a victory, even though he claimed he had actually won a strong majority of the vote.*

*The runoff election was scheduled for May 28, but the government soon made it clear that Fujimori was taking no chances on allowing Toledo to win. The government unleashed a torrent of propaganda through the pro-Fujimori newspapers and television stations—including reports that Toledo was an alcoholic and had an illegitimate daughter. After analyzing the conduct of the first round of elections, the OAS observer team in mid-May called for postponing the second round until the middle of June, saying there was not enough time to ensure a valid election. Toledo adopted the call for a postponement, and when Fujimori refused to change the date, Toledo announced on May 18 that he was withdrawing from the race. Toledo urged his supporters to nullify their ballots by writing on them: "No to fraud." In its final report before the election, the OAS said the process "is far from one that could be considered free and fair" and refused to observe the vote.*

On election day, Fujimori was declared the victor with about 50.8 percent of the vote. Toledo had 16.7 percent, and nearly all the remaining ballots were blank or nullified. Speaking at an enormous protest rally in Lima, Toledo said he would lead continuing protests in hopes of forcing Fujimori to back down and allow an "honest" election.

Toledo quickly won influential support from the Clinton administration, which attempted to build a consensus within the OAS for a demand that Fujimori allow new elections under close international supervision. But old traditions in Latin America—including a reluctance by governments to criticize each other and a resentment of U.S. intervention—proved to be more important factors than a desire to promote democracy in Peru. The OAS took no serious action to protest the election, and Fujimori was inaugurated for his third term as president on July 27.

In his inaugural address, Fujimori made little mention of several reform recommendations that an OAS delegation had presented in late June, including judicial and electoral reforms and new standards for guaranteeing human rights and freedom of the press. Fujimori did say that he would introduce legislation to reform the intelligence and security services, but he offered no details.

Three people were killed in demonstrations protesting Fujimori's inauguration. On July 27, the night before the inaugural, an estimated 80,000 people attended a peaceful protest rally in Lima; observers said it was the largest mass rally in the country's history.

## A Storm Sweeps In

Fujimori had little time to enjoy his third term. Early in September, news reports linked intelligence chief Montesinos to a complex scheme under which 10,000 AK-47 assault rifles purchased in Jordan by Peruvian military agents were shipped to the Revolutionary Armed Forces of Colombia, the largest of two guerrilla groups in neighboring Colombia. Fujimori and Montesinos claimed to have uncovered the arms smuggling deal; reportedly unbeknownst to Fujimori, Montesinos had been directly involved in the deal all along.

A Lima television station on September 14 broadcast a videotape of a meeting between Montesinos and an opposition member of Congress, Alberto Kouri. In that meeting, Montesinos handed Kouri $15,000 in exchange for his promise to support Fujimori. The broadcast of the videotape appeared to confirm what critics had alleged for many years: Montesinos was the linchpin of Fujimori's presidency, the man who had ensured the backing of the military and had kept opposition politicians in check. By the same token, the unmasking of Montesinos rapidly undermined support for both him and Fujimori within the military. According to news reports, some of Peru's military leaders urged both men to step aside, and on September 16 Fujimori complied. In a nationally televised address, Fujimori said he would call new presidential elections, but would not be a candidate himself. However, he made no announcement about the status of Montesinos, who dis-

*appeared from public view and then sought asylum in Panama, which was denied.*

*Opposition leaders celebrated Fujimori's announcement and called on him to resign immediately in favor of a transition government that would hold new elections. Within a few days they learned that Fujimori had no plans for an early departure. The president said elections would be held in April 2001 but his successor would not take office until July 28, 2001, a delay of ten months. "I have a mandate to govern and I will continue governing," Fujimori said.*

*When rumors surfaced that Montesinos and some top military leaders were planning a coup, Fujimori announced a nationwide manhunt for Montesinos, who returned from Panama on October 23 and went into hiding. Fujimori forced his military commanders to resign on October 28, but the political crisis surrounding him continued to build as government prosecutors began investigating charges that Montesinos had stashed millions of dollars in secret foreign bank accounts.*

*In mid-November the Peruvian congress—for many years a reliable rubber stamp for the president—ousted a leader who had been a Fujimori ally and installed Paniagua in her place. At about the same time, Fujimori left Peru for a summit meeting in Brunei of the Asia-Pacific Economic Cooperation forum. Rather than returning home via Panama, as planned, he headed on to Japan. On November 19 Fujimori told aides that he would resign, and a day later he faxed a resignation letter to the Peruvian congress. But the congress on November 21 rejected the resignation letter and instead passed a resolution declaring the presidency vacant and Fujimori "morally unfit" to hold it. In the meantime, Fujimori's two vice presidents had both resigned under pressure, clearing the way for Paniagua to take over as acting president after having served as the leader of congress for just one week.*

*In his inaugural address on November 22, Paniagua pledged to make "the restoration of democracy" his primary task as president. Paniagua promised an investigation into charges of government corruption, but he ignored calls from the audience of "Justice for Fujimori." Paniagua named Perez de Cuellar as prime minister of a coalition government; the appointment apparently came as a surprise to the eighty-year-old Perez de Cuellar, who had lived for several years in Paris but who said he would accept the post. Paniagua also fired most of the country's top military leaders, and on December 31 prosecutors arrested the former armed forces chief, General Jose Villaneuva, on corruption charges.*

*On December 11 the Japanese government announced it had determined that Fujimori held Japanese citizenship, even though he had lived in Peru all his life. Under Japanese law, that meant that Fujimori could not be extradited to Peru against his will to face any criminal charges that might be brought against him. A committee of the Peruvian congress investigating corruption charges against Montesinos had said it needed testimony from Fujimori—a move widely seen as opening the possibility for an indictment of Fujimori himself.*

*Meanwhile, the Peruvian government continued to search for Monte-
sinos, who had been reported at various locations in South America. To help
with its search, the government in late December launched a site on the
Internet with photographs and descriptions of Montesinos and an artist's
rendering of how he might appear with a beard.*

*Following is the text of a speech delivered by Valentin Paniagua
after his inauguration on November 22, 2000, as acting president of Peru. The document was obtained from the Internet at
http://www.peruemb.org/frupdate.html.*

Today a new era is born. A stage of Peruvian history ends as another begins.
Faith exhilarates the spirits of the Nation; and illusion, excessive perhaps,
shakes Peruvians as a whole. We all want to believe that there is a new task
and THERE IS, modest perhaps, but greatly consequential to the Nation's
development.

This illusion is neither fruit of any one passion for the political environment
nor a demagogic enchantment. As strange as it may seem, it is a feeling born
from a deep conviction: the need to extol, praise and consolidate the Constitution as a norm of life in our daily coexistence.

As Francisco de Paula Gonzales and Vigil said in the historical constitutional accusation to President Gamarra: "Nothing is small, everything contained in the Constitution is great and sacred. . . ." Such understanding of
the value of the Constitution inspired our national hero "El Caballero de los
Mares," we symbolically uphold his stance—the proclamation according to
which he acknowledged no caudillo other than the Constitution.

This is precisely what we want to affirm, as inspiration-source for the task
we have set out to fulfill, in these short eight months incumbent upon us
pursuant to Article 115 of the Constitution. Indeed, the task is to decisively
contribute to the democratic re-construction and re-institutionalization undertaken by the various sectors at the dialogue table assembled by OAS,
which this Congress has put into effect by means of fundamental laws. The
mere legal rite of improving or amending laws cannot fulfill this task. In fact,
because it is democratic, it must be inspired by coalition, dialogue and the
search for consensus.

Likewise, it must be based on solid ethical and political principles that en-
lighten and guide each step of this fundamental task. Nothing can be more
appropriate for this commitment than to recall the ancestral Andean Triple
Order, not only to vindicate our legitimate Peruvian roots but also to project
inspiration in the edification of our future, without which it would be impossible to consolidate. Thus, we proclaim and appropriate the Inca's principles
and ethics of industriousness, truthfulness and honesty.

Moreover, this difficult task imposed upon us by the current historical environment must, in the first place, rely on the help of exceptional men who

genuinely embody the finest values of our community. Therefore, I am pleased to announce to the Nation that Ambassador Javier Perez de Cuéllar has been appointed as Prime Minister to the Government of National Union and Reconciliation.

The term of office that I shall preside is short, too short to try to impart new courses in the economy. However, I cannot refrain from indicating some basic goals inspiring its administration.

First, it is imperative to attain fiscal balance, as basic element of economic stability. To do so, we shall adopt the necessary measures to restructure expenditure and items of expenditure in sectors that under present circumstances are of little priority or of no priority at all, bearing in mind the need to maintain indispensable items of social expenditure and those related to public investments.

In the same sense, we will review and pay close attention to our external debt structure and, after the pertinent technical evaluations, we will multilaterally plan for ways to adapt to our real economic and social capacities payments thereof. But, I reiterate, there will be no surprises or unilateral decisions in those acts, just the negotiation and firm determination of the government I preside.

Nobody argues on the urgent need to increase national and foreign investments, which lately have decreased unfortunately. Therefore, and because investments are an indispensable element in the attainment of economic growth and increase in job offers, we shall adopt, in a coherent manner, every technical measure that may be required by the tax and financial system.

We will evaluate the results of the privatization process of public companies and carefully analyze the fate of the US$ 9.2 Billion obtained from the sales. Consequently, we shall adopt the pertinent measures as to encourage private investments for the fair and decentralized development of the country.

Now that so many hopes have been kindled, we shall try to proceed to move forward in the decentralization process that for so many years Peruvian towns have demanded. Municipalities will not be seen as government agencies nor will political interests influence the much-needed co-operation of the Executive.

I am conscious that if our country does not undergo a much-needed decentralization process, our democracy and national development will continue to be weak. I hope the new budget, to be yet approved by Congress, grants minimum economic autonomy to remote Peruvian towns, enough to foster local progress by means of an appropriate transfer of resources.

This government's foremost responsibility is, by unequivocal constitutional mandate, to summon to elections. Having this been done already, we ratify and declare that this will be the main task to which we will fervently be devoted to.

Firstly, by zealously guaranteeing that no public agency shall interfere with the electoral process. Secondly, by closely co-operating with organizations related to the election process so that they may fulfill their goals. Thirdly, by pledging to uphold public order and freedom from social unrest as the previous and indispensable condition for Peruvians to freely and independently cast their votes knowing that their choice will be scrupulously respected.

As I have already indicated, this Transitory Government's term is short, hence it shall require every sector and institutions' co-operation. Convinced of the submission of the Armed Forces and the Police to uphold constitutional order, domestic and foreign peace is secured. In addition, so are international commitments and obligations binding Peru, as domestic legal certainty is secured thanks to the independence with which the Judiciary, the Public Ministry and the Constitutional Courts must act.

In this transitional stage, the co-operation of national and foreign industrialist is required more than ever to enable transit to the next government without having to affect projects or economic initiatives already in motion. The government will act with equanimity, transparency and responsibility, avoiding to compromise the success of efforts that may damage the economic stability.

The democratic Constitution is a collective effort. Thus, I summon all sectors of the country. I specifically request the co-operation of young people who have disinterestedly fought for democracy and with whom I have shared so many years of academic concerns. Likewise, I request the understanding of labor and social union organizations to enable the fluid and dynamic transit towards a genuinely democratic government.

In short, I summon all Peruvians, including housewives who are burdened by the sufferings generated by the economic crisis, to tell them that time has come for the constitutional re-institutionalization of Peru based on dialogue and coalition.

Nobody can feel excluded. I know that even our political adversaries, whose discrepancies we salute and respect, agree with the purposes encouraging us. This is why I am convinced that this Government may make coalition and dialogue the means to guarantee national union.

I would like to sincerely thank every political sector, including our adversaries whom in midst of the storm we have lived through these past days, have had the greatness to wish us success and offered collaboration, which of course I accept and welcome for the good of our Mother country.

Finally, I would like to thank representatives of friendly Nations, whom with their presence ratify old and honorable historical ties. Likewise, I would like to thank the people for giving us their support and enthusiasm these past few days. I am absolutely convinced that under this environment we may be able to guide the country through the path of progress, turning into reality the motto wedged by our founding fathers as a promise and bet for the future of Peru: FIRM AND HAPPY FOR THE SAKE OF UNION.

# UN HUMAN RIGHTS COMMISSIONER
# ON MIDDLE EAST VIOLENCE
## November 27, 2000

*Hopes that a lasting peace between Israel and the Palestinians would be achieved in 2000 were dashed by the eruption into violence of long-simmering hatreds and frustrations. After U.S. president Bill Clinton tried, and failed, to broker a comprehensive peace deal between Israeli prime minister Ehud Barak and Palestinian leader Yasir Arafat, violence exploded in Israel and the occupied territories at the end of September. Stone-throwing Palestinians clashed with heavily armed Israeli security forces, setting off an incessant series of attacks and counterattacks that lasted through the rest of the year. By year's end, more than 385 people had been killed in the violence. The overwhelming majority—about 325—were Palestinians, according to the Palestine Red Crescent Society. Forty-three Israeli Jews and 13 Israeli Arabs also were killed, according to the Israeli Defense Forces. The violence was the most sustained conflict between Israelis and Palestinians since the Palestinian uprising, or "Intifada," which lasted from 1987 to 1993.* (Peace negotiations, p. 494)

*Palestinian leaders said the violence was the consequence of pent-up frustration among the more than 3 million stateless Palestinians, who for more than a half-century had seen their national aspirations thwarted. For seven years, since the opening of direct peace talks between Israel and Palestinian leaders in Oslo, Norway, Palestinians had waited for an agreement that would give them control over their homelands in exchange for lasting peace with Israel. The long-running negotiations had produced some benefits for the Palestinians—most importantly the creation of a Palestinian Authority based in the Gaza Strip and Palestinian control over about 42 percent of the Israeli-occupied West Bank of the Jordan River. But the vast majority of Palestinians continued to live in poverty and tens of thousands were crowded into UN-run refugee camps around the region. By late 2000 it was clear that many Palestinians had come to doubt the value of peace negotiations and, in frustration, were once again turning to violence as a means of achieving their goals.*

*Frightened by the sudden upsurge of violence, Israelis responded with harsh measures. Security forces fired rubber-coated bullets and tear gas at protesters, many of whom were children. The government prevented Palestinians from traveling between their homes in Gaza and the West Bank to jobs in Israel, a move that put thousands of people out of work and seriously damaged Israel's own economy. Ultimately, the government launched specific attacks against individual Palestinian leaders who were seen as fomenting the violence; that campaign succeeded in killing an estimated twenty Palestinian paramilitary commanders.*

*In a hard-hitting report reviewing her visit to the region in November, Mary Robinson, the United Nations High Commissioner on Human Rights, said she had found "two peoples who are linked by history and geography, but are currently separated by a wide and growing gap in their perceptions of each other. The violence in recent months has resulted in a hardening of positions, with little willingness on either side to understand or accept" the other.*

*The violence also killed, at least for the time being, any chance for a final "land-for-peace" deal between the two sides. Right through the end of the year, Clinton attempted to mediate an agreement that would give Palestinians control of nearly all the Israeli-occupied West Bank in return for Palestinian security pledges that would guarantee a permanent peace. But the violence helped destabilize the political position of Prime Minister Barak, who had offered far-reaching concessions to the Palestinians. In December he announced his resignation and called new elections for February 2001. That election was almost certain to be won by rightist leader Ariel Sharon, a staunch opponent of all previous peace agreements between Israel and its Arab neighbors.*

## The Palestinian Uprising

*The triggering event—if not the ultimate cause—for the Palestinian uprising was a September 28 visit by Sharon to the plaza outside the Al Aksa mosque in Jerusalem's Old City. The area was considered holy ground both by Jews, who called it the Temple Mount, and by Muslims, who called it the Noble Sanctuary. Sharon, the leader of the rightist Likud Party in parliament, had obtained permission from the Israeli police to lead a Likud delegation to the plaza. Sharon insisted that his visit was merely intended to signal that Jews had the right to visit the site, which he said was a sovereign part of Israel. But the act was a provocative one in the eyes of Palestinians, who considered Sharon responsible for the 1982 massacre of several hundred Palestinians at two refugee camps in Lebanon. Moreover, Palestinians viewed Sharon's action as reinforcing the refusal by many Israelis to cede sovereignty over any part of east Jerusalem to the Palestinian Authority.*

*Dozens of Palestinian protesters were wounded during clashes with Israeli security forces immediately after Sharon's visit. The level of violence escalated the following day, when Israeli police fired rubber-coated bullets at stone-throwing protesters in the Temple Mount area, killing six and wounding as many as two hundred. September 30, the first day of the Jewish new year, marked a turning point of another kind, as the violence spread into the Palestinian-controlled Gaza Strip and throughout much of the West Bank.*

*One incident, filmed by a French television crew, quickly became a worldwide symbol of the terror of the violence. At the entrance to Netzarim, a Jewish settlement in the Gaza Strip, a Palestinian man and his twelve-year-old son were caught in a gun battle between Palestinians and Israeli security forces. Terrified, the father and son tried to hide behind a large cement container, and the father cried out, appealing for a halt in the shooting. But his appeal was in vain. According to numerous witnesses, both were hit by Israeli gunfire, and the boy, Muhammad al-Dirra, slumped dead against his father, who was seriously wounded. A Palestinian Red Crescent ambulance driver who tried to rescue the pair also was killed in the crossfire. Film of the incident was broadcast locally and around the world, further inflaming Palestinian passions and sparking international denunciations of Israeli security tactics. The boy and the ambulance driver were among a dozen Palestinians killed that day; his father was among several dozen wounded.*

*Yet another milestone in the conflict was reached a day later, on October 1, when Jews and Israeli Arabs clashed in several Arab-populated towns in northern Israel. Those clashes were especially significant because the Arabs were Israeli citizens, unlike the stateless Palestinians, and many were moderates who had long worked within the Israeli political system. Writing in the newspaper* Maariv, *one well-known Israeli Arab—former soccer star Rifat Turk—vented his anguish at the violence against his "brothers," the Palestinians. "Even if you are a person who has spent your whole life trying to act in moderation, you discover at times like this that under your skin, with a power that surprises even you, a great rage resides."*

*At the same time, the course of events was undermining the political position of the Israeli peace movement—Jews who had long advocated compromise with the Palestinians. Arafat's refusal to accept Barak's concessions at Camp David seemed to demonstrate, even for the staunchest peace advocates, the limits of trying to negotiate with the Palestinians. Arafat's unwillingness, or inability, to stem the street violence gave renewed urgency to Israeli security concerns and cast new doubt on the Palestinian leader's reliability as a partner in peace.*

*A cease-fire on October 3 lasted only a few hours before Palestinians resumed their rioting (in response, they said, to Israel's failure to withdraw security forces from key points), and the now-familiar cycle of stone throwing and gun battles ensued. On October 4 Secretary of State Madeleine K. Albright mediated talks in Paris between Barak and Arafat in an attempt to win agreement on a formal cease-fire and the resumption of peace talks. Arafat refused to sign a cease-fire accord because it did not meet his demand for an international inquiry into the causes of the violence.*

*A "day of rage" on October 6 successfully vented Palestinian anger but also resulted in nine more Palestinian deaths in Gaza, the West Bank, and*

*Jerusalem. Rioting, gun battles, and various efforts to negotiate a cease-fire continued for the next ten days. On October 12 a Palestinian mob killed two Israeli army reserve soldiers and dragged their bodies through the streets. A photograph of a Palestinian waving his hands, bloody from one of the Israeli bodies, captured world attention and served as a counterpoint to the earlier image of the Palestinian boy killed in Gaza. In retaliation, Israeli helicopters fired missiles at several Palestinian targets.*

*On October 16, Clinton and Egyptian president Hosni Mubarak hosted a summit meeting at the Egyptian resort town of Sharm el-Sheik. There, for two days Arafat and Barak met with Clinton, Mubarak, Jordan's King Abdullah, and UN Secretary General Kofi Annan. On the evening of October 17 Clinton announced that Barak and Arafat had agreed to stop the violence and explore ways of restarting the peace talks. Clinton said the two leaders also had agreed on terms for an international inquiry into the causes of the violence, which had been Arafat's key demand. Clinton later named former senator George Mitchell to head the inquiry; Mitchell's panel was expected to issue a report in 2001.*

*The Sharm el-Sheik summit appeared to help calm the level of violence for two days, but an upsurge of fighting on October 20 led Barak to threaten to suspend the process of peace talks begun at Oslo seven years earlier. Meeting in Cairo the following day, Arab leaders blamed Israel for the violence and the lack of progress in the peace talks. Their only substantive action, however, was to declare a joint suspension of economic relations with Israel. Barak responded on October 22 by formally suspending Israel's participation in the peace talks—a step that had only symbolic importance because there were no talks to suspend.*

*The violence continued throughout the rest of the year but on a more episodic basis than during the first month after Sharon's fateful visit to the Temple Mount. In most cases, an attack by one side brought swift retaliation from the other. The tit-for-tat equation was imbalanced only by the fact of the overwhelming superiority of weapons held by the Israeli military. Palestinians used automatic weapons and car bombs, as well as slingshots, but the Israeli government was able to respond with jet fighters, helicopters, and laser-guided missiles. In one particularly gruesome episode, a armored school bus used to transport the children of Jewish settlers in the Gaza Strip came under a mortar attack on November 20; a teacher and a maintenance man were killed, and three children were severely wounded. In retaliation, Israel launched missile attacks against Palestinian targets in Gaza, including offices of Arafat's Palestinian Authority.*

*On several occasions during the last two months of the year, Israeli forces targeted individual Palestinians who were considered responsible for violent attacks. One of the most highly publicized incidents came on November 9 when an army helicopter fired a missile on a car occupied by a Palestinian paramilitary commander, Hussein Obaiyat, killing him and two women who were nearby. Palestinians denounced these killings as "state terrorism," but Israeli authorities defended them as necessary "punishment" for violence against Israeli citizens.*

## International Condemnations

*The disproportionate ratio of casualties led most international observers to blame Israel for using excessive force to combat Palestinian protests. International human rights organizations and various UN agencies repeatedly argued that Israel violated international legal standards by using live ammunition, helicopters, missiles, and other weapons of war against protesters, many of them children armed only with stones and slingshots.*

*The UN first acted on October 7, when the Security Council approved a resolution condemning Israel's "excessive use of force" against the Palestinians. The United States abstained on that resolution. Two weeks later, on October 19, the UN Commission on Human Rights narrowly adopted an Arab-sponsored resolution, over U.S. objections, strongly condemning the "indiscriminate use of force in violation of international humanitarian law by the Israeli occupying power." That language referred to the fact that the UN considered Israel's occupation, since 1967, of the West Bank to be illegal under international law. The UN General Assembly adopted a similar resolution on October 20, again over U.S. objections. Israeli diplomats rejected all the UN resolutions as unbalanced because they attacked Israeli actions without mentioning what Israel considered to be Palestinian provocations.*

*A more comprehensive assessment of the Israeli-Palestinian violence came in a report issued November 27 by Mary Robinson, the United Nations High Commissioner on Human Rights. Robinson, a former president of Ireland, visited the Middle East November 8–16 and said she found the human rights situation, especially in Palestinian areas, to be "bleak." Robinson said Palestinians faced a reality of "grinding, petty humiliations, discrimination and inequalities which were ultimately dehumanizing."*

*Among Israelis, she said, there was "a preoccupation with security, born of a strong sense of isolation and of being set upon from all sides." Robinson reported that she was especially shocked to learn that Palestinian radio stations had broadcast calls for "the killing of all Jews." Robinson called for the establishment of an international commission to monitor developments in Israel, Gaza, and the West Bank.*

*The UN's special coordinator for the Middle East, Norwegian diplomat Terje Rod Larsen, issued a report on December 5 arguing that two months of violence and Israeli restrictions had devastated the Palestinian economy. "Three years of progress have been wiped out in two months of conflict," Larsen said. Larsen reported that the Palestinian economy had lost more than $500 million in lost wages and exports, representing 10 percent of the entire year's total for the 3 million Palestinians in Gaza and the West Bank. About one-third of adult Palestinians were unemployed and nearly half were living on less than $2 a day, Larsen said. That stood in contrast to Israel's per capita annual income of about $18,000, the highest in the Middle East.*

### *Israel's Political Infighting*

*The street battles between Palestinians and Israeli security forces were mirrored, although in a nonviolent fashion, in the struggle for power within the Israeli political establishment. Even before the Camp David negotiations in July, Barak had lost his working majority in the Israeli parliament and had been able to govern only through a series of political deals that temporarily balanced the interests of the country's numerous factions.*

*During the first month of the Palestinian uprising, Barak had a somewhat free hand because the parliament was in recess. The return of parliament on October 30 put new pressure on Barak, starting with several no-confidence motions filed by Arab representatives. Barak survived those motions, but on November 20 the ultra-Orthodox Shas Party, which had supported his government in exchange for government funding of party-run social programs, announced that it would withdraw its backing.*

*On December 9 Barak announced that he would resign, a move that would trigger a new election for prime minister, but not for parliament. Barak's move was aimed at heading off a challenge by the man considered to be his most formidable opponent—Benjamin Netanyahu, the former prime minister who Barak had defeated in May 1999. Under Israeli election rules, Netanyahu could not run in a special election for prime minister because he was no longer a member of parliament. Even so, Netanyahu attempted to convince the parliament to dissolve itself, a move that would enable him to run. Netanyahu's maneuvering failed, and on December 19 he withdrew from the race. That left Likud leader Sharon as Barak's challenger in the election, which was scheduled for February 2001. Campaigning on the slogan, "Only Sharon can bring peace," he was running well ahead of Barak at year's end in public opinion polls and seemed all but certain to become Israel's new prime minister.*

> *Following are excerpts from a report, released November 27, 2000, by Mary Robinson, the United Nations High Commissioner on Human Rights, with observations from her visit earlier that month to Israel, the Israeli-occupied territories, Egypt, and Jordan. The document was obtained from the Internet at http://www .unhchr.ch/Huridocda/Huridoca.nsf/TestFrame/b620f0b58038 e34cc12569a7003e368a?Opendocument.*

[Paragraphs 1 through 18 reviewed the mandate of the UN Commission on Human Rights and discussed the itinerary of the High Commissioner's visit to the Middle East November 8–16, 2000.]

## III. General Observations

19. The human rights situation in the occupied Palestinian territories is bleak. The civilian population feels besieged by a stronger power prepared

to use its superior force against demonstrations and stonethrowing by adolescents. During the course of the visit the violence escalated, with more shooting—including so-called drive-by shootings—on the Palestinian side and the use of rockets and heavy machine-gun fire on the Israeli side. At each meeting in the occupied Palestinian territories pleas for international protection or for some form of international monitoring presence were voiced.

20. In the occupied Palestinian territories, discussions concerning the present crisis and its impact on human rights were linked to the reality of the occupation itself. That reality was described by Palestinians as one of grinding, petty humiliations, discrimination and inequalities which were ultimately dehumanizing. It was explained that the anger and frustration of the present Intifada stemmed from lack of implementation of the key United Nations resolutions, especially General Assembly resolutions 181 (II) and 194 (III) and Security Council resolution 242 (1967), the continuing encroachment on land for settlements, and what was perceived as a peace process which had not addressed the Palestinian claims of a State with East Jerusalem as its capital and some recognition of the right of return of refugees.

21. Perhaps the strongest and most troubling impression taken away by the High Commissioner from her visit to Israel and the occupied Palestinian territories was that of two peoples who are linked by history and geography, but are currently separated by a wide and growing gap in their perceptions of each other. The violence of recent months has resulted in a hardening of positions, with little willingness on either side to understand or accept the narrative of the other.

22. Amongst Israelis there is a preoccupation with security, born of a strong sense of isolation and of being set upon from all sides. This can easily be understood in terms of Israeli and Jewish history. However, it is not appreciated or allowed for by a Palestinian people who see only Israel's overwhelming military superiority and experience its readiness to use it. Israelis with whom the High Commissioner met, including many who deeply believe in the peace process, said they felt shell-shocked by the recent breakdown of negotiations at a time when, to them, a comprehensive settlement had seemed so close. Amongst Palestinians, on the other hand, the predominant sentiment was that the process of the past seven years had delivered little or nothing to them. Whilst Israelis point to the building of economic links as a positive sign, Palestinians see the same process as increasing the dependence of the occupied territories and their vulnerability to exploitation by Israel during periods of crisis.

23. The High Commissioner was offered different views about the origins of the present cycle of violence, including on the significance of the visit of Mr. Ariel Sharon to the Temple Mount/Haram Al-Sharif, and on whether the current Intifada is a spontaneous popular uprising or an orchestrated strategy. The High Commissioner referred repeatedly to her mandate, which addresses the underlying human rights causes of the conflict. Such an approach acknowledges the long-standing and unresolved grievances of the Palestinian

people, many of whom are now third-generation refugees. It must also be understood, as it is by many Israelis, that Palestinians, including Arabs who have Israeli citizenship, have suffered and continue to suffer from serious discrimination. An inescapable conclusion is that much of the present situation has to do with the daily reality of life under the occupation, including what Palestinians see as the numerous daily humiliations imposed upon them, often deliberately, but sometimes through bureaucratic indifference towards people who lack political power. However, in discussing root causes, it must also be acknowledged that over an extended period the right of Israelis to "security of person" (Universal Declaration of Human Rights, article 3) has been threatened. This persistent insecurity has given rise to many of the problems which now lie at the heart of the human rights situation in the occupied Palestinian territories and Israel.

24. A related problem is that of hate speech and incitement. Numerous examples were cited to the High Commissioner during her visit and evidence was clearly visible on the walls of Palestinian houses and Israeli settlements. The High Commissioner was struck, for example, by the deep hurt caused by the accusation that Palestinian parents were forcing their children into the line of fire to achieve martyrdom. Similarly, she was shocked by calls broadcast on Palestinian television and radio urging the killing of all Jews. At this very difficult time it is incumbent upon leaders on both sides to avoid inciting racial and religious animosities and to condemn such incitement when it does occur within their communities. The High Commissioner believes that the forthcoming World Conference against Racism, Racial Discrimination, Xenophobia and Related Intolerance will provide an opportunity for reflection and reconciliation, which political leaders and members of civil society alike should begin to prepare for.

## IV. Human Rights Situation in the Occupied Palestinian Territories

25. While in the occupied Palestinian territories, the High Commissioner received information from numerous sources alleging serious violations of human rights, both in relation to recent events and more long-term systematic abuses originating from the occupation itself. Also alleged was a failure on the part of Israel to adhere to international humanitarian law, in particular the 1949 Fourth Geneva Convention relative to the protection of civilians in time of war, whose applicability to the occupied territories has been repeatedly reaffirmed by United Nations bodies, including the Security Council, the General Assembly and the Commission on Human Rights. Particular areas of concern with regard to recent developments included: excessive and disproportionate use of force, including alleged attacks on medical personnel; the arbitrary destruction of property; the effects on Palestinian residents of Israeli settlement activity, including restrictions on freedom of movement; the serious economic impact on the residents of the occupied territories; the violations of the human rights of children; and restrictions on access to humanitarian assistance.

## Excessive use of force

26. The most persistent allegation brought to the attention of the High Commissioner was that Israeli security forces have engaged in excessive force, disproportionate to the threat faced by their soldiers. A wide range of observers, including United Nations representatives, expressed the strong view that the very high number of casualties, combined with the nature of the injuries being sustained, including by young people, could only be consistent with a military response which was both excessive and inappropriate. With only minor regional variations, this pattern was, said the observers, repeated in different locations throughout the affected areas.

27. The High Commissioner had requested a meeting with the Israeli Defense Forces (IDF). The meeting was facilitated by Israel and took place at Ben Gurien Airport on 13 November prior to her flight to Cairo. It is described in some detail in paragraphs 66 to 71 below but, as it offered an opportunity to hear the Israeli perspective on the allegations of excessive use of force, the relevant comments or a reference to the relevant paragraphs are inserted in the present section of the report.

28. In an attempt to disperse the demonstrations, the Israeli military authorities have used live ammunition, rubber coated steel bullets and tear gas, all of which have resulted in deaths and injuries amongst the Palestinians. Heavier weapons have also been used, including rockets fired by infantry and from helicopters, armoured vehicles which have been deployed throughout the Gaza Strip and the West Bank, and heavy machine guns. The use of heavy weapons has raised the incidence of death and injury amongst non-combatants and, indeed, several such deaths occurred during the period of the High Commissioner's visit.

29. A high percentage of the injuries sustained by Palestinians have been to the upper part of their body, including a large number of eye injuries, some caused by the firing of "rubber" bullets at close range. The result is often the loss of an eye, but can also be severe brain damage or death. In subsequent discussions senior IDF representatives accepted the potential lethalness of "rubber" bullets, and also that of tear gas, if used in a confined area, as has been alleged.

30. When asked about the reported injuries, senior IDF officers told the High Commissioner (see paras. 69–70 below) that the methods and weapons employed by the IDF in dealing with the present crisis are carefully calibrated according to the nature of the threat being faced and, in particular, that live fire, whether from small arms or heavier weapons, has only been directed at those who have used firearms or petrol bombs in attacks against Israeli forces.

31. While in the Gaza Strip, the High Commissioner visited Shifa Hospital, the largest hospital in Gaza with 650 beds and 8 operating theatres. The High Commissioner met with 45 patients, including boys and girls under 18 and their relatives. A 15-year-old, now a paraplegic, informed the High Commissioner that he was shot by Israeli soldiers while he was demonstrating and throwing stones in the industrial zone close to Erez checkpoint. He had joined other teenagers after school to express his anger following the death of one

of his schoolmates the previous day. A 14-year-old wounded in the arm and leg explained that he had gone to throw stones in revenge after a classmate had been shot and blinded in both eyes, and the doctor accompanying the High Commissioner confirmed he had treated this other boy. The High Commissioner heard numerous anecdotal accounts of shootings involving Palestinians who, it was said, could not have been involved in any form of protest activity, for example, an elderly man who was shot twice near the door of his house and a pregnant woman who was shot whilst on the roof of her house. See paragraphs 69 and 70 below for the IDF response on rules of engagement and child casualties.

32. The Minister of Health of the Palestinian Authority, Dr. Riadh Al-Zaanoun, told the High Commissioner that by his estimates some 6,958 persons (3,366 in the West Bank and 3,592 in the Gaza Strip) had been wounded during the period 29 September-9 November 2000 and that 1,016 Palestinians had been injured in Israel. Of those injured, he said, 40 per cent were under the age of 18. According to the Minister, the types of ammunition responsible for injuries were as follows: rubber bullets (41 per cent); live bullets (27 per cent); tear gas (27 per cent); and others, including rockets (11 per cent).

33. The Palestinian Red Crescent Society estimates that 236 Palestinians were killed and 9,353 injured during the period 29 September–23 November. During the period 27 September–23 November, Israeli official sources estimate that 30 Israelis were killed and 375 were injured. Estimates are disputed by the parties.

## Impact on children

34. According to the Red Cross/Red Crescent, as of 20 November, 86 children (aged 18 and under) had been killed and over 3,000 injured, two to three hundred of whom, it is estimated, will have permanent disabilities. According to the same source, hundreds of Palestinian children have been obliged to abandon their homes in order to escape the violence. The destruction of family dwellings has left more than a thousand children without homes, often in situations of food shortage and without access to medical care.

35. The current situation in the West Bank and Gaza Strip has had a serious impact on the Palestinian education system. The High Commissioner visited two schools in the Gaza Strip and one school in Ramallah where she was briefed by teachers on the consequences of the current situation for Palestinian pupils. She was told that since the beginning of October more than 40 schools have been closed or are unable to operate owing to curfews or closures. Other schools, such as one visited by the High Commissioner in the Gaza Strip, have been damaged by gunfire and the premises abandoned, requiring that several thousand children be fitted into other schools if possible.

36. In discussions with directors of preparatory schools and educators, as well as delegations of children in Gaza and Ramallah, the High Commissioner was told that many children suffer from psychological and social problems as a direct consequence of the current situation. Children themselves explained to the High Commissioner their fear of leaving their homes or, in some cases,

of going back to their homes, and of difficulties sleeping. According to UNICEF, only about 1 per cent of adolescents in Gaza have actually engaged in demonstrations or attacks against Israeli military positions. However, teachers have reported that the rest of the students who have remained at their studies have nevertheless been mentally distracted or emotionally affected by the events in the street, with the result that their educational performance has deteriorated.

## Medical personnel

37. An aspect of particular concern is the allegation that the medical condition of many of the victims has suffered, with some deaths, as a consequence of their being denied access to timely medical assistance. Reportedly, Palestinian ambulances and medical personnel have been prevented from discharging their normal responsibilities. During the High Commissioner's visit to Gaza, her vehicle was unable to proceed along the main north-south road because of an exchange of gunfire on the road ahead which had left two Israeli soldiers at a checkpoint seriously wounded and two Palestinians dead in their vehicle. The High Commissioner witnessed the fact that two ambulances were not permitted to attend to the Palestinian casualties.

38. Very serious allegations were made of attacks by Israeli security forces on medical personnel and ambulances. The High Commissioner was informed about the case of a Palestinian Red Crescent Society ambulance driver, Bassam Al-Balbisi, who had been killed while trying to approach 12-year-old Mohammad Al-Dura and his father in order to move them into an ambulance. According to Palestinian officials, 45 ambulances had been attacked by Israeli forces in Jerusalem and the West Bank and 23 in the Gaza Strip. The High Commissioner was told that nine ambulances had been put out of service owing to damage between 29 September and 9 November.

## Destruction of property

39. In the Gaza Strip, the High Commissioner visited Rafah refugee camp and surrounding areas where she was able to inspect a number of private houses and apartments that had been heavily damaged by gunfire and/or rocket attack, particularly at night. The owner of one house in Rafah told the High Commissioner that she had been obliged to leave her house, within a few minutes, when she realized that an Israeli tank had already started to destroy part of the house. A farm owner told the High Commissioner that Israeli soldiers had destroyed his greenhouses and his family residence during the night of 29 October. Water wells have reportedly also been destroyed in actions carried out by settlers or Israeli forces. The High Commissioner saw that a number of fields of fruit-bearing trees, particularly olive trees, had been cleared in the occupied regions. The High Commissioner was told that, in many cases, these orchards and fields represented the entire livelihood of dozens of families.

40. According to the IDF (see sect. V below), the clearances and demolitions were carried out as matter of military necessity because these structures or plantations had been used as cover by Palestinian gunmen. The IDF told the High Commissioner that the doctrine of military necessity meant that com-

pensation was not payable in these circumstances. Israeli officials told the High Commissioner that military action carried out in the Palestinian areas often took place at night, because this was the time when Palestinian gunfire most often occurred.

## Settlements

41. At the best of times relations between Israeli settlers and Palestinians are extremely sensitive and tense. At times of crisis the settlements can become a catalyst for violence. Amongst the main concerns raised by the Palestinian interlocutors were the privileged position settlements enjoy with respect to land and water for domestic and agricultural use, the negative impact on surrounding Palestinian communities, the fact that settlers are heavily armed and live in barrier-enclosed areas protected by the IDF and that separate roads have been created for settlers alone which are prohibited to Palestinians. The concerns raised with the High Commissioner by three Israeli families living in Gilo whom she met at Ben Gurion Airport on 15 November are set out at paragraph 71 below.

42. In Gaza, Israeli installations to protect settlements there are located on the main road through Gaza and have become the focus for stone throwing and shooting by Palestinians, with severe retaliation by the Israeli military. It was strongly represented to the High Commissioner that if these military installations and heavy armoury were to move off the highway and closer to the settlements being protected this could ease tension. The IDF analysis was that the protection role could only be discharged from the present positions (see paras. 69–70 below).

43. Following her visit to the refugee camp at Rafah the High Commissioner was driven along a settlement road and was surprised to be shown further expansions of settlements taking place.

44. The High Commissioner visited the city of Hebron, one of the biggest administrative units in the occupied Palestinian territories in terms of area and population, and went into the Israeli controlled part of Hebron known as H2 in the company of officials of the Temporary International Presence in Hebron (TIPH). Since the first week of October, the IDF has imposed a curfew on 30,000 Palestinians living in the H2 zone, which has had an enormous impact on the enjoyment by Palestinian residents of their basic human rights. As a result of the curfew, thousands of families and their children live under virtual house arrest, confined to their homes for all but a few hours per week. During the hours when the curfew is not imposed the use of motor vehicles by Palestinian residents is forbidden, requiring residents to walk considerable distances to purchase food supplies, as shops in the Hebron H2 zone are also affected by the curfew.

45. Workers from the Hebron H2 zone have been prevented from reaching their places of work, whether in Israel or in the occupied territories. Restrictions on freedom of movement make it increasingly difficult for the Palestinians in the H2 zone to meet their most basic needs, such as food supplies and medical care, and Palestinian children cannot attend school. In this regard, the High Commissioner was informed that 32 schools had been closed since

the beginning of the events, preventing some 15,000 pupils from exercising their right to education.

46. The curfew does not apply to the 300 to 400 Israeli settlers living in the H2 zone of the city and the settler school remains open. To ensure the safety of those settlers, the IDF maintains a large presence in that part of Hebron (700 soldiers according to the IDF; 2,000 according to another source). Three schools and several Palestinian houses in the H2 zone have been taken over by the IDF and turned into military posts.

47. At a meeting with the Mayor of Hebron, the Minister for Transport and other officials in the H1 zone of Hebron (under the Palestinian Authority), the High Commissioner was told that, since October, 20 Palestinians had been killed in Hebron, of whom 5 were under 18 years of age, and that many houses, stores and facilities had been damaged, without compensation. Allegations were made that settlers were involved in violence against and harassment of Palestinian residents, with the tacit consent of the IDF.

48. IDF representatives told the High Commissioner that their presence was necessary to secure the safety of the settler community, which had been subjected to regular fire from Palestinian gunmen.

## Freedom of movement

49. An effective closure of the occupied territories has been applied since the beginning of October and the movement of the population there continues to be heavily restricted. The High Commissioner's own travel between Israel and the occupied territories, and within the occupied territories, afforded an opportunity to assess the immediate impact of these restrictions. It was noted that, while road closures impact heavily on Palestinians, there exists a parallel road network, established by the Government of Israel, known as the bypass roads, exclusively for the use of Israeli settlers and the authorities, enabling them to travel freely.

50. In discussions with senior IDF representatives, the High Commissioner called for a lifting or easing of the closures. The response from the senior officer responsible for IDF operations in the occupied territories was that the closures were a necessary security measure. An explicit linkage was drawn between the closures and the release in October, by the Palestinian Authority, of some 80 prisoners who had been held in Palestinian custody and who are considered by the Israeli authorities to pose a major security threat to Israel. The High Commissioner was told that if the Palestinian Authority were to reincarcerate these 80 prisoners then the closures would be lifted the same day.

## Freedom of religion

51. The High Commissioner met Muslim and Christian leaders representing the Palestinian and Armenian communities in East Jerusalem. They told the High Commissioner that the Israeli authorities continued to deny Palestinians full access to holy sites, including the Al-Aqsa Mosque and the Church of the Holy Sepulchre.

52. Since the beginning of October, access to the Al-Aqsa Mosque has been denied to Muslims, even religious leaders, under the age of 45 years. As a re-

sult, only one tenth of the usual number of worshippers currently have access to Al-Aqsa. Representatives of both communities expressed the wish to have full responsibility for their own holy places, which is currently denied by the Israeli authorities. They complained also of disrespectful behaviour by Israeli troops stationed at the holy sites. In discussing the need for religious tolerance, they explained to the High Commissioner their shared vision of Jerusalem as encompassing "one city, two peoples and three religions" and stressed the universal character of the city and the necessity to maintain its spiritual soul.

53. The High Commissioner relayed these views to the Israeli authorities in her subsequent discussions with them. In particular, she expressed her concern that restrictions on access to the holy sites could result in increased tension during the coming month of Ramadhan. The Israeli authorities told the High Commissioner that the restrictions were necessary to prevent armed extremists from occupying the holy sites, which would necessitate an Israeli military response. They argued that the degree of control over holy sites currently given to Palestinians was greater than that which had been accorded to Jewish communities prior to the creation of the State of Israel. In some cases where Palestinians had been entrusted with the protection of holy sites, such as Joseph's Tomb, these sites had subsequently been desecrated.

## Economic impact

54. The United Nations development and humanitarian agencies operating in Jerusalem and Gaza provided comprehensive briefings to the High Commissioner on the impact that the current situation, particularly the closures, is having on the enjoyment by Palestinians of their economic rights and their right to development. They explained that the seriousness of the economic situation required that they put development programmes on hold and concentrate on emergency response and relief.

55. Approximately 128,000 Palestinian workers, normally employed in Israel, are currently barred from travelling to their workplaces. The movement of Palestinians within the occupied territories is severely restricted under the strict internal closure imposed, for instance, on the various parts of the West Bank.

56. According to the Israeli Ministry of Defence figures, the restrictions affect 20 per cent of the Palestinian workforce and some 35 per cent of total salary income. According to the Office of the United Nations Special Coordinator, unemployment had tripled since the beginning of October, which translates into a loss of household income of some 10 to 11 million dollars per day. While most reports indicated that there were adequate supplies of food within the occupied territories, the means with which to purchase food, medicines and other basic necessities are rapidly becoming exhausted as affected families use the last of their savings.

57. United Nations studies also report a 50 per cent reduction in normal economic activity within the territories themselves. Restrictions on the movement of Palestinians within the West Bank have had economic consequences. Another serious factor has been the restriction on the import of raw materials,

particularly cement. The ban on the movement of cement has effectively brought construction, normally the single largest industry in the occupied territories, to a standstill.

58. According to a Ministry of Defence briefing provided to the High Commissioner, loss of confidence among Israelis has also had a major effect on economic conditions in the occupied territories. In 1999, some 100,000 Israelis travelled to the territories for commercial reasons, generating income of $500 million. Cooperative projects in industrial zones along the "green line" between Israel and the territories had resulted in the completion of 25 factories but since the start of the Intifada, three of these factories have been burned and an industrial estate attacked, with the result that investor confidence has plummeted. The Ministry representatives also stated that the effects of the closures have been exacerbated in some cases by the reluctance of Palestinian Authority officials to cooperate with Israeli security processes at border checkpoints.

59. According to an International Monetary Fund (IMF) briefing provided to the High Commissioner, a factor which has aggravated the economic impact of the closures and other restrictions has been the failure of the Israeli authorities to make available to the Palestinian Authority in a timely manner certain tax revenues owed to it under existing agreements, which has affected the capacity of the Palestinian Authority to pay salaries to its employees.

60. Although the adverse economic consequences of the current situation are being felt most acutely in the occupied Palestinian territories, they have also had a negative impact on the Israeli economy.

## Humanitarian access

61. Access is a major preoccupation for all humanitarian organizations operating in the occupied territories. Of particular concern are the restrictions imposed on the movement of United Nations local Palestinian staff, who make up the vast majority of United Nations employees in the occupied territories.

62. The High Commissioner was informed that because of the closures, emergency evacuation of seriously injured civilians for treatment abroad is difficult. Restrictions on access also affect the import of donations of humanitarian goods and equipment from abroad. Imports into Gaza involve unloading of the cargo of every truck originating from Israel at the Gaza/West Bank entry checkpoints and reloading onto other trucks for onward delivery. United Nations agencies have reported difficulties in obtaining clearance for emergency health kits.

63. The Ministry of Defence indicated that it was doing everything possible to facilitate humanitarian access to the occupied territories. During October alone, the Ministry representatives said, requests from some 80 countries had been processed in relation to medical supplies, blankets and sophisticated hospital equipment. A special coordination centre had been set up in order to bypass the usual bureaucratic channels and close liaison had been established with the Palestinian Authority.

64. The High Commissioner, in her subsequent discussions with senior IDF representatives, raised the specific issue of UNRWA medical supplies that had

been blocked in Jerusalem. The IDF representatives indicated that this type of cargo should not be the subject of any restriction and they undertook to facilitate its delivery.

# V. Visit to Israel

65. The High Commissioner's visit to Israel allowed her to address general human rights issues and hear the views of a wide range of Israeli citizens and organizations, both Jewish and Arab. However, given the current situation, most discussions focused on the human rights situation in the occupied territories. The following paragraphs reflect the Israeli perspective on the situation.

## Excessive use of force

66. On 13 November, following her visits to Gaza, Hebron and Ramallah, the High Commissioner discussed, with the Israeli authorities, the use of force by the IDF and other security forces. The High Commissioner expresses her appreciation for the very frank and informative meeting with the senior IDF officers responsible for security, intelligence, legal issues, weapons development and public affairs, which the government facilitated.

67. The IDF officers outlined their view of the genesis of the present situation—a view which was shared by other Israeli government officials. In brief, the view was put that the current Intifada had been launched as a deliberate strategy of the Palestinian leadership. On offer at Camp David had been a Palestinian State, with reference made to both a right of return and a negotiated division of Jerusalem. According to the IDF, the Palestinian leadership, unwilling to make the difficult political compromises required, had ignited what it hoped would be a "CNN war" in which Palestinian losses would rally the support of the Muslim world and sway public opinion in the West. The aim was to increase international pressure on Israel to make further concessions. The ultimate goal was a Kosovo-style intervention force to protect "Palestinian territory," rather than "Palestinian people," thereby achieving a resolution without having to go to the negotiating table.

68. In terms of the pattern of the violence, the IDF officers described as typical a situation which commenced with stone throwing but which quickly escalated into armed attacks. Whereas the previous Intifada had almost exclusively featured stone throwers, who were dealt with using riot control techniques, the Palestinians were now armed and many incidents featured a lethal mix of stone throwers and shooters. It was stated that out of 5,085 attacks on Israeli settlements, some 1,400 had involved live fire, including machine gun fire or the use of firebombs.

69. The IDF officers said that, according to their rules of engagement, attackers who use live ammunition could be shot by soldiers and sharpshooters deployed for that purpose. Nevertheless, they said, the IDF was only using 2 per cent of its military force. The High Commissioner was told that most of those killed over recent weeks had been armed attackers, shot after opening fire on Israeli positions. Some, however, had been killed in the crossfire, by one side or the other. Asked about the number of child casualties, the IDF

officers responded that they were unable to indicate ages and numbers as the IDF generally had no access to the dead and wounded on the Palestinian side. However, they felt that the numbers reported were exaggerated and told the High Commissioner that the Tanzeem militia recruited and armed children.

70. Asked why the IDF reportedly often resorts to the use of live ammunition instead of non-lethal weapons, the IDF officers indicated that the military tactics being employed against them influenced the types of weapons the IDF could employ. They explained to the High Commissioner that Israel was concerned to reduce the number of casualties. So-called less-than-lethal weapons (which can still kill at short ranges or high concentrations) such as plastic coated bullets, tear gas and water cannons are only effective at a range of 50-100 metres. But at this range troops are vulnerable to live fire. The IDF have over the last few months field-tested dozens of weapons but have concluded that less-than-lethal weapons effective to a range of 200 metres do not currently exist. As a consequence, new weapons systems are being developed which, the IDF hope, will soon be deployed to control crowds effectively at longer ranges with little or no risk of serious injury.

71. Before leaving Israel on 15 November, the High Commissioner met at Ben Gurion Airport with three families from Gilo, a Jewish settlement on the outskirts of Jerusalem, who described nightly gunfire directed at their homes from a neighbouring Palestinian area. They also expressed concern that this resulted in heavy retaliation by the Israeli side, causing an intolerable situation for all civilians. They had had good relations with their Arab neighbours and were appalled at how the situation had deteriorated. Their families had lived in Gilo for upwards of 20 years and they did not see themselves as settlers. They urged the need to stop the violence and return to political dialogue.

### Investigations; compensation for damage

72. Matters which the High Commissioner pursued with IDF representatives were the issue of how the use of lethal force was investigated by the IDF, what punishments were available for improper or excessive use of such force, and how many investigations had been conducted to date and with what result.

73. She was told that, unlike the situation during the previous Intifada, when the Israeli army was in full control of the occupied Palestinian territories, there was currently no policy of routine investigation into the use of lethal force. Investigations could, however, be carried out internally if there was a particular reason to suspect that improper conduct had taken place. It was explained that that decision had arisen from the IDF evaluating that the current situation could be described as a state of "active warfare." In that situation the rules of war applied and soldiers were not required to account for each shot fired. In any case, the IDF representatives said, the number of shots being fired made such a policy impractical. Reference was also made to the practical difficulties of investigating incidents in areas under Palestinian Authority control. Another consequence of the IDF decision about the state of "active warfare" was that compensation would no longer be made for the mili-

tary use of private property, as it had been in the past. Asked about the destruction of houses and orchards in the occupied Palestinian territories, the IDF representatives advised the High Commissioner that there was no question of compensation as, under the rules of war, those areas had been cleared as a matter of military necessity because they had been used as cover by Palestinian gunmen.

74. The IDF representatives added that the new assessment of their current legal situation would normally also affect their own rules of engagement. In the present case, however, a decision had been taken to maintain the same rules of engagement as applied in previous Intifada, in order not to increase the number of casualties. The IDF representatives made the point that double standards were being applied in relation to the Palestinian side which was not under international scrutiny about its rules of engagement or its policy on investigating shootings and violations of human rights. The IDF representatives referred to the lynching of two Israeli soldiers in Ramallah.

## Situation of Arab Israelis

75. The situation of Arab Israeli citizens was raised at a meeting between representatives of Israeli NGOs and the High Commissioner as a specific human rights problem, albeit one which could not be entirely separated from the general situation in the occupied territories. Representatives of a number of Israeli NGOs indicated that Israeli Arabs, who represent 20 per cent of the State's population, had faced decades of neglect and discrimination on the part of the Israeli authorities.

76. Representatives of the Ministry of Foreign Affairs told the High Commissioner that the Government of Israel was taking measures to promote the integration of Israeli Arabs into Israeli society and to guarantee their rights as full citizens. Most Israeli interlocutors, including officials, acknowledged, however, that Israeli Arabs had suffered disadvantage and discrimination and that there was still some way to go in achieving full equality for that community. The President of the Supreme Court, Chief Justice Aharon Barak, briefed the High Commissioner on judicial action taken by the Supreme Court with respect to issues of equality, including decisions granting Arabs the right to purchase land in Israel. He also outlined the liberal approach adopted by his court concerning issues such as standing and jurisdiction in civil cases, which enabled NGOs to bring suits on behalf of aggrieved persons.

77. Most of the Arab Israelis whom the High Commissioner met described their situation as one of exclusion, prejudice, official hostility and routine humiliation. Since 28 September, however, the threat of violence which has engulfed many of their communities has become the primary concern of Arab Israelis. There was a sense of frustration that their problems were perhaps less well recognized than those of Palestinians living in the occupied territories.

78. Arab Israeli NGO representatives told the High Commissioner that, following the street demonstrations that took place in Arab cities and villages in Israel at the end of September and beginning of October, the security forces

had responded with brutality and excessive force, using live ammunition, tear gas and plastic coated bullets, in contrast to the more moderate tactics employed against Jewish protesters. This had led to the deaths of 13 Arab Israeli citizens. Many more had been injured and more than 1,000 arrested. A particular concern was the manner in which detention policy was being implemented. Many arrests, including of minors, were being carried out during night-time raids on homes. Once arrested, Arab detainees, including minors, were, according to these sources, far more likely to be held in custody without bail until the conclusion of their trials. It was asserted that this pattern was the result of a deliberate policy of discrimination against Arab Israelis on the part of the Attorney General's Office and the State Prosecutor's Office. It was further asserted that this policy extended to appealing every decision to release Palestinian detainees, which did not apply where Jewish detainees were concerned. Concern was expressed that the courts had largely acquiesced to these policies, with the result that large numbers of young Arab Israelis remained in detention. This issue was raised by the High Commissioner with the State Attorney General who indicated that she would look into the situation of young detainees.

## Israeli Commission of Inquiry

79. On 11 November, the Government of Israel decided to establish a State commission of inquiry to inquire into the clashes, since 29 September, between the security forces and Israeli citizens in which 13 Arabs were killed and hundreds of people injured. The Commission, composed of three members, will be chaired by a justice of the Supreme Court. The Judicial Commission of Inquiry Law gives this Commission full power to subpoena and obtain information from anyone it deems may be able to assist in its inquiry. Witnesses who testify before it enjoy full immunity. Its mandate is to investigate how the events developed, determine the facts and draw conclusions. The Commission of Inquiry will decide for itself whether to publish its findings. It will not address cases which occurred in the occupied Palestinian territories or cases involving non-Israeli citizens.

80. Some Arab Israeli NGOs have welcomed the establishment of the Commission of Inquiry, while regretting that time was lost by the Government in establishing initially a more limited "examining committee." Others have expressed scepticism as to whether it will adequately address the issues.

## National human rights commission

81. Recent events in Israel have underlined the need to strengthen national mechanisms for the protection and promotion of human rights, especially in the area of non-discrimination. In this context, the High Commissioner noted the positive steps being taken towards the establishment of an independent national human rights commission.

82. During the High Commissioner's meeting with the Minister of Justice and representatives of civil society such as human rights lawyers, academics and experts, the Minister reiterated his commitment to establish a human

rights commission. He mentioned that the Minerva Center for Human Rights at the Hebrew University of Jerusalem had undertaken to carry out research on national human rights institutions and to recommend a model for an Israeli institution. In the first stage of the project, the research team examined international guidelines and the legislative and administrative structure, function and modes of operation of human rights institutions in other countries. The NGO community had also been consulted when the proposal was being drawn up and their concerns, ideas and suggestions had been discussed with the research team.

83. Following these consultations the research team will prepare a draft report which will be distributed for comments among government officials, academic institutions and the NGO community. The final proposal, which will incorporate the responses on the draft report, will be presented to the Minister of Justice by March 2001. The High Commissioner was advised that the proposal will include recommendations on the relationship between the human rights commission and the Parliament and the Government, as well as existing executive bodies, such as the State Comptroller, the Ombudsman and the recently established Commission for Equal Rights for People with Disabilities. The final report will present the amendments needed to current legislation and recommend draft implementing legislation.

84. The High Commissioner offered the services of her Special Adviser on National Human Rights Institutions to assist the Government in its efforts towards the establishment of a national commission. On 17 November, the High Commissioner wrote to the Minister of Justice reiterating this offer. . . .

[Paragraphs 85 through 89 reviewed the High Commissioner's visits to Egypt and Jordan, where she discussed the violence in the Israeli-occupied territory with senior government officials and leaders of the Arab League.]

## VIII. Conclusions and Recommendations

90. The High Commissioner came away from her visit deeply concerned about the serious deterioration of the human rights situation in the occupied territories and Israel and at the terrible cost in terms of human lives. It is vital that both parties renew efforts to halt the current dangerous escalation.

91. Mindful of the urgent and widespread calls for international protection made to her during her visit to the occupied territories, the High Commissioner believes that every effort should be made to explore the feasibility of establishing an international monitoring presence.

92. The only path to lasting peace and stability is through peaceful negotiation, which calls for courage and responsibility on the part of the leadership of both sides. When she met with Chairman Arafat in Gaza on 15 November, the High Commissioner asked him if he would publicly call for an end to the shooting by Palestinians. Later the same day he called on Palestinians to stop firing on Israeli targets from zone "A" of the occupied territories. In discussions with senior IDF officers, the High Commissioner also urged a withdrawal of Israeli military forces from some of their forward positions and a lowering of the military profile in the occupied territories. She continues to believe that

some specific steps in that direction by the IDF could help to break the present cycle of violence.

93. The High Commissioner believes that a peaceful and stable future in the region can only be achieved on the basis of a framework conforming to the requirements of international human rights and humanitarian law. Full application of the international human rights standards set out in the Universal Declaration of Human Rights and the two Human Rights Covenants is essential.

94. The High Commissioner recalls that the General Assembly and the Commission on Human Rights have repeatedly reaffirmed the de jure applicability of the 1949 Fourth Geneva Convention relative to the Protection of Civilians in Time of War to the occupied Palestinian territories. Article 1 of the Convention places a duty on all the High Contracting Parties "to respect and to ensure respect" of the provisions of the Convention "in all circumstances." It would be appropriate for the High Contracting Parties to assume their responsibility under the Convention.

95. Another way in which the international community can assist is through the work of the task force established under the terms of the Sharm El Sheikh Agreement.

96. The High Commissioner would urge that the following specific steps be taken in order to stop the escalation of violence:

- The security forces of both sides should act in full conformity with the Code of Conduct for Law Enforcement Officials and the Basic Principles on the Use of Force and Firearms by Law Enforcement Officials. Whenever force is used the principle of proportionality has to be applied and all necessary measures have to be taken to avoid loss of life or injury to civilians or damage to civilian property.
- The construction of new settlements should cease and those located in heavily populated Palestinian areas should be removed. As well as protecting settlers, the Israeli security forces should also protect Palestinians from violence perpetrated by Israeli settlers.
- All cases of the use of lethal force on both sides should be investigated and subjected to the processes of justice in order to avoid impunity.
- Compensation should be provided to the victims of unlawful use of force, including for the loss of property.
- Curfews should be imposed only in extreme circumstances and as a last resort. In no case should curfews be used as a punitive measure. In cases where a curfew is imposed, it should be done in consultation with the local communities with a view to limiting the adverse impact on the human rights of those affected.
- The enjoyment of economic rights within the occupied Palestinian territories, including the right to development, should be protected.
- All holy sites and access to them by all faiths should be respected.
- The Israeli authorities should ensure freedom of movement of international and national staff of United Nations agencies and facilitate access by them to those in need of assistance.

Cooperation with the United Nations agencies is vital to ensure effective humanitarian assistance in the occupied Palestinian territories.

97. The High Commissioner will:

- Continue, through her office in the occupied Palestinian territories, to assist the Palestinian Authority to build up its institutional capacity in the area of the rule of law;
- Offer the services of her Special Adviser on National Human Rights Institutions to assist the Government of Israel in its efforts towards the establishment of a national human rights commission;
- Provide the necessary secretariat support for actions undertaken by the Commission on Human Rights, and its mechanisms, in the implementation of the resolution adopted at its fifth special session;
- Stand ready to facilitate dialogue between the human rights bodies of Israel and the Palestinian Authority, Palestinian and Israeli NGOs, and other representatives of civil society in order to enhance mutual understanding;
- Urge the international community to support the work of United Nations agencies in the occupied Palestinian territories and, in this context, contribute generously to the different resource mobilization initiatives currently under way including those of the World Food Programme, UNICEF, the World Health Organization and UNRWA.

# UN SECRETARY GENERAL ON THE POLITICAL SITUATION IN HAITI
## November 28 and December 27, 2000

*Jean-Bertrand Aristide, a charismatic former president of Haiti seen as a hero by many of the nation's impoverished people, engineered his return to political power in a series of elections that were widely criticized by international observers. But Aristide paid a heavy price for his apparent determination to gain power through flawed elections. International agencies withheld about $500 million in aid for Haiti, the poorest country in the Western Hemisphere. The United Nations, which for years had tried to help Haiti establish the functioning elements of a civil society, gave up in frustration. Conceding that it could not deal with rampant violence in Haiti, the UN announced on November 28 that it would pull its most visible mission out of the country on February 6, 2001—the day before Aristide was scheduled to return to office.*

*In the closing days of 2000, President Bill Clinton extracted a written promise from Aristide to correct the most flagrant of the electoral abuses, to initiate government reforms, and to include opposition leaders in a government coalition. But Clinton was himself about to leave office, and it was far from clear how much effort the incoming administration of George W. Bush was willing to devote to Haiti's seemingly endless problems. Moreover, the political situation in Haiti was so polarized that opposition leaders appeared more anxious to destabilize Aristide's government than to work with it.*

### Background to a Difficult Year

*A nation of nearly 8 million people, Haiti shared the island of Hispaniola with the Dominican Republic. Neither country was prosperous, but the Dominican Republic was an oasis of stability and economic progress in comparison with its neighbor. In 1999, according to the World Bank, the Dominican Republic had a per capita annual income of about $1,900; in Haiti, the average was about $1 a day. A UN report issued in August said that more than 70 percent of the Haitian workforce was unemployed* *and that more than 70 percent of the nation's income came from foreign aid and remittances sent by émigrés living in the United States and other countries.*

*Throughout much of the first half of the twentieth century, Haiti was under the direct or indirect control of the United States. Then, from 1957 until 1986, Francois Duvalier (known as "Papa Doc") and his son Jean-Claude (known as "Baby Doc") ran Haiti as personal fiefdoms. Aristide, a former priest who had gained fame with his fierce advocacy on behalf of the poor, won Haiti's first-ever free presidential election in 1990. Seven months later, the military ousted him in a coup, and he fled into exile. Aristide's supporters claimed at the time that the coup was sponsored, or at least supported, by the United States, but no solid evidence of U.S. involvement was ever made public.*

*In 1994 President Clinton sent 20,000 U.S. soldiers into Haiti to oust the military coup leaders and restore Aristide to power. Aristide proved to be an autocratic leader, and in 1995 he sought to circumvent a constitutional prohibition on seeking a second term. When that attempt failed, Aristide chose a protege, Renee Preval, as his successor. Like Aristide, Preval seemed to have little taste for working with the institutions of a democratic government. Election irregularities in 1997 led to the resignation of Preval's prime minister. The legislature refused to approve a new prime minister until new elections were held, and so Preval dissolved the legislature in January 1999 and governed by decree. It was widely assumed that Aristide remained the real power in Haitian politics, even though he was no longer in office.* (U.S. intervention, Historic Documents of 1994, p. 436)

*Clinton withdrew the last remaining U.S. troops in 1999, although the United States continued to support a UN program that helped establish and train a new national police force in Haiti. Clinton often cited his intervention in Haiti as a U.S. foreign policy "success." But Republican leaders in Congress opposed the intervention and drew attention to the many failings of the Aristide and Preval governments. By the late 1990s Haiti had become a major transit point for international narcotics traffickers based in Colombia and other South American countries, a development that gave Republican critics additional ammunition for their attacks on Clinton's policy.* (Colombia drug issue, p. 840)

*Escalating domestic criticism and the continued failures of the Preval government led the Clinton administration to join with France and other bilateral aid donors in halting about $500 million in pending international aid to Haiti until legislative elections were held. Under that pressure, Preval agreed to call elections for the two-chamber legislature in May.*

## Legislative Elections

*The events leading to the May 21 legislative elections was marred by the type of political violence that had been common in Haiti for decades. Two events in April were especially disturbing. First, on April 3, gunmen assassinated Haiti's best known and most respected journalist, Jean Dominique,*

*owner of Radio Haiti-Inter. A sharp-tongued advocate for the poor, Domi-
nique had been an ally of President Preval. The government arrested several
men in connection with the killing, but as of the end of the year little hard
information had emerged about the case. On April 8, the day of Dominique's
funeral, a mob of about one hundred people attacked and burned the headquarters of an opposition party, the Space for Dialogue. Party leader Evans
Paul went into hiding after some members of the mob threatened to kill him.*

*Despite these ominous signs, the May 21 voting was remarkably peace-
ful, with a strong majority of registered voters going to the polls. But irregularities soon surfaced: on the evening after the voting, armed men stole
ballots in some precincts; many ballots were counted at police stations without poll watchers present; and boxes of ballots were dumped in the streets
of the capital, Port-au-Prince. A delegation of election observers appointed
by the Organization of American States (OAS) said the voting had been
compromised by serious irregularities, and opposition parties charged extensive fraud. The government refused to investigate the fraud charges, but
police did arrest more than thirty opposition leaders, including at least two
legislative candidates.*

*The counting of votes proved to be the most controversial aspect of the
elections. Under Haiti's constitution, if no legislative candidate in a district
won a majority of 50 percent plus one, the top two candidates would face
each other in a runoff. But after the voting, the government's election commission changed the rules for determining the basis of a majority victory,
thus allowing ten senate candidates from Aristide's party to be declared
winners without having to compete in a second round. That action meant
that Aristide's party captured eighteen of the nineteen contested Senate
seats, giving it a majority of the twenty-seven seat chamber. The president
of the national electoral council, who opposed that decision, fled to the
United States in mid-June, saying he had been told he would be killed if
he did not cooperate.*

*The United States and the OAS pressured the government to reverse its
stance on the issue, but the government refused. In response, OAS election
monitors boycotted the second round of voting on July 9 and declared the
election to be "fundamentally flawed." The United States, France, and other
countries then stepped up the pressure on the government by saying that international aid would not be resumed until the disputed senate seats were
put to a second round of voting. One immediate consequence was a halt
of U.S. aid that had been planned for Haiti's presidential election in late
November.*

*In mid-October OAS deputy secretary general Luigi Einaudi held meet-
ings in Port-au-Prince with leading figures from the government, Aristide's
Lavalas Party, and opposition parties. Einaudi tried, but failed, to settle the
election controversy and win agreement on standards for the presidential
election. With the failure of those talks, the major opposition parties announced that they would boycott the presidential election.*

*During the period between elections, Congress stiffened U.S. policy against the Haitian government. Congress passed, and Clinton signed, legislation barring aid to the government until the State Department determined that Haiti's legislative elections were "free and fair" and the White House drug policy office certified that the Haitian government had no links to international narcotics dealers.*

## *Presidential Election*

*Facing no significant opposition, Aristide easily won the November 26 voting, receiving—according to the elections council—2.6 million votes, or nearly 92 percent of all ballots cast. The council put the turnout at 68 percent of eligible voters, but most diplomats and news organizations estimated the actual turnout at just 10 to 20 percent. The victory gave Aristide and his party control of the executive branch, all but one of the twenty-seven senate seats, and about 80 percent of the assembly.*

*In a news conference the day after the election—his first since 1994—Aristide struck a conciliatory note. He said he did not intend to become a dictator and appealed to opposition parties to join his government. "To have a peaceful Haiti, the opposition is indispensable," he said. "It is part of our democratic fate."*

*Despite Aristide's words, his electoral tactics proved to be the last straw for the UN. Secretary General Kofi Annan on November 28 made public a report to the General Assembly in which he recommended "with regret" the ending of the United Nations International Civilian Support Mission in Haiti when its mandate expired on February 6, 2001. "A combination of rampant crime, violent street protests, and incidents of violence targeted at the international community could severely limit the ability of [the mission] to fulfill its mandate," Annan said. The mission, which began functioning only in June, was a scaled-back version of a much larger UN program that for several years had attempted to build social services and governmental structures in Haiti. Annan said other UN agencies, including the United Nations Development Program, would continue their economic development and humanitarian aid programs in Haiti.*

*On December 1 Clinton wrote a letter to Aristide reminding him of the 1994 U.S. intervention that restored him to the presidency and emphasizing the importance of maintaining democracy in Haiti. At Clinton's request, Aristide met with Anthony Lake, Clinton's former national security adviser, later in December and reportedly agreed to a series of U.S. demands on elections and other issues. Aristide sent Clinton a letter with his pledges, and the White House on December 28 issued a statement revealing Aristide's commitments. According to that statement, Aristide promised to "rectify the problems associated with" the May 21 legislative elections, to create a "credible" elections council, to "enhance" cooperation with the United States antinarcotics programs (including allowing U.S. Coast Guard boats to patrol Haitian coastal waters), to professionalize the police force and judiciary, to protect human rights, and to appoint a "broad-based government."*

*In his letter, Aristide said: "I confirm my commitment to the points made therein, confident that they will help strengthen the ties between our two nations where democracy and peace will flourish." Clinton administration officials said the test of Aristide's commitment would be whether he followed through on his promises, especially the pledge to hold new elections for the ten disputed senate seats. At year's end the incoming Bush administration had given no indications of what its policy toward Haiti might be.*

*Following are the "Observations" from the report, "The Situation of Democracy and Human Rights in Haiti," submitted by United Nations Secretary General Kofi Annan on November 9, 2000, to the UN General Assembly (and made public on November 28), in which he described the political situation in Haiti and recommended the termination of the United Nations International Civilian Mission in Haiti (MICAH), which had provided logistical aid to the Haitian government. The second document is a letter, dated December 27, 2000, written by Haiti's president-elect, Jean-Bertrand Aristide, to President Bill Clinton, accompanied by a list of eight points referred to in his letter. The first document was obtained from the Internet at http://www.un.org/documents/ga/docs/55/a55618.pdf; the second document was not available on the Internet at the time of publication.*

# ANNAN'S REPORT TO THE GENERAL ASSEMBLY

[Paragraphs 1 through 33 reviewed the events in Haiti leading up to the November 27 presidential elections.]

## VIII. Observations

34. The political polarization of Haiti was highlighted by the Inter-American Commission of Human Rights, which visited Port-au-Prince from 21 to 25 August. In a statement issued at the end of the visit, the Commission stated that the most critical and worrying aspect of the current human rights situation in Haiti was the deterioration of the political climate to such a point that no consensus seemed to exist about the ways in which to consolidate the country's fledgling democracy. In his most recent report, the independent expert of the Commission on Human Rights on the situation of human rights in Haiti pointed out that Haiti suffered from an enormous lack of a culture of democracy, which must be reduced if democracy were truly to be strengthened and political stability ensured in that country, which seemed to have gone from one crisis to another since the restoration of democracy.

35. A disturbing element of this polarization is the widely held perception among opponents of Fanmi Lavalas [Lavalas Family, the ruling political

party]—shared by many former supporters—that the party might establish a dictatorial and repressive regime if, as is widely expected, Mr. [Jean-Bertrand] Aristide once again assumes the presidency. On the other hand, it is very evident that Mr. Aristide enjoys the loyalty of broad sectors of the urban and rural poor. The disinclination of the parties to work towards a compromise is a fundamental cause of the polarization.

36. The negative perception of Mr. Aristide's party seems to be a factor in the opposition's reluctance to enter into a dialogue. Many in the opposition seem to hope that, under the pressure of international isolation and internal unrest, Fanmi Lavalas will somehow disintegrate and that compromise is therefore unnecessary. The consequences of this attitude can be seen in Haiti's political stalemate, soon to enter its fourth year. Its costs can be witnessed in the increasingly desperate situation of the country's poor, unprotected from the impact of external factors, such as rising oil prices and some aspects of globalization.

37. In my previous report, I stressed the fact that Haitian authorities had flouted the views of OAS [Organization of American States], the International Organization of la Francophonie, CARICOM [Caribbean Community], bilateral partners, domestic electoral monitors and other civil society groupings, as well as the United Nations, in particular the concern of members of the Security Council. In refusing to recalculate the erroneous Senate results, some Haitian leaders have violated basic norms of democratic governance and fair play. In recent weeks, as opportunity after opportunity to reach common ground has been missed, there have been suggestions by critics that these leaders are further isolating Haiti, and ensuring it pariah status. This isolation is apt to grow, as a Parliament has been seated whose legitimacy is in doubt, rendering unlikely the early resumption of international assistance.

38. A further indication of the deteriorating political situation is the charge that high-ranking officers within HNP [National Police of Haiti] were plotting a coup d'état, although evidence has not been presented. Already demoralized by poor working conditions and a climate of impunity, HNP is increasingly the target of those who would use the force for their own political ends. It bears recalling that public security is central to the lives of all citizens and that an independent police force, which respects the rights of citizens, is indispensable to any democratic society.

39. It was with considerable reluctance that the United Nations withdrew the team of experts which was providing technical assistance to CEP [Permanent Electoral Council], the government's elections commission] after supporting for several years Haiti's efforts to ensure conditions adequate to the free exercise of the franchise. This most recent technical assistance project began nearly one year ago, and was expected to last through the presidential elections scheduled for the end of 2000. It aimed also to train a new Permanent Electoral Council, which will be charged with organizing elections over the next decade. After intensive examination of Haiti's current electoral council and its practice, it was decided that requisite standards had not been met, necessitating the withdrawal of United Nations support.

40. While denying the Government direct international assistance, so as to send a political message, Haiti's bilateral donors hope to avoid hurting the Haitian population by channelling aid through non-governmental organizations. However, directly or indirectly, the Haitian economy and population will inevitably suffer. The swings of international assistance from government to non-governmental organizations and back, according to the legitimacy of the government of the day, have disrupted long-term development in the past. Assistance provided through non-governmental organizations may partially alleviate hardship but the Government is a necessary partner for poverty reduction and health programmes. Likewise, the kinds of programmes needed to revive development—such as infrastructural projects and schemes to reinforce the police and overhaul the judicial system—require strong, governmental measures. Furthermore, the failure of the Haitian authorities to address the concerns of the political parties and the international community has so far prevented Haiti from regaining access to the international financial assistance that has been suspended for the past three years. These factors, and the overall political crisis, have been largely responsible for the fall in the gourde, which has hit the poor hard by triggering a rapid rise in the price of foodstuffs and other basic commodities.

41. In the absence of any solution to the crisis, popular discontent seems likely to mount in response to the rising prices and increasing poverty, and may lead to further turmoil. A combination of rampant crime, violent street protests and incidents of violence targeted at the international community could severely limit the ability of MICAH to fulfil its mandate. Its capacity to function effectively has already been adversely affected by the withdrawal or reduction of once-important bilateral programmes of assistance in the areas of justice and public security. At bottom, MICAH support is contingent upon legitimate counterparts who enjoy the esteem of the Haitian people and that of the international community.

42. In this climate of political turmoil and instability, and with national counterparts often lacking or distracted by political concerns, it will be necessary to devise new forms of technical assistance that might better allow the United Nations system to continue supporting the Haitian people. It is my view, therefore, in the light of the conditions in Haiti, that a renewal of the mandate of MICAH is not advisable, and it is with regret that I recommend that the Mission be terminated when its mandate draws to an end on 6 February 2001. In preparation, discussions have already commenced among UNDP [United Nations Development Program], MICAH and the Friends of the Secretary-General for Haiti, in consultation with other members of the United Nations system, with the aim of designing a programme of assistance to the Haitian people that is commensurate with the country's political realities and absorption capacity.

43. Overall, it is imperative that the country's political leaders and civil society engage in a constructive dialogue so as to address the needs of one of the most impoverished populations in the world and create an enabling environment for international financial and developmental assistance. I hardly need emphasize that a well-functioning, multi-party system is essential to demo-

cratic governance. Political turmoil has produced plummeting economic indicators, which in turn has led to a deteriorating security situation. Firm action to stop this downward spiral is long overdue. It should be emphasized that, in the absence of such steps, the misery of Haiti's long-suffering poor majority will only be exacerbated.

44. The Friends of the Secretary-General for Haiti deserve gratitude for their advice and cooperation, which have been a key element throughout United Nations activities in Haiti. I shall count on their counsel in the future. I am grateful to the Member States which have contributed to the Trust Fund for MICAH—Canada, Norway and the United States of America. I would like to commend the efforts of my representative, Alfredo Lopes Cabral and all MICAH personnel, for their work in difficult and challenging circumstances.

# ARISTIDE'S LETTER TO CLINTON

Dear President Clinton:

Season's greetings to you and to your family.

What a pleasure it was to see our good friend Tony Lake and Ambassador [Donald] Steinberg last week. We spent a very productive two days working and preparing the attached document. I confirm my commitment to the points made therein, confident that they will help strengthen the ties between our two nations where democracy and peace will flourish."

As the new year rapidly approaches, we wish you all the best in your new endeavors.

Sincerely,
Jean-Bertrand Aristide

President-elect Aristide agreed to:

1. Rapid rectification of the problems associated with the May 21 elections through run-offs for disputed Senate seats or by other credible means. . . .
2. Creation of a credible new provisional electoral council (CEP) in consultation with opposition figures to rectify the problems associated with the disputed Senate seats.
3. Enhance substantially cooperation to combat drug trafficking, including implementation of money-laundering legislation and expansion of maritime cooperation, building on the October 1997 agreement [an anti-narcotics agreement between the United States and Haiti], in order to allow access for U.S. Coast Guard and anti-drug operations in Haitian waters. Strengthen efforts, in collaboration with the U.S. and Dominican Republic [DR] governments, to interdict trafficking across Haitian/DR border.
4. Nominate capable and respected officials for senior security positions, including within the HNP [Haitian National Police]. Ensure that there is no interference in the professional work and conduct of the HNP by

members of Parliament and others. Take steps to enhance the professionalism and independence of judicial system.

5. Strengthen democratic institutions and protection of human rights trough the establishment of a semi-permanent OAS [Organization of American States] commission to facilitate dialogue among Haitian political, civic, and business leaders and through international monitoring of the protection of human rights.

6. Seek to install a broad-based government including "technocrats" and members of the opposition.

7. Initiate new dialogue with international financial institutions concerning sound budgetary proposals and economic reforms to enhance free markets and promote private investment. Such measures will be aimed at reducing poverty and stimulating growth.

8. Negotiate agreement for repatriation of illegal migrants [Haitians who had emigrated illegally to the United States].

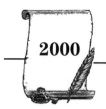

# December

# VICENTE FOX ON HIS INAUGURATION
# AS PRESIDENT OF MEXICO
## December 1, 2000

*The seventy-one year domination of Mexican political life by one political party came to a surprising end in 2000 with the election as president of an opposition candidate, Vicente Fox. A former businessman and governor of the state of Guanajuato, Fox won 43 percent of the vote July 2, 2000, in a three-man race, decisively defeating the candidate of the Institutional Revolutionary Party (known as the PRI), which had controlled the federal government with an iron hand since 1929. Fox took office on December 1 and immediately plunged into a formidable agenda that included ending a long-running insurgency in the southern state of Chiapas, curtailing the corruption that had become embedded in Mexican politics, and providing economic benefits for the roughly 40 million Mexicans (out of a total population of 100 million) living in poverty.*

*Perhaps the new president's greatest challenge would be taking charge of a government that—as long as anyone could remember—had seemed to be the permanent property of one political party. Moreover, Fox's center-right National Action Party (known as the PAN) failed to win control of either chamber of congress, making it likely that Fox would be forced into extensive bargaining to get his legislative proposals enacted. In the months between the election and his inauguration, Fox worked closely with the outgoing president, Ernesto Zedillo.*

## Background to the Election

*After the collapse of the Soviet Union at the end of 1991, and the resulting loss of power by the Soviet Communist Party, the PRI became the longest-serving ruling party in the world. Every seven years its appointed candidates had won the presidency, and in every legislative election its members had won a majority of seats in the senate and chamber of deputies. For all practical purposes, the PRI and the Mexican national government were one and the same. Each PRI president selected his successor through a process known as* el dedazo, *or "the tapping."*

*Founded by generals who had led Mexico's 1917 revolution, the PRI in its early years had been the force that created a strong central government, built the physical infrastructure of modern Mexico, and delivered social services to the poor. But over time the party lost its revolutionary cast and became a conservative institution based on the government bureaucracy and the reliable votes of rural farmers and peasants. In1968 police killed several hundred protesting students in the Tlatelolco neighborhood of Mexico City—an act that opened the party to criticism as a dictatorship. Responding to a deep recession in the 1980s, business leaders poured money and energy into the NAP, which for decades had been a fringe party associated with the Catholic Church. PAN chipped away at the PRI's iron grip on state and local governments and won its first state governorship in 1989. The leftist Party of the Democratic Revolution, headed by Cuauhtemoc Cardenas, gained control of the capital, Mexico City. Until Zedillo took office, the PRI's response to these political challenges was to use fraud and intimidation to win elections.*

*The 2000 election was widely considered the cleanest and fairest in Mexican history. That was because in 1996 Zedillo had won congressional approval of electoral reforms, including public financing of campaigns and the creation of an elections agency independent of the government and the PRI. A Yale-educated economist from outside the PRI mainstream, Zedillo had campaigned for the presidency on a promise of political reform, and he kept his word. Fox's party had protested many of the reforms at the time, but ultimately it and other minority parties were the ones to benefit. Unlike all his predecessors, Zedillo did not choose his successor by* el dedazo. *Instead, he set in motion a party primary, although he did make clear that Fransico Labastida was his favored candidate, and Labastida got the nomination.*

*On the evening of Fox's victory, it was Zedillo—not the losing PRI candidate—who appeared on national television to concede the election. Zedillo came close to portraying his party's stunning defeat as a good thing for the country. "Today we have shown for all to see that ours is a nation of free men and women who believe in the means of democracy and law to achieve progress," he said.*

## From Coca-Cola to Politics

*Fox, who turned fifty-eight on election day, grew up on a large ranch in Guanajuato but spent one year attending a Jesuit academy in Prairie du Chien, Wisconsin. As a young man Fox went to work for Coca-Cola, eventually rising to become head of the company's Mexican operations in 1975. He quit Coca-Cola in 1979—declining, he said, a promotion that would have forced him to move to Florida—and returned to the family ranch. Fox won a seat in congress in 1988, representing the NAP. As a legislator, Fox earned a reputation as a maverick, voting some of the time on the side of the business-oriented party he represented but at other times in support of positions taken by the PRI or leftist parties. After an unsuccessful run for governor of Guanajuato in 1991, Fox tried again in 1995 and won. In 1998, taking advantage of Zedillo's electoral reforms, Fox resigned as governor and began campaigning for the presidency.*

*An energetic man comfortable in both business suits and casual clothing,*

*Fox campaigned as a populist outsider. He aimed his multiple messages at a broad audience, from the country's business elite, to the urban middle class, to the rural farmers who long had been the PRI's base. Exit polls on election day showed that Fox's appeal was greatest among young, well-educated voters whose chief concerns were corruption and the country's lack of democracy. Fox hired U.S. consultants to help with his campaign, including Dick Morris, who had helped craft Bill Clinton's presidential victories in 1992 and 1996.*

*As the election campaign neared its end, most polls appeared to indicate that the race between Fox and Labastida was tight, with leftist third-party candidate Cardenas drawing off support from both of them. Fox spent several days campaigning in the United States, hoping to win the support of Mexican immigrants still eligible to vote in their home country. But when the votes were counted, Fox scored a surprisingly solid victory, earning 43 percent of the vote, to 36 percent for Labastida and 17 percent for Cardenas.*

*Despite his breathtaking win, Fox's coattails were not strong enough to carry a sufficient number of his party members to seats in the national congress, which took office September 1. The NAP won 208 seats in the 500-member chamber of deputies, roughly the same number as the PRI. Likewise, the PAN won 46 seats in the 128-member senate, compared to 60 held by the PRI. As a consequence, it was clear that, to win approval of his programs, Fox and his party's legislative leaders would need to build coalitions with members of other parties—perhaps on an issue-by-issue basis.*

## *Getting Ready to Govern*

*Unlike every one of Mexico's previous presidents in recent decades, Fox could not count on a built-in bureaucracy to staff the top levels of government departments and carry out his policies. Instead, he announced shortly after his election that he would use head-hunting firms to help select cabinet ministers and other top officials. He quickly appointed a team of government outsiders, including business leaders, opposition politicians, and representatives of various advocacy groups. From the U.S. point of view, one of his most intriguing appointments was that of Jorge Castaneda, a leftist intellectual who had spent many years teaching and writing in the United States, as foreign minister.*

*In mid-September, Fox received a taste of the difficulties he would face taking charge of the government. A newspaper published transcripts of telephone conversations between Fox and a top aide, indicating that at least one of his telephones had been tapped during the election campaign. Government security services denied any involvement, but the incident served as a reminder of Mexico's past as a one-party state.*

*As Fox took office, Mexico's economy was in relatively good shape, having experienced growth averaging about 5 percent for five consecutive years. That stood in sharp contrast to the early months of Zedillo's tenure in late 1994 and early 1995, when the Mexican monetary unit, the peso, collapsed and the economy was spared a deep depression only through the intervention of the United States and the International Monetary Fund. Zedillo's*

*government in September paid off the last $3 billion installment of the emer-
gency loans from that period.*

*In the weeks between his election and inauguration, Fox issued a flurry
of proposals and traveled to more than a dozen countries to promote his vision of a reformed Mexico. Many of his ideas called for sweeping changes
in Mexican life, such as creating a million new jobs each year, eliminating
government corruption, and overhauling the police and judicial systems.
Many observers, including some of his advisers, warned that he ran the
danger of creating public expectations that he could not possibly fulfill. Even
so, many Mexicans seemed hopeful that Fox would at least try to make the
changes he advocated. "I don't think that everything he's promised is going
to happen in six years," Pedro Olivares, a shoeshiner in Mexico City told the
Associated Press. "But if he can do at least some of it, and then we get another president with the same mentality to follow him, that would be great."*

*In his inaugural address on December 1, Fox repeated many of the
themes that had won him support during the campaign, most notably cleaning up a government widely believed to be riddled with corruption. "The
fight against corruption begins today," he told his audience, which included
sixteen heads of state. Responding to complaints that his party represented
big business, Fox pledged to tackle poverty. "I cannot be satisfied as long as
there are children who have no schools, young people who have no future,
and elderly people who have no support," he said. "No one can be satisfied as
long as there are millions of families living in extreme poverty." To symbolize his stated commitment, Fox began his inaugural day by having
breakfast with several dozen street children in an impoverished neighborhood of Mexico City.*

*Fox also moved quickly to tackle one of the government's longest-running
problems: a seven-year rebellion by an Indian-based group, known as the
Zapatista National Liberation Army, in the southern state of Chiapas. Fox
promised a political, rather than military, solution to the conflict, and by
year's end it appeared possible that the government and rebels might soon
be engaging in serious negotiations for the first time in years.*

*The government won unexpectedly strong support for the first part of its
budget package. On December 26, the Chamber of Deputies overwhelmingly
approved a revenue bill, sending a signal that Fox might be succeeding in
building the coalitions he needed to govern.*

*Following are excerpts from the speech delivered December 1,
2000, by Vicente Fox upon his inauguration as president of Mexico. The document was obtained from the Internet at http://world
.presidencia.gob.mx/?Orden=Leer&Tipo=Pe&Art=3.*

Honorable Congress of the Union:

I have assumed the great responsibility of serving as President of Mexico,
swearing to uphold the Constitution and the Laws that have arisen from it. I

have done so in good conscience and mindful of the moral values and principles to which I am committed.

I bring to this solemn ceremony not only my personal convictions, but also the dreams and aspirations for change of all the Mexican people.

I cannot fail to mention that I am taking office as head of the Executive Branch under new circumstances. The sovereign decision of those who voted on July 2nd was unprecedented.

No individual can claim all the credit for this achievement, but we cannot fail to recognize the contribution each has made.

On that day, millions of Mexican men and women from every part of the country came to cast their vote. All of us participated in this civic celebration.

For perhaps the first time in our history, no one arrived too late, nor were any left behind. Nothing hindered the free expression of our democratic will; no one died that day to make this possible. At the end of the day, the victory belonged to all of us.

Electoral institutions, political parties and their candidates also came to that celebration.

Then-President Ernesto Zedillo recognized the mandate expressed by citizens at the polls, and in the spirit of our republic, he facilitated the transition from his administration to the administration I head beginning today.

I am therefore proud to recognize the efforts of all of Mexico's men and women; together on July 2nd we renewed our political pact in a climate of civility and concord.

The presence of Heads of State and Government and the High-Level Diplomatic Delegations who are here with us today is a sign of confidence that enhances our prospects for change.

I would also like to express my gratitude for the presence of outstanding representatives of the world's political, economic and cultural life. Please accept our thanks and take back to your countries this expression of the Mexican people's appreciation and solidarity.

In the recent elections, the men and women of Mexico demonstrated our will and determination to use democratic principles as the basis for establishing a new foundation for the nation in the 21st century.

This democratic change—which entered its decisive phase on July 2nd—is the result of a long-held aspiration of society. It took shape during several decades through the sacrifice and efforts of many exceptional Mexican men and women who fought on various fronts to make what we now have possible.

I mention with reverence to Francisco I. Madero. His sacrifice in pursuit of democracy was not in vain. Today, at the close of one stage of our history marked by authoritarianism, his presence is again felt as a signpost that marks the path from which we must never stray.

I pay homage to the men and women who founded our political parties and organizations, to those who—aside from their personal victories—believed and taught others to believe in the triumph of a democratic Mexico; to those who spoke out on every street corner until they won this victory for democracy. . . .

In this new era of democratic practice, the President proposes and the

Congress disposes. That is the new reality for the Executive Branch in Mexico.

For many years our traditional "presidentialism" imposed its monologue. Today more than ever before, governing means dialogue; the nation's strength can no longer come from a single point of view, a single party or a single philosophy.

Today more than ever before, understanding, agreement and convergence among the various political, economic and social participants, among the various legitimate interests and diverse ideological visions, are necessary.

I call on all political parties to build, without prejudice, a dignified and transparent relationship without any subservience; I call them to a frank and spontaneous exchange of arguments and purposes with the new administration, so that together we can make progress in creating a legal framework for the process of change.

For my part, I will encourage a relationship based on ongoing negotiation with the parliamentary groups that participate here, so that in the process of working out areas of agreement and disagreement, we arrive at reforms that enhance the legitimacy of our public institutions and the decisions they make.

In this Inaugural Session, I affirm my administration's commitment to render accounts to this national body of representatives in as broad a scope and as frequently as is necessary.

I am directing Cabinet members to respond readily and promptly, week after week, to the needs of the Mexican Congress and its commissions.

Citizens demand better administration of justice. The Executive Branch I head will be a strong ally of those who favor consolidating the autonomy of the Federal Judicial Branch and the independence of those who serve in it.

On this solemn occasion, I pledge to do everything in my power to strengthen the ability of the federal jurisdictional entities so that they may determine the constitutionality of Mexico's laws and the legality of the acts of the Public Administration.

I am honored to assume by constitutional mandate the post of Commander in Chief of the Armed Forces. With honor and dignity, Mexico's soldiers have been true to the nation from the moment they have taken on their duties.

Their loyalty to Mexico, their strict fulfillment of their constitutional duties, their exemplary action in fighting drug trafficking and in civil defense, and their respect for our country's political processes have provided a fundamental guarantee for democracy.

The great challenge involved in the Reform of the State lies in inaugurating a new political future after 71 years. We must therefore be bold in order to break free of old paradigms, inertia, and the recurrence of a political culture that viewed agreement as an act of capitulation and similar political viewpoints as full proof that someone had been co-opted.

Only by clearing the way for an era of far-reaching democratization of our national life can the reform of the State meet society's expectations for change.

This requires a program proposal based on consensus, long-term in scope, whose feasibility is not dependent on a circumstantial agreement.

The cause of many of our problems lies in the excessive concentration of power. The reform of the State must assure that the exercise of power in an ever more balanced and democratic manner is reinforced.

It must also assure Mexico's political modernization by means of ensuring the fully effective Rule of Law, equity in the distribution of wealth, rationality in the government's administrative structure, full institutionalization of the exercise of public power, broad social participation in its decision-making, and preparation for confronting the challenges of globalization.

Alternating parties in power will not in and of itself complete the transition process. I invite all of you who have duties related to directing the reform of the State to work together with us so that we can propose to the nation the initiatives needed to effect substantive change in our political system. Let us proceed sensibly, with the courage to destroy all vestiges of authoritarianism and to build a genuine democracy.

The Constitution that guides us has been distorted by excessive amendments. We need to reconstitute our long-term national consensus around a supreme law of the land consistent with our best traditions and the requirements of the 21st century.

Political stability and democratic change affect each other. It is practically impossible to isolate ourselves without losing effectiveness, and it is an illusion to believe that one can occur without the other.

Together we must find the formula for engaging in all the changes that the nation demands, without losing our effectiveness in conducting the government.

In order to guarantee both an effective democracy and democratic effectiveness, I am making the commitment to promote seven key reforms that I gathered during my presidential campaign and that represent the Mexican people's mandate for change.

One reform will consolidate the democratic progress we have made so that all people may speak freely and be heard. One reform will create progress in the fight against poverty and for social equality, so that no mother lacks enough money to buy milk for her children.

An educational reform that will assure the development of better human capital and that no young person in our country—no matter how poor he or she may be—fails to complete his or her education due to a lack of resources.

A reform that will guarantee economic growth with stability, so that our young people will never again have to leave their homes and immigrate to another country.

A reform that decentralizes Federal powers and resources, in order to give the states, municipalities and communities greater vitality.

A reform that assures transparency and accountability in the work of governing, in order to eliminate corruption and deception.

A reform that combats our lack of safety and does away with impunity, so that every family may sleep peacefully.

We cannot set policy if we worship our differences. Political and ideological differences are an integral part of all democratic societies; rather than dividing us, they enrich us.

We must make this positive view a basic premise of our new life together in Mexico, in order to move from a polarizing pluralism to a fully civilized relationship among the different political participants.

We have an entire history to build ahead of us, which we must begin constructing on the basis of a purposeful dialogue and within the framework of a mature relationship among political participants; we must conduct this struggle ethically and respectfully and not as part of a battle for power.

Let us realistically accept that the country's full democratization is a national cause that is unlikely to emerge from isolated partisan initiatives.

We are all limited by the relative strength of the parties, which means that no single form of political expression will be able to promote any change independently of others.

Intransigence, visions no one shares and absolute truths have no place in a pluralistic society. Tolerance is essential to consolidating the pluralism of our society and for advancing to a transition in which methods, goals, phases and time periods are agreed on.

Changing the party is in power is not the only issue at stake in the next six years. Something much more significant and profound is also at risk: the hope of millions of Mexican men and women.

This is where the process of democratic convergence shows its true historic value and its ethical, moral and political sustenance. That is the real challenge at this stage of transition: responding to the hopes of all men and women through the interaction of the nation's various social and political forces.

Like many of you in this chamber—and those of you throughout our country as well—I grew up on a ranch, on an *ejido*. All of us in rural areas know that the best crops come from hybrids of several seeds, because even nature gains its greatest strength in diversity.

That is how those of us who are farmers provide better feed for our cattle and how workers forge stronger metals.

All the men and women in this Congress, all those who hear and see us throughout the nation, we must all understand that diversity is the foundation of our future, of our ideas, our energy, and our labor, which are the bricks, the pick and the shovel, the tempered steel for constructing the new Mexico.

Strict respect for the freedom of expression is an indispensable guarantee of democratic development; its preservation is the responsibility, first, of any democratic State.

I firmly believe that the communications media arise from this freedom and that they can only fulfill their ethical responsibility to inform society if this freedom exists.

My administration will show absolute respect for that fundamental freedom to inform and dissent. We will listen and respond to citizens' scrutiny expressed in public opinion.

I have adopted a new ethic that overcomes the historic evil of a official culture that favored the control and manipulation of information about political matters to the detriment of that information's timeliness and veracity. . . .

Opening up politics and the exercise of power to participation and control from the grassroots, its base, will be a central objective of my administration.

I accept the people's mandate to consolidate democracy through methods that involve direct democracy, such as plebiscite, referendum and popular initiative.

In a politically modern system, those instruments, duly regulated, enable citizens to express their feelings in a precise way and provide orientation that is beneficial.

The society we want requires ending all forms of discrimination. We will carry out our commitment to eliminate all forms of discrimination against and exclusion of minority groups.

The goal is for the differences between one human being and another to be only those that indicate his or her commitment to freedom, justice and brotherhood.

We Mexicans aspire and deserve to live with the certainty of a society of laws in which the government's example makes the legal order a reality of civic life.

Arbitrary action and deficiencies in applying the law are the cause of many of our social ills. In Mexico, the use of violence has been the prerogative of the Government, rather than of the State. More than a few coercive actions of the State have been motivated by the political benefit of an official or group in power.

Personal enmity or political differences with those who unlawfully hold power have been frequent causes of common citizens becoming the victims of the State's use of force.

Use of spy or monitoring equipment or intimidation methods against parties, labor unions, social organizations, political figures or opinion leaders is not a valid means of governing and preserving the State's political security.

If a Government needs to investigate what people are thinking, it is because it is not listening.

My administration will not tolerate the continued unpenalized use of these practices. Repression will never again be the means of resolving political differences. My administration will not divert security agencies to dissuade our critics or to neutralize our opponents unless the State lacks information essential to national security.

The perils that befall the collective security of our citizens, risks to national security, and natural or human disasters that we must anticipate and prevent never arise from the exercise of freedom.

Mexico will no longer be held up as a bad example in matters of human rights. We will protect human rights as never before, respecting them as never before and seeking a culture that repudiates any violation and punishes the guilty.

Corruption has left the Government's credibility with society at a very low ebb. Arrogance and arbitrary behavior make up the remainder of its image. These excesses mean that the public agenda still includes society's demand that moral authority be reinstated in the exercise of government.

The solution is not merely more laws or tougher laws. Above all, we need laws to be enforced within a framework of complete certainty. That is the best alternative.

I will combat these ills with all the rigor and authority of the law, with all the power of the President of the Republic, but also with the simple and powerful force of example.

My administration's decisions will be consistent with our history, but I will not allow the past to determine the destiny and prospects of Mexico's future. History is made by looking always forward, but no relation to the past is healthy if it is not based on the truth.

Without replacing the processes of administration of justice and law enforcement, I propose to open what has remained closed in sensitive episodes of our recent history and to investigate what has not been resolved though steps that address the majority of Mexicans' demand for the truth.

Society's justified indignation cannot be stifled. Highly placed corrupt officials of the past, present and future will be held accountable; for them there will be no wiping the slate clean and starting over.

There will be no pious amnesia regarding those who have broken the law, nor will we tolerate those who seek to continue exercising privileges that are unacceptable today.

However, no action related to the past will be motivated by any resentment, vengeance, desire for personal vindication or the wish to reinterpret history.

We will give no quarter to crime. We will not rest until we live in safety, without fear or anxiety, until we enjoy life without assaults and ill treatment.

We will tackle the seemingly insoluble problem of a lack of public safety with the strength of the law and our institutions, but also with measure that do away with extreme inequality and marginalization.

Police action that is disconnected from its social context runs the risk of being seen as repression, and no purpose is served by resorting to authoritarianism when criminal behavior is not solely the result of the weakness of police forces. No police force is capable of containing hunger and unemployment.

Objectively recognizing reality without distortions or complacency is a basic prerequisite for improving it. Although the main macroeconomic variables are stable, we have not yet fulfilled the long-held desire to moderate extreme wealth and extreme poverty.

No doubt, I am taking office as the economy is operating well, but with a budget that has little room to maneuver to respond to our enormous social deficiencies.

Throughout my election campaign, I saw great human and natural potential going to waste throughout the country: children without schools, young people without a future or prospects for advancement; family disintegration, marginalization and discrimination; highly trained professionals and technicians with no alternative to unemployment or underemployment; single mothers with no education who are the sole breadwinners for their households; elderly people without support or resources with which to live out the last stage of their lives in peace.

The government's accumulated responsibility is enormous in social matters. The least bit of common sense tells us how false the thesis is that claims we must curb people's living standards for the sake of economy's health.

I emphatically maintain that social justice is part of an efficient economy, not its adversary. It is time we recognized that everything cannot be solved by the State, nor can everything be solved by the market.

In other words, it is neither all for the State, nor for the individual alone.

I believe that the vote for democracy is inseparable from the vote for social equity.

We can close our eyes to extreme poverty and marginalization; we can live with more crime, less water, fewer forests and a more contaminated environment.

We can pretend not to see corruption, poverty and unemployment. If we do so, we are betraying those who have fought for change.

Mexico no longer wants nor is able to survive amid islands of wealth and prosperity surrounded by oceans of extreme poverty.

For a long time now, millions of Mexican men and women have been bearing the heavy burden of marginalization and poverty. Those who suffer in this way have just demands to make to society, to the State and to my administration.

I am convinced that the economy must recover its moral and humanistic dimensions, which give it meaning and direction. I am also convinced that a society's quality of life is measured not only by its ability to generate wealth, but above all by its equity in the distribution of wealth.

I will work with everyone and for everyone, but I will seek always to address first the needs of those who have been waiting for justice for time immemorial, and the needs of those who daily suffer from extreme poverty, neglect, ignorance and violence.

Education . . . we're getting there, calm down now. . . .

Quality education, employment and regional development are the levers to remove, once and for all, the signs of poverty which are inequity, injustice, discrimination and exclusion.

We owe a debt to the indigenous communities which we must settle: the original peoples of these lands continue to suffer an intolerable situation of injustice and inequality.

I promised during my campaign, and today I reiterate: as Constitutional President of the Republic I have been, am and will be committed to new relations between the indigenous peoples and the Mexican State. I shall work tirelessly until this is achieved.

I will implement programs, which they themselves will administer, aimed at improving their communities.

I reiterate clearly and unequivocally that this task is and will be, from this moment on, the direct responsibility of the President of the Republic; that in fulfilling this commitment, I will take the lead. However, every effort will be insufficient without the full and constant participation of the indigenous peoples themselves and their representatives in national deliberations, proposals and decisions.

Brothers and Sisters of the indigenous communities,

To my friends of the indigenous peoples:

Allow me to address you in a special way. In a special way so that it is the future is a flourishing one.

As President of Mexico, I responsibly pledge to create conditions that make possible the ongoing participation of each and every one of you, of your communities and your peoples, in building the legal frameworks that guarantee, within the National State, the full exercise of your autonomy and your self-determination in national unity, so that the future is a flourishing one.

Never again a Mexico without you!

In Mexico and in Chiapas there will be a new dawn!

In Chiapas, actions, not hollow words, will be the backbone of a new federal and presidential policy that leads to peace.

I pledged my word to send to this Honorable Congress . . . a bill . . . which summarizes the spirit of the San Andrés Accords [an agreement between the government and Zapatista rebels in Chiapas, never implemented]. This will be the first act of my administration related to this Congress. Next Tuesday, you will have this bill here. I call upon the legislators, the political forces and parties, to deliberate with full responsibility on the capital topic embodied in that document: that of the State, society and Mexico's indigenous peoples.

In the rural sphere, we will seek to ensure that campesinos can make progress with the resources produced by their work and not with those the government may give them. We are going to move on from inefficient subsidies to productive supports that generate wealth.

Education will form the backbone of development. I ratify my promise to make every effort to raise the budget for education, because it is here that we invest in our nation's future. . . .

The children, the dear children of Mexico will be our priority, the justification for all our efforts. This morning I had a breakfast of delicious tamales with homeless children. I saw abandonment and injustice in their faces.

When I assume before the people of Mexico each of the commitments I make, facing the nation, the memory of those children whom I promised not to fail is in my mind.

Today I say to all those little Mexican girls and boys that I will not fail them. Mexico's future cannot be built outside the realm of more than half of its population.

Women—the majority of whom are committed to work two shifts a day, their job and attending to their homes and families—demand spaces and opportunities equal to their dedication and passion. It is my conviction to respond to these demands.

My administration will conduct itself with a gender perspective. It will foster a cultural transformation that recognizes values and promotes measures to facilitate the full integration of women into all spheres of national activity. In this commitment I will pledge all the power of the Presidency I assume today.

My administration's Economic Program calls for a genuine commitment to stability and growth. We are not going to play with macroeconomic variables. We are going to act with complete discipline.

We do not want Pyrrhic victories in the fight against poverty. Artificial measures for well-being end up by confiscating the result of everyone's work and by postponing the well-being to which we aspire.

We will maintain macroeconomic stability, because it represents the order without which what has been earned is lost. But we will work to turn it into tangible and specific benefits in the pockets of every Mexican man and woman.

The Economic Program we propose calls for effective and prudent participation by the government, so as to promote equity between regions, companies and households.

The program includes a business development policy for small, very small and medium-scale companies and a policy of economy, with a social rationale for very small companies, for the self-employed.

We are going to emancipate Mexican men and women with lower incomes from a legal and institutional credit system that discriminates against them.

I share the aspiration of building relations of respect, dialogue and common objectives with workers and their unions.

There are many goals we must meet, beginning with a gradual but sustained increase in workers' living standards.

But there are no magic solutions. We need to raise productivity, create wealth and distribute it at the same time.

My administration wants to support this effort by updating labor legislation to consolidate rights, promote employment, foster training, productivity and competitiveness, and thus provide new channels for union life. . . .

We will promote before this Congress the opening to investment, in order to safeguard fiscal resources so we can invest them in hospitals, schools, development of indigenous communities and the fight against poverty. That is where fiscal resources should be used.

Within the current constitutional framework, PEMEX [the state-owned oil company] will continue as the exclusive property of the nation. It should nevertheless be recognized that PEMEX is dealing with strong administrative, budgetary and regulatory rigidity that prevents it from developing into an efficient and competitive company.

Today I affirm that PEMEX will be transformed into a company managed with criteria of efficiency and subject to criteria in the vanguard worldwide; that PEMEX will be managed honestly. It will also be a company with sensitivity for the regions, states and municipalities in which it operates.

Globalization is the hallmark of our times, but we must reconcile it with Mexico's interests.

In the sphere of foreign policy, we reject any attempt at interference in our internal affairs, we condemn any intention to enforce an extra-territorial criterion in the application of laws of third parties.

We are opposed to unilateral views and to any treatment that infringes the highest rule of international law: sovereign equality under international law, sovereign equality among nations.

My administration will not leave our dear migrants, our heroic migrants, on their own, nor our companies in the face of abuses of authority or unfair international trade practices.

We will ensure that the talent we have throughout the world, in our Embassies and Consulates, becomes the best ally of their rights and a true lever of our country's economic development.

One of the things that hurts most is to see how every year hundreds of thousands of Mexicans, many of them well trained, have to emigrate to the United States and Canada—many, very many of them from Guanajuato, indeed; and from Chiapas, and Tabasco, Mexico City, Jalisco, Zacatecas, and Chihuahua and from the whole country to the United States and Canada—to find work and opportunities there which are denied to them in their own country.

To all of them I reiterate my commitment to safeguard their rights abroad and during their return to Mexico. Here we will do the essential, and we will work to ensure that they will soon find here the opportunities they went in search of, because Mexico needs them all.

Today I propose to democratize access to public health services, to have a system in which the beneficiaries have a voice in the decisions that affect them, and greater freedom in choosing the service provider, until we reach the point where every family can choose its own doctor. If on July 2nd Mexican men and women could choose their own President, I do not see why they cannot choose their own doctor.

The change involves providing financial protection in the area of health care for the entire population, so that at the end of this six-year term all Mexican families have basic health insurance. It also means that public health-care services should be provided not only with quality, but also with the respect, warmth and sensitivity that we all want to see. . . .

I disagree completely with the old expression that power is not to be shared. With that idea local bosses, centralism, authoritarianism and all the other pernicious forms of exercising public functions have been adopted. I will share power and also the responsibilities.

I am the depository of Executive Power, not its owner. I will never raise myself above the framework of the democratic origin of the office I have received; it will never be my purpose to concentrate power, but to gain moral authority in its exercise.

I will not be a President who can do everything. The times when the President of Mexico was omnipresent on the national scene will end with us.

It is no longer a single person or a government that is responsible for the destiny of the nation. All of us, in our daily labors, have a role to play in this great struggle in favor of Mexico. . . .

I am and will continue to be bound by my campaign pledges, and I will adhere to them without reservation.

Mexicans aspire to a government that serves their interests sensitively and from close at hand. I will listen obediently to their voice. I will nourish my sensibilities with intense communication with organizations, groups and social sectors.

I feel a great responsibility faced with the expectations of all Mexican men and women, particularly young people and children. There is only one way to meet their expectations: work hard, starting today. . . .

Building the Mexico of the future is not the task of one person. We need the work and commitment of all men and women, each at his or her own battlefront, but working always with passion and love for our homeland.

It is not enough to vote and then abandon political participation. The responsibility does not exclude anyone. On the contrary, true, profound and radical change will come from all of us or it will not come at all.

Let us put aside pessimism and apathy. Let us be optimists while still keeping our feet on the ground. Let us build the future with realism and joy, and day by day let us turn our present, ours and that of our families, into a better future for all men and women.

It is in our hands and within our reach, with the efforts of all, we will all be better for it. Let us start today.

We have inherited backlogs, and we have work to do and problems to solve before us. The challenge is great, but it should not intimidate us—there is no reason for it to do so.

July 2nd awakened intense emotions in us and strengthened our love for Mexico.

With this triumph we have first of all gained a new spirit to face the challenges of the future. Let us never lose it. Let us live it to the full every day, seeking always to be better and keeping the flame of hope alive.

Today, we are all responsible for complying with the mandate we gave ourselves in that exemplary election; a mandate for change to install, to establish a democratic exercise of power. It is in our hands and within our reach, and we will all be better for it.

I am and will continue to be obliged to continue the effort of this great nation, I am obliged to continue and to work with passion for those who gave us our homeland, for those who built the Mexico we have today and for those who dreamed of that different, successful and triumphant Mexico.

Thank you.

# UN SECRETARY GENERAL ON THE WAR IN CONGO
## December 6, 2000

*A war in the Democratic Republic of the Congo—by far the biggest con-
flict anywhere in the world at the turn of the century—dragged on through
2000 with little prospect for a peaceful resolution. Six of Congo's neighbors,
along with three major rebel groups and at least two dozen armed militias,
were battling for control of Africa's third largest country. Many observers
called the conflict Africa's "World War" because so many countries were involved. The war was deadlocked at the end of the year, and the situation was
extremely unstable.*

*In a report to the United Nations Security Council on December 6, Secre-
tary General Kofi Annan estimated that 16 million people—about one-third
of Congo's population—were critically short of food because of the war. Of
those, Annan said, 2 million had been forced from their homes; some had
fled into neighboring countries, but hundreds of thousands were homeless
within their own country. Estimates of the number of people killed in the war
ranged widely, from several hundred thousand to more than 1.5 million.*

*The UN pressed all year—unsuccessfully—for the combatants to comply
with a peace agreement signed in August 1999. The chief stumbling block
was Congo's embattled president, Laurent Kabila, whose actions betrayed
an understanding that an end to the war likely would bring an end to his
days in power.*

*The war in Congo (formerly known as Zaire) began in August 1998 when
two of the country's eastern neighbors, Rwanda and Uganda, invaded in
hopes of ousting Kabila from power. Ironically, both countries had been the
principal backers of Kabila in 1997 when he lead a rag-tag rebel army that
drove out Zaire's longtime corrupt dictator Mobutu Sese Seko. Now threatened himself, Kabila received military support from several neighbors, most
importantly Angola and Zimbabwe.*

*By 2000 Congo was essentially divided in half, with most of the north
and the east controlled by Rwanda, Uganda, Burundi, and the rebel forces
aligned with them; most of the south and the west were controlled by remnants of Kabila's army, various militias, and the armies of Angola, Zim-*

*babwe, and Namibia. Even North Korea had troops in Congo, serving as advisers to Kabila's army. Weapons and war materiel were flown into Congo from all over the world—paid for by the looting of Congo's vast natural resources, including diamonds, gold, oil, and timber. Those riches were prime attractions for all the participants, who took them as the spoils of war.* (Mobutu ouster, Historic Documents of 1997, p. 877; Congo war background, Historic Documents of 1999, p. 645)

## *Battling for Position*

*The Congo war had become a quagmire from which none of the participants appeared able—or even willing—to extract themselves. Each of the outside nations had its own motives for intervening in the war, and after two years of fighting none of those participants had fully achieved its aims. Rwanda and Uganda still hoped to oust Kabila from power and to continue their control of the eastern portions of the country, from which they hoped to reap enormous economic benefits. Angola and Zimbabwe also were profiting from deals that gave them mining concessions as payment for supporting Kabila; the leader of each country also had domestic political reasons for staying involved in Congo. Moreover, various rebel groups and local militias throughout the country had used the war as an excuse to plunder their regions. Of all the actors, Kabila seemed to have the least incentive to end the war. Without it he would have virtually no power base and no resources to confront the country's underlying economic and social problems. According to most assessments, Kabila was more willing to allow the country to be split into two or more pieces than to share power with opponents in a united Congo.*

*In the midst of the fighting, the UN and the Organization of African Unity attempted to sponsor political discussions between the various internal factions in Congo. Known as the Inter-Congolese Dialogue, the discussions were to have been a key component of the 1999 peace agreement all parties had signed in Lusaka, Zambia. African leaders had named Sir Ketumile Masire, a former president of Botswana who had wide international respect, to serve as moderator of the dialogue. But Kabila refused to participate and accused Masire of favoring his political opponents in Congo. Kabila also brutally suppressed political opposition in the limited areas under his direct control, most importantly the capital, Kinshasa.*

*Another major element of the Lusaka agreement—the introduction of a UN peacekeeping force—also was thwarted by the continued intransigence of the warring parties. The UN Security Council in 1999 approved a small mission of military observers to determine when and how to send in a larger peacekeeping force, initially planned to have 5,537 members. The first military observers arrived in September 1999, and by late 2000 the UN had 224 of them in various parts of the country. The Security Council on December 14 extended the mandate of the UN mission until June 15, 2001, and doubled the number of military observers to 500. But at year's end it seemed unlikely that the full-fledged peacekeeping force would be deployed anytime soon.*

*Throughout the year Annan and African leaders made repeated efforts to get the warring parties to comply with the Lusaka peace accord they had signed in 1999. Their efforts produced a series of interim agreements in April, November, and December, calling on the armies to "disengage" and pull back from the front lines. At various times some of the participants withdrew some of their forces from the fighting. A number of the outside parties—including Zimbabwe, which was undergoing domestic political turmoil, and Angola, which was more interested in combating its own rebel insurgency—began talking about pulling their troops out of Congo.*

*Annan told the Security Council he was hopeful that all sides would respect the latest disengagement agreement, signed December 6, so that UN peacekeepers could begin the task of enforcing a permanent cease-fire. Annan also said that he would not send peacekeepers until there was a peace to keep. "The main problem in the Congo is that agreements have never been respected," he told reporters during a trip to Africa on December 9. "The [Lusaka] cease-fire has been violated consistently, even right from the beginning."*

*Adding to the complexity of the war was the tendency of the two major anti-Kabila allies, Rwanda and Uganda, to battle each other. The allies fought three major battles over the city of Kisangani, a key outpost on the Congo River in the northern part of the country. The latest battle, in June, killed more than 600 civilians (according to the International Red Cross) and destroyed much of the city. In response, a frustrated UN Security Council on June 17 passed a resolution demanding that Rwanda and Uganda withdraw their forces from Congo or face the possibility of sanctions. The resolution also called on the two countries to pay for the damage they caused in Kisangani.*

### A Humanitarian Disaster

*While armies and militias battled for position, millions of Congolese civilians suffered the consequences of the war. Annan's December 6 report, along with the reporting of various news organizations and humanitarian agencies, painted a picture of a country in a state of near collapse. Aside from the war and the pillaging of natural resources associated with it, virtually all aspects of a normal economy had come to a halt. In the Kinshasa region, Annan said it was estimated that about 70 percent of the 7 million residents survived on less than $1 a day for food. "Some 18 percent of children in the inner city and over 30 percent in the outskirts suffer from chronic malnutrition," he reported.*

*The situation was especially desperate in two eastern provinces, North Kivu and South Kivu, which were under the control of militias associated with Rwanda and Uganda. In the Kivus—as well as in several other areas of eastern Congo—the regional aspects of the war were complicated by decades-old ethnic conflicts, the most important of which was between the Hutu and the Tutsi. The Tutsi-led government of Rwanda had initiated the war, at least in part, to seek revenge against Hutu guerillas based in Congo who had been responsible for a 1994 genocide in Rwanda that had killed at least 500,000 Tutsi. Despite the needs of the civilian population, the security situation was so bad that most international aid agencies had pulled out of the Kivus, leaving tens of thousands of people with no reliable source of food or other supplies.* (Rwanda genocide, Historic Documents of 1999, p. 860)

*Following are excerpts from a report submitted December 6, 2000, by United Nations Secretary General Kofi Annan to the UN Security Council in which he described the situation in the Democratic Republic of the Congo. The document was obtained from the Internet at http://www.un.org/Depts/dhl/docs/s20001156.pdf.*

[Paragraphs 1 through 55 reviewed political and diplomatic efforts during the year to resolve the war and the status of the United Nations Organization Mission in the Democratic Republic of the Congo, known as MONUC].

## V. Humanitarian affairs

55. The humanitarian situation in the Democratic Republic of the Congo has continued to deteriorate. At the end of November, the Office for the Coordination of Humanitarian Affairs estimated that the number of displaced persons was around 2 million, with less than one half receiving humanitarian assistance. In addition, UNHCR [United Nations High Commissioner for Refugees] reports that the number of Congolese refugees in the Congo has reached 100,000 and as many as 20,000 may have fled to the Central African Republic. Owing to the fighting and other difficulties, humanitarian assistance could not reach a significant proportion of these refugees. In response to a request from the United Nations High Commissioner for Refugees, MONUC has agreed in principle to provide logistics support to efforts to gain access and deliver assistance to them.

56. Over the past six months, Equateur province [in western Congo] has been affected by massive displacements of populations, either to neighbouring countries or to areas in the province considered to be more secure. The United Nations humanitarian agencies have recently launched a major initiative in Equateur province to deliver the urgently needed lifesaving support to over 400,000 war-affected persons. Agencies involved in this operation have, however, encountered serious problems in obtaining government clearances to operate in southern Equateur.

57. The number of persons in critical need of food in the Democratic Republic of the Congo remains at an estimated 16 million, or roughly 33 per cent of the country's population. The uprooting of rural populations and isolation from their traditional food sources, together with the declining economic situation, continue to be the underlying causes of this troubling situation. The situation is aggravated at Kinshasa, where it is estimated that 70 per cent of the population of seven million live on less than US$1 per day for food. Some 18 per cent of children in the inner city and over 30 per cent in the outskirts

suffer from chronic malnutrition. The food deficit of Kinshasa for the ongoing year is estimated at one million tons. A number of factors contribute to the crisis in the capital, including the swelling population caused by the war, a deterioration of the road infrastructure, inadequate food supply from Equateur and the eastern provinces, a scarcity of fuel and overvaluation of the official exchange rate.

58. The health situation in the country has also continued to decline, with less than 37 per cent of the population having access to essential medical facilities. Less than 47 per cent of the population is estimated to have access to safe drinking water. In addition to epidemic outbreaks of cholera, meningitis, dysentery and malaria, the World Health Organization (WHO) has reported the emergence and re-emergence of serious illnesses, such as haemorrhagic fever. Women and children are among the vulnerable groups most affected by the crisis.

59. The war, poor sanitary conditions among displaced populations and residents, and malnutrition have created a fertile ground for the outbreak and spread of numerous illnesses and infectious diseases, including those that are sexually transmitted. There are 20,000 new cases of HIV [the virus that caused AIDS] this year, according to the national AIDS programme, adding to the figure of one million infected adults, which includes at least 600,000 women. There are an estimated 680,000 orphans with AIDS, whose parents have died of the disease.

60. In the Kivus [North and South Kivu provinces, in eastern Congo], the increased security risk to health personnel has forced the suspension of humanitarian operations by some agencies, further increasing the vulnerability of displaced persons and residents. Armed groups continue to attack civilians, causing numerous casualties and rendering travel in the area extremely dangerous.

61. On 4 and 5 October, the inter-agency and donor country meetings were held at Geneva to consider the humanitarian response strategy to be adopted in the Democratic Republic of the Congo. Donors called for enhanced coordination and stressed that humanitarian action should be broadened and deepened, as should cooperation with local structures. At the meeting attended by my Special Representative, three main themes came to light: the need to allocate more resources to existing humanitarian projects, the need to reach more people through a more flexible humanitarian action response with the objective of saving more lives, and the need to increase the capacity of international humanitarian agencies working in the Democratic Republic of the Congo to manage an enhanced response.

62. The consolidated appeal for the Democratic Republic of the Congo for 2001 was launched at the end of November; US$ 139.5 million was requested to address the critical humanitarian needs of the war-affected populations. The appeal seeks to provide household food security and health interventions at the local community level, as well as initiatives at the national level, such as immunization days and transport corridors for essential medicines and food supplies.

63. A United Nations inter-agency mission, consisting of senior represen-

tatives of the Office for the Coordination of Humanitarian Affairs, UNDP, the United Nations Children's Fund (UNICEF), UNHCR, the World Food Programme (WFP), the Food and Agriculture Organization of the United Nations (FAO) and WHO, visited the Democratic Republic of the Congo from 20 to 24 November to examine ways of improving the coordination of humanitarian relief operations in the country. The mission report and recommendations were presented to the Executive Committee on Humanitarian Assistance on 4 December.

64. MONUC has prepared and submitted an aide-mémoire which is to be presented to the Security Council and which proposes the strengthening of the humanitarian mandate of the Mission and requests the allocation of programme funds to support a series of projects. The most notable of the projects is a request for US$ 2. 5 million to provide air logistics support with MONUC aircraft to humanitarian agencies in the Congo. This support could come in the form of an appeal by the Security Council to Member States to contribute to a trust fund established for such projects. Until funds are in place, MONUC could make an important contribution to relieving humanitarian suffering in this country by being able to use the existing funds and resources of the Mission, especially the many MONUC aircraft with their considerable under-utilized capacity, in support of humanitarian work. This would also contribute to the central peacekeeping mandate of the Mission by increasing under-standing and trust of the Mission by the people of the country and by all parties concerned. At its meeting held at Lusaka on 29 November, the Political Committee adopted an agreement aimed at improving the humanitarian situation of populations at risk, which included guaranteed access to them.

## VI. Human rights

65. The human rights situation throughout the territory of the Democratic Republic of the Congo continued to give cause for grave concern. The situation in the eastern provinces is particularly troubling, owing to the absence of governmental structures in rebel-controlled areas. Arbitrary arrests, illegal detention, forced deportation and ill-treatment have been used to harass and intimidate the population, human rights groups, church associations and non-governmental organizations. In addition, the dire economic situation has led soldiers and gangs of armed men to resort to extortion and looting, thus creating an atmosphere of insecurity and terror among vulnerable groups.

66. Recent months have seen an increase in leadership struggles in the rebel movements, rising inter-ethnic rivalries and increasing resentment among Congolese ethnic groups vis-à-vis the Tutsi in general. These developments have put the civilian population in greater danger than previously reported. There has also been a marked increase in the number of warlords in remote areas who have engaged in a pattern of systematically destroying the institutions of civil society, and manipulating the regions' clan system and ethnic groups against each other. The violence between opposing members of the Hema and Lendu tribes in the north-eastern region of the Democratic Republic of the Congo is particularly worrisome and civilian casualties are mounting.

67. The Mayi-Mayi militia [in the Kivu provinces] and predominantly Hutu

armed groups have continued to commit widespread human rights abuses. They have regularly attacked villages, forced people to hand over their belongings and killed them if they refuse to do so. In this context, the high incidence of murder of women and children of Rwandan origin should be noted. It has also been reported that Hutu armed groups use rape as a weapon of war.

68. In government-controlled territory, despite the authorities' stated commitment to a moratorium on the death penalty and the establishment of a military court appeals chamber, executions continue to take place, albeit at a reduced rate. There are also no indications that the military court system will be reformed. The system was established to try cases regarding abuses by military and police officers, and armed robbery. Civilians such as journalists and political opponents continue, however, to be tried by these courts for other crimes, in breach of international law. Moreover, notwithstanding the use of death penalty sentences, defendants appearing before military courts have no right of appeal and in some cases, no legal representation.

69. The prohibition of political parties continues, with only those parties newly registered with the Government being allowed to function, a justification for the arbitrary arrest and detention of persons affiliated with non-registered political parties. Although the Ministry of Information had announced its intention to introduce a law abolishing imprisonment for press offences, reports indicate that journalists and human rights activists continue to suffer attacks, intimidation and imprisonment. An important radio and television station, Radio-Television Kin-Malebo (RTKM), was nationalized on the basis that it had secret ties to the rebellion. Its employees have been subjected to harassment and arrest. These targeted restrictions on freedom of expression and freedom of association are completely at odds with fundamental human rights.

70. During her visit from 1 to 3 October, the United Nations High Commissioner for Human Rights [Mary Robinson] met with President [Laurent] Kabila. The High Commissioner identified a number of human rights violations that the Government had to address in order to conform with Congolese law and international human rights standards and norms. She sought the immediate release of 253 political prisoners, many of them journalists and human rights activists, who have yet to benefit from the general amnesty law. She demanded the abolition of the Court of Military Order and the suspension of the death penalty and executions; she raised the issue of administrative detentions and the prohibition of torture, the rights of the accused and respect for fundamental human rights even in times of war, while referring to relevant United Nations resolutions, international treaties ratified by the Democratic Republic of the Congo and the Lusaka Ceasefire Agreement.

71. While the Government of the Democratic Republic of the Congo made commitments to respect human rights and take the actions specified by the High Commissioner, no enforcement action has been taken to end those abuses and to establish a system of accountability and rule of law. The Court of Military Order is still being used to punish those suspected of collaborating with the rebel movements. On 9 October, the Court sentenced to death a former director of the security service, Ndjango Mfungazam, for allegedly passing on information to the rebels. On 30 October, a former Commandant of FAC [the

Armed Forces of Congo] was arrested by the President of the Military Court for allegedly plotting to overthrow the Government. Several members of his ethnic group in FAC and the opposition parties are reported to have disappeared from their homes.

## VII. Child protection aspects

72. The situation of children has continued to be of serious concern. The education situation in the eastern provinces remains disastrous, with between 40 per cent and 50 per cent of school-aged children out of school and prone to becoming targets for forced recruitment into the armed forces or militia groups that operate in the region. According to recent reports, between 15 per cent and 30 per cent of newly recruited combatants are children under 18 years of age, with a substantial number less than 12 years old.

73. On 15 May, RCD [the Congolese Rally for Democracy, an anti-Kabila rebel group] issued an instruction establishing an inter-departmental commission on the demilitarization, demobilization and reintegration of child soldiers. The commission, however, has yet to be established. On 15 and 16 November, the local radio and television station at Goma broadcast an appeal from the head of RCD, inviting parents to allow their children to be recruited into the movement's military forces. The Governor of North Kivu Province reiterated the call on 19 November, urging that children be enrolled for local defence. Following reports of the recruitment of children aged 13 to 17 years at Rutshuru on 19 November, my Special Representative contacted the RCD leadership, drawing its attention to these violations of the Convention on the Rights of the Child.

74. MONUC and the UNICEF offices at Kinshasa and Kampala are closely following the matter and have contacted the relevant authorities. As a result of joint advocacy efforts by MONUC and UNICEF, RCD-ML has recently taken steps towards setting up a coordination unit for the demilitarization, demobilization and reintegration process in areas under its control. Similar advocacy directed at MLC [Movement for the Liberation of Congo, an anti-Kabila rebel group] is planned.

75. MONUC has received confirmation of the cross-border deportation of recruited Congolese children from the Bunia, Beni and Butembo region to Uganda after the August "mutiny" of troops against the leadership of RCD-ML. In line with Council resolution 1304 (2000), the cross-border recruitment and abduction of children is strongly condemned.

76. President Kabila signed a decree on 6 June ordering the demobilization and reintegration of vulnerable groups, including child soldiers. Despite the positive reaction from the international community and the willingness shown by donor countries to assist in implementation of the decree, no substantial progress has been recorded. The national coordination unit for the demilitarization, demobilization and reintegration of vulnerable groups, including child soldiers, is still to be set up by the Government.

77. During the reporting period, the two MONUC child protection advisers have undertaken field trips to Bukavu, Kabalo, Kindu, Isiro, Kananga and Bunia to meet with all child protection partners and obtain first-hand infor-

mation on children affected by the conflict. These trips have also provided the opportunity to train MONUC military observers with regard to child protection issues. . . .

[Paragraphs 78 through 84 discuss efforts to monitor the exploitation of natural resources in Congo, the proposed budget for the UN mission in Congo, and the next steps for deployment of military observers in that mission.]

## XI. Observations and recommendations

85. The past two months has witnessed intense diplomatic activity in support of the peace process in the Democratic Republic of the Congo. I welcome the personal initiatives of heads of State in the region and commend their dedication and perseverance in efforts to put the peace process back on track. I also commend the role that OAU [Organization of African Unity] has continued to play in this regard.

86. Despite substantial compliance with the ceasefire in most parts of the Democratic Republic of the Congo, fighting has occurred in Equateur and Katanga provinces. This fighting not only complicated and imperilled ongoing peace efforts but, since the clashes occurred in border areas, threatened to spill over into the Congo and the Central African Republic to the north and into Zambia to the south. At the same time, the highly volatile environment in the Kivus marked by frequent and violent attacks by the non-signatory armed groups [local militias that had not signed the 1999 Lusaka cease-fire accord] has continued to be a most serious concern.

87. The situation around Kisangani has shown some improvement, and I welcome the restoration of calm there after the outbreaks of fighting in June. Security Council resolution 1304 (2000), however, in which the Council demanded the withdrawal of Rwandan and Ugandan forces from the territory of the Democratic Republic of the Congo without further delay, in conformity with the timetable of the Lusaka Agreement and the Kampala disengagement plan of 8 April, has yet to be implemented in full. By the same resolution, the Council, acting under Chapter VII of the [United Nations] Charter, made a number of other demands on the parties, including cooperation with the deployment of MONUC and full engagement in the national dialogue process. These demands also have yet to be met.

88. In view of the situation summarized above, I recommend that the Security Council extend the mandate of MONUC for a further six months, until 15 June 2001. During that period, in order to monitor and verify the parties' implementation of the ceasefire and disengagement plans adopted at Maputo and Lusaka, MONUC should, as a first step, deploy additional military observers, accompanied by the necessary medical, aviation, riverine and logistical support units. A deployment of this kind could be effected within the current mandate approved by the Council in resolution 1291 (2000), and with the mandate described in paragraph 84 above.

89. In principle, I would also be prepared subsequently, with the guidance of the Security Council, to recommend that infantry units be deployed in support of the military observers, if conditions both required and permitted such deployment. At the appropriate juncture, I would accordingly submit to the

Council an updated concept of operations, taking into account developments on the ground and the precise nature of the tasks that the troops would realistically be able to perform. I have requested the [UN] Secretariat to continue to liaise closely with potential troop-contributing countries in order to ascertain their continued readiness to provide the necessary personnel and specialized units.

90. At the same time, however, it is clear that broader agreement needs to be reached on the key questions that have so far not been resolved. In my view, the best way of doing so would be to build on the valuable diplomatic initiatives taken in recent weeks and to provide a framework and a stimulus for their follow-up. I am therefore considering the type of action that the United Nations could take to help to achieve this result.

91. The objective of this meeting would be to focus on the underlying questions at the core of the conflict that have yet to be satisfactorily resolved. These include the withdrawal of foreign forces; the disarmament and demobilization of armed groups; the security of the borders of Rwanda, Uganda and Burundi with the Democratic Republic of the Congo; the return of refugees in safety; the inter-Congolese dialogue; and regional economic reconstruction and cooperation.

92. It may be necessary to consider the establishment of a permanent mechanism to pursue genuine and workable arrangements for attaining these objectives. In order to ensure that the measures under discussion were practical and likely to enjoy the support of the Security Council, it would be necessary for the United Nations to support and participate in such a mechanism.

93. Finally, I wish to express my deep appreciation to my Special Representative, to the Force Commander, and to all the military and civilian personnel of MONUC for the strenuous efforts that they continue to make, often under adverse conditions, to help to restore peace to the Democratic Republic of the Congo.

# JUSTICE DEPARTMENT REPORT
# ON THE DEATH PENALTY
## December 10, 2000

*Capital punishment—which had surfaced only occasionally as a signifi-
cant public issue since the Supreme Court restored it in 1976—suddenly
came under broad attack during 2000. Journalistic investigations and academic studies raised new questions about the fairness and competence of
the nation's criminal justice system in capital cases, and there were several
prominent defections from the ranks of death penalty supporters. Opinion
polls also showed a drop in public support for the death penalty, although a
strong majority continued to believe it was necessary.*

*The states in 1999 executed 98 people, according to a report issued De-
cember 10, 2000, by the U.S. Justice Department. That was the highest number since 1951, when 105 were put to death. The number fell back to 85 in
2000—but that still was the second-highest number for any single year
since 1976.* (Previous report, Historic Documents of 1999, p. 828)

### Growing Concern About the Death Penalty

*In the quarter-century since the Supreme Court revived the death pen-
alty, the practice had enjoyed wide public support and had been criticized
primarily by liberals, civil rights groups, and some churches. But as the
number of executions rose dramatically during the 1990s—and as new evidence arose that dozens of people had been wrongfully convicted of capital
crimes—some previous supporters of capital punishment began raising
questions or even expressing opposition to it.*

*Perhaps the most important change of heart was by Illinois governor
George Ryan, a Republican, who said on January 31, 2000, that he was imposing a moratorium on executions in his state, which had executed twelve
people since reviving the death penalty in 1977. Ryan acted after the Chicago Tribune and journalism students at Northwestern University separately published reports showing that at least thirteen people in Illinois had
been wrongly convicted in capital crimes; all were released from death row
after proving their innocence. "I can only draw one conclusion: Our system
is broken," Ryan said. Ryan on March 9 named a fourteen-member panel to*

*review the state's use of the death penalty. Former U.S. district court judge Frank McGarr chaired the panel, and among its members were former U.S. senator Paul Simon and novelist Scott Turow. The panel had not finished its work as of the end of the year.*

*Examinations of the death penalty were under way in six other states: Arizona, Indiana, Maryland, Nebraska, North Carolina, and Virginia. Death penalty opponents also scored a significant public relations victory during the year in New Hampshire, historically one of the nation's most conservative states. The state House of Representatives voted on March 9 to repeal the death penalty, and the Senate followed suit on May 18. But Governor Jeanne Shaheen, a Democrat, vetoed the bill on May 19, arguing that some crimes were so heinous that the perpetrators should be punished by death.*

*Several prominent conservatives also voiced concerns about capital punishment. Pat Robertson, a religious broadcaster who had run for president in 1988, in April called for a moratorium on the death penalty, saying he believed it had been administered in a fashion that discriminated against minorities and the poor. Conservative columnist George Will also voiced doubts about the death penalty. Representative Henry J. Hyde, the Illinois Republican who chaired the House Judiciary Committee, said he was one of many death penalty supporters who "have had our confidence shaken" by evidence that dozens of death row inmates were innocent.*

*Public opinion surveys taken during the year showed that a strong majority of Americans still supported the death penalty, at least in certain cases. A* Newsweek *poll in June showed support at 73 percent, which the magazine said was "down only slightly" from previous surveys in the past five years. A survey in February by the Gallup Poll found 66 percent approving of capital punishment, down from support levels ranging from 71 percent to as high as 80 percent in the 1990s.*

*Despite the new concerns about the death penalty, there were some trends in the opposite direction. The Florida legislature on January 7 cleared legislation to speed the appeals process so inmates could be executed more quickly. Among other things, the bill tightened filing deadlines for appeals and limited the number of appeals that could be filed in capital cases. Governor Jeb Bush called the new law a "historic piece of legislation that will be much more respectful of family members and victims of these heinous crimes." The Florida Supreme Court later overturned the new law as unconstitutional.*

## *Reports on Death Penalty Cases*

*Several reports issued during the year provided new factual ammunition for the cause of death penalty opponents. Perhaps the broadest study, released June 12, found that about two-thirds of court appeals in death penalty cases between 1973 and 1995 were successful. Columbia University law professor James Liebman, lead author of the report, "A Broken System: Error Rates in Capital Cases, 1973–1995," said the result showed that most capital cases "are so seriously flawed that they have to be done over again." Liebman and fellow researchers examined 4,578 appeals and found that*

*68 percent of capital convictions were reversed on appeal. The reversal rate varied sharply from state to state; for example, 73 percent of cases studied in Florida were reversed, but only 18 percent of Virginia's cases were reversed. In most cases where the death penalty was reversed, defendants were given lesser sentences after retrial, the study showed. Death penalty supporters disputed Liebman's conclusions, insisting that his study showed that the criminal justice system worked as intended and did, in fact, protect the rights of defendants.*

*Another study detailed the cases of sixty-seven people who had been released from death row between 1992 and 1999 when DNA evidence showed they were innocent. Issued in February, the study, "Actual Innocence," cited several reasons for the convictions of those who were later released, including representation by incompetent lawyers and the use of testimony by victims that turned out to have been in error. The book's authors were Jim Dwyer, a columnist for the* New York Daily News, *and lawyers Barry Scheck and Peter Neufeld, who headed the Innocence Project at the Benjamin N. Cardozo School of Law in New York.* Newsweek *reported in its June 12 issue that eighty-seven people had been released from death row since the resumption of the death penalty in 1976.*

*Finally, Attorney General Janet Reno on September 12 issued a report showing that minorities had been disproportionately represented in capital cases in federal courts. Since 1995, the study found, 80 percent of the 682 defendants who faced federal charges involving the death penalty were minorities. U.S. attorneys recommended the death penalty for 183 defendants—74 percent of whom were minorities—during that period. Reno said she was "sorely troubled" by the findings and ordered a review of the issue by U.S. attorneys. "We must ensure that all defendants who come into our system are treated in a fair and just manner," Reno said. She noted that the report had not challenged the guilt of those convicted of federal capital crimes—just the reasons for the overwhelming preponderance of minorities in that group.*

*President Bill Clinton cited the Justice Department report in delaying what was to have been the first execution in a federal prison since 1963. Juan Raul Garza, who had been sentenced in 1993 for the murder of three drug traffickers in Texas, was supposed to be executed in November. On December 6 Clinton ordered a six-month reprieve for Garza to allow for a study of racial and geographic disparities in the imposition of death sentences.*

## *Focus on Texas*

*Much of the year's attention concerning the death penalty was focused on Texas, for two reasons: Texas routinely executed far more people than any other state (accounting for nearly half of the nation's total for 2000), and its governor, George W. Bush, was the Republican Party's leading presidential candidate, and eventually the president-elect. In June the* Chicago Tribune *published a detailed critique of the state's use of the death penalty, especially the 131 executions that had taken place since Bush became governor in 1995. The newspaper reported that about one-third of those convicted in*

*Texas capital cases during Bush's governorship had been defended by lawyers who were later disbarred, suspended, or sanctioned by the bar association in some other way. Attorneys representing forty of the capital case defendants had presented just one witness or no evidence at all during the sentencing procedures, the newspaper reported.*

*In response to the* Tribune's *reports, Bush defended his state's use of the death penalty. "I've said it once and I've said it a lot, that in every case, we've adequately answered innocence or guilt," he said. "If you're asking me whether or not as to the innocence or guilt or if people have had adequate access to the courts in Texas, I believe they have. They've had full access to the courts. They've had full access to a fair trial."*

*Another report condemning the Texas record on the death penalty came out October 15 from the Texas Defender Service, a nonprofit agency that represented death row inmates. That report detailed numerous cases in which appeals court judges had failed to hold hearings and cited forty-one cases in which prosecutors "intentionally distorted the truth-seeking process." The report also focused considerable attention on the role played by James Grigson, a psychiatrist who had testified for the prosecution in nearly four hundred capital cases. The report said Grigson had been expelled from membership in the American Psychiatric Association in 1995 for "arriving at psychiatric diagnoses without first having examined the individuals in question." The conclusions of the report were disputed by a representative of the state District and County Attorneys Association.*

*Bush faced two highly controversial death penalty cases in mid-year that focused national attention on his state's heavy reliance on capital punishment. The first case came in June when Bush granted his first-ever reprieve to Ricky McGinn, who had been convicted in 1994 of raping and killing his twelve-year-old stepdaughter, so McGinn could undergo DNA testing that had been unavailable at the time of his conviction. The testing later failed to clear McGinn, and he was executed September 27.*

*Also in June, Bush refused to halt the execution of Gary Graham, who had been convicted of killing a man during a 1981 robbery of a supermarket. Graham had been convicted on the strength of an account by one witness who said she saw him at the scene of the crime, in a dark parking lot. Graham's attorneys presented new evidence that they said had been overlooked at the time of the original trial. But the Supreme Court refused to hear the case, Bush declined to intervene, and Graham was executed June 23.*

## Supreme Court cases

*In two decisions issued in 2000, the U.S. Supreme Court limited the ability of federal courts to intervene in state death penalty cases. Both decisions were made by the 5–4 margin that in recent years had become standard in controversial cases.*

*The first ruling, issued April 18, came in a Virginia case,* Williams v. Taylor. *The Court upheld language in a 1996 law, the Anti-Terrorism and Effective Death Penalty Act (PL 104–132), in which Congress tried to block federal judges from overturning death penalty convictions by state courts. Passed in response to the 1995 bombing of the federal building in Oklahoma City, that law said federal judges must defer to state courts in death penalty cases if they concluded the state decision was not "unreasonable." Despite that ruling, the Court, on a 6–3 vote, threw out the death sentence of convicted murderer Terry Williams and ordered a new sentencing hearing for him.*

*In a second ruling, on June 12, the Supreme Court ruled that a federal district court judge could not set aside the death sentence of another Virginia man, Bobby Lee Ramdass. In that case,* Ramdass v. Angelone, *the federal judge had overturned a decision by the Virginia Supreme Court that allowed the death sentence for Ramdass even though he had been barred from telling jurors he would be ineligible for parole if he was sentenced to life in prison. In their decision, the U.S. Supreme Court majority upheld the Virginia Supreme Court action.*

## *Death Penalty Report*

*In its annual report on the death penalty, issued December 10, the Justice Department noted that southern states—most notably Texas and Virginia—led the nation in capital punishment during 1999. Texas, with thirty-five executions, and Virginia, with fourteen, together accounted for exactly half of the 1999 total. In 1998 the two states had executed thirty-three people, just short of half of that year's nationwide total of sixty-eight. Texas in 2000 set a one-year record for executions by any one state—forty.*

*Other states with multiple executions during 1999 were Missouri (nine), Arizona (seven), Oklahoma (six), Arkansas (four), North Carolina (four), South Carolina (four), Alabama (two), California (two), and Delaware (two). Florida, Illinois, Indiana, Kentucky, Louisiana, Nevada, Ohio, Pennsylvania, and Utah each executed one person.*

*One striking finding in the report was that those executed during 1999 had spent an average of eleven years and eleven months on death row—an average of thirteen months longer than those who had been executed during 1998. Analysts said it was not clear whether that change represented a trend or was just a one-year occurrence.*

*At the end of 1999, according to the Justice Department report, 3,527 people were on death row, including 50 women. The youngest inmate on death row was eighteen and the oldest was eighty-four.*

*Following are excerpts from the report, "Capital Punishment 1999," released December 10, 2000, by the Department of Justice's Bureau of Justice Statistics. The document was obtained from the Internet at http://www.ojp.usdoj.gov/bjs/abstract/cp99.htm.*

Twenty States executed 98 prisoners during 1999. The number executed was 30 greater than in 1998 and was the largest annual number since the

105 executed in 1951. The prisoners executed during 1999 had been under-sentence of death an average of 11 years and 11 months, 13 months more than that for inmates executed in 1998.

At yearend 1999, 3,527 prisoners were under sentence of death. California held the largest number on death row (553), followed by Texas (460), Florida (365), and Pennsylvania (230). Twenty were under a Federal death sentence.

During 1999, 32 States and the Federal prison system received 272 prisoners under sentence of death. Texas (48 admissions), California (43), North Carolina (24) and Florida (20) accounted for half of those sentenced to death in 1999.

During 1999, 98 men were executed: 61 whites, 33 blacks, 2 American Indians, and 2 Asians. The executed inmates included 9 Hispanics (8 white and 1 American Indian). Ninety-four of the executions were carried out by lethal injection; 3, by electrocution; and 1, by lethal gas.

From January 1, 1977, to December 31, 1999, 598 executions took place in 30 States. Sixty-four percent of the executions occurred in 5 States: Texas (199), Virginia (73), Florida (44), Missouri (41), and Louisiana (25).

## Capital punishment laws

At yearend 1999 the death penalty was authorized by 38 States and the Federal Government. During 1999 no State enacted new legislation authorizing capital punishment.

## Statutory changes

During 1999, 9 States revised statutory provisions relating to the death penalty. Most of the changes involved additional aggravating circumstances and procedural amendments.

By State, the changes were as follows:

Alabama—Added to the criminal code as aggravating circumstances murder of two or more persons in the course of one "scheme" and murder that was one of a series of intentional killings committed by the defendant.

Colorado—Added as an aggravating factor any Class 1 felony committed "because of the victim's race, color, ancestry, religion, or national origin."

Kansas—Revised the code of criminal procedure. Changes became effective 7/1/99. Kansas added language to keep confidential the identity of persons carrying out the execution and providing for certification that substances used in the execution will "result in death in a swift and humane manner" Kansas legislators revised the statute designating witnesses to the execution: witnesses must be at least 18 years old; the Secretary of Corrections may select 10 witnesses, including family members of the victim; the identity of a witness cannot be divulged by anyone other than the witness himself; any witness may be barred from attending for security reasons. Kansas also amended its procedural code for issuance of orders by the courts regarding implementation of the execution.

Nevada—Added to both the definition of first degree murder and the list of aggravating factors murder committed on school property or in any venue related to a school-sponsored activity when the "perpetrator" intended to cause death or substantial bodily harm to more than one person by means of a weapon, device or course of action that would normally be hazardous to the lives of more than one person." These changes became effective 10/1/99.

New Jersey—Amended an aggravating factor, felony murder, to include any murder where the victim had a domestic violence restraining order filed against the defendant.

Oregon—Amended its procedural code. The changes became effective 10/23/99. Oregon revised the procedures for issuing and carrying out a death warrant. The revisions established guidelines for a death warrant hearing, which will include a review of the offender's mental competency. Another procedural amendment set forth circumstances under which a person other than the defendant may file for post-conviction relief on behalf of the defendant. Oregon amended its procedural guidelines pertaining to appointment of counsel for indigent defendants and a defendant's right to waive counsel. The amendment also added a provision insulating licensed health care professionals from disciplinary action stemming from their participation in an execution. Lawmakers added a provision requiring that any documents filed on behalf of the defendant are to be served personally to the defendant by providing a copy to the defendant's current custodian.

Pennsylvania—Revised provisions of the capital statute to clarify the exact time period in which the Pennsylvania Supreme Court is required to provide the Governor with a complete record of court proceedings and its opinion and order in death penalty cases.

Texas—Amended the Texas Code of Criminal Procedure to allow during the sentencing phase of a capital trial, upon written request of the defendant's attorney, a court instruction to the jury that any person not sentenced to death will be sentenced to life imprisonment and will not be eligible for parole until the actual time served by the offender equals 40 years.

Wyoming—Amended an aggravating factor to include among capital felonies murder in the commission of abuse of a child under 16 years of age.

## Automatic review

Of the 38 States with capital punishment statutes at yearend 1999, 36 provided for review of all death sentences regardless of the defendant's wishes. The Federal death penalty procedures did not provide for automatic review after a sentence of death had been imposed.

In Arkansas, case law held that the supreme court review the trial court record for error in capital cases (*State v. Robbins*, 1999). Such review is independent of a defendant's right to waive appeals.

In South Carolina the defendant had the right to waive sentence review if the defendant was deemed competent by the court (*State v. Torrence*, 1996). In Mississippi the question of whether a defendant could waive the right to automatic review of the sentence had not been addressed. In Wyoming neither statute nor case law clearly precluded a waiver of appeal.

While most of the 36 States authorized an automatic review of both the conviction and sentence, Idaho, Indiana, Kentucky, Oklahoma, and Tennessee required review of the sentence only. In Idaho review of the conviction had to be filed through appeal or forfeited. In Indiana and Kentucky, a defendant could waive review of the conviction.

The review is usually conducted by the State's highest appellate court regardless of the defendant's wishes. If either the conviction or the sentence was vacated, the case could be remanded to the trial court for additional proceedings or for retrial. As a result of retrial or resentencing, a death sentence could be reimposed.

## Method of execution

As of December 31, 1999, lethal injection was the predominant method of execution (34 States).

Eleven States authorized electrocution; 4 States, lethal gas; 3 States, hanging; and 3 States, a firing squad.

Sixteen States authorized more than 1 method—lethal injection and an alternative method—generally at the election of the condemned prisoner; however, 5 of these 16 stipulated which method must be used, depending on the date of sentencing; 1 authorized hanging only if lethal injection could not be given; and if lethal injection is ever ruled unconstitutional, 1 authorized lethal gas, and 1 authorized electrocution.

The Federal Government authorizes the method of execution under two different laws. Offenses prosecuted under 28 CFR, Part 26, mandate lethal injection, while those prosecuted under the Violent Crime Control act of 1994 (18 U.S.C. 3596) call for the method of the State in which the conviction took place.

## Minimum age

In 1999 seven jurisdictions did not specify a minimum age for which the death penalty could be imposed.

In some States the minimum age was set forth in the statutory provisions that determine the age at which a juvenile may be transferred to criminal court for trial as an adult. Fourteen States and the Federal system required a minimum age of 18. Seventeen States indicated an age of eligibility between 14 and 17.

## Characteristics of prisoners under sentence of death at yearend 1999

Thirty-seven States and the Federal prison system held a total of 3,527 prisoners under sentence of death on December 31, 1999, an increase of 62, or 1.8% more than at the end of 1998.

The Federal prison system count rose from 19 at yearend 1998 to 20 at yearend 1999. Three States reported 39% of the Nation's death row population:

California (553), Texas (460), and Florida (365). Of the 39 jurisdictions with statutes authorizing the death penalty during 1999, New Hampshire had no one under a capital sentence, and Kansas, South Dakota, Colorado, New Mexico, and Wyoming had 4 or fewer.

Among the 38 jurisdictions with prisoners under sentence of death at yearend 1999, 19 had more inmates than a year earlier, 11 had fewer inmates, and 8 had the same number. California had an increase of 41, followed by North Carolina (15). Florida had the largest decrease (10).

During 1999 the number of black inmates under sentence of death rose by 25; the number of whites increased by 31; and the number of persons of other races rose from 59 to 65.

The number of Hispanics sentenced to death rose from 315 to 325 during 1999. Thirty-three Hispanics were received under sentence of death, 14 were removed from death row, and 9 were executed. Three-quarters of the Hispanics were held in 3 States: California (107), Texas (100), and Florida (34).

During 1999 the number of women sentenced to be executed increased from 49 to 50. Three women were received under sentence of death and two were removed from death row.

Women were under sentence of death in 18 States. More than half of all women on death row at yearend were in California, Texas, Florida, and North Carolina.

Among inmates under sentence of death on December 31, 1999, for whom information on education was available, three-fourths had either completed high school (38%) or finished 9th, 10th, or 11th grade (38%). The percentage who had not gone beyond eighth grade (14%) was larger than that of inmates who had attended some college (10%). The median level of education was the 11th grade.

Of inmates under a capital sentence and with reported marital status, more than half had never married; more than a fifth were married at the time of sentencing; and a fifth were divorced, separated, or widowed.

Among all inmates under sentence of death for whom date of arrest information was available, about half were age 20 to 29 at the time of arrest for their capital offense; 13% were age 19 or younger; and less than 1% were age 55 or older.

The average age at time of arrest was 28 years. On December 31, 1999, 37% of all inmates were age 30 to 39, and 69% were age 25 to 44. The youngest offender under sentence of death was age 18; the oldest was 84.

### Entries and removals of persons under sentence of death

Between January 1 and December 31, 1999, 32 State prison systems reported receiving 271 prisoners under sentence of death; the Federal Bureau of Prisons received 1 inmate. Half of the inmates were received in 4 States: Texas (48), California (43), North Carolina (24), and Florida (20).

All 272 prisoners who had been received under sentence of death had been convicted of murder. By gender and race, 155 were white men, 103 were black men, 4 were American Indian men, 6 were Asian men, 1 was a self-identified

Hispanic male, 2 were white women, and 1 was a black woman. Of the 272 new admissions, 33 were Hispanic men.

Twenty-one States reported a total of 88 persons whose sentence of death was overturned or removed. Appeals courts vacated 48 sentences while upholding the convictions and vacated 31 sentences while overturning the convictions. Florida (22 exits) had the largest number of vacated capital sentences. Illinois reported two commutations of death sentences; Alabama, Arkansas, Maryland, Missouri, North Carolina, and Virginia each reported one. Illinois removed one inmate when the Governor granted him a pardon.

As of December 31, 1999, 58 of the 88 persons who were formerly under sentence of death were serving a reduced sentence, 17 were awaiting a new trial, 9 were awaiting resentencing, 1 was found not guilty upon retrial, 2 had all capital charges dropped, and 1 had no action taken after being removed from under sentence of death.

In addition, 24 persons died while under sentence of death in 1999. Nineteen of these deaths were from natural causes—5 in Florida, 4 in Tennessee, 3 in Texas, 2 in Pennsylvania, and 1 each in Ohio, Alabama, Georgia, North Carolina, and Arizona. Two suicides occurred—1 each in Alabama and Florida. Two inmates were killed by other inmates—1 each in New Jersey and Mississippi. One inmate in Florida died from injuries received during an altercation with a correctional officer.

From 1977, the year after the Supreme Court upheld the constitutionality of revised State capital punishment laws, to 1999, a total of 5,985 persons entered prison under sentence of death. During these 23 years, 598 persons were executed, and 2,240 were removed from under a death sentence by appellate court decisions and reviews, commutations, or death.

Among individuals who received a death sentence between 1977 and 1999, 2,956 (49%) were white, 2,453 (41%) were black, 483 (8%) were Hispanic, and 93 (2%) were of other races. The distribution by race and Hispanic origin of the 2,240 inmates who were removed from death row between 1977 and 1999 was as follows: 1,156 whites (52%), 922 blacks (41%), 130 Hispanics (6%), and 32 persons of other races (1%). Of the 598 who were executed, 334 (56%) were white, 211 (35%) were black, 43 (7%) were Hispanic, and 10 (2%) were of other races.

## Criminal history of inmates under sentence of death in 1999

Among inmates under a death sentence on December 31, 1999, for whom criminal history information was available, 64% had past felony convictions, including 8% with at least one previous homicide conviction.

Among those for whom legal status at the time of the capital offense was reported, 40% had an active criminal justice status. Less than half of these were on parole, and a quarter were on probation. The others had charges pending, were incarcerated, had escaped from incarceration, or had some other criminal justice status.

Criminal history patterns differed by race and Hispanic origin. More blacks (68%) than whites (62%) or Hispanics (58%) had a prior felony conviction.

About the same percentage of blacks (9%), whites (8%), and Hispanics (7%) had a prior homicide conviction. A slightly higher percentage of Hispanics (24%) or blacks (19%) than whites (16%) were on parole when arrested for their capital offense.

Since 1988, data have been collected on the number of death sentences imposed on entering inmates. Among the 3,448 individuals received under sentence of death during that time, about 1 in every 7 entered with 2 or more death sentences. . . .

## Executions

During 1999 Texas carried out 35 executions; Virginia executed 14 persons; Missouri, 9; Arizona, 7; Oklahoma, 6; Arkansas, North Carolina, and South Carolina, 4 each; Alabama, California, and Delaware, 2 each; and Florida, Illinois, Indiana, Kentucky, Louisiana, Nevada, Ohio, Pennsylvania, Utah, and Washington, 1 each. The inmate executed in Ohio was the first executed in that State since 1963. All persons executed in 1999 were male. Fifty-three were white; 33 were black; 9 were Hispanic; 1 was American Indian; and 2 were Asian.

From 1977 to 1999, 6,365 prisoners were under death sentences for varying lengths of time. The 598 executions accounted for 9% of those at risk. A total of 2,240 prisoners (35% of those at risk) received other dispositions. About the same percentage of whites (11%), blacks (8%), and Hispanics (9%) were executed. Somewhat larger percentages of whites (37%) and blacks (35%) than Hispanics (26%) were removed from under a death sentence by means other than execution.

Among prisoners executed from 1977 to 1999, the average time spent between the imposition of the most recent sentence received and execution was nearly 10 years. White prisoners had spent an average of 9½ years, and black prisoners, 10½ years. The 98 prisoners executed in 1999 were under sentence of death an average of 11 years and 11 months.

For the 598 prisoners executed between 1977 and 1999, the most common method of execution was lethal injection (438). Other methods were electrocution (144), lethal gas (11), hanging (3), and firing squad (2). . . .

# SUPREME COURT ON FLORIDA ELECTION VOTE RECOUNT
## December 12, 2000

*By a 5–4 vote divided along conservative-liberal lines, the Supreme Court on December 12, 2000, put an end to the five-week dispute over the presidential election results in Florida and effectively elected Republican George W. Bush as the nation's forty-third president. The decision stopped the manual count of several thousand contested ballots that had been ordered by the Florida Supreme Court, leaving Bush the certified winner by 537 votes of the state's twenty-five electoral votes, enough to give him the presidency. Although the U.S. Supreme Court sent the case back to the Florida court for further consideration, the decision left Vice President Al Gore's attorneys little maneuvering room to pursue his challenge, and the Democratic nominee conceded the election to Bush on December 13. It was a painful decision for Gore, who had won the nationwide popular vote by approximately 577,000 votes. (Bush, Gore speeches, p. 1025)*

*The Court's decision capped the most extraordinary period in U.S. presidential politics in more than a century. The November 7 election left Gore with 267 electoral votes—just 3 short of the 270 needed under the Constitution for election as president. Bush had 246 electoral votes coming out of the election. In doubt were Florida's 25 electoral votes, which would provide the margin of victory. There Bush had a slim advantage, and for five weeks lawyers and partisans for the two sides clashed in the courts, at local elections headquarters, and even in the streets. Bush sought to preserve his slim lead by erecting legal roadblocks to the recounting of thousands of ballots that were in dispute. Needing every vote he could get, Gore demanded that all disputed votes be counted.*

*Throughout the ordeal, the nation and the world watched as election workers peered at ballots looking for signs of voter intent, and as judges struggled with Florida's sometimes conflicting laws to determine the state legislature's intent. It was the closest the United States had come to a constitutional crisis over a presidential election since 1876, when an election dispute dragged on for months and was finally resolved by a contentious vote in the House of Representatives.*

*In the end Bush won because he had two important allies working in tandem: the calendar and the Supreme Court. Under a federal law enacted in 1887, a state's electors had to be selected by December 12 if they were to be free from challenge in the U.S. Congress. Although nothing in the law prevented electors from being selected after December 12—in 1960 Hawaii did not select its electors until January 4—the Bush team argued that the Florida legislature had intended December 12 to be the deadline for selecting electors. Bush's attorneys then used every legal maneuver they could muster to prevent or delay voter recounts until this deadline had passed and it was too late to overturn the Bush lead. As the December 12 date approached, the final arbiter of whether additional votes would be counted was the Supreme Court, which for the first time in U.S. history found itself in the position of being able to determine who would become president. On the key decision in the case of* Bush v. Gore, *the Court's five most conservative justices sided with Bush, the conservative candidate, and the four most liberal justices sided with Gore, the liberal candidate.*

*The coincidence of this split did not go unremarked. Editorial writers and legal experts said that the Court should have refused to review the dispute and left it for Congress to resolve. By injecting the Supreme Court into a political issue, the Court had weakened its own legitimacy as well as Bush's claim to the White House, those critics said. John Paul Stevens, one of the dissenting justices, said the Court's ruling "can only lend credence to the most cynical appraisal of the work of judges throughout the land." Another dissenter, Justice Stephen G. Breyer, referred to the Court action as "this self-inflicted wound." Nor did it escape public notice that the Republican nominee who had campaigned on states' rights had turned to the federal judiciary to overrule the Florida state courts or that his promises of inclusion did not extend to disputed ballots cast primarily by blacks, the urban poor, and the elderly.*

*Although most Americans accepted the Court's decision and Gore's concession calmly, it remained to be seen to what extent the controversy had damaged the public's trust in its governing institutions and in the electoral process. Some observers predicted that the incident would discourage voter turnout in the future, especially among African-Americans and other minorities who were already skeptical about the voting process. Several news organizations immediately announced plans to perform their own recounts of the Florida ballots, while politicians and election officials across the country promised to review election laws and procedures to prevent similar situations in the future.*

*On December 14 Florida governor Jeb Bush announced that he was creating a special task force to investigate the integrity of Florida's election process. He also said he would welcome an investigation by the U.S. Commission on Civil Rights into allegations into voting irregularities, including incidents of intimidation directed at black voters. Bush, the younger brother of the president-elect, and Florida secretary of state Katherine Harris, an acknowledged Bush supporter, had been accused by Gore partisans of using their offices to help thwart the recount.*

## The First Phase: Protesting the Count

Pollsters and political pundits had predicted that the presidential race would be close, but no one could have predicted the precise, sometimes bizarre, twists and turns that would occur before the outcome of the 2000 election was determined. The dispute over Florida's ballots began early on election evening, November 7, when television networks first projected that Gore would win Florida and then put the state back into the undecided column. Early in the morning of November 8, both Bush and Gore were projected to be within reach of an electoral college majority—with Florida's twenty-five electoral votes enough to clinch the victory for either candidate. After several news organizations declared Bush the winner in Florida, Gore called him to concede. A half hour later, the Gore campaign determined Florida was too close to call, and Gore called Bush to retract his concession.

After the first statewide count, which did not include thousands of absentee ballots, Bush was ahead by 1,784 votes out of more than 6 million cast statewide. A mandatory machine recount of the close vote whittled Bush's lead down to 327 votes. By this time Democratic voters in several counties were complaining about broken voting machines and confusing ballots that may have caused them to vote for a candidate other than Gore. Many voters said there was so much confusion and such long lines at some precincts that they left without voting. Some black voters said that police roadblocks prevented then from even getting to the polls. On November 10, three days after the balloting was completed and with the presidential election outcome still uncertain, the Gore campaign formally asked for a manual recount of the ballots in the four Florida counties where most of the complaints originated. The following day, the Bush campaign filed suit in federal district court to stop the recounts.

For the next ten days the dispute centered on the secretary of state's certification of the vote, with the Bush forces pushing election officials to hold to certification deadlines established in state law and the Gore forces trying to extend those deadlines so that the manual recounts could be completed. The recount process was slow, as vote counters wrangled over whether to count the "hanging chads" and "dimples" left in ballots that were not cleanly punched through by the voting machines. Election officials in Miami-Dade County eventually abandoned their recount because they did not think they could meet a court-imposed deadline. Vote counters in Palm Beach and Broward counties continued, despite uncertainties about whether their efforts would ever be counted in the state's final tally. In at least one case, vote counters were threatened by Republican partisans monitoring the count.

On November 18 absentee ballots were counted, raising Bush's official lead to 930 votes. But the Florida Supreme Court had barred the secretary of state from certifying the election until it could hear arguments on whether the ballots counted by hand should be included in the final tally. On November 21 the seven-member court unanimously ruled that the hand counts had to be included and extended the deadline for certification of the vote from November 14 to November 26. Bush immediately appealed the de-

*cision to the U.S. Supreme Court, arguing that the Florida Supreme Court had violated federal election law by rewriting the state election law after the election had taken place. In the first of several controversial decisions involving the recount, the U.S. Supreme Court agreed on November 24 to review the case.*

## The Second Phase:
## Contesting the Certification

*The second, or contest, phase of the dispute began November 26, when Harris certified Bush the winner with 537 votes. The following day Gore filed suit in state court, contesting the results of the certification on the grounds that there were still enough uncounted votes to change the outcome of the election. Throughout this phase the Gore attorneys argued that the will of the people could not be fully known until all the ballots were counted; while the Bush attorneys argued that recounts using different standards were unfair and a violation of the Constitution's equal protection clause.*

*On December 1 the U.S. Supreme Court heard arguments in the suit brought by Bush challenging the extended certification deadline. Three days later, on December 4, the Court issued an unsigned opinion setting aside the Florida Supreme Court's decision extending the deadline for manual recounts and asked the Florida court to clarify two issues regarding its original decision. On the same day, Florida judge N. Sanders Sauls rejected Gore's suit contesting the election results.*

*Gore appealed Sauls's ruling to the state supreme court. By a 4–3 decision on December 8 the state supreme court ordered an immediate manual recount of all the "undervotes"—some 45,000 ballots that had not been counted because machines had not detected a vote for president. The ruling revived Gore's flagging hopes for the White House and sent Bush's lawyers back to the U.S. Supreme Court, where they sought a stay of the recount while they appealed the state supreme court ruling. On December 9 the Court granted the stay and agreed to hear the appeal. On December 11 the Court heard oral argument, and on December 12, at about 10:00 P.M., it handed down its historic ruling.*

## The Decision: Equal Protection
## Under a Deadline

*The majority opinion was unsigned, but it was obvious from the four dissents that the main opinion had been supported by the five conservative justices—Chief Justice William H. Rehnquist, and Justices Sandra Day O'Connor, Anthony M. Kennedy, Antonin Scalia, and Clarence Thomas. Rehnquist wrote a concurring opinion that was joined by Scalia and Thomas. Justices Stevens, Breyer, David H. Souter, and Ruth Bader Ginsburg each wrote dissents that were joined in part by the other dissenters. Court reporters said the unsigned or "per curiam" Court opinion appeared to be largely the work of O'Connor and Kennedy, neither of whose name ap-*

*peared on any of the signed opinions. O'Connor and Kennedy were the most moderate justices on the Court and often were the decisive votes in close cases. The majority opinion itself appeared to be a failed effort at finding a compromise that would draw the support of both liberal and conservative justices. In its main finding, the majority ruled that the state supreme court's failure to establish uniform standards for manually counting the undervotes denied Florida voters their constitutionally guaranteed right to equal protection of the laws.*

*Breyer and Souter indicated in their dissents that they, too, were troubled by the equal protection problems associated with standards that varied from county to county and even among teams of counters. Whereas Breyer and Souter would have sent the case back to the state supreme court with instructions to establish uniform standards and proceed with the recount, the majority said there was no time for that to happen before December 12, the deadline for the state to obtain the so-called safe harbor for its electors protecting them from challenge in Congress. Because the Florida Supreme Court held that the state legislature had intended to obtain that safe harbor, the majority said, the remedy proposed by the dissenters to extend the count beyond that deadline "contemplates action in violation of the Florida election code" and was therefore inappropriate.*

*In their separate opinions, the four dissenters argued that the federal questions involved were insubstantial and the Court should never have agreed to review the case in the first place. "Of course, the selection of the President is of fundamental national importance," Breyer wrote. "But that importance is political, not legal. And this Court should resist the temptation unnecessarily to resolve tangential legal disputes, where doing so threatens to determine the outcome of the election." Stevens was blunter in his criticism: "What must underlie petitioners' entire federal assault on the Florida election procedures is an unstated lack of confidence in the impartiality and capacity of the state judges who would make the critical decision if the vote count were to proceed. Otherwise their position is without merit," Stevens wrote.*

*In their concurring opinion, Rehnquist, Scalia, and Thomas acknowledged that "in most cases, comity and respect for federalism compel us to defer" to state courts on interpretations of state law. But the three justices said there were a "few exceptional cases in which the Constitution imposes a duty or confers a power on a particular branch of a state's government" and thus presented a "federal question" that was appropriate for the Supreme Court to address. Bush v. Gore was one of those exceptional cases, Rehnquist wrote, because it involved a presidential election, and because the Constitution specifically delegated authority to oversee presidential elections to state legislatures. Having justified their intervention in the case, the three then found the state supreme court's interpretation of the Florida election law to be "absurd."*

*Both Stevens and Ginsburg rejected the equal protection argument advanced by the majority. "We live in an imperfect world, one in which thou-*

sands of votes have not been counted," Ginsburg said. "I cannot agree that the recount adopted by the Florida court, flawed as it may be, would yield a result any less fair or precise than the certification that preceded that recount." All four dissenters lambasted the majority for hinging the outcome of the case on the December 12 safe-harbor deadline. No state was required to meet that deadline, Souter said. The only penalty for failing to meet it was loss of the safe harbor and "even that determination is to be made, if made anywhere, in the Congress."

Although the impact of the Supreme Court's controversial ruling on the courts and on the legitimacy of Bush's presidency could not be assessed for years to come, legal experts warned that the majority's application of equal protection notions to the voting booth may have opened a big can of worms. Even though the majority explicitly stated that its ruling was limited to the case before it, said Kathleen Sullivan, dean of Stanford University Law School, "theoretically any voter in America going to court tomorrow" could challenge differences in the voting procedures in the same state or county under the equal protection clause. Someone, for example, could protest the use of punch-card machines in one precinct and optical scanners in another, she said. A. E. Dick Howard, a professor at the University of Virginia Law School, agreed that the "spirit and philosophy of the equal protection discussion [in the Bush v. Gore ruling] would be one that could invite other attacks in other contexts. Once an idea is unleashed, it's not easily cabined. . . . I'm not prepared to say the court can keep that particular genie in the bottle."

> Following are excerpts from the unsigned majority opinion, a concurring opinion, and four dissenting opinions, in the case of Bush v. Gore, in which the Supreme Court by a vote of 5–4 ruled on December 12, 2000, that the Florida Supreme Court had failed to guarantee equal protection of the laws when it ordered a manual count of several thousand disputed votes cast in the presidential election and ruled further that the error could not be remedied in time to meet a December 12 deadline for selecting electors. The decision had the effect of naming Republican George W. Bush, governor of Texas, the president-elect of the United States. The document was obtained from the Internet at http://frwebgate.access.gpo.gov/supremecourt/00-949_dec12.fdf.

No. 00–949

| George W. Bush, et al., Petitioners<br>v.<br>Albert Gore, Jr., et al. | On writ of certiorari<br>to the Florida<br>Supreme Court |

[December 12, 2000]

PER CURIAM.

# I

On December 8, 2000, the Supreme Court of Florida ordered that the Circuit Court of Leon County tabulate by hand 9,000 ballots in Miami-Dade County. It also ordered the inclusion in the certified vote totals of 215 votes identified in Palm Beach County and 168 votes identified in Miami-Dade County for Vice President Albert Gore, Jr., and Senator Joseph Lieberman, Democratic Candidates for President and Vice President. The Supreme Court noted that petitioner, Governor George W. Bush asserted that the net gain for Vice President Gore in Palm Beach County was 176 votes, and directed the Circuit Court to resolve that dispute on remand. The court further held that relief would require manual recounts in all Florida counties where so-called "undervotes" had not been subject to manual tabulation. The court ordered all manual recounts to begin at once. Governor Bush and Richard Cheney, Republican Candidates for the Presidency and Vice Presidency, filed an emergency application for a stay of this mandate. On December 9, we granted the application, treated the application as a petition for a writ of certiorari, and granted certiorari.

. . . On November 8, 2000, the day following the Presidential election, the Florida Division of Elections reported that petitioner, Governor Bush, had received 2,909,135 votes, and respondent, Vice President Gore, had received 2,907,351 votes, a margin of 1,784 for Governor Bush. Because Governor Bush's margin of victory was less than "one-half of a percent . . . of the votes cast," an automatic machine recount was conducted under . . . the Florida Election Code, the results of which showed Governor Bush still winning the race but by a diminished margin. Vice President Gore then sought manual recounts in Volusia, Palm Beach, Broward, and Miami-Dade Counties, pursuant to Florida's election protest provisions. A dispute arose concerning the deadline for local county canvassing boards to submit their returns to the Secretary of State (Secretary). The Secretary declined to waive the November 14 deadline imposed by statute. The Florida Supreme Court, however, set the deadline at November 26. We granted certiorari and vacated the Florida Supreme Court's decision, finding considerable uncertainty as to the grounds on which it was based. On December 11, the Florida Supreme Court issued a decision on remand reinstating that date. On November 26, the Florida Elections Canvassing Commission certified the results of the election and declared Governor Bush the winner of Florida's 25 electoral votes. On November 27, Vice President Gore, pursuant to Florida's contest provisions, filed a complaint in Leon County Circuit Court contesting the certification. He sought relief pursuant to §102.168 (3) (c), which provides that "[r]eceipt of a number of illegal votes or rejection of a number of legal votes sufficient to change or place in doubt the result of the election" shall be grounds for a contest. The Circuit Court denied relief, stating that Vice President Gore failed to meet his burden of proof. He appealed to the First District Court of Appeal, which certified the matter to the Florida Supreme Court.

Accepting jurisdiction, the Florida Supreme Court affirmed in part and reversed in part. The court held that the Circuit Court had been correct to reject Vice President Gore's challenge to the results certified in Nassau County and his challenge to the Palm Beach County Canvassing Board's determination that 3,300 ballots cast in that county were not, in the statutory phrase, "legal votes." The Supreme Court held that Vice President Gore had satisfied his burden of proof . . . with respect to his challenge to Miami-Dade County's failure to tabulate, by manual count, 9,000 ballots on which the machines had failed to detect a vote for President ("undervotes"). Noting the closeness of the election, the Court explained that "[o]n this record, there can be no question that there are legal votes within the 9,000 uncounted votes sufficient to place the results of this election in doubt." A "legal vote," as determined by the Supreme Court, is "one in which there is a 'clear indication of the intent of the voter.'" The court therefore ordered a hand recount of the 9,000 ballots in Miami-Dade County. Observing that the contest provisions vest broad discretion in the circuit judge to "provide any relief appropriate under such circumstances," the Supreme Court further held that the Circuit Court could order "the Supervisor of Elections and the Canvassing Boards, as well as the necessary public officials, in all counties that have not conducted a manual recount or tabulation of the undervotes . . . to do so forthwith, said tabulation to take place in the individual counties where the ballots are located." The Supreme Court also determined that Palm Beach County and Miami-Dade County, in their earlier manual recounts, had identified a net gain of 215 and 168 legal votes, respectively, for Vice President Gore. Rejecting the Circuit Court's conclusion that Palm Beach County lacked the authority to include the 215 net votes submitted past the November 26 deadline, the Supreme Court explained that the deadline was not intended to exclude votes identified after that date through ongoing manual recounts. As to Miami-Dade County, the Court concluded that although the 168 votes identified were the result of a partial recount, they were "legal votes [that] could change the outcome of the election." The Supreme Court therefore directed the Circuit Court to include those totals in the certified results, subject to resolution of the actual vote total from the Miami-Dade partial recount.

The petition presents the following questions: whether the Florida Supreme Court established new standards for resolving Presidential election contests, thereby violating Art. II, §1, cl. 2, of the United States Constitution and failing to comply with 3 U.S.C. §5, and whether the use of standardless manual recounts violates the Equal Protection and Due Process Clauses. With respect to the equal protection question, we find a violation of the Equal Protection Clause.

## II

### [A omitted]

### B

The individual citizen has no federal constitutional right to vote for electors for the President of the United States unless and until the state legislature chooses a statewide election as the means to implement its power to appoint members of the Electoral College. This is the source for the statement in *McPherson v. Blacker* (1892) that the State legislature's power to select the manner for appointing electors is plenary; it may, if it so chooses, select the electors itself, which indeed was the manner used by State legislatures in several States for many years after the Framing of our Constitution. History has now favored the voter, and in each of the several States the citizens themselves vote for Presidential electors. When the state legislature vests the right to vote for President in its people, the right to vote as the legislature has prescribed is fundamental; and one source of its fundamental nature lies in the equal weight accorded to each vote and the equal dignity owed to each voter. The State, of course, after granting the franchise in the special context of Article II, can take back the power to appoint electors. . . .

The right to vote is protected in more than the initial allocation of the franchise. Equal protection applies as well to the manner of its exercise. Having once granted the right to vote on equal terms, the State may not, by later arbitrary and disparate treatment, value one person's vote over that of another. . . .

There is no difference between the two sides of the present controversy on these basic propositions. Respondents say that the very purpose of vindicating the right to vote justifies the recount procedures now at issue. The question before us, however, is whether the recount procedures the Florida Supreme Court has adopted are consistent with its obligation to avoid arbitrary and disparate treatment of the members of its electorate.

Much of the controversy seems to revolve around ballot cards designed to be perforated by a stylus but which, either through error or deliberate omission, have not been perforated with sufficient precision for a machine to count them. In some cases a piece of the card—a chad—is hanging, say by two corners. In other cases there is no separation at all, just an indentation. The Florida Supreme Court has ordered that the intent of the voter be discerned from such ballots. For purposes of resolving the equal protection challenge, it is not necessary to decide whether the Florida Supreme Court had the authority under the legislative scheme for resolving election disputes to define what a legal vote is and to mandate a manual recount implementing that definition. The recount mechanisms implemented in response to the decisions of the Florida Supreme Court do not satisfy the minimum requirement for non-arbitrary treatment of voters necessary to secure the fundamental right. Florida's basic command for the count of legally cast votes is to consider the "intent of the voter." This is unobjectionable as an abstract proposition and a starting principle. The problem inheres in the absence of specific standards to ensure its equal application. The formulation of uniform rules to determine intent based on these recurring circumstances is practicable and, we conclude, necessary.

. . . The want of those rules here has led to unequal evaluation of ballots in various respects. As seems to have been acknowledged at oral argument, the standards for accepting or rejecting contested ballots might vary not only from county to county but indeed within a single county from one recount team to another. . . .

The State Supreme Court ratified this uneven treatment. It mandated that the recount totals from two counties, Miami-Dade and Palm Beach, be included in the certified total. The court also appeared to hold *sub silentio* that the recount totals from Broward County, which were not completed until after the original November 14 certification by the Secretary of State, were to be considered part of the new certified vote totals even though the county certification was not contested by Vice President Gore. Yet each of the counties used varying standards to determine what was a legal vote. Broward County used a more forgiving standard than Palm Beach County, and uncovered almost three times as many new votes, a result markedly disproportionate to the difference in population between the counties. In addition, the recounts in these three counties were not limited to so-called undervotes but extended to all of the ballots. The distinction has real consequences. A manual recount of all ballots identifies not only those ballots which show no vote but also those which contain more than one, the so-called overvotes. Neither category will be counted by the machine. This is not a trivial concern.

At oral argument, respondents estimated there are as many as 110,000 overvotes statewide. As a result, the citizen whose ballot was not read by a machine because he failed to vote for a candidate in a way readable by a machine may still have his vote counted in a manual recount; on the other hand, the citizen who marks two candidates in a way discernable by the machine will not have the same opportunity to have his vote count, even if a manual examination of the ballot would reveal the requisite indicia of intent. Furthermore, the citizen who marks two candidates, only one of which is discernable by the machine, will have his vote counted even though it should have been read as an invalid ballot. The State Supreme Court's inclusion of vote counts based on these variant standards exemplifies concerns with the remedial processes that were under way.

That brings the analysis to yet a further equal protection problem. The votes certified by the court included a partial total from one county, Miami-Dade. The Florida Supreme Court's decision thus gives no assurance that the recounts included in a final certification must be complete. Indeed, it is respondent's submission that it would be consistent with the rules of the recount procedures to include whatever partial counts are done by the time of final certification, and we interpret the Florida Supreme Court's decision to permit this. . . . The press of time does not diminish the constitutional concern. A desire for speed is not a general excuse for ignoring equal protection guarantees.

In addition to these difficulties the actual process by which the votes were to be counted under the Florida Supreme Court's decision raises further concerns. That order did not specify who would recount the ballots. The county canvassing boards were forced to pull together ad hoc teams comprised of judges from various Circuits who had no previous training in handling and interpreting ballots. Furthermore, while others were permitted to observe, they were prohibited from objecting during the recount.

The recount process, in its features here described, is inconsistent with the minimum procedures necessary to protect the fundamental right of each voter in the special instance of a statewide recount under the authority of a single state judicial officer. Our consideration is limited to the present circumstances, for the problem of equal protection in election processes generally presents many complexities.

The question before the Court is not whether local entities, in the exercise of their expertise, may develop different systems for implementing elections. Instead, we are presented with a situation where a state court with the power to assure uniformity has ordered a statewide recount with minimal procedural safeguards. When a court orders a statewide remedy, there must be at least some assurance that the rudimentary requirements of equal treatment and fundamental fairness are satisfied. Given the Court's assessment that the recount process underway was probably being conducted in an unconstitutional manner, the Court stayed the order directing the recount so it could hear this case and render an expedited decision. The contest provision, as it was mandated by the State Supreme Court, is not well calculated to sustain the confidence that all citizens must have in the outcome of elections. The State has not shown that its procedures include the necessary safeguards. . . .

Upon due consideration of the difficulties identified to this point, it is obvious that the recount cannot be conducted in compliance with the requirements of equal protection and due process without substantial additional work. It would require not only the adoption (after opportunity for argument) of adequate statewide standards for determining what is a legal vote, and practicable procedures to implement them, but also orderly judicial review of any disputed matters that might arise. . . .

The Supreme Court of Florida has said that the legislature intended the State's electors to "participat[e] fully in the federal electoral process," as provided in 3 U.S.C. §5.

That statute, in turn, requires that any controversy or contest that is designed to lead to a conclusive selection of electors be completed by December 12. That date is upon us, and there is no recount procedure in place under the State Supreme Court's order that comports with minimal constitutional standards. Because it is evident that any recount seeking to meet the December 12 date will be unconstitutional for the reasons we have discussed, we reverse the judgment of the Supreme Court of Florida ordering a recount to proceed. Seven Justices of the Court agree that there are constitutional problems with the recount ordered by the Florida Supreme Court that demand a remedy. The only disagreement is as to the remedy.

Because the Florida Supreme Court has said that the Florida Legislature intended to obtain the safe-harbor benefits of 3 U.S.C. §5, JUSTICE BREYER's proposed remedy—remanding to the Florida Supreme Court for its ordering of a constitutionally proper contest until December 18—contemplates action in violation of the Florida election code, and hence could not be part of an "appropriate" order authorized by Fla. Stat. §102.168 (8) (2000). . . .

None are more conscious of the vital limits on judicial authority than are the members of this Court, and none stand more in admiration of the Constitution's design to leave the selection of the President to the people, through their legislatures, and to the political sphere. When contending parties invoke the process of the courts, however, it becomes our unsought responsibility to resolve the federal and constitutional issues the judicial system has been forced to confront. The judgment of the Supreme Court of Florida is reversed, and the case is remanded for further proceedings not inconsistent with this opinion.

Pursuant to this Court's Rule 45.2, the Clerk is directed to issue the mandate in this case forthwith.

*It is so ordered.*

CHIEF JUSTICE REHNQUIST, with whom JUSTICE SCALIA and JUSTICE THOMAS join, concurring.

We join the per curiam opinion. We write separately because we believe there are additional grounds that require us to reverse the Florida Supreme Court's decision.

# I

We deal here not with an ordinary election, but with an election for the President of the United States. . . .

In most cases, comity and respect for federalism compel us to defer to the decisions of state courts on issues of state law. That practice reflects our understanding that the decisions of state courts are definitive pronouncements of the will of the States as sovereigns. Of course, in ordinary cases, the distribution of powers among the branches of a State's government raises no questions of federal constitutional law, subject to the requirement that the government be republican in character. . . . But there are a few exceptional cases in which the Constitution imposes a duty or confers a power on a particular branch of a State's government. This is one of them.

Article II, §1, cl. 2, provides that "[e]ach State shall appoint, in such Manner as the Legislature thereof may direct," electors for President and Vice President. Thus, the text of the election law itself, and not just its interpretation by the courts of the States, takes on independent significance. . . . A significant departure from the legislative scheme for appointing Presidential electors presents a federal constitutional question.

3 U.S.C. §5 informs our application of Art. II, §1, cl. 2, to the Florida statutory scheme, which, as the Florida Supreme Court acknowledged, took that statute into account. Section 5 provides that the State's selection of electors "shall be conclusive, and shall govern in the counting of the electoral votes" if the electors are chosen under laws enacted prior to election day, and if the selection process is completed six days prior to the meeting of the electoral college. . . .

If we are to respect the legislature's Article II powers, therefore, we must ensure that postelection state-court actions do not frustrate the legislative desire to attain the "safe harbor" provided by §5.

In Florida, the legislature has chosen to hold statewide elections to appoint the State's 25 electors. Importantly, the legislature has delegated the authority to run the elections and to oversee election disputes to the Secretary of State (Secretary), and to state circuit courts. Isolated sections of the code may well admit of more than one interpretation, but the general coherence of the legislative scheme may not be altered by judicial interpretation so as to wholly change the statutorily provided apportionment of responsibility among these various bodies. In any election but a Presidential election, the Florida Supreme Court can give as little or as much deference to Florida's executives as it chooses, so far as Article II is concerned, and this Court will have no cause to question the court's actions. But, with respect to a Presidential election, the court must be both mindful of the legislature's role under Article II in choosing the manner of appointing electors and deferential to those bodies expressly empowered by the legislature to carry out its constitutional mandate.

In order to determine whether a state court has infringed upon the legislature's authority, we necessarily must examine the law of the State as it existed prior to the action of the court. Though we generally defer to state courts on the interpretation of state law . . . there are of course areas in which the Constitution requires this Court to undertake an independent, if still deferential, analysis of state law. . . .

This inquiry does not imply a disrespect for state courts but rather a respect for the constitutionally prescribed role of state legislatures. To attach definitive weight to the pronouncement of a state court, when the very question at issue is whether the court has actually departed from the statutory meaning, would be to abdicate our responsibility to enforce the explicit requirements of Article II.

## II

Acting pursuant to its constitutional grant of authority, the Florida Legislature has created a detailed, if not perfectly crafted, statutory scheme that provides for appointment of Presidential electors by direct election. Under the statute, "[v]otes cast for the actual candidates for President and Vice President shall be counted as votes cast for the presidential electors supporting such candidates." The legislature has designated the Secretary of State as the "chief election officer," with the responsibility to "[o]btain and maintain uniformity in the application, operation, and interpretation of the election laws."

The state legislature has delegated to county canvassing boards the duties of administering elections. Those boards are responsible for providing results to the state Elections Canvassing Commission, comprising the Governor, the Secretary of State, and the Director of the Division of Elections. . . .

After the election has taken place, the canvassing boards receive returns from precincts, count the votes, and in the event that a candidate was defeated by .5% or less, conduct a mandatory recount. The county canvassing boards must file certified election returns with the Department of State by 5 p. m. on the seventh day following the election. The Elections Canvassing Commission must then certify the results of the election. The state legislature has also provided mechanisms both for protesting election returns and for contesting certified election results. . . . Any protest must be filed prior to the certification of election results by the county canvassing board. Once a protest has been filed, "the county canvassing board may authorize a manual recount." If a sample recount . . . "indicates an error in the vote tabulation which could affect the outcome of the election," the county canvassing board is instructed to: "(a) Correct the error and recount the remaining precincts with the vote tabulation system; (b) Request the Department of State to verify the tabulation software; or (c) Manually recount all ballots." In the event a canvassing board chooses to conduct a manual recount of all ballots, [state law] prescribes procedures for such a recount.

. . . The grounds for contesting an election include "[r]eceipt of a number of illegal votes or rejection of a number of legal votes sufficient to change or place in doubt the result of the election." Any contest must be filed in the appropriate Florida circuit court, and the canvassing board or election board is the proper party defendant. [Florida law] provides that "[t]he circuit judge to whom the contest is presented may fashion such orders as he or she deems necessary to ensure that each allegation in the complaint is investigated, examined, or checked, to prevent or correct any alleged wrong, and to provide any relief appropriate under such circumstances." In Presidential elections, the contest period necessarily terminates on the date set by 3 U.S.C. §5 for concluding the State's "final determination" of election controversies.

In its first decision . . , the Florida Supreme Court extended the 7-day statutory certification deadline established by the legislature. This modification of the code, by lengthening the protest period, necessarily shortened the contest period for Presidential elections. Underlying the extension of the certification deadline and the shortchanging of the contest period was, presumably, the clear implication that certification was a matter of significance: The certified winner would enjoy presumptive validity, making a contest proceeding by the losing candidate an uphill battle. In its latest opinion, however, the court empties certification of virtually all legal consequence during the contest, and in doing so departs from the provisions enacted by the Florida Legislature. The court determined that canvassing boards' decisions regarding whether to recount ballots past the certification deadline (even the certification deadline established by Harris I) are to be reviewed de novo, although the election code clearly vests discretion whether to recount in the boards, and sets strict deadlines subject to the Secretary's rejection of late tallies and monetary fines for tardiness. . . . Moreover, the Florida court held that all late vote tallies arriving during the contest period should be automatically included in the certification regardless of the certification deadline (even the certification deadline established by Harris I), thus virtually eliminating both the deadline and the Secretary's discretion to disregard recounts that violate it.

Moreover, the court's interpretation of "legal vote," and hence its decision to order a contest-period recount, plainly departed from the legislative scheme. Florida statutory law cannot reasonably be thought to require the counting of improperly marked ballots. Each Florida precinct before election day provides instructions on how properly to cast a vote, §101.46; each polling place on election day contains a working model of the voting machine it uses, §101.5611; and each voting booth contains a sample ballot, §101.46. In precincts using punch-card ballots, voters are instructed to punch out the ballot cleanly. . . .

No reasonable person would call it "an error in the vote tabulation," or a "rejection of legal votes," when electronic or electromechanical equipment performs precisely in the manner designed, and fails to count those ballots that are not marked in the manner that these voting instructions explicitly and prominently specify. The scheme that the Florida Supreme Court's opinion attributes to the legislature is one in which machines are required to be "capable of correctly counting votes," but which nonetheless regularly produces elections in which legal votes are predictably not tabulated, so that in close elections manual recounts are regularly required. This is of course absurd. The Secretary of State, who is authorized by law to issue binding interpretations of the election code, rejected this peculiar reading of the statutes. . . . The Florida Supreme Court, although it must defer to the Secretary's interpretations, . . . rejected her reasonable interpretation and embraced the peculiar one.

But as we indicated in our remand of the earlier case, in a Presidential election the clearly expressed intent of the legislature must prevail. And there is no basis for reading the Florida statutes as requiring the counting of improperly marked ballots, as an examination of the Florida Supreme Court's textual analysis shows. . . . The State's Attorney General (who was supporting the Gore challenge) confirmed in oral argument here that never before the present election had a manual recount been conducted on the basis of the contention that "undervotes" should have been examined to determine voter intent. For the court to step away from this established practice, prescribed by the Secretary of State, the state official charged by the legislature with "responsibility to . . . [o]btain and maintain uniformity in the application, operation, and interpretation of the election laws," §97.012 (1), was to depart from the legislative scheme.

## III

The scope and nature of the remedy ordered by the Florida Supreme Court jeopardizes the "legislative wish" to take advantage of the safe harbor provided by 3 U.S.C. §5. December 12, 2000, is the last date for a final determination of the Florida electors that will satisfy §5. Yet in the late afternoon of December 8th—four days before this deadline—the Supreme Court of Florida ordered recounts of tens of thousands of so-called "undervotes" spread through 64 of the State's 67 counties. This was done in a search for elusive—perhaps delusive—certainty as to the exact count of 6 million votes. But no one claims that these ballots have not previously been tabulated; they were initially read by voting machines at the time of the election, and thereafter reread by virtue of Florida's automatic recount provision. No one claims there was any fraud in the election. The Supreme Court of Florida ordered this additional recount under the provision of the election code giving the circuit judge the authority to provide relief that is "appropriate under such circumstances."

Surely when the Florida Legislature empowered the courts of the State to grant "appropriate" relief, it must have meant relief that would have become final by the cut-off date of 3 U.S.C. §5. In light of the inevitable legal challenges and ensuing appeals to the Supreme Court of Florida and petitions for certiorari to this Court, the entire recounting process could not possibly be completed by that date. . . .

As the dissent noted: "In [the four days remaining], all questionable ballots must be reviewed by the judicial officer appointed to discern the intent of the voter in a process open to the public. Fairness dictates that a provision be made for either party to object to how a particular ballot is counted. Additionally, this short time period must allow for judicial review. I respectfully submit this cannot be completed without taking Florida's presidential electors outside the safe harbor provision, creating the very real possibility of disenfranchising those nearly 6 million voters who are able to correctly cast their ballots on election day.". . . Given all these factors, and in light of the legislative intent identified by the Florida Supreme Court to bring Florida within the "safe harbor" provision of 3 U.S.C. §5, the remedy prescribed by the Supreme Court of Florida cannot be deemed an "appropriate" one as of December 8.

It significantly departed from the statutory framework in place on November 7, and authorized open-ended further proceedings which could not be completed by December 12, thereby preventing a final determination by that date.

For these reasons, in addition to those given in the per curiam, we would reverse.

JUSTICE STEVENS, with whom JUSTICE GINSBURG AND JUSTICE BREYER join, dissenting.

The Constitution assigns to the States the primary responsibility for determining the manner of selecting the Presidential electors. . . . When questions arise about the meaning of state laws, including election laws, it is our settled practice to accept the opinions of the highest courts of the States as providing the final answers. On rare occasions, however, either federal statutes or the Federal Constitution may require federal judicial intervention in state elections. This is not such an occasion.

The federal questions that ultimately emerged in this case are not substantial. Article II provides that "[e]ach State shall appoint, in such Manner as the Legislature thereof may direct, a Number of Electors." It does not create state legislatures out of whole cloth, but rather takes them as they come—as creatures born of, and constrained by, their state constitutions. Lest there be any doubt, we stated over 100 years ago in *McPherson v. Blacker* (1892), that "[w]hat is forbidden or required to be done by a State" in the Article II context "is forbidden or required of the legislative power under state constitutions as they exist." In the same vein, we also observed that "[t]he [State's] legislative power is the supreme authority except as limited by the constitution of the State." The legislative power in Florida is subject to judicial review pursuant to Article V of the Florida Constitution, and nothing in Article II of the Federal Constitution frees the state legislature from the constraints in the state constitution that created it. Moreover, the Florida Legislature's own decision to employ a unitary code for all elections indicates that it intended the Florida Supreme Court to play the same role in Presidential elections that it has historically played in resolving electoral disputes. The Florida Supreme Court's exercise of appellate jurisdiction therefore was wholly consistent with, and indeed contemplated by, the grant of authority in Article II.

It hardly needs stating that Congress, pursuant to 3 U.S.C. §5, did not impose any affirmative duties upon the States that their governmental branches could "violate." Rather, §5 provides a safe harbor for States to select electors in contested elections "by judicial or other methods" established by laws prior to the election day. Section 5, like Article II, assumes the involvement of the state judiciary in interpreting state election laws and resolving election disputes under those laws. Neither §5 nor Article II grants federal judges any special authority to substitute their views for those of the state judiciary on matters of state law.

Nor are petitioners correct in asserting that the failure of the Florida Supreme Court to specify in detail the precise manner in which the "intent of the voter," is to be determined rises to the level of a constitutional violation. We found such a violation when individual votes within the same State were weighted unequally . . . but we have never before called into question the substantive standard by which a State determines that a vote has been legally cast. And there is no reason to think that the guidance provided to the factfinders, specifically the various canvassing boards, by the "intent of the voter" standard is any less sufficient—or will lead to results any less uniform—than, for example, the "beyond a reasonable doubt" standard employed everyday by ordinary citizens in courtrooms across this country.

Admittedly, the use of differing substandards for determining voter intent in different counties employing similar voting systems may raise serious concerns. Those concerns are alleviated—if not eliminated—by the fact that a single impartial magistrate will ultimately adjudicate all objections arising from the recount process. Of course, as a general matter, "[t]he interpretation of constitutional principles must not be too literal. We must remember that the machinery of government would not work if it were not allowed a little play in its joints." *Bain Peanut Co. of Tex. v. Pinson* (1931) (Holmes, J.). If it were otherwise, Florida's decision to leave to each county the determination of what balloting system to employ—despite enormous differences in accuracy—might run afoul of equal protection. So, too, might the similar decisions of the vast majority of state legislatures to delegate to local authorities certain decisions with respect to voting systems and ballot design. Even assuming that aspects of the remedial scheme might ultimately be found to violate the Equal Protection Clause, I could not subscribe to the majority's disposition of the case. As the majority explicitly holds, once a state legislature determines to select electors through a popular vote, the right to have one's vote counted is of constitutional stature. As the majority further acknowledges, Florida law holds that all ballots that reveal the intent of the voter constitute valid votes. Recognizing these principles, the majority nonetheless orders the termination of the contest proceeding before all such votes have been tabulated. Under their own reasoning, the appropriate course of action would be to remand to allow more specific procedures for implementing the legislature's uniform general standard to be established.

In the interest of finality, however, the majority effectively orders the disenfranchisement of an unknown number of voters whose ballots reveal their intent—and are therefore legal votes under state law—but were for some reason rejected by ballot-counting machines. It does so on the basis of the deadlines set forth in Title 3 of the United States Code. But, as I have already noted, those provisions merely provide rules of decision for Congress to follow when selecting among conflicting slates of electors. They do not prohibit a State from counting what the majority concedes to be legal votes until a bona fide winner is determined. Indeed, in 1960, Hawaii appointed two slates of electors and Congress chose to count the one appointed on January 4, 1961, well after the Title 3 deadlines. . . . Thus, nothing prevents the majority, even if it properly found an equal protection violation, from ordering relief appropriate to remedy that violation without depriving Florida voters of their right to have their votes counted. As the majority notes, "[a] desire for speed is not a general excuse for ignoring equal protection guarantees." Finally, neither in this case, nor in its earlier opinion in *Palm Beach County Canvassing Bd. v. Harris*, did the Florida Supreme Court make any substantive change in Florida electoral law. Its decisions were rooted in long-established precedent and were consistent with the relevant statutory provisions, taken as a whole. It did what courts do—it decided the case before it in light of the legislature's intent to leave no legally cast vote uncounted. In so doing, it relied on the sufficiency of the general "intent of the voter" standard articulated by the state legislature, coupled with a procedure for ultimate review by an impartial judge, to resolve the concern about disparate evaluations of contested ballots. If we assume—as I do—that the members of that court and the judges who would have carried out its mandate are impartial, its decision does not even raise a colorable federal question.

What must underlie petitioners' entire federal assault on the Florida election procedures is an unstated lack of confidence in the impartiality and capacity of the state judges who would make the critical decisions if the vote count were to proceed. Otherwise, their position is wholly without merit. The endorsement of that position by the majority of this Court can only lend credence to the most cynical appraisal of the work of judges throughout the land. It is confidence in the men and women who administer the judicial system that is the true backbone of the rule of law. Time will one day heal the wound to that confidence that will be inflicted by today's decision. One thing, however, is certain. Although we may never know with complete certainty the identity of the winner of this year's Presidential election, the identity of the loser is perfectly clear. It is the Nation's confidence in the judge as an impartial guardian of the rule of law. I respectfully dissent.

JUSTICE SOUTER, with whom JUSTICE BREYER joins and with whom JUSTICE STEVENS and JUSTICE GINSBURG join with regard to all but Part C, dissenting.

The Court should not have reviewed either *Bush v. Palm Beach County Canvassing Bd.* or this case, and should not have stopped Florida's attempt to recount all undervote ballots by issuing a stay of the Florida Supreme Court's orders during the period of this review. If this Court had allowed the State to follow the course indicated by the opinions of its own Supreme Court, it is entirely possible that there would ultimately have been no issue requiring our review, and political tension could have worked itself out in the Congress following the procedure provided in 3 U.S.C. §15. The case being before us, however, its resolution by the majority is another erroneous decision.

As will be clear, I am in substantial agreement with the dissenting opinions of JUSTICE STEVENS, JUSTICE GINSBURG and JUSTICE BREYER. I write separately only to say how straightforward the issues before us really are.

There are three issues: whether the State Supreme Court's interpretation of the statute providing for a contest of the state election results somehow violates 3 U.S.C. §5; whether that court's construction of the state statutory provisions governing contests impermissibly changes a state law from what the State's legislature has provided, in violation of Article II, §1, cl. 2, of the national Constitution; and whether the manner of interpreting markings on disputed ballots failing to cause machines to register votes for President (the undervote ballots) violates the equal protection or due process guaranteed by the Fourteenth Amendment. None of these issues is difficult to describe or to resolve.

## A

The 3 U.S.C. §5 issue is not serious. That provision sets certain conditions for treating a State's certification of Presidential electors as conclusive in the event that a dispute over recognizing those electors must be resolved in the Congress under 3 U.S.C. §15. Conclusiveness requires selection under a legal scheme in place before the election, with results determined at least six days before the date set for casting electoral votes. But no State is required to conform to §5 if it cannot do that (for whatever reason); the sanction for failing to satisfy the conditions of §5 is simply loss of what has been called its "safe harbor." And even that determination is to be made, if made anywhere, in the Congress.

## B

The second matter here goes to the State Supreme Court's interpretation of certain terms in the state statute governing election "contests." The issue is whether the judgment of the state supreme court has displaced the state legislature's provisions for election contests: is the law as declared by the court different from the provisions made by the legislature, to which the national Constitution commits responsibility for determining how each State's Presidential electors are chosen? . . .

Bush does not, of course, claim that any judicial act interpreting a statute of uncertain meaning is enough to displace the legislative provision and violate Article II; statutes require interpretation, which does not without more affect the legislative character of a statute within the meaning of the Constitution. What Bush does argue, as I understand the contention, is that the interpretation of §102.168 was so unreasonable as to transcend the accepted bounds of statutory interpretation, to the point of being a nonjudicial act and producing new law untethered to the legislative act in question.

The starting point for evaluating the claim that the Florida Supreme Court's interpretation effectively rewrote §102.168 must be the language of the provision on which Gore relies to show his right to raise this contest: that the previously certified result in Bush's favor was produced by "rejection of a number of legal votes sufficient to change or place in doubt the result of the election."

None of the state court's interpretations is unreasonable to the point of displacing the legislative enactment quoted. As I will note below, other interpretations were of course possible, and some might have been better than those adopted by the Florida court's majority; the two dissents from the majority opinion of that court and various briefs submitted to us set out alternatives. But the majority view is in each instance within the bounds of reasonable interpretation, and the law as declared is consistent with Article II.

## 1

The statute does not define a "legal vote," the rejection of which may affect the election. The State Supreme Court was therefore required to define it, and in doing that the court looked to another election statute, dealing with damaged or defective ballots, which contains a provision that no vote shall be disregarded "if there is a clear indication of the intent of the voter as determined by a canvassing board." The court read that objective of looking to the voter's intent as indicating that the legislature probably meant "legal vote" to mean a vote recorded on a ballot indicating what the voter intended.

It is perfectly true that the majority might have chosen a different reading. . . . But even so, there is no constitutional violation in following the majority view; Article II is unconcerned with mere disagreements about interpretive merits.

## 2

The Florida court next interpreted "rejection" to determine what act in the counting process may be attacked in a contest. Again, the statute does not define the term. The court majority read the word to mean simply a failure to count. That reading is certainly within the bounds of common sense, given the objective to give effect to a voter's intent if that can be determined. . . .

## 3

The same is true about the court majority's understanding of the phrase "votes sufficient to change or place in doubt" the result of the election in Florida. The court held that if the uncounted ballots were so numerous that it was reasonably possible that they contained enough "legal" votes to swing the election, this contest would be authorized by the statute. While the majority might have thought (as the trial judge did) that a probability, not a possibility, should be necessary to justify a contest, that reading is not required by the statute's text, which says nothing about probability. Whatever people of good will and good sense may argue about the merits of the Florida court's reading, there is no warrant for saying that it transcends the limits of reasonable statutory interpretation to the point of supplanting the statute enacted by the "legislature" within the meaning of Article II. . . .

## C

It is only on the third issue before us that there is a meritorious argument for relief, as this Court's Per Curiam opinion recognizes. It is an issue that might well have been dealt with adequately by the Florida courts if the state proceedings had not been interrupted, and if not disposed of at the state level it could have been considered by the Congress in any electoral vote dispute. But because the course of state proceedings has been interrupted, time is short, and the issue is before us, I think it sensible for the Court to address it.

Petitioners have raised an equal protection claim (or, alternatively, a due process claim . . . in the charge that unjustifiably disparate standards are applied in different electoral jurisdictions to otherwise identical facts. It is true that the Equal Protection Clause does not forbid the use of a variety of voting mechanisms within a jurisdiction, even though different mechanisms will have different levels of effectiveness in recording voters' intentions; local variety can be justified by concerns about cost, the potential value of innovation, and so on. But evidence in the record here suggests that a different order of disparity obtains under rules for determining a voter's intent that have been applied (and could continue to be applied) to identical types of ballots used in identical brands of machines and exhibiting identical physical characteristics (such as "hanging" or "dimpled" chads).

I can conceive of no legitimate state interest served by these differing treatments of the expressions of voters' fundamental rights. The differences appear wholly arbitrary. In deciding what to do about this, we should take account of the fact that electoral votes are due to be cast in six days. I would therefore remand the case to the courts of Florida with instructions to establish uniform standards for evaluating the several types of ballots that have prompted differing treatments, to be applied within and among counties when passing on such identical ballots in any further recounting (or successive recounting) that the courts might order.

Unlike the majority, I see no warrant for this Court to assume that Florida could not possibly comply with this requirement before the date set for the meeting of electors, December 18.

. . . To recount these [ballots] manually would be a tall order, but before this Court stayed the effort to do that the courts of Florida were ready to do their best to get that job done. There is no justification for denying the State the opportunity to try to count all disputed ballots now. I respectfully dissent.

JUSTICE GINSBURG, with whom JUSTICE STEVENS joins, and with whom JUSTICE SOUTER and JUSTICE BREYER join as to Part I, dissenting.

# I

THE CHIEF JUSTICE acknowledges that provisions of Florida's Election Code "may well admit of more than one interpretation." But instead of respecting the state high court's province to say what the State's Election Code means, THE CHIEF JUSTICE maintains that Florida's Supreme Court has veered so far from the ordinary practice of judicial review that what it did cannot properly be called judging. . . . I might join THE CHIEF JUSTICE were it my commission to interpret Florida law. But disagreement with the Florida court's interpretation of its own State's law does not warrant the conclusion that the justices of that court have legislated. There is no cause here to believe that the members of Florida's high court have done less than "their mortal best to discharge their oath of office," and no cause to upset their reasoned interpretation of Florida law. . . .

The extraordinary setting of this case has obscured the ordinary principle that dictates its proper resolution: Federal courts defer to state high courts' interpretations of their State's own law. This principle reflects the core of federalism, on which all agree. . . .

THE CHIEF JUSTICE's solicitude for the Florida Legislature comes at the expense of the more fundamental solicitude we owe to the legislature's sovereign.

Were the other members of this Court as mindful as they generally are of our system of dual sovereignty, they would affirm the judgment of the Florida Supreme Court.

# II

I agree with JUSTICE STEVENS that petitioners have not presented a substantial equal protection claim. Ideally, perfection would be the appropriate standard for judging the recount. But we live in an imperfect world, one in which thousands of votes have not been counted. I cannot agree that the recount adopted by the Florida court, flawed as it may be, would yield a result any less fair or precise than the certification that preceded that recount. . . .

Even if there were an equal protection violation, I would agree with JUSTICE STEVENS, JUSTICE SOUTER, and JUSTICE BREYER that the Court's concern about the December 12 date is misplaced. Time is short in part because of the Court's entry of a stay on December 9, several hours after an able circuit judge in Leon County had begun to superintend the recount process. More fundamentally, the Court's reluctance to let the recount go forward . . . ultimately turns on its own judgment about the practical realities of implementing a recount, not the judgment of those much closer to the process.

. . . In sum, the Court's conclusion that a constitutionally adequate recount is impractical is a prophecy the Court's own judgment will not allow to be tested. Such an untested prophecy should not decide the Presidency of the United States.

I dissent.

JUSTICE BREYER, with whom JUSTICE STEVENS and JUSTICE GINSBURG join except as to Part I–A–1, and with whom JUSTICE SOUTER joins as to Part I, dissenting.

The Court was wrong to take this case. It was wrong to grant a stay. It should now vacate that stay and permit the Florida Supreme Court to decide whether the recount should resume.

# I

The political implications of this case for the country are momentous. But the federal legal questions presented, with one exception, are insubstantial.

# A

## 1

The majority raises three Equal Protection problems with the Florida Supreme Court's recount order: first, the failure to include overvotes in the manual recount; second, the fact that all ballots, rather than simply the undervotes, were recounted in some, but not all, counties; and third, the absence of a uniform, specific standard to guide the recounts. As far as the first issue is concerned, petitioners presented no evidence, to this Court or to any Florida court, that a manual recount of overvotes would identify additional legal votes. The same is true of the second, and, in addition, the majority's reasoning would seem to invalidate any state provision for a manual recount of individual counties in a statewide election.

The majority's third concern does implicate principles of fundamental fairness. The majority concludes that the Equal Protection Clause requires that a manual recount be governed not only by the uniform general standard of the "clear intent of the voter," but also by uniform subsidiary standards. . . . I agree that, in these very special circumstances, basic principles of fairness should have counseled the adoption of a uniform standard to address the problem. In light of the majority's disposition, I need not decide whether, or the extent to which, as a remedial matter, the Constitution would place limits upon the content of the uniform standard.

## 2

Nonetheless, there is no justification for the majority's remedy, which is simply to reverse the lower court and halt the recount entirely. An appropriate remedy would be, instead, to remand this case with instructions that, even at this late date, would permit the Florida Supreme Court to require recounting all undercounted votes in Florida, including those from Broward, Volusia, Palm Beach, and Miami-Dade Counties, whether or not previously recounted prior to the end of the protest period, and to do so in accordance with a single-uniform substandard.

The majority justifies stopping the recount entirely on the ground that there is no more time. In particular, the majority relies on the lack of time for the Secretary to review and approve equipment needed to separate undervotes.

But the majority reaches this conclusion in the absence of any record evidence that the recount could not have been completed in the time allowed by the Florida Supreme Court. The majority finds facts outside of the record on matters that state courts are in a far better position to address. Of course, it is too late for any such recount to take place by December 12, the date by which election disputes must be decided if a State is to take advantage of the safe harbor provisions of 3 U.S.C. §5.

Whether there is time to conduct a recount prior to December 18, when the electors are scheduled to meet, is a matter for the state courts to determine. And whether, under Florida law, Florida could or could not take further action is obviously a matter for Florida courts, not this Court, to decide. . . .

By halting the manual recount, and thus ensuring that the uncounted legal votes will not be counted under any standard, this Court crafts a remedy out of proportion to the asserted harm. And that remedy harms the very fairness interests the Court is attempting to protect. The manual recount would itself redress a problem of unequal treatment of ballots. As JUSTICE STEVENS points out, the ballots of voters in counties that use punch-card systems are more likely to be disqualified than those in counties using optical-scanning systems. According to recent news reports, variations in the undervote rate are even more pronounced. . . . Thus, in a system that allows counties to use different types of voting systems, voters already arrive at the polls with an unequal chance that their votes will be counted. I do not see how the fact that this results from counties' selection of different voting machines rather than a court order makes the outcome any more fair. Nor do I understand why the Florida Supreme Court's recount order, which helps to redress this inequity, must be entirely prohibited based on a deficiency that could easily be remedied.

**B**

The remainder of petitioners' claims, which are the focus of the CHIEF JUSTICE's concurrence, raise no significant federal questions. I cannot agree that the CHIEF JUSTICE's unusual review of state law in this case is justified by reference either to Art. II, §1, or to 3 U.S.C. §5.

Moreover, even were such review proper, the conclusion that the Florida Supreme Court's decision contravenes federal law is untenable. . . .

**II**

Despite the reminder that this case involves "an election for the President of the United States," no preeminent legal concern, or practical concern related to legal questions, required this Court to hear this case, let alone to issue a stay that stopped Florida's recount process in its tracks. With one exception, petitioners' claims do not ask us to vindicate a constitutional provision designed to protect a basic human right. Petitioners invoke fundamental fairness, namely, the need for procedural fairness, including finality. But with the one "equal protection" exception, they rely upon law that focuses, not upon that basic need, but upon the constitutional allocation of power. Respondents invoke a competing fundamental consideration—the need to determine the voter's true intent. But they look to state law, not to federal constitutional law, to protect that interest.

Neither side claims electoral fraud, dishonesty, or the like. And the more fundamental equal protection claim might have been left to the state court to resolve if and when it was discovered to have mattered. It could still be re- solved through a remand conditioned upon issuance of a uniform standard; it does not require reversing the Florida Supreme Court. Of course, the selection of the President is of fundamental national importance. But that importance is political, not legal. And this Court should resist the temptation unnecessarily to resolve tangential legal disputes, where doing so threatens to determine the outcome of the election.

The Constitution and federal statutes themselves make clear that restraint is appropriate. They set forth a road map of how to resolve disputes about electors, even after an election as close as this one. That road map foresees resolution of electoral disputes by state courts. See 3 U.S.C. §5 (providing that, where a "State shall have provided, by laws enacted prior to [election day], for its final determination of any controversy or contest concerning the appoint- ment of . . . electors . . . by judicial or other methods," the subsequently cho- sen electors enter a safe harbor free from congressional challenge). But it nowhere provides for involvement by the United States Supreme Court. To the contrary, the Twelfth Amendment commits to Congress the authority and re- sponsibility to count electoral votes. A federal statute, the Electoral Count Act, enacted after the close 1876 Hayes-Tilden Presidential election, speci- fies that, after States have tried to resolve disputes (through "judicial" or other means), Congress is the body primarily authorized to resolve remaining disputes. . . .

Given this detailed, comprehensive scheme for counting electoral votes, there is no reason to believe that federal law either foresees or requires reso- lution of such a political issue by this Court. Nor, for that matter, is there any reason to . . . think [that] the Constitution's Framers would have reached a dif- ferent conclusion. Madison, at least, believed that allowing the judiciary to choose the presidential electors "was out of the question." The decision by both the Constitution's Framers and the 1886 Congress to minimize this Court's role in resolving close federal presidential elections is as wise as it is clear.

However awkward or difficult it may be for Congress to resolve difficult electoral disputes, Congress, being a political body, expresses the people's will far more accurately than does an unelected Court. And the people's will is what elections are about.

. . . I think it not only legally wrong, but also most unfortunate, for the Court simply to have terminated the Florida recount. Those who caution judicial re- straint in resolving political disputes have described the quintessential case for that restraint as a case marked, among other things, by the "strangeness of the issue," its "intractability to principled resolution," its "sheer momentous- ness . . . which tends to unbalance judicial judgment," and "the inner vulner- ability, the self-doubt of an institution which is electorally irresponsible and has no earth to draw strength from." Those characteristics mark this case.

At the same time, as I have said, the Court is not acting to vindicate a fundamental constitutional principle, such as the need to protect a basic human liberty. No other strong reason to act is present. Congressional statutes tend to obviate the need. And, above all, in this highly politicized matter, the appearance of a split decision runs the risk of undermining the public's confidence in the Court itself. That confidence is a public treasure. It has been built slowly over many years, some of which were marked by a Civil War and the tragedy of segregation. It is a vitally necessary ingredient of any successful effort to protect basic liberty and, indeed, the rule of law itself. We run no risk of returning to the days when a President (responding to this Court's efforts to protect the Cherokee Indians) might have said, "John Marshall has made his decision; now let him enforce it!" But we do risk a self-inflicted wound—a wound that may harm not just the Court, but the Nation.

I fear that in order to bring this agonizingly long election process to a definitive conclusion, we have not adequately attended to that necessary "check upon our own exercise of power," "our own sense of self-restraint." *United States v. Butler* (1936) (Stone, J., dissenting). Justice Brandeis once said of the Court, "The most important thing we do is not doing." What it does today, the Court should have left undone. I would repair the damage as best we now can, by permitting the Florida recount to continue under uniform standards. I respectfully dissent.

# GORE CONCESSION SPEECH, BUSH VICTORY SPEECH
## December 13, 2000

*In a graceful speech that put an end to thirty-six days of uncertainty about the future leadership of the United States, Vice President Al Gore conceded the 2000 presidential election to Republican Texas governor George W. Bush. Gore's nationally televised concession speech came on the evening of December 13, 2000, just one day after the Supreme Court of the United States voted 5–4 to stop a manual count of thousands of contested votes in Florida. Gore's decision to end further challenges in the state gave Florida's twenty-five electoral votes—and the presidency—to Bush, who was ahead by 537 votes in the official count. On December 18, electors cast 271 votes for Bush and 266 for Gore, ratifying Bush as the president-elect. (One "faithless elector" pledged to Gore abstained to protest the District of Columbia's lack of voting representation in Congress.) Gore had won the national popular vote by some 577,000 votes. (Supreme Court ruling, p. 999)*

*"Let there be no doubt," Gore said, "while I strongly disagree with the Court's decision, I accept it. . . . And tonight, for the sake of our unity as a people and the strength of our democracy, I offer my concession." An hour later, Bush addressed the nation for the first time as president-elect. He paid tribute to Gore and called on Americans to reconcile their political differences and move forward in unity. "Our nation must rise above a house divided," Bush said from the chamber of the Texas House of Representatives. "Americans share hopes and goals and values far more important than any political disagreements. Republicans want the best for our nation. So do Democrats. Our votes may differ, but not our hopes."*

*For Americans and for nations around the globe, the two speeches were a powerful reaffirmation of the peaceful transition of power that took place in the United States since George Washington first turned over the presidency to John Adams in 1796. Only three presidents before Bush had won the presidency without winning the popular vote—John Quincy Adams (also the only other son of a former president to win the office) in 1824, Rutherford B. Hayes in 1876, and Benjamin Harrison in 1888. None of the three won a second term, although all three sought reelection.*

*Although Gore's lead in the popular vote was slim, in 1960 and 1968 the vote was even closer. In 1960 John F. Kennedy led Richard Nixon by 115,000 votes; in 1968 Nixon beat Hubert H. Humphrey by 511,000 votes. But the winners of the popular votes in those elections also won the electoral college vote decisively. In the 2000 election the loser of the popular vote won the presidency in the electoral college by a single vote after being declared the winner by 537 votes in a state where several thousand ballots that might have changed the outcome remained uncounted.*

## Gore's Decision to Concede

*Even after the Supreme Court announced its controversial decision on December 12, some of Gore's advisers counseled him to continue the fight to have all the Florida ballots counted. The ruling had left one small opening that some of Gore's attorneys thought might be exploited to Gore's advantage. But the vice president's political advisers questioned whether the country would tolerate a prolonged dispute and the uncertainty of not knowing who would take the oath of office on January 20, 2001. Gore reportedly spent much of the night sifting through his options. At 10:00 A.M. on December 13, his campaign manager, William Daley, issued a two-sentence statement indicating that Gore was calling a halt to his campaign and would address the nation that evening.*

*In his speech Gore candidly admitted his disappointment in the outcome of the election and referred to the "continuing differences" between the two parties. But he called on all Americans, particularly those who supported his campaign, to unite behind Bush. "While we yet hold and do not yield our opposing beliefs," Gore said, "there is a higher duty than the one we owe to political party. This is America and we put country before party. We will stand together behind our new president."*

*"This has got to be excruciatingly painful" for Gore, retiring senator Bob Kerrey (D-Neb.) told the* New York Times. *"There's a lot of ifs, ands, or buts for him that could have made him president." One of those "ifs" was the third-party candidacy of consumer advocate Ralph Nader, who ran under the progressive Green Party banner and drew more than 90,000 votes in Florida. According to exit polls, about one-third of those who voted for Nader said they would have voted for Gore had Nader not been in the race. Democrats who before November 7 had begged Nader to quit the presidential election to avoid throwing the election to Bush now blamed the consumer advocate for costing the Democrats the White House.* (Nader candidacy, p. 895)

*Many Democrats blamed Gore for running an inept campaign, noting that a stronger run not only might have captured the presidency but returned the Democrats to the majority in Congress. As a result of the election, the Senate was evenly divided, with Republicans holding the balance of power by virtue of the Republican vice president's authority to break tie votes. The Republicans had a nine-seat majority in the House. Gore failed to win his own state of Tennessee or President Bill Clinton's home state of Arkansas. Victories in either of those states would have given Gore enough electoral college votes to win the election. Some Democrats, reportedly in-*

*cluding Clinton, said Gore could have made more effective use of the presi-dent during the campaign despite Clinton's liabilities among some voters. Others said Gore failed to capitalize on the achievements of the Clinton ad-ministration, particularly the strong economy that had produced millions of new jobs, low unemployment, and low inflation for nearly ten years.*

*Although the last three Democrats to lose a presidential election—George McGovern in 1972, Walter F. Mondale in 1984, and Michael S. Dukakis in 1988—were never again serious contenders for the office, Gore appeared to leave the door open to making another run for the presidency in 2004. In his concession speech, he said he did not know what he would do next but that he planned to spend some time mending fences "literally and figuratively" in Tennessee. He also said that his one regret was "that I didn't get the chance to stay and fight for the American people over the next four years."*

## The Bush Transition

*In his subdued victory speech, Bush too called on Americans to put aside their political differences and unite behind his presidency. In return, he promised to be the president "of every single American, of every single race and every background. Whether you voted for me or not, I will do my best to serve your interests, and I will work to earn your respect."*

*Given the continuing questions about the legitimacy of his elevation to the presidency, the lack of a clear mandate from the voters, and the paper-thin Republican majorities in Congress, political pundits predicted that Bush would have to "govern from the middle"—that is, select Cabinet mem-bers and advance legislative proposals that could attract support from mod-erates on both sides of the aisles. Some speculated that Bush would be forced, for example, to trim back his proposed massive tax cut and to choose Cabi-net members that would pass muster with at least some Democrats as well as Republicans.*

*Early actions of the Bush transition team indicated that the conventional wisdom was wrong and that the president-elect was prepared to govern as if he had won a landslide victory and the voters had soundly endorsed his campaign platform. "The governor is committed to the programs on which he ran," Ari Fleischer, Bush's transition spokesman, told the* Washington Post *in mid-December. "The ability to govern and enact an agenda derives more from the actions of the officeholder than from the margins of an elec-tion." Even before the election was resolved, Bush himself indicated an un-willingness to compromise on the main points of his campaign platform. "I feel one of the reasons I'm sitting here is because of the agenda, and it was a clear agenda," Bush said at the beginning of December.*

*Bush's early Cabinet selections indicated that he did not feel obligated to appeal only to the political middle. The Cabinet members Bush had chosen by the end of the year included women, African Americans, Hispanics, and Asians. One, Norman Minetta, a former member of the U.S. House from California, was a Democrat. Some of Bush's picks were political moderates, such as Colin Powell, the retired army general that Bush named to head the State Department, and Christie Whitman, the governor of New Jersey who was tapped to head the Environmental Protection Agency. But other choices seemed calculated to appeal primarily to political conservatives. Chief among these was former senator John Ashcroft (R-Mo.), who had lost his bid for reelection to the Senate in November. One of the Republican Party's leading social conservatives, Ashcroft was a staunch foe of abortion rights and an equally staunch supporter of the death penalty. His nomination was immediately attacked by blacks and others who were still angry with Ashcroft for his role in defeating the nomination for a federal judgeship of a black state judge in Missouri in 1999. The nomination seemed certain to alienate the black community, which was already upset because a large proportion of the uncounted disputed votes in Florida had been cast by African Americans. Conservative leaders said they were delighted with Ashcroft's nomination; liberal organizations vowed to challenge the nomination at Senate confirmation hearings.*

*Following are the texts of speeches delivered December 13, 2000, by Vice President Al Gore conceding the 2000 presidential election to Texas governor George W. Bush and by Bush a short time later asking the American people to put politics aside and unite behind his presidency. The documents were obtained from the Internet at http://www.democrats.org/election2000/gore121300/index.html and http://www.rnc.org/newsroom1/1214_103.htm.*

# GORE'S CONCESSION SPEECH

Just moments ago, I spoke with George W. Bush and congratulated him on becoming the 43rd president of the United States. And I promised I wouldn't call him back this time.

I offered to meet with him as soon as possible, so that we can start to heal the divisions of the campaign, and the contest through which we have just passed.

Almost a century and a half ago, Sen. Stephen Douglas told Abraham Lincoln, who had just defeated him for the presidency, "Partisan feeling must yield to patriotism. I am with you, Mr. President, and God bless you."

In that same spirit, I say to President-elect Bush that what remains of partisan rancor must now be put aside. And may God bless his stewardship of this country.

Neither he nor I anticipated this long and difficult road. Certainly, neither of us wanted it to happen. Yet it came. And now it has ended, resolved as it must be resolved—through the honored institutions of our democracy.

Over the library of one of our great law schools is inscribed the motto: "Not under man but under God and law." It is the ruling principle of American freedom, the source of our democratic liberties; I have tried to make it my guide throughout this contest, as it has guided America's deliberations of all the complex issues of the past five weeks.

Now the U.S. Supreme Court has spoken. Let there be no doubt: While I strongly disagree with the Court's decision, I accept it. I accept the finality of this outcome, which will be ratified next Monday in the Electoral College. And tonight, for the sake of our unity as a people and the strength of our democracy, I offer my concession.

I also accept my responsibility, which I will discharge unconditionally—to honor the new president-elect, and do everything possible to help him bring Americans together in fulfillment of the great vision that our Declaration of Independence defines, and that our Constitution affirms and defends. Let me say how grateful I am to all those who supported me—and supported the cause for which we have fought.

Tipper and I feel a deep gratitude to Joe and Hadassah Lieberman, who brought passion and high purpose to our partnership—and opened new doors not just for our campaign, but for our country.

This has been an extraordinary election. But in one of God's unforeseen paths, this belatedly broken impasse can point us all to a new common ground. For its very closeness can serve to remind us that we are one people, with a shared history and a shared destiny.

Indeed, that history gives us many examples of contests as hotly debated, as fiercely fought, with their own challenges to the popular will.

Other disputes have dragged on for weeks before reaching resolution. And each time, both the victor and the vanquished have accepted the result peacefully, and in a spirit of reconciliation.

So let it be with us.

I know that many of my supporters are disappointed. I am, too. But our disappointment must be overcome by our love of country.

And I say to our fellow members of the world community: Let no one see this contest as a sign of American weakness. The strength of American democracy is shown most clearly through the difficulties it can overcome.

Some have expressed concern that the unusual nature of this election might hamper the next president in the conduct of his office. I do not believe it need be so.

President-elect Bush inherits a nation whose citizens will be ready to assist him in the conduct of his large responsibilities. I personally will be at his disposal.

And I call on all Americans—I particularly urge all who stood with us—to unite behind our next president.

This is America. Just as we fight hard when the stakes are high, we close ranks and come together when the contest is done.

And while there will be time enough to debate our continuing differences, now is the time to recognize that that which unites us is greater than that which divides us.

While we yet hold and do not yield our opposing beliefs, there is a higher duty than the one we owe to political party.

This is America, and we put country before party. We will stand together behind our new president.

As for what I'll do next, I don't know the answer to that one yet. Like many of you, I'm looking forward to spending the holidays with family and old friends. I know I'll spend time in Tennessee and mend some fences—literally and figuratively.

Some have asked whether I have any regrets, and I do have one regret: that I didn't get the chance to stay and fight for the American people for the next four years. Especially for those who need burdens lifted and barriers removed. Especially for those who feel their voices have not been heard.

I heard you—and I will not forget.

I've seen America in this campaign. And I like what I see. It's worth fighting for. And that's a fight I'll never stop.

As for the battle that ends tonight, I do believe, as my father once said, that no matter how hard the loss, defeat may serve as well as victory to shake the soul and let the glory out.

So for me, this campaign ends as it began: with the love of Tipper and our family; with faith in God and in the country I have been so proud to serve, from Vietnam to the vice presidency; and with gratitude to our truly tireless campaign staff and volunteers, including all those who worked so hard in Florida for the last 36 days.

Now the political struggle is over. And we turn again to the unending struggle for the common good of all Americans, and for those multitudes around the world who look to us for leadership in the cause of freedom.

In the words of our great hymn, "America, America, let us crown thy good with brotherhood, from sea to shining sea."

And now, my friends, in a phrase I once addressed to others—it is time for me to go.

Thank you, and good night. And God bless America.

## BUSH'S VICTORY SPEECH

Thank you all. Thank you very much. Good evening, my fellow Americans. I appreciate so very much the opportunity to speak with you tonight.

Mr. Speaker, Lieutenant Governor, friends, distinguished guests, our country has been through a long and trying period, with the outcome of the presidential election not finalized for longer than any of us could ever imagine.

Vice President Gore and I put our hearts and hopes into our campaigns. We both gave it our all. We shared similar emotions, so I understand how difficult this moment must be for Vice President Gore and his family.

He has a distinguished record of service to our country as a congressman, a senator and a vice president.

This evening I received a gracious call from the vice president. We agreed to meet early next week in Washington, and we agreed to do our best to heal our country after this hard-fought contest.

Tonight I want to thank all the thousands of volunteers and campaign workers who worked so hard on my behalf.

I also salute the vice president and his supporters for waging a spirited campaign. And I thank him for a call that I know was difficult to make. Laura and I wish the vice president and Sen. [Joseph I.] Lieberman and their families the very best.

I have a lot to be thankful for tonight. I'm thankful for America, and thankful that we were able to resolve our electoral differences in a peaceful way.

I'm thankful to the American people for the great privilege of being able to serve as your next president.

I want to thank my wife and our daughters for their love. Laura's active involvement as first lady has made Texas a better place, and she will be a wonderful first lady of America.

I am proud to have Dick Cheney by my side, and America will be proud to have him as our next vice president.

Tonight I chose to speak from the chamber of the Texas House of Representatives because it has been a home to bipartisan cooperation. Here in a place where Democrats have the majority, Republicans and Democrats have worked together to do what is right for the people we represent.

We've had spirited disagreements. And in the end, we found constructive consensus. It is an experience I will always carry with me, an example I will always follow.

I want to thank my friend, House Speaker Pete Laney, a Democrat, who introduced me today. I want to thank the legislators from both political parties with whom I've worked.

Across the hall in our Texas capitol is the state Senate. And I cannot help but think of our mutual friend, the former Democrat lieutenant governor, Bob Bullock. His love for Texas and his ability to work in a bipartisan way continue to be a model for all of us.

The spirit of cooperation I have seen in this hall is what is needed in Washington, D.C. It is the challenge of our moment. After a difficult election, we must put politics behind us and work together to make the promise of America available for every one of our citizens.

I am optimistic that we can change the tone in Washington, D.C.

I believe things happen for a reason, and I hope the long wait of the last five weeks will heighten a desire to move beyond the bitterness and partisanship of the recent past.

Our nation must rise above a house divided. Americans share hopes and goals and values far more important than any political disagreements.

Republicans want the best for our nation, and so do Democrats. Our votes may differ, but not our hopes.

I know America wants reconciliation and unity. I know Americans want progress. And we must seize this moment and deliver.

Together, guided by a spirit of common sense, common courtesy and common goals, we can unite and inspire the American citizens.

Together, we will work to make all our public schools excellent, teaching every student of every background and every accent, so that no child is left behind.

Together we will save Social Security and renew its promise of a secure retirement for generations to come.

Together we will strengthen Medicare and offer prescription drug coverage to all of our seniors.

Together we will give Americans the broad, fair and fiscally responsible tax relief they deserve.

Together we'll have a bipartisan foreign policy true to our values and true to our friends, and we will have a military equal to every challenge and superior to every adversary.

Together we will address some of society's deepest problems one person at a time, by encouraging and empowering the good hearts and good works of the American people.

This is the essence of compassionate conservatism, and it will be a foundation of my administration.

These priorities are not merely Republican concerns or Democratic concerns; they are American responsibilities.

During the fall campaign, we differed about the details of these proposals, but there was remarkable consensus about the important issues before us: excellent schools, retirement and health security, tax relief, a strong military, a more civil society.

We have discussed our differences. Now it is time to find common ground and build consensus to make America a beacon of opportunity in the 21st century.

I'm optimistic this can happen. Our future demands it, and our history proves it. Two hundred years ago, in the election of 1800, America faced another close presidential election. A tie in the Electoral College put the outcome into the hands of Congress.

After six days of voting and 36 ballots, the House of Representatives elected Thomas Jefferson the third president of the United States. That election brought the first transfer of power from one party to another in our new democracy.

Shortly after the election, Jefferson, in a letter titled "Reconciliation and Reform," wrote this: "The steady character of our countrymen is a rock to which we may safely moor; unequivocal in principle, reasonable in manner. We should be able to hope to do a great deal of good to the cause of freedom and harmony."

Two hundred years have only strengthened the steady character of America. And so as we begin the work of healing our nation, tonight I call upon that character: respect for each other; respect for our differences; generosity of spirit, and a willingness to work hard and work together to solve any problem.

I have something else to ask you, to ask every American. I ask for you to pray for this great nation. I ask for your prayers for leaders from both parties. I thank you for your prayers for me and my family, and I ask you to pray for Vice President Gore and his family.

I have faith that with God's help we as a nation will move forward together as one nation, indivisible. And together we will create an America that is open, so every citizen has access to the American dream; an America that is educated, so every child has the keys to realize that dream; and an America that is united in our diversity and our shared American values that are larger than race or party.

I was not elected to serve one party, but to serve one nation.

The president of the United States is the president of every single American, of every race and every background.

Whether you voted for me or not, I will do my best to serve your interests and I will work to earn your respect.

I will be guided by President Jefferson's sense of purpose, to stand for principle, to be reasonable in manner, and above all, to do great good for the cause of freedom and harmony.

The presidency is more than an honor. It is more than an office. It is a charge to keep, and I will give it my all.

Thank you very much and God bless America.

# FEDERAL TRADE COMMISSION ON THE AOL-TIME WARNER MERGER
## December 14, 2000

*The worlds of "old" media and "new" media came together as never before in 2000 with a corporate merger that created the world's biggest communications company. America Online (AOL), the world's largest Internet service, and Time Warner, one of the biggest producers of movies, music recordings, books, and magazines, joined forces in a deal that had the potential to change the distribution and marketing of communications services for years to come. U.S. and European regulators approved the merger after adding conditions intended to protect consumers and thwart unfair competition.*

*The merger creating AOL Time Warner Inc. was the biggest and most controversial of dozens of major corporate mergers announced during the year. Other mergers that were proposed or completed in 2000 would bring together some of the most familiar names in American business, including Chevron and Texaco, United Airways and US Air, and Nabisco and Phillip Morris. One controversial merger did not happen as planned: the Justice Department and the European Union (EU) successfully blocked a merger between long-distance telephone carriers WorldCom (itself the product of numerous mergers in the 1980s and 1990s) and Sprint.*

### AOL-Time Warner

*The January 10 announcement of the merger of AOL and Time Warner represented a major coup for AOL, a company that had been in business for just fifteen years and had seen numerous obituary notices written about it—prematurely, it turned out—during the mid-1990s. The purchase was made possible by AOL's enormous market value, which had soared, along with other Internet-related companies, during the late 1990s. On January 10, AOL had a total market value of $189.6 billion, dwarfing that of Time Warner's $129 billion, despite the fact that the latter was a much larger company. The value of the transaction was variously estimated at $165 billion to $183 billion; whichever figure was used, in dollar terms it was by far the biggest merger in U.S. history.*

*Just six weeks after the merger was announced, Wall Street investors began selling off high-technology companies such as AOL. On the day the merger was announced, AOL stock closed at $72.63 a share. AOL share prices fell immediately and kept falling most of the rest of the year. By mid-December the stock stood at $50, a decline of 31 percent, putting the company's total market value at $130.2 billion. Time Warner stock also suffered during the year, but to a lesser degree. The company's shares traded at $92.25 on the day the merger was announced; in mid-December they stood at $74.40, a drop of 19 percent, for a total market value of $98.7 billion. The combined value of the two firms had fallen $89.7 billion in ten months.* (High-tech stock sell-offs, p. 302)

*AOL was by far the biggest provider of Internet access service in the world; as of 2000 it had more than 26 million subscribers. It already had acquired two major Internet rivals: CompuServe and Netscape. Time Warner was the second-biggest cable television service in the United States, with 12.6 million customers, second only to AT&T. Time Warner also owned some of the best-known media products in the country:* Time, Sports Illustrated, *and* People *magazines; the Warner Brothers movie and television studio; Cable News Network; and Home Box Office.*

*The enormous size and sweeping nature of the deal ensured that it would encounter opposition. Leading consumer groups and some of the most important media and technology companies in the United States filed objections to the proposed merger, including AT&T, Microsoft Corporation, and the Walt Disney Company. Time Warner heightened public concern about the deal and drew increased attention from federal regulators, when for two days in May it blocked ABC programming from about 3.5 million homes. The action was the result of a contractual dispute between Time Warner and ABC's parent company, Walt Disney. Many observers worried that Time Warner's use of such strong-arm tactics against another major corporation could be a harbinger of how an even bigger AOL Time Warner might use its enormous market power to bludgeon competitors both large and small.*

*The deal faced three major regulatory reviews, by the Federal Trade Commission (FTC), the Federal Communications Commission (FCC), and the EU. The Europeans were the first to act, approving the merger on October 11 after forcing Time Warner to drop its plan to acquire the British-based record label, the EMI Group.*

*In the United States, attention focused on the FTC, which had broad authority to block the merger on antitrust grounds. Several FTC members, including chairman Robert Pitofsky, had signaled that they were deeply concerned about several aspects of the merger. The agency's main concern was that the combined company might prohibit other Internet providers— AOL's competitors—from offering their services over Time Warner's cable system.*

*After negotiations that took several months, the FTC approved the merger on December 14, based on AOL Time Warner's acceptance of several conditions. A key condition was that the company allow at least three other Internet service providers to use each of its local cable systems. In a move to comply with that requirement, the company on November 20 signed a deal allowing EarthLink (the number two Internet access provider) to use Time Warner cable lines in the major markets it served (such as New York City and Los Angeles). The FTC approved that deal and required AOL Time Warner to offer arrangements at least as favorable as that one to other Internet providers in smaller markets.*

*The FTC also required the company to allow competition in an emerging market called "interactive television" service, which would allow consumers to buy products even as they were being advertised. Under the order, AOL Time Warner was required to allow competing companies to provide that service over its cable systems. Similarly, the FTC required AOL to offer a type of high-speed Internet access over telephone lines, known as "digital subscriber lines" (DSL), in places where the company also was offering Internet access over cable lines.*

*The FTC regulation came in the form of a "consent agreement" under which AOL Time Warner pledged to abide by the restrictions for a period of five years. The FTC said it would appoint a "monitor trustee" to observe the company's compliance with the decree. Announcing the order, FTC chairman Pitofsky said the order was "intended to ensure that this new medium, characterized by openness, diversity, and freedom, will not be closed down as a result" of a major merger.*

*Representatives of consumer groups and corporate rivals to AOL Time Warner expressed satisfaction with the FTC restrictions. Gene Kimmelman, a co-director of Consumers Union, praised the FTC for going beyond what other government agencies had done in terms of opening access to cable services. The decision, he said, "has finally required cable monopolies to open their wires to high-speed Internet competition." That view was challenged by a spokesman for the cable television industry, however, who said the FTC's rules would not apply to any company other than AOL Time Warner. Preston Padden, chief Washington lobbyist for Walt Disney, expressed satisfaction with the FTC's requirement that AOL Time Warner allow competition on the interactive television market. Noting the FTC's appointment of a trustee to monitor AOL Time Warner's compliance with the rules, Padden told the* New York Times: *"I don't see how we can ask for much more assurance."*

*The FCC gave final regulatory approval to the AOL Time Warner merger on January 11, 2001, one year and one day after the merger was announced. The key action in the FCC review centered around a popular AOL service known as "instant messaging," which allowed users to send instant notes to one another; the service was expected to become a format for Internet users to swap music, video clips, and other files. At the time of the FCC review, AOL did not allow other companies to provide instant messaging over their systems. In its decision, the FCC said that if AOL decided to add new features to its instant messaging service—such as video teleconferencing—it then would have to allow at least one competitor to use its system; within 180 days after signing a contract with that competitor, AOL would have to allow two other competitors into its system. The FCC allowed AOL to seek a waiver from the instant messaging requirement if significant competition developed for that service or if it could prove that competitor's services were not technically compatible.*

*The five FCC commissioners approved the merger on a unanimous vote, but two commissioners opposed the restrictions. One, Michael K. Powell, was generally thought to be in line for the commission chairmanship under the incoming administration of President George W. Bush. Powell had voted in the case even though his father, retired general and secretary-of-state designate Colin Powell, was a member of the AOL board of directors. The younger Powell said he saw no conflict of interest.*

## Other Communications Mergers

*The AOL Time Warner merger was just the biggest of several moves toward consolidation in the Internet and communications industries during the year. Lycos, one of the most important Internet "portal" sites, became the first major U.S. Internet firm to be purchased by a foreign company (Terra Networks, of Spain). Vivendi, a French media conglomerate, and Canada's Seagram conglomerate (owner of Universal Studios) said in July that they would merge to form another giant media company that many observers said could be a strong competitor to AOL Time Warner. The $44 billion Vivendi-Seagram merger overcame its chief regulatory hurdle on October 14 when it was approved by the executive commission of the EU.*

*Two major mergers of U.S. telecommunications companies were approved by regulators during the year, but a third was blocked. The approved mergers were between AT&T (the long-distance carrier) and MediaOne Group Inc., one of the nation's largest cable television companies. Approved on May 25 by the FCC, the $58 billion deal created the nation's biggest cable and broadband access company. The nation's biggest telephone company emerged from a merger between Bell Atlantic and the GTE Corporation. Bell Atlantic, which provided local telephone service for all of the northeast and mid-Atlantic states, later changed its name to Verizon.*

*The Justice Department and the EU both acted to block a merger of long-distance telephone carriers WorldCom and Sprint Corporation. WorldCom had purchased the MCI Corporation in 1998 and controlled about 20 percent of the nation's long-distance market. Sprint had about 8 percent of the market. In a complaint filed on June 28, the Justice Department said that because the two companies were competitors, their $129 billion merger would reduce competition in the long-distance and Internet service markets. Faced with such strong opposition, the companies withdrew their proposed merger on July 14.*

## Other Major Mergers

*Continuing a trend toward consolidation of the oil industry, Chevron announced a plan on October 16 to purchase Texaco, creating the world's fourth largest oil company. The combined company would be known as*

*Chevron Texaco; its combined revenues in 1999 were $66.5 billion. The world's largest oil company, Exxon Mobil, was the product of a merger in 1998, and the third largest, BP Amoco, was the result of a 1999 merger. The number two firm was Royal Dutch/Shell.*

*Some of the best-known American consumer food brands were involved in major corporate mergers during the year. In a deal announced June 25, Phillip Morris—a tobacco company that owned Kraft Foods, producer of such items as Maxwell House coffee, Post cereals, and Jell-O—purchased Nabisco, famous for its snack foods, such as Oreo cookies, Ritz crackers, and LifeSavers candy. The FTC approved the purchase on December 7 after ordering the combined company to sell several small food operations.*

*Two giant Minneapolis food companies—General Mills and Pillsbury—on July 17 announced plans to join forces. General Mills brands included such breakfast cereals as Cheerios, and other food lines including Betty Crocker products, Green Giant vegetables, and Haagen-Daz ice cream. Pillsbury's most famous product was its ready-to-bake cookies and breads.*

*A major step toward consolidation of the airline industry seemed possible with the announcement that UAL Corporation (the parent of United Airlines, the nation's largest air carrier) would purchase most of US Airways Inc. The Justice and Transportation Departments were examining the proposed merger at year's end. Several major competitor airlines, including American, Continental, and Delta, had asked the government to block the merger because it would give United excessive control over several routes, including the profitable East Coast to London route.*

*The world's biggest pharmaceutical company developed from the merger of two British giants, Glaxo Wellcome and SmithKline Beecham. The makers of such products as Zantac, Geritol, and Tums, the firms announced their merger in January; it had a value of $182 billion. The FTC, which had jurisdiction because the companies had significant shares of the U.S. drug market, approved the merger on December 18, after requiring the combined company to sell several product lines. British courts approved the merger two days later.*

> *Following are excerpts from an "analysis" document released November 14, 2000, by the Federal Trade Commission, as an explanation of a "consent agreement" and "decision and order" issued that same day that gave approval, with certain conditions, to the proposed merger between America Online Inc. and Time Warner Inc. The document was obtained from the Internet at http://www.ftc.gov/os/2000/12/aolanalysis.pdf.*

# I. Introduction

The Federal Trade Commission ("Commission") has accepted for public comment from America Online, Inc. ("AOL") and Time Warner Inc. ("Time

Warner") (collectively "Proposed Respondents") an Agreement Containing Consent Orders ("Proposed Consent Agreement"), including the Decision and Order ("Proposed Order"). The Proposed Respondents have also reviewed a draft complaint. The Commission has now issued the complaint and an Order to Hold Separate ("Hold Separate Order"). The Proposed Consent Agreement intends to remedy the likely anticompetitive effects arising from the merger of AOL and Time Warner.

## II. The Parties and the Transaction

AOL is the world's leading internet service provider ("ISP"), providing access to the internet for consumers and businesses. AOL operates two ISPs: America Online, with more than 25 million members; and CompuServe, with more than 2.8 million members. AOL also owns several leading Internet products including AOL Instant Messenger, ICQ, Digital City, MapQuest, and MoviePhone; the AOL. com and Netscape. com portals; the Netscape 6, Netscape Navigator and Communicator browsers; and Spinner. com and NullSoft's Winamp, leaders in Internet music.

Time Warner is the nation's second largest cable television distributor, and one of the leading cable television network providers. Time Warner's cable systems pass approximately 20.9 million homes and serve approximately 12.6 million cable television subscribers, or approximately 20% of U.S. cable television households. Time Warner, or its principally owned subsidiaries, owns leading cable television networks, such as HBO, Cinemax, CNN, TNT, TBS Superstation, Turner Classic Movies and Cartoon Network. Time Warner also owns, directly or through affiliated businesses, a wide conglomeration of entertainment or media businesses. Time Warner's holdings include leading magazine franchises, such as Time, People and Sports Illustrated; copyrighted music from many of the world's leading recording artists that it produces and distributes through a family of established record labels, such as Warner Bros. Records, Atlantic Records, Elektra Entertainment and Warner Music International; the unique and extensive film and animation libraries owned or managed by Warner Bros. and New Line Cinema; and trademarks, such as the Looney Tunes characters, Batman and The Flintstones; the WB Network, a national broadcasting network; and Internet websites, such as CNN. com. Time Warner is the majority owner of Road Runner (the trade name of ServiceCo, LLC), the second largest provider of cable broadband ISP service in the U. S., serving more than 1.1 million subscribers. Road Runner has an exclusive contract to provide cable broadband ISP service via Time Warner's cable systems through December 2001.

On January 10, 2000, AOL and Time Warner entered into an Agreement and Plan of Merger (the "merger"), pursuant to which Time Warner common stockholders will receive 1.5 shares of the combined AOL Time Warner ("combined company," or "AOL Time Warner") for each share of Time Warner common stock they hold. AOL common stockholders will receive one share of common stock of AOL Time Warner for each share of AOL common stock they hold.

## III. The Proposed Complaint

According to the complaint the Commission intends to issue, AOL's merger with Time Warner will have anticompetitive effects in three relevant product markets: (1) the market for broadband Internet access; (2) the market for residential broadband Internet transport services, or last mile access; and (3) the market for interactive television ("ITV") services.

AOL is the dominant narrowband ISP. Its narrowband customer base positions AOL to become a significant broadband ISP competitor as well. Time Warner provides broadband Internet access through Road Runner, a partially owned subsidiary in which it has a controlling interest. AOL and Road Runner are two of the most significant broadband ISP competitors in Time Warner cable areas. According to the Commission's draft complaint, the relevant broadband ISP markets are or are likely to become highly concentrated as a result of the merger, and the merger will increase the ability of the combined firm to unilaterally exercise market power in Time Warner cable areas and throughout the United States. Moreover, new entry is not likely to be timely or sufficient to prevent the combined firm from exercising market power.

In the market for broadband Internet transport services, the Commission's complaint alleges that cable television lines and digital subscriber lines ("DSL") are the two principal means of providing last mile access for broadband ISPs to the customers. Satellite and fixed wireless technologies also provide last mile access, but consumers do not view them as viable alternatives for DSL or cable broadband access. Currently, AOL's principal means of providing broadband access to its subscribers is through DSL, and every broadband subscriber it signs represents a lost revenue opportunity for cable broadband providers. AOL's merger with Time Warner will reduce its incentives to promote and market broadband access through DSL in Time Warner cable areas, adversely affecting DSL rollout in those areas and nationally, and will increase AOL Time Warner's ability to exercise unilateral market power in those areas.

According to the Commission's complaint, ITV combines television programming with Internet functionality. Cable television lines have distinct competitive advantages over DSL in providing ITV services to broadband customers. AOL recently launched AOL TV, a first generation ITV service, and is well positioned to become the leading ITV provider. Local cable companies will play the key role in enabling the delivery of ITV services. After the merger, AOL Time Warner will have incentives to prevent or deter rival ITV providers from competing with AOL's ITV service. Thus, the merger could enable AOL to exercise unilateral market power in the market for ITV services in Time Warner cable areas, which also affects the ability of ITV providers to compete nationally.

## IV. Terms of the Proposed Order

The Proposed Order is effective for a term of five years and resolves the Commission's antitrust concerns with the merger as discussed below.

## A. Broadband Internet Access Services

Under the terms of the Proposed Order, before Time Warner can make AOL's broadband ISP service available in certain identified cable divisions representing over 70 percent of Time Warner's cable customers ("Identified Cable Divisions") [the identified cable divisions to which this provision applies are: New York City, Tampa Bay, Central Florida, Houston, Raleigh/Fayetteville, Western Ohio, Northern Ohio, Charlotte, Los Angeles, Milwaukee, Greensboro, Hawaii, Cincinnati, San Antonio, Syracuse, Kansas City, South Carolina, Columbus, Rochester, Albany, and any other cable division with 300,000 subscribers or more that is controlled by Respondents], Time Warner must first make available cable broadband service offered by Earthlink, Inc. pursuant to an agreement between Time Warner and Earthlink that the Commission has evaluated and approved.

In addition, Respondents cannot begin to advertise or promote AOL's broadband ISP service to subscribers in a cable division until Earthlink's competing ISP service is available to subscribers in that cable division or Earthlink advertises or promotes its service in that cable division, whichever occurs first. These provisions ensure that a competing ISP service, which is not affiliated with AOL Time Warner, is available to subscribers in most Time Warner cable areas at the same time that AOL introduces its cable broadband ISP service. It does not prevent Time Warner from conducting tests involving a limited number of subscribers that are purely for technological and operational implementation purposes, rather than for commercial purposes.

Within 90 days of making AOL's broadband ISP service available to subscribers, Time Warner must enter into agreements to carry at least two other non-affiliated broadband ISPs to provide cable broadband ISP services in the Identified Cable Divisions. The non-affiliated ISPs, and Time Warner's agreements with them, must receive the prior approval of the Commission. If Time Warner fails to enter into such agreements within this time period, the Commission may appoint a trustee who will have the authority to enter into such agreements on Time Warner's behalf. These agreements must also receive the prior approval of the Commission. These agreements must be on terms comparable to either the Earthlink agreement, or any agreement between AOL and another cable system to provide AOL's cable broadband ISP service over that cable system. [This provision applies to the following cable systems: Adelphia, AT&T, Cablevision, Charter, Comcast, and Cox.]

In Time Warner's other cable divisions, Time Warner must enter into cable broadband ISP service agreements that have received the prior approval of the Commission with at least three other non-affiliated ISPs that have received the prior approval of the Commission within 90 days of making AOL's cable broadband ISP service available in each such division. If Time Warner fails to enter into such agreements within this time period, the Commission may appoint a trustee who will have the authority to enter into such agreements, which will be subject to the prior approval of the Commission. These agreements must be on terms comparable to either another alternative cable broadband ISP service agreement between a broadband ISP and the Proposed

Respondents approved by the Commission, or any agreement between AOL and another cable system to provide AOL's cable broadband ISP service over that cable company's system.

The Proposed Order requires Time Warner to include several provisions in the agreements it negotiates with the non-affiliated ISPs. Specifically:

- Time Warner must include a most favored nation ("MFN") clause in all alternative cable broadband ISP service agreements submitted to the Commission for approval. The MFN must provide that if AOL executes a cable broadband ISP service agreement with another cable system operator, Respondents must provide a copy of the agreement with that cable system operator to a Monitor Trustee appointed by the Commission; give notice of the execution of the agreement to each non-affiliated ISPs that is a party to an alternative cable broadband ISP service agreement approved by the Commission; and give the non-affiliated ISPs the ability to convert to all of the rates and terms in the cable system operator's agreement;

- Time Warner must also include in all alternative cable broadband ISP service agreements submitted to the Commission for approval a requirement that if Proposed Respondents makes available different levels of service to their affiliated ISPs, they must make those levels of service available to non-affiliated ISPs;

- Time Warner must also include in all alternative cable broadband ISP service agreements submitted to the Commission for approval a requirement that if Proposed Respondents make available any network flow monitoring data or usage accounting to any of their affiliated ISPs , they must make that same data or accounting available to non-affiliated ISPs;

- Time Warner must also include in all alternative cable broadband ISP service agreements, at the option of the non-affiliated ISP, a requirement that disputes concerning compliance with the rates, terms, and conditions of that agreement shall be submitted to binding arbitration; and

- If requested by a non-affiliated ISP, Time Warner must provide the non-affiliated ISPs with the same point of connection within Time Warner's cable divisions that Time Warner provides to affiliated ISPs. This provision is intended to ensure that Time Warner may not discriminate against non-affiliated ISPs by providing them with a less-advantageous connection point to its network than it provides to AOL.

If any of the alternative cable broadband ISP service agreements approved by the Commission is for a term that terminates prior to expiration of the Proposed Order (i. e., five years from the date the Proposed Order becomes final), the Proposed Order requires Time Warner to enter into an additional alternative cable broadband ISP service agreement with a non-affiliated ISP, subject to the Commission's approval, that must take effect immediately upon the expiration of the original agreement. If the original alternative cable broadband ISP service agreement is for a term of at least three years, Time Warner must offer the non-affiliated ISP that is a party to that agreement an option to renew the agreement for at least two years.

If Time Warner terminates any of the alternative cable broadband ISP service agreements approved by the Commission before the expiration of the Proposed Order, the Proposed Order requires Time Warner to enter into an additional alternative cable broadband ISP service agreement with a non-affiliated ISP, subject to the Commission's approval, which must take effect immediately upon the expiration of the original agreement.

If any non-affiliated ISP terminates its alternative cable broadband ISP service agreement approved by the Commission before the expiration of the Proposed Order, or if the non-affiliated ISP ceases to make its ISP service available to subscribers in a particular identified cable division, Time Warner must enter into an additional alternative cable broadband ISP service agreement with a non-affiliated ISP, subject to the Commission's approval, within 90 days after the original non-affiliated cable broadband ISP service is no longer available to subscribers.

In addition to the broadband ISP service agreements described above, the Proposed Order also requires Time Warner to negotiate and enter into arms' length, commercial agreements with any other non-affiliated ISP that seeks to provide cable broadband ISP service on Time Warner's cable system. Time Warner may decline to enter into such negotiations or agreements or impose rates, terms, or conditions based on cable broadband capacity constraints, other cable broadband technical limitations, or cable broadband business considerations, but only so long as it makes such determinations without discrimination on the basis of affiliation and not on the basis of the impact on Proposed Respondents' ISPs (including, but not limited to a decrease in subscribers of Proposed Respondents' ISPs).

The purpose of these provisions is to ensure that a full range of content and services from non-affiliated ISPs is available to subscribers; prevent discrimination by Proposed Respondents as to non-affiliated ISPs on the basis of affiliation, which would interfere with the ability of the non-affiliated ISP to provide a full range of content and services; and remedy the lessening of competition in the market for broadband ISP service as alleged in the Commission's complaint.

## B. Interactive Television and Other Internet Services

Section III of the Proposed Order prohibits Time Warner from interfering in any way with content passed along the bandwidth contracted for and being used by non-affiliated ISPs in compliance with their agreements with Proposed Respondents. The Proposed Order also prohibits Time Warner from discriminating on the basis of affiliation in the transmission or modification of content that Time Warner has contracted to deliver to subscribers over its cable systems. The Proposed Order specifically prohibits Time Warner from interfering with the ability of a subscriber to use, in conjunction with ITV services provided by a non-affiliated entity, interactive signals, triggers, or other content that the Proposed Respondents have agreed to carry. If Time Warner has agreed to transmit ITV signals or interactive triggers that AOL subscribers can use, it cannot block transmission of such ITV signals or triggers to subscribers using a competing ITV service. In addition, the Proposed Order prohibits the Proposed Respondents from entering into any agreement with any other cable system that would interfere with the ability of the other cable system to enter into agreements with non-affiliated ISPs or ITV providers.

The Proposed Order also requires the Proposed Respondents to provide the Commission with all complaints from any non-affiliated broadband ISP relating to the failure of the Proposed Respondents to make content available. The Proposed Order also requires the Proposed Respondents to notify the Commission whenever a television programmer complains that the Proposed Respondents have failed to carry interactive triggers, signals or content through its cable systems.

## C. Broadband Transport Services

Section IV of the Proposed Order requires AOL to charge the same or comparable price for its DSL service to subscribers in Time Warner cable areas where AOL cable broadband ISP service or Road Runner is available as AOL charges for its DSL service in areas in which neither AOL cable broadband ISP service nor Road Runner is available. However, AOL may charge different prices for its DSL service to the extent such pricing differences reflect any actual cost differences for DSL transmission services. The Proposed Respondents must include a description of these cost differences in the reports they are required to submit to the Commission.

The Proposed Order also requires AOL to market and promote its DSL services to subscribers in Time Warner cable areas where AOL cable broadband ISP service or Road Runner is available at the same or comparable level and in the same or comparable manner as it markets and promotes DSL services to subscribers in areas in which neither AOL cable broadband ISP service nor Road Runner is available.

## D. Monitor Trustee Provisions

The Proposed Consent Order authorizes the Commission to appoint a Monitor Trustee to monitor compliance with the Order at any time after the Proposed Respondents sign the Consent Agreement. The Proposed Consent Order provides the Monitor Trustee with the power and authority to monitor the Proposed Respondents' compliance with the terms of the Proposed Consent Order, and full and complete access to personnel, books, records, documents, and facilities of the Proposed Respondents to fulfill that responsibility. In addition, the Monitor Trustee may request any other relevant information that relate to the Proposed Respondents' obligations under the Proposed Consent Order. The Proposed Consent Order precludes Proposed Respondents from taking any action to interfere with or impede the Monitor Trustee's ability to perform his or her responsibilities or to monitor compliance with the Proposed Consent Order.

The Monitor Trustee may hire such consultants, accountants, attorneys, and other assistants as are reasonably necessary to carry out the Monitor Trustee's duties and responsibilities. The Proposed Consent Order requires the Proposed Respondents to bear the cost and expense of hiring these assistants.

## E. Trustee Provisions

The Proposed Consent Order provides that the Commission may appoint a trustee to enter into broadband agreements with non-affiliated ISPs in two instances. First, if the Proposed Respondents have failed to enter into agreements with two additional ISPs in the Identified Cable Divisions within 90 days of making an affiliated ISP available to subscribers, the Commission may appoint a trustee to enter into an agreements, subject to the prior approval of the Commission. The trustee shall, for an additional 90 days, offer to enter into agreements with non-affiliated ISPs that are comparable, taken as a whole, to (1) the Earthlink agreement; or (2) any broadband agreement AOL enters into with any other cable system operator. The trustee's obligation is to ensure that at least two non-affiliated ISPs are available on the Time Warner system in these divisions in addition to Earthlink.

The Commission may also appoint a trustee to enter into agreements in other Time Warner cable divisions if the Proposed Respondents fail to enter into agreements with at least three non-affiliated ISPs that the Commission approves within 90 days of making any affiliated ISP available. The trustee shall, for an additional 90 days, offer to enter into agreements with non-affiliated ISPs that are comparable, taken as a whole, to (1) any other broadband agreement with a non-affiliated ISP for carriage on any Time Warner cable system; or (2) any broadband agreement AOL enters into with any other cable system operator. The trustee's obligation is to ensure that at least three non-affiliated ISPs are available on the Time Warner cable systems in these divisions.

## F. Order to Hold Separate

In addition to the Proposed Order, the Commission also issued an Order to Hold Separate ("Hold Separate Order"). The purpose of the Hold Separate Order is to prevent interim harm to competition and to prevent AOL from gaining a competitive first mover advantage through a relationship with Road Runner.

The Hold Separate Order requires the Proposed Respondents to hold AOL and Road Runner separate in each Identified Cable Division until they have made an affiliated ISP available to broadband customers in that Identified Cable Division. The Hold Separate Order expressly prohibits AOL and Road Runner from, among other things, cross or joint promotional activities, joint or cooperative advertising, and any steps to benefit, directly or indirectly, from each other's business activities.

The Commission may appoint a trustee to monitor compliance with the terms of the Hold Separate Order.

# V. Opportunity for Public Comment

The Proposed Consent Agreement has been placed on the public record for 30 days for receipt of comments by interested persons. Comments received during this period will become part of the public record. After thirty days, the Commission will again review the Proposed Consent Agreement and the comments received and will decide whether or not to make the Proposed Order final.

By accepting the Proposed Agreement subject to final approval, the Commission anticipates that the competitive problems alleged in the complaint will be resolved. The purpose of this analysis is to invite public comment on the Proposed Consent Agreement, to aid the Commission in its determination of whether it should make final the Proposed Order contained in the agreement. This analysis is not intended to constitute an official interpretation of the Proposed Order, nor is it intended to modify the terms of the Proposed Order in any way.

# NATIONAL INTELLIGENCE COUNCIL ON WORLD TRENDS IN 2015
## December 18, 2000

*The United States almost certainly would remain the dominant economic and military power into the second decade of the twenty-first century, but its overall influence in the world might start to wane. Russia would continue to deteriorate as a society, and Japan might begin to fade from the top ranks of the world's economic powers, but China and India likely would become increasingly influential in global economic and political terms. Globalization—the booming worldwide trade in goods and financial services—would remain the world's most important economic trend and would lift many nations out of poverty. Even so, dozens of countries and hundreds of millions of people around the world, including most of sub-Saharan Africa, would be left behind. Poverty, AIDS, environmental degradation, overpopulation in urban areas, terrorism, and shortages of water would become increasingly important and dangerous factors in world affairs.*

*These were some of the broad conclusions contained in a sweeping assessment of where the world might be headed between the years 2000 and 2015. The view was provided by the National Intelligence Council, a research arm of the Central Intelligence Agency (CIA), in consultation with experts from more than a dozen U.S. universities and research institutions.* Called Global Trends 2015: A Dialogue about the Future with Nongovernmental Experts, *the study was an updated version of a similar exercise, conducted in 1997, that looked to the future of 2010.*

*CIA officials cautioned that the study did not constitute a firm prediction of what would happen in the world during the 2000–2015 period, and it certainly was not an endorsement by the U.S. intelligence community of many of the trends that were identified. But the review was intended "to stimulate U.S. policymakers to think beyond their 'in-boxes,'" John Gannon, National Intelligence Council chairman said in an introductory letter.*

### The United States in the World

*Nearly all of the study focused on countries other than the United States, but its analysis did provide some intriguing glimpses into the U.S. role in the world in the first two decades of the twenty-first century. At least through 2015 the U.S. economy would remain by far the biggest in the world, challenged only by the combined strength of European Union nations, the study said. Moreover, the U.S. military would remain the strongest in the world, and it probably would become even more powerful relative to that of any other country. Because of its dedication to research, the United States would remain "in the vanguard of the technological revolution from information to biotechnology and beyond."*

*All these trends would seem to suggest a comfortable position for the United States. But a somewhat different picture emerged from four "alternative global futures" that were discussed during two workshops involving several dozen experts from the government and nongovernmental agencies. In one scenario, globalization continued as a positive influence that broadened and deepened economic growth in most of the world, helped improve governance and the delivery of social services, and contributed to a reduction of international tension and conflict. Under a second scenario, globalization benefited only a minority of the world's "elites," disparities in economic growth became more obvious, population pressures caused intensified competition for scarce natural resources, and the collapse of many governments led to greater international conflict. A third scenario highlighted increasing competition between and within what were called the three "dominant" regions of the world (Europe, Asia, and the Americas), with a particular emphasis on European and Asian resistance to U.S. leadership. In the fourth scenario, described as a "post-polar world," a gradual stagnation of the U.S. economy led the United States to withdraw its troops from Europe and to focus on affairs at home and in the Western Hemisphere, while China became more assertive and provoked a confrontation with Japan.*

*All four scenarios had common themes—including the failure of some regions of the world to benefit from globalization and the necessity of effective national governments and international cooperation. Another notable trend, the study's authors noted, was that in all four scenarios, even the optimistic ones, "U.S. global influence wanes" as other countries improved their economies and challenged Washington's dominance in international affairs.*

### Russia, China, and Japan

*Aside from sub-Saharan Africa, the study's most pessimistic assessments dealt with Russia and other countries that formerly were part of the Soviet Union. Throughout the early part of the twenty-first century, the study said, Russia would continue to struggle unsuccessfully with the negative consequences of seven decades of communist rule: economic stagnation, environmental degradation, widespread corruption, a collapsed health system, and a military much too extravagant for the nation to support. The central questions, the study said, were whether Russia could adjust "its expectations for world leadership to its dramatically reduced resources" and whether it made that adjustment "in a way that preserves rather than up-*

*sets regional stability." The "critical factor" in the answer to those questions would be the manner of Russia's government; on that question, the study offered a pessimistic assessment that the country's "general drift is . . . toward authoritarianism, though not to the extreme extent of the Soviet period." Ukraine, the nations of the Caucasus region (Georgia, Armenia, and Azerbaijan), and other former Soviet republics in Central Asia would suffer negative consequences from Russia's troubles. But all those nations would fight to maintain their recently won independence from Moscow and some would be influenced strongly by the actions of other nations, such as Iran, China, India, and Turkey.* (Russian politics, p. 171)

*The study repeatedly used the word* unknowables *in reference to China. It was likely that China's economy would continue to grow (although possibly not at the 7 percent average annual rate of the 1990s), the study said. But the country faced "an array of political, social, and economic pressures that will increasingly challenge the regime's legitimacy, and perhaps its survival." Among those challenges, the study said, were the "structural changes" that would be required when China became a member of the World Trade Organization (WTO), possibly in 2001. When it joined the WTO and opened its economy to the brisk winds of international trade, China would be required to shut down or privatize many of its massive state-owned enterprises and reduce subsidies for millions of farmers. Such changes would pose enormous risks for the communist rulers in Beijing, who for nearly two decades had sought to introduce capitalist elements into the economy while maintaining a rigidly authoritarian style of government.* (China and the WTO, p. 213)

*Japan, China's main rival for influence within Asia, also faced significant uncertainties, mostly about its economy, the study said. It was unclear whether Japan would undertake the "structural reforms"—such as modernizing its corrupt banking system and loosening the ties between government and big business—that most experts said were necessary to revive the country's economy. Japan had suffered a recession for much of the 1990s, and in 2000 was experiencing only weak economic growth. Even if its economic performance improved in the early part of the twenty-first century, the study said, Japan's "relative importance in the global economy will decrease" as China, India, and other countries grew.* (Japanese recession, Historic Documents of 1998, p. 532)

## Other Regional Concerns

*Two inherently unstable regions of the world—the Middle East and South Asia—were almost certain to remain in that category through 2015, the study said. In fact, the study suggested that both regions could become even more unstable and dangerous than in the past. Countries in both regions had fought numerous wars in the half-century following World War II, and while the study did not predict new wars, it offered little encouragement that permanent peace was at hand.*

*The Middle East (broadly defined to include North Africa as well as the entire area of the eastern Mediterranean and Persian Gulf) likely would face a variety of pressures, most notably the need to provide jobs, housing, and public services for rapidly growing populations. In most countries of the region, the study said, more than half of the population was under twenty years of age in 2000; that trend would continue well into the new century. Lacking strong educational systems and resilient economies, these countries faced increasing political instability unless they modernized; and if they modernized, their autocratic regimes could tumble. The study offered little in the way of optimism on the question of Israel's relations with its Arab neighbors, including the Palestinians. At best, it argued, Israel would have achieved a "cold peace" with only limited social, economic, or cultural ties in the region.* (Middle East issues, pp. 494, 930)

*South Asia probably would continue to be one of the most dangerous spots on the planet, the study suggested. The Indian economy was likely to develop rapidly on a base of information technology (the country already was a leading center of research in that area). But half of India's 1 billion people would remain in "dire poverty," the study said, and so a "widening gulf" between poor and wealthy regions would cause domestic strife. India's rival Pakistan likely would face even more severe internal stresses, the result of decades of "political and economic mismanagement, divisive politics, lawlessness, corruption, and ethnic friction." Confronted with a growth of Islamic extremism, the Pakistani government probably would lose effective control of much of the country, the study said. In that context, the fact that both India and Pakistan had developed nuclear weapons would pose continuing dangers well into the century.* (Indian and Pakistani nuclear tests, Historic Documents of 1998, p. 326)

*The Korean peninsula also would remain a worrisome danger spot, the report said. If capitalist South Korea and communist North Korea decided to merge, the process could take more than a decade and would consume South Korea's energies and resources. If the move toward unification failed, North Korea could resume its drive to build nuclear weapons and ballistic missiles.* (Korean issues, pp. 359, 866)

*Even under the most optimistic scenarios, most of sub-Saharan Africa likely would be left behind as the rest of the world experienced economic growth and the benefits of information technology. The study noted that many countries in the region were being ravaged by AIDS (which had reduced average life spans and was leaving tens of millions of orphans), ethnic conflict, and corrupt governments. South Africa and Nigeria would remain the region's dominant economic powers, but both needed to improve the lives of their own citizens and could not be expected to be "economic locomotives and stabilizers" for their neighbors.* (Africa issues, pp. 63, 753, 978, 1072)

*The study suggested a somewhat similar scenario for Latin America. Three countries—Brazil, Mexico, and Chile—likely would continue to grow and prosper. But many others—most notably the Andean states of Bolivia, Columbia, Ecuador, and Peru—would remain impoverished and victimized by drug traffickers, guerrillas, and unstable or authoritarian governments.* (Colombia drug war, p. 840)

## *Other Transnational Trends*

*The study's often discouraging findings on economic and political trends were matched by a review of other troubling issues that cut across national and even regional boundaries. One of the most widespread problems in this category was the lack of water in much of the world. By 2015, the study said, more than 3 billion people (nearly half the world's population) would live in countries classified as "water-stressed." The main areas of water shortages were Africa, northern China, the Middle East, and South Asia. International competition for water resources could become a source of conflict, for the first time in world history, the study said. As potential trouble spots, the study noted that Turkey was building dams and irrigation projects on the Tigris and Euphrates rivers that would reduce water flows into Iraq and Syria, and Egypt was building a major water-diversion project that could the reduce flow of the Nile River in Ethiopia and Sudan.*

*Environmental degradation, including deforestation and air and water pollution, would become an increasingly urgent problem, especially in the developing world, the study said. Large urban centers, such as Beijing, Lagos, Mexico City, and Sao Paulo would face "severe air and water quality problems" as their populations continued to grow. The study offered little hope for serious reductions in global emissions of greenhouse gases, which most scientists believed were responsible for an increase in temperatures known as "global warming." Economic and population pressures would lead emissions of those gases to increase "substantially," rather than decline, as had been called for in United Nations agreements in 1992 and 1997.* (Global warming, p. 337)

*Criminal organizations and networks, including narcotics traffickers, would become increasingly powerful by 2015. "They will form loose alliances with one another, with smaller criminal entrepreneurs, and with insurgent movements for specific operations," the study warned. "They will corrupt leaders of unstable, economically fragile or failing states, insinuate themselves into troubled banks and businesses, and cooperate with insurgent political movements to control substantial geographic areas." In one especially frightening observation, the study warned of increased risks that organized criminal groups would traffic in nuclear, biological, and chemical weapons—especially if countries that produced those weapons were unable to control them.*

*Following in the footsteps of numerous other studies, the CIA analysis warned that the United States was likely to be an inviting target for terrorist groups, most notably those based in the Middle East and Southwest Asia. Terrorists would continue to attack U.S. military and diplomatic facilities overseas and likely would expand their targets to include American citizens and U.S.-owned companies. Terrorist groups and so-called rogue nations, such as Iraq or North Korea, could be expected to try to attack the United States with a short- or medium-range missile armed with a biological, chemical, or nuclear warhead, the study warned.* (Terrorism studies, p. 277)

*Following are excerpts from* Global Trends 2015: A Dialogue about the Future with Nongovernmental Experts, *made public December 18, 2000, by the Central Intelligence Agency. The study was conducted by the National Intelligence Council, a research arm of the CIA, in cooperation with experts from U.S. universities and research institutes. The document was obtained from the Internet at http://www.cia.gov/cia/publications/globaltrends2015/index .html.*

# Overview

Over the past 15 months, the National Intelligence Council (NIC), in close collaboration with US Government specialists and a wide range of experts outside the government, has worked to identify major drivers and trends that will shape the world of 2015.

The key drivers identified are:

(1) Demographics.
(2) Natural resources and environment.
(3) Science and technology.
(4) The global economy and globalization.
(5) National and international governance.
(6) Future conflict.
(7) The role of the United States.

In examining these drivers, several points should be kept in mind:

- No single driver or trend will dominate the global future in 2015.
- Each driver will have varying impacts in different regions and countries.
- The drivers are not necessarily mutually reinforcing; in some cases, they will work at cross-purposes.

Taken together, these drivers and trends intersect to create an integrated picture of the world of 2015, about which we can make projections with varying degrees of confidence and identify some troubling uncertainties of strategic importance to the United States. . . .

## The Drivers and Trends

### Demographics

World population in 2015 will be 7.2 billion, up from 6.1 billion in the year 2000, and in most countries, people will live longer. Ninety-five percent of the increase will be in developing countries, nearly all in rapidly expanding urban areas. Where political systems are brittle, the combination of population growth and urbanization will foster instability. Increasing lifespans will have significantly divergent impacts.

- In the advanced economies—and a growing number of emerging market countries—declining birthrates and aging will combine to increase health care and pension costs while reducing the relative size of the working population, straining the social contract, and leaving significant shortfalls in the size and capacity of the work force.
- In some developing countries, these same trends will combine to expand the size of the working population and reduce the youth bulge—increasing the potential for economic growth and political stability.

## Natural Resources and Environment

Overall food production will be adequate to feed the world's growing population, but poor infrastructure and distribution, political instability, and chronic poverty will lead to malnourishment in parts of Sub-Saharan Africa. The potential for famine will persist in countries with repressive government policies or internal conflicts. Despite a 50 percent increase in global energy demand, energy resources will be sufficient to meet demand; the latest estimates suggest that 80 percent of the world's available oil and 95 percent of its gas remain underground.

- Although the Persian Gulf region will remain the world's largest single source of oil, the global energy market is likely to encompass two relatively distinct patterns of regional distribution: one serving consumers (including the United States) from Atlantic Basin reserves; and the other meeting the needs of primarily Asian customers (increasingly China and India) from Persian Gulf supplies and, to a lesser extent, the Caspian region and Central Asia.
- In contrast to food and energy, water scarcities and allocation will pose significant challenges to governments in the Middle East, Sub-Saharan Africa, South Asia, and northern China. Regional tensions over water will be heightened by 2015.

## Science and Technology

Fifteen years ago, few predicted the profound impact of the revolution in information technology. Looking ahead another 15 years, the world will encounter more quantum leaps in information technology (IT) and in other areas of science and technology. The continuing diffusion of information technology and new applications of biotechnology will be at the crest of the wave. IT will be the major building block for international commerce and for empowering nonstate actors. Most experts agree that the IT revolution represents the most significant global transformation since the Industrial Revolution beginning in the mid-eighteenth century.

- The integration—or fusion—of continuing revolutions in information technology, biotechnology, materials science, and nanotechnology will generate a dramatic increase in investment in technology, which will further stimulate innovation within the more advanced countries.

- Older technologies will continue lateral "sidewise development" into new markets and applications through 2015, benefiting US allies and adversaries around the world who are interested in acquiring early generation ballistic missile and weapons of mass destruction (WMD) technologies.
- Biotechnology will drive medical breakthroughs that will enable the world's wealthiest people to improve their health and increase their longevity dramatically. At the same time, genetically modified crops will offer the potential to improve nutrition among the world's one billion malnourished people.
- Breakthroughs in materials technology will generate widely available products that are multi-functional, environmentally safe, longer lasting, and easily adapted to particular consumer requirements.
- Disaffected states, terrorists, proliferators, narcotraffickers, and organized criminals will take advantage of the new high-speed information environment and other advances in technology to integrate their illegal activities and compound their threat to stability and security around the world.

## The Global Economy and Globalization

The networked global economy will be driven by rapid and largely unrestricted flows of information, ideas, cultural values, capital, goods and services, and people: that is, globalization. This globalized economy will be a net contributor to increased political stability in the world in 2015, although its reach and benefits will not be universal. In contrast to the Industrial Revolution, the process of globalization is more compressed. Its evolution will be rocky, marked by chronic financial volatility and a widening economic divide.

- The global economy, overall, will return to the high levels of growth reached in the 1960s and early 1970s. Economic growth will be driven by political pressures for higher living standards, improved economic policies, rising foreign trade and investment, the diffusion of information technologies, and an increasingly dynamic private sector. Potential brakes on the global economy—such as a sustained financial crisis or prolonged disruption of energy supplies—could undo this optimistic projection.
- Regions, countries, and groups feeling left behind will face deepening economic stagnation, political instability, and cultural alienation. They will foster political, ethnic, ideological, and religious extremism, along with the violence that often accompanies it. They will force the United States and other developed countries to remain focused on "old-world" challenges while concentrating on the implications of "new-world" technologies at the same time.

## National and International Governance

States will continue to be the dominant players on the world stage, but governments will have less and less control over flows of information, technology, diseases, migrants, arms, and financial transactions, whether licit or illicit, across their borders. Nonstate actors ranging from business firms to nonprofit organizations will play increasingly larger roles in both national and international affairs. The quality of governance, both nationally and internationally, will substantially determine how well states and societies cope with these global forces.

- States with competent governance, including the United States, will adapt government structures to a dramatically changed global environment—making them better able to engage with a more interconnected world. The responsibilities of once "semiautonomous" government agencies increasingly will intersect because of the transnational nature of national security priorities and because of the clear requirement for interdisciplinary policy responses. Shaping the complex, fast-moving world of 2015 will require reshaping traditional government structures.
- Effective governance will increasingly be determined by the ability and agility to form partnerships to exploit increased information flows, new technologies, migration, and the influence of nonstate actors. Most but not all countries that succeed will be representative democracies.
- States with ineffective and incompetent governance not only will fail to benefit from globalization, but in some instances will spawn conflicts at home and abroad, ensuring an even wider gap between regional winners and losers than exists today.

Globalization will increase the transparency of government decision-making, complicating the ability of authoritarian regimes to maintain control, but also complicating the traditional deliberative processes of democracies. Increasing migration will create influential diasporas, affecting policies, politics and even national identity in many countries. Globalization also will create increasing demands for international cooperation on transnational issues, but the response of both states and international organizations will fall short in 2015.

## Future Conflict

The United States will maintain a strong technological edge in IT-driven "battlefield awareness" and in precision-guided weaponry in 2015. The United States will face three types of threats:

- Asymmetric threats in which state and nonstate adversaries avoid direct engagements with the US military but devise strategies, tactics, and weapons—some improved by "sidewise" technology—to minimize US strengths and exploit perceived weaknesses;
- Strategic WMD threats, including nuclear missile threats, in which (barring significant political or economic changes) Russia, China, most likely North Korea, probably Iran, and possibly Iraq have the capability to strike the United States, and the potential for unconventional delivery of WMD by both states or nonstate actors also will grow; and

- Regional military threats in which a few countries maintain large military forces with a mix of Cold War and post-Cold War concepts and technologies.

The risk of war among developed countries will be low. The international community will continue, however, to face conflicts around the world, ranging from relatively frequent small-scale internal upheavals to less frequent regional interstate wars. The potential for conflict will arise from rivalries in Asia, ranging from India-Pakistan to China-Taiwan, as well as among the antagonists in the Middle East. Their potential lethality will grow, driven by the availability of WMD, longer-range missile delivery systems and other technologies.

Internal conflicts stemming from religious, ethnic, economic or political disputes will remain at current levels or even increase in number. The United Nations and regional organizations will be called upon to manage such conflicts because major states—stressed by domestic concerns, perceived risk of failure, lack of political will, or tight resources—will minimize their direct involvement.

Export control regimes and sanctions will be less effective because of the diffusion of technology, porous borders, defense industry consolidations, and reliance upon foreign markets to maintain profitability. Arms and weapons technology transfers will be more difficult to control.

- Prospects will grow that more sophisticated weaponry, including weapons of mass destruction—indigenously produced or externally acquired—will get into the hands of state and nonstate belligerents, some hostile to the United States. The likelihood will increase over this period that WMD will be used either against the United States or its forces, facilities, and interests overseas.

## Role of the United States

The United States will continue to be a major force in the world community. US global economic, technological, military, and diplomatic influence will be unparalleled among nations as well as regional and international organizations in 2015. This power not only will ensure America's preeminence, but also will cast the United States as a key driver of the international system.

The United States will continue to be identified throughout the world as the leading proponent and beneficiary of globalization. US economic actions, even when pursued for such domestic goals as adjusting interest rates, will have a major global impact because of the tighter integration of global markets by 2015.

- The United States will remain in the vanguard of the technological revolution from information to biotechnology and beyond.
- Both allies and adversaries will factor continued US military pre-eminence in their calculations of national security interests and ambitions.
- Some states—adversaries and allies—will try at times to check what they see as American "hegemony." Although this posture will not trans-

late into strategic, broad-based and enduring anti-US coalitions, it will lead to tactical alignments on specific policies and demands for a greater role in international political and economic institutions.

Diplomacy will be more complicated. Washington will have greater difficulty harnessing its power to achieve specific foreign policy goals: the US Government will exercise a smaller and less powerful part of the overall economic and cultural influence of the United States abroad.

- In the absence of a clear and overriding national security threat, the United States will have difficulty drawing on its economic prowess to advance its foreign policy agenda. The top priority of the American private sector, which will be central to maintaining the US economic and technological lead, will be financial profitability, not foreign policy objectives.
- The United States also will have greater difficulty building coalitions to support its policy goals, although the international community will often turn to Washington, even if reluctantly, to lead multilateral efforts in real and potential conflicts.
- There will be increasing numbers of important actors on the world stage to challenge and check—as well as to reinforce—US leadership: countries such as China, Russia, India, Mexico, and Brazil; regional organizations such as the European Union; and a vast array of increasingly powerful multinational corporations and nonprofit organizations with their own interests to defend in the world.

## Key Uncertainties: Technology Will Alter Outcomes

Examining the interaction of these drivers and trends points to some major uncertainties that will only be clarified as events occur and leaders make policy decisions that cannot be foreseen today. We cite eight transnational and regional issues for which the future, according to our trends analysis, is too tough to call with any confidence or precision.

- **These are high-stakes, national security issues that will require continuous analysis and, in the view of our conferees, periodic policy review in the years ahead.**

## Science and Technology

We know that the possibility is greater than ever that the revolution in science and technology will improve the quality of life. What we know about this revolution is exciting. Advances in science and technology will generate dramatic breakthroughs in agriculture and health and in leap-frog applications, such as universal wireless cellular communications, which already are networking developing countries that never had land-lines. What we do not know about the S&T revolution, however, is staggering. We do not know to what extent technology will benefit, or further disadvantage, disaffected national populations, alienated ethnic and religious groups, or the less developed countries. We do not know to what degree lateral or "side-wise" technology will increase the threat from low technology countries and groups. One certainty is that progression will not be linear. Another is that as future technologies emerge, people will lack full awareness of their wider economic, environmental, cultural, legal, and moral impact—or the continuing potential for research and development.

Advances in science and technology will pose national security challenges of uncertain character and scale.

- Increasing reliance on computer networks is making critical US infrastructures more attractive as targets. Computer network operations today offer new options for attacking the United States within its traditional continental sanctuary—potentially anonymously and with selective effects. Nevertheless, we do not know how quickly or effectively such adversaries as terrorists or disaffected states will develop the tradecraft to use cyber warfare tools and technology, or, in fact, whether cyber warfare will ever evolve into a decisive combat arm.
- Rapid advances and diffusion of biotechnology, nanotechnology, and the materials sciences, moreover, will add to the capabilities of our adversaries to engage in biological warfare or bio-terrorism.

## Asymmetric Warfare

As noted earlier, most adversaries will recognize the information advantage and military superiority of the United States in 2015. Rather than acquiesce to any potential US military domination, they will try to circumvent or minimize US strengths and exploit perceived weaknesses. IT-driven globalization will significantly increase interaction among terrorists, narcotraffickers, weapons proliferators, and organized criminals, who in a networked world will have greater access to information, to technology, to finance, to sophisticated deception-and-denial techniques and to each other. Such asymmetric approaches—whether undertaken by states or nonstate actors—will become the dominant characteristic of most threats to the US homeland. They will be a defining challenge for US strategy, operations, and force development, and they will require that strategy to maintain focus on traditional, low-technology threats as well as the capacity of potential adversaries to harness elements of proliferating advanced technologies. At the same time, we do not know the extent to which adversaries, state and nonstate, might be influenced or deterred by other geopolitical, economic, technological, or diplomatic factors in 2015.

## The Global Economy

Although the outlook for the global economy appears strong, achieving broad and sustained high levels of global growth will be contingent on avoiding several potential brakes to growth. These include:

**The US economy suffers a sustained downturn.** Given its large trade deficit and low domestic savings, the US economy—the most important driver of recent global growth—is vulnerable to a loss of international confidence in its growth prospects that could lead to a sharp downturn, which, if long lasting, would have deleterious economic and policy consequences for the rest of the world.

**Europe and Japan fail to manage their demographic challenges.** European and Japanese populations are aging rapidly, requiring more than 110 million new workers by 2015 to maintain current dependency ratios between the working population and retirees. Conflicts over social services or immigration policies in major European states could dampen economic growth.

**China and/or India fail to sustain high growth.** China's ambitious goals for reforming its economy will be difficult to achieve: restructuring state-owned enterprises, cleaning up and transforming the banking system, and cutting the government's employment rolls in half. Growth would slow if these reforms go off-track. Failure by India to implement reforms would prevent it from achieving sustained growth.

**Emerging market countries fail to reform their financial institutions.** Many emerging market countries have not yet undertaken the financial reforms needed to help them survive the next economic crisis. Absent such reform, a series of future economic crises in emerging market countries probably will dry up the capital flows crucial for high rates of economic growth.

**Global energy supplies suffer a major disruption.** Turbulence in global energy supplies would have a devastating effect. Such a result could be driven by conflict among key energy-producing states, sustained internal instability in two or more major energy-producing states, or major terrorist actions.

## The Middle East

Global trends from demography and natural resources to globalization and governance appear generally negative for the Middle East. Most regimes are change-resistant. Many are buoyed by continuing energy revenues and will not be inclined to make the necessary reforms, including in basic education, to change this unfavorable picture.

- Linear trend analysis shows little positive change in the region, raising the prospects for increased demographic pressures, social unrest, religious and ideological extremism, and terrorism directed both at the regimes and at their Western supporters.
- Nonlinear developments—such as the sudden rise of a Web-connected opposition, a sharp and sustained economic downturn, or, conversely, the emergence of enlightened leaders committed to good governance— might change outcomes in individual countries. Political changes in Iran in the late 1990s are an example of such nonlinear development.

## China

Estimates of developments in China over the next 15 years are fraught with unknowables. Working against China's aspirations to sustain economic growth while preserving its political system is an array of political, social, and economic pressures that will increasingly challenge the regime's legitimacy, and perhaps its survival.

- The sweeping structural changes required by China's entry into the World Trade Organization (WTO) and the broader demands of economic globalization and the information revolution will generate significantly new levels and types of social and economic disruption that will only add to an already wide range of domestic and international problems.

Nevertheless, China need not be overwhelmed by these problems. China has proven politically resilient, economically dynamic, and increasingly assertive in positioning itself for a leadership role in East Asia. Its long-term military program in particular suggests that Beijing wants to have the capability to achieve its territorial objectives, outmatch its neighbors, and constrain US power in the region.

- We do not rule out the introduction of enough political reform by 2015 to allow China to adapt to domestic pressure for change and to continue to grow economically.

Two conditions, in the view of many specialists, would lead to a major security challenge for the United States and its allies in the region: a weak, disintegrating China, or an assertive China willing to use its growing economic wealth and military capabilities to pursue its strategic advantage in the region. These opposite extremes bound a more commonly held view among experts that China will continue to see peace as essential to its economic growth and internal stability.

## Russia

Between now and 2015, Moscow will be challenged even more than today to adjust its expectations for world leadership to its dramatically reduced resources. Whether the country can make the transition in adjusting ends to means remains an open and critical question, according to most experts, as does the question of the character and quality of Russian governance and economic policies. The most likely outcome is a Russia that remains internally weak and institutionally linked to the international system primarily through its permanent seat on the UN Security Council. In this view, whether Russia can adjust to this diminished status in a manner that preserves rather than upsets regional stability is also uncertain. The stakes for both Europe and the United States will be high, although neither will have the ability to determine the outcome for Russia in 2015. Russian governance will be the critical factor.

## Japan

The first uncertainty about Japan is whether it will carry out the structural reforms needed to resume robust economic growth and to slow its decline relative to the rest of East Asia, particularly China. The second uncertainty is whether Japan will alter its security policy to allow Tokyo to maintain a stronger military and more reciprocal relationship with the United States. Experts agree that Japanese governance will be the key driver in determining the outcomes.

## India

Global trends conflict significantly in India. The size of its population—1.2 billion by 2015—and its technologically driven economic growth virtually dictate that India will be a rising regional power. The unevenness of its internal economic growth, with a growing gap between rich and poor, and serious questions about the fractious nature of its politics, all cast doubt on how powerful India will be by 2015. Whatever its degree of power, India's rising ambition will further strain its relations with China, as well as complicate its ties with Russia, Japan, and the West—and continue its nuclear standoff with Pakistan.

## Key Challenges to Governance: People Will Decide

*Global Trends 2015* identifies governance as a major driver for the future and assumes that all trends we cite will be influenced, for good or bad, by decisions of people. The inclusion of the United States as a driver—both the US Government as well as US for-profit and nonprofit organizations—is based on the general assumption that the actions of nonstate actors as well as governments will shape global outcomes in the years ahead.

An integrated trend analysis suggests at least four related conclusions:

## National Priorities Will Matter

- To prosper in the global economy of 2015, governments will have to invest more in technology, in public education, and in broader participation in government to include increasingly influential nonstate actors. The extent to which governments around the world are doing these things today gives some indication of where they will be in 2015.

## US Responsibilities Will Cover the World, Old and New

- The United States and other developed countries will be challenged in 2015 to lead the fast-paced technological revolution while, at the same time, maintaining military, diplomatic, and intelligence capabilities to deal with traditional problems and threats from low-technology countries and groups. The United States, as a global power, will have little choice but to engage leading actors and confront problems on both sides of the widening economic and digital divides in the world of 2015, when globalization's benefits will be far from global.

## US Foreign Priorities Will be More Transnational

- International or multilateral arrangements increasingly will be called upon in 2015 to deal with growing transnational problems from economic and financial volatility; to legal and illegal migration; to competition for scarce natural resources such as water; to humanitarian, refugee, and environmental crises; to terrorism, narcotrafficking, and weapons proliferation; and to both regional conflicts and cyber threats. And when international cooperation—or international governance—comes up short, the United States and other developed countries will have to broker solutions among a wide array of international players—including governments at all levels, multinational corporations, and nonprofit organizations.

## National Governments Will be More Transparent

- To deal with a transnational agenda and an interconnected world in 2015, governments will have to develop greater communication and collaboration between national security and domestic policy agencies. Interagency cooperation will be essential to understanding transnational threats and to developing interdisciplinary strategies to counter them. Consequence management of a biological warfare (BW) attack, for example, would require close coordination among a host of US Government agencies, foreign governments, US state and municipal governments, the military, the medical community, and the media. . . .

# CLINTON ADMINISTRATION ON THE PRIVACY OF MEDICAL RECORDS
## December 20, 2000

*Capping a five-year effort, the Clinton administration on December 20, 2000, announced sweeping regulations intended to protect the privacy of medical records held by the health care industry. When fully in effect by 2002, the regulations would prohibit health care providers, insurance companies, pharmacies, and other entities from disclosing medical files about patients without obtaining their consent in advance. The regulations were strongly supported by groups advocating consumer protections and privacy rights but were opposed by much of the health care industry. The regulations were subject to review by the incoming Bush administration.*

*Congress kicked off a debate over medical records privacy in 1996 when it passed the Health Insurance Portability and Accountability Act, better known as the Kennedy-Kassebaum bill (PL 104–191), which made it easier for Americans to keep their health insurance after changing jobs. Little noticed by the public at the time were two provisions in the law dealing with medical records. One required the health care industry to maintain medical records in a uniform electronic format; the purpose was to ease the sharing of information among doctors, hospitals, insurance companies, and others. To protect the confidentiality of those records, the law also established a procedure under which Congress promised to develop privacy standards within three years, by August 21, 1999. After that date, the task would be turned over to the executive branch. The Republican-controlled Congress missed its three-year deadline, and in November 1999 the Clinton administration used its authority under the 1996 law to propose regulations preventing the unauthorized disclosure of most—but not all—medical records. During the next year, the Department of Health and Human Services (HHS) said it received more than 50,000 comments on the proposed regulations.* (Early debate on medical records privacy, Historic Documents of 1997, p. 580)

### The Final Regulations

*In general, the new regulations announced on December 20 by President Bill Clinton and Health and Human Services Secretary Donna E. Shalala required health care providers to obtain advance consent from patients before disclosing information in their medical files to other parties. The rule applied to doctors, hospitals, health insurance companies, pharmacies, and most other institutions that had access to patient medical records. These entities could ask a patient to sign a blanket consent form authorizing what were called "routine disclosures"—such as the sharing of information between a doctor and the hospital where a patient was being treated, or between a health care provider and the patient's insurance company. Patients would have to give specific authorization, on a case-by-case basis, for "nonroutine" disclosures, such as the release of medical information to employers, banks, or companies that sold medical products and services.*

*The final version of the regulations was considerably stronger than had been proposed just one year earlier. The original version had applied only to records in electronic format, but the final rules covered all types of medical records, including paper files and oral communications. The original rule had applied only to nonroutine disclosures, but the final rule required advance consent for routine disclosures as well.*

*The regulation gave patients the legal right to view and make copies of their medical records and to request correction of mistakes. In most cases, patients also would have a right to learn who had gained access to their records. The regulation also prohibited health care providers and insurance companies from requiring patients to agree to nonroutine disclosures of their records as a condition of receiving treatment.*

*The regulation established civil and criminal penalties for violations. The most severe penalty, a fine of up to $250,000 and a maximum ten-year prison sentence, would be imposed for obtaining or disclosing health care information with the intent to sell, transfer, or use it for "commercial advantage, personal gain, or malicious harm." Among the exemptions to the general requirement for advance patient consent were some law enforcement purposes, identification of the body of a deceased person, and judicial procedures.*

*"For the first time, all Americans—no matter where they live, no matter where they get their health care—will have protections for their most private personal information, their health records," Shalala said in announcing the new rules.*

## The Debate over Medical Privacy

*Privacy advocates had pushed for the regulations on two grounds. In general, they argued that the need for privacy had grown with the widespread computerization of medical records. In the past, a HHS "fact sheet" noted, most medical records were kept in file cabinets in doctors' offices and were not readily accessible to insurance companies, banks, or other potential users. But once they were put into computerized formats, records could be shared almost instantly without a patient's consent. On a related issue, privacy advocates said that in recent years an unknown number of people had stopped seeking treatment or were withholding information from their doc-*

*tors because they feared that employers, banks, and others would discover their medical problems, such as alcohol or drug abuse. "Medical information is the most intimate information people have, and it's important that the individual control that information," Ron Welch, a legal consultant for the American Civil Liberties Union told the* Washington Post.

*Supporters said the regulations also had become necessary because Congress in 1999 had passed legislation (PL 106–102) allowing banks to buy or establish other "financial services" businesses, such as stock brokerage firms and insurance companies. As a consequence, a patient might find himself applying for a mortgage or consumer loan to a bank that also owned his health insurance company, and the two entities could share his medical information without his knowledge.*

*In announcing the regulation, President Clinton pointed to another issue that was attracting increasing attention: the marketing of pharmaceuticals and other medical products to consumers based on information in their medical records. "Recently, expectant mothers who haven't even told their friends the good news are finding sales letters for baby products in their mailboxes," he said. "That's wrong. Under these rules, it will also be illegal."*

*Representatives of the health care industry said they agreed with the need to protect the privacy of medical records, but many complained that the regulations would impose difficult administrative burdens. In particular, representatives for hospitals and insurance companies objected to a rule allowing patients to ask health care providers to restrict how their medical records were used or to revoke their consent to having their records shared. Industry representatives said it would be difficult and costly to keep track of the various consent forms required for the disclosure of each patient's records.*

*Health care industry officials also objected to the fact that the regulations did not overturn rules imposed by states that in some cases were even tougher. In effect, the rules established a national minimum standard but allowed states to impose stricter rules about the disclosure of medical records. "Without uniformity, the regulations are going to cause more, not less, confusion," Chip Kahn, president of the Health Insurance Association of America, told the Associated Press.*

*The Clinton administration and the health care industry also disputed the potential cost of the regulations. In its announcement, HHS estimated that the health care industry would spend about $17.6 billion over a ten-year period to comply with the regulations. But that cost would be more than offset by savings of nearly $30 billion, over the same period, resulting from the congressionally imposed uniform standards for the keeping of medical records, HHS said. Health care industry officials disputed both figures, saying the administration had underestimated the potential costs and overestimated the potential savings. For example, Melinda R. Hatton, vice president of the American Hospital Association, said her hospitals would have to spend $22 billion over five years to comply with the privacy rules.*

*What was not clear by the end of the year was the position of the incom-*

*ing administration of George W. Bush. Before the November election Bush's campaign had issued a position paper that generally supported the privacy of medical records but offered no specifics. Responding to the Clinton administration announcement, several of Bush's aides said the new administration would review the new regulation after taking office.*

*Following is the text of a "fact sheet" from the Department of Health and Human Services outlining details of regulations governing the privacy of medical records, announced on December 20, 2000, by President Bill Clinton and HHS Secretary Donna E. Shalala. The document was obtained from the Internet at   http://www.hhs.gov/news/press/2000pres/00fsprivacy/html.*

*Overview: Each time a patient sees a doctor, is admitted to a hospital, goes to a pharmacist or sends a claim to a health plan, a record is made of their confidential health information. For many years, the confidentiality of those records was maintained by our family doctors, who kept our records sealed away in file cabinets and refused to reveal them to anyone else. Today, the use and disclosure of this information is protected by a patchwork of state laws, leaving large gaps in the protection of patients' privacy and confidentiality. There is a pressing need for national standards to control the flow of sensitive patient information and to establish real penalties for the misuse or disclosure of this information.*

*President Clinton and Congress recognized the need for national patient record privacy standards in 1996 when they enacted the Health Insurance Portability and Accountability Act of 1996 (HIPAA). That law gave Congress until August 21, 1999, to pass comprehensive health privacy legislation. After three years of discussion in Congress without passage of such a law,*

*HIPAA provided HHS [Department of Health and Human Services] with the authority to craft such privacy protections by regulation. Following the principles and policies laid out in the recommendations for national health information privacy legislation the Administration submitted to Congress in 1997, the Administration drafted regulations to guarantee patients new rights and protections against the misuse or disclosure of their health records and the President and Secretary Donna E. Shalala released them in October of last year. During an extended comment period, HHS received, electronically or on paper, more than 52,000 communications from the public.*

*This final rule provides the first comprehensive federal protection for the privacy of health information. However, because of the limitations of the HIPAA statute, these protections do not fully achieve the Administration's goal of a seamless system of privacy protection for all health information. Members of both parties in Congress will need to pass meaningful, comprehensive privacy protection for American patients that would extend the reach of the standards being finalized today to all entities that hold personal health information.*

## Covered Entities

As required by HIPAA, the final regulation covers health plans, health care clearinghouses, and those health care providers who conduct certain financial and administrative transactions (e.g., electronic billing and funds transfers) electronically.

## Information Protected

All medical records and other individually identifiable health information held or disclosed by a covered entity in any form, whether communicated electronically, on paper, or orally, is covered by the final regulation.

## Components of the Final Rule

The rule is the result of the Department's careful consideration of every comment and reflects a balance between accommodating practical uses of individually identifiable health information and rendering maximum privacy protection of that information.

## Consumer Control Over Health Information

Under this final rule, patients have significant new rights to understand and control how their health information is used.

- Patient education on privacy protections. Providers and health plans are required to give patients a clear written explanation of how they can use, keep, and disclose their health information.
- Ensuring patient access to their medical records. Patients must be able to see and get copies of their records, and request amendments. In addition, a history of most disclosures must be made accessible to patients.
- Receiving patient consent before information is released. Patient authorization to disclose information must meet specific requirements. Health care providers who see patients are required to obtain patient consent before sharing their information for treatment, payment, and health care operations purposes. In addition, specific patient consent must be sought and granted for non-routine uses and most non-health care purposes, such as releasing information to financial institutions determining mortgages and other loans or selling mailing lists to interested parties such as life insurers. Patients have the right to request restrictions on the uses and disclosures of their information.
- Ensuring that consent is not coerced. Providers and health plans generally cannot condition treatment on a patient's agreement to disclose health information for non-routine uses.
- Providing recourse if privacy protections are violated. People have the right to complain to a covered provider or health plan, or to the Secretary, about violations of the provisions of this rule or the policies and procedures of the covered entity.

## Boundaries on Medical Record Use and Release

With few exceptions, an individual's health information can be used for health purposes only.

- Ensuring that health information is not used for non-health purposes. Patient information can be used or disclosed by a health plan, provider or clearinghouse only for purposes of health care treatment, payment and operations. Health information cannot be used for purposes not related to health care—such as use by employers to make personnel decisions, or use by financial institutions—without explicit authorization from the individual.
- Providing the minimum amount of information necessary. Disclosures of information must be limited to the minimum necessary for the purpose of the disclosure. However, this provision does not apply to the transfer of medical records for purposes of treatment, since physicians, specialists, and other providers need access to the full record to provide best quality care.
- Ensuring informed and voluntary consent. Non-routine disclosures with patient authorization must meet standards that ensure the authorization is truly informed and voluntary.

## Ensure the Security of Personal Health Information

The regulation establishes the privacy safeguard standards that covered entities must meet, but it leaves detailed policies and procedures for meeting these standards to the discretion of each covered entity. In this way, implementation of the standards will be flexible and scalable, to account for the nature of each entity's business, and its size and resources. Covered entities must:

- Adopt written privacy procedures. These must include who has access to protected information, how it will be used within the entity, and when the information would or would not be disclosed to others. They must also takes steps to ensure that their business associates protect the privacy of health information.
- Train employees and designate a privacy officer. Covered entities must provide sufficient training so that their employees understand the new privacy protections procedures, and designate an individual to be responsible for ensuring the procedures are followed.
- Establish grievance processes. Covered entities must provide a means for patients to make inquiries or complaints regarding the privacy of their records.

## Establish Accountability for Medical Records Use and Release

Penalties for covered entities that misuse personal health information are provided in HIPAA.

- Civil penalties. Health plans, providers and clearinghouses that violate these standards would be subject to civil liability. Civil money penalties are $100 per incident, up to $25,000 per person, per year, per standard.

- Federal criminal penalties. There would be federal criminal penalties for health plans, providers and clearinghouses that knowingly and improperly disclose information or obtain information under false pretenses. Penalties would be higher for actions designed to generate monetary gain. Criminal penalties are up to $50,000 and one year in prison for obtaining or disclosing protected health information; up to $100,000 and up to five years in prison for obtaining protected health information under "false pretenses"; and up to $250,000 and up to 10 years in prison for obtaining or disclosing protected health information with the intent to sell, transfer or use it for commercial advantage, personal gain or malicious harm.

## Balancing Public Responsibility with Privacy Protections

After balancing privacy and other social values, HHS is establishing rules that would permit certain existing disclosures of health information without individual authorization for the following national priority activities and for activities that allow the health care system to operate more smoothly. All of these disclosures have been permitted under existing laws and regulations. Within certain guidelines found in the regulation, covered entities may disclose information for:

- Oversight of the health care system, including quality assurance activities
- Public health
- Research, generally limited to when a waiver of authorization is independently approved by a privacy board or Institutional Review Board
- Judicial and administrative proceedings
- Limited law enforcement activities
- Emergency circumstances
- For identification of the body of a deceased person, or the cause of death
- For facility patient directories
- For activities related to national defense and security

The rule permits, but does not require these types of disclosures. If there is no other law requiring that information be disclosed, physicians and hospitals will still have to make judgments about whether to disclose information, in light of their own policies and ethical principles.

### Special Protection for Psychotherapy Notes

Psychotherapy notes (used only by a psychotherapist) are held to a higher standard of protection because they are not part of the medical record and never intended to be shared with anyone else. All other health information is considered to be sensitive and treated consistently under this rule.

### Equivalent Treatment of Public and Private Sector Health Plans and Providers

The provisions of the final rule generally apply equally to private sector and public sector entities. For example, both private hospitals and government agency medical units must comply with the full range of requirements, such as providing notice, access rights, requiring consent before disclosure for routine uses, establishing contracts with business associates, among others.

## Changes from the Proposed Regulation

[This section describes changes made from the original regulation that had been proposed by HHS in November 1999.]

- Providing coverage to personal medical records in all forms. The proposed regulation had applied only to electronic records and to any paper records that had at some point existed in electronic form. The final regulation extends protection to all types of personal health information created or held by covered entities, including oral communications and paper records that have not existed in electronic form. This creates a privacy system that covers virtually all health information held by hospitals, providers, health plans and health insurers.
- Requiring consent for routine disclosures. The final rule requires most providers to obtain patient consent for routine disclosure of health records, in addition to requiring special patient authorization for non-routine disclosures. The earlier version had proposed allowing these routine disclosures without advance consent for purposes of treatment, payment and health care operations (such as internal data gathering by a provider or health care plan). However, most individuals commenting on this provision, including many physicians, believed consent for these purposes should be obtained in advance, as is typically done today. The final rule retains the new requirement that patients must also be provided detailed written information on privacy rights and how their information will be used.
- Allowing disclosure of the full medical record to providers for purposes of treatment. For most disclosures, such as information submitted with bills, covered entities are required to send only the minimum information needed for the purpose of the disclosure. However, for purposes of treatment, providers need to be able to transmit fuller information. The final rule gives providers full discretion in determining what personal health information to include when sending patients' medical records to other providers for treatment purposes.
- Protecting against unauthorized use of medical records for employment purposes. Companies that sponsor health plans will not be able to access the personal health information held by the plan for employment-related purposes, without authorization from the patient.

## Cost of Implementation

Recognizing the savings and cost potential of standardizing electronic claims processing and protecting privacy and security, the Congress provided in HIPAA 1996 that the overall financial impact of the HIPAA regulations reduce costs. As such, the financial assessment of the privacy regulation includes the ten-year $29.9 billion savings HHS projects for the recently released electronic claims regulation and the projected $17.6 billion in costs projected for the privacy regulation. This produces a net savings of approximately $12.3 billion for the health care delivery system while improving the efficiency of health care as well as privacy protection.

### Preserving Existing, Strong State Confidentiality Laws

Stronger state laws (like those covering mental health, HIV infection, and AIDS information) continue to apply. These confidentiality protections are cumulative; the final rule sets a national "floor" of privacy standards that protect all Americans, but in some states individuals enjoy additional protection. In circumstances where states have decided through law to require certain disclosures of health information for civic purposes, we do not preempt these mandates. The result is to give individuals the benefit of all laws providing confidentiality protection as well as to honor state priorities.

### The Need for Further Congressional Action

HIPAA limits the application of our rule to the covered entities. It does not provide authority for the rule to reach many persons and businesses that work for covered entities or otherwise receive health information from them. So the rule cannot put in place appropriate restrictions on how such recipients of protected health information may use and re-disclose such information. There is no statutory authority for a private right of action for individuals to enforce their privacy rights. We need Congressional action to fill these gaps in patient privacy protections.

### Implementation of the Final Regulation

The final regulation will come into full effect in two years. The regulation will be enforced by HHS' Office for Civil Rights, which will provide assistance to providers, plans and health clearinghouses in meeting the requirements of the regulation. . . .

# UN SECURITY COUNCIL RESOLUTION ON SIERRA LEONE
## December 22, 2000

*Guerrillas in the West African nation of Sierra Leone—said to be responsible for the deaths and grisly mutilations of tens of thousands of people during a decade-long war—on May 1, 2000, captured and held five hundred United Nations peacekeepers for nearly a month. The incident humiliated the UN and symbolized its difficulty in mounting complex peacekeeping operations without adequate funding or logistical support. Rather than monitoring a realistic peace agreement, the UN mission found itself actively fighting the guerrillas whom, many observers said, never intended to keep the pledges they made in a 1999 accord.*

*The Sierra Leone operation was a major test of the UN's ability to mount a large-scale peacekeeping force in the wake of recent reports documenting spectacular failures by peacekeepers in Rwanda, Bosnia, and elsewhere. At year's end the Sierra Leone mission had nearly 12,500 troops and military observers to enforce the peace in a country slightly larger than West Virginia. The UN Security Council was considering a recommendation by Secretary General Kofi Annan that the force be expanded to 20,500 peacekeepers—by far the largest of any currently mounted by the UN. After visiting Sierra Leone in October, eleven ambassadors representing countries on the Security Council wrote that helping the country "is a challenge that the UN and the international community as a whole should gather the collective will to meet. It is a small country, rich in natural resources—not the least of which are its resilient and hopeful people, who have been let down too many times by their own leaders and by influences and circumstances beyond their control." (Report on UN peacekeeping, p. 642)*

*As with most of Africa's conflicts at the turn of the century, the war in Sierra Leone involved more than just one country. The Sierra Leone guerrillas depended heavily on Charles Taylor, the president of neighboring Liberia, for financial and political backing. Nigeria was the leader among several West African countries that had sent large contingents of troops into Sierra Leone, over a period of several years, to try to stop the war. Neigh-*

*boring Guinea was suffering the disastrous consequences of hosting many thousands of refugees who had fled from the fighting in Sierra Leone. The situation in Guinea appeared to be worsening during the latter part of the year as the Sierra Leone guerrillas began attacking civilians there. At year's end Guinea and Liberia also were trading accusations about cross-border raids into each other's territory. In a December 22 report to the Security Council, Annan warned that the fighting along the borders between Sierra Leone, Guinea, and Liberia "could have grave repercussions not only for the situation in Sierra Leone but also for the whole region" of West Africa.*

## *Background to the War*

*Although it involved a tiny country, the war in Sierra Leone had generated big headaches for the world, and especially for West Africa, since it broke out in 1991. The war was launched by a guerrilla group, the Revolutionary United Front (RUF), which sought to depose the elected civilian government. Amid attempts by the UN and other international organizations to broker a peace agreement, elections in February 1996 were won by Ahmed Tejan Kabbah, a former UN official. Kabbah was ousted in a military coup a year later, but in 1998 a military force sent by Nigeria and other West African countries dumped the military regime, pushed the guerrillas into remote positions in the north and east of the country, and reinstalled Kabbah as president.*

*Supported by elements of the national army, the guerrillas regathered their strength later in 1998 and in December launched a massive attack on Freetown, the capital, managing to take control of most of the city during January 1999.*

*The guerrillas financed their operations with proceeds from Sierra Leone's diamond mines, which they controlled. According to reports by international observers, the RUF sold diamonds on the international market through Liberia, whose president, Taylor, took a significant cut of the profits. Starting in the late 1990s, the guerrillas used terror as their primary war tactic, methodically lopping off the hands, arms, feet, and even lips of thousands of civilians.*

*Under pressure from Nigeria, which wanted to pull its troops from Sierra Leone, the UN in mid-1999 negotiated a peace agreement, signed by the government and guerrillas in Lome, Togo. The Clinton administration played a central role in achieving that agreement through the intervention of civil rights leader Jesse Jackson, who was serving as President Bill Clinton's special envoy for Africa. The accord granted amnesty to the guerrillas, including RUF leader Foday Sankoh. The agreement also gave the guerrillas several cabinet positions, the most important of which was the ministry in charge of natural resources—in effect giving the rebels legal custody of the diamond mines they already controlled.*

*The granting of amnesty to guerrillas responsible for terrorizing Sierra Leone's civilian population generated widespread international criticism. In response, UN officials said the guerrillas would not lay down their arms unless amnesty was offered. Moreover, the UN said the amnesty applied only within Sierra Leone, so that Sankoh could be subject to arrest for war crimes if he traveled to other countries.*

*U.S. secretary of state Madeleine K. Albright visited Freetown in October 1999 and met privately with Sankoh. The guerrilla leader, she said later, was "delivering the right message"—that he was committed to ending the war. But it soon became clear that Sankoh and his guerrillas had little intention of carrying out the terms of the Lome peace accord. Even as the UN laid plans for a peacekeeping force to monitor the accord, the guerrillas stepped up their attacks on civilians and consolidated their control of about half of the country.*

## Peacekeepers Captured

*The first elements of a 6,000-man UN peacekeeping force, known as the United Nations Mission in Sierra Leone (UNAMSIL), arrived in Sierra Leone in April 2000. Within weeks, the force was embroiled in one of the most serious crises in the five decades of UN peace missions. The crisis began in late April when Nigeria pulled out most of the troops that had constituted the former West African peacekeeping mission in Sierra Leone. At the same time, the UN peacekeepers—who were still in the process of getting organized—attempted to assert their right under the peace agreement to patrol guerrilla positions in the diamond-mining area around Koidu in eastern Sierra Leone. On April 29 the UN mission commander told reporters that he was ready to dispatch a contingent of Zambian troops to Koidu. Two days later, in a dispute over several rebel fighters who had surrendered their weapons to the UN, RUF guerrillas captured about five hundred UN peacekeepers, all from African nations.*

*Annan asked the United States, France, and Great Britain to organize a rapid reaction force to rescue the peacekeepers, but Washington and Paris refused. The Clinton administration agreed to transport troops of other nations to Sierra Leone—but Annan rejected the offer when the Defense Department insisted on payment at rates higher than what commercial carriers were charging. Washington's other response to the crisis was to dispatch Jesse Jackson to Freetown to help negotiate the release of the captured peacekeepers. But the government in Freetown—angered by Jackson's statements expressing sympathy with guerrilla leader Sankoh—refused to guarantee his safety, and Jackson withdrew.*

*Only the British, the former colonial rulers of Sierra Leone, responded positively to Annan's appeal and sent about 1,000 marines and paratroopers to Freetown. Although their primary mission was to evacuate British citizens, the British troops helped stabilize the situation until the UN was able to get reinforcements from India, Nigeria, Russia, and other countries. Britain also kept about six hundred troops in Sierra Leone through the rest of the year to train the country's ragged army and help rebuild its military facilities.*

*For the UN, the embarrassment of having its troops captured by rebels was compounded by the need to turn for help to Liberian president Taylor—*

*a former rebel leader in his own country who had actively supported the Sierra Leone guerrillas. Taylor arranged to win the release of the peacekeepers in several stages beginning on May 14. The last eighty-five captive peacekeepers were released May 28.*

*In the middle of the May crisis, an armed supporter of the government captured Sankoh in a Freetown neighborhood. He was turned over to the government, which held him in prison under the protection of British paratroopers. The RUF later named another commander, Issa Sessay, to succeed Sankoh, but UN officials said he did not appear to have full control over the guerrilla armies.*

*Reporting on the crisis to the Security Council, Annan directly blamed Sankoh and his RUF guerrillas, saying their actions had raised new questions about their willingness to abide by the Lome peace agreement. Annan called on the international community "to bring economic and political as well as military pressure to bear" on the guerrillas.*

*In a British-sponsored attempt to get at the root of the conflict, the Security Council on July 5 voted to impose an international ban on trade in diamonds from Sierra Leone. The ban was to remain in effect for eighteen months or until the Freetown government regained control over the nation's diamond mines and established a system to certify the origin of diamonds.*

*The Security Council took another step to pressure the guerrillas on August 14 when it voted to create a special court to prosecute those who committed war crimes and other "crimes against humanity" during the war in Sierra Leone. The council's resolution specified that the court was to include legal officers from Sierra Leone. UN officials said Sankoh almost certainly would be a prime target for prosecution by the new court.*

*In the months after the peacekeepers were released, the situation within Sierra Leone remained static, with the UN forces and the national army controlling Freetown and surrounding regions and the guerrillas retaining their lock on about half of the country, including the diamond-producing regions. Under international pressure, the RUF guerrillas on November 10 signed a cease-fire agreement that committed them to allow free access to territory they held by UN troops, civilians, and international aid workers. But by the end of the year UN officials and other observers said the guerrillas had not met their obligations under that agreement.*

## Bolstering the UN Force

*The hostility of rebel forces may have been the most dangerous challenge the UN peacekeepers faced in Sierra Leone, but it was far from the only challenge. As had been the case in many previous peacekeeping operations, the UN had trouble securing adequate funding for the mission, and troops from different countries arrived with varying levels of training and equipment. Moreover, observers said the peacekeepers were stymied for months by a series of disagreements between Major General Vijay Jetley, the Indian general appointed by UN headquarters to run the force, and the Nigerian officers whose forces composed a major element of the force. Annan sought to resolve the discord in September by asking the Indian government to replace the commander. In response, New Delhi announced that it would withdraw its 3,000 troops from the UN force—but over a period of time so the UN would be able to find replacements. Jordan also said it would withdraw its 1,600 troops in the peacekeeping force.*

*Hoping to force some progress, ambassadors from eleven countries represented on the Security Council visited Sierra Leone and other countries in the region in October. In their report, made public on October 16, the ambassadors called for a strengthened UN peacekeeping force by accepting offers by Nigeria and other West African countries to provide additional troops. "Only a sustained and effective military instrument, with the capability to extend its reach throughout the country and following clear political and military objectives, can maintain pressure on RUF and create incentives for dialogue and disarmament," the ambassadors wrote. They said most of the principals of the controversial 1999 Lome peace agreement "remain valid"—so long as the RUF rebels were dislodged from their control of the diamond-producing areas.*

*In reports to the Security Council on October 31 and December 15, Annan proposed to boost the force in Sierra Leone to 20,500 troops, making it the largest of the 15 UN peacekeeping missions in the world. But Annan also acknowledged that he had been unable to convince UN member countries to send enough troops to reach the goal. In a concession to reality, and despite the call by Security Council ambassadors for a strengthened force, the full council sidestepped the issue in a December 22 resolution that extended the mandate of the current force in Sierra Leone through March 2001. The council urged nations "in a position to do so seriously to consider contributing peacekeeping forces for Sierra Leone."*

> *Following is the text of Resolution 1334, adopted by the United Nations Security Council on December 22, 2000, extending the mandate of a UN peacekeeping force in Sierra Leone until March 31, 2000. The document was not available on the Internet at the time of publication.*

# Resolution 1334 (2000)

## Adopted by the Security Council at its 4253rd meeting, on 22 December 2000

*The Security Council,*

*Recalling* its resolutions 1270 (1999) of 22 October 1999, 1289 (2000) of 7 February 2000, 1313 (2000) of 4 August 2000, 1317 (2000) of 5 September 2000, 1321 (2000) of 20 September 2000, the statement of its President of 3 November 2000 (S/PRST/2000/31), and all other relevant resolutions and the statements of its President concerning the situation in Sierra Leone,

*Having considered* the report of the Secretary-General of 15 December 2000 (S/2000/1199),

1. *Expresses* its continued concern at the continuing fragile situation in Sierra Leone and neighbouring States;

2. *Takes note* of the ceasefire agreement signed in Abuja on 10 November 2000 between the Government of Sierra Leone and the Revolutionary United Front (RUF) (S/2000/1091), *expresses* its concern at the failure of the RUF fully to meet their obligations under the agreement, and *calls* on them to give a more convincing demonstration of commitment to the ceasefire and the peace process;

3. *Recalls* that the main objective of the United Nations Mission in Sierra Leone (UNAMSIL), as set out in its resolution 1313 (2000) and confirmed in the concept of operations proposed by the Secretary-General in his report of 24 August 2000 (S/2000/832), remain to assist the efforts of the Government of Sierra Leone to extend State authority, restore law and order and further stabilize the situation progressively throughout the entire country and to assist in the promotion of the political process, leading to a renewed disarmament, demobilization and reintegration programme where possible, and *reiterates* that, to that end, the structure, capability, resources and mandate of UNAMSIL require appropriate strengthening;

4. *Commends* the continued efforts of the Secretary-General in that regard to seek further firm commitments of troops for UNAMSIL, *strongly urges* all States in a position to do so seriously to consider contributing peacekeeping forces for Sierra Leone, and *expresses* its appreciation to those States who have already made such offers;

5. *Expresses* its intention, in that context, following consultations with troop-contributing countries, to respond promptly to any additional specific recommendations made my the Secretary-General in the next period on the force strength and tasks of UNAMSIL;

6. *Decides* to extend the present mandate of UNAMSIL until 31 March 2001;

7. *Decides* to remain actively seized of the matter.

# CUMULATIVE INDEX, 1996–2000

## A

# J